UNIVERSITY CASEBOOK SERIES®

FEDERAL INCOME TAXATION

PRINCIPLES AND POLICIES

EIGHTH EDITION

MICHAEL J. GRAETZ
Columbia Alumni Professor of Tax Law
Columbia Law School
Justus S. Hotchkiss Professor Emeritus
Yale Law School

DEBORAH H. SCHENK
Marilynn and Ronald Grossman Professor of Law Emerita
New York University School of Law

ANNE L. ALSTOTT
Jacquin D. Bierman Professor in Taxation
Yale Law School

FOUNDATION
PRESS

© 1940, 1946, 1950, 1954, 1955, 1960, 1966, 1976, 1985, 1988, 1995, 2001, 2002 FOUNDATION PRESS
© 2005, 2009 THOMSON REUTERS/FOUNDATION PRESS
© 2013 by LEG, Inc. d/b/a West Academic Publishing
© 2018 LEG, Inc. d/b/a West Academic
    444 Cedar Street, Suite 700
    St. Paul, MN 55101
    1-877-888-1330

Printed in the United States of America

ISBN: 978-1-64020-680-9

To our students
M.J.G.
D.H.S.
A.L.A.

PREFACE TO EIGHTH EDITION

This whole book is but a draught—nay, but the draught of a draught. Oh, Time, Strength, Cash and Patience!

—HERMAN MELVILLE,
MOBY DICK, CH. 32.

March 1, 2018, the day this edition of the coursebook went to the printers, marked the 105th anniversary of the effective date of the U.S. income tax. The first income tax act was signed by President Wilson on October 3, 1913, as part of the Underwood-Simmons Tariff Act, and was made retroactive. Congress has enacted tax legislation virtually every year since then—sometimes one act and sometimes dozens of pieces of legislation in a single year. The Congress, the courts, and the Internal Revenue Service all collaborate to ensure that any book designed for teaching a basic course in Federal Income Taxation can never be more than a draft of a draft. Today, no area of law seems more susceptible to change than federal taxation. Consider the following:

The first income tax act was fifteen pages and contained only a few provisions. "The Code" came into existence in 1939 when Congress codified previous acts. The Code currently contains about 2000 provisions affecting individuals and businesses. As of March 2018, the Code was more than four times longer than *War and Peace* and considerably harder to parse. The regulations are over 15,000 pages long.

The first income tax form was released in 1914 and it was three pages with a single page of instructions. For 2017 an individual filing the income tax Form 1040 could file a return with 79 lines, with 12 additional schedules. The schedules refer you to 27 additional worksheets. The instructions to the Form 1040 filled 107 pages of rather small type. In addition to Form 1040, there are many additional forms that can be used by individuals, ranging from commonly used forms (e.g. Form 8283 for noncash charitable contributions) to the truly arcane (Form T for Forest Activities Schedule) and another 293 pages of instructions.

Meanwhile, the courts have decided nearly 45,000 tax cases. Hundreds of tax bills are introduced in Congress each year. Most of them go nowhere, but this century, Congress has passed dozens of major tax acts, not counting legislation affecting Social Security, railroad retirement, unemployment compensation, tariffs and customs duties, or the public debt limit. Since the last edition of this casebook was published, there have been significant changes to the Code, most notably in the more than 500 pages of amendments to the code in the important tax reduction legislation signed by the president in December 2017, formerly known as the "Tax Cuts and Jobs Act of 2017."

Obviously it is impossible—and we think unwise—for a course introducing the income tax to try to instruct students about every detail of these developments. This book is about the fundamental concepts and forces shaping the income tax, not just current events. That is why this edition reflects surprising continuity with its ancestor edition, Griswold's Cases on Federal Taxation. That book, initially published nearly 80 years ago in 1940, was the first law school coursebook devoted exclusively to federal taxation. It appeared at a time when most of the operative statutory provisions were phrased in general terms and many of the basic concepts of federal taxation had not yet matured. Most law schools taught federal taxation only as part of a course that also covered state and local taxation. Nevertheless, this text retains much of the overarching organization that Erwin Griswold first brought to the subject. The subsequent adoption of this structure by most income tax coursebooks is a tribute to Griswold's insights into how the subject of federal taxation should be taught.

The mass of detail that has been added to the statute and the regulations and the burgeoning case law in the intervening seven decades has, of course, required a substantial rethinking of the purposes of an introductory course in federal taxation and, hence, of this coursebook. For one thing, the details have become so voluminous and the changes so frequent that the student must necessarily strive to understand the fundamental concepts and currents rather than to memorize particular rules. The practice of tax law has become more specialized, and most law schools offer a number of advanced courses in taxation. The student in an introductory course therefore must attain some familiarity not only with the statute, the regulations, and the cases but also with the trends in the tax law, the prospects for change, and the fundamental policy issues that inform such changes. Successful tax lawyering involves responding to new and unforeseeable rules and therefore demands a strong conceptual understanding of income tax principles and policies. Likewise, the nonspecialist needs to be introduced to these fundamental concepts of income taxation, if only to be able intelligently to recognize and monitor his or her clients' tax problems.

The composition of this book has also been influenced by the increasing use of the tax law as an instrument of social and economic policy. The income tax is not merely a revenue-raising device to finance the goods and services provided by the government. The decisions as to what to tax, and when, increasingly affect the direction, growth, and overall condition of our economy and the allocation and distribution of resources within our society.

For these reasons, this volume devotes substantial attention to the general principles and policies of federal taxation. Thus, cases have been supplemented with excerpts from congressional reports, administrative pronouncements, and commentaries and analyses of tax issues. In addition, there are explanatory notes introducing fundamental concepts of tax law and shorter notes following the principal cases.

This edition nevertheless continues to reflect the pedagogical perspective developed in Erwin Griswold's original volume, the preface of which stated:

Here is an opportunity, almost unique * * *, to study a complete and self-contained system. Here is an opportunity to come into contact with perhaps our most experienced administrative agency. Here is an opportunity to deal with a statute, not as some excrescence on the common law, but as the law, to trace its growth, to learn how it is given meaning and how that meaning changes. Here is an opportunity to deal with authoritative judicial decisions—or at least, and perhaps more important, to consider how far they are authoritative. * * * Here as elsewhere it is understanding and knowledge of the process that is sought.

These opportunities are no less present in this volume than they were in its ancient predecessor.

This edition retains much of the chapter organization of its predecessors. The first chapter contains the basic policy and procedural aspects of income taxation. This chapter includes a brief history of taxation in the United States, an introduction to income tax terminology, and a discussion of the roles of Congress, the executive, and the courts. Subsequent chapters explore the topics "What Is Income?," "Deductions and Credits," "Whose Income Is It?," "Capital Gains and Losses," and "When Is It Income?". Of course, tax problems rarely can be placed into such discrete categories. Hence, there is some overlap of subjects within the chapters. Chapter 4, for example, now takes up in some detail the important special deduction applicable to "qualified business income," added by the 2017 legislation. Chapter 6 provides a description of the important concepts and considerations involving the taxation of deferred compensation and tax-favored savings for retirement. In its exploration of the relationship of Roth IRAs (nondeductible, excludable) to traditional IRAs (deductible, includible), it provides important context intended to fix concepts regarding the value of tax deferral and the time value of money that are explored in earlier chapters. Chapter 8 contains a brief introduction to corporate tax shelters along with materials on the ethical responsibilities of tax lawyers, thereby providing an appropriate context for analysis and discussion of the ethical issues that tax lawyers face. The Appendix contains tables of present values.

As every teacher of taxation knows well, it has become increasingly difficult to teach an introduction to federal taxation in a single semester, even in a 48-hour course. Compromises between breadth of coverage and treating materials in depth are ever more necessary. Most instructors have learned to maintain realistic expectations as to what can reasonably be accomplished in the first course and to assume that students with a genuine interest in taxation will take additional courses in the subject.

This volume continues the layered approach of the prior editions. By selecting from the materials available here, teachers can decide which aspects of income tax law and policy to emphasize and which to skim or omit in an introductory course. This volume surely contains enough material to teach not only a four-hour basic course in federal income taxation, but also an additional three-hour course designed to pursue certain issues in greater detail than is possible in the basic course. This means that the instructor must exercise considerable selectivity in teaching any single course from this book. Instructors who wish to cover more ground might consider relying on students to read some of the more straightforward materials without significant classroom discussion.

Designing courses inherently involves personal priorities and choices. The precise materials assigned will depend upon each teacher's choices of where to delve deeply into substantive law and policy issues as well as how to trade off in-depth discussions and general coverage. We have attempted here to provide sufficiently comprehensive, interesting, and flexible materials to allow teachers to make a wide variety of successful selections.

Federal income taxation is, of course, primarily a statutory course. In addition to this text, the student will need a current edition of at least selected sections of the Internal Revenue Code and probably some sections of the Income Tax Regulations. A number of publishers now produce one volume editions of selected statutory and regulatory provisions that may be used along with this text.

Citations and footnotes have been freely omitted. We have numbered the footnotes in the cases consecutively even where we have omitted footnotes. Dissenting and concurring opinions frequently have been omitted; however, the existence of these opinions generally has been noted to enable students to find them by consulting the original sources. When brief excerpts from opinions have been used, the page reference typically has been omitted.

Preparation of a book of this sort produces many debts. Of course, we are indebted to Erwin Griswold, whose first six editions of his predecessor book were used by a substantial number of American law students. We also wish to thank both the students and faculty who have used prior editions; the comments and criticisms and the syllabuses so many shared with us greatly influenced this edition. In this edition, we have been joined by Anne Alstott, the Jacquin D. Bierman Professor in Taxation at Yale Law School, an especially gifted writer and teacher, who has won teaching awards at both Columbia and Yale Law Schools. Rick D'Avino also provided important and timely suggestions regarding the material on new section 199A. In addition to all of those who labored on prior editions to whom we remain indebted, we thank especially Benjamin Thomson, a student at Columbia Law School, who labored tirelessly and with great care on this edition.

MICHAEL J. GRAETZ
DEBORAH H. SCHENK
ANNE L. ALSTOTT

March 2018

SUMMARY OF CONTENTS

TABLE OF CONTENTS

TABLE OF CASES

The principal cases are in bold type.

TABLE OF INTERNAL REVENUE CODE SECTIONS

TABLE OF TREASURY REGULATIONS

TABLE OF INTERNAL REVENUE RULINGS

The principal rulings are in bold type.

TABLE OF MISCELLANEOUS RULINGS

UNIVERSITY CASEBOOK SERIES®

FEDERAL INCOME TAXATION

PRINCIPLES AND POLICIES

EIGHTH EDITION

CHAPTER 1

INTRODUCTION TO FEDERAL TAXATION

Taxation is the process by which a government transfers resources (almost always money) from the private to the public sector. Individual citizens often resist sacrificing their private wealth to the public fisc, but—even though a broad anti-tax attitude is now common in American politics—the citizenry at large demands that government provide goods and services, such as roads and bridges, disability and retirement insurance, education, and national defense, all of which ultimately must be financed through taxation. This fundamental conflict—between the public's demand for government provision of goods and services and each person's desire to minimize his own tax burden—works its way through the political process to affect dramatically both the nation's tax laws and government expenditures.

In deciding whom to tax, what to tax, and when, Congress routinely makes fundamental social and economic judgments. Tax policy decisions often affect the general condition of the economy, its direction, and growth. Tax provisions also have a major impact on the use of specific resources: who works and who doesn't, how much the nation spends on this or that and for whom. Today's income tax, for example, makes it cheaper for people to own their own homes than to rent, gives a break to families with one spouse who stays at home rather than those with both husband and wife in the job market, and makes it less costly for some people to marry, but cheaper for others to divorce or remain unmarried. Federal alcohol taxes favor wine drinkers over beer drinkers, and both over people who prefer whiskey.

The most fundamental issues of public policy are sometimes raised when Congress enacts tax laws, and the Internal Revenue Code is laden with legislative judgments about social policy. Even the nation's founders recognized that taxation was a "means for shaping the national economy, bringing foreign nations to fair commercial terms, regulating morals, and realizing . . . social reforms"—thereby taking a thoroughly modern view of taxation.[1] Issues of equity in taxation raise issues of justice generally. Asking how much revenue to take from various classes of individuals in our society is one way of asking how much economic inequality society will tolerate.

But even this view of the political role of taxation is too narrow. John Hampden's refusal to pay "ship money" to Charles I of England raised a

---

[1] Sidney Ratner, Taxation and Democracy in America 18 (1942), citing Wesley C. Mitchell, A History of the Greenbacks (1903).

tax issue, but it also raised a fundamental question of the proper balance of power between the monarch and Parliament that profoundly affected the structure of English government. A tax issue also sparked the Revolutionary War. And the gesture chosen by Henry David Thoreau, and later by Vietnam War protesters, to question the validity of government action was a refusal to pay taxes.

Taxation long has been a primary link between the people and their government. In the United States today, more people file tax returns than vote in presidential elections, and the politics of taxation influences electoral debate at every level of office seeking. A French finance minister once called taxation the art of plucking the goose with the least amount of squawking. Now we hear lots of squawking.

In the summer of 1988 George H.W. Bush sought the presidency with the slogan: "Read my lips: no new taxes!" Many political pundits said that breaking this pledge in the deficit reduction agreement of 1990 was Bush I's political undoing in the 1992 election. His son George W. Bush went one better in the 2000 election, promising a tax cut that he convinced Congress to deliver in May 2001. Today no politician seems completely free from fear of political reprisals for suggesting tax increases.

Resistance to taxes is as American as apple pie and can be traced back to the nation's birth. We have always been a tax-hating people. And whenever we have recognized that new taxes or increases in old ones are unavoidable, we always have strived to impose them on someone else. In 1928, when the income tax was just a teenager, a Treasury tax official characterized tax lawmaking as a "group contest in which powerful interests vigorously endeavor to rid themselves of present or proposed tax burdens."[2] Decades later, Russell Long, the Democrat from Louisiana who served as Chairman of the Senate Finance Committee, captured this sentiment nicely when he offered this ditty as the first principle of tax reform: "Don't tax you. Don't tax me. Tax the fellow behind the tree." In 1992, Dan Rostenkowski, then Chairman of the House Ways and Means Committee, added a second stanza, in light of the globalization of the world economy: "Don't tax you. Don't tax me. Tax the companies across the sea."

In the nation's infancy, when adequate revenues could be produced by tariffs, battles were principally among regions in an effort both to shift tax burdens to others and to protect local industries from competition. These kinds of battles still ring familiar two centuries later; for example, in 2017 high-tax "Blue" states fought (with only limited success) to avoid repeal of the itemized deductions for state and local taxes to fund lower tax rates championed by "Red" state Republicans. Today, regions battle, industries battle, labor and business interests battle; efforts to shift tax burdens to others abound.

---

[2]   T.S. Adams, "Ideals and Idealism in Taxation," 18 Am.Econ.Rev. 1 (1928).

In tax legislation, personal interests and ideologies conspire to produce arguments for action, justifications for inaction, and rationalizations for things done or left undone. Ideology and self-interest generally have little respect for facts, and the abuse and misuse of facts is a standard weapon of the advocates' arsenal. Unfortunately, when Congress is making tax policy, information and misinformation often serve simply as tools for argument. There is a glut of factual controversy, what economists label "empirical uncertainty," about the effects of taxation. Even the most fundamental factual questions about the effects of tax legislation often lack definitive answers. For example, despite almost a century of experience, we still do not know for sure what combination of people actually pays the corporate income tax: shareholders, consumers, employees, all owners of capital. Firm belief about the consequences of tax policy, however, is omnipresent. Whenever adequate facts do not exist or are controversial, the task of advocates in the political process is made easier. The role of objective policy analysts, if there are such rare, endangered beasts, diminishes.

At a minimum, the anti-tax attitude of the public that has dominated federal policy since the late 1970s has postponed serious consideration of tax policy issues that are fundamental to our nation's future economic well-being: is the current mix of taxes appropriate to the economic conditions that we face both domestically and internationally in the 21st century? How can we raise the necessary revenues in a manner that is fair to and facilitates the well-being of the U.S. people in the global economy and at the same time encourages savings and investment, and nurtures economic growth?

Politicians' fear of increasing taxes—coupled with their unwillingness to limit government spending—made deficits of unprecedented size the dominant fiscal event of the late 20th and early 21st centuries, in the process shattering the promise of the tax limitation movement: that stemming the supply of tax revenues would constrain government spending and reduce government size. Instead, federal public spending continued to grow, and deficits swelled. With a robust economy, federal deficits gave way to surpluses in the late 1990s, and public policy shifted to the question whether to cut taxes, pay down the public debt, or do a bit of both. The period of surpluses was short-lived, however, and by 2002 the federal government was running significant deficits once again. By 2018 the deficit was over $660 billion and the federal debt held by the public exceeded $14.7 trillion. These numbers will grow larger due to large tax cuts enacted in 2017 and as the baby boom generation continues to retire and become eligible for Social Security and Medicare.

Whatever the long- or short-term fiscal outlook, the goals of the nation's tax and fiscal policies will be what they always have been: to facilitate growth of the nation's economy and to do justice in the distribution of the burdens and benefits of government, while raising revenues adequate to finance government's expenditures.

And tax policy inevitably will be constrained by the difficulties of achieving political majorities. The tax provisions in force today reflect no more than yesterday's political compromises, but the underlying structural and policy conflicts have changed little over time. A student of taxation must understand the current tax law and the process for making it; this requires insights into timeless policy and political conflicts and the institutional mechanisms for resolving them. The output itself—the nation's tax law—lives in perpetual motion.

This chapter provides an introduction to the income tax by (1) briefly summarizing the history of taxation in the United States, (2) describing the magnitude and sources of current tax collections, (3) introducing some basic income tax terminology, (4) examining the dominant criteria for evaluating tax systems and tax provisions, (5) exploring "tax expenditure" analysis, and (6) describing the roles of the three branches of government in the formulation and operation of the tax laws.

SECTION 1.   BRIEF HISTORY OF TAXATION IN THE UNITED STATES

Early Taxes

In 1791, the first Secretary of the Treasury, Alexander Hamilton, convinced Congress to impose taxes on distilled spirits and carriages "more as a measure of social discipline than as a source of revenue."[3] Hamilton had the financial purpose of raising money to pay the small national debt, but, more importantly, he wanted the tax imposed to advance and secure the power of the new federal government. This distilled spirits tax produced the "Whiskey Rebellion" of 1794, a tax resistance movement led by farmers of western Pennsylvania and including others from Maryland, Virginia, and North Carolina, who—being consumers as well as producers of substantial quantities of whiskey—regarded themselves as the targets of the tax. In July 1794, about 500 tax protesters burned a tax collector's home and soon thereafter, with the approval of Congress, George Washington sent 13,000 troops into the troubled area. This ended the rebellion. Suppressing these tax protesters demonstrated the ability of the recently formed federal government to enforce its revenue laws within the states. In so doing, it served to secure the power of the national government and to fulfill, at least temporarily, Hamilton's policies.

The carriage tax produced the first Supreme Court case to consider the constitutional validity of an exercise of the taxing power, and the tax was upheld in Hylton v. United States, 3 U.S. (3 Dall.) 171 (1796), on the ground that it was not a "direct tax" required to be apportioned among

---

[3]   Samuel E. Morrison, Oxford History of the United States 1783–1917, at 182 (1927).

the states by population under Article 1, Section 2, clause 3 of the Constitution.

The first "commissioner of the revenue" was appointed on May 8, 1792. Soon thereafter, taxes were imposed on snuff, sugar, auction sales, legal instruments, and bonds. In addition, a direct tax was enacted in 1798 on real property—houses and land—as well as a tax of fifty cents on all slaves between the ages of twelve and fifty. Like the taxes on distilled spirits, these two taxes proved both unpopular and difficult to collect, and, along with opposition to the Alien and Sedition Acts, contributed to Thomas Jefferson's presidential victory over John Adams in 1800.

In 1802, at the initiative of President Jefferson and his Treasury Secretary Albert Gallatin, all internal taxes (except a tax on salt) were repealed, reflecting Jefferson's determination to reduce federal taxes and expenditures and the national debt. The connection between death and taxes—made famous in an oft-quoted remark describing them as the only two certain events, first attributed to Benjamin Franklin in 1789—became all too real shortly thereafter, as the nation's major changes in tax policies began their long pattern of accompanying wars.

The War of 1812 demonstrated the risks of Jefferson's policy of relying entirely on tariffs as the sole source of federal government finance. This war also offered the nation's first proof that higher rates need not necessarily produce higher revenues: a doubling of tariff rates in 1812 raised half the pre-enactment revenues in 1814 due to the wartime decline in imports. During this war, virtually all the previous federal taxes were revived, inaugurating the country's acceptance of the adage "an old tax is a good tax."

A Century of Tariffs

A peacetime deluge of imports the following year led domestic manufacturers to embrace additional protectionism, and the Tariff Act of 1816 raised duties on imports to a new high. By 1817, the fiscal situation of the federal government had so improved that the wartime taxes were all repealed, and the federal government did not again require revenues from internal taxes until the Civil War. During the interim, the government financed all its activities from customs duties and sales of public lands. Indeed, trade tariffs remained the most significant single source of federal revenues until 1894. Thus, although Congress had raised some revenues from taxes on internal sources since the first days of the Union, tariffs produced the bulk of the money required to finance federal expenditures for most of the nation's first century.

The federal government's reliance on tariffs as its principal funding source initially suited both the young nation's manufacturers and farmers. High duties on imports served to protect the country's manufacturers from foreign competition and imposed little or no burden on the farmers, who were largely self-sufficient from items they produced themselves. Do not think, however, that tariffs avoid imposing burdens similar to those that accompany taxation. Tariffs produce higher prices, for both imported and domestically produced goods that are subject to these duties, and therefore impose significant burdens on consumers, similar to those associated with sales or excise taxes, but varying depending on the linkage between the tariff schedule and each family's mix of purchases of goods and services.

The Civil War Income Tax

The need to finance the Civil War gave rise in 1861 to a direct tax on real property apportioned among the states by population and on July 1, 1862, President Lincoln signed the first income tax imposed by the federal government. It applied to all income in excess of $600, and taxed amounts up to $10,000 at a 3 percent rate with income exceeding that amount taxed at 5 percent. The constitutionality of the income tax was sustained in Springer v. United States, 102 U.S. 586 (1880), against the contention that it was a direct tax that should be apportioned among the states. The 1862 Act also imposed taxes on inheritances in excess of $1,000 with rates graduated from .75 percent to 5 percent depending on how close a relative the beneficiary was to the decedent.

The income tax was increased in 1864—with the top rate doubled to 10 percent—reduced in 1867 and again in 1870, when the inheritance tax was repealed, and was repealed in 1872 during the Grant administration when the federal government enjoyed large budget surpluses. During this time, James A. Garfield proved himself a thoroughly modern politician by railing in 1867 against the income tax he had avidly supported in 1865 and subsequently riding a conservative tide to become President in 1880.

Tariff issues dominated the Presidential campaigns of both 1888 and 1892. Tariffs were increased to an average rate of nearly 50 percent in the McKinley Tariff Act of 1890. But by 1894 it had become apparent that further tariff increases would be counterproductive and that only a decrease in tariff rates would increase revenues.

The next war—with Spain over Cuba and the Philippines—which established the United States as a major world power, demanded additional revenues, and the War Revenue Act of 1898 doubled alcohol and tobacco taxes, enacted a wide range of new excise taxes, and reenacted an inheritance tax. But the usual pattern prevailed, and these taxes were all repealed in 1902 after the crisis had passed.

After intense controversy, the income tax was reinstated at the insistence of the Democrats in 1894 to compensate for the reduction in tariffs anticipated to result from the 1894 Tariff Act. The tax was modeled after the Civil War income tax and imposed a rate of 2 percent on all income over $4,000. In an innovation that since has been lost, gifts and inheritances were taxed as income to the recipient. Contrary to its prior determination in 1880 that the Civil War income tax was constitutionally permissible, in 1895 the Supreme Court struck down the entire income tax as a direct tax not apportioned among the states in conformity with the Constitution. Pollock v. Farmers' Loan & Trust Co., 158 U.S. 601 (1895). That decision was highly controversial, with the Court's majority suffering accusations that they had forgotten they were a court and not a legislature—something courts often are accused of forgetting. The case ultimately led to the adoption of the Sixteenth Amendment in 1913, which permits Congress to tax income "from whatever source derived."

The Twentieth Century: Expansion and Entrenchment of Income and Wage Taxes

Two years before the ratification of the Sixteenth Amendment, the Supreme Court sustained the constitutional validity of the corporation excise tax of 1909, the forerunner of the general income tax. The Tariff Act of 1909 had imposed a tax of 1 percent on corporate net incomes in excess of $5,000. The Supreme Court upheld this tax on the ground that it was an "excise tax" on the privilege of doing business as a corporation rather than a direct tax on property. Flint v. Stone Tracy Co., 220 U.S. 107 (1911).[4]

The Sixteenth Amendment was ratified February 3, 1913, and it took Congress only until October 3 of that year to enact a tax on the net income of individuals and corporations that was retroactive to March 1. The Supreme Court sustained the income tax enacted in 1913 under the explicit power the Sixteenth Amendment granted to Congress to impose income taxes. Brushaber v. Union Pacific Railroad Co., 240 U.S. 1 (1916).

Congress also enacted taxes on estates in 1916 and enacted a tax on gifts in 1924 (which was repealed in 1926 and reinstated in 1932), and the Supreme Court upheld both taxes. These are the predecessors of the modern estate and gift taxes.

During the period 1925–1932, Secretary of the Treasury Andrew Mellon became a role model for President Ronald Reagan by lowering the top income tax rate from its previous high of 73 percent, when he took office in 1921, to 25 percent in 1925. (Six decades later in 1981, President Reagan started three points lower, at 70 percent, and ended three points higher, at 28 percent in 1986.) The period of a 25 percent top rate, which lasted from 1925 to 1932, was something of a mixed economic bag: times were very good for a while; then times became very bad. During the subsequent five decades from 1932 to 1982—also a period of some very good years and some bad ones—the top rate never dropped below 63 percent and was as high as 94 percent. Nevertheless, the notion that a

---

[4]   This case is notable now chiefly because of its quaint constitutional distinction between the "subject" (doing business in the corporate form) and the "measure" (income) of a tax—a distinction that also served to uphold the estate tax as an excise on the transfer of property rather than a direct tax on wealth.

low maximum tax rate is critical to the American economy has become an article of unshakeable faith in many quarters.

By 1932, the Depression had so depleted its revenues that the federal government was experiencing large and growing deficits. In these pre-Keynesian days, agreement was universal that taxes had to be raised. As a result, the Revenue Act of 1932 enacted a major tax increase that served only to prolong the Depression.

From his first days as President, Franklin Delano Roosevelt preached from a populist's hymnal, railing against the rich and big business, but in tax legislation at least, his bark was generally far worse than his bite. In 1936, President Roosevelt proposed a major change in corporate income taxes, but Congress refused to go along, and instead enacted a new tax on undistributed corporate profits, which was soon reduced to less than one-tenth of its original rate, and was phased out by the Revenue Act of 1938. From then until taxes were raised to finance the Second World War—with the notable exception of the Social Security revisions of 1939—annual tax legislation was of little general importance.

The Enactment of Social Security

Clearly the most significant tax legislation of the years between the First and Second World Wars was the Social Security Act of 1935 and its amendments in 1939. This legislation created the federal retirement, disability, and unemployment insurance system, financed by a flat-rate payroll tax on a specified amount of wages. The system of benefits paid for by this tax is progressive, providing greater wage replacement for lower-wage retirees.

Originally, the Social Security tax rate was set at 1 percent of wages to grow to 5 percent, split evenly between employees and their employers. Today the combined tax rate on employers and employees exceeds 12 percent and an additional tax of nearly 3 percent of wages is imposed to pay for hospital insurance under Medicare. The share of federal revenues supplied by these payroll taxes has grown substantially over time; in recent years it has ranged from 35 to 40 percent. Counting both the employers' and employees' shares of those taxes, more than 65 percent of American households now pay more in payroll (and self-employment) taxes than in income taxes. Nevertheless, with the retirement of the baby boom generation and Americans living longer, payroll tax revenues are expected to be inadequate to pay currently legislated Social Security benefits in the decades ahead.

Extension of the Income Tax to Most Americans

The First World War secured for the income tax an important place in this nation's fiscal system, and the Second World War converted this levy from its initial limited scope into a tax on the masses. Although it has long served as the nation's principal source of revenue—and greatest cause of springtime headaches—the income tax originally was imposed at low rates and applied to fewer than 400,000 individuals. It was not until World War II that the income tax came to be paid by most Americans. Income tax rates reached their peak of 94 percent during that era. Following the Second World War, taxes—as usual following a war—began to decline, but that trend came to an end with legislation in 1950 and 1951 to finance the Korean War. Beginning with the election of President Kennedy in 1960, the use of tax policy as a short-term economic stimulus became commonplace, and since the early 1960s, the government has frequently used tax policy to stimulate economic growth.

The Tax Reform of 1986

With considerable hyperbole, the Tax Reform Act of 1986 was widely heralded as the most significant tax change since the income tax was extended to the masses during the Second World War. The 1986 Act was the result of an uneasy political marriage of conservatives' desire for low tax rates and liberals' desire for a broad tax base. Both sides of this compromise immediately came under attack. Its stability, therefore, was precarious from the outset, and although it put an end to a debilitating and escalating tax shelter industry for individuals, it ultimately failed to produce a markedly better tax system. By removing or reducing certain tax provisions that had produced very unequal rates of tax on different investments, however, the 1986 legislation did—for a short while at least—improve the economic efficiency of investment decisions and made the economy somewhat more productive. The 1986 legislation achieved some simplification for low- and some moderate-income taxpayers, but these gains soon were eroded by subsequent legislation. The rate-reducing and base-broadening contours of the 1986 Act were mimicked throughout the industrialized world. The ink was barely dry on the 1986 legislation, however, before the compromise began to unravel.

Since the 1990s, Presidents and Congress have used the income tax the way a mother might employ chicken soup: as a magic elixir to solve all the nation's economic and social difficulties. If the nation has a problem in access to education, child care affordability, health insurance coverage, or financing of long-term care, to name just a few, an income tax deduction or credit seems to be the politicians' answer.

As its coverage has broadened and its missions have grown more numerous, the income tax has grown more cumbersome. Extraordinary complexity continues to be an income tax hallmark, in no small measure due to the efforts by policymakers to accommodate a variety of competing purposes, although the taxation of business and investment income is inherently complicated. This nation's tax law is now more than seven times longer than Tolstoy's *War and Peace* and considerably harder to parse.

The most important aspect of the 1986 Act—the decision to strengthen the income tax rather than to replace it with a consumption tax—also was challenged beginning in the 1990s. Several Republican candidates for president in 1996 and Republican members of the House leadership throughout the 1990s urged that the income tax be replaced by some form of consumption tax: a sales tax, a value-added tax, or a so-called flat tax. The presidential election campaign of 2004 again brought forth renewed proposals to change the income tax and in 2016, House Republicans published a "Blueprint" for tax reform that would have substituted a unique form of consumption tax for the corporate income tax, but this proposal was abandoned in 2017. While the central role of the income tax seems likely to continue, its exact form remains up for grabs.

The Beginning of the Twenty-First Century: Tax Cuts and Deficits

In 2001, Alan Greenspan, then Chairman of the Federal Reserve, told the Senate that projected surpluses were so large that the federal government would soon pay off all its debt and would then have to begin investing in corporate stock, a prospect he abhorred. The good news is that this problem has been solved.

Acting on President George W. Bush's campaign promise, in 2001, Congress enacted tax cut legislation to be phased in during the years 2001–2010. This legislation reduced income tax rates, increased income tax allowances for children and education, and repealed the estate tax, effective in 2010. In a cynical move made to comply with budget resolutions, this law rescinded all its tax reductions at the end of 2010 unless extended in subsequent legislation. The result was a crazy quilt pattern of phase-ins and phase-outs that was the product of pure politics and arcane budget rules. Congress again cut taxes in 2003, once again lowering individual rates, providing marriage penalty relief, and increasing allowances for children. The 2003 Act also contained generous provisions for business and lowered the rates on capital gains and dividends. A handful of Senate Democrats had thought they had secured victory by insisting on a budget resolution that limited the 2001 tax cuts to $1.3 trillion over the coming decade rather than the $1.6 trillion that President Bush had proposed, but with all of the timing gimmicks, the 2001 and 2003 tax laws ended up costing closer to $3 trillion than $1 trillion during the decade that followed.

Despite the widespread anticipation of fundamental tax reform, Congress decided to pursue an exercise in brinksmanship by extending the 2001 and 2003 tax cuts in December 2010 for two additional years. Then, Congress also reinstated the federal estate tax (which had been repealed for 2010 only) with a top rate of 40 percent and an exemption of $5 million per person, indexed for inflation.

During the financial crisis in 2008 Congress passed an economic stimulus bill that enacted and expanded a number of "temporary" tax benefits for individuals and businesses. All of these provisions ultimately were extended to December 31, 2012 as well. As part of the 2010 deal to extend these tax cuts two more years, Congress also enacted a temporary payroll tax holiday.

Congress is a big fan of temporary tax breaks—if they only last a year, only a year's revenue is counted as lost. And a provision that is about to expire attracts the attention of lobbyists and (their wealthy clients) who will benefit from its retention and, therefore, be especially generous in their political contributions. These provisions are known as "extenders" and in recent years there have been about 60 that are scheduled to expire at the end of every year. There is little precedent, however, for letting the extenders expire.

The confluence of the huge problems Congress created for itself with temporary tax laws all came together on December 31, 2012. Despite fears that delay would roil the markets and have a negative effect on the economy, Congress waited until late on New Year's Eve 2012 to pass legislation that made most of the Bush tax cuts permanent except for very high-income taxpayers. It also extended almost all the extenders for another year. Despite this "solution," Congress often continues to punt, wrangling over raising taxes or cutting spending.

The 2017 Tax Legislation

During his 2016 campaign for the presidency, Donald Trump promised substantial tax cuts for both individuals and businesses and in April 2017, he presented to the American people a one-page statement of his tax revision principles and another half page outlining some specific goals. (This was a sharp contrast to Ronald Reagan's 489-page description in May 1985 of his tax reform proposals, which ultimately led to the 1986 Tax Reform Act.) Then, in late September 2017, the White House released a nine-page "Unified Framework for Fixing Our Broken Tax Code," again calling for substantial cuts in taxes on business and individual income. This document had been agreed to by a group of Republican leaders calling themselves the "Big Six." The group included President Trump's Treasury Secretary and National Economic Council Director, the Chairman of the Ways and Means Committee, the Chairman of the Senate Finance Committee, the Speaker of the House and the Majority Leader of the Senate. A few weeks later, on November 3, 2017, the House Ways and Means Committee Chairman, Kevin Brady of Texas, released proposed legislation containing 425 pages of amendments to the Internal Revenue Code, which he labeled the "Tax Cuts and Jobs Act."

Less than two months after that, on December 22, 2017, President Trump signed into law the most sweeping tax revision in decades. This law went through Congress with unprecedented speed—by comparison, the 1986 Tax Reform had taken 53 weeks. The 2017 legislation lowered the corporate tax rate from 35 percent to 21 percent, adopted an unprecedented special rate for business income reported on individual returns (discussed in Chapter 4), and revised substantially the way the United States taxes income earned abroad by U.S. multinational companies. The 2017 law also lowered tax rates for individuals, nearly doubled the standard deduction, significantly increased credits for children, and cut back on numerous deductions, including, most notably, for state and local taxes, personal exemptions, and business expenses of employees (discussed in Chapter 3). The new law also doubled the estate tax exception to $11 million ($22 million for a married couple).

Unlike major tax legislation in the past, the new law was enacted on a purely partisan basis with only Republican votes. It passed the Senate with a 51–48 vote and the House 227 to 203. Some Democrats immediately began calling for legislation to "repeal and replace" the new law. Importantly, unlike prior unsuccessful efforts of both the Obama Administration and the Republican Ways and Means Chairman, there was no attempt to keep the 2017 legislation revenue neutral. Instead, Republicans adopted a budget resolution that permitted the 2017 tax law to lose $1.5 trillion of revenue between 2018 and 2027. But, in a replay of 2001, Congress was unwilling to limit the size of its tax cuts to that level and instead terminated virtually all of the individual income tax changes at the end of 2025 (changes which had been estimated to cost nearly $800 billion from 2018 through 2025). Republican congressional leaders, of course, expected that these tax cuts, like those enacted in 2001, would be extended by a future Congress. By 2027, extending all of these provisions is estimated to cost close to an additional $200 billion a year. Federal deficits are expected to exceed $1 trillion annually by 2019, and without major changes in taxes or spending will exceed an unsustainable level of 5 percent or more of GDP by 2022. At a minimum, this means that, despite the massive change in 2017, the tax law continues to be unstable.

The termination of many of the changes of the 2017 law, along with the speed with which it was enacted, have made the Internal Revenue Code even more difficult to parse. Numerous provisions that were repealed or changed significantly are treated in the law as "suspended." This creates special challenges for students (as well as coursebook editors). In a final wrinkle, the statute, which had been labeled the "Tax Cuts and Jobs Act" in both the House and the Senate, lost this name due to an obscure ruling of the Senate parliamentarian. Like the fans of the enormously talented late artist formerly known as "Prince," many commentators on the 2017 legislation continue to refer to it as the "TCJA." We, however, have chosen here to call it simply the 2017 legislation or the 2017 tax act.

As this brief history indicates, taxation plays a central role in U.S. public policy and is always on the congressional agenda. Congress has passed some form of tax legislation nearly every year for the last five decades. Taxation is increasingly important in political elections and a topic of concern to average Americans. Taxation has gone from a way for Alexander Hamilton to secure the power of the federal government to one of the most important issues facing the country.

SECTION 2.   CURRENT TAXES IN THE UNITED STATES

The Internal Revenue Code of 1986 imposes all federal internal revenue taxes. The 1986 Code superseded the Internal Revenue Code of 1954, which, in turn, had superseded the Internal Revenue Code of 1939. These codes have imposed more than 50 kinds of taxes. The major taxes are the corporate and individual income taxes and the payroll tax. In addition, there are estate and gift taxes and a large number of excise taxes. Over time excise taxes have been imposed on a wide variety of goods, from liquor and cigarettes to oleomargarine and playing cards, and on the manufacture of many articles, including tires, toilet preparations, automobiles, and gasoline, and on telegraph, telephone, radio, and cable messages.

Figure 1.1
Total Federal Revenue vs. Total Federal Outlays
as a Percentage of Gross Domestic Product
1950 to 2016

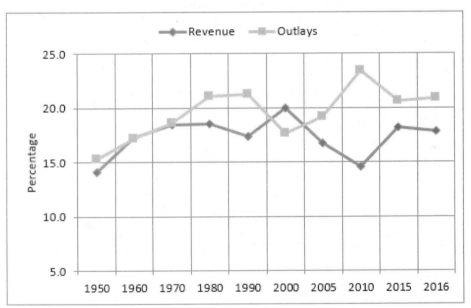

http://www.whitehouse.gov/omb/budget/Historicals Table 1.2

Even though the overall federal tax level has remained relatively constant as a percentage of total national output over a long period of time, with fluctuations due largely to the state of the economy, the share of Social Security and Medicare employment taxes has increased dramatically relative to GDP, changing substantially the composition of U.S. taxes. Indeed, the most important development in the federal tax structure in the past 60 years has been the growth of the payroll tax to finance social welfare programs, particularly Social Security. These taxes have risen from 10 percent of total budget receipts in 1953 to 34 percent in 2016. The impact of this increase has been especially dramatic for low- and middle-income workers, and the promise of future benefits—particularly upon retirement—has not served to offset the public and political perception that the wages of the middle class are being overtaxed.

Some economists claim that the current method of funding Social Security may be having an adverse effect on the nation's level of private savings, although whether this is actually occurring is quite controversial. In 2004 President Bush proposed to "privatize" part of Social Security by permitting some taxpayers to direct a portion of their Social Security payments into private savings accounts. But this proposal went nowhere in part because the government would need to borrow substantial amounts to cover distributions to current retirees since current Social Security payments are used to fund distributions to retirees.

Figure 1.2
Total Federal/State/Local Receipts vs.
Total Federal/State/Local Expenditures as a
Percentage of Gross Domestic Product
1950 to 2016

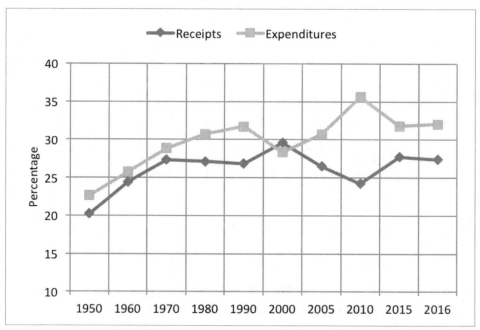

http://www.whitehouse.gov/omb/budget/Historicals Table 14.3

In contrast to the growth in taxes on wages, the past 50 years have witnessed a sharp decline in the percentage of total revenues generated by the corporate income tax. The corporate tax produced 30.3 percent of federal revenues in 1954, but only 9.2 percent in 2016.

The individual income tax, however, has remained a relatively steady source of federal revenues, producing 42.4 percent of the total in 1954, 45.4 percent in 1986, and 47.3 percent in 2016.

The excise taxes have generated relatively little controversy (and therefore are rarely studied in law school tax courses). Many of these taxes, such as those on tobacco and liquor, are collected routinely on a clearly defined product from a small number of taxpayers (often manufacturers). Whatever their economic merit, many excise taxes meet the test of raising significant sums at low administrative costs.

Some comparative figures of federal receipts are given in the following table:

SOURCES OF FEDERAL REVENUES
Table 1–1: 1800–1985*
(Amounts in Millions of Dollars)

Year	Customs	Income Taxes	Other	Total Receipts
1800	9.1		1.7	10.8
1870	194.5	37.8	179.0	411.3
1900	233.2		334.0	567.2
1920	322.9	3,945.0	2,427.1	6,695.0
1930	587.00	2,411.0	1,180.0	4,178.0
1940	349.0	2,125.0	2,791.0	5,265.0
1950	407.0	26,204.0	12,832.0	39,443.0
1960	1,105.0	62,209.0	29,178.0	92,492.0
1970	2,430.0	123,241.0	67,136.0	192,807.0
1975	3,676.0	163,007.0	112,407.0	279,090.0
1980	7,174.0	308,669.0	201,269.0	517,112.0
1985	12,079.0	395,862.0	326,147.0	734,088.0

* Because of changes in accounting procedures, the figures for recent years are not wholly comparable with those for earlier years. The chief difference is in the figure for "total receipts," which now includes the figures for federal trust funds, such as the Social Security and highway trust funds.

Table 1–2: 1990–2016
(Amounts are in Millions of Dollars)

Year	Excise Taxes	Income Taxes	Estate & Gift Taxes	Payroll Taxes	Total Receipts
1990	27,139	650,245	11,762	367,219	1,056,366
1995	44,981	850,201	15,144	465,405	1,375,732
2000	68,865	1,211,751	29.010	652,852	2,025,191

Year	Excise Taxes	Income Taxes	Estate & Gift Taxes	Payroll Taxes	Total Receipts
2005	73,094	1,206,004	24,764	794,125	2,153,611
2010	66,909	1,089,986	18,885	864,814	2,162,724
2015	76,457	1,784,565	19,119	1,019,263	2,899,405
2016	74,532	1,740,856	21,337	1,070,578	2,907,303

Source: Statistics of Income, Internal Revenue Service,
https://www.irs.gov/statistics/soi-tax-stats-collections-and-refunds-
by-type-of-tax-irs-data-book-table-1

The graph that follows depicts the levels of the individual income tax, the corporate income tax, and payroll taxes as a percentage of total federal revenues for the 81-year period 1935–2016:

Figure 1.3
Sources of Federal Revenue, as Percentages
of Federal Revenue, 1935–2016

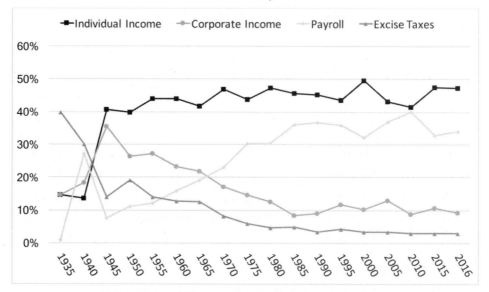

https://www.whitehouse.gov/omb/budget/Historicals

In addition to federal taxes, taxes in the United States also are levied by state and local governments, with each state or locality administering and enforcing its own tax laws. The fiscal arrangements among the three levels of government are complex. Each raises revenue on its own, but there is also a substantial intergovernmental flow of revenue. The following graph compares total government receipts and total federal receipts for the period 1954–2016:

Figure 1.4
Total Federal Receipts vs. Total Government Receipts
1950 to 2016

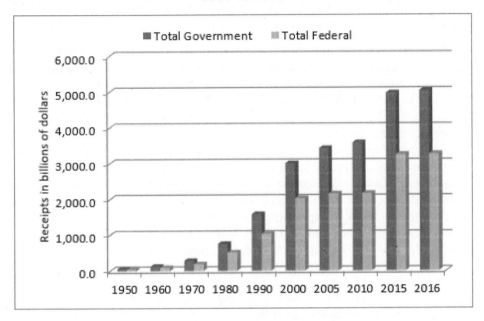

http://www.whitehouse.gov/omb/budget/Historicals Table 14.1

At the state level, the sales tax and the income tax are the main sources of tax revenue. This represents a dramatic shift from the earlier part of this century when almost half of state tax revenues came from property taxes. Five states have no sales tax and seven states have no individual income taxes. The structure of state taxation varies. Most state income tax schemes resemble the federal system. State rates are, of course, lower than federal rates. Some states use the amount reported on the federal return as the starting point for completing state returns. Many individual and business taxpayers are required to file more than one state tax return.

Sales taxes are collected by vendors at the point of sale. A variety of exemptions and rate differentials across the states add to the complexity of sales tax systems. For example, many states attempt to soften the regressivity of sales taxes by exempting certain essentials like food or medicine. Sales tax rates now range from 2.9 percent to 7.25 percent (combined with average local sales tax, the top rates sometimes exceed 10 percent); by comparison, in the 1930s when the first state sales taxes were adopted, the top rate was 3 percent. Sales taxes have come to play an increasing fiscal role for state governments, one that varies more from state to state than it did in the past.

At the local level, the major source of tax revenue is still the property tax, imposed primarily on real property and on business inventory and equipment. There is great variability in the assessments of property of equal value even within the same state, and underassessment seems to be "the rule rather than the exception." As a result, the property tax is the subject of widespread criticism, and there has been some tendency by local governments to diversify their revenue sources by imposing local sales or income taxes if state law allows it.

Although the populace often complains about high taxes, taxes in the United States are lower as a percentage of gross domestic product than in many other countries. When one adds state and local taxes to the federal take, total U.S. taxes are about 26.2 percent of GDP. This is low by international standards—the average for Organization for Economic Cooperation and Development ("OECD") countries is about 34 percent, with a range from 17 to 46 percent. In the OECD, only Chile, Turkey, Mexico and Ireland enjoy total taxes lower as a percentage of GDP than the United States. But other countries' spending patterns are also different, especially with regard to health and education, where the government's share of spending is much higher than in the United States. The table and graphs below, which were derived from statistics collected by the OECD, show the relative percentages over time:

Table 1-3
Tax Revenues as a Percentage of GDP
United States and Selected Trading Partners
1995 to 2015

Country	1995	2000	2005	2010	2015
U.S.	26.5	28.2	25.9	23.5	26.2
Canada	34.8	34.8	32.2	30.6	32.0
France	41.9	43.1	42.8	42.0	45.2
Germany	36.2	36.2	33.9	35.0	37.1
Italy	38.6	40.6	39.1	41.9	43.3
Japan	26.4	26.6	27.3	27.6	30.7
U.K.	29.8	32.8	32.5	32.5	32.5

Source: https://stats.oecd.org/Index.aspx?DataSetCode=REV

Figure 1.5
Total Tax Revenue as a Percentage of Gross Domestic Product
U.S. and OECD Countries (on Average)
1990 to 2015

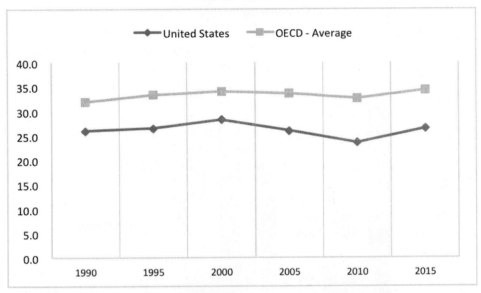

Source: https://stats.oecd.org/Index.aspx?DataSetCode=REV#

The United States relies more heavily on income and payroll taxes than do our trading partners, many of whom use consumption taxes, in particular value added taxes, more extensively.

Table 1–4
Type of Tax as Percentage of Total Tax Revenues
2015

Type of Tax	Canada	France	Germany	Italy	Japan*	UK	US
Indiv. Income	36.8	18.9	26.7	26.2	18.9	27.9	40.8
Corp. Income	9.8	4.6	4.7	4.8	12.9	7.5	8.3
Payroll	17.3	14.6	37.9	30.2	39.7	18.6	23.7
Property	11.8	8.9	2.9	6.4	8.5	12.5	10.4
Goods/ Services	23.2	24.4	27.2	27.1	19.8	32.9	16.8
Other	0.1	2.5	0.0	4.0	0.3	0.0	0.0

* Data for Japan is from 2014

Source: https://stats.oecd.org/Index.aspx?DataSetCode=REV#

Figure 1.6
Taxes as a Percentage of Gross Domestic Product
U.S. and OECD Countries (on Average)
Individual, Corporate, Social Security, Property,
and Goods and Services Taxes
2014

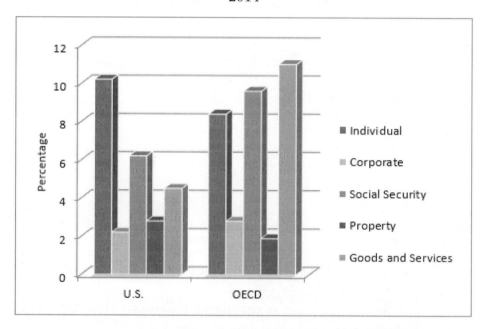

Source: https://stats.oecd.org/Index.aspx?DataSetCode=REV#

The composition of the tax base reflects important policy decisions. In general, excise and payroll taxes are often earmarked to fund specific expenditures: for example, our payroll taxes fund retirement, disability, and survivors insurance under the Social Security system and hospital insurance for the elderly under Medicare. General revenue needs are more likely to be funded by income or consumption taxes. Total federal revenues have increased over time in both real and nominal terms because national output—GDP—has grown consistently over a long period of time. See Figure 1.1, supra at page 13. The important point here is that economic growth has long been the engine of federal revenues—not changes in the kinds or rates of tax, or a dramatically more burdensome federal tax structure.

Note on the Distribution of Income and Income Taxes

Income is distributed quite unequally in the United States, and over the last five decades, it grew considerably more unequal. First, a greater share of total wages has been going to highly-skilled, -trained, and -educated workers at the top of the income distribution. This is due both to a shift away from goods-producing industries, which had provided relatively high wage opportunities for relatively low-skilled workers, to technical services industries, which disproportionately employ college graduates, and within-industry shifts in labor demand away from less-educated workers. Other factors are the decline in the proportion of workers who belong to unions, intensifying global competition, and the increasing use of temporary or part-time workers. Second, changes in family composition and living arrangements have increased the differences in families' incomes. Here, the key factor is the shift away from higher income married-couple households toward single-parent households, especially where the head of household has only a high school education or less. Others attribute today's greater inequality to the decline of policies developed during the New Deal and World War II, such as policies supporting unions, the extent of employer provision of health and retirement benefits, and changing norms with respect to pay inequality.

Students are often surprised at the levels of income at various percentiles of the income distribution. In 2016, for example, according to the Census Bureau, median household income in the United States was $59,039. Twenty percent of households had income of $24,002 or less; 80 percent had income of $121,018 or less. Income of $225,251 or more put a household in the top 5 percent. This is about the income of a young associate at a large urban law firm.

Income for tax purposes is calculated differently from the Census Bureau's measure of household income, but tax data show a similar dispersion of income. The dispersion of after-tax income is a bit more equal than pretax income because the U.S. tax system is somewhat progressive. The individual income tax is quite progressive, as the following data from tax returns filed in 2015, published in the IRS *Statistics of Income Bulletin*, demonstrates:

Table 1-5
Dispersion of After-Tax Income
2014

	Returns (millions)	AGI (billions)	Total tax	Tax as % of AGI
Less than $20,000	47.7	270.0	6.6	2.4%
$20,000–$50,000	45.0	1,489.3	87.1	5.8%
$50,000–$100,000	32.2	2,303.6	223.5	9.7%
$100,000–$200,000	17.5	2,361.8	308.9	13.1%
$200,000–$500,000	5.0	1,419.8	263.0	18.5%
$500,000–$1M	.8	562.6	141.4	25.1%
$1M–$10M	.5	858.3	245.6	28.6%

	Returns (millions)	AGI (billions)	Total tax	Tax as % of AGI
Over $10M	.02	505.7	126.3	25.0%
Total	148.6	9,771.0	1,402.4	14.4%

Source: https://www.irs.gov/pub/irs-soi/14inintaxreturns.pdf

Note that returns with income above $200,000 accounted for 16.0 percent of the returns filed, 58.4 percent of the total income, and paid 77.4 percent of the income tax. Although the income tax is quite progressive, it has done little to eliminate the "income gap."

The top 0.8 percent of households collectively earned considerably more after-tax income than the bottom 44.8 percent of households and paid 41 percent of income taxes in 2015.

SECTION 3.   INTRODUCTION TO INCOME TAX TERMINOLOGY

This section offers an overview of some of the tax terminology to be used throughout this book. It is important for students to acquire a general familiarity with these terms and concepts early in their study of taxation; the details are provided subsequently.

Income tax is generally computed by multiplying *taxable income*—that is, *gross income* minus certain *deductions*—by the appropriate *tax rates*. This tax is then reduced by any allowable tax *credits* to determine the amount due.

Gross income has been broadly defined by the Code and the Supreme Court to encompass "all income from whatever source derived." Thus, an individual's income may include not only wages, commissions, and other compensation for services, but also dividends, lottery winnings, discharges of indebtedness, and so forth. Congress has expressly excluded some receipts, however, that otherwise might be characterized as income—for example certain fringe benefits provided by an employer to its employees, such as health insurance. Income includes not only cash receipts, but also receipts in the form of services, property, or payments to third parties on the taxpayer's behalf.

Gross income also includes *gains* derived from the sale of securities, real estate, works of art, and other tangible and intangible property. The amount of gain generally is the excess of the price at which the taxpayer sold the property over the price at which she purchased the property. For example, a taxpayer who bought a share of stock for $50 and later sold it for $70 would realize a $20 taxable gain and a $50 nontaxable return of capital. The portion of the sales proceeds that the taxpayer may recover without incurring tax liability is called her *basis* in the property. The owner's *adjusted basis* in a purchased asset typically is her purchase price adjusted upward or downward to reflect subsequent expenditures or tax benefits attributable to the asset. If the adjusted basis exceeds the sales price, there is a *loss,* which sometimes may be taken into account for tax purposes. Gains and losses are not taken into account as they accrue over time, but only when they are *realized* by a sale or other disposition of the property. Gross income issues are examined in Chapter 2.

Various provisions of the Code allow or disallow the *deduction* of certain expenditures in the computation of taxable income. For individuals, a distinction is made between expenses incurred in the production of business income, which are often deductible, and personal expenses, which generally are not deductible. Only a few of the latter are deductible without regard to a profit-seeking motive—including, for example, home mortgage interest, certain state taxes up to a limit, medical expenses, and charitable deductions—the so-called *itemized deductions.* First, certain expenses (generally business expenses) are subtracted by individuals from gross income to obtain *adjusted gross income.* Then either the *standard deduction* or *itemized deductions* are subtracted from adjusted gross income to obtain taxable income. The standard deduction is a flat amount specified by the Code that varies with marital status, which the taxpayer may deduct regardless of actual expenses. If taxpayers are entitled to itemized deductions in excess of the standard deduction, they will claim the itemized deductions rather than the standard deduction. Itemized deductions are defined as all allowable deductions other than the deductions allowable in arriving at adjusted gross income. Taxpayers generally prefer deductions from gross income to deductions from adjusted gross income, since they benefit from the latter only when they total more than the applicable standard deduction. In addition, certain itemized deductions can be claimed only when they exceed a percentage of adjusted gross income; by reducing adjusted gross income, a larger itemized deduction sometimes may be claimed. Adjusted gross income, the standard deduction, and itemized deductions are concepts applicable to individual taxpayers; corporations simply subtract all allowable deductions from gross income to obtain taxable income.

Some expenditures incurred in the production of income (for example, the cost of a building) cannot be deducted immediately in the year paid or accrued. Instead, the expenditure must be *capitalized*—that is, added to the taxpayer's adjusted basis in the property with respect to which the expense was incurred. The taxpayer may recover some of these capital expenditures over a period of years by means of annual deductions for *depreciation* or *amortization;* he may recover other expenditures only upon the sale of the asset, when they will serve to reduce the gain (or increase the loss) he realizes. The following simple example illustrates this principle: a taxpayer pays $30,000 to obtain a piece of land and another $100,000 to construct a factory on the land. Neither expenditure is immediately deductible from income. The structure is a depreciable asset whose cost may be recovered over the first

39 years of its productive life in accordance with a prescribed schedule of annual depreciation deductions. The land, on the other hand, is a nondepreciable asset whose cost may be recovered only upon its sale by the taxpayer. Although the dollar amount of deductions may be the same regardless of when they are allowed to be taken, taxpayers often prefer earlier deductions because of the resulting opportunity to defer tax liability on an offsetting amount of income and to earn interest on the taxes saved. The 2017 legislation allows an immediate deduction for the purchase of certain "qualified property," which includes, for example, machinery and the costs of producing movies or television shows. Deductions are considered in Chapter 3.

The Code accords special tax treatment to *capital gains* and *capital losses* arising from the sale of certain (usually investment) property that the taxpayer has held for a specified period. For individual taxpayers, long-term capital gains (as well as dividends) are taxed at more favorable rates than ordinary income. Capital losses are deductible to a more limited extent than ordinary losses, and generally are allowed to offset only $3,000 a year of an individual's ordinary income, such as wages or interest. Taxpayers seek to characterize an asset as "capital" or "ordinary" depending on whether its disposition produces a profit or a loss. This distinction between capital and ordinary gains and losses involves numerous Code sections and has generated quite a large body of complicated case law. The treatment of capital gains and losses is considered in detail in Chapter 5, but an awareness that capital gains are treated favorably and that deductions of capital losses are limited is assumed throughout.

Once taxable income is determined, the *tax rates* are applied. Individuals calculate their tax according to one of four tax-rate tables that depend on their filing status (married filing jointly, married filing separately, head of household, or single). The 2017 legislation added a new deduction from taxable income for up to 20 percent of certain business income earned by a sole proprietor or as a partner or shareholder in a partnership, limited liability company, or Subchapter S corporation. This deduction is equivalent to a 20 percent reduction in the tax rates on such income and is discussed in Chapter 4. The income tax is *progressive* in that the rate of tax applied to an individual's income increases as income increases. Although the income tax has always been somewhat progressive, the degree of progressivity has varied considerably. Prior to 1964, the rates applicable to individuals ranged from 11 percent to 90 percent. Currently these rates range from 10 percent to 37 percent and are found in § 1. The standard deduction, the rate tables, and certain other amounts specified in the Code are all adjusted for inflation.

It is important to distinguish between the *average rate* of tax applicable to taxable income as a whole and the *marginal rate* applicable to the last dollar of taxable income. Imagine a tax system in which taxpayers paid tax at a rate of 25 percent of their taxable income up to $20,000 and a rate of 50 percent on all taxable income above $20,000. We can now compute the tax of a taxpayer with $50,000 of taxable income:

Tax:	.25 × 20,000	=	$5,000
	.50 × 30,000	=	$15,000
			$20,000

Average rate = 40 percent (20,000/50,000).

Marginal rate = 50 percent (rate of tax on last dollar of taxable income).

Suppose this taxpayer is entitled to a $5,000 deduction for business expenses. He will save tax at his marginal rate of 50 percent even though his average rate is 40 percent. His tax bill will go down by $2,500 and, consequently, his average tax rate will go down.

Gross Income			$50,000
Deduction		−	($5,000)
Taxable Income			$45,000
Tax	.25 × 20,000	=	5,000
	.50 × 25,000	=	12,500
			$17,500

Average rate = 38.89 percent (17,500/45,000).

Marginal rate = 50 percent.

The tax savings of additional dollars of deduction and the tax cost of additional income always should be evaluated at the relevant marginal tax rate.

Tax sometimes can be saved by shifting income to a taxpayer in a lower marginal tax bracket or shifting deductions to a taxpayer in a higher bracket. Chapter 4 discusses this shifting. A similar strategy also applies to changes in one taxpayer's marginal rate from year to year. It is to the taxpayer's advantage to report a gain in a year when her marginal tax bracket is low. Moreover, if tax rates and the timing of non-tax cash outlays do not change, it is better to pay a dollar of tax in the future than now. The longer the tax payment can be deferred, the greater the advantage to the taxpayer who can invest the money and earn interest during the interval. This idea is captured in the concept of present discounted value, which is the value now of money to be received or paid at some future time. Timing issues recur throughout this book and are reviewed in Chapter 6. A table of present values is set forth in the Appendix.

Taxpayers may reduce their tax liability by the amount of any *credits* for which they are eligible. A credit represents a direct reduction in tax in the amount of the allowable credit, while a deduction represents a reduction in taxable income that, in turn, reduces tax liability by the amount of the allowable deduction multiplied by the taxpayer's marginal rate. Thus, a deduction is of greater dollar value to taxpayers with greater taxable income, while a credit provides generally similar reductions in tax to all taxpayers. Most credits are nonrefundable, which means they only offset tax liability. A few, like the earned income credit and a portion of the child tax credit, are refundable, and for those, the taxpayer receives a refund to the extent the credit exceeds the tax liability. Consider, for example, the different effects of a credit and a deduction on the tax liabilities of A, who has taxable income of $550,000, and B, who has taxable income of $9,500. A $1,000 deduction would decrease A's tax liability by $370 ($1,000 multiplied by A's marginal tax rate of 37 percent), but would decrease B's tax liability by only $100 ($1,000 multiplied by B's marginal tax rate of 10 percent). A $200 credit would reduce the tax liability of both A and B by $200. The difference between the effects of credits and deductions becomes more pronounced as the difference between the bottom and top tax rates widens.

Summary. The description above illustrates the computation of income tax liability. The following five steps summarize that computation. The references to the relevant Internal Revenue Code sections provided parenthetically here are—as you will soon learn— merely a starting point in the determination of the tax. Other Code sections often alter the general rules provided in this section.

STEP ONE: Calculate *gross income* (§ 61).

STEP TWO: Subtract *"above-the-line"* deductions (enumerated in § 62). The resulting figure is known as *adjusted gross income* (§ 62).

STEP THREE: Subtract *"below-the-line"* deductions[5] = *either* the *standard deduction* or *itemized deductions* (start with §§ 63 and 67). The resulting figure is known as *taxable income* (§ 63). (If the special deduction for certain business income of individuals is available, reduce taxable income by the allowable amount.)

STEP FOUR: Apply the *tax rate schedules* (found in § 1) to *taxable income* to determine tentative tax liability.

STEP FIVE: Subtract from tentative *tax liability* any available *tax credits*. Bear in mind the important distinction between deductions and credits; deductions reduce

---

[5] The personal exemption is a below-the-line deduction taken in addition to either the standard deduction or itemized deductions. (§ 151). The amount of the personal exemption was set to zero for tax years 2018 through 2025 by the 2017 legislation to partially offset the increased standard deduction and child tax credit.

income, while credits directly reduce tax liability. The remaining amount is final tax liability.

A second tax computation is required of certain individuals who otherwise might pay little or no tax as a result of so-called items of tax preference that reduce their tax liability. This *alternative minimum tax* (AMT) imposes tax on a broader income tax base that is reduced by fewer deductions, exclusions, and credits than the regular base. The impact of the AMT was substantially reduced by the 2017 legislation, and it has no impact at all for taxpayers with income below its exemption level of $109,400 for a married couple in 2018. The exemption is not fully phased out for a married couple until AMT income reaches $1 million. The minimum tax provisions were intended to improve the fairness of the income tax by ensuring that taxpayers cannot reduce their tax liabilities to zero by combining tax preferences, exclusions, deductions, or credits, but this is achieved only at the cost of considerable complexity. Since the minimum tax must be paid whenever it is greater than the regular tax for which the individual otherwise would be liable, many taxpayers engage in tax planning and tax computations under both the AMT and regular provisions. The AMT provisions can be found in §§ 55–59 of the Code. Given its complexity and limited scope, the AMT is not considered further in this book.

The income tax is assessed on an annual basis. The *taxable year* for most individuals and many businesses is simply the calendar year. Income or loss typically is allocated to one taxable year or another according to one of the two basic methods of accounting. The *cash method* generally includes items in income in the year in which they are received and allows items as deductions in the year in which they are paid. The *accrual method* includes items in income when earned, regardless of when they are actually received, and generally allows items as deductions in the year in which they are incurred, regardless of when they actually are paid. Most individuals and many service businesses use the cash method, while manufacturing, wholesale and retail, and other corporations typically use the accrual method. (The 2017 legislation expanded the ability of many small businesses to use the cash method.) Tax accounting is the subject of Chapter 7.

While the taxation of entities is not generally the subject of this coursebook, it is helpful to know the basic federal income tax treatment of various entities. Corporations, trusts, and estates generally are treated under the Internal Revenue Code as distinct taxpaying entities (although trusts and estates do not pay tax on income currently distributed to beneficiaries). Partnerships, limited liability companies, and certain privately held corporations (known as S corporations), in contrast, are generally treated as conduits through which the income or losses of the business flow to the partners (or shareholders) to be included in their individual returns.

Beginning in 2018, corporations are taxed at a flat rate of 21 percent. No deduction is allowed a corporation for income distributed as dividends to its shareholders; hence, these distributions sometimes are said to incur "double taxation"—once at the corporate level, and again at the shareholder level—to the extent that both parties are subject to tax. The lower rate on dividends received by individuals was enacted in 2003 to reduce the combination of the individual and corporate taxes.

The undistributed income of trusts and estates is taxed under a separate rate schedule. Trust income, however, may remain taxable to a grantor who retains a reversionary interest in the trust or who has certain powers under the trust instrument.

Filling in the details of this introduction to tax terminology is the task of the remainder of this book. As quickly will become clear, this chore frequently becomes quite complex.

SECTION 4.   WHY TAX INCOME?

Note Introducing Criteria for Evaluating Taxes

How do we decide whether a particular tax is "good" or "bad"? There is widespread agreement that the criteria to be used in evaluating taxes are equity, efficiency, and simplicity. There is considerably less agreement, however, as to the precise meaning of these criteria and the relative priorities that they should be accorded, as well as to such underlying facts as the effect of a tax on people's behavior.

The Equity Criterion. Tax equity requires that those with greater ability to pay taxes should pay more tax. It follows that those with equal ability to pay taxes should pay equal amounts of tax. In other words, for a tax to be "fair," it should not impose significantly different burdens on those in similar economic circumstances.

This requires a determination of what are "similar economic circumstances" so that we can determine the identity of equals. The tax base is used to implement that criterion. Our current tax base is "income." Alternative bases are discussed in a Note infra at page 36. Thus, in an income tax, people with the same income ordinarily would pay the same amount of tax regardless of the source and use of their income, while people with greater income would pay greater amounts of that income in tax. (The first prong of this test often is termed "horizontal equity" while the second is termed "vertical equity.") The succeeding Note discusses justifications for a progressive rate structure.

Even assuming that Congress has agreed on the appropriate distribution of the tax burden and that income best measures ability to pay, there remains the difficult chore of defining income. Chapter 2 explores the parameters of the tax law's definition of "income." In principle, the definition of income should be such that those with equal ability to pay should be taxed the same and those with unequal ability to pay should be taxed differently.

It is also important that a tax system be perceived to be fair by the populace. If it is not, noncompliance may be widespread.

Finally, the distributional criterion suggested here—that people with greater ability to pay (as measured by income) should bear greater tax burdens is itself controversial. For example, some people claim that ability to pay is better measured by consumption or wealth and, therefore, that is what should be taxed. Others contend that equity should be based on one's capacity to pay taxes, so that, for example, people with equal capacities to earn income should be taxed the same. And for some, distributional concerns should focus on equality of opportunity rather than the distribution of income.

The Efficiency Criterion. The efficiency criterion rests on the assumption that, left to themselves, individuals will act to maximize their well-being. If that is true, then taxes that alter people's behavior will reduce total well-being. Hence, economists sometimes state that efficiency requires that a tax interfere as little as possible with the allocation of goods and services that would occur in a market economy in the absence of taxes. In some fundamental sense, describing economic efficiency this way is nonsensical because a market economy cannot function in the absence of government, which in turn must be financed through taxation. Moreover, the hypothesis that people act to maximize total well-being would hold true only under certain idealized circumstances. Still, even in a world that does not meet these conditions, people are rightly concerned with potential reductions in the economy's ability to satisfy consumer demands because taxes change people's incentives to engage in important economic activities, such as work, savings, domestic or foreign investment, risk taking, or consumption.

Almost all taxes have efficiency costs, that is, they are non-neutral, because they will change the incentives to engage in various activities and this is likely to affect people's behavior and thus the allocation of resources. Sometimes Congress may consciously use a tax to affect behavior or to reallocate resources. But often the distortions are undesirable. There are two essential questions: how does a tax or a tax rule lead people to change their behavior? Why is the change desirable or objectionable? The first of these questions is empirical, the second normative. Generally, a "good" tax is thought to be one that has as few efficiency costs as possible (given the need to satisfy other criteria, such as equity).

The efficiency criterion sometimes has other meanings. A tax often is said to be efficient when it promotes economic growth and inefficient when it inhibits such growth. Finally, efficiency sometimes refers to the extent to which incentive provisions provide benefits to taxpayers other than the intended beneficiaries. Where, for example, an unintended third party receives a benefit, or where the intended beneficiary receives less than the government loses in tax revenue, the tax provision is said to be inefficient.

On some important issues of tax policy, the norms of equity and efficiency are in harmony. For example, both economic efficiency and equity generally support uniform treatment of various sources and uses of income under an income tax. In other circumstances, however, equity and efficiency conflict. For example, equity might support taxing income when economic efficiency would imply taxing consumption or wages. Likewise, the disincentive for earning income may be increased under a progressive rate structure that applies higher rates to greater amounts of income, but a society's sense of tax justice may demand such progressivity.

The Simplicity Criterion. Simplicity often is viewed not as a separate norm, but as a feature of any tax system that is both equitable and efficient. Complex tax rules are inefficient because taxpayers must divert time from other activities in order to calculate their taxes (or to earn the money to pay for professional or computer tax assistance) and because the government must maintain a large agency to interpret these complex rules and to ensure that taxes are calculated correctly.

Moreover, complexity is inequitable because taxpayers with equal abilities to pay may have different tax burdens because of their unequal abilities to understand or manipulate the tax rules. Generally, wealthier citizens are better able to turn tax ambiguities and complicated rules to their advantage in minimizing tax. Ambiguity and uncertainty also have a tendency to reward the most aggressive adversaries in a self-assessment system of reporting income tax liability such as ours where only a small percentage of returns filed each year are audited by the Internal Revenue Service. Of course, one would never intentionally design a tax system to benefit its strongest adversaries and penalize those most diligent in trying to comply with its requirements.

Adam Smith stated well the simplicity criterion: "The tax which each individual is bound to pay ought to be certain, and not arbitrary. The time of payment, the manner of payment, and the quantity to be paid ought to be clear and plain to the contributor, and to every other person. * * * Every tax ought to be levied at the time or in the manner in which it is most likely to be convenient for the contributor to pay it."

Unfortunately, the Internal Revenue Code—our nation's tax law—is extraordinarily complex. In a far simpler time long ago, Albert Einstein regarded the federal income tax as the hardest thing in the world to understand. Completing his own return, Einstein reputedly remarked, "This is too difficult for a mathematician. It takes a philosopher." More than sixty years ago, the renowned Judge Learned Hand expressed his frustration with the complexity of our tax laws:

In my own case the words of such an act as the Income Tax, for example, merely dance before my eyes in a meaningless procession: cross-reference to cross-reference, exception upon exception—couched in abstract terms that offer no handle to seize hold of—leave in my mind only a confused sense of some vitally important, but successfully concealed, purport, which it is my duty to extract, but which is within my power, if at all, only after the most inordinate expenditure of time.

Learned Hand, The Spirit of Liberty 213 (1952).

As you study the current Internal Revenue Code, you too will quickly become convinced that it is not simple. You should try to understand why it is so complex. Professor David Bradford described three kinds of complexity: compliance, transactional, and rule complexity. David F. Bradford, Untangling the Income Tax 266–67 (1986). The most easily understood is "rule complexity," which refers to the problems of understanding and interpreting the law. Rule complexity emanates not only from statutes, but also from administrative rules (regulations and rulings) and case law. If one cannot understand her obligations (or cannot afford to pay someone to explain them), a rule that covers all the contingencies may be unenforceable.

"Compliance complexity" is the complexity that one encounters in complying with the law, that is, keeping the required records and filling out the appropriate forms. Any tax that requires extensive recordkeeping and perhaps professional tax assistance for ordinary citizens cannot be described as simple. Compliance complexity also refers to the government's ability to administer the law.

"Transactional complexity" is the complexity that arises when taxpayers organize their affairs to minimize taxes. It is created any time the tax law treats similar economic transactions differently. For example, in a particular transaction, the difference between a sale and a lease may be economically insignificant, but may have dramatically different tax consequences. Since the stakes are often quite high, a premium is placed on the form of the transaction. Furthermore, the taxation of business and investment income is inherently complicated because the transactions themselves are complex.

The complexity of the tax law is fair game for the jabs of politicians and pundits alike who delight at ridiculing 200-word sentences in the Internal Revenue Code. Simplifying the tax law, however, has proven to be a daunting political task. Despite universal complaints about complexity, there is no effective political constituency for tax simplification, and when Congress must choose between a simplification of the tax law and a complex alternative that either produces additional revenue or is claimed to increase economic efficiency or tax equity, the quest for simplification far too often is abandoned. Thus, complexity will continue to be a hallmark of our tax system.

The Special Problems of Economic Globalization. A nation's ability to impose taxes through a carefully structured compromise among the norms of equity, economic efficiency, and simplicity is severely limited by both flexibility in legal arrangements and the internationalization of economic activity. Because capital, in particular, is extremely mobile across international boundaries, national sovereignty over tax policy is threatened. For example, a nation's view of tax fairness may demand high and steeply progressive rates on capital income, but its ability to implement such a policy can be thwarted by citizens shifting wealth into foreign corporations and other entities employing that capital abroad. If a nation competing for capital investment reduces its taxes on capital or capital income to make such investment more attractive, an international race to the bottom—a "beggar thy neighbor" policy—can result and in the process undermine each nation's independent tax equity goals.

Issues of international taxation are not taken up in this introduction to income taxation, but international conflicts in applying tax policy norms to transactions that cross national borders inevitably must be faced. And these conflicts not only determine the economic burdens that may apply to the individuals who supply the capital for such transactions, but also produce debates about the appropriate sharing of tax revenues among the countries involved. The system of international taxation that governs transactions in today's modern global economy, which is characterized by instantaneous communication and capital transfers, is in substantial part a relic from the early part of the 20th century, a time that predates both transoceanic flights and telephone calls. Improving this archaic system may well prove the greatest tax policy challenge of our time.[6] Meanwhile, our national ability to collect revenues with fairness and economic efficiency is becoming more difficult. The 2017 Act included major revisions to the U.S. system of taxing international business income.

Note: Why Progressive Income Tax Rates?

Although the federal income tax has always had a progressive rate structure, the degree of support for progressivity has varied over time. Some academics and policymakers have suggested replacing the progressive income tax rates with a flat-rate tax. Some of these proposals would dramatically redistribute the tax burden from upper-income individuals to middle- and lower-income individuals. It therefore seems appropriate to reassess the arguments for progressivity that have recurred over time.

First, progressive rates are defended as essential to taxation based on ability to pay. This requires one to accept that those with larger incomes are better able to pay taxes than those with smaller incomes. The standard assumption is that equal amounts of income are not of

---

[6] For one of the authors' views, see Michael J. Graetz Follow the Money: Essays on International Taxation, available for free download at documents.law.yale.edu/follow-the-money.

equal value to all recipients. Instead, the incremental value of additional income is assumed to decline as income rises; for example, an additional $100 means less to a person earning $100,000 than to a person earning $10,000 and less to either of them than to a person earning $1,000.

This argument is criticized on the ground that the importance of particular preferences to individual taxpayers cannot be measured objectively. Indeed, there is little reason to assume that the progressive rate schedule is systematically related to the declining marginal utility of income.

Second, progressive rates are defended as a deliberate mechanism for reducing economic inequalities. The progressive income tax, however, has in fact done relatively little to reduce economic disparities in American society.

Third, progressive rates are said to be necessary to produce proportionality of the overall tax burden by offsetting the effects of other, more regressive taxes (such as federal payroll and excise taxes, state and local sales taxes, and perhaps property taxes).

Finally, some analysts defend progressive rates on the ground that the benefits of government expenditures increase progressively with income and wealth. This assertion seems to require acceptance of the view that governmental expenditures on international affairs, national defense, and public order are of special importance to those who are well off. Moreover, today many large government expenditures, particularly transfers through Social Security, Medicare, and Medicaid, benefit the less well-off. For example, taking benefits into account, the Social Security system is progressive even though it is financed by a flat-rate payroll tax applicable to wages up to a specified ceiling.

The appropriate distributions of income and wealth, and the appropriate redistributive role of taxation, are controversial issues ultimately grounded in individual value judgments. In 1953, law professors Walter Blum and Harry Kalven attempted to demonstrate that the case for progressive taxation was "stubborn but uneasy," concluding:

> It is hard to gain much comfort from the special arguments * * * constructed on notions of benefit, sacrifice, ability to pay, or economic stability. The case has stronger appeal when progressive taxation is viewed as a means of reducing economic inequalities. But the case for more economic equality, when examined directly, is itself perplexing. And the perplexity is greatly magnified for those who in the quest for greater equality are unwilling to argue for radical changes in the fundamental institutions of the society.[7]

---

[7]   Walter Blum & Harry Kalven, The Uneasy Case for Progressive Taxation 103–04 (1953). Professor Blum, in a 1982 retrospective, concluded: "In the 1950's the case for progressive taxation was not easy. Subsequent developments in our society have made it no less, and

Compare the response of Professor Boris Bittker:

> I cannot accept the argument that advocacy of socially-prescribed constraints on economic inequality is so inconsistent with a free market that it constitutes, or should if logically pursued lead to, "radical changes in the fundamental institutions of the society." * * * The case for progressive taxation is "uneasy" but it seems no more uneasy than the case for proportionality or for preferring one tax base over another.[8]

Bittker thus questioned the assumption that progressivity "must meet the burden of proof." He found support for his position in an anecdote offered by Dan T. Smith, former assistant secretary of the Treasury and professor of finance at Harvard. Smith had visited a one-room Montana schoolhouse and asked three children what would be a fair tax on a family with an income of $5,000 if a family with an income of $2,000 paid a tax of $200:

> The first child said, "500 dollars," thereby showing a predisposition for proportional burdens and perhaps a desire to make use of a newly acquired familiarity with percentages. A second child immediately disagreed, with the comment that the payment should be more than 500 dollars because "each dollar isn't so important" to the family with the larger income. A third child agreed but with the reservation that the additional tax over 500 dollars shouldn't be "too much more or they won't work so hard."

In 1998, one of the authors of this book repeated Mr. Smith's experiment in his daughter's fifth grade classroom, and, remarkably, the first three students to speak gave answers identical to the Montana children, in exactly the same order. The intuitions about progressive taxation of the children of the 1990s in a New Haven, Connecticut school mirrored precisely those of Montana school children in the 1960s. After learning that their answers were identical to those of Montana children three decades earlier, many students commented on how "cool," "neat," "amazing," and weird that was. One student concluded, "I guess that must be fair if both of the schools got the same answers," echoing Mr. Smith's earlier comment that "elaborate theoretical structures concerning diminishing utility and incentives and disincentives are all really refinements of the quasi-intuitive opinions of these children and may not lead to any greater certainty."[9]

These two experiments might serve as a caution to those who believe that the American public will regard as fair replacing a progressive tax

---

perhaps even more uneasy." Walter Blum, "Revisiting the Uneasy Case for Progressive Taxation," 60 Taxes 16, 21 (1982).

[8]   Charles Galvin & Boris I. Bittker, The Income Tax: How Progressive Should It Be? 56, 58 (1969).

[9]   Id. at 30–31 (citing Dan T. Smith, "High Progressive Tax Rates: Inequity and Immorality?", 20 U. Fla. L. Rev. 451–52 (1968)).

on income with a flat-rate tax on consumption. That sentiment seems likely to last only until the second child speaks.

Indeed, the analytical starting point of most critics of progressive taxation is highly questionable.[10] They begin with the presumption that the market rewards the strong and fails to reward only the lazy, weak, or undeserving. Since they regard income and wealth as manifestations of merit, they see little reason for taxing such income or wealth in order to fund government programs or redistribution to others.

The assumption that the market distribution is "just" creates the necessity for "making a case" for progressive taxation, indeed for any taxation at all. But there are several reasons not to regard market distributions as inherently fair or as presumptively just.

First, even when the market is functioning perfectly, returns to both capital and labor inputs depend on the demand for the product or service being produced. People who supply capital or labor to endeavors where demand proves strong will do very well; people who work or risk their capital in endeavors where demand proves weak will do badly. These rewards depend on factors outside an individual's control. For example, the enormous demand to follow the life of Kim Kardashian has made her a very wealthy woman. If public tastes were to improve and demand for her services were to decrease, her income would decline dramatically without regard to any change in her ability or work effort.

Second, most production is based on the joint use of different resources provided by different people. It is usually impossible, as an ethical matter, to determine which person produces what share of the total output.

Third, market returns to capital and labor are attributable in part to social conditions. The existence of public institutions—for example, laws and law-enforcement mechanisms—affects returns to private actors. It therefore might be appropriate to ask what portion of returns to labor and capital should be attributed to society rather than to the individual.

Fourth, returns to capital and labor are dramatically affected by luck—for example, being born into a family of wealth and education rather than a family of poverty and ignorance. The empirical evidence shows that much of the wealth of the truly rich is attributable to inherited wealth and enormous one-shot gains. Both of these sources of great wealth are typically "morally arbitrary."

This litany is intended to call into question the typical starting point of people who attack the moral validity of progressive taxation by simply assuming that the market distributes rewards to people who deserve them and denies rewards to people who do not. Little of what we own is attributable to individual merit alone. All receipts are joint products,

---

[10] The material that follows is adapted from Michael Graetz, "To Praise the Estate Tax, Not to Bury It," 93 Yale L.J. 259 (1983).

both individual and societal. Because individual and social characteristics are both essential to their joint outcome, there is simply no means by which a percentage of individual and social "desert" can be calculated.

The justification for a market distribution of income and wealth therefore must rely not on ethics, but on economic efficiency and consumer and producer sovereignty. This reflects the belief that a market economy avoids waste and improves the standard of living even for those with a lesser distributional share as well as the view that minimal governmental interference in the market increases freedom of choice and liberty generally.

Four separate liberties seem to be affected by any change in the market's distribution of income and wealth through taxation. The first is the liberty of consumer sovereignty: people's right to watch TV shows about Kim Kardashian's life and buy products she endorses if they wish. The second is the liberty of producer sovereignty: Kim Kardashian's right to either shun or bask in the limelight based on the amount she would be able to retain after taxes. These two important liberties are not constrained by progressivity in taxation.

The third liberty is Kim Kardashian's right to keep all that she earns based on her celebrity, and the fourth is the right of her heirs to keep whatever of those payments she does not expend before her death. These liberties are not nearly so absolute. Moreover, there are also important conflicting liberties at stake—most significantly, the liberty interests of descendants of other people to start off with a rough equality of opportunity and of initial wealth.

The case for progressive taxation thus becomes far easier when one rejects the strong presumption that preserving the market distribution of income and wealth is necessarily linked to fairness or freedom. Accepting the need for progression does not, however, necessarily require accepting a progressive income tax. For example, some commentators regard the combination of consumption and wealth taxes as superior to a progressive income tax alone.

Note on Alternative Tax Bases

The tax levied is the tax rate multiplied by the tax base. Income is only one of several possible bases for the imposition of tax. For example, state and local and foreign governments often impose tax on consumption (for example, by means of a sales or value-added tax) or on wealth (for example, by means of property taxes and taxes on wealth transferred by gift or at death). This Note considers various bases that might provide a significant long-term source of federal revenues.

Perhaps the most economically efficient tax would be a so-called head tax. A flat tax on each adult American above the poverty level in the amount of $5,000 would raise $1.5 trillion dollars to fund federal expenditures—assuming 300 million people were taxed. Unlike payroll, consumption, wealth, or income taxes, the amount of a head tax would not vary with work effort or earnings, consumption, savings, risk taking, or investment. A person could lawfully avoid the tax only by dying, emigrating, or becoming poor, so a head tax would have minimal impact in changing people's behavior. Despite the appeal of tax avoidance, very few would commit suicide and only a few more might emigrate; the principal behavioral effect would be other efforts to evade the tax. A head tax is manifestly unfair, however, because it ignores people's different abilities to pay, and such a tax has never seriously been proposed in the United States.

In 1987, however, after winning a third term, the government of British Prime Minister Margaret Thatcher proposed a head tax on all adults—labeled a "poll tax" and euphemistically referred to as a "community charge"—to replace local residential property taxes. Despite considerable opposition on the ground that a tax should not be imposed with such disregard for variations in people's ability to pay, the tax was enacted in 1988 and put into effect in Scotland in 1989 and in England and Wales in 1990. The British poll tax was justified by the argument that equal taxation of all people within the taxing jurisdiction would promote greater political oversight by the citizenry of the spending decisions of local government units. This elevation of concerns for economic efficiency over equity proved a political disaster for Mrs. Thatcher and led to her being replaced as the head of Britain's Conservative party in November, 1990. The tax produced protests, civil unrest, and widespread refusals to pay. As many as one-fifth of all taxpayers required a summons to be issued before making payment.[11] The poll tax experience—which apparently married inept implementation to poor policy—made the extremely unpopular local property taxes seem positively benign. This political lesson from across the Atlantic proves both the necessity of public acceptance for tax reform to be successful and the folly of taking the recommendations of the economists too literally.

A tax theoretically could be based on the extent to which people benefit from government goods and services. This concept is currently embodied in the user fees assessed on campers at national parks and, more loosely, in the gasoline tax used to build and maintain federal highways. There are major obstacles, both theoretical and practical, to extending this "benefit theory" to the financing of general government services. One is the difficulty of ascertaining the extent and intensity of taxpayers' demands for and use of each public program. How could defense expenditures, for example, be allocated among taxpayers based on the benefit that each receives? The benefit principle clearly would be inappropriate to transfer programs (such as Social Security, Food

---

[11] See Peter Smith, "Lessons from the British Poll Tax Disaster," 44 Nat'l Tax J. 421 (1991).

Stamps, Medicaid, and other welfare programs) that are, by definition, redistributive. Some might argue, however, that higher income individuals benefit when conditions are less dire for lower income individuals.

Many people feel that everything but the air they breathe (and sometimes even that) is subjected to tax by some level of government. As we have all come to know through experience, virtually any product or transaction can be taxed, and politicians therefore enjoy limitless potential to do mischief in deciding whom and what to tax. In addition, within any tax, there are myriad possible variations on the amount of tax that can be imposed as specific circumstances change. Moreover, in taxation—unlike other practices, such as discrimination in employment—the Constitution offers people no real protection against the whims of the politicians. The legislative playground frequently produces complexities, unfairness, and economic waste, all of which serve to reinforce the public's anti-tax sentiments.

In sharp contrast to the freedom politicians enjoy in determining how, when and where to impose taxes, financial reality severely limits the kinds of taxes that can serve effectively to finance the expenditures of government. All the governments of the world—including the United States—generally are financed by only three or four kinds of taxes: taxes on income, wages, consumption, or wealth. This is no accident. Income, wages, consumption, and wealth are the four general tax bases sufficiently robust to produce the revenues required that also generally can be said to satisfy the dominant criterion of a good tax, namely that it be fair—that the tax be connected in some way to a person's ability to pay. This basic principle of tax fairness was stated well more than two centuries ago by Adam Smith: "The subjects of every state ought to contribute towards the support of government, as nearly as possible in proportion to their respective abilities." Ability to pay has been measured historically in a variety of ways, although the task has always been essentially the same: to find some way to measure people's relative capacity to finance their government. In medieval England, for example, the tax collector counted the number of windows to determine the homeowner's taxpaying capacity. Perhaps tax avoidance explains the label "The Dark Ages."

In modern times, each of these four broad tax bases—wages, consumption, income, and wealth—has been considered potentially capable of satisfying the ability-to-pay criterion. In the United States today, income and wage taxes are together the major sources of federal revenues—accounting for 90 percent of all federal revenues—while consumption and wealth taxes have largely been left to state and local governments as a source of finance.

These four tax bases are linked to one another in a variety of ways. Wages, for example, are a form of income as well as a source of consumption and wealth. Wealth is one use of income and a source of both income and consumption. Income is derived from both wages and wealth and income is used for both consumption and wealth creation.

In terms of sources, an income tax base includes both income from labor and income from capital; in terms of uses, an income tax base includes savings as well as consumption. On the contrary, a consumption tax base exempts income that people save from taxation and, bequests aside, imposes a burden more like a wage tax than an income tax. See Alvin C. Warren Jr., "How Much Capital Income Taxed Under an Income Tax Is Exempt Under a Cash Flow Tax?", 52 Tax L. Rev. 1 (1996).

Sometimes arguments for one of these tax bases over another are advanced by asserting "first principles" of fairness in taxation. Probably the most famous among these is John Stuart Mill's proposition that consumption taxes are the most fair because they tax only what individuals have removed from the common societal pool for their own personal consumption. Others claim income to be a superior tax base because it allows the government to claim a share of the returns from both the labor and capital of its citizens and residents—a share of the nation's total output—output that was made possible because of the existence of a variety of government institutions, including such diverse activities, for example, as the protection of property rights through the courts, public education, police and fire protection, and national defense.

Over a person's lifetime, she will spend (or consume) all of the income that she does not accumulate as wealth or transfer to others as gifts or bequests. Obviously, if one were willing to adopt a lifetime perspective to measure people's abilities to pay, a combination of a consumption tax and a wealth tax—or a consumption tax that treats gifts and bequests as consumption—might be quite good substitutes for a tax on income.

Indeed, many who would replace the current income taxes with consumption taxes argue that a lifetime perspective demonstrates that a consumption tax is fairer than an income tax because it treats equally people who consume identical amounts over their lifetimes in contrast to an income tax, which (by taxing income that is both spent and saved) taxes people who consume early in their lifetimes less heavily than those who postpone consumption by saving until later in life.

To the contrary, if fairness in taxation—taxing in accord with people's relative abilities to pay—should be measured over a shorter time horizon, an income tax base is a more comprehensive measure of a person's ability to pay than either wages or consumption. Although most observers agree that some averaging of progressive rates over a time horizon longer than one year is warranted, some analysts argue for an annual measuring rod of peoples' relative ability to pay since governments must collect taxes at least as frequently as annually.

This debate about the proper time horizon for assessing ability to pay will never be resolved to the satisfaction of the opposing camps; an annual period is no doubt too short for assessing people's relative capacity or ability to pay taxes, and a lifetime is probably too long given the contingencies and uncertainties of personal, political, and economic affairs. Some intermediate period over which the ups and downs of income or consumption can be averaged is probably best, but selecting such a time horizon is inevitably arbitrary, thereby shifting this dispute from the moral high ground of arguing about a "true" measure of fairness onto the quagmire of political compromise and debate. Nevertheless, it is revealing that in the income versus consumption tax debate, proponents of consumption taxes tend to emphasize claims grounded in economic efficiency, while income tax adherents stress fairness arguments.

Consumption taxes in the United States consist of selective excise taxes at the federal level and of retail sales taxes at the state and local levels. In Europe, consumption taxes usually take the form of value-added taxes. A value-added tax typically is collected at each stage of the production process as goods and services move from suppliers, to manufacturers, to wholesalers, to retailers. Sales taxes, in contrast, generally are collected only at the retail level.

These consumption taxes often are imposed at a single rate. Thus, they are proportional with respect to consumption but regressive with respect to income. That is because high-income people tend to devote a smaller percentage of their income to consumption than do lower-income people. Value-added or sales taxes can be made proportional with respect to income, however, if certain consumption items—such as food, housing, and medicine—are excluded from tax or through other provisions designed to reduce burdens on consumption by the poor. In 2016, a unique form of consumption tax (used nowhere in the world) was proposed by House Republicans in their "Blueprint" for tax reform, but the proposal was abandoned in 2017.

The federal employment taxes are the most significant wage taxes levied in the United States. Wage taxes exempt from taxation capital and the income from capital, and consumption taxes sometimes are viewed as similar in this regard. Consequently, many economists have concluded that wage and consumption taxes are less inhibitive of savings and capital formation, and therefore are more conducive to economic growth, than are wealth and income taxes. This perception has contributed to the growing use of wage and consumption taxes at all levels of government. For example, social insurance taxes generated only 10 percent of federal revenues in 1954 but 34 percent of federal revenues by 2016. Proposals for a national sales tax—typically in the form of a value-added tax—resurface every several years.

The same factor that has caused some to embrace wage and consumption taxes on grounds of efficiency has caused others to reject these taxes on grounds of equity: these taxes fail to take into account ability to pay based on the accumulation of capital or on income derived from capital. A person who consumes more may have a greater ability to pay than a person who consumes less, and a person who earns higher wages may have a greater ability to pay than a person who earns lower wages. But neither of these measures in isolation may provide an accurate index of overall economic well-being; consider, for example, the very wealthy person who lives frugally and earns no wages.

Wealth taxes, which are imposed on capital accumulation, offer one means of assuring that taxation is based on ability to pay. One lingering legacy of the constitutional requirement that revenues from direct taxes must be apportioned to the states in accordance with their population, however, is that the federal government does not impose a periodic tax on wealth. Instead, transfers of wealth by gift or bequest have been subject to so-called transfer taxes, better known as estate and gift taxes, which generally account for only 1 percent of federal revenues. The threshold amounts for imposition of these taxes have been set high enough that these taxes have not been a concern for nine out of ten Americans; indeed, the estate tax in recent years applied only to the wealthiest 0.2 percent of Americans who die each year. With the 2017 doubling of the estate tax exemption to more than $22 million for a married couple (indexed for inflation), the tax will apply to only a handful of our nation's wealthiest citizens. However, the federal estate and gift taxes historically have made a significant contribution to the overall progressivity of the tax system. The other major example of wealth taxation in this country is the local property tax, which typically is imposed only on real estate, automobiles, and certain tangible business property.

As you study the materials in this book, ask yourself whether our current federal income tax has, in fact, become a "hybrid" that is part wage or consumption tax and part income tax. Many provisions of the Internal Revenue Code have the effect of taxing income from capital more favorably than income from services or of excluding capital income from the tax base entirely. The hybrid nature of the tax reflects a congressional desire to base taxation on ability to pay, while not unduly inhibiting savings, capital formation, and economic growth.

The case for income as a tax base—rather than other bases discussed in this Note—ultimately is grounded in notions of equity. Notwithstanding its shortcomings, the federal income tax has come to symbolize the nation's commitment to just taxation based on ability to pay. One should not lose sight of this symbolic function of the income tax even while recognizing that there may be considerable dispute about what constitutes greater ability to pay, about the appropriate relationship between greater ability and greater tax burden, and about the appropriate trade-offs among equity, efficiency, and simplicity.

SECTION 5.   THE TAX EXPENDITURE BUDGET

Excerpt from Estimates of Federal Tax Expenditures for Fiscal Years 2016–2020*

Staff of the Joint Committee on Taxation. January 30, 2017.

I.   THE CONCEPT OF TAX EXPENDITURES

Overview

Tax expenditures are defined under the Congressional Budget and Impoundment Control Act of 1974 (the "Budget Act") as "revenue losses attributable to provisions of the Federal tax laws which allow a special exclusion, exemption, or deduction from gross income or which provide a special credit, a preferential rate of tax, or a deferral of tax liability." Thus, tax expenditures include any reductions in income tax liabilities that result from special tax provisions or regulations that provide tax benefits to particular taxpayers.

Special income tax provisions are referred to as tax expenditures because they may be analogous to direct outlay programs and may be considered alternative means of accomplishing similar budget policy objectives. Tax expenditures are similar to direct spending programs that function as entitlements to those who meet the established statutory criteria.

Estimates of tax expenditures are prepared for use in budget analysis. They are a measure of the economic benefits that are provided through the tax laws to various groups of taxpayers and sectors of the economy. The estimates also may be useful in determining the relative merits of achieving specific public goals through tax benefits or direct outlays. It is appropriate to evaluate tax expenditures with respect to cost, distributional consequences, alternative means of provision, and economic effects and to allow policymakers to evaluate the tradeoffs among these and other potentially competing policy goals.

The legislative history of the Budget Act indicates that tax expenditures are to be defined with reference to a normal income tax structure (referred to here as "normal income tax law"). The determination of whether a provision is a tax expenditure is made on the basis of a broad concept of income that is larger in scope than "income" as defined under general U.S. income tax principles. The Joint Committee staff uses its judgment in distinguishing between those income tax provisions (and regulations) that can be viewed as a part of normal income tax law and those special provisions that result in tax expenditures. A provision traditionally has been listed as a tax expenditure by the Joint Committee staff if there is a reasonable basis

---

*   [Ed. Note: These estimates do not reflect the changes made by the 2017 Act.]

for such classification and the provision results in more than a de minimis revenue loss. * * *

Some provisions in the Internal Revenue Code ("the Code") provide for special tax treatment that is less favorable than normal income tax law. Examples of such provisions include (1) the denial of deductions for certain lobbying expenses, (2) the denial of deductions for certain executive compensation, and (3) the two-percent floor on itemized deductions for unreimbursed employee expenses. Tax provisions that provide treatment less favorable than normal income tax law and are not related directly to progressivity are called negative tax expenditures.

* * *

II.   MEASUREMENT OF TAX EXPENDITURES

Tax Expenditure Calculations Generally

A tax expenditure is measured by the difference between tax liability under present law and the tax liability that would result from a recomputation of tax without benefit of the tax expenditure provision. Taxpayer behavior is assumed to remain unchanged for tax expenditure estimate purposes.

* * *

Each tax expenditure is calculated separately, under the assumption that all other tax expenditures remain in the Code. If two or more tax expenditures were estimated simultaneously, the total change in tax liability could be smaller or larger than the sum of the amounts shown for each item separately, as a result of interactions among the tax expenditure provisions.

Year-to-year differences in the calculations for each tax expenditure reflect changes in tax law, including phaseouts of tax expenditure provisions and changes that alter the definition of the normal income tax structure, such as the tax rate schedule, the personal exemption amount, and the standard deduction. For example, the dollar level of tax expenditures tends to increase and decrease as tax rates increase and decrease, respectively, without any other changes in law. * * *

If a tax expenditure provision were eliminated, Congress might choose to continue financial assistance through other means rather than terminate all Federal assistance for the activity. If a replacement spending program were enacted, the higher revenues received as a result of the elimination of a tax expenditure might not represent a net budget gain. A replacement program could involve direct expenditures, direct loans or loan guarantees, regulatory activity, a mandate, a different form of tax expenditure, or a general reduction in tax rates. * * *

Tax Expenditures versus Revenue Estimates

A tax expenditure calculation is not the same as a revenue estimate for the repeal of the tax expenditure provision for three reasons. First, unlike revenue estimates, tax expenditure calculations do not incorporate the effects of the behavioral changes that are anticipated to occur in response to the repeal of a tax expenditure provision. Second, tax expenditure calculations are concerned with changes in the reported tax liabilities of taxpayers. Because tax expenditure analysis focuses on tax liabilities as opposed to Federal government tax receipts, there is no concern for the short-term timing of tax payments. Revenue estimates are concerned with changes in Federal tax receipts that are affected by the timing of all tax payments. * * *

Tax Expenditure Estimates By Budget Function, Fiscal Years 2016–2020 (Billions of dollars)*
(Numbers are total amounts for the five-year period for both individuals and corporations)

National Defense	38.6
International Affairs	699.0
General Science, Space, and Technology	69.1
Energy	98.6
Natural Resources and Environment	12.3
Agriculture	13.0
Commerce and Housing	
Financial Institutions	14.4
Insurance Companies	34.1
Housing	
Mortgage Interest	357.0
Property Taxes (homes)	180.0
Exclusion of Capital Gains on Sale of Homes	166.3
Low Income Housing	45.1
Other Housing	43.7
Other Business and Commerce	
Reduced Rate on Dividends/Capital Gains	677.7
Exclusion of Capital Gains at Death	179.4
Carryover Basis on Gifts	17.0
Installment Sales	40.3
Like Kind Exchanges	90.2
Reduced Rate on Corporate Taxes	15.9
Deduction for Domestic Production Activity Income	102.1

---

   * [Ed. Note: Certain "negative tax expenditures" (also known as tax penalties, see page 260 infra), are listed here and indicated by a * and a negative number. Those not specifically listed are netted with the tax expenditures.]

Section 179 Expensing	248.2
Other Business and Commerce	58.8
Equipment Depreciation in Excess of Alternative	65.7
* Surtax on Net Investment Income	−151.6
Transportation	33.8
Community and Regional Development	12.4
Education, Training, Employment, and Social Services	
Education and Training	
College Tax Credits	98.2
Charitable Deductions	54.2
Exclusion of Scholarships and Fellowships Income	19.5
Deduction for Interest on Student Loans	11.9
Parental Exemption for Students	23.0
Other Education and Training	47.6
Employment	
Fringe Benefits	40.2
Cafeteria Plans	168.8
ESOPs	15.5
Meals and Lodging	16.1
Other Employment	27.3
*Limit on Deductible Compensation	−4.3
*Other Tax Penalty Provisions	−6.6
Social Services	
Child Credit	270.5
Charitable Contributions	230.5
Child Care	21.8
Adoption Credit and Foster Care	4.0
Health	
Employer-provided Health Insurance Premiums	863.1
Self-employed Insurance Premiums	31.2
Medical and Long-term Care Deduction	56.6
Workers' Comp (medical benefits)	26.1
Health Savings Accounts	15.0
Bond Interest	13.5
Charitable Contributions to Health Organizations	28.7
Subsidies to Insurance Exchanges	326.6
Other Health	36.3

Income Security

Exclusion of life insurance	128.3
Workers' Comp (disability and survivors payments)	15.8
Damages for Personal Injury	8.6
Standard Deduction for the Blind and Elderly	18.7
Earned Income Tax Credit	373.4
Casualty and Theft Losses	2.1
Pension Contributions (Employer Plans)	1,007.9
IRAs/Keoughs	193.4
Employee Life Insurance	21.5
Employee Accident and Disability Insurance	23.1
Other Income Security	7.5

Social Security and Railroad Retirement	213.8
Veteran's Benefits and Services	54.3

General Purpose Fiscal Assistance

State and Local Bonds	194.7
State and Local Tax Deduction	368.8
Deferral of Interest on Savings Bonds	6.4

Tax expenditures are not distributed equally across income classes. The tax expenditure budget also provides information on the distribution of various expenditures. The tables below indicate how the Joint Committee on Taxation distributes some of the more popular tax expenditures to income classes (based on 2016 data). As expected, expenditures intended to benefit low- and middle-income taxpayers are used primarily by those income classes.

Home Mortgage Interest Deduction

Income Class	# of Returns (Thousands)	Amount ($Mil)
Below $10,000	6	2
$10,000 to $20,000	138	40
$20,000 to $30,000	350	132
$30,000 to $40,000	668	337
$40,000 to $50,000	1,153	602
$50,000 to $75,000	4,692	3,650
$75,000 to $100,000	5,074	5,538
$100,000 to $200,000	14,597	24,853

Income Class	# of Returns (Thousands)	Amount ($Mil)
$200,000 and over	7,178	29,782
Total	33,856	64,935

Charitable Contribution Deduction

Income Class	# of Returns (Thousands)	Amount ($Mil)
Below $10,000	2	<0.5
$10,000 to $20,000	107	9
$20,000 to $30,000	348	57
$30,000 to $40,000	710	155
$40,000 to $50,000	1,214	305
$50,000 to $75,000	4,805	1,703
$75,000 to $100,000	5,221	2,662
$100,000 to $200,000	15,180	11,929
$200,000 and over	8,208	40,727
Total	35,795	57,547

Earned Income Tax Credit

Income Class	# of Returns (Thousands)	Amount ($Mil)
Below $10,000	5,105	5,218
$10,000 to $20,000	9,062	28,389
$20,000 to $30,000	5,240	17,896
$30,000 to $40,000	3,856	10,409
$40,000 to $50,000	3,010	6,405
$50,000 to $75,000	2,922	4,641
$75,000 to $100,000	236	311
$100,000 to $200,000	8	20
$200,000 and over	0	0
Total	29,439	73,290

NOTES

(A) *A Continuing Debate.* There are some critics of the tax expenditure approach. The most common complaint is that it is impossible to define a "normal" tax base. The following comment by Boris Bittker is typical:

> The trouble is that * * * any system of income taxation is an aggregation of decisions about a host of structural issues. * * * As to these, one could lock forty tax experts in a room for forty days, and get no agreement—except as a surrender to hunger or boredom * * *. For such issues, every man can create his own set of "tax expenditures," but it will be no more than his collection of disparities between the income tax law as it is, and as he thinks it ought to be. Such compilations would be interesting, but I do not know how we can select one of them for inclusion in the National Budget.

Boris I. Bittker, Accounting for Federal "Tax Subsidies" in the National Budget, 22 Nat'l Tax J. 244 (1969).

Yet despite decades of criticism, the concept endures. Professor Bittker objected to the tax expenditure concept because of the inherent difficulty of defining the "correct model." But it is not necessary to agree on an "official model" to make use of tax expenditure analysis. One does need a referent (a tax expenditure is a provision that deviates from the referent). But although the referent may be an ideal income tax, it does not necessary have to be an ideal income tax. For example, the referent could exclude certain items on administrative grounds that probably would be included in an "ideal tax."

It is clear that Congress does use tax preferences in lieu of direct grants or loans. What are the pros and cons of this behavior? It is equally clear that the line between what is part of a "normal" income tax and what is a tax expenditure is not always obvious. For example, the exclusion from income of scholarships is not listed in the tax expenditure budget, but other subsidies for education are included. As you go through subsequent materials in this book, it is sometimes helpful to ask whether the provision under study is appropriately classified as a tax expenditure or as a proper provision in developing a definition of income. This distinction may affect whether a deduction or credit is more appropriate.

(B) *Upside-Down Subsidies.* As the Joint Committee has noted, the originator of the tax expenditure concept was Stanley Surrey. One of his objections to tax expenditures was the way they provided a larger tax benefit to those in higher brackets than to those in lower brackets. The following excerpt from congressional testimony he gave in 1972 nicely illustrates upside-down subsidies.

> [C]onsider the tax expenditure program for housing represented by the deductibility of mortgage interest and property taxes paid on owner-occupied homes, listed as items under [Commerce] and Housing. This is a program of assistance estimated at about [$95.7 billion, fiscal 2017]. The translation of the tax language in which the program is framed and the assistance provided—a *deduction* in computing taxable income—tells us first that the wealthier the

individual the greater is his assistance under the program. This is because the higher the individual's income and thus the higher the individual's income tax rate, the larger is the tax benefit—the tax reduction—brought about by the deduction. * * * [A]n individual or family whose income is so low that they are not required to pay an income tax—their income being below their personal exemptions and standard deduction—does not receive any financial assistance, for deductions benefit only taxpayers and not non-taxpayers. * * *

The process of translation thus gives us the contours of the tax expenditure program for housing—contours that are quite different from the housing assistance programs formulated in direct expenditure terms. But the contrast—and hence the nature of the task of analysis in expenditure terms—can only be appreciated after the translation is made. It is only then that we can really ask the crucial question of how does this tax expenditure program measure up as an "expenditure" program. For then we can restate the tax program as a direct expenditure program and ask whether such a program represents a desirable policy.

The translation and consequent restatement of a tax expenditure program in direct expenditure terms [often] shows an upside-down result utterly at variance with usual expenditure policies.

(C) *Some Additional Features of Tax Expenditures.* Unlike direct expenditures that can be eliminated only by outright repeal, tax expenditures can be eliminated in two ways—by either repealing the tax expenditure or repealing the tax. Thus, the tax expenditure budget would go to zero if income taxes were repealed.

In some cases, taxpayers make imaginative use of tax expenditures and structural tax provisions to enjoy "negative tax rates" that not only reduce the tax on the favored transaction to zero but also achieve an additional reduction. In such cases, the tax laws encourage transactions that would not be made in a world of no taxes. The distinction should be noted between tax preferences that encourage these economically inefficient transactions and tax preferences that reduce barriers to otherwise efficient transactions. This important distinction is often lost in discussions of tax expenditures. This matter is considered in a variety of contexts in subsequent chapters of this book.

Congress can also use rules and regulations rather than tax or direct subsidies to affect the market. For example, Congress could prohibit the distribution of federal funds to any municipality that does not adopt housing code regulations requiring a specified energy efficiency in homes. Or it could establish production quotas and maximum prices for storm windows and insulation in order to reduce prices and increase output. It could create a new federal crime for failure to insulate residences. It could require that all purchasers of housing would receive an "energy efficiency certificate" so purchasers could estimate the cost of heating and cooling the home. What are the advantages and disadvantages of these alternatives?

(D) *Tax Penalty Budget.* A "tax penalty budget" would include the revenue Congress is collecting by adopting provisions that increase the tax base above the normative tax base or the referent. The Joint Committee has begun to include calculations of this revenue for some tax penalties, which it calls "negative tax expenditures."

SECTION 6.   AN OVERVIEW OF THE TAXING PROCESS

The relative impact of the three branches of government—the legislature, the executive, and the judiciary—on the formulation of tax policy has varied over time. Resolution of constitutional issues was critical in the early days of the income tax. The judiciary, performing its traditional function in interpreting the Constitution, was of foremost importance. But since the constitutional validity of the income tax was settled by the ratification of the Sixteenth Amendment in 1913, the general authority of the Congress in the field of taxation has not been significantly challenged. Congress, in turn, has delegated substantial powers to Treasury. Today, the courts function principally to review legal determinations by Treasury.

A pessimist might describe the process as follows: (1) Congress amends the Internal Revenue Code; (2) Treasury interprets the amendment; (3) taxpayers with a financial interest in the outcome disagree with Treasury's interpretation and litigate the issue; (4) after considerable time has passed, one circuit court of appeals agrees with the taxpayers; (5) another circuit court of appeals agrees with the IRS; (6) the Supreme Court denies certiorari and Congress ignores the issue—confusion reigns or (6) the Supreme Court grants certiorari and resolves the conflict; (7) Congress disagrees with the Supreme Court's interpretation and amends the statute; (8) go back six places to (2) above.

The process for formulating tax law is considered in the materials that follow. The section focuses in turn on the legislative, administrative, and judicial processes.

A. CONSTITUTIONAL PROVISIONS

In the early days of the income tax, there were some important constitutional hurdles, and perhaps there will be others in times to come. Currently, however, constitutional issues do not seem nearly as important as they did at an earlier time. The relevant constitutional provisions follow:

Article I, Section 2, clause 3:

"Representatives and direct Taxes shall be apportioned among the several States which may be included within this Union, according to their respective Numbers, which shall be determined by adding to the whole Number of free Persons, including those bound to Service for a

Term of Years, and excluding Indians not taxed, three-fifths of all other Persons."*

Article I, Section 7, clause 1:

"All Bills for raising Revenue shall originate in the House of Representatives; but the Senate may propose or concur with amendments as on other Bills."

Article I, Section 8, clause 1:

"The Congress shall have Power To lay and collect Taxes, Duties, Imposts and Excises, to pay the Debts and provide for the common Defence and general Welfare of the United States; but all Duties, Imposts and Excises shall be uniform throughout the United States; * * *."

Article I, Section 9, clauses 4 and 5:

"No Capitation, or other direct, Tax shall be laid, unless in Proportion to the Census or Enumeration herein before directed to be taken.

"No Tax or Duty shall be laid on Articles exported from any State."

Article I, Section 10, clauses 2 and 3:

"No State shall, without the Consent of the Congress, lay any Imposts or Duties on Imports or Exports, except what may be absolutely necessary for executing its inspection Laws: and the net Produce of all Duties and Imposts, laid by any State on Imports, or Exports, shall be for the Use of the Treasury of the United States; and all such Laws shall be subject to the Revision and Controul of the Congress.

"No State shall, without the Consent of Congress, lay any Duty of Tonnage, * * * "

Fifth Amendment:

"No person shall be held to answer for a capital, or otherwise infamous crime, unless on a presentment or indictment of a Grand Jury, except in cases arising in the land or naval forces, or in the Militia, when in actual service in time of War or public danger; nor shall any person be subject for the same offence to be twice put in jeopardy of life or limb; nor shall be compelled in any criminal case to be a witness against himself, nor be deprived of life, liberty, or property, without due process of law; nor shall private property be taken for public use, without just compensation."

Tenth Amendment

"The powers not delegated to the United States by the Constitution, nor prohibited by it to the States, are reserved to the States respectively, or to the people."

---

* [Ed. Note: The part of this clause relating to the method of apportionment was amended by the Fourteenth Amendment, clause 2, and as to taxes on income by the Sixteenth Amendment, which is quoted below.]

Sixteenth Amendment

"The Congress shall have power to lay and collect taxes on incomes, from whatever source derived, without apportionment among the several States, and without regard to any census or enumeration."

Note on the Constitutional Tax Provisions

The provision of Article I, Section 2, which insists that "direct taxes shall be apportioned among the several states" was rather clearly intended to prevent the more heavily populated manufacturing states from financing the federal government's spending by imposing land taxes that would disproportionately burden the farming states, although even today much mystery still attends the question what—if anything, in addition to a land tax or a head tax—is a direct tax. In the 2012 Supreme Court decision upholding the Affordable Care Act (known generally as "Obamacare") as a constitutional exercise of taxing power, Chief Justice Roberts described capitation, real property and personal property taxes as direct taxes and implied, but did not state, that no other tax is a direct tax. National Federation of Independent Business v. Sebelius, 567 U.S. 519 (2012). As the history section of this Chapter described, in 1895, the Supreme Court construed this direct tax clause to hold unconstitutional—without apportionment to the states based on their population—the federal income tax of 1894. That decision was reversed by the adoption of the Sixteenth Amendment in 1913, which permits Congress to tax income "from whatever source derived."

Notwithstanding the striking down of the 1894 income tax, the broad discretion of Congress in the tax field generally has been accepted by the Supreme Court. In particular, the Supreme Court began to acknowledge Congress' broad power to enact such tax statutes beginning in the late 1930s when it became more accommodating of economic regulations generally. This new attitude was made evident, for example, in Sunshine Anthracite Coal Co. v. Adkins, 310 U.S. 381 (1940), which upheld a tax on coal producers who refused to join a code established by the Bituminous Coal Commission. The Court declared:

> Clearly this tax is not designed merely for revenue purposes. In purpose and effect it is primarily a sanction to enforce the regulatory provisions of the Act. But that does not mean that the statute is invalid and the tax unenforceable. Congress may impose penalties in aid of the exercise of any of its enumerated powers. * * *

This view perhaps reached its apogee in *NFIB v. Sebelius*, when the Supreme Court upheld the constitutionality of various provisions of the Health Care and Education Reconciliation Act of 2010 and the Patient Protection and Affordable Care Act of 2010. That legislation mandated that most Americans purchase health insurance and imposed a penalty for failure to do so. Chief Justice John Roberts treated the penalty as a "tax," thus constitutionally permitted under Congress' power to tax. Unlike most taxes, which are imposed for buying something (like as sales tax or excise tax) or for earning something (like an income tax), the health insurance "tax" was imposed for not doing something (not buying health insurance). The law in question had called it a penalty, rather than a tax, even though payments would be made to the IRS. This mandate or "tax" was effectively repealed in the 2017 legislation by setting the penalty to zero.

With an important but now archaic exception dealing with the taxation of stock dividends (which we shall examine in Chapter 2), constitutional challenges to the income tax statute have generally failed, and after the constitutional validity of the income tax was settled by the ratification of the Sixteenth Amendment in 1913, the authority of the Congress in the field of taxation has not been significantly challenged. Indeed, today the Constitution seems to stop where the Internal Revenue Code begins.

Consider the "origination" clause, Article I, Section 7, clause 1, which states: "All Bills for raising Revenue shall originate in the House of Representatives; but the Senate may propose or concur with amendments as on other Bills." In 1982, the House of Representatives passed a minor piece of tax legislation that, in three pages of statutory language, would have lowered revenues by less than $1 billion over the subsequent five-year period. When this legislation got to the Senate, its entire substance was deleted and replaced with more than 500 pages of statutory amendments to the Internal Revenue Code that were estimated to raise about $100 billion during the next three years. The Senate Amendment was accepted virtually intact by a House-Senate conference, was passed by both chambers of Congress, and signed by President Reagan.

Disgruntled taxpayers challenged the constitutional validity of this legislation on the ground that, since the House bill would have reduced revenues, this measure to raise revenues originated in the Senate, in violation of the origination clause. The several courts of appeals that heard these cases all found them without merit and upheld the legislation. Since these cases had not produced a conflict in the lower courts, the Supreme Court saw no need to hear this issue and refused to grant certiorari.

In effect, this episode renders the origination clause a nullity, with no practical significance whatsoever. As one commentator put it:

> To be sure, the House can prevent the Senate from taking any action on taxation by refraining from originating *any* tax legislation; but even if the Senate were allowed to originate a tax bill, it could not become law without House concurrence, so it hardly matters which chamber acts first. Since it takes two to

tango, what difference does it make whose foot first touches the ballroom floor?[12]

In 1983, the Supreme Court performed an almost equivalent evisceration of the uniformity clause of Article 1, Section 8, which mandates that "all Duties, Imposts and Excises shall be uniform throughout the United States," by upholding, in a unanimous opinion, an exemption for Alaskan oil from the Crude Oil Windfall Profits Tax Act of 1980. United States v. Ptasynski, 462 U.S. 74 (1983). The Court concluded that the exemption was not designed to grant Alaska any "undue preference," but rather was supported by geographic differences that legitimately—and constitutionally—could be taken into account by the Congress in fashioning tax legislation.

In a surprising—if not shocking—development, a panel of the D.C. Circuit in 2006 held that damages awarded for emotional distress, which Congress had explicitly included in income, were not income within the meaning of the Sixteenth Amendment. Murphy v. Internal Revenue Service, 460 F.3d 79 (D.C. Cir. 2006). The opinion failed to consider or even mention Congress' power "to lay and collect Taxes" under Article I, Section 8. Following this opinion, which provoked a tsunami of criticism, the Justice Department fully briefed the constitutional issues in its petition for rehearing en banc. In an unusual move, the panel itself decided to rehear the case and, although it did not entirely abandon its earlier opinion, held that the amount would be taxed (as gross income under § 61 of the Code) based on Congress' Article I, Section 8 power since this was not a "direct tax" that had to be apportioned to the states. Murphy v. Internal Revenue Service, 493 F.3d 170 (D.C. Cir. 2007). Since the panel did not want to confess that it had been wrong in its first opinion, the second opinion is hardly a model of constitutional clarity. Generally, experts have responded with a shoulder shrug, commenting that "all's well that ends well."

Taken together, all of the modern decisions—along with other constitutional events that are beyond the scope of this text—suggest that, at least at this moment in our constitutional history, there are few serious procedural or substantive constitutional impediments on congressional power in enacting tax legislation. Exceptions occur only when the tax law interferes with such fundamental rights as the freedoms of speech or religion granted by the First Amendment or the guarantees of equal protection under the Fifth and Fourteenth Amendments. Today constitutional questions play a relatively minor role in federal taxation. Notwithstanding the bump in the road from the first *Murphy* opinion, constitutional challenges to tax legislation frequently are heard but almost never upheld.

---

[12] Boris I. Bittker, "Constitutional Limits on the Taxing Power of the Federal Government," 41 Tax Law. 3 (1987)

B. THE LEGISLATIVE PROCESS

Note on the Process for Enacting Tax Legislation

The Constitution grants Congress the power "To lay and collect Taxes, Duties, Imposts and Excises." This congressional power over tax legislation constitutionally is limited only by the President's veto, which, of course, can be overridden by a two-thirds vote of each house.

Despite the emphasis in the Constitution on congressional responsibility, much tax legislation is initiated by the President. Responsibility for tax policy and tax administration generally is vested in the Department of the Treasury. The Secretary of the Treasury delegates to the Internal Revenue Service responsibility for the administration of tax laws, but not for the formulation of tax policy. That job is assigned to the Assistant Secretary for Tax Policy, who oversees a relatively small staff of lawyers, economists, statisticians, and econometricians, who are engaged in the development of tax policy and legislation for the administration. The staff regularly consults with others in the Treasury Department, including the IRS, and with other government departments and agencies. The White House staff also plays an important role because the President retains final authority over tax policy within the administration.

The Constitution provides that all revenue bills shall originate in the House of Representatives and thus, tax legislation often is first considered by the Committee on Ways and Means. Established in 1789, the Ways and Means Committee is one of the oldest House committees. It exercises jurisdiction over legislation concerning taxes, tariffs, foreign trade policy, welfare and health insurance, the level of the public debt, and the Social Security system. Congressional consideration of a major or controversial tax proposal thus often begins with a public hearing held by the Ways and Means Committee or one of its subcommittees. If the administration has initiated the measure, the Secretary of the Treasury is usually the first witness to appear, followed by other administration representatives and then by witnesses from the public. After public hearings, the Ways and Means Committee generally holds "mark-up" sessions on the proposal to determine the details of the bill. In considering the 2017 legislation, the tax writing committees held no public hearings but instead went directly to mark-up. The bill, accompanied by a report describing the bill and outlining reasons for the Ways and Means Committee's action, goes to the House for debate. Tax bills are often sent to the floor under a rule permitting very few, if any, amendments, although that determination is made by the House Rules Committee.

After the bill is approved, the process is repeated in the Senate. The counterpart of the House Ways and Means Committee is the Senate Finance Committee. The Finance Committee sometimes does not wait to act on a House bill, but rather holds its own hearings and often works on a bill while the House bill is working its way through the process. The Senate rules provide for unlimited debate when a tax bill is considered on the floor, and generally permit any senator to move to delete or modify any part of the bill or to add new provisions. Under the rules of the Senate, a 60-vote majority is sometimes necessary to pass tax legislation. In some cases the Senate may enact tax legislation with only a simple 51-vote majority under a process known as budget reconciliation. If, however, such a bill loses revenue in years subsequent to the budget period (usually ten years), it is subject to a point of order (known as the Byrd rule) that blocks the legislation and can only be overridden by a 60-vote majority.

When the Senate version of the bill differs from the House version—as it almost always does—the revised bill is returned for House consideration. Though the House may accept the changes made by the Senate, it ordinarily will ask for a conference of senior members of the House and Senate to reconcile the differences. In the conference committee, the House and Senate members each vote on the issues as a unit, the vote of each chamber being controlled by a majority vote of that side. The Conference Committee sometimes adds provisions that were in neither the House nor the Senate bills.

Once agreement has been reached, a conference report is issued containing the statutory changes and briefly explaining the conference result. The report is presented separately to the Senate and House. Each must either accept or reject the conference version; no amendments are allowed. If approved by both bodies, the bill is sent to the President for signature or veto.

In 1996 President Clinton signed legislation permitting a partial line item veto, which permitted him, after signing a spending or tax bill, to send to Congress a separate message that lists the items he wishes to veto. Those items were deemed automatically rescinded by Congress unless it passed a bill to overturn some or all of them. President Clinton used this authority to cancel two provisions in the Taxpayer Relief Act of 1997. The beneficiaries of the tax breaks challenged the constitutionality of the line item veto and the Supreme Court agreed. It held that the Constitution did not give the President the authority to create a law whose text was not voted on by either the House or the Senate and presented to the President for his signature. Clinton v. City of New York, 524 U.S. 417 (1998).

NOTES

(A) *Joint Committee on Taxation.* The Joint Committee on Taxation, established in 1926 and made up of members of both houses, meets only about three times a year. The primary importance of the JCT is to provide status for its professional staff of lawyers, economists, accountants, and statistical analysts. See §§ 8001–8023 for the organization and functions of the Joint Committee. The Committee provides assistance to both the House Ways and Means Committee and the Senate Finance Committee, and is responsible for estimating the revenue effects of legislative proposals and enacted legislation for the Congress. The JCT produces reports analyzing proposed legislation before and after a bill is enacted. The staff often produces a "General Explanation" of a new law, an important document of legislative history.

(B) *The Code Itself.* The *first* matter to consider in *any* tax case is: what are the exact words of the statute? There is no use in a lawyer's thinking great thoughts about a tax problem unless the thoughts are firmly based on the controlling statute. A certain amount of "common law" of federal taxation has developed and judicial decisions are often very important, but federal taxation is not a common law subject.

The basic statute is the Internal Revenue Code of 1986, which has been amended virtually every year since it was adopted. Earlier statutes may be important, however, in showing the history and development of the provisions now contained in the Code—the story of "the Government's [often futile] endeavor to keep pace with the fertility of invention" of taxpayers' lawyers.[13]

The provisions of the Internal Revenue Code vary greatly in terms of substantive scope, specificity, and drafting style. The student must acquire an ability to deal with the Code in its many vagaries and to parse its complexities.

(C) *Legislative History.* Since the chief problems in federal taxation relate to the application and construction of statutes, it is important to be familiar with the materials that may shed light on these questions. They include:

Committee Reports. The reports of the House Ways and Means Committee, the Senate Finance Committee, and the conference committees provide useful explanations of the provisions of a revenue bill and the reasons for the changes in the law. In addition to the committee reports on legislation, there are other reports on tax issues; the most significant of these are reports issued by the staff of the Joint Committee on Taxation.

Hearings. A record is published of the public hearings before the congressional committees. The hearings occasionally yield material that is useful in considering tax questions. On-line databases, such as those maintained by Tax Analysts, often contain statements submitted at congressional hearings and sometimes unofficial hearing transcripts.

Statements on the Floor of Congress. The debates in Congress, recorded in the Congressional Record, are sometimes of moment in the construction of tax statutes.

(D) *Gucci Gulch.* There has long been concern about the disproportionate influence of so-called "special interests" on the tax legislative process. See, e.g., the 1957 article by Stanley Surrey, "The Congress and the Tax Lobbyist—How Special Tax Provisions Get Enacted,"

---

[13] The phrase comes from Justice Cardozo in Burnet v. Wells, 289 U.S. 670, 676 (1933).

70 Harv. L. Rev. 1145 (1957). For an account of how an unusual coalition managed in 2001 to get Congress to temporarily repeal the federal estate tax, which had been a part of the tax law since 1916, see Michael J. Graetz & Ian Shapiro, *Death by a Thousand Cuts: The Fight over Taxing Inherited Wealth* (Princeton University Press, 2006). More recently, the advent of political action committees ("PACs") with enormous influence over campaign funding has intensified concerns that special interests now dominate the tax legislative process. Enormous sums of money are contributed to members of the tax writing committees of Congress.

When Congress has tax legislation on its agenda, the halls of Capitol Hill are lined with "Gucci-clad" lobbyists, each urging defeat or passage of special provisions that would benefit their clients. Their victories and defeats in the Tax Reform Act of 1986 are described in Jeffrey H. Birnbaum and Alan S. Murray, *Showdown at Gucci Gulch: Lawmakers, Lobbyists, and the Unlikely Triumph of Tax Reform* (1987).

As a counterpoint to the vast sums of money contributed to members of the tax writing committees of Congress, consider the following comments concerning the retirement of George Lefcoe from the Los Angeles County Regional Planning Commission, excerpted from Kaplan, "When He Missed the Ham, He Quit," Los Angeles Times, January 25, 1987 at Part VIII, Page 2:

> [Lefcoe] did say that a mistake might have been that he retired before, and not after, Christmas. "I really missed the cards from engineers I never met, the wine and cheese from development companies I never heard of and, especially, the Honeybaked ham from, of all places, Forest Lawn [a well-known Los Angeles mortuary and cemetery], even though the company was never an applicant before the commission when I was there," Lefcoe said.

> "But because I miss them is why I think it was a good idea I resigned," he added. "I do not think it is wise to stay in public office for too long a time." Lefcoe used the ham from Forest Lawn as an illustration:

> "My first Christmas as a commissioner—when I received the ham— I tried to return it at once, though for the record, I did not because no one at Forest Lawn seemed authorized to accept hams, apparently not even for burial. My guess is that no one of the many public servants who received the hams ever had tried to return it," said Lefcoe.

> "When I received another ham the next Christmas, I gave it to a worthy charity," Lefcoe recalled. "The next year, some worthy friends were having a party, so I gave it to them. The next year I had a party and we enjoyed the ham."

> "In the fifth year, about the 10th of December," said Lefcoe, "I began wondering, where is my ham? Why is it late?"

> Lefcoe sighed and laughed. "So much for the seduction of public officials. It was then I thought it was time to retire, though it took me two more hams and three years to finally do it."

C. THE ADMINISTRATION OF THE TAX LAWS

Note on Tax Administration

Organization of the Internal Revenue Service. From the time of the Civil War, the agency charged with collecting internal taxes was known as the Bureau of Internal Revenue. In 1953, the name was changed to the Internal Revenue Service. Its principal officer is the Commissioner of Internal Revenue, who is nominated by the President and confirmed by the Senate.

The IRS is an extremely large agency, having a budget of approximately $12 billion and employing nearly 83,000 people. In 2016, the IRS processed 244 million returns and supplemental forms and collected $2.9 trillion in tax revenues. The average administrative cost of collecting each $100 of revenue was 35 cents. About 1.2 million returns filed in 2015 were audited, comprising 0.7 percent of individual returns and 1.1 percent of corporate returns.

The central supervisory office where the top officers work, called the National Office, is located in Washington, D.C. The IRS has over 700 field offices located around the United States and in foreign countries. The chief legal advisor to the Commissioner is the Chief Counsel, whose office is responsible for preparing regulations, overseeing tax litigation, and writing rulings. There are regional counsel as well, who are primarily responsible for litigation in the Tax Court. The large field offices are headed by a District Director, and a Regional Commissioner supervises the district offices within each region. Regional Service Centers generally are responsible for collecting taxes and processing tax returns.

Congress has expressly given authority, in many places in the Code, "to the Secretary or his delegate." Much of the power of the Secretary of the Treasury with respect to taxes has been delegated to the Commissioner, and the Commissioner, in turn has, delegated his authority to various officers in the Service. See §§ 7802–7809.

Concerned that the organizational structure of the IRS made it ill-equipped to efficiently collect revenue under an increasingly complex tax code, Congress passed the Internal Revenue Service Restructuring and Reform Act of 1998. The Act provided for a complete reorganization of the IRS and established within the Treasury Department an IRS Oversight Board. In addition to the Treasury Secretary, the Commissioner, and a full-time federal employee, the board has six private members. The Board is to oversee the IRS in administration, management, conduct, and execution of the tax laws. The Act also created the post of Treasury Inspector General for Tax Administration, whose job is to evaluate IRS programs and operations and to ferret out fraud, abuse, or misconduct within the IRS.

Treasury Regulations. Congress has delegated substantial rulemaking power to the Treasury. Section 7805(a) provides that "the

Secretary shall prescribe all needful rules and regulations for the enforcement" of the internal revenue laws. For decades there had been some confusion about the deference that applies to Treasury regulations and even whether the deference was the same as that applied to other areas of the law. The Supreme Court ended that confusion in Mayo Foundation for Medical Education & Research v. United States, 562 U.S. 44 (2011). It rejected "tax exceptionalism" and found that there was no separate deference test for tax. It applied the standard from Chevron U.S.A., Inc. v. National Resources Defense Council, Inc., 467 U.S. 837 (1984), to all cases in which "it appears that Congress delegated authority to the agency generally to make rules carrying the force of law, and that the agency interpretation claiming deference was promulgated in the exercise of that authority."

Additional rulemaking authority is also delegated to Treasury by specific Code sections. See, e.g., § 25A (delegating to Treasury authority to "prescribe such regulations as may be necessary or appropriate" to interpret the rules with respect to the credit for education expenses). Regulations issued under such broad delegations of legislative authority are virtually always binding on taxpayers.

The regulations are quite extensive in scope and detail. They usually are designated by a number that includes the relevant Code section (for example, § 1.61–2 is a regulation under § 61 of the Code). There are many references to regulations in this book, but no effort has been made to include comprehensive citations.

The Secretary of the Treasury has delegated the authority to issue regulations to the Commissioner of Internal Revenue, subject to the approval of the Assistant Secretary of the Treasury for Tax Policy. Typically, a regulation is published in the Federal Register as a notice of proposed rulemaking. Comments from the public are received, and often a public hearing is held, before final regulations are published as a Treasury Decision ("T.D."). When time is limited and the need for guidance is immediate, regulations are sometimes issued as temporary regulations without following the notice of rulemaking procedures. In response to the increased use of temporary regulations, Congress enacted a provision that "sunsets" or terminates them after three years if no final regulations are issued. § 7805(e). Previously, temporary regulations remained in force until permanent regulations were issued.

After narrowly losing *NFIB v. Sebelius* (see supra page 52), opponents engaged in other litigation aimed at the Affordable Care Act. One effort was to undermine the subsidies the Act provides to low- and moderate-income families enabling them to purchase health insurance. At issue was a regulation that interpreted a provision of the Act that provided tax credits for insurance purchased on "an exchange established by the State." The IRS interpreted that phrase to cover federal exchanges established when states did not set up such exchanges. In deciding whether the regulation should be upheld, the Supreme Court declined to apply *Chevron*. King v. Burwell, 576 U.S. ___, 135 S. Ct. 2480 (2015). The majority reasoned that this issue was of "deep economic and political significance" and that Congress would have done so expressly had it wished to "delegate this decision to the IRS, which has no expertise in crafting health insurance policy of this sort." Thus, the Court saw no need to defer to the IRS despite the acknowledged ambiguity of the statute. The Court did find, however, that the IRS interpretation was the only reasonable interpretation of the statute. That means that it would be impossible for a subsequent administration to simply rewrite the regulations to change the result, something that would be possible under *Chevron*. The tax credit for insurance premiums is no different from many other subsidies and spending programs enacted in the tax law (see the discussion on tax expenditures). Does this decision portend less deference under *Chevron* when laws are ambiguous and the issues are outside the IRS's natural expertise?

Revenue Rulings and Revenue Procedures. In addition to the Regulations, the Service publishes a large volume of revenue rulings and revenue procedures. A revenue ruling is the Commissioner's "official interpretation of the law" and generally is binding on revenue agents and other IRS officials. The IRS states that taxpayers generally may rely on published revenue rulings in determining the tax treatment of their own transactions that arise out of similar facts and circumstances. Courts typically give revenue rulings less weight than regulations, but many courts accord them considerable respect.

Revenue procedures typically reflect the contents of internal management documents, but also may announce practice and procedures for the guidance of the public. From time to time, however, the IRS has issued revenue procedures stating IRS policy on substantive issues. See, e.g., Rev. Proc. 72–18, 1972–1 C.B. 740 (setting forth guidelines for disallowing interest deductions when taxpayers hold tax-exempt state and local bonds). When the IRS chooses to issue a substantive revenue procedure rather than a revenue ruling, the substantive rules set forth in the revenue procedure may be of doubtful validity; there may not have been sufficient support within the IRS to issue a revenue ruling—an "official interpretation of the law."

Private Rulings and Determination Letters to Taxpayers. Taxpayers sometimes can obtain rulings (generally referred to as "private" or "letter" rulings) and determination letters from the Internal Revenue Service. The first Revenue Procedure issued each year provides the procedures for requesting a ruling. Rev. Proc. 2018–1 defines a "letter ruling" as a "written determination issued to a taxpayer by an [IRS] office in response to the taxpayer's written inquiry, filed prior to the filing of returns * * * about its status for tax purposes or the tax effects of its acts or transactions."

A "determination letter" is a written statement, issued by a District Director in response to a taxpayer's written inquiry, that applies the principles and precedents previously announced by the National Office to a particular set of facts. When the question involves a novel issue, a determination letter will not be issued.

Private rulings and other administrative guidance are available to the public although certain identifying information is deleted. Section 6110(k)(3) provides that these written determinations are to have no precedential value, but taxpayers routinely cite private rulings when it is advantageous to do so and courts occasionally cite them as reflecting the IRS position. The basic tension here is between fairness to similarly situated taxpayers and the administrative necessity to give only a relatively low level of review to private rulings within the IRS.

NOTES

(A) *Administrative Announcements.* Revenue rulings and revenue procedures are published in the weekly Internal Revenue Bulletin. Until 2008, the material in the weekly issues was gathered together semi-annually into a publication titled the Cumulative Bulletin (cited as "C.B."). The IRS also publishes technical information releases (known as TIRs), press releases, pamphlets, tax forms and instructions, and other documents and pronouncements. The Cumulative Bulletin also contains IRS acquiescences or non-acquiescences in Tax Court decisions, Treasury decisions, executive orders, legislative histories, and other related items. The rulings and procedures and many other Service announcements also are found in privately-published tax services and in computer databases.

(B) *Retroactivity.* Section 7805(b) gives Treasury the power to decide whether regulations, rulings, or changes in regulations or rulings are to be retroactive in effect. This section is stated in the reverse form from normal administrative practice, viz, in such a way as to make "retroactive" rulemaking the norm with provision for discretionary prospective relief.

This is an important power, and determinations whether to make pronouncements or changes retroactive are quite frequent. The courts generally have upheld the power unless the Commissioner has abused his discretion. The Courts seldom have considered abuses of discretion to occur, usually only when they perceive unfairness to affected taxpayers. The classic example is International Business Machines Corp. v. United States, 343 F.2d 914 (1965), cert. denied 382 U.S. 1028 (1966), in which the court ruled that the IRS could not apply an unfavorable ruling retroactively when it had previously given a favorable ruling to the taxpayer's competitor.

In addition to the technical questions raised by § 7805(b), there is a difficult policy issue as to when taxpayers should be entitled to rely on a tax law remaining unchanged. Can Congress, for example, enact tax laws that will explicitly apply retroactively? In 1993 and 2001, for example, Congress changed the rate structure and applied it retroactively to the beginning of the year. For a general discussion of the policy considerations relating to retroactive changes in the tax laws, see Michael J. Graetz, "Legal Transitions: The Case of Retroactivity in Income Tax Revision," 126 U. Pa.

L. Rev. 47 (1977); Michael J. Graetz, "Retroactivity Revisited," 98 Harv. L. Rev. 1820 (1985).

(C) *Application of the Administrative Procedure Act.* Relying on the Supreme Court decision in *Mayo Foundation for Medical Education & Research v. United States*, see supra page 60, the D.C Circuit held that the Administrative Procedure Act applies to the IRS, just like any other federal agency. Cohen v. United States, 650 F.3d 717 (D.C. Cir. 2011). The APA exempts interpretative regulations from its notice-and-comment rules, but legislative regulations must follow those rules. The status of temporary regulations under the APA is less clear. See Intermountain Insurance Service of Vail v. Commissioner, 134 T.C. 211 (2010), where Judge Halpern dissented on the grounds that temporary regulations in question violated the APA, a question not considered by the majority.

The fact that the APA clearly applies to tax rulemaking has provoked challenges to regulations that otherwise might have received *Chevron* deference and has brought into question the way regulations are issued. In Altera v. Commissioner, 145 T.C. 91 (2015), the Tax Court invalidated a regulation because Treasury's explanation of its decision in the preamble was inadequate and therefore failed the "reasoned decision-making standard" imposed by courts under the APA. That preamble failed to disclose Treasury's findings and failed to adequately address the comments it had received during the notice and comment period. If upheld (Altera is on appeal to the Ninth Circuit), Treasury may have to reform the process for issuing regulations if it expects *Chevron* deference.

(D) *Freedom of Information Act.* Until the mid-1970s, the IRS made little information available to the public. In response to several lawsuits brought by Tax Analysts under the Freedom of Information Act, the IRS subsequently agreed to release all private letter rulings, technical advice memoranda, General Counsel Memoranda (legal advice on proposed revenue rulings, private letter rulings, and technical advice memoranda), and Actions on Decisions (attorneys' recommendations whether to appeal adverse Tax Court or District Court decisions). Other lawsuits resulted in the release of audit guidelines, the Closing Agreement Handbook (which sets forth rules, procedures, and guidelines for IRS personnel in entering into certain agreements with taxpayers), and Treasury bill reports (which state Treasury's position on proposed legislation).

The IRS also reversed prior practice whereby people could submit comments on proposed regulations with a request that they be kept confidential. All comments on proposed regulations are now subject to public inspection and copying. Substantial portions of the Internal Revenue Manual are now available and can be very helpful to practitioners.

Before making public certain written determinations, information is deleted, including: (1) the taxpayer's name and other identifying characteristics, (2) commercial or financial information that is privileged or confidential, (3) trade secrets, (4) classified matter, (5) information specifically exempted by statutes, (6) information relating to bank regulations, (7) matters relating to personal privacy, and (8) certain geological and geophysical information. In 2000, Congress enacted legislation prohibiting the IRS from releasing information pertaining to certain agreements between taxpayers and the IRS, including closing agreements, certain "refiling agreements," and information arising under treaty obligations.

What limitations, if any, should be imposed upon the publication requirement? Would you extend the publication requirement to audit tolerances, investigative techniques, and other law enforcement materials?

(E) *Disclosure of Tax Return Information.* Section 6103 of the Code generally provides that tax returns and related information cannot be disclosed except under the following specific conditions: (1) to congressional committees, (2) to the President, (3) to the Justice Department, (4) to certain officials of state and local governments, (5) with respect to judicial and administrative tax proceedings, (6) to federal officers or employees involved in the administration of federal laws other than the tax law, (7) to the General Accounting Office, (8) to people designated by the taxpayer, and (9) to other persons having a material interest in the amount of tax due. Are there any situations where you would require disclosure of tax returns? Of publicly held corporations? Of elected officials? Of your own tax return?

(F) *Stopping Pandora.* In 1997 President Clinton signed the Taxpayer Browsing Protection Act, which makes the unauthorized browsing of taxpayer's returns by federal or state employees a crime. Congress apparently was moved to act after the press extensively reported on activities of two curious IRS employees. The First Circuit overturned the conviction of Richard Czubinski, a contact representative for the IRS Boston office (and a member of the Ku Klux Klan) who made it a habit of browsing the returns of people he knew, although he failed to do anything with the information. The court found browsing "reprehensible," but ruled that it did not rise to the level of a crime. United States v. Czubinski, 106 F.3d 1069 (1st Cir. 1997). According to the April 4, 1997 edition of the Chicago Sun-Times, Czubinski's motive was curiosity. "It's human nature to be curious" he said. "That's why we're so far advanced technologically. . . . It was just like, if you go into somebody's home, have you ever looked in the medicine cabinet?"

Robert M. Patterson, a computer "inputter" on the graveyard shift in the Memphis IRS office, was simply trying to get ahead in his job. Claiming he was not adequately trained, he regularly looked up the returns of famous people (and other people with the same names) in order to get computer experience. Although charged with falsely obtaining Social Security numbers, he was acquitted.

Note on Administrative Resolution of Tax Disputes

The Filing of a Tax Return. Under our self-assessment system, taxpayers make the initial determination of their tax liability. Section 6012 of the Code requires that every individual who has gross income in excess of a certain level must file a tax return. See § 6012(a)(1), which sets the level as the sum of the taxpayer's exemption amount (zero from 2018 to 2025) plus the standard deduction. Section 6012 also requires all corporations subject to income taxation and all estates and trusts with gross income of $600 or more to file returns. Most individuals report their income on a calendar-year basis and must file their returns by April 15 of the following year, but extensions of time until August 15 are routinely permitted.

Taxpayers are subject to a penalty if they fail to file their return by the due date. Although taxpayers often rely on tax preparers or accountants to file the return, they are personally responsible for making sure it is filed. For example, Mo Vaughn got caught looking and was slapped with a penalty for failing to file his returns for two years. (For those who are not baseball aficionados, the "Hit Man" was the American League MVP for the Boston Red Sox in 1995.) Vaughn turned his financial affairs over to a financial advisor and an accountant who not only did not file his tax returns for two years, but also embezzled $3 million from him. Vaughn struck out with the Sixth Circuit when he tried to argue that the embezzlement was a reasonable cause for not filing his tax returns. The court noted that the duty to file was non-delegable and rejected his reasonable cause argument. Vaughn v. United States, 635 Fed. Appx. 216 (6th Cir. 2015).

In 2010, the IRS issued a notice requiring large corporations to reveal so-called "uncertain tax positions." Corporations that issue audited financial statements are required to file a schedule of uncertain tax positions ("Schedule UTP") with their tax returns. Announcement 2010–30, 2010–19 I.R.B. 668. Uncertain positions are those for which the taxpayer has recorded a reserve in an audited financial statement. Under financial accounting rules (known as Fin. 48), taxpayers must record a reserve in audited financial statements for any tax position that is not "more likely than not to be sustained," and for any portion of a tax position that is not greater than 50 percent likely of being realized upon ultimate settlement with the Service. In layman's terms, that means any position the taxpayer expects to lose if the IRS finds out about it. Lest you think a corporation would not enter into a transaction where it expected to lose, consider United States v. Textron Inc., 577 F.3d 21 (1st Cir. 2009), where the taxpayer claimed a work product privilege for tax accrual papers describing the taxpayer's tax reserves. The taxpayer assessed the Service's likelihood of success on some "uncertain positions" as 100 percent.

Final payment of tax for the year is required with the return, but, in most cases, the bulk of the tax liability has already been collected by the IRS through withholding or estimated tax payments. Employers are required to withhold income and payroll taxes from the wages and salaries of employees, to deposit the withheld taxes regularly, and, by January 31 of the following year, to give the employee a statement of the wages paid and the taxes withheld—the Form W-2. Certain gambling winnings and dividend and interest income, where required information has not been submitted, are also subject to withholding. See §§ 3401–

3406. Quarterly payment of estimated tax is required from individuals who receive income, such as business income, interest, or dividends, that is not subject to withholding. There are significant penalties for failing to pay estimated tax. See § 6654.

About 75 percent of all individual tax liability is paid through withholding. Much of the balance is secured through estimated tax payments. The filing of a return is, therefore, principally a reconciliation of the amount withheld or paid as an estimate with the taxpayer's final determination of tax liability for the year. An additional payment to the government or a refund to the taxpayer is then made. Because many taxpayers do not base their withholding on the full exemptions to which they are entitled, there is a large amount of overwithholding and as a result, most taxpayers who have only wage income receive refunds.

IRS Review of Returns. Review of the taxpayer's self-assessment of tax liability begins with a computerized check of the tax return for mathematical mistakes. If such mistakes are found, the taxpayer is billed or additional tax is refunded. The IRS also performs computerized matching of information returns, such as Form 1099 reports of interest and dividend payments, and employers' reports of wages, with the taxpayers' returns. In addition, some returns are selected for audit. The specific criteria for selecting returns for audit are not made public, but the IRS focuses the bulk of its audit efforts on returns that are likely to produce significant amounts of revenue. Thus, the IRS audits a higher percentage of returns of individuals with high incomes and a significant percentage of returns of large corporations. In 2016, for example, 10.46 percent of individuals with income of $5 million to $10 million were audited compared with 0.62 percent of individuals with income of $100,000 to $200,000. The audit rate for very large corporations was 78 percent. Returns also are selected for audit if they contain certain questionable deductions, such as unusually large itemized deductions or a disproportionate ratio of expenses to income. Certain occupations and professions are subjected to greater scrutiny. Section 6103(b)(2) permits the IRS to refuse to disclose to taxpayers the standards used for the selection of tax returns for audit or the data used in developing audit standards.

In 2016 the percentage of individual tax returns audited had fallen to 0.7 percent, the lowest level in more than a decade. The limited ability of the IRS to audit tax returns, coupled with the ever-increasing complexity of the income tax law, has given rise to a significant compliance problem known as the "audit lottery." Many corporations and individuals have adopted an "opening bid" philosophy, resolving every issue in favor of paying less, on the assumption that they will not be audited or that, if they are audited, the revenue agent will miss or compromise certain issues. At worst, they will pay the taxes due plus interest. Congress has enacted severe penalties to try to deal with this "compliance gap."

A taxpayer who prevails in a tax case in federal court can be awarded reasonable litigation costs if the position of the government is not "substantially justified." Under certain conditions, the taxpayer may recover reasonable administrative costs incurred after the date on which the first letter of proposed deficiency that allows the taxpayer an opportunity for administrative review is sent. § 7430(a)(1).

The Audit and Administrative Appeals Process. An audit can be a "correspondence audit," where the taxpayer is asked to mail material to the local district office, an "office audit," where the taxpayer must personally appear at the district office with any material requested, or a "field audit," where the IRS official examines the taxpayer's books and other relevant material at the taxpayer's home or place of business. In the case of a field audit, the taxpayer should determine whether the examining officer is a "revenue agent" or a "special agent." Special agents investigate potential criminal charges, and taxpayers have different rights in dealing with special agents.

If the taxpayer does not agree with the IRS determination of tax liability on audit, he will receive a "30-day letter" from the IRS that explains his options for further administrative review of the dispute. Most disputes are settled administratively. If there is no settlement or if the taxpayer decides to forgo any administrative review, she may request a "statutory deficiency" notice (known as a 90-day letter because the taxpayer then has only 90 days to file a petition in the Tax Court). If the taxpayer fails to respond to the 30-day letter, she will receive a 90-day letter.

Section 7121 of the Code authorizes the Secretary or his delegate to make binding "closing agreements" with respect to past or future tax liability. Closing agreements are final except where fraud, malfeasance, or misrepresentation of a material fact can be shown. In some cases, the IRS may require a taxpayer to enter into a closing agreement as a condition to obtaining a ruling.

NOTES

(A) *Statute of Limitations.* The IRS generally has three years from the filing of a tax return to send a 90-day letter. § 6501(a). The period is six years if the taxpayer omits an amount from gross income that exceeds 25 percent of the gross income on the return unless there is disclosure. § 6501(e). If no return is filed or the return is false or fraudulent with an intent to evade tax, the time to send a notice is unlimited. § 6501(c). The statute of limitations may be extended by the taxpayer in writing; taxpayers usually agree to do so when requested by the IRS because a failure to agree will result in the immediate issuance of a deficiency letter that is probably erroneous.

The taxpayer has three years from the date a return was filed (or two years from the time the tax was paid, whichever is later) to file for a refund. § 6511. If the taxpayer has filed a waiver to assessment, he also may file a refund claim within the extension plus six months.

(B) *Taxpayer Bills of Rights.* The so-called Taxpayer Bills of Rights, which probably should be given an award for the most exaggerated legislative title, were responses to taxpayer concerns with tax penalties and perceived IRS abuses. At the most basic level, the Taxpayer Bill of Rights of 1988 requires the IRS to prepare and disseminate a comprehensive and comprehensible statement explaining taxpayer rights and IRS duties at virtually every stage of the tax administrative process. This Taxpayer Bill of Rights was not as effective as Congress had hoped. So it enacted another one. And, as part of the Internal Revenue Service Restructuring and Reform Act of 1998, Congress added additional taxpayer protections.

One of the more nerve-wracking experiences for any taxpayer is an "interview" with the IRS. The IRS now must conduct examinations at reasonable times and places. § 7605. It is generally not reasonable, for example, to force a small business owner to close shop in order to attend an interview. Taxpayers may record interviews, and the Service may record an interview if the IRS official informs the taxpayer prior to the interview and upon request provides the taxpayer with the transcript or recording. § 7521(a). Taxpayers are now empowered to stop an interview in order to consult with an "authorized representative." § 7521(b)(2). For this purpose, an authorized representative includes an attorney, CPA, or any other person allowed to represent a taxpayer before the IRS.

The IRS frequently provides taxpayers with advice that turns out to be incorrect. The IRS must abate any portion of a penalty that is attributable to a mistake in written advice from the Service. § 6404(f). Since § 6404(f) applies only to written advice, a taxpayer who relies on inaccurate advice given by the IRS over the phone may be out of luck.

The 1998 IRS restructuring legislation created a new National Taxpayer Advocate who is to help taxpayers who suffer hardships because of action taken by the IRS.

(C) *Levies and Liens.* Section 6331 provides generally that the IRS may levy on a taxpayer's property if taxes remain unpaid ten days after notice and demand for payment. Unless the collection of tax is in jeopardy, however, the IRS must give the taxpayer notice of the proposed levy and wait thirty days after the notice before it levies on the property. § 6331(d)(2). The notice that precedes the levy must be in simple, nontechnical language and must give the taxpayer information on how to avoid or challenge the levy. § 6331(d)(4). The Service also is required to release a levy if it is causing economic hardship because of the taxpayer's financial status or if certain other conditions are met, for example, the taxpayer has made arrangements to pay the tax on the installment method.

The exemptions from levy for certain personal property are currently $9,380, § 6334(a)(2), and $4,690 for business books and tools, § 6334(a)(3). These numbers are adjusted for inflation. Weekly wages equal to the taxpayer's standard deductions and personal exemptions (if any) are exempt from levy. § 6334(d). Some public assistance payments are exempt altogether, such as unemployment benefits, supplemental security income, and worker's compensation. § 6334(a)(4), (7), and (11). A taxpayer's principal residence cannot be seized without prior judicial approval.

(D) *Anyone Can Be Hassled by the Tax Collector.* While the IRS and other tax collection agencies try to be thoughtful and evenhanded in their administration of the tax law, overreaching is inevitable. Consider the following two stories:

In 1987 newspapers throughout the land reported the saga of one Gary D. Keefer, a 12-year-old whose life savings of $10.35 was seized by the IRS to settle a tax debt owed by his parents. Keefer's parents apparently were delinquent on a $200 monthly overdue tax bill and Gary's account was seized because his mother's Social Security number was on it. Keefer's first salvo was a letter to President Reagan, stating: "Greetings from Virginia. I regret to inform you that there is once again trouble in the colonies." Reagan did not answer, but after many phone calls, the IRS returned Gary's $10.35. On August 4, 1987, the IRS announced that it will no longer ask banks to seize accounts with balances under $100 and will freeze temporarily—rather than seize—any accounts that bear a name in addition to the delinquent taxpayer. Bless the children.

A footnote to this story. Sympathizers of Gary, including patrons of the New Paradise Lounge in Madison, Wisconsin, sent him checks for $10.35 and his account grew. Proving further his perspicacity, Gary said, "The IRS is going to want to tax all of that as income. A piggy bank is awfully inviting, considering they can just go into your account and take it again."

Finally, a tax professor (who for obvious reasons prefers to remain anonymous) reports the following encounter with an IRS revenue agent. The agent, on a question of deductions for medical expenses, was presented canceled checks and evidence that no reimbursement by insurance had occurred. "Not enough," he said, "I need a letter from your doctor indicating dates of treatment, etc."

"What!!" replied Professor X. "Why do you need more?"

The agent turned smugly to the table behind his desk and patted the Internal Revenue Code benignly. "It's in this book; we just have to go by this book," he said.

Professor X, who had not yet identified his line of work, felt a surge of adrenaline. The agent had patted a book he knew something about. Cloaking his voice now with sugar and innocence, the professor asked, "Could I just see what it says?"

The agent promptly flipped the Code open to the contemporaneous recordkeeping requirements of § 274(d). Almost leaping from his seat, the professor noted that § 274(d) was directed at entertainment expenses and a few other specific items, but not medical expenses.

Undaunted, the revenue agent replied, "It may say 'travel and entertainment,' but it means everything."

The professor reports that he then hired an accountant who cost him several thousand dollars to obtain a "no change" letter regarding his tax return from the IRS.

(E) *Tax Penalties.* Unlike some systems, in which the government determines the amount of tax due and sends the taxpayer a bill, the first formal determination of tax liability occurs when taxpayers themselves file their tax returns. The "voluntary" compliance demanded by "self-assessment" depends upon a variety of motivations ranging from the fear of being caught to the pleasure of participating in the democratic process. Justice Holmes wrote, "I like to pay taxes. With them I buy civilization." But his is distinctly a minority view. Compare Justice Stone, writing for the Court in Carmichael v. Southern Coal & Coke Co., 301 U.S. 495, 522 (1937): "A tax is not an assessment of benefits. It is * * * a means of distributing the burden of the cost of government."

Should taxpayers, when "self-assessing" the tax due, attempt to sit as a judge, resolving doubtful questions of law and fact according to "legislative intent," or as an adversary, resolving each doubtful issue in their own favor? Most taxpayers do the latter in addition to playing the audit lottery. On occasion, however, a fraudulent return is filed.

Alarmed by the extent of noncompliance, the proliferation of tax shelters and the audit lottery, Congress substantially revised the penalty structure of the Code to try to increase the economic costs of cheating. The tax return accuracy penalty is found in § 6662, which imposes a 20 percent penalty on any portion of an underpayment of tax that is attributable to (1) negligence or disregard of rules or regulations, (2) substantial understatement of income tax liability, or (3) valuation misstatement. § 6662(b). No penalty is imposed with respect to any portion of an underpayment if the taxpayer establishes that there was reasonable cause for that portion of the underpayment and that the taxpayer acted in good faith. § 6664(c).

The penalty for a substantial understatement of income tax is imposed where the underpayment of tax exceeds the greater of 10 percent of the correct tax liability or $5,000 ($10,000 in the case of a corporation). § 6662(d)(1)(A). No penalty is imposed on an understatement to the extent that it is attributable to a position with respect to which (1) "substantial authority" exists, or (2) the relevant facts concerning tax treatment are "adequately disclosed" on the return or an attached statement and there is a reasonable basis for the opinion.

The substantial authority standard is less stringent than a "more likely than not" standard (where there is a greater than 50 percent chance that the position will be upheld), but more stringent than a reasonable basis standard. Reg. § 1.6662–4(d)(2). The regulations define substantial authority to include the Internal Revenue Code and other statutes, proposed, temporary, and final regulations, tax treaties and their official explanations, court cases, committee reports and certain other legislative history, including explanations by the Joint Committee on Taxation, private letter rulings, technical advice memoranda, IRS information and press releases, and IRS notices and other announcements published in the Internal Revenue Bulletin. Treatises, legal periodicals, legal opinions, or opinions rendered by tax professionals are not authority. Reg. § 1.6662–4(d)(3)(iii). Authority for the tax treatment of an item is substantial if the weight of authorities supporting it is substantial in relation to the weight of authorities supporting contrary treatment. Reg. § 1.6662–4(d)(3)(i). A taxpayer may have substantial authority for a position that is supported only by a well-reasoned construction of the applicable statutory provision. Reg. § 1.6662–4(d)(3)(ii). The penalty also may be avoided if the taxpayer acts in good faith and has reasonable cause. § 6664(c).

The accuracy penalty also is triggered by substantial income tax valuation misstatements, substantial overstatements of pension liabilities, and substantial estate or gift tax valuation understatements. § 6662(e), (f), and (g). Understatements attributable to these causes are not reduced by the existence of substantial authority or by adequate disclosure.

Taxpayers who evade their tax obligations with criminal intent are subject to prosecution under various criminal provisions of the Code. §§ 7201 *et seq.* In addition, if any portion of an underpayment of tax is attributable to "fraud," the Code provides a civil penalty equal to 75 percent of the portion of the underpayment that is due to fraud. § 6663.

Tax preparers, which can include lawyers who provide tax advice used to prepare a return, can be subject to penalty if there is an understatement of tax liability on the return.

IRS employees have their own penalty—they can be fired. Federal law mandates termination of any IRS employee found to have willfully understated his federal tax liability, unless such understatement is due to reasonable cause and not willful neglect. Consider Benjamin Agbaniyaka, an IRS agent. Mr. Agbaniyaka took a deduction for losses on his African arts and crafts business that turned out to be more of a hobby. See § 183, discussed infra at page 385. First the IRS challenged his deductions. Then they met in court, and he lost his case. 94 T.C.M. 350. Then the IRS fired him. Finally, the Federal Circuit rejected his grievance complaint. 484 Fed. Appx. 545. An IRS agent is apparently expected to know the law he is paid to enforce.

In 2015, Congress gave the government another weapon. The Fixing America's Surface Transportation Act of 2015 allows the IRS to request that the State Department revoke the passport of any one with a "seriously delinquent tax debt" (greater than $50,000).

(F) *Interest.* Interest rates on tax underpayments are determined twice a year. The rate is generally the recent short-term Federal rate plus 3 percent and interest accrues on a compounded daily basis. §§ 6621, 6662. Interest accrues from the date the tax was owed, usually the return filing date. Interest is not suspended while litigation is pending in the Tax Court.

(G) *The Tax Gap.* While there is substantial compliance with the tax law—particularly for a "voluntary" tax system—there is also a significant amount of noncompliance. The "tax gap" for any year is the amount of tax liability faced by taxpayers that is not paid on time, either because a return is not filed, the taxpayer under-reports the amount of income, or the taxpayer does not pay the entire amount owed. The IRS estimates that the voluntary compliance rate—the percentage of total tax revenues paid on a timely basis—for 2008–2010 was 83.7 percent. The IRS estimate of the average annual tax gap for that period was $458 billion of which $387 billion was attributable to under-reporting. Compliance is highest where there is withholding or third-party information reporting. For example, only 1 percent of wages and salaries for which there is withholding were under-reported. Of course, all of these estimates should be viewed with skepticism; if the IRS really knows this much about the tax gap, why doesn't the agency close it?

D. THE ROLE OF THE JUDICIARY IN TAX MATTERS

When the administrative process fails to produce agreement between the IRS and the taxpayer, the taxpayer may litigate through any of three procedural avenues. This array of alternatives, and the consequences of choosing one or another, cannot be explained in terms of a rational tax judicial system but only as a matter of history.

Note on the Judicial Process in Tax Cases

District Courts. The taxpayer, on receipt of a notice of deficiency from the IRS, may pay the deficiency assessed, file a claim for a refund, and bring suit to enforce that claim in the appropriate district court under 28 U.S.C.A. § 1346. If the taxpayer loses, he may appeal to the proper court of appeals and ultimately petition the Supreme Court for a writ of certiorari.

The Claims Court. The taxpayer may pay the deficiency, file a claim for a refund, and bring suit to enforce that claim in the Court of Federal Claims under 28 U.S.C.A. § 1491. If she loses in the Claims Court, she may take an appeal to the Court of Appeals for the Federal Circuit.[14] The suit must be filed within two years after the Service has denied the claim for refund. § 6532(a).

The Tax Court. The taxpayer may refuse to pay the deficiency and, within 90 days of receipt of the notice of deficiency, petition the Tax Court for review under §§ 7441–7478 of the Code. Either she or the Service may obtain review of a Tax Court decision in the appropriate court of appeals, §§ 7481–7487, and ultimately petition the Supreme Court for review. (Section 7463 provides for a simplified and relatively informal optional procedure for "small" tax cases, involving $50,000 or less.)

Prior to 1924, there was no method to obtain judicial review of an IRS determination of tax liability without first paying the tax. Congress then established the Tax Court's predecessor, the Board of Tax Appeals, as "an independent agency in the executive branch." In 1942, the Board's name was changed to the Tax Court of the United States; in 1969, Congress established the Tax Court as an Article I court, exercising the legislative power of Congress, as distinguished from an Article III court, exercising powers under the judicial article of the Constitution. Article I courts are more limited in jurisdiction than Article III courts, and Article

---

[14] The Federal Circuit was created in 1982. Prior to that, its jurisdiction resided in the United States Court of Claims.

I judges do not enjoy life tenure as do Article III judges. Judges on the Tax Court are appointed to 15-year terms.

The Tax Court's role and operations are unique to the tax law and often as unfamiliar to experienced tax practitioners as to beginning law students. The following comments of Tax Court Judge Mary Ann Cohen to the University of Southern California Tax Institute provide helpful insights into the court's operations.

> * * * Tax lawyers sometimes forget that the Tax Court is a trial court, bound by the evidence in the case before it and the applicable statutes as written by Congress. * * *

> Tax Court opinions are often difficult to read from beginning to end because of compliance with the statutory admonition that "it shall be the duty of the Tax Court . . . to include in its report upon any proceeding its findings of fact or opinion or memorandum opinion." Judges sometimes write opinions and include voluminous facts because of the possibility of appeal. * * *

> For these reasons, opinions sometimes seem replete with minutiae and invite the reader to skip over the portion labeled "findings of fact" and to read only the discussion under the heading "opinion." But the detailed facts or the procedural history of the case may well explain a surprising result and [this material] is probably there so that prior or subsequent cases may be distinguished if the same result is not appropriate in other cases.

> In that regard it is important to understand and keep in mind the distinction between opinions published in the official Tax Court reports and memorandum opinions published privately by commercial publishers. Only the former are officially recognized as precedents where the full impact of *stare decisis* is felt binding on the court, although most lawyers and some judges will regularly cite memorandum opinions, especially in analogous fact situations. The so-called division opinions published by the court are those that the chief judge designates as deciding a significant issue of law not previously decided, whereas memorandum opinions generally are entirely factual or merely apply settled law to the facts of the case before the court. Thus classification of an opinion as a memorandum opinion may itself be a signal that the case should not be relied on in other circumstances as establishing a rule of law. Of course, if the facts of a case are similar to those in a reported memorandum opinion, the advocate who likes the result should argue that the situations are indistinguishable and the advocate who does not like the result should urge that it be limited to the facts of the case in which it was reached. You, of course, should not say that it is "merely a memorandum opinion of Judge X."

I should acknowledge that memorandum opinions or even bench opinions may sometimes become significant because of appellate action. The famous *Duberstein* case was a memorandum opinion in the Tax Court. * * *

Another aspect of the court that sometimes is not well understood is the relationship between the trial judge hearing the case and the court conference of all 19 judges entitled to vote on a case. The Tax Court is unique in this melding process by which the report of the judge becomes the opinion of the court. The chief judge is central to the process. * * * When a judge tries a case on a trial session, usually in one of approximately sixty places of trial away from Washington, D.C., and unless a bench opinion is rendered at the close of trial, a written report must be prepared. * * * When the trial judge has completed the report, it is sent to the chief judge. By statute, section 7460(b), "the report of the division shall become the report of the Tax Court within 30 days after such report by the division, unless within such period the chief judge has directed that such report shall be reviewed by the Tax Court." The parties have no right to affect this action or inaction by the chief judge.

* * * Past chief judges have adopted rules of thumb by which certain categories of cases will be referred to the court conference for review. * * * The categories include cases invalidating a treasury regulation, overruling a prior case, or re-examining an issue where we have been reversed by a court of appeals in a circuit other than the one in which the case before the court arises.

[Y]ou cannot discount a case because it has not been court reviewed. Any published opinion is the opinion of the Tax Court unless and until it has been overruled. The result reached may have seemed so clearly right and noncontroversial to the chief judge that the consumption of judicial time in the court review process was unwarranted. On the other hand, a case designated as a memorandum opinion by the chief judge may have been regarded as either clearly right and noncontroversial under established law or may involve a unique set of facts not likely to be seen again and therefore not regarded as establishing any precedent.

The Courts of Appeals. Tax Court and district court decisions are reviewable by the court of appeals for the circuit in which these lower courts sit, and Claims Court decisions are reviewable by the Federal Circuit. Section 7482(a) provides for appellate review of Tax Court decisions "in the same manner and to the same extent as decisions of the district Courts in civil actions tried without a jury." The 13 different circuits are not bound by one another's decisions, and the Tax Court and district courts are bound only by the decisions of the circuit to which the case may be appealed. Consequently, the outcome of a tax case often depends on the circuit in which the trial court is situated; inconsistent holdings among the circuits are not uncommon. The strategy for tax litigators often includes choosing the tribunal with the most favorable precedents.

Supreme Court Review. Review by the Supreme Court in federal cases is ordinarily only by writ of certiorari. 28 U.S.C.A. § 1245(1). Certiorari is granted in only a small proportion of the federal tax cases in which it is sought—recently far less than 10 percent. Most but not all of these writs are granted on the government's petition.

NOTES

(A) *The* Golsen *Rule.* When a Tax Court decision has been reversed by a court of appeals, the decision of the court of appeals is, of course, controlling in the particular case. Should the Tax Court also defer to that decision in cases reviewable by other courts of appeals? What should it do in the case of another taxpayer who can take his appeal to the same court of appeals?

In Golsen v. Commissioner, 54 T.C. 742 (1970), affirmed on the merits, 445 F.2d 985 (10th Cir. 1971), the full Tax Court announced that it would follow the decision of a court of appeals whenever the taxpayer's appeal would lie to that circuit. The Tax Court was faced with the problem of a case involving two or more taxpayers, appealable to more than one circuit in Kast v. Commissioner, 78 T.C. 1154 (1982). The court followed Ninth Circuit precedent to grant summary judgment in favor of the seven taxpayers whose cases were appealable to that circuit. But the court, citing its disagreement with the Ninth Circuit, refused to grant summary judgment to the one taxpayer whose case was appealable elsewhere.

(B) *"Acquiescence" and "Non-Acquiescence."* After the Commissioner has lost a case in the Tax Court, he may decide, for one reason or another, not to seek further review. He may, for example, conclude that the decision against the IRS is correct. In that event, he may decide to publish his "acquiescence" in the decision. This is done by including the case in a list of "acquiescences" in the Internal Revenue Bulletins. The Commissioner's formal "acquiescence" amounts to instructions to all Treasury employees that the decision is to be followed. Thus, it has much the same effect as a revenue ruling.

However, the Commissioner, even though he does not appeal, may announce his "non-acquiescence" in the decision. This, too, is published in the Internal Revenue Bulletin. The procedure of "non-acquiescence" causes some misunderstanding. If the Commissioner does not agree with the decision, why does he not appeal? In the first place, the decision whether to appeal is made by the Solicitor General, who may have refused to follow the Commissioner's recommendation. Or the Commissioner himself may have recommended against an appeal on the grounds that the case is unimportant or factually weak so that review of the issue by an appellate court should await some other case where the facts are better for the government.

A "non-acquiescence" has something of the status of a revenue ruling against the taxpayer and means that Treasury personnel will not apply the Tax Court's decision. The taxpayer, however, can probably win if he takes his case to the Tax Court unless the case has factual differences, or is appealed, or is affected by an intervening appeal of a similar case.

(C) *Score One for Pyrrhus.* The decades-old judicially created rule that the taxpayer has the burden of proof in tax cases was curtailed by Congress in the Internal Revenue Service Restructuring and Reform Act of 1998. Now the government has the burden of proof in a judicial proceeding as to a factual issue if the taxpayer introduces credible evidence relevant to determining her tax liability. In order to shift the burden of proof to the government, the taxpayer must (1) comply with any substantiation requirements imposed by the Code, (2) maintain records required by the Code and regulations, and (3) cooperate with IRS requests for meetings, information, documents, and the like, including exhausting her administrative remedies. Large corporations, partnerships, and trusts continue to have the burden of proof. Despite the enormous amount of "pro-taxpayer" publicity that accompanied this change, it actually affects only a tiny fraction of the millions of taxpayers filing returns and seems likely to affect the outcome of very few cases, if any. It does create, however, the prospect of some additional litigation over whether the taxpayer really "cooperated," and may make IRS agents somewhat more aggressive in obtaining information during audits.

As this idea was winding its way through Congress, nearly 100 tax law professors sent the tax writing committees a letter indicating that this was a very bad idea that would "make tax controversies more expensive, more intrusive, and more inconvenient for taxpayers" and also "would erode federal revenues, require higher appropriations for tax enforcement and make tax disputes more acrimonious." We suspect that the legislation has turned out to be neither as bad as opponents predicted nor the victory for the American people that its proponents claim. On the other hand, unlike Goldilocks' porridge, it doesn't seem "just right" either.

(D) *The Three Branches of Government.* If Congress does not like a tax decision of a court (including the Supreme Court), it can simply amend the statute. After all, taxation is purely statutory and Congress can amend provisions at any time and has done so frequently in response to judicial decisions. But what if Treasury does not like a judicial interpretation of the statute? Can it issue regulations that do not follow the judicial decision? Recall that regulations are entitled to *Chevron* deference. See page 60 supra.

Note on the Anti-Injunction Act and Standing Requirements

Anti-Injunction Act. The courts often have been asked to resolve tax-related controversies that raise the sorts of constitutional or, at least, political issues with respect to which the judiciary may be less inclined to defer to the expertise of the executive branch. The impetus for increased judicial scrutiny of tax policy frequently has been provided by the IRS treatment of tax-exempt organizations. The Supreme Court has tempered this judicial activism, however, by its strict construction of standing requirements and the Anti-Injunction Act § 7421 of the Code.

In Bob Jones University v. Simon, 416 U.S. 725 (1974), the Court held that the Anti-Injunction Act barred an action to enjoin the IRS from revoking a ruling letter that previously had declared the plaintiff university tax-exempt and eligible for deductible charitable contributions despite its refusal to admit black students. The Supreme Court declared that the Act, which provides that "no suit for the purpose of restraining the assessment or collection of any tax shall be maintained in any court," was applicable to the action because the university was seeking to restrain the collection of its own income, FICA, and FUTA (employment) taxes, as well as the income taxes of its donors, who would be denied charitable contribution deductions under the IRS action. Thus, the university could avoid the inhibitions of the Anti-Injunction Act only by establishing both irreparable injury and certainty of success on the merits; here, the Court found that Bob Jones University had failed to prove that "under no circumstances could the government ultimately prevail."

The Court emphasized that "this is not a case where an aggrieved party has no access at all to judicial review" since an assessment of tax eventually could be contested by the university or a donor in the Tax Court or the federal district courts. The university subsequently litigated the issue in a suit for the refund of $21 in unemployment taxes. In Bob Jones University v. United States, 461 U.S. 574 (1983), the Supreme Court denied tax exemptions to religious schools that engage in racially discriminatory practices. For the case, see infra at page 472.

The Supreme Court recognized in the first *Bob Jones University* case that "serious problems" may be suffered by organizations whose tax exemption is revoked by the IRS. Similar concerns motivated legislation that now provides for declaratory judgment proceedings in the Tax Court, the Court of Federal Claims, or the Federal District Court for the District of Columbia to resolve controversies over an IRS determination or failure to make a determination with respect to an organization's tax-exempt status. See § 7428. A limited number of additional declaratory judgment procedures also have been authorized by Congress. See, e.g., § 7478, providing the Tax Court exclusive jurisdiction to hear cases of actual controversy involving an IRS determination (or failure to make a determination) whether interest on a prospective obligation of a state or local government is exempt from the federal income tax.

The taxpayers who initiated the litigation in which the Supreme Court upheld the constitutionality of the penalty for failure to purchase health insurance in the "Obamacare" legislation sought an injunction to prevent enforcement of the penalty. National Federation of Independent Business v. Sebelius, 567 U.S. 519 (2012). The Court held this provision to be a "tax" for constitutional purposes, but not for purposes of the Anti-Injunction Act, which would have barred this lawsuit if held applicable.

Standing. In Simon v. Eastern Kentucky Welfare Rights Organization, 426 U.S. 26 (1976), the Supreme Court held that the Eastern Kentucky Welfare Rights Organization did not have standing to challenge an IRS ruling that exempted hospitals from tax as charitable institutions even though they provided no indigent care facilities or services. The Court held that neither the organization nor its indigent members could show the "actual injury" necessary to establish standing. The Court repeatedly characterized as "speculative" the connection between the plaintiffs' injuries and the challenged actions of the IRS; for example, the court characterized as "speculative" the inference that the hospitals were so dependent on their tax exemption that they would change their treatment policies rather than forgo tax-exempt status.

It is almost impossible to obtain standing to challenge an IRS decision *not* to collect additional taxes. This difficulty was made clear by the Supreme Court in Allen v. Wright, 468 U.S. 737 (1984). The Court denied standing to a group of parents of black public school children who sought to bring a class action suit against the IRS attempting to challenge IRS grants of tax exemption to racially discriminatory schools. The Court held that the parents' claim of injury was not "fairly traceable" to the government conduct challenged as unlawful, and that the parents therefore lacked standing. The Court further stated that the links in the "chain of causation" between the challenged IRS conduct and the asserted injury were too weak to sustain the parents' standing since it was speculative whether withdrawal of tax exemption would lead the schools to change their segregationist policies.

In dissenting in *Allen,* Justice Stevens (joined by Justice Blackmun) referred to statements in *Bob Jones University* as well as to language in Regan v. Taxation With Representation of Washington, 461 U.S. 540, 544 (1983), that a tax exemption is a form of subsidy administered through the tax system. Through what he described as a "restatement of elementary economics," Stevens explained why the grant of such a subsidy by the government could arguably be deemed causative of an injury to the black parents for purposes of standing analysis. Justice Stevens also dismissed the majority's invocation of separation of powers, believing the question of IRS' administrative policy to be well within the competence of the judiciary. (Justice Brennan filed a separate dissent.)

After many court proceedings, standing was denied to various individuals and organizations who sued to challenge the tax-exempt status of the Roman Catholic Church asserting that the church's anti-abortion activities violated the Code's prohibition against lobbying by tax-exempt organizations. In re United States Catholic Conference, 885 F.2d 1020 (2d Cir. 1989), cert. denied 495 U.S. 918 (1990). See also Apache Bend Apartments, Ltd. v. United States, 987 F.2d 1174 (5th Cir. 1993), in which the court held that taxpayers who did not benefit from extensive transition rules enacted as part of the 1986 Act lacked standing to challenge their constitutionality.

Most standing cases deal with the issue of whether federal taxpayers have standing to object to an expenditure of federal funds simply because they are taxpayers. In Cuno v. DaimlerChrysler, the Court held that state taxpayers also lack standing to challenge a state fiscal decision that benefits another taxpayer on the ground that it might affect their tax liability. 547 U.S. 1147 (2006).

Congressmen fare no better in obtaining standing to challenge tax legislation. The Supreme Court held that six Congressmen who voted against the Line Item Veto Act had no standing to challenge its constitutionality because they had no particularized and personal injury. Raines v. Byrd, 521 U.S. 811 (1997).

In Flast v. Cohen, 392 U.S. 83 (1968), the Court carved out a narrow exception to the general rule against federal taxpayer standing. A taxpayer asserting an Establishment Clause claim under the First Amendment has standing to challenge a law authorizing the use of federal funds that allegedly violates that clause. The Court has been reluctant to extend the exception. For example, in Hein v. Freedom from Religion Foundation, 551 U.S. 587 (2007), taxpayers challenged conferences organized by the White House Office of Faith-Based and Community Initiatives at which they alleged officials of this office promoted religious community groups over secular ones. Holding that the taxpayers lacked standing, a plurality of the Court found that the *Flast* exception applied only to challenges directed at exercises of congressional power under the Taxing and Spending Clause, and did not apply to the use of funds appropriated for the general discretionary use of the Executive Branch. Because the expenditures were not expressly authorized by any specific congressional enactment, the Court said the action lacked a nexus between taxpayer status and the type of legislative enactment challenged.

In Freedom from Religion Foundation, Inc. v. Lew, 773 F.3d 815 (7th Cir. 2014), the foundation and its atheist co-presidents challenged the constitutionality under the First Amendment of § 107, which exempts any housing allowance provided to a "minister of the gospel." First, the court found that they lacked standing because they suffered no direct harm. The *Flast* exception did not apply because taxpayers do not have standing to challenge tax expenditures. The plaintiffs received a housing allowance from their employer and, not being ministers, they were subject to tax. Thus, they argued they were denied a benefit based on religion. Because the plaintiffs had not claimed the exemption, the court rejected the argument that they were denied its benefit. The court implied that the plaintiffs might have had standing if they had claimed the exemption and subsequently been denied by the IRS. That is exactly what they did, and in October 2017, a federal district court judge in Wisconsin held that § 107 is unconstitutional. Gaylor v. Mnuchin, 278

F.Supp.3d. 1081 (W.D. Wis. 2017). The government, of course, has appealed.

NOTES

(A) *Why Wait?* What is to be gained by waiting until suits are filed by those more directly injured by IRS actions? Can it fairly be said that any person who is willing to bear the expenses of litigation will pursue the case "with the kind of vigor that the Article III 'case or controversy' standard requires"? Tax Analysts and Advocates v. Schultz, 376 F. Supp. 889 (D.D.C. 1974).

(B) *The South Carolina Case.* In South Carolina v. Regan, 465 U.S. 367 (1984), the Court permitted a state to invoke its original jurisdiction to decide a question concerning the tax liability of those who would buy bonds from the state. In *South Carolina,* the state wanted the Court to decide the constitutionality of § 103(j) (now § 149) of the Code, which denies owners of state and municipal bonds issued after June 30, 1983, an exclusion for interest unless the issuer has put the obligation in registered form. Although the nominal tax liability under this provision falls on bondholders, issuers would likely bear a portion of the economic consequences of taxation by having to pay higher interest rates. South Carolina in effect claimed *jus tertii* standing to assert its bondholders' rights to avoid tax liability, largely because its own material stakes were closely tied to the bondholders.

In upholding South Carolina's right to sue, the Supreme Court distinguished the *Bob Jones University* case, on the grounds that the loss of tax-exempt status produced some direct liability under the federal unemployment tax that would enable Bob Jones University to obtain post-assessment judicial review of their constitutional claims. In contrast, South Carolina would not owe any taxes to the federal government, no matter what the tax status of its bonds, and had only its bondholders' liability to contest.

Seizing on the non-direct-access opening, the *South Carolina* Court created a new exception to the Anti-Injunction Act. A majority believed that the exception extended to all cases where a person asserted only the tax claims of third parties and therefore had no power to bring a refund suit. It discounted the possibility that bondholders could vindicate the state's interests.

Having swept aside the Anti-Injunction Act, the Court did not look for positive congressional authorization for the suit to proceed. Perhaps it believed no inquiry was necessary, as the case met the requirements of the Court's original jurisdiction, the state had a clear economic interest in the litigation, and the cause of action could be implied directly from the Constitution.

Is it the Court's view that the state's showing of direct economic harm is simply a more important claim than, for example, the *Allen* plaintiffs' allegations concerning the nature of their harms? Constitutional history suggests the opposite, but distinguishing the cases on "causation" grounds seems tenuous indeed.

(C) *An Ombudsman?* If the IRS chooses not to enforce a provision of the Code, or interprets it in a clearly erroneous way favorable to the taxpayer, who could challenge the decision? The standing cases seem to suggest that it is virtually impossible to obtain judicial review of IRS determinations that are favorable to the taxpayers whose financial interests are at stake.

The Taxpayer Advocate is like an ombudsman for taxpayers. How would allowing the Taxpayer Advocate to sue compare to a general grant of standing to public interest law firms, other public interest organizations, and groups of plaintiffs such as those in *Allen*?

CHAPTER 2

WHAT IS INCOME?

There is no universally accepted definition of income for the purpose of levying an income tax.

Laymen find it hard to believe that there are major problems in defining income. They are used to thinking in terms of cash wages and salaries, which are easily identified and clearly income. In fact, wages and salaries account for the great bulk of income—however defined—in the U.S. economy; other items like interest and dividends are also easily identified. So it may be fairly said that most of the dollars identified as income in the total economy will be the same under any definition of income.

But as one approaches the edges of the concept of income, there is a substantial grey area. It is small compared with the bulk of income, but this grey area * * * is the focus of much controversy. There is an extensive literature on the subject, beginning before the turn of the century and continuing to the present, with no consensus except that particular definitions may be more practical in certain circumstances than in others.

U.S. Treasury Dep't, Blueprints for Tax Reform 21 (1977).

The term "income" is not defined in the Code or the Regulations. Although a number of courts have attempted to define income, more than a century of experience with a federal income tax has not produced an acceptable definition. Nevertheless, scholars have devoted a great deal of thought to the question, "What is income?" It is valuable to compare some of the definitions proposed by economists with the concept of income for tax purposes developed by Congress, the Internal Revenue Service, and the courts. A sampling from the economic literature is set out below:

Robert Haig, "The Concept of Income," in The Federal Income Tax 1, 7 (1921): "Income is the money value of the net accretion to one's economic power between two points of time."

William Hewett, The Definition of Income and its Application in Federal Taxation 22–23 (1925): "Net individual income is the flow of commodities and services accruing to an individual through a period of time and available for disposition after deducting the necessary costs of acquisition."

Henry C. Simons, Personal Income Taxation 50 (1938): "Personal income may be defined as the algebraic sum of (1) the market value of rights exercised in consumption and (2) the change in the value of the store of property rights between the beginning and end of the period in question."

Richard Posner, Economic Analysis of Law 535 (1998): "The broadest definition of income would be all pecuniary and nonpecuniary receipts, including not only leisure and other nonpecuniary income from household production but also gifts, bequests and prizes."

The Simons definition, which is considered a refinement of the Haig definition, is the most widely accepted and is usually referred to as the Haig-Simons definition of income. It is used by many economists and lawyers as a basis for testing the equity of the income tax. Simons himself, however, noted that the definition would not serve for all purposes and without modification would not describe a workable tax base.

It is not clear that a generally accepted economic definition of income should be accepted by Congress, the Service, and the courts for tax purposes. The selection of income as the base implies that income should provide a measure of an individual's ability to pay tax and any definition should serve to further that purpose. Furthermore, the concept of income must be sufficiently practical to be administered by the IRS.

Gross income is defined in § 61 of the Code as "all income from whatever source derived." So according to the Code, income is income (echoing Gertrude Stein who insisted that "a rose is a rose is a rose is a rose.") Section 61 also includes a non-inclusive list of specific items included in gross income. Sections 71–90 of the Code are concerned with additional items specifically included in gross income, and §§ 101–150 specifically exclude certain items from gross income. But the items cataloged are not an exhaustive list of the receipts included in gross income, and the Service and the courts have attempted to further determine what is within the contours of "income." In Eisner v. Macomber, 252 U.S. 189, 207 (1920), the Supreme Court attempted to define income:

Income may be defined as the gain derived from capital, from labor, or from both combined, provided it be understood to include profit gained through a sale or conversion of capital assets. * * *

This definition of income, while often quoted, was abandoned long ago as being too narrow. For example, it would not include windfalls. The Supreme Court tried again in Commissioner v. Glenshaw Glass Co., 348 U.S. 426 (1955), when it found that punitive damages were included in gross income.

This Court has frequently stated that [the statutory language of the predecessor to § 61] was used by Congress to exert in this field "the full measure of its taxing power." * * * Congress applied no limitations as to the source of taxable receipts, nor restrictive labels as to their nature. * * * Here we have instances of *undeniable accessions to wealth, clearly realized, and over* *which the taxpayers have complete dominion.* * * * We would do violence to the plain meaning of the statute and restrict a clear legislative attempt to bring the taxing power to bear upon all receipts constitutionally taxable were we to say that the payments in question here are not gross income.

This definition stands for the proposition that "income" should be broadly construed in the absence of a specific congressional directive to the contrary.

In determining *what* is income, we do not focus just on receipts. It is also appropriate to determine *which deductions* are allowed in measuring taxable income. We also must determine *whose* income it is and *when* it is taxable. As you will see, these are not always clearly separated issues; they shade into one another. Nevertheless, the classification is useful and it has been followed as an organizing principle of this book.

The primary focus of this Chapter is the first question: What is income? Often there is no question as to *who* has received the benefit or *when* it was received. The fundamental question is which receipts or benefits are income.

SECTION 1.   COMPENSATION FOR SERVICES

Section 61 requires that compensation for services be included in gross income. Thus, wages, salaries, fees, commissions, fringe benefits, and similar items are income. Compensation received in the form of royalties, or as a percentage of profits, is also income. It is not necessary that there be an employer-employee relationship; tips, legal and medical fees, and jury fees are all compensation for services includible in gross income. Generally, the form of payment does not affect the inclusion of compensation in gross income. Thus, for example, compensation would include stock, notes, or other property transferred for services; the amount of the income is the fair market value of the transferred property. § 1.61–2(d) and § 83. There are, however, many important exceptions that are considered in this Section.

Not all payments to employees are compensation; the question is whether the payment was compensatory in nature. Sometimes specific Code provisions exclude from gross income certain payments by employers to or for the benefit of employees even if compensatory. This Section of the Chapter provides illustrations of the general rule and its exceptions and limitations.

A. FORM OF RECEIPT

Old Colony Trust Co. v. Commissioner

Supreme Court of the United States, 1929. 279 U.S. 716.

■ MR. CHIEF JUSTICE TAFT delivered the opinion of the Court.

* * *

The facts certified to us are substantially as follows:

William M. Wood was president of the American Woolen Company during the years 1918, 1919, and 1920. In 1918 he received as salary and commissions from the company $978,725, which he included in his federal income tax return for 1918. In 1919 he received as salary and commissions from the company $548,132.87, which he included in his return for 1919.

August 3, 1916, the American Woolen Company had adopted the following resolution, which was in effect in 1919 and 1920:

"Voted: That this company pay any and all income taxes, State and Federal, that may thereafter become due and payable upon the salaries of all the officers of the company * * * to the end that said persons and officers shall receive their salaries or other compensation in full without deduction on account of income taxes, State or Federal, which taxes are to be paid out of the treasury of this corporation."

This resolution was amended on March 25, 1918, as follows:

"Voted: That, referring to the vote passed by this board on August 3, 1916, in reference to income taxes, State and Federal, payable upon the salaries or compensation of the officers and certain employees of this company, the method of computing said taxes shall be as follows, viz.:

" 'The difference between what the total amount of his tax would be, including his income from all sources, and the amount of his tax when computed upon his income excluding such compensation or salaries paid by this company.' "

Pursuant to these resolutions, the American Woolen Company paid to the collector of internal revenue Mr. Wood's federal income and surtaxes due to salary and commissions paid him by the company, as follows:

Taxes for 1918 paid in 1919	$681,169.88
Taxes for 1919 paid in 1920	$351,179.27

The decision of the Board of Tax Appeals here sought to be reviewed was that the income taxes of $681,169.88 and $351,179.27 paid by the American Woolen Company for Mr. Wood were additional income to him for the years 1919 and 1920.

* * *

[The first portion of the opinion, in which the jurisdiction of the federal courts to review decisions of the Board of Tax Appeals was sustained, is omitted.]

Coming now to the merits of this case, we think the question presented is whether a taxpayer, having induced a third person to pay his income tax or having acquiesced in such payment as made in discharge of an obligation [of his], may avoid the making of a return thereof and the payment of a corresponding tax. We think he may not do so. The payment of the tax by the employers was in consideration of the services rendered by the employee, and was a gain derived by the employee from his labor. The form of the payment is expressly declared to make no difference. * * *. It is therefore immaterial that the taxes were directly paid over to the government. The discharge by a third person of an obligation [of his] is equivalent to receipt by the person taxed. The * * * taxes were imposed upon the employee, * * * the taxes were actually paid by the employer and * * * the employee entered upon his duties in the years in question under the express agreement that his income taxes would be paid by his employer. This is evidenced by the terms of the resolution passed August 3, 1916, more than one year prior to the year in which the taxes were imposed. The taxes were paid upon a valuable consideration, namely, the services rendered by the employee and as part of the compensation therefor. We think, therefore, that the payment constituted income to the employee. * * *

Nor can it be argued that the payment of the tax * * * was a gift. The payment for services, even though entirely voluntary, was nevertheless compensation within the statute. This is shown by the case of Noel v. Parrott (C.C.A.) 15 F.2d 669. There it was resolved that a gratuitous appropriation equal in amount to $3 per share on the outstanding stock of the company be set aside out of the assets for distribution to certain officers and employees of the company, and that the executive committee be authorized to make such distribution as they deemed wise and proper. The executive committee gave $35,000 to be paid to the plaintiff taxpayer. The court said * * *:

"In no view of the evidence, therefore, can the $35,000 be regarded as a gift. It was either compensation for services rendered, or a gain or profit derived from the sale of the stock of the corporation, or both; and, in any view, it was taxable as income."

It is next argued against the payment of this tax that, if these payments by the employer constitute income to the employee, the employer will be called upon to pay the tax imposed upon this additional income, and that the payment of the additional tax will create further income which will in turn be subject to tax, with the result that there would be a tax upon a tax. This, it is urged, is the result of the government's theory, when carried to this logical conclusion, and results in an absurdity which Congress could not have contemplated.

In the first place, no attempt has been made by the Treasury to collect further taxes, upon the theory that the payment of the additional taxes creates further income, and the question of a tax upon a tax was not before the Circuit Court of Appeals, and has not been certified to this Court. We can settle questions of that sort when an attempt to impose a tax upon a tax is undertaken, but not now. * * * It is not, therefore, necessary to answer the argument based upon an algebraic formula to reach the amount of taxes due. The question in this case is, "Did the payment by the employer of the income taxes assessable against the employee constitute additional taxable income to such employee?" The answer must be "Yes."

■ [The dissent by JUSTICE MCREYNOLDS is omitted.]

NOTES

(A) *A "Tax on a Tax"?* In Old Colony, the government assessed a deficiency on the original amount paid to the taxpayer by his employer and in litigation did not raise the issue of a tax on a tax. Was the government's concession necessary or desirable? If the employer agreed to pay all taxes owed, could it have computed the exact amount of the total tax? See Rev. Proc. 81–48, 1981–2 C.B. 623 and Rev. Rul. 86–14, 1986–1 C.B. 304, both of which require pyramiding of federal income and employment taxes under current law.

(B) *Tax-Inclusive Base.* Section 275 denies any deduction for federal income taxes. Therefore, the federal income tax is imposed on a "tax-inclusive" basis: The amount of tax is included in the amount of taxable income to which rates are applied. Our current withholding system reflects this. The tax is levied on the gross amount of compensation even though the employee receives a net amount after the appropriate amount of tax has been withheld and sent to the government. If federal taxes were deductible, the income tax would be imposed on a "tax-exclusive" basis. Whether the federal income tax is deductible or not is simply a matter of the rate of tax. Tax-inclusive rates can be converted into tax-exclusive rates (and vice versa) by the following formulas:

$$r_e = \frac{r_i}{1 - r_i} \quad \text{and } r_i = \frac{r_e}{1 + r_e}$$

The following table illustrates some tax-inclusive and tax-exclusive rates:

Tax-Inclusive Rates	Equivalent Tax-Exclusive Rates
24%	32%
37%	59%

Tax-Inclusive Rates	Equivalent Tax-Exclusive Rates
40%	$66^2/_3$%
50%	100%
75%	300%
83%	488%

For example, assume an employer wants to pay a salary yielding $30,000 in after-tax income to an employee who is taxable at a 24 percent tax-inclusive rate. Applying the 24 percent rate to the $30,000 of income produces $7,200 of tax, which in turn (at a 24 percent rate) would produce $1,728 of tax, $415 of tax, $100 of tax, $24 of tax, $6 of tax, $1 of tax and some additional pennies for a total of $9,474. (These numbers are rounded to the nearest dollar. Those who insist on mathematical precision and are concerned with Zeno's paradox should look at § 7504). Alternatively, the corresponding tax-exclusive rate of 32 percent would also produce a tax of $9,474. The same result would be obtained by applying the 24 percent tax-inclusive rate to a before-tax income of $39,474. The $9,474 tax liability would represent the entire pyramid discussed in *Old Colony*. Algebraically, if an employer wants to pay a specific amount after taxes, the net salary (N) equals the gross salary (G) minus the tax due, which is the gross salary times the tax rate (t). So: $N = G - Gt$ or $N = G(1-t)$, so $G = N/(1-t)$. Thus at a 24 percent rate, to pay a $30,000 net salary, the employer must pay 30,000/(1–.24) or $39,474.

In contrast to income taxes, sales taxes generally are applied on a tax-exclusive basis. In his 2016 presidential campaign, however, Senator Ted Cruz proposed a tax on consumption but advanced a tax-inclusive rate of 16 percent (equivalent to a tax-exclusive rate of 19.05 percent). Why might a politician prefer a tax-inclusive rather than a tax-exclusive rate?

(C) *Progressivity.* Note that the 1918 amendment in *Old Colony* whereby the company agreed to pay the difference between the employee's total tax and the tax on his non-company income had the effect of "stacking" the employee's salary (on which the company paid tax) on top of his other income. Given a progressive rate schedule, the company thus paid the highest marginal rate of tax. Compare this result to an agreement that computed the tax by stacking non-company income on top of the company salary; under this agreement, the company would calculate the employee's tax liability at the lowest marginal rate. An alternative plan might have required the company to pay a proportion of the employee's total tax equal to the ratio of the company salary to his total income; here the company would pay tax based on the employee's average tax rate. The 1918 agreement was to the employee's benefit when it was adopted, and stacking wages on which the company would pay tax on top of other income would always be to the employee's benefit under a progressive rate schedule.

The distinction between marginal and average rates of tax is important. The *marginal rate* is the rate that applies to additional dollars of taxable income, and therefore is the rate that affects tax decisions at the margin. The marginal rate tells you how much an additional dollar of income or deduction will change your tax liability. In a progressive rate schedule, marginal tax rates increase as income increases. Often marginal rates are referred to as tax "brackets." The *average tax rate* is the total tax liability divided by income. Typically, taxable income is used as the denominator for calculating average tax rates, but sometimes other concepts of income—adjusted gross income or some estimate of "economic income"—are used. Average rates measure taxpayers' overall tax burdens and are frequently used to compare tax rates across taxpayers.

(D) *Other Benefits. Old Colony* is not limited to taxes paid by the employer. In theory, any in-kind benefit transferred as compensation for services rendered is income, although Congress has chosen to exempt certain benefits. The employer, for example, could pay the employee's rent or pay school tuition for an employee's child. Generally, the employer's payment of the employee's obligation is equivalent to the receipt of the amount of the obligation. See, e.g., O'Malley v. Commissioner, 91 T.C. 352 (1988) (payment of legal fees); Tennessee Securities, Inc. v. Commissioner, 674 F.2d 570 (6th Cir. 1982) (payment on guarantee of taxpayer's loan).

(E) *A Tax on a Tax Break.* State and local governments commonly use targeted tax breaks to encourage economic development. Should the value of these incentives count as income to the taxpayer? In Maines v. Commissioner, 144 T.C. 123 (2015), the court held that refundable state tax credits to a business are taxable income for federal tax returns, but only to the extent that they exceed state tax liability. The court seems to conclude that credits are not accessions to wealth when they merely reduce state tax liability, but when in excess of the state tax liability, they are.

B. FRINGE BENEFITS

Introductory Note on Fringe Benefits

The term "fringe benefits" is loosely used to describe in-kind benefits transferred to an employee. They may be additional compensation or they may be essential to the performance of the employee's job. An example of the former is an all-expenses-paid vacation and an example of the latter is chalk used by a school teacher. Most fringe benefits fall somewhere in between. They are transferred because the employee has performed services for the employer and thus they have a compensatory element, but they also are often for the benefit of the employer and important in enabling the employee to do her job.

Which of the following would be "income"? Suppose the employer installs a drinking fountain or supplies free sodas? Suppose air conditioning is provided? What if very expensive art is hung in an executive's office? What about free uniforms furnished to janitors? Or free suits furnished to law firm associates? What about a free limousine that brings an executive to work and back? Or a van that takes workers home who finish work at 2 a.m.? Suppose free parking is provided? Suppose employees are allowed to use a gym on the business premises?

Suppose country club dues are paid by the employer? What about health or life insurance? What if only highly-paid employees were eligible for perks? Would it make a difference if the employer reimbursed the employee for any of these items? Would the result be the same if the employer simply paid additional compensation and expected employees to pay for the items?

Many fringe benefits are not subject to the income tax under current law—not because they are not income, but because Congress has chosen to treat them specially. Fringe benefits excluded from the income tax generally also are excluded from the definition of "wages" under the federal payroll taxes, including Social Security tax. In recent years, fringe benefits, including health and pension benefits, have accounted for an increasing percentage of employee compensation. They also are one of the largest tax expenditures. The most important of these are described in the following Section.

1.   TAX EXPENDITURE FRINGE BENEFITS

Several fringe benefits are eligible for specific statutory exclusion from gross income. All of them constitute "income" in an economic sense and thus none can be justified on tax policy grounds. Rather, they must be defended as accomplishing some nontax policy objective.

Note on the Exclusion of Employer-Provided Health Insurance

Section 106 excludes employer contributions to accident and health plans from the gross income of employees. Under this provision, the cost of employer-provided disability or medical insurance is not taxable to employees whether the employer provides the protection through an insurance company or on a self-financed basis. If an employee purchases accident or health insurance himself, no deduction is provided (except to the limited extent an itemized medical expense deduction might be available, see page 483 infra), but the proceeds in the event of sickness or disability are not taxed. § 104(a)(3).

Section 104 also excludes from gross income compensation for injuries or sickness in the form of workers' compensation, disability pensions, received as a result of active service in the military, foreign service, Coast Guard, or Public Health Service, and disability payments received by civilian government employees for injuries attributable to terrorist attacks.

Section 105 excludes benefits paid under an employer's accident and health plan for the medical expenses of employees and their families as well as for permanent disfigurement or "loss of use of a member or function of the body." Sick pay, however, is taxable. Self-insured medical reimbursement plans established by employers must not discriminate in terms of eligibility or benefits in favor of highly-paid employees, officers, or shareholders. § 105(h)(2). Lump sum payments to employees on the termination of a health and accident plan are taxable as compensation.

In 2010, the Affordable Care Act made major changes to the U.S. health care insurance system, including to the tax code. A major aim of the new law was to extend benefits to the uninsured, and to that end the legislation created health-insurance exchanges, or marketplaces, where individuals and families could buy policies. A new refundable tax credit in § 36B assists low-income purchasers in paying their premiums. The goal of the credit is to ensure that qualifying individuals do not spend more than a specific percentage of their incomes on health insurance premiums, but the terms of the statute are almost incomprehensively complex.

Another goal of the Affordable Care Act was to avoid the problem of adverse selection, which can raise prices and suppress participation in a health insurance market. Insurance works by pooling costs, and it works best when high- and low-risk patients are in the pool together. Adverse selection occurs when young and healthy people decline to buy insurance, leaving only sick people in the pool. Prices must then rise to cover the higher costs of the sicker population. The price increase may drive additional healthy people out of the market, which leads to another round of price increases. To encourage widespread participation in the insurance pools, the legislation included the famous (or infamous) individual mandate, a tax provision found in § 5000A, which imposes a penalty (termed a "shared responsibility payment") on taxpayers who lack insurance for themselves or for a dependent.

In 2017, the maximum penalty for a year without insurance was $695 per person or, if less, 2.5 percent of household income in excess of the tax threshold (that is, the sum of the standard deduction and the personal exemptions). But the 2017 tax legislation set the penalty to zero beginning in 2019, effectively repealing the individual mandate. Religious objectors, undocumented aliens, prisoners, members of Native American tribes, and some hardship cases are exempt. The individual mandate was upheld by the Supreme Court against a constitutional challenge in National Federation of Independent Business v. Sebelius, 567 U.S. 519 (2012). But the individual mandate was repealed by the 2017 tax law. The repeal was estimated to raise more than $300 billion in the following decade but to increase the number of uninsured by 4 million in 2019 and 13 million in 2027.

The political controversy in the United States over health insurance has been especially contentious in recent years, but whether and how to attempt to provide nearly every American with health coverage has long been controversial. Prior to World War II, there was remarkably little private health insurance in the United States; only 9 percent of the population enjoyed such coverage in 1940. By 1950, half of the U.S. population was covered by private health insurance, largely because employment-based health insurance had become a desirable form of paying wages—it was exempt from wartime wage control limitations. Federal income and payroll tax exemptions further stimulated employment-based health insurance as a way of compensating workers. Employer-based coverage, however, has experienced a steady decline that began in the 1980s. In 1979, for example, 82 percent of full-time civilian employees had employer-sponsored health insurance. That number had declined to 73 percent in little more than a decade and in 2017 was about 55 percent. About 47 percent of workers in firms with less than 10 employees enjoy employer-sponsored health insurance, compared to 80 percent of workers with 1,000 or more employees. Part-time workers are far more likely not to be insured by their employers than full-time workers.

The exclusion for employer-provided health care benefits is one of the largest tax expenditures but has been widely criticized by policy makers across the political spectrum. Consider the analysis provided by the Congressional Budget Office in 2013:

Congressional Budget Office, Options for Reducing the Deficit: 2014–2023, Reduce Tax Preferences for Employment-Based Health Insurance (2013)

Current Law. * * * The favorable tax treatment of employment-based health insurance is the largest single tax expenditure by the federal government. * * * Excluding employment-based health insurance from both income and payroll taxes will cost the government $248 billion in 2013, CBO estimates. In addition, the federal government incurs a tax expenditure of about $6 billion a year by allowing self-employed people to deduct the costs of health insurance from their taxable income for the individual income tax (though not for payroll taxes).

* * *

Effects of the Current Tax Treatment. The tax subsidy for employment-based health insurance reduces the problem of "adverse selection," in which less healthy people are more likely to buy health insurance (or to buy specific types of plans) than healthier people are. Adverse selection can cause health insurance markets to break down or to operate inefficiently. Most people would be willing to pay an insurance premium that was somewhat higher than their expected costs for health care in order to avoid the financial risks from unexpected and costly health problems. However, it is difficult and expensive for insurers to determine, and tailor their premiums to, an individual's expected health care costs.

In markets where everyone pays the same premium, health insurance tends to attract enrollees with above-average costs, for whom insurance provides more benefit, and to be less attractive to people with below-average costs, for whom insurance provides less benefit. Thus, in the absence of subsidies or a mandate to purchase coverage, markets for health insurance usually end up offering limited coverage (which less healthy people do not find as appealing), denying coverage to people with high expected costs (to the extent that insurers can determine them), charging high premiums (to cover the costs of less healthy enrollees), or some combination of those outcomes. * * *

Employment-based health insurance limits those market problems in several ways. Employers generally select a workforce on the basis of criteria other than health care costs, so most workforces consist of a mix of healthier and less healthy people. Therefore, pooling risks across a workforce (and its family members) reduces the variability of average health care spending for the group. The current tax exclusions encourage employers to offer health insurance; in turn, when employers pay a large share of premiums, employees' share tends to be small relative to their expected health care costs, which encourages them to buy insurance and thereby reduces adverse selection. * * *

The Affordable Care Act made several changes to health insurance markets that, together, will substantially reduce the traditional problems in individual markets discussed above, thus weakening the rationale for subsidizing employment-based insurance:

- The new insurance exchanges will enable individuals and families to buy insurance if they lack other sources of coverage that are deemed affordable. * * *

- Most legal U.S. residents will be required to obtain insurance coverage or potentially be liable for a penalty tax. [Ed. Note: This is the individual mandate, which was effectively repealed by the 2017 legislation.]

- Insurance purchased individually (through the exchanges or directly from insurers) will be available on a guaranteed-issue basis—meaning that policies will be offered to all applicants regardless of their health status—and premiums will not be allowed to vary according to policyholders' health status or sex. In addition, variation in premiums by age will be limited. (Without the subsidies and the requirement to obtain insurance, those provisions alone would increase adverse selection in the market for individually purchased insurance.)

Although the current tax preferences for employment-based health insurance reduce adverse selection, those preferences also encourage workers to favor health care over other goods and services they could purchase and thus contribute to the growth of health care spending. That outcome occurs because the tax exclusions encourage employers to compensate their workers with a combination of health insurance coverage and cash wages rather than entirely with cash wages. And because the value of the tax subsidy increases with an insurance plan's premium, * * * enrollment is especially encouraged in plans that cover a greater number of services, cover more expensive services, or require enrollees to pay a smaller share of the costs of the services they receive. As a result, people use more health care—and health care spending is higher—than would otherwise be the case. * * *

Another concern about the tax exclusions arises from how their subsidy is distributed among workers at different income levels. The value of the exclusions is generally larger for workers with higher income, partly because those workers face higher income tax rates (although they may face lower rates of payroll taxation) and partly because they are more likely to work for an employer that offers coverage. Because larger subsidies go to higher-income workers, who are more likely to buy insurance even without the tax exclusions, and smaller subsidies go to lower-income workers, who are less likely to purchase coverage, the exclusions do not yield the maximum gains in insurance coverage for the tax dollars forgone. Thus, the tax exclusions are an inefficient means of increasing the number of people who have health insurance, and they are regressive in the sense of giving larger benefits to people with higher income. * * *

NOTES

(A) *Distribution of the Tax Expenditure.* The following figure shows that the exclusion for employer-provided health insurance disproportionately benefits higher-income households:

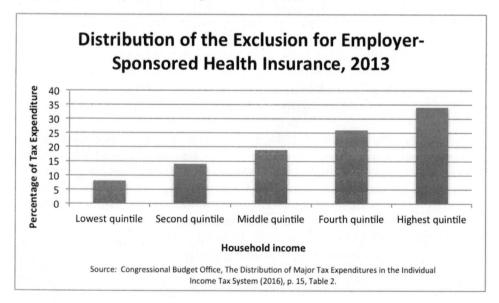

Distribution of the Exclusion for Employer-Sponsored Health Insurance, 2013

Source: Congressional Budget Office, The Distribution of Major Tax Expenditures in the Individual Income Tax System (2016), p. 15, Table 2.

(B) *The Cadillac Tax.* The Affordable Care Act enacted a new tax that cuts back on the tax benefits for employer-provided health insurance. Section 4980I imposes an excise tax on so-called "Cadillac" plans, defined as those whose total value (including premiums paid by workers and by employers) exceeds certain thresholds. The thresholds are $10,200 for single coverage and $27,500 for family coverage, with slightly higher thresholds for retirees ages 55 to 64. The excise tax is equal to 40 percent of the excess of the cost of the Cadillac plan and the applicable threshold. The Congressional Budget Office notes that, if employers and workers do not change their coverage in response to the tax, roughly one out of every five people enrolled in an employment-based health plan in 2018 would be subject to the tax. The CBO predicts, however, that many employers will shift to cheaper (and more limited) health insurance plans to avoid the Cadillac tax. Congress, however, postponed this tax again in January 2018 as part of an agreement to keep the federal government open. Many members of Congress have proposed repealing it, but, so far, they have not garnered the necessary votes.

(C) *Reform Options*. Critics of the exclusion for employer-provided health insurance have suggested a variety of options that would make the provision more progressive. One option is to cap the exclusion at a specific dollar amount (perhaps varying by taxpayer age). Another option is to phase out the exclusion for higher-income people. A third option would convert the exclusion to a tax credit, which could be made refundable.

(D) *Obstacles to Reform*. Although policy makers across the political spectrum have criticized the exclusion, reform faces several political obstacles. Many workers are happy with the health insurance coverage provided by their employers and are fearful of any change. Other workers, including unionized workers, have bargained for compensation packages that include health insurance benefits assumed to be tax-free. Including the value of the insurance in workers' income would subject workers to an unexpected tax increase, lowering their after-tax pay. The complexity of the health care system is itself also a barrier to reform, because any new system would produce winners and losers across a variety of constituencies, including taxpayers, employers, and insurance companies. In 2017, for instance, the Trump Administration and the Republican Congress found themselves unable to assemble a political coalition to repeal and replace the Affordable Care Act, although they did repeal the individual mandate as part of the 2017 tax act.

(E) *The Tax on Indoor Tanning*. In what might be viewed as a nod towards health care prevention but surely was just a grab for a bit of revenue, Congress also imposed a 10 percent excise tax on indoor tanning services. In its infinite wisdom it excluded tanning beds that were part of "health" clubs but not those located in stand-alone tanning salons. And while ultraviolent tanning is taxed, spray-on tans are not. Tanning salons, expecting their clients to flee to gyms, thought that installing some exercise equipment among the tanning beds might do the trick. But the IRS quickly issued regulations that permit the exclusion only for "qualified physical fitness facilities," which apparently does not include a tanning salon with treadmills.

Note on Other Tax Expenditure Fringe Benefits

Among the largest tax expenditures are those that subsidize retirement savings. Sections 401–404 and 410–416 provide favorable tax treatment for "qualified" pension, profit-sharing, and stock bonus plans. Employees are not taxed on these plans until they receive payments, usually in retirement, although employers receive immediate deductions for contributions to fund the retirement benefits. In addition, the pension trust or fund that accumulates contributions and income to fund the retirement benefits is tax-exempt. The Code also contains provisions that allow employees to make contributions to retirement savings plans in lieu of receiving cash salary and, by doing so, to receive tax savings comparable to those available to employer-sponsored qualified pension plans. See, e.g., §§ 401(k) and 403(b). Tax-preferred retirement income plans suffer some of the same problems as beset employer-provided health insurance: they tend to provide greater benefits to higher earners and to employees of larger firms. In the case of retirement income, however, the universal coverage of Social Security, whose benefits are skewed in favor of lower-wage workers, provides a universal baseline of retirement security for all. The income taxation of deferred compensation is taken up in Chapter 6.

In addition, employers who maintain a qualified pension plan can provide tax-free retirement planning services to their employees. § 132(a)(7).

The Code also provides tax benefits for a limited amount of employer-provided life insurance. Generally, if the employer pays life insurance premiums on the life of an employee and the employee's estate or family is the beneficiary, the employer's premium payments are income to the employee. See, e.g., Frost v. Commissioner, 52 T.C. 89 (1969). Where the employer or a charity is the beneficiary, the premium payments are not taxable to the employee. Rev. Rul. 68–99, 1968–1 C.B. 193.

An employee may exclude, however, the value of premiums on a limited amount of group term life insurance provided by an employer. Under § 79, an exclusion from income for group term life insurance premiums paid by an employer is provided for the premiums on an aggregate of $50,000 of insurance. The cost of the excess over $50,000 is subject to tax. Employer payments to group term life insurance plans are eligible for exclusion from employees' income only if the plans do not discriminate in favor of key employees with respect to eligibility or benefits. § 79(d). Similar nondiscrimination rules apply to the other benefits described below.

While one might think that Congress has included this exclusion in order to encourage employers to provide group insurance, it is not clearly so. The Regulations long contained a provision under which premiums paid on group term life insurance policies for employees were not taxable.

Although this exclusion presumably was designed to apply to modest premium payments on relatively small insurance policies covering all or most of a company's employees, the regulatory exclusion was stated in general terms without any limit in amount and without any requirement against discriminatory application. It is likely that this provision was based on a de minimis principle, plus the fact that the individual employee's premium would be small and perhaps also difficult to compute.

Tax expenditure fringes also include payments made by an employer for the care of dependents of its employees. These payments are excluded from the employee's income by § 129. The exclusion is limited to $5,000 a year ($2,500 for married individuals filing separately). The definitional limitations closely parallel those for the dependent care credit discussed infra at page 280. Much dependent care is provided by way of cafeteria plans (see note C infra).

NOTES

(A) *Educational Benefits.* An employee can exclude up to $5,250 a year for amounts paid by her employer under a "qualified educational assistance program." Educational assistance includes tuition, fees and books but does not include living expenses. § 127. (Other tax benefits for education are provided through deductions and credits and are described in Chapter 3 at page 445.)

(B) *Adoption Assistance.* Amounts paid under a qualified adoption assistance program provided by an employer are excludible to the extent they are used in connection with the employee's adoption of a child. § 137. The maximum amount excludible is $10,000 and is phased out for employees whose adjusted gross income exceeds $150,000. The exclusion is not available to an employee whose AGI exceeds $190,000. These limits are indexed for inflation. Qualified expenses include adoption fees, attorney fees, and court fees. Taxpayers who pay adoption expenses themselves are able to take a credit for the expenses, subject to the same limitations. See § 23.

(C) *Cafeteria Plans.* Plans that allow employees to select from a group of employer-provided nontaxable fringe benefits have become known as "cafeteria plans." These are considered a valuable compensation device, since the platter of benefits can be selected to reflect the tastes of the particular employee. Section 125 excludes from employee income employer contributions to certain nondiscriminatory cafeteria plans. An employee may choose only among excludable fringe benefits and cash. § 125(d)(1)(B). If the benefits are concentrated on key employees, they will be taxed as if they had received cash. One notable aspect of cafeteria plans is that if the employee does not use the amount elected, he loses it. For example if the employee elects $2,500 of child care reimbursement and only uses for $2,000 for child care, the remaining $500 of compensation is lost. Section 125(i)(1) limits the amount of health spending that an employee can exclude from income under a cafeteria plan to $2,500 a year, adjusted for inflation.

Note on Evaluating Fringe Benefits

The Code creates a large incentive for employers to pay compensation in the form of tax-free fringe benefits. An employee subject to a 37 percent marginal tax rate is indifferent as to receiving $63 of desirable tax-free fringe benefits or $100 of taxable wages, but would prefer $64 of tax-free benefits to $100 of cash. Employers, needless to say, would prefer paying $64 of benefits to $100 of wages. (As Chapter 3 will detail, the costs of either the benefits or the cash usually are deductible by the employer, regardless of whether they are included in the employees' income). As marginal income tax rates rise, the incentive to substitute tax-free benefits for cash salary increases. (Remember that in addition to the income tax, Social Security taxes exceeding 12 percent also apply to most salaries below $127,200 (in 2017, a number that is indexed each year for inflation) and Medicare taxes of nearly 3 percent are levied on all wages. The examples in this book generally ignore the payroll taxes.)

Equity. Tax-free fringe benefits raise a number of tax policy concerns, including equity issues. If A receives $15,000 cash and B receives $10,000 cash and $5,000 of tax-free airfare, they are not taxed the same even though they may be in the same economic position. This is said to violate horizontal equity because two taxpayers in the same economic situation are taxed differently. In reality, because the airfare is not taxed, B's employer may provide less. Thus, B might receive only $3,150 of benefits, and although he received $1,850 less than A, he would have the same after-tax benefit as A if both are taxed at 37 percent. In that case A and B would be in the same economic position after tax as well. If this occurs, it appears that the tax preference inured to the benefit of the employer who has been able to pay less compensation. It is possible, however, that the employer may pass through the lower costs by reducing prices to customers. The idea that the "incidence" of a tax or tax exception can burden or benefit a party other than the one nominally affected is very important and will come up again.

Another equity concern is that untaxed benefits are more valuable and often have been more available to employees in higher tax brackets. Moreover, untaxed fringes may be disproportionately available depending upon the employee's industry or occupation.

Efficiency. Issues of economic efficiency also are involved because the failure to tax benefits induces employers to offer, and employees to select, wage and benefit packages very different from those that they would obtain without the tax benefits. Suppose in the above example, that the employer is willing to offer $5,000 cash compensation or $5,000 in free airfare and, because the cost is the same, is indifferent between the two. If B is not particularly fond of flying, he would choose the $5,000 cash. But assume that the cash is taxable and the airfare is not. If B takes the cash, he will have $3,150 left after paying tax at a 37 percent rate. So long as the air travel is worth more to him than $3,150 (even if it is not worth $5,000), he will choose the airfare. Suppose the airfare is worth only $4,000 to him, although it costs the employer $5,000 to provide it. In that case despite the $1,850 in tax reduction, the employee gains only $850. Economists call the wasted $1,000 a "deadweight loss." But keep in mind that Congress might knowingly prefer this distortion, if, for example, it wanted to provide an incentive to a failing airline industry. There is, however, a cost. If the income tax is to raise a certain amount of revenue, exclusion of fringe benefits requires higher tax rates. Even if the exclusion from income of fringe benefits were defended as a type of rate reduction on labor income, corresponding to exclusion of certain types of capital income, it would be fairer and more efficient to exclude a portion of labor income from tax for all taxpayers regardless of the form in which it is received.

Complexity. The taxation of fringe benefits has been troublesome since the beginning of the income tax in 1913 and has proven to be surprisingly complex. There are two principal reasons for this complexity. First is the inherent difficulty—as a matter both of theory and of administration of the tax laws—in distinguishing in-kind compensation from goods or services related to an employee's work that also provide the employee incidental economic benefits. For example, a free book would constitute noncash compensation to most employees, but might constitute a noncompensatory incident of employment to a book critic.

As noted previously, the concept of income is not self-defining. It is clear that excluding all noncash compensation from income, while simple, would very quickly produce a barter economy for labor income. On the other hand, taxing any economic benefit, no matter how closely related to an employee's work, would violate public perceptions of fairness and would dramatically increase the costs of tax compliance for both the government and taxpayers. Drawing the line between these two unacceptable extremes, however, is necessarily controversial and often arbitrary. Fringe benefit taxation therefore is subject to inevitable controversy and periodic change.

Change itself is an additional source of complexity. Many exclusions of "work-related" fringe benefits originated in administrative practice and judicial decisions in the early days of the income tax, when tax rates were low and the income tax was largely confined to upper-income people. By the time a fringe benefit, perhaps long ignored by tax administrators as de minimis, had become an important component of employees' compensation, workers had come to regard the income exclusion as an entitlement.

The second source of complexity is Congress' unwillingness to accept the principle that all noncash compensation designed to reward the employee for services rendered should be subject to income tax. The exclusion from gross income of a number of fringe benefits reflects a variety of policies unrelated to the measurement of income. As we have seen, these exclusions include employer-provided life and health insurance, health, accident, and death benefits, dependent care assistance, and some benefits provided to members of the Armed Forces.

Statutory Provisions. The complexity of fringe benefit taxation is reflected in the relevant statutory provisions. Section 61 includes compensation in income, including fringe benefits, and the regulations provide that if services are paid for other than in money, the fair market value of the property or services taken in payment must be included in income. Reg. § 1.61–2(d). Statutory authority for taxing fringe benefits also is found in § 83. Although the original purpose of that section was to tax income received as compensation through restricted stock plans, the language is much broader.

Numerous fringe benefits are specifically excluded from income. In addition to those discussed above, Section 132 excludes eight or more categories of work-related fringe benefits—an expansion of the four originally excluded in 1984. Section 132, which should be studied carefully, was added to the Code to provide much greater certainty in the taxation of common fringe benefits, but it is not clear if work-related benefits not meeting the tests of § 132 otherwise might be excludable because they are not "income." In addition to § 132, there are a variety of other specific statutory exclusions for fringe benefits. Section 119 excludes certain work-related meals and lodging. Section 117(d) deals with tuition reduction plans for employees of educational institutions.

Substitute Taxation. The 2017 tax legislation disallows employer deductions for several major categories of fringe benefits. Section 274 now disallows business deductions for entertainment and qualified transportation fringes under § 132. § 274(a) and (*l*). The legislation disallows 50 percent of certain meals on the business premises of the employer, effective in 2018. § 274(n). And, beginning in 2026, the 2017 tax act eliminates all deductions for meals provided for the convenience of the employer and excludable under either § 119 or § 132(e)(2).

These changes reflect a strategy known as substitute taxation. Instead of taxing these fringes to the employee who receives them, the new rules (in effect) tax the employer by denying a deduction that would otherwise be allowed. Consider the table below, which assumes that a worker receives $100 in cash or an excludable fringe worth $100. As the table shows, the most tax-advantageous arrangement is the excludable fringe that is deductible by the employer.

	Employer tax	Employee tax	Net taxable income in the system
Ordinary compensation or taxable fringe (includible by the employee and deductible by the employer)	($100)	$100	$0
Excludable fringe with employer deduction	($100)	$0	($100)
Excludable fringe with no employer deduction	$0	$0	$0

However, substitute taxation works perfectly only when employers and employees face the same marginal tax rate. When marginal tax rates differ, the disallowance of the employer's deduction will over- or undercompensate the Treasury for the exclusion enjoyed by the worker. For example, as of 2018, the new top corporate tax rate is 21 percent and the new top individual tax rate is 37 percent. With this combination of tax rates, the fringe benefit is still preferable to cash compensation even if it is not deductible by the corporation. That is because the exclusion saves the employee $37 in taxes, while the denied deduction costs the employer only $21.

Why might Congress choose substitute taxation rather than outright repeal of these fringe benefits? In some cases, it may be administratively simpler to deny an employer a deduction. Taxing workers on meals in a company cafeteria, for instance, might be difficult because the company would have to track which workers ate in the cafeteria and the value of their meals. Denying a deduction to the employer may be much simpler in that context.

But it is also possible that politics enters into the equation as well. When exclusions remain on the books, perhaps Congress can still take credit for, say, subsidizing environmentally-sound practices like public transit, even though the subsidy has been dramatically reduced or eliminated by substitute taxation of the employer.

2.   WORK-RELATED FRINGE BENEFITS

Section 132 now governs the tax treatment of fringe benefits provided by employers in the workplace and not covered by a specific provision such as the exclusion for employer-provided health insurance.

The legislative history of Section 132, part of which is reproduced below, expresses the aims of the legislation.

Excerpt from Report of the Committee on Ways and Means on the Tax Reform Act of 1983
H.R. Rep. No. 98–432, at 286, 1983.

In providing statutory rules for exclusion of certain fringe benefits for income and payroll tax purposes, the committee has attempted to strike a balance between two competing objectives.

First, the committee is aware that in many industries, employees may receive, either free or at a discount, goods and services which the employer sells to the general public. In many cases, these practices are long established, and have been treated by employers, employees, and the IRS as not giving rise to taxable income. Although employees may receive an economic benefit from the availability of these free or discounted goods or services, employers often have valid business reasons, other than simply providing compensation, for encouraging employees to avail themselves of the products which they sell to the public. For example, a retail clothing business will want its salespersons to wear, when they deal with customers, the clothing which it seeks to sell to the public. In addition, the fact that the selection of goods and services available from a particular employer usually is restricted makes it appropriate to provide a limited exclusion, when such discounts are generally made available to employees, for the income employees realize from obtaining free or reduced-cost goods or services. The committee believes, therefore, that many present practices under which employers may provide to a broad group of employees, either free or at a discount, the products and services which the employer sells or provides to the public do not serve merely to replace cash compensation. These reasons support the committee's decision to codify the ability of employers to continue these practices without imposition of income or payroll taxes.

The second objective of the committee's bill is to set forth clear boundaries for the provision of tax-free benefits. * * * [T]he administrators of the tax law have not had clear guidelines in this area, and hence taxpayers in identical situations have been treated differently. The inequities, confusion, and administrative difficulties for businesses, employees, and the IRS resulting from this situation have increased substantially in recent years. * * *

In addition, the committee is concerned that without any well-defined limits on the ability of employers to compensate their employees tax-free by using a medium other than cash, new practices will emerge that could shrink the income tax base significantly, and further shift a disproportionate tax burden to those individuals whose compensation is in the form of cash. A shrinkage of the base of the social security payroll tax could also pose a threat to the viability of the social security system.

* * * Finally, an unrestrained expansion of noncash compensation would increase inequities among employees in different types of businesses, and among employers as well.

The nondiscrimination rule is an important common thread among the types of fringe benefits which are excluded under the bill from income and employment taxes. Under the bill, most fringe benefits may be made available tax-free to officers, owners, or highly compensated employees only if the benefits are also provided on substantially equal terms to other employees. The committee believes that it would be fundamentally unfair to provide tax-free treatment for economic benefits that are furnished only to highly paid executives. Further, where benefits are limited to the highly paid, it is more likely that the benefit is being provided so that those who control the business can receive compensation in a nontaxable form; in that situation, the reasons stated above for allowing tax-free treatment would not be applicable. Also * * * some commentators argue that the current situation—in which the lack of clear rules for the tax treatment of nonstatutory fringe benefits encourages the non-reporting of many types of compensatory benefits—has led to non-reporting of types of cash income which are clearly taxable under present-law rules, such as interest and dividends.

In summary, the committee believes that * * * the bill substantially improves the equity and administration of the tax system.

NOTES

(A) *The Expansion (and Contraction) of Excludable Fringes.* Subsequently Congress added additional excludible fringe benefits to § 132, including certain transportation costs, moving expense reimbursements, retirement planning services, and certain benefits provided to the military. Transportation expenses include commuter vans, transit passes, parking, and bicycle commuting costs. Originally the amount of parking that could be excluded was significantly higher than the amount of commuter vans or transit passes but Congress subsequently equalized the amounts (currently $255, adjusted for inflation).

In the 2017 tax act, Congress repealed the exclusions for bicycle commuting and for moving expenses, applicable between 2018 and the end of 2025. § 132(f)(8) and (g)(2). Members of the Armed Forces on active duty may still exclude moving reimbursements (but may not commute tax-free by bicycle) during this period. It is tempting to try to divine Congressional intent here: why eliminate the exclusion for cyclists and movers but not for subway and van riders? The changes likely reflect only the search for revenue as the 2017 Congress worked to put together a tax bill that would meet budget rules limiting the extent to which legislation can add to the deficit.

(B) *Substitute Taxation.* The 2017 tax legislation disallows the employer's deduction for § 132 qualified transportation fringes other than bicycle commuting, rather than taxing these fringes to the employee. (As described in Note (A), the exclusion for bicyclists was repealed.) The 2017 Act also taxes these fringes at the corporate rate (now 21 percent) when provided by tax exempt organizations. See § 512(a)(7).

———————

Whether an expenditure by an employer is a working condition fringe excludable under § 132(d) typically turns on whether the employee could deduct the item as an ordinary and necessary business expense under § 162. That section of the Code will be explored in detail in Chapter 3, but the following case demonstrates the kinds of issues that arise under § 132(d).

Townsend Industries, Inc. v. United States

United States Court of Appeals, Eighth Circuit, 2003. 342 F.3d 890.

■ BOWMAN, CIRCUIT JUDGE:

This is a case about the taxability of business and entertainment expenses spent on a Canadian fishing trip. After the Internal Revenue Service determined that the per-employee cost of Townsend Industries' annual fishing trip was wages, it assessed deficiencies against the company for the 1996 and 1997 tax years. Townsend paid a portion of the deficiency and filed a * * * suit seeking a refund. After a bench trial, the District Court found in favor of the Government [that] expenses involved in the trips were employee wages within the meaning of the Internal Revenue Code, and ruled that a portion of these wages should have been withheld for income tax and Social Security and Medicare taxes. Townsend appeals that decision, and we reverse. * * *

Townsend Industries, based in Altoona, Iowa, manufactures the T-51, a product that allows offset printers to produce two-color documents in a single pass * * *. For the last forty years, Townsend has gathered its salespeople for an annual, two-day meeting at its headquarters * * *. Following that meeting, the company has sponsored a four-day expense-paid fishing trip to a resort in Ontario, Canada * * *. Aside from a dinner at which the company owner * * * and its CEO * * * spoke about the state of the company, the employees and salespeople spent their time largely as they wished (though the vast majority fished). Nevertheless, business discussions were conducted on an on-going basis during the trip.

The question of whether the per-employee cost of the trips amounted to taxable wages and whether Townsend should have withheld a portion of these costs turns on whether each employee could have deducted these costs as business expenses. A taxpayer may exclude certain fringe benefits from his or her gross income and thereby avoid paying income tax on these benefits. Section 132(d) of the Internal Revenue Code excludes "working condition fringe" benefits from an individual's wages and provides that " 'working condition fringe' means any property or services provided to an employee of the employer to the extent that, if the employee paid for such property or services, such payment would be allowable as a deduction under section 162 or 167." * * *

What [the] statutes and regulations boil down to is a requirement that Townsend prove that its fishing trips were reasonable and necessary business expenses that were directly related to, or associated with, the active conduct of Townsend's business. Further, Townsend must demonstrate its business purpose by showing: that it had more than a general expectation of deriving some income or other trade or business benefit from the trip; that its employees actively engaged in business meetings, negotiations, discussions, or other bona fide business transactions; and that the principal character of the combined business and entertainment was the active conduct of Townsend's trade or business. * * *

The District Court determined that Townsend failed to establish a business purpose and ruled in favor of the Government. * * * We disagree with the District Court's holding that the evidence presented at trial failed to establish a business purpose for Townsend's 1996 and 1997 trips.

Simply put, the testimony elicited at trial clearly established that the 1996 and 1997 trips were business trips and that Townsend properly excluded the trip expenses from its employees' gross income. * * *

In the first place, we cannot agree that District Court's conclusion that the voluntary nature of the trips rendered them an undeductible business expense. Although the trips were voluntary, nearly all of the Townsend employees who testified felt an obligation to attend and some felt that it was part of their job. Moreover, Robert Townsend, the owner, testified that while he felt it would be antithetical to his business philosophy to make the trips mandatory, he and other senior management "definitely encourage" employees to attend and that "[w]hat we want to do is to get them to go, and we do lean on them." * * *

Dean Evans, the chief engineer, added that he felt a responsibility to attend and that, for his part, he did not even look forward to the event:

> I like the environment up there. It's very beautiful, but it's actually the culmination of a year's worth of work, because the fishing trip is where we launch products, introduce it to our staff, and so it's a pretty tough time. Usually we've been at it pretty hard to get it done at that particular date, so it's trying times.

* * * [A] number of witnesses testified that in 1996 many discussions focused on the need to introduce a new model to compete with the Ryobi 3302 press and that in 1997, the new Anniversary Edition (AE) press was introduced. * * * In addition to testimony about the Anniversary Edition press, many witnesses testified about discussions regarding the complexity of the T-51 press and problems that customers, employees, and salespeople (who also repaired the machine) had with its 800 parts.

* * * Many witnesses also testified that the fishing trips were a unique opportunity for the national sales team to interact with the Townsend employees who manufacture and assemble the intricate parts and those who send out replacement parts.

Another particularly telling piece of evidence that buttresses our conclusion that Townsend met its burden and established a bona fide business purpose for its trips is the fact that Townsend stopped including its plastics division in the annual trip in 1994, three years before Townsend sold the division. * * * This decision, to our minds, indicates that Townsend clearly had a specific business purpose for these trips. If Townsend was merely providing a free vacation to its salespeople and employees, it would not have mattered if they continued to include the plastics division.

* * * Contrary to the District Court's conclusion that Townsend merely had a general "expectation to derive uncertain future benefits, particularly in the way of improved comradery [sic] and relations among its employees and sales personnel," * * * we conclude that Townsend had a realistic expectation to gain concrete future benefits from the trip based on its knowledge of its own small company, its knowledge of the utility of interpersonal interactions that probably would not occur but for the trip, and its knowledge of its own past experience. As such, the trips and their expenses qualified as working condition fringe benefits under § 132 and a bona fide business expense under §§ 162 and 274 of the Internal Revenue Code. * * *

Nor do we think the present case is like Hippodrome Oldsmobile, Inc. v. United States, 474 F.2d 959 (6th Cir. 1973), a case in which the parties conceded that "the company customers entertained [on the boat] were not subjected to any specific exposure to taxpayer's products or suggestion that they buy them while being thus entertained" and that the taxpayer was merely using the boat to generate future good will. * * * In the case at hand, as we have noted, the employees and salespeople were exposed to Townsend products, a new Townsend product was initiated and subsequently introduced during the years in question, complaints and suggestions were discussed about current Townsend products, and Townsend business practices were discussed at length. Given this evidence, we conclude this was not a case where the taxpayer had no specific business purpose and was merely trying to generate good will. * * *

Accordingly, the decision of the District Court is reversed and the matter remanded with instructions to enter judgment in favor of Townsend Industries.

NOTES

(A) *Employers' Entertainment Deductions Disallowed.* The result in *Townsend Industries* remains valid: workers may exclude (and firms need not withhold income and payroll taxes on) the value of the fishing trip. The 2017 tax legislation altered the tax picture for such trips, however, by eliminating the employer's deduction for activities that constitute "entertainment, amusement, or recreation." § 274(a). The new rule would not affect the workers' exclusion. But it would presumably require Townsend to allocate the costs of future fishing trips between (nondeductible) "recreation" and (deductible) travel and lodging. Such allocations may be difficult, because hotels and resorts (and fishing lodges) do not typically separate the value of (nondeductible) recreation from the cost of (deductible) accommodations. Could the IRS argue that the full cost of a trip for employees to a luxury fishing cabin constitutes a nondeductible expenditure on employee "recreation"?

As Chapter 3 describes, Congress in 2017 repealed the deduction for employee business expenses, but the statute explicitly makes clear that this change does not affect the scope of the exclusion of working condition fringes under § 132.

(B) *Distinguishing Excludable Fringes from Taxable Compensation.* Section 132 represents an effort to develop fringe benefit rules that distinguish "working condition benefits" from "in-kind compensation." The former usually are regarded as primarily for the benefit of the employer and therefore not includible in the income of the employee. Thus, an essential prerequisite for exclusion should be the existence of a substantial noncompensatory business purpose on the part of the employer for providing the good or service in question to its employees. A good or service should not be excluded unless it is related to the employee's work and is something ordinarily useful to someone in the employee's position. A benefit provided at the employer's place of business would be more likely to be characterized as a working condition fringe than a benefit provided outside the business premises.

How well does § 132 conform to these principles? Pay attention also to § 119, § 132(b), and (c). How are the following items treated under § 132?

Question 1: A law firm at which Jane is a summer associate gives her tickets to a Broadway show, which she attends with two other summer associates. What if the firm, instead, gives Jane $125, and she uses the money to buy a ticket and attend the show on her own?

Question 2: JetBlue allows its employees to ride for free on any of its routes by reserving a seat at least 30 days prior to the departure date. Is the value of a free trip taken by Employee A included in her income?

Question 3: Suppose that Apple gives its employees a 50 percent discount. Employee C buys a $4000 MacBook (which cost Apple $2800) for $2000. How much income does C have as a result of this purchase? What if the discount is available only to executives?

Distinguishing between working condition fringes and compensation is particularly difficult because in many cases the fringe benefits are intended to be a form of compensation, designed to attract and retain employees. Consider all the fringes provided to the employees of Google. Those who work at the company's headquarters, the Googleplex, reportedly receive free haircuts, use of gyms, swimming pools, and pool tables, as well as free dry cleaning. An employee can eat breakfast, lunch, and dinner free in one of many cafes and in between can consume treats in the many snack rooms. Are these items for the convenience of the employer or the employee? Consider this statement from executive chairman Eric Schmidt: "The goal is to strip away everything that gets in our employees' way . . . . Let's face it: programmers want to program, they don't want to do their laundry. So we make it easy for them to do both."

(C) *Valuation.* What is the amount of income when a fringe benefit is includible in the employee's gross income? The cost to the employer, the fair market value or the subjective value to the employee? The basic rule is that the amount is the fair market value. Reg. § 1.61–2(d). The regulations define fair market value as "the amount that an individual would have to pay for the particular fringe benefit in an arm's length transaction." Reg. § 1.61–21(b)(2).

This may lead to results that might be considered unfair. Suppose the employee receives something that is of little value to him, for example, the non-skier who is given a trip to Aspen. The value might be discounted to reflect the possibility that employees might have purchased something else had they received cash or because the item received had less value to them. See Turner v. Commissioner, 13 T.C.M. 462 (1954), where (in a case decided long before § 132 was enacted) the court refused to require the taxpayer to include the market value of a free trip to South America. The court stated:

> The winning of the tickets did not provide them with something which they needed in the ordinary course of their lives and for which they would have made an expenditure in any event, but merely gave them an opportunity to enjoy a luxury otherwise beyond their means. Their value to the petitioners was not equal to their retail cost.

Turner is an unusual case. Usually, the courts require taxpayers to use the fair market value in valuing receipt of in-kind items. Generally it would not be feasible to permit taxpayers to prove that a receipt is worth less to them than market value. Rather than taking seriously employee allegations that they would have said to their employers, "Please, don't give me that Mercedes," an income tax generally must include such goods or services in employees' income at their objective fair market value and rely on employees to negotiate for cash when they really prefer it. Of course, an employee generally can reject a benefit and forgo tax.

Suppose the item is more valuable to the recipient than it is to other taxpayers. For example, assume a law professor would rather read the Internal Revenue Code than any other book and receives a free copy. Would it be appropriate to include the excess value in income? Economists describe this excess of satisfaction from property over its market price as consumer surplus. Is it ever practical to tax consumer surplus?

Are there situations where using fair market value as the touchstone creates inequities? Suppose an executive is allowed to travel free on a space-available basis on the company jet. The value of a seat on a private jet (or the employer's cost of providing the seat) might be ten times higher than the cost of a first class ticket to the same destination. The regulations provide special rules for certain situations. See, e.g., Reg. § 1.61–21(g) (rules for valuing flights on noncommercial aircraft).

(D) *Nondiscrimination.* As the excerpt from the Ways and Means Committee Report notes, in some cases, § 132 places great weight on a nondiscrimination requirement to insure equity. See § 132(e)(2) and (j). Nondiscrimination rules are also found in § 117(d) and § 274(e)(4). Would vertical equity be achieved by providing each employee the same dollar amount of nontaxable fringe benefits? By providing each employee nontaxable fringes as the same proportion of total compensation?

(E) *Frequent Fliers.* Suppose an employee takes a business trip and his airfare is paid by the employer. The airline awards the employee frequent flier miles, which the employee uses for a personal trip. Do these transactions have any federal income tax consequences? Is there a Code section that clearly dictates the tax treatment of frequent flier miles awarded to customers? If not, what is the economic substance of their frequent flier miles?

In 2002 the IRS announced that it will not assert that a taxpayer has gross income because he has received or used frequent flier miles attributable to business travel. Announcement 2002–18, 2002–10 I.R.B. 10. The Service noted that there are many unanswered questions with respect to the miles and until it can figure out the answers, the miles will go untaxed.

But then in early 2012 Citibank issued statements to its customers indicating that miles handed out as part of a promotion for opening a bank account were taxable. After press reports, the IRS issued a statement that said, "when frequent flyer miles are provided as a premium for opening a financial account, it can be a taxable situation subject to reporting under current law." Despite the lack of clarity in that statement, the IRS appeared to agree with Citibank. The Tax Court agreed with the IRS, holding that the miles received for opening a bank account were taxable. Shankar v. Commissioner, 143 T.C. 140 (2014). Taxpayers might also receive frequent flyer miles as a prize. In 2015 United Airlines awarded a million miles to a hacker who located holes in its security system. United indicated that it valued the award at two cents a mile. That works out to a federal tax bite on $20,000 of income, for this "bug bounty," which of course must be paid in cash, not miles. Assuming the miles are taxable, what value should the account holder report? The value of the miles or the value of the ticket purchased with the miles? Does it matter that the amount an airline charges an institutional customer is about half the price it charges individuals? And what if the recipient never uses the miles and they expire?

(F) *Alternatives.* Contrast § 132 with a 1977 Treasury proposal to exclude only items required as a condition of a particular job. Why not just assume that all fringe benefits—other than working condition fringes—are part of the bargain between employers and employees and include their fair market value in employee's income?

Another possibility is an excise tax on the value of such benefits. The disallowance of a deduction can be the equivalent of an excise tax. How might such an excise tax rate be chosen? See § 4977, which allows employers to elect a 30 percent excise tax on certain "excess fringe benefits" in lieu of taxation to employees under § 132.

(G) *Benefits Provided to Other than an Employee.* Although the general language of § 132 applies only to benefits provided by an employer to an employee, there are many instances where "employee" is very broadly defined. For example, no-additional-cost service and qualified employee discount fringes can be excluded by family members of employees. § 132(h). Parents of airline employees get their own exclusion. § 132(h)(3). The regulations treat independent contractors as employees for purposes of working condition fringes, and family members as employees for purposes of on-site athletic facilities. Reg. § 1.132–1(b). And anyone can exclude a de minimis fringe. Reg. § 1.132–1(b)(4). Where does the IRS get the authority to exclude de minimis fringes provided to non-employees? See § 132(n). Why should the parents of airline employees get tax-free air travel while a Greyhound bus driver would have to pay tax on a free ticket provided to his parents? Folklore has it that former Ways and Means Chairman Dan Rostenkowski added § 132(h)(3) to the Code because two of his daughters were flight attendants.

(H) *Interest-Free Loans.* Generally, an interest-free (or low-interest) loan from an employer to an employee will be recharacterized to reflect economic reality. The employer/lender is treated as charging a market rate of interest (established by the statute) and making a payment of some or all of that amount to the employee/borrower. This payment is treated as compensation. The employee is then deemed to transfer the amount of the payment to the employer as interest. § 7872. Loans between individuals of $10,000 or less are generally excluded unless one of the principal purposes of the transaction is tax avoidance. Similar rules apply to gifts and certain transactions between corporations and shareholders. For further discussion of § 7872, see page 761 infra.

(I) *Benefits Not from Employers.* What is the appropriate tax treatment of benefits provided by a non-employer that are not covered by § 132? Suppose, for example, a law firm associate visits a firm client and the client pays her parking fee and buys her lunch? What if a prospective employer pays a law student's airfare to interview with a firm? See Rev. Rul. 63–77, 1963–1 C.B. 177.

––––––––

The next case deals with a transfer by a nonemployer.

United States v. Gotcher

United States Court of Appeals, Fifth Circuit, 1968. 401 F.2d 118.

■ THORNBERRY, CIRCUIT JUDGE:

In 1960, Mr. and Mrs. Gotcher took a twelve-day expense-paid trip to Germany to tour the Volkswagen facilities there. The trip cost

$1372.30. His employer, Economy Motors, paid $348.73, and Volkswagen of Germany and Volkswagen of America shared the remaining $1023.53. Upon returning, Mr. Gotcher bought a twenty-five percent interest in Economy Motors, the Sherman, Texas Volkswagen dealership, that had been offered to him before he left. Today he is President of Economy Motors in Sherman and owns fifty percent of the dealership. Mr. and Mrs. Gotcher did not include any part of the $1372.30 in their 1960 income. The Commissioner determined that the taxpayers had realized income to the extent of the $1372.30 for the expense-paid trip and asserted a tax deficiency of $356.79, plus interest. * * * The district court, sitting without a jury, held that the cost of the trip was not income or, in the alternative, was income and deductible as an ordinary and necessary business expense. 259 F. Supp. 340. We affirm the district court's determination that the cost of the trip was not income to Mr. Gotcher ($686.15); however, Mrs. Gotcher's expenses ($686.15) constituted income and were not deductible.

Section 61 of the Internal Revenue Code of 1954 * * * defines gross income as income from whatever source derived and specifically includes fifteen items within this definition. The court below reasoned that the cost of the trip to the Gotchers was not income because an economic or financial benefit does not constitute income under section 61 unless it is conferred as compensation for services rendered. This conception of gross income is too restrictive since it is well-settled that section 61 should be broadly interpreted and that many items, including non-compensatory gains, constitute gross income.

Sections 101–123 specifically exclude certain items from gross income. Appellant argues that the cost of the trip should be included in income since it is not specifically excluded by sections 101–123, reasoning that section 61 was drafted broadly to subject all economic gains to tax and any exclusions should be narrowly limited to the specific exclusions. This analysis is too restrictive since it has been generally held that exclusions from gross income are not limited to the enumerated exclusions. Moreover, the Supreme Court in Rudolph v. United States, 1962, 370 U.S. 269, has indicated, in concurring and dissenting opinions to dismissing the writ of certiorari as improvidently granted, that sections 101–123 are not exhaustive. * * *

In determining whether the expense-paid trip was income within section 61, we must look to the tests that have been developed under this section. The concept of economic gain to the taxpayer is the key to section 61. * * * This concept contains two distinct requirements: There must be an economic gain, and this gain must primarily benefit the taxpayer personally. In some cases, as in the case of an expense-paid trip, there is no direct economic gain, but there is an indirect economic gain inasmuch as a benefit has been received without a corresponding diminution in wealth. Yet even if expense-paid items, as meals and lodging, are received by the taxpayer, the value of these items will not be gross income, even though the employee receives some incidental benefit, if the meals and lodging are primarily for the convenience of the employer. See *Rule* * * * § 119.

* * *

The trip was made in 1959 when VW was attempting to expand its local dealerships in the United States. The "Buy American" campaign and the fact that the VW people felt they had a "very ugly product" prompted them to offer these tours of Germany to prospective dealers. * * * In 1959, when VW began to push for its share of the American market, its officials determined that the best way to remove the apprehension about this foreign product was to take the dealer to Germany and have him see his investment first-hand. It was believed that once the dealer saw the manufacturing facilities and the stability of the "new Germany" he would be convinced that VW was for him. Furthermore, VW considered the expenditure justified because the dealer was being asked to make a substantial investment of his time and money in a comparatively new product. Indeed, after taking the trip, VW required him to acquire first-class facilities. * * * Apparently these trips have paid off since VW's sales have skyrocketed and the dealers have made their facilities top-rate operations under the VW requirements for a standard dealership.

The activities in Germany support the conclusion that the trip was oriented to business. * * * There is ample support for the trial judge's *business* finding that a substantial amount of time was spent touring VW facilities and visiting local dealerships. VW had set up these tours with local dealers so that the travelers could discuss how the facilities were operated in Germany. Mr. Gotcher took full advantage of this opportunity and even used some of his "free time" to visit various local dealerships. Moreover, at almost all of the evening meals VW officials gave talks about the organization and passed out literature and brochures on the VW story.

Some of the days were not related to touring VW facilities, but that fact alone cannot be decisive. The dominant purpose of the trip is the critical inquiry and some pleasurable features will not negate the finding of an overall business purpose. * * * Since we are convinced that the agenda related primarily to business and that Mr. Gotcher's attendance was prompted by business considerations, the so-called sightseeing complained of by the Government is inconsequential. * * * Indeed, the district court found that even this touring of the countryside had an indirect relation to business since the tours were not typical sightseeing excursions but were connected to the desire of VW that the dealers be persuaded that the German economy was stable enough to justify investment in a German product. We cannot say that this conclusion is clearly erroneous. Nor can we say that the enthusiastic literary style of the brochures negates a dominant business purpose. It is the business reality of the total situation, not the colorful expressions in the literature, that controls. Considering the record, the circumstances prompting the trip, and the objective achieved, we conclude that the primary purpose of the trip was to induce Mr. Gotcher to take out a VW dealership interest.

The question, therefore, is what tax consequences should follow from an expense-paid trip that primarily benefits the party paying for the trip. In several analogous situations the value of items received by employees has been excluded from gross income when these items were primarily for the benefit of the employer. Section 119 excludes from gross income of an employee the value of meals and lodging furnished to him for the convenience of the employer. Even before these items were excluded by the 1954 Code, the Treasury and the courts recognized that they should be excluded from gross income. Thus it appears that the value of any trip that is paid by the employer or by a businessman primarily for his own benefit should be excluded from gross income of the payee on similar reasoning. * * *

In the recent case of Allen J. McDonell, 26 T.C.M. 115, Tax Ct.Mem. 1967–18, a sales supervisor and his wife were chosen by lot to accompany a group of contest winners on an expense-paid trip to Hawaii. In holding that the taxpayer had received no income, the Tax Court noted that he was required by his employer to go and that he was serving a legitimate business purpose though he enjoyed the trip. The decision suggests that in analyzing the tax consequences of an expense-paid trip one important factor is whether the traveler had any choice but to go. Here, although taxpayer was not forced to go, there is no doubt that in the reality of the business world he had no real choice. The trial judge reached the same conclusion. He found that the invitation did not specifically order the dealers to go, but that as a practical matter it was an order or directive that if a person was going to be a VW dealer, sound business judgment necessitated his accepting the offer of corporate hospitality. So far as Economy Motors was concerned, Mr. Gotcher knew that if he was going to be a part-owner of the dealership, he had better do all that was required to foster good business relations with VW. Besides having no choice but to go, he had no control over the schedule or the money spent. VW did all the planning. In cases involving noncompensatory economic gains, courts have emphasized that the taxpayer still had complete dominion and control over the money to use it as he wished to satisfy personal desires or needs. Indeed, the Supreme Court has defined income as accessions of wealth over which the taxpayer has complete control. Commissioner of Internal Revenue v. Glenshaw Glass Co. Clearly, the lack of control works in taxpayer's favor here.

McDonell also suggests that one does not realize taxable income when he is serving a legitimate business purpose of the party paying the expenses. * * * Thus, the rule is that the economic benefit will be taxable to the recipient only when the payment of expenses serves no legitimate corporate purpose. * * * The decisions also indicate that the tax consequences are to be determined by looking to the primary purpose of the expenses and that the first consideration is the intention of the payor. The Government in argument before the district court agreed that whether the expenses were income to taxpayers is mainly a question of the motives of the people giving the trip. Since this is a matter of proof, the resolution of the tax question really depends on whether Gotcher showed that his presence served a legitimate corporate purpose and that no appreciable amount of time was spent for his personal benefit and enjoyment.

* * *

The corporate-executive decisions indicate that some economic gains, though not specifically excluded from section 61, may nevertheless escape taxation. They may be excluded even though the entertainment and travel unquestionably give enjoyment to the taxpayer and produce indirect economic gains. When this indirect economic gain is subordinate to an overall business purpose, the recipient is not taxed. We are convinced that the personal benefit to Mr. Gotcher from the trip was merely incidental to VW's sales campaign.

As for Mrs. Gotcher, the trip was primarily a vacation. She did not make the tours with her husband to see the local dealers or attend discussions about the VW organization. This being so the primary benefit of the expense-paid trip for the wife went to Mr. Gotcher in that he was relieved of her expenses. He should therefore be taxed on the expenses attributable to his wife. * * * Nor are the expenses deductible since the wife's presence served no bona fide business purpose for her husband. Only when the wife's presence is necessary to the conduct of the husband's business are her expenses deductible under section 162. * * * Also, it must be shown that the wife made the trip only to assist her husband in his business. A single trip by a wife with her husband to Europe has been specifically rejected as not being the exceptional type of case justifying a deduction. * * *

Affirmed in part; reversed in part.

■ JOHN R. BROWN, CHIEF JUDGE (concurring):

* * *

Attributing income to the little wife who was neither an employee, a prospective employee, nor a dealer, for the value of a trip she neither planned nor chose still bothers me. If her uncle had paid for the trip, would it not have been a pure gift, not income? Or had her husband out of pure separate property given her the trip would the amount over and above the cost of Texas bed and board have been income? I acquiesce now, confident that for others in future cases on a full record the wife, as now does the husband, also will overcome.

NOTES

(A) *Gotcher and § 132.* If *Gotcher* were decided today, would the result be the same? Presumably the portion of Gotcher's trip paid for by Economy

Motors, his employer, would be covered by § 132, thanks to § 132(d), but not that paid for by Volkswagen, which was never his employer. Should both portions be treated the same?

The *Gotcher* court emphasized that the taxpayer "had no real choice" but to take the trip and to follow the planned itinerary. What is the relevance of the taxpayer's lack of control over funds expended by the employer for the employee's personal consumption? Suppose a travel agency requires an employee to take an all-expenses-paid two-week trip to Paris with the itinerary selected by the employer? What if an employer orders an employee to take a prepaid vacation in order to improve his efficiency at work?

(B) *Spouse's Expenses.* Regardless of the test adopted, should the same test also apply to a spouse? The *Gotcher* court suggests that the motive of the person paying for the trip is determinative rather than Gotcher's purpose for travel. Is that correct? Is the court's determination that the value of Mrs. Gotcher's trip is taxable consistent with its view that Volkswagen's motive is determinative?

In United States v. Disney, 413 F.2d 783 (9th Cir. 1969), Roy Disney and his wife were reimbursed by his employer, Walt Disney Productions, for expenses incurred on certain of his business trips. The court found it was necessary for Mrs. Disney to accompany her husband and that she assisted his performance of business duties. The court held that reimbursement of Mrs. Disney's expenses was includible in gross income, but allowed the Disneys to deduct these expenses as business expenses under § 162.

It is now significantly more difficult to deduct the cost of a spouse's travel expenses. Section 274(m)(3) provides that travel expenses are deductible for a spouse or dependent only if the spouse is an employee of the taxpayer, there is a bona fide business purpose, and the expenses otherwise would have been deductible. While it might have been relatively easy to add Mrs. Disney to the payroll, it will not be possible for most businesses to do so. Suppose a corporation or a law firm, for example, picks up the expenses for a non-employee spouse who travels to a meeting and attends dinners with other spouses. Does either spouse have taxable income? Reg. § 1.132–5(t) provides that even if the employer cannot deduct the spouse's expenses, the employee can exclude the reimbursement so long as the spouse's presence had a bona fide business purpose. This is another example of "substitute taxation."

3.   MEALS AND LODGING

Note on the Exclusion of Meals and Lodging

In the early versions of the income tax regulations and in a number of early rulings, the Bureau of Internal Revenue exempted from gross income meals and lodging furnished to employees in a variety of circumstances "for the convenience of the employer." These included board and lodging furnished seamen aboard ship, O.D. 265, 1 C.B. 71 (1919), living quarters furnished to employees for the convenience of the employer, Reg. § 45, Art. 33, T.D. 2992, 2 C.B. 76 (1920), and certain cash payments for "supper money," O.D. 514, 2 C.B. 90 (1920).

Benaglia. In Benaglia v. Commissioner, 36 B.T.A. 838 (1937), a manager of two deluxe Hawaiian resorts and a golf club and his wife occupied a suite of rooms and took meals free of charge at the hotel, "entirely for the convenience" of the employer. The Commissioner argued that the fair market value of the meals and lodging, $7,845, was income. The Board of Tax Appeals disagreed, stating:

> [P]etitioner's residence at the hotel was not by way of compensation for services, not for his personal convenience, comfort or pleasure, but solely because he could not otherwise perform the services required of him. * * * His duty was continuous and required his presence at a moment's call. * * * Under such circumstances, the value of meals and lodging is not income to the employee, even though it may relieve him of an expense which he would otherwise bear.

The majority accepted the employer's statement that the manager could not perform his job without living in the hotel suite since his job required his presence at a moment's call. The dissenting judge was far more skeptical that acceptance of a suite of rooms in one of the world's most luxurious hotels was really for the convenience of the employer. He noted that the taxpayer managed the other hotel and the golf club without living there and was away from Honolulu for over five months for the year in question.

The Commissioner subsequently followed the *Benaglia* case and permitted certain meals and lodging furnished to an employee to be excluded from income. They had to be furnished "for the convenience of the employer" and could not represent compensation for services rendered.

Section 119. Section 119, added by the 1954 Code, was the first legislative treatment of the problem. This provision provides that an employee may exclude from income "the value of any meals * * * furnished to him * * * by his employer for the convenience of the employer, but only if * * * the meals are furnished on the business premises of the employer * * *." Taxpayers may also be able to exclude from income the value of meals and lodging furnished to their immediate families.

The Supreme Court in Commissioner v. Kowalski, 434 U.S. 77 (1977), refused to permit New Jersey state troopers to exclude cash reimbursements that they received for meals eaten at restaurants while they were on duty. The Court noted that "meals" requires an in-kind transfer, not cash. Furthermore, the meals were not eaten on the business premise of the employer since the troopers ate in private restaurants. The dissent argued that § 119 did not explicitly distinguish between cash and in-kind provisions and also accepted the troopers' argument that the employer's business premise was the state of New Jersey and thus the troopers were on duty wherever they happened to be. They also were more sympathetic to the argument that it was inequitable to let the military exclude meals but not "the paramilitary New Jersey state troopers." Compare Christey v. United States, 841 F.2d 809 (8th Cir. 1988) (permitting state troopers to deduct as ordinary and necessary business expenses under § 162(a) the costs of meals that they were required to eat at public restaurants adjacent to the highway while they were on duty). The treatment of deductions is taken up subsequently in Chapter 3, but it is worth noting here that the 2017 legislation repealed the deduction for employee business expenses.

Section 119 is a good example of a statutory provision that uses everyday terms that have special meanings in the tax context. The notes below consider what is meant by "meals and lodging," "business premises," and "the convenience of the employer."

Meals and Lodging. Section 119 excludes meals and lodging. As *Kowalski* makes clear, a cash payment or cash reimbursement to an employee is not excludable under § 119. Thus, an employee on call who is reimbursed for the sandwich he brings to his desk is taxed, but the employee whose employer brings the sandwich to the desk is not taxed. Any fear that the employee could spend the cash for something other than the meal could be alleviated by requiring the employee to account to the employer.

What are the tax consequences (after *Kowalski*) of supper money provided to law firm associates who work at night? Recipients should check Reg. § 1.132–6. In American Airlines, Inc. v. United States, 204 F.3d 1103 (Fed. Cir. 2000), the court held that $50 American Express vouchers given to employees to use for meals while traveling were not excluded as a de minimis fringe under § 132(e). As a practical matter, the employees could use the vouchers at any time.

Business Premises. The requirement that the meals and lodging be on the business premises was designed to eliminate controversy, but it has not been completely successful. Consider the following cases:

The president of a Japanese subsidiary of a U.S. corporation was provided a large company-owned house in a prestigious Tokyo location. The Court of Claims in Adams v. United States, 585 F.2d 1060 (Ct.Cl.1978), rejected a literal reading of § 119 and imposed a "functional rather than a spatial test." In holding that the lodging was excluded from the president's gross income, the court emphasized that the company had built the house specifically for its presidents, with facilities for a home office and substantial business entertaining, that the company president had lived there for 15 years and that the house had become associated with the company, and that the taxpayer was required to live in the house and to perform various business activities there after working hours. The court concluded that the house served important business functions of the company and therefore was part of its business premises. The Service took a similar approach in ruling that state governors are not required to include in gross income the fair market value of their official residences. Rev. Rul. 75–540, 1975–2 C.B. 53.

These results should be contrasted with Hargrove v. Commissioner, T.C. Memo 2006–159. The taxpayers were civilian employees of a U.S. defense facility in Australia and were required to accept lodging as a condition of their employment. The homes where the taxpayers lived were in a town 22 miles from the defense facility. No taxpayer performed any work for the contractor at his home and thus the court held that the homes were not the "business premises" of the employer.

Convenience of Employer. The regulations for § 119 provide that meals are provided for the convenience of the employer only if there is a "substantial noncompensatory purpose." The statute requires that lodging must be a condition of employment as well. Will a requirement that the employee live in a particular residence suffice? Suppose a couple requires a nanny to occupy a room in their home, but she is only expected to work fixed hours? Suppose a university president is required to live in the president's house located in a suburb several miles from an urban campus? Does "convenience of the employer" mean that the lodging or meals are essential to the functioning of the business or simply helpful?

Generally, a requirement that an employee be "on call" after business hours establishes that the lodging or meals are for the convenience of the employer. Another way to establish that meals are for the convenience of the employer is to adopt a policy that precludes employees from eating away from the employer's business premise during reasonable meal hours. Ann. 99–77, 1999–32 I.R.B. 243, indicated that the IRS would accept the employer's judgment about restricting the ability of the employees to leave for meals, regardless of the reason, so long as the policy is actually enforced.

In 1998, Congress amended Section 119 to provide that *all* meals furnished to employees at a place of business are treated as furnished for the convenience of the employer if more than one-half of the employees to whom meals are provided are furnished the meals for the convenience of the employer. This provision was the work of a Nevada Congressman who was a former casino official and the son of the CEO of Circus Circus. Want to guess whom this obscure provision benefits? Apparently large casinos in Las Vegas permit most of their employees to eat in subsidized or free cafeterias. Although it was clear that the meals served to food service employees were for the convenience of the employer, that was not true for exotic dancers and lion tamers. This created an employee relations imbroglio in that the hash slingers got to exclude their free hamburgers while the performers did not. Enter the lobbyists. Through a complex interaction of Sections 119, 132, and 274 (that you do not want to wade through), Congress agreed to the amendment, which essentially provides companies that serve meals to its employees a 100 percent deduction for a fringe benefit that is not taxable to the employees. But that still left employees having to argue that the meals were furnished for the convenience of the employer simply because they had to remain on the premises during their entire shift. The Ninth Circuit dealt them a winning hand. Holding that *Kowalski* does not require that the employee must accept the meals in order to properly perform his duties, the court found the stay-on-the premises policy was sufficient. The court noted that the IRS argument that accepting the meals had to be necessary to perform the specific duties of the employee would "render the test virtually impossible to satisfy; only restaurant critics and dieticians could meet such a test." Boyd Gaming Corp. v. Commissioner, 177 F.3d 1096 (9th Cir. 1999).

NOTES

(A) *Substitute Taxation and the Countdown to 2026.* The tax act of 2017 limited employers' deductions for meals (but not lodging) excludable under § 119. Beginning in 2018, such meals will be only 50 percent deductible. § 274(n). Beginning in 2026, however, such meals will be entirely nondeductible. § 274(*o*). The disallowance of the deduction will raise the tax cost of having workers eat their meals on the premises. The long lead time on the change might be intended to permit employers to adjust their working conditions to take this change into account. The long lead time may also have political advantages for members of Congress seeking contributions: which employers do you suppose will lobby heavily between now and 2026 to extend the deduction?

(B) *Schmoozing and Section 119.* The New York Times reported that Ellen Futter, the president of New York's Museum of Natural History, lives rent-free in a $5 million apartment purchased when she joined the institution. And Ms. Futter is not alone. The Times also reported that Glenn Lowry, the director of the Museum of Modern Art, lives in a $6 million condo in the tower atop the museum. According to the Times, neither of these museum heads pay federal income tax on the value of living rent-free in their luxurious surroundings. Presumably, the ground for the exclusion is § 119, raising the question whether such apartments constitute the "business premises" of the employer and whether the museum heads are required to accept the lodging for the convenience of the employer. The Times reports that the museums justify the exclusion because the apartments function as business premises used for meetings and schmoozing with donors. By contrast, according to the newspaper, the heads of the Getty Museum and Carnegie Hall report their free housing as taxable income, apparently taking a different view of § 119.

(C) *Sections 107 and 134.* Note Section 107, which exempts from gross income the rental value of a parsonage or a rental allowance paid to a minister. In Gaylor v. Mnuchin, 278 F. Supp. 3d 1081 (W.D. Wis. 2017), a district court judge in Wisconsin held that the § 107(2) exclusion from gross income of "a rental allowance" paid to "a minister of the gospel" as "part of his compensation" violates the Establishment Clause of the First Amendment since it has no secular purpose—relying on the statement by the sponsor of the legislation that the provision "was needed to 'fight against' a 'godless and anti-religious world movement'." A previous decision by the same judge had been reversed by the Seventh Circuit on the ground that plaintiffs did not have standing to sue. Freedom from Religion Foundation v. Lew, 773 F.3d 815 (7th Cir. 2014), reversing 983 F. Supp. 2d 1051 (W.D. Wis. 2013). In this subsequent case, the plaintiffs, married co-presidents of the Freedom from Religion Foundation, had been paid a "housing allowance" by the foundation, excluded it from income, and sued for a refund after the Service denied the exclusion, thereby obtaining standing to challenge the constitutionality of § 107(2). This will make it difficult for the Seventh Circuit and perhaps even the Supreme Court to avoid deciding the constitutional issue.

See also § 134, which excludes from gross income benefits to military personnel that were excludable from gross income as of September 9, 1986. The Regulations have long granted an exemption for quarters furnished to military personnel and to commutation in lieu of quarters. Is there any tax policy justification for these exclusions?

(D) *Is the Exclusion Justified?* Is it good tax policy to exclude from an employee's income the value of items furnished by the employer, such as meals and lodging, which the employee necessarily would otherwise purchase out of after-tax income? If the meals and lodging are for "the convenience of the employer," is this forced consumption? Should it matter if the consumption is different from that which a taxpayer would normally prefer, for example, meals at a fancy hotel or on a merchant marine ship? Note that § 119 also excludes meals and lodging provided to the employee's spouse or dependents, presumably because it is difficult to allocate the cost of meals and lodging provided to family members.

Note on Section 83

Section 83 provides additional authority for taxing benefits received by a taxpayer in connection with the performance of services. In addition, that section indicates when such benefits should be taxed and in what amount.

In some instances a taxpayer acquires goods or services at a price below the general market price. For example, a purchaser acquires a valuable antique from a junk shop dealer unaware of its value. This so-called bargain purchase is not subject to tax. Where, however, a taxpayer is permitted to purchase property or services at a price below fair market value because the seller is compensating the purchaser for services, the purchaser has gross income in the amount of the discount. § 83(a). The general rule of § 83 also provides that if a person receives property in return for the performance of services, and if the property is nontransferable and subject to a substantial risk of forfeiture at the time of transfer, then the property is treated as still owned by the transferor and no income is realized by the transferee. When the forfeiture risk is removed or the property becomes transferable, the fair market value of the property at that time, less any amount originally paid for it, is includible in income by the person who performed the services. Section 83(c)(1) provides that property is subject to a substantial risk of forfeiture if full enjoyment of the property is conditioned upon the future performance of substantial services by an individual. Section 83(b) permits a taxpayer to elect to include the property in gross income when received even though it is subject to a substantial risk of forfeiture or is nontransferable. Although he must report income on the receipt of the property, he has no further income when the property vests.

The employer is entitled to take a deduction under § 162 for the compensation in the year in which the employee includes the property in income. § 83(h). A divided Tax Court held that in order for the employer to take a deduction, the employees must actually have reported the receipt of the property on their tax returns. A failure to do so deprives the employer of the deduction. Venture Funding, Ltd. v. Commissioner, 110 T.C. 236 (1998). Section 83 is discussed further in Chapter 6.

SECTION 2.   IMPUTED INCOME

Note on Imputed Income

Suppose in exchange for legal services performed by a lawyer, a house painter paints the lawyer's house. Or an individual who owns an apartment building receives a work of art from an artist in exchange for his rent-free use of an apartment. Both the lawyer and the house painter have gross income equal to the fair market value of the services received. The apartment owner includes the value of the painting in income and the artist has income equal to the fair rental value of the apartment. Rev. Rul. 79–24, 1979–1 C.B. 60.

Suppose, however, that the lawyer paints his own house. The benefits derived from labor on one's own behalf or the benefits from the ownership of property are commonly referred to as "imputed income." Economists generally regard imputed income as income that should be taxed, but these benefits usually are not treated as income for tax purposes. Although the failure to tax imputed income creates inequities and inefficiencies, the practical difficulties in subjecting imputed income to tax make taxation unlikely.

The exclusion of imputed income results in similarly situated taxpayers paying different tax. Assume that Bill and Jill each own a dog. Bill works overtime and earns $10, which he uses to pay someone to walk his dog. Jill leaves work on time and walks her own dog. Bill and Jill are in the same economic situation, but Bill will pay tax on $10 more income than Jill does.

The exclusion of imputed income also produces inefficiencies by causing taxpayers to make economic choices different from those that they would have made in a no-tax world. Returning to the lawyer and the house painter, assume the lawyer earns $500 an hour and it will cost him

$400 to have his windows painted, a one hour job. If he works for an hour, he will have only $315 left after taxes, assuming a 37 percent tax rate. Thus, the lawyer may paint the windows himself even though he may prefer to work as a lawyer and his work as a lawyer results in greater productivity.

There are a number of reasons for the failure to tax imputed income. The conceptual difficulty with taxing imputed income is determining where to stop. Does the person who shaves himself have imputed income equal to the value of a shave by a barber? What about a person who reads a book rather than have someone read it to him? Can leisure be thought of as a type of imputed income? Presumably someone who chooses leisure values it by the income that she would have earned had she chosen to work instead. Should income be measured by the amount that a person could earn, rather than what is actually earned? Should a law professor be taxed on the salary she could have earned by practicing on Wall Street? How could we justify taxing services performed by the taxpayer for himself, but not taxing leisure?

There are also practical difficulties in taxing imputed income. Putting aside the political wisdom of legislating a rule that no one would understand or accept, there are valuation and recordkeeping problems. If I comb my hair and do a lousy job, would my income be the value of a comb-out by a stylist or of my own weak attempt? Would sloppy housekeepers have less income than fastidious ones? Do fastidious housekeepers really have more ability to pay taxes than sloppy ones? Imagine the privacy concerns if the Service had to enforce compliance with a rule that required the taxpayer to account for services performed for one's self.

Although we may think the failure to tax the value of walking one's dog or combing one's hair is of academic interest only, the failure to tax the services provided by homemakers has undoubtedly influenced the decisions of some women to stay at home rather than to enter the work force. Many homemakers cannot earn sufficient income after taxes to pay for an equivalent amount of domestic services. Thus, there is an incentive for one spouse to perform untaxed domestic services. There is a problem of fairness as well. Both spouses of couple AB work outside the home and earn a total of $50,000. They pay $10,000 for domestic help. Only one spouse of couple CD works outside the home and earns $40,000 and the other spouse is a homemaker. Couple AB's taxable income exceeds couple CD's by $10,000 even though they have no economic advantage. Domestic services rendered by homemakers to their families is the largest source of imputed income from services. Since taxing the imputed income from domestic services is impractical and unlikely, are there alternatives? One clearly unacceptable alternative is to provide a deduction to the person who pays someone else to perform any services he could have performed for himself. Such a deduction for personal consumption would allow many taxpayers to eliminate their taxable income and would seriously erode the income tax base. An alternative approach is to allow a tax credit or deduction for families in which both spouses work. Congress did provide for such a deduction for a time. But this may create disparity with the single person who must pay for household services.

It is sometimes very difficult to distinguish imputed income from services that should be taxed. Consider the following definition of imputed income:

> a flow of satisfactions from durable goods owned and used by the taxpayer, or from goods and services arising out of the personal exertions of the taxpayer on his own behalf. Imputed income is non-cash income or income in kind. But all non-cash income, or income in kind, is not * * * imputed income. For example, where income in kind is received in return for services rendered, we have an ordinary market transaction without a transfer of cash but with a direct monetary valuation implied. * * * [The] distinguishing characteristic [of imputed income] is that it arises outside of the ordinary processes of the market.

Donald B. Marsh, "The Taxation of Imputed Income," 58 Pol. Sci. Q. 514 (1943).

The courts have been somewhat inconsistent in their treatment of imputed income. In Morris v. Commissioner, 9 B.T.A. 1273 (1928), acq. VII–2 C.B. 75, the Board of Tax Appeals held that the value of farm products consumed by the owners of the farm is not income, stating:

> To include the value of such products, even if [the value] could be determined, * * * to a farmer as compensation would * * * include in income something which Congress did not intend should be so regarded. If products of a farm consumed thereon are income to the producer, it would seem to follow that the rental value of the farmer's home, the gratuitous services of his wife and children, and the value of the power derived from draft animals owned by the farmer and used without cost should also be so considered. It is obvious that such items are comparable to the rental value of a private residence, which has never been regarded as income or as a factor in the determination of tax liability.

Compare Dicenso v. Commissioner, 11 B.T.A. 620 (1928), holding that the owner of a grocery store must include in income groceries used for home consumption. In Commissioner v. Minzer, 279 F.2d 338 (5th Cir. 1960), the Fifth Circuit held that an insurance agent was taxable on the usual commission payable on a policy on his own life even if he simply remitted the premiums to the insurance company after subtracting the commission. The court found that he performed the same services for himself that he performed for other insureds. Compare Benjamin v. Hoey, 139 F.2d 945 (2d Cir. 1944), where a partner in a brokerage firm received, as part of his share of partnership profits, commissions on transactions for his own account. The Court held that there was no income from these transactions. In Worden v. Commissioner, 2 F.3d 359 (10th Cir. 1993), an insurance agent was not taxable where he sold first-year coverage on life insurance policies at cost, and remitted only the net premium to the company because he waived his commission in contracts with the clients.

The most significant form of imputed income from property is the imputed rental value of owner-occupied homes. Consider two taxpayers each with $500,000 to invest. The first puts his money in a bank and earns $30,000 a year (6 percent) in interest income. The second purchases a home for $500,000 that she occupies—a home with an annual rental value of $30,000. The first taxpayer has $30,000 of taxable interest income; the second has no gross income from her investment. Note that the exclusion of imputed income on owner-occupied housing not only treats these two taxpayers differently, but also creates an incentive to invest in a home rather than an asset that produces taxable investment income. Note that this incentive exists regardless of the treatment of interest paid on home mortgages or property taxes, issues that are discussed in Chapter 3.

For a while, Britain taxed imputed income from owner-occupied housing, although such income has never been taxed in the United States. The Treasury Department has included such income in measuring "family economic income," which it uses as a measure to classify families by income levels in evaluating the distribution of taxes and proposed tax changes among people at different levels of income. But even this limited use of imputed income is not well understood by the media, politicians, or the public.

SECTION 3.   GIFTS AND BEQUESTS, PRIZES, AND SCHOLARSHIPS

A. GIFTS

Commissioner v. Duberstein
Supreme Court of the United States, 1960. 363 U.S. 278.

[Two cases were decided in this opinion. No. 376, Commissioner v. Duberstein, involved a Cadillac car given to Duberstein by Berman because Duberstein had been helpful in suggesting customers to Berman. There was no prior arrangement for compensation, and Duberstein did not expect to be paid. The Court of Appeals held that this was not income, reversing the Tax Court.

In No. 546, Stanton v. United States, the taxpayer had been comptroller of Trinity Church and manager of its real estate. He resigned in 1942. The directors then voted him "a gratuity" of $20,000. There was no enforceable right or claim for any such payment. The Court of Appeals held that this was income, reversing the District Court.]

■ MR. JUSTICE BRENNAN delivered the opinion of the Court.

* * *

First. The Government suggests that we promulgate a new "test" in this area to serve as a standard to be applied by the lower courts and by the Tax Court in dealing with the numerous cases that arise.[6] We reject this invitation. We are of opinion that the governing principles are necessarily general and have already been spelled out in the opinions of this Court, and that the problem is one which, under the present statutory framework, does not lend itself to any more definitive statement that would produce a talisman for the solution of concrete cases. The cases at bar are fair examples of the settings in which the problem usually arises. They present situations in which payments have been made in a context with business overtones—an employer making a payment to a retiring employee; a businessman giving something of value to another businessman who has been of advantage to him in his business. In this context, we review the law as established by the prior cases here.

The course of decision here makes it plain that the statute does not use the term "gift" in the common law sense, but in a more colloquial sense. This Court has indicated that a voluntary executed transfer of his property by one to another, without any consideration or compensation therefor, though a common-law gift, is not necessarily a "gift" within the meaning of the statute. For the Court has shown that the mere absence of a legal or moral obligation to make such a payment does not establish that it is a gift. Old Colony Trust Co. v. Commissioner, 279 U.S. 716, 730. And, importantly, if the payment proceeds primarily from "the constraining force of any moral or legal duty," or from "the incentive of anticipated benefit" of an economic nature, Bogardus v. Commissioner, 302 U.S. 34, 41, it is not a gift. And, conversely, "[w]here the payment is in return for services rendered, it is irrelevant that the donor derives no economic benefit from it." Robertson v. United States, 343 U.S. 711, 714.[7] A gift in the statutory sense, on the other hand, proceeds from a "detached and disinterested generosity," Commissioner of Internal Revenue v. LoBue, 351 U.S. 243, 246 (1956); "out of affection, respect, admiration, charity or like impulses." Robertson v. United States [343 U.S. at 714]. And in this regard, the most critical consideration, as the Court has agreed in the leading case here, is the transferor's "intention." Bogardus v. Commissioner, 302 U.S. 34, 43. * * *

---

[6]   The Government's proposed test is stated: "Gifts should be defined as transfers of property made for personal as distinguished from business reasons."

[7]   The cases including "tips" in gross income are classic examples of this. See, e.g., Roberts v. Commissioner, 176 F.2d 221.

The Government says that this "intention" of the transferor cannot mean what the cases on the common-law concept of gift call "donative intent." With that we are in agreement, for our decisions fully support this. Moreover, the *Bogardus* case itself makes it plain that the donor's characterization of his action is not determinative—that there must be an objective inquiry as to whether what is called a gift amounts to it in reality. 302 U.S., at 40. * * *

Second. The Government's proposed "test," while apparently simple and precise in its formulation, depends frankly on a set of "principles" or "presumptions" derived from the decided cases, and concededly subject to various exceptions; and it involves various corollaries, which add to its detail. Were we to promulgate this test as a matter of law, and accept with it its various presuppositions and stated consequences, we would be passing far beyond the requirements of the cases before us, and would be painting on a large canvas with indeed a broad brush. The Government derives its test from such propositions as the following: That payments by an employer to an employee, even though voluntary, ought, by and large, to be taxable; That the concept of a gift is inconsistent with a payment's being a deductible business expense; That a gift involves "personal" elements; That a business corporation cannot properly make a gift of its assets. The Government admits that there are exceptions and qualifications to these propositions. We think, to the extent they are correct, that these propositions are not principles of law but rather maxims of experience that the tribunals which have tried the facts of cases in this area have enunciated in explaining their factual determinations. * * * The taxing statute does not make nondeductibility by the transferor a condition on the "gift" exclusion; nor does it draw any distinction, in terms, between transfers by corporations and individuals, as to the availability of the "gift" exclusion to the transferee. The conclusion whether a transfer amounts to a "gift" is one that must be reached on consideration of all the factors. * * *

Third. Decision of the issue presented in these cases must be based ultimately on the application of the fact-finding tribunal's experience with the mainsprings of human conduct to the totality of the facts of each case. The nontechnical nature of the statutory standard, the close relationship of it to the data of practical human experience, and the multiplicity of relevant factual elements, with their various combinations, creating the necessity of ascribing the proper force to each, confirm us in our conclusion that primary weight in this area must be given to the conclusions of the trier of fact. * * *

This conclusion may not satisfy an academic desire for tidiness, symmetry and precision in this area, any more than a system based on the determinations of various factfinders ordinarily does. But we see it as implicit in the present statutory treatment of the exclusion for gifts, and in the variety of forums in which federal income tax cases can be tried. If there is fear of undue uncertainty or overmuch litigation,

Congress may make more precise its treatment of the matter by singling out certain factors and making them determinative of the matter, as it has done in one field of the "gift" exclusion's former application, that of prizes and awards. * * * But the question here remains basically one of fact, for determination on a case-by-case basis. * * *

One consequence of this is that appellate review of determinations in this field must be quite restricted. Where a jury has tried the matter upon correct instructions, the only inquiry is whether it cannot be said that reasonable men could reach differing conclusions on the issue. * * * Where the trial has been by a judge without a jury, the judge's findings must stand unless "clearly erroneous." * * * And Congress has in the most explicit terms attached the identical weight to the findings of the Tax Court. I.R.C. § 7482(a).

Fourth. A majority of the Court is in accord with the principles just outlined. And, applying them to the *Duberstein* case, we are in agreement, on the evidence we have set forth, that it cannot be said that the conclusion of the Tax Court was "clearly erroneous." It seems to us plain that as trier of the facts it was warranted in concluding that despite the characterization of the transfer of the Cadillac by the parties and the absence of any obligation, even of a moral nature, to make it, it was at bottom a recompense for Duberstein's past services, or an inducement for him to be of further service in the future. We cannot say with the Court of Appeals that such a conclusion was "mere suspicion" on the Tax Court's part. To us it appears based in the sort of informed experience with human affairs that factfinding tribunals should bring to this task.

As to *Stanton,* we are in disagreement. To four of us, it is critical here that the District Court as trier of fact made only the simple and unelaborated finding that the transfer in question was a "gift." To be sure, conciseness is to be strived for, and prolixity avoided, in findings; but, to the four of us, there comes a point where findings become so sparse and conclusory as to give no revelation of what the District Court's concept of the determining facts and legal standard may be. * * * For all that appears, the District Court may have viewed the form of the resolution or the simple absence of legal consideration as conclusive. While the judgment of the Court of Appeals cannot stand, the four of us think there must be further proceedings in the District Court looking toward new and adequate findings of fact. In this, we are joined by MR. JUSTICE WHITTAKER, who agrees that the findings were inadequate, although he does not concur generally in this opinion.

Accordingly, in No. 376, the judgment of this Court is that the judgment of the Court of Appeals is reversed, and in No. 546, that the judgment of the Court of Appeals is vacated, and the case is remanded to the District Court for further proceedings not inconsistent with this opinion.

It is so ordered.

■ MR. JUSTICE HARLAN concurs in the result in No. 376. In No. 546, he would affirm the judgment of the Court of Appeals for the reasons stated by MR. JUSTICE FRANKFURTER.

■ MR. JUSTICE WHITTAKER, agreeing with *Bogardus* that whether a particular transfer is or is not a "gift" may involve "a mixed question of law and fact," 302 U.S., at 39, concurs only in the result of this opinion.

■ MR. JUSTICE DOUGLAS dissents, since he is of the view that in each of these two cases there was a gift under the test which the Court fashioned nearly a quarter of a century ago in Bogardus v. Commissioner, 302 U.S. 34.

■ [The opinion of JUSTICE BLACK concurring in No. 376 (Duberstein) and dissenting in No. 546 (Stanton) is omitted.]

■ MR. JUSTICE FRANKFURTER, concurring in the judgment in No. 376 and dissenting in No. 546.

As the Court's opinion indicates, we brought these two cases here * * * primarily on the Government's urging that, in the interest of the better administration of the income tax laws, clarification was desirable for determining when a transfer of property constitutes a "gift" and is not to be included in income for purposes of ascertaining the "gross income" under the Internal Revenue Code. * * *

Despite acute arguments at the bar and a most thorough reexamination of the problem on a full canvass of our prior decisions and an attempted fresh analysis of the nature of the problem, the Court has rejected the invitation of the Government to fashion anything like a litmus paper test for determining what is excludable as a "gift" from gross income. Nor has the Court attempted a clarification of the particular aspects of the problem presented by these two cases, namely, payment by an employer to an employee upon the termination of the employment relation and non-obligatory payment for services rendered in the course of a business relationship. While I agree that experience has shown the futility of attempting to define, by language so circumscribing as to make it easily applicable, what constitutes a gift for every situation where the problem may arise, I do think that greater explicitness is possible in isolating and emphasizing factors which militate against a gift in particular situations.

Thus, regarding the two frequently recurring situations involved in these cases—things of value given to employees by their employers upon the termination of employment and payments entangled in a business relation and occasioned by the performance of some service—the strong implication is that the payment is of a business nature. The problem in these two cases is entirely different from the problem in a case where a payment is made from one member of a family to another, where the implications are directly otherwise. No single general formulation appropriately deals with both types of cases, although both involve the question whether the payment was a "gift." While we should normally suppose that a payment from father to son was a gift, unless the contrary is shown, in the two situations now before us the business implications are so forceful that I would apply a presumptive rule placing the burden upon the beneficiary to prove the payment wholly unrelated to his services to the enterprise. The Court, however, has declined so to analyze the problem. * * *

The Court has made only one authoritative addition to the previous course of our decisions * * * that it is "for the triers of the facts to seek among competing aims or motives the ones that dominated conduct." All this being so in view of the Court, it seems to me desirable not to try to improve what has "already been spelled out" in the opinions of this Court but to leave to the lower courts the application of old phrases rather than to float new ones and thereby inevitably produce a new volume of exegesis on the new phrases.

Especially do I believe this when factfinding tribunals are directed by the Court to rely upon their "experience with the mainsprings of human conduct" and on their "informed experience with human affairs" in appraising the totality of the facts of each case. Varying conceptions regarding the "mainsprings of human conduct" are derived from a variety of experiences or assumptions about the nature of man, and "experience with human affairs," is not only diverse but also often drastically conflicting. What the Court now does sets factfinding bodies to sail on an illimitable ocean of individual beliefs and experiences. This can hardly fail to invite, if indeed not encourage, too individualized diversities in the administration of the income tax law. I am afraid that by these new phrasings the practicalities of tax administration, which should be as uniform as is possible in so vast a country as ours, will be embarrassed. By applying what has already been spelled out in the opinions of this Court, I agree with the Court in reversing the judgment in Commissioner v. Duberstein.

But I would affirm the decision of the Court of Appeals for the Second Circuit in Stanton v. United States. * * *

NOTES

(A) *Subsequent History.* On remand of *Stanton,* the District Court, sitting without a jury, held that the payment made to Stanton was a gift. The Second Circuit affirmed, finding that the decision was not clearly erroneous. Stanton v. United States, 186 F. Supp. 393 (E.D.N.Y. 1960), affirmed 287 F.2d 876 (2d Cir. 1961). Does it make sense that Duberstein's receipt was taxable and Stanton's was exempt?

Section 102(c) (added to the Code subsequently) provides that the gift exclusion does not apply to any transfer from an employer to an employee. A personal relationship is irrelevant. See Williams v. Commissioner, 120 F.App'x 289 (10th Cir. 2005) (fact that employer and employee were "close personal friends" does not matter). Does that mean an employee is taxable on receipt of a birthday or wedding gift from her employer? What about § 132(a)(4)? Would § 102(c) cover the relationship in *Duberstein*?

Apparently Berman had claimed a deduction even though Duberstein attempted to exclude the Cadillac as a gift. Section 274(b) provides a maximum deduction of $25 for business gifts that are excludable under § 102. The payor generally would prefer to take a business deduction, defeating a claim of nonbusiness or donative intent. The volume of these cases declined after this section was enacted in 1962. Why would § 274(b) have no effect on the *Stanton* situation?

(B) *The Duberstein Approach*. How much guidance does the *Duberstein* approach provide to lower courts? Are there any limitations on the trier of fact?

Is a diversity of outcomes (or more pointedly, inconsistency of outcomes) in common situations troublesome? Is there an explanation for Duberstein's loss and Stanton's victory or is this simply the outcome of tax cases being litigated in many forums?

While almost all cases involving gifts cite the "detached and disinterested generosity" language of *Duberstein,* it is not entirely clear what the words mean. In Goodwin v. United States, 67 F.3d 149 (8th Cir. 1995), the court noted:

> Many courts nevertheless give talismanic weight to a phrase used more casually in the *Duberstein* opinion—that a transfer to be a gift must be the product of "detached and disinterested generosity." It is the rare donor who is completely "detached and disinterested." To decide close cases using this phrase requires careful analysis of what detached and disinterested means in different contexts. Thus, the phrase is more sound bite than talisman.

In *Goodwin*, a church made substantial gifts to its minister by gathering cash contributions made anonymously by church members, which were then presented on behalf of the entire congregation by church leaders. The court refused to simply look at the intention of the actual donors to see if they acted out of disinterested generosity. Instead it examined other factors such as the fact that the minister was paid a small salary and the regularly scheduled "special gifts" provided a reasonable salary.

How much assistance does *Duberstein* provide to a lawyer advising a client? How does a donee determine whether the donor has the requisite intent? Why is the donor's intent relevant? Can a donee have a "gift" from an unknown donor? Does a panhandler who collects coins from subway passengers have income? Would it matter if the person who puts the coin in the cup does so out of pity or to encourage the panhandler to move on or with gratitude for the panhandler's saxophone playing? Does performance by the donee matter? If Dad purchases a car for Son when he makes the honor roll, does Son have income?

Would the government's proposed test in *Duberstein* be more workable?

For an example of how the discretion conferred by *Duberstein* haunts the tax law, see Yang v. Commissioner, T.C. Summ. Op. 2008–156. The Tax

Court decided that the $10,500 the taxpayer received from her boyfriend was a gift, rather than payment for services. Although the taxpayer did some cooking and cleaning for her boyfriend, she was not his formal employee. Nevertheless, her boyfriend issued her a statement that she had income and deducted the $10,500 he paid her as a business deduction. (What a nice guy.) The court found that the taxpayer had not actually worked for her boyfriend and the payments were made "with 'detached and disinterested generosity' out of his affection for her at the time."

(C) *Some Tips.* Tips are taxable income. See Reg. § 1.61–2(a). Collection of income tax on tip income has proven difficult, however. Tip reporting requirements for employers have increased the likelihood of collection. See §§ 6053(c) and 6722.

In Olk v. United States, 536 F.2d 876 (9th Cir. 1976), cert. denied, 429 U.S. 920 (1976), the court found that "tokes" received by a craps dealer from casino patrons were income, noting that the payments were motivated by superstition rather than by detached or disinterested generosity. Although the court noted that the amount, regularity, and equal division of the tokes among dealers all indicated that dealers regarded them as compensation for services, that factor does not appear to be relevant under *Duberstein*. The court also noted: "Tribute to the gods of fortune which it is hoped will be returned bounteously soon can only be described as an 'involved and intensely interested' act."

Consider this photo from https://www.good.is/articles/libertarian-tip-tax-free-gift-restaurants:

The photo prompted debate among tax academics who ultimately agreed that this ploy was unsuccessful in its effort to transform a taxable tip into a nontaxable gift.

(D) *Bagging the Swag.* What started as "gifts" to actresses to make them shine on Oscar night morphed into a full-fledged bidding war. Fashion designers competed to have winners and presenters appear on the red carpet in their dresses and jewels. Remarks in interviews that this kind of "product placement" was extraordinarily valuable defeated any possibility that the designers were acting out of disinterested generosity. Several days before the Oscars are awarded, the Commissioner often wishes the nominees good luck and reminds them that the six-figure goodie bags provided by a variety of sponsors are taxable income. He points out that "movie stars face the same tax obligations as ordinary Americans." Despite the taxes, in 2012, for example, nominees who did not take home a statuette received a swag bag filled with items that ranged from a $35 bottle of hand sanitizer with a bejeweled sleeve to a $16,000 African safari.

(E) *Political Contributions.* In Revenue Ruling 68–512, 1968–2 C.B. 41, the Service held that political contributions are not taxable to a political candidate to the extent used for expenses of a political campaign. However, any amount diverted for personal use is taxable.

What is the underlying theory of the ruling? What Code section enables the Service to reach this result? Congress subsequently affirmed this ruling, noting that if a payment satisfies a legal obligation of the candidate, including an obligation for federal income taxes, it is a diversion for personal use. See S.Rep. No. 93–1357, 93d Cong., 2d Sess. 31 (1974).

In Loren-Maltese v. Commissioner, 104 T.C.M (CCH) 115 (2012), the Court found that Loren-Maltese had failed to report over $350,000 in political contributions she used for personal purposes while town president of Cicero, Illinois, the Chicago suburb that was home to legendary tax evader Al Capone. She used some of the campaign funds to purchase herself a brand-new Cadillac. The IRS proved that Loren-Maltese committed fraud in her understatement of income. It did not help her case that Loren-Maltese had already been convicted of defrauding Cicero of over $10 million. If the exclusion of political contributions is based on § 102, what difference does it make how the funds are used? Is it the court's view that these "gifts" are made conditional on their being used for campaign expenditures? Do you believe that large campaign contributions are made out of "detached and disinterested generosity"?

(F) *Support and Government Transfer Payments.* Support provided by family members, like intrafamily gifts, is not included in gross income. There is no specific statutory authority for this rule, but the Service has never sought to tax family support.

It also has been the general policy of the Service to exclude from income most government benefits and other welfare payments. For example, the IRS has ruled that Social Security payments, unemployment compensation, benefit payments to the blind, and other assistance payments are not includible in the gross income of the recipient. See, e.g., Rev. Rul. 70–280, 1970–1 C.B. 13 (unemployment benefits); Rev. Rul. 70–217, 1970–1 C.B. 12 (Social Security payments); Rev. Rul. 57–102, 1957–1 C.B. 26 (state aid to the blind). It is clear, however, that Congress can choose to tax such benefits.

See, e.g., § 85 (taxing unemployment payments). Other payments that are not need-based have typically been subject to tax. See, e.g., Rev. Rul. 85–39, 1985–1 C.B. 21 (taxing "dividend" payments to Alaska residents out of state's oil income). The general welfare exclusion does not apply to businesses. For example, in Revenue Ruling 2005–46, 2005–30 IRB 1, the IRS held that disaster relief payments made under a state program providing grants for uncompensated losses were taxable. Disaster relief payments to individuals, however, are generally excluded. § 139.

What is the justification for excluding these payments from income? If welfare payments were taxed, would the government simply have to increase welfare? Is there any merit to the contention that if the government taxed such benefits, it would merely be paying with one hand and taking back with another? Does the exclusion result in different treatment for similarly situated taxpayers? The case for taxing transfer payments that are wage replacements or deferred compensation can easily be supported on equity grounds. What about other in-kind benefits like free medical care or legal services, police protection, maintained highways, etc.?

(G) *Bequests.* Like gifts, bequests are excluded from income under § 102, and, as with gifts, questions sometimes arise whether a particular transfer (or class of transfers) qualifies as an excludable bequest. For example, an attorney may not exclude the amount of a legacy received under the will of a client in lieu of payment of legal fees during the client's lifetime. See e.g., Wolder v. Commissioner, 493 F.2d 608 (2d Cir. 1974) where the attorney had contracted to perform all legal services that his client would require during her lifetime in exchange for her promise to bequeath to him certain shares of stock or their equivalent. The Commissioner asserted that the fair market value of the property was taxable compensation for services, while the attorney countered that the legacy was excludable under § 102, even though some consideration had flowed from beneficiary to decedent. The Tax Court held for the Commissioner and the Second Circuit affirmed on the ground that the parties had merely agreed to postpone payment for legal services, stating: "A transfer in the form of a bequest was the method that the parties chose to compensate Mr. Wolder for his legal services, and that transfer is therefore subject to taxation, whatever its label . . . may be."

In Miller v. Commissioner, 53 T.C.M. 962 (1987), A and B agreed to take care of C for the rest of his life. C agreed to leave all of his personal property to A and B, stating that this was in payment for their services. The Tax Court ruled that the amount was taxable as income to A and B.

(H) *Policy Reasons for the Exclusion of Gifts.* An individual who works is taxed, but one who lives off the munificence of others is not taxed. What is the rationale for not taxing gifts as income? If it is difficult to distinguish between support and gifts, does this justify not taxing gifts?

Consider the three possible ways to treat gifts under an income tax: (1) the gift might be deducted from the income of the donor and included in the income of the donee, (2) the gift might be included in the income of the donor and also in the income of the donee, or (3) the gift might be included in the income of the donor but excluded from the income of the donee.

The first of these treatments taxes the person who uses the gift for personal consumption. The second treatment taxes the person with the wherewithal to make the gift as well as the person who uses the gift for consumption. The third treatment is that of the income tax, at least with respect to property with no unrealized appreciation at the time the gift is made.

Under the first and third options, there is no additional income tax on the transfer of wealth from one taxpayer to another. There may be, however, an estate or gift tax. The income tax burdens under those two alternatives, however, will tend to differ with a progressive rate structure, depending on whether or not the marginal tax rate of the donee is higher or lower than the marginal tax rate of the donor. Typically, marginal rates of donors are higher than those of donees, at least at the time of the transfer. (Children under age 18 may be taxed at their parents' tax rates. § 1(g).) Under the second option, the consumption financed by the gift, in effect, is taxed twice, to both the donor and the donee.

B. PRIZES AND AWARDS

Note on Prizes and Awards

The recipient of a prize or award generally includes the prize in income even if the transfer was gratuitous. Regulation § 1.102–1(a) has long provided that the gift exclusion under § 102 does not apply to prizes and awards. Under § 74, certain prizes are excludable from income if they are not retained by the recipient. The award must be in recognition of religious, charitable, scientific, educational, artistic, literary or civic achievement; the recipient must have taken no action to enter the contest; the recipient must not be required to render substantial future services; and the prize or award must be transferred to charity. § 74(b).

Given that a recipient must donate the prize to charity, why is there any need for limitation on the types of excludable prizes? In many cases, if the recipient were forced to include the prize in income, there would be an offsetting charitable deduction. The current rule, however, permits the recipient of certain prizes to transfer them to a charity without the adverse tax consequence that would occur if the recipient were subject to one of the limitations on the amount of deductible charitable contributions.

NOTES

(A) *Oprah's Pontiacs.* The IRS has always taken the position that game show winners must report their earnings and prizes. Since that creates a hardship for those who win, sponsors usually do not mention the obligation. Consider Oprah Winfrey who has made a habit of giving away prizes to her audience. She started the 2004 season by giving a fully loaded Pontiac G6 to everyone who attended the first show. Although Pontiac announced they were covering the taxes, it turned out they were paying only the sales taxes.

After weeks of bad publicity, Oprah started giving away cash to cover the income taxes as well. Then she discovered that she needed to give away cash to cover the taxes on the cash, and then she discovered . . . you get the idea. The Daily Show had great fun with this incident. See http://www.cc.com/video-clips/6efkkk/the-daily-show-with-jon-stewart-wheels-of-misfortune.

(B) *Other Winners*. Other winners try different tactics. In March of 2007 a furniture store in Boston promised that everyone who purchased furniture during the following six weeks would have their entire purchase price refunded if the Red Sox won the World Series. The Sox beat the odds and won the 2007 World Series. The furniture store refunded millions to customers who ended up with free furniture. At the urging of the store, the IRS announced that the customers owed no tax, asserting that the refunds were a purchase price reduction. How is this 100 percent discount different from the cars that Oprah gave away?

(C) *Olympic Prizes*. In the summer of 2016 after the U.S. Olympic team garnered a slew of gold medals, a brief political firestorm erupted when the press reported that the medals and the prize money medalists received were taxable. Responding to Olympic fever, Congress enacted § 74(d) to exempt the prizes and medals from tax. The swimmer Michael Phelps, for example, won five gold medals, one silver, and $140,000 in prize money in the 2016 Summer Olympics.

Section 74(d) limits the exclusion to prizes from the "United States Olympic Committee" so athletes who are resident in the United States, and therefore taxable in the United States, who compete successfully and receive prizes or prize money from other nations' Olympic Committees must pay U.S. income tax on these awards.

Section 74(d) also provides that the inclusion for Olympic prizes and prize money does not apply if the taxpayer has other qualified gross income of more than $1 million. This, of course, means that the National Basketball Association players who typically garner Olympic gold must include the value of their medals and prize money in income. So must other athletes who earn more than $1 million in the year of the Olympics from product endorsements. Michael Phelps may be one; news reports estimate his endorsement income to be $12 million in 2016. Note that the $1 million figure is a "cliff," unusual in the tax law: If an Olympic prize winning athlete has only $1 million of other adjusted gross income, her prizes and prize money are tax-exempt; if the athlete's adjusted gross income is $1,000,001 or more the entire winnings are taxed.

(D) *Other Athletes*. Colleges and universities routinely provide their student-athletes rewards for winning. For example, in 2011, Auburn University spent about $750,000 on conference and national championship rings for its players and other football-related members of the school's athletic department. Professional sports teams often spend much more on rings for athletes, coaches, and others close to the team. Those prizes are taxable to the recipients.

(E) *Nobel and Pulitzer Prizes*. Is there a principled reason why Olympic athletes should exclude their medals and prize money? Are they different from Pulitzer Prize winners or Nobel Laureates? In 1995, five American Nobel Laureates in science sent the following letter to President Clinton (the letter was reprinted in Tax Notes Today, a daily tax news service, on July 27, 1995):

Dear Mr. President:

> The undersigned American Nobel Laureates of 1994 greatly appreciate your and Mrs. Clinton's kindness to invite us to the White House for a reception in our honor. As much as a Nobel Prize is a most rewarding personal recognition, we strongly feel that it also reflects acknowledgment of the continuing strength of American Science and its achievements.
>
> * * *
>
> We perhaps may be allowed to raise a point concerning the Nobel Prizes. According to the Nobel Foundation the US is the only Western country that taxes the prizes. We understand that even the gold medals we are to receive in Stockholm are being taxed by their weight. This is a relatively new policy, introduced in only 1986 during a previous administration. The tax on income from a few Nobel Prizes cannot make much difference for the Treasury but restoring their former tax-free status would show the world that the United States government and the American people do appreciate scientific achievement and do agree that it should receive proper recognition.
>
> We hope that you will agree, Mr. President, that the present policy should be rescinded and that the tax-free status of Nobel Prizes should be restored. We hope that this can be done in a retrospective manner as from October 1, 1994, preferably by an Executive Order or by initiation of Legislative Action if needed. We would very much appreciate your favorable consideration of this matter.

How should the President—or the Treasury's Assistant Secretary for Tax Policy—respond?

C. SCHOLARSHIPS AND FELLOWSHIPS

Note on the Exclusion of Scholarships

The exclusion for scholarships and fellowships under § 117 is limited to amounts used by degree candidates for "qualified tuition and related expenses." Qualified expenses are (1) tuition and fees for enrollment or attendance by a student enrolled in a school and (2) fees, books, supplies, and equipment required for the course of study. The recipient is not required to trace dollars of scholarship aid to these particular uses; an exclusion is allowed to the extent that the scholarship or grant received does not exceed these amounts. There is no exclusion for grant or scholarship money used for room and board. The exclusion applies only if the terms of the grant or scholarship do not earmark or designate its use for nonqualified expenses and do not specify that the funds cannot be used for tuition or course-related expenses.

Any portion of a "scholarship" received for teaching, research, or other services required as a condition for receiving the scholarship is not excludable. § 117(c). Thus, amounts received for teaching are taxable whether the compensation takes the form of a paycheck, tuition reduction, or a scholarship. Note that the Service has emphasized the necessity of a *quid pro quo*. In Revenue Ruling 77–263, 1977–2 C.B. 47, the Service held that an athletic scholarship is excludable if the scholarship "does not require the student to participate in a particular sport, requires no particular activity in lieu of participation, and does not cancel if the student cannot participate."

Why should scholarships be excluded from gross income? If a student works part-time, she will pay her tuition with after-tax dollars. If an individual obtains a student loan rather than a scholarship, the loan is not income at the time of receipt, but it will be repaid out of after-tax income. In certain circumstances if the loan is forgiven, the cancellation of indebtedness income is excluded. § 108(f), discussed infra at page 198.

If scholarships were taxed, should the value of higher education at state schools provided free or at reduced cost to state residents also be taxed as income? What about a gift from a parent used to pay tuition?

A limited amount of educational assistance provided through an employer-funded plan is exempt from tax. § 127. Certain taxpayers can deduct a limited amount of education expenses. § 221, discussed infra at page 361.

SECTION 4.   CAPITAL APPRECIATION AND RECOVERY OF BASIS

Note Introducing the Concepts of Capital Recovery and Basis

Section 61 provides that gross income means income from "whatever source derived," and inherent in the concept of "income" is the notion of net gain. Thus, if A purchases property for $1,000, and it yields no income while he holds it, he must sell it for more than $1,000 to have income or profit. If he sells it for less than $1,000, he has a loss. If he sells it for $1,000, he has merely experienced a "recovery of capital" and does not have any net gain or loss.

In determining income in the context of a business selling its inventory, the regulations distinguish gross income from gross receipts. Thus, § 1.61–3(a) of the Regulations states that " 'gross income' means the total sales less the costs of goods sold." The Supreme Court recognized this distinction in 1918, when it ruled that, absent any statutory provision authorizing an offset against gross receipts, the income concept implied a deduction for the cost of goods sold. In Doyle v. Mitchell Brothers Co., 247 U.S. 179 (1918), Justice Pitney stated, at 185:

> Whatever difficulty there may be about a precise and scientific definition of "income", it imports * * * something entirely distinct from principal or capital either as a subject of taxation or as a measure of the tax; conveying rather the idea of gain or increase * * * * Understanding the term in this natural and obvious sense, it cannot be said that a conversion of capital assets invariably produces income. If sold at less than cost, it produces rather loss or outgo. * * * In order to determine whether there has been gain or loss, and the amount of the gain, if any, we must withdraw from the gross proceeds an amount sufficient to restore the capital value that existed at the commencement of the period under consideration.

The Code currently reaches this result as follows: Section 61(a)(3) includes in income "gains derived from dealings in property." Section 1001 describes a *gain* as the excess of the *amount realized* from the sale over the taxpayer's *basis* for the property. In the preceding example, the amount realized is the sales price, and the taxpayer's basis is $1,000. *Basis* is a term of art in the tax law. Section 1012 provides that the basis of property is usually its cost to the taxpayer, except as otherwise provided. How basis is determined in a variety of contexts is discussed in the next Note. It is important to understand that basis is the technical mechanism by which taxpayers are allowed to recover their capital investment when they sell property. The determination of the "amount realized," the "adjusted basis" and thus, the amount of gain or loss, is in many cases far more difficult than the above discussion would suggest. A more detailed discussion of the taxation of gain or loss on the disposition of property is found in Chapter 5, which deals with capital gains and losses.

The problems would be hard enough if our system measured gain or loss at the end of each year. But the reckoning of gross income from the ownership of property can take many years, because accounting for gain or loss generally is postponed until property is sold. Thus, there is a significant distinction between the tax concept of "income" and "economic income," which may increase or diminish as the market value of property changes. Rather than requiring a taxpayer to estimate the change in value of his assets each year and to include that amount in income (or to deduct any losses), the Code generally taxes only "realized" gains. The realization requirement, which calls for a realization event before gain is taken into income, is discussed infra at page 148.

The tax-free recovery of capital is a fundamental aspect of income measurement, and the timing and mechanism for recovering capital is one of the most important issues in designing an income tax. Although taxpayers are taxed only on income, and thus will be able to recover capital tax free, the *timing* of the capital recovery is extremely important.

There are basically three ways in which the taxpayer accounts for costs. First, some expenditures for the production of income are treated as *immediately deductible expenses;* the costs are said to be "expensed." If there is enough income to offset the deductions, the tax-free recovery of such income-producing expenses is immediate. Other expenses must be *capitalized* and the purchase price or cost taken into account only when the asset is sold or exchanged. In the case of stock, for example, the cost or basis is taken into account only when the stock is sold or exchanged. Dividend income received while the stock is held is taxed without any offset for the capital invested. Finally, other assets may be *depreciated;* that is, periodic deductions are allowed for the asset's cost. Suppose a cab driver purchases a $30,000 cab for her business. The $30,000 cost of the cab must be capitalized, but periodic deductions will be allowed for depreciation. For example, if the cab was useful in her business for five years, she might be permitted to take one-fifth of her cost or $6,000 a year as a depreciation deduction. The determination whether costs are immediately deductible or must be capitalized is discussed in Chapter 3, infra at page 318. The rules for determining the tax allowance for depreciation also are considered in detail in Chapter 3.

It is critical to understand that so long as a tax-free recovery of capital is allowed, the same total net income will be taxed over the entire period the asset is held, but there may be great variations in annual income depending upon the timing of the offset for capital recovery. If taxable income can be deferred to later years through faster deductions for capital expenditure, the accompanying postponement of taxes is generally to the taxpayer's advantage. Thus tax deferral is one of the principal tax planning functions. We return to the issue of deferral throughout the course. We next explore in more detail the concepts of basis and realization.

Note on the Determination of the Basis of Property

Basis of Purchased Property. The basis of property is its cost, except as otherwise provided. § 1012. This rule is simple where a taxpayer purchases a piece of property for cash—her basis is the amount of cash paid. Where the taxpayer receives property in exchange for services and the value of the property is included in gross income, her basis is the fair market value of the property received. Reg. § 1.61–2(d)(2)(i). In effect, it is as if the employee had received compensation in cash and had used the cash to purchase the property. The term "tax cost" is sometimes used to describe the basis of property that was not purchased, but whose fair market value the taxpayer included in income.

Basis generally is cost even if the taxpayer has "underpaid" or "overpaid" for the property. If the property is purchased at less than its fair market value, the purchaser takes a cost basis and is not taxed on the gain until she disposes of the property at its fair market value. Similarly, if the taxpayer overpays for property, the basis is the amount paid, and the loss will be realized only when she sells the property for its fair market value. Sometimes, however, a bargain purchase occurs as a result of a relationship between the parties. For example, an employer might allow an employee to purchase an asset at less than the market value as a form of compensation. A bargain purchase also might occur between companies and their shareholders as a substitute for dividends or between landlords and tenants as a substitute for rent or between family members as a way of making a gift. In general, courts will examine the facts and circumstances in an effort to recharacterize the transaction to reflect its substance. Often, the substance of the transaction is the sale of property in exchange for cash and services. Where a bargain purchase is in substance a substitute for salary, the amount of price reduction is included in income and the purchaser is treated as acquiring the asset for fair market value. The cost basis of the asset would then be its recharacterized purchase price: the amount actually paid plus the amount included in income as salary. For example, if Employee is permitted to purchase stock worth $100 for $80, Employee would be taxed on $20 of compensation and his basis in the stock would be $100. (Contrast this example to the situation where the employee receives the stock subject to forfeiture. See the discussion of § 83, supra at page 121.)

Basis also must be determined where the taxpayer acquires property in exchange for other property. Generally, an arm's length transaction will involve an exchange of properties of equal value and any difference in the values of the properties exchanged will be accounted for by the transfer of cash. The exchange usually will be a "realization" event and any gain or loss on either side of the transaction will be "recognized." As to the basis of the property purchased, courts have construed cost to mean the value of the property received. See, e.g. Philadelphia Park Amusement Co. v. United States, 126 F. Supp. 184 (Ct.Cl.1954) (holding that where the value of the property given up differs from the value of the property received, the taxpayer's basis in the property received is its value).

[handwritten margin note: Basis is determined by cost. Cost = whatever I gave for it]

There are a number of instances where the taxpayer acquires property in a transaction where gain or loss is not "recognized." Where such "nonrecognition" provisions apply, recognition of gain or loss generally is postponed until the taxpayer's investment is significantly altered. Almost always, there are special basis rules that apply when the taxpayer has entered into a nonrecognition transaction. These rules are considered in some detail in Chapter 5.

Finally, the basis of property acquired with borrowed funds is considered infra at page 199.

Basis of Property Acquired by Gift. Section 1015 provides that, for all gifts and transfers in trust since 1921, the basis of property for computing gain in the hands of a donee shall be the same as the basis in the hands of the donor. This treatment is commonly known as "carryover basis" or technically as "transferred basis." § 7701(a)(42) and (43). This carryover basis provision reflects a congressional determination not to tax accrued income at the time of a gift, but to preserve the basis so that the tax is triggered on subsequent disposition. The basis for determining loss, however, is either the donor's basis or the fair market value at the time of the gift, whichever is lower. For example, suppose Mom buys property for $100, she gives it to her son when it is worth $150, and he subsequently sells it for $175. The son's basis is $100; thus, when the asset is sold, he will report a $75 gain: the $50 gain that had accrued at the time of the gift as well as the $25 appreciation that accrued while he held the asset. If, however, the value of the property was $80 at the time of the gift and the son subsequently sold it for $75, he would recognize only a $5 loss. The loss of $20 that had accrued by the date of the gift would disappear. Suppose the value of the property at the date of the gift was $50 and the son sold it for $75? See Reg. § 1.1015–1(a)(2).

The Supreme Court upheld the constitutionality of requiring the donee to pay tax on the gain accrued by the donor. Taft v. Bowers, 278 U.S. 470 (1929). Of course, the donee did not question the appropriateness of receiving a basis in the gifted property when she had no cost.

In combination, the basis rules for gifts permit the transfer of tax on accrued gains to the donee, but not the transfer of the tax benefit of losses. (Note that § 267 disallows losses on sales between related parties.) Which should be of more concern, gains or losses? Does it matter if the donor and donee are in different income tax brackets?

What if a taxpayer cannot establish the donor's basis? See § 1015(a), which provides that the donee must attempt to attain such facts from the donor and if impossible, the basis will be the fair market value at the date the property was acquired by the donor.

Basis of Property Acquired from a Decedent. The basis rules are quite different when a taxpayer acquires property from a decedent. Section 1014 provides that the basis of property acquired from a decedent is "the fair market value of the property at the date of the decedent's death." This section apparently reflects a policy decision that death is an inappropriate time to tax accrued gain on property passing to others from the decedent. The result of this decision is a "stepped-up" (or stepped-down) basis for the transferee and the accrued gain (or loss) on the property will never be subjected to income tax (or available to reduce tax).

Because so much appreciation on property transferred at death escapes income tax, proposals to eliminate the stepped-up basis rule have been advanced for many years. Proponents of reform argue that § 1014 is inequitable because it produces a different tax burden depending on whether a decedent's estate is composed of unrealized appreciation or of previously taxed income. In addition, proponents argue that a carryover basis provision or an income tax on appreciation at death would mitigate the so-called "lock-in" effect that occurs when owners of appreciated property, aware of the stepped-up basis that will be given to their heirs under § 1014, refuse to sell appreciated property prior to death. Many analysts contend that the repeal of the step-up in basis would eliminate the advantage of holding assets until death. A carryover basis rule, however, might amplify the "lock-in" effect, because once an asset passes to a beneficiary, he might become particularly reluctant to sell it, since he would have to pay tax on gain that accrued during the decedent's lifetime as well as any gain that accrued subsequently. In the 1970s, Congress enacted a carryover basis provision, but compromises embodied in the provision resulted in an enormously complex set of rules. Ultimately, Congress repealed this provision before it became effective. In 2001 Congress again enacted a carryover basis provision for certain assets transferred at death, but this provision took effect only for one year in 2010 before it was repealed.

Transfers for Release of Marital Rights. Where the taxpayer receives property in exchange for a release of marital rights in a prenuptial agreement, the gain on the release of the marital rights is not recognized and the recipient takes a fair market value basis in the property. See *Farid-Es-Sultaneh*, infra at page 513. The transfer of property between spouses or between former spouses incident to a divorce is treated somewhat similarly to a gift with a carryover of the transferor's basis and no gain taxed or loss allowed until the recipient sells the property. See § 1041.

Note on Adjusted Basis

Events subsequent to the acquisition of property may require "adjustments to basis" before gain or loss is determined. See §§ 1001(a), 1011, 1016. These adjustments reflect the history of the asset in the hands of the taxpayer or, in the case of a "transferred basis," the history of the asset in the hands of another person or asset whose basis has been "carried over." Capitalized expenditures, untaxed receipts, and certain losses are reflected as adjustments to basis. Depreciation also requires adjustments to basis. In general, such adjustments increase basis to reflect capital expenditures and reduce basis to reflect the tax benefits allowed to taxpayers while they hold the property. Further detail is provided by the regulations under § 1016.

Note on Allocation of Basis

Where a taxpayer sells less than her whole interest in an asset, it may be difficult to allocate basis to the portion sold and the portion retained. Early recovery of basis defers the realization of income, while late basis recovery can accelerate gross income for tax purposes.

When a person acquires property and then sells part of it, there are two possible ways to handle the transaction: (1) She could apply the amount realized against the basis for the entire property, and not report any gain until the aggregate amount realized exceeds her entire basis, or

(2) she could allocate the basis of the whole between the part sold and the part retained in some reasonable manner, and compare the amount realized with the portion of the total basis allocated to the part sold. Reg. § 1.61–6(a) provides that when a portion of property is sold, the basis must be divided among the parts. Furthermore, the gain or loss on each component part must be determined at the time of the sale of each part and cannot be deferred until the entire property has been sold. See, e.g., Gladden v. Commissioner, 262 F.3d 851 (9th Cir. 2001) (allocation of basis to water rights associated with land). For example, if a person buys Blackacre and later sells a portion of it, the portion sold and the portion retained must be appraised and the original basis allocated to the two portions in proportion to their values at the time of acquisition. Allocation of basis is routinely required when a single price is paid for a building and land held for investment or used in a trade or business. The taxpayer can depreciate the basis allocated to the building but not to the land.

It is occasionally impossible to allocate basis in a reasonable way. In that case, the consideration received on the sale may be credited against the basis for the entire property. For example, if the taxpayer receives an amount for an easement that affects the entire property, the basis of the entire property is offset against the payment and the basis is reduced. Consider the following example based on the case of Inaja Land Co. v. Commissioner, 9 T.C. 727, 735 (1947):

In 1940, a taxpayer paid $100 to buy land and the fishing rights on a river in order to establish a fishing club. In 2003, the taxpayer received $20 in settlement of a lawsuit against a city up river that had polluted the river. In 2005, the taxpayer sold the fishing club for $120.

The taxpayer's overall gain (amounts received minus amounts paid) is $40 (i.e., $120 + $20 − $100). If that total gain ultimately is to be taxed, the decision to include or not include the $20 of damages in income in 2003 must affect the measurement of subsequent gain. The income tax uses the concept of basis for this purpose.

Suppose the taxpayer can prove that $5 of the $100 originally paid to establish the fishing club was for the right to have a river free of pollution by the city. In that case, the amount of gain (amount realized minus basis) taxable in 2003 would presumably be $15 (i.e., $20 − $5). As the taxpayer used $5 of basis in 2003, there would remain $95 of basis to be subtracted from the amount realized in 2005, when the taxable gain would be $25 (i.e., $120 − $95), so the total amount of gain taxed over the years would be $40.

Suppose that the full $20 of damages is taxed in 2003. In that case, the $100 basis would remain unchanged and amount taxed in 2005 would be $20 (i.e., $120 − $100), so the total amount of gain taxed would again be $40.

Suppose finally that the $20 receipt is not taxed in 2003. In order to tax the total gain of $40 when the taxpayer sells the fishing club in 2005, the taxpayer's basis would be reduced in 2003 by the $20 amount received but excluded in 2003 (i.e., $100 − $20 = $80). With this adjustment to basis the full $40 would be taxed in 2005 (i.e., $120 amount realized minus the $80 basis).

The key point here is to understand the relationship between taxation (or not) of a receipt and the way basis is adjusted and taken into account in future transactions. The assumption of the example was that we wanted ultimately to tax the full $40 of gain. Consider the basis consequences of the decision not to tax the $20 receipt in 2003 if we assume that this portion of the taxpayer's gain should never be taxed. In such a case, the $20 would be excluded from income without any reduction in basis.

Determination of basis also can be difficult where the taxpayer has acquired similar assets at different times. Problems often occur with the sale of securities. If a taxpayer cannot adequately identify the lot from which the stock sold or transferred was taken, the stock sold will be charged against the earliest lots of such stock acquired by the taxpayer to determine basis and gain or loss. A taxpayer who can adequately identify the assets to be sold will be able to escape the possibly unfavorable consequences of this "first-in, first-out" rule. Reg. § 1.1012–1(c).

In a part-gift, part-sale transfer, the transferor generally can allocate basis to the portion of the transfer that constitutes a sale. For example, suppose Mom sells property with an adjusted basis of $80 and a value of $100 to Son for $75. Regulation § 1.1015–4 provides that the initial basis of the transferee is the greater of the amount paid by the transferee for the property or the transferor's basis under § 1015(d). Thus, the son's basis is $80. For determining a subsequent loss, however, the basis is never greater than the fair market value of the property at the time of the transfer. When, however, a taxpayer makes a part-gift, part-sale to a charity, § 170(e) and Reg. § 1.1011–2 require an allocation of basis between the gift and sale portions in proportion to their respective values. In the above example, if Mom sold the property to a charity for three-fourths of its value and gifted the remainder, $60 of Mom's basis (three-quarters of $80) would be allocated to the sale, producing a $15 gain. Mom would have made a charitable contribution of $25, the difference between the value of the property and the purchase price. Is there any reason for having different rules, depending only on the identity of the donee? Consider that in the case of the gift to the son, the carryover basis means that the gain will be taxed when the son sells the property.

Hort v. Commissioner

Supreme Court of the United States, 1941. 313 U.S. 28.

■ MR. JUSTICE MURPHY delivered the opinion of the Court.

We must determine whether the amount petitioner received as consideration for cancellation of a lease of realty in New York City was ordinary gross income as defined in § 22(a) of the Revenue Act of 1932 (47 Stat. 169, 178), and whether, in any event, petitioner sustained a loss through cancellation of the lease which is recognized in § 23(e) of the same Act (47 Stat. 169, 180).

Petitioner acquired the property, a lot and ten-story office building, by devise from his father in 1928. At the time he became owner, the premises were leased to a firm which had sublet the main floor to the Irving Trust Co. In 1927, five years before the head lease expired, the Irving Trust Co. and petitioner's father executed a contract in which the latter agreed to lease the main floor and basement to the former for a term of fifteen years at an annual rental of $25,000, the term to commence at the expiration of the head lease.

In 1933, the Irving Trust Co. found it unprofitable to maintain a branch in petitioner's building. After some negotiations, petitioner and the Trust Co. agreed to cancel the lease in consideration of a payment to petitioner of $140,000. Petitioner did not include this amount in gross income in his income tax return for 1933. On the contrary, he reported a loss of $21,494.75 on the theory that the amount he received as consideration for the cancellation was $21,494.75 less than the difference between the present value of the unmatured rental payments and the fair rental value of the main floor and basement for the unexpired term of the lease. He did not deduct this figure, however, because he reported other losses in excess of gross income.

The Commissioner included the entire $140,000 in gross income, disallowed the asserted loss, made certain other adjustments not material here, and assessed a deficiency. The Board of Tax Appeals affirmed. 39 B.T.A. 922. The Circuit Court of Appeals affirmed per curiam on the authority of Warren Service Corp. v. Helvering, 110 F.2d 723. 112 F.2d 167. Because of conflict with Commissioner v. Langwell Real Estate Corp., 7 Cir., 47 F.2d 841, we granted certiorari limited to the question whether, "in computing net gain or loss for income tax purposes, a taxpayer [can] offset the value of the lease canceled against the consideration received by him for the cancellation". 311 U.S. 641.

Petitioner apparently contends that the amount received for cancellation of the lease was capital rather than ordinary income and that it was therefore subject to [the sections] which govern capital gains and losses. Further, he argues that even if that amount must be reported as ordinary gross income he sustained a loss which § 23(e) authorizes him to deduct. We cannot agree.

The amount received by petitioner for cancellation of the lease must be included in his gross income in its entirety. Section 22(a), * * * expressly defines gross income to include "gains, profits, and income from * * * rent, * * * or gains or profits and income derived from any source whatever". Plainly this definition reached the rent paid prior to cancellation just as it would have embraced subsequent payments if the lease had never been canceled. *It would have included a prepayment of the discounted value of unmatured rental payments whether received at the inception of the lease or at any time thereafter.* Similarly, it would have extended to the proceeds of a suit to recover damages had the Irving Trust Co. breached the lease instead of concluding a settlement. * * * That the amount petitioner received resulted from negotiations ending in cancellation of the lease rather than from a suit to enforce it cannot alter the fact that basically the payment was merely a substitute for the rent reserved in the lease. So far as the application of § 22(a) is concerned, it is immaterial that petitioner chose to accept an amount less than the strict present value of the unmatured rental payments, rather than to engage in litigation, possibly uncertain and expensive.

[margin note: GI Rule]

The consideration received for cancellation of the lease was not a return of capital. We assume that the lease was "property" whatever that signifies abstractly. Presumably the bond in Helvering v. Horst, 311 U.S. 112, and the lease in Helvering v. Bruun, 309 U.S. 461, were also "property" but the interest coupon in *Horst* and the building in *Bruun* nevertheless were held to constitute items of gross income. Simply because the lease was "property" the amount received for its cancellation was not a return of capital, quite apart from the fact that "property" and "capital" are not necessarily synonymous in the Revenue Act of 1932 or in common usage. Where, as in this case, the disputed amount was essentially a substitute for rental payments which § 22(a) expressly characterizes as gross income, it must be regarded as ordinary income, and it is immaterial that for some purposes the contract creating the right to such payments may be treated as "property" or "capital".

[margin note: ordinary income]

For the same reasons, that amount was not a return of capital because petitioner acquired the lease as an incident of the realty devised to him by his father. Theoretically, it might have been possible in such a case to value realty and lease separately and to label each a capital asset. * * * But that would not have converted into capital the amount petitioner received from the Trust Co. since [the statute] would have required him to include in gross income the rent derived from the property, and [the statute] does not distinguish rental payments and a payment which is clearly a substitute for rental payments.

We conclude that petitioner must report as gross income the entire amount received for cancellation of the lease without regard to the claimed disparity between that amount and the difference between the present value of the unmatured rental payments and the fair rental value of the property for the unexpired period of the lease. The cancellation of

[margin note: Holding]

the lease involved nothing more than relinquishment of the right to future rental payments in return for a present substitute payment and possession of the leased premises. Undoubtedly it diminished the amount of gross income petitioner expected to realize, but to that extent he was relieved of the duty to pay income tax. Nothing in [the statute] indicates that Congress intended to allow petitioner to reduce ordinary income actually received and reported by the amount of income he failed to realize. * * * We may assume that petitioner was injured insofar as the cancellation of the lease affected the value of the realty. But that would become a deductible loss only when its extent had been fixed by a closed transaction. Regulations No. 77, Art. 171, p. 46; United States v. White Dental Mfg. Co., 274 U.S. 398.

The judgment of the Circuit Court of Appeals is affirmed.

NOTES

(A) *Basis.* In the Court's view, what is Hort's basis in the lease? It is implicit in the Court's decision (although certainly not explicit) that his entire basis in the property was allocated to the land and building. Does this seem appropriate in light of the factual circumstances of the case? Might a different result be called for if, for example, the taxpayer purchased a building with an outstanding lease with a rent far in excess of the rental value of the property? Remember, in *Hort* the building was inherited in 1928 subject to the lease, and the lease was canceled in 1933. Something bad happened to the U.S. economy during that interval. Under current law, no portion of the basis of property acquired subject to a favorable lease may be allocated to the lease. § 167(c)(2).

Purchase of a lease only, without acquiring any ownership in the building, however, does give the purchaser a basis in the lease equal to the amount paid. Assume, for example, that a law firm, which had leased floors of an office building, decides to move and, because its rents are below market, is able to sell its lease to another law firm. The purchaser of the lease would have a basis in the lease equal to its cost.

(B) *Other Issues.* In addition to issues of basis, *Hort* raises questions of characterizing gain as capital gain or ordinary income, and this aspect of the case is considered infra at page 608.

SECTION 5.   THE REALIZATION REQUIREMENT

Note Introducing the Realization Requirement

As prior sections of this Chapter have made clear, amounts do not need to be received in cash to be included in gross income under § 61. The fair market value of property received is often included in income at the time of receipt. On the other hand, the Code normally does not include unrealized appreciation in income. Thus, gains and losses in the value of property generally are reflected in taxable income only when "realized." For example, if the taxpayer buys a painting for $100 and it increases in value to $1,000, she has no income until the painting is sold. Similarly, if she bought the painting at an auction and it turns out to be worth $5,000 more than she paid for it, the $5,000 gain will not be income until the painting is sold. As the succeeding cases indicate, however, the time of realization is not always crystal clear.

The non-taxation of unrealized appreciation is one of the most fundamental aspects of the federal income tax. The realization requirement provides taxpayers with considerable flexibility in the timing of taxation of gains and losses. This ability to accelerate or postpone gains and losses is one of the major tools of tax planning. In periods of high interest rates and high tax rates, the tax stakes of deferring income or accelerating deductions are magnified. As will be seen throughout this book, the realization requirement often produces tremendous complexity, primarily because taxpayers try to arrange their affairs to take advantage of deferral. Important consequences often turn on arbitrary and insignificant distinctions and this is one of the major problems with our income tax. In fact, Harvard Law Professor William Andrews described the realization requirement as the "Achilles heel" of the income tax. See William Andrews, "The Achilles' Heel of the Comprehensive Income Tax," in New Directions in Federal Tax Policy for the 1980s (Charls Walker, ed. 1983).

Despite the problems created by the realization requirement, including the potential for abuse, it is widely believed to be a necessary evil. The realization requirement is justified on the grounds that periodic taxation of accrued gains (and losses) would cause three problems that, in the view of the Treasury, "taken together, appear insurmountable": "(1) [t]he administrative burden of annual reporting; (2) the difficulty and costs of determining asset values annually; and (3) the potential hardship of obtaining the funds to pay taxes on accrued but unrealized gains." U.S. Treasury Dep't, Blueprints for Tax Reform 82–83 (1977). There also would be no political support for the taxation of what are commonly viewed as "paper gains." For a detailed discussion of the problems with the realization rule and the arguments why it cannot be abandoned, see Deborah H. Schenk, "A Positive Account of the Realization Rule," 57 Tax L. Rev. 355 (2004).

Although these concerns are sufficiently serious that we are not likely to abandon the realization requirement, some scholars (and occasionally Congress) have come to realize that these problems do not apply to all assets and all situations. For example, it is relatively easy to determine the value of some assets annually. Some commentators have suggested taxing unrealized gains and losses of securities traded on major stock exchanges. Furthermore, administrative, valuation, and cash flow problems are present on the receipt of any in-kind benefit, and yet we generally do not exempt in-kind transfers from tax. In addition, liquidity cannot be the only concern. Taxpayers could too easily avoid tax if the rule was that income is never realized until cash is received. The failure to include in-kind amounts in income at the time of receipt would give taxpayers too much control over the timing of tax liabilities and large incentives to exchange property or services in lieu of cash. (Taxpayers who use the accrual method of accounting, for example, are routinely required to include amounts in income before cash is received. See Chapter 7.)

Congress has made some inroads on the realization requirement. For example, bondholders are required to include in income annually an interest amount, known as "original issue discount" that is not payable until the bond matures and is redeemed. (Original issue discount is discussed infra at page 756.) Another case is § 1256, which deals with the taxation of certain financial instruments including commodities futures contracts. Section 1256 requires holders of such instruments to account annually for gains and losses without regard to realization ("mark-to-market" taxation). Section 1256 (and its companion provision § 1092) are discussed at page 401. Further deviations from the realization requirement are often proposed, particularly with respect to financial instruments.

Despite these limited changes, the realization requirement continues to play an important role in the income tax and to present serious questions of equity and efficiency. In many instances, the requirement violates horizontal equity. Consider A who earns $1,000 in salary and B who owns a building that increases in value from $50,000 to $51,000 during the taxable year. Each has $1,000 of economic income, but only A will be taxed currently. Although B ultimately may pay tax on the income when he disposes of the property, he enjoys the tax benefit of deferral. The incentive to acquire assets that produce unrealized, and therefore untaxed, appreciation distorts investment decisions. If a taxpayer in a 30 percent tax bracket has the choice to invest $10,000 in a bond accruing 10 percent annual interest or a share of stock that increases in value 10 percent a year, he is likely to choose the latter. At the end of two years, the taxpayer with the bond will have $11,450 (the value of the bond at an after-tax rate of return of 7 percent—10 percent reduced by the 30 percent tax). If the taxpayer with the stock sells it, he will have $11,470 (the stock will have increased in value to $11,000 in the first year and to $12,100 in the second year, producing a $2,100 gain, which, if taxed at 30 percent, would result in $630 in taxes). Ignoring risk, in order to attract a buyer, the interest rate on the bond will have to increase. Actually, throughout most of our history, the tax rate on the stock has been less than the rate on bond interest (due to lower rates on capital gains), creating an even wider disparity.

The following cases illustrate the difficulty in determining when there has been a realization event. We will return to this subject throughout the book.

Cesarini v. United States

United States District Court, N.D.Ohio, 1969. 296 F. Supp. 3,
affirmed 428 F.2d 812 (6th Cir. 1970).

■ YOUNG, DISTRICT JUDGE. [Plaintiffs purchased a used piano for $15 in 1957. In 1964 they found $4,467 in cash in the piano. They paid the tax on that sum in their 1964 return and sued for a refund, claiming that the windfall was not includible in gross income under § 61.]

After a consideration of the pertinent provisions of the Internal Revenue Code, Treasury Regulations, Revenue Rulings, and decisional law in the area, this Court has concluded that the taxpayers are not entitled to a refund of the amount requested * * *.

The starting point in determining whether an item is to be included in gross income is, of course, Section 61(a) of Title 26 U.S.C.A., and that section provides in part:

> "Except as otherwise provided in this subtitle, *gross income means all income from whatever source derived,* including (but not limited to) the following items: * * * " (Emphasis added.)

Subsections (1) through (15) of Section 61(a) then go on to list fifteen items specifically included in the computation of the taxpayer's gross income, and Part II of Subchapter B of the 1954 Code (Sections 71 et seq.) deals with other items expressly included in gross income. While neither of these listings expressly includes the type of income which is at issue in the case at bar, Part III of Subchapter B (Sections 101 et seq.) deals with items specifically *excluded* from gross income, and found money is not listed in those sections either. This absence of express mention in any of the code sections necessitates a return to the "all income from whatever source" language of Section 61(a) of the code, and the express statement there that gross income is "not limited to" the following fifteen examples. Section 1.61–1(a) of the Treasury Regulations, the corresponding section to Section 61(a) in the 1954 Code, reiterates this broad construction of gross income, providing in part:

> "Gross income means all income from whatever source derived, unless excluded by law. *Gross income includes income realized in any form,* whether in money, property, or services. * * * " (Emphasis added.)

The decisions of the United States Supreme Court have frequently stated that this broad all-inclusive language was used by Congress to exert the full measure of its taxing power under the Sixteenth Amendment to the United States Constitution. Commissioner of Internal Revenue v. Glenshaw Glass Co., 348 U.S. 426, 429 (1955) * * *.

In addition, the Government in the instant case cites and relies upon an I.R.S. Revenue Ruling which is undeniably on point:

> "The finder of treasure-trove is in receipt of taxable income, for Federal income tax purposes, to the extent of its value in United

IRS Rev Rul

Treasure-trove

States currency, for the taxable year in which it is reduced to undisputed possession." Rev. Rul. 61, 1953–1, Cum.Bull. 17.

The plaintiffs argue that the above ruling does not control this case for two reasons. The first is that subsequent to the Ruling's pronouncement in 1953, Congress enacted Sections 74 and 102 of the 1954 Code, § 74 expressly *including* the value of prizes and awards in gross income in most cases, and § 102 specifically *exempting* the value of gifts received from gross income. From this, it is argued that Section 74 was added because prizes might otherwise be construed as non-taxable gifts, and since no such section was passed expressly taxing treasure-trove, it is therefore a gift which is non-taxable under Section 102. This line of reasoning overlooks the statutory scheme previously alluded to, whereby income from all sources is taxed unless the taxpayer can point to an express exemption. Not only have the taxpayers failed to list a specific exclusion in the instant case, but also the Government *has* pointed to express language covering the found money, even though it would not be required to do so under the broad language of Section 61(a) and the foregoing Supreme Court decisions interpreting it.

* * *

Although not cited by either party, and noticeably absent from the Government's brief, the following Treasury Regulation appears in the 1964 Regulations, the year of the return in dispute:

"§ 1.61–14   Miscellaneous items of gross income.

"(a) In general. In addition to the items enumerated in section 61(a), there are many other kinds of gross income * * *. *Treasure trove, to the extent of its value in United States currency, constitutes gross income for the taxable year in which it is reduced to undisputed possession.*"

Identical language appears in the 1968 Treasury Regulations, and is found in all previous years back to 1958. * * * This Court is of the opinion that Treas.Reg. § 1.61–14(a) is dispositive of the major issue in this case if the $4,467.00 found in the piano was "reduced to undisputed possession" in the year petitioners reported it, for this Regulation was applicable to returns filed in the calendar year of 1964. * * *

[The portions of the opinion holding that the cash was income in the year found and not the year the piano was purchased and that the amount was taxable as ordinary income and not as capital gain have been omitted.]

NOTES

(A) *Other Treasures.* Would Mrs. Cesarini have had gross income if, instead of finding cash in the piano, she had discovered a diamond ring worth $5,000? If she had discovered that the piano was a Steinway Concert Grand worth $5,000 more than she paid for it? Suppose she discovered that one of the keys was solid gold and worth $5,000?

Suppose a taxpayer purchases a house and subsequently, while digging in the backyard, unexpectedly uncovers a huge reserve of natural gas. What if he uncovered a chest of gold coins? Suppose he discovered an underground stream with gold nuggets?

(B) *Undisputed Possession.* Suppose the taxpayer is unable to reduce the item to "undisputed possession" because it does not belong to him? Where the taxpayer converts or uses the money for his own benefit, it is clearly taxable even if he later must return it. Consider the case of William H. Irvin. A short time after being discharged from the Army, Irvin went to a lonely road and prayed that he would become self-sufficient. His prayers were answered shortly thereafter, when the Army, which owed him $183.69, mistakenly issued a Treasury check in the amount of $836,939.19. Irvin testified that he thought the check was a nontaxable miracle and proceeded to spend $340,000 before the government detected the error. Miracle or not, the check was taxable. United States v. Irvin, 67 F.3d 670 (8th Cir. 1995). Suppose Irvin returns the money? It is deductible when paid. This issue is discussed infra at page 184.

(C) *Baseballs.* On September 8, 1998 Mark McGwire hit his 62d home run of the season, breaking Roger Maris' season record. The ball was caught by Cardinals groundskeeper Tim Forneris; under baseball rules, he was free to keep the ball. Forneris, however, promptly returned the ball to McGwire, saying it belonged in the Hall of Fame. And that is where McGwire sent it.

On September 27, 1998 Philip Ozersky paid $40 to attend the Cardinals baseball game in which Mark McGwire hit his 70th home run, setting the record. Ozersky caught the ball. In 1999 he sold it at an auction for $3,005,000 (Ozersky collected $2.7 million after the auction fee).

On Tuesday August 7, 2007, Barry Bonds hit his 756th home run, breaking Hank Aaron's career total record. The ball was caught by a guy from Queens named Matt Murphy who had stopped in San Francisco on his way to an Australian vacation. He paid $13 at the gate for his ticket. Press reports indicated that the ball was worth at least $500,000. Murphy told a Daily News reporter that "he had won the lottery." Later in the year he sold the ball for $752,467.

In July 2011 Christian Lopez used a $65 ticket given to him by his girlfriend as a birthday gift to attend the Yankees game where Derek Jeter blasted his 3000th MLB hit. Lopez was the lucky guy who caught it. He was whisked away by security and according to some news reports, was asked by the Yankees what he wanted for the ball. He asked for the opportunity to return the ball to Jeter personally and for a few signed baseballs, forgoing the opportunity to sell the ball for a possible $1 million. The Yankees showered him with free tickets and team memorabilia worth about $60,000. He also received his own baseball card and a 2009 World Series ring. Two businessmen said they would pay $50,000 towards Lopez's $150,000 student loans. The owner of a NYC sporting goods store staged a "Christian Lopez

Week" and transferred 5 percent of the proceeds of Yankees merchandise to Lopez. And a beer company offered to pay his potential tax bill.

Do any of these lucky guys have income? If so, when? Might any of the receipts be excluded as gifts? After the game where McGwire set the record, the IRS issued a press release stating that a fan who catches and returns a home run baseball does not have income. It based this conclusion on an analogy to the tax law principles "that apply when someone immediately declines a prize or returns unsolicited merchandise." It noted that the tax consequences might be different if the fan retained the ball for sale.

Despite the possible tax consequences, ball hawks continue to try to snag balls that create records. In 2015, Zack Hample caught Alex Rodriguez's 3,000th base hit. Although he apparently planned initially to sell it or keep it, after two weeks of negotiations with the Yankees, he gave it back to A-Rod and the Yankees made a $150,000 contribution to a charity supported by Hample along with tickets, paraphernalia, and other perks. Does the fact that Hample did not immediately return the ball mean that he has income? If so, should he have a charitable deduction?

(Lest you think that there are more important things to study, you might want to know that former Senate Finance Committee Chairman William Roth fumed that the mere possibility that one of these baseballs might be taxed is "a prime example of what is wrong with our current tax code." For a time, the kinds of questions asked above were common fodder for law school tax exams.)

Haverly v. United States

United States Court of Appeals, Seventh Circuit, 1975. 513 F.2d 224,
cert. denied 423 U.S. 912 (1975).

■ HASTINGS, SENIOR CIRCUIT JUDGE. This case presents for resolution a single question of law which is of first impression: whether the value of unsolicited sample textbooks sent by publishers to a principal of a public elementary school, which he subsequently donated to the school's library and for which he claimed a charitable deduction, constitutes gross income to the principal within the meaning of Section 61 of the Internal Revenue Code of 1954 * * *

During the years 1967 and 1968 Charles N. Haverly was the principal of the Alice L. Barnard Elementary School in Chicago, Illinois. In each of these years publishers sent to the taxpayer unsolicited sample copies of textbooks which had a total fair market value at the time of receipt of $400. The samples were given to taxpayer for his personal retention or for whatever disposition he wished to make. The samples were provided, in the hope of receiving favorable consideration, to give taxpayer an opportunity to examine the books and determine whether they were suitable for the instructional unit for which he was responsible. The publishers did not intend that the books serve as compensation.

In 1968 taxpayer donated the books to the Alice L. Barnard Elementary School Library. The parties agreed that the donation entitled the taxpayer to a charitable deduction under 26 U.S.C. § 170, in the amount of $400, the value of the books at the time of the contribution.

The parties further stipulated that the textbooks received from the publishers did not constitute gifts within the meaning of 26 U.S.C. § 102 since their transfer to the taxpayer did not proceed from a detached and disinterested generosity nor out of affection, respect, admiration, charity or like impulses.

not gift
§102

Taxpayer's report of his 1968 income did not include the value of the textbooks received, but it did include a charitable deduction for the value of the books donated to the school library. The Internal Revenue Service assessed a deficiency against the taxpayer representing income taxes on the value of the textbooks received. Taxpayer paid the amount of the deficiency, filed a claim for refund and subsequently instituted this action to recover that amount.

The amount of income, if any, and the time of its receipt are not issues here since the parties stipulated that if the contested issue of law was decided in the taxpayer's favor, his taxable income for 1968 as determined by the Internal Revenue Service would be reduced by $400.00.

* * * The district court issued a memorandum opinion which held that receipt of the samples did not constitute income. Haverly v. United States, N.D.Ill., 374 F. Supp. 1041 (1974). The court subsequently ordered, in accordance with its decision, that plaintiffs recover from the United States the sum of $120.40 plus interest. The United States appeals from that judgment. We reverse.

Trial

Section 61(a) of Title 26 of the United States Code provides: "Except as otherwise provided in this subtitle, gross income means all income from whatever source derived, including (but not limited to) the following items:" The section thereafter enumerates fifteen items none of which, the government concedes, encompass the receipt of sample textbooks. The taxpayer concedes that receipt of the books does not fall within any of the specific exclusions from gross income set out in Sections 101 through 124 of Title 26. The only question remaining is whether the value of the textbooks received is included within "all income from whatever source derived."

The Supreme Court has frequently reiterated that it was the intention of Congress "to use the full measure of its taxing power" and "to tax all gains except those specifically exempted." James v. United States, 366 U.S. 213, 218–219 (1961). The Supreme Court has also held that the language of Section 61(a) encompasses all "accessions to wealth, clearly realized, and over which the taxpayers have complete dominion." Id. at 219; Commissioner v. Glenshaw Glass Co., 348 U.S. 426, 431 (1955).

There are no reported cases which have applied these definitions of income to the question of the receipt of unsolicited samples. The parties have cited to the court a number of cases applying income definitions to other fact situations. We have considered these cases, but we find them of no particular assistance in resolving the question before us. In view of the comprehensive conception of income embodied in the statutory language and the Supreme Court's interpretation of that language, we conclude that when the intent to exercise complete dominion over unsolicited samples is demonstrated by donating those samples to a charitable institution and taking a tax deduction therefor, the value of the samples received constitutes gross income.

The receipt of textbooks is unquestionably an "accession to wealth." Taxpayer recognized the value of the books when he donated them and took a $400 deduction therefor. Possession of the books increased the taxpayer's wealth. Taxpayer's receipt and possession of the books indicate that the income was "clearly realized." Taxpayer admitted that the books were given to him for his personal retention or whatever disposition he saw fit to make of them. Although the receipt of unsolicited samples may sometimes raise the question of whether the taxpayer manifested an intent to accept the property or exercised "complete dominion" over it, there is no question that this element is satisfied by the unequivocal act of taking a charitable deduction for donation of the property.

The district court recognized that the act of claiming a charitable deduction does manifest an intent to accept the property as one's own. It nevertheless declined to label receipt of the property as income because it considered such an act indistinguishable from other acts unrelated to the tax laws which also evidence an intent to accept property as one's own, such as a school principal donating his sample texts to the library *without* claiming a deduction. We need not resolve the question of the tax consequences of this and other hypothetical cases discussed by the district court and suggested by the taxpayer. To decide the case before us we need only hold, as we do, that when a tax deduction is taken for the donation of unsolicited samples the value of the samples received must be included in the taxpayer's gross income.

This conclusion is consistent with Revenue Ruling 70–498, 1970–2 Cum.Bull. 6, in which the Internal Revenue Service held that a newspaper's book reviewer must include in his gross income the value of unsolicited books received from publishers which are donated to a charitable organization and for which a charitable deduction is taken. This ruling was issued to supersede an earlier ruling, Rev. Rul. 70–330, 1970–1 Cum.Bull. 14, that mere retention of unsolicited books was sufficient to cause them to be gross income.

The Internal Revenue Service has apparently made an administrative decision to be concerned with the taxation of unsolicited samples only when failure to tax those samples would provide taxpayers with double tax benefits. It is not for the courts to quarrel with an agency's rational allocation of its administrative resources.

In light of the foregoing, the judgment appealed from is reversed and the case is remanded to the district court with directions to enter judgment for the United States.

NOTES

(A) *Double Dipping.* The Service's objection to excluding the books from income and allowing a tax deduction for the contribution of the books to charity can be seen from the following example: Assume T's salary is $60,000, he sells the books for $1,000, and donates the $1,000 to the charity. T would have $61,000 of gross income ($60,000 salary plus the $1,000 from the sale of the books) and a charitable contribution deduction that would reduce taxable income to $60,000. But if the books were donated directly to charity, T would have taxable income of $59,000 ($60,000 salary minus the charitable deduction). T would be allowed a deduction for something whose value was never included in income.

What would have been the tax consequences if Haverly had sold the books rather than giving them to charity? What is his basis in the books? What if he had simply put them on his bookshelf? Suppose he had used them to prepare for class? What is the theory of *Haverly*? Is giving the books to charity a realization event, but receiving them is not? As the Court notes, in Revenue Ruling 70–498, 1970–2 C.B. 6, the IRS ruled that books received by a newspaper book reviewer are taxable only if the taxpayer donates them to charity and claims a deduction. (As Chapter 3 at page 466 describes, the kind of double benefit claimed by Mr. Haverly is widely available for charitable gifts of appreciated securities and real estate.)

(B) *Other Freebies.* What if, instead of books, Haverly had received and consumed unsolicited samples of toothpaste or soap? Would it matter whether the sample was an item that he ordinarily would purchase with after-tax income or an item he uses in his business? What difference would it make if, instead of a sample of toothpaste, the taxpayer received a coupon entitling him to a 50-cent discount on toothpaste?

Eisner v. Macomber

Supreme Court of the United States, 1920. 252 U.S. 189.

■ MR. JUSTICE PITNEY delivered the opinion of the court.

[Mrs. Macomber owned 2,200 shares in Standard Oil of California, which in 1916 issued a pro rata dividend of additional stock equal to 50 percent of the outstanding shares, increasing the number of her shares to 3,300 without increasing her proportionate ownership interest in the company.]

This case presents the question whether, by virtue of the Sixteenth Amendment, Congress has the power to tax, as income of the stockholder and without apportionment, a stock dividend. * * *

It arises under the Revenue Act of September 8, 1916, * * * which, in our opinion * * * plainly evinces the purpose of Congress to tax stock dividends as income.

* * *

In Pollock v. Farmers' Loan & Trust Co., 158 U.S. 601, * * * it was held that taxes upon rents and profits of real estate and upon returns from investments of personal property were in effect direct taxes upon the property from which such income arose, imposed by reason of ownership; and that Congress could not impose such taxes without apportioning them among the States according to population, as required by Art. I, § 2, cl. 3, and § 9, cl. 4, of the original Constitution.

Afterwards, and evidently in recognition of the limitation upon the taxing power of Congress thus determined, the Sixteenth Amendment was adopted, in words lucidly expressing the object to be accomplished: "The Congress shall have power to lay and collect taxes on incomes, from whatever source derived, without apportionment among the several States, and without regard to any census or enumeration."

* * *

In order, therefore, that the clauses cited from Article I of the Constitution may have proper force and effect, save only as modified by the Amendment, and that the latter also may have proper effect, it becomes essential to distinguish between what is and what is not "income," as the term is there used; and to apply the distinction, as cases arise, according to truth and substance, without regard to form. * * *

The fundamental relation of "capital" to "income" has been much discussed by economists, the former being likened to the tree or the land, the latter to the fruit or the crop; the former depicted as a reservoir supplied from springs, the latter as the outlet stream, to be measured by its flow during a period of time. For the present purpose we require only a clear definition of the term "income," as used in common speech, in order to determine its meaning in the Amendment; and, having formed also a correct judgment as to the nature of a stock dividend, we shall find it easy to decide the matter at issue.

After examining dictionaries in common use * * * we find little to add to the succinct definition adopted in two cases arising under the Corporation Tax Act of 1909 (Stratton's Independence v. Howbert, 231 U.S. 399, 415; Doyle v. Mitchell Bros. Co., 247 U.S. 179, 185)—"Income may be defined as the gain derived from capital, from labor, or from both combined," provided it be understood to include profit gained through a sale or conversion of capital assets. * * *

Brief as it is, it indicates the characteristic and distinguishing attribute of income essential for a correct solution of the present controversy. The Government, although basing its argument upon the definition as quoted, placed chief emphasis upon the word "gain," which was extended to include a variety of meanings; while the significance of the next three words was either overlooked or misconceived. *"Derived—from—capital";* * * * Here we have the essential matter: *not* a gain *accruing to* capital; not a *growth* or *increment* of value *in* the investment; but a gain, a profit, something of exchangeable value *proceeding from* the property, *severed from* the capital, however invested or employed, and *coming in,* being *"derived,"*—that is, *received* or *drawn by* the recipient (the taxpayer) for his *separate* use, benefit and disposal—*that* is income derived from property. Nothing else answers the description.

The same fundamental conception is clearly set forth in the Sixteenth Amendment—"incomes from whatever source derived"—the essential thought being expressed with a conciseness and lucidity entirely in harmony with the form and style of the Constitution.

Can a stock dividend, considering its essential character, be brought within the definition? * * * [A stock dividend] does not alter the preexisting proportionate interest of any stockholder or increase the intrinsic value of his holding or of the aggregate holdings of the other stockholders as they stood before. The new certificates simply increase the number of the shares, with consequent dilution of the value of each share.

* * *

Far from being a realization of profits of the stockholder, [a stock dividend] tends rather to postpone such realization, in that the fund represented by the new stock has been transferred from surplus to capital, and no longer is available for actual distribution.

The essential and controlling fact is that the stockholder has received nothing out of the company's assets for his separate use and benefit; on the contrary, every dollar of his original investment, together with whatever accretions and accumulations have resulted from employment of his money and that of the other stockholders in the business of the company, still remains the property of the company, and subject to business risks which may result in wiping out the entire investment. Having regard to the very truth of the matter, to substance and not to form, he has received nothing that answers the definition of income within the meaning of the Sixteenth Amendment.

* * *

It is said that a stockholder may sell the new shares acquired in the stock dividend; and so he may, if he can find a buyer. It is equally true that if he does sell, and in doing so realizes a profit, such profit, like any other, is income, and so far as it may have arisen since the Sixteenth Amendment is taxable by Congress without apportionment. The same would be true were he to sell some of his original shares at a profit. But if a shareholder sells dividend stock he necessarily disposes of a part of his capital interest, just as if he should sell a part of his old stock, either before or after the dividend. What he retains no longer entitles him to the same proportion of future dividends as before the sale. His part in the control of the company likewise is diminished. Thus, if one holding $60,000 out of a total of $100,000 of the capital stock of a corporation should receive in common with other stockholders a 50 per cent stock dividend, and should sell his part, he thereby would be reduced from a majority to a minority stockholder, having six-fifteenths instead of six-tenths of the total stock outstanding. * * * Yet, without selling, the shareholder, unless possessed of other resources, has not the wherewithal to pay an income tax upon the dividend stock. Nothing could more clearly show that to tax a stock dividend is to tax a capital increase, and not income, than this demonstration that in the nature of things it requires conversion of capital in order to pay the tax.

* * *

Conceding that the mere issue of a stock dividend makes the recipient no richer than before, the Government nevertheless contends that the new certificates measure the extent to which the gains accumulated by the corporation have made him the richer. There are two insuperable difficulties with this: In the first place, it would depend upon how long he had held the stock whether the stock dividend indicated the extent to which he had been enriched by the operations of the company; unless he had held it throughout such operations the measure would not hold true. Secondly, and more important for present purposes, enrichment through increase in value of capital investment is not income in any proper meaning of the term.

* * *

It is said there is no difference in principle between a simple stock dividend and a case where stockholders use money received as cash dividends to purchase additional stock contemporaneously issued by the corporation. But an actual cash dividend, with a real option to the stockholder either to keep the money for his own or to reinvest it in new shares, would be as far removed as possible from a true stock dividend, such as the one we have under consideration, where nothing of value is taken from the company's assets and transferred to the individual ownership of the several stockholders and thereby subjected to their disposal.

* * *

[The Sixteenth] Amendment applies to income only, and what is called the stockholder's share in the accumulated profits of the company is capital, not income. As we have pointed out, a stockholder has no individual share in accumulated profits, nor in any particular part of the assets of the corporation, prior to dividend declared.

Thus, from every point of view, we are brought irresistibly to the conclusion that neither under the Sixteenth Amendment nor otherwise has Congress power to tax without apportionment a true stock dividend

* * * as income of the stockholder. The Revenue Act of 1916, in so far as it imposes a tax upon the stockholder because of such dividend, contravenes the provisions of Article I, § 2, cl. 3, and Article I, § 9, cl. 4, of the Constitution, and to this extent is invalid notwithstanding the Sixteenth Amendment.

Judgment affirmed.

■ MR. JUSTICE HOLMES, dissenting. * * * I think that the word "incomes" in the Sixteenth Amendment should be read in "a sense most obvious to the common understanding at the time of its adoption." * * * The known purpose of this Amendment was to get rid of nice questions as to what might be direct taxes, and I cannot doubt that most people not lawyers would suppose when they voted for it that they put a question like the present to rest. * * *

■ MR. JUSTICE DAY concurs in this opinion.

■ MR. JUSTICE BRANDEIS, dissenting. Financiers, with the aid of lawyers, devised long ago two different methods by which a corporation can, without increasing its indebtedness, keep for corporate purposes accumulated profits, and yet, in effect, distribute these profits, among its stockholders. One method is a simple one. The capital stock is increased; the new stock is paid up with the accumulated profits; and the new shares of paid-up stock are then distributed among the stockholders pro rata as a dividend. * * * The other method is slightly more complicated. Arrangements are made for an increase of stock to be offered to stockholders pro rata at par, and, at the same time, for the payment of a cash dividend equal to the amount which the stockholder will be required to pay to the company, if he avails himself of the right to subscribe for his pro rata of the new stock. If the stockholder takes the new stock, as is expected, he may endorse the dividend check received to the corporation and thus pay for the new stock. In order to ensure that all the new stock so offered will be taken, the price at which it is offered is fixed far below what it is believed will be its market value. If the stockholder prefers ready money to an increase of his holdings of stock, he may sell his right to take new stock pro rata, which is evidenced by an assignable instrument. In that event the purchaser of the rights repays to the corporation, as the subscription price of the new stock, an amount equal to that which it had paid as a cash dividend to the stockholder.

* * *

It is conceded that if the stock dividend paid to Mrs. Macomber had been made by the more complicated method * * * [it] would have been taxable. * * * But it is contended that, because the simple method was adopted * * *, the new stock is not to be deemed income. * * * If such a different result can flow merely from the difference in the method pursued, it must be because Congress is without power to tax as income * * * the stock received * * *; for Congress has, by the provisions in the

Revenue Act of 1916, expressly declared its purpose to make stock dividends, by whichever method paid, taxable as income. * * *

Hitherto powers conferred upon Congress by the Constitution have been liberally construed, and have been held to extend to every means appropriate to attain the end sought. In determining the scope of the power the substance of the transaction, not its form has been regarded. * * * Is there anything in the phraseology of the Sixteenth Amendment or in the nature of corporate dividends which should lead to a departure from these rules of construction and compel this court to hold, that Congress is powerless to prevent a result so extraordinary as that here contended for by the stockholder? * * *

NOTES

(A) *Terminology.* A "dividend" generally can be thought of as a distribution of cash or property based on the ownership of stock. (If you insist on technical perfection, take a glance at §§ 301 and 316 for the conditions under which a "distribution" will be taxed as a "dividend.") Usually a distribution is in cash, but corporations sometimes distribute other assets. A "stock dividend" is a distribution of additional shares of stock in the distributing corporation based on shareholders' outstanding ownership. Thus, if a corporation declares a stock dividend of 10 percent, it will distribute 10 new shares of stock for every 100 shares owned. After a stock dividend, there are more shares outstanding (110 percent in the example), but each shareholder's proportionate ownership interest remains the same until some shareholders begin buying or selling shares. It has long been clear that a cash dividend is gross income under § 61; the question in the case was whether a stock dividend—Mrs. Macomber received additional shares of stock and no cash at all—triggers tax.

It is clear that if one owns and holds shares of stock in a corporation that has earned and retained income, the shareholder has not realized income even though the value of her stock has appreciated due to the additional retained earnings. It is also clear that Mrs. Macomber would have been taxed had she received a cash dividend that she then used to purchase more shares of Standard Oil. Why? Because she received cash rather than a distribution of the shares of stock? When will Mrs. Macomber's unrealized appreciation in the Standard Oil Company be taxed?

Although the general principles announced in *Macomber* have been subjected to qualification, the result of the case is expressly provided by the law today. A simple pro rata "common on common" stock dividend, in which the stockholder receives shares identical to those producing the dividend and has no option to choose cash, produces no taxable income. § 305. The rules governing other kinds of stock dividends are quite complex, reflecting the variety of potential transactions between a corporation and its shareholders.

(B) *Constitutional Nature of the Realization Requirement.* In no case since *Macomber* has the Supreme Court ruled that a federal revenue statute violated the Sixteenth Amendment, although in the two decades following the decision, the Court reaffirmed the constitutional basis of the holding.

See, e.g., Edwards v. Cuba Railroad Co., 268 U.S. 628 (1925); Helvering v. Independent Life Ins. Co., 292 U.S. 371, 378–79 (1934). Although the Court has not overruled *Macomber,* it has confined the decision to its facts. See Commissioner v. Glenshaw Glass Co., 348 U.S. 426 (1955). The Ninth Circuit has held that the mark-to-market rules found in § 1256 (relating to certain financial instruments) are constitutional. Murphy v. United States, 992 F.2d 929 (9th Cir. 1993). The continuing vitality of *Macomber* as a constitutional precedent is dubious.

Cottage Savings Ass'n v. Commissioner

Supreme Court of the United States, 1991. 499 U.S. 554.

■ JUSTICE MARSHALL delivered the opinion of the Court.

The issue in this case is whether a financial institution realizes tax-deductible losses when it exchanges its interests in one group of residential mortgage loans for another lender's interests in a different group of residential mortgage loans. We hold that such a transaction does give rise to realized losses.

Petitioner Cottage Savings Association (Cottage Savings) is a savings and loan association (S & L) formerly regulated by the Federal Home Loan Bank Board (FHLBB). Like many S & L's, Cottage Savings held numerous long-term, low-interest mortgages that declined in value when interest rates surged in the late 1970's. These institutions would have benefited from selling their devalued mortgages in order to realize tax-deductible losses. However, they were deterred from doing so by FHLBB accounting regulations, which required them to record the losses on their books. Reporting these losses consistent with the then-effective FHLBB accounting regulations would have placed many S & L's at risk of closure by the FHLBB.

The FHLBB responded to this situation by relaxing its requirements for the reporting of losses. In a regulatory directive known as "Memorandum R-49," dated June 27, 1980, the FHLBB determined that S & L's need not report losses associated with mortgages that are exchanged for "substantially identical" mortgages held by other lenders. The FHLBB's acknowledged purpose for Memorandum R-49 was to facilitate transactions that would generate tax losses but that would not substantially affect the economic position of the transacting S & L's.

This case involves a typical Memorandum R-49 transaction. On December 31, 1980, Cottage Savings sold "90% participation interests" in 252 mortgages to four S & L's. It simultaneously purchased "90% participation interests" in 305 mortgages held by these S & L's.[3] All of the loans involved in the transaction were secured by single-family

---

[3] By exchanging merely participation interests rather than the loans themselves, each party retained its relationship with the individual obligors. Consequently, each S & L continued to service the loans on which it had transferred the participation interests and made monthly payments to the participation-interest holders.

homes, most in the Cincinnati area. The fair market value of the package of participation interests exchanged by each side was approximately $4.5 million. The face value of the participation interests Cottage Savings relinquished in the transaction was approximately $6.9 million.

On its 1980 federal income tax return, Cottage Savings claimed a deduction for $2,447,091, which represented the adjusted difference between the face value of the participation interests that it traded and the fair market value of the participation interests that it received. As permitted by Memorandum R-49, Cottage Savings did not report these losses to the FHLBB * * * *

Rather than assessing tax liability on the basis of annual fluctuations in the value of a taxpayer's property, the Internal Revenue Code defers the tax consequences of a gain or loss in property value until the taxpayer "realizes" the gain or loss. The realization requirement is implicit in § 1001(a) of the Code * * * As this Court has recognized, the concept of realization is "founded on administrative convenience." Under an appreciation-based system of taxation, taxpayers and the Commissioner would have to undertake the "cumbersome, abrasive, and unpredictable administrative task" of valuing assets on an annual basis to determine whether the assets had appreciated or depreciated in value. * * *

Section 1001(a)'s language provides a straightforward test for realization: to realize a gain or loss in the value of property, the taxpayer must engage in a "sale or other disposition of [the] property." The parties agree that the exchange of participation interests in this case cannot be characterized as a "sale" under § 1001(a); the issue before us is whether the transaction constitutes a "disposition of property." The Commissioner argues that an exchange of property can be treated as a "disposition" under § 1001(a) only if the properties exchanged are materially different. The Commissioner further submits that, because the underlying mortgages were essentially economic substitutes, the participation interests exchanged by Cottage Savings were not materially different from those received from the other S & L's. Cottage Savings, on the other hand, maintains that any exchange of property is a "disposition of property" under § 1001(a), regardless of whether the property exchanged is materially different. Alternatively, Cottage Savings contends that the participation interests exchanged were materially different because the underlying loans were secured by different properties.

We must therefore determine whether the realization principle in § 1001(a) incorporates a "material difference" requirement. If it does, we must further decide what that requirement amounts to and how it applies in this case. We consider these questions in turn.

Neither the language nor the history of the Code indicates whether and to what extent property exchanged must differ to count as a "disposition of property" under § 1001(a). Nonetheless, we readily agree with the Commissioner that an exchange of property gives rise to a realization event under § 1001(a) only if the properties exchanged are "materially different." The Commissioner himself has by regulation construed § 1001(a) to embody a material difference requirement:

"Except as otherwise provided * * * the gain or loss realized from the conversion of property into cash, or from the exchange of property for other property differing materially either in kind or in extent, is treated as income or as loss sustained." Treas.Reg. § 1.1001–1. * * *

Precisely what constitutes a "material difference" for purposes of § 1001(a) of the Code is a more complicated question. The Commissioner argues that properties are "materially different" only if they differ in economic substance. To determine whether the participation interests exchanged in this case were "materially different" in this sense, the Commissioner argues, we should look to the attitudes of the parties, the evaluation of the interests by the secondary mortgage market, and the views of the FHLBB. We conclude that § 1001(a) embodies a much less demanding and less complex test.

* * * We must look to the case law from which the test derives and which we believe Congress intended to codify in enacting and reenacting the language that now comprises § 1001(a). * * *

We start with the classic treatment of realization in Eisner v. Macomber. [The Court's description of Eisner v. Macomber is omitted.]

In three subsequent decisions—United States v. Phellis, 257 U.S. 156 (1921); Weiss v. Stearn, 265 U.S. 242 (1924); and Marr v. United States, 268 U.S. 536 (1925)—we refined Macomber's conception of realization in the context of property exchanges. In each case, the taxpayer owned stock that had appreciated in value since its acquisition. And in each case, the corporation in which the taxpayer held stock had reorganized into a new corporation, with the new corporation assuming the business of the old corporation. While the corporations in Phellis and Marr both changed from New Jersey to Delaware corporations, the original and successor corporations in Weiss both were incorporated in Ohio. In each case, following the reorganization, the stockholders of the old corporation received shares in the new corporation equal to their proportional interest in the old corporation.

The question in these cases was whether the taxpayers realized the accumulated gain in their shares in the old corporation when they received in return for those shares stock representing an equivalent proportional interest in the new corporations. In Phellis and Marr, we held that the transactions were realization events. We reasoned that because a company incorporated in one State has "different rights and powers" from one incorporated in a different State, the taxpayers in Phellis and Marr acquired through the transactions property that was "materially different" from what they previously had. United States v. Phellis, 257 U.S., at 169–173; see Marr v. United States, supra, at 540–542 (using phrase "essentially different"). In contrast, we held that no realization occurred in Weiss. By exchanging stock in the predecessor corporation for stock in the newly reorganized corporation, the taxpayer did not receive "a thing really different from what he theretofore had." Weiss v. Stearn, supra, at 254. As we explained in Marr, our determination that the reorganized company in Weiss was not "really different" from its predecessor turned on the fact that both companies were incorporated in the same State. See Marr v. United States, supra, at 540–542 (outlining distinction between these cases).

Obviously, the distinction in Phellis and Marr that made the stock in the successor corporations materially different from the stock in the predecessors was minimal. Taken together, Phellis, Marr, and Weiss stand for the principle that properties are "different" in the sense that is "material" to the Internal Revenue Code so long as their respective possessors enjoy legal entitlements that are different in kind or extent. * * * No more demanding a standard than this is necessary in order to satisfy the administrative purposes underlying the realization requirement in § 1001(a). See Helvering v. Horst, 311 U.S. at 116. For, as long as the property entitlements are not identical, their exchange will allow both the Commissioner and the transacting taxpayer easily to fix the appreciated or depreciated values of the property relative to their tax bases.

In contrast, we find no support for the Commissioner's "economic substitute" conception of material difference. According to the Commissioner, differences between properties are material for purposes of the Code only when it can be said that the parties, the relevant market (in this case the secondary mortgage market), and the relevant regulatory body (in this case the FHLBB) would consider them material. Nothing in Phellis, Weiss, and Marr suggests that exchanges of properties must satisfy such a subjective test to trigger realization of a gain or loss.

Moreover, the complexity of the Commissioner's approach ill serves the goal of administrative convenience that underlies the realization requirement. In order to apply the Commissioner's test in a principled fashion, the Commissioner and the taxpayer must identify the relevant market, establish whether there is a regulatory agency whose views should be taken into account, and then assess how the relevant market participants and the agency would view the transaction. The Commissioner's failure to explain how these inquiries should be conducted further calls into question the workability of his test. * * *

Under our interpretation of § 1001(a), an exchange of property gives rise to a realization event so long as the exchanged properties are "materially different"—that is, so long as they embody legally distinct entitlements. Cottage Savings' transactions at issue here easily satisfy this test. Because the participation interests exchanged by Cottage Savings and the other S & L's derived from loans that were made to different obligors and secured by different homes, the exchanged interests did embody legally distinct entitlements. Consequently, we conclude that Cottage Savings realized its losses at the point of the exchange.

The Commissioner contends that it is anomalous to treat mortgages deemed to be "substantially identical" by the FHLBB as "materially different." The anomaly, however, is merely semantic; mortgages can be substantially identical for Memorandum R-49 purposes and still exhibit "differences" that are "material" for purposes of the Internal Revenue Code. Because Cottage Savings received entitlements different from those it gave up, the exchange put both Cottage Savings and the Commissioner in a position to determine the change in the value of Cottage Savings' mortgages relative to their tax bases. Thus, there is no reason not to treat the exchange of these interests as a realization event, regardless of the status of the mortgages under the criteria of Memorandum R-49. * * *

NOTES

(A) Cottage Savings *Oral Argument.* When he was serving as Acting Solicitor General, Chief Justice John Roberts argued on behalf of the government in *Cottage Savings* before the Supreme Court. You can listen to the oral argument at http://www.oyez.org/cases/1990–1999/1990/1990_89_1965.

(B) *Aftermath of* Cottage Savings. The scope of *Cottage Savings* is not certain. Both of the tests for realization considered by the Court—changes in economic vs. legal aspects—have difficulties. Any such general rule for triggering realization on an exchange of assets or liabilities has the potential both to create tax planning opportunities to accelerate losses or defer gains and at the same time to create traps for the unwary. (One example of the planning efforts can be found in Chapter 8.)

(C) *Leasehold Improvements.* Suppose a taxpayer leases land to a tenant who constructs a building that will pass to the lessor at the termination of the lease. When should the landlord realize the gain attributable to the tenant's improvements? When the tenant constructs the improvements? Ratably over the remaining lease term as periodic rent? At the end of the lease when the landlord gains possession of the building? Or only when the landlord sells the property and improvements? In Helvering v. Bruun, 309 U.S. 461 (1940), the Supreme Court held that the landlord had income when he gained possession of the building. Section 109 now provides, however, that the lessor does not include in income on the termination of the lease the value of the leasehold improvements constructed by the lessee unless the improvements are intended as a rent substitute. By virtue of § 1019, the landlord's basis is unaffected, so that the value of the improvements will be taxed on disposition because a lower basis yields increased gain (or decreased loss).

SECTION 6.   ANNUITIES AND LIFE INSURANCE

The concepts of realization, basis, and cost recovery are further illustrated by the tax treatment of annuities and life insurance. Annuities are governed by § 72 of the Code. Regulations issued under that provision cover both annuities and life insurance proceeds paid while the insured is still living. Section 101 and the regulations thereunder govern life insurance proceeds paid on account of the death of the insured. Other forms of retirement savings are covered in Chapter 6.

A.   ANNUITIES

Note on the Taxation of Annuities

When a person transfers money or other property and receives from the transferee a promise to pay certain sums at intervals, the amount so paid is likely to be an annuity. It is clearly an annuity if the period of payment is measured by a life or lives. It may be an annuity if it is for a fixed period of years. Annuities often relate to a person's life expectancy. For example, you can buy an annuity that will pay you $1,000 each year for the rest of your life. The seller will use a table of average life expectancies to decide what you should pay for such an annuity. An individual may wish to provide for a constant flow of income after retirement. He might then purchase an annuity for a fixed premium that would pay him a constant sum each month from age 65 until his death. The amount of the premium will be determined by (1) the individual's life expectancy and (2) the return the insurance company expects to receive from investing the premium. The amount actually received by the individual under such an arrangement will depend on how long he lives.

Allocating the Cost. For tax purposes, the annuitant has income to the extent he receives more than he paid for the annuity. The investment in the annuity is, in effect, his "basis," which is recovered as annuity payments are received. It is therefore necessary to determine what portion of each payment is treated as tax-free recovery of basis and what portion is the taxable return on the investment.

Suppose the taxpayer purchases an annuity for $267.30 that will pay $100 a year for three years (an interest rate of 6 percent). It is clear that the total income from this transaction is $32.70, the excess of the $300 received over the $267.30 paid. The question is how this income is allocated to each of the three years of the annuity. There are several methods that might be used to determine the income tax consequences of annuity payments:

(1) There might be no tax on the receipts until the aggregate of receipts equaled the amount paid, after which everything would be taxable. Thus, basis would be recovered first. This was the method used before there was any special provision for taxing annuities. See Burnet

v. Logan, 283 U.S. 404, 414 (1931). In the above example, the taxpayer would report nothing for the first two years and $32.70 in the third year.

(2) A portion of each annuity payment could be treated as a recovery of investment and a portion could be treated as a taxable return. This is the approach of § 72, under which the entire amount that is expected to be received under the annuity is compared to the amount paid for the annuity. A ratable portion of each payment received is excluded from income in an amount expected to restore the capital in full when the final payment is received. The amount of payment excluded from income is determined by the "exclusion ratio," where the numerator is the investment in the contract and the denominator is the expected return. § 72(b). In the example above, the exclusion ratio is 89.1 percent ($267.30/$300) and 89.1 percent of each $100 payment is a recovery of capital. Thus, the taxpayer would report $10.90 each year or $32.70 total.

(3) The third method is best seen by comparing the annuity to a bank account. Suppose a bank paid 6 percent interest on savings accounts, and the taxpayer put $267.30 into the bank and withdrew $100 at the end of each of the following three years. In a year, she would earn $16.04 of taxable interest, resulting in $283.34 in the account. If she then withdrew $100, she would still have $183.34 in the bank. After another year, she would earn $11 of taxable interest on the $183.34, for a total of $194.34. After withdrawing $100, she would have $94.34 in the bank. In a year, that sum would earn $5.66 of taxable interest, for a total of $100, which she would withdraw.

Beginning of Year Balance	Interest	Total	Withdrawal	Year-End Balance
$267.30	$16.04	$283.34	$100	$183.34
183.34	11.00	194.34	100	94.34
94.34	5.66	100.00	100	0

If the taxpayer makes a loan of $267.30 at a 6 percent rate of interest to be paid back $100 a year for three years, the annual loan payments would be taxed just as the bank account above. A simple annuity works the same way, i.e., if 6 percent were an appropriate market rate of interest, the taxpayer could buy an annuity for $267.30. The annuity could be taxed just as the interest on a bank account or a loan would be: $16.04 of income in Year 1, $11 of income in Year 2 and $5.66 of income in Year 3 or $32.70 total.

It is the timing of the income inclusions that is important. Although the aggregate income reported is the same, the present value of the tax liabilities under the first and second methods are of course less than they are under the third method. (The concept and calculation of present value is described in detail in the Appendix.)

Deferred Annuities. Suppose the taxpayer purchases an annuity with payments to begin at some point in the future, for example, at retirement. During the period between the purchase date and the date when annuity payments begin, interest accrues on the annuity and typically the insurance company treats it as a return on the purchaser's investment. The interest, however, is not taxable to the annuitant as it accrues as it would be in the case of a bank account or a loan, but rather is taxed to the annuitant as he receives payment. § 72(b). This timing difference between the income inclusions of annuities and other economically similar transactions has produced efforts to disguise bank deposits, mutual funds, and other arrangements as annuities. It is possible, for example, to buy an annuity with investment returns similar to a mutual fund, where the amounts distributed under the contract depend on the investment results. Counter-moves by Congress and the IRS have led to extraordinary complexity. See, e.g., §§ 817(h) (requiring an account on which an annuity is based to be diversified), 72(q) and (u).

Under prior law, a withdrawal of an amount prior to the annuity starting date was treated as a return of capital and thus tax-free until the taxpayer's entire investment had been received. Insurance companies marketed these annuities, primarily because of the benefits of the tax deferral of the interest and the favorable treatment of early withdrawals. Apparently interested in protecting this tax advantage only when it fulfills long-term retirement goals, but not short-term investments, Congress added § 72(e), which treats cash withdrawals including borrowed funds before the annuity starting date as income to the extent the cash value of the contract exceeds the owner's investment. Thus, when cash is withdrawn, interest is taxed first. In addition, § 72(q) imposes a penalty on amounts withdrawn before retirement. The penalty is 10 percent of the amount includible in income. The penalty does not apply if the payments are made after the annuitant has reached age 59½ or if by reason of the annuitant's death. Note that neither of these rules changes the deferral of interest if there is no early withdrawal.

Why should annuities be treated more favorably than other investments producing interest? Why doesn't Congress just tax an annuity as the interest accrues and avoid this complexity? From time to time, Treasury has proposed taxing the annuitant currently on the interest on the grounds that the investment income is similar to that earned on other savings vehicles, that the rules favor insurance companies over other financial institutions, and that generally only high-income people with disposable income are able to take advantage of the rules.

While an annuity is clearly taxed favorably as compared to a bank account, it is not clear it is advantageous compared to a mutual fund that invests in stock. Recall that gains are not taxed until realized and may be taxed at more favorable capital gains rates. See page 148 supra and page 559 infra. Further, unrealized appreciation at death escapes income tax entirely. In contrast all distributions from an annuity are ordinary income and there is no basis step-up at death.

There are other tax-favored vehicles for specific investment purposes that are treated even more favorably than annuities, individual retirement accounts, for example. IRAs are taken up in Chapter 6. Section 529, for another example, provides that the earnings on deposits in qualified state educational savings programs are generally not taxed either when they are earned or when distributed. Interest on U.S. government savings bonds can be included in income either as it accrues or when the bond is surrendered. § 454(c).

Mortality Gains and Losses. When the annuity is payable each year of a person's life, it is not certain from the outset how much will be received. The statute provides that, in such a case, the aggregate amount to be received, for determining the exclusion ratio, is based on the life expectancy of the person or persons whose lives measure the period of the annuity. § 72(c)(3). Of course, the actual payments may be more or less than the amount determined based on the life expectancies. When the annuitant outlives the life expectancy, he is said to have a mortality gain on which he is taxed. § 72(b)(2). Since basis has been fully recovered, future payments would be fully taxable. Where the annuitant dies prior to the expectancy, he has a mortality loss and is able to deduct his unrecovered investment on his last income tax return. § 72(b)(3). In contrast mortality gains and losses on life insurance, discussed below, are neither taxable nor deductible. Annuities were given the same treatment prior to 1986. Is there a policy reason why they should be treated differently? With an annuity, mortality gains occur when the annuitant outlives her life expectancy; with life insurance the gains occur if the insured dies young. Perhaps Congress thought it would be easier to explain the tax in the annuity case. Possibly so, but it might be just as difficult to explain why an 80-year old widow is subject to tax when she reaches her life expectancy. See Note (A) following the description of life insurance below.

The previous discussion has focused on the basis recovery rule of § 72(b). The case that follows involves the special basis recovery rules of § 72(d) for annuity distributions from qualified retirement plans.

Zedaker v. Commissioner

United States Tax Court, 2011. T.C. Summ. Op. 2011–64.

■ ARMEN, SPECIAL TRIAL JUDGE: * * * * [T]he issue for decision is whether respondent correctly determined that petitioners were required to report in gross income $13,311 of a $19,100 retirement annuity distribution for 2008. As explained in greater detail below, we hold that petitioners were so required, and we shall therefore grant respondent's Motion For Summary Judgment.

Background

* * *

Before 1986 petitioner was a teacher for the State of California, and during her tenure as a teacher she made contributions to and accumulated interest in the California State Teachers' Retirement System (CalSTRS). In 1986 petitioner withdrew all of her contributions and accumulated interest from her CalSTRS account and paid the appropriate Federal income tax on the amount withdrawn.

In 1991 petitioner returned to teaching and redeposited $149,553.01 into her CalSTRS account.

Petitioner subsequently retired from teaching, and on July 1, 2004, her CalSTRS retirement annuity became effective. In 2004 petitioner attained the age of 60.

As of August 1, 2006, petitioner's CalSTRS monthly annuity benefit was $1,524.46, which monthly benefit would continue for petitioner's lifetime.

During 2008 petitioner received a gross distribution of $19,100 from her CalSTRS account. CalSTRS reported on a Form 1099-R, Distributions From Pensions, Annuities, Retirement or Profit-Sharing Plans, IRAs, Insurance Contracts, etc., the $19,100 gross distribution and indicated thereon a taxable amount of $13,311.

On their 2008 Federal income tax return, petitioners did not report any of the $19,100 gross distribution in gross income.

In a notice of deficiency respondent determined, inter alia, that petitioners failed to report $13,311 of the $19,100 distribution in gross income.

* * *

Includability of Annuity Payments

Section 72(a) generally requires that any amount received as an annuity be included in gross income. Section 72(d) allows taxpayers to exclude the benefits that represent a return of their own investment in a qualified employer retirement plan under the simplified method for recovery of investment. The simplified method excludes from gross income the amount of any monthly annuity payment that does not exceed the amount obtained by dividing the taxpayer's contribution to the plan by the number of anticipated payments. Sec. 72(d)(1)(B). If the age of the annuitant on the annuity starting date is more than 55 but not more than 60, the number of anticipated payments is 310. Sec. 72(d)(1)(B)(iii).

Respondent contends that petitioners may exclude from gross income each month $482.43 (i.e., $149,553.01/310 = $482.43) of petitioner's annuity payment from CalSTRS under the simplified method in section 72(d). Therefore, respondent contends that petitioners are entitled to a yearly exclusion of $5,789.16 (i.e., $482.43/mo. x 12 mos.), or, in other words, petitioners must report in gross income $13,311 of the $19,100 gross distribution (i.e., $19,100–$5,789.16 = $13,310.84).

In contrast, petitioners argue that under the simplified method it will take 25 years for petitioner to recover her investment in the contract, at which time petitioner would be 90 years old and beyond her life expectancy. Therefore, petitioners argue that fairness dictates a more reasonable approach, and they suggest that the Court adopt the "first in, first out" formula advocated by the AARP. Under this formula, petitioners argue that all payments received under the annuity contract would be tax free until petitioner had recovered her $149,553.01 initial investment; thereafter, the full amount of all payments received by petitioner would be subject to income tax. Petitioners argue that under this method petitioner would recoup her initial investment within 8 years.

We are cognizant of the inequity that petitioners perceive in the application of the simplified method under the circumstances of their case. The result that petitioners request was available to taxpayers whose annuity starting date was on or before July 1, 1986, when the predecessor to the current section 72(d) provided a 3-year basis recovery rule under certain circumstances. However, this provision was repealed by the Tax Reform Act of 1986, Pub.L. 99–514, sec. 1122(c)(1), (h)(1)–(7), 100 Stat. 2467, 2470.

Petitioners should understand that the Tax Court is a court of limited jurisdiction and that we are not at liberty to make decisions based solely in equity. In other words, absent some constitutional defect, we are constrained to apply the law as written, and we may not rewrite the law because we may deem its " 'effects susceptible of improvement' ". Accordingly, petitioners' appeal must, in this instance, be addressed to their elected representatives. "The proper place for a consideration of petitioner's complaint is in the halls of Congress, not here."

Petitioners impress us as conscientious taxpayers who take their tax responsibilities seriously and try to follow the rules. Unfortunately for them, we are constrained by the law, as discussed above, to hold that they are required to include in gross income $13,311 of the $19,100 gross distribution from CalSTRS.

NOTE

What Counts as Investment in the Contract? Other attempts to reduce the taxable portion of an annuity distribution involve efforts to show a higher "investment in the contract," which would make more of the distribution a tax-free return of basis. In Tobias v Commissioner, 110 T.C.M. 222 (2015), the taxpayers had sold securities at a significant loss and used the proceeds to purchase an annuity. After cashing in the annuity, they claimed on their tax returns that their investment was the total they had paid for the annuity *plus* the loss on their sale of the securities. The Tax Court found no support for this treatment and held that the taxpayers were not entitled to add the earlier capital loss to their basis in the annuity. Should it matter that the Tobiases "made no money" on the sale of the securities and investment in the annuity, taken together?

Other taxpayers have been more creative. The retiree in Nordtvedt v. Commissioner, 116 T.C. 165 (2001) decided to increase his basis in the annuity by the amount of inflation since he purchased it. Mr. Nordtvedt offered no justification in the Code, or anywhere else, for his adjustment and the Tax Court rejected his changes. Does Mr. Nordtvedt have a policy argument to make here? Should investment gains be taxed as income if they merely represent inflation, not an increase in buying power? See also Reg. § 1.72–4 and § 1.72–6.

B. LIFE INSURANCE PROCEEDS

Note on the Preferential Treatment of Life Insurance Savings

Life insurance generally consists of two elements.[1] The first is "pure insurance"—protection against the event of death during the period of coverage. The insured (or someone else) pays a premium in return for which a specified sum will be paid to his survivors in the event of his death. This generally is referred to as "term insurance." Term insurance involves essentially a gamble of the insurance premium on the odds that the insured will live through the term or period covered by the insurance. If the insured survives the period, his beneficiaries do not collect on the policy, and they "lose" their insurance gamble. But if the insured dies during the period covered by the term insurance, his beneficiaries receive the value for which his life was insured. Term insurance thus represents a bet against the mortality averages through which the insured endeavors to provide for his heirs.

Most actual insurance, however, combines such pure term insurance with a savings element. The size of the savings component relative to the pure (or term) insurance component varies. In some life insurance contracts (for example, one or five-year term policies), the savings element is small; in others (for example, whole life policies), it may be quite large.

The savings element easily can be seen in "ordinary life insurance" which involves the payment of a uniform annual premium throughout the life of the insured and matures at death. The annual premium (per dollar of coverage) of annual term insurance would rise over time because of the increasing likelihood of death. Eventually the cost of the term coverage would become quite burdensome. Ordinary life insurance provides a mechanism to maintain a uniform premium.

---

[1] This description of life insurance is drawn largely from Charles E. McLure, Jr. "The Income Tax Treatment of Interest Earned on Savings in Life Insurance" in Joint Economic Committee, the Economics of Federal Subsidy Programs: A Compilation of Papers, 92d Cong., 2d Sess. 370B92, July 15, 1972.

A uniform premium payable throughout the life of the insured (or over some specified shorter period) exceeds the actuarial cost of term insurance in the early years of the policy creating a reserve. The reserve is invested by the insurance company and increases over time because of interest earnings and because the premiums exceed the actuarial cost of insurance in the early years of the policy. Because the reserve will provide a portion of the benefit on death, the amount of additional insurance that must be purchased each year declines as the reserve increases. Thus, although the cost per dollar of term insurance increases with age, the annual premium can continue to be sufficient.

The savings element, represented by the reserve accumulation, becomes apparent if one compares purchasing whole life insurance to purchasing pure term insurance and investing the difference in cost in a bank account or other investment vehicle.

Earnings on savings invested in most kinds of interest-bearing assets are subject to income tax, either as they accrue or as they are realized. (An important exception is interest earned on investments in state and local bonds, discussed infra at page 226.) Thus, interest on corporate bonds and on savings accounts with banks and savings and loan associations is taxable in the year earned. On the other hand, interest earned on the savings element of life insurance is largely or totally excluded from federal income taxation.

In addition to earnings on savings, life insurance policies can also yield mortality gains or losses. In the case of term life insurance, for example, the insured is said to have a mortality loss when he outlives the term of his policy. This is a loss because the insured paid premiums for the insurance, but the policy never paid out. On the other hand, when an insured dies within the term of the policy, or sooner than expected by the actuarial tables, there is a mortality gain on the policy because the payout on death is greater than the premium paid in. Note that the opposite is true for annuities, where mortality gain on the contract increases with the life of the annuitant.

The basic rule about life insurance proceeds is that amounts paid "by reason of the death of the insured" are not subject to income tax— regardless of the amount of gain that actually may be involved. § 101(a). Thus, the interest earned on savings through life insurance, or any other return on the taxpayer's investment, and any mortality gain or loss are free of income tax if received by reason of the death of the insured. This remains true even if the insured has borrowed against the policy in his lifetime. If the owner of the policy has purchased the policy from a prior holder, then the amount excluded from income is limited to the amount paid for the policy plus premiums paid by the owner. § 101(a)(2). These transactions must be reported to the IRS. § 101(a)(3). Proceeds received on the termination of a cash value policy through surrender, rather than because of death of the insured, are taxable to the extent that they exceed the total cost of the policy.

Because of the exclusion of investment earnings, the attractiveness of life insurance rises with a taxpayer's marginal tax rate, and hence with income level and wealth. In order to get this exemption, however, it is necessary to purchase some insurance as well as the investment component of life insurance. Except to provide liquid assets in the event of death, the very wealthy may be less in need of life insurance than those in the lower and middle income groups; therefore, so long as the insurance component is relatively significant, the wealthy might find the pure insurance and investment package relatively unattractive because of the expenditure required for the pure risk component. For example, for taxpayers in the highest tax brackets, state and local bonds may be more attractive than cash value life insurance, because municipal bonds do not require a (possibly unwanted) expenditure on pure insurance protection and tend to allow more financial flexibility.

NOTES

(A) *Policy of the Exclusion.* Unlike annuities, mortality gains and losses on life insurance are ignored for tax purposes. This might be justified for both life insurance and annuities because, in the aggregate, the mortality gains and losses even out. Suppose for example, three individuals A, B, and C purchase $3,000 of term insurance for one year, each paying a premium of $1,000. Assume further that the life insurance company expects that one will die within the year. If A dies, he has a mortality gain of $2,000 (the $3,000 insurance payout less $1,000 recovery of capital). B and C each have a mortality loss of $1,000. The mortality gains and losses wash out and thus, ignoring them for tax purposes could be defended as "rough justice." Taxing mortality gains when someone dies young might seem harsh.

Interest earned on the savings in cash value life insurance, however, clearly receives preferential income tax treatment. Earnings on other types of savings are typically taxed. What arguments would you advance for the preferential treatment of savings through life insurance? Is life insurance an especially important form of savings since it provides death benefits in the event of the untimely death of the insured and savings for retirement if the insured does not die early?

(B) *Case Law Requirement of Insurance Risk.* A person bought a life insurance policy and a life annuity contract at the same time, paying a single premium for the two contracts. The single premium was equal to the face value of the insurance contract. The taxpayer could not have bought the life insurance contract separately. He made his daughter beneficiary of the life insurance policy and assigned the policy to her after it was issued. The Treasury ruled that since the required purchase of the annuity contract eliminated any risk to the insurer of premature death of the insured, the life policy was not insurance, and the proceeds were not excludable from gross income under § 101(a). Rev. Rul. 65–57, 1965–1 C.B. 56. See also Helvering v. Le Gierse, 312 U.S. 531, 539 (1941) ("risk shifting and risk distributing" are the heart of insurance).

(C) *Payments Before Death.* Congress amended Section 101 in 1996 to permit the exclusion of death benefits paid out to terminally ill insureds. Similarly, amounts received by a terminally ill taxpayer from the sale or assignment of any portion of a death benefit under a life insurance contract to a qualified person are also excluded from gross income. The purpose of this exclusion is to permit terminally ill patients to obtain the benefits of their insurance policy tax-free when they need it most, before death when expenses are high.

SECTION 7.   TRANSACTIONS INVOLVING BORROWED FUNDS

The income tax treatment of borrowing and lending is one of the most complex and conceptually difficult aspects of income taxation. The taxation of loans raises problems of universal application. Tax planners have contributed greatly to the confusion and complexity by taking advantage of the difficulty of distinguishing loans from other transactions that have similar economic consequences but dramatically different tax consequences. Thus, they have structured legal relationships as loans when favorable tax consequences flow from that characterization and as something else—for example, leases, or ownership interests—when a loan would produce less favorable tax consequences.

This Section is an introduction to some of the issues that arise in answering the question "what is income?" when loans are involved. But issues affecting the taxation of borrowing and lending will occur throughout the book. More detail about the deductibility of interest payments is found in Chapter 3, which deals with deductions and credits. Lending and borrowing transactions also raise questions about when income should be recognized and deductions should be allowed and many of those issues are deferred until Chapter 7. In addition, loans raise issues of assignment and allocation of income and deductions and some of these issues are taken up in Chapters 3 and 4. Finally, the tension between interest income, which is considered ordinary income, and capital gain is considered in Chapter 5.

A borrower does not realize income upon receipt of a loan, regardless of how the loan proceeds are used. Similarly, he has no deduction when he makes principal payments on the loan. Likewise, the lender does not have a deductible loss upon making the loan and does not realize income on the repayment of the loan principal. Loans are assets to lenders and their repayment is a recovery of capital. These results are appropriate because there is no change in the net worth of either party. It may be useful to refer to the lender and borrower's balance sheets. The increase in the borrower's assets is offset by an equivalent liability to repay. When the borrower pays off the loan, his assets decrease, but so do his liabilities. When the lender makes a loan, the decrease in the lender's assets from transferring cash to the borrower is offset by the borrower's promise to pay. In entering into an arm's length transaction, the parties have merely exchanged one form of property for another—that is, a sum of money for a promise to repay that sum at a future date. As time passes, the lender will earn income on the transaction in the form of interest, a payment for the use or forbearance of money.

Suppose the borrower does not pay back the loan. If his debt is paid by another, he would have income under *Old Colony Trust Co.* (at page 86), or it might be a nontaxable gift. If, however, the debt is subsequently cancelled for less than its face value, the borrower is considered to have income. § 61(a)(12). For example, a taxpayer whose $10,000 debt is cancelled on payment of $7,000 generally is deemed to have $3,000 cancellation of indebtedness income. (The lender in a business context will typically have a deduction for the $3,000 loss as a bad debt. Bad debt deductions are taken up in Chapter 3.) As the following case demonstrates, people who have embezzled or extorted funds from another sometimes have attempted to exclude the proceeds as "borrowing."

A. ILLEGAL INCOME

Collins v. Commissioner

United States Court of Appeals, Second Circuit, 1993. 3 F.3d 625.

■ CARDAMONE, CIRCUIT JUDGE:

Collins was employed as a ticket vendor and computer operator at an Off-Track Betting (OTB) parlor in Auburn, New York. OTB runs a network of 298 betting parlors in New York State that permit patrons to place legal wagers on horse races without actually going to the track. Operating as a cash business, OTB does not extend credit to those making bets at its parlors. It also has a strict policy against employee betting on horse races. Collins, an apparently compulsive gambler, ignored these regulations and occasionally placed bets on his own behalf in his computer without paying for them. Until July 17, 1988 he had always managed to cover those bets without detection. On that date, appellant decided he "would like some money" and on credit punched up for himself a total of $80,280 in betting tickets.

* * *

[After betting on 10 races] Collins was behind $38,105 for the day. At the close of the races Collins put his $42,175 in winning tickets in his OTB drawer and reported his bets and his losing ticket shortfall to his supervisor, who until then had not been aware of Collins' gambling activities. She called the police, and in police custody Collins signed an affidavit admitting what he had done. On October 27, 1988 he pled guilty to one count of grand larceny. * * *

A.   General Principles

In addressing the argument Collins raises regarding the tax treatment of his illegal actions, we believe it useful to set out initially the basic principles underlying the definition of gross income. Internal Revenue Code § 61 defines gross income broadly as "all income from whatever source derived." It then categorizes 15 common items that constitute gross income, a list that includes interest, rents, royalties, salaries, annuities, and dividends, among others. Gross income, as § 61 specifically states, is "not limited to" the enumerated items.

Defining gross income as "all income" is admittedly somewhat tautological. In the early days of the tax code, the Supreme Court recognized this problem and attempted to provide a more workable and perhaps somewhat more limited definition for the term. It defined income in Eisner v. Macomber, 252 U.S. 189 (1920), " 'as gain derived from capital, from labor, or from both combined,' provided it be understood to include profit gained through a sale or conversion of capital assets * * *."

It soon became evident that this definition created more problems than it solved. Under the Eisner formulation questions arose as to whether gains from cancellation of indebtedness or embezzlement— which do not fall neatly into either the labor or capital categories— constituted gross income. * * * Acknowledging the defects in the *Eisner* definition, the Supreme Court began to steer away from it. For example, in United States v. Kirby Lumber Co., 284 U.S. 1, 3 (1931), it held that gains from the retirement of corporate bonds by their issuer at less than their issuing price were includible in gross income. Justice Holmes, writing for the Court, reached this conclusion despite the fact that the gains were not clearly derived from either capital or labor. In so doing he adverted to the futility of attempting to capture the concept of income and encapsulate it within a phrase.

The Court finally abandoned the stilted capital-labor formulation of gross income and jettisoned its earlier attempts to define the term in Commissioner v. Glenshaw Glass Co., 348 U.S. 426, 430–31 (1955). There the taxpayers had received treble damage awards from successfully prosecuting antitrust suits. They argued that two-thirds of these awards constituted punishment imposed on the wrongdoer and, under the gross income definition of Eisner, this punitive portion of the damages could not be treated as income derived from either labor or capital. In rebuffing this proposition, the Court ruled the damage awards taxable in their entirety. It cast aside *Eisner*'s definition of income stating that it was "not meant to provide a touchstone to all future gross income questions." Instead the Court stated, "Congress applied no limitations as to the source of taxable receipts, nor restrictive labels as to their nature." The legislature intended to simply tax "all gains," which the Court effectively described as all "accessions to wealth, clearly realized, and over which the taxpayers have complete dominion."

Since *Glenshaw Glass* the term gross income has been read expansively to include all realized gains and forms of enrichment, that is, "all gains except those specifically exempted." Under this broad definition, gross income does not include all moneys a taxpayer receives. It is quite plain, for instance, that gross income does not include money acquired from borrowings. Loans do not result in realized gains or enrichment because any increase in net worth from proceeds of a loan is offset by a corresponding obligation to repay it.

This well-established principle on borrowing initially gave rise to another nettlesome question on how embezzled funds were to be treated. The Supreme Court once believed that money illegally procured from another was not gross income for tax purposes when the acquiror was legally obligated, like a legitimate borrower, to return the funds. See Commissioner v. Wilcox, 327 U.S. 404, 408–09 (1946). In Rutkin v. United States, 343 U.S. 130, 136–38 (1952), the Court partially and somewhat unsatisfactorily abandoned that view, holding that an extortionist, unlike an embezzler, was obligated to pay tax on his ill-gotten gains because he was unlikely to be asked to repay the money.

Rutkin left the law on embezzlement in a murky state. This condition cleared in James v. United States, 366 U.S. 213, 218 (1961). There the Court stated unequivocally that all unlawful gains are taxable. It reasoned that embezzlers, along with others who procure money illegally, should not be able to escape taxes while honest citizens pay taxes on "every conceivable type of income." Id. at 221. Thus, under *James*, a taxpayer has received income when she "acquires earnings, lawfully or unlawfully, without the consensual recognition, express or implied, of an obligation to repay and without restriction as to their disposition * * *." Id. at 219. This income test includes all forms of enrichment, legal or otherwise, but explicitly excludes loans.

Distinguishing loans from unlawful taxable gains has not usually proved difficult. Loans are identified by the mutual understanding between the borrower and lender of the obligation to repay and a bona fide intent on the borrower's part to repay the acquired funds. Accordingly, in Buff v. Commissioner, 496 F.2d 847, 849 (2d Cir.1974), we found an embezzler who confessed to his crime and within the same year signed a judgment agreeing to make repayment had received a taxable gain as opposed to a loan because he never had any intention of repaying the money. The embezzler's expressed consent to repay the loan, we determined, "was not worth the paper it was written on." The mere act of signing such a consent could not be used to escape tax liability.

It is important to note, in addition, that though an embezzler must under the *James* test include as taxable income all amounts illegally acquired, the taxpayer may ordinarily claim a tax deduction for payments she makes in restitution. Such a deduction is available for the tax year in which the repayments are made. *See* § 165(c); *James*, 366 U.S. at 220. * * *

B.   Principles Applied

With this outline of the relevant legal principles in mind, we have little difficulty in holding that Collins' illegal activities gave rise to gross income. Under the expansive definitions of income advanced in *Glenshaw Glass* and *James*, larceny of any kind resulting in an unrestricted gain of moneys to a wrongdoer is a taxable event. Taxes may be assessed in the year in which the taxpayer realizes an economic benefit from his actions. In this case, Collins admitted to stealing racing tickets from OTB on July 17, 1988. This larceny resulted in the taxpayer's enrichment: he had the pleasure of betting on horses running at the Finger Lakes Race Track. Individuals purchase racing tickets from OTB because these tickets give them the pleasure of attempting to make money simply by correctly predicting the outcomes of horse races. By punching up tickets on his computer without paying for them, Collins appropriated for himself the same benefit that patrons of OTB pay money to receive. This illegally-appropriated benefit, as the tax court correctly concluded, constituted gross income to Collins in 1988.

The taxpayer raises a series of objections to this conclusion. He first insists that such a holding cannot be correct because at the end of the day he was in debt by $38,105. He asserts that a tax is being assessed on his losses rather than on any possible gain. What may seem at first glance a rather anomalous result is explained by distinguishing between Collins' theft and his gambling activities. Collins took illegally acquired assets and spent them unwisely by betting on losing horses at a racetrack.

Although the bets gave rise to gambling losses, the taxpayer gained from the misappropriation of his employer's property without its knowledge or permission. The gambling loss is not relevant to and does not offset Collins' gain in the form of opportunities to gamble that he obtained by virtue of his embezzlement. Collins' situation is quite the same as that of any other individual who embezzles money from his employer and subsequently loses it at the racetrack. Such person would properly have his illegally-acquired assets included in his gross income. Further, taxpayer would not be able to deduct gambling losses from theft income because the Internal Revenue Code only allows gambling losses to offset gambling winnings. See § 165(d). Collins is being treated the same way.

The taxpayer next contends his larceny resulted in no taxable gain because he recognized that he had an obligation to repay his employer for the stolen tickets. He posits that recognition of a repayment obligation transformed a wrongful appropriation into a nontaxable transaction. In effect, Collins tries to revive pre-*James* law under which an embezzler's gain could be found nontaxable due to the embezzler's duty to repay stolen funds. Yet, the Supreme Court has clearly abandoned the pre-

James view and ruled instead that only a loan, with its attendant "consensual recognition" of the obligation to repay, is not taxable. See *James*, 366 U.S. at 219. There was no loan of funds, nor was there any "consensual recognition" here: OTB never gave Collins permission to use betting tickets. * * * His unilateral intention to pay for the stolen property did not transform a theft into a loan within the meaning of *James*. * * *

The taxpayer then avers this case is analogous to Gilbert v. Commissioner, 552 F.2d 478 (2d Cir.1977), in which we found a consensual recognition of the obligation to repay despite the absence of a loan agreement. Taxpayer Edward Gilbert, as president and a director of E.L. Bruce Company, acquired on margin a substantial personal stake in the stock of a rival company, Celotex Corporation, intending to bring about a merger between Celotex and E.L. Bruce. The stock market declined after Gilbert bought these shares, and he was required to meet several margin calls. Lacking personal funds to meet these obligations, Gilbert instructed the corporate secretary of E.L. Bruce to make $1.9 million in margin payments on his behalf. A few days later, Gilbert signed secured promissory notes to repay the funds; but, the corporation's board of directors refused to ratify Gilbert's unauthorized withdrawal, demanded his resignation, and called in his notes. The board also declined to merge with Celotex, and soon thereafter the Celotex stock that Gilbert owned became essentially worthless. Gilbert could not repay his obligations to E.L. Bruce, and he eventually pled guilty to federal and state charges of unlawfully withdrawing funds from the corporation.

The IRS claimed that Gilbert's unauthorized withdrawal of funds constituted income to the taxpayer. It asserted that there was no consensual recognition of a repayment obligation because E.L. Bruce Company's board of directors was unaware of and subsequently disapproved Gilbert's actions. Citing the highly atypical nature of the case, we held that Gilbert did not realize income under the James test because (1) he not only "fully" intended but also expected "with reasonable certainty" to repay the sums taken, (2) he believed his withdrawals would be approved by the corporate board, and (3) he made prompt assignment of assets sufficient to secure the amount he owed. These facts evidenced consensual recognition and distinguished *Gilbert* from the more typical embezzlement case where the embezzler plans right from the beginning to abscond with the embezzled funds.

Plainly, none of the significant facts of *Gilbert* are present in the case at hand. Collins, unlike Gilbert, never expected to be able to repay the stolen funds. He was in no position to do so. The amount he owed OTB was three times his annual salary—a far cry from Gilbert, where the taxpayer assigned to the corporation enough assets to cover his unauthorized withdrawals. Also in contrast to Gilbert, Collins could not have believed that his employer would subsequently ratify his transactions. He knew that OTB had strict rules against employee betting. Moreover, while Gilbert was motivated by a desire to assist his corporation, Collins embezzled betting tickets because he wanted to make some money. Collins' purpose makes this a garden variety type of embezzlement case, not to be confused with a loan. *Gilbert* is therefore an inapposite precedent.

Finally, appellant complains of the root unfairness and harshness of the result, declaring that the imposition of a tax on his July 17 transaction is an attempt to use the income tax law to punish misconduct that has already been appropriately punished under the criminal law. Although we are not without some sympathy to the taxpayer's plight, we are unable to adopt his claim of unfairness and use it as a basis to negate the imposition of a tax on his income. The Supreme Court has repeatedly emphasized that taxing an embezzler on his illicit gains accords with the fair administration of the tax law because it removes the anomaly of having the income of an honest individual taxed while the similar gains of a criminal are not. See *James*, 366 U.S. at 218; *Rutkin*, 343 U.S. at 137–38. Thus, there is no double penalty in having a taxpayer prosecuted for the crime that resulted in his obtaining ill-gotten gains and subsequently being required to pay taxes on those illegal gains. Such is not an unduly harsh result because Internal Revenue Code § 165 provides that once the taxpayer makes restitution payments to OTB or its insurer, he will be able in that year to deduct the amount of those payments from his gross income. *See* § 165(c).

* * *

Having determined that the July 17 transaction resulted in a taxable gain to Collins, we next consider how that gain should be measured. It is well-settled that income received in a form other than cash is taxed at its fair market value at the time of its receipt. * * *

Based on this measure the value of Collins' tickets was the price at which they would have changed hands between legitimate bettors and OTB. This price was the retail price or face value of the tickets. Accordingly, the Tax Court properly found that the stolen tickets were worth $80,280, their retail price, and this amount was correctly included in the taxpayer's gross income, as a gain from theft. From that figure Collins was entitled to a deduction for restitution he made to OTB in 1988. Collins returned to his till on July 17 winning tickets with a face value of $42,175.

* * *

NOTES

(A) *A Bad Day at the Races*. Collins had a stupendously bad day at the races. Here is how the Tax Court (64 T.C.M. 557, 557–559) described his bets at the Finger Lakes Race Track in Farmington, NY:

> Petitioner was a compulsive gambler * * *. When he had [bet] on prior occasions, petitioner either ended up ahead or lost a small

amount, which he covered without being detected by anyone at OTB.

Petitioner appears to have employed a variant of a technique for betting on horseraces in which he bet on the favorite (the horse with the lowest odds) in each race, increasing the amount of each subsequent bet until he would pick a winner, which would recoup his prior losses and provide a modest surplus. This time, however, petitioner encountered a series of losses that caused his gambling fever to spiral out of control.

He started by placing three $20 bets on one horse in the first race * * *. He bet on this horse to win, place (finish second or better), and show (finish third or better), for total bets of $60. This horse did not finish among the top three. Petitioner then tried to recoup his $60 loss by betting $40 in the second race on one horse to win, place, and show, for total bets of $120. This horse also failed to run in the money.

Petitioner bet a total of $600 on the third race, repeating the pattern of dividing his bets equally among win, place, and show bets on the same horse. * * * He lost again.

Petitioner bet a total of $1,500 on the fourth race and lost. He skipped the fifth race, but bet another $1,500 on the sixth race and lost. He bet $7,500 on the seventh race and $15,000 on the eighth. Both times he lost.

With two races left that day, petitioner owed OTB $26,280. He bet $25,500 on the ninth race. His horse came in third, so one of his three $8,500 bets paid off, but it paid only $8,925.

By the 10th race, petitioner was down $42,855. He made three bets totaling $28,500 on one horse in the 10th race. He finally caught the winner, which paid a total of $33,250 on his three bets. But petitioner still was behind $38,105, and the racing day was over. Petitioner's bets had totaled $80,280.

(B) *Getting Caught Quickly Does Not Solve the Tax Problem.* What if the embezzler is caught while he still has some or all of the money? The taxpayer/embezzler is entitled to a deduction in the year in which he actually repays or forfeits the illegally obtained gains. In Ianniello v. Commissioner, 98 T.C. 165 (1992), the taxpayer, known as "Matty the Horse," was convicted of a RICO violation for skimming restaurant receipts. The court held that the receipts were taxable income even though title to the receipts vested in the United States immediately. Thus, the taxpayer has income in the year of embezzlement, followed by a deduction in the year of forfeiture. Note that the taxes the IRS collects generally are paid out of the funds that otherwise would be returned to the victim. The government's claim for taxes takes priority over the victim's claim for the stolen property. See § 6321.

(C) *Illegal Income.* The fact that gain arises out of illegal activity does not result in its exclusion from income. For example, in United States v. Sullivan, 274 U.S. 259 (1927), the Supreme Court held that the income of a bootlegger was subject to tax notwithstanding its illegal origin. The Court stated: "We see no reason * * * why the fact that a business is unlawful should exempt it from paying the taxes that if lawful it would have to pay."

(D) *Constitutional Implications.* The taxation of illegal income raises several questions of constitutional dimensions. The Supreme Court has held that the requirement that an individual disclose illegal income on a tax return does not constitute compulsory self-incrimination under the Fifth Amendment. In *United States v. Sullivan*, supra, the Court said:

> If the form of the return provided called for answers that the defendant was privileged from making he could have raised the objection in the return, but could not on that account refuse to make any return at all.

If the taxpayer has income from drug dealing, for example, he is required to file a return and required to disclose the amount of taxable income, but is not required to reveal its source.

In Couch v. United States, 409 U.S. 322 (1973), the Supreme Court rejected the taxpayer's attempt to invoke her Fifth Amendment claim of self-incrimination against an IRS summons directing her to produce business and tax records in the possession of her accountant. The Court emphasized the "personal" nature of the Fifth Amendment privilege, noting that the privilege "adheres basically to the person, not to information that may incriminate him." Notwithstanding these decisions, however, the precise scope of the self-incrimination privilege in connection with tax return information remains uncertain.

(E) *Enforcement of Nontax Criminal Laws.* From time to time, criminal tax violations have been used principally to enforce nontax criminal statutes. The two most famous instances involve Al Capone's criminal tax conviction, his only criminal conviction, and the resignation of Spiro Agnew as Vice President of the United States following a plea of nolo contendere to a criminal tax charge for failure to report income from bribes and kickbacks.

The use of federal tax laws to enforce state criminal laws was criticized by Justice Black in his dissenting opinion in Rutkin v. United States, 343 U.S. 130, 140–41 (1952):

> To all intents and purposes, bootleggers and gamblers are engaged in going businesses and make regular business profits which should be taxed * * *. However, in my judgement it stretches previous tax interpretations too far to classify the sporadic loot of an embezzler, an extortioner or a robber as taxable earnings gained from a business, trade or profession. I just do not think Congress intended to treat the plunder of such criminals as theirs.

> It seems illusory to believe, as the majority apparently does, that the burden on honest American taxpayers will be lightened by a governmental policy of pursuing extortioners in futile efforts to collect income taxes. I venture the guess that this one trial has cost United States taxpayers more money than the Government will collect in taxes from extortioners in the next twenty-five years. If this statute is to be interpreted on the basis of what is financially best for honest taxpayers, it probably should be construed so as to

save money by eliminating federal prosecutions of state crimes under the guise of punishing tax evaders.

* * *

[Today's decision gives] Washington more and more power to punish purely local crimes such as embezzlement and extortion. [It] illustrates an expansion of federal criminal jurisdiction into fields of law enforcement heretofore wholly left to states and local communities. I doubt if this expansion is wise from the standpoint of the United States or the states.

Is it wrong for the federal government to use enforcement of the tax law to convict individuals who have engaged in nontax crimes? Should it matter whether a state or federal crime is involved?

B. DISCHARGE OF INDEBTEDNESS

In an early case, the Supreme Court found that a corporation had taxable discharge of indebtedness income when it repurchased in the market at less than par bonds that had been issued earlier in the year at par. Kirby Lumber Co. had issued more than $12 million of its own bonds for cash. Subsequently, that same year it repurchased in the market some of these bonds for about $137,000 less than it had received when the bonds were issued. The court held that this difference was income to Kirby Lumber. United States v. Kirby Lumber Co., 284 U.S. 1 (1931). The *Kirby Lumber* principle is codified in § 61(a)(12), which provides that gross income includes "income from discharge of indebtedness." This result could be reached by either of two approaches. Using a balance sheet analogy, taxation becomes appropriate when the net worth of the taxpayer is increased by the cancellation of indebtedness—that is, the liability is erased without decreasing assets. This approach suggests that taxation may not be warranted if there is no increase in net worth; for example, if the taxpayer is insolvent before and after the transaction. Under a second view, immediate inclusion in income of the loan proceeds was not required on the grounds that the loan will be repaid. If the loan is not repaid in full, the failure to repay is a taxable event. Under this theory, characterization of the original transaction as a loan may be critical. Because imposing tax on borrowers who are unable to repay their debts in full sounds harsh, Section 108 contains a number of statutory exceptions to the *Kirby Lumber* rule and to § 61(a)(12), some of which are discussed in the next case and the notes following.

Where the original consideration for the borrower's debt is not cash equal to the face amount of the debt, the courts have sometimes had difficulty determining if there is cancellation of indebtedness income, as the following case illustrates.

Zarin v. Commissioner

United States Tax Court, 1989. 92 T.C. 1084.

■ COHEN, JUDGE: * * * * David Zarin (petitioner) occasionally stayed at Resorts International Hotel, Inc. (Resorts), in Atlantic City. * * * In June 1978, petitioner applied to Resorts for a $10,000 line of credit to be used for gambling. After a credit check, which included inquiries with petitioner's banks and "Credit Central," an organization that maintains records of individuals who gamble in casinos, the requested line of credit was granted, despite derogatory information received from Credit Central.

The game most often played by petitioner, craps, creates the potential of losses or gains from wagering on rolls of dice. When he played craps at Resorts, petitioner usually bet the table limit per roll of the dice. Resorts quickly became familiar with petitioner. At petitioner's request, Resorts would raise the limit at the table to the house maximum. * * *

By November 1979, petitioner's permanent line of credit had been increased to $200,000. Despite this increase, at no time after the initial credit check did Resorts perform any further analysis of petitioner's creditworthiness. Many casinos extend complimentary services and privileges ("comps") to retain the patronage of their best customers. Beginning in the late summer of 1978, petitioner was extended the complimentary use of a luxury three-room suite at Resorts. Resorts progressively increased the complimentary services to include free meals, entertainment, and 24-hour access to a limousine. * * *

Once the line of credit was established, petitioner was able to receive chips at the gambling table. Patrons of New Jersey casinos may not gamble with currency, but must use chips provided by the casino. Chips may not be used outside the casino where they were issued for any purpose.

Petitioner received chips in exchange for signing counter checks, commonly known as "markers." The markers were negotiable drafts payable to Resorts drawn on petitioner's bank. The markers made no reference to chips, but stated that cash had been received.

Petitioner had an understanding with Gary Grant, the credit manager at Resorts, whereby the markers would be held for the maximum period allowable under New Jersey law, which at that time was 90 days, whereupon petitioner would redeem them with a personal check. At all times pertinent hereto, petitioner intended to repay any credit amount properly extended to him by Resorts and to pay Resorts in full the amount of any personal check given by him to pay for chips or to reduce his gambling debt. Between June 1978 and December 1979, petitioner incurred gambling debts of approximately $2.5 million. Petitioner paid these debts in full. * * *

After [problems with the state casino control commission arose], Resorts began a policy of treating petitioner's personal checks as "considered cleared." Thus, when petitioner wrote a personal check it was treated as a cash transaction, and the amount of the check was not included in determining whether he had reached his permanent credit limit. * * *

By January 1980, petitioner was gambling compulsively at Resorts. Petitioner was gambling 12–16 hours per day, 7 days per week in the casino, and he was betting up to $15,000 on each roll of the dice. Petitioner was not aware of the amount of his gambling debts.

On April 12, 1980, Resorts increased petitioner's permanent credit line to $215,000, without any additional credit investigation. During April 1980, petitioner delivered personal checks and markers in the total amount of $3,435,000 that were returned to Resorts as having been drawn against insufficient funds. On April 29, 1980, Resorts cut off petitioner's credit. Shortly thereafter, petitioner indicated to the Chief Executive Officer of Resorts that he intended to repay the obligations.

On November 18, 1980, Resorts filed a complaint in New Jersey state court seeking collection of $3,435,000 from petitioner based on the unpaid personal checks and markers. On March 4, 1981, petitioner filed an answer, denying the allegations and asserting a variety of affirmative defenses.

On September 28, 1981, petitioner settled the Resorts suit by agreeing to make a series of payments totaling $500,000. Petitioner paid the $500,000 settlement amount to Resorts in accordance with the terms of the agreement. The difference between petitioner's gambling obligations of $3,435,000 and the settlement payments of $500,000 is the amount that respondent alleges to be income from forgiveness of indebtedness.

* * *

Income From the Discharge of Indebtedness

Rule

In general, gross income includes all income from whatever source derived, including income from the discharge of indebtedness. Sec. 61(a)(12). Not all discharges of indebtedness, however, result in income. See sec. 1.61–12(a), Income Tax Regs., "The discharge of indebtedness, in whole or in part, *may* result in the realization of income." The gain to the debtor from such discharge is the resultant freeing up of his assets that he would otherwise have been required to use to pay the debt. See United States v. Kirby Lumber Co., 284 U.S. 1 (1931).

issue

Respondent contends that the difference between the $3,435,000 in personal checks and markers that were returned by the banks as drawn against insufficient funds and the $500,000 paid by petitioner in settlement of the Resorts suit constitutes income from the discharge of indebtedness. Petitioner argues that the settlement agreement between

Resorts and himself did not give rise to such income because, among other reasons, the debt instruments were not enforceable under New Jersey law and, in any event, the settlement should be treated as a purchase price adjustment that does not give rise to income from the discharge of indebtedness.

price adj

Enforceability

* * *

Petitioner received credit of $3,435,000 from Resorts. He treated these amounts as a loan, not reporting any income on his 1980 tax return. * * * The parties have stipulated that he intended to repay the amounts received. Although Resorts extended the credit to petitioner with the expectation that he would continue to gamble, theoretically petitioner could have redeemed the chips for cash. Certainly if he had won, rather than lost, at gambling, the amounts borrowed would have been repaid.

Petitioner argues that he did not get anything of value when he received the chips other than the "opportunity to gamble," and that, by reason of his addiction to gambling, he was destined to lose everything that he temporarily received. Thus, he is in effect arguing, * * * that the settlement merely reduced the amount of his loss and did not result in income.

reduce loss

We have no doubt that an increase in wealth from the cancellation of indebtedness is taxable where the taxpayer received something of value in exchange for the indebtedness.

We conclude here that the taxpayer did receive value at the time he incurred the debt and that only his promise to repay the value received prevented taxation of the value received at the time of the credit transaction. When, in the subsequent year, a portion of the obligation to repay was forgiven, the general rule that income results from forgiveness of indebtedness, section 61(a)(12), should apply.

Legal enforceability of an obligation to repay is not generally determinative of whether the receipt of money or property is taxable. James v. United States, 366 U.S. 213, 219 (1961).

Here the timing of recognition was set when the debt was compromised. The amount to be recognized as income is the part of the debt that was discharged without payment. The enforceability of petitioner's debts under New Jersey law did not affect either the timing or the amount and thus is not determinative for Federal income tax purposes. We are not persuaded that gambling debts should be accorded any special treatment for the benefit of the gambler—compulsive or not.

holding

* * *

Disputed Debt

Petitioner also relies on the principle that settlement of disputed debts does not give rise to income. * * * Prior to the settlement, the amount of petitioner's gambling debt to Resorts was a liquidated amount. * * * There is no dispute about the amount petitioner received. The parties dispute only its legal enforceability, i.e., whether petitioner could be legally compelled to pay Resorts the fixed amount he had borrowed. A genuine dispute does not exist merely because petitioner required Resorts to sue him before making payment of any amount on the debt. In our view, petitioner's arguments concerning his defenses to Resorts' claim, which apparently led to Resorts' agreement to discount the debt, are overcome by (1) the stipulation of the parties that, at the time the debt was created, petitioner agreed to and intended to repay the full amount, and (2) our conclusion that he received full value for what he agreed to pay, i.e., over $3 million worth of chips and the benefits received by petitioner as a "valued gambling patron" of Resorts.

Deductibility of Gambling Losses

In several different ways, petitioner argues that any income from discharge of his gambling debt was income from gambling against which he may offset his losses; thus, he argues, he had no net income from gambling.

Section 165(d) provides that "Losses from wagering transactions shall be allowed only to the extent of the gains from such transactions." Neither section 165(d) nor section 1.165–10, Income Tax Regs., defines what items are included as gains from wagering transactions. The regulation, however, provides that wagering losses "shall be allowed as a deduction but only to the extent of the gains *during the taxable years* from such transactions." (Emphasis supplied.) Petitioner incurred gambling losses in 1980, but his gain from the discharge of his gambling debts occurred in 1981. That gain is separate and apart from the losses he incurred from his actual wagering transactions. We have no evidence of his actual wagering gains and losses for either year. If we were to effectively allow petitioner to deduct the value of the lost chips from the value of the discharged debt, we would ignore annual accounting and undermine section 165(d) by in effect allowing gambling losses in excess of gambling winnings.

Purchase Money Debt Reduction

Petitioner argues that the settlement with Resorts should be treated as a purchase price adjustment that does not give rise to income from the discharge of indebtedness. * * * All gambling must be done with chips provided by the casino. Such chips are property which are not negotiable and may not be used to gamble or for any other purpose outside the casino where they were issued. Respondent argues that petitioner actually received "cash" in return for his debts. * * *

For a reduction in the amount of a debt to be treated as a purchase price adjustment under section 108(e)(5), the following conditions must be met: (1) The debt must be that of a purchaser of property to the seller which arose out of the purchase of such property; (2) the taxpayer must be solvent and not in bankruptcy when the debt reduction occurs; and (3) except for section 108(e)(5), the debt reduction would otherwise have resulted in discharge of indebtedness income. * * *

In addition to the literal statutory requirements, the legislative history indicates that section 108(e)(5) was intended to apply only if the following requirements are also met: (a) The price reduction must result from an agreement between the purchaser and the seller and not, for example, from a discharge as a result of the bar of the statute of limitations on enforcement of the obligation; (b) there has been no transfer of the debt by the seller to a third party; and (c) there has been no transfer of the purchased property from the purchaser to a third party. * * *

It seems to us that the value received by petitioner in exchange for the credit extended by Resorts does not constitute the type of property to which section 108(e)(5) was intended to or reasonably can be applied. Petitioner argued throughout his briefs that he purchased only "the opportunity to gamble" and that the chips had little or no value. We agree with his description of what he bargained for but not with his conclusion about the legal effect.

Petitioner [asserts he] purchased the opportunity to gamble as he received chips in exchange for his markers. * * * Petitioner [also asserts that] in entering into the gaming transactions with Resorts, [he] did not receive any item of tangible value. In support of an argument that "A debt incurred by a casino patron to acquire gambling opportunity is not a typical commercial debt and as such should not be treated as a typical commercial debt," petitioner argues:

> In addition to the character of the gambling debt being different than a typical commercial debt, the Petitioner-Resorts gambling transactions did not occur in the normal commercial debtor-creditor relationship in which a debtor borrows funds from a creditor and uses the loan proceeds elsewhere or uses the funds as purchase money for which he acquires something of value. Petitioner received gambling chips from Resorts. He then promptly gambled and lost the entire amount of chips at Resorts. Petitioner received no consideration from Resorts and was, in fact, $500,000 poorer from his transactions, while Resorts parted with nothing. * * * Accordingly, the only value represented by the chips is their potential income earning power. * * *

The "opportunity to gamble" would not in the usual sense of the words be "property" transferred from a seller to a purchaser. The terminology used in section 108(e)(5) is readily understood with respect to tangible property and may apply to some types of intangibles. Abstract concepts of property are not useful, however, in deciding whether what petitioner received is within the contemplation of the section. * * *

We conclude that petitioner's settlement with Resorts cannot be construed as a "purchase-money debt reduction" arising from the purchase of property within the meaning of section 108(e)(5).

■ TANNENWALD, J., dissenting: The foundation of the majority's reasoning is that Mr. Zarin realized income in an amount equal to the amount of the credit extended to him because he was afforded the "opportunity to gamble." Based upon that theory, the majority concludes that Mr. Zarin is seeking to reduce the amount of his loss. * * *

I think it highly significant that in all the decided cases involving the cancellation of indebtedness, the taxpayer had, in a prior year when the indebtedness was created, received a nontaxable benefit clearly measurable in monetary terms which would remain untaxed if the subsequent cancellation of the indebtedness were held to be tax free. Such is simply not the case herein. The concept that petitioner received his money's worth from the enjoyment of using the chips (thus equating the pleasure of gambling with increase in wealth) produces the incongruous result that the more a gambler loses, the greater his pleasure and the larger the increase in his wealth. Under the circumstances, I think the issue of enforceability becomes critical. In this connection, the repeated emphasis by the majority on the stipulation that Mr. Zarin intended to repay the full amount at the time the debt was created is beside the point. If the debt was unenforceable under New Jersey law, that intent is irrelevant.

In resolving that issue, I think it significant that because the debts involved herein were unenforceable *from the moment that they were created,* there was no freeing up of petitioners' assets when they were discharged, see United States v. Kirby Lumber Co., supra, and therefore there was no increase in petitioners' wealth that could constitute income. Cf. Commissioner v. Glenshaw Glass Co., supra. This is particularly true in light of the fact that the chips were given to Mr. Zarin with the expectation that he would continue to gamble and, therefore, did not constitute an increase in his wealth when he received them in the same sense that the proceeds of a non-gambling loan would. * * *

■ JACOBS, J., dissenting: In my opinion, petitioner's obligation to Resorts was void ab initio, and therefore, I would first hold that petitioner realized income (herein referred to as chip income) in 1980 (a year at issue) to the extent of the value of the chips received.

It is apparent that petitioner left the chips he obtained through the extension of credit by Resorts on Resorts' gambling tables. For had he won, his markers undoubtedly would have been paid, and this case would not be before us. Accordingly, I would next hold that the amount of petitioner's losses from wagering activities in 1980 equaled or exceeded the amount of chip income.

I recognize that section 165(d) limits losses from wagering transactions to the extent of gains from such transactions. In my opinion, for purposes of section 165(d), the chip income constitutes gain from a wagering transaction, because no such income would have been realized but for the wagering transactions in which petitioner's losses occurred. Thus, I would hold that petitioner is entitled to deduct in 1980 his gambling losses to the extent of the chip income.

While I believe the preceding analysis resolves the tax consequences of petitioner's transaction with Resorts, I feel compelled to address the majority's holding that petitioner had income from discharge of gambling indebtedness in 1981.

Section 61(a)(12) provides that gross income includes income from the discharge of indebtedness. However, as the majority recognizes, not all discharges of indebtedness result in income.

In my opinion, for tax purposes, an unenforceable debt is a contradiction in terms, an oxymoron. It is like shooting craps without dice. For interest on indebtedness to be deductible under section 163, it is well recognized that the indebtedness must be enforceable. I am unable to discern why the majority imposes a different rule for the inclusion of discharge of indebtedness income. Accordingly, for 1981, I would hold petitioner did not realize discharge of indebtedness income.

The result reached by the majority is tantamount to taxing petitioner on his losses.

■ RUWE, J., dissenting: Although I agree with much of the majority's reasoning in this case, I dissent from that portion of the opinion which holds that section 108(e)(5) is inapplicable to the transaction at issue. I find no support in the language of the statute or the accompanying legislative history for the majority's determination that the gambling chips purchased by petitioner do not constitute "property" for purposes of section 108(e)(5). Because I believe that petitioner acquired "property" from the casino on credit and subsequently negotiated a reduction of his debt to the casino, I would apply section 108(e)(5) in this case.

NOTES

(A) *More Theories.* The Third Circuit overruled the Tax Court. 916 F.2d 110 (3d Cir. 1990). Agreeing with a comment in Judge Jacobs' dissent, the Appeals Court said that one cannot have cancellation of indebtedness income without indebtedness. Under § 108(d)(1), indebtedness of the taxpayer is defined as indebtedness for which the taxpayer is liable or subject to which the taxpayer holds property. The court held that since Zarin's loan was unenforceable under New Jersey law and the chips were not property to which a debt related, there was no indebtedness to be cancelled. Alternatively, the court applied the so-called contested liability doctrine, under which, if a taxpayer disputes the amount of a debt, a subsequent settlement is treated as the actual amount of indebtedness. The dissenting judge found that the casino was selling for cash "the exhilaration and the potential for profit inherent in games of chance." Zarin made this purchase on credit in exchange for which Resorts provided chips that entitled him to participate in Resorts' gambling activity on the same basis as others who had paid cash. To not tax Zarin, it argued, was incompatible with the fundamental principle that "anything of commercial value received by a taxpayer is taxable unless expressly excluded from gross income."

The Tax Court stuck to its original position in *Zarin* in Rood v. Commissioner, 71 T.C.M. 3125 (1996), and held that a patron who gambled on credit had income when the casino discharged his debt. Unlike *Zarin*, the court found that the debt was not in dispute and thus Rood had discharge of indebtedness income when he settled with the casino for less than the amount he owed. The Eleventh Circuit affirmed in a per curiam opinion. 122 F.3d 1078 (11th Cir. 1997). The Third Circuit's decision in *Zarin* was also criticized by the Tenth Circuit, which disagreed that the contested debt doctrine applied. Preslar v. Commissioner, 167 F.3d 1323 (1999) ("A total denial of liability is not a dispute touching upon the amount of the underlying debt.")

The numerous opinions in *Zarin* do not exhaust the possibilities as to how to approach this case. For example, one could argue that Zarin should not be taxed on the full value of his income because of the offsetting negative utility of his gambling addiction. See Daniel N. Shaviro, "The Man Who Lost Too Much: *Zarin v. Commissioner* and the Measurement of Taxable Consumption," 45 Tax L. Rev. 215 (1990). Alternatively, Zarin might have no income because this is simply a bargain purchase of consumption that should not be taxable. See Joseph M. Dodge, "*Zarin v. Commissioner:* Musings About Debt Cancellations and 'Consumption' in an Income Tax Base," 45 Tax L. Rev. 677 (1990). Or perhaps Zarin has no income because his failure to pay for his chips was a recovery of his prior nondeductible gambling losses and under the tax benefit rule, the recovery is exempt. See Calvin H. Johnson, "*Zarin* and the Tax Benefit Rule: Tax Models for Gambling Losses and the Forgiveness of Gambling Debts," 45 Tax L. Rev. 697 (1990).

Suppose Zarin had received the ultimate bargain purchase—Resorts gave him $2.5 million in chips with which to gamble and he could keep his winnings and did not need to pay anything back if he lost. Would he have had gross income in either case? Suppose instead Zarin had run up a $2.5 million tab at the hotel in lodging and meal costs, never paid it and ultimately Resorts wrote it off. Should this unpaid-for consumption be taxable?

(B) *Comparing* Collins *and* Zarin. Students and commentators are often sympathetic to Zarin, although they have little trouble concluding that Collins, supra at page 178, had income when he gambled and lost with OTB money. In both cases the inability to offset the income (whether from embezzlement or cancellation of indebtedness) with gambling losses, due to the limitation of § 165(d), means that both of these losers may have to pay income tax. Is the difference in results—income to Collins, no income to Zarin—justifiable?

Collins relied on the Third Circuit's decision in *Zarin* to argue that the stolen tickets were essentially valueless for tax purposes. He insisted that like Zarin he stole opportunities to gamble and that his stolen racing tickets—like Zarin's gambling chips—had no intrinsic economic value. The court was not sympathetic to Collins' claim, and distinguished *Zarin:*

> [W]e observe that the statement in Zarin regarding the value of the casino's gambling chips was offered as part of the appellate court's interpretation of the narrow income exclusion provision of § 108(d) of the Code. * * * We are not convinced that the Third Circuit's reasoning is applicable outside the context of § 108 and the specific facts of that case where nothing was stolen and there was no embezzlement. * * * Zarin may have been written differently had the Third Circuit been confronted with the separate question of whether to include as gross income under § 61 the face value of stolen gambling opportunities.

(C) *Insolvency Exception.* Although cancellation of indebtedness often results in income to the debtor, there are a number of important exceptions. They have emerged largely as a response to the perceived harshness of imposing a tax on debtors at a time when they have not received cash income and under circumstances where the very fact giving rise to taxable income— a cancellation of indebtedness for less than its face value—may well suggest that the debtor is in a precarious financial condition.

If a taxpayer who is insolvent or who is the subject of bankruptcy proceedings settles with his creditors at a discount, § 108(a) permits him to exclude the debt cancellation from income to the extent of his insolvency. The amount excluded is limited to the extent to which his liabilities exceed his assets. For example, a taxpayer who has liabilities of $20,000 and assets of $13,000 discharges his $20,000 debt with a payment of $12,000. Although $8,000 of his liabilities are thus forgiven, he has only $1,000 of discharge of indebtedness income. The difference between his liabilities and his assets, $7,000 in this case, is excluded from income. The quid pro quo is that the taxpayer must reduce certain tax benefits (for example, net operating loss carryovers) or the basis in his property by the amount of the debt cancellation. § 108(b).

Note that other forms of income received by insolvent taxpayers are taxable to them. See, e.g., Parkford v. Commissioner, 133 F.2d 249 (9th Cir. 1943), which held that salary paid to an insolvent individual is income. Should there be a general exclusion for all income of insolvent taxpayers? If not, why is cancellation of indebtedness income different?

(D) *Lost Deductions.* Section 108(e)(2) excludes from income the discharge of a debt if its payment would have given rise to a deduction. This puts the taxpayer in the same position he would have been in had the discharge of the debt been included in income and a deduction allowed for it.

(E) *Purchase Price Reduction.* If the seller of specific property reduces the debt of the buyer arising out of the purchase, the reduction is treated by both parties as an adjustment of the purchase price. § 108(e)(5). Suppose for example, A owes B $10,000 for property he acquired from B that later turns out to be a lemon. A and B settle by agreeing that A owes B only $7,000. A has no income on the settlement, but his purchase price (and basis) for the property is now $7,000. This provision does not apply if the purchaser is insolvent or the subject of bankruptcy proceedings, if the seller has transferred the debt to a third party or if the purchaser has transferred the property to a third party. The § 108(e)(5) provision is very similar to the contested liability doctrine used by the Third Circuit in *Zarin* and was urged in the Tax Court dissent of Judge Ruwe. Either approach eliminates COD income when the buyer and seller of goods or services reduce the debt as a purchase price adjustment.

The reduction of the principal amount of an undersecured nonrecourse debt that arose in connection with the sale of property by the holder of the debt (who was not the seller) results in COD income because the debt reduction is not treated as a purchase price adjustment. For example, suppose a taxpayer borrowed $200,000 to purchase a building. At a time when the building is worth only $150,000, the lender agrees to reduce the principal amount to $150,000. The taxpayer has $50,000 of COD income.

(F) *Corporate Debt to Shareholder.* If a shareholder forgives a debt owed him by a corporation, § 108(e)(6) treats this as if the corporation had satisfied the debt with an amount of money equal to the shareholder's basis in the debt. Thus, in the usual case, where the shareholder's basis is equal to the face amount of the debt, the corporation would have no discharge of indebtedness income.

(G) *Corporate Stock Issued in Exchange for Debt.* Section 108(e)(8) provides that a corporation that is not insolvent or in bankruptcy proceedings realizes discharge of indebtedness income when it issues stock in cancellation of its debt to the extent that the value of the stock is less than the principal amount of the debt.

(H) *Discharge of Indebtedness Treated as Gift.* Despite the Supreme Court's ruling in Helvering v. American Dental Co., 318 U.S. 322 (1943), that a gratuitous cancellation of indebtedness in a business context was a gift excluded from income, it now seems clear that in a commercial setting, a discharge of indebtedness is not a gift. The Senate Finance Committee in its report on the Bankruptcy Tax Act of 1980 expressed its intention that "there will not be any gift exception in a commercial context (such as a shareholder-corporation relationship) to the general rule that income is realized on the discharge of indebtedness."

In a noncommercial setting, such as a loan between family members, a discharge may be treated as a gift excludable under § 102. If a party who is related to the debtor acquires the debt from an unrelated party, the debt is treated as acquired by the debtor, which may result in COD income to the debtor and the debtor is treated as issuing a new debt to the related party. § 108(e)(4). (For the definition of related party, see § 267(b)).

(I) *John Oliver Arranges for Cancellation of Medical Debt.* On June 5, 2016, John Oliver on HBO's "Last Week Tonight" announced that a company he had formed had purchased nearly $15 million of outstanding medical debt for about $60,000. His company then transferred the debt to a charitable organization that forgave the debt. See the clips at: https://ripmedicaldebt. org/the-miracle-of-debt-forgiveness-on-hbos-last-week-tonight-with-john-oliver/. David S. Miller of the Proskauer law firm, which represented, on a pro bono basis, RIP Medical Debt, the charity that actually forgave the debt, claimed that since the charity forgave the debt out of "detached and disinterested generosity," the debtors have no cancellation of indebtedness income because the forgiveness was a gift. See http://www.proskauertax talks.com/2016/06/last-week-tonight-debt-forgiveness/. But is this right? What is the value of the gift? John Oliver's corporation could only value its gifts of the debt to the charity at the $60,000 purchase price in determining its charitable deduction. Could David Zarin have avoided his cancellation of indebtedness income by having his sister purchase his $3.5 million debt for $500,000 and then forgiving it? See § 108(e)(4).

Does § 108(e)(2) shelter the debt from tax because the medical expenses that gave rise to the debt are deductible under § 213? Notice that the limitations in § 213 (and the existence of the standard deduction) mean that many of the 9,000 people whose debt was forgiven would not actually have been able to deduct their medical expenses. So the application of § 108(e)(2) turns on whether the IRS interprets § 108(e)(2) to require that the expenditure giving rise to the debt must actually be deductible by the taxpayer or allowable as a deduction ignoring the limitations. If the latter, Oliver's gambit was successful. Would a similar ploy work for student debt? (See Note M below.)

The preceding paragraphs demonstrate that John Oliver's efforts raise more complex tax issues than he described on his show. But, of course, for those debtors who were insolvent, § 108(a) clearly excludes the debt forgiveness from income.

(J) *Qualified Principal Residence Indebtedness.* Until 2017, home owners could exclude discharge of indebtedness income arising from the discharge of acquisition indebtedness on a principal residence. §§ 108(a)(1)(E) and 108(h). The acquisition indebtedness was capped at $2 million. The provision arose out of the home mortgage crisis of 2008 and, after several extensions, expired at the end of 2016. The law provided relief for owners when the value of their home plummeted below the mortgage on the house. Absent this provision, home owners not only face foreclosure and eviction but also taxable COD income. For example, assume a taxpayer bought a home for $300,000 paying $60,000 cash and obtaining a $240,000 loan secured by the home. The home declines in value to $200,000. Although the taxpayer is solvent, his financial position is such that the bank reduces the principal amount of the mortgage to $200,000. The taxpayer has $40,000 of COD income unless the reduction occurred while the provision was in effect, in which case he was able to exclude that amount from gross income. In such case, he reduced his basis in the property by the same amount.

(K) *Qualified Farm Indebtedness.* Under certain circumstances, gross income does not include the discharge of "qualified farm indebtedness." The incurably curious should consult §§ 108(a)(1)(C) and 108(g).

(L) *Real Estate Business Debt.* Those interested in the power of lobbyists should take a look at § 108(a)(1)(D). This provision permits individual taxpayers to elect to exclude from gross income the discharge of real property business indebtedness in exchange for reducing the basis of property. The mortgage must be either acquisition indebtedness or have been incurred or assumed before 1993. This exception was intended to benefit those who suffered when the real estate market crashed and the value of unoccupied office buildings and shopping malls plummeted in the late 1980s and early 1990s.

(M) *Student Loan Forgiveness.* Section 108(f) provides that gross income does not include any amount from the forgiveness of certain student loans (generally made by a government agency), provided the forgiveness is contingent on the student working for a certain period of time in certain professions for any of a broad class of employers (e.g., providing health care services to a nonprofit organization). The 2017 Act amended § 108(f) also to exclude from income discharges of student debt on account of the death or total permanent disability of the student. (This provision is scheduled to expire at the end of 2025, but seems likely to be extended.) Gross income also does not include forgiveness of student loans made by tax-exempt charities (such as universities) where a condition of the loan is that the student (or former student) must fulfill a public service requirement. The statute defines this as an occupation or working in an area with unmet needs so long as the work is performed for or under the direction of a tax-exempt charitable organization or a government entity. The proceeds of the loan can be used to pay tuition and expenses or to refinance outstanding student loans. This latter rule would cover lawyers who participate in public service student loan programs that require them to work for a public service organization or the government for a period of time. Generally, under these programs a portion of the student loan is forgiven each year the student works in a public interest job. Under § 108(f), there is no taxable income when the law school forgives the loan. Rev. Rul. 2008–34, 2008–2 C.B. 76, confirmed that this provision applies to these kinds of law school loan forgiveness programs, including those that permit refinancing of law school debt. While law students may enjoy favorable tax treatment when loans are forgiven, others are not so lucky. Why should some student loan forgiveness be taxed and other exempt?

Recall that scholarships are exempt from tax but only to the extent they do not exceed tuition and related expenses. Free room and board provided by a university would be subject to tax. What if a law student uses the proceeds of a student loan to pay rent and subsequently has the loan forgiven via a loan forgiveness program?

(N) *Discharge of Interest.* What if the creditor simply forgives the accrued interest rather than the principal of the debt? Does this constitute discharge of indebtedness income? The Tax Court has held that it does not matter whether the cancelled debt constitutes principal or interest; either is taxable unless an exception applies. Payne v. Commissioner, 95 T.C.M. 1253 (2008) affirmed in an unpublished opinion, 2010–1 U.S.T.C. ¶ 50,132 (8th Cir. 2009). If the interest was nondeductible personal interest, § 108(e)(2) would not apply. However, if the interest is deductible home mortgage interest, it would. The borrowers received the principal in the form of cash proceeds but never received the forgiven interest. Does the rationale for taxing discharged debts apply to interest? If not, does some other theory support taxation?

As if debtors with COD income do not have enough tax problems, consider the plight of Robert Melvin. He paid a firm $2,126 to reduce his $13,084 credit card debt with Chase to $4,579 (i.e. the fee was 25 percent of the savings). Nevertheless he had COD income of the entire $8,505 reduced debt. Melvin v. Commissioner, 98 T.C.M. 159 (2009).

SECTION 8.   THE EFFECT OF DEBT ON BASIS AND AMOUNT REALIZED

Note on Acquisition and Disposition of Property Encumbered by Debt

This Section deals with the treatment of debt used to purchase or carry assets. Where a taxpayer purchases an asset for cash, the basis, as described earlier, is equal to the cash paid. Many taxpayers finance acquisitions with debt, however, and the basis of such assets must be determined in order to assess the tax consequences—such as depreciation deductions and the amount realized on a disposition of the assets.

There are two general types of borrowing: (1) recourse debt, where the borrower is personally liable for repayment of the debt, and (2) nonrecourse debt, where the borrower is not personally liable and the lender can look only to the assets that secure the debt for repayment. On default of a recourse debt, the lender can look not only to any asset securing the debt, but also to the borrower's other assets for repayment. On default of a nonrecourse debt, the lender can obtain satisfaction of the obligation only from the property securing the debt. If, when a nonrecourse loan comes due, the value of the property is adequate to satisfy the amount owed, the lender will be paid in full. If, on the other hand, the value of the property is inadequate to satisfy the debt—either because the property declined in value after the loan was made or because the property was overvalued at the time of the loan—the lender, not the borrower, will suffer the economic loss. Where the borrower has other financial resources, the economic consequences will be quite different than if the borrower had been personally liable. The borrower's lack of personal liability might arise in a variety of ways. For example, the lender might agree that the loan will be nonrecourse; a straw or dummy might be used in the conveyance; the purchaser might take property subject to a mortgage without assuming personal liability; or guarantees or other similar arrangements might protect the borrower from personal liability.

The appropriate tax treatment of borrowed amounts in determining basis and amount realized is a serious issue for the income tax. The classic case of Crane v. Commissioner, 331 U.S. 1 (1947), established as a general principle that recourse and nonrecourse debt will be treated alike. A loan, whether recourse or nonrecourse, is included in the basis of the asset it finances. This creates parity between a purchaser who borrows from a bank and pays the seller cash and a purchaser who uses seller financing. Thus, if A acquires a building for $1 million by paying $100,000 in cash and assuming a $900,000 mortgage, his basis is $1 million whether he borrows the $900,000 from a bank or the seller or assumes an outstanding $900,000 mortgage on the property. When property is sold (or otherwise disposed of), any balance of the recourse or nonrecourse debt is included in the amount realized. Thus, if B purchases A's building for $1.1 million by transferring $300,000 cash and assuming the mortgage with an outstanding principal amount of $800,000, A's amount realized is $1.1 million.

The combination of these rules creates a significant benefit for the taxpayer. First, if the property is eligible for depreciation deductions, including the borrowed amount in basis enables a taxpayer to recover costs that she has not yet paid or assumed directly. Second, if the money for buying the property is borrowed through a nonrecourse mortgage for which the taxpayer has no personal liability, it may be possible for her to recover through depreciation putative acquisition costs for which she may never have to put up any of her own money. Third, although the amount of the outstanding debt will be included in the taxpayer's amount realized on an eventual sale (offsetting the earlier depreciation deductions), the taxpayer enjoys the time value of the tax savings from the depreciation deductions. For example, suppose A purchases property for $100,000, giving the seller a nonrecourse note calling for no principal payments for 20 years. A has a $100,000 basis and takes $100,000 in depreciation deductions over the 20-year life of the property. Assuming A's marginal tax rate is 37 percent, she will save $37,000 in taxes from these depreciation deductions. Her basis will be reduced by the deductions so that at the end of 20 years, her adjusted basis will be zero. Suppose the seller forecloses at that time because A makes no principal payment. The amount realized will be the outstanding principal of the debt or $100,000 and A will have a gain of like amount. Assuming A's marginal tax rate remains 37 percent, she will owe $37,000 in taxes. Although the total deductions equal the gain on the foreclosure, A has enjoyed the tax benefits of the depreciation well in advance of the time when she must pay tax on the gain. The typical loan, of course, will not defer all payments of principal for as long as 20 years, so the foregoing is a somewhat extreme example of the deferral potentially available, but the principle it illustrates holds and the amounts borrowed may be far greater.

In the *Crane* case, which is described further in the *Tufts* case below, the taxpayer had inherited an apartment building subject to a nonrecourse mortgage equal to the value of the property. Applying the predecessor of § 1014, she originally calculated her basis as equal to the value of the building without reduction for the mortgage. Over the course of six years, she deducted about a tenth of this figure as depreciation. She made no payments on the mortgage and, in the face of a foreclosure threat, she sold the building, subject to the mortgage, for a small cash sum. The Court rejected her claim that the nonrecourse debt should not have counted in calculating her basis and that the amount she realized on the sale should not include her relief from the mortgage obligation. Instead the Court ruled that, in calculating basis, a taxpayer must treat a nonrecourse mortgage as equivalent to a cash investment, and that, in determining the amount realized on disposition of property, the taxpayer must include relief from the obligation to repay the nonrecourse debt.

The principal effect of the government's "victory" in *Crane* was to increase and accelerate the amount of depreciation deductions allowed to owners of property financed from debt. If, as Beulah Crane had argued, property was defined as "equity," she would have been entitled to zero depreciation while she held the property.

In a famous footnote (famous in some quarters at least), number 37, the *Crane* court left open the question whether the transfer of property subject to a nonrecourse mortgage in excess of the value of the property securing it should produce the same results. That issue is resolved in the following case.

Commissioner v. Tufts

Supreme Court of the United States, 1983. 461 U.S. 300.

■ JUSTICE BLACKMUN delivered the opinion of the Court.

Over 35 years ago, in Crane v. Commissioner, 331 U.S. 1 (1947), this Court ruled that a taxpayer, who sold property encumbered by a nonrecourse mortgage (the amount of the mortgage being less than the property's value), must include the unpaid balance of the mortgage in the computation of the amount the taxpayer realized on the sale. The case now before us presents the question whether the same rule applies when the unpaid amount of the nonrecourse mortgage exceeds the fair market value of the property sold.

Crane Rule

issue

I

On August 1, 1970, respondent Clark Pelt, a builder, and his wholly owned corporation, respondent Clark, Inc., formed a general partnership. The purpose of the partnership was to construct a 120-unit apartment complex in Duncanville, Tex., a Dallas suburb. Neither Pelt nor Clark, Inc., made any capital contribution to the partnership. Six days later, the partnership entered into a mortgage loan agreement with the Farm & Home Savings Association (F & H). Under the agreement, F & H was committed for a $1,851,500 loan for the complex. In return, the partnership executed a note and a deed of trust in favor of F & H. The partnership obtained the loan on a nonrecourse basis: neither the partnership nor its partners assumed any personal liability for repayment of the loan. Pelt later admitted four friends and relatives, respondents Tufts, Steger, Stephens, and Austin, as general partners. None of them contributed capital upon entering the partnership.

The construction of the complex was completed in August 1971. During 1971, each partner made small capital contributions to the partnership; in 1972, however, only Pelt made a contribution. The total of the partners' capital contributions was $44,212. In each tax year, all partners claimed as income tax deductions their allocable shares of ordinary losses and depreciation. The deductions taken by the partners in 1971 and 1972 totalled $439,972. Due to these contributions and deductions, the partnership's adjusted basis in the property in August 1972 was $1,455,740.

In 1971 and 1972, major employers in the Duncanville area laid off significant numbers of workers. As a result, the partnership's rental income was less than expected, and it was unable to make the payments due on the mortgage. Each partner, on August 28, 1972, sold his partnership interest to an unrelated third party, Fred Bayles. As consideration, Bayles agreed to reimburse each partner's sale expenses up to $250; he also assumed the nonrecourse mortgage.

On the date of transfer, the fair market value of the property did not exceed $1,400,000. Each partner reported the sale on his federal income tax return and indicated that a partnership loss of $55,740 had been sustained.[1] The Commissioner of Internal Revenue, on audit, determined that the sale resulted in a partnership capital gain of approximately $400,000. His theory was that the partnership had realized the full amount of the nonrecourse obligation.[2]

Relying on Millar v. Commissioner, 577 F.2d 212, 215 (CA3), cert. denied 439 U.S. 1046 (1978), the United States Tax Court, in an unreviewed decision, upheld the asserted deficiencies. 70 T.C. 756 (1978). The United States Court of Appeals for the Fifth Circuit reversed, 651 F.2d 1058 (1981). That court expressly disagreed with the Millar analysis, and, in limiting Crane v. Commissioner, supra, to its facts, questioned the theoretical underpinnings of the Crane decision. We granted certiorari to resolve the conflict. 456 U.S. 960 (1982).

II

Section 752(d) of the Internal Revenue Code of 1954, 26 U.S.C. § 752(d), specifically provides that liabilities incurred in the sale or exchange of a partnership interest are to "be treated in the same manner

---

[1] The loss was the difference between the adjusted basis, $1,455,740, and the fair market value of the property, $1,400,000. On their individual tax returns, the partners did not claim deductions for their respective shares of this loss. In their petitions to the Tax Court, however, the partners did claim the loss.

[2] The Commissioner determined the partnership's gain on the sale by subtracting the adjusted basis, $1,455,740, from the liability assumed by Bayles, $1,851,500, [leaving as a] resulting figure, $395,760 * * *.

as liabilities in connection with the sale or exchange of property not associated with partnerships." Section 1001 governs the determination of gains and losses on the disposition of property. Under § 1001(a), the gain or loss from a sale or other disposition of property is defined as the difference between "the amount realized" on the disposition and the property's adjusted basis. Subsection (b) of § 1001 defines "amount realized": "The amount realized from the sale or other disposition of property shall be the sum of any money received plus the fair market value of the property (other than money) received." At issue is the application of the latter provision to the disposition of property encumbered by a nonrecourse mortgage of an amount in excess of the property's fair market value.

A

In Crane v. Commissioner, supra, this Court took the first and controlling step toward the resolution of this issue. Beulah B. Crane was the sole beneficiary under the will of her deceased husband. At his death in January 1932, he owned an apartment building that was then mortgaged for an amount which proved to be equal to its fair market value, as determined for federal estate tax purposes. The widow, of course, was not personally liable on the mortgage. She operated the building for nearly seven years, hoping to turn it into a profitable venture; during that period, she claimed income tax deductions for depreciation, property taxes, interest, and operating expenses, but did not make payments upon the mortgage principal. In computing her basis for the depreciation deductions, she included the full amount of the mortgage debt. In November 1938, with her hopes unfulfilled and the mortgagee threatening foreclosure, Mrs. Crane sold the building. The purchaser took the property subject to the mortgage and paid Crane $3,000; of that amount, $500 went for the expenses of the sale.

Crane reported a gain of $2,500 on the transaction. She reasoned that her basis in the property was zero (despite her earlier depreciation deductions based on including the amount of the mortgage) and that the amount she realized from the sale was simply the cash she received. The Commissioner disputed this claim. He asserted that Crane's basis in the property, under [the predecessor of] § 1014 of the 1954 Code * * * was the property's fair market value at the time of her husband's death, adjusted for depreciation in the interim, and that the amount realized was the net cash received plus the amount of the outstanding mortgage assumed by the purchaser.

In upholding the Commissioner's interpretation * * * the Court observed that to regard merely the taxpayer's equity in the property as her basis would lead to depreciation deductions less than the actual physical deterioration of the property, and would require the basis to be recomputed with each payment on the mortgage. 331 U.S., at 9–10. The Court rejected Crane's claim that any loss due to depreciation belonged to the mortgagee. The effect of the Court's ruling was that the taxpayer's basis was the value of the property undiminished by the mortgage. Id., at 11.

The Court next proceeded to determine the amount realized under [the predecessor of] § 1001(b) of the 1954 Code. * * * In order to avoid the "absurdity," of Crane's realizing only $2,500 on the sale of property worth over a quarter of a million dollars, the Court treated the amount realized as it had treated basis, that is, by including the outstanding value of the mortgage. To do otherwise would have permitted Crane to recognize a tax loss unconnected with any actual economic loss. The Court refused to construe one section of the Revenue Act so as "to frustrate the Act as a whole."

Crane, however, insisted that the nonrecourse nature of the mortgage required different treatment. The Court, for two reasons, disagreed. First, excluding the nonrecourse debt from the amount realized would result in the same absurdity and frustration of the Code. Id., at 13–14. Second, the Court concluded that Crane obtained an economic benefit from the purchaser's assumption of the mortgage identical to the benefit conferred by the cancellation of personal debt. Because the value of the property in that case exceeded the amount of the mortgage, it was in Crane's economic interest to treat the mortgage as a personal obligation; only by so doing could she realize upon sale the appreciation in her equity represented by the $2,500 boot. The purchaser's assumption of the liability thus resulted in a taxable economic benefit to her, just as if she had been given, in addition to the boot, a sum of cash sufficient to satisfy the mortgage.

In [footnote 37], pertinent to the present case, the Court observed:

> "Obviously, if the value of the property is less than the amount of the mortgage, a mortgagor who is not personally liable cannot realize a benefit equal to the mortgage. Consequently, a different problem might be encountered where a mortgagor abandoned the property or transferred it subject to the mortgage without receiving boot. That is not this case."

Id., at 14, n. 37.

B

This case presents that unresolved issue. We are disinclined to overrule Crane, and we conclude that the same rule applies when the unpaid amount of the nonrecourse mortgage exceeds the value of the property transferred. Crane ultimately does not rest on its limited theory of economic benefit; instead, we read Crane to have approved the Commissioner's decision to treat a nonrecourse mortgage in this context as a true loan. This approval underlies Crane's holdings that the amount of the nonrecourse liability is to be included in calculating both the basis and the amount realized on disposition. That the amount of the loan exceeds the fair market value of the property thus becomes irrelevant.

When a taxpayer receives a loan, he incurs an obligation to repay that loan at some future date. Because of this obligation, the loan proceeds do not qualify as income to the taxpayer. When he fulfills the obligation, the repayment of the loan likewise has no effect on his tax liability.

Another consequence to the taxpayer from this obligation occurs when the taxpayer applies the loan proceeds to the purchase price of property used to secure the loan. Because of the obligation to repay, the taxpayer is entitled to include the amount of the loan in computing his basis in the property; the loan, under § 1012, is part of the taxpayer's cost of the property. Although a different approach might have been taken with respect to a nonrecourse mortgage loan,[5] the Commissioner has chosen to accord it the same treatment he gives to a recourse mortgage loan. The Court approved that choice in Crane, and the respondents do not challenge it here. The choice and its resultant benefits to the taxpayer are predicated on the assumption that the mortgage will be repaid in full.

When encumbered property is sold or otherwise disposed of and the purchaser assumes the mortgage, the associated extinguishment of the mortgagor's obligation to repay is accounted for in the computation of the amount realized. * * * Because no difference between recourse and nonrecourse obligations is recognized in calculating basis,[7] Crane teaches that the Commissioner may ignore the nonrecourse nature of the obligation in determining the amount realized upon disposition of the encumbered property. He thus may include in the amount realized the amount of the nonrecourse mortgage assumed by the purchaser. The rationale for this treatment is that the original inclusion of the amount of the mortgage in basis rested on the assumption that the mortgagor incurred an obligation to repay. Moreover, this treatment balances the

---

[5] The Commissioner might have adopted the theory, implicit in Crane's contentions, that a nonrecourse mortgage is not true debt, but, instead, is a form of joint investment by the mortgagor and the mortgagee. On this approach, nonrecourse debt would be considered a contingent liability, under which the mortgagor's payments on the debt gradually increase his interest in the property while decreasing that of the mortgagee. * * * Because the taxpayer's investment in the property would not include the nonrecourse debt, the taxpayer would not be permitted to include that debt in basis. * * *

We express no view as to whether such an approach would be consistent with the statutory structure and, if so, and Crane were not on the books, whether that approach would be preferred over Crane's analysis. We note only that the Crane Court's resolution of the basis issue presumed that when property is purchased with proceeds from a nonrecourse mortgage, the purchaser becomes the sole owner of the property. 331 U.S., at 6. Under the Crane approach, the mortgagee is entitled to no portion of the basis. Id., at 10, n. 28. The nonrecourse mortgage is part of the mortgagor's investment in the property, and does not constitute a co-investment by the mortgagee. * * *

[7] The Commissioner's choice in Crane "laid the foundation stone of most tax shelters," Bittker, Tax Shelters, Nonrecourse Debt, and the Crane Case, 33 Tax.L. Rev. 277, 283 (1978), by permitting taxpayers who bear no risk to take deductions on depreciable property. Congress recently has acted to curb this avoidance device by forbidding a taxpayer to take depreciation deductions in excess of amounts he has at risk in the investment. * * * Real estate investments, however, are exempt from this prohibition. § 465(c)(3)(D) * * *. Although this congressional action may foreshadow a day when nonrecourse and recourse debts will be treated differently, neither Congress nor the Commissioner has sought to alter Crane's rule of including nonrecourse liability in both basis and the amount realized.

fact that the mortgagor originally received the proceeds of the nonrecourse loan tax free on the same assumption. Unless the outstanding amount of the mortgage is deemed to be realized, the mortgagor effectively will have received untaxed income at the time the loan was extended and will have received an unwarranted increase in the basis of his property.[8] The Commissioner's interpretation of § 1001(b) in this fashion cannot be said to be unreasonable.

C

The Commissioner in fact has applied this rule even when the fair market value of the property falls below the amount of the nonrecourse obligation. Treas.Reg. § 1.1001–2(b), 26 CFR § 1.1001–2(b) (1982); Rev. Rul. 76–111, 1976–1 Cum.Bull. 214. Because the theory on which the rule is based applies equally in this situation, * * * [w]e have no reason, after Crane, to question this treatment.[11]

Respondents received a mortgage loan with the concomitant obligation to repay by the year 2012. The only difference between that mortgage and one on which the borrower is personally liable is that the mortgagee's remedy is limited to foreclosing on the securing property.

---

[8]   * * * Our analysis applies even in the situation in which no deductions are taken. It focuses on the obligation to repay and its subsequent extinguishment, not on the taking and recovery of deductions. * * *

[11]   Professor Wayne G. Barnett, as amicus in the present case, argues that the liability and property portions of the transaction should be accounted for separately. Under his view, there was a transfer of the property for $1.4 million, and there was a cancellation of the $1.85 million obligation for a payment of $1.4 million. The former resulted in a capital loss of $50,000, and the latter in the realization of $450,000 of ordinary income. Taxation of the ordinary income might be deferred under § 108 by a reduction of respondents' bases in their partnership interests.

Although this indeed could be a justifiable mode of analysis, it has not been adopted by the Commissioner. Nor is there anything to indicate that the Code requires the Commissioner to adopt it. We note that Professor Barnett's approach does assume that recourse and nonrecourse debt may be treated identically.

The Commissioner also has chosen not to characterize the transaction as cancellation of indebtedness. We are not presented with and do not decide the contours of the cancellation-of-indebtedness doctrine. We note only that our approach does not fall within certain prior interpretations of that doctrine. In one view, the doctrine rests on the same initial premise as our analysis here—an obligation to repay—but the doctrine relies on a freeing-of-assets theory to attribute ordinary income to the debtor upon cancellation. See Commissioner v. Jacobson, 336 U.S. 28, 38–40 (1949); United States v. Kirby Lumber Co., 284 U.S. 1, 3 (1931). According to that view, when nonrecourse debt is forgiven, the debtor's basis in the securing property is reduced by the amount of debt canceled, and realization of income is deferred until the sale of the property. * * * Because that interpretation attributes income only when assets are freed, however, an insolvent debtor realizes income just to the extent his assets exceed his liabilities after the cancellation. Lakeland Grocery Co. v. Commissioner, 36 B.T.A. 289, 292 (1937). Similarly, if the nonrecourse indebtedness exceeds the value of the securing property, the taxpayer never realizes the full amount of the obligation canceled because the tax law has not recognized negative basis.

Although the economic benefit prong of Crane also relies on a freeing-of-assets theory, that theory is irrelevant to our broader approach. In the context of a sale or disposition of property under § 1001, the extinguishment of the obligation to repay is not ordinary income; instead, the amount of the canceled debt is included in the amount realized, and enters into the computation of gain or loss on the disposition of property. According to Crane, this treatment is no different when the obligation is nonrecourse: the basis is not reduced as in the cancellation-of-indebtedness context, and the full value of the outstanding liability is included in the amount realized. Thus the problem of negative basis is avoided.

This difference does not alter the nature of the obligation; its only effect is to shift from the borrower to the lender any potential loss caused by devaluation of the property.[12] If the fair market value of the property falls below the amount of the outstanding obligation, the mortgagee's ability to protect its interests is impaired, for the mortgagor is free to abandon the property to the mortgagee and be relieved of his obligation.

This, however, does not erase the fact that the mortgagor received the loan proceeds tax-free and included them in his basis on the understanding that he had an obligation to repay the full amount. See Woodsam Associates, Inc. v. Commissioner, 198 F.2d 357, 359 (C.A.2 1952). When the obligation is canceled, the mortgagor is relieved of his responsibility to repay the sum he originally received and thus realizes value to that extent within the meaning of § 1001(b). From the mortgagor's point of view, when his obligation is assumed by a third party who purchases the encumbered property, it is as if the mortgagor first had been paid with cash borrowed by the third party from the mortgagee on a nonrecourse basis, and then had used the cash to satisfy his obligation to the mortgagee.

> Moreover, this approach avoids the absurdity the Court recognized in Crane. Because of the remedy accompanying the mortgage in the nonrecourse situation, the depreciation in the fair market value of the property is relevant economically only to the mortgagee, who by lending on a nonrecourse basis remains at risk. To permit the taxpayer to limit his realization to the fair market value of the property would be to recognize a tax loss for which he has suffered no corresponding economic loss.[13] Such a result would be to construe "one section of the Act * * * so as * * * to defeat the intention of another or to frustrate the Act as a whole." 331 U.S., at 13.

In the specific circumstances of Crane, the economic benefit theory did support the Commissioner's treatment of the nonrecourse mortgage as a personal obligation. The footnote in Crane acknowledged the limitations of that theory when applied to a different set of facts. Crane

---

[12] In his opinion for the Court of Appeals in *Crane*, Judge Learned Hand observed: "[The mortgagor] has all the income from the property; he manages it; he may sell it; any increase in its value goes to him; any decrease falls on him, until the value goes below the amount of the lien. . . . When therefore upon a sale the mortgagor makes an allowance to the vendee of the amount of the lien, he secures a release from a charge upon his property quite as though the vendee had paid him the full price on condition that before he took title the lien should be cleared. . . ." 153 F.2d 504, 506 (C.A.2 1945).

[13] In the present case, the Government bore the ultimate loss. The nonrecourse mortgage was extended to respondents only after the planned complex was endorsed for mortgage insurance under §§ 221(b) and (d)(4) of the National Housing Act, 12 U.S.C. § 17151(b) and (d)(4) * * *. After acquiring the complex from respondents, Bayles operated it for a few years, but was unable to make it profitable. In 1974, F & H foreclosed, and the Department of Housing and Urban Development paid off the lender to obtain title. In 1976, the Department sold the complex to another developer for $1,502,000. The sale was financed by the Department's taking back a note for $1,314,800 and a nonrecourse mortgage. To fail to recognize the value of the nonrecourse loan in the amount realized, therefore, would permit respondents to compound the Government's loss by claiming the tax benefits of that loss for themselves.

also stands for the broader proposition, however, that a nonrecourse loan should be treated as a true loan. We therefore hold that a taxpayer must account for the proceeds of obligations he has received tax-free and included in basis. Nothing in either § 1001(b) or in the Court's prior decisions requires the Commissioner to permit a taxpayer to treat a sale of encumbered property asymmetrically, by including the proceeds of the nonrecourse obligation in basis but not accounting for the proceeds upon transfer of the encumbered property. * * *

[The Court's discussion rejecting the taxpayer's argument that § 752 expressly requires a different result for partnership dispositions is omitted.]

IV

When a taxpayer sells or disposes of property encumbered by a nonrecourse obligation, the Commissioner properly requires him to include among the assets realized the outstanding amount of the obligation. The fair market value of the property is irrelevant to this calculation. We find this interpretation to be consistent with Crane v. Commissioner, 331 U.S. 1 (1947), and to implement the statutory mandate in a reasonable manner. * * *

The judgment of the Court of Appeals is therefore reversed.

It is so ordered.

■ JUSTICE O'CONNOR, concurring.

I concur in the opinion of the Court, accepting the view of the Commissioner. I do not, however, endorse the Commissioner's view. Indeed, were we writing on a slate clean except for the *Crane* decision, I would take quite a different approach—that urged upon us by Professor Barnett as *amicus*.

Crane established that a taxpayer could treat property as entirely his own, in spite of the "co-investment" provided by his mortgagee in the form of a nonrecourse loan. That is, the full basis of the property, with all its tax consequences, belongs to the mortgagor. That rule alone, though, does not in any way tie nonrecourse debt to the cost of property or to the proceeds upon disposition. I see no reason to treat the purchase, ownership, and eventual disposition of property differently because the taxpayer also takes out a mortgage, an independent transaction. In this case, the taxpayer purchased property, using nonrecourse financing, and sold it after it declined in value to a buyer who assumed the mortgage. There is no economic difference between the events in this case and a case in which the taxpayer buys property with cash; later obtains a nonrecourse loan by pledging the property as security; still later, using cash on hand, buys off the mortgage for the market value of the devalued property; and finally sells the property to a third party for its market value.

The logical way to treat both this case and the hypothesized case is to separate the two aspects of these events and to consider, first, the ownership and sale of the property, and, second, the arrangement and retirement of the loan. Under Crane, the fair market value of the property on the date of acquisition—the purchase price—represents the taxpayer's basis in the property, and the fair market value on the date of disposition represents the proceeds on sale. The benefit received by the taxpayer in return for the property is the cancellation of a mortgage that is worth no more than the fair market value of the property, for that is all the mortgagee can expect to collect on the mortgage. His gain or loss on the disposition of the property equals the difference between the proceeds and the cost of acquisition. Thus, the taxation of the transaction *in property* reflects the economic fate of the *property*. If the property has declined in value, as was the case here, the taxpayer recognizes a loss on the disposition of the property. The new purchaser then takes as his basis the fair market value as of the date of the sale. * * *

In the separate borrowing transaction, the taxpayer acquires cash from the mortgagee. He need not recognize income at that time, of course, because he also incurs an obligation to repay the money. Later, though, when he is able to satisfy the debt by surrendering property that is worth less than the face amount of the debt, we have a classic situation of cancellation of indebtedness, requiring the taxpayer to recognize income in the amount of the difference between the proceeds of the loan and the amount for which he is able to satisfy his creditor. 26 U.S.C. § 61(a)(12). The taxation of the financing transaction then reflects the economic fate of the loan.

The reason that separation of the two aspects of the events in this case is important is, of course, that the Code treats different sorts of income differently. A gain on the sale of the property may qualify for capital gains treatment, §§ 1202, 1221 * * * while the cancellation of indebtedness is ordinary income, but income that the taxpayer may be able to defer. §§ 108, 1017 * * *. Not only does Professor Barnett's theory permit us to accord appropriate treatment to each of the two types of income or loss present in these sorts of transactions, it also restores continuity to the system by making the taxpayer-seller's proceeds on the disposition of property equal to the purchaser's basis in the property. Further, and most important, it allows us to tax the events in this case in the same way that we tax the economically identical hypothesized transaction.

Persuaded though I am by the logical coherence and internal consistency of this approach, I agree with the Court's decision not to adopt it judicially. We do not write on a slate marked only by Crane. The Commissioner's longstanding position, Rev. Rul. 76–111, 1976–1 C.B. 214, is now reflected in the regulations. Treas.Reg. § 1.1001–2, 26 CFR § 1.1001–2 (1982). In the light of the numerous cases in the lower courts including the amount of the unrepaid proceeds of the mortgage in the proceeds on sale or disposition, * * * it is difficult to conclude that the Commissioner's interpretation of the statute exceeds the bounds of his discretion. As the Court's opinion demonstrates, his interpretation is defensible. One can reasonably read § 1001(b)'s reference to "the amount realized *from* the sale or other disposition of property" (emphasis added) to permit the Commissioner to collapse the two aspects of the transaction. As long as his view is a reasonable reading of § 1001(b), we should defer to the regulations promulgated by the agency charged with interpretation of the statute. * * * Accordingly, I concur.

NOTES

(A) *The Taxpayer Is Still Ahead.* By resolving the ambiguity of *Crane*'s footnote 37 and making clear the symmetrical treatment of mortgage indebtedness in basis and amount realized, *Tufts* demonstrates that the *total amount* of income from such property transactions will be the same whether the mortgage debt is included in both basis and amount realized or excluded from both. The difference between the two rules is a question of timing of tax liabilities. The ability to obtain accelerated and larger depreciation deductions offsets the inclusion of the deductions in income on disposition. Even if the taxpayer's marginal tax rate has not changed, the subsequent increase in tax liability by the amount of the earlier reduction is not adequate to make either the government or taxpayers indifferent. The deferral of tax is of major advantage to taxpayers because the present value of the future tax liability is less than its nominal value. *Crane* served as the foundation of tax shelter investments based on increasing the amount of tax deferred through borrowing or "leverage." The value of deferral is discussed infra at page 313.

(B) *The "Joint Venture" Analysis.* In Footnote [3] of *Tufts* the Court raises but does not adopt a joint venture analysis of an acquisition of property with debt. The Court felt constrained by its earlier decision in *Crane,* which treated the borrower as the sole owner of the property. The *Crane* court was clearly influenced by its view that depreciation deductions reflect wear and tear of the asset rather than a recovery of the taxpayer's capital investment. If, however, the Court had regarded depreciation as a device for the recovery of the taxpayer's actual investment in the property, depreciation might be allowed only to a taxpayer who suffers an economic loss due to the decline in the value of the property over time. That, of course, does not describe an owner of property subject to a nonrecourse mortgage. The lender who provides the nonrecourse mortgage bears this economic risk and thus might be entitled to basis in the property and depreciation deductions.

The lender, however, is not exactly like a participant in a joint venture because, unless he has an "equity kicker," he will not enjoy the benefits if the property appreciates in value. The borrower/"owner" has something akin to an option—he can walk away without further loss if the property declines in value, but will retain the property and enjoy the benefits if it increases in value. The question who should be treated as the "owner" of the property and thus who should have basis is quite difficult. The *Crane* rule, therefore, influences not only timing, but also the allocation of income and deductions among taxpayers by treating loans differently from other economically similar transactions.

The *Crane* rule also may affect the amount of gain treated as ordinary income or capital gain. This is taken up in Chapter 5. The following case reveals the potential for abuse resulting from the *Crane* rule.

Estate of Franklin v. Commissioner

United States Court of Appeals, Ninth Circuit, 1976. 544 F.2d 1045.

■ SNEED, CIRCUIT JUDGE:

This case involves another effort on the part of the Commissioner to curb the use of real estate tax shelters. In this instance he seeks to disallow deductions for the taxpayers' distributive share of losses reported by a limited partnership with respect to its acquisition of a motel and related property. These "losses" have their origin in deductions for depreciation and interest claimed with respect to the motel and related property. These deductions were disallowed by the Commissioner on the ground either that the acquisition was a sham or that the entire acquisition transaction was in substance the purchase by the partnership of an option to acquire the motel and related property on January 15, 1979. The Tax Court held that the transaction constituted an option exercisable in 1979 and disallowed the taxpayers' deductions. Estate of Charles T. Franklin, 64 T.C. 752 (1975). We affirm this disallowance although our approach differs somewhat from that of the Tax Court.

The interest and depreciation deductions were taken by Twenty-Fourth Property Associates (hereinafter referred to as Associates), a California limited partnership of which Charles T. Franklin and seven other doctors were the limited partners. The deductions flowed from the purported "purchase" by Associates of the Thunderbird Inn, an Arizona motel, from Wayne L. Romney and Joan E. Romney (hereinafter referred to as the Romneys) on November 15, 1968.

Under a document entitled "Sales Agreement," the Romneys agreed to "sell" the Thunderbird Inn to Associates for $1,224,000. The property would be paid for over a period of ten years, with interest on any unpaid balance of seven and one-half percent per annum. "Prepaid interest" in the amount of $75,000 was payable immediately; monthly principal and interest installments of $9,045.36 would be paid for approximately the first ten years, with Associates required to make a balloon payment at the end of the ten years of the difference between the remaining purchase price, forecast as $975,000, and any mortgages then outstanding against the property.

The purchase obligation of Associates to the Romneys was nonrecourse; the Romneys' only remedy in the event of default would be forfeiture of the partnership's interest. The sales agreement was recorded in the local county. A warranty deed was placed in an escrow account, along with a quitclaim deed from Associates to the Romneys, both documents to be delivered either to Associates upon full payment of the purchase price, or to the Romneys upon default.

The sale was combined with a leaseback of the property by Associates to the Romneys; Associates therefore never took physical possession. The lease payments were designed to approximate closely the principal and interest payments with the consequence that with the exception of the $75,000 prepaid interest payment no cash would cross between Associates and Romneys until the balloon payment. The lease was on a net basis; thus, the Romneys were responsible for all of the typical expenses of owning the motel property including all utility costs, taxes, assessments, rents, charges, and levies of "every name, nature and kind whatsoever." The Romneys also were to continue to be responsible for the first and second mortgages until the final purchase installment was made; the Romneys could, and indeed did, place additional mortgages on the property without the permission of Associates. Finally, the Romneys were allowed to propose new capital improvements which Associates would be required to either build themselves or allow the Romneys to construct with compensating modifications in rent or purchase price.

In holding that the transaction between Associates and the Romneys more nearly resembled an option than a sale, the Tax Court emphasized that Associates had the power at the end of ten years to walk away from the transaction and merely lose its $75,000 "prepaid interest payment." It also pointed out that a *deed* was never recorded and that the "benefits and burdens of ownership" appeared to remain with the Romneys. Thus, the sale was combined with a leaseback in which no cash would pass; the Romneys remained responsible under the mortgages, which they could increase; and the Romneys could make capital improvements. The Tax Court further justified its "option" characterization by reference to the nonrecourse nature of the purchase money debt and the nice balance between the rental and purchase money payments.

Our emphasis is different from that of the Tax Court. We believe the characteristics set out above can exist in a situation in which the sale imposes upon the purchaser a genuine indebtedness within the meaning of section 167(a), Internal Revenue Code of 1954, which will support both interest and depreciation deductions. * * *

In none of [the cases sustaining such transactions], however, did the taxpayer fail to demonstrate that the purchase price was at least approximately equivalent to the fair market value of the property. Just such a failure occurred here. The Tax Court explicitly found that on the basis of the facts before it the value of the property could not be estimated. 64 T.C. at 767–768.[4] In our view this defect in the taxpayers' proof is fatal.

Reason supports our perception. An acquisition such as that of Associates if at a price approximately equal to the fair market value of the property under ordinary circumstances would rather quickly yield an equity in the property which the purchaser could not prudently abandon. This is the stuff of substance. It meshes with the form of the transaction and constitutes a sale.

No such meshing occurs when the purchase price exceeds a demonstrably reasonable estimate of the fair market value. Payments on the principal of the purchase price yield no equity so long as the unpaid balance of the purchase price exceeds the then existing fair market value. Under these circumstances the purchaser by abandoning the transaction can lose no more than a mere chance to acquire an equity in the future should the value of the acquired property increase. While this chance undoubtedly influenced the Tax Court's determination that the transaction before us constitutes an option, we need only point out that its existence fails to supply the substance necessary to justify treating the transaction as a sale *ab initio*. It is not necessary to the disposition of this case to decide the tax consequences of a transaction such as that before us if in a subsequent year the fair market value of the property increases to an extent that permits the purchaser to acquire an equity.

---

[4]   The Tax Court found that appellants had "not shown that the purported sales price of $1,224,000 (or any other price) had any relationship to the actual market value of the motel property. . . . " 64 T.C. at 767.

Petitioners spent a substantial amount of time at trial attempting to establish that, whatever the actual market value of the property, Associates acted in the good faith *belief* that the market value of the property approximated the selling price. However, this evidence only goes to the issue of sham and does not supply substance to this transaction. "Save in those instances where the statute itself turns on intent, a matter so real as taxation must depend on objective realities, not on the varying subjective beliefs of individual taxpayers." * * *

In oral argument it was suggested by the appellants that neither the Tax Court nor they recognized the importance of fair market value during the presentation of evidence and that this hampered the full and open development of this issue. However, upon an examination of the record, we are satisfied that the taxpayers recognized the importance of presenting objective evidence of the fair market value and were awarded ample opportunity to present their proof; appellants merely failed to present clear and admissible evidence that fair market value did indeed approximate the purchase price. Such evidence of fair market value as was relied upon by the appellants, viz. two appraisals, one completed in 1968 and a second in 1971, even if fully admissible as evidence of the truth of the estimates of value appearing therein, does not require us to set aside the Tax Court's finding. As the Tax Court found, the 1968 appraisal was "error-filled, sketchy" and "obviously suspect." 64 T.C. at 767 n. 13. The 1971 appraisal had little relevancy as to 1968 values. On the other side, there existed cogent evidence indicating that the fair market value was substantially less than the purchase price. This evidence included (i) the Romneys' purchase of the stock of two corporations, one of which wholly-owned the motel, for approximately $800,000 in the year preceding the "sale" to Associates ($660,000 of which was allocable to the sale property, according to Mr. Romney's estimate), and (ii) insurance policies on the property from 1967 through 1974 of only $583,200, $700,000, and $614,000. 64 T.C. at 767–768.

Given that it was the appellants' burden to present evidence showing that the purchase price did not exceed the fair market value and that he had a fair opportunity to do so, we see no reason to remand this case for further proceedings.

Authority also supports our perception. It is fundamental that "depreciation is not predicated upon ownership of property *but rather upon an investment in property.* * * * " No such investment exists when payments of the purchase price in accordance with the design of the parties yield no equity to the purchaser. * * * In the transaction before us and during the taxable years in question the purchase price payments by Associates have not been shown to constitute an *investment in the property.* Depreciation was properly disallowed. Only the Romneys had an investment in the property.

Authority also supports disallowance of the interest deductions. This is said even though it has long been recognized that the absence of personal liability for the purchase money debt secured by a mortgage on the acquired property does not deprive the debt of its character as a bona fide debt obligation able to support an interest deduction. * * * However, this is no longer true when it appears that the debt has economic significance only if the property substantially appreciates in value prior to the date at which a very large portion of the purchase price is to be discharged. Under these circumstances the purchaser has not secured "the use or forbearance of money." * * * Nor has the seller advanced money or forborne its use. * * * Prior to the date at which the balloon payment on the purchase price is required, and assuming no substantial increase in the fair market value of the property, the absence of personal liability on the debt reduces the transaction in economic terms to a mere chance that a genuine debt obligation may arise. This is not enough to justify an interest deduction. To justify the deduction the debt must exist; potential existence will not do. For debt to exist, the purchaser, in the absence of personal liability, must confront a situation in which it is presently reasonable from an economic point of view for him to make a capital investment in the amount of the unpaid purchase price. * * * Associates, during the taxable years in question, confronted no such situation. Compare Crane v. Commissioner, 331 U.S. 1, 11–12 (1947).

Our focus on the relationship of the fair market value of the property to the unpaid purchase price should not be read as premised upon the belief that a sale is not a sale if the purchaser pays too much. Bad bargains from the buyer's point of view—as well as sensible bargains from buyer's, but exceptionally good from the seller's point of view—do not thereby cease to be sales. * * * We intend our holding and explanation thereof to be understood as limited to transactions substantially similar to that now before us.

Affirmed.

NOTES

(A) *Don't Take Your Parents.* A tax law professor informs us that the Thunderbird Inn has been renamed a number of times. He says it is now the Mountain Side Inn. TripAdvisor ranks that establishment as number 30 out of 30 hotels and motels in Williams, Arizona. On that website, one reviewer described the inn as "filthy, old, run down," adding, "This is a place where you wish to go to bed fully dressed." Another reviewer added: "Horrible hotel. . .very dirty ants and roaches everywhere. Owners and employees are very rude. A place to avoid." Both the overvaluation tax scam and the motel seem like things to avoid.

(B) *Options.* The Tax Court had held that the payment by the partnership was in substance an option and not a loan. Under this recharacterization of the transaction, the partnership was treated as having the right, but not the obligation, to purchase the property after ten years by paying the amount in the balloon payment note. (This is a "call option"; an option to sell at a fixed price is a "put option.") The $75,000 payment that the parties labeled "prepaid interest" was treated by the Tax Court as the "premium" or price for the option. An option may be exercised, sold to a third party, or allowed to lapse or terminate. The tax law treats options as separate property with the price (or premium) as its basis. If the option is exercised, its basis becomes part of the basis of the property purchased. Thus, under the Tax Court's approach, the Romneys would continue to have been treated as the owner of the motel until the partnership exercised the option, if it ever did. The partnership would have a separate capital asset—an option—with a basis of $75,000. Only if the partnership actually exercised the option and became the owner of the motel would it have been permitted to take depreciation deductions. This is a very different approach to the transaction than that taken by the circuit court. Which do you think better reflects the "substance" of the transaction?

(C) *Treatment of Basis.* Where at the time of purchase the amount of a nonrecourse loan exceeds the value of the property securing it, should the indebtedness be excluded completely from basis, or rather be limited to the value of the property?

The Service, following *Estate of Franklin,* takes the position that an inadequately secured nonrecourse loan generally is too contingent to merit characterization as indebtedness and hence will not allow any portion of the loan to be considered an acquisition cost includible in basis. Rev. Rul. 77–110, 1977–1 C.B. 58. See also Rev. Rul. 84–5, 1984–1 C.B. 32 (denying interest deductions on a 30-year nonrecourse obligation with a large final "balloon" payment on the grounds that the obligation "does not constitute a valid indebtedness") A number of courts have explicitly agreed with the entire exclusion of undersecured nonrecourse loans from basis. See, e.g., Brannen v. Commissioner, 722 F.2d 695 (11th Cir. 1984); Brountas v. Commissioner, 692 F.2d 152 (1st Cir. 1982).

In Pleasant Summit Land Corp. v. Commissioner, 863 F.2d 263 (3d Cir. 1988), cert. denied sub nom. Commissioner v. Prussin, 493 U.S. 901 (1989), the Third Circuit disagreed with the conclusion of *Estate of Franklin* that all depreciation and interest deductions should be disallowed whenever nonrecourse debt significantly exceeds the fair market value of property on acquisition. Instead the court allowed the taxpayer to deduct depreciation and interest attributable to the portion of the nonrecourse debt that did not exceed the fair market value of the property. The court reasoned that the creditor has no incentive to foreclose if the debtor offers to settle the debt for the fair market value and thus, it was appropriate to regard that amount of the debt as genuine. The *Pleasant Summit* approach has not been followed. It was explicitly rejected by the Second, Fifth, and Ninth Circuits. See, e.g., Lebowitz v. Commissioner, 917 F.2d 1314 (2d Cir. 1990) (rejecting *Pleasant Summit*).

(D) Tufts *and* Franklin *Reconciled. Tufts* should be understood as holding only that a taxpayer must treat a nonrecourse mortgage consistently when he accounts for basis and amount realized. Thus, in an *Estate of Franklin* situation, where the amount of the mortgage exceeds the fair market value of the property securing it when the debt was first incurred, the mortgage is not included in the basis and thus will not be included in the amount realized on disposition, generally foreclosure. In the *Tufts* situation, where the value of the security exceeded the debt initially, the debt is included in the basis and likewise is included in the amount realized on foreclosure, even if the amount of debt then exceeds the fair market value of the property.

Generally, where there is an unrelated third party lender, the *Estate of Franklin* issue will not arise. A commercial lender, for example, will not extend nonrecourse debt where the value of the underlying security is insufficient. The seller of the property, however, is not so constrained because he does not actually transfer cash to the borrower. (Furthermore, as we shall see in Chapter 7, because of the installment sale rules, the seller reports no gain unless he actually receives payment on the debt).

What if a purchaser assumes a nonrecourse mortgage that exceeds the security? Reconsider the facts in *Tufts*. What is the basis of the purchaser from Tufts who assumed the $1.8 million nonrecourse mortgage and agreed to reimburse Tufts and his partners for the sale expenses when the "fair market value" of the property was only $1.4 million? Since the purchaser was an unrelated third party, is what he paid (the assumption of the debt and the reimbursement of the expenses) really the fair market value? Or is the debt excluded from his basis under *Franklin* because the value of the security is less than the debt? Justice O'Connor's concurring opinion in *Tufts* assumes the purchaser's basis would be the fair market value at the date of sale (as in *Pleasant Summit Land Corp.*) and states that "Professor Barnett's theory . . . restores continuity to the system by making the taxpayer-seller's proceeds on the disposition of property equal to the purchaser's basis in the property."

(E) *Comparison of Discharge of Indebtedness Income and Gain.* A taxpayer who settles a debt at a discount generally has discharge of indebtedness income. United States v. Kirby Lumber Co., 284 U.S. 1 (1931). Where a taxpayer disposes of property secured by the debt, the debt is included in the amount realized. As *Tufts* indicates, this is true regardless of the value of the underlying security so long as the debt is nonrecourse. Where the debt is recourse, however, the transaction is bifurcated if the amount of the indebtedness exceeds the value of the property. Where a taxpayer transfers property with a fair market value that exceeds the basis, but is less than the outstanding debt, the amount realized is the value of the property and the extent to which it exceeds the basis is gain. Any excess debt that is discharged is income from the discharge of indebtedness. Reg. § 1.1001–2(c) (Ex. 8). If the Court had followed the approach preferred by Justice O'Connor, nonrecourse and recourse debt would be treated consistently. This may be important if the sale of the property would produce a capital gain or if the discharge of indebtedness income is excluded from income by virtue of § 108, where, for example, the debtor is insolvent. The extent to which the fair market value of the property exceeds the basis is a taxable gain even if the debtor is insolvent. See Gehl v. Commissioner, 102 T.C. 784 (1994), aff'd in unpublished opinion, 50 F.3d 12 (8th Cir. 1995).

For example, suppose A has property with an adjusted basis of $10, that is subject to a *recourse* mortgage of $45. At a time when the fair market value of the property is $30, the lender forecloses. The disposition of the property will satisfy $30 of the debt and the borrower will have a $20 gain. If the lender is unable to obtain assets to satisfy the remainder of the debt, A will have $15 of discharge of indebtedness income. If the debt were *nonrecourse*, the amount realized would include the entire debt and A would have $35 of gain. Generally, the amount received on a foreclosure sale is treated as the amount realized.

Where a taxpayer is discharged from all or a portion of a nonrecourse liability, but does not dispose of the collateral, there is discharge of indebtedness income. There is no effect on the basis of the property used as security. Note, however, that if the debt reduction is considered a reduction of the purchase price of the asset, there is no cancellation of indebtedness income under § 108(e)(5).

The interplay of these provisions is nicely illustrated by Preslar v. Commissioner, 167 F.3d 1323 (10th Cir. 1999). The Preslars bought a ranch financed by a local bank. They subdivided and sold lots and turned the proceeds over to the bank to pay down the debt. The bank was declared insolvent and the FDIC took over the loan. When it refused to accept lot sale contracts, the Preslars made no more payments. Ultimately, they settled and their total payments on a $1 million debt were $550,000. The Preslars argued that they had no discharge of indebtedness income because the debt was disputed. (Recall the discussion of the disputed liability doctrine in *Zarin*, supra at page 187. The Tenth Circuit ruled that the mere fact that the taxpayers challenged the enforceability of the debt does not automatically shield them from income on the resolution of the debt. The underlying amount of the debt was not in dispute, only the method of payment. The court also held that § 108(e)(5) did not apply because neither the bank nor the FDIC was the seller of the property. The result was that the Preslars had $450,000 of discharge of indebtedness income and retained their original cost basis.

(F) *Borrowing in Excess of Basis.* Suppose A purchases real estate for $50,000 at a time when the market value of this asset is $100,000, A takes out a nonrecourse loan for $80,000 secured only by the real estate. Does A have income? In Woodsam Associates, Inc. v. Commissioner, 198 F.2d 357 (2d Cir. 1952), the court held that a loan, even when secured only by untaxed appreciation in property, does not constitute realized income to the borrower. The borrowing is not a realization event. The taxpayer (in a role reversal, having to do with a corporate tax provision) had argued that the loan, which allowed the borrower to receive cash without assuming any personal obligation to repay, constituted a partial disposition of the property that resulted in a realization of gain. *Woodsam* is another example of a timing advantage. The borrower does not include the amount of the loan in her basis because it is not an acquisition cost. She will either pay off the loan or, if it is assumed or discharged, it will be included in her amount realized. In the meantime, however, the taxpayer has the use of the borrowed money without any tax liability.

Suppose the taxpayer builds up additional equity in property and obtains post-acquisition indebtedness, either a second mortgage or an equity loan. The debt is not included in basis because it is not part of the "cost" of acquisition. § 1012. If, however, the taxpayer uses the proceeds to add to or improve the property, the amount expended would increase basis. § 1016. On disposition, regardless of whether the debt was included in basis, the outstanding amount of the indebtedness would be included in the amount realized. This reflects the fact that the taxpayer withdrew an amount of cash equal to the principal of the loan, which was not taxed on receipt under *Woodsam*.

(G) *Contingent Liabilities.* As the opinion in *Estate of Franklin* intimates, a loan should not increase basis where it is unclear whether the borrower will ever actually make principal payments. Thus, contingent liabilities are not included in basis until payment is made. For example, where the purchaser of a business agrees to pay the seller a percentage of profits, his basis does not include this liability until payments are made. Albany Car Wheel Co. v. Commissioner, 40 T.C. 831 (1963), aff'd per curiam, 333 F.2d 653 (2d Cir. 1964).

SECTION 9.   DAMAGES

The nature of the injury for which compensation is made determines the tax consequences of damages received by the taxpayer. It is sometimes difficult, but essential, to distinguish between business and personal damages because the Code provides preferential treatment for certain personal damages.

A. DAMAGES TO BUSINESS INTERESTS

Note on Business Damages

The tax consequences of a compensatory damages award or reimbursement depend on the tax treatment of the item for which the reimbursement is intended to substitute.

In Raytheon Production Corp. v. Commissioner, 144 F.2d 110, 113–14 (1st Cir. 1944), cert. denied 323 U.S. 779 (1944), the court of appeals further detailed the principles governing the taxation of business damages:

Damages recovered in an antitrust action are not necessarily nontaxable as a return of capital. As in other types of tort damage suits, recoveries which represent a reimbursement for lost profits are income. * * * The reasoning is that since the profits would be taxable income, the proceeds of litigation which are their substitute are taxable in like manner.

Damages for violation of the antitrust acts are treated as ordinary income where they represent compensation for loss of profits. * * *

The test is not whether the action was one in tort or contract but rather the question to be asked is "In lieu of what were the damages awarded?" * * * Where the suit is not to recover lost profits but is for injury to good will, the recovery represents a return of capital and, with certain limitations * * * is not taxable.

* * *

Since the suit was to recover damages for the destruction of the business and good will, the recovery represents a return of capital. Nor does the fact that the suit ended in a compromise settlement change the nature of the recovery; "the determining factor is the nature of the basic claim from which the compromised amount was realized."

* * *

But, to say that the recovery represents a return of capital in that it takes the place of the business good will is not to conclude that it may not contain a taxable benefit. Although the injured party may not be deriving a profit as a result of the damage suit itself, the conversion thereby of his property into cash is a realization of any gain made over the cost or other basis of the good will prior to the illegal interference.

Raytheon presented no evidence to establish the basis in its lost goodwill. Since a zero basis was determined for the goodwill, the entire amount recovered for its destruction was realized income.

Where the taxpayer receives an amount to compensate him for the loss of property that has an adjusted basis, the amount of income equals the amount by which the amount received exceeds his adjusted basis. For example, if the taxpayer's truck that he uses in his business has a basis of $10,000 and is destroyed and the tortfeasor gives him $15,000, he has income to the extent that amount exceeds his adjusted basis, or $5,000. The taxation of that income may sometimes be deferred in instances of "involuntary conversions" when the proceeds are reinvested in similar assets. See the discussion of § 1033 in Chapter 5 at page 648.

Where the taxpayer receives an amount to compensate for lost profits, he has no basis (usually because his costs have been deducted) and thus the entire amount is taxable. Similarly, punitive damages are entirely taxable. In Commissioner v. Glenshaw Glass Co., 348 U.S. 426 (1955), the Court held that money received as punitive damages for fraud or as the punitive two-thirds portion of a treble damage recovery must be included in gross income under § 61. In that opinion, which is widely quoted for its definition of income, quoted supra at page 84, the Court also said:

> The mere fact that the payments were extracted from the wrongdoers as punishment for unlawful conduct cannot detract from their character as taxable income to the recipients. Respondents concede, as they must, that the recoveries are taxable to the extent that they compensate for damages actually incurred. It would be an anomaly that could not be justified in the absence of clear congressional intent to say that a recovery for actual damages is taxable but not the additional amount extracted as punishment for the same conduct which caused the injury. And we find no such evidence of intent to exempt these payments.

Where the taxpayer settles a claim for damages, what she is being compensated for must be determined. In Revenue Procedure 67–33, 1967–2 C.B. 659, the Service established procedures for determining tax liability for settlement of claims for damages. The tax treatment of settlements, like the tax treatment of damages, depends on the treatment of the amounts for which the settlement is a substitute. To the extent the settlement is attributable to a taxpayer's claim for the trebling of actual damages, therefore, it will be included in the taxpayer's gross income. But no amount will be attributed to punitive damages if the taxpayer can reasonably establish that actual damages exceeded the amount of the settlement (less legal expenses). In allocating the settlement amount between compensation for lost profits (taxable as ordinary income) and restoration of capital (treated as recovery of basis or, if in excess of basis, perhaps capital gain), however, the tax-free recovery cannot exceed the adjusted basis of the assets involved in the suit. The basis of the assets must be decreased to reflect the restoration of capital resulting from the settlement.

Section 186 permits taxpayers to reduce their taxable damages to reflect earlier losses that they have not been able to deduct fully (for example, because they had insufficient income at the time the injury occurred and net operating loss carryovers expired before they could use the deductions). This provision was intended to prevent injured parties who could not realize the benefit of loss deductions from being exposed to full tax liability for the compensation they received. It allows a deduction in the amount of the lesser of the compensation received (minus legal expenses) or the unrecovered losses sustained from the injury. Recoveries may be deducted only in the amount of actual economic injury; no deduction is permitted for punitive damages or for the noncompensatory two-thirds of treble damage antitrust awards. Reg. § 1.186–1.

B. DAMAGES FOR PERSONAL INJURY

Note on Damages for Personal Injuries

The need to distinguish between personal and business damages is occasioned by § 104(a)(2), which excludes from income "the amount of any damages received (whether by suit or agreement and whether as lump sums or as periodic payments) on account of personal physical injuries or illness." This task is complicated by the fact that tort law, which generates compensation eligible for the § 104 exclusion, usually is indifferent to the personal-business distinction or the distinction between damages for physical or emotional injuries. Prior to 1996, § 104(a)(2) excluded "the amount of any damages received * * * on account of personal injuries or sickness." This simple language led to a tremendous amount of litigation, primarily revolving around nonphysical personal injuries and punitive damages.

After decades of struggle by the lower courts to determine whether a particular injury—such as defamation or age discrimination—was a personal injury, the Supreme Court twice entered the fray to try to craft a definition. See United States v. Burke, 504 U.S. 229 (1992) (holding that back pay received on account of sex discrimination was taxable because personal injury involves only tort-like rights); Commissioner v. Schleier, 515 U.S. 323 (1995) (holding that back pay received on account of age discrimination was not on account of a personal injury). The decision to interpret personal injury to mean tort-like injuries did little to quell the controversies given the increasing coalescence of tort and contract claims. In 1996, Congress substantially narrowed the scope of § 104 by limiting the exclusion to personal *physical injury*. Thus, amounts received for defamation, sexual harassment, age discrimination, racial discrimination, and the like—some of which previously had been excludible—are now taxable.

Section 104(a) also provides that emotional distress is not to be treated as "physical injury" or "sickness." Damages not in excess of the amount paid for medical care attributable to emotional distress are, however, excludible, presumably on the ground that medical expenses are deductible. Legislative history indicates that damages for physical injury or sickness resulting from emotional distress (headaches, insomnia) may not be excluded but damages for emotional distress resulting from physical injury may be. Legislative history also indicates that damages from loss of consortium or emotional distress arising from a physical injury to one's spouse are excluded.

If a settlement or judgment fails to specify exactly why the damages are being paid, it is left to the taxpayer and the IRS to figure out what amounts are paid on account of personal injury and what is paid for something else. That leads to a lot of second-guessing. Basketball fans—who are old enough—may recall the memorable 1997 Chicago Bulls-Timberwolves game where Dennis Rodman came flying off the court and kicked one of the photographers on the sidelines in the groin. Rodman was suspended and fined and the photographer was taken to the hospital. He subsequently sued and settled for $200,000. The photographer claimed the entire $200,000 was paid for the physical injury but the court did not buy that. Pointing out that the settlement agreement included provisions that prevented the two from disparaging or defaming each other and estopped the photographer from publicizing the incident or assisting in a criminal prosecution, the court found that $80,000 was paid for reasons other than physical injury. It basically ignored a provision that provided for $200,000 to be paid to Rodman if the photographer breached the defamation or confidentiality provisions, finding that the remaining $120,000 was attributable to the physical injury from the kick in the groin. Amos v. Commissioner, 86 T.C.M. 663 (2003).

Unlike awards for business damages for lost profits, an award for lost wages arising out of physical injury is excludible under § 104(a)(2). Rev. Rul. 85–97, 1985–2 C.B. 50.

Although at one time the IRS had taken the position that the broad language "amounts received on account of personal injury" excluded punitive damages, it subsequently changed its mind. After taxpayers won several cases in which the courts held that punitive damages were excludible, Congress amended § 104 to make it clear that all punitive damages are taxable. The Supreme Court ruled that the prior language did not exclude punitive damages. O'Gilvie v. United States, 519 U.S. 79 (1996).

Legislation enacted in 2015 excluded from taxation restitution or civil damages awarded for a wrongful conviction. Amounts received for physical injury attributable to the incarceration were already excluded but restitution for the incarceration itself previously had been taxable. The provision was made retroactive for those who claimed a refund within a year of enactment. See § 139F.

NOTES

(A) *Physical Injuries.* Because Section 104(a) excludes only damages for physical injuries, there is an incentive to try to link physical symptoms to emotional or non-physical injury. For example, in Lindsey v. Commissioner, 422 F.3d 684 (8th Cir. 2005), the court held that physical manifestations of underlying emotional distress for which damages were received did not give rise to excludible income because the settlement agreement provided for payments for damage to "emotions, reputation and character." The line between physical sickness arising from emotional distress and emotional distress arising from physical injury or sickness is not always clear. In Domeny v. Commissioner, the taxpayer was able to exclude a settlement payment received from her former employer. The taxpayer had suffered numerous physical problems from multiple sclerosis. She was fired and suffered further physical ailments. The court found that the payment was for physical injury. 90 T.C.M. 2047 (2010). The taxpayer in Blackwood v. Commissioner, however, failed to convince the court that there was physical injury or sickness. She suffered from depression and relapsed when she lost her job, suffering insomnia, migraines, vomiting and back pain. The court required her to include the settlement payment from her employer because it found that she actually suffered from emotional distress, not physical injury. 104 T.C.M. 27 (2012). Legislative history indicates that Congress considers symptoms of emotional distress, such as insomnia, headaches, and stomach aches, as not physical injuries or sickness. Apparently none of them ever had a migraine.

If there is no physical injury, payments for emotional distress, no matter how extreme, are taxable. In Stadnyk v. Commissioner, 96 T.C.M. 278 (2008), aff'd in an unpublished opinion, 367 Fed. Appx. 586 (6th Cir. 2010), the taxpayer purchased a used car with a personal check but the car broke down within minutes of leaving the dealer. Although she tried to contact the dealer, her calls were ignored. She asked the bank to stop payment on the check for "dissatisfied purchase" but instead the bank stamped it as "insufficient funds." The car dealer filed a criminal complaint, the taxpayer was arrested, handcuffed, strip-searched, placed in a holding pen, and indicted for passing a bad check. The bank eventually paid her damages of $49,000, which she excluded from income. Despite the humiliation, emotional distress, and loss of reputation, the taxpayer conceded she suffered no physical injury and the court found that being handcuffed and searched was not per se a physical injury.

The IRS has ruled that compensation awarded under a federal statute to victims of human trafficking is not taxable. Notice 2012–12, 2012–6 I.R.B. 365. In addition to restitution for medical expenses for physical and psychological injury, the state also provides for reimbursement for travel, housing, and child care expenses. The Notice cites no authority for the proposition that the compensation is not taxable.

(B) *Interest*. With the exception of certain tax-exempt interest (which is discussed in the next Section), interest generally is taxable to the recipient. Because the injury may occur long before payment is made by the tortfeasor, the parties may agree that the settlement amount should include interest on the amount of damages from the time of injury. Some state statutes mandate that interest accrue on the award before it is paid. The Tenth Circuit determined that pre-judgment interest was not excludible because it was not "damages received on account of personal injury." Rather it was to compensate the victim for the lost time value of money. Brabson v. United States, 73 F.3d 1040 (10th Cir. 1996). This interpretation puts the taxpayer in the same position he would have been in had he received the excludible damages on the date of the injury and invested the proceeds in an asset or account paying interest.

Suppose the injured party and the tortfeasor simply agree on a lump-sum amount of "damages," which is to be paid several years after the injury.

If they do not explicitly state that the amount reflects a time value element, is anything taxable? In Delaney v. Commissioner, 99 F.3d 20 (1st Cir. 1996), the court determined that a portion of the damages was nonexcludable prejudgment interest even though a settlement reached during the appeals process stated "No interest. No costs." The court clerk had added prejudgment interest to the jury award. If, however, no interest is stated, periodic payments are excluded under § 104(a) even though a portion of each payment is the economic equivalent of interest. E.g., Rev. Rul. 79–220, 1979–2 C.B. 74 (recipient of annuity in satisfaction of a personal injury claim can exclude entire amount).

(C) *Jury Instructions as to Exclusion of Damage Awards.* In Norfolk and Western Ry. Co. v. Liepelt, 444 U.S. 490 (1980), a wrongful death case arising out of the Federal Employers' Liability Act, the Supreme Court held that the jury should be instructed that "your award will not be subject to any income taxes and you should not consider such taxes in fixing the amount of your award." The plaintiff's expert witness had computed the amount of pecuniary loss at about $302,000, and the jury awarded damages of $775,000. The majority assumed that most jurors would be sufficiently "tax conscious" to assume the award would be taxable and therefore would increase the amount of the award by the "imaginary tax" they expected would be due. The Court concluded that the requested instruction was brief and easily understood by the jury, would not be prejudicial to either party, and would "merely eliminate an area of doubt or speculation that might have an improper impact on the computation of damages." Such an instruction "can certainly help by preventing the jury from inflating the award and thus overcompensating the plaintiff on the basis of an erroneous assumption that the judgment will be taxable."

In a vigorous dissent (joined by Justice Marshall), Justice Blackmun argued that "by mandating adjustment of the award by way of reduction for [taxes] on his earnings, the Court appropriates for the tortfeasor a benefit intended to be conferred on the victim or his survivors." Justice Blackmun suggested that Congress had two likely purposes in not taxing wrongful death awards:

> First, [that it] is simply not worthwhile to enact a complex and administratively burdensome system in order to approximate the tax treatment of the income if, in fact, it had been earned over a period of time by the decedent. Second, Congress may have intended to confer a humanitarian benefit on the victim or victims of the tort.

* * *

> Whichever of these concerns it was that motivated Congress, transfer of the tax benefit to the * * * tortfeasor-defendant is inconsistent with that purpose.

Assume, in *Norfolk and Western Ry. Co. v. Liepelt* that the jury would have awarded $300,000 of damages with an instruction and $775,000 without such an instruction. If Congress, in fact, intended the first purpose suggested by Justice Blackmun, to approximate the tax treatment if the income had been earned over a period of time, then the appropriate award is the after-tax income stream. Is Justice Blackmun correct that this appropriates the tax savings to the tortfeasor? If the jury was blissfully ignorant of § 104, presumably they would award the before-tax income stream. In that case, can it be said that the failure to give an instruction about the excludability of damage awards would impose an additional and unwarranted "penalty" on tortfeasors by requiring damages greater than necessary to make the victim whole?

On the other hand, suppose Congress had the second purpose mentioned by Justice Blackmun, "to confer a humanitarian benefit on the victim." The implication is that Congress intended to put the victim in a better position than he would have been in had he not suffered the injury and received the compensation as salary, for example. In that case, would the failure to give the instruction penalize or benefit the victim?

(D) *Policy Justifications for Exclusion.* A number of justifications have been offered for the § 104 exclusion, none of which is entirely satisfactory.

Taxing an award for pain and suffering is offensive. Some have asserted that taxing a recovery due to pain and suffering is offensive and the victim should be assisted rather than taxed. This might be a justification for a tax expenditure, but § 104 then is a peculiar way to accomplish it. There clearly are items exempted by § 104 that do not involve pain and suffering.

A recovery for expenses should not be taxed. If a taxpayer incurred expenses and is reimbursed for them, there should be no income (unless he took a deduction in a prior year). In theory, this justifies excluding expenses that otherwise would be deductible, such as medical expenses, but, as Chapter 3 describes, many taxpayers are unable to deduct their medical expenses because of various limitations. It certainly does not justify excluding wages, which otherwise would be taxed.

A recovery of human capital should not be taxed. If an award is a replacement of human capital, it should not be taxed because the taxpayer has no gain; he has an offsetting economic loss. Thus, payments received for a lost limb, for example, should be exempt. This is akin to a property recovery, although in a property recovery the taxpayer would have no income only if his basis were deemed to be equal to the amount received. It is possible—although mysterious and without statutory authority—that a taxpayer is born with a basis in his body, reputation, etc. The Supreme Court has held, for example, that a spouse has a basis in marital rights equal to their value. United States v. Davis, 370 U.S. 65, 73 n.7 (1962). If this is Congress' reason for exempting recoveries, § 104 creates an inequity for a victim without insurance or one who is unable to recover from the tortfeasor: the taxpayer who loses an arm but receives no recovery has no deduction for a loss of human capital. Furthermore, a taxpayer has no loss for a decline in value of his human capital.

Recoveries for nontaxable items should be tax-free. In many circumstances, a recovery is to compensate the taxpayer for a loss of an item which is itself nontaxable. For example, possessing good health, the use of one's body, enjoying one's reputation, privacy, civil rights, and the freedom from harassment and discrimination are all "psychic benefits" that are untaxed. Recall the discussion on the failure to tax imputed income from services. The payment made by the tortfeasor can be likened to a transfer equal to the imputed income stream from these items that would be untaxed. If this were correct, § 104 is too narrow since it results in taxation of payments for nonphysical injury. There is an essential difference, however: imputed income generally is untaxed due to the absence of a market transaction. The services are not taxed because we would have trouble identifying or valuing them. When the taxpayer converts the services into cash, however, she is taxed. Perhaps, then, when the taxpayer converts body parts or reputation, for example, into cash, she should be taxed. In United States v. Garber, 589 F.2d 843 (5th Cir. 1979), reversed in part on rehearing, 607 F.2d 92 (5th Cir. 1979), the Fifth Circuit held that income derived from the sale of blood plasma is taxable, whether giving blood is classified as a personal service or as the sale of a product. The court held that the substantial amount the taxpayer received for her blood, which contained a rare antibody, was taxable because it produced an economic gain not excluded by statute. Section 104(a)(2) was held not to be applicable.

(E) *Disaster Relief.* Congress occasionally chooses to provide special tax benefits to those who have been injured in combat or disasters or to those who lost property in a federally-declared disaster area. In 2002, for example, Congress enacted generous benefits to those affected by the September 11 terrorist attack. It forgave the federal income tax liabilities for 2000 and 2001 for all those who died in the September 11 attack, as well as the anthrax attacks in the fall of 2001, and the Oklahoma City bombing in 1995. If the victim's tax liability was less than $10,000, the difference was paid to the victim's estate. Also excluded from income are disaster relief payments, disability payments, employer death benefits paid to survivors' families, and payments made by the federal September 11 Victims' Compensation Fund. In 2003 Congress extended this tax relief to astronauts who lost their lives on a space mission, including those who perished in the Columbia space shuttle explosion. In 2017, Congress passed tax relief legislation that eliminated the penalty for early withdrawal of 401(k) retirement savings and the 10 percent floor on casualty loss deductions for victims of all federal disasters declared in 2016, a year of large hurricanes and wildfires in California. The relief also adopts tax credits to encourage employers affected by the hurricanes to keep employees on the payroll.

(F) *Denial of Deductions for Certain Settlements of Sexual Abuse Claims.* The 2017 legislation added a new provision denying business deductions for any settlement, payout or attorney's fees relating to sexual abuse or harassment if such payments are subject to a nondisclosure agreement. See § 162(q).

SECTION 10. TAX-EXEMPT INTEREST

Section 103 generally excludes from income interest on state and local obligations. Such a tax exemption has been provided ever since the federal income tax was adopted in 1913.

The exemption allows state and local governments to pay lower rates of interest on their debt than that paid on taxable corporate bonds of comparable risk. For example, if the market rate of interest is 10 percent on a comparable corporate bond, a municipality could pay only 6.3 percent on its debt and a purchaser in a 37 percent marginal tax bracket would be indifferent between the municipal and the corporate bond, since the after-tax interest rate on the corporate bond would be 6.3 percent. The municipal bond is sometimes said to be subject to an implicit tax due to the reduction in interest. In the above example, the bond is subject to an implicit tax of 37 percent. Although the federal government forfeits the 3.7 percent differential, the state or local government saves the same amount. Taking into account the implicit tax, there is no violation of horizontal equity since the two taxpayers with the same economic income receive the same after-tax return.

Historically, the ratio of yields on tax-exempt issues to taxable issues has generally been about 75 percent, but in some years it has been more than 90 percent. The ratio of yields has varied in response to the general availability of credit, the demand for credit, and the relative demand of state and local governments for credit in the total market. If high-income taxpayers do not purchase the entire tax-exempt bond market, the ratio of the yields on tax-exempt bonds to taxable bonds must rise. In the above example, a taxpayer in the 22 percent bracket would not purchase the municipal bond with a 6.3 percent interest rate because his after-tax yield on the taxable 10 percent corporate bond would be 7.8 percent. Thus, in order to attract purchases by 22 percent-bracket taxpayers, the municipality would need to pay at least 7.8 percent. Notice that a 37 percent-bracket taxpayer who purchased a 7.8 percent municipal bond would receive a 1.5 percentage point windfall—an amount not needed to get him to purchase the bond. As a result of high ratios of tax-exempt to taxable bond yields, high-income taxpayers otherwise subject to high income tax rates (who constitute a major portion of the market for tax-exempt state and local securities) often receive significantly greater tax benefits than necessary for them to prefer tax-exempt to taxable bonds. On the 7.8 percent bond purchased by the 37 percent taxpayer, the federal government will lose the 3.7 percent that it would have received had the taxpayer purchased a 10 percent taxable bond, but the state or local government would receive only a 2.2 percent interest-savings benefit. Thus, the subsidy can be said to be inefficient because it provides benefits to third parties (i.e., the high-income investors) in addition to the benefits to the local government; the revenue cost to the federal government is substantially greater than the savings in interest costs to state and local governments.

Aid to state and local governments would be more efficient if the interest on the bonds was taxable and the holder was entitled to a tax credit. In fact, the windfall to high-income investors could be totally eliminated if the credit was itself treated as taxable interest. There are now a number of examples of bonds with these characteristics. See § 54A (Credit to Holders of Qualified Tax Credit Bonds). Under § 54A(f), the credit is treated as taxable interest and under § 54A(i), ownership of the bond and entitlement to the credit can be separated. The latter provision is important because the credit is not refundable.

It would also be efficient for the state or local government to issue bonds paying the taxable interest rate and the federal government to send a subsidy check to the bond issuer. At one time a state or local government could do just that. When a local government issued bonds paying taxable interest, it received a subsidy from the federal government equal to 35 percent of the interest paid (i.e. keyed to the then-top 35 percent tax rate). These so-called "Build America Bonds," which were part of the 2009 stimulus program, were very popular with local governments and investors. A total of more than $181 billion in bonds were sold during the 21 months the program was in effect.

Distributional Aspects of the Tax Exemption. It is clear that if the present tax exemption were eliminated, the entire burden would not be borne by the purchasers of taxable state and local bonds, who, as a statutory matter, would pay the tax on the interest from the bonds. Elimination of the tax exemption undoubtedly would require higher interest rates for state and local bonds. The benefits of the tax exemption, in effect, are shared by the bondholders and the taxpayers of state and local governments and thus, both would also share the burden of the elimination of the tax exemption.

But descriptions of the distributional effects that would result from repeal of the tax exemption often ignore the effects on interest rates.[2] The sharing of benefits of the tax exemption between bond owners and state and local governments is not taken into account in determining the burdens of such repeal. According to a 2013 Tax Policy Center report, excluding the interest savings to state and local governments, nearly 90 percent of the benefits from the tax exemption accrue to the taxpayers with incomes in the top quintile of income. But when the interest saving is taken into account, the benefits from the tax exemption would appear to be spread far more evenly through the income classes. About half of the benefits would flow to individuals with adjusted gross incomes of $20,000 or less, and less than one-third of the revenue loss benefits individuals with adjusted gross incomes over $100,000.[3]

---

[2] This discussion is based on Michael J. Graetz, "Assessing the Distributional Effects of Income Tax Revision: Some Lessons from Incidence Analysis," 4 J. of Legal Studies 351 (1975).

[3] These figures are based on the assumption that state and local governments will finance the increased interest costs that would result from repeal of the tax exemption through general revenues. They are a rough approximation of a distribution of benefits from the tax exemption. They are based on the assumption that 70 percent of the revenue loss from the tax exemption would be reflected in lower interest costs to state and local governments and that this 70 percent benefits income classes of individuals in proportion to their burdens of general state and local tax revenues. In other words, it assumes that repeal of the exemption would increase interest costs to state and local governments and that these governments would finance the increased interest costs out of general revenues. Of course, the impact of repeal of the exemption would

Would you expect to see a similar shifting of other income tax benefits from one party to another? Can you think of examples?

Constitutional Implications. Although there is a body of opinion that regards it as unconstitutional for the federal government to tax interest paid by state and local governments, recent decisions of the Supreme Court have made it clear that the Constitution grants Congress power to repeal the tax exemption for interest in state and local bonds. In South Carolina v. Baker, 485 U.S. 505 (1988), the Court upheld a provision that taxes interest on state and local bonds unless the bonds are issued in registered (as opposed to bearer) form. The Court rejected the argument that the statute interfered with the state's right to borrow, made borrowing more expensive, and therefore impaired its exercise of sovereign powers.

Some Limitations on Tax-Exempt Bonds. Primarily as a response to the increasing issuance of bonds by state and local governments to finance activities other than general government operations or governmentally owned and operated facilities, Congress has substantially limited the issuance of such bonds. Sections 141–150 contain restrictions on the general exclusion for certain types of private activity or industrial development bonds, arbitrage bonds, and other special types of bonds.

An arbitrage bond is one used by a state or local government to acquire other securities with a higher rate of return. This return would not be taxed to the government because it is tax-exempt. Section 148 imposes severe restrictions on these bonds, so that in most cases the interest on the bond would not be tax-exempt. § 103(b)(2).

An industrial development bond (IDB) is often used as a way to attract a business to a state or locality. The local government is simply a conduit. It borrows the funds, in order to obtain the tax exemption, but the payment of the debt service on the bond is the responsibility of the user of the facility acquired with the bond proceeds. Alarmed at the increasing use of these private activity bonds, Congress limited their use when (1) more than 10 percent of the proceeds is for direct or indirect use in a trade or business of anyone other than a governmental unit (with certain further restrictions); or (2) more than 5 percent of the proceeds of the issue is used to make or finance loans to entities other than state or local governments. § 141(b). Bonds that are used for traditional public activities—such as schools, roads and bridges, and sewers—continue to be exempt without limitation. There are also a number of exceptions to the private activity bond limitations, for example, where the proceeds are used to provide airports, docks and wharves, mass commuting facilities, qualified residential rental projects, facilities for the furnishing of electric

---

vary from state to state but no attempt has been made to take interstate differences into account. The lowering of the top rate from 70 percent in the 1970s to 37 percent today has increased the share of the tax benefits going to state and local governments, so the 70 percent number may now be a bit low, but the principle of the illustration holds.

energy or gas, local district heating or cooling facilities, or high-speed intercity rail facilities. § 142(a). In addition, certain mortgage bonds, small issue bonds, student loan bonds, redevelopment bonds, and bonds where the proceeds are to be used by a charity are also exempt. Other exceptions can be found in §§ 143–147. These arcane rules are of mindboggling complexity and typically left to tax-exempt bond specialists.

Congress has also used the tax exemption to provide below-market financing for specific targeted areas. For example, after the terrorist attacks of 2001, Congress created the Liberty Bond program with $8 billion in tax-exempt funds to rebuild lower Manhattan. Before the exemption expired at the end of 2011 a substantial portion of the funds were used to rebuild office buildings. The developer of the World Trade Center received almost $3 billion through the program, Goldman Sachs financed construction of its headquarters with about $1.5 billion, and Bank of America received $650 million.

Tax-Exempt Bonds of Universities. State and local governments are not the only entities eligible to issue tax-exempt debt. Entities such as hospitals and colleges and universities, which are tax-exempt organizations under § 501(c)(3) can also issue tax-exempt bonds for certain purposes. See § 145. Harvard University, to take a prominent example, had about $2.9 billion of tax-exempt bonds outstanding as of June 30, 2016. The University then also had about $2.2 billion of taxable debt outstanding. While many factors beyond tax status can affect the interest rate on bonds, comparing the average rates of tax-exempt bonds and taxable bonds here gives a good approximation of the benefit to the university. Harvard saved about $23.2 million in 2016 because of its ability and capacity to issue tax-exempt bonds. Assuming a 7.6 percent return, providing that $23.2 million would have required an additional university endowment of $305 million. (Harvard's annual returns on its endowment averaged about 7.6 percent from 2013 through 2017.) Is extending the advantage of issuing tax-exempt bonds to institutions like Harvard University sound policy?

In 2010, Harvard issued two sets of bonds with similar terms, one taxable, the other tax-exempt. (The tax-exempt debt was officially issued by the Massachusetts government on Harvard's behalf, as what are known as revenue bonds.) The market rates for these bonds at the time they were issued were approximately 4.9 percent and 4.0 percent, respectively. This difference implies that the tax rate of the marginal purchaser was 18.4 percent. (A 4.9 percent return subject to a tax rate of 18.4 percent produces an after-tax return of 4.0 percent.)

U.S. Treasury Bonds. The interest on federal bonds, unlike that on state and local bonds is generally subject to tax. There is one exception. Section 135 exempts the interest on certain U.S. savings bonds to the extent the proceeds are less than college tuition and fees for the taxpayer, her spouse or dependents. This exclusion is phased out for married couples with income exceeding $60,000 ($40,000 for a single taxpayer), with these numbers adjusted for inflation after 1990. § 135(b)(2)(B). The actual use of the funds is not traced so that the taxpayer could use other resources to pay for college.

Tax Expenditure Considerations. The tax exemption for general purpose bonds provides an unlimited subsidy. In general, there is no limitation on the number of bonds issued or the amount a state or local government may borrow. Furthermore, the federal government does not exercise control over what projects are funded with general purpose bonds or which states or municipalities are subsidized. It has seemed highly unlikely that Congress would pass an unlimited direct subsidy for local governments. Are there advantages or disadvantages of a subsidy in the form of tax exemption?

CHAPTER 3

DEDUCTIONS AND CREDITS

This Chapter discusses questions that arise in reducing gross income to taxable income by subtracting allowable deductions. Many deductions are necessary to measure income accurately. The deduction for ordinary and necessary business expenses, § 162, is essential if we are to tax net income. Other deductions are not necessary to obtain an accurate measurement of net income, but rather are tax subsidies for certain activities or investments. An example is the immediate write-off for expenses to remove architectural and transportation barriers to the handicapped and elderly found in § 190. Certain deductions, however, are very difficult to categorize. For example, tax experts have hotly debated whether the charitable deduction and medical deduction are subsidies or whether they are needed to properly determine net income.

A deduction is closely related to an exclusion from income; both remove amounts from taxable income. A deduction of an item related to personal consumption may have the same effect as an exclusion from income. If, for example, a taxpayer receives $10,000 of salary and a $1,000 excludable fringe benefit, he will have the same net economic and taxable income if he receives $11,000 of salary and spends $1,000 on a benefit that produces a deduction. As we shall see, in many cases a taxpayer will prefer an exclusion to a deduction because of limits imposed on deductions.

For corporations, allowable deductions serve to reduce gross income to taxable income; for individuals, the computation of taxable income is more cumbersome. The first computational step for individuals is to subtract those deductions allowable in reducing gross income to "adjusted gross income" (AGI) as defined in § 62. Then AGI is reduced to "taxable income" by subtracting the larger of the standard deduction or "itemized deductions." § 63(c). Itemized deductions are, in some cases, fully allowable. In others, they are allowable only to the extent of certain related types of income or only to the extent they exceed certain floors—typically, specified percentages of AGI.

Tax legislation in 2017 added layers of complexity because of Congress' decision to terminate virtually all of the new law's provisions at the end of 2025 to comply with Senate budget rules. Although the clear intention was for these provisions ultimately to become permanent, the statute instead "suspends" certain deductions between 2018 through the end of 2025. At the end of that period, the numerous rules of the pre-2017 law spring back to life in 2026 (unless Congress re-enacts the changes). For example, during this eight-year period, certain "miscellaneous itemized deductions," are disallowed. § 67(g). But, absent further legislation, those deductions will be allowable again in 2026, subject to the "two-percent floor," which provides that only the amount of miscellaneous itemized deductions that exceeds 2 percent of the taxpayer's AGI may be deducted. § 67(a). The 2017 act also suspended deductions for state and local income and property taxes in excess of $10,000 and for personal exemptions, among other items. The temporary nature of the 2017 changes not only creates difficulty for coursebook authors, but it also makes the very complex Internal Revenue Code significantly more difficult to parse.

In addition to deductions that reduce taxable income, this Chapter also considers several income tax credits that offset tax liability. A dollar of tax credit saves a dollar of taxes, while a dollar of deduction saves a fraction of that amount, depending on the taxpayer's tax bracket. For example, a $100 deduction for a taxpayer in the 25 percent bracket saves $25 in taxes whereas a $100 credit saves $100 in taxes regardless of the taxpayer's rate bracket. Typically, a tax credit is allowed only for a specified percentage of the expenditure that qualifies for the credit.

Generally, a taxpayer can use deductions only to the extent of her income for the taxable year. In some cases, the deductions are preserved and carried over to be used in a succeeding taxable year. In other situations, the deductions are lost. Similarly, a credit that is usable only to the extent of the tax liability for the taxable year is nonrefundable. A few credits are refundable, meaning that the taxpayer will receive a check from the government even if he has no tax liability. Some credits can be carried over to a succeeding year. As with deductions, Congress in 2017 made important changes to tax credits, most notably child tax credits, but again these changes expire at the end of 2025 and prior law returns, absent new legislation.

One of the major issues in connection with deductions is timing, especially those deductions relating to capitalization of costs and their recovery, such as through depreciation allowances. Timing issues are extremely important both to tax policy and tax planning. Indeed, as will be detailed subsequently, acceleration of a deduction may be equivalent to a full or partial exclusion of the income generated by the deductible expense.

Is there is a constitutional right to deductions? Could Congress deny all deductions and impose a tax on gross income? Would a tax on gross income constitute a direct tax on wealth that must be apportioned among the states? Or does the Sixteenth Amendment doom such an argument? See Helvering v. Independent Life Insurance Co., 292 U.S. 371, 381 (1934) ("Unquestionably Congress has power to condition, limit or deny deductions from gross income in order to arrive at the net that it chooses to tax."). See also Pedone v. United States, 151 F. Supp. 288, 291 (Ct.Cl.1957) (Congress may "provide that certain costs, the incurring of which is in violation of law or public policy, shall be disregarded in computing gains.").

Courts often state that deductions should be narrowly construed. The usual phrase is "an income tax deduction is a matter of legislative grace and the burden of clearly showing the right to the claimed deduction is on the taxpayer." Interstate Transit Lines v. Commissioner, 319 U.S. 590, 593 (1943). It is true that the taxpayer bears the burden of proving his right to a deduction, but the question should not be approached in terms of a "narrow" construction or "legislative grace." The clear intent of Congress to impose the tax on "taxable income" requires recognition of deductions as well as gross income. When Congress wants to limit deductions, it can do so explicitly.

SECTION 1.   BUSINESS EXPENSES

Note on Ordinary and Necessary Business Expenses

There are a number of Code sections that provide for a deduction for expenses or losses incurred by a business. The primary provision is § 162, which allows a deduction for "all the ordinary and necessary expenses paid or incurred during the taxable year in carrying on any trade or business." This section permits a wide-ranging number of deductions, most of which are commonplace and noncontroversial. The regulations give as examples of deductible business expenses employee wages, annual insurance premiums on business assets, office rent, utilities, and the like.

Section 162 permits deductions only in connection with a trade or business. Section 212 formally permits individuals to deduct "ordinary and necessary" expenses stemming from income-producing activities that do not qualify as a trade or business. Section 212 was Congress' response to Higgins v. Commissioner, 312 U.S. 212 (1941), in which the Supreme Court held that an investor could not treat the management of his own investments as a trade or business and therefore could not deduct the salaries of his assistants, office rent, and similar outlays.

However, thanks to the tax act of 2017, § 212 is a dead letter for the eight tax years from 2018 through the end of 2025. Section 212 is one of the miscellaneous itemized deductions disallowed during that period. § 67(g). Absent further changes, however, beginning in 2026 § 212 will regain its usual form: it applies only to individuals and generally is only a deduction from AGI to obtain taxable income; consequently, the taxpayer must have itemized deductions that exceed the standard deduction in order to take advantage of § 212 expenses. As of 2026, § 212 expenses will be miscellaneous itemized deductions subject to the 2 percent limitation, discussed above. See also page 269 infra.

As if this statutory scheme were not complicated enough, there is an exception: § 212 deductions attributable to rents and royalties are deductible from gross income in determining AGI and, therefore, are not miscellaneous itemized deductions. § 62(a)(4). These deductions continue to be allowed.

These distinctions (as well as others, see, e.g., §§ 163(d), 166(d), 172(d)(4), 469, 1221, and 1231) make it important to know whether an activity is a "trade or business" or an income-producing activity. In Commissioner v. Groetzinger, 480 U.S. 23 (1987), the Supreme Court held that a professional gambler engages in a trade or business if "involved in the activity with continuity and regularity" and with the primary purpose of earning income or profit, even if there is no sale of goods or services. The Seventh Circuit has noted that a taxpayer cannot simply call itself a "business" and make it so:

> The concept of "trade or business" is plastic, CIR v. Groetzinger * * *, but it hardly follows that anything goes. The taxpayers take a "magic words" approach to the subject: if the * * * documents contain the right language, then all is well. The [question is] whether the [taxpayers] reasonably anticipated availing themselves of the privileges they possessed on paper. That is the right question; pen and ink divorced from reasonable business expectations do not a "trade or business" make.

Levin v. Commissioner, 832 F.2d 403, 406 (7th Cir. 1987) (holding that passive investors in a partnership to develop "bacon board dispensers" were not entitled to a research deduction because they had no intention of going into business).

Sections 165(a) and (c) permit deductions for losses incurred in a trade or business or in a profit-seeking activity. In practice the distinction between § 162 and § 165 can become blurred.

The cases and materials presented here do not exhaust the issues arising under § 162, but they do illustrate the more important issues. Section 162 permits a deduction for "all the ordinary and necessary expenses paid or incurred during the taxable year in carrying on any trade or business." Three types of general questions have arisen: (1) To what extent does the phrase "ordinary and necessary" imply that there is a class of nondeductible business expenses? (2) What distinguishes a "trade or business" expense from a personal expense? (3) What separates a deductible expense from a capital outlay?

The latter two questions are essential in defining net income. In contrast, deciding that some expenses are "extraordinary" or "unnecessary," even though they are not capital expenditures and are expended to advance the taxpayer's business, is a departure from the concept of net income in pursuit of some other policy.

The *Welch* case, which follows, is widely cited as putting flesh on the meaning of the phrase "ordinary and necessary;" *Gilliam*, which follows *Welch*, is less typical.

Welch v. Helvering

Supreme Court of the United States, 1933. 290 U.S. 111.

■ MR. JUSTICE CARDOZO delivered the opinion of the Court.

The question to be determined is whether payments by a taxpayer, who is in business as a commission agent, are allowable deductions in the computation of his income if made to the creditors of a bankrupt corporation in an endeavor to strengthen his own standing and credit.

In 1922 petitioner was the secretary of the E.L. Welch Company, a Minnesota corporation, engaged in the grain business. The company was adjudged an involuntary bankrupt, and had a discharge from its debts. Thereafter the petitioner made a contract with the Kellogg Company to purchase grain for it on a commission. In order to reestablish his relations with customers whom he had known when acting for the Welch Company and to solidify his credit and standing, he decided to pay the debts of the Welch business so far as he was able. In fulfilment of that resolve, he made payments of substantial amounts during five successive years. * * * The Commissioner ruled that these payments were not deductible from income as ordinary and necessary expenses, but were rather in the nature of capital expenditures, an outlay for the development of reputation and good will. The Board of Tax Appeals sustained the action of the Commissioner (25 B.T.A. 117), and the Court of Appeals for the Eighth Circuit affirmed. 63 F.2d 976. The case is here on certiorari.

"In computing net income there shall be allowed as deductions * * * all the ordinary and necessary expenses paid or incurred during the taxable year in carrying on any trade or business." [citing predecessors of § 162.]

We may assume that the payments to creditors of the Welch Company were necessary for the development of the petitioner's business, at least in the sense that they were appropriate and helpful. McCulloch v. Maryland, 4 Wheat. 316. He certainly thought they were, and we should be slow to override his judgment. But the problem is not solved when the payments are characterized as necessary. Many necessary payments are charges upon capital. There is need to determine whether they are both necessary and ordinary. Now, what is ordinary, though there must always be a strain of constancy within it, is nonetheless a variable affected by time and place and circumstance. Ordinary in this context does not mean that the payments must be habitual or normal in the sense that the same taxpayer will have to make them often. A lawsuit affecting the safety of a business may happen once in a lifetime. The counsel fees may be so heavy that repetition is unlikely. Nonetheless, the expense is an ordinary one because we know from experience that payments for such a purpose, whether the amount is large or small, are the common and accepted means of defense against attack. * * * The situation is unique in the life of the individual affected, but not in the life of the group, the community, of which he is a part. At such times there are norms of conduct that help to stabilize our judgment, and make it certain and objective. The instance is not erratic, but is brought within a known type.

The line of demarcation is now visible between the case that is here and the one supposed for illustration. We try to classify this act as ordinary or the opposite, and the norms of conduct fail us. No longer can we have recourse to any fund of business experience, to any known business practice. Men do at times pay the debts of others without legal obligation or the lighter obligation imposed by the usages of trade or by neighborly amenities, but they do not do so ordinarily, not even though the result might be to heighten their reputation for generosity and opulence. Indeed, if language is to be read in its natural and common meaning * * *, we should have to say that payment in such circumstances instead of being ordinary is in a high degree extraordinary. There is nothing ordinary in the stimulus evoking it, and none in the response. Here, indeed, as so often in other branches of the law, the decisive distinctions are those of degree and not of kind. One struggles in vain for any verbal formula that will supply a ready touchstone. The standard set up by the statute is not a rule of law; it is rather a way of life. Life in all its fullness must supply the answer to the riddle.

The Commissioner of Internal Revenue resorted to that standard in assessing the petitioner's income, and found that the payments in controversy came closer to capital outlays than to ordinary and necessary expenses in the operation of a business. His ruling has the support of a presumption of correctness, and the petitioner has the burden of proving it to be wrong. * * * Unless we can say from facts within our knowledge that these are ordinary and necessary expenses according to the ways of conduct and the forms of speech prevailing in the business world, the tax must be confirmed. But nothing told us by this record or within the sphere of our judicial notice permits us to give that extension to what is ordinary and necessary. Indeed, to do so would open the door to many bizarre analogies. One man has a family name that is clouded by thefts committed by an ancestor. To add to his own standing he repays the stolen money, wiping off, it may be, his income for the year. The payments figure in his tax return as ordinary expenses. Another man conceives the notion that he will be able to practice his vocation with greater ease and profit if he has an opportunity to enrich his culture. Forthwith the price of his education becomes an expense of the business, reducing the income subject to taxation. There is little difference between these expenses and those in controversy here. Reputation and learning are akin to capital assets, like the good will of an old partnership. * * * For many, they are the only tools with which to hew a pathway to success. The money spent in acquiring them is well and wisely spent. It is not an ordinary expense of the operation of a business.

Many cases in the federal courts deal with phases of the problem presented in the case at bar. To attempt to harmonize them would be a futile task. They involve the appreciation of particular situations, at times with borderline conclusions. * * *

The decree should be

Affirmed.

NOTES

(A) *The Ordinary and Necessary Standard.* Does "life in all its fullness" supply an answer to the riddle of the meaning of "ordinary and necessary"? "Ordinary" and "necessary" are terms of art; it is quite clear that an expense that is neither "ordinary" nor "necessary" in the dictionary sense may still be deductible.

Although the Court in Deputy v. du Pont, 308 U.S. 488, 494 (1940), says that "ordinary" has the "connotation of normal, usual, or customary," it also notes that an expense can be ordinary even though it happens only once in a person's life. It must be, however, common or a frequent occurrence in the type of business involved. Does this mean that the first taxpayer to incur a particular business expense may not deduct it? "Necessary" does not mean essential; it appears to mean appropriate and helpful for the development of the taxpayer's business.

Others have interpreted *Welch* to mean that a capital expenditure is not an ordinary and necessary business deduction. This principle is codified in § 263, which explicitly prohibits a deduction under § 162 for capital expenditures. The Service had argued in *Welch* that the expenses "came closer to capital outlays than to ordinary and necessary expenses in the operation of a business." Perhaps the Court could have decided *Welch* without reference to the "ordinary and necessary" language simply by applying the predecessor of § 263 to this expenditure and denying a deduction on the ground that it was capital. The Supreme Court in Commissioner v. Tellier, infra at page 254, suggests that "this is the principal function of the term 'ordinary.' " Capital expenditures are treated infra at page 309.

(B) *Deduction for Payment of Another's Expenses. Welch* has not led to a general rule that forbids taxpayers from deducting all reimbursements of another's losses. Where such payments are made to protect the payor's own business, they are frequently deductible. If, however, the payor incurs the expense due to a moral obligation, there is no deduction. For example, in Friedman v. Delaney, 171 F.2d 269 (1st Cir. 1948), a lawyer made a payment on behalf of a client when the client would not pay the amount for which the lawyer had settled a case. The lawyer felt that the payment was a moral obligation, although it was not legally enforceable. The court held that the payment was not deductible. In perhaps a one-of-a-kind case, the Tax Court ruled in favor of the late country singer Conway Twitty when he deducted payments made to investors in his restaurant. Jenkins v. Commissioner, 47 T.C.M. 238 (1983). Although the restaurant served unusual Twitty Burgers—beef topped by pineapple slices deep fried in onion ring batter—it went belly up after two years. The court determined that Twitty made the payments to protect his personal business reputation as a country music performer and apparently accepted his testimony that his fans insisted on integrity. The judge who wrote the opinion, himself an amateur singer, performed his self-penned "Ode to Conway Twitty" when he announced the result. The IRS announced its non-acquiescence in the case in "Ode to Conway Twitty: Reprise." AOD 1984–22 (Mar. 23, 1984).

In Capital Video Corp. v. Commissioner, 311 F.3d 458 (1st Cir. 2002), a corporation paid the legal fees of its sole shareholder who was convicted of conspiracy in a scheme to avoid taxes that should have been paid on "tribute payments" made by the shareholder to a Gambino family capo for his help in fending off extortion attempts. The corporation argued that the business— distribution of pornographic tapes and a show called "Night Dreams" in Las Vegas—would have been in danger if the shareholder had been convicted. The court found that the payments of the legal fees did not have sufficient business relationship with the protection or promotion of Capital Video's business.

Gilliam v. Commissioner

United States Tax Court, 1986. 51 T.C.M. 515.

■ CHABOT, JUDGE: * * * Gilliam is, and was at all material periods, a noted artist. His works have been exhibited in numerous art galleries throughout the United States and Europe * * * In addition, Gilliam is, and was at all material periods, a teacher of art. On occasion, Gilliam lectured and taught art at various institutions.

Gilliam accepted an invitation to lecture and teach for a week at the Memphis Academy of Arts in Memphis, Tennessee. On Sunday, February 23, 1975, he flew to Memphis to fulfill this business obligation.

Gilliam had a history of hospitalizations for mental and emotional disturbances and continued to be under psychiatric care until the time of his trip to Memphis.

Before his Memphis trip, Gilliam created a 225-foot painting for the Thirty-fourth Biennial Exhibition of American Painting at the Corcoran Gallery of Art (hereinafter sometimes referred to as "the Exhibition"). The Exhibition opened on Friday evening, February 21, 1975. In addition, Gilliam was in the process of preparing a giant mural for an outside wall of the Philadelphia Museum of Art for the 1975 Spring Festival in Philadelphia. The budget plans for this mural were due on Monday, February 24, 1975.

On the night before his Memphis trip, Gilliam felt anxious and unable to rest. * * * On Sunday, February 23, 1975 * * * he boarded American Airlines flight 395 at Washington National Airport, Washington, D.C., bound for Memphis. About one and one-half hours after the airplane departed Washington National Airport, Gilliam began to act in an irrational manner. He talked of bizarre events and had difficulty in speaking. According to some witnesses, he appeared to be airsick and held his head. Gilliam began to feel trapped, anxious, disoriented, and very agitated. Gilliam said that the plane was going to crash and that he wanted a life raft. Gilliam entered the aisle and, while going from one end of the airplane to the other, he tried to exit from three different doors. Then Gilliam struck * * * another passenger, several times with a telephone receiver. Gilliam also threatened the navigator and a stewardess, called for help, and cried * * *.

On arriving in Memphis, Gilliam was arrested by Federal officials. On March 10, 1975, Gilliam was indicted. * * * Gilliam entered a plea of not guilty to the criminal charges. * * * [T]he district court granted Gilliam's motion for a judgment of acquittal by reason of temporary insanity. Petitioners paid $8,250 and $8,600 for legal fees in 1975 and 1976.

Petitioners contend that they are entitled to deduct the amounts paid in defense of the criminal prosecution and in settlement of the related civil claim under section 162. Petitioners maintain that the instant case is directly controlled by our decision in Dancer v. Commissioner, 73 T.C. 1103 (1980). According to petitioners, "[t]he clear holding of Dancer is * * * that expenses for litigation arising out of an accident which occurs during a business trip are deductible as ordinary and necessary business expenses." Respondent contends that the legal fees paid are not deductible under either section 162 or section 212 because the criminal charges against Gilliam were neither directly connected with nor proximately resulted from his trade or business and the legal fees were not paid for the production of income. Respondent maintains that "the criminal charges which arose as a result of * * * [the incident on the airplane], could hardly be deemed 'ordinary,' given the nature of [Gilliam's] profession." Respondent contends "that the provisions of section 262 control this situation." We agree with respondent that the expenses are not ordinary expenses of Gilliam's trade or business. * * * In Deputy v. du Pont, the Supreme Court set forth a guide for application of the statutory requirement that the expense be "ordinary", as follows (308 U.S. at 494–497):

> Ordinary has the connotation of normal, usual, or customary. To be sure, an expense may be ordinary though it happen but once in the taxpayer's lifetime * * * Yet the transaction which gives rise to it must be of common or frequent occurrence in the type of business involved. Hence, the fact that a particular expense would be an ordinary or common one in the course of one business * * * does not necessarily make it such in connection with another business. One of the extremely relevant circumstances is the nature and scope of the particular business out of which the expense in question accrued.

Gilliam is a noted artist and teacher of art. It undoubtedly is ordinary for people in Gilliam's trades or businesses to travel (and to travel by air) in the course of such trades or businesses; however, we do not believe it is ordinary for people in such trades or businesses to be involved in altercations of the sort here involved in the course of any such travel. The travel was not itself the conduct of Gilliam's trades or businesses. Also, the expenses here involved are not strictly a cost of Gilliam's transportation. Finally, it is obvious that neither the altercation nor the expenses were undertaken to further Gilliam's trades or businesses.

We conclude that Gilliam's expenses are not ordinary expenses of his trades or businesses.

It is instructive to compare the instant case with Dancer v. Commissioner, supra, upon which petitioners rely. * * * In Dancer, the taxpayer was driving an automobile; he caused an accident which resulted in injuries to a child. The relevant expenses were the taxpayer's payments to settle the civil claims arising from the accident.

In Dancer, we stated as follows:

> It is true that the expenditure in the instant case did not further petitioner's business in any economic sense; nor is it, we hope, the type of expenditure that many businesses are called upon to pay. Nevertheless, neither factor lessens the direct relationship between the expenditure and the business. Automobile travel by petitioner was an integral part of this business. * * * As unfortunate as it may be, lapses by drivers seem to be an inseparable incident of driving a car. Costs incurred as a result of such an incident are just as much a part of overall business expenses as the cost of fuel.

Dancer is distinguishable.

NOTES

(A) *Carrying on a Trade or Business.* As *Gilliam* states, an expense must be incurred in carrying on a trade or business in order to be deductible under § 162. Note that the court says that the travel itself was not the conduct of Gilliam's business. Suppose at the lecture in Memphis Gilliam had slugged someone who had disparaged his art? Could he have deducted expenses in connection with that altercation? This issue is closely related to distinguishing between personal and business expenses, which is discussed infra at page 270.

(B) *Sports Fines.* In 2007, the NFL imposed a fine of $500,000 on Coach Bill Belichick of the New England Patriots for spying on the opposing team's defensive signals. Roger Goodell, the Commissioner of the NFL, wrote to the Patriots that the spying was a "calculated and deliberate attempt to avoid long-standing rules designed to encourage fair play and promote honest competition on the playing field." Would such a fine be deductible under the tests set forth in *Gilliam*? Cheating certainly happens fairly frequently in sports. Indeed, the NFL fined the Patriots as a team in 2015 over the so-called Deflategate scandal, which alleged that the team had deliberately underinflated footballs in a championship game. And cheating of this kind seems clearly business-related, rather than personal. Note that Section 162(f) would not apply (because that section limits only deductions for fines imposed by governments, not the NFL).

(C) *Legal Expenses.* Although one might argue that litigation costs are inherently profit motivated, at least whenever money will change hands as a result of the litigation, the courts have not provided such generous tax treatment for legal fees. In United States v. Gilmore, 372 U.S. 39 (1963), the taxpayer sought to deduct legal expenses incurred in contesting a divorce property settlement. The Court developed an "origin of the claim" test to distinguish deductible from nondeductible litigation expenses; the spouse's claim originated in the marital relationship, so the costs of opposing it were personal and nondeductible.

Where the litigation is criminal rather than civil, the courts have made deductibility turn on the origin of the government's charges. Taxpayers may deduct only the cost of defending against prosecutions that stem from profit-seeking activities. Compare Commissioner v. Tellier infra at page 254 (deduction allowed for unsuccessful defense against securities act violations by underwriter), with Hylton v. Commissioner, 32 T.C.M. 1238 (1973) (no deduction for successful defense against murder charges resulting from domestic dispute).

A. REASONABLE ALLOWANCE FOR SALARIES

Exacto Spring Corporation v. Commissioner

United States Court of Appeals, Seventh Circuit, 1999. 196 F.3d 833.

■ POSNER, CHIEF JUDGE. This appeal from a judgment by the Tax Court requires us to interpret and apply § 162(a)(1), which allows a business to deduct from its income its "ordinary and necessary" business expenses, including a "reasonable allowance for salaries or other compensation for personal services actually rendered." In 1993 and 1994, Exacto Spring Corporation, a closely held corporation engaged in the manufacture of precision springs, paid its cofounder, chief executive, and principal owner, William Heitz, $1.3 and $1.0 million, respectively, in salary. The Internal Revenue Service thought this amount excessive, that Heitz should not have been paid more than $381,000 in 1993 or $400,000 in 1994, * * * The Tax Court * * * found that the maximum reasonable compensation for Heitz would have been $900,000 in the earlier year and $700,000 in the later one. * * *

In reaching its conclusion, the tax court applied a test that requires the consideration of seven factors: "(1) the type and extent of the services rendered, (2) the scarcity of qualified employees, (3) the qualifications and prior earning capacity of the employee, (4) the contributions of the employee to the business venture, (5) the net earnings of the employer, (6) the prevailing compensation paid to employees with comparable jobs, and (7) the peculiar characteristics." It is apparent that this test, though it or variants of it (one of which has the astonishing total of 21 factors), * * * are encountered in many cases, * * * leaves much to be desired—being, like many other multi-factor tests, "redundant, incomplete, and unclear." * * *

To begin with, it is nondirective. No indication is given of how the factors are to be weighed in the event they don't all line up on one side. And many of the factors, such as the type and extent of services rendered, the scarcity of qualified employees, and the peculiar characteristics of the employer's business, are vague.

Second, the factors do not bear a clear relation either to each other or to the primary purpose of section 162(a)(1), which is to prevent dividends (or in some cases gifts), which are not deductible from corporate income, from being disguised as salary, which is. Suppose that an employee who let us say was, like Heitz, a founder and the chief executive officer and principal owner of the taxpayer rendered no services at all but received a huge salary. It would be absurd to allow the whole or for that matter any part of his salary to be deducted as an ordinary and necessary business expense even if he were well qualified to be CEO of the company, the company had substantial net earnings, CEOS of similar companies were paid a lot, and it was a business in which high salaries are common. The multifactor test would not prevent the Tax Court from allowing a deduction in such a case even though the corporation obviously was seeking to reduce its taxable income by disguising earnings as salary. The court would not allow the deduction, but not because of anything in the multi-factor test; rather because it would be apparent that the payment to the employee was not in fact for his services to the company. Treas. Reg. § 1.162–7(a).

Third, the seven-factor test invites the Tax Court to set itself up as a superpersonnel department for closely held corporations, a role unsuitable for courts. * * * The test * * * invites the court to decide what the taxpayer's employees *should* be paid on the basis of the judges' own ideas of what jobs are comparable, what relation an employee's salary should bear to the corporation's net earnings, what types of business should pay abnormally high (or low) salaries, and so forth. The judges of the Tax Court are not equipped by training or experience to determine the salaries of corporate officers; no judges are.

Fourth, since the test cannot itself determine the outcome of a dispute because of its nondirective character, it invites the making of arbitrary decisions based on uncanalized discretion or unprincipled rules of thumb. The Tax Court in this case essentially added the IRS's determination of the maximum that Mr. Heitz should have been paid in 1993 and 1994 to what he was in fact paid, and divided the sum by two. It cut the baby in half. One would have to be awfully naive to believe that the seven-factor test generated this pleasing symmetry.

Fifth, because the reaction of the Tax Court to a challenge to the deduction of executive compensation is unpredictable, corporations run unavoidable legal risks in determining a level of compensation that may be indispensable to the success of their business.

The drawbacks of the multi-factor test are well illustrated by its purported application by the Tax Court in this case. With regard to factor (1), the court found that Heitz was "indispensable to Exacto's business" and "essential to Exacto's success." Heitz is not only Exacto's CEO; he is also the company's chief salesman and marketing man plus the head of its research and development efforts and its principal inventor. The company's entire success appears to be due on the one hand to the research and development conducted by him and on the other hand to his marketing of these innovations (though he receives some additional compensation for his marketing efforts from a subsidiary of Exacto). The court decided that factor (1) favored Exacto.

Likewise factor (2), for, as the court pointed out, the design of precision springs, which is Heitz's specialty, is "an extremely specialized branch of mechanical engineering, and there are very few engineers who have made careers specializing in this area," let alone engineers like Heitz who have "the ability to identify and attract clients and to develop springs to perform a specific function for that client. * * * It would have been very difficult to replace Mr. Heitz." Notice how factors (1) and (2) turn out to be nearly identical.

Factors (3) and (4) also supported Exacto, the court found. "Mr. Heitz is highly qualified to run Exacto as a result of his education, training, experience, and motivation. Mr. Heitz has over 40 years of highly successful experience in the field of spring design." And his "efforts were of great value to the corporation." So factor (4) duplicated (2), and so the first four factors turn out to be really only two.

With regard to the fifth factor—the employer's (Exacto's) net earnings—the tax court was noncommittal. Exacto had reported a loss in 1993 and very little taxable income in 1994. But it conceded having taken some improper deductions in those years unrelated to Heitz's salary. After adjusting Exacto's income to remove these deductions, the court found that Exacto had earned more than $1 million in each of the years at issue net of Heitz's supposedly inflated salary.

The court was noncommittal with regard to the sixth factor— earnings of comparable employees—as well. The evidence bearing on this factor had been presented by expert witnesses, one on each side, and the court was critical of both. The taxpayer's witness had arrived at his estimate of Heitz's maximum reasonable compensation in part by aggregating the salaries that Exacto would have had to pay to hire four people each to wear one of Heitz's "hats," as chief executive officer, chief manufacturing executive, chief research and development officer, and chief sales and marketing executive. * * * [S]alaries are determined not by the method of comparable worth but, like other prices, by the market, which is to say by conditions of demand and supply. * * *

The Internal Revenue Service's expert witness sensibly considered whether Heitz's compensation was consistent with Exacto's investors' earning a reasonable return (adjusted for the risk of Exacto's business), which he calculated to be 13 percent. * * *

What is puzzling is how disallowing deductions and thus increasing the taxpayer's tax bill could increase the investors' return. What investors care about is the corporate income available to pay dividends or be reinvested; obviously money paid in taxes to the Internal Revenue Service is not available for either purpose. The reasonableness of Heitz's compensation thus depends not on Exacto's taxable income but on the corporation's profitability to the investors. * * * Both parties, plus the Tax Court, based their estimates of investors' returns on the after-tax income shown on Exacto's tax returns * * * rather than on Exacto's real profits. * * * The approach is inconsistent with a realistic assessment of the investors' rate of return, but as no one in the case questions it we shall not make an issue of it.

Finally, under factor (7) ("peculiar characteristics"), the court first and rightly brushed aside the IRS's argument that the low level of dividends paid by Exacto (zero in the two years at issue, but never very high) was evidence that the corporation was paying Heitz dividends in the form of salary. The court pointed out that shareholders may not want dividends. They may prefer the corporation to retain its earnings, causing the value of the corporation to rise and thus enabling the shareholders to obtain corporate earnings in the form of capital gains taxed at a lower rate than ordinary income. The court also noted that while Heitz, as the owner of 55 percent of Exacto's common stock, obviously was in a position to influence his salary, the corporation's two other major shareholders, each with 20 percent of the stock, had approved it. They had not themselves been paid a salary or other compensation, and are not relatives of Heitz; they had no financial or other incentive to allow Heitz to siphon off dividends in the form of salary.

Having run through the seven factors, all of which either favored the taxpayer or were neutral, the court reached a stunning conclusion: "We have considered the factors relevant in deciding reasonable compensation for Mr. Heitz. On the basis of all the evidence, we hold that reasonable compensation for Mr. Heitz" was much less than Exacto paid him. The court's only effort at explaining this result when Heitz had passed the seven-factor test with flying colors was that "we have balanced Mr. Heitz' unique selling and technical ability, his years of experience, and the difficulty of replacing Mr. Heitz with the fact that the corporate entity would have shown a reasonable return for the equity holders, after considering petitioners' concessions." But "the fact that the corporate entity would have shown a reasonable return for the equity holders" after the concessions is on the same side of the balance as the other factors; it does not favor the Internal Revenue Service's position. The government's lawyer was forced to concede at the argument of the appeal that she could not deny the possibility that the Tax Court had pulled its figures for Heitz's allowable compensation out of a hat.

The failure of the Tax Court's reasoning to support its result would alone require a remand. But the problem with the court's opinion goes deeper. The test it applied does not provide adequate guidance to a rational decision. We owe no deference to the tax court's statutory interpretations, its relation to us being that of a district court to a court of appeals, not that of an administrative agency to a court of appeals. The federal courts of appeals, whose decisions do of course have weight as authority with us even when they are not our own decisions, have been moving toward a much simpler and more purposive test, the "independent investor" test. * * * We applaud the trend and join it.

Because judges tend to downplay the element of judicial creativity in adapting law to fresh insights and changed circumstances, the cases * * * prefer to say * * * that the "independent investor" test is the "lens" through which they view the seven (or however many) factors of the orthodox test. But that is a formality. The new test dissolves the old and returns the inquiry to basics. The Internal Revenue Code limits the amount of salary that a corporation can deduct from its income primarily in order to prevent the corporation from eluding the corporate income tax by paying dividends but calling them salary because salary is deductible and dividends are not. (Perhaps they should be, to avoid double taxation of corporate earnings, but that is not the law.) In the case of a publicly held company, where the salaries of the highest executives are fixed by a board of directors that those executives do not control, the danger of siphoning corporate earnings to executives in the form of salary is not acute. The danger is much greater in the case of a closely held corporation, in which ownership and management tend to coincide; unfortunately, as the opinion of the Tax Court in this case illustrates, judges are not competent to decide what business executives are worth.

There is, fortunately, an indirect market test, as recognized by the Internal Revenue Service's expert witness. A corporation can be conceptualized as a contract in which the owner of assets hires a person to manage them. The owner pays the manager a salary and in exchange the manager works to increase the value of the assets that have been entrusted to his management; that increase can be expressed as a rate of return to the owner's investment. The higher the rate of return (adjusted for risk) that a manager can generate, the greater the salary he can command. If the rate of return is extremely high, it will be difficult to prove that the manager is being overpaid, for it will be implausible that if he quit if his salary was cut, and he was replaced by a lower-paid manager, the owner would be better off; it would be killing the goose that lays the golden egg. The service's expert believed that investors in a firm like Exacto would expect a 13 percent return on their investment. Presumably they would be delighted with more. They would be *overjoyed* to receive a return more than 50 percent greater than they expected— and 20 percent, the return that the tax court found that investors in Exacto had obtained, is more than 50 percent greater than the benchmark return of 13 percent.

When, notwithstanding the CEO's "exorbitant" salary (as it might appear to a judge or other modestly paid official), the investors in his company are obtaining a far higher return than they had any reason to expect, his salary is presumptively reasonable. We say "presumptively" because we can imagine cases in which the return, though very high, is not due to the CEO's exertions. Suppose Exacto had been an unprofitable company that suddenly learned that its factory was sitting on an oil field, and when oil revenues started to pour in its owner raised his salary from $50,000 a year to $1.3 million. The presumption of reasonableness would be rebutted. There is no suggestion of anything of that sort here and likewise no suggestion that Mr. Heitz was merely the titular chief executive and the company was actually run by someone else, which would be another basis for rebuttal.

The government could still have prevailed by showing that while Heitz's salary may have been no greater than would be reasonable in the circumstances, the company did not in fact intend to pay him that amount as salary, that his salary really did include a concealed dividend though it need not have. This is material (and the "independent investor" test, like the multifactor test that it replaces, thus [is] incomplete, though invaluable) because any business expense to be deductible must be, as we noted earlier, a bona fide expense as well as reasonable in amount. The fact that Heitz's salary was approved by the other owners of the corporation, who had no incentive to disguise a dividend as salary, goes far to rebut any inference of bad faith here, which in any event the Tax Court did not draw and the government does not ask us to draw.

Reversed.

NOTES

(A) *Reasonable Allowance.* If the language "a reasonable allowance for salaries or other compensation" were not in the Code, would the result in *Exacto Spring* have been any different? Since the general language of § 162 would surely permit a deduction for salaries, the more specific language generally is thought to limit the deduction for salaries that exceed a reasonable amount. Why is such a limitation necessary? Legislative history indicates that the language originally was added to permit taxpayers to take deductions for salaries greater than the amounts actually paid to employees in order to reduce the World War I excess profits tax. See Erwin Griswold, "New Light on 'A Reasonable Allowance for Salaries'," 59 Harv.L. Rev. 286 (1945).

Despite its original purpose, the language has come to serve as a check on salary deductions where the taxpayer is attempting to substitute compensation for a nondeductible expenditure. There are two general situations where it might be appropriate to recharacterize the "unreasonable salary" as something else. Corporate earnings distributed to shareholders as dividends are taxed twice, once at the corporate level and again at the shareholder level. This "double taxation" is unusual; profits of trusts, partnerships, and proprietorships generally are taxed only once, whether distributed or retained. Amounts paid by corporations to employees as salary, however, are deductible to the corporation and are taxed only to the employee. A payment is taxed twice if the corporation is denied a deduction (because the amount is "unreasonable") while the recipient nevertheless must include the amount in income. Since a single tax at the individual level is always less than two levels of tax, regardless of rates, there is an incentive for a corporation to give a shareholder/employee salary rather than a dividend distribution. An amount paid to a shareholder that does not actually represent compensation for services rendered is, under our system, subject to double, rather than single taxation.

Today, however, the double taxation of corporate income is essentially limited to large publicly held companies. Closely held enterprises can be formed as limited liability companies, which escape corporate tax since the tax law treats them as partnerships, or can elect Subchapter S status, which also avoids any corporate-level tax. The only closely held businesses now subject to the corporate tax are corporations that fail to convert to pass-through form because they might have to pay the tax on unrealized appreciation of their assets, or for some other reason. Even though the statute itself draws no distinction between publicly and closely held corporations, the IRS never challenges as unreasonable—no matter how large—salaries paid to executives of large publicly held companies, where the double corporate tax has its principal force. Corporate governance mechanisms, independent directors, and shareholder rights, along with the stock market itself, presumably are thought to guard against the payment of unreasonable amounts to executives. But at today's levels, it seems likely that a portion of many executives' salaries is a diversion of amounts that otherwise would be paid to shareholders as dividends. And the amounts at stake are far greater than those at issue in cases like *Exacto Spring*. This may be why Congress has limited deductions for salaries to certain corporate executives under § 162(m) discussed in Note (D) below.

Income transferred by gift is also taxed once to the donor, who is not allowed a deduction, but not again to the donee who enjoys the § 102 exclusion. Thus, there is no question of double taxation. But where two employees are related, there is an incentive to overcompensate the taxpayer in the lower bracket to minimize the total taxes on the two family members. Similarly, putting a family member on the corporate payroll may permit the taxpayer to make support payments out of pretax income.

If the disguised salary is unreasonable, how does that affect the taxation of the recipient? A shareholder is taxed on the receipt of a dividend, albeit at a lower rate than salary income. § 61(a)(7). A gift, however, is excluded. But see § 102(c). Would the donor have the requisite disinterested generosity? See Smith v. Manning, 189 F.2d 345 (3d Cir. 1951) (payments made by owner to daughters who worked in the business that were held to be unreasonable could not be treated as excludible gifts because there was no donative intent).

In the 2017 legislation, Congress enacted a special 20 percent reduction in taxable income for self-employed proprietors and owners of interests in pass-through businesses, such as partnerships, limited liability companies, and Subchapter S corporations. § 199A. This tax break does not apply to "reasonable compensation" in certain cases. § 199A(c)(4). This constraint may substantially increase the litigation over what constitutes "reasonable compensation." Section 199A is discussed further in Chapter 4 at page 535.

Except where a gift or dividend is masquerading as salary or where the 20 percent reduction in taxable income for flow-through businesses is at stake, why should the IRS or the courts question the reasonableness of the amount of compensation? What policy is served by a general limitation on salary deductions? Why should the Service second guess a business judgment as to salary? As the court points out in *Exacto Spring*, one result of the factors approach is to set the court up as a "superpersonnel department," substituting the court's judgment as to what is a reasonable salary for that of the business. The court may have an entirely different view about an individual's worth than does the market. It may also bring to the decision some questionable judgments. Consider Thomas A. Curtis, M.D., Inc. v. Commissioner, 67 T.C.M. 1958 (1994). The Service questioned the payment of roughly $500,000 in salary to Ellen Curtis, a registered nurse with extensive training, who organized and ran the business, which provided psychiatric treatment and reports to the court with respect to worker's compensation cases. The court detailed Ms. Curtis' training, background, and work hours (60–70 per week). It also noted that she had set up the six-office operation, hired all the psychologists, and supervised the 60–80 employees. Among other laudatory statements, the court said, "Ms. Curtis' efforts have been a primary reason for the corporation's success" and "[i]n the case at hand, the importance of Ms. Curtis' role cannot be questioned," and her "vision * * * and ability * * * have been of paramount importance." Nevertheless, without really explaining its decision, the court found that only $239,000 of Ms. Curtis' salary was reasonable. Her husband, *Dr.* Curtis (the corporation's other shareholder), was paid an identical salary but the IRS failed to question its reasonableness. The taxpayer argued that the IRS had "taken an inconsistent position by questioning Ms. Curtis' amount of compensation but not the compensation paid to Dr. Curtis," contending that the IRS position "is 'antediluvian' and constitutes sexual discrimination." The Tax Court said it would not look behind the IRS's decision to challenge the salary of only the female nurse and not the male doctor.

(B) *Absence of Dividends.* A failure to pay dividends is an important, although not conclusive factor. The IRS has rejected an approach that would require a reasonable return on capital, Rev. Rul. 79–8, 1979–1 C.B. 92, but a number of courts have noted that an absence of dividends is troubling. See, e.g., Charles McCandless Tile Service v. United States, 422 F.2d 1336 (Ct.Cl.1970). In *McCandless,* the Court of Claims held that even though compensation paid to two shareholder-employees was reasonable in amount, the payments "necessarily" contained disguised dividends because the closely held corporation had been profitable but had never paid dividends since its formation. This holding has been referred to as the "automatic dividend" rule. It has been criticized by commentators and rejected by other courts. As Judge Posner notes in *Exacto Spring,* investors may prefer (perhaps for tax reasons) that the corporation retain and reinvest its earnings and therefore would neither demand nor want that earnings be distributed as dividends. The incentive for a corporation to retain earnings rather than distribute them as dividends to shareholders has been increased by the 2017 reduction of the corporate tax rate from 35 to 21 percent.

Other courts have continued to look at the factors criticized in the principal case, but have viewed them from the perspective of an investor. In Dexsil Corp. v. Commissioner, 147 F.3d 96 (2d Cir. 1998), the Court of Appeals vacated and remanded a Tax Court decision holding a part of compensation paid to Ted Lynn, the company's founder, key officer, and its majority shareholder, to be unreasonable because the Tax Court had failed to assess "the entire tableau from the perspective of an independent investor." The Second Circuit stated:

> The independent investor test is not a separate autonomous factor; rather, it provides a lens through which the entire analysis should be viewed. * * * Thus, if the company's earnings on equity, when viewed in relation to such factors as the company's overall performance and levels of compensation, "remain at a level that would satisfy an independent investor, there is a strong indication that management is providing compensable services and that profits are not being siphoned out of the company disguised as salary."

The Tax Court refused to follow the independent investor test, Menard, Inc. v. Commissioner, 89 T.C.M. 656 (2005), but was reversed by the Seventh Circuit. 560 F.3d 620 (7th Cir. 2009). Judge Posner, again writing for the court, found a $20 million salary payable to the CEO and majority shareholder reasonable because the company's rate of return on equity for the year was 18.8 percent, more than much bigger competitors. The court noted that no shareholder seemed to have complained about receiving "only" an 18.8 percent return and that the uncontradicted evidence was that Menard was a workaholic. The court gave short shrift to the concerns of the Tax Court that Menard had an agreement to repay his bonus if it was disallowed by the IRS and that his bonus "looked" like a dividend. It also said that the facts that no dividends had been paid at all, that the salary was paid at year end, and that no outside advice was sought on compensation, were all irrelevant. Judge Posner thought it much more important that Menard's salary structure was quite risky—if the company had a bad year, Menard would have earned only $157,000 (as he noted, less than a federal judge). On average, he speculated, Menard's salary was probably quite less than the $20 million for the year in question. Finally Posner criticized the IRS for focusing only on "salary," failing to take into account other forms of compensation like options and severance, in comparing Menard to the CEOs of Home Depot and Lowe's (Menard, Inc.'s competitors). Unlike the Second and Seventh Circuits, the First, Ninth, and Tenth Circuits have declined to follow the independent investor test and instead rely on the traditional multi-part factor test rejected in *Exacto Spring*. Eberl's Claim Service, Inc. v. Commissioner, 249 F.3d 994 (10th Cir. 2001), aff'g 77 T.C.M. 2336 (1999); Haffner's Service Stations, Inc. v. Commissioner, 326 F.3d 1 (1st Cir. 2003); Metro Leasing and Development Corp. v. Commissioner, 376 F.3d 1015 (9th Cir. 2004). The Fifth Circuit has reaffirmed use of the multi-factor test without referring to the alternative test. Brewer Quality Homes, Inc. v. Commissioner, 122 Fed.Appx. 88 (5th Cir. 2004) (unpublished opinion).

Judge Posner doesn't always find that the "independent investor" test is met. In Mulcahy, Pauritsch, Salvador & Co. v. Comm'r, 680 F.3d 867 (7th Cir. 2012), his majority opinion held that the consulting fees paid to entities owned by owner-employees of an accounting firm were, in fact, disguised dividends and not reasonable compensation. These fees reduced the net income of the firm to effectively zero on revenue between $5 million and $7 million. The independent investor test was not met because, "judging by the salaries received by the founding shareholders, the firm was doing fine" yet was generating no return for equity investors. The court noted that the independent investor test is not helpful when dealing with a small professional services firm without meaningful capital against which to judge the return. However, the firm in this case had "physical capital to support some 40 employees in multiple branches, and [ ] intangible capital in the form of client lists and brand equity—and capital in a solvent firm generates earnings." Judge Posner also rejected the taxpayer's argument that the fees could not be dividends because they were allocated to the owners based on hours worked rather than capital contributed.

The *McCandless* rule, thus, may not be dead. What if the salary is reasonable in amount but the employer does not have the requisite compensatory intent? Suppose one of the employer's motives is to avoid paying nondeductible dividends? In O.S.C. & Associates, Inc. v. Commissioner, 187 F.3d 1116 (9th Cir. 1999), the court held that to be deductible, the employer's purpose for making the payments must be compensatory. In *O.S.C. & Associates*, the corporation adopted an incentive compensation plan and payments were made to two shareholder-employees according to their stock ownership. The court determined that most of the payments were disguised dividends, intended to be a distribution of excess profits, even though the total amount did not exceed an amount determined by the IRS to be reasonable compensation. Thus, even if the compensation is reasonable, it will not be deductible unless the employer possesses the necessary compensatory intent.

(C) *Repayment of Unreasonable Salary.* Suppose the employee is required to repay any salary that is held to be unreasonable. At least one court has implied that a repayment agreement is evidence of "unreasonableness." Charles Schneider & Co. v. Commissioner, 500 F.2d 148, 155 (8th Cir. 1974). But see Rev. Rul. 69–115, 1969–1 C.B. 50 (allowing a deduction where the repayment is made pursuant to an agreement entered into prior to the payment). (Recall, however, that no deduction is allowed for employee business expenses paid or incurred between 2018 and the end of 2025 under the 2017 legislation.)

(D) *Executive Compensation.* Section 162(m) denies a deduction for compensation in excess of $1 million paid to the principal executive officer, the principal financial officer, or any of the three other most highly compensated officers of a publicly held corporation. The 2017 tax act substantially strengthened the § 162(m) disallowance by eliminating exceptions for commissions and performance-based compensation. Under prior law, many corporations were able to avoid the $1 million limitation by structuring executive compensation to fall within those exceptions. The 2017 act also expanded the coverage of § 162(m) to certain large, privately-held corporations.

Is a provision such as § 162(m) appropriate in an income tax? If a business determines that $2 million is the proper salary for an executive, why should the government disallow a deduction? If compensation is a necessary business expense and very few deductions are likely to be denied, why would Congress adopt such a provision? Note that § 162(m) does not apply to compensation paid to anyone other than corporate executives. Thus, there is no limitation on salaries paid to doctors, lawyers, professional athletes, or rock stars. Does this distinction make sense?

(E) *Undercompensation.* Section 162(a)(1) has not been interpreted to prevent undercompensation. Suppose, for example, a shareholder/employee is not adequately compensated. This might be done when the corporate tax rate is less than the individual rate and the shareholder had no need to withdraw funds for the foreseeable future. In that case, the income would be shifted to the lower-taxed corporation. In the case of a pass-through entity, the incentive may be to undercompensate a high bracket shareholder or partner in order to shift income to a related shareholder or partner. The Service has the authority to prevent the shift. See §§ 706, 1366(e). Shareholders and partners also have an incentive to convert compensation income into dividends or a partnership draw in order to avoid the Social Security and Medicare taxes and in some cases to obtain the 20 percent reduction in taxable income available to flow-through businesses. Furthermore, dividends currently are taxed at a lower rate than compensation.

(F) *Payments Other than Salaries.* The issue whether a payment that is denominated as an item deductible under § 162 is actually a nondeductible expense arises in other contexts as well. See, e.g., Tulia Feedlot, Inc. v. United States, 513 F.2d 800 (5th Cir. 1975), where a corporation was not allowed to deduct under § 162 a payment to a shareholder for personally guaranteeing a corporate loan. The court found the payment was a dividend even though the corporation needed the loan and the fee was reasonable in relation to existing interest rates. Cf. Tulia Feedlot, Inc. v. United States, 3 Cl.Ct. 364 (1983) (holding such fees deductible where company was unable to obtain financing without the shareholders' guarantees); Fong v. Commissioner, 48 T.C.M. 689 (1984) (denying deduction for similar fees).

Payments that are denominated as rent, but that are, in fact, dividends or gifts are not deductible. It also is well established that excessive rent paid to a related lessor will be disallowed. Is the problem whether the payment is excessive or whether the payment is for something other than rent?

B.   EXPENSES CONTRARY TO PUBLIC POLICY

Commissioner v. Tellier

Supreme Court of the United States, 1966. 383 U.S. 687.

■ MR. JUSTICE STEWART delivered the opinion of the Court.

The question presented in this case is whether expenses incurred by a taxpayer in the unsuccessful defense of a criminal prosecution may qualify for deduction from taxable income under § 162(a) of the Internal Revenue Code of 1954, which allows a deduction of "all the ordinary and necessary expenses paid or incurred during the taxable year in carrying on any trade or business * * * " The respondent, Walter F. Tellier, was engaged in the business of underwriting the public sale of stock offerings and purchasing securities for resale to customers. In 1956 he was brought to trial upon a 36-count indictment that charged him with violating the fraud section of the Securities Act of 1933 and the mail fraud statute, and with conspiring to violate those statutes. He was found guilty on all counts and was sentenced to pay an $18,000 fine and to serve four and a half years in prison. The judgment of conviction was affirmed on appeal. In his unsuccessful defense of this criminal prosecution, the respondent incurred and paid $22,964.20 in legal expenses in 1956. He claimed a deduction for that amount on his federal income tax return for that year. The Commissioner disallowed the deduction and was sustained by the Tax Court. T.C.Memo. 1963–212, 22 CCH Tax Ct.Memo. 1062. The Court of Appeals for the Second Circuit reversed in a unanimous *en banc* decision, 342 F.2d 690, and we granted certiorari. 382 U.S. 808. We affirm the judgment of the Court of Appeals.

There can be no serious question that the payments deducted by the respondent were expenses of his securities business under the decisions of this Court, and the Commissioner does not contend otherwise. * * *

The Commissioner also concedes that the respondent's legal expenses were "ordinary" and "necessary" expenses within the meaning of § 162(a). Our decisions have consistently construed the term "necessary" as imposing only the minimal requirement that the expense be "appropriate and helpful" for "the development of the [taxpayer's] business." Welch v. Helvering, 290 U.S. 111, 113. The principal function of the term "ordinary" in § 162(a) is to clarify the distinction, often difficult, between those expenses that are currently deductible and those that are in the nature of capital expenditures, which, if deductible at all, must be amortized over the useful life of the asset. Welch v. Helvering, supra, at 113–16. The legal expenses deducted by the respondent were not capital expenditures. They were incurred in his defense against charges of past criminal conduct, not in the acquisition of a capital asset. Our decisions establish that counsel fees comparable to those here involved are ordinary business expenses, even though a "lawsuit affecting the safety of a business may happen once in a lifetime." Welch v. Helvering, supra, at 114.

It is therefore clear that the respondent's legal fees were deductible under § 162(a) if the provisions of that section are to be given their normal effect in this case. The Commissioner and the Tax Court determined, however, that even though the expenditures meet the literal requirements of § 162(a), their deduction must nevertheless be disallowed on the ground of public policy. That view finds * * * no support * * * in any regulation or statute or in any decision of this Court, and we believe no such "public policy" exception to the plain provisions of § 162(a) is warranted in the circumstances presented by this case.

We start with the proposition that the federal income tax is a tax on net income, not a sanction against wrongdoing. That principle has been firmly imbedded in the tax statute from the beginning. One familiar facet of the principle is the truism that the statute does not concern itself with the lawfulness of the income that it taxes. Income from a criminal enterprise is taxed at a rate no higher and no lower than income from more conventional sources. "[T]he fact that a business is unlawful [does not] exempt it from paying the taxes that if lawful it would have to pay." United States v. Sullivan, 274 U.S. 259, 263. * * *

With respect to deductions, the basic rule, with only a few limited and well-defined exceptions, is the same. During the Senate debate in 1913 on the bill that became the first modern income tax law, amendments were rejected that would have limited deductions for losses to those incurred in a "legitimate" or "lawful" trade or business. Senator Williams, who was in charge of the bill, stated on the floor of the Senate that

> "[T]he object of this bill is to tax a man's net income; that is to say, what he has at the end of the year after deducting from his receipts his expenditures or losses. It is not to reform men's moral characters; that is not the object of the bill at all. The tax is not levied for the purpose of restraining people from betting on horse races or upon 'futures,' but the tax is framed for the purpose of making a man pay upon his net income, his actual profit during the year. The law does not care where he got it from, so far as the tax is concerned, although the law may very properly care in another way." 50 Cong.Rec. 3849.

The application of this principle is reflected in several decisions of this Court. As recently as Commissioner v. Sullivan, 356 U.S. 27, we sustained the allowance of a deduction for rent and wages paid by the operators of a gambling enterprise, even though both the business itself and the specific rent and wage payments there in question were illegal under state law. In rejecting the Commissioner's contention that the illegality of the enterprise required disallowance of the deduction, we held that, were we to "enforce as federal policy the rule espoused by the Commissioner in this case, we would come close to making this type of business taxable on the basis of its gross receipts, while all other business would be taxable on the basis of net income. If that choice is to be made, Congress should do it." Id., at 29. * * *

Deduction of expenses falling within the general definition of § 162(a) may, to be sure, be disallowed by specific legislation, since deductions "are a matter of grace and Congress can, of course, disallow them as it chooses." * * * But * * * only where the allowance of a deduction would "frustrate sharply defined national or state policies proscribing particular forms of conduct" have we upheld its disallowance. * * * Further, the "policies frustrated must be national or state policies evidenced by some *governmental* declaration of them." * * * Finally, the "test of nondeductibility always is the severity and immediacy of the frustration resulting from allowance of the deduction." Tank Truck Rentals v. Commissioner, 356 U.S. 30, 35. In that case, as in Hoover Motor Express Co. v. United States, 356 U.S. 38, we upheld the disallowance of deductions claimed by taxpayers for fines and penalties imposed upon them for violating state penal statutes; to allow a deduction in those circumstances would have directly and substantially diluted the actual punishment imposed.

The present case falls far outside that sharply limited and carefully defined category. No public policy is offended when a man faced with serious criminal charges employs a lawyer to help in his defense. That is not "proscribed conduct." It is his constitutional right. In an adversary system of criminal justice, it is a basic [tenet] of our public policy that a defendant in a criminal case have counsel to represent him.

Congress has authorized the imposition of severe punishment upon those found guilty of the serious criminal offenses with which the respondent was charged and of which he was convicted. But we can find no warrant for attaching to that punishment an additional financial burden that Congress has neither expressly nor implicitly directed. To deny a deduction for expenses incurred in the unsuccessful defense of a criminal prosecution would impose such a burden in a measure dependent not on the seriousness of the offense or the actual sentence imposed by the court, but on the cost of the defense and the defendant's particular tax bracket. We decline to distort the income tax laws to serve a purpose for which they were neither intended nor designed by Congress.

The judgment is affirmed.

NOTES

(A) *Other Cases.* In *Tank Truck Rentals v. Commissioner,* discussed in the principal case, the Supreme Court refused to permit a trucking company to deduct fines levied by Pennsylvania for violation of its weight limits. Surrounding states had much higher limits, which meant that the truckers faced three choices: (1) drive around Pennsylvania at great expense; (2) carry light loads at greater proportional costs; or (3) violate the weight limit. The last of these choices was the universal industry practice. The state did not require overweight trucks to unload or impose any nonmonetary penalties, and its own regulatory agency required the companies to record the fines on their books as business expenses. Nevertheless, the Court found that allowance of a deduction for these expenses would undermine Pennsylvania's weight limit policy; the fines therefore did not qualify as ordinary and necessary business expenses.

In *Commissioner v. Sullivan,* also discussed in *Tellier* and decided the same day as *Tank Truck,* the Court allowed a deduction for salaries and rents paid by a bookmaker, even though the applicable state law made these payments a separate criminal offense. The Court explained that salaries and rent were part of the "normal" costs of doing business. Could a state be said to have a policy forbidding bookmakers to pay salary and rents? If so, why are these expenses any more ordinary and necessary than those at stake in *Tank Truck?*

(B) *Statutory Provisions.* Perhaps in response to the confusion created by these cases, Congress amended § 162 to specifically deny five types of expenditures: (1) fines or similar penalties paid to a government (or at the direction of a government) for the violation of any law, § 162(f); (2) a portion of treble damage payments under the antitrust laws following a related criminal conviction (or plea of guilty or nolo contendere), § 162(g); (3) bribes or kickbacks paid to public officials, § 162(c)(1); (4) bribes or referral fees for Medicaid and Medicare patients, § 162(c)(3); and (5) any other illegal bribe, kickback, or payment under any law if such law is generally enforced and it subjects the payor to a criminal penalty or the loss of license or privilege to engage in a trade or business, § 162(c)(2).

In 2017, the Congress extended the § 162(f) disallowance to payments made to (or at the direction of) certain nongovernment entities that exercise self-regulatory powers, including the major stock and futures exchanges and other entities to be specified in regulations. § 162(f)(5).

(C) *Settlements in Cases of Sexual Harassment Involving Nondisclosure Agreements.* In 2017, public outrage erupted when the *New York Times* revealed that Hollywood producer Harvey Weinstein had paid large sums to a number of women to settle and suppress claims of sexual harassment and sexual assault. According to the *Times,* Weinstein's lawyers had often required women receiving settlements to agree not to disclose the circumstances of the settlement. Following the Weinstein story, many more cases of sexual harassment by powerful men came to light.

As part of the 2017 Act, in an apparent effort to discourage such nondisclosure agreements, the Congress enacted § 162(q), which denies a deduction for any settlement related to sexual harassment or sexual abuse if the settlement is subject to a nondisclosure agreement. The provision also disallows attorneys' fees "related to such a settlement."

It seems clear that the Congress intended the new rules to penalize payors of such settlements, rather than recipients. However, some tax lawyers have pointed out that the statutory language could be read literally to deny settlement recipients a deduction for their own attorneys' fees.

(D) *Vitality of Common Law Public Policy Exception.* Congress apparently intended that the provisions of § 162 denying deductions for payments that were deemed to violate public policy be exclusive. "Public policy, in other circumstances, generally is not sufficiently clearly defined to justify the disallowance of deductions." See Staff of the Joint Committee on Taxation, General Explanation of the Tax Reform Act of 1969, 91st Cong., 1st Sess. 233–35 (1969). See also Reg. § 1.162–1(a): "A deduction for an expense * * * which would otherwise be allowable under section 162 shall not be denied on the grounds that allowance of such deduction would frustrate a sharply defined public policy. See section 162(c), (f), and (g) * * *." Most courts have so found, but not all. The Sixth Circuit, which seems genuinely confused about the public policy limitation, disallowed a deduction for a kickback that did not violate either state or federal law or subject the payor to loss of its business license. Car-Ron Asphalt Paving Co., Inc. v. Commissioner, 758 F.2d 1132 (6th Cir. 1985). The taxpayer paid $90,000 in kickbacks to the supervisor of construction of a shopping mall that secured about $1 million in contracts for the company. In the previous year, however, the same court permitted another taxpayer to deduct similar payments to the same individual. Raymond Bertolini Trucking Co. v. Commissioner, 736 F.2d 1120 (6th Cir. 1984). The panel in *Car-Ron* neither overruled *Bertolini* nor did it forthrightly explain the difference between the cases. The majority distinguished the earlier case by saying that the Tax Court had found the payments in *Car-Ron* were not necessary, even though the Tax Court's definition of "necessary" in this case seemed to include only "essential" expenses—a definition that is clearly wrong as a matter of law and that, in any event, seemed to have been met in the case. The good news is that the recipient of the kickbacks was convicted for federal tax fraud for failing to report the kickbacks as income, a conviction that probably never would have occurred if the payments had not been revealed by Bertolini and Car-Ron deducting them.

In Nacchio v. United States, 824 F.3d. 1370 (Fed. Cir. 2016), rev'g 115 Fed. Cl. 195 (2014), the Federal Circuit held that Mr. Naccio was barred by § 162(f) from deducting $44 million in insider trading profits that he had to disgorge as part of his sentence. The court asks "whether Nacchio's criminal forfeiture is a "fine or similar penalty" under § 162(f), or if allowing a deduction in these circumstances would otherwise frustrate public policy", which suggests that there might be some public policy exceptions that exist at common law, outside of § 162. However, the analysis focuses entirely on whether the payment at issue was a "fine or similar penalty", and never reaches the question whether the common law public policy doctrine has continuing validity.

(E) *Other Public Policy Limitations.* The general public policy limitation lives on, however, in other Code sections. The courts have imported into § 165 the limitation on the deductibility of losses that would "frustrate sharply defined national or state policies proscribing particular types of conduct" (the language of *Tellier*). See, e.g., King v. United States, 152 F.3d 1200 (9th Cir. 1998). After being caught in a drug sting, the taxpayer voluntarily led the FBI to a large sum of money buried on his ranch that he had procured from selling marijuana. Assured by the FBI that they would turn the money over to the IRS, the taxpayer thought he had satisfied his obligation to the government and filed a return reporting the stash as income and then taking a loss deduction. But he was wrong. Forfeiting the money to the FBI did not eliminate the tax liability; the court held he was not entitled to a loss deduction because it would violate public policy.

Gullible Mr. Mazzei gave $20,000 to someone who claimed to have a machine that reproduced money. The man was about to demonstrate the machine to the victim when the man's confederates burst into the room impersonating law enforcement officers. They took Mr. Mazzei's cash on the pretext of seizing evidence of counterfeiting. The IRS disallowed Mazzei's theft loss. A majority of the Tax Court agreed, holding that allowing a deduction to Mazzei under these circumstances would frustrate public policy because the loss bore a "direct relationship" to what the taxpayer had believed to be an illegal act. Mazzei v. Commissioner, 61 T.C. 497 (1974). A dissenting opinion argued that Congress had intended to reserve for itself the power to limit deductions on public policy grounds. See also Notice 2004–27, 2004–1 C.B. 782, in which the IRS denied a theft loss for a change in stock value caused by corporate wrongdoing.

Treasury also has issued regulations stating that taxpayers may not deduct under § 212 (investment expenses) or § 471 (inventory costs) items that would be nondeductible under § 162. Regs. §§ 1.212–1(p), 1.471–3(d).

(F) *Questions on the Margins of Statutory Language.* Notwithstanding the legislative efforts to make more precise the contours of the disallowance of business deductions on public policy grounds, the courts continue to struggle at the margins. For example, in True v. United States, 894 F.2d 1197 (10th Cir. 1990), a pipeline company was not entitled to deduct a civil penalty assessed for an oil leak under the Federal Water Pollution Control Act. The court upheld the validity of Reg. § 1.162–21(b)(1), which provides that civil as well as criminal penalties are subject to § 162(f). See also Reg. § 1.162–21(b)(2), which states that "compensatory" damages paid to the government are not "fines or penalties." Were the fines in *Tank Truck* compensatory or retributive penalties? At least one court has refused to make such distinctions. In Colt Industries, Inc. v. United States, 880 F.2d 1311 (Fed. Cir. 1989), the court held that no distinction could be drawn between compensatory and retributive civil penalties. It refused to permit the taxpayer to deduct payments made to settle a suit with the Environmental Protection Agency, saying that ascertaining whether payments were compensatory would require the courts to determine the underlying purpose of every civil penalty. In *True,* supra, the Tenth Circuit took a different approach, finding that if there are "deterrent and retributive function[s]" to a penalty, it cannot be deducted even if it also has "compensatory and remedial aspects."

In Huff v. Commissioner, 80 T.C. 804 (1983), the Tax Court distinguished nondeductible civil penalties "imposed for purposes of enforcing the law and as punishment for the violation thereof" from deductible civil penalties "imposed to encourage prompt compliance with a requirement of the law or as a remedial measure to compensate another party for expenses incurred as a result of the violation." The former were considered "similar" to criminal penalties while the latter were not. The civil penalties imposed in this case were not deductible because the Supreme Court of California had characterized them as designed to penalize past illegal conduct.

(G) *Payments to Third Parties.* Because § 162(f) prohibits deductions only for fines or penalties paid to a government (or, as described above, certain self-regulatory bodies), damages or payments made to a private party for a violation of law or for violating private rules are typically deductible. Where, however, the payments to private parties are akin to a fine, deduction has been disallowed. See, e.g., Rev. Rul. 81–151, 1981–1 C.B. 74 (corporate officer who caused the corporation to make illegal campaign contributions resulting in a fine could not deduct restitution he was required to make to corporation). Similarly, restitution made to the victims of fraud or theft is not deductible where the repayment serves a punitive purpose. Kraft v. United States, 991 F.2d 292 (6th Cir. 1993). In Allied-Signal Inc. v. Commissioner, 54 F.3d 767 (3d Cir. 1995) (unpublished opinion), the court refused to permit a corporation to deduct the contribution it made to an environmental endowment fund in lieu of paying a fine for releasing toxic chemicals. A company that makes a court-ordered charitable contribution in lieu of a criminal fine may not take a business deduction under § 162 or a charitable deduction under § 170. The IRS regards the contribution as a nondeductible fine under § 162(f) and not gratuitous as required for deductibility under § 170. Rev. Rul. 79–148, 1979–1 C.B. 93.

(H) *Tax Penalties.* The denial of a deduction for a business expense that is contrary to public policy can be seen as a "tax penalty" (or excise tax). These provisions are the reverse of tax expenditure provisions, discussed supra at page 42. They are departures from the net income concept; business expenses ought to be deductible in defining income in an income tax. The practical effect of the denial varies with the taxpayer's marginal tax rate, rather than with the importance of the underlying policy goal. This sentiment seems consistent with the next-to-last sentence of *Tellier.* Is the Court consistent when it suggests two paragraphs earlier that allowing a deduction for fines would dilute the punishment? Is a tax penalty less objectionable if Congress carved out the exception to the net income concept or if the courts take the initiative?

Olive v. Commissioner

United States Court of Appeals, Ninth Circuit, 2015. 792 F.3d 1146.

■ GRABER, CIRCUIT JUDGE:

Petitioner Martin Olive appeals the Tax Court's decision assessing deficiencies and penalties for tax years 2004 and 2005, which arise from Petitioner's operation of the Vapor Room Herbal Center ("Vapor Room"), a medical marijuana dispensary in San Francisco. * * * *

Established in 2004, the Vapor Room provides its patrons a place where they can socialize, purchase medical marijuana, and consume it using the Vapor Room's vaporizers. The Vapor Room sells medical marijuana in three forms: dried marijuana leaves, edibles, and a concentrated version of THC. Customers who purchase marijuana at the Vapor Room pay varying costs, depending on the quantity and quality of the product and on the individual customer's ability to pay.

The Vapor Room is set up much like a community center, with couches, chairs, and tables located throughout the establishment. Games, books, and art supplies are available for patrons' general use. The Vapor Room also offers services such as yoga, movies, and massage therapy. Customers can drink complimentary tea or water during their visits, or they can eat complimentary snacks, including pizza and sandwiches. The Vapor Room offers these activities and amenities for free.

Each of the Vapor Room's staff members is permitted under California law to receive and consume medical marijuana. Petitioner purchases, for cash, the Vapor Room's inventory from licensed medical marijuana suppliers. Patrons who visit the Vapor Room can buy marijuana and use the vaporizers at no charge, or they can use the vaporizers (again, at no charge) with marijuana that they bought elsewhere. Sometimes, staff members or patrons sample Vapor Room inventory for free. When staff members interact with customers, occasionally one-on-one, they discuss illnesses; provide counseling on various personal, legal, or political matters related to medical marijuana; and educate patrons on how to use the vaporizers and consume medical marijuana responsibly. All these services are provided to patrons at no charge.

Petitioner filed business income tax returns for tax years 2004 and 2005, which reported the Vapor Room's net income during those years as $64,670 and $33,778, respectively. Although Petitioner reported $236,502 and $417,569 in Vapor Room business expenses for 2004 and 2005, the Tax Court concluded that § 280E of the Internal Revenue Code precluded Petitioner from deducting any of those expenses. . . .

The Internal Revenue Code provides that, for the purpose of computing taxable income, an individual's or a business's "gross income" includes "all income from whatever source derived," including "income derived from business." I.R.C. § 61(a)(2). The Code further allows a business to deduct from its gross income "all the ordinary and necessary expenses paid or incurred during the taxable year in carrying on [the] trade or business." Id. § 162(a). But there are exceptions to § 162(a). . . . One such exception applies when the "amount paid or incurred during the taxable year" is for the purpose of "carrying on any trade or business . . .consist[ing] of trafficking in controlled substances." Id. § 280E. Although the use and sale of medical marijuana are legal under California state law, see Cal. Health & Safety Code § 11362.5, the use and sale of marijuana remain prohibited under federal law, see 21 U.S.C. § 812(c).

We turn first to the text of I.R.C. § 280E. * * * * To determine whether Petitioner may deduct the expenses associated with the Vapor Room, then, we must decide whether the Vapor Room is a "trade or business [that] consists of trafficking in controlled substances * * * prohibited by Federal law."

We start with the phrase "trade or business." The test for determining whether an activity constitutes a "trade or business" is "whether the activity 'was entered into with the dominant hope and intent of realizing a profit.'" *United States v. Am. Bar Endowment*, 477 U.S. 105, 110 n.1 (1986) (quoting *Brannen v. Comm'r*, 722 F.2d 695, 704 (11th Cir. 1984)); see also *Vorsheck v. Comm'r*, 933 F.2d 757, 758 (9th Cir. 1991) (per curiam) (applying the same standard to § 162(a) deductions). The parties agree, and the Tax Court found, that the only income-generating activity in which the Vapor Room engaged was its sale of medical marijuana. The other services that the Vapor Room offered— including, among other things, the provision of vaporizers, food and drink, yoga, games, movies, and counseling—were offered to its patrons at no cost to them. The only activity, then, that the Vapor Room "entered into with the dominant hope and intent of realizing a profit," . . .was the sale of medical marijuana. Accordingly, Petitioner's "trade or business," for § 162(a) purposes, was limited to medical marijuana sales.

Given the limited scope of Petitioner's "trade or business," we conclude that the business consist[ed] of trafficking in controlled substances . . . prohibited by Federal law." The income-generating activities in which the Vapor Room engaged consisted solely of trafficking in medical marijuana which, as noted, is prohibited under federal law. Under § 280E, then, the expenses that Petitioner incurred in the course of operating the Vapor Room cannot be deducted for federal tax purposes.

Petitioner's argument relies primarily on the phrase "consists of," rather than on the phrase "trade or business." According to Petitioner, the use of the words "consists of" is most appropriate "when a listing is meant to be exhaustive"; the word "consisting," he argues, is not synonymous with the word "including." Relying on that proposition, Petitioner contends that, for § 280E purposes, a business "consists of" a service only when that service is the *sole* service that the business provides. Because the Vapor Room provides caregiving services *and* sells medical marijuana, Petitioner concludes that his business does not "consist of" either one alone and therefore does not fall within the ambit of § 280E.

To support that line of reasoning, Petitioner cites the Tax Court's decision in Californians Helping to Alleviate Medical Problems, Inc. v. Commissioner (*CHAMP*), 128 T.C. 173 (2007). His reliance on *CHAMP* is misplaced. In *CHAMP*, the petitioner's income-generating business included the provision not only of medical marijuana, but also of "extensive" counseling and caregiving services. *Id.* at 175.The Tax Court noted that the business's "primary purpose was to provide caregiving services to its members" and that its "secondary purpose was to provide its members with medical marijuana." *Id.* at 174. The court found, after considering the "degree of economic interrelationship between the two undertakings," that the petitioner was involved in "more than one trade or business." *Id.* at 183. That is not the case here. Petitioner does not provide counseling, caregiving, snacks, and so forth for a separate fee; the only "business" in which he engages is selling medical marijuana.

An analogy may help to illustrate the difference between the Vapor Room and the business at issue in *CHAMP*. Bookstore A sells books. It also provides some complimentary amenities: Patrons can sit in comfortable seating areas while considering whether to buy a book; they can drink coffee or tea and eat cookies, all of which the bookstore offers at no charge; they can obtain advice from the staff about new authors, book clubs, community events, and the like; they can bring their children to a weekend story time or an after-school reading circle. The "trade or business" of Bookstore A "consists of" selling books. Its many amenities do not alter that conclusion; presumably, the owner hopes to attract buyers of books by creating an alluring atmosphere. By contrast, Bookstore B sells books but also sells coffee and pastries, which customers can consume in a cafe-like seating area. Bookstore B has two "trade[s] or business[es]," one of which "consists of" selling books and the other of which "consists of" selling food and beverages.

Petitioner's arguments related to congressional intent and public policy are similarly unavailing. He contends that I.R.C. § 280E should not be construed to apply to medical marijuana dispensaries because those dispensaries did not exist when Congress enacted § 280E. Congress added that provision, he maintains, to prevent street dealers from taking a deduction. According to Petitioner, Congress could not have intended for medical marijuana dispensaries, now legal in many states, to fall within the ambit of "items not deductible" under the Internal Revenue Code. We are not persuaded.

That Congress might not have imagined what some states would do in future years has no bearing on our analysis. It is common for statutes to apply to new situations. And here, application of the statute is clear. . . . Application of the statute does not depend on the illegality of marijuana sales under state law; the only question Congress allows us to ask is whether marijuana is a controlled substance "prohibited by Federal law." I.R.C. § 280E. If Congress now thinks that the policy embodied in § 280E is unwise as applied to medical marijuana sold in conformance with state law, it can change the statute. We may not.

* * * *

AFFIRMED.

NOTES

(A) *Legislative Intent.* The legislative history emphasizes that Congress did not intend to bar drug traffickers from offsetting the cost of obtaining drugs against the receipts of their illegal business. The language of § 280E is much broader. Is there a justification for the distinction between the cost of goods sold and the other expenses of running an illegal business?

Even if § 280E does not prevent a deduction for the cost of goods sold, it may be disallowed for other reasons. In Beck v. Commissioner, T.C. Memo. 2015–149, the Tax Court noted that the owner of a medical marijuana dispensary in California could not take a deduction for the cost of goods sold because the goods (i.e. the marijuana) had been seized by the federal DEA and therefore had not been "sold." The court also held that § 280E precluded a loss deduction under § 165 for the seized marijuana. And for good measure, the court imposed an accuracy-related penalty for filing a return with a negligent disregard of the rules.

(B) *Effective Tax Rate.* In 2005 Olive reported net income of $33,778 and had business expenses of $417,569. Because he was unable to deduct his business expenses, he owed tax on $451,347. An effective tax rate measures taxes paid as a percentage of economic profit. Can you figure out the effective tax rate on his economic income of $33,778? Is this kind of penalty justified for an activity that is legal under state law?

(C) *Other Crimes.* The expenses of other illegal profit-seeking ventures are deductible. For example, John DiFronzo was the "crew chief" in a crime syndicate that attempted to control gaming operations of the Rincon Band of Mission Indians. He paid a lawyer $50,000 to defend him but he was convicted anyway of participating in a criminal venture. The Tax Court permitted him to deduct his legal fees, finding that he had a "genuine intention of making a profit." DiFronzo v. Commissioner, 75 T.C.M. 1693 (1998). Why should only drug dealers lose their business deductions? Should operators of illegal businesses be taxed on gross receipts rather than net income?

C. LOBBYING EXPENSES

Notes on Lobbying Expenses

History. One of the earliest uses of the "ordinary and necessary" requirement as a basis for denying business deductions involved expenses for lobbying, propaganda, and campaign contributions. The Supreme Court upheld regulations disallowing such deductions in Textile Mills Securities Corp. v. Commissioner, 314 U.S. 326 (1941), which rejected a deduction for the costs of persuading Congress to compensate foreign businesses that had lost property during World War I under the Trading with the Enemy Act. In Cammarano v. United States, 358 U.S. 498 (1959), the Court reaffirmed the regulations and refused to permit a beer distributor to deduct the costs of opposing a referendum that would have abolished private alcohol distribution in the state.

Today, § 162(e) prohibits the deduction of expenses incurred in lobbying federal or state legislators, lobbying local government branches, such as a city council, or certain executive branch officials. Lobbying is defined (1) influencing legislation, (2) participation in, or intervention in, any political campaign on behalf of (or in opposition to) any candidate for public office, (3) any attempt to influence the general public, or segments thereof, with respect to elections, legislative matters, or referendums, or (4) any direct communication with a certain executive branch officials. There is, however, a de minimis exception: If a taxpayer's total in-house lobbying expenditures do not exceed $2,000, they are deductible.

Constitutional Limitations. The limitations on deductibility contained in § 162(e) mean that taxpayers may not deduct some indisputably business-related expenses solely because they involve politics. Justice Douglas, concurring in *Cammarano,* appeared troubled by the possibility that singling out political expenses for nondeductibility might constitute a violation of the First Amendment. He concluded that no constitutional problems existed, however, because "[d]eductions are a matter of grace, not of right;" moreover, he found that nondeductibility reflects "a complete hands-off policy on the part of government [that] is at times the only course consistent with First Amendment rights." Cammarano v. United States, 358 U.S. 498, 515 (1959). Does departure from the rule that nonpersonal, noncapital business expenses normally are deductible reflect a "hands-off" policy? Is nondeductibility justified on the ground that an opposite rule would favor political activity by pro-business interests? Is it appropriate for government to restrict the political power of the wealthy to enhance the power of the less wealthy?

Charities eligible for deductible contributions face substantial limits on the extent of legislative lobbying that they may undertake. These rules are discussed infra at page 481. In Regan v. Taxation With Representation, 461 U.S. 540 (1983), the Court upheld these restrictions against First Amendment and equal protection attacks. By characterizing the charitable exemption as a kind of subsidy, the Court fit the limitations within the principle that the government may not penalize, but need not subsidize, the exercise of free speech. This characterization also permitted the Court to apply a less demanding form of equal protection scrutiny; the Court therefore could uphold as rational the different treatment of lobbying by business, charitable, and veterans' groups.

Advertising vs. Other Efforts to Influence the Public. The Treasury regulations interpreting § 162(e) distinguish between deductible institutional or goodwill advertising and nondeductible efforts to influence the public on particular issues of legislative significance. Reg. § 1.162–20. How easy is it to separate the presentation of "views on economic, financial, social, or other subject of a general nature" from propaganda on matters of particular legislative significance? May an oil company deduct the costs of newspaper ads contending that gasoline price controls are economically unsound? May an electric utility deduct advertisements detailing the benefits of nuclear power?

In Geary v. Commissioner, 235 F.3d 1207 (9th Cir. 2000), Geary, a police officer, took a puppet, Officer O'Smarty, to work in order to improve his relationship with the community. (This did not take place in NYC.) Forbidden from patrolling with the puppet, Geary formed a committee to put the issue on the local ballot and advertised in voting materials. The measure was approved and O'Smarty went back on the beat, but Geary lost his deduction. The advertising was intended to influence the general public and thus was nondeductible.

"Neutrality." Even with restrictions, does § 162(e) give businesses an advantage over individuals? Assume that a group of milk producers is lobbying to obtain a $20,000 increase in milk prices. What is the maximum amount that the producers would spend to lobby for such legislation if such expenses were deductible? If they were nondeductible? How much would a citizens group spend to oppose the legislation if such expenses were deductible? Nondeductible? Would your answers to the preceding question change if the lobbying was related to a business's effort to obtain a substantial loan from the government at favorable interest rates? An especially favorable federal income tax provision?

D. EMPLOYEE BUSINESS EXPENSES

Note on Employee Business Expenses

The tax act of 2017 draws a sharp line between employee business expenses that are reimbursed by an employer and those that are not. In general, reimbursed expenses are deductible (meaning that the employee includes the reimbursement in income and deducts the expense), while unreimbursed expenses are not deductible during the period from 2018 through the end of 2025.

Deriving this distinction from the language of the Code isn't easy, but it's a productive exercise in statutory discovery (or, if you prefer, an illustration of extreme legal complexity). The first step is to note that expenses incurred by an employee in connection with a trade or business are deductible under § 162, provided they are ordinary and necessary.

Performing your job is considered the trade or business of an employee. Quite often the issue is whether the expenses are actually personal in nature. This issue is discussed in detail infra at page 270. Professional expenses such as supplies, dues to professional societies and unions, subscriptions to professional journals, and the expenses incurred in using an automobile to make business calls are (in principle) deductible, but read on! (As discussed before, these rules also determine whether a benefit provided to an employee is deductible as a working condition fringe. See § 132(d).)

The second, critical step is to distinguish between employee business expenses deducted "above the line" and those taken as itemized deductions. Employer-reimbursed expenses are deductible above the line, which means the employee may deduct them even if she takes the standard deduction. § 62(a)(2)(A). The employee, however, must provide substantiation to the person providing reimbursement and cannot be reimbursed for more than the deductible expense. § 62(c).

Unreimbursed expenses are, again in theory, deductible as itemized deductions if the employee itemizes (i.e., does not take the standard deduction). But not really! Keep reading.

The third step is to apply § 67, which limits (between 2018 and the end of 2025) all "miscellaneous itemized deductions." Section 67(a) defines "miscellaneous itemized deductions" by exclusion, detailing what is not a miscellaneous itemized deduction. Excluded are the itemized deductions for interest, taxes, casualty and wagering losses, charitable donations, medical expenses, and several other deductions. The result is that § 67 applies to unreimbursed employee business expenses and investment expenses under § 212.

Now for the final step: while § 67(a) appears to permit the deduction of miscellaneous itemized deductions in excess of 2 percent of AGI, those deductions are disallowed under § 67(g) for tax years 2018 through 2025.

The result is that a taxpayer with $100,000 of salary and $2,500 of unreimbursed employee business expenses can deduct none of her expenses during the eight-year disallowance period. However, absent further change, beginning in 2026, she will be able to deduct the amount that exceeds 2 percent of her AGI, here $500, as an itemized deduction. In no year is the remaining $2,000 deductible.

The limitations on the deduction for employee business expenses will have the heaviest impact on workers who pay for their own expenses. Consider a worker who earns $100,000 in salary but pays for his own travel and supplies, totaling $25,000. Under prior law (and again after 2025), he would be allowed to deduct $23,000 in expenses, reporting taxable income of $77,000. Between 2018 and 2025, however, he will pay tax on all $100,000—even though he is no richer.

Workers facing tax increases of this kind will predictably try one of two tax "fixes." One is to persuade the employer to reimburse expenses, so that they become deductible. The worker in the example above would be better off if he lowered his salary to $75,000 and accepted $25,000 in employer reimbursements: after all, $75,000 is his true compensation.

A second tax workaround would be to recharacterize the employee as an independent contractor. Independent contractors are treated as business owners and so can deduct their expenses above the line, as explained above. (As discussed in Chapter 4, the tax legislation of 2017 also includes a special tax break for businesses that adds an extra incentive for reclassifying workers as independent contractors.) We have seen examples of independent contractors (or self-employed business owners if you prefer) before: the taxpayers in the *Welch* and *Gilliam* cases earlier in this chapter, for example, were both independent contractors.

This tax "fix," however, isn't necessarily an easy or advantageous one. First, the courts and the IRS have developed substantive standards distinguishing employees from independent contractors. See Rev. Rul. 87–41, 1987–1 C.B. 296, listing twenty factors to be taken into account, including whether the service provider performs according to instructions, training, and supervision of the "contractor." The more instruction, training, and supervision provided, the more likely the IRS is to treat the relationship as one of employment. On the other hand, as with other multi-factor tests that we have seen before, the classification of a worker as an employee or an independent contractor is often uncertain and controversial. For example, whether your dog's walker is an employee or an independent contractor may depend on whether you tell her specifically what time and where to walk your dog and who supplies the pooper-scooper or doggie bags. A New York Uber driver who uses her own car, chooses her own hours, and also drives for Lyft is almost certainly an independent contractor, not an employee. Many people who describe themselves as employees when asked by the Census are actually independent contractors under the tax law, and the percentage of workers filing their taxes as self-employed has increased from about 13 percent of all workers in 2000 to more than 16 percent in 2012, even without the significant tax advantages to self-employed workers provided in the 2017 tax legislation.

In addition to increased deductions for business expenses, a bona fide reclassification as an independent contractor may make a worker eligible for a deduction that, in effect, lowers their income tax rate by 20 percent. See § 199A, discussed in Chapter 4. At the same time, however, independent contractors may lose some state labor law protections available only to employees, but some states may apply different standards than the IRS.

The unfavorable treatment of employee business expenses does not affect the exclusion of fringe benefits, discussed in Chapter 2. Where an employee's business expenses are paid by the employer, the payment can be excluded from income. Section 132(d) defines as a working condition fringe benefit any "property or services provided to an employee of the employer to the extent that, if the employee paid for such property or services, such payment would be allowable as a deduction under section 162 or 167." Must the employee include in income any working condition fringe that would not be deductible because of the § 67(f) disallowance of miscellaneous itemized deductions? The regulations, issued under prior law, indicate that the 2 percent limitation of § 67(a) can be ignored for purposes of § 132. Reg. § 1.132–5(a)(vi). And the 2017 law contains a similar rule that makes clear that the disallowance of all miscellaneous itemized deductions between 2018 and the end of 2025 has no effect on § 132(d).

Congress occasionally treats certain professions preferentially by permitting employees to deduct unreimbursed expenses "above the line" Section 62(a)(2)(D) permits full-time teachers to deduct up to $250 in unreimbursed expenses for classroom supplies. In 2017, the House proposed to repeal that deduction, but after unfavorable press coverage and political blowback, the final bill preserved it. Section 62(a)(2)(E) provides an above-the-line deduction for the transportation, meals, and lodging expenses of National Guard and Reserve members who travel away from home more than 100 miles (and stay overnight) to attend National Guard and Reserve meetings.

The elimination of the deduction for miscellaneous itemized deductions also applies to deductions taken under § 212, as noted above at page 235. This can lead to the taxpayer's tax bill being larger than her net income. This bizarre result is illustrated nicely by the situation where a plaintiff pays his attorney on a contingency basis. Suppose the litigation arises in connection with the plaintiff's employment. The amount of the judgment or settlement paid to the attorney as a fee would be an itemized deduction, disallowed between 2018 and the end of 2025 by § 67. In almost all cases the plaintiff would lose the deduction and would be taxed on the full amount of the proceeds, even though she typically would pay one-third of the amount to her lawyer. See Commissioner v. Banks, 543 U.S. 426 (2005). Congress has permitted a deduction for attorneys' fees and court costs in civil rights suits and in whistleblower cases. § 62(a)(20) and (21). Attorneys' fees and costs for other employee recoveries, however, are taxable.

Congress justified the 2 percent floor on simplicity grounds, thereby confirming Will Rogers' famous adage that when Congress makes a joke, it's a law. Essentially, the 2 percent floor was added to raise revenue, as was the eight-year elimination of all miscellaneous itemized deductions by the 2017 tax act. However, the adverse treatment of miscellaneous itemized deductions may promote some simplification by eliminating the recordkeeping burden for taxpayers and the auditing burden for the IRS. Disallowing all or a percentage of income-producing expenses, however, often means that more than net income is taxed. Do the attendant simplification benefits warrant such a departure from basic income tax principles?

The 2017 tax act eliminated an additional complicating factor—the so-called 3 percent "haircut." For tax years before 2017, and again after 2025, § 68 caps the total amount of certain itemized deductions for high bracket taxpayers (generally, those with AGI over $300,000 for taxpayers filing jointly or $250,000 for individual taxpayers, with these amounts indexed for inflation). Above those income levels, the Code reduced itemized deductions (other than medical expenses, investment interest, gambling, and casualty losses) by 3 percent of the excess AGI. The reduction could not exceed 80 percent of the deductions.

In theory, § 68 will spring back to life in 2026, but past political experience suggests that Congress often extends popular tax benefits. When the 3 percent haircut did apply, it operated essentially to reduce the benefit of itemized deductions as income rises. The effect was the same as raising the top marginal tax rate on the affected taxpayers without changing the nominal tax rates listed in § 1. Why do you suppose Congress chose to disguise a change to the top rates in this manner?

SECTION 2.   DISTINCTION BETWEEN DEDUCTIBLE BUSINESS OR INVESTMENT EXPENSES AND NONDEDUCTIBLE PERSONAL, LIVING OR FAMILY EXPENSES

Note Introducing the Business or Investment— Personal Consumption Distinction[1]

Since an individual can at once obtain income and satisfy personal needs, the line between deductible and nondeductible expenses is often hard to draw. Some business expenses have little or no personal connection, but most personal expenses can be linked, at least tenuously, to business. Taxpayers often find ways to mix personal pleasure with potentially deductible business. Under prior law, the annual congregation of corporate jets at the Kentucky Derby and the Super Bowl was not accidental. The 2017 tax act, however, eliminated deductions for entertainment expenses and so may crimp the style of corporate entertainers.

Still, we would have difficulty performing our jobs or other income-producing tasks if we did not eat, obtain housing, or take an occasional vacation. Thus, much basic consumption performs some "income-producing" function. Money often is spent not only to provide personal satisfaction but also to make more money. Marvin Chirelstein accurately assesses the difficulty of the tax collector's task when he observes that

---

[1]   Much of the material in this note is taken from Michael J. Graetz, "Expenditure Tax Design" in What Should Be Taxed: Income or Expenditure? 222–27 (Joseph Pechman ed., 1979).

"the notion of a sharp division between pleasure-seeking and profit-seeking is alien to human psychology and essentially unrealistic."[2]

Boris Bittker has remarked on the dilemma in greater detail:

There is, unfortunately, no theoretically satisfactory boundary between business expenses that provide incidental personal benefits and personal expenditures that incidentally serve business purposes. No matter how generously the Code defines business expenses in an effort to insure that all business-related expenses can be deducted, there will always be some non-deductible items beyond the line that contribute in some way to the production of income, whether it is the basic cost of living—one cannot work, after all, unless one is fed and housed—or the cost of luxuries that contribute to the taxpayer's willingness to work and to his initiative and reliability while on the job. On the other hand, no matter how severely the term "business expense" is defined, many items will continue to qualify for deduction although they confer "personal" benefits on the taxpayer. Taxpayers may be forbidden to deduct entertainment expenses because they are suspected of enjoying dinners and theater parties with their business customers, for example, but even the most puritanical definition of business expense is not likely to prevent self-employed taxpayers from deducting the cost of air conditioning their offices, upholstering their swivel chairs, or adding gadgets to their telephones, even if they derive personal pleasure from these amenities.[3]

Chirelstein's and Bittker's emphasis on indeterminacy is in sharp contrast to Daniel Halperin's conclusion:

The position that a deduction ought to be allowed for all income-generating expenses, while quite correct, is really beside the point. If such expenditures actually provide personal satisfaction, the amount of such satisfaction ought to be included in income. The fairest income tax would take account of income from "whatever source derived." On-the-job entertainment, traveling expenses and other expenditures which but for their connection with income-generating activities would be considered to provide personal satisfaction should not be distinguished from other forms of enjoyment.

An indirect way of taxing these benefits is to deny a deduction to the extent personal satisfaction has been obtained from the expenditure. If satisfaction were equal to cost, this approach would suggest complete disallowance. This reasoning is the foundation of [my] conclusion * * * that, assuming perfect

---

[2]   Marvin A. Chirelstein, Federal Income Taxation: A Law Student's Guide to the Leading Cases and Concepts 106 (10th ed., 2005).

[3]   Boris Bittker, "Income Tax Deductions, Credits and Subsidies for Personal Expenditures," 16 J. Law and Econ. 203–04 (1973).

information and absence of administrative problems, a deduction should be permitted only to the extent that the costs incurred exceed the personal benefit obtained. The proposal does not, therefore, represent a challenge to the right to a deduction for expenditures intended to produce income.

Despite [measurement difficulties] * * * it is not necessary to have complete assurance that personal satisfaction equals cost in order to make this assumption for purposes of taxation. While undoubtedly this will lead to overtaxation in some circumstances, such a result is far more acceptable than the understatement of income which results from ignoring the personal benefit. Of course, there will be many circumstances in which the matter is completely in doubt, and some sort of arbitrary allocation or partial taxation may be the best solution available.[4]

Notwithstanding the conceptual difficulties, the income tax law must distinguish business from personal expenses. If personal expenses could be deducted, personal consumption would be omitted from the tax base; in contrast, if business deductions were not allowed, gross income, not net income, would be taxed. The problems of equity and efficiency that emerge from the necessity of drawing the business-personal line are quite similar to those that emerge in connection with fringe benefits. (In fact, an employee's fringe benefit may be a self-employed person's business deduction.)

Unwarranted business deductions would permit taxpayers to finance personal consumption from pretax rather than after-tax dollars. To a taxpayer subject to a 37 percent marginal tax rate, a $50 fully deductible meal has the same after-tax cost as a $31.50 nondeductible meal. Allowing business deductions for personal consumption produces both horizontal and vertical inequities; taxpayers with similar incomes have different abilities to obtain these deductions depending on their occupations, while taxpayers with higher income often have more opportunities to obtain these deductions than do people with lower incomes. Such deductions also induce a misallocation of resources as spending flows toward deductible forms of consumption.

For many years, the struggle to distinguish deductible business or investment expenses from nondeductible personal, family, or living expenses was left to the IRS and the courts. More recently, however, Congress has responded to what it perceives as abuses by imposing restrictions on or disallowing certain deductions. In 2017, Congress disallowed all business deductions for entertainment; under prior law, entertainment had been deductible if sufficiently business-related. Congress has also limited certain mixed-motive expenses in order to raise

---

[4] Daniel Halperin, "Business Deduction for Personal Living Expenses: A Uniform Approach to an Unsolved Problem," 122 U.Pa. L. Rev. 859 (1974).

revenue. See, e.g., § 280A (disallowing deduction of certain expenses in connection with home office and vacation homes), § 280F (limiting depreciation deductions and investment tax credits for "luxury" automobiles and personal property not used primarily for business purposes), § 183 (limiting deductions with respect to "activities not engaged in for profit.")

Meals and travel expenses, in particular, may have a large consumption element. While staying in a Motel 6 and eating McDonald's on the road may not seem like luxury, staying in the Four Seasons and eating at Chez Panisse certainly is. Congress has, in a Solomon-like move, limited the deductibility of business meals to 50 percent. § 274(n).

In the absence of statutory rules, the IRS and the courts have applied various tests for deductibility. These tests are not uniform; they depend on the type of expenses involved. For some expenses, the courts allow the deduction whenever the expense is appropriate and helpful to the taxpayer's business or income-producing activity. For other expenses, courts disallow the deduction unless the taxpayer's "primary purpose" in incurring the expense was profit-seeking (or, in some cases, unless the expense would not have been made "but for" a business or investment motive). The courts occasionally require that the taxpayer's expenditures be "reasonable" even if they were clearly incurred for profit-oriented rather than personal reasons. Courts sometimes have allowed a deduction only for the "additional expenses" due to the needs of the taxpayer's business or income-producing activities. Expenses sometimes are allocated between business and personal use, with deduction permitted only for the amount allocated to business use. Some types of expense have been regarded by the courts as "inherently personal" and nondeductible even if shown to enhance profit-making activity. It is difficult to know when the courts will apply any of these tests. The cost of haircuts, for example, is nondeductible under the "inherently personal" test, but the cost of books is deductible if "appropriate and helpful" to the taxpayer's business. In some cases, the IRS, in regulations, has provided specific, and somewhat arbitrary rules for the deduction of certain mixed-motive expenses. Neither the IRS nor the courts, however, has developed an overarching theory.

Because logical reasoning often will not provide the answer, there is no substitute for examining the precedents or regulations relating to the particular type of expense at issue. Many of the rules are illustrated in the materials that follow. Sometimes the question is made more difficult by issues of timing, for example, whether an expenditure is a currently deductible "expense" or a nondeductible capital expenditure. In reading the materials that follow, reflect upon the following questions: Should a single test govern the line between profit-seeking and personal expenses, or are multiple tests desirable or at least inevitable? Are some tests clearly superior to others?

In theory there are two possible approaches: the deduction should be equal to the amount that would have been spent for business purposes or the deduction should be limited to the amount, if any, by which the expenditure exceeds the personal benefit. Is it possible to view the tests described in this note as attempts to achieve one of these results as nearly as possible given imperfect information? Consider whether the law has evolved from favoring the first approach to a greater recognition of the second.

Pevsner v. Commissioner

United States Court of Appeals, Fifth Circuit, 1980. 628 F.2d 467.

■ SAM D. JOHNSON, CIRCUIT JUDGE:

This is an appeal by the Commissioner of Internal Revenue from a decision of the United States Tax Court. The tax court upheld taxpayer's business expense deduction for clothing expenditures in the amount of $1,621.91 for the taxable year 1975. We reverse.

Since June 1973 Sandra J. Pevsner, taxpayer, has been employed as the manager of the Sakowitz Yves St. Laurent Rive Gauche Boutique located in Dallas, Texas. The boutique sells only women's clothes and accessories designed by Yves St. Laurent (YSL), one of the leading designers of women's apparel. * * *

As manager of the boutique, the taxpayer is expected by her employer to wear YSL clothes while at work. In her appearance, she is expected to project the image of an exclusive lifestyle and to demonstrate to her customers that she is aware of the YSL current fashion trends as well as trends generally. Because the boutique sells YSL clothes exclusively, taxpayer must be able, when a customer compliments her on her clothes, to say that they are designed by YSL. In addition to wearing YSL apparel while at the boutique, she wears them while commuting to and from work, to fashion shows sponsored by the boutique, and to business luncheons where she represents the boutique. * * *

Although the clothing and accessories purchased by the taxpayer were the type used for general purposes by the regular customers of the boutique, the taxpayer is not a normal purchaser of these clothes. * * *

Although taxpayer's employer has no objection to her wearing the apparel away from work, taxpayer stated that she did not wear the clothes during off-work hours because she felt that they were too expensive for her simple everyday lifestyle. * * * Taxpayer did admit at trial, however, that a number of the articles were things she could have worn off the job and in which she would have looked "nice."

* * *

The principal issue on appeal is whether the taxpayer is entitled to deduct as an ordinary and necessary business expense the cost of purchasing and maintaining the YSL clothes and accessories worn by the taxpayer in her employment as the manager of the boutique. This determination requires an examination of the relationship between Section 162(a) of the Internal Revenue Code of 1954, which allows a deduction for ordinary and necessary expenses incurred in the conduct of a trade or business, and Section 262 of the Code, which bars a deduction for all "personal, living, or family expenses." Although many expenses are helpful or essential to one's business activities—such as commuting expenses and the cost of meals while at work—these expenditures are considered inherently personal and are disallowed under Section 262. * * *

The generally accepted rule governing the deductibility of clothing expenses is that the cost of clothing is deductible as a business expense only if: (1) the clothing is of a type specifically required as a condition of employment, (2) it is not adaptable to general usage as ordinary clothing, and (3) it is not so worn. Donnelly v. Commissioner, 262 F.2d 411, 412 (2d Cir. 1959).[3]

In the present case, the Commissioner stipulated that the taxpayer was required by her employer to wear YSL clothing and that she did not wear such apparel apart from work. The Commissioner maintained, however, that a deduction should be denied because the YSL clothes and accessories purchased by the taxpayer were adaptable for general usage as ordinary clothing and she was not prohibited from using them as such. The tax court, in rejecting the Commissioner's argument for the application of an objective test, recognized that the test for deductibility was whether the clothing was "suitable for general or personal wear" but determined that the matter of suitability was to be judged subjectively, in light of the taxpayer's lifestyle. Although the court recognized that the YSL apparel "might be used by some members of society for general purposes," it felt that because the "wearing of YSL apparel outside work would be inconsistent with * * * [taxpayer's] lifestyle," sufficient reason was shown for allowing a deduction for the clothing expenditures.

[The court's discussion of the Tax Court's reliance on a similar case, Yeomans v. Commissioner, 30 T.C. 757 (1958) (where the taxpayer was allowed to deduct expensive work clothing not suitable to her lifestyle) is omitted.]

Notwithstanding the tax court's decision in *Yeomans,* the Circuits that have addressed the issue have taken an objective, rather than subjective, approach. * * * Under an objective test, no reference is made to the individual taxpayer's lifestyle or personal taste. Instead, adaptability for personal or general use depends upon what is generally accepted for ordinary street wear.

---

[3]   When the taxpayer is prohibited from wearing the clothing away from work a deduction is normally allowed. See Harsaghy v. Commissioner, 2 T.C. 484 (1943). However, in the present case no such restriction was placed upon the taxpayer's use of the clothing.

The principal argument in support of an objective test is, of course, administrative necessity. The Commissioner argues that, as a practical matter, it is virtually impossible to determine at what point either price or style makes clothing inconsistent with or inappropriate to a taxpayer's lifestyle. Moreover, the Commissioner argues that the price one pays and the styles one selects are inherently personal choices governed by taste, fashion, and other unmeasurable values. Indeed, the tax court has rejected the argument that a taxpayer's personal taste can dictate whether clothing is appropriate for general use. * * * An objective test, although not perfect, provides a practical administrative approach that allows a taxpayer or revenue agent to look only to objective facts in determining whether clothing required as a condition of employment is adaptable to general use as ordinary street wear. Conversely, the tax court's reliance on subjective factors provides no concrete guidelines in determining the deductibility of clothing purchased as a condition of employment.

In addition to achieving a practical administrative result, an objective test also tends to promote substantial fairness among the greatest number of taxpayers. As the Commissioner suggests, it apparently would be the tax court's position that two similarly situated YSL boutique managers with identical wardrobes would be subject to disparate tax consequences depending upon the particular manager's lifestyle and "socio-economic level." This result, however, is not consonant with a reasonable interpretation of Sections 162 and 262.

For the reasons stated above, the decision of the tax court * * * is

Reversed.

NOTES

(A) *Clothing.* The Tax Court had permitted Ms. Pevsner to deduct the cost of her clothes, apparently being much more sympathetic to her claim that she would not wear the clothes outside of work. The court found that the question of suitability was a subjective one to be answered by the taxpayer. If the taxpayer had prevailed, what kinds of clothing would be deductible? Suits worn by laid-back attorneys? The Fifth Circuit accepted the Commissioner's objective test: If the clothing was adaptable for general usage, it was not deductible. This test is derived from several rulings that permit a deduction for "uniforms" if (1) they are specifically required as a condition of employment and (2) they are not adaptable to general wear. Rev. Rul. 70–474, 1970–2 C.B. 34; Rev. Rul. 67–115, 1967–1 C.B. 30.

The extent to which the fisc might be raided if taxpayers were permitted to treat clothing, grooming, and the like as a deductible business expense is nicely illustrated by Irwin v. Commissioner, 72 T.C.M. 1148 (1996). Pennel Phlander Irwin, author of the unpublished novels "Great Woods Poppy" and "Positively People," attempted to deduct many of life's costs including a television, a hot tub, the expenses of traveling to his mother's funeral, his daughter's dorm expenses at college, and the costs of his home. He explained to the court: "For fiction writing all personal experiences and observations are all business experiences and observations. * * * (Example: Upon awaking in the morning the toiletry and dressing process carried out by myself, and observed in others, is research whose end observations are included in the fictional writing for similar actions carried on by the various characters; and therefore, different grooming products would be justifiable research expenses as well as different clothing that conveys fit and feel.)" The following exchange from the trial transcript gives the flavor of Irwin's approach to research and its relationship to his tax return:

> The Court: Mr. Irwin, please explain your research expenses.

> Irwin: * * * Interview research expenses are incurred when I am trying to gain information on different types of subject matter. For instance, Scott Keithley is listed under interview research materials. Scott Keithley happens to be a dentist, and I was getting information on dental hygiene and dental practice, which I learned about firsthand.

> The Court: Was he your dentist?

> Irwin: Scott Keithley? Yes. So part of the service I'm paying for—

> The Court: * * * What did Scott Keithley do for you? Did he clean your teeth?

> * * *

> Irwin: Okay, well, when I'm paying for a service, I prefer—I pay for the physical service as well as for the information that person provides. * * *

Irwin chose not to deduct all food and toiletries however, in part so that he would not have to reveal the contents of works in progress. Despite his largess, the court found all the expenses inherently personal and not deductible. The Ninth Circuit affirmed. 131 F.3d 146 (1997).

In Nicely v. Commissioner, 92 T.C.M. 134 (2006), the Tax Court refused to permit the taxpayer, a welder, to deduct the cost of his Rocky Wolverine work boots because they were suitable for general or personal use. How did the judge know that? Mr. Nicely, who appeared pro se, showed up for the trial wearing the boots. In Hamper v. Commissioner, T.C. Summ. Op. 2011–17, the court denied a deduction for the costs of what a TV news anchor described as "conservative business clothing unsuitable for everyday wear." The judge may have been influenced by the fact that her "work" purchases included loungewear, a robe, cotton bikini and thong underwear, and evening wear.

Would a better alternative be to assume that all costs of clothing and grooming are inherently personal and thus nondeductible? To whom would that be unfair? Perhaps someone who derived no pleasure from the activity and for whom the expenses played a substantial role in her trade or business. A piano soloist required to wear formal attire? See W.J. Fisher v. Commissioner, 23 T.C. 218 (1954) (permitting a deduction for tuxedos). A professional tennis player who wears out court shoes every three weeks? See

Mella v. Commissioner, 52 T.C.M. 1216 (1986) (denying a deduction and rejecting taxpayer's statement that tennis pros do not wear tennis shoes off the court). A model whose hair is styled? See Wilson v. Commissioner, 32 T.C.M. 407 (1973) (denying a deduction because styling provided personal benefits). A soldier whose fatigues cannot be worn off duty? See Rev. Rul. 67–115, 1967–1 C.B. 30 (allowing deduction for fatigues that do "not merely take the place of articles required in civilian life"). Is it important that (almost) everyone purchases clothes for work and incurs grooming expenses? Is it fair that a lawyer can deduct a legal pad but a tennis pro cannot deduct court shoes?

As we have discussed, Congress in 2017 eliminated deductions for employee business expenses, but the question whether the expense is deductible under § 162 remains important in determining whether a benefit provided by an employer is an excludable working condition fringe benefit under § 132(a)(3) and (d). So, could Ms. Pevsner avoid paying for her YSL attire out of after-tax dollars if her employer provided such clothing to her as a fringe benefit? Which, if any, of the exclusions of § 132 would apply?

(B) *The Inherently Personal Standard.* Are there some expenses that are so "inherently personal" that no deduction should be allowed? In Trebilcock v. Commissioner, 64 T.C. 852 (1975), aff'd 557 F.2d 1226 (6th Cir. 1977), the court disallowed deductions for payments by a businessman to a minister for business and personal advice based on prayer. A similar result was reached in Fred W. Amend Co. v. Commissioner, 55 T.C. 320 (1970), aff'd 454 F.2d 399 (7th Cir. 1971), where a businessman hired a Christian Science practitioner who provided spiritual guidance on both business and personal matters. In both cases, the courts disallowed deduction on the ground that the expenditures were "inherently personal in nature." Would it have made any difference if other similar businesses "ordinarily" consulted ministers or Christian Science practitioners? Would it have made any difference if the advice given via prayer and spiritual counseling always resulted in significantly increased profits? If they had received identical advice from a "business consultant," would the payment of the consultant's fee have been deductible? The court in *Trebilcock* noted that "all benefits provided by ministers are inherently personal by nature." Are benefits provided by sports psychologists inherently personal? By aerobics teachers? Stress managers? Does the inherently personal standard provide much guidance? See Kelly v. Commissioner, 62 T.C.M. 1406 (1991). The taxpayer, a CPA who did tax work, sought to deduct the cost of athletic equipment he acquired to build up the stamina needed for a tax practice. The court, rejecting the taxpayer's inherently believable position, found the exercise equipment inherently personal.

Joseph Calarco, a drama professor and playwright, also attempted to deduct newspaper subscriptions, video rentals, and theatre tickets, which he claimed were all business-related, since these quotidian activities helped him to produce art. The Tax Court disagreed, finding the expenditures all personal, but to prove drama can be found anywhere, the judge wrote the opinion as a three-act play complete with prologue, epilogue, and two dozen footnotes referencing the role taxes have played in the theater. Calarco v. Commissioner, 2004 WL 1616387 (unpublished opinion).

Another professor attempted to deduct the cost of home Internet service and a professional library of books, CDs and DVDs among other unreimbursed expenses. The professor claimed that "individuals holding such terminal degrees [a doctorate] bear a lifelong burden of 'developing knowledge, finding knowledge, exploring, [and] essentially self-educating.'" The court, however, found that using the Internet in pursuit of general knowledge by a college professor was more in the nature of a personal expense. As for the books, the court pointed out that some of the collection did not seem relevant to a communications professor or his wife, a college librarian, for example, "The Cat Owners Manual," "The Girl Who Couldn't Fly," and "The Groucho Marx Collection." Tanzi v. Commissioner, 112 T.C.M. 210 (2016).

(C) *Comparison to Fringe Benefits.* Reconsider § 132. Does the exclusion of § 132(a)(3) for "working condition fringes" defined in § 132(d) as property or services, which, if paid for by the employee, would be deductible under § 162, simply shift the inquiry to the employee level? In Henderson v. Commissioner, 46 T.C.M. 566 (1983), the Tax Court denied a deduction for a $35 framed print and a $35 plant purchased by a South Carolina assistant attorney general for her office, finding they were personal expenses. If Ms. Henderson had been assigned an office with a print and a plant, would she have had income? It is likely that the answer is no. How can that be reconciled with § 132(d)?

(D) *Public Employees.* Although, in general, a trade or business expense must be profit-seeking, a limited exception has been carved out for public employees. In Frank v. United States, 577 F.2d 93 (9th Cir. 1978), a businessman who also worked as a virtually uncompensated aide to a United States Senator was allowed to deduct food, lodging, and transportation expenses for trips taken on the Senator's behalf. In some years, the taxpayer's expenses were more than thirty times his salary as an aide. The court recognized that not every public office could be considered a trade or business, but concluded that a position that entailed "a definite work assignment" and was not undertaken "as a tax dodge" would qualify as a trade or business and its expenses could be deducted. See also Rev. Rul. 84–110, 1984–2 C.B. 35, which interprets § 7701(a)(26) to provide an exception for public officeholders to the requirement of a profit motive for a trade or business.

(E) *Unreimbursed Expenses.* The courts tend to be suspicious of any expense paid by an employee not reimbursed by the employer, presumably on the ground that if it were sufficiently appropriate and helpful, the employer would have covered the cost. For example, in Tesar v. Commissioner, 73 T.C.M. 2709 (1997), the taxpayer—a high school math teacher and an apparent comic book fanatic—attempted to deduct almost $30,000 he spent on 16,000 comic books he bought for the school comic book club. Although the Service argued that the expense was not ordinary—because other teachers/sponsors commonly bought only snacks—and not necessary because he did not have to sponsor a club, the taxpayer appears to have lost his deduction because he took all the comics with him when he left his job.

(F) *Domestic Services and Child Care*. Prior to the adoption of § 21, taxpayers argued that the cost of child care during work hours was an ordinary and necessary expense in carrying on a trade or business. In Smith v. Commissioner, 40 B.T.A. 1038 (1939), aff'd per curiam 113 F.2d 114 (2d Cir. 1940), the court held that such amounts paid by a two-earner married couple were "inherently personal" and were not deductible. In effect, the court treated the decision to have a child as an "inherently personal" one, without which no child care expenses would have been incurred. Although there previously had been a deduction for child care expenses, § 21 currently provides a tax credit for qualifying child care expenses. Taxpayers with adjusted gross income of $15,000 or less may offset tax liability by 35 percent of their employment-related dependent care expenses. That percentage is reduced one percentage point for each additional $2,000 of adjusted gross income of the taxpayer, until it reaches 20 percent for taxpayers with AGI above $43,000. The amount of creditable expenses is limited to the income of the lower-earning spouse or, in the case of a single person, to earned income. Students are deemed to earn a limited amount of income. There is a ceiling on creditable expenses of $3,000 for one dependent and $6,000 for more than one. Thus, the credit cannot exceed $1,050 for one dependent or $2,100 for two or more dependents. The credit is not refundable if the taxpayer has insufficient tax liability to take full advantage of it. While the credit seems generous, very few low income taxpayers will be able to take advantage of it and virtually no one would get the maximum credit. For example, a single mother with two children who earns only $15,000 is not likely to pay a babysitter $6,000, and even if she does, she has no tax liability against which to offset any credit.

Is the child care credit appropriately classified as a tax expenditure or is it necessary to a proper measurement of income? Does the phase-down of the credit and the overall dollar limitation inform your answer? Do the following distinctions lend support to either view? (1) The credit is limited to expenses incurred for dependents under age 13. (2) Expenses of sending a child to preschool are deductible, but elementary school tuition is not. (3) The cost of overnight camp is ineligible for the credit, but the expense of day camp is creditable. (4) Not all expenses incurred while the taxpayer is employed are deductible. They must enable the taxpayer to work. But see Brown v. Commissioner, 73 T.C. 156 (1979) (employment motive need not be exclusive or even dominant). How effective is the language of § 21(b)(2)(A), which permits a deduction for expenses "but only if such expenses are incurred to enable the taxpayer to be gainfully employed"? (5) So long as there is a qualifying individual in the home, expenses for "household services" are creditable.

Consider also § 129, which permits an employee to exclude up to $5,000 in any taxable year in dependent care costs covered by or provided by the employer. The maximum amount of the dependent care credit under § 21 is reduced by the amounts excluded under § 129. Is § 129 consistent with the policy reflected in § 21?

Recall that the imputed income from child care services provided by the taxpayer is not subject to tax. See page 123 supra. Is that consistent with the policy of § 21?

Section 45F permits a credit for employer-provided child care facilities. Employers receive a credit equal to 25 percent of qualified expenses for child care for employees and 10 percent of expenses for child care resource and referral services. The maximum credit is $150,000 each taxable year.

Section 23 permits an adopting parent to take a credit of up to $10,000 for expenses incurred in adopting a minor child who is not the child of a spouse. Qualified expenses include court costs, adoption fees, and attorney expenses. Taxpayers who adopt a "special needs child" are automatically entitled to the full amount of the credit regardless of how much they spend. The credit phases out for taxpayers with adjusted gross income between $150,000 and $190,000. The cap and the phase-out amounts are adjusted for inflation. Expenses reimbursed by an employer are not eligible for the credit. The credit is not refundable but can be carried forward for five years.

A. TRAVEL EXPENSES

1. TRANSPORTATION EXPENSES

Note on Transportation Expenses

Transportation expenses, such as air fare, taxicab fare or the cost of operating a car, generally are deductible when the taxpayer is traveling on business. This may be the cost of traveling from one city to another, but it also may be the cost of traveling from one business engagement to another within one metropolitan area. For example, cab fare from the taxpayer's law firm to the courthouse would be deductible.

Commuting. These deductions should be contrasted with the rule that the cost of commuting from home to work and back are nondeductible personal expenses. Reg. § 1.162–2(e). This rule has been defended on the grounds that the work location is fixed and the decision to live beyond walking distance is a personal one. In Commissioner v. Flowers, 326 U.S. 465 (1946), the taxpayer lived in Jackson, Mississippi and worked in Mobile, Alabama and tried to deduct the travel expenses incurred in commuting between the two cities, including meals and hotel accommodations in Mobile. The Supreme Court held that the additional expenses, including the commuting expenses, were not deductible. The Court stated that the "expense must be incurred in pursuit of business," which means that there must be a direct connection between the expenditure and the carrying on of the taxpayer's business. The Court concluded that the traveling expenses were not incurred in pursuit of the business of the taxpayer's employer. The Court found that the sole cause of the expense was the taxpayer's personal desire to reside in Jackson, "a factor irrelevant" to the employer's business since where one chooses to live is generally a matter of personal convenience.

A strict denial of commuting deductions avoids difficult factual inquiries, but may seem unfair where the taxpayer cannot avoid commuting (for example, if she works at a weapons testing facility in the desert) or incurs significant additional expenses. Even though the disallowance of commuting deductions is well settled, questions have remained about special commuting costs that some taxpayers must incur because of the nature of their work.

Commuting and Transportation Fringes. In general, employer reimbursements for commuting costs constitute income to the employee; § 132(d) does not apply because the amount would not be deductible if paid by the employee. However, the regulations permit the cost of transportation provided by the employer to employees paid on an hourly basis to be valued at $1.50 (regardless of actual value) if the transportation is furnished solely due to unsafe conditions. Unsafe conditions exist if a reasonable person would not consider it safe to walk or take public transportation at the applicable time of day. Reg. § 1.61–21(k).

Section 132(f) provides a limited exclusion to employees for qualified transportation fringes, as defined in § 132(f). Until the 2017 tax act, such fringes were also deductible by the employer. However, § 274(a)(4) and (*l*) now deny the deduction. This change in law may discourage employers from offering such fringes, which include transit passes, parking, and commuter highway vehicles. Congress also disallowed any other deduction for employees' commuting expenses, unless necessary for safety.

When it comes to bicycle commuting, however, the fringe rules are reversed during the eight years from 2018 through 2025. Employers may deduct the cost of providing qualified bicycle commuting reimbursements. § 274(*l*). But employees must include the value in income. § 132(f)(8).

Tools of the Trade. In a per curiam opinion, the Supreme Court in Fausner v. Commissioner, 413 U.S. 838 (1973), carved out an exception for "[a]dditional expenses [that] may at times be incurred for transporting job-required tools and material to and from work." In Revenue Ruling 75–380, the IRS asserted that it would permit a deduction "for only the portion of the cost of transporting the work implements by the mode of transportation used which is in excess of the cost of commuting by the same mode of transportation without the work implements." It illustrated this position with the following example:

A taxpayer commuted to and from work by public transportation before the taxpayer had to carry necessary work implements. It cost $2 per day to commute to and from work. When it became necessary to carry the implements to and from work, it cost $3 per day to drive a car and an additional $5 per day to rent a trailer in which the implements were carried. The allowable deduction would be the $5 per day additional expense that the taxpayer incurred in renting the trailer to carry the work implements.

Under this formulation, what expense would the IRS approve other than the cost of renting a trailer? Suppose an employer ordered an employee to take 50 pounds of documents home to read over the weekend. If the employee took a cab rather than his usual mode of travel, the cab fare would not be deductible. But if the employee took the subway and put the documents in the cab, the cab fare would be deductible.

Working and Driving. In Pollei v. Commissioner, 877 F.2d 838 (10th Cir. 1989), the court ruled that police officers, who began active patrol when they left home, were engaged in their jobs while driving to and from the stationhouse. Therefore, the commuting expenses allocable to that time were deductible. The government argued that allowing this deduction would lead to a flood of claims from people who during their commute work on dictaphones or telephones. The court, however, found that the nature of police work allowed it to be distinguished.

Can a meaningful line be drawn between the police officer in this case and a lawyer, who while driving to work, telephones a client or listens to educational tapes?

Commuting to Temporary Employment. The IRS has promulgated the following rules: (1) A taxpayer may deduct daily transportation expenses incurred in going between the taxpayer's residence and a temporary work location outside the metropolitan area where the taxpayer lives and normally works. Generally, however, daily transportation expenses incurred in going between the taxpayer's residence and a temporary work location within the metropolitan area are nondeductible commuting expenses. (2) If a taxpayer has one or more regular work locations away from the taxpayer's residence, the taxpayer may deduct daily transportation expenses incurred in going between the taxpayer's residence and a temporary work location in the same trade or business, regardless of the distance. (3) If a taxpayer's residence is the taxpayer's principal place of business within the meaning of § 280A(c)(1)(A), the taxpayer may deduct daily transportation expenses incurred in going between the residence and another work location in the same trade or business, regardless of whether the other work location is regular or temporary and regardless of the distance. Rev. Rul. 99–7, 1999–1 C.B. 361. A temporary place of business is a location at which the taxpayer performs services on an irregular or short-term basis (usually days or weeks). Rev. Rul. 90–23, 1990–1 C.B. 28.

Thus, if a self-employed accountant drives from her house to her office, and subsequently travels to see a client, the cost of traveling to the office is a nondeductible commuting expense while the cost of traveling from the office to the client is deductible. If she drives from her house to see a regular client before going to the office, the cost is deductible. Is this rational? Should all commuting expenses be allowed as a deduction, or should trips from the taxpayer's residence always be disallowed?

Suppose a worker is required to use a car for business purposes during working hours. Can the cost of getting the car (and not coincidentally the driver/employee) to work be deducted? In an aptly named case, Fillerup v. Commissioner, 55 T.C.M. 362 (1988), the court permitted a doctor to deduct the cost of driving his Mercedes from one hospital to another, but not the cost of driving to the first hospital.

Luxury Expenses. Even when a taxpayer travels on business, the style of transportation may be so luxurious as to produce clear personal benefits. Nevertheless, Congress has acted to limit deductions in only a few cases. Deductions for "luxury" water travel (i.e., cruise ships) are limited to twice the highest per diem allowable to employees of the executive branch of the U.S. government while away from home but serving in the United States. § 274(m). Section 280F limits deductions for "luxury" car expenses.

2.   FOOD AND LODGING

Section 162(a)(2) allows a deduction for travel expenses incurred "while away from home in the pursuit of a trade or business." Deductible expenses include not only transportation but also meals and lodging "while away from home." Travel expenses reimbursed by the employer (as well as those incurred by self-employed individuals) are deductible from gross income under § 62(a)(2)(A). Unreimbursed employee travel expenses are not deductible (between 2018 and the end of 2025) under § 67(g); if this rule is not extended, in 2026 and afterward, they will be subject to the 2 percent floor. In United States v. Correll, 389 U.S. 299 (1967), the Supreme Court upheld the Commissioner's rule that the phrase "away from home" does not include any trip not requiring "sleep or rest" no matter how far the taxpayer travels. The Court concluded that the Commissioner's "overnight" rule for deductions of meals has "achieved not only ease and certainty of application, but also substantial fairness" by placing "all one-day travelers on a similar tax footing, rather than discriminating against intra-city travelers and commuters."

Does an "overnight" requirement aid in the basic determination whether meals should be deductible? In Bissonnette v. Commissioner, 127 T.C. 124 (2006), the court permitted a deduction for meals a ferry boat captain ate during a six-hour layover in a harbor during a one-day, 17-hour sea trip. The demanding job required rest, which the captain did on a cot on the boat. Meals eaten during a one-hour layover were not deductible. In Rev. Rul. 75–168, 1975–1 C.B. 58, the Service permitted deduction of a truck driver's expenses for meals and lodging during eight-hour layovers provided so that he could sleep or rest, but disallowed deduction of the cost of meals purchased during layovers of approximately one-half hour.

If a taxpayer takes the first shuttle from Washington to New York and the last shuttle back the same day, eating breakfast, lunch, and dinner in New York, the cost of the meals is not deductible. If, however, the taxpayer spends the night in New York, returning to Washington early the following day, all three meals are deductible. Note that the taxpayer bears any extra cost of eating in restaurants if she does not stay overnight. The airfare, however, would be deductible in either case. Since § 162(a)(2) is not applicable if the taxpayer returns home the same day, what provision permits the deduction of the airfare? What does this suggest about the purposes of § 162(a)(2)?

The following case further explores what is meant by "away from home in the pursuit of a trade or business."

Hantzis v. Commissioner

United States Court of Appeals, First Circuit, 1981. 638 F.2d 248,
cert. denied, 452 U.S. 962 (1981).

■ LEVIN H. CAMPBELL, CIRCUIT JUDGE.

The Commissioner of Internal Revenue (Commissioner) appeals a decision of the United States Tax Court that allowed a deduction under 26 U.S.C. § 162(a)(2) (1976) for expenses incurred by a law student in the course of her summer employment. * * *

In the fall of 1973 Catharine Hantzis (taxpayer) * * * entered Harvard Law School in Cambridge, Massachusetts, as a full-time student. During her second year of law school she sought unsuccessfully to obtain employment for the summer of 1975 with a Boston law firm. She did, however, find a job as a legal assistant with a law firm in New York City, where she worked for ten weeks beginning in June 1975. Her husband, then a member of the faculty of Northeastern University with a teaching schedule for that summer, remained in Boston and lived at the couple's home there. At the time of the Tax Court's decision in this case, Mr. and Mrs. Hantzis still resided in Boston.

On their joint income tax return for 1975, Mr. and Mrs. Hantzis reported the earnings from taxpayer's summer employment ($3,750) and deducted [under § 162] the cost of transportation between Boston and New York, the cost of a small apartment rented by Mrs. Hantzis in New York and the cost of her meals in New York ($3,204). * * *

The Commissioner disallowed the deduction on the ground that taxpayer's home for purposes of section 162(a)(2) was her place of employment and the cost of traveling to and living in New York was therefore not "incurred * * * while away from home." The Commissioner also argued that the expenses were not incurred "in the pursuit of a trade or business." Both positions were rejected by the Tax Court, which found that Boston was Mrs. Hantzis' home because her employment in New York was only temporary and that her expenses in New York were "necessitated" by her employment there. The court thus held the expenses to be deductible under section 162(a)(2).

In asking this court to reverse the Tax Court's allowance of the deduction, the Commissioner has contended that the expenses were not incurred "in the pursuit of a trade or business." We do not accept this argument; nonetheless, we sustain the Commissioner and deny the deduction, on the basis that the expenses were not incurred "while away from home."

I.

Section 262 of the Code * * * declares that "except as otherwise provided in this chapter, no deductions shall be allowed for personal, living, or family expenses." Section 162 provides less of an exception to this rule than it creates a separate category of deductible business expenses. This category manifests a fundamental principle of taxation: that a person's taxable income should not include the cost of producing that income. * * *

The test by which "personal" travel expenses subject to tax under section 262 are distinguished from those costs of travel necessarily incurred to generate income is embodied in the requirement that, to be deductible under section 162(a)(2), an expense must be "incurred . . . in the pursuit of a trade or business." In *Flowers* the Supreme Court read this phrase to mean that "[t]he exigencies of business rather than the personal conveniences and necessities of the traveler must be the motivating factors." 326 U.S. at 474. Of course, not every travel expense resulting from business exigencies rather than personal choice is deductible; an expense must also be "ordinary and necessary" and incurred "while away from home." 26 U.S.C. § 162(a)(2) (1976); *Flowers,* 326 U.S. at 470. But the latter limitations draw also upon the basic concept that only expenses necessitated by business, as opposed to personal, demands may be excluded from the calculation of taxable income.

With these fundamentals in mind, we proceed to ask whether the cost of taxpayer's transportation to and from New York, and of her meals and lodging while in New York, was incurred "while away from home in the pursuit of a trade or business."

II.

The Commissioner has directed his argument at the meaning of "in pursuit of a trade or business." He interprets this phrase as requiring that a deductible traveling expense be incurred under the demands of a trade or business which predates the expense, i.e., an "already existing" trade or business. Under this theory, section 162(a)(2) would invalidate the deduction taken by the taxpayer because she was a full-time student before commencing her summer work at a New York law firm in 1975 and so was not continuing in a trade or business when she incurred the expenses of traveling to New York and living there while her job lasted.[3] The Commissioner's proposed interpretation erects at the threshold of deductibility under section 162(a)(2) the requirement that a taxpayer be engaged in a trade or business *before* incurring a travel expense. Only if that requirement is satisfied would an inquiry into the deductibility of an expense proceed to ask whether the expense was a result of business exigencies, incurred while away from home, and reasonable and necessary.

Such a reading of the statute is semantically possible and would perhaps expedite the disposition of certain cases. Nevertheless, we reject it as unsupported by case law and inappropriate to the policies behind section 162(a)(2).

* * *

Nor would the Commissioner's theory mesh with the policy behind section 162(a)(2). As discussed, the travel expense deduction is intended to exclude from taxable income a necessary cost of producing that income. Yet the recency of entry into a trade or business does not indicate that travel expenses are not a cost of producing income. To be sure, the costs incurred by a taxpayer who leaves his usual residence to begin a trade or business at another location may not be truly *travel* expenses, i.e., expenses incurred while "away from home," see infra, but practically, they are as much incurred "in the pursuit of a trade or business" when the occupation is new as when it is old.

* * *

Accordingly, we turn to the question whether, in the absence of the Commissioner's proposed threshold limit on deductibility, the expenses at issue here satisfy the requirements of section 162(a)(2) as interpreted in Flowers v. Commissioner.

III.

As already noted, *Flowers* construed section 162(a)(2) to mean that a traveling expense is deductible only if it is (1) reasonable and necessary, (2) incurred while away from home, and (3) necessitated by the exigencies of business. Because the Commissioner does not suggest that Mrs. Hantzis' expenses were unreasonable or unnecessary, we may pass directly to the remaining requirements. Of these, we find dispositive the requirement that an expense be incurred while away from home. As we think Mrs. Hantzis' expenses were not so incurred, we hold the deduction to be improper.

The meaning of the term "home" in the travel expense provision is far from clear. When Congress enacted the travel expense deduction now codified as section 162(a)(2), it apparently was unsure whether, to be

---

[3] The taxpayer has not argued that being a law student constitutes a trade or business and so we do not address the issue. See generally Reisinger v. Commissioner, 71 T.C. 568 (1979); Rev. Rul. 68–591, 1968–2 C.B. 73.

deductible, an expense must be incurred away from a person's residence or away from his principal place of business. * * * This ambiguity persists and courts, sometimes within a single circuit, have divided over the issue. * * * It has been suggested that these conflicting definitions are due to the enormous factual variety in the cases. * * * We find this observation instructive, for if the cases that discuss the meaning of the term "home" in section 162(a)(2) are interpreted on the basis of their unique facts as well as the fundamental purposes of the travel expense provision, and not simply pinioned to one of two competing definitions of home, much of the seeming confusion and contradiction on this issue disappears and a functional definition of the term emerges.

We begin by recognizing that the location of a person's home for purposes of section 162(a)(2) becomes problematic only when the person lives one place and works another. Where a taxpayer resides and works at a single location, he is always home, however defined; and where a taxpayer is constantly on the move due to his work, he is never "away" from home. * * * However, in the present case, the need to determine "home" is plainly before us, since the taxpayer resided in Boston and worked, albeit briefly, in New York.

We think the critical step in defining "home" in these situations is to recognize that the "while away from home" requirement has to be construed in light of the further requirement that the expense be the result of business exigencies. The traveling expense deduction obviously is not intended to exclude from taxation every expense incurred by a taxpayer who, in the course of business, maintains two homes. Section 162(a)(2) seeks rather "to mitigate the burden of the taxpayer who, *because of the exigencies of his trade or business, must* maintain two places of abode and thereby incur additional and duplicate living expenses." * * *

Consciously or unconsciously, courts have effectuated this policy in part through their interpretation of the term "home" in section 162(a)(2). Whether it is held in a particular decision that a taxpayer's home is his residence or his principal place of business, the ultimate allowance or disallowance of a deduction is a function of the court's assessment of the reason for a taxpayer's maintenance of two homes. If the reason is perceived to be personal, the taxpayer's home will generally be held to be his place of employment rather than his residence and the deduction will be denied. * * *

If the reason is felt to be business exigencies, the person's home will usually be held to be his residence and the deduction will be allowed. * * * We understand the concern of the concurrence that such an operational interpretation of the term "home" is somewhat technical and perhaps untidy, in that it will not always afford bright line answers, but we doubt the ability of either the Commissioner or the courts to invent an unyielding formula that will make sense in all cases. The line between personal and business expenses winds through infinite factual permutations; effectuation of the travel expense provision requires that any principle of decision be flexible and sensitive to statutory policy.

Construing in the manner just described the requirement that an expense be incurred "while away from home," we do not believe this requirement was satisfied in this case. Mrs. Hantzis' *trade or business* did not require that she maintain a home in Boston as well as one in New York. Though she returned to Boston at various times during the period of her employment in New York, her visits were all for personal reasons. It is not contended that she had a business connection in Boston that necessitated her keeping a home there; no professional interest was served by maintenance of the Boston home—as would have been the case, for example, if Mrs. Hantzis had been a lawyer based in Boston with a New York client whom she was temporarily serving. The home in Boston was kept up for reasons involving Mr. Hantzis, but those reasons cannot substitute for a showing by *Mrs.* Hantzis that the exigencies of *her* trade or business required *her* to maintain two homes. Mrs. Hantzis' decision to keep two homes must be seen as a choice dictated by personal, albeit wholly reasonable, considerations and not a business or occupational necessity. We therefore hold that her home for purposes of section 162(a)(2) was New York and that the expenses at issue in this case were not incurred "while away from home."

We are not dissuaded from this conclusion by the temporary nature of Mrs. Hantzis' employment in New York. Mrs. Hantzis argues that the brevity of her stay in New York excepts her from the business exigencies requirement of section 162(a)(2) under a doctrine supposedly enunciated by the Supreme Court in Peurifoy v. Commissioner, 358 U.S. 59 (1958) (per curiam).[13] The Tax Court here held that Boston was the taxpayer's home because it would have been unreasonable for her to move her residence to New York for only ten weeks. At first glance these contentions may seem to find support in the court decisions holding that, when a taxpayer works for a limited time away from his usual home, section 162(a)(2) allows a deduction for the expense of maintaining a second home so long as the employment is "temporary" and not "indefinite" or "permanent." * * *

---

[13] In *Peurifoy,* the Court stated that the Tax Court had "engrafted an exception" onto the requirement that travel expenses be dictated by business exigencies, allowing "a deduction for expenditures * * * when the taxpayer's employment is 'temporary' as contrasted with 'indefinite' or 'indeterminate.' " 358 U.S. at 59. Because the Commissioner did not challenge this exception, the Court did not rule on its validity. It instead upheld the circuit court's reversal of the Tax Court and disallowance of the deduction on the basis of the adequacy of the appellate court's review. The Supreme Court agreed that the Tax Court's finding as to the temporary nature of taxpayer's employment was clearly erroneous. Id. at 60, 61.

Despite its inauspicious beginning, the exception has come to be generally accepted. Some uncertainty lingers, however, over whether the exception properly applies to the "business exigencies" or the "away from home" requirement. * * * In fact, it is probably relevant to both.

                          * * *

Because we treat these requirements as inextricably intertwined, * * * we find it unnecessary to address this question; applied to either requirement, the temporary employment doctrine affects the meaning of both.

The temporary employment doctrine does not, however, purport to eliminate any requirement that continued maintenance of a first home have a business justification. We think the rule has no application where the taxpayer has no business connection with his usual place of residence. If no business exigency dictates the location of the taxpayer's usual residence, then the mere fact of his taking temporary employment elsewhere cannot supply a compelling business reason for continuing to maintain that residence. Only a taxpayer who lives one place, works another and has business ties to *both* is in the ambiguous situation that the temporary employment doctrine is designed to resolve. In such circumstances, unless his employment away from his usual home is temporary, a court can reasonably assume that the taxpayer has abandoned his business ties to that location and is left with only personal reasons for maintaining a residence there. Where only personal needs require that a travel expense be incurred, however, a taxpayer's home is defined so as to leave the expense subject to taxation. * * * Thus, a taxpayer who pursues temporary employment away from the location of his usual residence, but has no business connection with that location, is not "away from home" for purposes of section 162(a)(2). * * *

On this reasoning, the temporary nature of Mrs. Hantzis' employment in New York does not affect the outcome of her case. She had no business ties to Boston that would bring her within the temporary employment doctrine. By this holding, we do not adopt a rule that "home" in section 162(a)(2) is the equivalent of a taxpayer's place of business. Nor do we mean to imply that a taxpayer has a "home" for tax purposes only if he is already engaged in a trade or business at a particular location. Though both rules are alluringly determinate, we have already discussed why they offer inadequate expressions of the purposes behind the travel expense deduction. We hold merely that for a taxpayer in Mrs. Hantzis' circumstances to be "away from home in the pursuit of a trade or business," she must establish the existence of some sort of business relation both to the location she claims as "home" and to the location of her temporary employment sufficient to support a finding that her duplicative expenses are necessitated by business exigencies. This, we believe, is the meaning of the statement in *Flowers* that "[b]usiness trips are to be identified *in relation to* business demands and the traveler's business headquarters." 326 U.S. at 474 (emphasis added). On the uncontested facts before us, Mrs. Hantzis had no business relation to Boston; we therefore leave to cases in which the issue is squarely presented the task of elaborating what relation to a place is required under section 162(a)(2) for duplicative living expenses to be deductible.

Reversed.

 ■ KEETON, DISTRICT JUDGE, concurring in the result.

Although I agree with the result reached in the court's opinion, and with much of its underlying analysis, I write separately because I cannot join in the court's determination that New York was the taxpayer's home for purposes of 26 U.S.C. § 162(a)(2). In so holding, the court adopts a definition of "home" that differs from the ordinary meaning of the term and therefore unduly risks causing confusion and misinterpretation of the important principle articulated in this case.

In adopting section 162(a)(2), Congress sought "to mitigate the burden of the taxpayer who, because of the exigencies of his trade or business, must maintain two places of abode and thereby incur additional and duplicate living expenses."

* * *

In the present case, the taxpayer does not contend that she maintained her residence in Boston for business reasons. Before working in New York, she had attended school near her home in Boston, and she continued to do so after she finished her summer job. In addition, her husband lived and worked in Boston. Thus, on the facts in this case, I am in agreement with the court that the taxpayer's deductions must be disallowed because she was not required by her trade or business to maintain both places of residence. However rather than resting its conclusion on an interpretation of the language of section 162(a)(2) taken as a whole, which allows a deduction for ordinary and necessary expenses incurred "while away from home in the pursuit of trade or business," the court reaches the same result by incorporating the concept of business-related residence into the definition of "home," thereby producing sometimes, but not always, a meaning of "home" quite different from ordinary usage.

* * *

The court enters [the] conflict among circuits with a "functional" definition of home not yet adopted by any other circuit. I read the opinion as indicating that in a dual residence case, the Commissioner must determine whether the exigencies of the taxpayer's trade or business require her to maintain both residences. * * * If so, the Commissioner must decide that the taxpayer's *principal residence* is her "home" and must conclude that expenses associated with the secondary residence were incurred "while away from home," and are deductible. If not, as in the instant case, the Commissioner must find that the taxpayer's *principal place of business* is her "home" and must conclude that the expenses in question were not incurred "while away from home." The conclusory nature of these determinations as to which residence is her "home" reveals the potentially confusing effect of adopting an extraordinary definition of "home."

* * *

The result reached by the court can easily be expressed while also giving "home" its ordinary meaning, and neither Congress nor the Supreme Court has directed that "home" be given an extraordinary meaning in the present context. * * *

In analyzing dual residence cases, the court's opinion advances compelling reasons that the first step must be to determine whether the taxpayer has business as opposed to purely personal reasons for maintaining both residences. This must be done in order to determine whether the expenses of maintaining a second residence were, "necessitated by business, as opposed to personal, demands," * * * and were in this sense incurred by the taxpayer "while away from home in pursuit of trade or business." Necessarily implicit in this proposition is a more limited corollary that is sufficient to decide the present case: When the taxpayer has a business relationship to only one location, no traveling expenses the taxpayer incurs are "necessitated by business, as opposed to personal demands," regardless of how many residences the taxpayer has, where they are located, or which one is "home."

* * *

NOTES

(A) *The "Away-from-Home" Test.* The obvious task of § 162(a)(2) is to distinguish everyday living expenses from those occasioned by business travel. Does the phrase "away from home" adequately differentiate business from personal expenses? The current rule essentially ignores the personal consumption element of business travel, unless the food and lodging are lavish and extravagant, a limitation seldom, if ever, applied.

(B) *A House Is Not Necessarily a Home.* The Service's position is that a taxpayer's "home" for purposes of § 162(a)(2) is the taxpayer's regular or principal place of business. If the taxpayer has no principal place of business, then his "tax home" is his regular place of abode. Rev. Rul. 75–432, 1975–2 C.B. 60. Several Courts of Appeals have adopted this position. See, e.g., Markey v. Commissioner, 490 F.2d 1249 (6th Cir. 1974). The Second Circuit, however, has concluded that your house is indeed your home. Using the approach that a taxpayer's residence is his home, the court shifted the focus to whether the expenses were required in pursuit of business. Rosenspan v. United States, 438 F.2d 905 (2d Cir. 1971). As the concurring opinion of Judge Keeton suggests, the court in *Hantzis* seems to create a "third way." While several courts have rejected the IRS approach (which seems easier to apply), the taxpayers still generally have lost. Should the court first consider when its approach will make a difference before deciding to complicate the law? Can you think of any circumstances where the approach will be determinative? See Note (G) below.

If the taxpayer has no regular abode, there is no deduction. In Wirth v. Commissioner, 61 T.C. 855, 859 (1974), the court disallowed any deduction for an itinerant salesman without a regular home because there must be substantial continuing expenses that will be duplicated by expenditures made when the taxpayer is required to travel elsewhere for business purposes.

Reiterating the *Flowers* holding that travel must be required by the exigencies of business to be deductible, former Alaska Governor and former

Vice-Presidential candidate Sarah Palin had to pay taxes on almost $17,000 of per diem payments she received while staying at her home in Wasilla, AK. Alaska allowed the payments since Juneau is the governor's "duty station." Palin had collected per diems for 312 days spent at her own home during the first 19 months in office. Although originally the state had not treated the reimbursements as income, it reversed itself after the Presidential campaign and found that the costs of staying in her home were not legitimate business expenses. If Wasilla/Anchorage was considered Palin's tax home, then she would not be away from home when she worked there. Thus, her living expenses would not be deductible and the reimbursements would be includible.

(C) *Multiple Businesses.* Suppose Hantzis had worked part-time during the school year at the Boston office of the New York City firm where she spent the summer? Would it make any difference if she had returned to the job during her third year? Would it matter how much she earned or how many hours she worked in Boston? Note that Hantzis netted, after expenses, $546, for her 10 weeks in New York, far less than the minimum wage. Even if she had retained a "tax home" in Boston, would her expenses be "necessitated by business exigencies"?

Where a taxpayer has two businesses, it is clear that she can deduct the costs of traveling between them and meals and lodging when she is away from home. Is she always "away from home"? Or is she in that status in only one location? The Service's position is that "home" is the principal place of business and thus meals and lodging can be deducted only when the taxpayer is at her minor place of business. Rev. Rul. 63–82, 1963–1 C.B. 33. In Rev. Rul. 75–432, 1975–2 C.B. 60, the IRS applied this rule to seasonal workers, such as baseball players, who alternate between two bases every year.

In Barrett v. Commissioner, 114 T.C. M. 398 (2017), the Tax Court allowed a deduction for a video producer's travel from his home in Las Vegas to Washington, D.C. where he spent a couple of months a year in hotels or rental apartments finishing the videos in his client's studio. The Court accepted his testimony that he did most of the work in his Las Vegas home so it, and not D.C., was his principal place of business.

(D) *Temporary vs. Indefinite Employment.* Where a taxpayer leaves his regular place of work to take a temporary job at another location, the taxpayer may treat his regular residence or place of employment as "home" and deduct the costs of food and lodging at his temporary job. If the duration of the new job is "indefinite," however, the taxpayer may not deduct his expenses. Section 162(a) provides that the taxpayer is not treated as being temporarily away from home if the period of employment exceeds one year. The IRS has interpreted this to mean that expenses attributable to employment which is realistically expected to last for more than a year are not deductible regardless of how long the employment actually lasts. Expenses relating to employment expected to last for less than a year that in fact does last for less than a year are deductible, but if the expectation changes, only the expenses until that date are deductible. Rev. Rul. 99–7, 1999–1 C.B. 361. A taxpayer who is temporarily away from home on business for 370 days, for example, would be able to deduct none of her travel expenses. If you were out of town "temporarily" assigned to a case, what should you consider doing on the 364th day?

The Tax Court has followed this distinction, allowing a deduction only for expenses if the duration of the new job is temporary rather than indefinite. In Wilbert v. Commissioner, 553 F.3d 544 (7th Cir. 2009), Judge Posner ridiculed this distinction, noting: "The problem with the Tax Court's distinction is that work can be, and usually is, both temporary and indefinite, as in [a] lawyer example. A lawsuit he is trying in London might settle on the second day, or last a month; his sojourn away from his office will therefore be both temporary *and* indefinite. Indeed *all* work is indefinite and much "permanent" work is really temporary." Instead he relied on the *Flowers* holding "that unless the taxpayer has a business rather than a personal reason to be living in two places he cannot deduct his traveling expenses if he decides not to move." In *Wilbert* the taxpayer was a mechanic who had been laid off from his job with Northwest Airlines in Minneapolis. Within a several month period, he exercised seniority rights to bump another mechanic in Chicago until he was bumped by a more senior mechanic, whereupon he bumped his way to Anchorage and then New York City before getting a position back in Anchorage from which he was laid off. The Seventh Circuit held he had no business reason to be "living in" both Minneapolis and the other locations and thus denied the deduction.

(E) *Two-Earner Families.* As *Hantzis* illustrates, two-earner families can face particular problems as a result of the "tax home" concept. See, e.g., Daly v. Commissioner, 662 F.2d 253 (4th Cir. 1981), in which a salesman maintained a home in Virginia near his wife's place of employment, but spent most of his time in and around Philadelphia where many of his customers were located. Reversing a panel decision, the en banc court held that Philadelphia was the taxpayer's "home" for purposes of § 162(a)(2) and disallowed deductions for travel between Philadelphia and Virginia and for meals and lodging consumed in Philadelphia. The decision not to live separately from his wife was considered personal. A concurring opinion argued for legislative reform to accommodate the particular problems of working couples.

(F) *Mixed Personal-Business Trips.* Once the taxpayer establishes a "tax home," he must be away from that home "in pursuit of a trade or business." If a trip is for mixed business and personal reasons, travel costs are deductible only if the trip is primarily for business purposes. The relative amount of time spent on business as opposed to pleasure is important, but not determinative, as to the primary purpose. Suppose a doctor attends a continuing education program for physicians at a ski resort, attends classes from 8–10 a.m. and skis for the rest of the day? (See § 274(c) for special rules relating to foreign travel.)

(G) *Duplication.* Why should meals and lodging ever be deductible? Although the IRS has steadfastly tried to apply a mechanical rule to determine when the taxpayer is away from home, the courts increasingly look to the purpose behind the deduction. In the view of the First Circuit, a taxpayer may deduct expenses when business reasons require him to duplicate expenses. See Andrews v. Commissioner, 931 F.2d 132 (1st Cir.

1991), where a taxpayer spent several months of the year operating a pool construction business in Massachusetts and the rest of the year maintaining a stable of race horses in Florida. The court rejected the Service's argument that he was never away from home because he had two tax homes, finding that he had one tax home and could deduct his duplicate expenses while away on business. It is difficult, however, to see how food expenses could be duplicative. An individual must have food and lodging whether she engages in business or not, although the price of these items might rise as business constraints limit her choices. To the extent the expense substitutes for, rather than duplicates, personal consumption, it might be classified as inherently personal. Alternatively, why not limit deductions for meals to verifiable "additional expenses?" Another alternative is to disallow a deduction for a portion of the food expenses. See 274(n), discussed infra at page 301. Consider also the excludability of meals under § 119, discussed supra at page 117, and their deductibility as business entertainment, infra in the next Section.

B. BUSINESS MEALS

Moss v. Commissioner

Tax Court of the United States, 1983. 80 T.C. 1073.

■ WILBUR, JUDGE: * * *

Petitioner is a partner in a Chicago law firm that met every business day in 1976 and 1977 at the Café Angelo for lunch. Current litigation problems, scheduling, assignments, and settlement of cases were discussed at that time. The firm paid for the meals of those lawyers who ate during the firm meetings. The issue for decision is whether petitioner may deduct his share of those expenses in calculating his taxable income.

Petitioner contends that the luncheon meeting expenses are deductible under section 162 as ordinary and necessary business expenses. * * * Respondent, conversely, claims that the lunches are a personal and therefore nondeductible expense. We agree with respondent.

The broad purpose of the Internal Revenue Code is to tax all accessions to wealth, "from whatever source derived." Sec. 61(a). The goal being to tax income, business expenses reduce taxable income. Sec. 162. Funds spent on personal consumption, on the other hand, are not deductible. Sec. 262. The boundary line dividing personal expenses from business expenses, often obscurely marked, has been a fertile field of battle. * * * In close contests, it is essential to bear in mind that the provisions of section 262 take priority over section 162.

The expense in question is close to that evanescent line dividing personal and business expenses. From the perspective of the partnership, the lunches were a cost incurred in earning their income. The lawyers needed to coordinate assignments and scheduling of their case load, and the noon hour was a logical, convenient time at which to do so. They considered the meeting to be part of their working day, not as an hour of reprieve from business affairs. The individuals did not feel free to make alternate plans, or to eat elsewhere. For this firm, petitioner argues, the meeting was both ordinary and necessary.

The Commissioner focuses not on the circumstances bringing the partnership together each day, but rather on the fact that the individuals were eating lunch while they were together. Rather than to section 162, he looks to section 262, and the regulations which specifically categorize meals as personal expenses. Sec. 1.262–5, Income Tax Regs. The respondent, in essence, argues that while the meeting may have been ordinary and necessary to the business, the outlay was for meals, a personal item.

The dual nature of the business lunch has long been a difficult problem for legislators and courts alike. The traditional view of the courts has been that if a personal living expense is to qualify under section 162, the taxpayer must demonstrate that it was "different from or in excess of that which would have been made for the taxpayer's personal purposes." Sutter v. Commissioner, 21 T.C. 170, 173 (1953).[9]

Following the *Sutter* formula, numerous taxpayers have attempted to deduct the cost of meals eaten under unusual or constraining circumstances. The claims have been denied almost invariably. See, e.g., Fife v. Commissioner, 73 T.C. 621 (1980) (attorney may not deduct cost of meals eaten in restaurants due to late client meetings); Ma-Tran Corp. v. Commissioner, 70 T.C. 158 (1978) (corporation may not deduct cost of officer's locally consumed meals absent travel or compliance with section 274); Drill v. Commissioner, 8 T.C. 902 (1947) (construction worker cannot deduct cost of dinners on nights he worked overtime). Daily meals are an inherently personal expense, and a taxpayer bears a heavy burden in proving they are routinely deductible.

Petitioner relies on Wells v. Commissioner, 626 F.2d 868 (9th Cir. 1980), affg. without published opinion T.C.Memo. 1977–419, in support of his position. In *Wells,* we denied a deduction claimed by a public defender for the cost of occasional lunch meetings with his staff. The Court noted, however, that in a law firm, "an occasional luncheon meeting with the staff to discuss the operation of the firm would be regarded as an 'ordinary and necessary expense.'" We note, first, that this statement is dictum in a memorandum opinion, and thus not

---

9   * * * The present circumstances do not require an exploration of the dimensions of our opinion in Sutter v. Commissioner, 21 T.C. 170 (1953). We note, however, that in the case of business meals, *Sutter* permits a deduction where the expense is "different from *or* in excess of" the personal expenditure the taxpayer would otherwise have made. This language is in the disjunctive. Business meals have received extensive congressional consideration through the years. Accordingly, Congress is presumed to be aware of the administrative practice permitting the entire expense of a business meal to be deducted without fragmentation. In essence, where a proper business purpose and relationship are established, the expenses are presumed to be different from one the taxpayer would normally have made.

controlling. Second, that case referred to occasional lunches, a far cry from the daily sustenance involved in the case at bar. Even assuming that *Wells* is of any assistance to petitioner, we need not decide where the line between these two cases should be drawn, for we are convinced that outlays for meals consumed 5 days per week, 52 weeks per year would in any event fall on the nondeductible side of it.

The only recent cases where deductions were allowed for meals taken on a regular basis were Sibla v. Commissioner, 611 F.2d 1260 (9th Cir. 1980), affg. 68 T.C. 422 (1977), and Cooper v. Commissioner, 67 T.C. 870 (1977). Those cases involved Los Angeles firemen who were required to contribute to a meal fund for each day they were on duty, regardless of whether they ate or even were present at the fire station. This Court allowed them to deduct the expense under section 162; a concurring opinion would have allowed the expense by analogy to section 119. Cooper v. Commissioner, supra at 874–876. On appeal, the Ninth Circuit approved of both theories, stating that because the taxpayer's situation was both unusual and unique, the expense was business rather than personal.

The decision by the Ninth Circuit implies that similar considerations are involved in determining whether a meal is a business expense under section 162 and whether the value of a meal supplied by an employer should be included in gross income under section 61. Section 119 provides a limited exception to section 61 by allowing an employee to exclude such amounts if the meal is furnished on the business premises for the convenience of the employer. The cases decided under section 119 have focused on the degree to which the employee's actions are restricted by his employer's demands. * * * Language referring to compliance with the demands of one's employer can also be found in section 162 cases decided by this Court. * * *

Petitioner relies on this notion of restriction in contending that the cost of the lunches, like the cost of the firehouse mess in *Sibla* and *Cooper,* should be deductible. He argues that the attorneys "considered the luncheon meetings as a part of their regular work day," and that the firm incurred the expense "solely for the benefit of its practice and not for the personal convenience of its attorneys."

Petitioner has not explained, however, how this "restriction" is any different than that imposed on an attorney who must spend his lunch hour boning up on the Rules of Civil Procedure in preparation for trial or reading an evidence book to clarify a point that may arise during an afternoon session. In all these cases, the lawyer spends an extra hour at work. The mere fact that this time is given over the noon hour does not convert the cost of daily meals into a business expense to be shared by the Government.

* * *

In agreeing with the Commissioner on this point, we are well aware that business needs dictated the choice of the noon hour for the daily meeting. In a very real sense, these meetings contributed to the success of the partnership. But other costs contributing to the success of one's employment are treated as personal expenses. Commuting is obviously essential to one's continued employment, yet those expenses are not deductible as business expenses. * * *

In the instant case, we are convinced that petitioner and his partners and associates discussed business at lunch, that the meeting was a part of their working day, and that this time was the most convenient time at which to meet. We are also convinced that the partnership benefited from the exchange of information and ideas that occurred.

But this does not make his lunch deductible any more than riding to work together each morning to discuss partnership affairs would make his share of the commuting costs deductible. If only the four partners attended the luncheons, petitioner's share of the expenses (assuming they were coequal partners) would have corresponded to his share of the luncheons. This is not an occasion for the general taxpayer to share in the cost of his daily sustenance. Indeed, if petitioner is correct, only the unimaginative would dine at their own expense.

* * *

■ STERRETT, J., concurring: I concur in the result in this particular case, but I want to make it clear that I do not view this opinion as disallowing the cost of meals in all instances where only partners, co-workers, etc., are involved. We have here findings that the partners met at lunch because it was "convenient" and "convenient" 5 days a week, 52 weeks a year.

■ TANNENWALD, FAY, GOFFE, WHITAKER, KORNER, SHIELDS, HAMBLEN, and COHEN, JJ., agree with this concurring opinion.

NOTES

(A) *Employer-Subsidized Meals.* The *Sutter* case, cited in *Moss,* is the leading case disallowing deductions for regular business meals. In Christey v. United States, 841 F.2d 809 (8th Cir. 1988), however, the Eighth Circuit Court of Appeals permitted state troopers to deduct as ordinary and necessary business expenses under § 162(a) the cost of meals that they were required to eat at public restaurants adjacent to the highway while they were on duty. By treating such expenses as deductible employee business expenses, the court achieved results somewhat similar, but not precisely identical, to the exclusion under § 119 that the Supreme Court rejected in *Kowalski,* which is discussed at page 117 supra.

Are the lunches of the associates at Moss's law firm taxable to them? Omitted Footnote 13 of *Moss* indicates that the meals may be compensation. Might they be excludable under § 119? Would the answer be different if the meals were provided on the business premises? According to the October 28,

1986 edition of the Chicago Tribune, the Moss law firm subsequently hired its favorite waiter at Café Angelo to cook meals in a new dining room at the firm. Is there any reason why the results under § 119 and § 162 should be different?

Consider also § 132(e)(2) for what appears to be an alternative means of providing employer-subsidized meals.

(B) *The Client's Meal.* How do you think the Tax Court would view a case where a law partner eats lunch with a client and pays for both meals? The cost of the client's meal would be deductible under § 274(a) if it is "directly related" or "associated with the active conduct of a trade or business." Legislative history indicates that a business meal is directly related to the active conduct of the taxpayer's trade or business if (1) the taxpayer has more than a general expectation of deriving income or a specific business benefit; (2) the taxpayer engaged in business discussions during or directly before or after the meal or entertainment; and (3) the principal reason for the expense was the active conduct of the taxpayer's trade or business.

In addition, § 274(d) imposes substantiation rules, requiring the taxpayer to retain adequate documentation. This rule effectively repealed the so-called *Cohan* rule, which had allowed approximations of the amount of expenditures when there was evidence of a deductible expenditure in some amount. See Cohan v. Commissioner, 39 F.2d 540 (2d Cir. 1930); Reg. § 1.274–5(c)(3). See also Rev. Proc. 83–71, 1983–2 C.B. 590, which provides that taxpayers may claim a specified amount per day for meals instead of substantiating the actual cost of each meal.

Would you expect these requirements to significantly limit the number of client meals that are deductible?

(C) *The Taxpayer's Meal.* May the taxpayer who accompanies the client to dinner deduct his own meal? See Rev. Rul. 63–144, 1963–2 C.B. 129, which provides in part as follows:

> 31. Question: Several of these questions and answers refer to the cost of a taxpayer entertaining a business customer at lunch or dinner. To what extent is the cost of the taxpayer's own meal deductible?
>
> Answer: Judicial decisions under established law, applying the statutory rules that deductions are not allowed for personal expenses, hold that a taxpayer cannot obtain a deduction for the portion of his meal cost which does not exceed an amount he would normally spend on himself. The Service practice has been to apply this rule largely to abuse cases where taxpayers claim deductions for substantial amounts of personal living expenses. The Service does not intend to depart from this practice.

Why should the taxpayer's own meal be deductible if he eats with a client? *Moss* was affirmed by the Seventh Circuit. 758 F.2d 211 (7th Cir. 1985). Writing for the court, Judge Posner noted:

Suppose a theatrical agent takes his clients out to lunch at the expensive restaurants that the clients demand. Of course he can deduct the expense of their meals, from which he derives no pleasure or sustenance, but can he also deduct the expense of his own? He can, because he cannot eat more cheaply; he cannot munch surreptitiously on a peanut butter and jelly sandwich brought from home while his client is wolfing down tournedos Rossini followed by soufflé au grand marnier. No doubt our theatrical agent, unless concerned for his longevity, derives personal utility from his fancy meal, but probably less than the price of the meal. He would not pay for it if it were not for the business benefit; he would get more value from using the same money to buy something else; hence the meal confers on him less utility than the cash equivalent would.

Why should the taxpayer's meal be deductible if he eats with a client, but not if he eats with a co-worker? Judge Posner explained that dichotomy:

[I]t is undeniable that eating together fosters camaraderie and makes business dealings friendlier and easier. It thus reduces the costs of transacting business, for these costs include the frictions and the failures of communication that are produced by suspicion and mutual misunderstanding, by differences in tastes and manners, and by lack of rapport. A meeting with a client or customer in an office is therefore not a perfect substitute for a lunch with him in a restaurant. But it is different when all the participants in the meal are coworkers, as essentially was the case here (clients occasionally were invited to the firm's daily luncheon, but Moss has made no attempt to identify the occasions). They know each other well already; they don't need the social lubrication that a meal with an outsider provides—at least don't need it daily. If a large firm had a monthly lunch to allow partners to get to know associates, the expenses of the meal might well be necessary, and would be allowed by the Internal Revenue Service * * *. But Moss's firm never had more than eight lawyers (partners and associates), and did not need a daily lunch to cement relationships among them.

(D) *No Deduction for Entertainment Expenses.* Beginning in 2018, Congress flatly prohibited the deduction of entertainment. Off-limits now (in terms of deductibility) are sports tickets, theater tickets, and club dues. The new prohibition replaces an array of rules that imposed special restrictions on hunting lodges and sky boxes at sporting events (among other items).

(E) *Conventions.* Concerned that nominally business-motivated foreign travel, particularly conventions held at resorts, had substantial potential for abuse, Congress imposed special limitations on foreign conventions. No deduction is allowed for expenses allocable to a convention, seminar, or similar meeting held outside the North American area unless, taking into account certain factors, it is "as reasonable" for the meeting to be held outside the North American area as within it. (The North American area includes the United States, its possessions, Canada, Mexico, and the Trust Territory of the Pacific Islands and, in certain circumstances, the countries of the Caribbean.) § 274(b)(3) and (6). The factors that will be taken into account are: (1) the purpose of the meeting and its activities; (2) the purposes and activities of the sponsoring groups; and (3) the residence of the active members of the sponsoring groups and the places at which other meetings have been held. Expenses for conventions reasonably held outside North America are treated like any other business expense and not disallowed unless they are extravagant.

In general, the expenses of attending a convention in the United States (even if at a ski resort or oceanside paradise) are deductible. Under the 2017 tax act, any entertainment is nondeductible. Presumably, taxpayers will have to allocate convention costs among deductible items (meals, transportation, and lodging) and nondeductible entertainment. Interesting questions of interpretation are likely to follow: is, say, a paid speech to conventiongoers by a former President "entertainment" or part of the business program?

What is the logic of rules that would permit a deduction for attendance at a convention of U.S. swimming pool dealers in Alaska but not for high school art teachers in France?

(F) *The 50 Percent Disallowance.* A more direct attack on the personal element of meals and entertainment is found in § 274(n), which now limits the deduction to 50 percent of cost. This provision is intended, in a rough way, to reflect Congress' judgment that an element of personal consumption is inherent in such meals and is a reaction to the public sentiment that government is subsidizing expense account living. In effect, Congress arbitrarily treats the consumption as one-half the cost of the meal. The report of the Senate Finance Committee, S. Rep. No. 313, 99th Cong., 1st Sess. 68 (1986) (discussing an amendment that had limited the deduction to 80 percent) noted:

> The committee believes that present law, by not focusing sufficiently on the personal-consumption element of deductible meal and entertainment expenses, unfairly permits taxpayers who can arrange business settings for personal consumption to receive, in effect a Federal tax subsidy for such consumption that is not available to other taxpayers. * * * For example, when executives have dinner at an expensive restaurant following business discussions and then deduct the cost of the meal, the fact that there may be some bona fide business connection does not alter the imbalance between the treatment of those persons, who have effectively transferred a portion of the cost of their meal to the Federal Government, and other individuals, who cannot deduct the cost of their meals.

> The significance of this imbalance is heightened by the fact that business travel and entertainment often may be more lavish than comparable activities in a nonbusiness setting. * * * This disparity is highly visible, and contributes to public perceptions that the tax system is unfair.

The 50 percent limitation also applies to meals while away from home overnight on business. It does not apply to, among other things: traditional recreational meal expenses for employees, such as a holiday party or summer outing, meals fully taxed to the recipient as compensation, and meals sold to customers (e.g., a restaurant can fully deduct the cost of meals sold to patrons). § 274(e).

A case involving the Boston Bruins hockey team nicely illustrates the interaction of the employer's deduction for meals and the employee's exclusion (as well as telling you more about the life of a professional hockey team than you ever wanted to know, including the gastric requirements of the players). The Bruins contracted with hotels in the cities where away games were played to provide meals to players and staff and asserted that the 50 percent limitation of § 274(n) did not apply. The Bruins relied on § 274(n)(2)(B), which provides an exception if the meals qualify as a de minimis fringe under § 132(e). Meals are considered a de minimis fringe if, among other tests, the facility where the meals are eaten is located on or near the business premises of the employer and the annual revenue derived from the facility normally equals or exceeds the direct operating costs of the facility. § 132(e)(2). As to that second test, the regulations provide that it is met if the employer can determine that the meals were excludible under § 119. That section requires that the meals must be provided on the employer's business premise for the convenience of the employer. Assuming you are still following this, it all boiled down to whether the hotels where the team ate could reasonably be treated as the Bruins' business premise. The Tax Court found that an employer's business premise is a place where employees perform a significant portion of their duties or where the employer conducts a significant portion of business. In what will probably come as a surprise to hockey fans, the court found that a significant portion of the Bruins' business was conducted in the ballrooms of hotels around the country. Among the business reasons cited were ensuring the employees' nutritional needs were met so that they could perform at peak levels, providing consistent meals to avoid gastric issues during the game, and the limited time to prepare for a game in each city given the "hectic" hockey season schedule. Jacobs v. Commissioner, 148 T.C. No. 24 (2017).

Beginning in 2026, the 2017 legislation cuts back on the tax benefits of meals provided as fringe benefits excludable by employees. Specifically, employers may not deduct the costs of meals excludable under § 132(e)(2) (certain on-premises eating facilities) or provided for the convenience of the employer. § 274(*o*).

If a taxpayer is reimbursed for the cost of business meals (and makes an adequate accounting), the 50 percent limitation applies to the one who makes the reimbursement, not the taxpayer. Thus, for example, if a law firm separately bills and is reimbursed by a client for meal expenses, the client, and not the law firm, is subject to the 50 percent limitation on these expenses. Likewise, an employee who spends amounts on business-related meals and is reimbursed by his employer is not taxed on this amount, but the employer is allowed to deduct only 50 percent of the cost of the meals. Reg. § 1.62–2(h).

If the employee is not reimbursed by the employer, no deduction is permitted between 2018 and the end of 2025. § 67(g). Without further change, in years afterward (as under prior law), the expenses for meals and entertainment will be subject to not only the 50 percent limitation, but also the 2 percent floor of § 67.

(G) *Reform Strategy.* Considerations of equity seem to dominate efforts to restrict entertainment and business meal deductions. The most equitable result would be to prohibit a deduction for the personal consumption portion of a meal or entertainment expense. Congress seems to recognize the folly of actually inquiring about the personal consumption component of business meal and entertainment expenses and instead has adopted a number of arbitrary rules, most recently, in 2017, by disallowing all entertainment expenses while still permitting a 50 percent deduction for most business meals. What do you think is the best strategy for dealing with business meals and entertainment? Does a flat prohibition reflect Congress' judgment as to what are helpful costs in trying to maximize profits?

Despite the limitations, the liberal allowance of the deduction for meals is in sharp contrast to the restrictions on deduction of many other business-related costs, such as work clothing and commuting. Is the case for characterizing expenditures as "inherently personal" stronger or weaker for entertainment than for work clothing or grooming?

Is it important that high income individuals generally are thought to capture most of the benefits of the meal and entertainment deductions? Note that if a law firm partner takes a client/friend to dinner and the theater, the costs are deductible, but if a blue-collar laborer has a hot dog at the ball game with a co-worker, the cost is not deductible even if they talk about their jobs during the seventh-inning stretch.

The 2017 tax bill's disallowance of entertainment deductions may have an adverse economic impact on certain sectors of the economy and certain regions (hint: Las Vegas and Atlantic City may be hit). Charles Clotfelder has offered the following estimate of the economic effects of disallowing business deductions for travel and entertainment:

> Proposals to limit deductibility * * * would undoubtedly cause sharp declines in employment in hotels, restaurants, and some entertainment sectors. The * * * estimates * * * imply that halving the deduction for entertainment could cause spending on entertainment by proprietorships to drop by 50 percent.

Charles Clotfelder, "Tax-Induced Distortions and the Business-Pleasure Borderline: The Case of Travel and Entertainment," 73 Am.Econ.Rev. 1053 (1983). Whether or not Clotfelder's estimates are accurate, some shifting of the sort he describes will no doubt occur as a result of the disallowance of the entertainment deductions.

C. HOME OFFICE EXPENSES

Popov v. Commissioner

United States Court of Appeals, Ninth Circuit, 2001. 246 F.3d 1190.

■ HAWKINS, CIRCUIT JUDGE:

This case concerns the continuing problem of the home office deduction. We conclude, on the facts of this case, that a professional musician is entitled to deduct the expenses from the portion of her home used exclusively for musical practice.

Facts and Procedural Background

Katia Popov is a professional violinist who performs regularly with the Los Angeles Chamber Orchestra and the Long Beach Symphony. She also contracts with various studios to record music for the motion picture industry. In 1993, she worked for twenty-four such contractors and recorded in thirty-eight different locations. These recording sessions required that Popov be able to read scores quickly. The musicians did not receive the sheet music in advance of the recording sessions; instead, they were presented with their parts when they arrived at the studio, and recording would begin shortly thereafter. None of Popov's twenty-six employers provided her with a place to practice.

Popov lived with her husband Peter, an attorney, and their four-year-old daughter Irina, in a one-bedroom apartment in Los Angeles, California. The apartment's living room served as Popov's home office. The only furniture in the living room consisted of shelves with recording equipment, a small table, a bureau for storing sheet music, and a chair. Popov used this area to practice the violin and to make recordings, which she used for practice purposes and as demonstration tapes for orchestras. No one slept in the living room, and the Popovs' daughter was not allowed to play there. Popov spent four to five hours a day practicing in the living room.

In their 1993 tax returns, the Popovs claimed a home office deduction for the living room and deducted forty percent of their annual rent and twenty percent of their annual electricity bill. The Internal Revenue Service ("the Service") disallowed these deductions, and the Popovs filed a petition for redetermination in the Tax Court.

The Tax Court concluded that the Popovs were not entitled to a home office deduction. Although "practicing at home was a very important component to [Popov's] success as a musician," the court found that her living room was not her "principal place of business." In the court's view, her principal places of business were the studios and concert halls where she recorded and performed, because it was her performances in these places that earned her income. * * *

Analysis

The Internal Revenue Code allows a deduction for a home office that is exclusively used as "the principal place of business for any trade or business of the taxpayer." 26 U.S.C. § 280A(c)(1)(A). The Code does not define the phrase "principal place of business."

A.   The Soliman Tests

Our inquiry is governed by Commissioner v. Soliman, 506 U.S. 168 (1993), the Supreme Court's most recent treatment of the home office deduction. In Soliman, the taxpayer was an anesthesiologist who spent thirty to thirty-five hours per week with patients at three different hospitals. None of the hospitals provided Soliman with an office, so he used a spare bedroom for contacting patients and surgeons, maintaining billing records and patient logs, preparing for treatments, and reading medical journals.

The Supreme Court denied Soliman a deduction for his home office, holding that the "statute does not allow for a deduction whenever a home office may be characterized as legitimate." Id. at 174. Instead, courts must determine whether the home office is the taxpayer's principal place of business. Although the Court could not "develop an objective formula * * *," the Court stressed two primary considerations: "the relative importance of the activities performed at each business location and the time spent at each place." Id. at 174–75. We address each in turn.

1.   Relative Importance

The importance of daily practice to Popov's profession cannot be denied. Regular practice is essential to playing a musical instrument at a high level of ability, and it is this level of commitment that distinguishes the professional from the amateur.[3] Without daily practice, Popov would be unable to perform in professional orchestras. She would also be unequipped for the peculiar demands of studio recording: The ability to read and perform scores on sight requires an acute musical intelligence that must be constantly developed and honed. In short, Popov's four to five hours of daily practice lay at the very heart of her career as a professional violinist.

Of course, the concert halls and recording studios are also important to Popov's profession. Without them, she would have no place in which to perform. Audiences and motion picture companies are unlikely to flock to her one-bedroom apartment. In Soliman, the Supreme Court stated that, although "no one test is determinative in every case," "the point where goods and services are delivered must be given great weight in determining the place where the most important functions are performed." Id. at 175. The Service places great weight on this statement, contending that Popov's performances should be analogized to the

---

[3]   One who doubts this might consult George Bernard Shaw's famous observation that "hell is full of musical amateurs." George Bernard Shaw, Man and Superman act 3 (1903).

"service" of delivering anesthesia that was at issue in Soliman; these "services" are delivered in concert halls and studios, not in her apartment.

We agree with Popov that musical performance is not so easily captured under a "goods and services" rubric. The German poet Heinrich Heine observed that music stands "halfway between thought and phenomenon, between spirit and matter, a sort of nebulous mediator, like and unlike each of the things it mediates—spirit that requires manifestation in time, and matter that can do without space."[4] Heinrich Heine, Letters on the French Stage (1837), quoted in Words about Music: A Treasury of Writings 2 (John Amis & Michael Rose eds., 1989). Or as Harry Ellis Dickson of the Boston Symphony Orchestra explained more concretely:

> A musician's life is different from that of most people. We don't go to an office every day, or to a factory, or to a bank. We go to an empty hall. We don't deal in anything tangible, nor do we produce anything except sounds. We saw away, or blow, or pound for a few hours and then we go home. It is a strange way to make a living!

Harry Ellis Dickson, Gentlemen, More Dolce Please (1969), quoted in Drucker v. Comm'r, 715 F.2d 67, 68–69 (2d Cir. 1983).

It is possible, of course, to wrench musical performance into a "delivery of services" framework, but we see little value in such a wooden and unblinking application of the tax laws. Soliman itself recognized that in this area of law "variations are inevitable in case-by-case determinations." * * * We believe this to be such a case. We simply do not find the "delivery of services" framework to be helpful in analyzing this particular problem. Taken to extremes, the Service's argument would seem to generate odd results in a variety of other areas as well. We doubt, for example, that an appellate advocate's primary place of business is the podium from which he delivers his oral argument, or that a professor's primary place of business is the classroom, rather than the office in which he prepares his lectures.

We therefore conclude that the "relative importance" test yields no definitive answer in this case, and we accordingly turn to the second prong of the Soliman inquiry.

2.   Amount of Time

Under *Soliman*, "the decisionmaker should . . . compare the amount of time spent at home with the time spent at other places where business activities occur * * * This factor assumes particular significance when," as in this case, "comparison of the importance of the functions performed at various places yields no definitive answer to the principal place of

---

[4]   Although not, perhaps, without practice space.

business inquiry." Id.[5] In *Soliman*, the taxpayer spent significantly more time in the hospitals than he did in his home office. In this case, Popov spent significantly more time practicing the violin at home than she did performing or recording.[6]

This second factor tips the balance in the Popovs' favor. They are accordingly entitled to a home office deduction for Katia Popov's practice space, because it was exclusively used as her principal place of business.

Holding

* * * *

C. Conclusion

For the foregoing reasons, the Tax Court's denial of the Popovs' home office deduction is reversed.

AFFIRMED

NOTES

(A) *Principal Place of Business Exception.* The general rule is that no deduction is permitted for a "home office." Section 280A, however, permits such a deduction in very limited circumstances, that is, where the office is the taxpayer's "principal place of business." As *Popov* illustrates, it is often not easy to determine what constitutes a principal place of business. The Supreme Court in *Commissioner v. Soliman,* discussed in *Popov*, looked to two factors: relative importance of the location and the amount of time spent there, and put great weight on the location where goods and services are delivered. Judge Hawkins gives short shrift to that factor. Is it really so *Soliman* difficult to determine where Popov's services are delivered? Assuming Hawkins simply thought the test produced bad results, is he free to ignore this Supreme Court interpretation of "principal place of business"?

(B) *Administrative Activities.* The *Soliman* decision was controversial, particularly with small business, who persuaded Congress that the decision had created havoc. Section 280A now provides that a home office can qualify as a principal place of business if the taxpayer uses the office to conduct administrative or management activities and there is no other fixed location of the business where the taxpayer conducts substantial administrative or

---

[5] Justices Thomas and Scalia concurred in Soliman, but noted that the Court provided no guidance if the taxpayer "spent 30 to 35 hours at his home office and only 10 hours" at the hospitals. 506 U.S. at 184 (Thomas, J., concurring) (Which factor would take precedence? The importance of the activities undertaken at home . . . ? The number of hours spent at each location? I am at a loss, and I am afraid the taxpayer, his attorney, and a lower court would be as well.") Id.

[6] The Service argues that the evidence is unclear as to "how much time Mrs. Popov spent practicing at home as opposed to the time she spent performing outside of the home." It is true that the evidence is not perfectly clear and that the Tax Court made no specific comparative findings. However, the Tax Court found that she practiced four to five hours a day in her apartment. If we read this finding in the light most generous to the Service and assume that she only practiced four hours a day 300 days a year, Popov would still have practiced 1200 hours in a year. She testified that she performed with two orchestras for a total of 120–140 hours. If she spent a similar amount of time recording, she would still be spending about five hours practicing for every hour of performance or recording. The only plausible reading of the evidence is that Popov spent substantially more time practicing than she did performing or recording.

management activities. Does this change help Popov? Why do you suppose the change was limited to "administrative or management activities"?

(C) *Exclusive Use.* Section 280A(c)(1) requires that the portion of the house claimed as a home office be used exclusively for that purpose. In Sengpiehl v. Commissioner, 75 T.C.M. 1604 (1998), the Tax Court denied a deduction for a dining room even though it was used exclusively for legal practice during working hours because family members occasionally used it for meals after working hours. Popov claimed that the living room in her one-bedroom apartment was off-limits to her four-year old daughter. Does that seem credible?

(D) *Other Requirements.* Section 280A permits a taxpayer to deduct expenses of a home office where it is used by patients, clients, or customers in meeting with the taxpayer. In Green v. Commissioner, 707 F.2d 404 (9th Cir. 1983), the court refused to allow a deduction for a home office used exclusively to receive telephone calls from clients.

The deductible home office expenses are limited to the gross income from the use of the home office less deductions associated with the residence that are allowable regardless of use (such as mortgage interest, real property taxes, and casualty losses) and other deductible expenses attributable to the business (such as the cost of supplies and wages paid to others). In effect, then, home office deductions may not exceed the net income from the activity. Disallowed deductions may be carried forward to succeeding years, subject to continuing application of the gross income limit. These mechanics are not easy to follow and small businesses operated in a home objected to the complexity. In 2013 the IRS announced that taxpayers had the option of deducting $5 a square foot for up to 300 square feet ($1500 maximum). This would largely be in lieu of depreciation.

(E) *Rationale.* Legislative history suggests two reasons for the enactment of § 280A. First, prior law often allowed a business deduction for expenses attributable to the home even though no additional costs resulted from the business use. The typical case was a taxpayer/employee who occasionally read work-related material in an armchair in the family den and deducted the costs of maintaining the den. Second, the various standards applied by the courts and the IRS were considered confusing to taxpayers. Congress perceived a "great need for definitive rules." Section 280A and the cases interpreting that provision seem to demonstrate that this latter purpose has not been achieved. Is this failure the result of faulty statutory draftsmanship or the incredible variety of facts and circumstances? Might the results have been clearer if Congress had sacrificed some equity for greater simplicity? For example, what if no deduction at all was available for a home office? Or might the results have been clearer if Congress had enacted rules even more detailed than § 280A? Would explicitly requiring taxpayers to prove "additional or incremental" expenses be more definitive or simpler? Would it be fair? Or would such a rule merely shift the nature of the controversies rather than eliminating or reducing them? If so, does this make you terminally pessimistic about a "simple" income tax? Wildly optimistic about the prospects of making a good living practicing tax law?

(F) *Vacation Homes.* Section 280A also applies to vacation homes. A "vacation home" essentially is a dwelling unit used by the taxpayer for more than the greater of 14 days or 10 percent of the number of days the unit is rented. § 280A(d)(1). If so classified, the taxpayer pro-rates expenses other than interest and taxes and can deduct these expenses up to the amount of rent reduced by the appropriate share of interest and taxes. § 280A(c)(5). If the unit is used for personal purposes for less than the specified number of days, pro rata deductions are allowed. § 280A(e). There is a de minimis exception for those who use the property for personal purposes for a sufficient amount of time, but rent the property for less than 15 days. § 280A(g). The owner forfeits any deductions other than interest and taxes, but need not include the rental income. Consider the owner of a home in Louisville who each year rents it only for the first weekend in May to Derby enthusiasts for $10,000. Is there a rationale for not taxing this income?

(G) *Listed Property.* Dual use property is not limited to home offices and vacation homes. Cars and computers often serve both functions. Congress has tackled the problem with respect to these items quite differently than it did with respect to homes. Section 280F limits depreciation deductions and lease payments with respected to "listed property," which includes vehicles, boats, airplanes, and computers. Generally, any listed property, other than automobiles, which is used more than 50 percent for business is exempt from the limitations.

Valuation is a particularly difficult problem for fringe benefits that provide both personal and business use and thus § 280F has been controversial. At one time the section required employers to include cell phones distributed to employees as a taxable fringe and employees were required to keep detailed records of all calls made on these cell phones that indicate which calls are business and which calls are personal. This produced a storm of protest since no one keeps such logs and besides, who knows what the cost of a single call on a cell phone costs. Congress eventually threw in the towel and removed cell phones from the definition of listed property. The IRS subsequently decided that a cell phone provided to an employee for a substantial noncompensatory purpose—like being available to speak to clients at all hours—was a nontaxable working condition fringe and that personal use was a de minimis fringe (see page 102 supra).

SECTION 3.   THE DISTINCTION BETWEEN DEDUCTIBLE BUSINESS OR INVESTMENT EXPENSES AND NONDEDUCTIBLE CAPITAL EXPENDITURES

Taxpayers account for their business or investment costs in one of three ways. Some expenditures for the production of income, such as those previously discussed in this chapter, are deductible; the costs are said to be "expensed." Provided there is enough income to offset the deductions, the tax-free recovery of such income-producing expenses is immediate. Other expenses must be "capitalized" and the cost taken into account only when the asset is disposed of in the future. Other assets may be capitalized and then "depreciated"; that is, deductions are allowed for the asset's cost over a period of time. The determination whether costs are immediately deductible or must be capitalized is the subject of this Section.

Section 263 specifically disallows deduction of a "capital expenditure." When an amount must be capitalized, it is added to the taxpayer's basis in the asset with respect to which the expenditure is incurred. This amount either will be recovered when the asset is sold or over some period of time during which the asset is held, through a series of deductions called depreciation or amortization. Distinguishing deductible business or investment expenses from nondeductible capital expenditures can be as difficult as distinguishing business expenses from personal expenses. The distinction is nevertheless essential to an income tax. If all expenditures made for business or investment purposes were immediately deductible, the tax would be imposed on consumption, rather than income. In a tax where consumption is the base, all savings and investment would be subtracted from receipts to measure an individual's consumption during the taxable period. Under a consumption tax, therefore, a deduction would be allowed immediately for all business and investment expenditures, including such classic capital expenditures as purchased shares of stock, equipment, and real estate. In an income tax, those expenditures are deducted over time or recovered when assets are sold. The difference is timing but that is crucially important. The importance of this distinction can be demonstrated by the equivalence, under certain conditions, of immediate deduction of a capital investment to exemption from tax of the income from the investment. The relationship between immediate deduction of capital expenditures and the exemption of the yield is examined in the Note on Tax Deferral, which follows.

Tax planners are well aware of the distinction between nondeductible capital expenditures and deductible business or investment expenses. If an expenditure that should be capitalized is permitted to be deducted immediately, the taxpayer will postpone tax liability on the income offset by the deduction. Especially in times of high interest rates, such tax deferrals are very valuable to taxpayers.

In 2017, Congress greatly expanded the availability of immediate expensing. Rather than a blanket repeal of the capitalization requirement, however, Congress chose to retain the capitalization rules but to enact favorable cost recovery rules to certain taxpayers, for certain investments, and in certain years. Some of these are set to expire in the mid- to late 2020s. The new cost recovery rules are explained in more detail in Section 4, at page 343, infra.

In addition, if long-term capital gains are treated preferentially while long-term capital losses are not as readily deductible as ordinary losses, the total tax may be very different depending on whether an expense is treated as deductible or a capital expenditure. These two advantages—deferral of tax and conversion of ordinary income into capital gains—are the chief functions of tax planning; for example, they were central features of "tax shelters" used in the 1980s to enable high income taxpayers to reduce their tax liability substantially. Both Congress and the courts have struggled to define the line between deductible expenses and capital expenditures to prevent taxpayers from inappropriately using deferral and conversion to reduce income. This Section concerns the kinds of expenditures that must be capitalized. It is important to remember that when capitalization is required, the taxpayer will be permitted to account for his cost; the issue is when. Because the advantage of an immediate deduction is much greater than offsetting sales proceeds with the taxpayer's cost when an asset is sold, or even allowing deductions for the cost during the time the asset is held through depreciation, the stakes are quite high.

A. TAX DEFERRAL—THE TAX IMPACT OF THE CAPITALIZATION REQUIREMENT

Before turning to the specific rules for distinguishing deductible expenses and capital expenditures and for recovering capital expenditures over time, it is worthwhile to examine in greater detail the impact of income tax timing decisions on both taxpayers and the government. In Chapter 2, we explored the concept that a taxpayer is entitled to a tax-free recovery of capital. The timing and mechanism for recovering capital is one of the most important issues in designing an income tax. Although the same total net income will be taxed over the period the asset is held, income will vary depending on the timing of the offset for capital recovery.

To make this point clear, consider the following example:

Example: Assume T purchases an asset for $10,000 that will produce $3,000 of income each year for five years and then at the end of Year 5 will be worthless and disposed of. Consider three possible tax treatments for the recovery of the cost of the asset: (1) immediate expensing, (2) depreciation of equal amounts over the five-year period, and (3) cost recovery only when the asset is disposed of.

Case 1 (Immediate Expensing)

	Year 1	Year 2	Year 3	Year 4	Year 5
Gross Income	$3,000	$3,000	$3,000	$3,000	$3,000
Deductions	10,000	0	0	0	0
Net Income	(7,000)	3,000	3,000	3,000	3,000

Case 2 (Ratable Depreciation)

	Year 1	Year 2	Year 3	Year 4	Year 5
Gross Income	$3,000	$3,000	$3,000	$3,000	$3,000
Deductions	2,000	2,000	2,000	2,000	2,000
Net Income	1,000	1,000	1,000	1,000	1,000

Case 3 (Recovery on Disposition)

	Year 1	Year 2	Year 3	Year 4	Year 5
Gross Income	$3,000	$3,000	$3,000	$3,000	$3,000
Deductions	0	0	0	0	10,000
Net Income	3,000	3,000	3,000	3,000	(7,000)

The total net income for the five-year period is $5,000 in each of the three cases, but the allocation of taxable gain or loss to each year, and therefore, the timing of tax payments is very different. The precise stream of tax payments depends on the rules for deducting losses. If the total deduction for any year exceeds the income, there is a loss. Such losses generally may be used to offset other unrelated income. For example, in Case 1, the taxpayer might use the $7,000 loss in Year 1 to offset dividend income. In some cases, losses from one type of activity cannot be used against other income. If the taxpayer has no income in a particular year against which to offset the loss, the taxpayer may be able to carry forward or carry back the loss to offset income from other years. If there is no income during the entire statutory period when losses are eligible for carryover, the recovery of capital deductions may be useless to the taxpayer. A detailed discussion of the deductibility of losses begins infra at page 378.

Assuming that the losses in the above example reduce taxes in the year that they occur (Year 1 in Case 1 and Year 5 in Case 3), at a 30 percent marginal tax rate, the tax results for each case would be as follows:

Tax Liability

	Year 1	Year 2	Year 3	Year 4	Year 5	Total	Present Value (8 percent)
Case 1	$(2,100)	$900	$900	$900	$900	$1,500	$815
Case 2	300	300	300	300	300	1,500	1,198
Case 3	900	900	900	900	(2,100)	1,500	1,551

Given the flat rate of tax assumed in the example, the total tax for the five-year period is the same in each case, $1,500 (30 percent x $5,000). But the stream of payments is quite different. If the stream of tax payments is discounted to present value, assuming an 8 percent interest rate (and that tax payments are made at the end of each year), Case 1 is best for the taxpayer and Case 3 is the worst. This example should make clear that timing differences will produce significant variations in the real tax burdens in the three cases.

The Note that follows explores in greater detail the value of tax deferral. Here, we treat the value of tax deferral alone, putting aside for the moment the prospects for "conversion" from combining ordinary deductions with capital gains and for "tax arbitrage" or "leverage" from combining borrowing with exclusions from income or accelerated or immediate deductions (an issue that was briefly described in connection with the *Tufts* case, supra at page 201, and that will be examined further in subsequent materials).

Note on Tax Deferral[5]

The ability to accelerate deductions, and thereby defer tax, is of major advantage to taxpayers. In some instances, deferral may exempt income from tax permanently; for example, most property held until death is given a stepped-up basis equal to its fair market value. In other cases, deferral may cause income to be taxed at lower rates, for example, when the taxpayer is subsequently in a lower tax bracket or when the income is eligible for favorable capital gains treatment. Tax deferral is valuable even if the tax on the income in a later year is identical in amount to the tax saved from a deduction in an earlier year. In some ways, the deferral advantage is well understood. It is clear that you would be wealthier if the IRS allowed you to wait until 2015 to pay $100,000 of taxes owed for 2012. You could put the $100,000 in the bank and earn interest, or invest it in other productive assets, or pay off a loan and avoid interest expenses. The value of postponing tax by deferring income or accelerating deductions depends upon tax rates, interest rates, and the length of deferral. The following paragraphs attempt to describe and quantify the benefits of tax deferral by analogies to (1) an interest-free loan, (2) tax forgiveness, and (3) a tax-free return on the amount invested. The third is the most difficult to understand.

(a) Some Examples

1. *Equivalence to an Interest-Free Loan.*

One way to think of the value of deferral is by analogy to an interest-free loan. Assume a taxpayer T in a 50 percent tax bracket invests $100 in an asset that will be sold in ten years and that will produce ordinary income at the time of sale. If the cost could be deducted in the year of acquisition, the immediate deduction would save T $50 in taxes. When sold, the asset will produce $100 more ordinary income than if the cost of

---

[5]   This note is largely adapted from materials found in Stanley S. Surrey, "The Tax Reform Act of 1969—Tax Deferral and Tax Shelters," 12 Bost. Coll. Ind. & Comm. L. Rev. 307 (1971); William Andrews, "A Consumption-Type or Cash Flow Personal Income Tax," 87 Harv. L. Rev. 1113, 1123–28 (1974); Michael Graetz, "Implementing a Progressive Consumption Tax," 92 Harv. L. Rev. 1575, 1597–23 (1979); and conversations with Daniel I. Halperin and Alvin C. Warren, Jr.

the asset had been capitalized because the basis is zero; thus, T will repay, at the time of sale, the $50 of tax saved in the year of acquisition. It is as if the government made a ten-year interest-free loan of $50 to T. (The amount of the loan depends upon the taxpayer's tax bracket, and its duration depends upon the length of deferral.)

2.   *Equivalence to a Reduction of Tax Rates or Tax Forgiveness.*

In the above example, T arranges to defer $50 of tax for ten years. Assume that the market rate of interest on T's borrowing, saving or lending is 12 percent (or 6 percent after tax). If T puts $27.92 in the bank at a 12 percent interest rate, he will have accumulated $50 at the end of ten years after withdrawing enough money each year to pay taxes (at a 50 percent rate) on each year's interest income. The ten-year deferral is thus the equivalent of paying only $27.92 in taxes in the initial year. The difference of $22.08 in taxes is, in effect, forgiven, and T's tax rate effectively has been reduced from 50 percent to 27.9 percent.

This is just another way of saying that the interest-free loan is worth $22.08 to T—the present value of after-tax earnings of 6 percent in interest each year for ten years. This equivalence can be seen by assuming that borrowing the $50 would have cost T 12 percent interest, or $6 a year. Assuming a tax deduction is allowed for interest, the $6 interest before tax would cost $3 a year after tax. T thus saves a total of $30 in interest costs by virtue of the immediate deduction (the "interest-free loan"). Expressed in terms of the present value of money, the acceleration of the deduction from year ten to year one is worth $22.08 to T. (This amount was computed by applying a discount rate of 6 percent to the total $30 interest costs, assuming T can borrow at that after-tax rate.)

3.   *The Immediate Deduction-Yield Exemption Equivalence.*

The tax savings that occur when the cost of an investment is deductible immediately, under certain conditions, can be described as equivalent to disallowing the deduction initially but exempting from tax the income from the investment.

The concept originated in an article by Professor E. Cary Brown more than 60 years ago, and appears in the standard public finance texts.[6] Although difficult to grasp—and only true under limited conditions—this equivalence often provides a useful analytical tool. The equivalence also helps to explain the relationship between income taxes and consumption taxes.

Here we approach this equivalence first by setting out some examples to demonstrate the relationship of immediate deduction and exemption of the yield, then by outlining the conditions (or assumptions)

[6]   E. Cary Brown, "Business-Income Taxation and Investment Incentives," in Income, Employment and Public Policy: Essays in Honor of Alvin E. Hansen 330–416 (1948). See also Stanley S. Surrey, Pathways to Tax Reform 123 (1973); Carl S. Shoup, Public Finance 302 (1969).

necessary for the equivalence to hold, and finally by demonstrating its implications for the distinction between income taxes and consumption taxes.

Example 1: Consider a taxpayer who pays $100 for Greenacre, which is sold five years later for $200. The tax rate is 30 percent.

Capitalized Expenditure

If the purchase price is capitalized, the 30 percent tax reduces the investor's rate of profit from 100 to 70 percent as expected.

	Year 1 Investment	Year 5 Disinvestment	Profit	Rate of Profit
Pre-tax	$100	$200	$100	100%
Tax (reduction)		30*		
After-tax	100	170	70	70%

* This amount is computed as follows: Amount realized of $200 less basis of $100 equals gain of $100, which is taxed at 30 percent for a tax of $30.

Immediately Deductible Capital Cost
Same Pre-tax Investment

If the $100 purchase price can be deducted in the year of purchase, there is an immediate tax savings of $30, so the taxpayer's net investment is only $70. As before the investment doubles, even after taxes, by year 5. There is no difference between the pre-tax and after-tax rate of profit.

	Year 1 Investment	Year 5 Disinvestment	Profit	Rate of Profit
Pre-tax	$100	$200	$100	100%
Tax (reduction)	(30)	60*		
After-tax	70	140	70	100%

* This amount is computed as follows: Amount Realized of $200 less zero basis equals gain of $200, which is taxed at 30 percent for a tax of $60.

Immediately Deductible Capital Cost
Same After-tax Investment

Assume now that the taxpayer wanted to increase his investment in Greenacre using not only his $100, but also the tax savings from deducting the purchase price. He would be able to invest $143 in Greenacre and would have $200 after paying taxes in year 5.

	Year 1 Investment	Year 5 Disinvestment	Profit	Rate of Profit
Pre-tax	*$143	$286	$143	100%
Tax (reduction)	**(43)	***86		
After-tax	100	200	100	100%

* The pre-tax investment is calculated as follows: The post-tax investment of $100 is divided by one minus the tax rate [$100/(1–t) = $100/(1–.3) = $143].

** The tax savings is 30 percent x the $143 investment or $43.

*** This amount is calculated as follows: The amount realized of $286 less a basis of zero equals a gain of $286, which is taxed at 30 percent rate for a tax of $86.

The after-tax rate of profit of 100 percent, when the purchase price of Greenacre is deducted immediately is equal to the pre-tax profit of 100 percent, the same result as if there is no tax. In other words, with expensing, the pre-tax and after-tax rates of return are the same.

Example 2: The Treasury Department has described the value of deferral in a slightly different fashion, stating that "permitting the capital cost of an asset to be expensed has the effect of exempting the income from ownership of the asset from taxation." The Treasury used the following example to illustrate the point:[7]

> An intuitive explanation of this somewhat surprising result takes the following form: A $1,000 asset will generate some stream of revenue over its life; if the cost is expensed and the tax rate is 48 percent, the net cost of the asset to the owner * * * is only $520, after tax. However, in the future, each $1 of revenue will be taxed fully, with no allowance for depreciation, leaving $0.52 of net return on the $520 investment, the same ratio as $1 to $1,000 as if there were no tax. Incidentally, in those cases, as in minerals taxation, where the total present value of expensing and depletion deductions may actually exceed the cost of the investment, the effective tax rate is negative. That is, in some instances the tax rate equivalent of an investment tax incentive is a tax rate less than zero.

Example 3:[8] Assume a taxpayer with $1,000, who faces a tax rate of 50 percent, could invest the $1,000 in a tax-exempt savings account that yielded 10 percent annually and have $100 to consume each year after taxes. If that taxpayer could instead invest $2,000 in a deductible asset or account (by virtue of $1,000 in tax savings from the deduction) that yielded a fully taxable return of 10 percent, this also would leave the investor $100 to consume each year after taxes. Withdrawal of the

---

[7]   The quotation and example are from a 1970 Treasury Department Study on Tax Depreciation Policy, set forth at 116 Cong.Rec. 6963–75 (daily ed. July 23, 1970). Both are reproduced and discussed in Surrey, supra note 1, at 313.

[8]   This example is from American Bar Association, Section of Taxation, Simplification Committee, "Report on the Bradley-Gephardt and Kemp-Kasten Bills," 38 Tax Law. 381 (1985).

balances from the accounts would leave the taxpayer with $1,000 after taxes in both cases, because the $2,000 amount would be fully taxable as a result of the previous deduction of that amount.

(b) Conditions for the Equivalence to Hold.

A number of conditions are necessary for the immediate deduction-yield exemption equivalence to hold.[9] For example:

(i)   The applicable tax rates must remain constant—rates can be neither progressive nor change over time. Tax, therefore, is saved from the deduction and collected at an identical rate on the earnings from an asset immediately deducted and on amounts received at the close of the transaction (whether by the disposition of the asset or by some other event.)

(ii)   The deduction must produce an immediate tax savings equal to the taxpayer's marginal rate multiplied by the deduction. This means that the deduction must offset income from other sources and cannot be either lost or delayed by carryover requirements.

(iii) The tax savings is assumed to be invested so as to yield a return identical to that of the original investment. It is assumed that the opportunities for investment at the assumed rate of return are unlimited.

The government may be regarded as automatically becoming a joint venturer in the taxpayer's investment by permitting its immediate deduction. In effect, the government invests a percentage equal to the taxpayer's marginal tax rate in the deductible venture. For example, if the taxpayer's marginal rate is 37 percent, the taxpayer receives an initial tax savings of 37 percent of the investment, and the government receives 37 percent of the gain or contributes 37 percent of the loss.

(c) An Implication of the Equivalence: The Difference Between an Income Tax and an Expenditure (or Progressive Consumption) Tax Is Only Timing.

Under a consumption tax, all investments would be immediately deductible; consumption would be determined by subtracting all savings and investments from all receipts. The equivalence of an immediate deduction of investments to an exemption of their yield has led a number of commentators to note that a consumption tax does not reduce the before-tax return from investments. The Meade Commission, for example, has stated:

It is indeed the characteristic feature of [a consumption] tax as contrasted with an income tax that, at any given constant rate of tax, the former will make the rate of return to the saver on his reduced consumption equal to the rate of return which can

---

[9]   For a slightly different statement of the formal conditions in the economics literature, see Graetz, supra note 1, at 1602.

be earned on the investment which his savings finances, whereas the income tax will reduce the rate of return to the saver below the rate of return which the investment will yield.[10]

Professor Alvin Warren has used the equivalence to demonstrate that a consumption tax can be viewed as exemption of all capital income from tax and therefore as equivalent to a wage tax.[11]

In any event, this analysis of tax deferral confirms the need under an income tax to distinguish immediately deductible expenses from capital expenditures, notwithstanding the difficulties of doing so. The analysis also suggests that too rapid deduction of capital expenditures may seriously undermine the income tax. The expansion of immediate expensing in the 2017 tax act, discussed in detail in Section 4, thus can be seen as a partial move away from income taxation and toward consumption taxation, at least in the case of favored assets and taxpayers.

Finally, as each of the three approaches illustrates, tax deferral can be of great value to taxpayers. For a large part of the history of the income tax, those responsible for tax policy overlooked the immense revenue losses that can result from tax deferral alone. Some efforts to redress this problem have occurred in recent times. These basic issues will be explored further in the next Section in connection with the rules for distinguishing capital expenditures from deductible expenses and the provisions for the recovery of capital, and also in connection with the treatment of deferred compensation and individual retirement accounts (IRAs) discussed in Chapter 6. Many opportunities for the deferral of tax still exist; the deduction of expenses that should be capitalized is but one important example.

Note Introducing the Distinction Between Deductible Expenses and Capital Expenditures

Certain categories of expenditures are routinely required to be capitalized. These include expenditures to purchase an asset, including financial assets, such as stock or bonds, real estate, tangible personal property, such as machinery and equipment, and intangible assets, such as contracts and patents. It also includes the costs of constructing an asset, such as a building. Similarly, the costs incurred by a company in raising capital by issuing debt or stock or of reorganizing a company's capital structure are capital expenditures. Likewise, the costs of entering

---

[10] Institute for Fiscal Studies, the Structure and Reform of Direct Taxation 37 (United Kingdom, 1978) (also known as the "Meade Report" after the Chairman of the Commission that prepared the Report.)

[11] Alvin C. Warren, Jr., "Fairness and a Consumption-Type or Cash Flow Personal Income Tax," 88 Harv.L. Rev. 931 (1975). This equivalence between a consumption tax and a wage tax ignores the potential effect of the former on returns from pre-existing capital investments that had not been deductible. It also depends on the assumption described above about investment of the tax savings from a deduction for savings.

into a new trade or business or of acquiring the stock or assets of a new trade or business are capital expenditures. In these cases, the issues that arise tend to be factual. For example, is an expenditure made in order to enter a new trade or business or to expand an existing trade or business? Sometimes disputes also arise over what costs must be capitalized. The most difficult legal issues, however, tend to occur in connection with expenditures for operating or expanding an existing business.

The materials that follow provide an introduction to and overview of the kinds of questions that arise. In general the materials move from circumstances where the case for capitalization is relatively clear to more controversial circumstances. One general idea is that expenditures that produce income beyond the current taxable year should be capitalized. But consider the following statement by Judge Posner in Encyclopaedia Britannica v. Commissioner, 685 F.2d 212 (7th Cir. 1982)

> If one really takes seriously the concept of a capital expenditure as anything that yields income, actual or imputed, beyond the period (conventionally one year * * *) in which the expenditure is made, the result will be to force the capitalization of virtually every business expense. It is a result courts naturally shy away from. * * * It would require capitalizing every salesman's salary, since his selling activities create goodwill for the company and goodwill is an asset yielding income beyond the year in which the salary expense is incurred. The administrative costs of conceptual rigor are too great.

Thus, the courts sometimes ask whether the immediate or long-term benefits dominate. They also weigh the administrative costs of capitalization versus expensing. Courts are also more willing to allow deduction of recurring rather than nonrecurring expenditures.

The question whether particular expenditures must be capitalized became more contentious following the Supreme Court's decision in *INDOPCO v. Commissioner*, set forth at page 323 infra, which used very broad language in requiring the capitalization of intangible assets with future benefits. The IRS national office and Treasury personnel often asserted that the *INDOPCO* case did not change the longstanding principles for determining whether an expenditure is capital or deductible. Many IRS agents and litigators, however, regarded the *INDOPCO* decision as an invitation to capitalize any expenditure that is likely to produce a "significant future benefit" and urged capitalization of expenditures that businesses had previously deducted without challenge. The Tax Court largely agreed with this reading of *INDOPCO*, but the courts of appeals reversed some of the Tax Court's decisions. In response to the confusion and controversy, Treasury issued regulations providing guidance with respect to capitalization.

B. ACQUISITION AND DISPOSITION OF ASSETS

Nondeductible capital expenditures typically include the acquisition of business or investment assets that will last longer than the taxable year. Thus, a taxpayer can immediately deduct the purchase of a legal pad, but must capitalize the cost of machinery and equipment, land and buildings, and intangibles such as stocks and bonds. Although the principle is easily stated, its application is not always easy, as the following notes illustrate.

NOTES

(A) *Costs of Acquiring Tangible Property.* The regulations provide that a taxpayer must capitalize the costs of acquiring real or personal tangible property. This would include not only the amount paid for the property—such as land, buildings, equipment—but also the transaction costs. Reg. § 1.263(a)–2T. The costs of defending or perfecting title must also be capitalized. Transaction costs are the amounts spent to investigate and pursue the acquisition of property and would include an appraisal of the property, negotiation fees, attorney fees, broker commissions, transfer taxes, and other costs that facilitate the acquisition of the property. Transaction costs do not include employee compensation. For example, if the taxpayer used an in-house attorney to provide the legal services to acquire a building, the attorney's compensation would not need to be capitalized into the cost of the building. If, however, the taxpayer hired a third party attorney to provide legal services, the amount paid to the attorney would need to be capitalized into the cost of the building. The regulations contain a de minimis provision.

(B) *Costs of Constructing Property.* Suppose instead of purchasing property, the taxpayer constructs it. What is the proper treatment of the taxpayer's construction costs? In order to provide parity with the purchaser of property, the costs of constructing a capital asset must be capitalized. Reg. § 1.263(a)–2T. Costs that otherwise would be deductible, such as wages paid to construction workers, must be capitalized and included in the asset's basis when they are paid in connection with the construction of property or property acquired for resale. § 263A. The recovery of such costs then depends on the applicable rules governing depreciation or amortization of the constructed asset.

For some expenses, this result follows from the explicit language of § 263(a)(1), which disallows a deduction for "[a]ny amount paid out for new buildings or for permanent improvements or betterments made to increase the value of any property or estate." The treatment of other costs is not so clear. For example, in Commissioner v. Idaho Power Co., 418 U.S. 1 (1974), a public utility used equipment for the construction of its own facilities. It depreciated the equipment over a ten-year useful life, the appropriate period then for the equipment. The Commissioner argued that under § 263, insofar as the equipment was used in constructing capital facilities, depreciation deductions should be disallowed and the disallowed amounts added to the taxpayer's adjusted basis in the new facilities. The adjusted basis of the facility (which would include the cost of using the equipment) would be depreciated over its useful life, then 30 years or more. The Supreme Court upheld the Commissioner's position, stating (at 418 U.S. 13–14):

> There can be little question that other construction-related expense items, such as tools, materials, and wages paid construction workers, are to be treated as part of the cost of acquisition of a capital asset. The taxpayer does not dispute this. Of course, reasonable wages paid in the carrying on of a trade or business qualify as a deduction from gross income. Section 162(a)(1) of the 1954 Code, 26 U.S.C. § 162(a)(1). But when wages are paid in connection with the construction or acquisition of a capital asset, they must be capitalized and are then entitled to be amortized over the life of the capital asset so acquired. * * *

> Construction-related depreciation is not unlike expenditures for wages for construction workers. The significant fact is that the exhaustion of construction equipment does not represent the final disposition of the taxpayer's investment in that equipment; rather, the investment in the equipment is assimilated into the cost of the capital asset constructed. * * * The taxpayer's own accounting procedure reflects this treatment, * * * on its books the construction-related depreciation was capitalized * * *. By the same token, this capitalization prevents the distortion of income that would otherwise occur if depreciation properly allocable to asset acquisition were deducted from gross income currently realized. * * *

> An additional pertinent factor is that capitalization of construction-related depreciation by the taxpayer who does its own construction work maintains tax parity with the taxpayer who has its construction work done by an independent contractor. The depreciation on the contractor's equipment incurred during the performance of the job will be an element of cost charged by the contractor for his construction services, and the entire cost, of course, must be capitalized by the taxpayer having the construction work performed.

The rule of *Idaho Power* was codified in § 263A, which generally requires capitalization of virtually all indirect costs, in addition to all direct costs, allocable to the construction or production of real property or tangible personal property. Section 263A imposes specific rules with respect to certain items, but it also gives the IRS the authority to allocate other direct and indirect costs. See Noël B. Cunningham & Deborah H. Schenk, "How to Tax the House That Jack Built," 43 Tax L. Rev. 447 (1988).

(C) *Costs of Shareholder Litigation.* In Woodward v. Commissioner, 397 U.S. 572 (1970), the Supreme Court addressed the treatment of expenses incurred by a taxpayer in so-called appraisal litigation. The taxpayer, a shareholder in an Iowa corporation, had a legal duty to buy out shares held by minority shareholders. The parties litigated over the value of the stock, and the taxpayer incurred attorneys', accountants', and appraisers' fees. The taxpayer tried to deduct the costs, but the Court held that the fees had to be capitalized into the basis of the shares of stock purchased.

(D) *Capitalization to Avoid "Conversion."* The decision whether an expense is required to be capitalized or is deductible immediately may affect the total amount of income that will be characterized as capital gain (or loss) as opposed to ordinary gain (or loss). Since capital gains are taxed less heavily than ordinary income, a deduction of expenses against ordinary income, combined with the taxation of the gain at favorable capital gains rates, can result in extraordinary tax savings. For example, in United States v. Regan, 410 F.2d 744 (9th Cir.), cert. denied, 396 U.S. 834 (1969), a taxpayer was prohibited from amortizing and deducting the cost of building access roads to timber, which produced capital gain when sold. The following example demonstrates the potential for "negative" tax rates from "conversion," that would have occurred if the taxpayer had been permitted to deduct the cost of building the roads:

Assume that the timber cost $10,000, that the only additional expense was a road costing $7,500, and that the timber would be sold for $19,000. Assume that a marginal tax rate of 37 percent applies to the taxpayer's ordinary income and that the taxpayer's capital gains are taxed at 20 percent. The total pre-tax profit on the transaction would be $1,500 ($19,000 sales price minus $10,000 cost of timber and minus $7,500 cost of road). Applying the favorable 20 percent rate to this profit would produce a tax liability of $300. But if the cost of the road were deducted, the result would be as follows:

(1) Allowing a deduction of $7,500 for the road at the taxpayer's 37 percent marginal rate would produce a tax savings of $2,775.

(2) The profit on the sale of timber would be $9,000 ($19,000 sales price minus $10,000 basis—since the cost of the road was deducted, it would not be added to basis). This gain would be taxed at a 20 percent rate, producing a tax liability of $1,800.

(3) The total tax effect would be a tax savings of $2,775 from the deduction of the cost of the road and a tax liability of $1,800 from the capital gain on the timber sale. Thus, there would be a net tax of negative $975 on a $4,000 economic profit when there should have been a $300 tax at the favorable capital gains rate.

There are many instances where taxpayers take ordinary deductions while holding an asset that will qualify for capital gain on sale. Generally, the IRS questions the deductions or attempts to deny capital gains treatment only where the expenditures are at least arguably capital in nature.

(E) *Costs of Disposition.* The typical costs of disposing of property—for example, a broker's selling commission—are not deductible under §§ 162 or 212 as ordinary and necessary business or investment expenses. Rather they are capitalized and are offset against the amount realized, thereby reducing the amount of gain or increasing the loss from the asset's disposition. See Reg. § 1.263(a)–1T. Thus, if the asset qualifies for capital gain treatment, the broker's commission will reduce that gain rather than offset ordinary income. This rule is favorable to taxpayers now that deductions under § 212 have been eliminated from 2018 to the end of 2025. In general, the nondeductibility of § 212 expenses (see the discussion at page 235) may lead taxpayers to attempt to capitalize as many expenses as possible into the basis of investment assets, thus permitting greater cost recovery, even if deferred until sale.

C. ACQUISITION OF INTANGIBLE ASSETS OR BENEFITS

The courts have had difficulty determining the appropriate treatment of expenditures with respect to intangibles. There are usually two issues: When should the existence of a future benefit require capitalization of the expenditures and where there is a future benefit, what transaction costs should be deemed to "facilitate" the creation of the future benefit, such that they should be capitalized?

INDOPCO, Inc. v. Commissioner
Supreme Court of the United States, 1992. 503 U.S. 79.

■ JUSTICE BLACKMUN delivered the opinion of the Court. [The petitioner, formerly National Starch, was the target of a friendly takeover by Unilever and incurred significant investment banking and legal fees as well as other acquisition expenses which it sought to deduct as ordinary and necessary business expenses.]

In this case we must decide whether certain professional expenses incurred by a target corporation in the course of a friendly takeover are deductible by that corporation as "ordinary and necessary" business expenses under § 162(a) of the federal Internal Revenue Code.

* * *

Section 162(a) of the Internal Revenue Code allows the deduction of all the "ordinary and necessary expenses paid or incurred during the taxable year in carrying on any trade or business." In contrast, § 263 of the Code allows no deduction for a capital expenditure—an amount paid out for new buildings or for permanent improvements or betterments made to increase the value of any property or estate. The primary effect of characterizing a payment as either a business expense or a capital expenditure concerns the timing of the taxpayer's cost recovery: While business expenses are currently deductible, a capital expenditure usually is amortized and depreciated over the life of the relevant asset, or, where no specific asset or useful life can be ascertained, is deducted upon dissolution of the enterprise. * * * Through provisions such as these, the Code endeavors to match expenses with the revenues of the taxable period to which they are properly attributable, thereby resulting in a more accurate calculation of net income for tax purposes.

* * *

In exploring the relationship between deductions and capital expenditures, this Court has noted the familiar rule "that an income tax deduction is a matter of legislative grace and that the burden of clearly showing the right to the claimed deduction is on the taxpayer." * * * The notion that deductions are exceptions to the norm of capitalization finds support in various aspects of the Code. Deductions are specifically enumerated and thus are subject to disallowance in favor of capitalization. See §§ 161 and 261. Nondeductible capital expenditures, by contrast, are not exhaustively enumerated in the Code; "rather than providing a complete list of nondeductible expenditures," * * * § 263 serves as a general means of distinguishing capital expenditures from current expenses.

* * *

National Starch contends that the decision in [Commissioner v.] Lincoln Savings [403 U.S. 345 (1971)] * * * announced an exclusive test for identifying capital expenditures, a test in which "creation or enhancement of an asset" is a prerequisite to capitalization, and deductibility under § 162(a) is the rule rather than the exception. * * * We do not agree, for we conclude that National Starch has overread Lincoln Savings. * * *

not necessary

Lincoln Savings stands for the simple proposition that a taxpayer's expenditure that "serves to create or enhance * * * a separate and distinct" asset should be capitalized under § 263. It by no means follows, however, that only expenditures that create or enhance separate and distinct assets are to be capitalized under § 263. We had no occasion in Lincoln Savings to consider the tax treatment of expenditures that * * * did not create or enhance a specific asset, and thus the case cannot be read to preclude capitalization in other circumstances. In short, Lincoln Savings holds that the creation of a separate and distinct asset well may be a sufficient but not a necessary condition to classification as a capital expenditure. * * *

factor

Although the mere presence of an incidental future benefit—*some future aspect*—may not warrant capitalization, a taxpayer's realization of benefits beyond the year in which the expenditure is incurred is undeniably important in determining whether the appropriate tax treatment is immediate deduction or capitalization. * * * Indeed, the text of the Code's capitalization provision, § 263(a)(1), which refers to "permanent improvements or betterments," itself envisions an inquiry into the duration and extent of the benefits realized by the taxpayer.

holding

In applying the foregoing principles to the specific expenditures at issue in this case, we conclude that National Starch has not demonstrated that the investment banking, legal, and other costs it incurred in connection with Unilever's acquisition of its shares are deductible as ordinary and necessary business expenses under § 162(a).

Although petitioner attempts to dismiss the benefits that accrued to National Starch from the Unilever acquisition as "entirely speculative" or "merely incidental," * * * the Tax Court's and the Court of Appeals' findings that the transaction produced significant benefits to National Starch that extended beyond the tax year in question are amply supported by the record.

Reasoning

* * *

Courts long have recognized that expenses such as these, incurred for the purpose of changing the corporate structure for the benefit of future operations are not ordinary and necessary business expenses. * * *

NOTES

(A) *Separate and Distinct Asset.* Prior to *INDOPCO,* some courts had interpreted the Court's opinion in *Lincoln Savings* as requiring a separate and distinct asset as a prerequisite for capitalization. The *INDOPCO* Court rejected that interpretation, holding that capitalization could be required without a separate and distinct asset but gave little indication under what circumstances capitalization would be required.

Treasury regulations under § 263 clarify that, in the absence of a separate and distinct asset, capitalization is not required unless the type of asset is listed in the regulations or in future published guidance by the IRS. Treasury also adopted a definition of "separate and distinct asset." The term means "a property interest of ascertainable and measurable value in money's worth that is subject to protection under applicable State, Federal or foreign law and the possession and control of which is intrinsically capable of being sold, transferred or pledged . . . separate and apart from a trade or business." Reg. § 1.263(a)–4(b)(3). Is the definition helpful or sensible?

Those regulations by listing certain assets continue prior law with respect to the acquisition costs of most intangibles. The cost of acquiring stock, financial instruments, leases, and intellectual property rights, for example, must be capitalized. Taxpayers also must capitalize the costs of many created intangibles, such as amounts paid to obtain or modify contract rights or amounts paid to defend or perfect title. The regulations specifically exempt the costs of package design, amounts paid to develop computer software, and fees paid to a consultant to build goodwill, all of which might be capital expenditures but for the regulations.

(B) *Future Benefit.* Regulations under § 263 indicate that not all expenditures that produce a future benefit must be capitalized. Reg. § 1.263(a)–4(b). A good example is advertising. Historically, advertising and promotional expenses generally have been deducted despite the fact that a particular ad campaign might last several years. See, e.g., Rev. Rul. 68–561, 1968–2 C.B. 117 (permitting a natural gas company to deduct costs of an advertising campaign incurred as part of a program to increase gas consumption).

To quell fears that *INDOPCO* would require capitalization of expenses commonly deducted, the Service announced that the decision did not affect the longstanding treatment of advertising costs. Rev. Rul. 92–80, 1992–2 C.B. 7, stating: "Only in the unusual circumstance where advertising is directed towards obtaining future benefits significantly beyond those traditionally associated with ordinary product advertising or with institutional or goodwill advertising, must the costs of that advertising be capitalized." See also Reg. § 1.263(a)–1(*l*), Example 7 (permitting deduction of advertising expenses in connection with a product launch). This lack of consistency with respect to INDOPCO-type expenses creates an incentive for taxpayers to argue that their expenditures are in the nature of advertising. In Robinson Knife Manufacturing Company, Inc. v. Commissioner, 97 T.C.M. 1037 (2009), the taxpayer paid license fees to label its knives and kitchen tools as "Oneida" and "Pyrex." It tried to deduct the fees as advertising expenses incurred to enhance the marketability of its products. The court agreed with the IRS that the fees had to be capitalized into inventory because the design approval and quality control elements of the licensing agreements benefited the taxpayer in the development and production of the kitchen tools marketed with the licensed trademarks.

(C) *Transaction Costs.* The regulations require that a taxpayer must capitalize only those transaction costs that "facilitate" the acquisition, creation, or enhancement of an intangible that itself must be capitalized. This would include amounts paid to investigate or pursue a transaction, such as fees for attorneys, accountants, and appraisers. There are two significant exceptions, however. The first is a de minimis exception; generally if the transaction costs are less than $5,000, none of them must be capitalized.

The second and much more important exception is for employee compensation and overhead costs. One of the most hotly contested questions after *INDOPCO* was the extent to which salaries needed to be capitalized. The IRS had asserted that in-house costs, such as the salary paid to a corporate officer whose job included evaluating intangibles for acquisition had to be capitalized. Compare Wells Fargo & Co. v. Commissioner, 224 F.3d 874 (8th Cir. 2000) (permitting executive salaries to be deducted), with Lychuk v. Commissioner, 116 T.C. 374 (2001) (requiring capitalization of salaries of employees whose sole task was to check creditworthiness of potential borrowers for automobile loans). In some circumstances the courts agreed but in others they struggled to continue the historical treatment of compensation. The government was under a good deal of pressure by the business community to end the uncertainty. Bowing to what it described as administrative necessity, Treasury exempted all overhead costs and employee compensation but not payments to independent contractors from capitalization. For example, a company can expense the costs of an in-house staff even if the employees spend all their time negotiating the acquisition of intangibles whose costs must be capitalized. Treasury appeared to adopt the rationale of PNC Bancorp, Inc. v. Commissioner, 212 F.3d 822 (3d Cir. 2000), which held that "normal and routine" expenses could be deducted.

(D) *Corporate Reorganizations. INDOPCO* itself involved expenses incurred by a target company in completing a corporate takeover and takeover expenses were at issue in number of subsequent cases. The regulations are not nearly so broad with respect to the capitalization of this type of expense as INDOPCO would imply. They require capitalization of expenses to "facilitate" takeovers and reorganizations, but carve out many expenses. "Inherently facilitative" costs are always capitalized. These include appraisals, tax advice, structuring the transaction, regulatory and shareholder approvals, and the costs of conveying the property. Other costs must be capitalized only if they occur after a bright-line date, the earlier of an agreement between the acquirer and the target or board authorization. For example, informal advice before the bright line date is deductible. In no case must in-house salaries be capitalized. This rule follows a distinction made by the Eighth Circuit in *Wells Fargo*. The court held that expenses incurred before the "final decision" to merge were deductible "investigatory" expenses of an ongoing business but that the fees incurred after that date were incurred to "facilitate consummation" of the merger transaction and therefore must be capitalized.

National Starch, the company involved in *INDOPCO*, incurred its expenses in completing a friendly takeover. The Court does not mention a hostile takeover. In A.E. Staley Manufacturing Co. v. Commissioner, 119 F.3d 482 (7th Cir. 1997), the Seventh Circuit permitted the taxpayer to deduct the fees in unsuccessfully fighting a hostile takeover. The court rejected the Tax Court's position that the hostile nature of the takeover did not distinguish the case from *INDOPCO*. Rather, it found that Staley, unlike National Starch, did not create a new asset or add future value. Because the fees were not to facilitate a change in ownership but to protect the existing structure, the court applied what it described as a longstanding rule that costs incurred to defend a business were deductible. The regulations provide the same result.

Suppose a corporation pays a large retainer each year to have a major law firm on call for the purpose of fighting any hostile takeover. Each year the retainer is applied against routine legal fees, including the acquisition of capital assets. Is the retainer deductible? In Dana Corp. v. United States, 174 F.3d 1344 (Fed. Cir. 1999), the taxpayer paid the law firm Wachtell, Lipton $100,000 each year to ensure that Wachtell would not represent a hostile company in a takeover attempt. For the first eight years, Wachtell performed minimal or no legal services, but kept the retainer. In two subsequent years, Dana Corp. completed a takeover of another company. In each case, Wachtell provided legal representation and Dana credited the $100,000 retainer against the fees owed. The court rejected Dana's argument that $100,000 of the legal fees was an ordinary and necessary expense of preventing a takeover. The court reasoned that it was more appropriate to look at the transaction to which the legal fees actually related rather than the original motive for incurring the fee and therefore the retainer must be capitalized as the cost of acquiring a capital asset.

(E) INDOPCO *"Overruled"?* The regulations under § 263 in many instances permit deduction of expenses that produce a future benefit, expenses that INDOPCO would appear to require to be capitalized. Treasury stated that it intended the regulations to displace prior rulings and case law. Can Treasury "overrule" the Supreme Court's opinion? Recall the discussion in Chapter 1, supra at page 59, about the deference given to Treasury regulations. See also Nat'l Cable & Telecomms. Ass'n v. Brand X Internet Servs., 545 U.S. 967 (2005) ("only a precedent holding a statute to be unambiguous forecloses a contrary agency construction.") Is § 263 unambiguous?

(F) *The "One-Year" Guidepost.* As the Court notes in *INDOPCO,* the capitalization requirement is in part concerned with accurately matching a taxpayer's income and expenses to measure net income for the relevant period of time. Thus, where an expenditure is expected to produce income over a period of time rather than only in the current year, capitalization, accompanied by a recovery of capital as the income is earned, is thought to reflect each year's income more accurately than immediate deduction of the expenditure.

This is the notion behind a line of cases, of which *INDOPCO* is an example, that deal with expenditures that do not involve the acquisition, construction, or manufacture of a separate asset. Capitalization, nevertheless, is sometimes required if the expenditure is expected to produce benefits beyond the year in which the expenditure occurred. On the other hand, if the economic benefit will be exhausted by the expiration of the current period, immediate deduction results in the proper measure of current net income.

The one-year rule is often blurred with tax accounting requirements, including the rule of § 446(b) that the taxpayer's method of accounting must "clearly reflect income." This rule is considered in the chapter on accounting provisions, Chapter 7.

A generous version of the one-year rule is now found in the regulation dealing with the capitalization of intangibles. Reg. § 1.263(a)–4(f) permits deduction of payments whose benefit lasts 12 months after the taxpayer first realizes a benefit or the end of the taxable year following the taxable year in which the payment was made, whichever is shorter. This would include prepayments for rents, interest, and licenses. Is this rule consistent with *INDOPCO?*

(G) *Expenses with Respect to a New Business.* The usual issue raised with respect to expenses incurred in entering a new business is whether an expense was incurred to maintain an existing business or to change or expand to a new business. If the former, the expense would be deductible or capitalized under the rules previously discussed; if the latter it usually must be capitalized.

Income tax law has had considerable difficulty with the treatment of expenses that would be deductible by an ongoing business but that are incurred prior to the time the business becomes a "going concern." In general, start-up costs or expenditures incurred prior to entering a new business have been required to be capitalized. For example, in Richmond Television Corp. v. United States, 345 F.2d 901 (4th Cir. 1965), vacated and remanded on another issue, 382 U.S. 68 (1965), the court required capitalization of job training and related expenses incurred before the company obtained its operating license from the Federal Communications Commission and began broadcasting. The court held that Richmond Television was not "carrying on a trade or business" until the license was obtained. Likewise, in a widely-followed decision, Frank v. Commissioner, 20 T.C. 511 (1953), the taxpayer sought to deduct travel and legal expenses incurred in the search for and investigation of newspaper and radio properties. The deduction under the predecessor of § 162(a) was disallowed on the grounds that the statute presupposed an existing business with which the taxpayer was connected. The taxpayer's expenses were characterized as investigatory and preparatory to entering a business and therefore not deductible.

Although § 212 does not require that the taxpayer be "carrying on a trade or business" as § 162 does, the courts have held that the pre-opening expenses doctrine applies as well to § 212. See, e.g., Sorrell v. Commissioner, 882 F.2d 484 (11th Cir. 1989) (investor services fee paid by a limited partnership prior to commencing business must be capitalized); Fishman v. Commissioner, 837 F.2d 309 (7th Cir. 1988) (pre-opening expenses including rentals must be capitalized).

The controversy over whether an expense is a start-up expense is mitigated to some extent by § 195, which permits taxpayers to deduct up to $5,000 of start-up expenses in the year the business or activity begins. The deduction is phased out and is eliminated if expenses exceed $55,000. If an election is made, the remaining expenses are deducted over a 15-year period. (Expenses to purchase intangible assets of an existing business also are amortized over a 15-year period under § 197.) See infra at page 349. See also Note (I) below. Since the amortization period is identical it may not be necessary to characterize the expenditure. Start-up expenditures include expenditures in connection with the investigation or creation of an active trade or business that would be deductible if incurred in connection with the operation of an existing trade or business, as well as expenditures incurred in connection with a § 212 activity in "anticipation of such activity becoming an active trade or business." § 195(c)(1).

The requirement that start-up expenses be deductible if incurred by an existing business has caused controversy and limits the benefits of the deduction. The question when an active trade or business begins is left to the regulations. The IRS has interpreted this to mean that expenditures incurred as part of a general search for, or an investigation of, an active trade or business—for example, expenditures paid to determine whether to enter a new business and which new business to enter—are investigatory costs that are start-up expenditures eligible for deduction under § 195. Costs incurred in the attempt to acquire a specific business are capital in nature and thus generally must be capitalized. Rev. Rul. 99–23, 1999–10 C.B. 998.

(H) *Expenses of an Ongoing Business.* Courts have struggled with the distinction between expanding an existing business and entering a new business. As indicated above, courts and the IRS have been more willing to allow deduction of expenses attributable to the former, but those attributable to the latter must be capitalized. For example, the courts of appeal split on whether expenses in connection with new bank branches must be capitalized. In Central Texas Savings & Loan Association v. United States, 731 F.2d 1181 (5th Cir. 1984), the Fifth Circuit held that the expenditures made to investigate and establish new branches had to be capitalized. The Fourth Circuit, on the other hand, held that such expenses could be deducted immediately because they were incurred in expanding the bank's existing business. NCNB Corp. v. United States, 684 F.2d 285 (4th Cir. 1982). The court in NCNB relied on a number of cases that allowed banks an immediate deduction for the costs of initiating bank card services. See, e.g., Colorado Springs National Bank v. United States, 505 F.2d 1185 (10th Cir. 1974) (permitting deduction because bank was not entering into a new business but merely carrying on its old business of lending in a new way). The Eleventh Circuit, in requiring capitalization of the expenses of acquiring the stock of a new subsidiary, noted the anomaly that would result if the cost of a subsidiary must be capitalized, but the cost of a branch could be deducted. Ellis Banking Corp. v. Commissioner, 688 F.2d 1376 (11th Cir. 1982).

To some extent, the diversity of results in these cases turned on differing interpretations of the Supreme Court's holding in Commissioner v. Lincoln Savings & Loan Association, 403 U.S. 345 (1971), which seemed to require the existence of a new asset for capitalization. The separate asset requirement of *Lincoln Savings* was overruled by *INDOPCO v. Commissioner,* supra at page 323, thereby clouding somewhat the value of these cases as precedents, although the IRS has cited them, along with *Briarcliff Candy*, discussed below, favorably in a number of post-*INDOPCO* revenue rulings. In addition to the *Lincoln Savings* precedent, the courts in *NCNB* and *Central Texas Savings* looked to the nonrecurring nature of the expenses and the life of the new branches to determine if the expenditures should be capitalized. Which approach do you think would better serve the purposes of the capitalization requirement? Should expenses of such expansions normally be immediately deductible?

In Briarcliff Candy Corp. v. Commissioner, 475 F.2d 775 (2d Cir. 1973), the taxpayer, a manufacturer, wholesaler, and retailer of candy, expended more than $300,000 reorganizing its sales force, entering into franchise contracts with retailers, and advertising its products. The Second Circuit, while describing the capital-deductible boundary as "imprecise," permitted a deduction of these expenses, emphasizing that they were related to an advertising and promotional campaign, where deduction is the norm.

(I) *Amortization.* In cases in which the expenditure does not create a separate and distinct asset, but nevertheless must be capitalized, the taxpayer supposedly accounts for the cost by amortizing it over its useful life. The taxpayer has the burden of proving the appropriate useful life for amortization. Unless the useful life can be determined with reasonable accuracy, the regulations provide that a 15-year life can be used in most circumstances. Reg. § 1.167(a)–3(b).

(J) *The Nonrecurring Expenditure Standard.* In Encyclopaedia Britannica, Inc. v. Commissioner, 685 F.2d 212 (7th Cir. 1982), the taxpayer decided to publish a book, titled The Dictionary of Natural Sciences, which it ordinarily would have prepared in-house. Being temporarily short-handed, however, it hired David-Stewart Publishing Company to do all necessary research work and to prepare, edit, and arrange the manuscript. The contract contemplated that David-Stewart would turn over a complete manuscript that would be copyrighted, published, and sold by Encyclopaedia Britannica and, in exchange, David-Stewart would receive advances against the royalties that Encyclopaedia Britannica expected to earn from the book.

Encyclopaedia Britannica treated these advances as ordinary and necessary business expenses deductible in the years when they were paid, though it had not yet obtained any royalties. The IRS disallowed the deductions, but the Tax Court held that the expenditures were for "services" rather than for the acquisition of an asset and could be deducted immediately. The opinion by Judge Posner, reversing the Tax Court, emphasized the nonrecurring quality of the expenditure although he also referred to the one-year rule as a reason for requiring capitalization.

Encyclopaedia Britannica suggests that nonrecurring expenses are more likely to be required to be capitalized. But it is sometimes very difficult to determine whether an expense is recurring. Under the regulations some expenses, such as employee compensation, are clearly recurring and would be deductible. Treasury considered a general rule allowing deductions for recurring expenditures but ultimately decided not to include it in the regulations.

D. DEDUCTIBLE REPAIRS VS. NONDEDUCTIBLE REHABILITATION OR IMPROVEMENTS

A frequently disputed issue is whether the expenses of repairing or improving an existing asset must be capitalized or are immediately deductible. In general, expenses associated with preserving assets and keeping them in efficient operating condition are deductible as repairs under §§ 162 (or § 212, subject to the 2 percent floor and elimination of the deduction between 2018 and the end of 2025), and expenditures for replacement of property or "permanent" improvements made to increase the value or prolong the life of property are capital expenditures, similar to the purchase of a new asset. See Reg. § 1.162–4. Of course any repair increases the value of an unrepaired building and prolongs its life. What the regulations must mean is that the "repair" does not prolong the original expected life of the assets. For example, if the taxpayer purchases a building with a useful life of 30 years, he expects that there will be maintenance costs that will be necessary to actually produce 30 years of productive use.

The IRS has attempted to clarify the distinction between deductible repairs and capital improvements in the following Revenue Ruling and in the regulations discussed in the note that follows the Ruling. The regulations provide that whether a "repair" prolongs the original expected life of the assets is based on a determination of the appropriate "unit of property." For example, installing a new engine in an airplane must be capitalized if the appropriate "unit of property" is an engine but not necessarily if it is the entire plane. The question what constitutes a unit of property has been the most controversial aspect of the regulations.

For instance, in Rev. Rul. 2001–4, 2001–1 C.B. 295, the IRS considered, in some detail, the various kinds of maintenance that are routinely performed on commercial aircraft. The ruling noted that:

Any properly performed repair, no matter how routine, could be considered to prolong the useful life and increase the value of the property if it is compared with the situation existing immediately prior to that repair. Consequently, courts have articulated a number of ways to distinguish between deductible repairs and non-deductible capital improvements. For example, in *Illinois Merchants Trust Co. v. Commissioner*, 4 B.T.A. 103, 106 (1926), acq., V–2 C.B. 2, the court explained that repair and maintenance expenses are incurred for the purpose of keeping the property in an ordinarily efficient operating condition over its probable useful life for the uses for which the property was acquired. Capital expenditures, in contrast, are for replacements, alterations, improvements, or additions that appreciably prolong the life of the property, materially increase its value, or make it adaptable to a different use.

The Service ruled that the expenses of "heavy maintenance" on aircraft could be deducted, even though the maintenance involved the replacement of many airframe parts and took place only once every eight years. The ruling did, however, require capitalization of improvements including the replacement of a "significant portion" of the skin panels on the fuselage and the installation of fire detection systems, a ground proximity warning system, and an air phone system. The ruling also required the capitalization of the costs of replacing "major components" and "substantial structural parts" on an airplane that substantially extended the airplane's useful life.

NOTES

(A) *Treasury Regulations.* As with the rules relating to capitalization in connection with intangible assets, the question whether an expenditure is a deductible repair or a nondeductible capital expenditure has long troubled both taxpayers and the Treasury. When taxpayers own large quantities of equipment or other depreciable property, the stakes are often quite high, even though only the timing of deductions is at issue, since the capitalized costs can be depreciated. These determinations often turn on the facts. For example, in the leading case, Plainfield-Union Water Co. v. Commissioner, 39 T.C. 333 (1962), the cleaning and cement lining of a water main was held not to increase the useful life, strength, value, or capacity of the main, and therefore were deductible. The court said the proper time to ask the key question whether the expenditure increased the property's useful life or materially increased its value was immediately prior to the condition that necessitated the repair. The court stated: "An expenditure which returns property to the state it was in before the situation prompting the expenditure arose, and which does not make the relevant property more valuable, more useful, or longer lived is usually deemed a deductible repair. A capital expenditure is generally considered to be a more permanent increment in the longevity, utility or worth of the property."

Despite the intensely factual nature of these inquiries, Treasury has produced comprehensive regulations that will provide more certainty. The regulations require capitalization of an expenditure that "improves" a unit of property. An amount paid is an improvement if it results in a betterment to the unit of property, restores the unit of property, or adapts the property to a new or different use. An expenditure is a "betterment" only if it (1) ameliorates a material condition or defect that either existed prior to the taxpayer's acquisition of the property or arose during the production of the property, whether or not the taxpayer was aware of the condition or defect at the time of acquisition or production; (2) results in a material addition (including a physical enlargement, expansion, or extension) to the property; or (3) results in a material increase in capacity, productivity, efficiency, strength, or quality of the property or the output of the property. An amount is paid to adapt a property to a new or different use if the adaptation is not consistent with the taxpayer's intended ordinary use of the property at the time originally placed in service by the taxpayer. An important aspect of the regulations is what constitutes a unit of property. All components of property that are functionally interdependent comprise a single unit of property. So, for example, an air-conditioning system would be a separate unit and whether a repair would constitute a capital expenditure would depend on whether it resulted in a betterment to the air conditioning system, not the entire building. Treasury has mandated that costs to provide specific building systems—such as heating systems, security, and elevators—must be capitalized. Whether an expenditure results in an improvement is a difficult question and depends on the facts and circumstances. Treasury has provided numerous examples in the regulations for guidance. See Treas. Reg. § 1.162–3, § 1.162–4 and § 1.263(a)–1 to –3.

The regulations also provide a safe harbor for routine maintenance of property other than buildings. Routine maintenance, such as cleaning, and replacement of parts, is not an improvement to a property and is deductible. If the maintenance is expected to be performed more than once during the lifetime of the property, it is treated as routine. Under a de minimis rule, materials and supplies are not considered to be a unit of property, and generally are deductible to the extent the cost is less than $100 and are reasonably expected to be consumed in 12 months or less.

(B) *Environmental Cleanup.* In Rev. Rul. 94–38, 1994–1 C.B. 35, the IRS permitted a taxpayer to deduct costs incurred to clean up hazardous waste attributable to its manufacturing operations. The ruling held that soil remediation expenses need not be capitalized because they merely brought the land back to its state before the contamination. The IRS said the appropriate test was to compare the status of the asset after the expenditure to the status before the condition arose that created the need for the expenditure. The costs of constructing groundwater treatment facilities, however, had to be capitalized. In another ruling, the IRS noted that *INDOPCO* does not affect the deduction for incidental repairs "even though they have some future benefit." In Rev. Rul. 94–12, 1994–1 C.B. 36. In Rev. Rul. 98–25, 1998–1 C.B. 998, the costs of removing, cleaning, and disposing of old underground storage tanks and filling and monitoring new underground storage tanks were held to be deductible business expenses under § 162. In Rev. Rul. 2004–18, 2004–8 I.R.B. 509, the IRS required the taxpayer to capitalize into the costs of its inventory the costs incurred to clean up hazardous waste at its manufacturing plant. In Revenue Ruling 2005–42, 2005–28 I.R.B. 67, the Service provided specific examples of environmental remediation costs that must be capitalized as inventory costs.

The courts have refused to extend the rule in Rev. Rul. 94–38 to cases where the taxpayer purchases contaminated property rather than contaminates the property itself. Dominion Resources, Inc. v. United States, 219 F.3d 359 (4th Cir. 2000); United Dairy Farmers, Inc. v. United States, 267 F.3d 510 (6th Cir. 2001). The courts reasoned that deduction was inappropriate in the latter case because the expenses put the property in usable condition as opposed to keeping the property in such condition.

(C) *Temporary Expensing.* The 2017 legislation took much of the pressure off the distinction between deductible repairs and capital expenditures during the period from 2018 through 2022 by allowing 100 percent bonus depreciation (discussed at page 348) for most purchases of tangible personal property, such as machinery or other equipment. And § 179 now allows immediate deduction of up to $1 million for even broader categories of assets purchased by relatively small businesses. These changes mean that, at least for a while, controversies over repairs versus capital expenditures will occur mainly in connection with real estate.

E.   EXPENSES THAT INVOLVE BOTH THE PERSONAL-BUSINESS AND CAPITAL-NONCAPITAL BOUNDARIES: JOB-SEEKING AND EDUCATION EXPENSES

1.   JOB-SEEKING EXPENSES

Revenue Ruling 75–120
1975–1 C.B. 55.

* * *

[I]t is now the position of the Service that expenses incurred in seeking new employment in the same trade or business are deductible under § 162 of the Code if directly connected with such trade or business as determined by all the objective facts and circumstances.

However, such expenses are not deductible if an individual is seeking employment in a new trade or business even if employment is secured. If the individual is presently unemployed, his trade or business would consist of the services previously performed for his past employer if no substantial lack of continuity occurred between the time of the past employment and the seeking of the new employment. Such expenses are not deductible by an individual where there is a substantial lack of continuity between the time of his past employment and the seeking of new employment, or by an individual seeking employment for the first time. Such expenses are not deductible under section 212(1) of the Code which applies only to expenses incurred with respect to an existing profit-seeking endeavor not qualifying as a trade or business.

NOTES

(A) *New Trade or Business.* What is the rationale for not permitting a deduction when an employee seeks employment in a new trade or business? Is it merely a statutory interpretation question as to the meaning of "carrying on a trade or business" or is there a policy distinction? Drawing this line puts pressure on the definition of a "new" trade or business and results in rather arbitrary distinctions. For example, a corporate executive in the oil industry who incurs costs in looking for a job as an executive in the retailing industry can deduct the costs, but a lawyer who incurs similar costs in looking for a teaching position cannot. In Davis v. Commissioner, 65 T.C. 1014, 1019 (1976), in deciding whether an education expenditure qualified the taxpayer for a "new trade or business," the Tax Court described itself as applying a "commonsense approach":

> If substantial differences exist in the tasks and activities of various occupations or employments, then each such occupation or employment constitutes a separate trade or business.

Why should fees paid to an employment agency by a graduate of Harvard Business School seeking her first job not be deductible? Does § 195 allow the amortization of job-seeking or education expenses for a new trade or business? Should it? In Snell v. Commissioner, 38 T.C.M. 635 (1979), the taxpayer incurred expenses of a nonrefundable entrance fee, deed preparation, and a trip to London for a personal interview to become a member of Lloyd's of London. The Tax Court disallowed the taxpayer's deduction of expenses, but allowed him to amortize them over his life expectancy. The taxpayer's assertion that he intended to resign in seven years was not enough to establish a shorter useful life for the membership. Compare Harman v. Commissioner, 72 T.C. 362 (1979) (initiation fee paid to become a member of the New York Stock Exchange added to the cost basis of the membership, but not amortized).

Job-seeking and education expenses often are linked because both raise the new vs. old business issue. The notes following the next case explore this issue further.

(B) *Expenses of Seeking Public Office.* In McDonald v. Commissioner, 323 U.S. 57 (1944), the court held that a state judge could not deduct assessments that had to be paid to a political party fund if the taxpayer was to obtain the support of the party organization for his election campaign. The court held that if campaign expenditures were to be deductible, the policy should be more clearly stated by Congress. See also Nichols v. Commissioner, 511 F.2d 618 (5th Cir. 1975), where the Fifth Circuit, sitting en banc, held that a candidate for judicial office could not deduct a fee enabling him to be placed on a ballot for a primary election. Five judges dissented.

The Tax Court reaffirmed its *McDonald* position in Estate of Rockefeller v. Commissioner, 83 T.C. 368 (1984), where it denied a deduction under § 162 for $550,160 of legal fees and other expenses paid by Nelson Rockefeller in connection with investigations and hearings for his confirmation as Vice President of the United States. The Tax Court rejected the argument that "holding public offices" constitutes a single trade or business and instead viewed the office of Vice President as a "unique position * * * with vastly different tasks, activities, and responsibilities from the offices previously held by Mr. Rockefeller."

2.   EDUCATION EXPENSES

Wassenaar v. Commissioner

United States Tax Court, 1979. 72 T.C. 1195.

■ SIMPSON, JUDGE.

The Commissioner determined a deficiency of $521 in the petitioner's Federal income tax for 1973. The issue[ ] for decision [is]: Whether the petitioner may deduct as an ordinary and necessary business expense the cost of his masters of law degree in taxation * * *

The petitioner graduated from Wayne State University Law School (Wayne State) in Detroit, Mich., in June 1972. He served on law review while at Wayne State in both 1971 and 1972, and although he was a member of the board of editors, his services were no different from those of any other law review member. His duties included editing legal material, checking sources of legal articles, and writing legal articles. He received compensation for such services from Wayne State in the amounts of $845 in 1971 and $1,314 in 1972.

From June to September 1971, the petitioner worked for the law firm of Warner, Norcross & Judd (Warner firm). He prepared legal memorandums, drafted legal documents, and consulted with clients in the presence of an attorney from the firm. He received $2,920 from the Warner firm as compensation for his services that summer.

The petitioner was not employed during the summer following his graduation from law school; instead, he prepared for the Michigan bar, which he took in July 1972. However, he continued to search for employment with a law firm during such period. In October 1972, he passed the bar exam, but he was not formally admitted to the Michigan bar until May of 1973.

In September 1972, the petitioner began courses in the graduate law program in taxation at New York University (NYU), and he graduated with a masters degree in taxation in May 1973. * * * The petitioner's principal residence was Holland, Mich., while he lived in New York to attend NYU during the year in issue. Following his graduation from NYU, the petitioner returned to Detroit to commence employment with the law firm of Miller, Canfield, Paddock & Stone (Miller firm).

From 1963 until his beginning law school at Wayne State, the petitioner held numerous positions and worked for numerous employers.

In 1965, he was employed by the Sunday School Guide Publishing Co., the city of Holland, Mich., the Capital Park Motel in Lansing, Mich., and the Motor Wheel Corp. in Lansing, Mich. He worked for the city of Holland, Fleetwood Furniture, and H. J. Heinz Co. in 1966. The petitioner was employed by three employers in 1967—the Klaasen Printing Co., Fleetwood Furniture, and Wiersma Construction Co. In 1968, he worked for General Electric Co., and he worked for Lear Siglar Co. in 1969.

On his Federal income tax return for 1973, the petitioner deducted the expenses he incurred while attending NYU as an employee business expense. In his notice of deficiency, the Commissioner disallowed the deduction on the ground that such expenses were not ordinary and necessary expenses paid or incurred in connection with any trade or business. * * *

The first issue for decision is whether the petitioner may deduct as an ordinary and necessary expense incurred in his trade or business the expense for tuition, books, meals, lodging, and other miscellaneous items paid by him while he obtained his masters degree in taxation.

The petitioner contends that for more than 10 years prior to 1973, he was in a trade or business of "rendering his services to employers for compensation." He contends that he was engaged in the trade or business of "analyzing and solving legal problems for compensation" while he worked on the law review at Wayne State, while he worked for the Warner firm, and later while he worked for the Miller firm. He maintains that the graduate courses in taxation helped maintain and improve his skills in that work. On the other hand, the Commissioner takes the position that the petitioner never began the practice of law until the summer of 1973 and that his attendance at NYU was merely the completion of his program of education preparatory to the practice of law. In the alternative, the Commissioner argues that the petitioner's expenses for travel and meals and lodging are not deductible since he was not "away from home" while attending NYU.

Section 162(a) allows a deduction for all the ordinary and necessary expenses of carrying on a trade or business, including amounts expended for education. Deductible educational expenses under section 162(a) may include expenditures for tuition and books as well as amounts for travel and meals and lodging while the taxpayer is away from home. (Reg. § 1.162–5(e)(1).) Reg. § 1.162–5(a)(1) expressly allows a deduction for those educational expenditures which maintain or improve skills "required by the individual in his employment or other trade or business." Whether education maintains or improves skills required by the taxpayer in his trade or business is a question of fact. Moreover, the taxpayer must be established in the trade or business at the time he incurs an educational expense to be able to deduct such expense under section 162. See *Jungreis v. Commissioner*, 55 T.C. 581, 588 (1970).

The petitioner artfully attempts to characterize his trade or business as "analyzing and solving legal problems for compensation," and he received compensation for the performance of such services. Nevertheless, it is clear that the petitioner's intended trade or business at the time he attended NYU was that of an attorney, with an emphasis on the law of taxation. We observe that he enrolled in the masters in taxation program at NYU directly from law school, and there was thus an uninterrupted continuity in his legal education. Although the work the petitioner performed before his graduation from law school and NYU was admittedly of a legal nature, such work in no way constituted his being engaged in the practice of law. Before his admission to the bar in May of 1973, he was not authorized to practice law as an attorney. Therefore, his expenses at NYU were not incident to the trade or business of practicing law, and thus, he was not maintaining or improving the skills of that profession within the purview of Reg. § 1.162–5(a)(1). See, e.g., *Fielding v. Commissioner*, 57 T.C. 761 (1972) (medical school graduate was denied a business expense deduction for tuition cost of his residency since expenses were not incident to any profession that he previously practiced); *Horodysky v. Commissioner*, 54 T.C. 490 (1970) (taxpayer who had been a lawyer in Poland was denied a business expense deduction for cost of obtaining an American law school degree since he had no previous employment as a lawyer in this country).

Moreover, although the petitioner completed the requirements for admission to the bar in 1972, he was not formally admitted until May of 1973, and until that time, he could not engage in the practice of law. It is a well-established principle that being a member in good standing of a profession is not tantamount to *carrying on* that profession for the purpose of section 162(a). * * *

Because the petitioner had not practiced law as an attorney before his attendance at NYU, his situation is not analogous to that of other professionals who have been allowed educational expense deductions under section 162(a). In such cases, the taxpayer was already firmly established in his profession and was truly taking courses or attending a seminar for the purpose of maintaining or improving the skills of his profession. See *Coughlin v. Commissioner*, 203 F.2d 307 (2d Cir. 1953), revg. and remanding 18 T.C. 528 (1952) (attorney allowed business deduction for expenses incurred in attending NYU Tax Institute seminar); *Bistline v. United States*, 145 F. Supp. 802 (E.D. Idaho 1956), aff'd. per curiam on another issue 260 F.2d 80 (9th Cir. 1958) (attorney allowed a business deduction for expenses incurred in attending 2-week course in Federal taxation at the Practicing Law Institute); *Watson v. Commissioner*, 31 T.C. 1014 (1959) (doctor specializing in internal medicine allowed deduction under earlier regulations for courses in psychiatry since such courses helped him to better understand psychosomatic illnesses); *Furner v. Commissioner*, 393 F.2d 292 (7th Cir. 1968), revg. 47 T.C. 165 (1966) (teacher who took year off to secure masters degree was still carrying on a trade or business and allowed to deduct educational expenses); see also Reg. § 1.162–5(c).

In addition, the petitioner is also denied a deduction for his expenses at NYU by Reg. § 1.162–5(b)(3), which provides that educational expenses are not deductible if the education "is part of a program of study being pursued by him which will lead to qualifying him in a new trade or business." The petitioner's attendance at NYU was part of his "program of study" of becoming a lawyer, a trade or business in which he was not previously engaged before his attendance there. After his admission to the bar in May of 1973 and his completion of the program at NYU, he was authorized to and began the practice of law, a wholly different trade or business from any in which he had been previously engaged. * * *

The petitioner is also not entitled to an educational expense deduction on the theory that he was engaged in the trade or business of "rendering his services to employers for compensation." It is a well-established principle that educational expenses must bear a direct and proximate relation to the taxpayer's trade or business. * * * In *Carroll v. Commissioner*, 51 T.C. at 215, this Court stated that it is not sufficient that "the petitioner's education is helpful to him in the performance of his employment." The education must be more than tenuously related to the skills required in the taxpayer's occupation; it must be proximately related to such skills. We cannot accept the petitioner's argument that courses in the more advanced fields of tax law have any proximate relation to his past employment with the Sunday School Guide Publishing Co., Fleetwood Furniture, or the Capital Park Motel—some of his employers as many as 7 years before his attendance at NYU.

* * * Accordingly, we hold that the petitioner's expenses in obtaining a masters of law degree in taxation are not deductible as an ordinary and necessary business expense since he was not engaged in the trade or business of being an attorney at the time such expenses were incurred and since, therefore, he was not maintaining or improving the skills of such trade or business. Such expenses are nondeductible personal expenses. (Sec. 262.) * * *

NOTES

(A) *The Business-Personal Distinction*. All education involves an element that is personal: knowledge is imparted that may not be directly related to the production of income. The regulations distinguish between education that maintains or improves skills in a trade or business and education that leads to qualification for a new trade or business. How well does that test serve to distinguish between personal and business expenses? The regulations state that the nondeductible expenditures "are personal expenditures or constitute an inseparable aggregate of personal and capital expenditures." Why were Wassenaar's NYU Law School expenses not business-related? Suppose Wassenaar had practiced tax law long enough to earn money to go to graduate school? Should that matter?

(B) *Capital Expenditure Analysis.* Why should any education expense be immediately deductible even if it is directly related to a trade or business? Education provides a "permanent" benefit lasting far beyond the taxable year. The distinction between qualification for a new business and maintenance of skills for an old business corresponds to the requirement that start-up expenses be capitalized. If so, why not capitalize education expenses and amortize them? Over what period of time? When should the recovery of costs begin? What result would be appropriate if the education expense was personal in nature?

(C) *When Does a Trade or Business Begin?* As a technical matter, education expenses are not deductible unless they are "incurred in carrying on" a trade or business. Expenses that are incurred prior to beginning a business or career are not deductible. The level of activity necessary to establish a trade or business is an oft-litigated question. Compare *Wassenaar* with Ruehmann v. Commissioner, 30 T.C.M. 675 (1971), where an individual was permitted to deduct the costs of a master's degree program at Harvard Law School he began within months of his graduation from law school. Unlike Wassenaar, Ruehmann worked the summer after graduating from law school and thus was engaged in the practice of law prior to entering the graduate program. The Commissioner also conceded that the LL.M. program, through which Ruehmann took business law courses, did not prepare Ruehmann for a new trade or business.

In Ford v. Commissioner, 56 T.C. 1300 (1971), aff'd 487 F.2d 1025 (9th Cir. 1973), the taxpayer worked as a substitute teacher before and while pursuing a graduate degree in anthropology. He also taught English, Spanish, and history full-time for one semester. Then he spent a year in Norway during which he studied Norwegian, linguistic analysis, and cultural anthropology. He returned to the United States to become a full-time teacher of high school English and social studies. The court allowed him to deduct the expense of his Norwegian education. The six dissenters argued that the taxpayer had not been carrying on the trade or business of teaching prior to the trip but instead in Norway was pursuing studies for a new trade as an anthropologist. Even granting the taxpayer's teaching status, however, the dissenters maintained that the purpose of the trip was primarily personal rather than to maintain or improve his skills as a teacher.

If the taxpayer were to change from teaching English and social studies in high school to teaching physics, would he remain within the same trade or business? See Reg. § 1.162–5(b)(3)(i) (stating that an employee's change of duties is not a new trade or business).

(D) *Minimum Educational Requirements.* The regulations do not permit a taxpayer to deduct minimum education requirements for "qualification in his employment or other trade or business." Thus, education that qualifies the taxpayer for a new trade or business is not deductible even if the taxpayer never intended or never did enter the new business. Reg. § 1.162–5(b)(2).

In Toner v. Commissioner, 71 T.C. 772 (1979), the taxpayer worked as a teacher in a parochial elementary school. The minimum education required by her employer was a high school diploma, but teachers without a bachelor's degree also were required to earn six hours of college credit each year. Teachers in the public elementary schools generally were required to have a bachelor's degree in order to begin teaching. While teaching, the taxpayer took fifteen college hours, received her degree, and claimed a deduction for the educational expenses. The Tax Court denied the deductions, finding that the degree met the minimum educational requirement "for qualification in his employment" as expressed in the regulations. The seven dissenters argued that the language of the regulation should be controlled by the "requirements of the employer," not the standards of the profession (the public school system). In addition, the dissent argued that teaching in the public schools would not be a new trade or business within the meaning of Reg. § 1.162–5(b)(3). The Third Circuit reversed under reasoning similar to the Tax Court dissents. Toner v. Commissioner, 623 F.2d 315 (3d Cir. 1980).

The courts and the Service have had a great deal of difficulty determining what is a new trade or business. Lawyers have not fared well. See, e.g., Sharon v. Commissioner, 66 T.C. 515 (1976), aff'd 591 F.2d 1273 (9th Cir. 1978), cert. denied, 442 U.S. 941 (1979) (New York attorney could not deduct the expenses incurred in studying for and taking the California bar exam because the practice of law in California was a new business, but the expenses could be amortized over his life expectancy); Rev. Rul. 75–412, 1975–2 C.B. 62 (the holder of a foreign law degree cannot deduct a law school course necessary to take a state bar exam because it would enable him to become a U.S. lawyer); Johnson v. United States, 332 F. Supp. 906 (E.D.La. 1971) (lawyer could not deduct the expense of attending graduate school to obtain an LL.M. in taxation because it prepared him for a new business, i.e. being a tax lawyer); O'Donnell v. Commissioner, 62 T.C. 781 (1974), aff'd 519 F.2d 1406 (7th Cir. 1975) (CPA could not deduct costs of attending law school even though he was already in the business of being a "tax accounting professional").

On the other hand, MBA students have had more luck in convincing the courts that the degree is not the minimum requirement for any particular profession and thus a recipient is not qualified for a new trade or business. In Allemeier v. Commissioner, 90 T.C.M. 197 (2005), a salesman of mouth guards to athletes was permitted to deduct the cost of an MBA because the degree was not a condition precedent at his place of employment and he was not qualified to perform significantly different tasks and activities after he earned his degree. On the other hand, in Foster v. Commissioner, T.C. Summ. Op. 2008–22, the court denied a deduction for the costs of the MBA degree because the taxpayer previously had worked as an engineer and moved to a marketing position after completing the degree. In Link v. Commissioner, 90 T.C. 460 (1988), aff'd 869 F.2d 1491 (6th Cir. 1989), the taxpayer was denied a deduction for the expenses of obtaining an MBA because he had worked for only one summer after graduating from college. Taking a long view and examining the taxpayer's activities since high school, the court found that his employment was a "temporary hiatus between academic endeavors" that was "more in the nature of a sporadic and isolated deviation from his 'career' as a student."

In Kopaigora v. Commissioner, T.C. Summ. Op. 2016–35, the taxpayer claimed a deduction for the costs of his executive MBA program. The IRS argued that he was not eligible for the deduction because, as a result of losing his job, he did not carry on his trade or business through the tax year. The petitioner successfully argued that he remained established in the field because, during his unemployment, he continued to look for similar work, and his next job was in the same field. The Court accepted a broad definition of his field, management and finance, which included both the hotel manager role and his next job as a vice president at a financial services firm. This broad definition also allowed the taxpayer to overcome the argument that the executive MBA is a general degree which does not improve specific job skills by showing that most of his classes were in management or finance.

This line drawing is often quite arbitrary. Compare, for example, *Sharon* and Robinson v. Commissioner, 78 T.C. 550 (1982) (licensed practical nurse cannot deduct the cost of nursing school that will qualify her to be a registered nurse), with Rev. Rul. 71–58, 1971–1 C.B. 55 (a teacher in one state may deduct the cost of courses necessary to qualify to teach in another state) and Reg. § 1.162–5(b)(3) (Ex. 4) (psychiatrist may deduct the cost of study at a psychoanalytic institute that will qualify him to practice psychoanalysis).

(E) *General Self-Improvement.* Although all education has aspects of general self-improvement, in some cases that aspect is so predominant that a deduction is denied. Generally, the costs of obtaining an undergraduate degree or taking "college" courses is not deductible, in part because it is the minimum education requirement for so many businesses, but also because there is a large personal consumption element that would be helpful to any trade or business. But see Glasgow v. Commissioner, 31 T.C.M. 310 (1972), aff'd 486 F.2d 1045 (10th Cir. 1973), in which a Baptist minister was allowed to deduct the cost of obtaining a college degree. The court found that the study for this degree maintained skills—such as public speaking, English, drama, accounting, psychology, history, and education—that are required for a pastor to carry out his varied duties effectively.

(F) *Travel Expenses.* Although travel expenses in connection with otherwise deductible education are themselves deductible, there is no deduction for travel as education. § 274(m)(2). Thus, although traveling in Europe visiting art museums may improve the skills of an art history teacher, the travel is not deductible.

(G) *Employer Subsidies.* An employee whose education costs are subsidized through an educational assistance program has no gross income even if he would not have been able to deduct the costs if he had paid it himself. Section 127 permits an employee to exclude reimbursement of undergraduate or graduate school expenses paid by his employer. Only $5,250 may be excluded each taxable year. Reg. § 1.162–5 is designed to distinguish between the costs of producing income and personal consumption. Section 127 is a tax expenditure designed to subsidize the cost of education.

F. OPTION TO DEDUCT OR CAPITALIZE

In a number of situations, Congress has given the taxpayer the option of deducting items otherwise required to be capitalized or capitalizing items otherwise deductible. Current examples where deduction is permitted include: § 173 (circulation expenses), § 175 (soil and water conservation), § 190 (costs of removing architectural and transportation barriers for persons with disabilities), and § 198 (certain environmental cleanup costs).

A taxpayer who is likely to have no income against which to take a deduction would prefer to capitalize rather than deduct expenses that otherwise would be deductible. Section 266, for example, permits a taxpayer to capitalize otherwise deductible interest, taxes, and carrying charges with respect to property.

Should the decision whether expenses will be capitalized or immediately deducted be left to the taxpayer? What results would you expect from allowing taxpayers to determine whether various expenditures should be capitalized or deducted? The decision to deduct rather than capitalize produces, at a minimum, a deferral of tax that otherwise would be paid currently. How would the availability of a capital gains preference on the sale of the asset affect your decision whether to provide an option to deduct currently expenses that ordinarily would be capitalized?

SECTION 4.   RECOVERY OF CAPITAL EXPENDITURES

The prior Section of this Chapter focused on the distinction between immediate deduction and capitalization. We now consider in detail the principal mechanisms for recovery of capitalized expenditures over a number of years: depreciation, amortization, and depletion. The following materials illustrate that the precise timing of such deductions the tax law permits has varied dramatically from time to time and with the kind of asset at issue. This Section also considers the role of several special tax credits available to businesses. Historically, the most important of these has been the investment tax credit, in effect from time to time in various forms from 1962 to 1986.

The 2017 tax act made a major change, enacting new rules that permit immediate expensing of certain property by certain taxpayers in certain years. Most of these provisions expire at the end of 2026 or 2027. The sunset of these expensive provisions was intended, in part, to meet Senate rules limiting tax cuts that produce deficits.

The 2017 act's piecemeal and time-limited approach to cost recovery, described in more detail below, will motivate a great deal of tax planning. As soon as the 2017 bill took its final form, taxpayers (and their tax lawyers, of course) began to plan to purchase the most tax-advantaged assets in the most tax-advantaged years. The 2017 tax act also creates a high degree of uncertainty, since it is possible, even highly likely, that some of the benefits will be extended. But extension is not a sure bet, and lobbying surely will affect which benefits are extended and for whom. Tax uncertainty can be costly for taxpayers, who may accelerate, defer, or forgo transactions due to the inability to plan for tax effects. But someone likely benefits from uncertainty: what do you suppose are the political advantages of this selective and time-limited approach?

A. DEPRECIATION AND AMORTIZATION

Note on Depreciation and Amortization

An allowance for depreciation has been a part of the tax law since the enactment of the corporate income tax in 1909. With the exception of salaries, depreciation has long been the largest single deduction on corporate tax returns. The history of the annual depreciation allowance has been marked by frequent change and considerable controversy.

Section 167 of the Code permits as a depreciation deduction a "reasonable allowance for the exhaustion, wear and tear (including a reasonable allowance for obsolescence)" of assets used in a trade or business or held for the production of income. Note that no depreciation allowance is provided for assets acquired for personal use, since to do so would undermine the prohibition against the deduction of personal expenses.

Section 168 provides a mandatory system of depreciation (the Accelerated Cost Recovery System or "ACRS") for tangible personal property and real property. In addition, the calculation of depreciation on various assets for purposes of the individual alternative minimum tax is performed according to different rules. Some taxpayers therefore have to contend with two separate depreciation systems. The AMT is described very briefly in Chapter 1.

The depreciation deduction allows taxpayers in determining taxable income to deduct an allocable part of the cost of business or investment assets that have a limited life. As we have seen, Section 162 authorizes taxpayers to deduct from income each year (to "expense") regularly recurring business or income-producing expenditures such as repairs, consumable supplies, heat, electricity, and salaries and wages. The cost of a machine is also an expense of doing business that must be offset against gross income if the taxpayer is to recover its capital investment. Since the machine has a life that extends over a period of years, however, under § 263 its cost must be capitalized and usually recovered over a number of years.

An allocation of costs to the related income is essential to the clear reflection of income. The cost of the machine should not be deducted entirely in the year of acquisition because that would understate income for that year. Neither should the deduction of the cost be spread over too long a period because income then would be overstated during the actual productive life of the machine. The depreciation deduction is, in principle, intended to allocate the cost of the machine over the proper period of time.

As noted above, § 168 now provides a mandatory depreciation system for certain property. However, as we will see, the 2017 tax act greatly expanded opportunities for immediate expensing. Before turning to current law in detail, the history of its development is described.

Economic Depreciation. It has been demonstrated that "economic depreciation"—which would allow deduction for the actual decline in an asset's value during the taxable period—would provide "appropriate" results under an income tax. Such a depreciation system would more properly measure net economic income for each period and would impose an effective rate of tax equal to the statutory rate for all assets. Economic depreciation would not distort taxpayers' choices among assets to be used in the production of income; taxpayers would acquire the same assets under an income tax as they would in the absence of an income tax.[12] Thus, economic depreciation can serve as a useful analytical benchmark to assess actual income tax rules.

The income tax, however, has never attempted to measure economic depreciation. Such measurement would be impossible as a practical matter because of the need to measure annually the change in value of a massive number of business and investment assets. For administrative reasons, Congress and the IRS have long endeavored to establish a single depreciation schedule to be used when an asset is first placed in service and followed throughout its useful life. Finally, depreciation allowances often have been used not just to measure income, but also to increase the overall level of investment in plant and equipment for fiscal and economic policy reasons.

Income Tax Rules. The annual depreciation allowance is applied to the *depreciable base*. This is usually the property's basis, which is determined under § 1011. Basis is often cost, but as discussed supra at page 140, other rules sometimes apply. The depreciable base includes any capital expenditures that have been added to basis under § 1016. The basis is reduced periodically by the amount of allowable depreciation. The result, referred to as adjusted basis, thus reflects the recovery of the taxpayer's capital investment over time. Depreciation deductions increase the gain or decrease the loss realized by the taxpayer on disposition.

The depreciation allowance depends on the depreciation *rate*. This rate is a function of both the *method* of depreciation and of the depreciation period, which generally is referred to as the *recovery period*. The recovery method may (or may not) be a function of the asset's "useful life."

---

[12] This result was demonstrated in Paul Samuelson, "Tax Deductibility of Economic Depreciation to Insure Invariant Valuations," 72 J. Pol. Econ. 604 (1964).

The simplest method of allocating the cost of an asset over the recovery period is the *straight line method.* Under this method, the cost of an asset is allocated in equal amounts over its useful life. Thus, a $100 asset with an estimated ten-year life would be depreciated under the straight line method at the rate of 10 percent or $10 in each of the ten years.

The *declining balance method* allocates a larger portion of the cost to the earlier years and a lesser portion to the later years. Under this method, a constant percentage is used, but it is applied each year to the (declining) amount remaining after the depreciation of previous years has been charged off. The double declining balance method (so named, because it uses double the straight line rate) would depreciate a $100 ten-year asset in amounts of $20 in the first year (twice 10 percent, or 20 percent x $100), $16 in the second year (20 percent x the balance of $80), $12.80 in the third year (20 percent x the balance of $64), and so on. Because the property would not be fully depreciated in ten years under this method, the declining balance method is generally only used while it produces more depreciation than the straight line method. Methods like the declining balance method that result in larger depreciation charges in the earlier years are often referred to as *accelerated depreciation.*

Determining the recovery period or useful life of an asset is necessarily an estimate or a prognostication of the period of time during which the asset will be economically productive. For administrative reasons, this estimate of useful life must be made when the asset is placed in service and, therefore, must take into account future events that are often unpredictable. These include engineering and economic factors, technological developments in the industry, future market conditions, and other variables.

The *salvage value* of an asset is the amount the taxpayer would expect to recover when he stops using the asset for the production of income. Theoretically, the portion of the taxpayer's cost allocable to salvage value should not be depreciated. This, however, requires an estimate of salvage value when an asset is first placed in service, even if the asset is expected to be used in the business for many years. Frequent controversies about the amount of salvage value have led Congress to ignore salvage value limitations and permit the entire cost of an asset to be depreciated. § 168(b)(4).

Brief History of Depreciation. Until the early 1960s, most assets were depreciated using the straight line method. For more than 20 years after the introduction of the corporate tax in 1909, taxpayers generally were free to determine the useful lives of their assets. This changed, however, as a result of the wrongheaded desire to raise revenue during the Depression. In 1934, the Treasury Department shifted the burden of proof as to depreciable lives to the taxpayer. Thereafter, useful life was determined largely by reference to standardized lives prescribed by the IRS. The taxpayer had a heavy burden of proof to sustain any shorter life on individual assets, and there was frequent controversy as to proper depreciation allowances.

In 1954, Congress first authorized the use of accelerated depreciation, and in 1962, the Service produced a fundamental change in the means of determining useful lives by promulgating a list of guideline lives for 75 broad classes of assets, mostly based on the industries in which the assets were used. These lives, which were shorter than those previously used, were meant to simplify depreciation accounting and to provide a stimulus for investment. In 1971, Congress adopted an Asset Depreciation Range (ADR) system that allowed taxpayers to select useful lives from a range, generally 20 percent above or below the guideline lives. The guideline lives so promulgated, now referred to as class lives, are the starting point for the current depreciation system.

In 1981, Congress took yet another step toward accelerating depreciation by providing for the recovery of capital costs over periods that generally were far shorter than the useful lives of prior law. For example, the cost of eligible personal property was recovered over a 15-year, 10-year, 5-year, or 3-year period, depending on the type of property. Most eligible personal property was in the 5-year class. The depreciation schedule that was generally in effect under the 1981 rules was constructed to approximate the benefits of a 150 percent declining balance method for the early years and the straight line method for the later years. For real property, the statute provided for a table in accordance with the use of a 175 percent declining balance schedule.

Current Rules. Under the current system, depreciable assets are assigned to recovery classes. There are ten recovery periods with class lives from three years to 50 years. § 168(c). Property is classified as 3-year property, 5-year property, etc. based on class lives. § 168(e). For example, most personal property with a guideline class life of more than four years but less than 10 years is classified as 5-year property, which not surprisingly is depreciated over a 5-year recovery period. Residential rental property is in the 27.5-year class, and commercial real property is in the 39-year class.

ACRS prescribes one of three depreciation methods for each class of property. Property in the 3-year, 5-year, 7-year, and 10-year classes is depreciated using the 200 percent declining balance method. The taxpayer switches to a straight line method that allocates the cost ratably over the remaining recovery period in the year in which that method produces a larger deduction. § 168(b)(1). Property in the 15-year and 20-year classes is depreciated using the 150 percent declining balance method, with a switch to the straight line method in the year that straight line recovery produces a larger deduction. § 168(b)(2). Straight line depreciation must be used for real estate. § 168(b)(3). The taxpayer may elect to use the straight line method for any class of property. § 168(b)(3)(C) and (b)(5).

Because property is seldom purchased on the first day of the year or disposed of on the last day of the year, some rule must be adopted to determine the depreciation allowance when the property is not used for the entire year. For personal property, a half-year convention is used, meaning that one-half year's depreciation is allowed in both the year of acquisition and the year of disposition, regardless of how long the taxpayer actually held the property. Whether the taxpayer purchased a machine on March 20 or September 20, he would take one-half of the total depreciation allowance for the year of purchase. § 168(d)(1). Obviously, there is an advantage to purchasing property late in the year. To prevent excessive gaming, the Code provides that when the taxpayer purchases a significant amount of depreciable property in the last quarter, a mid-quarter convention applies, meaning the property is deemed to have been purchased at the midpoint of the quarter. Note that this will actually increase the depreciation deduction for property put into service in the first half of the year. § 168(d)(3). For real property, a mid-month convention is used, meaning the taxpayer takes one-half a month's depreciation for the month of acquisition and disposition. If, for example, real property was placed in service on October 20, the taxpayer would take a depreciation allowance for 2½ months of the first year. § 168(d)(2).

Immediate Expensing. The tax act of 2017 expanded two opportunities for taxpayers to take immediate deductions for the full cost of certain property. (Recall the earlier note on the benefits of tax deferral that explains why this is important.)

The first is so-called "bonus depreciation," originally enacted as an economic stimulus in response to 9/11. The rules now permit taxpayers to deduct in the first year 100 percent of the cost of certain property (generally, property with a life of less than 20 years) if placed in service between September 2017 and January 1, 2023. The first-year "bonus" deduction phases down to 80 percent in 2024, 60 percent in 2025, 40 percent in 2026, and 20 percent in 2027, before disappearing entirely in 2028. § 168(k).

Like many other provisions of the 2017 act, the generosity of bonus depreciation phases down over time to meet Senate budget rules limiting the extent to which legislation can add to the deficit. How do you suppose taxpayers will react to the announced phasedown? If you had a client planning to buy business equipment some time in the mid-2020s, what would you advise her to do?

The 2017 tax act provides a major expansion of bonus depreciation. After September 11, 2001 and again for several years after the economic downturn of 2008, Congress permitted businesses of any size to deduct 50 percent of the adjusted basis of most tangible personal property acquired during the applicable year. Since the ACRS depreciation system is already highly front-loaded for personal property, bonus depreciation permitted businesses to deduct a substantial portion of the cost in the year or acquisition.

Proponents of bonus depreciation regard it as an effective stimulus to business investment, which they believe provides more economic bang for the buck than alternative forms of business tax reduction. In contrast to a general reduction in corporate tax rates, for example, bonus depreciation can be limited to property newly placed in service or even to particular types of investments. Detractors focus primarily on the fact that bonus depreciation is available only for limited categories of investment—principally business equipment—and therefore induces a shift away from other sectors of the economy where the cost of investing is not so heavily subsidized. A more general complaint is that the accelerated write-offs favors capital-intensive over labor-intensive industries.

Empirical evidence suggests that bonus depreciation was not very effective in providing short-term economic stimulus compared to alternative policies like cuts in payroll taxes and increases in unemployment benefits.

The second favorable expensing regime is § 179, which now permits a taxpayer to elect to deduct immediately ("expense") the cost of certain tangible business property up to $1 million per year. The benefit applies to tangible personal property used in business (but not generally to real property) and is available only to taxpayers whose annual total investment in qualified property is $2.5 million or less. The deduction is phased out dollar for dollar for taxpayers who place in service such property exceeding the cap in any one taxable year.

The effect of § 179 is to permit many small businesses to deduct the cost of business assets rather than to capitalize them. Unlike § 168(k), which permits full expensing only through 2023, the 100 percent deduction in § 179 is permanent. What would you advise a business to do that had already purchased $2.5 million of § 179 property during a taxable year and was contemplating purchasing $50,000 more? Does this provision always encourage the purchase of more business assets?

Amortization of Intangibles. Any ongoing business typically has what accountants call "goodwill," which is the excess of the value of the business over the value of its tangible assets. A popular coffee shop, for instance, might have tangible assets (tables, chairs, an espresso machine) worth just $100,000, but the business as a whole might sell for much more, say, $300,000. The $200,000 difference is often described as "goodwill," or "going concern value." Goodwill exists when the whole is greater than the sum of the parts—in this context, because businesses have intangible and hard-to-measure but still very real assets like reputation, customer loyalty, and branding.

Historically, when a taxpayer purchased a business, the portion of the purchase price allocated to goodwill was not depreciable. Taxpayers often argued that, in fact, they had purchased other intangible assets with a determinable useful life that could be depreciated. Examples included customer or subscriber lists, a trained workforce in place, and "core deposits" of financial institutions. The cases usually turned on costly expert evidence that a particular intangible had a value independent of goodwill and a limited useful life. See, e.g., Newark Morning Ledger Co. v. United States, 507 U.S. 546 (1993) (permitting amortization of a newspaper's list of subscribers where the taxpayer could prove the value and useful life of the asset but noting that the taxpayer's burden of proof "often will prove too great to bear").

Congress struck a blow for certainty by adopting rules to account for the cost of intangibles. In general, under § 197, most purchased intangibles, including goodwill, are amortized on a straight line basis over a 15-year period. This is something of a "rough justice" approach, sacrificing any attempt at accuracy for simplicity. Many intangibles will be amortized over a period that is either longer or shorter than their actual useful lives. But there is no longer any incentive to try to distinguish goodwill from other intangibles since both are now amortizable. Furthermore, there is no longer a need to determine (and ultimately litigate) the useful life of an asset since § 197 arbitrarily assigns a uniform useful life to intangibles. Section 197 does not apply to any intangible created by the taxpayer unless it was created in connection with the acquisition of a trade or business.

Although this provision has resulted in much simplification, in practice, § 197 itself is not simple. In addition to very complex rules defining a "section 197 intangible," there are complicated provisions dealing with the disposition of such an intangible before the recovery period expires, the acquisition of intangibles in nonrecognition transactions, the holding of intangibles in a pass-through entity, such as a partnership, and an election to apply the provision retroactively. Like the passive loss rules of § 469, § 197 is a good example of rule complexity coupled with transactional simplicity. That is, although § 197 appears on its face to be quite complex (an idea easily confirmed by quickly perusing it), it contributes to overall simplification by eliminating much transactional planning and litigation.

Start-up Expenses. As described above, a taxpayer may elect under § 195 to deduct a limited amount of start-up expenses in the year the business begins and amortize the remainder over 15 years. In addition, Section 248 permits a corporation and § 709 permits a partnership to elect to deduct up to $5,000 of organizational expenses, i.e., expenses incident to the formation of the entity. The deduction is phased out and is eliminated if expenses exceed $55,000. The remainder is amortized over 15 years.

NOTES

(A) *Recapture.* Current depreciation rules often provide a write-off of cost that exceeds economic depreciation (the actual decline in value). For example, suppose the taxpayer purchases an asset for $1,000, deducts $300 of depreciation and sells the asset for $800. The taxpayer's adjusted basis is

$700 and he will report $100 of gain, which represents the $100 in depreciation that exceeded the asset's actual $200 decline in value. Although, after taking the gain into account, the total amount of deductions equals the asset's economic depreciation, the taxpayer has enjoyed the time value of money, via taking depreciation in an earlier year and "paying it back" in a later year. Sections 1245 and 1250 provide that certain amounts previously deducted as depreciation will be "recaptured" in order to limit another potential advantage: the deduction of depreciation against ordinary income and the reporting of later gain as capital gain. The details of these provisions are treated in connection with the material on capital gains, infra in Chapter 5.

(B) *Property for Personal Use.* Section 167 permits depreciation only for assets used in a trade or business or an income-producing activity. Thus, there is no depreciation for property used for personal purposes. If an item is used for both personal and income-producing purposes (for example, renting out a floor of a personal residence or using a car for both business and personal purposes), the property's basis must be allocated between the business and personal uses. If personal use property is converted to business use, the basis for depreciation is the lesser of the fair market value of the property at the date of conversion or the property's adjusted basis. Reg. § 1.167(g)–1.

(C) *Land.* Land is not depreciable. Reg. § 1.167(a)–2. Buildings, however, are subject to depreciation. When land and buildings are bought together, as they often are, the purchase price (or other basis) must be allocated between land and buildings in proportion to their respective fair market values. Two justifications typically are offered for disallowing depreciation for the cost of land. The first is that land does not wear out or become obsolete. The second—which seems simply a different way of saying that land does not wear out—is that land has "no ascertainable useful life."

(D) *Antiques.* The IRS has taken the position that "valuable and treasured" works of art are not depreciable because they do not have a determinable useful life. Rev. Rul. 68–232, 1968–1 C.B. 79. Thus, under this rule, a professional musician who acquired a Stradivarius violin for performances would be unable to offset depreciation against his income. See Browning v. Commissioner, 890 F.2d 1084 (9th Cir. 1989), where the court found it impossible to believe that a 200-year-old violin had a remaining useful life of 12 years.

In striking contrast is Simon v. Commissioner, 103 T.C. 247 (1994). The court permitted the taxpayers—professional musicians—to depreciate two 19th century Tourte violin bows that they had purchased for $30,000 and $21,500. The court accepted evidence that the bows can suffer wear and tear and that they would become "unplayable" with use. The IRS argued that the bows, which were 175 years old at the time of purchase, had no ascertainable useful life. The court rejected the argument, explaining that useful life was irrelevant under current law. Under § 168, to be depreciable, property must be "recovery property," which means that the "property must be of a character subject to an allowance for depreciation." The court defined that to mean that it must "suffer exhaustion, wear and tear or obsolescence." In response to evidence the bows had appreciated in value substantially since purchased, the court stated that:

> depreciation accounting reflects the daily diminution in value of the underlying asset through other than market conditions. Accounting for changes in the values of depreciable property because of market conditions, on the other hand, is reportable as gain or loss upon the sale of the depreciable asset.

Should the logic of *Simon* apply only to assets that can be "used up" or subject to "wear and tear" through physical use? Suppose, for example, a business buys a collectible painting to hang on a wall. Should the business be allowed any deduction for depreciation?

Simon was affirmed by the Second Circuit. 68 F.3d 41 (2d Cir. 1995). The Third Circuit, in a related case, permitted the owner of a valuable bass violin to take depreciation deductions because the violin suffered wear and tear making it no longer usable, although it had increased in value. Liddle v. Commissioner, 65 F.3d 329 (3d Cir. 1995).

(E) *Automobiles.* Congress has adopted several provisions relating to the cost of automobiles, but they do not reflect any clear policy. Section 280F limits the amount of depreciation that can be taken on "luxury automobiles." The amount that can be taken as a deduction for depreciation in the first year of the recovery period is limited to $10,000. § 280F(a)(1)(A)(i). Automobiles subject to this limitation are passenger cars that weigh 6,000 pounds or less. In 2018, Congress increased the first year deduction limitation to $10,000, and increased the limitations in subsequent years. The bonus depreciation rules of § 168(k) permit, with limited exceptions, an additional first-year deduction of $8,000, for a total of $18,000 in the first year.

The Tesla Model X, which starts at nearly $80,000 and fits everyone's definition of a luxury car, may not be subject to these rules at all because its "gross vehicle weight rating" exceeds 6,000 pounds (which, by the way, makes it illegal to drive across the Brooklyn Bridge). The § 280F weight limit was intended to exempt farm and construction trucks, which are much less likely to be diverted to personal use. But § 280F was adopted before monster SUVs roamed the roads. Environmental critics were incensed that the entire cost of a Hummer, which weighs well over 6,000 pounds, could be written off under § 179 while a fuel-efficient hybrid could not. Responding to what Senator Grassley described as "an embarrassment," Congress added a provision that limits the deduction under that section to $25,000 for an SUV. The preference for Hummers (and Tesla Model Xs) remains, however, since the deduction under § 179 still exceeds the limitation on other luxury automobiles under § 280F.

(F) *Need for an Ownership Interest.* Only an owner of property who has a capital investment is entitled to depreciation deductions; the owner is thought to be the one who enjoys the economic benefits of ownership and bears the economic burden of the decline in value. Recall *Estate of Franklin*, supra at page 211 in which the court determined that the putative owners had no real economic investment in the property. The practical effect of the decision was to deny depreciation deductions to the taxpayers.

B. DEPLETION

Note on Depletion

In the case of mineral or oil and gas exploration and development, the capitalized costs of the income-producing property are recovered through allowances for depletion, a concept closely related to depreciation. Section 611 provides for a "reasonable allowance for depletion * * * according to the peculiar conditions in each case." Depletion allowances are used to reflect what portion of property has been removed from the ground and sold and what has been retained. Suppose, for example, a taxpayer purchases an oil well for $2 million and extracts and sells the oil. Although it is difficult or even impossible to estimate the total amount of oil that will be removed, at some point the well will run dry and become worthless.

There are two types of depletion allowance. The amount deductible is either "cost depletion" or "percentage depletion." Cost depletion estimates the total amount of natural resource in the property and allows deduction of its cost in proportion to each year's extractions. The taxpayer estimates the total number of units to be recovered (for example, barrels of oil) and each year deducts the basis per unit times the number of units sold. Thus, for example, if 100,000 barrels of oil were estimated as the total for a property, and 10,000 barrels were recovered, 10 percent of the basis would be deductible as cost depletion. Adjustments are made in succeeding years if new information changes the estimate.

"Percentage depletion," which has been in the tax law since 1924, allows the deduction of a specified percentage of the gross income from the property year after year without regard to the recovery of cost. It remains deductible even after the basis (the capital actually invested) has been recovered. Percentage depletion allowances range from 5 percent for gravel and sand, for example, to 22 percent for sulfur, uranium, and a host of other minerals. See § 613(b). Percentage depletion is limited to 50 percent of the taxable income from the property for minerals other than oil and gas. In 1975, following an energy crisis, which involved an embargo of shipments to the United States of foreign-produced oil and produced a substantial increase in the price of gasoline and other petroleum products and a boom in oil company profits, Congress repealed percentage depletion for oil and gas wells of major oil companies but preserved it for smaller oil producers, producers of natural gas, and miners of many minerals. See § 613A.

Although cost depletion is similar to depreciation, percentage depletion serves an additional purpose. Because it permits a taxpayer to deduct more than actual cost, it provides a subsidy for the activities to which it applies, and a stimulus to natural resource exploration and development.

Percentage depletion is calculated with respect to the "gross income from the property," which includes only the amount received for the extraction of the minerals, not the amount attributable to processing or manufacturing the minerals. See Reg. §§ 1.613–3, 1.613–4.

Only a taxpayer with an "economic interest" in the minerals is entitled to a depletion deduction. An economic interest is not limited to "ownership" of the minerals; other arrangements qualify. For example, in United States v. Swank, 451 U.S. 571 (1981), the Court held that a lessee under a mineral lease that could be terminated without cause by the lessor on 30 days notice had an economic interest. But a licensee who simply has the right to extract the minerals does not have an economic interest. See, e.g., Missouri River Sand Co. v. Commissioner, 774 F.2d 334 (8th Cir. 1985).

NOTES

(A) *Intangible Drilling Costs.* A deduction is allowed for so-called intangible drilling costs. When an oil well is drilled, there are a variety of expenses. Some relate to tangible property—a derrick, a shed, and so on. The costs of this property are recovered through depreciation deductions. But a large part of drilling expenses goes into the intangible costs of putting a hole in the ground. These include expenditures for items such as labor, fuel, repairs, hauling, and supplies. The taxpayer is given an option either to deduct immediately these costs—which typically amount to 65 to 85 percent of total drilling costs—or to capitalize and recover the costs through depletion. Intangible drilling costs normally are deducted since percentage depletion is a fixed deduction—relating to income—and is not limited to basis, so that deduction ordinarily is not any greater if intangible drilling costs are capitalized. The taxpayer thus is allowed to deduct production costs as well as percentage depletion. § 263(c); Reg. § 1.612–4. Those costs that are not immediately deductible must be deducted ratably over the 60 months following the expenditure. § 291(b).

(B) *Recapture.* Section 1254 provides that amounts deducted as intangible drilling expenses will be "recaptured" as ordinary income rather than capital gain when certain oil, gas, and geothermal properties are sold. Cost depletion deductions under § 611 are also subject to § 1254 recapture. Recapture is discussed generally in Chapter 5, infra at page 593.

(C) *Other Incentives.* The incentives provided to the oil and gas industry by percentage depletion and the deduction for intangible drilling costs are not the only tax benefits provided to the natural resources industry. Others include:

Exploration and Development Expenditures. Section 617 permits taxpayers to deduct currently certain expenditures incurred in the exploration or development of ores or minerals in the United States that otherwise would be capitalized into the depletable basis. A taxpayer who makes this election must recapture the deductions when the mine begins to produce, by including the deductions in income or reducing the income used to calculate the percentage depletion deduction.

Mine Development Expenditures. Section 616(a) allows the taxpayer to deduct all the expenses of developing a mine (other than an oil or gas well) after minerals have been discovered. Corporate taxpayers may deduct only 70 percent of mine development costs and the remaining 30 percent may be deducted ratably over a 60-month period. § 291(b)(1).

Reforestation Expenditures. Under § 194, a taxpayer can elect to amortize reforestation expenditures relating to qualified timber property over a 7-year period. The election is limited to $10,000 per taxable year.

(D) *Recycling.* Some commentators have suggested that the tax subsidies for exploration of natural resources—such as those discussed above—have created an incentive to waste natural resources and a disincentive for recycling them. Similar subsidies for recycling have been proposed to cure this alleged imbalance. Would you support such subsidies? Should the Code be amended to accomplish this result? If so, how? Consider § 168(m) (providing bonus depreciation for qualified reuse and recycling property) and § 30D(a)(2) (tax credit for certain plug-in electric vehicles).

SECTION 5.   INTEREST

A. THE GENERAL STRUCTURE OF THE INTEREST DEDUCTION

Note Providing an Overview of the Interest Deduction

Interest on borrowing by individuals and businesses historically has been deductible as an itemized deduction regardless of the use to which the borrowed funds were put. This principle has eroded over time until it seems to have become the exception rather than the rule. In the process, the income tax treatment of interest expenses has evolved from one of the simplest issues in the Code—when virtually all interest was deductible when paid or incurred—into one of the most complex. Tax legislation in 2017 added a new layer of complexity by limiting the deductibility of interest incurred by businesses. Today, the deductibility of interest turns on a number of factors, including the activities of the borrower and the purpose of the indebtedness—questions that invite tax planning and, fundamentally, are unanswerable since taxpayers generally borrow both to acquire new assets and to keep everything they have.

Interest expense should be regarded as a cost to the taxpayer of holding assets that are used in a business, for investment or for personal consumption. The proper treatment of interest is controversial because the taxation of assets financed with borrowed funds is uneven: The realization requirement precludes taxation of annual increases in asset values; imputed returns from housing and other assets used for consumption are not taxed; and a wide variety of both business and investment assets enjoy tax-favored treatment.

Business Interest. The 2017 tax act conferred major tax benefits on businesses, including immediate expensing for certain assets (see the discussion at page 348, supra). At the same time, the legislation limited some tax deductions previously available to businesses, including the interest deduction.

The new statutory scheme is complex. The general rule is that interest on indebtedness used to operate a trade or business is deductible like any other business expense, § 163(a), except in circumstances where interest is required to be capitalized, for example, when allocable to an asset the taxpayer is constructing, § 263A(f). However, § 163(j) now limits the interest deductible by businesses by generally limiting the deduction for "business interest" to the sum of business interest income and 30 percent of the taxpayer's "adjusted taxable income." Under the 2017 law, adjusted taxable income is essentially defined to equal earnings before interest, taxes, depreciation, and amortization (known as EBITDA) for taxable years beginning before January 1, 2022. After that date, the 2017 legislation would reduce adjusted taxable income by not adding back depreciation or amortization (making the limitation 30 percent of EBIT). Disallowed interest can be carried forward indefinitely.

For example, consider a business with $1 million in adjusted taxable income (before taking into account any business interest expense) and no business interest income. Under § 163(j), the business may deduct up to $300,000 in business interest each year.

The new limitation does not apply to "small" businesses, defined for this purpose as those with less than $25 million in gross receipts. § 163(j)(3).

In general, there is a sound policy reason for denying an interest deduction in a tax system that also permits immediate expensing. As the Note on Tax Deferral (supra, page 313) explains, an immediate deduction for capital expenditures is equivalent to exempting from tax the income from the asset in question. Thus, in a very real sense, the 2017 tax act reduced to zero the rate of income tax on business investments that can be immediately expensed. If the income tax rate is zero, it follows that no interest deduction should be permitted. Otherwise, the net tax burden on the investment would be less than zero.

The connection between the interest deduction limitation and immediate expensing also explains a special exception for the real estate industry. Some real estate businesses do not benefit significantly from immediate expensing, which (generally speaking) is limited to shorter-lived assets. Accordingly, the Code permits real estate businesses to elect to deduct interest without limitation, provided they also forgo immediate expensing. §§ 163(j)(7)(B), 168(g)(8).

Still, the complex line-drawing required by the new interest deduction limitation may invite tax planning. New § 163(j) leaves undefined key concepts, including how to allocate interest income and expense between business and investment income. § 163(j)(5), (6).

Investment Interest. The deduction of interest on debt incurred by individuals and properly allocable to investment property is limited to net investment income (with an indefinite carryforward of interest disallowed under this provision). § 163(d). Net investment income is total investment income less investment expenses. § 163(d)(4). Interest incurred in connection with a "passive activity" is not treated as investment interest but instead is subject to the rules of § 469, which limit the deduction of passive losses (discussed at page 424, infra). This investment interest limitation is somewhat analogous to requiring that investment interest be capitalized and deducted only as ordinary income is produced.

Section 163(d) was added to prevent both a mismatch of income and expense and conversion of ordinary income into capital gain. Suppose, for example, a taxpayer bought a growth stock paying no dividends for $30,000 and funded the purchase with debt. He paid $3,000 in interest for two years and then sold the stock for $40,000 at the beginning of the third year. His net profit is $4,000. Absent § 163(d), the interest would be deductible each year against ordinary income, but because of the realization requirement, the $10,000 gain would not be reported until the third year and then taxed at preferential capital gains rates.

Investment income does not include net capital gains or dividends unless the taxpayer forgoes the preferential rate on those items, which they may elect to do under § 163(d)(4). See § 1(h)(2). This rule prevents a taxpayer from deducting investment interest at the top ordinary rate to offset income that will be taxed at the lower capital gains or dividend rate.

Rents are generally treated as "passive income," not investment income. The adoption of the passive loss rules, see page 424 infra, and the lower rate on dividends seems likely to have increased the impact of § 163(d) since taxpayers are less likely to have fully taxed investment income to offset investment interest.

The amount of disallowed investment interest that can be carried forward to a succeeding year is not limited by the taxpayer's taxable income in the current year. Sharp v. United States, 14 F.3d 583 (Fed. Cir. 1993); Rev. Rul. 95–16, 1995–1 C.B. 9. Since there is no general carryover of an individual's interest expenses, this has the curious result of permitting the taxpayer to deduct more than would have been deductible had the limitations of § 163(d) never been enacted.

The matching of investment interest deductions with investment income creates a "basket" of income and expenses, analogous to the "basket" created by the matching of passive activity losses and income, discussed infra at page 424. As a result, some legitimate investment interest expenses may not be deductible in the year paid or incurred. This basket approach marks a shift away from a strict net income concept, under which noncapital expenses incurred in a profit-seeking activity would be fully deductible when paid or incurred.

The distinction between a business or an investment is important, for example, in connection with interest on debt used to purchase securities. Business interest is fully deductible, but if the taxpayer's activities in connection with the securities do not rise to the level of a business, the interest deduction is limited to the amount of investment income under § 163(d). The management of one's own securities investments typically is not a business. See, e.g., Estate of Yaeger v. Commissioner, 889 F.2d 29 (2d Cir. 1989). Even though the taxpayer made over 2,000 trades for his own account over a two-year period, and spent evenings and many days researching investments and placing orders, his activity was not a business. The critical factor, however, appeared to be that Yaeger did not churn his portfolio. The court noted that the two fundamental criteria distinguishing traders from investors are the length of the holding period and the source of the profit.

> Investors are engaged in the production of income. * * * Traders are those "whose profits are derived from the 'direct management of purchasing and selling.' " * * * Investors derive profit from the interest, dividends, and capital appreciation of securities. * * * They are "primarily interested in the long-term growth potential of their stocks." * * * Traders, however, buy and sell securities "with reasonable frequency in an endeavor to catch the swings in the daily market movements and profit thereby on a short term basis." * * * The activity of holding securities for a length of time to produce interest, dividends, and capital gains fits the abuse targeted by Section 163(d): investing for postponed income and current interest deduction.

Interest to Earn Tax-Exempt Income. The deduction of interest expended to earn tax-exempt or tax-preferred investment income has long been controversial. Congress has limited interest deductions in several of these contexts. For example, § 264 forbids deduction of interest on borrowing with respect to certain life insurance or annuity contracts; § 265(a)(2) prohibits deduction of interest on indebtedness to purchase or hold bonds that yield tax-exempt interest; §§ 1277 and 1282 defer the deduction of interest on indebtedness to purchase or hold certain bonds purchased at a discount until the "interest" income from the bond is taxed at maturity or upon disposition; and, as discussed above, § 163(d) limits the deduction of investment interest to investment income. Deductions of prepayments of interest are restricted, § 461(g); and interest incurred in connection with the construction of certain types of real property and tangible personal property must be capitalized and amortized, § 263A(f). Tax jargon uses the term "tax arbitrage" to describe deductions of interest in circumstances where related income is tax-exempt or tax-preferred. This issue is considered in some detail, infra at page 363.

Personal Interest. The propriety of interest deductions on borrowing for personal consumption has long been disputed. Some analysts regard interest charged on credit purchases of consumer goods and services simply as an additional element of the cost of consumption; as such, interest is no more entitled to deduction than is the rest of the item's price. A second view defends interest deductibility as necessary for equity between those who finance consumption purchases with debt and those who use their own assets. Taxpayers with investment assets producing taxable income could sell those assets and, for example, invest that equity in a residence, automobile, or other consumer good, the returns from which are not taxed. This suggests that the negative income—interest—of those who finance consumption with debt should be deductible to offset the advantage that otherwise would accrue to those who finance consumption with forgone earnings. The former can be said to be poorer, to have less ability to pay, than the latter.

Compare A who liquidates his $100,000 investment account and purchases a house and B who retains an identical account that earns $10,000, borrows $100,000, which he invests in a home, and pays $10,000 interest. If A and B were taxed on the imputed income on the use of the home, a deduction for B clearly would be appropriate as it would be a cost of producing taxable income; each then would have $10,000 of net income. Even without taxing imputed income, however, an interest deduction is necessary to create parity between A and B. Without an interest deduction, there would be a difference between the borrower-buyer B, who would have $10,000 of taxable income, and the cash buyer A, who would have no taxable income. This comparison might suggest a rule allowing a deduction of personal interest to the extent of investment income. Some would go further, however, and allow a deduction to C who has no investment account when he borrows to buy a house. Thus,

> the role of interest expense in income computation is analytically independent of the use to which the borrowed funds are put. The deductibility of interest expense follows simply from the fact that debt, a negative asset, is a source of negative income. In the logic of income computation, interest expense, however it arises in household or business finance, is properly deductible.[13]

Nevertheless, under § 163(h), personal nonbusiness interest generally is not deductible. Personal interest is defined by omission to

---

[13] Melvin I. White, "Proper Income Tax Treatment of Deductions for Personal Expense" in Tax Revision Compendium, Committee on Ways and Means 365–66 (1959).

include any interest that is *not*: (a) interest paid or incurred in connection with a trade or business (not including for this purpose the trade or business of performing services as an employee), (b) investment interest, (c) interest that would be deductible in connection with a § 469 passive activity, (d) "qualified residence interest" (as defined in § 163(h)(3) and discussed below), or (e) interest on certain deferred estate tax payments. Interest on an income tax deficiency is personal interest. See § 163(h)(1). This rule applies even where the income subject to the deficiency arose in a trade or business. E.g. Alfaro v. Commissioner, 349 F.3d 225 (5th Cir. 2003).

The Tax Court found that interest on indebtedness incurred as part of a divorce was not required to be treated per se as nondeductible personal interest. In Seymour v. Commissioner, 109 T.C. 279 (1997), the wife transferred an interest in stock, commercial property, and a home to the husband, who signed a promissory note and conveyed a mortgage secured by the home. The court found that the interest on the note was deductible. The recipient spouse could not use § 1041, which excludes marital transfers from tax, because the interest was not the marital property being transferred. Gibbs v. Commissioner, 73 T.C.M. 2669 (1997). If the interest had been unstated—that is, the amount to be transferred in the future was simply increased—the entire amount would be excluded under § 1041.

Home Mortgage Interest. The major exception to the disallowance of personal interest is the deduction allowed for home mortgage interest. Legislative history indicates that Congress believed that "encouraging home ownership is an important policy goal." Why would Congress want to provide an incentive for owning rather than renting a home? Recall B above who has a $100,000 bank account but borrows $100,000 to purchase a home. His interest deduction washes out his investment income. Compare him to C who uses the interest income from the account to pay $10,000 rent or D who uses the investment income to pay interest on a loan to purchase a car. C and D are taxed on $10,000 income. What is the justification for the difference?

The 2017 tax act permits the deduction of home mortgage interest on up to $750,000 of "acquisition indebtedness," defined as debt used to acquire, construct, or substantially improve either a principal residence or second home. That limitation applies from 2018 through the end of 2025, and during that period, no deduction is permitted for "home equity indebtedness," which is debt secured by a home incurred after the home is purchased. After 2025, however, absent further change, the prior rules spring back to life: at that point, interest would be deductible on up to $1 million of acquisition indebtedness and $100,000 of home equity indebtedness.

The Ninth Circuit has held that the § 163(h)(3) limitations on the deductibility of mortgage interest are applied on a per-taxpayer basis. Voss v. Commissioner, 796 F.3d 1051 (9th Cir. 2015). The taxpayer in the case, celebrity psychiatrist Charles Sophy, and his domestic partner owned homes as joint tenants but were not married. A married couple in the same situation would be limited to an interest deduction of half the amount of an unmarried couple. The issue in the case was one of statutory construction. Section 163(h)(3) limits the amount of interest deductible "per period" or taxable year. Rejecting the IRS contention that the deduction should be per residence, the court noted: "Residences do not have taxable years; only taxpayers do." If you and your spouse lived in California and had outstanding mortgages on your home(s) exceeding $750,000, how about divorcing in December and remarrying in January? See Revenue Ruling 76–255, page 507 infra.

The rules governing interest deductibility affect tax planning. Under prior law, and again after 2025, taxpayers may convert personal indebtedness into qualified residence indebtedness through home equity loans. The fungibility of money makes it virtually impossible to enforce limits on the deduction of interest incurred for certain purposes. Taxpayers may borrow against their residences to purchase consumer goods and circumvent the elimination of the deduction for consumer interest. Hence, this provision has granted a further advantage to homeowners as against renters. The economic downturn of 2007–2009, however, caused some overextended taxpayers who had shifted indebtedness to their residence to lose not only their credit ratings but also their homes.

Interest on Education Loans. Certain taxpayers may take an above-the-line deduction for up to $2,500 of interest paid on education loans. The indebtedness must be incurred to pay for college expenses for the taxpayer, the taxpayer's spouse, or a dependent. Expenses do not include scholarships, amounts received from educational assistance programs, or distributions from an education savings account, discussed at page 446 infra. The deduction is phased out for single taxpayers with income of $50,000 to $65,000 and married taxpayers with income of $100,000 to $130,000 (these numbers are indexed for inflation). See § 221. If a person who is not legally obligated to do so (for example, mom) pays the interest on behalf of the taxpayer who owes the interest (child), the payor is treated as making a gift to the recipient, who then is treated as paying the interest and gets the deduction. Reg. § 1.221–1(b)(4)(i).

Tracing Interest. Full deduction for interest has often been defended as necessary due to the administrative difficulties of tracing borrowed money to its use. For example, an individual might borrow money secured by investments to finance personal consumption, or might borrow against a personal residence to purchase investment assets. Borrowing to purchase an asset is really for two purposes: to acquire the new asset and to avoid disposing of assets already on hand. But, as indicated above, the Code currently disallows or limits interest deductions when indebtedness is used for certain purposes, and consequently requires tracing such indebtedness to its use. Alternatively, the law might require borrowing (and interest expense) to be allocated against all assets (see, e.g., § 265(b)(2)) although this, too, would be difficult administratively, or provide an ordering rule to treat certain expenditures as made with borrowed funds. Section 163(d)(1) (which allows interest to be deducted to the extent of fully taxed investment income) and § 263(f)(A)(ii) (providing rules for capitalizing interest) may be described as ordering rules. No one has yet offered a convincing rationale for preferring any of the three approaches.

Nevertheless, taxpayers frequently are required by the Code to "know" the purpose for which interest expense (and the related borrowing) was paid or incurred. As the foregoing discussion makes clear, a variety of provisions limit interest deductions based on the purpose of the loan. The Code requires the impossible; since money is fungible, there is no "correct" way to determine, with any degree of certainty, the purpose for which funds were borrowed. Obviously, the taxpayer borrows for the purpose of keeping everything she has and at the same time making whatever new expenditure is desired or required.

The impossibility of the task, however, has not deterred Congress or the regulation writers at the Treasury Department. See Temp. Reg. § 1.163–8T (tracing principles for allocation of loan proceeds to specific purposes) and § 1.163–10T(n) (definition of qualified residence interest). In general, the purpose of these rules is to tell taxpayers how to determine whether interest deductions will be disallowed or limited under § 163(d) (investment interest), § 163(h) (personal interest) or § 469 (passive activity interest), or fully deductible. "Qualified residence interest" is not subject to the tracing rules of Temp. Reg. § 1.163–8T at all, and other rules may trump these regulations by allocating interest to some other specific purpose, for example, to a trade or business purpose.

Generally, the rules determine the purpose of an interest expense by tracing loan proceeds to their use. It is the expenditure of the loan proceeds and (with the exception of qualified residence interest) not the security of the debt that governs. Thus, for example, if the taxpayer pledges an automobile as security for funds borrowed and used to buy corporate stock for investment, the interest paid on the loan is investment interest, and, contrariwise, if the taxpayer pledges corporate stock as security for loan proceeds that are used to buy an automobile for personal use, the interest expense on the loan is personal interest. Since investment and business interest may be deductible and personal interest is not, a well-informed taxpayer generally would arrange her affairs so as to use loan proceeds for investment or business purposes.

Compound interest and interest on funds borrowed to pay interest on other loans did not trouble the regulation writers; these are simply traced to the use of the original borrowing. Temp. Regs. §§ 1.163–8T(c)(2)(ii)(B) and 1.163–8T(c)(6)(ii). This approach, of course, works best when the lending institution forwards the loan proceeds directly to the seller of a particular asset. Fun can be had when the loan proceeds are paid to the taxpayer and commingled with other funds, for example, by being deposited in a bank account that contains other funds of the taxpayer. The regulations here provide that expenditures from bank accounts containing commingled funds are deemed to have been made first from borrowed funds and then from unborrowed funds, and proceeds from different loans (which, of course, may have differing interest rates) are used in the order that the loan proceeds are deposited. The order that checks are written generally determines the tracing of the use of proceeds, but for checks written on the same day, the taxpayer may designate the order, and a special rule allows taxpayers to designate any expenditure made within 15 days of the borrowing as the specific use of the funds. Temp. Reg. § 1.163–8T(c)(4).

For more fun than this, you will have to delve into the regulations yourself. Needless to say, the tracing approach of the regulations contains tax savings opportunities for those who plan their transactions carefully and tax increases or, more likely, random tax consequences for the unknowing or unwary and people with better ways to spend their time. Those who pay no attention at all seem likely to enjoy tax savings or tax increases depending upon their luck.

The drafters of these rules apparently believed that taxpayers have priorities in the sense that they first allocated their own funds and then decided whether or not to borrow for additional activities. As the above indicates, even if this position is correct, well-advised taxpayers will game the system. Other provisions in the Code rather than physically tracing funds appear to look to purpose, in effect inquiring what activity would be terminated if borrowing were reduced. See, e.g., § 265(a)(2). Another possible approach is to look to the security for the loan. See § 163(h)(3)(B).

B. INTEREST PAID TO EARN TAX-PREFERRED INCOME: THE PROBLEM OF "TAX ARBITRAGE"

Note on Tax Arbitrage

The treatment of assets and debt under the current income tax has resulted in a problem often labeled "tax arbitrage." This arises when assets eligible for favored tax treatment are acquired with debt.

Many income tax rules can be characterized as imposing a zero rate of tax on the income from important categories of assets. These have included investments in equipment, which, during the period of 1981–1986, essentially could be immediately expensed by a combination of accelerated cost recovery deductions and the investment tax credit, natural resource exploration and development, where immediate expensing is generally permitted, real estate, which prior to 1986 often produced negative income tax rates, owner-occupied houses, retirement savings, tax-exempt state and local bonds, and all assets held by tax-exempt organizations, such as pension funds or by taxable corporations with large operating losses. It has been estimated that in 1983 as much as 80 percent of the $10.5 trillion of assets held by individuals qualified for such favored treatment. Harvey Galper & Eugene Steuerle, "Tax Incentives for Savings," 2 Brookings Rev. 19–20 (Winter 1983).

A negative rate of tax can be achieved when a taxpayer can obtain both an interest deduction and the equivalent of a zero rate of tax on the income from the asset purchased with debt. Borrowing to purchase tax-exempt municipal bonds presents the classic case. Assume, for example, that a taxpayer subject to a 37 percent marginal tax rate simultaneously borrows at an interest rate of 8 percent to purchase municipal bonds yielding tax-exempt interest of 6 percent. Before tax, the transaction loses 2 percent. After tax, the net interest cost is 5.04 percent, which is 0.96 percentage point less than the after-tax yield of 6 percent. The 2 percent before-tax loss has become a 0.96 percent after-tax gain, a result that may be characterized as a negative tax.

Section 265(a)(2) bars tax arbitrage in such a case by disallowing interest deductions on borrowing to purchase or carry tax-exempt bonds. Section 163(d) likewise operates to disallow interest deductions on borrowing to purchase growth stocks that yield little or no current investment income.

Tax arbitrage also may occur where the Code allows immediate expensing of the cost of assets. This may be equivalent to exempting the yield from such an asset. See discussion supra at page 310. Viewed in this light, the 2017 limitations on business interest deductions may represent an attempt to limit tax arbitrage. See discussion supra at page 355. More subtle examples of tax arbitrage occur when the return from the asset takes the form of the use of the asset. For example, when a person owns a residence subject to a mortgage, the interest is deductible but the imputed rental value of the house is not included in taxable income.

In any circumstance where interest expense is entirely deductible and the income from the preferred asset is entirely excluded from income, taxpayers often will find that their total tax liability is negative—less than zero—on a fully leveraged investment. This may be true even when the transaction produces a gain before tax. As long as the after-tax rate of return on the preferred asset is greater than the after-tax rate of interest on the borrowing, the taxpayer will find such tax arbitrage profitable. See Eugene Steuerle, "Tax Arbitrage, Inflation, and the Taxation of Interest Payments and Receipts," 30 Wayne L. Rev. 991 (1984).

The problem of tax arbitrage, of course, would disappear if the income from the asset side of the above transaction were not subject to differential tax treatment—for example, if capital gains were not taxed more favorably than ordinary income and if gains were taxed when they accrue rather than when they are realized, if municipal bond interest were not exempt from tax, if depreciation were limited to economic depreciation, and if the imputed rental value of housing and home-equity financed consumer durables were not excluded from taxable income. It is unlikely, however, that these tax preferences will be repealed. If not, the only feasible means of preventing tax arbitrage (and negative tax rates) will be the disallowance of interest deductions in a wide variety of circumstances. This is probably the best explanation of many of the limitations on interest deductibility discussed in this Section.

Addressing Tax Arbitrage: Section 265(a)(2). Perhaps surprisingly, limitations intended to cabin tax arbitrage can also hinder the effectiveness of Congressionally-mandated tax subsidies. To see why, return to our earlier example of the taxpayer in the 37 percent bracket who borrows at 8 percent to purchase municipal bonds yielding tax-exempt interest income of 6 percent. As illustrated above, full deduction of interest produces an after-tax gain of 0.96 percent from a before-tax loss of 2 percent. Section 265(a)(2) maintains the before-tax loss by denying any deduction for interest; this ensures that taxpayers will not incur interest expense greater than the tax-exempt yield to purchase municipal bonds.

Recall, however, from our earlier discussion of the tax-exempt bonds, supra at page 226, that such bonds generally bear an "implicit tax" in that their interest rate is lower than taxable corporate bonds of equal risk, reflecting the tax advantage. Where that is the case, arguably the taxpayer should be permitted to deduct interest offset by this implicit income, which would have been taxed if received. Suppose a corporate bond carries an interest rate of 10 percent and a municipal bond of similar risk carries a 6.3 percent rate. The purchaser of the municipal bond "pays" an implicit tax of 37 percent, exactly the same as the actual tax paid by the purchaser of the corporate bond. If the holder of the corporate bond borrows at 5 percent to purchase the bond, his net after-tax return will be 3.15 percent (the net proceeds will be taxable at 37 percent since the interest is deductible). The purchaser of the municipal bond, who borrows at 5 percent to finance the bond, however, will have only a net after-tax return of 1.3 percent since he will enjoy no tax benefit from the interest.

Inhibiting borrowing to purchase tax-exempt bonds may reduce the volume of bonds purchased by high-bracket taxpayers. State and local governments then might pay greater interest on their bonds to attract lower-bracket investors and as a consequence increase the return to high-bracket investors who purchase the bonds with their own funds. Such windfall gains to high-bracket taxpayers are discussed at page 227, supra. If § 265(a)(2) were repealed, high-bracket taxpayers would enjoy after-tax profits as long as the yield on the tax-exempt bonds exceeded the after-tax cost of the borrowed funds. This would increase demand for tax-exempt bonds so that state and local government could pay lower rates of return on the bonds and thereby receive more of the benefits from the tax exemption.

The general point is that interest-disallowance provisions permit wealthy taxpayers to obtain relatively greater benefits from tax-favored assets because they can acquire tax-favored assets by liquidating their existing assets. This choice is not available to less wealthy taxpayers who would have to borrow the funds necessary to acquire the tax-favored assets. As indicated earlier in this Section, this is an important element of the general defense of the interest deduction.

The variety of limitations on interest deductions are controversial and often produce inconsistent results. The continuing ability to deduct home mortgage interest on indebtedness equal to the cost of two homes up to a total of $750,000 seems to be politically secure and not likely to be restricted through future "tax reform." On the other hand, the Code disallows deductions for interest on indebtedness for certain purposes and for much investment interest and requires capitalization of trade or business interest in a number of important circumstances. Targeted efforts to deal with tax arbitrage by limiting interest deductions seems likely to continue in the future and are guaranteed to produce uneven results and increased complexity.

NOTES

(A) *More Tracing.* As we have discussed, denying an interest deduction on indebtedness used for a specific purpose requires tracing the indebtedness to its use. Section 265(a)(2) requires the IRS to establish a direct connection between the taxpayer's borrowing and his purchasing or holding of tax-exempt securities. For example, interest on indebtedness where the proceeds are directly used to purchase tax-exempt debt is disallowed. The use of tax-exempt obligations as collateral for indebtedness is evidence of a purpose to carry the obligations. How can the IRS enforce this rule? On the other hand, the IRS does not consider the purchase of tax-exempt bonds at a time when the taxpayer holds a home mortgage as evidence of "carrying" the bonds. Rev. Proc. 72–18, 1972–1 C.B. 740.

(B) *Nonrecourse Liabilities.* Interest on a mortgage secured by real estate paid by the owner of the property is deductible even if there is no personal liability. Reg. § 1.163–1(b). Recall *Crane v. Commissioner*, supra at page 199, and *Commissioner v. Tufts*, supra at page 201, which confirmed that nonrecourse debt generally is treated the same as recourse debt for tax purposes.

(C) *Expenses to Produce Tax-Exempt Income.* Interest is not the only type of expense that could be used for arbitrage. Deducting any type of expense attributable to tax-exempt income also can create a negative rate of tax. Section 265(a)(1) generally prohibits the deduction of the expenses of producing tax-exempt income. See, e.g., Rev. Rul. 87–102, 1987–2 C.B. 78 (denying deduction for legal fees to obtain tax-exempt Social Security payments); Rugby Productions Ltd. v. Commissioner, 100 T.C. 531 (1993) (denying deduction for premiums on disability policy, the proceeds of which would have been exempt under § 104(a)(3)); Induni v. Commissioner, 990 F.2d 53 (2d Cir. 1993) (denying deduction for home mortgage interest where taxpayer received tax-exempt federal housing allowance). The regulations define exempt income as that exempt under a specific statutory provision and thus does not include items such as imputed income. Reg. § 1.265–1(b).

C. SHAMS AND TRANSACTIONS WITH NO "ECONOMIC PURPOSE"

Knetsch v. United States

Supreme Court of the United States, 1960. 364 U.S. 361.

■ MR. JUSTICE BRENNAN delivered the opinion of the Court.

This case presents the question of whether deductions from gross income claimed on petitioners' 1953 and 1954 joint federal income tax returns, of $143,465 in 1953 and of $147,105 in 1954, for payments made by petitioner, Karl F. Knetsch, to Sam Houston Life Insurance Company, constituted "interest paid * * * on indebtedness" within the meaning of § 23(b) of the Internal Revenue Code of 1939 * * * and § 163(a) of the Internal Revenue Code of 1954. * * * The Commissioner of Internal Revenue disallowed the deductions and determined a deficiency for each year. The petitioners paid the deficiencies and brought this action for refund in the District Court for the Southern District of California. The District Court rendered judgment for the United States, and the Court of Appeals for the Ninth Circuit affirmed, 272 F.2d 200. Because of a suggested conflict with the decision of the Court of Appeals for the Fifth Circuit in United States v. Bond, 258 F.2d 577, we granted certiorari, 361 U.S. 958.

On December 11, 1953, the insurance company sold Knetsch ten 30-year maturity deferred annuity savings bonds, each in the face amount of $400,000 and bearing interest at 2½% compounded annually. The purchase price was $4,004,000. Knetsch gave the Company his check for $4,000, and signed $4,000,000 of nonrecourse annuity loan notes for the balance. The notes bore 3½% interest and were secured by the annuity bonds. The interest was payable in advance, and Knetsch on the same day prepaid the first year's interest, which was $140,000. Under the Table of Cash and Loan Values made part of the bonds, their cash or loan value at December 11, 1954, the end of the first contract year, was to be $4,100,000. The contract terms, however, permitted Knetsch to borrow any excess of this value above his indebtedness without waiting until December 11, 1954. Knetsch took advantage of this provision only five days after the purchase. On December 16, 1953, he received from the company $99,000 of the $100,000 excess over his $4,000,000 indebtedness, for which he gave his notes bearing 3½% interest. This interest was also payable in advance and on the same day he prepaid the first year's interest of $3,465. In their joint return for 1953, the petitioners deducted the sum of the two interest payments, that is $143,465, as "interest paid * * * within the taxable year on indebtedness," under § 23(b) of the 1939 Code.

The second contract year began on December 11, 1954, when interest in advance of $143,465 was payable by Knetsch on his aggregate indebtedness of $4,099,000. Knetsch paid this amount on December 27, 1954. Three days later, on December 30, he received from the company cash in the amount of $104,000, the difference less $1,000 between his then $4,099,000 indebtedness and the cash or loan value of the bonds of $4,204,000 on December 11, 1955. He gave the company appropriate notes and prepaid the interest thereon of $3,640. In their joint return for the taxable year 1954 the petitioners deducted the sum of the two interest payments, that is $147,105, as "interest paid * * * within the taxable year on indebtedness," under § 163(a) of the 1954 Code.

The tax years 1955 and 1956 are not involved in this proceeding, but a recital of the events of those years is necessary to complete the story of the transaction. On December 11, 1955, the start of the third contract year, Knetsch became obligated to pay $147,105 as prepaid interest on an indebtedness which now totalled $4,203,000. He paid this interest on December 28, 1955. On the same date he received $104,000 from the company. This was $1,000 less than the difference between his indebtedness and the cash or loan value of the bonds of $4,308,000 at December 11, 1956. Again he gave the company notes upon which he prepaid interest of $3,640. Petitioners claimed a deduction on their 1955 joint return for the aggregate of the payments, or $150,745.

Knetsch did not go on with the transaction for the fourth contract year beginning December 11, 1956, but terminated it on December 27, 1956. His indebtedness at that time totalled $4,307,000. The cash or loan value of the bonds was the $4,308,000 value at December 11, 1956, which had been the basis of the "loan" of December 28, 1955. He surrendered the bonds and his indebtedness was canceled. He received the difference of $1,000 in cash.

The contract called for a monthly annuity of $90,171 at maturity (when Knetsch would be 90 years of age) or for such smaller amount as would be produced by the cash or loan value after deduction of the then existing indebtedness. It was stipulated that if Knetsch had held the bonds to maturity and continued annually to borrow the net cash value less $1,000, the sum available for the annuity at maturity would be $1,000 ($8,388,000 cash or loan value less $8,387,000 of indebtedness), enough to provide an annuity of only $43 per month.

The trial judge made findings that "[t]here was no commercial economic substance to the * * * transaction," that the parties did not intend that Knetsch "become indebted to Sam Houston," that "[n]o indebtedness of [Knetsch] was created by any of the * * * transactions," and that "[n]o economic gain could be achieved from the purchase of these bonds without regard to the tax consequences * * *." His conclusion of law, based on this Court's decision in Deputy v. du Pont, 308 U.S. 488, was that "[w]hile in form the payments to Sam Houston were compensation for the use or forbearance of money, they were not in substance. As a payment of interest, the transaction was a sham."

We first examine the transaction between Knetsch and the insurance company to determine whether it created an "indebtedness" within the meaning of § 23(b) of the 1939 Code and § 163(a) of the 1954 Code, or whether, as the trial court found, it was a sham. We put aside a finding by the District Court that Knetsch's "only motive in purchasing these 10 bonds was to attempt to secure an interest deduction."[2] As was said in Gregory v. Helvering, 293 U.S. 465, 469: "The legal right of a taxpayer to decrease the amount of what otherwise would be his taxes, or altogether avoid them, by means which the law permits, cannot be doubted * * *. But the question for determination is whether what was done, apart from the tax motive, was the thing which the statute intended."

When we examine "what was done" here, we see that Knetsch paid the insurance company $294,570 during the two taxable years involved and received $203,000 back in the form of "loans." What did Knetsch get for the out-of-pocket difference of $91,570? In form he had an annuity contract with a so-called guaranteed cash value at maturity of $8,388,000, which would produce monthly annuity payments of $90,171, or substantial life insurance proceeds in the event of his death before maturity. This, as we have seen, was a fiction, because each year Knetsch's annual borrowings kept the net cash value, on which any annuity or insurance payments would depend, at the relative pittance of $1,000.[3] Plainly, therefore, Knetsch's transaction with the insurance company did "not appreciably affect his beneficial interest except to reduce his tax * * *." Gilbert v. Commissioner, 2 Cir. 248 F.2d 399, 411 (dissenting opinion). For it is patent that there was nothing of substance to be realized by Knetsch from this transaction beyond a tax deduction. What he was ostensibly "lent" back was in reality only the rebate of a substantial part of the so-called "interest" payments. The $91,570 difference retained by the company was its fee for providing the facade of "loans" whereby the petitioners sought to reduce their 1953 and 1954 taxes in the total sum of $233,297.68. There may well be single premium annuity arrangements with nontax substance which create an

---

[2] We likewise put aside Knetsch's argument that, because he received ordinary income when he surrendered the annuities in 1956, he has suffered a net loss even if the contested deductions are allowed, and that therefore his motive in taking out the annuities could not have been tax avoidance.

[3] Petitioners argue further that in 10 years the net cash value of the bonds would have exceeded the amounts Knetsch paid as "interest." This contention, however, is predicated on the wholly unlikely assumption that Knetsch would have paid off in cash the original $4,000,000 "loan."

"indebtedness" for the purposes of § 23(b) of the 1939 Code and § 163(a) of the 1954 Code. But this one is a sham.

[The Court then rejected the taxpayer's argument that Congress had implicitly allowed deductions for such payments made prior to the 1954 enactment of § 264(a)(2), which denies a deduction for amounts paid on indebtedness incurred to purchase or carry single premium annuity contracts purchased after March 1, 1954.]

* * *

■ MR. JUSTICE DOUGLAS, with whom MR. JUSTICE WHITTAKER and MR. JUSTICE STEWART concur, dissenting. I agree with the views expressed by Judge Moore in Diggs v. Commissioner, 281 F.2d 326, 330–332, and by Judge Brown, writing for himself and Judge Hutcheson, in United States v. Bond, 258 F.2d 577.

It is true that in this transaction the taxpayer was bound to lose if the annuity contract is taken by itself. At least the taxpayer showed by his conduct that he never intended to come out ahead on that investment apart from this income tax deduction. Yet the same may be true where a taxpayer borrows money at 5% or 6% interest to purchase securities that pay only nominal interest; or where, with money in the bank earning 3%, he borrows from the self-same bank at a higher rate. His aim there, as here, may only be to get a tax deduction for interest paid. Yet as long as the transaction itself is not hocus-pocus, the interest charges incident to completing it would seem to be deductible under the Internal Revenue Code as respects annuity contracts made prior to March 1, 1954, the date Congress selected for terminating this class of deductions. 26 U.S.C.A. § 264. The insurance company existed; it operated under Texas law; it was authorized to issue these policies and to make these annuity loans. While the taxpayer was obligated to pay interest at the rate of 3½% per annum, the annuity bonds increased in cash value at the rate of only 2½% per annum. The insurance company's profit was in that 1-point spread.

Tax avoidance is a dominating motive behind scores of transactions. It is plainly present here. Will the Service that calls this transaction a "sham" today not press for collection of taxes* arising out of the surrender of the annuity contract? I think it should, for I do not believe any part of the transaction was a "sham." To disallow the "interest" deduction because the annuity device was devoid of commercial substance is to draw a line which will affect a host of situations not now before us and which, with all deference, I do not think we can maintain when other cases reach here. The remedy is legislative. Evils or abuses can be particularized by Congress. We deal only with "interest" as commonly understood and as used across the board in myriad transactions. Since

---

*   Petitioners terminated this transaction in 1956 by allowing the bonds to be cancelled and receiving a check for $1,000. The termination was reflected in their tax return for 1956. It might also be noted that the insurance company reported as gross income the interest payments which it received from petitioners in 1953 and 1954.

these transactions were real and legitimate in the insurance world and were consummated within the limits allowed by insurance policies, I would recognize them tax-wise.

NOTES

(A) *"Sham" vs. Tax Avoidance Motive.* Must a court find a "sham" in order to disallow interest deductions? Or will a "tax avoidance" motive or absence of any "business purpose" suffice?

In Goldstein v. Commissioner, 364 F.2d 734 (2d Cir. 1966), cert. denied, 385 U.S. 1005 (1967), a taxpayer who won $140,000 in the Irish Sweepstakes paid 4 percent interest to borrow money with which she purchased Treasury notes yielding annually about 1.5 percent interest income payable over a number of years. The taxpayer prepaid interest in the year she won the Sweepstakes and tried to deduct that prepayment. Although the taxpayer paid more interest than she would earn, the tax savings from, in effect, spreading the Sweepstakes winnings over a number of years would have made the transaction profitable. The court found no "sham" but nevertheless disallowed the interest deduction on the grounds that there was "no purposive reason, other than the securing of a deduction." The court then stated that allowing the deduction "would encourage transactions that have no economic utility and that would not be engaged in but for the system of taxes imposed by Congress."

What are the limits of the *Goldstein-Knetsch* analysis? Does *Goldstein* imply that the courts might deny interest deductions in any "tax arbitrage" situation?

Some courts have found no need to determine if transactions were fictitious, so long as there was no economic motive. For example, in Lifschultz v. Commissioner, 393 F.2d 232 (2d Cir. 1968), the court examined a transaction in which the taxpayers purchased bonds paying 2 7/8 percent by transferring his promissory note that called for 3 1/2 percent interest to a seller who did not own the bonds. The seller borrowed funds, which it used to purchase the bonds, using the bonds as collateral for the loan. The interest on the note was 4 percent. The court found it unnecessary to determine if the transactions were genuine because there was no realistic opportunity for profit. Since the bonds were U.S. treasury bonds near maturity, the only possibility for gain was if the bonds increased in value and such a fluctuation so close to maturity was unlikely. In examining an agreement involving the purchase and repurchase of Treasury bills, the Tax Court noted that "financing transactions will merit respect and give rise to deductible interest only if there is some tax-independent purpose of the transaction." Sheldon v. Commissioner, 94 T.C. 738, 752 (1990).

This "economic substance" doctrine has been used by the courts where the deduction the taxpayer seeks to take seems to fit within the literal language of the Code. The Service has used the doctrine to try to combat tax shelters with a good deal of success. See Chapter 8 infra.

(B) *Validity of Loan.* An important element of many "tax shelters" is the availability of an interest deduction. One way to attack the transaction is to question whether the indebtedness is valid. Recall *Estate of Franklin,* discussed supra at page 211, in which the Ninth Circuit refused to treat a "loan" that exceeded the value of the property when undertaken as valid indebtedness and therefore held the loan proceeds were not includible in the purchaser's basis. Another consequence of the court's finding that the debt was invalid was that interest deductions were denied. Thus, even if a transaction is not a "sham," interest deductions may be disallowed because the debt is invalid. See, e.g., Rev. Rul. 84–5, 1984–1 C.B. 32 (denying interest deductions on a 30-year nonrecourse obligation with a large final balloon payment on the grounds that the obligation "does not constitute a valid indebtedness"). Another strategy is to invalidate the entire transaction on the grounds that it lacks economic purpose (as the court did in *Knetsch*), which has the effect of eliminating the interest deduction. A third option is to recharacterize the transaction for tax purposes to better reflect its "economic reality" as the Tax Court did in *Estate of Franklin* when it recharacterized the "prepaid interest" as a payment to purchase an option.

D. WHAT IS INTEREST?

Note on Distinguishing Interest from Other Payments

Often it is difficult to know whether a particular payment is for interest or something else. The distinction will be crucial when interest is deductible but another characterization will produce no deduction.

The Supreme Court has defined interest as "the amount which one has contracted to pay for the use of borrowed money," Old Colony Railroad Co. v. Commissioner, 284 U.S. 552, 560 (1932), and as "compensation for the use or forbearance of money," Deputy v. du Pont, 308 U.S. 488, 498 (1940). The courts frequently have said that whether a payment is compensation for the use or forbearance of money is a factual determination, and that the labels or terminology used by the parties are not controlling. Nevertheless, points on home mortgages (a fee paid up front for obtaining the loan) are treated as interest. § 461(g)(2).

See also § 163(b), allowing an interest deduction under certain circumstances where carrying charges are imposed, even though the actual amount of interest cannot be determined, and § 216, which allows a tenant-stockholder in a cooperative building to deduct a pro rata share of interest (as well as property taxes).

Consider also § 7872, discussed at page 761 infra, which recharacterizes as interest amounts designated otherwise on a variety of no-interest or below-market interest transactions.

As evidence of the courts' reluctance to characterize as interest payments that are not labeled as such, consider Consolidated Edison Co. of N.Y., Inc. v. United States, 10 F.3d 68 (2d Cir. 1993). Con Ed accepted New York City's offer to prepay its real estate taxes and the prepayment extinguished its entire tax liability. Con Ed claimed that, in effect, the prepayment was a loan to the city, which the latter repaid with interest to Con Ed, that satisfied its tax liability. Since the "borrower" was a municipality, Con Ed attempted to exclude the discount as tax-exempt interest and deduct the entire real estate tax. The Court rejected the characterization. Although the court noted the appeal of this non-formalistic approach, it found that the discounts were compensation for the early payment of taxes and not "interest." It determined that the taxpayer was bound by the form of the transaction, which was not a "loan."

In Albertson's, Inc. v. Commissioner, 42 F.3d 537 (9th Cir. 1994), the court held that certain "additional amounts" paid to reflect the time value of money on compensation employees were entitled to currently but agreed to defer were not deductible as interest. The court determined that allowing a deduction for these amounts as interest would contravene the rules and policies with respect to the taxation of nonqualified deferred compensation, an issue taken up in Chapter 6. The IRS has ruled that credit card annual fees are not interest and therefore are not deductible. Rev. Rul. 2004–52, 2004–1 C.B. 973.

Distinguishing Debt from Equity. Allowing a deduction for interest paid on borrowing, but not for other payments to suppliers of capital, notably dividends paid to corporate equity suppliers, creates considerable controversy between taxpayers and the IRS as to whether particular payments are "interest." Lender-borrower relationships must be distinguished from other relationships, most importantly from those involving ownership. Moreover, deductible payments of interest must be distinguished from nondeductible payments of principal—a chore made more difficult in times of inflation.

In United States v. Mississippi Chemical Corp., 405 U.S. 298 (1972), the Supreme Court rejected the taxpayer farmers' arguments that "stock purchases" based directly on the amount of below-market interest payments due on loans were actually additional interest payments and therefore deductible. The Farm Credit Act required farmers who borrowed from cooperative banks to make quarterly purchases of bank stock, in proportion to the interest owed on the loans. This so-called Class C stock paid no dividends and was rarely transferable. Further, additional shares conferred no additional voting power, and Class C stock was redeemable only after all other classes of stock had been redeemed. All of these characteristics would make normal commercial stock undesirable and made the market for the Class C stock virtually nonexistent.

All in all, the required purchases of Class C stock economically resembled additional interest far more than typical equity purchases. Since the interest rates to farmers' cooperatives were lower than the market interest rates, and the amount of Class "C" stock required to be purchased was a percentage (15 percent) of the interest due, taxpayers' contention that their payments for the stock were for the "use or forbearance of money" seems persuasive. What weight would you give to the nonvoting character and nontransferability of the stock? The government conceded, and the Court agreed, that the stock was not worth the full $100 per share; the taxpayer contended that $99 of the $100 was interest. Would a more equitable result have been to permit an interest deduction for part of the $100, say $50? Would such a result be a proper construction of the statute?

Nevertheless, the Court rejected the taxpayers' effort to deduct $99 of every $100 stock purchase required as additional interest and held that the purported stock was indeed stock, noting Congress' goal of ensuring adequate bank capitalization and stability and continuity in the farm credit program. In one of those rather remarkable comments that give counsel something to quote when there is little of economic substance on their side, the Court remarked: "The taxpayers and the Government each allege that the other is looking at form rather than substance. At some point, however, the form in which a transaction is cast must have considerable impact." 405 U.S. at 311.

The *Mississippi Chemical* and *Knetsch* cases seem to reflect two quite different approaches by the Supreme Court to the question whether the form or substance of a transaction should govern for tax purposes. The problem of distinguishing between form and substance most frequently arises when, as in *Knetsch,* taxpayers select the form of economic transactions to minimize tax. This occurs in a variety of contexts, some of which are illustrated throughout this book. The courts routinely pay homage to the tax maxim that, absent explicit statutory provisions, the substance of a transaction, not its form, will determine its tax consequences, but there is considerable force to the Court's observation in *Mississippi Chemical* that the form of a transaction has considerable impact. Tax planning and tax administration routinely involve contests over moving that point.

Distinguishing Corporate Debt from Equity. The difficulties of distinguishing debt and equity transactions have long plagued the corporate income tax, which permits deduction of interest on debt but not of dividends on equity. Many cases have recharacterized "loans" as shareholders' contributions of capital, and thus recharacterized deductible "interest" payments as nondeductible dividends. The debt-equity distinction became increasingly important beginning in the 1980s. Companies then converted large amounts of equity capital into debt through a variety of financial transactions, including so-called leveraged buy-outs and leveraged recapitalizations. Conversely, cases also occasionally are encountered in which "dividends" payable on "stock" are held to be deductible as interest payments. The issue again became especially important this century when some U.S. corporations engaged in "inversion" transactions designed to shift to a structure with a foreign parent and in the process strip earnings out of the United States by paying interest on debt provided by the foreign parent.

The Tax Reform Act of 1969 attempted to respond to the difficulty of making such debt-equity distinctions by enacting § 385, which authorizes Treasury to prescribe by regulation how to ascertain whether an interest in a corporation is stock or debt. A number of relevant factors are listed in this Code section, but Treasury explicitly is not limited to these. The difficult determinations necessary to distinguish debt from equity were made no easier by delegating the task to Treasury. In October 2016, Treasury issued complex regulations under § 385 limiting the circumstances when a company can use related party debt to reduce its U.S. tax base. See also § 59A added by the 2017 legislation.

Distinguishing Interest from Principal. Because interest is often deductible and principal is not, it is important to be able to distinguish between the two. The designation by the parties of an amount as something other than interest, however, does not necessarily preclude an interest deduction. Conversely, the fact that the parties designate an amount paid as interest may not be decisive, especially if the parties are related or have different tax characteristics.

Suppose, for example, the buyer and seller contract on January 1 for the sale of property but the closing date can occur no later than August 1. In the interim, the purchaser will obtain a zoning variance. The purchaser makes a "down payment" on the contract date, which the seller will retain as liquidated damages if the sale does not close. The contract calls for an increase in the sales price to be calculated daily based on a market rate of interest from the contract date to the closing date. May the purchaser deduct this increase as "interest" or must it be treated as part of the cost of the property? In Halle v. Commissioner, 83 F.3d 649 (4th Cir. 1996), the court permitted a deduction. It rejected the Service's argument that the interest the purchaser held was akin to an option to purchase and the total payments represented the sales price when the option was exercised. The court disagreed, holding that even though the sale was contingent in the sense that it might not be completed, because the purchase price set on the contract date was equal to value, the payment was more in the nature of interest on a fixed obligation.

Sections §§ 1271–1278 also provide rules for allocating principal and interest on deferred-payment transactions. These provisions are treated in Chapter 7 at page 756, infra.

NOTES

(A) *Equity-Kicker Loans.* Unexpected and fluctuating rates of inflation beginning in the late 1960s resulted in wide swings in interest rates. In response, lenders devised new financing techniques involving varying or adjustable rates of interest, or in some instances, sharing between lender and borrower of any appreciation realized when the property securing the loan is sold. These "equity-kicker" loans, which have been quite common in real estate transactions, may permit the "lender" to obtain a variety of "equity-type" economic rights or risks, including:

(1) the right to share in appreciation of the property,

(2) the right to a portion of any cash flow generated by operation of the property,

(3) the risk of a decline in the value of the property because the "loan" is nonrecourse,

(4) the power to manage and control the property,

(5) the right to prohibit or insist upon sale or other disposition of the property, and

(6) the right to purchase the property at some future date.

Where financing arrangements provide the lender with such "equity-type" risks or rights, the IRS may argue for recharacterization of an arrangement labeled a "loan" as some form of equity, such as a joint venture or partnership interest. The cases generally have emphasized the parties' intent to enter into a debtor/creditor relationship (rather than a partnership or joint venture, for example) as the most critical factor in determining whether a "loan" will be recharacterized as "equity." However, the law in this area remains unsettled.

(B) *Distinguishing a Lender from an Owner.* The characterization of the transaction as a loan or a joint venture not only determines the availability of the interest deduction, but, since basis includes borrowed amounts, this characterization may also determine the amount of depreciation deductions allowable and who is allowed to deduct them.

The IRS and the courts often have relied on the parties' intent and their labels in determining whether a "loan" will be recharacterized as "equity" in order to assure consistent treatment on both sides of the transaction. Interest deductions to the "borrower" are interest income to the "lender"; allocation of the entire depreciable basis to the "borrower" defeats the "lender's" claim to any depreciation deductions. It was long thought that such "matching" of tax consequences without more would protect the federal fisc; thus, the IRS and the courts routinely accepted not only the taxpayers' characterization of the transaction as a loan but also their allocation of annual payments between interest and principal.

The "matching" approach does not suffice, however, where the tax characteristics of the parties are significantly different, such as when the "lender" is a tax-exempt entity or a corporation that is nontaxable because of excess losses. A tax-exempt organization suffers no adverse tax consequences from receiving ordinary interest income in lieu of capital gain or forgoing depreciation deductions. This cautions against undue reliance on the parties' intent, labels, and characterization of such transactions. There often will be no substitute for attempting to ascertain whether the "economic substance" of the transaction creates a debtor-creditor relationship or something more akin to a joint venture.

E. INFLATION AND THE INTEREST DEDUCTION

Note on Inflation and the Interest Deduction

Inflation is not systematically accounted for under the income tax; the fluctuating rates of inflation since the 1960s has created a variety of problems for the income tax. Congress has enacted a number of provisions designed to take inflation into account. See, e.g., § 1(f) (adjusting the rate brackets for inflation). None of them deals directly with assets or liabilities, although a variety of provisions have been enacted partly in response to inflation. For example, one of the justifications for rapid depreciation allowances and the preferential capital gain rate preference was to counterbalance inflation.

Meanwhile, problems caused by inflation with respect to debt have been largely ignored, although it is widely recognized that inflation results in overstatement of both interest income and interest deductions, a portion of which should be recharacterized as principal. For example, if a one-year loan of $10,000 has an interest rate of 9 percent, in the absence of inflation, the lender will have real income of $900 and the borrower will pay real interest of $900. If the inflation rate is 5 percent during that period, however, the lender has suffered a real loss of $500 because the borrower will repay $10,000, which is worth only $9,500 in Year 2 dollars. Similarly, the borrower has gained $500. In effect, the $10,000 principal of the loan was reduced by $500 due to the 5 percent inflation. One way to accurately treat this transaction is to give the lender a deductible loss of $500 and to tax the borrower on $500 of discharge of indebtedness income. Another alternative is to treat a portion of each interest payment as a return of principal. For example, the lender would treat $500 of the $900 payment by the borrower as principal and report only $400 of interest income; conversely, the borrower would deduct only $400 of interest expense. Adjusting for inflation would be quite complex.

Ignoring inflation's impact on the tax treatment of debt has largely been justified on the theory that the undertaxation of debtors (which results from overstating the interest deductions) in the aggregate will be compensated for by overtaxation of creditors (which results from overstating the interest income).[14] But this is unlikely to be true. The creditors are likely to be low-bracket taxpayers or tax-exempt and the borrowers are likely to be high-bracket taxpayers. Because the borrowers save more than the creditors pay in taxes, the fisc loses.

Congress' priorities in responding to the distortion of income caused by inflation no doubt reflect political considerations. Only the Treasury loses when Congress acts to reduce the inflationary overtaxation of owners of capital assets. Any effort to redress the overtaxation of lenders, however, would simultaneously require an effort to redress the

---

[14] In 1977, for example, Treasury justified its proposal to index assets but not debt on this ground. U.S. Treasury Dep't, Blueprints for Tax Reform (1977).

undertaxation of the far more numerous borrowers. Moreover, there has been little demand among lenders for Congress to take such actions. Taxable institutional lenders, such as banks and insurance companies, can shelter much of their overstated income, and tax-exempt lenders, such as pension funds and university endowment funds, are indifferent to income overstatement. Influential commentators have contributed to the imbalance by noting the practical difficulties of income tax indexing, particularly of indexing debt, and by focusing on the inhibiting effect of asset overtaxation on capital formation.

A 1984 Treasury Report to the President recommended rather comprehensive income tax adjustments for inflation. See 2 Treasury Dep't, Report to the President, Tax Reform for Fairness, Simplicity and Economic Growth 193–200 (1984). These included indexation of depreciation allowances, the basis of capital assets, and inventories. Interest would have been indexed for inflation by excluding a fractional amount of interest receipts from income and denying deduction of a corresponding fraction of interest payments. Congress did not adopt Treasury's proposal or any other when it considered comprehensive tax reform in 1986. For a comprehensive discussion of inflation, see Reed Shuldiner, Indexing the Tax Code, 48 Tax L. Rev. 537 (1993).

The failure of Congress to revise the taxation of debt to account for inflation, together with its capriciousness in revising the taxation of assets, has created an income tax that is often incapable of accurately measuring the income of asset owners, debtors, or creditors. Because Polonius' admonition to "neither a borrower nor a lender be" is universally ignored in modern American society, the wrong tax burden has been imposed on virtually every individual and corporation.

SECTION 6.   LOSSES

A. IN GENERAL

Section 165 of the Code permits deductions for certain losses not compensated for by insurance. Generally, § 165, consistent with §§ 162 and 212, allows deductions for losses incurred in connection with a trade or business or a transaction entered into for profit. See § 165(a), (c)(1) and (c)(2). There can be important tax differences, however, depending on whether a loss is a business loss or a loss arising from income-producing activities that fall short of a trade or business. The latter may be treated as capital losses and subject to limitations that do not apply to ordinary business losses. Losses that are connected with neither a trade or business nor a profit-seeking activity are personal in nature and generally not deductible. Section 165 allows a deduction, however, for certain personal casualty and theft losses. See § 165(c)(3), (d) and (e). Other sections of the Code deny deductions for losses in specific circumstances.

This Section organizes these specific limitations on deductions for losses into three categories: (1) losses that might be considered personal, (2) losses related to unrealized gains, and (3) tax shelter losses. Three limitations designed to enforce the nondeductibility of personal losses are considered by taking a slightly different look at the now familiar distinction between personal and income-producing activities. Limitations on deductions for gambling losses under § 165(d), and for so-called hobby losses under § 183, are treated first, followed by an examination of deductibility of casualty losses, the major exception to the general policy that losses incurred on assets related to personal consumption are not deductible. Next follows a discussion of loss deduction limitations that have been enacted to protect against taxpayers' efforts to take advantage of the realization requirement by realizing losses for tax purposes without fully parting with the asset, for example, by so-called wash sales (§ 1091), and sales to related parties (§ 267). Limitations to restrict a rather elaborate tax planning scheme, "straddles," which take advantage of the realization requirement, also are briefly described here. A detailed discussion of capital losses is postponed until Chapter 5.

The limitations on deductions for tax shelter losses—for example, the passive loss rules of § 469—are intended primarily to preclude taxpayers from using losses derived from tax shelter investments to reduce taxes on earned income and on investment income such as dividends and interest. These rules are described at the end of this Section.

Before turning to the various limitations on losses, the following Note considers the general issues of when and whether a loss exists and in what amount.

Note Discussing When and Whether a Loss Exists and in What Amount

1.   When Do Losses Occur?

As should be clear from prior materials, neither gains nor losses are taken into account for tax purposes as they accrue. Instead, they produce tax consequences only when they are realized. Thus, a mere decline in value is insufficient to create a loss for tax purposes. The time of realization is clear when property is sold, exchanged, or otherwise disposed of. But a taxpayer may dispose of property without actually suffering an economic loss, where he sells to a related party or where he is under an obligation to repurchase the property. For example, in Scully v. United States, 840 F.2d 478 (7th Cir. 1988), the court held there was no genuine economic loss arising from a sale of property between two trusts with the same fiduciaries and beneficiaries. This issue is discussed further infra at page 396. Losses sometimes are allowed when property becomes worthless, an issue that troubled the Supreme Court in the early days of the income tax. For example, in United States v. S.S. White Dental Manufacturing Co., 274 U.S. 398 (1927), the Court held that a loss was realized in 1918, when the German government seized the taxpayer's wholly-owned German branch, despite the possibility that some sort of claim might subsequently be presented against the German government. The Court said:

> The quoted regulations, consistently with the statute, contemplate that a loss may become complete enough for deduction without the taxpayer's establishing that there is no possibility of an eventual recoupment. * * * The Taxing Act does not require the taxpayer to be an incorrigible optimist.

Section 165(g) allows deduction for a loss when certain securities become worthless. In Boehm v. Commissioner, 326 U.S. 287 (1945), the Court held that a loss on a security was sustained when the security actually became worthless and not when the taxpayer in good faith believed that it had become worthless. In other words, an "objective" rather than a "subjective" test applies to this question. This test has produced many disputes. Section 6511(d) provides a seven-year statute of limitations for refund claims under § 165(g). The former three-year limit caused much litigation because the Commissioner often claimed the proper year for deducting the loss was a year barred by the statute.

The courts tend to fix the time of loss by looking to a "definitive" or "identifiable" event or to conduct indicating a "closed transaction" or "no reasonable prospect of recovery." The test is a "flexible practical one," not dependent upon "any single factor," thus requiring the courts to look to "realism and practicality" for the answer. The mere failure to use property is not enough, although it is not necessary to give up legal title. There must be some action evincing an intent to abandon property or the prospect of its recovery. Most cases have held that a loss deduction may not be taken on account of loss of goodwill until the taxpayer has disposed of the entire business. In general, no deduction is allowed for the loss of anticipated income.

2.   Amount of Loss Deduction

Although taxpayers think of losses in terms of market value, § 165(b) provides that the amount of the loss deduction is the adjusted basis of the property. The amount of deductible loss must be offset by the extent to which the taxpayer is partially compensated by insurance.

3.   The Distinction Between Business and Nonbusiness Profit-Seeking Losses

Business losses under § 165(c)(1) may receive more favorable tax treatment over time—in the form of net operating loss carryforwards provided by § 172—than investment or transaction-for-profit losses under § 165(c)(2). Trade or business losses are deductible from gross income rather than from adjusted gross income and therefore can be taken even if the taxpayer does not itemize deductions. § 62(a)(2). Section

165(c)(2) losses can be deducted in computing adjusted gross income only if they result from a sale or exchange of property or are attributable to property that produces rent or royalties. § 62(a)(3), (4). Otherwise, these loss deductions must be itemized and are allowed only if the taxpayer's total "allowable itemized deductions" exceed the standard deduction. Moreover, many nonbusiness losses are "capital losses" whose deductibility is limited, while business losses are more likely to be "ordinary losses" deductible in full against ordinary income. The definition and treatment of capital losses are considered in Chapter 5.

In 2017, the Congress further limited the business loss deductions available to noncorporate taxpayers. Section 461(*l*) now provides that individuals may deduct a maximum of $250,000 in "excess business losses" against nonbusiness income. Business losses that exceed that amount must be carried forward as a net operating loss.

Differences such as those described above can make it important to know whether a loss was incurred in business or a nonbusiness profit-seeking activity. For example, Reese v. Commissioner, 35 T.C.M. 1228 (1976) involved losses on the general contracting and financing of a manufacturing plant for a company of which the taxpayer was president, treasurer, chairman of the board of directors, and a principal stockholder. In finding that the loss was a nonbusiness loss, the court stated:

> In order for petitioner to qualify for a loss deduction under section 165(c)(1) the loss must be sustained in a trade or business. It is clear that the taxpayer may be engaged in more than one trade or business. * * * Whether the taxpayer's activities constitute a trade or business is a question of fact. * * *
>
> Petitioner was primarily engaged in the business of a corporate executive. Petitioner contends, however, that he was also engaged in another business—that of general contractor. * * * We must consequently determine whether his activities in regard to that project constituted a trade or business.
>
> Prior to [this] project petitioner admittedly had not been engaged as a general contractor nor was he so engaged on any subsequent project. Moreover, the record does not support a conclusion that petitioner did more than provide the financing for [this] project. In addition, no evidence regarding either the amount of time petitioner devoted to the project or specific tasks performed by petitioner in pursuit of the alleged trade or business was presented.
>
> Petitioner was clearly motivated by a desire to make a profit. The profit motive is in itself insufficient to transform financing activities into a trade or business. Thus, the loss is not deductible under section 165(c)(1) as a loss incurred in a trade or business. Nevertheless, since petitioner's primary motive was

to obtain a profit, the loss is deductible under section 165(c)(2) as a loss incurred in a transaction entered into for profit.

B. THE DISTINCTION BETWEEN PROFIT-SEEKING (OR BUSINESS) AND PERSONAL LOSSES

Note Introducing the Distinction Between Profit-Seeking (or Business) and Personal Losses

1.   In General

Section 165 denies a deduction for most personal losses. To a large extent, this rule corresponds to the rule of § 262 disallowing any deduction for personal expenses.

Under § 165, the problem of distinguishing nondeductible personal losses from deductible income-seeking losses sometimes arises with regard to residential property that has been used or offered for use for both purposes. In Austin v. Commissioner, 298 F.2d 583 (2d Cir. 1962), for example, the court asked whether the taxpayer's primary motive in acquiring and holding residential property was to earn a profit; the Second Circuit upheld the Tax Court's finding that a loss was not deductible because it was incurred on the sale of property "purchased by [the taxpayer] primarily for a residence and secondarily to generate a profit." The taxpayer had purchased a $28,000 home in Poughkeepsie, N.Y. in anticipation of his company's announced relocation from New York City. He immediately undertook a $40,000 renovation of the house. The company cancelled its relocation plans after the taxpayer had sold his previous home and moved into the new home. He immediately offered the home for sale and also offered it for rental one year later. When the house and land were finally sold, the taxpayer claimed a large loss deduction. In upholding the Tax Court's disallowance of the loss, the Second Circuit stated:

> The logical interrelationship of § 165 and § 262 [disallowing deductions for personal expenses] requires a decision as to which of the two motives was dominant, so that one or the other section can be applied. * * * This court has repeatedly held that, in determining the deductibility of a loss, the primary motive must be ascertained and given effect.

The same result typically is reached where the property first was acquired for rental purposes and so used, but then was used as a personal residence up to the time of the sale. This result also may be reached even though the taxpayer had ceased for some time before the sale to occupy the premises as a residence, had made efforts to rent it, and had expended substantial sums to place it in a more saleable condition. Is a loss deductible if the property was lived in, then rented for a period, and then sold? Reg. § 1.165–9(b)(1) permits a deduction if the property has been "appropriated to income-producing purposes."

When part of a property is used for one purpose and part for another, or when the same property is used at different times for different purposes, losses from the sale of the property must be allocated between the different uses. The deduction is allowed in proportion to the business or income-producing use in the same way that a taxpayer's basis in property is allocated between personal and business uses for calculating depreciation. For example, the taxpayer in Sharp v. United States, 199 F. Supp. 743 (D.Del.1961), aff'd per curiam 303 F.2d 783 (3d Cir. 1962), owned an airplane that cost $54,000. The airplane was used 75 percent for personal matters and 25 percent for business. The taxpayer took depreciation totaling $13,000 on one-fourth of the cost. The question was the amount of gain or loss realized by the taxpayer on the sale of the airplane for $35,000.

The taxpayer said that, since the cost was $54,000 and the depreciation allowed was $13,000, his adjusted basis was $41,000. Consequently, he claimed a loss of $6,000 when the plane was sold for $35,000. He did not contend that this loss was deductible. The government's contention was that three-fourths of the cost, or $40,500, was personal and remaining one-fourth, or $13,500, was business. The $13,000 depreciation was allocable only against this business portion of the plane, leaving an adjusted basis of $40,500 for the personal portion and $500 for the business portion. This produced a nondeductible loss of $14,250 on the personal portion and a taxable gain of $8,250 on the business portion ($8,750 less the $500 remaining basis on that portion). The court agreed.

2. Gambling Losses

A gambling loss is a classic example of a loss that is presumed to involve a component of personal consumption. To prevent taxpayers from using such consumption-related losses to reduce the tax otherwise payable on unrelated income and to permit the deduction of losses only when incurred in business or profit-seeking activities, § 165(d) allows gambling losses to be deducted only to the extent of gambling gains. This technique—limiting deductions to the amount of related income—has become quite common in the Code. Similar rules, for example, apply with respect to vacation homes (§ 280A), hobby losses (§ 183), and passive losses (§ 469). Hobby losses are considered infra at page 385 and passive losses at infra page 424.

NOTES

(A) *Proving Gambling Losses.* The issue most frequently litigated in gambling loss cases is the adequacy of the taxpayer's proof of his losses. For example, in Green v. Commissioner, 31 T.C.M. 592 (1972), the taxpayer submitted $23,680 in losing tickets, all allegedly purchased by him or on his behalf within a period of less than six weeks. The court noted that "[s]everal of the losing tickets submitted unmistakably bear heel marks," and disallowed a portion of the losses claimed. See also DeMonaco v.

Commissioner, 41 T.C.M. 718 (1981) (gambling losses disallowed; uncashed losing race tickets had no heel marks but were purchased at ticket windows to which taxpayer had no access, purchased at multiple windows for the same race, and were nonsequential). Sequential ticket numbers on clean tickets do not necessarily prove that the taxpayer did not "pick up the discarded stubs of disheartened bettors." See Norgaard v. Commissioner, 939 F.2d 874 (9th Cir. 1991) (disallowing a deduction to a taxpayer who presented a paper bag of such stubs to the trial court).

Gamblers often have inadequate records and attempt to rely on the so-called *Cohan* rule that permits a deduction based on estimates where the court believes that an expense actually was undertaken. Cohan v. Commissioner, 39 F.2d 540 (2d Cir. 1930), is a classic case in the tax law. In that case, the Board of Tax Appeals noted that George M. Cohan had spent considerable sums of money in entertaining actors, employees, and drama critics, but disallowed any deduction on the grounds that it was impossible to tell how much he had spent because his records were inadequate. The Second Circuit reversed in an opinion by Judge Learned Hand and instructed the Board to "make as close an approximation as it can." The case was expressly overruled for entertainment expenses by § 274 of the Code, which requires adequate records to support all entertainment expenses, but the *Cohan* rule lives on in other contexts. (Deductions for entertainment expenses are disallowed by the 2017 tax act.)

Rather than going to the time and trouble of picking up "the discarded stubs of disheartened bettors," the Daily Beast reports that gamblers can search Craigslist and eBay for losing track and lottery stubs for sale or rent. Apparently gamblers hold onto them so they can produce them if audited to justify the offsetting losses.[15]

(B) *Gambling Professionally.* The Supreme Court, in Commissioner v. Groetzinger, 480 U.S. 23 (1987), held that a professional gambler engages in a trade or business if "involved in the activity with continuity and regularity" and with the primary purpose of earning income or profit. A sporadic activity, a hobby, or an amusement diversion does not qualify. The Supreme Court viewed full-time, professional gambling to be as much of a profit-making enterprise as any other activity, for example, active trading of securities.

In cases following the *Groetzinger* decision, the Tax Court held that professional gamblers' gambling expenses are deductible under § 162 as ordinary and necessary business expenses, which permits them to be carried forward to other taxable years under § 172. The Congress reversed that rule in 2017: § 165(d) now provides that even professional gamblers cannot deduct expenses in excess of income. Still, professional gamblers may be eagerly awaiting 2026, when that disallowance is scheduled to sunset, and the Supreme Court's holding will again have important effect.

(C) *What Are Gambling Gains?* Section 165(d) provides that "losses from wagering transactions shall be allowed only to the extent of the gains from such transactions." Note that the statute does not say gambling

---

[15]   Source: www.thedailybeast.com/irs-scammed-with-losing-lotto-tickets.

"winnings." Does that mean that something other than winning bets might be used to offset gambling losses?

In Allen v. Commissioner, 976 F.2d 975 (5th Cir. 1992), the court refused to permit a blackjack dealer to offset "tokes" against his gambling losses. The court determined that the tokes were given to the dealer by the gambling patrons for services rendered and they did not constitute a wagering transaction. In Boyd v. United States, 762 F.2d 1369 (9th Cir. 1985), a professional poker player was not permitted to use his losses to offset the fees he was paid by the house to play cards as a shill.

In a somewhat surprising opinion, a taxpayer was permitted to offset gambling losses with the $2.5 million in comps (free cars) that he received from an Atlantic City casino. Libutti v. Commissioner, 71 T.C.M. 2343 (1996). Judge Laro interpreted "gains" to mean any increases to the gambler's wealth that arose out of wagering transactions. Recall that in *Zarin*, set out supra at page 187, one of the dissenting opinions argues that any income Zarin had when the debt was discharged should be offset against his gambling losses in the same year. Is the discharge of indebtedness income properly considered a gain from gambling transactions when the indebtedness occurs due to gambling activities?

1.   HOBBY LOSSES: LIMITED DEDUCTIBILITY OF EXPENSES INCURRED
      IN NOT-FOR-PROFIT ACTIVITIES

Section 183 is another provision designed to restrict the deduction of losses under § 165 to those incurred in the course of a business or profit-seeking activity. Losses incurred in the course of personal consumption are disallowed to the extent they exceed income from the activity. The "hobby loss" provisions of § 183 do not permit a deduction for a loss. Section 165(c), however, requires that losses be incurred in a business or in a transaction entered into for profit. Section 183 provides guidelines for determining whether an activity is entered into for profit.

Storey v. Commissioner

United States Tax Court, 2012. T.C. Memo. 2012–115.

■ KROUPA, JUDGE: * * * *

The primary issue is whether petitioner, a law firm partner and full-time attorney, was involved in the trade or business of film production under section 162 during the years at issue. We hold that she was engaged in the trade or business of film production during each of the years at issue and that she was engaged in this business for profit. * * * *

FINDINGS OF FACT

The deficiencies and penalties determined in this case relate entirely to petitioner's film production activity. She produced a documentary film entitled "Smile 'Til It Hurts: The Up With People Story" (Smile 'Til It Hurts). Smile 'Til It Hurts explores the peppy youth group Up With People, which began singing in the 1960s. * * * *

A. Prequel

Petitioner is the primary wage earner in her family. * * * * Petitioner earned a substantial income from her law practice during the years at issue, totaling over $1 million. Petitioner also has a strong interest in the arts. She directed theatrical productions in high school and maintained her involvement in theater even during law school. * * * *Years into their marriage, petitioner first learned that her husband had participated in Up With People as a teenager. Mr. Storey's involvement with this group sparked her interest in a topic that would ultimately become Smile 'Til It Hurts.

B. Lights, Camera . . .

* * * * Taking advantage of additional free time, she began to educate herself about filmmaking. Petitioner read extensively and took a sabbatical from her legal work to attend the New York Film Academy's (NY Academy) one-month filmmaking program to obtain hands-on experience. * * * * Petitioner also took filmmaking classes, including editing and DVD authorizing, at Scottsdale Community College.

* * *[P]petitioner went to an Up With People alumni meeting with her husband. It was then that a "light bulb went off." She negotiated the rights to all of the archival footage of Up With People. She hired * * * a video production company owner as a camera operator in 2004 to film interviews that petitioner conducted with Up With People alumni at a group reunion. With archival footage and some interviews under her belt, petitioner's filmmaking journey was underway.

C. Action!

Petitioner capitalized on the flexibility of her legal practice, working nights and weekends and taking off weeks as needed, to pursue her filmmaking journey. She began interviewing members of Up With People * * * and ultimately conducted 400 hours of interviews. She performed extensive research with Up with People * * *and hired a professional research firm to assist with the forensic accounting research.

Petitioner produced a 30-second promotional pitch (a "teaser") in 2004 and 2005. She produced the first trailer for Smile 'Til It Hurts in 2006 that was distributed in a packet with advertisements regarding petitioner's filmmaking team. That year, petitioner was accepted to attend the Sundance Institute's Independent Producers Conference (Sundance Conference) in late summer. Petitioner attended classes and benefited from networking opportunities* * *.

D. Publicity

Petitioner conducted screenings of the Smile 'Til It Hurts "rough cut" in test markets to identify necessary improvements to the film. She and her team revised the film using feedback from the screenings. * * * *As she was finalizing the film, petitioner attended the invitation-only Independent Film Producers' Independent Film Week Conference (IFW

Conference) in New York. The IFW Conference had a "rough cut lab" during which industry experts recommended improvements to the Smile 'Til It Hurts "rough cut." The IFW Conference also featured a "short" of Smile 'Til It Hurts and a private screening for film festival programmers and film distributors. Petitioner completed the final cut of Smile 'Til It Hurts in December 2008 and launched it the next month.* * * *

E.   Applause

Petitioner and Smile 'Til It Hurts received awards at some of the film festivals. * * * *Smile 'Til It Hurts has also been favorably reviewed in the press. * * * *

F.   Credits

Petitioner's successes were shared with a number of experts, both formal members of her Smile 'Til It Hurts team and professional acquaintances* * *

G.   The Fine Print

Armed with her experts' wisdom, petitioner leveraged her experience in her primary profession to comply with the extensive legal requirements and obligations of documentary film production. Petitioner obtained licenses for every second of the documentary film, including archival footage, music rights, photographs, newspaper clips and headlines. She obtained a formal written release to use each interviewee's image and statements on video. Petitioner obtained releases for the locations at which film was shot, [and] * * * also obtained extensive and varied insurance.

H.   Box Office Arrangements

Petitioner organized Storey Vision, LLC (Storey Vision), an Arizona limited liability company, in September 2005. Petitioner was the sole member and manager of Storey Vision, her film production company. She established a checking account, a savings account and a credit card for Storey Vision, each separate from any personal accounts.

Petitioner began to run numbers for Smile 'Til It Hurts in 2005 and first created a written business plan and timeline in 2006. She created written budgets for Smile 'Til It Hurts and modified them as her project progressed. * * * * Petitioner obtained loans for Storey Vision to finance Smile 'Til It Hurts * * *

Petitioner owns all of the rights to the film and continues to expect that she will make a profit. She anticipated sales to DVD viewers, cable outlets, television outlets and educational institutions like universities and libraries. She intended to sell regular DVDs for $19.95 and educational DVDs for $200 to $250. Petitioner received her first screening fee of $250 for the documentary film in March 2010 * * *

I.   Tracking the Numbers

Petitioner hired a bookkeeper to manage Storey Vision's finances * * * [who] prepared financial records during the years at issue for Storey Vision, including general ledgers, profit and loss statements, balance sheets, expense reports, business spending reports, petty cash ledgers and quick reports. Petitioner also retained an accounting firm* * * *.

Opinion

We begin by fleshing out the central plot to determine whether petitioner may deduct film production expenses paid or incurred during the years at issue under section 162(a). * * * * A taxpayer must conduct the activity with the requisite profit motive or intent for the activity to be considered a trade or business.

* * * * Respondent maintains petitioner was not engaged in the trade or business of being a film producer, and, accordingly, expenses incurred for the production of Smile 'Til It Hurts are not business expenses deductible under section 162(a). Rather, he argues, they are deductible only to the extent of the income derived from the activity under section 183. Because there was no income, respondent seeks to deny deductions for all expenses. * * * *

We structure our analysis of whether an activity is engaged in for profit around nine nonexclusive factors. Sec. 1.183–2(b), Income Tax Regs. The nine factors are: (1) the manner in which the taxpayer carried on the activity, (2) the expertise of the taxpayer or his or her advisers, (3) the time and effort expended by the taxpayer in carrying on the activity, (4) the expectation that the assets used in the activity may appreciate in value, (5) the success of the taxpayer in carrying on other similar or dissimilar activities, (6) the taxpayer's history of income or loss with respect to the activity, (7) the amount of occasional profits, if any, which are earned, (8) the financial status of the taxpayer, and (9) whether elements of personal pleasure or recreation are involved.

No factor or set of factors is controlling, nor is the existence of a majority of factors favoring or disfavoring a profit objective controlling. * * * The individual facts and circumstances of each case are the primary test, with greater weight to be given to objective facts than to the taxpayer's statement of intent. Moreover, certain factors may be given more weight than others because they are more meaningfully applied to the facts in this case. All nine factors do not necessarily apply in every case.

We begin with the first factor by considering whether petitioner carried on the film production activity in a businesslike manner. Factors that may indicate a profit objective include whether petitioner had a business plan, made changes in an effort to earn a profit, maintained complete and accurate books and records, and advertised the film. * * * * We find that this factor favors petitioner. * * * * Storey Vision maintained separate accounts and a business credit card. Storey Vision obtained commercial general liability coverage, an "entertainment package policy," and liability insurance for instances when petitioner shot film "on location." Petitioner hired a bookkeeper [and] retained an accounting firm to manage certain tax matters for her and for Storey Vision. Petitioner created a written business plan and * * * [and] obtained a business line of credit * * *.

Petitioner began marketing Smile 'Til It Hurts during the years at issue, even as the movie was being produced and finalized, and marketed it actively in later years. * * *Once Smile 'Til It Hurts was completed, she began actively marketing it by attending numerous film festivals selected after consulting her sales agent. * * * * Petitioner treated her reputation as a filmmaker with the same businesslike attention.

The second factor also favors her as petitioner developed her own expertise and sought guidance from industry experts. * * * *We find that petitioner sought to educate herself and received expert advice on her film production activity, and this weighs in favor of her argument that she carried on the activity in a businesslike manner and for profit.

The third factor focuses on the time and effort expended by the taxpayer in carrying on the activity. Petitioner spent numerous hours per week on her filmmaking activity during the years at issue. She billed 30 to 35 hours per week as an attorney and spent evenings and weekends on her Smile 'Til It Hurts project. Respondent emphasizes that petitioner was a partner at a law firm and suggests that her filmmaking activity could not rise to the level of a trade or business because she had a full-time job with significant responsibility. We disagree. Petitioner's position as a partner gave her flexibility to work on her filmmaking activity.

We have recognized that a taxpayer may engage in more than one trade or business at any one time. * * * * It is also well settled that the term "trade or business" includes the arts. Furthermore, petitioner engaged qualified professionals to work on her Smile 'Til It Hurts activity as well. The third factor favors petitioner as well.

Fourth, we weigh petitioner's expectation that the assets used in the filmmaking activity may appreciate. * * * * The value of the assets used in petitioner's Smile 'Til It Hurts activity is so closely tied to the larger question of profit potential for her activity that it limits the utility of this fourth factor. We will not put much weight on this factor. Instead we will treat it as slightly favoring petitioner to the extent that we view the praises and awards given to petitioner and Smile 'Til It Hurts as positive indications of potential value.

In considering the fifth factor, a taxpayer's previous success in similar activities may show that the taxpayer has a profit objective even though the current activity is presently unprofitable. A taxpayer's success in other, unrelated activities also may indicate a profit objective. Smile 'Til It Hurts is petitioner's first filmmaking endeavor. This factor is therefore of limited utility. She is, however, a successful attorney.

* * * * We treat petitioner's success as an attorney and accomplishments in the arts as favoring petitioner.

We examine the sixth and seventh factors, the taxpayer's history of income or losses with respect to the activity and amount of any occasional profits, in tandem. Respondent argues that petitioner's record of continuous losses from her filmmaking activity mandates a finding that she was not engaged in this activity for profit. Petitioner argues that while her efforts as a filmmaker have not proven profitable to date, her hard work will be rewarded with substantial income as Smile 'Til It Hurts is now complete, has received extensive praise and is being marketed* * *.

Petitioner did report a loss for each year of operation, and her income has been de minimis. Petitioner points us to two important facts in this case, however, that should be considered with respect to these losses. Losses during the initial or startup stage of an activity do not necessarily indicate that the taxpayer failed to conduct the activity for profit. The three years at issue were petitioner's fourth, fifth and sixth years of producing Smile 'Til It Hurts. She completed the film at the end of this period. We treat the years at issue as part of the startup phase because she needed to complete the film before she could sell it and, on the record, this period is not unreasonably long. * * * * We are not inclined to give much weight to the sixth and seventh factors in this instance because we find that petitioner was within a reasonable startup phase for her filmmaking activity during the years at issue.

Respondent argues that the eighth factor, the financial status of the taxpayer, negates petitioner's profit motive. He asserts that her significant income from her legal career is sufficient to offset her filmmaking losses while maintaining petitioners' lifestyle. This factor favors respondent.

The last factor looks to elements of personal pleasure or recreation. Petitioner admits that she enjoys both the practice of law and film production* * * We note, however, that petitioner's enjoyment of the filmmaking activity is not sufficient to cause the activity to be classified as a hobby if other factors indicate that she engaged in it for profit.

After considering all the facts and circumstances, we find that petitioner has shown that she engaged in her filmmaking activity for profit. We recognize some factors in this case that indicate the absence of a profit motive: petitioner has a history of losses, earns significant income from other sources and appears to enjoy filmmaking. These factors, however, are outweighed by the facts demonstrating that petitioner did engage in film production for profit. * * * *

NOTES

(A) *Mechanics of Section 183.* Section 183 has a rebuttable presumption that an activity was engaged in with the requisite profit motive if the activity produced profits for three out of five consecutive years ending with the year in question. If an activity cannot meet the presumption, a taxpayer may still attempt to prove the activity was engaged in for profit by using the regulation's factors, which are described in *Storey*.

This rebuttable presumption may be hard to meet in the early years of a business when start-up expenses will create losses. In Roberts v. Commissioner, 820 F.3d 247 (7th Cir. 2016), the taxpayer significantly ramped up a horse racing activity and incurred several years of losses before the IRS conceded it was a business. When the IRS challenged the deduction for the loss years, Judge Posner held the taxpayer was entitled to the loss deductions, noting that the IRS position "amounts to saying that a business's start-up costs are not deductible business expenses—that every business starts as a hobby and becomes a business only when it achieves a certain level of profitability." Even though the Judge Posner found that the nine factors in the regulation overwhelmingly favored the taxpayer, he commented that these factors were found in "a goofy regulation." Judge Posner's disdain for the nine-factor test of the regulations was hardly surprising. Then, he added: "A business that is in an industry known to attract hobbyists (and horse racing is that business par excellence), that loses large sums of money year after year that the owner of the business deducts from a very large income that he derives from other (and genuine) businesses or from trusts or from other conventional sources of income, is presumptively a hobby, though before deciding for sure, the court must listen to the owner's protestations of business motive." 820 F. 3d at 254.

If an activity is not engaged in for profit, certain deductions may be permitted in any event. First, a taxpayer may deduct those amounts that are deductible without regard to whether there was a profit motive, for example, taxes under § 164. Second, any amount that would have been deductible if there had been the requisite profit motive is deductible to the extent of gross income from the activity minus the first sort of deductions. The deduction may be disallowed, however. See § 67 and supra at page 267.

(B) *The Cases Turn on Their Facts*. Section 183 cases are highly fact-specific. What may be a profit-seeking activity for one taxpayer may not be for another. Compare Cornfeld v. Commissioner, 797 F.2d 1049 (D.C. Cir. 1986) (taxpayer had honest profit objective in connection with his aircraft leasing activities), with Worley v. Commissioner, 39 T.C.M. 1090 (1980) (no profit motive existed with respect to aircraft leasing). Furthermore, a taxpayer may have the proper motive one year and have abandoned it in a future year. See, e.g., Kartrude v. Commissioner, 925 F.2d 1379 (11th Cir. 1991) (stunt flier lacked proper profit motive although he previously had operated the activity as a business).

Dentists seem to have a lot of time on their hands. In Zdun v. Commissioner, 76 T.C.M. 278 (1998), aff'd per curiam 229 F.3d 1161 (9th Cir. 2000), the taxpayer attempted to combine a holistic dental practice with an organic apple orchard. When the latter lost money, he claimed it was part of the profitable dental practice because he sold the apples to his patients. The court found it was a separate activity not conducted for profit. The dentist in Morley v. Commissioner, 76 T.C.M. 363 (1998), was more successful. The court permitted him to deduct the losses from his Arabian horse breeding, remarking:

> Mr. Morley's work on the farm was difficult, and it often precluded him from spending time with his family. Mrs. Morley credibly testified that she and her children missed her husband and that she would have preferred it if Mr. Morley had been at home instead of working on the horse-breeding activity. Mr. Morley arrived home after dark, very tired, in a bad mood, and dirty with "a certain aroma" from his work on the farm. It appeared to the Court that Mrs. Morley resented the amount of time Mr. Morley spent on the horse-breeding activity and that she was unhappy that her husband came home every night dirty and smelly. We are not convinced that Mr. Morley would subject himself to such rigors solely for recreation or pleasure.

(C) *Tax Shelters.* Traditionally, the hobby loss problem involved activities that were unrelated to a taxpayer's primary business activities and that arguably provided a means of securing business deductions for what were in reality personal consumption expenditures. See, e.g., Whitecavage v. Commissioner, 96 T.C.M. 119 (2008) (denying a deduction for an IRS auditor's losses relating to breeding and racing greyhounds). Other cases have applied § 183 to tax shelters and represent an evolution of the original hobby loss concept. The use of § 183 as a weapon in the battles against tax shelters is discussed infra at page 422.

2.   CASUALTY LOSSES

Note on Casualty Losses

Section 165(c)(3) allows deductions for personal losses arising from "fire, storm, shipwreck, or other casualty, or from theft." Only uninsured casualty losses exceeding $100 are taken into account. Deductions for casualty losses equal to casualty gains are deductible from gross income. Excess casualty losses are limited to the amount that exceeds 10 percent of adjusted gross income and are deductible only as itemized deductions. § 165(h)(2). No deduction is permitted if the taxpayer does not file a timely insurance claim to the extent the policy would provide reimbursement.

The 2017 tax act restricts the deduction for individual casualty losses from 2018 through the end of 2025. During that period, a (net) casualty loss is permitted only if the loss is attributable to a disaster declared by the President under the Robert T. Stafford Disaster Relief and Emergency Assistance Act. In 2026, absent further change, the stated rules of § 165(c)(3) spring back to life.

The deduction for casualty and theft losses, when permitted, may seem at odds with the policy of disallowing personal losses, but the allowance may be motivated by ability-to-pay considerations. Suppose the taxpayer's $2,000 paycheck is stolen. Has the taxpayer therefore lost the opportunity to consume $2,000 or should he be taxed because he had the opportunity to consume $2,000 but was unable to do so? Is the answer different if he lost his paycheck?

The 10 percent floor ensures that only large and uninsured losses are deductible. Therefore, taxpayers who have sustained a severe, unexpected, and nonvolitional loss will bear less tax than other taxpayers who have not experienced such losses. The casualty loss rule is comparable to the medical expenses deduction, which is also limited to amounts in excess of 10 percent of AGI (reduced to 7.5 percent for 2017 and 2018). In each case, the loss or expense is considered to be largely beyond the taxpayer's control and not the result of a personal consumption choice, unlike gambling losses, where even very large net losses are not deductible. Some observers, however, regard the widespread availability of casualty insurance as adequate protection and would repeal the casualty loss deduction.

In prior years, a great deal of litigation occurred over the meaning of the word "casualty" in § 165(c)(3), particularly what is meant by "other casualty." For example, Kielts v. Commissioner, 42 T.C.M. 238 (1981), allowed a casualty loss deduction for the adjusted basis of a $20,000 diamond lost from a ring, based on expert testimony that the ring had suffered from a "fairly strong blow" on one side of the ring. Mrs. Kielts had absolutely no recollection of any such event. The court added, "absent willfulness, negligence has no bearing on whether a casualty has occurred." The same result was reached in White v. Commissioner, 48 T.C. 430 (1967), where the taxpayer irretrievably lost a diamond in her gravel driveway while shaking her hand in pain after a car door was slammed on it. The court concluded that the "events giving rise to the loss were 'sudden, unexpected, violent and not due to deliberate or willful actions'" by the taxpayer.

Suddenness may be necessary, but it is not sufficient. A mere decline in value does not give rise to a deduction unless there is actual physical damage. For example, two of O.J. Simpson's neighbors claimed a casualty loss due to the decline in value of their Brentwood properties because of the murders and the subsequent media attention and influx of onlookers. In each case, the deduction was denied because there was no physical damage to the property and because as the Tax Court put it, the claim was based on a long period of public attention "more akin to a steadily operating cause than to a casualty." Chamales v. Commissioner, 79 T.C.M. 1428 (2000); Caan v. United States, 99–1 U.S.T.C. ¶ 50,349 (C.D.Cal.1999).

The suddenness and physical damage requirements probably should be viewed as backstops to the realization requirement and depreciation rules. Recall that generally a taxpayer cannot take a deduction for the decline in value of property until the loss is "realized." Similarly, the depreciation deduction for ordinary wear and tear is unavailable for personal use property. A casualty deduction for anything less than a sudden event involving physical damage would circumvent these other limitations.

Amount of Loss. The amount of deduction on personal property is limited to the lesser of the fair market value before the casualty minus the fair market value after the casualty or the property's adjusted basis. § 1.165–7(b). Suppose, for example, the taxpayer's car is totally destroyed. The taxpayer paid $20,000 for the car, but at the time of the accident, it is worth only $8,000. The deductible loss is $8,000. The remaining $12,000 of basis is not a loss at all, but rather is attributable to the taxpayer's consumption, which is not deductible. On the other hand, suppose a painting worth $75,000 and purchased by the taxpayer for $30,000, is stolen. The deductible loss is $30,000. The remaining $45,000 represents untaxed appreciation.

It is necessary to disallow a loss deduction for unrealized gains in order to prevent the double benefit that otherwise would result since the gain was never taken into income. Treating the loss as an occasion for both the realization of gain and the deduction of the entire value of property would have the same effect in such circumstances as limiting the deduction to basis.

The amount of a casualty loss must be reduced by insurance or any other recovery. Reg. § 1.165–1(d)(2). If at the end of the taxable year in which the casualty occurs, there is a reasonable prospect of recovery, the taxpayer is not permitted to take a deduction.

NOTES

(A) *Theft Losses.* A theft loss is deductible in the year of discovery. Proving to the IRS that a theft loss occurred is often not straightforward. For example, in Krahmer v. United States, 810 F.2d 1145 (Fed. Cir. 1987), the Federal Circuit held that the taxpayer had not shown that he was entitled to a theft loss deduction when a painting he purchased that bore the signature of W.M. Chase turned out not to be an original Chase. The court stated that the existence of the forged signature is not sufficient as a matter of law, and that the taxpayer must "prove that the seller defrauded him by knowingly and intentionally misattributing the painting to the artist." Swell.

Victims of Bernard Madoff's Ponzi scheme fared better with the IRS than they did with the embezzler who bilked them out of their life savings. In Rev. Rul. 2009–9, 2009–1 C.B. 735, without mentioning Madoff by name, the IRS provided guidance with respect to the investors' losses. It ruled that the losses were theft losses, meaning that the year-of-discovery rule applied rather than the year that the theft occurred. Although treating the losses as theft losses, the IRS nevertheless let investors deduct them as losses incurred in transactions entered into for profit. Thus, they were not subject to the limitations on personal casualty and theft losses. Finally, they were treated as ordinary rather than capital losses so that the limitation on the deduction of capital losses (see page 563, infra) did not apply.

(B) *Section 123.* Section 123 of the Code excludes from gross income amounts received under an insurance contract to reimburse the taxpayer for living expenses when his residence is destroyed by fire or other casualty.

(C) *Public Policy Limitation.* A taxpayer is entitled to take a deduction even if the casualty results from her negligence, but not if it is intentional or results from gross negligence. In Blackman v. Commissioner, 88 T.C. 677 (1987), aff'd in an unpublished opinion 867 F.2d 605 (1st Cir. 1988), the Tax Court explained that permitting such a deduction would frustrate national or state public policy. The taxpayer returned to his home and found another man living with his wife. After quarreling, the taxpayer gathered some of his wife's clothes and set fire to them on the stove. Although he claimed to have tried to douse the fire, it spread and the house and most of its contents (but not all of the clothes) were destroyed. He was charged with arson and malicious destruction because he "did willfully and maliciously destroy, injure, deface and molest clothing." The court found Mr. Blackman's actions amounted to gross negligence and that to permit a deduction would frustrate the state's public policy against arson, burning, and domestic violence.

(D) *Insurance.* Does the tax deduction for casualty losses have any bearing on the desirability of maintaining insurance? If a taxpayer has no insurance, is the government acting as insurer? Does the answer to the previous question depend upon an individual's tax bracket? Should the premiums for insurance against destruction of one's personal possessions be deductible? Consider the following comments from Boris Bittker, "Income Tax Deductions, Credits, and Subsidies for Personal Expenditures," 16 J. Law & Econ. 193, 197–98 (1973):

> In a statistical sense, of course, destruction by fire is one of the hazards of home ownership, "voluntarily" assumed when the taxpayer chooses to buy a personal residence. But if a dog can distinguish between being kicked and being stumbled over, as Holmes asserted, we can properly distinguish between the minor frustrations of life—a cigarette burn in a rug, a dented fender, a quarter lost when fumbling for change to put in a parking meter—and major casualties ("sudden, unexpected, and unusual" events that do not "commonly occur in the ordinary course of day-to-day living)," (to quote a recent Revenue Ruling).

* * *

Casualties undeniably reduce the taxpayer's net worth—and should therefore presumptively reduce his income * * *.

A more cogent criticism of the casualty deduction is that taxpayers should be encouraged to insure against such losses and that the deduction mitigates the cost of neglecting this sensible precaution. Whatever its strength, this line of argument does not prove that a taxpayer whose uninsured home is destroyed by fire has the same "income" as an otherwise identical taxpayer whose house escapes. The first taxpayer's loss is real, no matter how stupid, pigheaded, or foolhardy his failure to insure. One might wish to deny him a deduction as a penalty for improvidence, as a warning to others, or as a mode of raising revenue; but these objectives should be openly acknowledged, not disguised as an effort to "define income" or to achieve horizontal equity.

Is the limitation on casualty loss deductions only to the extent they exceed 10 percent of adjusted gross income consistent with the position that Professor Bittker expresses? The 2017 legislation limiting casualty loss deductions to federally declared disasters? Is a floor based on a percentage of income preferable to a dollar amount limitation?

C. LIMITATIONS ON LOSSES TO PROTECT AGAINST ABUSES OF THE REALIZATION REQUIREMENT

Fender v. United States

United States Court of Appeals, Fifth Circuit, 1978. 577 F.2d 934.

■ AINSWORTH, CIRCUIT JUDGE:

Harris R. Fender, an experienced investment banker, established two trusts for his two sons and in 1969 the trusts had large capital gains from the sale of certain Continental Telephone stock. To offset those gains, Harris Fender, co-trustee of the trust, attempted to sell an installment of Bender Road Improvement District WW and SS Combination Tax and Revenue Bonds ("Bender Bonds") owned by the trusts. These bonds, along with the bond market as a whole, had substantially declined in value as a result of a rise in interest rates. The bonds were purchased by the trusts for the amount of $435,017 and had a par value of $445,000. Because the bonds were unrated, they could not be sold in the public bond market. On December 26, 1969, Fender completed an over-the-counter sale of the Bender Bonds to the Longview National Bank & Trust Company, Longview, Texas, for $225,000 (approximately 50% of par value) plus accrued interest. This resulted in a $106,258.35 loss for each of the trusts. At the time of the sale, Fender controlled 40.7% of the Longview National Bank's stock either individually or through the two trusts. Shortly thereafter, on January 15, 1970, the stock interest of Fender and the trusts in the Longview Bank increased to 50.15%. On February 6, 1970, 42 days after their transfer to the bank, the trusts repurchased the bonds from the bank for $224,735 (approximately 50.5% of par value) plus accrued interest. Both transactions were made at the fair market value of the bonds, though the bonds had limited marketability since they were unrated. The Internal Revenue Service disallowed the loss deduction claimed in connection with the transfer of the Bender Bonds and this litigation ensued.

A taxpayer is allowed a deduction for "any loss sustained during the taxable year * * *." I.R.C. § 165(a). However, not every transaction purporting to result in a loss is deductible. "Only a bona fide loss is allowable. Substance and not mere form shall govern in determining a deductible loss." Treas.Reg. § 1.165–1(b). The burden of showing that the loss was bona fide is on the taxpayer. See Rand v. Helvering, 8 Cir., 1935, 77 F.2d 450. Further, the district court's conclusion that the transfer of the Bender Bonds to the Longview Bank was a bona fide sale is a conclusion of law which this Court may fully review. * * *

In deciding to sell the Bender Bonds, the taxpayers were motivated by the possibility of tax avoidance. Standing alone such a motive is an insufficient basis for disallowing a deduction. The legal right of a taxpayer to decrease the amount of what would otherwise be his taxes, or to altogether avoid them, by means which the law permits, cannot be doubted. * * * But the question for determination is whether what was done, apart from the tax motive, was the thing which the statute intended. Gregory v. Helvering, 293 U.S. 465, 469 (1935). The circumstances of this case establish that the taxpayers did not in substance experience the loss that is necessary for a deduction under section 165, and that the sole purpose of the transaction was to create a tax loss in the year 1969.

Apart from the tax motive, there was no apparent reason for the taxpayers to sell the Bender Bonds. While increased interest rates had caused the market value of the bonds to decline, the issuer of the Bender Bonds remained financially sound and capable of continuing to pay current interest and the full par value of the bonds at maturity. Hence, a bondholder would experience no loss if the bonds were held to maturity. Although the trusts appeared to sustain a significant loss by transferring the bonds to the bank during a depressed bond market, the ability to repurchase these bonds meant that the trusts would eventually be paid their original investment in the bonds and would suffer no real loss from the sale.

Hence, in determining whether the taxpayers suffered a genuine loss in the alleged sale to the bank, we examine the circumstances to see whether the taxpayers were exposed to a real risk of not being able to repurchase the bonds in a short period of time and thus of not being able to recover the apparent loss from the December 26 sale to the bank. This, in turn, depends on whether the taxpayers were able effectively to control the Longview Bank sufficiently to assure a resale of the bonds to the trusts. In support of the loss deduction, Fender claims that there was no agreement for the trusts to repurchase the bonds from the bank.[3] Further, Fender contends that although the plaintiffs owned 50.15% of the bank's stock when the bonds were repurchased, the plaintiffs lacked sufficient control of the Longview Bank to assure the repurchase of the bonds when the bonds were initially sold to the bank since the plaintiffs then owned less than 50% of the bank's stock.[4]

---

[3]   Fender stated that there was an agreement that the Bender Bonds would not be resold to the trusts within 31 days of the sale. Such an agreement was necessary to prevent a deduction from being disallowed under the provisions of section 1091 of the Internal Revenue Code.

[4]   If the taxpayer had controlled more than 50% of the bank's stock, a deduction would automatically be disallowed as a sale to a related party. I.R.C. § 267(a)(1), (b)(2). However, section 267 is not an exclusive condition for denying a deduction. A deduction is also disallowed

This contention is invalid since a transaction may not be bona fide even if the seller does not completely control the buyer as he does in the situation where he owns a majority of the stock.

To divest a sale of its fundamental incident of finality plainly requires a controlled or sympathetic vendee. Such dominion might be * * * accomplished boldly through contracts or options to repurchase and the creation of fictitious entities or it might be * * * accomplished through the more subtle tie of affectionate interest found among families and friends, business or otherwise.

DuPont v. Commissioner of Internal Revenue, 3 Cir., 1941, 118 F.2d 544, 545, cert. denied, 314 U.S. 623 (1941). In DuPont v. Commissioner of Internal Revenue, two friends sold each other about the same amount of stock at a loss at the end of the year and repurchased the stock from one another at the start of the next year. Both sales were for the fair market value of the stock. Although the friends had no legal obligation to repurchase the stock, the court concluded that sufficient dominion existed to assure repurchase and thus to prevent bona fide sale. Another court denied a loss deduction to a taxpayer who sold and repurchased stock from one of his employees. See Rand v. Helvering, 8 Cir., 1935, 77 F.2d 450.

The circumstances of this case demonstrate that the taxpayers had sufficient influence over the Longview Bank to remove any substantial risk that the trusts would be unable to repurchase the Bender Bonds and thus eliminate the apparent loss on the sale to the bank. The taxpayers then controlled 40.7% of the bank's stock, the largest single block of stock. In addition, Fender had greatly assisted the bank recently in dealing with a series of financial difficulties. It appears that Longview Bank would not have agreed to the transaction absent a special relationship with Fender. The Bender Bonds were unrated and were of a maturity that the Longview Bank did not normally purchase. Another bank, Peoples National Bank, where Fender lacked similar influence, had refused to accept the offer to purchase the bonds. Further, since the Bender Bonds were unrated bonds and had limited marketability the Longview Bank would have had difficulty in selling the bonds to a buyer other than the taxpayers. Although the transaction was in the form of a sale to Longview Bank, the trusts allowed the money received from the sale to remain deposited in the Longview Bank until the bonds were repurchased. Finally, Norman Taylor, President of the Longview Bank at that time, in his deposition testified that the transaction was an

for any transaction which is not bona fide "even though section 267 does not apply to the transaction." Treas.Reg. 1.267(1)–1(c).

accommodation to Fender and that he understood that the trusts would repurchase the Bender Bonds within ninety days.[6]

Because the taxpayers had sufficient dominion over the Longview Bank to ensure that the apparent loss from the sale of Bender Bonds on December 26 could be recaptured through a repurchase of the bonds, we conclude that the taxpayers did not suffer a real economic loss as is necessary for a deduction under section 165.

NOTES

(A) *Has There Been a Loss?* Several provisions of the Code are designed to prevent the deduction of losses in circumstances where a loss has not actually been realized. In *Fender,* neither § 267 (transfer to a related party) nor § 1091 (wash sale) applied. These sections are discussed below. The court, however, finds that even where there are no statutory limitations, no loss is permitted unless there is a "bona fide sale." Is the court correct that the seller's control over the purchaser precludes a bona fide sale? Suppose interest rates had fallen and the value of the Bender bonds had risen. Could the bank, a regulated institution, have sold the bonds back to Fender at less than their market value? If there is an agreement to resell the property to its original owner, § 1091 would disallow the deduction. What if the agreement is informal or otherwise hidden from the Service? What evidence would indicate that there was no bona fide sale? Suppose T "parked" assets with A in exchange for $100,000 and six months later A "resold" the assets to T for $105,000?

(B) *Transactions Between Related Taxpayers.* Section 267 disallows deductions for losses from sales or exchanges of property, whether direct or indirect, between certain related people, such as family members or corporations and their majority (more than 50 percent) shareholders. What is the policy behind this provision? How easy would it be for the Commissioner to show whether there was a bona fide sale between such related persons and what the real price was? Suppose that a mother sells her son some property at a price lower than her purchase price. In general, loss deductions are not allowed until a loss is realized. Has the mother realized a loss in this situation? Is it appropriate to view the mother and son as a single economic unit for this purpose? Losses (as well as gains) between husbands and wives are also disallowed. See § 1041, discussed infra at page 511.

The seller's loss generally is lost permanently under § 267 because the purchaser's basis for computing loss when he sells the property is his cost. If, however, the related purchaser ultimately sells the property for a gain, he can reduce his gain to the extent of the related seller's disallowed loss. § 267(d). For example, suppose a mother sells property she purchased for $10,000 to her son for $6,000. Her $4,000 loss is disallowed. If, however, the son subsequently sells the property for $13,000, the son reports only $3,000

---

[6] The testimony of Norman Taylor, president of the bank and the only disinterested witness, indicates that an agreement to repurchase existed although the time and price for the repurchase was [sic] not fixed. * * *

gain (his $7,000 gain is offset by mom's $4,000 disallowed loss). For a similar rule in the case of property transferred by gift, see page 141, supra.

Several courts have found that the use of an intermediary results in a prohibited "indirect" sale. See, e.g., McWilliams v. Commissioner, 331 U.S. 694 (1947) (use of intermediary to effectuate sale to related party); Hassen v. Commissioner, 599 F.2d 305 (9th Cir. 1979) (foreclosure sale followed by prearranged but not binding repurchase by controlled corporation).

(C) *Wash Sales.* Section 1091 disallows a loss from a sale preceded or followed by a purchase of substantially identical securities (including options) within a 30-day period. The basis of the stock purchased is that of the stock sold, plus any additional amount paid on the repurchase, so that losses are deferred, not lost. For example, if the taxpayer sells for $500 a share of XYZ stock he purchased for $700 and repurchases a share of XYZ stock 15 days later for $550, the $200 loss on the sale is disallowed and the basis in his new share is $750. If the taxpayer repurchases the shares for less, his basis is reduced by the difference in the same manner. Similar rules apply to short sales of stock or securities. Note that § 1091 does not apply to gains nor does it apply if the securities are not "substantially identical." At year end, a taxpayer can sell a bond that has declined in value and purchase a similar bond from another issuer. Section 1091 will not prevent deduction of the loss because the issuers are not the same.

Is the approach of § 267, which permanently disallows the loss, or of § 1091, which defers the loss, more appropriate?

(D) *Capital Losses.* Probably the most important limitation on the deduction of losses is the restriction on the deduction of capital losses. Capital losses are deductible by individuals only to the extent of capital gains plus $3,000 of ordinary income. § 1211. Any capital losses not allowed in the current year may be carried forward indefinitely by individuals. § 1212. Capital losses are discussed in greater detail in Chapter 5.

Despite the limitation, taxpayers in many cases are able to deduct their losses while, at the same time, deferring their gains. This strategy, known as cherrypicking, is discussed infra at page 572.

(E) *Straddles.* Where a taxpayer retains related assets with unrealized gains, she can use tax losses to obtain optimum tax treatment, regardless of the effect on her overall economic position or the economic substance of the transactions. Straddles are an example of this ploy.

In a typical tax straddle, the taxpayer acquires offsetting positions in commodity futures contracts. For example, she might enter into contracts to both buy and sell the same quantity of January wheat. Any changes in the prices of the contracts will offset each other; a loss on the buy contract will offset any gain on the sell contract, so the taxpayer's economic position does not change. Each contract or "leg" of the straddle will show either a loss or gain. By selling one leg while holding the other, the taxpayers have been able to obtain two tax benefits: deferral and conversion.

To achieve deferral, the taxpayer sells the loss leg in the current tax year, while retaining the gain leg until the next year. Hence, the loss is accelerated while the offsetting gain is deferred. In a sophisticated straddle, the gain may be deferred almost perpetually by subsequent purchases of offsetting positions.

Net short-term gain is taxed at ordinary income rates, while long-term gain is taxed at lower, preferential rates. The holding period for long-term gain is one year. To achieve conversion,—i.e., the conversion of short-term capital gain into long-term capital gain—then, the taxpayer would hold the loss leg less than one year. He could use the short-term capital loss to shelter short-term capital gain (that otherwise would be taxed at the same rate as ordinary income) or a limited amount of ordinary income. The gain leg would be held more than a year, so that any gain eventually realized would be taxed at preferential long-term capital gain rates.

Section 1092 was enacted to address the straddle problem. In general, that section limits the deduction of losses from straddles to the amount by which losses exceed unrecognized gains on offsetting positions. If, however, the straddle is identified as such when acquired, no loss is allowed; the disallowed losses is added to the basis of the offsetting position. Section 1092 applies to certain commodity future contracts, and stock and stock option transactions where offsetting positions are held in similar or related properties. Complementing the straddle rules of § 1092 are the "mark-to-market" rules of § 1256. Section 1256 requires that any regulated futures contract, such as stock and commodities options, be "marked to market" at the end of the year, whether or not the taxpayer holds offsetting positions. That is, each such contract the taxpayer holds is treated as if it is sold at year's end. Gain or loss is fully recognized. Thus, under the mark-to-market rules, realized losses on investments subject to § 1256 are offset by unrealized gains so that only the net loss, if any, is available to reduce income from unrelated sources. See also §§ 1233, 1234, 1234A, and 1236. The mark-to-market rules of § 1256 provide a very limited accrual tax system.

The Service has applied the principle of § 1092 to transactions that are not explicitly covered by the straddle rules. Assume the taxpayer purchases two debt instruments at the same time. Each of them has a provision that the interest will be reset if a particular event occurs. If the event occurs, the interest on one note will go up and the interest on the other will go down and if the event does not occur, the opposite happens. On the reset date, the taxpayer sells the note whose value falls and holds the note that increases in value. The IRS held that the taxpayer cannot take a loss on the note that was sold. It did not realize an actual economic loss because the purported loss on the sale of one note was substantially offset by the unrealized gain in the other note. Rev. Rul. 2000–12, 2000–1 C.B. 744.

D. TAX SHELTER LOSSES

Investments in so-called tax shelters typically produce losses that can offset or "shelter" other income, such as wages, interest, or dividends that were neither produced by nor related to the income produced by the investment. A tax shelter combines various provisions of the Code to reduce taxes. In some cases, tax shelters result from tax benefits designed to encourage particular economic or social activities. In others, they result from basic structural provisions in the income tax system.

The materials that follow describe typical tax shelters and the methods used by the courts and Congress to combat their use. In the 1980s, tax shelters became ubiquitous and a significant percentage of the Tax Court's docket was tax shelter controversies. Because shelters threatened to undermine the tax base, Congress and the IRS began to wage war on shelters. The Service initially attacked transactions perceived to be without economic substance. When that failed to stem the tide, Congress responded with a variety of devices designed to limit tax shelter losses. After the 1986 Act, which contained a number of tax shelter limitations, the proliferation of shelters used by individuals abated. It is nevertheless useful to be familiar with the tax shelter phenomenon and the responses to it because the basic conflicts and structural issues remain and a study of tax shelters enables the student to perceive interrelationships within the Code and among seemingly discrete tax provisions. Finally, some of the issues that arose in connection with individual shelters have resurfaced in corporate tax shelters, which are discussed in Chapter 8, infra.

Note on Defining a Tax Shelter

Like pornography, a tax shelter is something that people know when they see it. The term has proved somewhat difficult to define, and whether an "abusive tax shelter" exists often depends upon who is watching.

Although the Code contains a number of technical tax shelter definitions, they all involve essentially the same characteristics. Tax shelters are passive investments; the investor typically is not actively involved in managing the activities. Tax shelter investments often are structured as limited partnerships in order to provide investors both the benefits of limited liability and conduit taxation (whereby the income and losses of the partnership are passed through to the partners). In general, a tax shelter may include any investment or transaction that produces a tax savings greater than that which would be appropriate given its economic income or loss. Tax shelter investments typically involve a mismatching of deductions and income to produce net losses that offset unrelated income. Alternatively, in some cases, the investment produces tax credits that shelter taxes that otherwise would be due on unrelated income.

Tax shelters have been grouped into two broad categories: (1) legitimate tax shelters and (2) abusive tax shelters. Legitimate tax shelters usually involve tax-favored investments clearly sanctioned by the tax laws, typically where tax benefits have been enacted expressly as incentives for particular activities (for example, oil exploration and real estate). In other cases, the result sought by taxpayers may be available under current law, but the tax preference is unintended.

Abusive tax shelters, on the other hand, typically involve transactions that, if the facts were known, would not be upheld in court. These investments enable taxpayers to take a reporting position for claiming deductions or credit that, while not ultimately allowable, may produce significant tax savings either because the return will not be examined by the IRS, or, if it is examined and the claimed deduction is disallowed, the tax will be deferred at a low interest cost. Abusive tax shelter investments are entered into primarily, if not exclusively, to reduce federal income tax liability. Often they yield negligible returns (and sometimes negative returns) before tax, but offer significant after-tax returns.

Tax shelters raise fairness concerns because they create horizontal inequities by permitting individuals with similar economic incomes to pay very different amounts of tax. They also decrease tax progressivity by reducing the tax burden of high income individuals. Tax shelters are inefficient because they often create incentives for taxpayers to engage in economically unproductive transactions. Even those activities that the government has sought to encourage through preferential tax treatment might be encouraged more effectively by alternative means, such as direct loans or subsidies. In addition, tax shelters may shift the ownership of certain assets from low-bracket individuals to high-bracket individuals who may be able to pay a higher price for assets. Because they can make better use of tax deductions, they may bid up the price of assets and force others out of business.

Finally, tax shelters are said to undermine taxpayer confidence in the fairness of the tax system and to encourage other forms of tax evasion and avoidance. When shelters proliferate, there are often calls for a more neutral tax system—one that is fairer and more economically efficient. Abusive tax shelter investments generate great concern among policymakers, enforcement officials, and taxpayers.

Note on Common Tax Shelter Techniques

Tax shelters rely on five basic techniques to reduce tax liability: income shifting, exemption, deferral, conversion, and leverage. (The last, in combination with exemption, deferral, or conversion, is often labeled arbitrage.) Each method is discussed in more detail elsewhere in this coursebook.

Income shifting involves structuring transactions to ensure that income, deductions, or credits are allocated among taxpayers in the manner that produces the lowest net tax liability. Generally, this means that deductions and credits are allocated to those in the highest brackets or to those who have offsetting income. Conversely, income is allocated to those in the lowest brackets, those who are tax-exempt, such as foreign taxpayers, or to those with expiring losses. Income shifting is explored at length in Chapter 4.

Furthermore, the income tax produces great incentives for undertaxed assets to be held by taxpayers subject to the highest marginal rates and for overtaxed assets, such as loans that produce taxable interest, to be held by low-bracket taxpayers and tax-exempt entities. Structural provisions of the Code, designed for a simpler era, allowed transactions to be planned to maximize arbitrage opportunities and thereby to achieve large tax savings.

Excessive or accelerated deductions create opportunities for taxpayers to have tax deductions that exceed current income from an investment. For example, during the 1980s, the tax savings generated by the combination of accelerated depreciation and the investment tax credit were likely to exceed the income produced by the asset in its early years. Profitable companies could use such tax losses to shelter other income, but new companies or companies with business losses were not able to use the increased deductions. Likewise, individuals with substantial amounts of unrelated income could use these deductions to shelter income, for example, when the losses were passed through to the individuals by a partnership.

Since the income tax is not refundable, taxable income is, in effect, a ceiling on the extent to which tax benefits can be obtained. One way to avoid that limitation is to sell the property to a taxpayer who can use all the tax benefits. In order to retain the ability to continue to use the property, the selling taxpayer would lease the property back. Because the rental payments generally were intended to cover all the purchaser's costs, the purchaser in a sale-leaseback was often merely purchasing tax benefits. The *Estate of Franklin* case, at page 211, supra, is an example of such a transaction. At one time, Congress provided for a fictionalized "safe-harbor leasing" of depreciable property that effectively sanctioned sales of the tax savings from depreciation and the investment tax credit by firms that could not benefit from them to firms that could. In response to the public outcry generated by widely publicized safe-harbor leases among major corporations, this provision was repealed. Taxpayers with unused losses, however, continued to use leasing to transfer benefits. The often tenuous distinction between a lender and an owner assumed overwhelming importance for tax purposes at the same time it was blurred for economic and legal purposes by new lending practices, especially equity participation.

Exemption involves receipt of economic income that is not subject to tax. Exemptions under current law include, for example, the exclusion of interest earned on state and local bonds, individual retirement accounts, and qualified employer pensions.

Deferral of tax from the current year to a future year is achieved by accelerating deductions and credits or by postponing recognition of income. Deferral often results from an investment that generates deductions in early years to offset unrelated income and that generates income, if at all, only in later years. For example, the taxpayer may take advantage of special provisions that allow the immediate deduction of capital expenditures that will produce income over a number of years.

Recall that the deferral of tax has been analogized to an interest-free loan from the government to the taxpayer. It also has been analogized to imposing tax currently but exempting from tax the earnings that are subsequently generated by investment of the amount that remains after tax. See the Note on Tax Deferral, supra at page 313.

Although Congress has attempted to curb the use of deferral by a variety of measures, major opportunities for deferral remain, for example, in the depreciation schedules for much equipment as well as in special provisions governing recovery of the costs of oil, gas, and mineral exploration and extraction.

Conversion of ordinary income into tax-preferred income typically is achieved where the investment generates both deductions against ordinary income and income that will be taxed at lower rates, for example, as long-term capital gains. This technique is discussed in Chapter 5.

Leverage is the use of borrowed funds to increase the size of deductible expenditures. The *Crane* rule, discussed supra at page 200, may allow the taxpayer to obtain deductions based not only on a cash investment but also on indebtedness incurred incident to the investment. For example, a taxpayer who is subject to income tax at a 37 percent rate makes a tax shelter investment of $100,000—$10,000 of his own funds and $90,000 in borrowed funds. If the investment produces a $40,000 tax loss in the first year, the taxpayer may save $14,800 in taxes on a $10,000 cash investment.

The ability to acquire large depreciation deductions for a comparatively small cash investment has long been an integral aspect of most tax shelters. The taxpayer may be able to use depreciation deductions on a large basis not only to offset any income from the property but also to offset unrelated income. Without borrowing, taxpayers may deduct only the amount of their investment; with borrowing, taxpayers may deduct much greater amounts and thereby recover their investments through tax savings in a short period of time. The tax cost of leverage is the gain to be realized from treating the unamortized mortgage balance as part of the amount realized when the investment is liquidated.

As discussed earlier in this chapter, the combination of leveraging and high deductions can even produce negative rates of tax. This point can be illustrated by an example that, for simplicity, uses immediate expensing of assets in lieu of other deductions.[16] Assume a tax rate of 40

---

[16] This example is derived from Alvin Warren & Alan Auerbach, "Transferability of Tax Incentives and the Fiction of Safe Harbor Leasing," 95 Harv.L. Rev. 1752 (1982); see also Calvin

percent, an interest rate of 10 percent, and a before-tax yield on investment of 10 percent. Without taxes, of course, there would be zero return from borrowing at 10 percent to finance an asset that yields 10 percent. In the current tax regime, however, assume the taxpayer borrows $60 to finance an investment of $100, which is immediately expensed for tax purposes. The $100 immediate deduction saves $40 in taxes, so the taxpayer has no out-of-pocket cost for the investment. From the $10 annual yield on the investment, he must pay interest of $6 and taxes of $1.60 ($10 income less $6 deductible interest leaves $4 taxable income taxed at 40 percent equals $1.60 taxes). This would leave him an annual after-tax return of $2.40 on a zero investment. Graduated rates further complicate the story but, in general, will tend to induce a concentration of tax-favored investments in the hands of upper-bracket taxpayers. Disallowing interest deductions would eliminate the profit in the above example. If the interest in the example were nondeductible, the tax would be $4 and the after-tax return zero ($4 of tax plus $6 of interest equal the $10 yield on the asset)—a result that we might expect given the taxpayer's out-of-pocket investment of zero. Note also, as indicated on page 226, supra, if the before-tax yield on the investment was reduced to 6 percent and the rate of interest on the loan remained 10 percent, the interest deduction would turn a pre-tax loss into a break-even investment after tax.

It is true that the taxpayer eventually may have to repay the loan or to recognize income from the cancellation of indebtedness. The present value of his loan, however, may be significantly less than the present value of his tax savings, especially if he is not obligated to make repayment until a date in the distant future. Moreover, the taxpayer may be able to deduct his interest payments—at least to the extent of his investment income—under § 163. The advantages of leverage are greatest where the taxpayer is not personally liable on the indebtedness. See the Note on Tax Arbitrage, supra at page 363.

Real estate is a good example of a tax shelter that often has combined the major tax shelter components: deferral, leverage, conversion of ordinary income into capital gain, and shifting of tax benefits to those who can best use them. Tax deferral was accomplished principally because the depreciation allowed for tax purposes was much more rapid than actual economic depreciation. Deductions were accelerated to a current year, while the investment was recovered (perhaps with some profit) in a subsequent taxable year. Real estate tax shelters were typically highly leveraged, i.e., a great percentage of the cost was financed with borrowed funds. This increased the taxpayer's basis for depreciation, which permitted deductions in excess of his equity in the property. These deductions often were converted into capital gains on a sale of the property, where the gain (the difference between the amount

Johnson, "Tax Shelter Gain: The Mismatch of Debt and Supply Side Depreciation," 61 Tex. L. Rev. 1013 (1983).

received and the depreciated basis) was eligible for preferential treatment. Shifting the tax benefit to investors who might best use them generally was accomplished through special partnership allocations or through sale-leaseback transactions.

1. JUDICIAL RESPONSE

Frank Lyon Co. v. United States
Supreme Court of the United States, 1978. 435 U.S. 561.

■ MR. JUSTICE BLACKMUN delivered the opinion of the Court.

This case concerns the federal income tax consequences of a sale-and-leaseback in which petitioner Frank Lyon Company (Lyon) took title to a building under construction by Worthen Bank & Trust Company (Worthen) of Little Rock, Ark., and simultaneously leased the building back to Worthen for long-term use as its headquarters and principal banking facility.

I

* * *

Lyon is a closely held Arkansas corporation engaged in the distribution of home furnishings, primarily Whirlpool and RCA electrical products. Worthen in 1965 was an Arkansas-chartered bank and a member of the Federal Reserve System. Frank Lyon was Lyon's majority shareholder and board chairman; he also served on Worthen's board. Worthen at that time began to plan the construction of a multistory bank and office building to replace its existing facility in Little Rock. About the same time Worthen's competitor, Union National Bank of Little Rock, also began to plan a new bank and office building. Adjacent sites on Capitol Avenue, separated only by Spring Street, were acquired by the two banks. It became a matter of competition, for both banking business and tenants, and prestige as to which bank would start and complete its building first.

Worthen initially hoped to finance, to build, and to own the proposed facility at a total cost of $9 million for the site, building, and adjoining parking deck. * * * Worthen's plan, however, had to be abandoned for two significant reasons:

  1. As a bank chartered under Arkansas law, Worthen legally could not pay more interest on any debentures it might issue than that specified by Arkansas law. But the proposed obligations would not be marketable at that rate.

  2. Applicable statutes or regulations of the Arkansas State Bank Department and the Federal Reserve System required Worthen, as a state bank subject to their supervision, to obtain prior permission for the investment in banking premises of any amount (including that placed in a real estate

subsidiary) in excess of the bank's capital stock or of 40% of its capital stock and surplus. * * * Worthen, accordingly, was advised by staff employees of the Federal Reserve System that they would not recommend approval of the plan by the System's Board of Governors.

Worthen therefore was forced to seek an alternative solution that would provide it with the use of the building, satisfy the state and federal regulators, and attract the necessary capital. In September 1967 it proposed a sale-and-leaseback arrangement. The State Bank Department and the Federal Reserve System approved this approach, but the Department required that Worthen possess an option to purchase the leased property at the end of the 15th year of the lease at a set price, and the federal regulator required that the building be owned by an independent third party.

Detailed negotiations ensued with investors that had indicated interest, namely, Goldman, Sachs & Company; White, Weld & Co.; Eastman Dillon; Union Securities & Company; and Stephens, Inc. Certain of these firms made specific proposals.

Worthen then obtained a commitment from New York Life Insurance Company to provide $7,140,000 in permanent mortgage financing on the building, conditioned upon its approval of the titleholder. At this point Lyon entered the negotiations and it, too, made a proposal. [Lyon was ultimately selected as the investor by Worthen and approved by the state and federal regulators, by First National City Bank for the construction financing, and by New York Life, as the permanent lender.]

In the meantime, on September 15, before Lyon was selected, Worthen itself began construction.

In May 1968 Worthen, Lyon, City Bank, and New York Life executed complementary and interlocking agreements under which the building was sold by Worthen to Lyon as it was constructed, and Worthen leased the completed building back from Lyon.

1.   Agreements between Worthen and Lyon. Worthen and Lyon executed a ground lease, a sales agreement, and a building lease.

Under the ground lease dated May 1, 1968, Worthen leased the site to Lyon for 76 years and 7 months through November 30, 2044. The first 19 months were the estimated construction period. The ground rents payable by Lyon to Worthen were $50 for the first 26 years and 7 months and thereafter in quarterly payments:

12/1/94 through 11/30/99	(5 years)—$100,000 annually
12/1/99 through 11/30/04	(5 years)—$150,000 annually
12/1/04 through 11/30/09	(5 years)—$200,000 annually

12/1/09 through 11/30/34   (25 years)—$250,000 annually

12/1/34 through 11/30/44   (10 years)—$ 10,000 annually.

Under the sales agreement dated May 19, * * *, Worthen agreed to sell the building to Lyon, and Lyon agreed to buy it, piece by piece as it was constructed, for a total price not to exceed $7,640,000, in reimbursements to Worthen for its expenditures for the construction of the building.

Under the building lease dated May 1, 1968, * * *, Lyon leased the building back to Worthen for a primary term of 25 years from December 1, 1969, with options in Worthen to extend the lease for eight additional 5-year terms, a total of 65 years. During the period between the expiration of the building lease (at the latest, November 30, 2034, if fully extended) and the end of the ground lease on November 30, 2044, full ownership, use, and control of the building were Lyon's, unless, of course, the building had been repurchased by Worthen * * *. Worthen was not obligated to pay rent under the building lease until completion of the building. For the first 11 years of the lease, that is, until November 30, 1980, the stated quarterly rent was $145,581.03 ($582,324.12 for the year). For the next 14 years, the quarterly rent was $153,289.32 ($613,157.28 for the year), and for the option periods the rent was $300,000 a year, payable quarterly * * *. The total rent for the building over the 25-year primary term of the lease thus was $14,989,767.24. That rent equaled the principal and interest payments that would amortize the $7,140,000 New York Life mortgage loan over the same period. When the mortgage was paid off at the end of the primary term, the annual building rent, if Worthen extended the lease, came down to the stated $300,000. Lyon's net rentals from the building would be further reduced by the increase in ground rent Worthen would receive from Lyon during the extension.[3]

The building lease was a "net lease," under which Worthen was responsible for all expenses usually associated with the maintenance of an office building, including repairs, taxes, utility charges, and insurance, and was to keep the premises in good condition, excluding, however, reasonable wear and tear.

Finally, under the lease, Worthen had the option to repurchase the building at the following times and prices:

---

[3] This, of course, is on the assumption that Worthen exercises its option to extend the building lease. If it does not, Lyon remains liable for the substantial rents prescribed by the ground lease. This possibility brings into sharp focus the fact that Lyon, in a very practical sense, is at least the ultimate owner of the building. If Worthen does not extend, the building lease expires and Lyon may do with the building as it chooses.

The Government would point out, however, that the net amounts payable by Worthen to Lyon during the building lease's extended terms, if all are claimed, would approximate the amount required to repay Lyon's $500,000 investment at 6% compound interest. Brief for United States 14.

> 11/30/80 (after 11 years)—$6,325,169.85
>
> 11/30/84 (after 15 years)—$5,432,607.32
>
> 11/30/89 (after 20 years)—$4,187,328.04
>
> 11/30/94 (after 25 years)—$2,145,935.00

These repurchase option prices were the sum of the unpaid balance of the New York Life mortgage, Lyon's $500,000 investment, and 6% interest compounded on that investment.

2.   Construction financing agreement. By agreement dated May 14, 1968, * * * City Bank agreed to lend Lyon $7,000,000 for the construction of the building. This loan was secured by a mortgage on the building and the parking deck, executed by Worthen as well as by Lyon, and an assignment by Lyon of its interests in the building lease and in the ground lease.

3.   Permanent financing agreement. By Note Purchase Agreement dated May 1, 1968, * * * New York Life agreed to purchase Lyon's $7,140,000 6¾% 25-year secured note to be issued upon completion of the building. Under this agreement Lyon warranted that it would lease the building to Worthen for a noncancelable term of at least 25 years under a net lease at a rent at least equal to the mortgage payments on the note. Lyon agreed to make quarterly payments of principal and interest equal to the rentals payable by Worthen during the corresponding primary term of the lease. The security for the note was a first deed of trust and Lyon's assignment of its interests in the building lease and in the ground lease. * * * Worthen joined in the deed of trust as the owner of the fee and the parking deck.

In December 1969 the building was completed and Worthen took possession. At that time Lyon received the permanent loan from New York Life, and it discharged the interim loan from City Bank. The actual cost of constructing the office building and parking complex (excluding the cost of the land) exceeded $10,000,000.

Lyon filed its federal income tax returns on the accrual and calendar year basis. On its 1969 return, Lyon accrued rent from Worthen for December. It asserted as deductions one month's interest to New York Life; one month's depreciation on the building; interest on the construction loan from City Bank; and sums for legal and other expenses incurred in connection with the transaction.

On audit of Lyon's 1969 return, the Commissioner of Internal Revenue determined that Lyon was "not the owner for tax purposes of any portion of the Worthen Building," and ruled that "the income and expenses related to this building are not allowable * * * for Federal income tax purposes." * * * He also added $2,298.15 to Lyon's 1969 income as "accrued interest income." This was the computed 1969 portion of a gain, considered the equivalent of interest income, the realization of which was based on the assumption that Worthen would exercise its option to buy the building after 11 years, on November 30, 1980, at the price stated in the lease, and on the additional determination that Lyon had "loaned" $500,000 to Worthen. In other words, the Commissioner determined that the sale-and-leaseback arrangement was a financing transaction in which Lyon loaned Worthen $500,000 and acted as a conduit for the transmission of principal and interest from Worthen to New York Life.

* * *

After trial without a jury, the District Court, in a memorandum letter-opinion setting forth findings and conclusions, ruled in Lyon's favor and held that its claimed deductions were allowable. * * * It concluded that the legal intent of the parties had been to create a bona fide sale-and-leaseback in accordance with the form and language of the documents evidencing the transactions. It rejected the argument that Worthen was acquiring an equity in the building through its rental payments. It found that the rents were unchallenged and were reasonable throughout the period of the lease, and that the option prices, negotiated at arm's length between the parties, represented fair estimates of market value on the applicable dates. It rejected any negative inference from the fact that the rentals, combined with the options, were sufficient to amortize the New York Life loan and to pay Lyon a 6% return on its equity investment. It found that Worthen would acquire an equity in the building only if it exercised one of its options to purchase, and that it was highly unlikely, as a practical matter, that any purchase option would ever be exercised. It rejected any inference to be drawn from the fact that the lease was a "net lease." It found that Lyon had mixed motivations for entering into the transaction, including the need to diversify as well as the desire to have the benefits of a "tax shelter."

The United States Court of Appeals for the Eighth Circuit reversed. 536 F.2d 746 (1976). It held that the Commissioner correctly determined that Lyon was not the true owner of the building and therefore was not entitled to the claimed deductions. It likened ownership for tax purposes to a "bundle of sticks" and undertook its own evaluation of the facts. It concluded, in agreement with the Government's contention, that Lyon "totes an empty bundle" of ownership sticks. * * * It stressed the following: (a) The lease agreements circumscribed Lyon's right to profit from its investment in the building by giving Worthen the option to purchase for an amount equal to Lyon's $500,000 equity plus 6% compound interest and the assumption of the unpaid balance of the New York Life mortgage.[5] (b) The option prices did not take into account

---

[5] Lyon here challenges this assertion on the grounds that it had the right and opportunities to sell the building at a greater profit at any time; the return to Lyon was not insubstantial and was attractive to a true investor in real estate; the 6% return was the minimum Lyon would realize if Worthen exercised one of its options, an event the District Court

possible appreciation of the value of the building or inflation.[6] (c) Any award realized as a result of destruction or condemnation of the building in excess of the mortgage balance and the $500,000 would be paid to Worthen and not Lyon.[7] (d) The building rental payments during the primary term were exactly equal to the mortgage payments.[8] (e) Worthen retained control over the ultimate disposition of the building through its various options to repurchase and to renew the lease plus its ownership of the site.[9] (f) Worthen enjoyed all benefits and bore all burdens incident to the operation and ownership of the building so that, in the Court of Appeals' view, the only economic advantages accruing to Lyon, in the event it were considered to be the true owner of the property, were income tax savings of approximately $1.5 million during the first 11 years of the arrangement.[10] Id. * * *[11] The court concluded * * *, that the transaction was "closely akin" to that in Helvering v. Lazarus & Co., 308 U.S. 252 (1939). "In sum, the benefits, risks, and burdens which [Lyon] has incurred with respect to the Worthen building are simply too insubstantial to establish a claim to the status of owner for tax purposes. * * * The vice of the present lease is that all of [its] features have been employed in the same transaction with the cumulative effect of depriving [Lyon] of any significant ownership interest." 536 F.2d at 754.

---

found highly unlikely; and Lyon would own the building and realize a greater return than 6% if Worthen did not exercise an option to purchase.

[6]   Lyon challenges this observation by pointing out that the District Court found the option prices to be the negotiated estimate of the parties of the fair market value of the building on the option dates and to be reasonable. * * *

[7]   Lyon asserts that this statement is true only with respect to the total destruction or taking of the building on or after December 1, 1980. Lyon asserts that it, not Worthen, would receive the excess above the mortgage balance in the event of total destruction or taking before December 1, 1980, or in the event of partial damage or taking at any time. Id., at 408–410, 411.

[8]   Lyon concedes the accuracy of this statement, but asserts that it does not justify the conclusion that Lyon served merely as a conduit by which mortgage payments would be transmitted to New York Life. It asserts that Lyon was the sole obligor on the New York Life note and would remain liable in the event of default by Worthen. It also asserts that the fact the rent was sufficient to amortize the loan during the primary term of the lease was a requirement imposed by New York Life, and is a usual requirement in most long-term loans secured by a long-term lease.

[9]   As to this statement, Lyon asserts that the Court of Appeals ignored Lyon's right to sell the building to another at any time; the District Court's finding that the options to purchase were not likely to be exercised; the uncertainty that Worthen would renew the lease for 40 years; Lyon's right to lease to anyone at any price during the last 10 years of the ground lease; and Lyon's continuing ownership of the building after the expiration of the ground lease.

[10]   In response to this, Lyon asserts that the District Court found that the benefits of occupancy Worthen will enjoy are common in most long-term real estate leases, and that the District Court found that Lyon had motives other than tax savings in entering into the transaction. It also asserts that the net cash after-tax benefit would be $312,220, not $1.5 million.

[11]   Other factors relied on by the Court of Appeals, 536 F.2d, at 752, were the allocation of the investment credit to Worthen, and a claim that Lyon's ability to sell the building to a third party was "carefully circumscribed" by the lease agreements. The investment credit by statute is freely allocable between the parties, § 48(d) of the 1954 Code, 26 U.S.C.A. § 48(d), and the Government has not pressed either of these factors before this Court.

We granted certiorari, 429 U.S. 1089 (1977), because of an indicated conflict with American Realty Trust v. United States, 498 F.2d 1194 (C.A.4 1974).

II

This Court, almost 50 years ago, observed that "taxation is not so much concerned with the refinements of title as it is with actual command over the property taxed—the actual benefit for which the tax is paid." Corliss v. Bowers, 281 U.S. 376, 378 (1930). In a number of cases, the Court has refused to permit the transfer of formal legal title to shift the incidence of taxation attributable to ownership of property where the transferor continues to retain significant control over the property transferred. E.g., Commissioner v. Sunnen, 333 U.S. 591 (1948); Helvering v. Clifford, 309 U.S. 331 (1940). In applying this doctrine of substance over form, the Court has looked to the objective economic realities of a transaction rather than to the particular form the parties employed. * * * Nor is the parties' desire to achieve a particular tax result necessarily relevant. * * *

In the light of these general and established principles, the Government takes the position that the Worthen-Lyon transaction in its entirety should be regarded as a sham. The agreement as a whole, it is said, was only an elaborate financing scheme designed to provide economic benefits to Worthen and a guaranteed return to Lyon. The latter was but a conduit used to forward the mortgage payments, made under the guise of rent paid by Worthen to Lyon, on to New York Life as mortgagee. This, the Government claims, is the true substance of the transaction as viewed under the microscope of the tax laws. Although the arrangement was cast in sale-and-leaseback form, in substance it was only a financing transaction, and the terms of the repurchase options and lease renewals so indicate. It is said that Worthen could reacquire the building simply by satisfying the mortgage debt and paying Lyon its $500,000 advance plus interest, regardless of the fair market value of the building at the time; similarly, when the mortgage was paid off, Worthen could extend the lease at drastically reduced bargain rentals that likewise bore no relation to fair rental value but were simply calculated to pay Lyon its $500,000 plus interest over the extended term. Lyon's return on the arrangement in no event could exceed 6% compound interest (although the Government conceded it might well be less * * *). Furthermore, the favorable option and lease renewal terms made it highly unlikely that Worthen would abandon the building after it in effect had "paid off" the mortgage. The Government implies that the arrangement was one of convenience which, if accepted on its face, would enable Worthen to deduct its payments to Lyon as rent and would allow Lyon to claim a deduction for depreciation, based on the cost of construction ultimately borne by Worthen, which Lyon could offset against other income, and to deduct mortgage interest that roughly would offset the inclusion of Worthen's rental payments in Lyon's income.

If, however, the Government argues, the arrangement was only a financing transaction under which Worthen was the owner of the building, Worthen's payments would be deductible only to the extent that they represented mortgage interest, and Worthen would be entitled to claim depreciation; Lyon would not be entitled to deductions for either mortgage interest or depreciation and it would not have to include Worthen's "rent" payments in its income because its function with respect to those payments was that of a conduit between Worthen and New York Life.

The Government places great reliance on Helvering v. Lazarus & Co., supra, and claims it to be precedent that controls this case. The taxpayer there was a department store. The legal title of its three buildings was in a bank as trustee for land-trust certificate holders. When the transfer to the trustee was made, the trustee at the same time leased the buildings back to the taxpayer for 99 years, with option to renew and purchase. The Commissioner, in stark contrast to his posture in the present case, took the position that the statutory right to depreciation followed legal title. The Board of Tax Appeals, however, concluded that the transaction between the taxpayer and the bank in reality was a mortgage loan and allowed the taxpayer depreciation on the buildings. This Court, as had the Court of Appeals, agreed with that conclusion and affirmed. It regarded the "rent" stipulated in the leaseback as a promise to pay interest on the loan, and a "depreciation fund" required by the lease as an amortization fund designed to pay off the loan in the stated period. Thus, said the Court, the Board justifiably concluded that the transaction, although in written form a transfer of ownership with a leaseback, was actually a loan secured by the property involved.

The *Lazarus* case, we feel, is to be distinguished from the present one and is not controlling here. Its transaction was one involving only two (and not multiple) parties, the taxpayer-department store and the trustee-bank. The Court looked closely at the substance of the agreement between those two parties and rightly concluded that depreciation was deductible by the taxpayer despite the nomenclature of the instrument of conveyance and the leaseback. See also Sun Oil Co. v. Commissioner, 562 F.2d 258 (C.A.3 1977) (a two-party case with the added feature that the second party was a tax-exempt pension trust).

The present case, in contrast, involves three parties, Worthen, Lyon, and the finance agency. The usual simple two-party arrangement was legally unavailable to Worthen. Independent investors were interested in participating in the alternative available to Worthen, and Lyon itself (also independent from Worthen) won the privilege. Despite Frank Lyon's presence on Worthen's board of directors, the transaction, as it ultimately developed, was not a familial one arranged by Worthen, but one compelled by the realities of the restrictions imposed upon the bank. Had Lyon not appeared, another interested investor would have been selected. The ultimate solution would have been essentially the same. Thus, the presence of the third party, in our view, significantly distinguishes this case from *Lazarus* and removes the latter as controlling authority.

III

It is true, of course, that the transaction took shape according to Worthen's needs. As the Government points out, Worthen throughout the negotiations regarded the respective proposals of the independent investors in terms of its own cost of funds. * * * It is also true that both Worthen and the prospective investors compared the various proposals in terms of the return anticipated on the investor's equity. But all this is natural for parties contemplating entering into a transaction of this kind. Worthen needed a building for its banking operations and other purposes and necessarily had to know what its cost would be. The investors were in business to employ their funds in the most remunerative way possible. And, as the Court has said in the past, a transaction must be given its effect in accord with what actually occurred and not in accord with what might have occurred. * * *

There is no simple device available to peel away the form of this transaction and to reveal its substance. The effects of the transaction on all the parties were obviously different from those that would have resulted had Worthen been able simply to make a mortgage agreement with New York Life and to receive a $500,000 loan from Lyon. Then *Lazarus* would apply. Here, however, and most significantly, it was Lyon alone, and not Worthen, who was liable on the notes, first to City Bank, and then to New York Life. Despite the facts that Worthen had agreed to pay rent and that this rent equaled the amounts due from Lyon to New York Life, should anything go awry in the later years of the lease, Lyon was primarily liable. No matter how the transaction could have been devised otherwise, it remains a fact that as the agreements were placed in final form, the obligation on the notes fell squarely on Lyon. Lyon, an ongoing enterprise, exposed its very business well-being to this real and substantial risk.

The effect of this liability on Lyon is not just the abstract possibility that something will go wrong and that Worthen will not be able to make its payments. Lyon has disclosed this liability on its balance sheet for all the world to see. Its financial position was affected substantially by the presence of this long-term debt, despite the offsetting presence of the building as an asset. To the extent that Lyon has used its capital in this transaction, it is less able to obtain financing for other business needs.

In concluding that there is this distinct element of economic reality in Lyon's assumption of liability, we are mindful that the characterization of a transaction for financial accounting purposes, on the one hand, and for tax purposes, on the other, need not necessarily be the same. * * * But in this case accepted accounting methods, as understood by the several parties to the respective agreements and as

416 DEDUCTIONS AND CREDITS   CHAPTER 3

applied to the transaction by others, gave the transaction a meaningful character consonant with the form it was given. Worthen was not allowed to enter into the type of transaction which the Government now urges to be the true substance of the arrangement. Lyon and Worthen cannot be said to have entered into the transaction intending that the interests involved were allocated in a way other than that associated with a sale-and-leaseback.

Other factors also reveal that the transaction cannot be viewed as anything more than a mortgage agreement between Worthen and New York Life and a loan from Lyon to Worthen. There is no legal obligation between Lyon and Worthen representing the $500,000 "loan" extended under the Government's theory. And the assumed 6% return on this putative loan—required by the audit to be recognized in the taxable year in question—will be realized only when and if Worthen exercises its options.

The Court of Appeals acknowledged that the rents alone, due after the primary term of the lease and after the mortgage has been paid, do not provide the simple 6% return which, the Government urges, Lyon is guaranteed. * * * Thus, if Worthen chooses not to exercise its options, Lyon is gambling that the rental value of the building during the last 10 years of the ground lease, during which the ground rent is minimal, will be sufficient to recoup its investment before it must negotiate again with Worthen regarding the ground lease. There are simply too many contingencies, including variations in the value of real estate, in the cost of money, and in the capital structure of Worthen, to permit the conclusion that the parties intended to enter into the transaction as structured in the audit and according to which the Government now urges they be taxed.

It is not inappropriate to note that the Government is likely to lose little revenue, if any, as a result of the shape given the transaction by the parties. No deduction was created that is not either matched by an item of income or that would not have been available to one of the parties if the transaction had been arranged differently. While it is true that Worthen paid Lyon less to induce it to enter into the transaction because Lyon anticipated the benefit of the depreciation deductions it would have as the owner of the building, those deductions would have been equally available to Worthen had it retained title to the building. The Government so concedes. * * * The fact that favorable tax consequences were taken into account by Lyon on entering into the transaction is no reason for disallowing those consequences.[15] We cannot ignore the reality that the tax laws affect the shape of nearly every business transaction.

---

[15] Indeed, it is not inevitable that the transaction, as treated by Lyon and Worthen, will not result in more revenues to the Government rather than less. Lyon is gambling that in the first 11 years of the lease it will have income that will be sheltered by the depreciation deductions, and that it will be able to make sufficiently good use of the tax dollars preserved thereby to make up for the income it will recognize and pay taxes on during the last 14 years of the initial term of the lease and against which it will enjoy no sheltering deduction.

* * * Lyon is not a corporation with no purpose other than to hold title to the bank building. It was not created by Worthen or even financed to any degree by Worthen.

The conclusion that the transaction is not a simple sham to be ignored does not, of course, automatically compel the further conclusion that Lyon is entitled to the items claimed as deductions. Nevertheless, on the facts, this readily follows. As has been noted, the obligations on which Lyon paid interest were its obligations alone, and it is entitled to claim deductions therefor under § 163(a) * * *.

As is clear from the facts, none of the parties to this sale and-leaseback was the owner of the building in any simple sense. But it is equally clear that the facts focus upon Lyon as the one whose capital was committed to the building and as the party, therefore, that was entitled to claim depreciation for the consumption of that capital. The Government has based its contention that Worthen should be treated as the owner on the assumption that throughout the term of the lease Worthen was acquiring an equity in the property. In order to establish the presence of that growing equity, however, the Government is forced to speculate that one of the options will be exercised and that, if it is not, this is only because the rentals for the extended term are a bargain. We cannot indulge in such speculation in view of the District Court's clear finding to the contrary. We therefore conclude that it is Lyon's capital that is invested in the building according to the agreement of the parties, and it is Lyon that is entitled to depreciation deductions, under § 167 * * *.

IV

We recognize that the Government's position, and that taken by the Court of Appeals, is not without superficial appeal. One, indeed, may theorize that Frank Lyon's presence on the Worthen board of directors; Lyon's departure from its principal corporate activity into this unusual venture; the parallel between the payments under the building lease and the amounts due from Lyon on the New York Life mortgage; the provisions relating to condemnation or destruction of the property; the nature and presence of the several options available to Worthen; and the tax benefits, such as the use of double declining balance depreciation, that accrue to Lyon during the initial years of the arrangement, form the basis of an argument that Worthen should be regarded as the owner of the building and as the recipient of nothing more from Lyon than a $500,000 loan.

We, however, as did the District Court, find this theorizing incompatible with the substance and economic realities of the transaction: the competitive situation as it existed between Worthen and Union National Bank in 1965 and the years immediately following; Worthen's undercapitalization; Worthen's consequent inability, as a matter of legal restraint, to carry its building plans into effect by a conventional mortgage and other borrowing; the additional barriers imposed by the state and federal regulators; the suggestion, forthcoming from the state regulator, that Worthen possess an option to purchase; the requirement, from the federal regulator, that the building be owned by an independent third party; the presence of several finance organizations seriously interested in participating in the transaction and in the resolution of Worthen's problem; the submission of formal proposals by several of those organizations; the bargaining process and period that ensued; the competitiveness of the bidding; the bona fide character of the negotiations; the three-party aspect of the transaction; Lyon's substantiality and its independence from Worthen; the fact that diversification was Lyon's principal motivation; Lyon's being liable alone on the successive notes to City Bank and New York Life; the reasonableness, as the District Court found, of the rentals and of the option prices; the substantiality of the purchase prices; Lyon's not being engaged generally in the business of financing; the presence of all building depreciation risks on Lyon; the risk, born by Lyon, that Worthen might default or fail, as other banks have failed; the facts that Worthen could "walk away" from the relationship at the end of the 25-year primary term, and probably would do so if the option price were more than the then-current worth of the building to Worthen; the inescapable fact that if the building lease were not extended, Lyon would be the full owner of the building, free to do with it as it chose; Lyon's liability for the substantial ground rent if Worthen decides not to exercise any of its options to extend; the absence of any understanding between Lyon and Worthen that Worthen would exercise any of the purchase options; the nonfamily and nonprivate nature of the entire transaction; and the absence of any differential in tax rates and of special tax circumstances for one of the parties—all convince us that Lyon has far the better of the case.[18]

In so concluding, we emphasize that we are not condoning manipulation by a taxpayer through arbitrary labels and dealings that have no economic significance. Such, however, has not happened in this case.

In short, we hold that where, as here, there is a genuine multiple-party transaction with economic substance which is compelled or encouraged by business or regulatory realities, is imbued with tax-independent considerations, and is not shaped solely by tax-avoidance features that have meaningless labels attached, the Government should honor the allocation of rights and duties effectuated by the parties. Expressed another way, so long as the lessor retains significant and

---

[18] Thus, the facts of this case stand in contrast to many others in which the form of the transaction actually created tax advantages that, for one reason or another, could not have been enjoyed had the transaction taken another form. See, e.g., Sun Oil Co. v. Commissioner, 562 F.2d 258 (C.A.3 1977) (sale-and-leaseback of land between taxpayer and tax-exempt trust enabled the taxpayer to amortize, through its rental deductions, the cost of acquiring land not otherwise depreciable). Indeed, the arrangements in this case can hardly be labeled as tax-avoidance techniques in light of the other arrangements being promoted at the time.

genuine attributes of the traditional lessor status, the form of the transaction adopted by the parties governs for tax purposes. What those attributes are in any particular case will necessarily depend upon its facts. It suffices to say that, as here, a sale-and-leaseback, in and of itself, does not necessarily operate to deny a taxpayer's claim for deductions.

The judgment of the Court of Appeals, accordingly, is reversed.

It is so ordered.

■ MR. JUSTICE WHITE dissents and would affirm the judgment substantially for the reasons stated in the opinion in the Court of Appeals for the Eighth Circuit. 536 F.2d 746 (1976).

■ MR. JUSTICE STEVENS, dissenting.

In my judgment the controlling issue in this case is the economic relationship between Worthen and petitioner, and matters such as the number of parties, their reasons for structuring the transaction in a particular way, and the tax benefits which may result, are largely irrelevant. The question whether a leasehold has been created should be answered by examining the character and value of the purported lessor's reversionary estate.

For a 25-year period Worthen has the power to acquire full ownership of the bank building by simply repaying the amounts, plus interest, advanced by the New York Life Insurance Company and petitioner. During that period, the economic relationship among the parties parallels exactly the normal relationship between an owner and two lenders, one secured by a first mortgage and the other by a second mortgage. If Worthen repays both loans, it will have unencumbered ownership of the property. What the character of this relationship suggests is confirmed by the economic value that the parties themselves have placed on the reversionary interest.

All rental payments made during the original 25-year term are credited against the option repurchase price, which is exactly equal to the unamortized cost of the financing. The value of the repurchase option is thus limited to the cost of the financing, and Worthen's power to exercise the option is cost-free. Conversely, petitioner, the nominal owner of the reversionary estate, is not entitled to receive *any* value for the surrender of its supposed rights of ownership. Nor does it have any power to control Worthen's exercise of the option.

"It is fundamental that 'depreciation is not predicated upon ownership of property *but rather upon an investment in property.*' No such investment exists when payments of the purchase price in accordance with the design of the parties yield no equity to the purchaser." Estate of Franklin v. Commissioner, 544 F.2d 1045, 1049 (C.A.9 1976) (citations omitted; emphasis in original). Here, the petitioner has, in effect, been guaranteed that it will receive its original $500,000 plus accrued interest. But that is all. It incurs neither the risk of depreciation,[4] nor the benefit of possible appreciation. Under the terms of the sale-leaseback, it will stand in no better or worse position after the 11th year of the lease—when Worthen can first exercise its option to repurchase—whether the property has appreciated or depreciated.[5] And this remains true throughout the rest of the 25-year period.

Petitioner has assumed only two significant risks. First, like any other lender, it assumed the risk of Worthen's insolvency. Second, it assumed the risk that Worthen might *not* exercise its option to purchase at or before the end of the original 25-year term.[6] If Worthen should exercise that right *not* to repay, perhaps it would *then* be appropriate to characterize petitioner as the owner and Worthen as the lessee. But speculation as to what might happen in 25 years cannot justify the *present* characterization of petitioner as the owner of the building. Until Worthen has made a commitment either to exercise or not to exercise its option, I think the Government is correct in its view that petitioner is not the owner of the building for tax purposes. At present, since Worthen has the unrestricted right to control the residual value of the property for a price which does not exceed the cost of its unamortized financing, I would hold, as a matter of law, that it is the owner.

I therefore respectfully dissent.

NOTES

(A) *Determining the Owner.* As *Frank Lyon* illustrates, many tax consequences (for example, who gets depreciation deductions) turn on who is the owner of the property. It is often difficult to determine the owner for tax purposes, particularly of property that is subject to an arrangement that the parties have characterized as a lease. The Service and the courts traditionally have attempted to distinguish between true leases, whereby the lessor owns the property for tax purposes, and conditional sales or financing arrangements, whereby the user of the property is the owner for tax purposes. The rules for making this distinction are not in the Code, but rather are contained in a series of revenue rulings, revenue procedures, and court decisions.

---

[4] Petitioner argues that it bears the risk of depreciation during the primary term of the lease, because the option price decreases over time. This is clearly incorrect. Petitioner will receive $500,000 plus interest, and no more or less, whether the option is exercised as soon as possible or only at the end of 25 years. Worthen, on the other hand, does bear the risk of depreciation, since its opportunity to make a profit from the exercise of its repurchase option hinges on the value of the building at the time.

[5] After the 11th year of the lease, there are three ways that the lease might be terminated. The property might be condemned, the building might be destroyed by act of God, or Worthen might exercise its option to purchase. In any such event, if the property had increased in value, the entire benefit would be received by Worthen and petitioner would receive only its $500,000 plus interest.

[6] The possibility that Worthen might not exercise its option is a risk for petitioner because in that event petitioner's advance would be amortized during the ensuing renewal lease terms, totaling 40 years. Yet there is a possibility that Worthen would choose not to renew for the full 40 years or that the burdens of owning a building and paying a ground rental of $10,000 during the years 2034 through 2044 would exceed the benefits of ownership.

Consider first the various factors that established—at least to the satisfaction of the Supreme Court—that the transaction in *Frank Lyon* was not a loan but a sale (followed by a leaseback). For example, what is the significance to this inquiry of the existence of competing bids on the acquisition of the building? Might not the parties have been competing only for the tax benefits incident to ownership of the building?

Of what importance is the fact that there were three parties to the transaction rather than only two? It is difficult to understand why the result should have differed if Lyon had possessed sufficient resources to construct the building without the assistance of New York Life. This distinction would appear to be relevant only in cases such as *Estate of Franklin,* supra at page 211, where the valuation of the property is an important issue.

What of the distant possibility that Worthen would go bankrupt or refuse to renew its lease in future years? Do not these risks assumed by Lyon more closely resemble those typically assumed by a lender of money rather than by a buyer of property? Does the Court do an adequate job of distinguishing the economic risks of an owner from those of a lender, such as a holder of a second mortgage? Is there any other way to separate the "substance" from the "form" of the transactions?

Note that the Court found support for its decision in the fact that "the Government is likely to lose little revenue" because the deductions taken by Lyon "would have been equally available to Worthen had it retained title to the building." Does this argue for a different result if Worthen and Lyon were taxed at different marginal rates? Perhaps if Worthen were tax-exempt because of operating losses? Consider also the following comment:

> One might say that Worthen and Lyon were in the same tax circumstances because both corporations were subject to the same schedule of tax rates under § 11 of the Internal Revenue Code. But that would be misleading. Worthen was in a "special tax circumstance" because it was a commercial bank. Commercial banks comprise the only class of taxpayers permitted to deduct the interest expenses incurred in holding state and local bonds that yield tax-exempt interest income. * * * [W]ithin limits commercial banks like Worthen can predict their taxable income, and they can alter it by shifting their mix of taxable and tax-exempt investments, while Lyon and other ordinary business corporations are less free to do so. Commercial banks can keep their taxable income below the level at which the maximum statutory rate (48 percent at the time of the Lyon-Worthen transaction) becomes applicable by carefully managing their investment portfolios. * * * It is not credible that Worthen and Lyon * * * were unaware of their differing tax needs and the way each might be helpful to the other at the expense of only the United States Treasury.

Bernard Wolfman, "The Supreme Court in the *Lyon*'s Den," 66 Cornell L. Rev. 1075, 1095–96, 1098 (1981).

The IRS has relied less on the form, and more on the substance of the transaction to determine who is the owner of property for tax purposes. A purported lease is required to have economic substance aside from the transfer of tax benefits.

In general, the owner of property must possess meaningful burdens and benefits of ownership as determined by the facts and circumstances. This inquiry focuses on which party experiences gains, or losses, when the property fluctuates in value. Thus, lease treatment may be denied, and the lessee will be treated as the owner, if the lessee has the option to acquire the property at the end of the lease for a price that is small in relation to the total lease payments or to the value of the property at the time the option is exercisable. In such cases, the lessor will be viewed as having transferred full ownership of the property in exchange for the rental payments because of the likelihood that the lessee will exercise the option. The IRS has issued two revenue procedures—Rev. Proc. 2001–28, 2001–1 C.B. 1156, and Rev. Proc. 2001–29, 2001–1 C.B. 1160—to provide objective guidelines for structuring leveraged leases of personal property. The courts, however, as *Frank Lyon* indicates, have not been as rigid as the IRS is in requiring a lessor to bear the economic burdens and benefits of ownership to qualify as an "owner" for tax purposes.

(B) *Subsequent Developments.* We have attempted to discover what happened to this bank building in the years since the Court's decision, but have had only limited success. Upon inquiry, the Pulaski County Clerk's office was unable to locate even the original transfer from Worthen to Frank Lyon Company. A clue that Worthen had exercised its option before the end of the first 25 years is provided by the fact that New York Life released its mortgage three months before the final option date in 1994. We know that Worthen changed its name to Boatmen's and acquired its competitor Union National Bank. By 1998 at the latest, Worthen owned the building which it sold to Argora Properties that year. Argora in 2003 sold it to SVP West Capital, which in 2006 sold it to 200 West Capitol for $10.2 million. We have had difficulty learning the building's history before 1998. We do know, however, that like many regional banks, Boatmen's was acquired by Nationsbank, which was itself acquired by Bank of America. So, if you are ever in Little Rock. . .

2.   SECTION 183

The IRS employed the limitations of § 183 (for deductions of losses on activities "not engaged in for profit") in its efforts to shut down tax shelters. For example, in Brannen v. Commissioner, 722 F.2d 695 (11th Cir. 1984), the court applied the multi-factor test of the § 183 regulations (see the *Storey* case supra at page 385) to disallow losses claimed by a doctor on an investment in a movie tax shelter partnership. Dr. Brannen had invested $20,000 for a promised $43,000 tax savings with respect to a movie aptly titled "Beyond the Law," a poorly dubbed "spaghetti western." The film opened and played briefly at the Red River Drive-In in Lubbock, Texas and showed also at other theaters in Texas, North Carolina, and South Carolina, but did not enjoy the protections of a U.S. copyright. The partnership had claimed depreciation deductions (and resulting losses) of $1,730,000 on the film, which earned a total of $17,180.02 in income.

Although the Service won a number of hobby loss decisions in addition to *Brannen*, § 183 did not prove to be an effective weapon against tax shelters. Inquiries into profit motive tend to turn on the particular facts of the case, and taxpayers were willing to try to prove that they had the requisite profit motive. Ultimately, § 183 did little or nothing to stem the tide of tax shelter litigation.

3.   THE "AT-RISK" LIMITATION OF SECTION 465

The advantages of leverage are greatest where the taxpayer is not personally liable on the indebtedness. By using nonrecourse debt, a tax shelter investment may produce tax losses (often from large depreciation deductions) for taxpayers who invest little of their own money in an asset and bear little genuine economic risk of loss.

The size of the tax benefit is exaggerated if the value of the property (and therefore the amount of the loan) is overstated. As previously noted, the IRS had been successful in disallowing deductions on investments financed with nonrecourse debt on the grounds that the purchase price was too inflated to permit the nominal buyer to obtain actual ownership of the property or that the debt was too contingent. See, e.g. *Estate of Franklin v. Commissioner*, supra at page 211. Because of the difficulty of making a careful inquiry as to value on a case-by-case basis and because nonrecourse debt made shelters attractive even where the value was not inflated, Congress decided to try a statutory attack.

Opportunities to obtain tax losses through nonrecourse financing were severely curtailed by the enactment of § 465. This provision allows the taxpayer to deduct losses on an investment only in the amount "at risk" with respect to that investment. § 465(a). A taxpayer is considered "at risk" only to the extent of (1) his investment of cash in the activity, (2) the adjusted basis of property contributed, (3) debt on which he is personally liable for repayment, and (4) the net fair market value of his personal assets that secure nonrecourse borrowings (apart from the investment). The taxpayer is not considered at risk with respect to losses for which he is guaranteed reimbursement. § 465(b). Deductions reduce the amount the taxpayer is considered to have at risk. If deductions and/or a decrease in the value of the collateral reduce the at-risk figure below zero, the taxpayer must recapture his deductions by including an offsetting amount in income. § 465(e).

Section 465 initially was limited to farming, oil and gas, motion pictures, and equipment leasing, but later was extended to all investments. The limitation applies to real estate activities as well, except for certain loans from parties actively engaged in the financing business, such as commercial banks. See § 465(b)(6).

Section 465 does not directly change the *Crane* rule and thus does not prohibit the inclusion of nonrecourse debt in basis. Rather, it limits loss deductions (including those due to depreciation) from the property to the amount the owner has at risk. Needless to say, § 465 inspired many creative tax plans to convert nonrecourse liabilities into loans where the taxpayer was considered "at risk" and even led to much substitution of recourse for nonrecourse financing.

4.   THE "PASSIVE LOSS" LIMITATION OF SECTION 469

When administrative and judicial efforts and various statutory provisions, including new penalties and compliance measures enacted in 1982 and 1984, failed to stem the tide of tax shelters, Congress responded in the 1986 Act with an extremely broad-based attack that limits the deduction of losses from "passive activities." This section was intended primarily to preclude taxpayers from using losses derived from tax shelter investments to reduce taxes on earned income and on investment income, such as interest and dividends. The passive loss rules are very complex, but they have been quite successful in shutting down tax shelters marketed to individuals. Since, despite its complexity, the statute does not define many of the critical statutory concepts, the regulations are extremely important.

The Mechanics. Section 469 provides that aggregate deductions from "passive activities" may be used only to offset the aggregate income from these activities. Passive activity losses in excess of passive activity income are not deductible, but may be carried forward to offset passive activity income of subsequent years. § 469(b). In effect, passive income and related deductions are placed in a separate "basket," and walled off from other forms of income. Passive activity losses therefore cannot shelter other forms of income.

Passive activities are defined by § 469(c) to include (1) the conduct of a trade or business in which the taxpayer does not materially participate and (2) rental activities.

Section 469 provides that a nonrental trade or business is a passive activity only if the taxpayer does not "materially participate" in the activity. The statute requires that the taxpayer be involved in the activity's operations on a "regular, continuous, and substantial" basis. The regulations provide six alternative tests for determining whether "material participation" exists. A taxpayer materially participates in the activity if she meets any of the following conditions: (1) she spends more than 500 hours per taxable year on the activity, (2) she performs substantially all of the activities performed by all of the individuals involved in the activity for a taxable year, (3) she spends more than 100 hours per taxable year on the activity where that equals or exceeds the participation of any other individual, (4) she has "significant participation" with respect to this activity (more than 100 hours, but less than that required for material participation) and her combined participation in all such activities exceeds 500 hours, (5) she materially participated in the activity for any five of the last ten prior taxable years, or (6) she materially participated in a "personal service activity" in any one of the three prior taxable years (where a "personal service activity" is a trade or business in which capital is not an income-producing factor). To further complicate things, a seventh alternative provides that the taxpayer may show material participation by "facts and circumstances" that demonstrate that she participates in the activity on a regular, continuous, and substantial basis. See § 469(h)(1) and § 1.469–5T.

The Regulations go on to provide that the work done to qualify under the above alternatives must be the type of work typically done by an owner of the activity and that the work may not be performed simply to avoid the passive loss rules. Work typically performed by investors, for example, such as reviewing financial statements, preparing summaries of finances or operations, or monitoring finances does not count. A limited partner is never treated as materially participating unless she spends more than 500 hours in the taxable year, meets the five-year or three-year material participation test, or is also a general partner. Participation in an activity for less than 100 hours a year can never constitute material participation unless the taxpayer performs substantially all of the activities associated with the business.

As if the material participation requirements of the Internal Revenue Code itself were lacking in complexity, the regulations have introduced the new concept of "significant participation activities" for the purpose of identifying a number of situations where a taxpayer will not be considered to have passive income. For example, if a taxpayer participates for more than 100 hours in an activity, but does not "materially participate," net income from the activity will not be treated as passive, even though losses from the activity are. See § 1.469–1T(f)(2)(i)(C). The purpose of this rule is to ensure that it will not be easy for a taxpayer to create passive income (which can be offset against other passive losses). The losses from significant participation activities will continue to be treated as passive. The government has been criticized for adopting a "heads we win, tails you lose" rule but it appears to be authorized by § 469(*l*)(3). The concern of the regulation writers is that a taxpayer with income would welcome a hard-to-achieve material participation standard while a taxpayer with losses would prefer that material participation be easy to achieve.

Another area of regulatory concern involves the definition of rental activities. A rental activity is passive even if the taxpayer participates materially in the management of the rental activity. § 469(c)(2). The regulations list a number of activities that will not constitute rental activities for purposes of the passive loss rules. See Reg. § 1.469–1(e)(3). For example, income from renting property for less than seven days will not be considered rent, nor will income from renting property for less than 30 days if significant personal services are provided.

These rules are substantially different with regard to real estate professionals. A rental real estate activity in which the taxpayer materially participates is not treated as passive if he meets certain eligibility requirements. Generally, the taxpayer must be involved in development, construction, acquisition, conversion, management, leasing, or brokering of the real property. Furthermore, the taxpayer must be involved on essentially a full-time basis: More than half of his services and more than 750 hours worth of services must be performed during the year in real estate businesses in which he materially participates. § 469(c)(7).

In the case of rental real estate activities, a special rule contained in § 469(i) provides that up to $25,000 of losses can be used against nonpassive income if the taxpayer is an "active participant." The $25,000 of allowable loss, however, is phased out beginning with taxpayers with adjusted gross income of $100,000 and is not available if AGI exceeds $150,000. This exception is designed to permit deduction of losses by some individuals with small scale rental activities who actively manage them. A favorite example is a New York firefighter who rents out a portion of her brownstone.

The definition of "activity" is important for two reasons. Material participation is defined with respect to each activity. Thus, if "activity" is narrowly defined, it may be difficult for a taxpayer to show material participation with respect to that activity. On the other hand, a narrow definition may make it easy for the taxpayer to completely dispose of an activity and thereby obtain the deduction of suspended losses. § 469(g).

The regulations use a facts-and-circumstances approach to identify a single activity. The primary factors that the regulations indicate will be used to treat several businesses as an activity are the types of businesses, common control, common ownership, geographical location, and business interdependence. § 1.469–4(c). Generally, a rental activity may not be grouped with another business and a real estate rental activity may not be grouped with an activity that rents personal property. § 1.469–4(d).

Passive activity income typically does not include "portfolio income," such as interest earned on bonds, dividends on stocks or income from other securities, annuities, or royalties. § 469(e)(1). Thus, passive losses cannot offset certain types of investment income. The distinctions between "portfolio" income, "passive activity" income, and "active" income are exceedingly complex. For example, the regulations provide that income from licensing intangible property will be treated as income from a trade or business, and hence not as passive income, only if the taxpayer receiving the royalties created the property or performed substantial services in its development or marketing.

The passive loss rules must be coordinated with the at-risk rules of § 465 and the capital loss provisions. In general, whether a loss is subject to the passive loss limitations of § 469 is determined after applying the at-risk limitations of § 465. The interaction of the capital loss limitations and the passive loss rules is not nearly so straightforward. In general, both rules are applied simultaneously. In determining the income or loss from a passive activity, capital gains and losses are treated the same as ordinary gains and losses. If a capital loss is suspended under the passive loss rules, it is not offset against capital gains. Capital gains and losses from passive activities that are not limited by § 469 are mixed with other capital gains and losses in calculating the limitations on the deduction of capital losses. Carryover rules generally operate similarly. See § 1.469–1(d). There are also instances where limitations on basis, for example, under the partnership provisions, interact with the passive loss rules. In general, if a loss is prohibited from being deducted under those basis rules, the loss is ignored under § 469 and a loss permitted by the § 469 rules is still subject to these other basis limitations. Further discussion of those rules here, however, would forever bar this course from being called "baby tax."

Policy Issues. The passive activity rules mark a major extension of a "basket" approach to income taxation. A basket approach also is illustrated by § 165(d)'s limitation of gambling loss deductions to gambling income and § 163(d)'s limitation of deductions for investment interest to investment income.

A "basket" approach generally divides income into certain categories or "baskets" and limits deductions against that income to expenses related in some manner to the production or receipt of that income. Inevitably, the use of baskets of income requires application of criteria to distinguish between different forms of income and "tracing rules" to match deductions to related income sources. As a practical matter, a "basket" approach introduces substantial complexities into the tax law because taxpayers often have flexibility to change the form of business and investment transactions and business and investment entities. For example, by changing a transaction from a "loan" to a "lease" with similar economic effects, interest income may be transformed into rents.

The use of baskets of income also in some circumstances will create a divergence between taxable and economic income. For example, a taxpayer who earns $10,000 of income in a passive activity but who has real economic expenses of $30,000 under § 469 would be able to deduct only one-third of the expenses in the year incurred. Carrying the losses forward would not fully compensate the taxpayer for the economic loss because of the cost of deferring the tax reduction. On the other hand, many tax shelter losses deducted by taxpayers against unrelated income under prior law were artificial losses generated by favorable tax rules, and did not reflect a genuine diminution in the taxpayer's economic income. Such losses, for example, often were due to accelerated depreciation. The passive loss rules restrict the availability of deductions for such artificial losses, but the trade-off may be restrictions on deductions for real economic losses.

Obviously, Congress has adopted a number of provisions trying to forestall the deduction of losses that either are not economic losses or are really personal losses. Those provisions, however, do not all do so in the same way. For example, § 183 disallows so-called hobby losses by denying losses that exceed income from an activity and § 469 similarly disallows passive losses that exceed income from passive activities. But § 469 permits the taxpayer to carryforward passive losses until there is income or the activity is sold, but losses from a "hobby" are not carried forward and thus are lost. That problem probably explains how the Romneys treated the losses from the partial ownership of the horse Rafalca. Ann Romney, wife of the 2012 Republican presidential candidate Mitt Romney, participated in dressage, an Olympic sport described by the New York Times as a sport where "horses costing up to seven figures execute pirouettes and other dancelike moves for riders wearing tails and top hats." Although Rafalca was ridden in the 2012 Olympics, dressage generally does not produce a big payoff. Hence the losses. The Romneys treated the ownership of Rafalca as a passive activity and thus the vast majority of their 2010 $77,000 loss on the horse was disallowed. But when they sell their ownership in the activity (i.e. Rafalca), the cumulative losses would be deductible. If they had treated ownership of Rafalca as a hobby, the losses would probably go unused. Peanuts for a couple who reported over $21 million of income in 2010, but apparently not too small for tax planning.

SECTION 7.   BAD DEBTS

Note on the Bad Debt Deduction

Code Requirements. A business bad debt is deductible in full as an ordinary loss. A partially worthless business debt can be deducted to the extent charged off by the taxpayer on his books. § 166(a). An individual may deduct a wholly worthless nonbusiness bad debt only as a short-term capital loss, which is not as valuable as an ordinary loss, since, unlike ordinary losses, capital losses can be deducted only to the extent of capital gains plus $3,000. § 166(d)(1). An individual may not deduct a partially worthless nonbusiness debt. Taxpayers always prefer business bad debts to nonbusiness bad debts, which can be deducted only as capital losses and only when entirely worthless. It is sometimes advantageous for a taxpayer to attempt to achieve deduction as a § 165 loss, instead of a bad debt. A nonbusiness profit-seeking transaction that produces a loss may be deductible against ordinary income under § 165. The Supreme Court has held that §§ 165 and 166 are mutually exclusive. Spring City Foundry Co. v. Commissioner, 292 U.S. 182 (1934). The treatment of capital losses is taken up in Chapter 5.

Cases Finding Dominant Business Motivation. The Supreme Court in United States v. Generes, 405 U.S. 93 (1972), held that the dominant motivation for the bad debt must be business-related. A significant business motivation will not suffice. The taxpayer in that case was a significant shareholder and president of a corporation to which he lent money. When the corporation defaulted, he claimed that he had made the loans to protect his job and salary. Finding a much more probable investment motivation, the Court disallowed a bad debt deduction.

The question whether a bad debt resulted from a loan made for a dominant business motive typically turns on the particular facts and circumstances, when both investment and business reasons are present. Contrast Hough v. Commissioner, 882 F.2d 1271 (7th Cir. 1989) (dominant motive in making loan to corporation was taxpayer's investment interest as a shareholder and not to protect business he received from corporation), with Garlove v. Commissioner, 24 T.C.M. 1049 (1965) (attorney made loans to client corporation of which he was a shareholder so that it would remain with him as a fee-paying client; dominant purpose was business-related).

The Trade or Business of Lending. In Estate of Bounds v. Commissioner, 46 T.C.M. 1209 (1983), the taxpayer made 16 loans to business and social acquaintances as well as to entities in which he had an investment interest. The Tax Court denied his deduction of five bad debts as business bad debts. The court rejected the taxpayer's claim that his lending activities were sufficiently extensive and continuous to place him in the trade or business of lending money, stating:

> The [taxpayer's] lending activities * * * lacked most of the attributes common to the carrying on of a trade or business. First of all, it does not appear that these activities occupied a substantial amount of the decedent's time and effort during this period. On the contrary, most of his time was divided between his duties as an employee and later a consultant * * * and, to a lesser extent, as an officer and director of several corporations. The [taxpayer] himself stated at trial that he devoted very little time to the making of loans. Such passive conduct is not at all characteristic of the operation of a trade or business. * * * The [taxpayer] did not advertise his lending activities and did not maintain what could fairly be considered a separate office for such activities. Moreover, he did not keep books and records reflecting his lending activities. For this reason, the [taxpayer] was unable to reconstruct his purported "business" activities with any degree of accuracy. These factors all weigh against him. * * * It is also enlightening that the [taxpayer] apparently did not consider himself in the money-lending business * * * as evidenced by the fact that he listed his occupation on his tax returns as that of executive * * *

> Although the occasional lending of large amounts of money indicates a hope of generating substantial income from such activity, it does not transform intermittent transactions into the operation of a trade or business any more than does the making

of large, isolated investments in the stock market. * * * We do not believe this is the "exceptional situation" where the [taxpayer's] lending activities were sufficiently extensive and continuous to elevate them to the status of a separate business.

Loans to Family and Friends. In his concurring opinion in *Generes,* noted above, Justice Marshall said that

> [t]he major congressional purpose in distinguishing between business and nonbusiness bad debts was to prevent taxpayers from lending money to friends or relatives who they knew would not repay it and then deducting against ordinary income a loss in the amount of the loan. * * * A related congressional purpose in enacting the predecessor of § 166 was "to put nonbusiness investments in the form of loans on a footing with other nonbusiness investments."

Compare Davis v. Commissioner, 60 T.C.M. 1256 (1990) (as there were no formal indicia of a loan such as interest, collateral, or documentation, advance was considered a gift), with Hunt v. Commissioner, 57 T.C.M. 919 (1989) (evidence indicated family transfer was a bona fide loan). See also Reg. § 1.166–1(c) (requiring a debt to be bona fide).

Should there be a deduction for bad debts arising out of personal loans to friends or relatives? Recall the tax treatment of a donor who simply gives money to a family member or friend. Should it make any difference if a loan to a family member bore adequate interest?

Was There a Loan? Did It Have Basis? Section 166 presupposes the existence of a bona fide debt. A debtor-creditor relationship must exist based on a valid and enforceable obligation to pay a fixed or determinable sum of money. Reg. § 1.166–1(c).

No deduction is allowed for a debt that was worthless when acquired. No bad debt deduction is allowed for a claim for unpaid wages or rent because such debts are treated as having a zero basis. These amounts would be fully included in income if collected, so the taxpayer's loss when they are unpaid is adequately reflected for tax purposes by excluding them from income. A deduction would add an unwarranted double benefit. See, e.g., Perry v. Commissioner, 92 T.C. 470 (1989), aff'd in an unpublished opinion 912 F.2d 1466 (5th Cir. 1990), cert. denied, 499 U.S. 938 (1991) (no bad debt deduction for unpaid alimony because wife has no basis in the obligation).

Loan Guarantees. A taxpayer who sustains a loss from guaranteeing a loan is treated in the same manner as a taxpayer who sustains a loss from a loan that she made directly. If the guaranty agreement relates to the guarantor's trade or business, the guarantor may treat the transaction as a business bad debt. If the guaranty agreement is unrelated to the guarantor's trade or business but related to a transaction entered into for profit, any resulting loss will be treated as a nonbusiness bad debt. Payments on loan guarantees based on personal motivation are not deductible. Reg. § 1.166–9. The taxpayer must have received reasonable consideration for making the guarantee and where the debtor is the taxpayer's spouse, dependent, or close relative, cash or property consideration must have changed hands.

The taxpayer obtains a deduction only in the year in which she actually makes payment on the guarantee and then only in the amount actually paid. A transfer of the guarantor's note does not give rise to a deduction. Black Gold Energy Corp. v. Commissioner, 99 T.C. 482 (1992).

Political Contributions. Section 271 specifically disallows deductions for the worthlessness of debts owed by a political party. This rule was designed to overcome a common practice whereby taxpayers loaned a large sum to a political organization and then deducted it as a bad debt. In this way, taxpayers obtained deductions for what were in substance nondeductible campaign contributions. The single exception to § 271 allows a deduction for worthless debts resulting from a bona fide sale of goods or services to a political party or campaign committee in the ordinary course of the seller's trade or business. This exception is permitted only if the taxpayer made substantial efforts to collect the debt and if more than 30 percent of its total business for the year in which the debt accrued was with political parties. See § 271(c).

In the 2008 presidential primaries, Republican Mitt Romney gave millions of dollars to his campaign, while Democrat Hillary Clinton loaned millions to hers. Clinton apparently was hoping that her donors ultimately would pick up the tab—and they no doubt would have if she had won. But, if she never collects, she and Romney will end up in the same boat—at least tax wise.

Voluntary Cancellation. A taxpayer who voluntarily cancels a debt is not entitled to a bad debt deduction. However, if the voluntary cancellation is for a business purpose, a deduction under § 162(a) may be taken.

Timing. Section 166(a) allows a deduction for "any debt which becomes worthless within the taxable year." This presents the often difficult question of determining the year in which the debt actually became worthless. The taxpayer must prove that the debt had some value at the beginning and none at the end of the year in which the deduction is claimed. Under the normal three-year statute of limitations, taxpayers would often lose deductions because they could not establish, or established too late, the year in which the worthlessness occurred. Since 1942, however, § 6511(d) has provided a special seven-year statute of limitations with respect to refund claims based on the deduction of bad debts. This usually enables the taxpayer to get a deduction in one of the seven years.

SECTION 8.   PERSONAL DEDUCTIONS

Taxpayers whose income is below a threshold amount are not thought to have the ability to pay income taxes. Some mechanism must be used to exempt them from the universe of taxpayers. Currently, three such devices are employed—the standard deduction, child tax credits, and to some extent the earned income credit. The standard deduction is available to all taxpayers and thus does not serve only to exempt low income taxpayers. The personal exemption was suspended by the 2017 act and child tax credits were expanded. For provisions designed principally to benefit presumably the least sophisticated citizens, these allowances are extraordinarily complex.

A. THE STANDARD DEDUCTION

A taxpayer may deduct either itemized deductions or a standard deduction. The latter is a flat amount that varies with marital status and may be taken regardless of whether the taxpayer actually had expenditures. § 63(c). By contrast, itemized deductions are a specific set of expenses, generally personal in nature. Since the standard deduction is the amount that taxpayers may deduct in lieu of itemized deductions, it effectively provides a floor for itemized deductions. In 2015, 70 percent of taxpayers with income took the standard deduction; almost all high income taxpayers itemize deductions rather than taking the standard deduction. Itemized deductions are discussed in the next Section.

The 2017 tax act increased the standard deduction substantially for all filing statuses (although the increases sunset at the end of 2025). As of 2018, the standard deduction is $24,000 for a married couple filing jointly, $18,000 for a head of household, and $12,000 for single taxpayers and for married individuals filing separately. § 63(c)(7). The standard deduction is indexed annually for inflation.

A larger standard deduction tends to simplify the tax-filing experience, since fewer taxpayers need to consult the rules on itemized deductions. At the same time, however, those who benefit from itemized deductions are often concerned. For example, charities who benefit from the itemized deduction for charitable contributions fear that less will be contributed by those who will no longer itemize deductions.

Additional amounts of standard deduction are allowed for people over age 65 and for the blind. Married taxpayers can each deduct an additional $1300 for each such status and unmarried taxpayers can deduct $1600 for each such status. § 63(f). (These amounts reflect statutory adjustments for inflation). Like the regular standard deductions, these additional allowances are not allowed to taxpayers who itemize deductions.

The standard deduction of an individual who can be claimed as a dependent by another taxpayer (see infra at page 435) is limited to the lesser of the usual standard deduction or the greater of $1050 or the individual's earned income plus $350. § 63(c)(5). These amounts also reflect inflation adjustments through 2017.

Some taxpayers are required to itemize deductions even if their deductions are less than the standard deduction. The standard deduction is not available, for example, to married taxpayers filing separate returns where either spouse itemizes deductions, to nonresident aliens, to U.S. citizens with income from U.S. possessions, and to estates, trusts, common trust funds, or partnerships.

There are two rationales typically offered for the standard deduction. First, it may be viewed as a substitute for itemized deductions for those taxpayers whose itemized deductions would be of relatively small amounts. Under this view, the standard deduction is justified on grounds of simplifying both tax administration and taxpayer recordkeeping. Taxpayers who do not itemize may not need to keep records and the IRS does not need to audit the standard deduction. Alternatively, the standard deduction may be viewed as an adjustment of the tax rate schedules. The amount of the standard deduction, in conjunction with the child credits (and certain other provisions such as the earned income tax credit), reflects Congress' determination of the level of income below which no tax should be imposed. In fact, for a while, the standard deduction was called the "zero bracket amount."

Policy arguments with respect to other provisions of the Code often turn on which of these two views of the standard deduction is being advanced. One often hears the argument—in the context of the charitable contribution deduction, for example—that providing only an itemized deduction for charitable contributions deprives nonitemizers of the benefit of the deduction. For example, the 2017 tax act, which raised the standard deduction for taxable years from 2018 through 2025, has the effect of excluding more taxpayers from claiming the charitable deduction, since fewer will now itemize.

If, however, the standard deduction is intended to substitute for itemized deductions for most taxpayers or to serve as a floor that itemized deductions must exceed to be allowed, this "unfairness" disappears. A taxpayer is a nonitemizer only if the total of his itemizable deductions is less than the standard deduction. Suppose a single taxpayer's total deductions, including charitable contributions, is $5,000. That taxpayer should be very happy with a standard deduction of $12,000. She can be viewed as getting $7,000 of "extra" deductions. The taxpayer's actual deductions are allowed, plus an extra amount that arises from the need to set the standard deduction at a level sufficiently high that the bulk of taxpayers will not itemize in order to achieve administrative and taxpayer recordkeeping simplifications. Under this view of the standard deduction, there should be no unfairness in failing to provide any charitable deduction (or other itemized deduction) for nonitemizers.

Of course, deductions available only as itemized deductions have no marginal incentive effects on nonitemizers. An itemized deduction for charitable contributions does not create similar incentives for itemizers and nonitemizers; if the itemizer and nonitemizer both increase their charitable giving, additional contributions save taxes for the former, but not for the latter. The nonitemizer takes only the standard deduction until her charitable giving is sufficient to make her an itemizer. Thus, whenever itemized deductions are intended to encourage particular behavior, there is a conflict between the incentive intentions of Congress and simplification concerns. Incentive considerations argue for making the deduction available to itemizers and nonitemizers alike, while simplification argues for limiting the deduction to itemizers. For example, the deductions for education expenses and interest on education loans, which are above-the-line deductions, available to nonitemizers. See pages 336 and 361 supra.

NOTE

Filing Status. A number of Code provisions (such as the standard deduction and the earned income credit) turn on the taxpayer's filing status. There are five possibilities: married filing jointly, married filing separately, surviving spouse, head of household, and single.

Married couples who choose to do so may combine income and deductions on one return. This is almost always more advantageous than married-filing-separately status. On the other hand, if the couple is not married and thus each files as a single taxpayer, their tax liability may be less in some circumstances, depending on the relative incomes of the two people. This dichotomy is discussed further in Chapter 4.

A taxpayer whose spouse has died in either of the two years preceding the current year continues to be treated as a married taxpayer. § 2(a). To qualify as a "surviving spouse," however, the taxpayer must maintain and reside in a household in which a dependent child resides for the entire taxable year. Congress apparently wanted to provide a transition from married filing jointly status to single status, but it is not clear why it thought a child was necessary.

Another intermediate status is "head of household;" the applicable rates and the amount of the standard deduction lie between those for a married couple and a single person. Such a taxpayer must be unmarried for federal tax purposes and must maintain a household in which she lives that is also the principal place of residence for more than one-half the taxable year of a qualifying child or a dependent. Alternatively, the taxpayer can maintain a separate residence for her mother or father so long as the parent qualifies as a dependent. § 2(b). "Maintaining a household" "child," "dependent," and "unmarried" are all words of art and the Code and regulations contain quite complex definitions.

B. PERSONAL EXEMPTION

As described in the preceding section the 2017 tax act increased the standard deduction for tax years from 2018 through 2025. For the same period, the act eliminated the deductions for personal exemptions. (Because this change was temporary, the statute sets the personal exemption amount at zero for the relevant years rather than eliminating the provision altogether.) § 151(d)(5). Personal exemptions, generally speaking, reduce tax liability to reflect family size. Thus, the effect of a larger standard deduction (which varies only based on the number of adults in the filing unit) and no personal exemption will be to reduce taxes on many smaller families but raise them on larger ones.

In 2026, the personal exemption is scheduled to return to life. The statute permits each taxpayer to deduct a personal exemption of $2,000 for herself and each dependent. § 151. The amount is indexed annually for inflation, and as of 2017 was $4,050. Husbands and wives filing joint returns are entitled to two personal exemptions; if they file separate returns one spouse may take an allowance for another spouse only if that spouse has no gross income and is not someone else's dependent.

The personal exemption allowed for a "dependent" follows definitions in § 152 to include a "qualifying child" or a "qualifying relative." A dependent generally must be a citizen or a resident of the United States or a contiguous country. § 152(b)(3). An individual who can be claimed as a dependent by another taxpayer cannot take an exemption for dependents. § 152(b)(1).

A taxpayer who can be claimed as a dependent by another taxpayer (usually a parent) cannot claim a personal exemption. The theory is that the exemption represents an amount spent on support that is unavailable to pay taxes. The person who actually pays the support should claim the deduction, not the person who receives the support. Amounts transferred as support generally are not includible in the income of the recipient. This rule mainly affects minor children with unearned income and college students who work part-time but are supported by their parents.

There is a phase out of personal exemptions for high income taxpayers that may return if personal exemptions are allowed to return in 2026.

Section 24 entitles a parent to a credit for each qualifying child who is under age 17 who is also the taxpayer's dependent. The 2017 tax act increased the child tax credit to $2,000 for taxable years from 2018 through 2025. The credit is phased out for taxpayers with AGI above $400,000 for married couples filing jointly (above $200,000 for all other taxpayers. The 2017 change doubles the size of the credit and allows it to higher-income taxpayers than before. However, these changes are scheduled to sunset at the end of 2025, when prior law's $1,000 credit amount and lower income thresholds are scheduled to apply. (This dramatic reduction of child credits seems unlikely to actually occur.)

Under the rules that apply from 2018 through 2025, the child tax credit is partially refundable to the extent of 15 percent of the taxpayer's earned income in excess of $2,500, up to a maximum of $1,400 per dependent. For example, suppose a couple with one child earned $15,000 and owed no taxes against which to offset the $2,000 in child credits due to other deductions and credits. They would still receive a check for $1,400 (§ 24(d)(1)(B) would permit $1,875 [15 percent x ($15,000 − $2,500)] to be refunded, but the overall cap of $1,400 would apply). The very poorest taxpayers, however, receive no credit, however, because a taxpayer with earned income of less than $2,500 who owes no taxes gets no credit. There are additional complexities for certain low-income taxpayers who also claim the earned income tax credit. For families with three or more children, the refundable credit is equal to the amount by which their Social Security taxes exceed their earned income tax credit (discussed infra at page 438) if that amount is greater than the above calculation.

NOTES

(A) *Qualifying Child.* The dependency exemption, the child tax credit, the dependent care credit, the head-of-household filing status, and the earned income tax credit all use the term "qualifying child." Prior to 2004, the term "child" had multiple definitions. In a small move towards simplicity, Congress adopted a uniform definition of qualifying child for these sections (not that the definition is simple or intuitive). A "child" is a (1) child of the taxpayer (son, daughter, stepson, or stepdaughter, including adopted and foster children), (2) a descendant of a child, or (3) a brother, sister, stepbrother, or stepsister of the taxpayer or their descendants. A "qualifying child" (1) must have the same principal place of abode as the taxpayer for more than half the year, (2) must be less than 19 years old, or if a student, less than 24 years old and must be younger than the person claiming the tax benefit, (3) cannot have filed a joint return with a spouse unless the return was filed only to obtain a refund, and (4) must not have provided more than half his or her own support. § 152(c).

It is possible of course that a qualifying child could be the dependent of more than one taxpayer. In that case there are a series of tie-breakers: The exemption goes to a parent or if no claimant is a parent, to the taxpayer with the highest adjusted gross income for the year. If both claimants are parents, the exemption goes to the parent with whom the child resided for the longest period of time during the year, and if even that results in a tie, the exemption goes to the parent with the highest adjusted gross income. § 152(c)(4). So much for simplicity.

But wait, there's more. If an individual's parents decline to claim an individual as a qualifying child, another taxpayer may claim that individual as a qualifying child. The other taxpayer may claim the individual as a qualifying child only if that taxpayer's AGI is higher than the AGI of either of the child's parents. The tiebreaker rules are triggered when two or more taxpayers can claim an individual as a qualifying child, regardless of whether they actually do.

(B) *Qualifying Relative.* Someone who fails to qualify as a qualifying child can still be a qualifying relative—but not vice versa. Relatives include a long list of individuals related by blood—child, descendants of children, siblings, parents (and step parents) and parent's ancestors, aunt, uncle, cousin, nieces and nephews, and various in-laws. But it also includes adopted and foster children as well as an unrelated individual who lives in the taxpayer's home as a member of the household. § 152(d)(2). A "qualifying relative" must have gross income less than the exemption amount (§ 151(d)), and receive more than half of his or her support from the taxpayer.

Section 152(f)(3) states that an unrelated individual is not a member of the household for exemption purposes if the relationship between the individual and the taxpayer is "in violation of local law." The Tax Court consequently has held that an individual cannot qualify as a dependent if his or her relationship to the taxpayer constitutes "cohabitation" in violation of a state statute. Peacock v. Commissioner, 37 T.C.M. 177 (1978).

(C) *Support.* The support test for a qualifying child is different from the support test for a qualifying relative: A qualifying child must not have provided more than half his or her own support. More than half of the support could come from someone else, such as a state agency. A qualifying relative must receive more than half her support from the taxpayer claiming her as a dependent. For example, a taxpayer cannot claim an allowance for a parent if more than half of the parent's support is paid by the government. (Thus, Social Security benefits and state old-age assistance are included in the support calculation. But insurance and Medicare payments are not. Turecamo v. Commissioner, 554 F.2d 564 (2d Cir. 1977).)

(D) *To-Do List: Wrap Gifts. Have Baby.* The tax law allows parents to claim a child credit for a child born at any point before the end of the tax year. This means babies born on New Year's Eve are generally more valuable for tax purposes than those born on New Year's Day. The following excerpt is from an article examining the family-planning consequences of this rule:

Unless you're a cynic, or an economist, I realize you might have trouble believing that the intricacies of the nation's tax code would impinge on something as sacred as the birth of a child. But it appears that you would be wrong.

In the last decade, September has lost its unchallenged status as the time for what we will call National Birth Day, the day with more births than any other. Instead, the big day fell between Christmas and New Year's Day in four of the last seven years—1997 through 2003—for which the government has released birth statistics. (The day was in September during the other years; conception still matters.) * * *

[T]o see if taxes were truly the culprit, [Harvard economist Amitabh] Chandra and another economist, Stacy Dickert-Conlin of Michigan State, devised some clever tests. They found that people who stood to gain the most from the tax breaks were also the ones who gave birth in late December most frequently. When the gains were similar, high-income parents—who, presumably, are more likely to be paying for tax advice—produced more December babies than other parents.

David Leonhardt, *To-Do List: Wrap Gifts. Have Baby.* David Leonhardt, N.Y. Times, Dec. 20, 2006, at C1.

C. EARNED INCOME TAX CREDIT

Note on the Earned Income Tax Credit

Section 32 provides a credit to low income individuals who have earnings. The credit is refundable, which means that people with no tax liability can receive a credit; they file a tax return to receive a cash payment.

In fiscal year 2017, the federal government spent more than $70 billion on EITC benefits for more than 25 million families. The EITC now ranks as the fourth-largest transfer program for low income families after Medicaid, SNAP (food stamps), and Supplemental Security Income (SSI). See Karen Spar and Gene Falk, Federal Benefits and Services for People with Low Income, Congressional Research Service, July 29, 2016.

Taxpayers eligible to take an EITC are (1) individuals with a qualifying child or (2) individuals between the ages of 25 and 65 who are not another taxpayer's dependent. For the definition of a qualifying child see Note (A) on page 436. For purposes of the EITC, however, a child can provide more than half of his or her own support.

The credit is a percentage of earned income, with both the credit percentage and the earned income varying with the number of children. The credit increases as earned income increases until it hits a maximum amount, and then is phased out by a percentage of the income exceeding the phase-out amount. The maximum amount and the phase-out amount are indexed for inflation.

For example, in 2017, a married couple with one qualifying child can claim a credit of 34 percent of the first $10,000 of earned income. The maximum credit for such a couple is $3,400 and is reduced by 15.98 percent of earned income in excess of $23,930. A married couple with one child receives no EITC once earned income is in excess of $45,207. The credit percentage for married taxpayers with two or more qualifying children is 40 percent and the maximum credit is $5,616. For taxpayers with three or more qualifying children, the maximum credit amount is increased to 45 percent of earned income, and the maximum EITC is $6,318. For a married couple with three or more qualifying children, the credit is phased out by $53,930 of earnings.

The credit is substantially less for individuals without children than it is for a taxpayer with a child. A childless couple receives a credit of 7.65 percent of the first $6,670 of earned income. The maximum credit is $510 and the credit is completely phased out at $20,600.

Note that these dollar amounts change annually thanks to inflation adjustments mandated by § 32(j). Each year, the IRS announces the updated amounts.

Figure 3.1. Earned Income Tax Credit for Married Couples, 2017

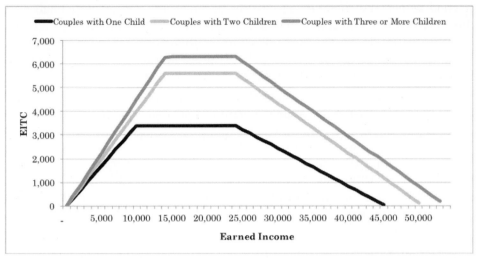

Both the EITC and the child tax credit (see page 435 supra) create an incentive to overstate earned income, contrary to most taxpayers' incentives to understate their income. The taxpayer in Cadet v. Commissioner, T.C. Summ. Op. 2015–39, claimed that she had net earnings of $17,190 from selling her children's clothes at a flea market. Reporting earnings of that amount entitled her to her child tax credits and an EITC that not only wiped out her tax liability but created a refund of almost $6,000. The Tax Court did not believe that she operated a used clothing business that created "earned income," which eliminated most of the two credits.

The phase-outs create the potential for large marriage penalties. For example, suppose a man and a woman, each earning $10,000 and each with one child get married. Before the wedding, each received an EITC of $3,400 or a total of $6,800. After marriage, they would receive one EITC of $5,616. Their taxes therefore increased by $1,184, simply by marrying. Although Congress has acted to alleviate the penalty by increasing the beginning and ending of the phase-out amounts for married couples, the problem remains.

The EITC originally was enacted primarily to reduce the burden of Social Security taxes on the working poor. It was used in 1986, in 1990, and again in 1993, however, to help remove people with poverty-level incomes from the income tax rolls and to provide a subsidy to low-wage workers. Many purposes are claimed for the EITC; in 1990, for example, the expansion of the EITC was claimed to be a means of increasing federal support for child care expenses of the working poor.

Increasingly, the EITC is seen not as a way to remove low-wage workers from the income tax rolls, but primarily as a way to help assure a minimum standard of living to the working poor. Thus, some have advocated the EITC as a form of a "negative tax" or a "wage subsidy" as the primary way to transfer government benefits to the working poor. Is it good to use the income tax system in this way? David Weisbach and Jacob Nussim argue that the choice between tax and spending programs should be based on the organizational advantages of each. David A. Weisbach and Jacob Nussim, "The Integration of Tax and Spending Programs," 113 Yale L.J. 955 (2004).

The EITC has become something of a pawn in the political battle over welfare. Those who favor government transfer payments generally support the EITC as a way to protect those below the poverty line, in part because of its pro-work character. Those who want to scale back transfer payments generally favor tightening eligibility requirements. For example, the 1996 Act adjusted the earned income and phase-out amounts upward to take inflation into account, but also provided that individuals who are not authorized to work in the United States cannot claim the credit.

The rules in § 32 are notably complex. Taxpayers must navigate a web of rules to determine whether they have a qualifying child; to calculate their earned income; and to detect whether they have "excessive investment income." The various eligibility rules have been thought necessary to prevent undeserving taxpayers from receiving unwarranted largess. For instance, the limitation on EITC awards to taxpayers with investment income over $2,200 was enacted to deny the credit to individuals who are wealthy but have low earned income. But the complexity also prevents some targeted beneficiaries from receiving the credit. For a critique of provisions affecting low income taxpayers and proposals for change, see Lawrence Zelenak, "Children and the Income Tax," 49 Tax L. Rev. 349 (1994); Ann L. Alstott, "The Earned Income Tax Credit and the Limitations of Tax-Based Welfare Reform," 108 Harv. L. Rev. 533 (1995). For a discussion of the economic effects of the EITC, see Nada Eissa and Hilary Hoynes, "Behavioral Responses to Taxes: Lessons from the EITC and Labor Supply," 20 Tax Policy and the Economy 73 (2006).

Baker v. Commissioner

United States Tax Court, 2006. 91 T.C.M. 949.

■ CHIECHI, JUDGE: * * * Petitioner and Deanna Wus (Ms. Wus) have a daughter A and a son C (collectively, the children). At a time not disclosed by the record, Ms. Wus purchased a double-wide trailer (trailer) located [in] Magnolia, Delaware. Ms. Wus, petitioner, and the children lived in the trailer for an undisclosed period of time prior to 2003. Sometime in 2002, Ms. Wus stopped residing in the trailer, but petitioner continued to live there until around mid-February 2003. Petitioner was unable to afford the payments for the mortgage loan, ground rent, and utilities with respect to the trailer after Ms. Wus stopped residing there.

[Mr. Baker moved several times in 2003. His last residence that year was a home his mother owned on Fox Road, referred to in the case as the Fox Road property.]

During 2003, petitioner, who worked as a plumber, and Ms. Wus were not married, lived in separate residences, and had no custody agreement concerning their daughter A who was four years old.

During 2003, Ms. Wus received public assistance for A's benefit from the State of Delaware, which listed Ms. Wus as the custodial parent of A. During that year, Medicaid, and not petitioner, provided healthcare benefits to A. During 2003, petitioner did not apply for food stamps or any other type of public assistance for his daughter A.

During 2003, petitioner and Ms. Wus each asked Rosemary Srase (Ms. Srase) to babysit the children at Ms. Srase's home. Ms. Srase was a longtime friend of petitioner and his mother who used to babysit petitioner when he was a child. Approximately two to three times a week during 2003, Ms. Srase usually babysat the children at her home for a few hours during the evenings. Occasionally during 2003, she babysat them during the daytime and overnight on weekends. During 2003, petitioner did not pay cash to Ms. Srase for babysitting the children for him. Instead, he did work for her at her home. Most of the time during 2003 that Ms. Srase babysat the children, she provided them with some food at her own expense. At no time during 2003 before petitioner moved to the Fox Road property did Ms. Srase babysit the children at petitioner's residence or personally observe them at petitioner's residence. When petitioner moved into the Fox Road property, Ms. Srase observed the children at that property.

On at least certain days during the period January 2 through March 31, 2003, the Dover Educational & Community Daycare Center (Daycare Center) provided daycare for the children. On most, but not all, of such days, Ms. Wus brought the children to, and petitioner picked them up from, the Daycare Center. On certain other days during the period January 2 through March 31, 2003, Ms. Wus brought the children to, and also picked them up from, the Daycare Center. On certain other days during that period, petitioner brought the children to, and also picked them up from, the Daycare Center. * * *

In petitioner's 2003 return, petitioner reported wages of $ 14,929, business income of $ 420 from Schedule C, Profit or Loss From Business, total income of $ 15,349, and adjusted gross income of $ 15,349. In petitioner's 2003 return, petitioner claimed (1) a dependency exemption deduction for his daughter A, (2) head of household filing status, (3) the earned income tax credit, (4) the child tax credit, and (5) the additional child tax credit.

In Ms. Wus's tax return for her taxable year 2003, Ms. Wus also claimed a dependency exemption deduction for her daughter A.

OPINION

* * * In support of his position with respect to each of the issues presented in this case, petitioner relies on his own testimony, the testimony of his mother, and the testimony of Ms. Srase, a longtime family friend who used to babysit petitioner when he was a child. We found the testimony of petitioner to be in material respects conclusory, vague, self-serving, and uncorroborated by reliable evidence. We found the testimony of petitioner's mother to be in material respects not based upon her personal knowledge, conclusory, and serving the interests of her son petitioner. We found the testimony of Ms. Srase to be in material respects not based upon her personal knowledge, conclusory, and serving the interests of her longtime friend petitioner. We are not required to, and we shall not, rely on the testimonies of petitioner, his mother, and Ms. Srase in order to establish petitioner's position with respect to the issues presented in this case. * * *

Petitioner and two other witnesses testified that * * * [A] lived with her father, the petitioner[,] from January 2003 until November 2003, when she went to live with her mother. They also testified that the mother took * * * [A] inconsistently on weekends for those ten months. * * *

[T]he record establishes that petitioner and Ms. Wus had no custody agreement with respect to either of the children for 2003. However, the State of Delaware reported to respondent that Ms. Wus, and not petitioner, was the claimed child's custodial parent. Moreover, the record is devoid of evidence that we find to be reliable establishing that A lived with her father from January until November 2003 or that he otherwise had physical custody of A for a portion of 2003 that is greater than the portion of such year during which Ms. Wus had physical custody of A.

Claimed Earned Income Tax Credit

Section 32(a)(1) permits an eligible individual an earned income credit against such individual's tax liability. * * * As pertinent here, section 32(c)(1)(A)(i) defines the term "eligible individual" to mean "any individual who has a qualifying child for the taxable year". The term "qualifying child" with respect to any taxpayer for any taxable year includes a daughter of the taxpayer who has the "same principal place of abode as the taxpayer for more than one-half of such taxable year". Sec. 32(c)(3)(A)(i) and (ii) and (B)(i)(I).

It is petitioner's position that his daughter A is a qualifying child for purposes of the earned income tax credit because she had the same principal place of abode as petitioner for more than one-half of his taxable year 2003. We found above that petitioner failed to show that for his taxable year 2003 he maintained as his home a household that constituted the principal place of abode, as a member of such household, of his daughter A for more than one-half of that year. On the record before us, we find that petitioner has failed to carry his burden of showing that for his taxable year 2003 A is a qualifying child for purposes of the earned income tax credit.[4] * * *

NOTES

(A) *Noncompliance and the EITC.* As *Baker* illustrates, the eligibility rules for the EITC can be difficult to apply in real-world situations. Government auditors have found that many taxpayers (like Mr. Baker) claim the EITC when they are not technically entitled to it. In 2009–2011, 29 percent of EITC benefits paid were estimated to be overclaims. Government Accountability Office, Refundable Tax Credits: Comprehensive Compliance Strategy and Expanded Use of Data Could Strengthen IRS's Efforts to Address Noncompliance.

In response to EITC noncompliance, Congress enacted § 32(k), which denies the EITC for 10 years to any taxpayer whose EITC was disallowed due to fraud (and for 2 years to any taxpayer whose EITC was disallowed due to reckless disregard of rules and regulations).

(B) *Tax Procedure and Low-Income Taxpayers.* As the *Baker* case illustrates, EITC claimants may lack legal representation and may be poorly prepared to litigate tax cases pro se. Some law schools have started tax clinics, which represent low-income taxpayers before the IRS and the courts. Some scholars have suggested that the Congress and the IRS should revamp tax procedures to address the situation of low-income taxpayers.

(C) *Who Pays Taxes?* The standard deduction and child credit (and the personal exemption if it returns in 2026 as scheduled) (and to a limited extent the earned income tax credit) are used to set the threshold for paying income taxes. The combination means that millions of Americans pay no income taxes at all. And many of those do not need to file a tax return unless they are claiming a refundable credit. The Urban-Brookings Tax Policy Center estimated that 46 percent of tax units would pay no federal income tax in 2018. This number varies as Congress adopts new legislation or as various credits expire. Only 17 percent, however, paid neither income nor payroll taxes. One might think that keeping taxpayers out of the taxpaying universe would make their lives less complicated and help with the IRS compliance burden, but most of these families have to file income tax returns to claim the credits and deductions that make them nontaxable. Some critics have argued, to the contrary, insisting that it is a civic responsibility to pay federal income taxes and that with little at stake, those who pay no taxes will press for more government spending or leave monitoring of congressional action to the wealthy whose interests tend to be quite different.

---

[4] Petitioner does not claim that he is entitled to the earned income tax credit under sec. 32(c)(1)(A)(ii). That section provides that a taxpayer with no qualifying child may nonetheless be eligible for the earned income tax credit, subject to the phase out limitations of sec. 32(a)(2), provided that the requirements of sec. 32(c)(1)(A)(ii) are satisfied. For taxable year 2003, the earned income tax credit is completely phased out if the individual who has no qualifying children and who is not married filing jointly has adjusted gross income that equals or exceeds $ 11,230. See sec. 32(b)(1)(A) and (2); Rev. Proc. 2002–70, 2002–2 C.B. 845, 847–848. The parties agree that petitioner has adjusted gross income of $ 15,349 for his taxable year 2003.

(D) *The Problem with Phase-outs.* Whenever phase-outs are used, such as in the child credit and the earned income credit, there is the potential for high effective marginal tax rates. Phase-outs are usually provided because Congress wants to provide a benefit to low- or middle-income taxpayers. When income reaches a certain level, the tax benefit, such as a credit, is no longer available. There are two ways to accomplish this. Suppose, for example, that Congress wanted to provide a $1,000 credit to families with children so long as the family's income does not exceed $25,000. A family with income of $24,999 would receive a $1000 credit. But if that family earned $1 more, they would owe $1000 more in taxes since they would lose the credit. That is known as a "cliff effect" and it is undesirable because of the high marginal effective tax rate and because of the disincentive it creates to earn that extra $1. For an example of such a cliff, see § 74(d). The other approach is to phase out the tax benefit over a larger range of incomes. This still results in high effective marginal rates, but the results are not so draconian. For example, assume that over a range of incomes, an additional $1 of income, causes the taxpayer to lose fifty cents in benefits. That marginal effective tax rate could be said to be 50 percent. The larger the range of income, the lower the effective rate, but the higher the revenue loss. When there are multiple phase-outs affecting the same taxpayer, the problem is even more complicated.

(E) *State EITC Programs.* Twenty-nine states and the District of Columbia have adopted their own add-on EITC programs. A low income family in California, for example, can claim the federal EITC plus an additional state EITC. The California add-on credit in 2016 ranges from a maximum of $217 for a childless worker to $2,706 for a worker with three qualifying children.

(F) *Single Taxpayers Without Children.* The maximum EITC allowable in 2018 to a single person with no children is $520. There has long been debate between Congressional Republicans and Democrats that this amount is too little to provide any real benefit to low-wage single workers, but the 2017 legislation failed to remedy this problem. Tax relief was provided instead by increasing the standard deduction and child credit.

D. CREDIT FOR THE ELDERLY AND DISABLED

Individuals who are 65 or older or who are permanently and totally disabled may qualify for a credit of 15 percent of their income up to a specified maximum. § 22(a). Such a credit (formerly the "retirement income credit") was added to the Code in 1954 because of concern that those receiving Social Security benefits, which generally are excluded from gross income, were favored over others receiving comparable forms of retirement income, which is includible in gross income.

The maximum amount of income against which the credit can be taken is $5,000 for single individuals and married couples where only one spouse is 65 or older, $7,500 for married couples where both spouses are 65 or older, and $3,750 for married individuals filing separately. The maximum for disabled individuals is the amount received as disability income.

The credit base is reduced dollar for dollar by any Social Security and Railroad Retirement benefits and other tax-exempt retirement income. The base also is reduced by 50 percent of the taxpayer's adjusted gross income in excess of $7,500 for single individuals, $10,000 for married individuals filing jointly and $5,000 for married individuals filing separately. § 22(c). As a result of these offsets, the expansions in Social Security coverage since the credit was first enacted, and the failure to index the thresholds, few elderly now benefit from this credit.

E. EDUCATION CREDITS

In recent years, Congress added several astonishingly complex credits designed to offset the cost of college tuition. Because these credits are often nonrefundable and are phased out at moderate levels of income, they are aimed primarily at middle-income taxpayers.

There are two education credits, the fancifully named American Opportunity Tax Credit and the Lifetime Learning Credit. The American Opportunity Tax Credit (which is also called the Hope Scholarship Credit) is a credit for the expenses of attending college for a taxpayer, spouse or dependent. § 25A(b). The credit is 100 percent of the first $2,000 of tuition and related expenses and 25 percent of the next $2,000. Thus, the maximum credit amount is $2,500. The credit applies to the first four years of college. The credit is phased out for single taxpayers with income between $80,000 and $90,000 ($160,000 to $180,000 for joint filers). Forty percent of the taxpayer's credit is refundable to the extent the taxpayer has no tax liability to offset the credit. A taxpayer whose unearned income is subject to the kiddie tax (see page 505, infra) cannot claim any portion of the credit as refundable.

Taxpayers also have the option of taking the equally fancifully named Lifetime Learning Credit. Unlike the American Opportunity Credit, the lifetime credit can be used for undergraduate or graduate education at any point in the taxpayer's (or spouse's or dependent's) life. An eligible student must attend at least half-time or be taking courses to acquire or improve job skills. The credit, which can be taken for an unlimited number of years, is 20 percent of tuition and fees up to $10,000. This credit is also phased out. § 25A(d). The credit is nonrefundable so that it is not available to anyone who does not owe taxes, which would be almost all low income families. Taxpayers must have significant amounts of income before they could use a $2000 credit.

A taxpayer is ineligible to take a deduction for education expenses for an individual if the taxpayer or any other person elects to take either the American Opportunity or Lifetime Credits for that individual. See the discussion of § 222. Because the amount of the benefits and the phase-out ranges for the credits and the deduction differ, taxpayers need to calculate all possibilities before deciding which provision to use.

As if choosing between the American Opportunity and the Lifetime Learning Credits and the education deduction were not complicated enough, taxpayers have a third option of contributing to a Coverdell Education Savings Account (sometimes called an education IRA). Up to $2,000 a year can be contributed to an investment account created to pay for education expenses, including fees, books, and room and board for a taxpayer, the taxpayer's spouse, or a dependent. The distributions from an education IRA may be used to pay for elementary and secondary school expenses as well as higher education. The use of an ESA is phased out for taxpayers filing jointly with an AGI between $190,000 and $220,000 ($95,000 to $110,000 for single taxpayers). § 530.

Distributions to a beneficiary from an education IRA are excludible from gross income. A taxpayer may claim an American Opportunity or Lifetime Credit and exclude distributions from an education IRA on behalf of the same student so long as the distributions are not used to pay the expenses for which the credit was claimed.

Taxpayers also have the option of contributing to qualified tuition programs maintained by all states and some colleges. Under these plans, a person (usually a parent or grandparent) contributes to an account that will be used to pay college tuition at any university or purchases tuition credits at a designated university. Both the earnings and distributions are exempt from the income of the beneficiary and the contributor. § 529. There is no income limitation on the use of 529 plans so they are particularly attractive to high income taxpayers. Since anyone can invest in any plan on behalf of any designated beneficiary, (e.g. Grandma in Kentucky can invest in New York's plan to benefit her grandson living in Washington), much competition has arisen between states for the billions of dollars that have been invested in the plans.

The Congress sweetened the tax benefits of § 529 plans in 2017 by permitting tax-free withdrawals of up to $10,000 for taxpayers who use the funds to pay for K–12 education in public, private, and parochial schools. § 529(c)(7).

A taxpayer can claim an American Opportunity or Lifetime Credit and exclude the proceeds of a qualified tuition account so long as the distribution is not used to pay the expenses for which the credit was claimed.

And if these options are not confusing enough, a taxpayer must also consider the effect using these provisions would have on any deduction for interest on education loans. See the discussion at page 361 supra.

In summary, there are eight tax breaks for current-year education expenses: Two tax credits, three deductions, and three exclusions from income. Five other provisions promote savings for college expenses. In 1987 there were only three provisions encouraging college expenditures or savings. The 1997 act alone added five provisions that were estimated to cost $41 billion over five years. Together they represented the largest increase in federal funding for higher education since the GI Bill.

And some political leaders continue to propose more tax breaks for higher education. This is not surprising. In recent decades, only health care costs have risen faster than the costs of higher education.

But the American public simply cannot comprehend the tax savings provided by these provisions, cannot know their eligibility requirements, cannot understand how they interact, and cannot maintain adequate records and reporting to qualify. Each provision has its own eligibility criteria and definition of qualified expenses. They do not even provide consistent treatment of room and board, books, supplies, sports expenses, non-academic fees or the class of relatives whose expenses may be taken into account. A student convicted of a felony for possession or distribution of a controlled substance is not eligible for one of the education credits but such a conviction is not a bar to another one. And this is just the tip of the iceberg. Is this any way for Congress to respond to a serious problem?

SECTION 9.   PERSONAL ITEMIZED DEDUCTIONS

As noted previously, taxpayers may deduct certain expenses— known as itemized deductions—if they exceed the standard deduction. We have already explored several itemized deductions, such as casualty losses, mortgage interest, and bad debts. This Section explores other deductions not related to a trade or business or income-producing activity.

Under the 2017 tax act, in 2026 the Code is again scheduled to place a cap on certain itemized deduction for high income taxpayers, defined as having AGI exceeding $300,000 (for married taxpayers filing jointly) or $250,000 in the case of single taxpayers. § 68. The 2017 act eliminates the § 68 disallowance from 2018 through 2025.

A. TAXES

Note on the Deduction for Taxes and the Foreign Tax Credit

The 2017 tax act made a major change to the Code by imposing a sharp (albeit temporary) limit on the longstanding deduction in § 164 for taxes paid to states, localities, and foreign governments. Section 164 historically has permitted deductions for the amount of certain tax payments to states and localities, to foreign countries and their political subdivisions, and to the federal government. Some taxes (for example, federal or state gasoline taxes) are deductible only if they are attributable to business or investment activity; other taxes (for example, state or local property taxes on one's residence) are deductible regardless of whether they are incurred in a personal or a profit-seeking context. In allowing deduction of state and local income and property taxes without regard to profit seeking, § 164 thus constitutes an exception to the general rule of § 262 that no deductions from income are allowed for "personal, living, or family expenses." The deduction for income and property taxes is not subject to the 2 percent AGI floor on "miscellaneous itemized deductions" (should it return in 2026 as scheduled.) § 67(b)(2).

Very generally, the 2017 legislation provides that, for tax years from 2018 through 2025, individuals may deduct a maximum of $10,000 in combined state and local property, income, and sales taxes. § 164(b)(6). The limitation contains a marriage penalty, since the $10,000 cap applies to both married couples filing jointly and to unmarried taxpayers. (The limitation is $5,000 for married individuals filing separate returns.)

Thus, for example, during the eight-year suspension period, a taxpayer who pays $7,000 in local property taxes and $8,000 in state income taxes can take a tax deduction of only $10,000 (compared to $15,000 under prior and, perhaps, future law).

The 2017 suspension does not apply to corporations or to foreign, state, and local taxes that are paid in connection with a trade or business or a § 212 activity.

Some taxes can never be deducted whether incurred in a personal or a profit-seeking context. These include the federal income tax itself as well as employees' Social Security taxes and estate, inheritance, and gift taxes imposed at the federal, state, and local levels. § 275. Taxes that are deductible only if incurred in connection with trade, business, or investment activity include federal excise taxes and customs duties, as well as, stock transfer taxes, gasoline taxes, and licensing fees.

State and Local Taxes on Real Property. The deduction (subject to the $10,000 cap described above) is allowable for "taxes imposed on interests in real property and levied for the general public welfare" but not for "taxes assessed against local benefits." § 164(c)(1). Renters cannot deduct an allocable portion of property taxes even if they are passed along to tenants under a state statute. Revenue Ruling 79–180, 1979–1 C.B. 95. Under prior law, and again beginning in 2026, foreign real property taxes are deductible; that deduction is eliminated during the eight-year period when the $10,000 cap also applies.

State and Local Taxes on Personal Property. A tax must meet three criteria in order to be deductible under § 164 (subject to the $10,000 cap described above) as a tax on personal property. First, the tax must be ad valorem, or based on the value of the property. Second, the tax must be imposed on an annual basis even if collected more or less frequently. Third, the tax must be on personal property. Reg. § 1.164–3(c).

For example, automobile registration fees may constitute deductible personal property taxes if based on the value of the car but not if based on its age, weight, or horsepower. If the fee is based on more than one of these factors, the taxpayer may deduct the portion that is attributable to the value of the vehicle.

State, Local, and Foreign Income, War Profits, and Excess Profits Taxes. No deduction is allowed for federal income taxes, but, as described supra at page 88, the disallowance of a deduction for the tax itself is simply a matter of tax rates being imposed on a tax-inclusive rather than tax-exclusive, base. Section 275 also bars employees from deducting their payroll taxes to fund Social Security. Employers can deduct their matching contributions so long as they represent a cost of producing income; however, a taxpayer cannot deduct Social Security taxes paid on behalf of a person employed for personal rather than business reasons. To achieve parity with employees, self-employed individuals are permitted to deduct one-half of their Social Security taxes.

The deduction for state, local, and foreign income taxes is subject to the $10,000 cap described above from 2018 through 2025. The sharp limitation on the deduction caused a political firestorm, because, for many taxpayers, the deduction for state and local income taxes has been their largest itemized deduction. According to the IRS, before 2018, almost all itemizers claimed a deduction for state and local taxes—income taxes (61 percent) and real estate taxes (34 percent) made up most of the deductions.

The eight-year cap on the § 164 deduction has a very different impact on taxpayers in different parts of the country. The disallowance will fall hardest on residents of states with relatively high income taxes, including California, New York, and New Jersey. Representatives of these states in Congress (including a number of Republicans) protested the change, but to no avail.

Politicians, particularly Democrats, were quick to point out that the § 164 cap will affect mostly "blue" states, that is, states that tend to have Democratic majorities in national elections. Section 164 does not, of course, formally discriminate based on political party, but because high-tax states tend to be Democratic, there is a noticeable political valence built into the deduction limit.

Following enactment of this limitation on deduction for state taxes, some states that will be most affected began considering changes in their revenue systems that might mitigate the impact of the change. On January 17, 2018, for example, the New York State Department of Finance published a Preliminary Report to the Governor discussing a number of options, including converting all or part of state income taxes into a deductible payroll tax on employers and allowing charitable contributions (deductible) in lieu of state income taxes. The Preliminary Report can be found at https://www.tax.ny.gov/pdf/stats/stat_pit/pit/preliminary-report-tcja-2017.pdf.

State and Local Sales Taxes. Section 164(b)(5) permits taxpayers to deduct either income taxes or state and local sales taxes. The provision mostly helps residents of states without income taxes (or with low income taxes). Taxpayers can deduct a presumptive amount based on tables issued by the IRS. A taxpayer who believes that his consumption is above average is apparently free to collect his thousands of receipts and deduct the actual amount. (Taxpayers in New Hampshire and much of Alaska get no benefit as those states have neither an income nor a general sales tax).

The Foreign Tax Credit. Income taxes of a foreign country, subject to certain important limitations, may be allowed as a credit against domestic income tax liability instead of as a deduction. See §§ 901–08; § 164(b)(3). This credit is designed to prevent double taxation of foreign source income. Its general effect is that foreign income is taxed at the higher of the foreign or the domestic rate. The credit typically is more beneficial than a deduction because U.S. tax liability is reduced dollar for dollar rather than based on the taxpayer's marginal domestic rate.

Capitalization Requirement. Certain state and local taxes incurred in connection with the acquisition or disposition of property must be capitalized. Such taxes are treated as a cost of acquisition and serve to increase the taxpayer's basis in the acquired property. Taxes paid on disposition decrease the amount realized. See the last sentence of § 164(a). The capitalization requirement does not apply to: (1) state, local, and foreign real property taxes, (2) state and local personal property taxes, (3) state, local, and foreign income taxes, or (4) the environmental tax of § 59A. § 164(a). See also § 263A which requires capitalization of costs (including taxes) in connection with the construction or production of certain types of real and personal property and with respect to inventory.

Tax Refunds. Taxpayers may be required to include in income the refund of a tax for which they claimed a deduction or credit in an earlier year. Congress has attempted to increase compliance with this previously ignored obligation by requiring state and local governments to file information returns reporting refunds to individuals of more than $10. See § 6050E. A refund must be included in income, however, only to the extent that the earlier tax payment served to reduce tax liability. See § 111. This is an application of the "tax benefit rule," discussed infra in Chapter 7 at page 685.

Note on Policies Regarding the Deductibility of Taxes

The 2017 tax act revitalized the debate over the deduction for taxes paid other than in an income-seeking context, and the 2026 expiration of the cap on such taxes will likely provide another occasion for debate, if it doesn't occur sooner. Proponents of the deduction have argued that the deduction produces a more accurate measurement of taxable income. For example, Boris Bittker contends that, because state and local tax payments are compelled rather than voluntary, the deduction "may therefore be defended as a mode of refining the concept of income." Boris Bittker, "Income Tax Deductions, Credits and Subsidies for Personal Expenditures," 16 J.L. & Econ. 193, 200–01 (1973).

Proponents of the deduction have also argued that state and local income taxes are a direct cost of earning income that will be taxed at the federal level. Like other costs, these taxes thus should be deductible since the federal income tax is imposed only on net income. (This would suggest repeal of the deduction for state and local property taxes because they are not a direct cost of earning income.)

By contrast, the Treasury has argued that the deduction for state and local taxes provides a federal subsidy for the public services provided by state and local governments that is not available when taxpayers acquire similar services by nondeductible private purchases. Treasury contended that voting at the polls and voting with one's "feet" provided sufficient voluntariness to justify taxation. See 2 Treasury Dep't, Report to the President, Tax Reform for Fairness, Simplicity and Economic Growth 62–68 (1984).

Evaluating the justification for the deduction should depend—at least in part—on the role of the deduction in the context of the entire system of intergovernmental financial assistance. State-local tax deductibility is but one of the three major methods by which the federal government subsidizes state-local activities. The other sources are grants-in-aid and the subsidy to borrowing through the exclusion of state and local bond interest from federal income taxation. State tax deductibility and the exclusion for bond interest may be less efficient than grants because they provide less than a dollar of revenue to state and local governments for each dollar of federal cost, but grants often require the state or local government to make expenditures specified by the federal government. By lowering the cost of state and local taxes, the deduction also may encourage state and local governments to impose higher taxes and provide more services than they would otherwise. Or they may replace nondeductible levies with deductible taxes. The deduction also has been challenged on equity grounds. Higher-income households are more likely than low- or moderate-income households to benefit from the deduction because they are more likely to itemize deductions and because the tax benefit increases as the marginal tax benefit increases.

B. CHARITABLE CONTRIBUTIONS

Since 1917, the income tax has allowed a deduction for charitable contributions. Section 170 allows a deduction for a transfer by an individual or a corporation of cash or, in some cases, for the fair market value of property transferred, but not for a contribution of services. The amount deductible is subject to a variety of limitations. Individuals generally are allowed a charitable contribution deduction of no more than

50 percent of adjusted gross income, or 60 percent in the case of cash contributions. § 170(b). (The cap is scheduled to fall back to 50 percent, as under prior law, in 2026.) § 170(b)(1)(G). Although Congress provides incentives for individuals to donate significant portions of their income to charities, it does not believe individuals should be permitted to eliminate their tax liability entirely by transferring all of the current year's income to charity. Certain gifts of appreciated property are limited to 30 percent of a taxpayer's adjusted gross income. Limitations are also imposed on gifts to private foundations. The charitable deduction is not subject to the 2 percent floor on miscellaneous itemized deductions of § 67, but is subject to the reduction of itemized deductions under § 68 (neither of which is in effect from 2018 to 2026).

A corporation's charitable deduction is limited to 10 percent of its taxable income. § 170(b)(2). Neither individuals nor corporations may deduct as a business expense charitable contributions in excess of the percentage limitations.

On occasion Congress temporarily changes the charitable contribution rules in order to encourage additional charitable giving. For example, in 2017 after Hurricanes Harvey, Irma, and Maria hit, Congress quickly passed legislation with various relief provisions. One of them suspended the limitations on the charitable deduction for contributions made for hurricane relief before the end of the year.

NOTES

(A) *Why Allow the Deduction?* Is the charitable deduction a tax expenditure? Some have argued that the choice to give property to a charity is itself a form of consumption and therefore the deduction is inappropriate. Others contend that a contribution deduction is justified by the fact that the amount given to charity will not be consumed by the taxpayer. Income generally is defined as the year's earnings that are available for consumption or savings. Is it appropriate to give a deduction to taxpayers who serve merely as conduits for funds to be consumed by someone else? Should the charity or the ultimate consumer be taxed instead of the donor? Would taxing the recipient of charitable largess be consistent with exempting other gifts from tax? Would it be administratively possible to tax the recipients? Many of those who benefit from charitable gifts are not subject to income tax because their income is below the taxable threshold. In such cases, it seems inappropriate to tax the amount of the gift at the donor's tax rate and a deduction for the donor seems justified. But many beneficiaries (such as patrons of the Metropolitan Opera or law students) would not be taxed at a zero rate. If the value of the benefit they receive from the contributed amounts cannot be taxed, why should the donor be allowed a deduction?

If a charitable deduction is an appropriate adjustment in measuring the donor's net income, is it appropriate to allow it only as an itemized deduction? Those who take a standard deduction are taxed on the dollars given to charity. From time to time, nonitemizers have been allowed to deduct a portion of charitable contributions that would have been deductible if they itemized, but even with the substantial increase in the standard deduction in 2017, no charitable deduction is now permitted for nonitemizers.

(B) *Efficiency of the Deduction.* Is the deduction an efficient means of encouraging gifts to charity? Economists differ on whether the deduction efficiently encourages gifts. Some believe that the deduction increases charitable giving by significantly more than the amount of lost revenue. Others believe that it may subsidize gifts that would have been made in any event.

To use an analogy, assume bread costs $2 a loaf. A buys three loaves of bread per week at a cost of $6. Suppose the price of bread falls to $1 a loaf. Which of the following describes A's likely behavior? Do you need more information?

(1)   A continues to buy three loaves, spending $3.

(2)   A gets six loaves for his $6.

(3)   The price of bread is so cheap that A substitutes bread for potatoes and buys ten loaves at $10 per week.

Similarly, if the charitable deduction reduces the cost of giving $1 to charity to 63 cents for a taxpayer in the 37 percent bracket, what is the likely behavior of a taxpayer who gave $3 to charity before taxes? Will he give $4.76, keeping his out-of-pocket costs at $3 or reduce his out-of-pocket costs to $1.89, maintaining the benefit to charity of $3? Conversely, once a charitable deduction is permitted, limiting or repealing the deduction will raise the price of the donation. What would be the effect on charitable contributions of retaining the deduction but lowering tax rates, as was done in 1986, 2001 and 2017? What would be the effect of raising the taxes rates, as was done in 2013?

In considering the equity and efficiency of the deduction, how would you assess the following alternatives:

(1)   Retain the charitable deduction;

(2)   Repeal the charitable deduction and replace it with a tax credit;

(3)   Repeal the charitable deduction and replace it with a matching grant program under which the federal government would provide the charity a direct grant equal to a specified percentage of the individual's gift;

(4)   Repeal the charitable deduction and lower tax rates generally to offset the revenue increase; or

(5)   Repeal the charitable deduction and replace it with direct federal subsidies.

1.   WHEN IS A TRANSFER TO A CHARITY A CONTRIBUTION?

Hernandez v. Commissioner

Supreme Court of the United States, 1989. 490 U.S. 680.

■ JUSTICE MARSHALL delivered the opinion of the Court.

Section 170 of the Internal Revenue Code of 1954 * * * permits a taxpayer to deduct from gross income the amount of a "charitable contribution." The Code defines that term as a "contribution or gift" to certain eligible donees, including entities organized and operated exclusively for religious purposes. We granted certiorari to determine whether taxpayers may deduct as charitable contributions payments made to branch churches of the Church of Scientology (Church) in order to receive services known as "auditing" and "training." We hold that such payments are not deductible.

I

Scientology was founded in the 1950's by L. Ron Hubbard. It is propagated today by a "mother church" in California and by numerous branch churches around the world. The mother church instructs laity, trains and ordains ministers, and creates new congregations. Branch churches, known as "franchises" or "missions," provide Scientology services at the local level, under the supervision of the mother church. Church of Scientology of California v. Commissioner, 823 F.2d 1310, 1313 (C.A.9 1987), cert. denied, 486 U.S. 1015 (1988).

Scientologists believe that an immortal spiritual being exists in every person. A person becomes aware of this spiritual dimension through a process known as "auditing." Auditing involves a one-to-one encounter between a participant (known as a "preclear") and a Church official (known as an "auditor"). An electronic device, the E-meter, helps the auditor identify the preclear's areas of spiritual difficulty by measuring skin responses during a question and answer session. Although auditing sessions are conducted one-on-one, the content of each session is not individually tailored. The preclear gains spiritual awareness by progressing through sequential levels of auditing, provided in short blocks of time known as "intensives."

The Church also offers members doctrinal courses known as "training." Participants in these sessions study the tenets of Scientology and seek to attain the qualifications necessary to serve as auditors. Training courses, like auditing sessions, are provided in sequential levels. Scientologists are taught that spiritual gains result from participation in such courses.

The Church charges a "fixed donation," also known as a "price" or a "fixed contribution," for participants to gain access to auditing and training sessions. These charges are set forth in schedules and prices vary with a session's length and level of sophistication. In 1972, for example, the general rates for auditing ranged from $625 for a 12½-hour auditing intensive, the shortest available, to $4,250 for a 100-hour intensive, the longest available. Specialized types of auditing required higher fixed donations: a 12½-hour "Integrity Processing" auditing intensive cost $750; a 12½-hour "Expanded Dianetics" auditing intensive cost $950. This system of mandatory fixed charges is based on a central tenet of Scientology known as the "doctrine of exchange," according to which any time a person receives something he must pay something back.. In so doing, a Scientologist maintains "inflow" and "outflow" and avoids spiritual decline.

The proceeds generated from auditing and training sessions are the Church's primary source of income. The Church promotes these sessions not only through newspaper, magazine, and radio advertisements, but also through free lectures, free personality tests, and leaflets. The Church also encourages, and indeed rewards with a 5% discount, advance payment for these sessions. The Church often refunds unused portions of prepaid auditing or training fees, less an administrative charge.

The petitioners in these consolidated cases each made payments to a branch church for auditing or training sessions. They sought to deduct these payments on their federal income tax returns as charitable contributions under § 170. Respondent Commissioner of the Internal Revenue Service (Commissioner or IRS) disallowed these deductions, finding that the payments were not charitable contributions within the meaning of § 170. * * *

For over 70 years, federal taxpayers have been allowed to deduct the amount of contributions or gifts to charitable, religious, and other eleemosynary institutions. Section 170, the present provision, was enacted in 1954; it requires a taxpayer claiming the deduction to satisfy a number of conditions. The Commissioner's stipulation in this case, however, has narrowed the statutory inquiry to one such condition: whether petitioners' payments for auditing and training sessions are "contribution[s] or gift[s]" within the meaning of § 170.

The legislative history of the "contribution or gift" limitation, though sparse, reveals that Congress intended to differentiate between unrequited payments to qualified recipients and payments made to such recipients in return for goods or services. Only the former were deemed deductible. The House and Senate Reports on the 1954 tax bill, for example, both define "gifts" as payments "made with no expectation of a financial return commensurate with the amount of the gift." S.Rep. No. 1622, 83d Cong., 2d Sess., 196 (1954); H.R.Rep. No. 1337, 83d Cong., 2d Sess., A44 (1954). Using payments to hospitals as an example, both Reports state that the gift characterization should not apply to "a payment by an individual to a hospital *in consideration of* a binding obligation to provide medical treatment for the individual's employees. It would apply only if there were no expectation of any *quid pro quo* from the hospital." S.Rep. No. 1622, supra, at 196 (emphasis added); H.Rep. No. 1337, supra, at A44 (emphasis added).

In ascertaining whether a given payment was made with "the expectation of any *quid pro quo*," the Internal Revenue Service (IRS) has customarily examined the external features of the transaction in question. This practice has the advantage of obviating the need for the IRS to conduct imprecise inquiries into the motivations of individual taxpayers. The lower courts have generally embraced this structural analysis.

In light of this understanding of § 170, it is readily apparent that petitioners' payments to the Church do not qualify as "contribution[s] or gift[s]." As the Tax Court found, these payments were part of a quintessential quid pro quo exchange: in return for their money, petitioners received an identifiable benefit, namely, auditing and training sessions. The Church established fixed price schedules for auditing and training sessions in each branch church; it calibrated particular prices to auditing or training sessions of particular lengths and levels of sophistication; it returned a refund if auditing and training services went unperformed; it distributed "account cards" on which persons who had paid money to the Church could monitor what prepaid services they had not yet claimed; and it categorically barred provision of auditing or training sessions for free. Each of these practices reveals the inherently reciprocal nature of the exchange.

Petitioners do not argue that such a structural analysis is inappropriate under § 170, or that the external features of the auditing and training transactions do not strongly suggest a quid pro quo exchange. * * * Petitioners argued instead that they are entitled to deductions because a quid pro quo analysis is inappropriate under § 170 when the benefit a taxpayer receives is purely religious in nature. Along the same lines, petitioners claim that payments made for the right to participate in a religious service should be automatically deductible under § 170.

We cannot accept this statutory argument for several reasons. First, it finds no support in the language of § 170. Whether or not Congress could, consistent with the Establishment Clause, provide for the automatic deductibility of a payment made to a church that either generates religious benefits or guarantees access to a religious service, that is a choice Congress has thus far declined to make. Instead, Congress has specified that a payment to an organization operated exclusively for religious (or other eleemosynary) purposes is deductible only if such a payment is a "contribution or gift." § 170(c). The Code makes no special preference for payments made in the expectation of gaining religious benefits or access to a religious service. * * *

Second, petitioners' deductibility proposal would expand the charitable contribution deduction far beyond what Congress has provided. Numerous forms of payments to eligible donees plausibly could be categorized as providing a religious benefit or as securing access to a religious service. For example, some taxpayers might regard their tuition payments to parochial schools as generating a religious benefit or as securing access to a religious service; such payments, however, have long been held not to be charitable contributions under § 170. * * * Taxpayers might make similar claims about payments for church-sponsored counseling sessions or for medical care at church-affiliated hospitals that otherwise might not be deductible. Given that, under the First Amendment, the IRS can reject otherwise valid claims of religious benefit only on the ground that a taxpayer's alleged beliefs are not sincerely held, but not on the ground that such beliefs are inherently irreligious, see United States v. Ballard, 322 U.S. 78 (1944), the resulting tax deductions would likely expand the charitable contribution provision far beyond its present size. We are loath to effect this result in the absence of supportive congressional intent.

Finally, the deduction petitioners seek might raise problems of entanglement between church and state. If framed as a deduction for those payments made in connection with a religious service, petitioners' proposal would force the IRS and the judiciary into differentiating "religious" services from "secular" ones. We need pass no judgment now on the constitutionality of such hypothetical inquiries, but we do note that "pervasive monitoring" for "the subtle or overt presence of religious matter" is a central danger against which we have held the Establishment Clause guards.

Accordingly, we conclude that petitioners' payments to the Church for auditing and training sessions are not "contribution[s] or gift[s]" within the meaning of that statutory expression.

[The Court rejects petitioners' constitutional claims based on the Establishment Clause and the Free Exercise Clause of the First Amendment. It finds that § 170 does not create an unconstitutional denominational preference by according disproportionately harsh tax status to those religions that raise funds by imposing fixed costs for participation in certain religious practices nor does § 170 threaten excessive governmental entanglement.]

■ JUSTICE O'CONNOR, with whom JUSTICE SCALIA joins, dissenting.

The Court today acquiesces in the decision of the Internal Revenue Service (IRS) to manufacture a singular exception to its 70-year practice of allowing fixed payments indistinguishable from those made by petitioners to be deducted as charitable contributions. Because the IRS cannot constitutionally be allowed to select which religions will receive the benefit of its past rulings, I respectfully dissent. * * *

It must be emphasized that the IRS' position here is not based upon the contention that a portion of the knowledge received from auditing or training is of secular, commercial, nonreligious value. * * * Here the IRS denies deductibility solely on the basis that the exchange is a *quid pro* *quo*, even though the quid is exclusively of spiritual or religious worth. The Government cites no instances in which this has been done before, and there are good reasons why.

When a taxpayer claims as a charitable deduction part of a fixed amount given to a charitable organization in exchange for benefits that have a commercial value, the allowable portion of that claim is computed by subtracting from the total amount paid the value of the physical benefit received. If at a charity sale one purchases for $1,000 a painting whose market value is demonstrably no more than $50, there has been a contribution of $950. The same would be true if one purchases a $1,000 seat at a charitable dinner where the food is worth $50. An identical calculation can be made where the quid received is not a painting or a meal, but an intangible such as entertainment, so long as that intangible has some market value established in a noncontributory context. Hence, one who purchases a ticket to a concert, at the going rate for concerts by the particular performers, makes a charitable contribution of zero even if it is announced in advance that all proceeds from the ticket sales will go to charity. The performers may have made a charitable contribution, but the audience has paid the going rate for a show.

It becomes impossible, however, to compute the "contribution" portion of a payment to a charity where what is received in return is not merely an intangible, but an intangible (or, for that matter a tangible) that is not bought and sold except in donative contexts so that the only "market" price against which it can be evaluated is a market price that always includes donations. Suppose, for example, that the charitable organization that traditionally solicits donations on Veterans' Day, in exchange for which it gives the donor an imitation poppy bearing its name, were to establish a flat rule that no one gets a poppy without a donation of at least $10. One would have to say that the "market" rate for such poppies was $10, but it would assuredly not be true that everyone who "bought" a poppy for $10 made no contribution. Similarly, if one buys a $100 seat at a prayer breakfast—receiving as the quid pro quo food for both body and soul—it would make no sense to say that no charitable contribution whatever has occurred simply because the "going rate" for all prayer breakfasts (with equivalent bodily food) is $100. The latter may well be true, but that "going rate" includes a contribution.

Confronted with this difficulty, and with the constitutional necessity of not making irrational distinctions among taxpayers, and with the even higher standard of equality of treatment among religions that the First Amendment imposes, the Government has only two practicable options with regard to distinctively religious quids pro quo: to disregard them all, or to tax them all. Over the years it has chosen the former course. * * *

The IRS reaffirmed its position in 1970, ruling that "[p]ew rents, building fund assessments and periodic dues paid to a church * * * are all methods of making contributions to the church and such payments are deductible as charitable contributions." Rev. Rul. 70–47, 1970–1

Cum.Bull. 49. Similarly, notwithstanding the "form" of Mass stipends as fixed payments for specific religious services, * * * the IRS has allowed charitable deductions of such payments. See Rev. Rul. 78–366, 1978–2 Cum.Bull. 241.

These rulings, which are "official interpretation[s] of [the tax laws] by the [IRS]," * * * flatly contradict the Solicitor General's claim that there "is no administrative practice recognizing that payments made in exchange for religious benefits are tax deductible."

There can be no doubt that at least some of the fixed payments which the IRS has treated as charitable deductions, or which the Court assumes the IRS would allow taxpayers to deduct, are as "inherently reciprocal," as the payments for auditing at issue here. In exchange for their payment of pew rents, Christians receive particular seats during worship services. * * * Similarly, in some synagogues attendance at the worship services for Jewish High Holy Days is often predicated upon the purchase of a general admission ticket or a reserved seat ticket. * * * Religious honors such as publicly reading from Scripture are purchased or auctioned periodically in some synagogues of Jews from Morocco and Syria. * * * Mormons must tithe ten percent of their income as a necessary but not sufficient condition to obtaining a "temple recommend," i.e., the right to be admitted into the temple. * * * A Mass stipend—a fixed payment given to a Catholic priest, in consideration of which he is obliged to apply the fruits of the Mass for the intention of the donor—has similar overtones of exchange. * * *

This is not a situation where the IRS has explicitly and affirmatively reevaluated its longstanding interpretation of § 170 and decided to analyze all fixed religious contributions under a quid pro quo standard. There is no indication whatever that the IRS has abandoned its 70-year practice with respect to payments made by those other than Scientologists. In 1978, when it ruled that payments for auditing and training were not charitable contributions under § 170, the IRS did not cite—much less try to reconcile—its previous rulings concerning the deductibility of other forms of fixed payments for religious services or practices. See Rev. Rul. 78–189, 1978–1 Cum.Bull. 68 (equating payments for auditing with tuition paid to religious schools).

Nevertheless, the Government now attempts to reconcile its previous rulings with its decision in these cases by relying on a distinction between direct and incidental benefits in exchange for payments made to a charitable organization. This distinction * * * recognizes that even a deductible charitable contribution may generate certain benefits for the donor. As long as the benefits remain "incidental" and do not indicate that the payment was actually made for the "personal accommodation" of the donor, the payment will be deductible. It is the Government's view that the payments made by petitioners should not be deductible under § 170 because the "unusual facts in these cases * * * demonstrate that the payments were made primarily for 'personal accommodation.'" Specifically, the Solicitor General asserts that "the rigid connection between the provision of auditing and training services and payment of the fixed price" indicates a quid pro quo relationship and "reflect[s] the value that petitioners expected to receive for their money."

There is no discernable reason why there is a more rigid connection between payment and services in the religious practices of Scientology than in the religious practices of the faiths described above. * * *

In my view, the IRS has misapplied its longstanding practice of allowing charitable contributions under § 170 in a way that violates the Establishment Clause. It has unconstitutionally refused to allow payments for the religious service of auditing to be deducted as charitable contributions in the same way it has allowed fixed payments to other religions to be deducted. Just as the Minnesota statute at issue in Larson v. Valente, 456 U.S. 228 (1982), discriminated against the Unification Church, the IRS' application of the *quid pro quo* standard here—and only here—discriminates against the Church of Scientology. I would reverse the decisions below.

NOTES

(A) *Hernandez Fallout.* In an unusual ruling the Service obsoleted an earlier ruling and held that the Church of Scientology and its related entities are tax-exempt churches and that contributions to them are deductible. The ruling did not mention *Hernandez,* which denied the deduction. Rev. Rul. 93–73, 1993–2 C.B. 75. The Service also entered into a closing agreement with the church, which was not made public.

Congress added its two cents when it added substantiation requirements to the Code in 1993. Section 170(f)(8) states that in providing a receipt the charitable donee should note if only "intangible religious benefits" were received, which are defined as a benefit "provided by an organization organized exclusively for religious purposes and which generally is not sold in a commercial transaction outside the donative context."

What if the benefit is religious education? In Sklar v. Commissioner, 282 F.3d 610 (9th Cir. 2002), the taxpayers attempted to deduct a portion of private school tuition for their children equal to the value of religious education received. The Appeals Court rejected any reliance on § 170(f) and instead followed *Hernandez.* The Sklars also argued that the IRS violated the Establishment Clause of the Constitution by permitting members of the Church of Scientology to deduct amounts paid for auditing but denying the deduction for the costs of religious education for other sects. Although the court remarked that it was impermissible for the IRS to withhold the closing agreement with the Church of Scientology and that such an agreement violates the Establishment Clause by favoring one religion, they nevertheless denied the Sklars their deduction. First, they were unwilling to order a deduction for all religious training absent Congressional approval and because the court believed doing so was unconstitutional. Second, they found that the Sklars had not made a "dual payment" whose cost exceeded the benefits of the secular education received. Thus, the court's findings with respect to the constitutionality of the *Hernandez* closing agreement became dicta.

(B) *Detached and Disinterested Generosity. Hernandez* is a difficult application of the longstanding rule that a charitable contribution is limited to the excess of the amount transferred to the charity over the value of any benefit received by the donor. For example, if one sends a contribution to the local public television station and receives an umbrella in return, the taxpayer must subtract the value of the umbrella from the amount contributed. The value to the donor is assumed to be the fair market value of whatever goods or services the donor receives. The cost to the donee of providing the goods and services is irrelevant. See, e.g., Rolfs v. Commissioner, 668 F.3d 888 (7th Cir. 2012) where the court denied a charitable deduction to taxpayers who donated their home to the local fire department for firefighting training. The court found that they received demolition services that exceeded the value of the donation.

Courts have increasingly supported the notion that a deductible charitable contribution must meet the *Duberstein* test ("detached and disinterested generosity," see page 125, supra) for what constitutes a gift. See, e.g., Babilonia v. Commissioner, 681 F.2d 678 (9th Cir. 1982), where the parents of figure skater Tai Babilonia attempted to deduct the costs of accompanying her to various international competitions as expenses incurred in performing services for a charitable organization. The deduction was denied on the ground that the taxpayers' primary purpose was to advance their daughter's career rather than to advance the Olympic team in general.

Suppose a taxpayer makes a purchase from an online retailer listed on the site of a Web-based "charity mall" and the mall makes a charitable contribution of 5 percent of the purchase price to a tax-exempt organization. Can the purchaser take a charitable deduction? Would it make any difference if the purchaser could choose the charity? Would it make a difference if the amount of the purchase was characterized as a rebate transferred to the purchaser who transfers it to the charity?

What if a taxpayer bids in an auction where the proceeds will be contributed to charity? In 2016 the Roman Catholic Archdiocese of New York offered a Fiat 500 Lounge with a list price of around $20,000 on the website of CharityBuzz.com. The winning bid was $300,000 for the so-called pope mobile in which Pope Francis rode while visiting New York City. The proceeds of the auction went to Catholic schools and charities. Can the winning bidder take a charitable deduction? Reg. § 1.170A–1(h)(4) provides: "A taxpayer may not treat an estimate of the value of goods or services as their fair market value if the taxpayer knows, or has reason to know, that such treatment is unreasonable."

The IRS has never attempted to tax less tangible returns, such a contribution to a college that results in the donor's name on a building. What if the donor's gift is contingent on the naming of a building, in other words a quid pro quo? Is this an example of the incidental benefits that *Hernandez* indicates do not preclude a charitable deduction?

The *Duberstein* standard is somewhat more difficult to apply where the donor is a business. For example, the Supreme Court applied the *Duberstein* test in United States v. American Bar Endowment, 477 U.S. 105 (1986), to disallow charitable deductions for payments to purchase insurance policies from a tax-exempt organization because the taxpayers were unable to show that they could have purchased comparable insurance policies elsewhere for less than the amount they paid.

In United States v. Transamerica Corp., 392 F.2d 522, 524 (9th Cir. 1968), the court held that a deduction could be taken where there was an indirect business benefit "such as one incidental to the public use or to public recognition of its act of generosity," but not where there was a direct economic benefit.

(C) *What Constitutes a Church?* Churches have a special status in the tax law, which is generally more favorable than that of other charitable organizations or even other religious organizations. For example, they are not subject to the private foundation rules, they are not subject to annual information filings, and there are restrictions on audits of churches. Determining whether an organization is a "church" is tricky because the statute fails to define the term. The IRS has listed fourteen factors to be considered. One is the existence of a regular congregation. Although no specific size is required, the Service rejects tax-exempt status for a congregation of one or two members or family members on the grounds that there is private inurement. A number of courts have developed an associational test to determine whether a religious organization is a church. Under this test an organization must include a body of believers who assemble regularly for communal worship. This apparently requires a brick-and-mortar building. An internet church where members regularly assembled at set times to worship as a virtual congregation was determined not to fulfill the associational role required to qualify a church. Foundation of Human Understanding v. United States, 614 F.3d 1383 (Fed. Cir. 2010). "The fact that all the listeners simultaneously received the Foundation's message over the radio or the Internet does not mean that those members associated with each other and worshiped communally." Is the court's failure to recognize a "church without walls" a reasonable interpretation of the meaning of "church" or is it a failure to recognize modern technology? Does the Church of Scientology, which conducts its religious practices in one-on-one settings, fail to qualify as a church? Should it?

While there are restrictions on what constitutes a church, it is surprisingly easy to establish one, as comedian John Oliver demonstrated when he set up the Church of the Perpetual Exemption and named himself "megareverend." He set up a website to collect donations in exchange for blessings. His "completely legal" satire was aimed at televangelists who "rake in millions" without paying taxes.

(D) *Seats at College Sporting Events.* The *Duberstein* gift analysis has been used to combat fundraising tactics that encourage giving for motives that could hardly be classified as "disinterested generosity." For example, colleges and universities often provide choice football or basketball seats to those who contribute in excess of a specific amount. The Code now disallows any charitable deduction whenever a contribution makes the donor eligible to obtain athletic tickets. § 170(*l*).

(E) *Gifts to Schools.* In Winters v. Commissioner, 468 F.2d 778 (2d Cir. 1972), the Second Circuit considered the deductibility of a couple's "contribution" of more than $2,000 to a church education fund that was used to support schools attended by their children. Although the taxpayers were active members of the church and were not required to pay tuition or otherwise to contribute to the schools, the court denied the deduction on the grounds that the gift was made with the "anticipation of economic benefit" rather than from "detached and disinterested generosity."

Revenue Ruling 83–104, 1983–2 C.B. 46, provides six examples of donations to private schools operated by charitable organizations. In each of the six situations, a taxpayer, who is a parent of a child who attends the school, makes a payment to the charitable organization operating the school. The cost of educating the child in the school is not less than the payments made by the parent to the organization. The ruling states:

> Whether a transfer of money by a parent to an organization that operates a school is a voluntary transfer that is made with no expectation of obtaining a commensurate benefit depends upon whether a reasonable person, taking all the facts and circumstances of the case into account, would conclude that enrollment in the school was in no manner contingent upon making the payment, that the payment was not made pursuant to a plan (whether express or implied) to convert nondeductible tuition into charitable contributions, and that receipt of the benefit was not otherwise dependent upon the making of the payment.

> In determining this issue, the presence of one or more of the following factors creates a presumption that the payment is not a charitable contribution: the existence of a contract under which a taxpayer agrees to make a "contribution" and which contains provisions ensuring the admission of the taxpayer's child; a plan allowing taxpayers either to pay tuition or to make "contributions" in exchange for schooling; the earmarking of a contribution for the direct benefit of a particular individual; or the otherwise unexplained denial of admission or readmission to a school of children of taxpayers who are financially able, but who do not contribute.

> In other cases, although no single factor may be determinative, a combination of several factors may indicate that a payment is not a charitable contribution: * * * (1) the absence of a significant tuition charge; (2) substantial or unusual pressure to contribute applied to parents of children attending a school; (3) contribution appeals made as part of the admissions or enrollment process; (4) the absence of significant potential sources of revenue for operating

the school other than contributions by parents of children attending the school; (5) and other factors suggesting that a contribution policy has been created as a means of avoiding the characterization of payments as tuition.

(F) *Gifts Earmarked for Individuals.* Ending a split among the circuits, the Supreme Court in Davis v. United States, 495 U.S. 472 (1990), denied the parents of missionaries of the Church of Jesus Christ of the Latter-Day Saints a deduction for payments used to support the missionary activities of their children. The Court noted that § 170 permits a deduction only if the contribution is made "to or for the use of" the charity. In *Davis,* the payments were made directly to the children and although the church required them to account for the funds, it had neither possession nor control of the funds. The Court concluded that: "a gift or contribution is 'for the use of' a qualified organization when it is held in a legally enforceable trust for the qualified organization or a similar legal arrangement."

The Court also rejected the parents' argument that the payments were deductible under Reg. § 1.170A–1(g), which permits the deduction of unreimbursed expenditures incident to the rendition of charitable services. The Court ruled that taxpayers may claim deductions only for expenditures undertaken in connection with their own contributions of services.

(G) *Gifts of Services.* Since 1920, the IRS has consistently maintained, and the courts have agreed, that a taxpayer cannot deduct the value of services rendered to charitable institutions. A person, however, may deduct unreimbursed out-of-pocket expenses incurred in connection with donating services to a charitable organization. See, e.g., McCollum v. Commissioner, 37 T.C.M. 1817 (1978), where the Tax Court allowed deductions for ski uniforms, ski equipment repairs, and lift tickets purchased by the taxpayer and his family, members of the National Ski Patrol, a voluntary organization engaged in policing ski slopes. The court was "unimpressed" with the IRS's argument that the deductions should be disallowed because the taxpayer "enjoyed skiing, enjoyed the work * * * and enjoyed the camaraderie of the other members of the ski patrol." Section 170(j) now provides that travel expenses (including meals and lodging) are not deductible unless there is "no significant element of personal pleasure, recreation, or vacation." Since many charitable activities involve an element of personal pleasure that limitation would seem to limit deductions. But legislative history indicates that "[i]n determining whether travel away from home involves a significant element of personal pleasure, recreation, or vacation, the fact that a taxpayer enjoys providing services to the charitable organization will not lead to denial of the deduction. That has been interpreted to mean that "the relevant inquiry is the extent and duration of the charitable services provided by the taxpayer, and not some quantum measure of pleasure derived by the taxpayer." Cavalaris v. Commissioner, 72 T.C.M. 46 (1996).

A taxpayer can claim a deduction for paying third parties to assist them in providing charitable services. See Rockefeller v. Commissioner, 676 F.2d 35 (2d Cir. 1982) (deduction permitted for salaries taxpayers paid to employees who provided services to charities that taxpayers supported).

In Lary v. United States, 787 F.2d 1538 (11th Cir. 1986), the court denied deduction for contributions of blood. The IRS had maintained that the contribution of blood was a service, but the Eleventh Circuit did not decide whether the contribution of blood was a service or a gift of property, noting that no charitable deduction would be available even in the latter case since the taxpayers could not prove the holding period or the basis of the blood or the amount or type of gain that would occur if the blood were sold rather than contributed. See the discussion of § 170(e) at page 467, infra.

Suppose the taxpayer is donating sperm? In Free Fertility Foundation v. Commissioner, 135 T.C. 21 (2010), the taxpayer created a non-profit corporation to provide his sperm free to women who requested it. Showing commendable discretion, the court did not consider whether the donation of sperm was a donation of property or services. Instead the court said the foundation did not qualify as a charity because the class of the taxpayer's beneficiaries was not sufficiently large to benefit the community as a whole. Although petitioner claimed that it was all women of child-bearing age, the court found it to be much smaller, i.e. only those who wanted this one man to be the sperm donor and who passed his selection process.

How does the failure to allow any deduction for services compare to the treatment the taxpayer would receive if he were compensated for the services and donated the payment to charity?

(H) *Substantiation.* Auctions of donated goods and services by charitable organizations have become commonplace. If a taxpayer bids $1,000 and wins a vacation at a ski resort, there is no charitable contribution at all unless the vacation normally sells for less than $1,000. Nevertheless, many purchasers of such items have deducted their purchases. In response, Congress strengthened substantiation requirements in an effort to curtail bogus charitable contributions. For gifts of $250 or more, the taxpayer must provide a written contemporaneous statement from the charity that includes information as to whether goods or services have been provided to the donor in exchange for the gift, and an estimate of their value. § 170(f)(8). A "contemporaneous statement" is one issued by the charity before the return is filed. Consider the plight of the Durdens who donated over $22,000 to their church in increments exceeding $250. The church sent them a year-end statement acknowledging their gifts. When the IRS asserted a deficiency a year later, the Durdens produced their cancelled checks and the letter from the church. The IRS rejected the evidence because the church's statement did not explicitly say that no goods or services had been provided. Since they had received nothing in return for their contribution, the Durdens got a second letter from the church with that statement added. Too late—the IRS said the letter was not "contemporaneous" and denied the entire deduction. The Tax Court agreed. Durden v. Commissioner, 103 T.C.M. 1762 (2012). Ouch!

Donations of property valued at more than $5,000 must include a form with an appraisal and certain other information, including the cost basis of the donated property. In RERI Holdings I v. Commissioner, 149 T.C. No. 1 (2017), a partnership whose principal investor was Stephen Ross, the owner of the Miami Dolphins and a major donor to the University of Michigan, gave an interest in property to the university and took a $33 million charitable deduction. The partnership had acquired the property seventeen months earlier for $3 million. The partnership attached the form to its return but omitted its cost basis. That omission, the Tax Court noted, failed to tip off the IRS, that something might be amiss with a claim that the property had increased in value $30 million over that period. The court denied the entire deduction.

For gifts of cash, regardless of size, the taxpayer must have a bank record (such as a cancelled check) or a written record from the donee showing the date and the amount of the contribution. That appears to eliminate a deduction for the dollars thrown in the ubiquitous Salvation Army kettles at Christmas.

2. GIFTS OF APPRECIATED PROPERTY

A taxpayer who gives appreciated property to charity generally does not realize gain, as she would have if she had sold the property for its fair market value. Nevertheless, the Code generally allows the taxpayer to deduct the full fair market value of the appreciated property. (A taxpayer also does not realize loss for tax purposes when depreciated property is given to charity; but the loss may be realized if she first sells the depreciated asset, realizing the loss for tax purposes, and then contributes the proceeds.)

The tax law thus confers a generous benefit on contributors of appreciated property. This benefit is limited by § 170(e), which, in some circumstances, reduces the charitable contribution by the amount of the unrealized gain.

The generous treatment of gifts of appreciated property to charity has long been a source of controversy. In 1984, for example, the Treasury recommended that the deduction for any charitable donation be limited to the lesser of the fair market value or the basis of the property, stating:

> The current treatment of certain charitable gifts of appreciated property is unduly generous and in conflict with basic principles governing the measurement of income for tax purposes. In other circumstances where appreciated property is used to pay a deductible expense, or where such property is the subject of a deductible loss, the deduction allowed may not exceed the taxpayer's adjusted basis plus any gain recognized. Thus, a taxpayer generally may not receive a tax deduction with respect to untaxed appreciation in property. The current tax treatment of certain charitable gifts departs from this principle by permitting the donor a deduction for the full value of the property, including the element of appreciation with respect to which the donor does not realize gain.

2 Treasury Dep't, Report to the President, Tax Reform for Fairness, Simplicity and Economic Growth 72–74 (1984).

Charities respond, however, that the deduction by donors for the fair market value of contributed appreciated property is essential to their continued well-being. Universities point out that while large gifts typically account for less than 5 percent of the number of gifts, large gifts of appreciated property account for nearly half of the total amount of donations received. The universities argue: "Even if granting a deduction for appreciated property favors the high-bracket taxpayer who can afford to make such gifts, this theoretical inequity is dwarfed by the benefits to higher education of the appreciated property rules and the potentially ruinous loss of private support that could result from change in those rules. * * * Making it more costly for a rich man to give money to charity does not make it less costly for a poor man to do so; such tax changes will only reduce the amount flowing to charity from those who can best afford it." Report of the Association of American Universities, Tax Reform and the Crisis of Financing Higher Education 8 (1973). For a good discussion of the problems with the failure to tax unrealized gains on the contribution of appreciated property to a charity, see Daniel Halperin, A Charitable Contribution of Appreciated Property and the Realization of Built-in Gains, 56 Tax L. Rev. 1 (2002).

NOTES

(A) *Section 170(e).* The amount of the charitable deduction for a donation of appreciated property depends on whether the recipient is a private foundation or a public charity, whether the appreciation would be taxed as capital gain or ordinary income if the property were sold, and whether the gift consists of tangible property or securities.

The deduction for a contribution of property to a public charity is generally the fair market value minus the amount of gain that would not have been long-term capital gain on a sale. If, however, the property is tangible personal property that will not be used by the donee in its charitable function, the deduction is the fair market value reduced by the full amount of the appreciation. Charitable contributions to public charities of appreciated securities or real estate therefore are deductible in full if they would produce long-term capital gain if sold. To make sure the charity will actually use donated tangible personalty, the deduction is limited to basis if the property is worth more than $5,000, the charity sells the property in the year of the contribution, and cannot certify that the related use has become impossible or impracticable. If the property is sold after the year of donation but within three years of the gift, the donor must recapture as ordinary income the excess of the deduction over her basis in the property. A contribution of any property other than marketable securities (defined in § 170(e)(5)) to a private foundation (defined in § 509) gives rise to a deduction equal to the fair market value of the property minus any capital gain or ordinary income—in other words, the deduction is generally limited to the basis of the property.

The taxpayer in Jones v. Commissioner, 560 F.3d 1196 (10th Cir. 2009), tried to claim a charitable deduction for the donation of discovery material he received as lead counsel for Timothy McVeigh, convicted of bombing a federal building in Oklahoma City. Although the disallowance of the deduction was largely based on the theory that the taxpayer did not actually own discovery material, the Tenth Circuit noted that discovery material is excepted from capital asset treatment by § 1221(a)(3)(B) and thus the charitable deduction would be limited to the taxpayer's basis. The court also pointed out that the taxpayer has no basis in the discovery material prepared for him.

The following four examples illustrate the application of § 170(e):

(1)   T contributes stock with an adjusted basis of $100 and a fair market value of $300 to the Red Cross, a public charity. If the stock has been held for more than a year, it would have produced long-term capital gain when sold and thus T's charitable deduction is $300. If the stock had been held for only six months, the $300 fair market value is reduced by the appreciation of $200, which would have been treated as a short-term capital gain had the stock been sold. Thus, T's deduction is limited to his basis of $100.

(2)   T contributes to the Red Cross a painting with an adjusted basis of $100 and a fair market value of $300. The Red Cross does not intend to hang the painting. Since T held the painting for more than a year, the appreciation would have been taxed as long-term capital gain if the painting had been sold. Because, however, the charity does not intend to use this tangible personal property in its charitable function, the deduction is limited to $300 minus the long-term capital gain of $200 or T's $100 basis.

(3)   T contributes the same painting to an art museum. If T held the painting for a year or less, the amount of the charitable deduction is only $100 because the fair market value is reduced by the short-term capital gain. If, however, T held the painting for more than a year, the deduction is the full $300 because the appreciation would be treated as long-term capital gain and the donee will use the painting in its charitable function. If, however, the museum sells the painting in the year of contribution, the deduction is limited to $100 unless it could certify that the related use is impractical. If the museum sells the painting two years after the contribution, the deduction would be $300, but in the year of sale the donor would recapture $200 as taxable income.

(4)   T contributes real estate with a basis of $100 and a fair market value of $300 to a private foundation. Because property other than marketable securities has been donated to a private foundation, the deduction is reduced by the full amount of the capital gain. Thus, T's deduction is $100.

Note that if the painting in (2) and (3) had been donated by the artist, the gain would have been ordinary income. See § 1221(a)(3). Regardless of the identity of the charity, the donation would have been the fair market value minus the ordinary income or $100. Note that a donee who receives the painting from the artist as a gift is treated the same as the artist under

§ 1221(a)(3). The painting in his hands is not a capital asset and the deduction is limited to basis under § 170(e).

The deduction for a contribution of a patent or other intellectual property is limited to the lesser of the adjusted basis of the property or its fair market value. A donor of such property is permitted to take an additional charitable deduction in the year of contribution and succeeding years of an amount equal to a percentage (decreasing over time) of the income generated by the property (reduced by the original deduction). § 170(m).

(B) *Tax Planning.* Charitable giving can be important in the tax planning of high-income taxpayers. Great care is necessary in counseling such individuals. Well-advised taxpayers, if they can, will make charitable contributions of appreciated stock, real estate, or other noncash assets qualifying for full deduction. You should try to understand why they do so, as well as why the advantages of doing so may be lost under § 170(e). The following example should clarify the underlying logic of § 170(e):

Assume that a person in the 37 percent bracket paid $2,000 for property that now has a market value of $10,000. The property is not as valuable to the taxpayer as $10,000 in cash because taxes will have to be paid if it is sold. If the property is sold and the taxpayer donates $10,000 cash, there is a net $ $2,100 benefit to the donor. The gain of $8,000 on the property is subject to a 20 percent capital gains tax or $1,600, which offsets the $3,700 value of the cash deduction ($10,000 x .37), which saves tax on other income. If the property is donated, the taxpayer enjoys the full benefit of the $10,000 deduction ($3,700) and pays no tax on the stock appreciation. (Some commentators, including representatives of charities, contend that a comparison between a charitable gift and sale is not apt because taxpayers instead could hold the property until death and avoid any tax on the appreciation under § 1014.)

The costs of giving cash and appreciated property would be the same if the gift to charity were a taxable event triggering payment of tax on the gain at the nominal rate. The deduction reduction of § 170(e) (in the limited situations where it applies) tends to accomplish such a goal indirectly. Instead of taxing the gain, § 170(e) reduces the charitable deduction by the amount that taxable income would be increased if the gain were taxable. If § 170(e) applies, the gain is not recognized, but the charitable deduction is reduced to the donor's basis. Notice that if the appreciated property is taxed at preferential rates and § 170(e) applies, selling generally produces a better result.

(C) *Valuation.* The value of a gift to a charity must be measurable with reasonable accuracy. The regulations state that the fair market value of property donated to a charity is the "price at which the property would change hands between a willing buyer and a willing seller, neither being under any compulsion to buy or sell and both having a reasonable knowledge of relevant facts." Reg. § 1.170A–1(c)(2).

The regulations contain extensive requirements for substantiation of charitable deductions greater than $5,000. § 1.170A–13(c). Among them is that an independent appraiser must value the property and a statement with the appraiser's signature must accompany the return. Joseph Mohamed, a prominent real estate developer and appraiser, donated $18.5 million of real estate to a charitable trust and took approximately $4 million in current deductions. He failed to read the tax form instructions, however, and did not include the required statement of an independent appraiser. Once an audit was started Mohamed obtained an independent appraisal that resulted in higher values than he had claimed. The IRS then realized that Mohamed had not attached the proper forms to his return and denied the entire deduction. The Tax Court, which upheld the IRS, was sympathetic to the taxpayer' plight but noted:

> We recognize that this result is harsh—a complete denial of charitable deductions to a couple that did not overvalue, and may well have *undervalued*, their contributions—all reported on forms that even to the Court's eyes seemed likely to mislead someone who didn't read the instructions. But the problems of misvalued property are so great that Congress was quite specific about what the charitably inclined have to do to defend their deductions, and we cannot in a single sympathetic case undermine those rules.

Mohamed v. Commissioner, 103 T.C.M. 1814 (2012).

Appraisals to establish the fair market value of charitable contributions—especially works of art—have produced many disputes between taxpayers and the IRS. Some tax shelter arrangements—involving buying at wholesale and giving at retail—have tried to inflate charitable deductions through overvaluation. The IRS has attempted to deal with the problem through such efforts as establishing an advisory group on the valuation of works of art. Congress further responded to the problem by mandating independent appraisals where the deduction exceeds a specific amount and by imposing new penalties on tax reductions due to overvaluations and on appraisers who deliberately inflate values. See § 6662(e) for rules dealing with valuation overstatements in the case of charitable contributions. See, e.g., Rev. Rul. 80–69, 180–1 C.B. 55 (disallowing deductions of gems donated 13 months after purchase for three times the "wholesale" purchase price.) Section 170(f)(11) provides that the taxpayer must include with the return a description of the property for any deduction of more than $500 where the property is not readily valued, and a qualified appraisal where the deduction exceeds $5,000.

Congress has severely limited a common scam involving donations of used cars. Many charities accepted cars that were then turned over to dealers for re-sale. Donors were told they could deduct the Blue Book value, which usually far exceeded the amount recouped by the charity on a subsequent sale. The deduction is now limited to the gross sales proceeds, an amount the charity must provide to the donor. Because of dealer commission and costs this can still substantially exceed the amount received by the charity. According to IRS data, car donations fell in value by 80 percent following the change in the law. With the end of the donated car scam, some taxpayers moved on to bigger game. A story in the *Washington Post* reports that big-game hunters were paying for hunting vacations by donating their mounted animals to museums and taking large charitable deductions. Many of the gifts found their way to the Wyobraska Wildlife Museum in Gering, Nebraska, whose website asked, "Are You Needing a Nice Tax Write-Off?" The museum stored hundreds of dusty trophy mounts in a railroad car before selling them off at auction for a small fraction of the $5 million in charitable deductions their donors took. Congress finally shut this ploy down by limiting the deduction to the lower of basis or fair market value and for purposes of determining basis only the actual costs of the taxidermy were included, not the costs of the hunt.

But, like a "whack-a-mole" game, as fast as Congress shuts down one scam, another pops up. For example, the taxpayer in Stamoulis v. Commissioner, T.C. Summ. Op. 2007–38, was an investment banker at Goldman Sachs who described herself as an "impulsive buyer." The court mused that some would find her annual clothing costs extravagant and noted that her wardrobe apparently changed constantly. According to her testimony, she routinely purchased designer clothing, wore it once or twice, and donated it to an upscale NYC thrift store. In the year in issue, based on her credit card statements, she spent $53,916 on clothing and $9,253 on shoes, out of her salary of $115,000. She claimed a charitable deduction for donated clothing of around $50,000. The taxpayer did not provide evidence of the original purchase price or the price at which the clothes were re-sold. (She guessed at the fair market value of a donated item and then doubled that to determine the original cost). Expressing "severe reservations" about the taxpayer's calculation of fair market value, and barely disguising its utter disbelief, the court permitted a deduction of about $9,000.

Ms. Stamoulis is not alone in taking a charitable deduction for bags of clothing given to a charity or dropped off at the Salvation Army. The IRS reported that in 2012 deductions of more than $12 billion were taken for clothing and household items. These claims are extremely difficult for the IRS to monitor even with substantiation requirements since taxpayers usually self-value all those contributions of last year's wide ties and platform shoes. In an attempt to stem the tide, Congress amended the rules to provide that no deduction can be taken unless the clothing is in at least good condition. Furthermore, it gave Treasury the power to issue regulations prohibiting a deduction for low-value items like "used socks and used undergarments." Unless thrift stores and the like prohibit donations of socks and T shirts with holes, it is hard to see how this measure will stem the tide. No doubt Ms. Stamoulis and others like her will claim *their* clothes are in top condition.

3.   TAX-EXEMPT ORGANIZATIONS

Note on Tax-Exempt Organizations

Organizations eligible for deductible charitable contributions are described in § 170(c) of the Code. These organizations—as well as certain other organizations whose donors are not entitled to charitable deductions under § 170—are also exempt from income tax under § 501.

Tax-exempt organizations that are eligible to receive deductible contributions are defined by § 170(c)(2) as follows:

> A corporation, trust, or community chest, fund, or foundation, * * * organized and operated exclusively for religious, charitable, scientific, literary, or educational purposes, or to foster national or international amateur sports competition (but only if no part of its activities involve the provision of athletic facilities or equipment), or for the prevention of cruelty to children or animals.

Regulation § 1.501(c)(3)–1(d)(2) provides that the term "charitable" is to be used in its generally accepted legal sense and is not limited by the enumeration in § 501(c)(3) of other tax-exempt purposes that may fall within the broad outlines of "charity" as developed by judicial decisions. Charity includes relief of the poor and distressed, advancement of religion, education or science, erection or maintenance of public buildings, monuments and works, lessening of the burdens of government, and promotion of social welfare by the reduction of neighborhood tensions, the elimination of prejudice or discrimination, the defense of human or civil rights, or the combating of community deterioration or juvenile delinquency. In Rev. Proc. 71–39, 1971–2 C.B. 575, the IRS allowed a tax exemption under § 501(c)(3) for public-interest law firms.

Considerable litigation has occurred over the conditions that organizations must meet in order to receive tax-exempt status and qualify for deductible gifts. The following case addresses that issue.

Bob Jones University v. United States

Supreme Court of the United States, 1983. 461 U.S. 574

■ CHIEF JUSTICE BURGER delivered the opinion of the Court.

We granted certiorari to decide whether petitioners, nonprofit private schools that prescribe and enforce racially discriminatory admissions standards on the basis of religious doctrine, qualify as tax-exempt organizations under § 501(c)(3) of the Internal Revenue Code of 1954.

I

* * * *

Bob Jones University is a nonprofit corporation located in Greenville, S.C. Its purpose is "to conduct an institution of learning . . . giving special emphasis to the Christian religion and the ethics revealed in the Holy Scriptures." The corporation operates a school with an enrollment of approximately 5,000 students, from kindergarten through college and graduate school. Bob Jones University is not affiliated with any religious denomination, but is dedicated to the teaching and propagation of its fundamentalist Christian religious beliefs. It is both a religious and educational institution. Its teachers are required to be devout Christians, and all courses at the University are taught according to the Bible. Entering students are screened as to their religious beliefs, and their public and private conduct is strictly regulated by standards promulgated by University authorities.

The sponsors of the University genuinely believe that the Bible forbids interracial dating and marriage. To effectuate these views, Negroes were completely excluded until 1971. From 1971 to May, 1975, the University accepted no applications from unmarried Negroes, but did accept applications from Negroes married within their race.

Following the decision of the United States Court of Appeals for the Fourth Circuit in McCrary v. Runyon, 515 F.2d 1082 (1975), aff'd, 427 U.S. 160 (1976), prohibiting racial exclusion from private schools, the University revised its policy. Since May 29, 1975, the University has permitted unmarried Negroes to enroll; but a disciplinary rule prohibits interracial dating and marriage. That rule reads:

There is to be no interracial dating.

1.   Students who are partners in an interracial marriage will be expelled.

2.   Students who are members of or affiliated with any group or organization which holds as one of its goals or advocates interracial marriage will be expelled.

3.   Students who date outside of their own race will be expelled.

4.   Students who espouse, promote, or encourage others to violate the University's dating rules and regulations will be expelled.

The University continues to deny admission to applicants engaged in an interracial marriage or known to advocate interracial marriage or dating. * * * *

On January 19, 1976, the IRS officially revoked the University's tax-exempt status, effective as of December 1, 1970, the day after the University was formally notified of the change in IRS policy. * * * *

The United States District Court for the District of South Carolina held that revocation of the University's tax-exempt status exceeded the delegated powers of the IRS, was improper under the IRS rulings and procedures, and violated the University's rights under the Religion Clauses of the First Amendment. 468 F.Supp. 890, 907 (1978). * * * *The Court of Appeals for the Fourth Circuit, in a divided opinion, reversed. 639 F.2d 147 (1980).

II

In Revenue Ruling 71–447, the IRS formalized the policy, first announced in 1970, that § 170 and § 501(c)(3) embrace the common law "charity" concept. Under that view, to qualify for a tax exemption pursuant to § 501(c)(3), an institution must show, first, that it falls within one of the eight categories expressly set forth in that section, and second, that its activity is not contrary to settled public policy.

Section 501(c)(3) provides that "[c]orporations . . . organized and operated exclusively for religious, charitable . . . or educational purposes" are entitled to tax exemption. Petitioners argue that the plain language of the statute guarantees them tax-exempt status. They emphasize the absence of any language in the statute expressly requiring all exempt organizations to be "charitable" in the common law sense, and they contend that the disjunctive "or" separating the categories in § 501(c)(3) precludes such a reading. Instead, they argue that, if an institution falls within one or more of the specified categories it is automatically entitled to exemption, without regard to whether it also qualifies as "charitable."
* * * *

It is a well-established canon of statutory construction that a court should go beyond the literal language of a statute if reliance on that language would defeat the plain purpose of the statute:

> The general words used in the clause . . . , taken by themselves, and literally construed, without regard to the object in view, would seem to sanction the claim of the plaintiff. But this mode of expounding a statute has never been adopted by any enlightened tribunal—because it is evident that, in many cases, it would defeat the object which the Legislature intended to accomplish. And it is well-settled that, in interpreting a statute, the court will not look merely to a particular clause in which general words may be used, but will take in connection with it the whole statute . . . and the objects and policy of the law. . . .
> Brown v. Duchesne, 19 How. 183, 194 (1857) (emphasis added).

Section 501(c)(3) therefore must be analyzed and construed within the framework of the Internal Revenue Code and against the background of the congressional purposes. Such an examination reveals unmistakable evidence that, underlying all relevant parts of the Code, is the intent that entitlement to tax exemption depends on meeting certain common law standards of charity—namely, that an institution seeking tax-exempt status must serve a public purpose and not be contrary to established public policy.

This "charitable" concept appears explicitly in § 170 of the Code. That section contains a list of organizations virtually identical to that contained in § 501(c)(3). It is apparent that Congress intended that list to have the same meaning in both sections. In § 170, Congress used the list of organizations in defining the term "charitable contributions." On its face, therefore, § 170 reveals that Congress' intention was to provide tax benefits to organizations serving charitable purposes. The form of § 170 simply makes plain what common sense and history tell us: in enacting both § 170 and § 501(c)(3), Congress sought to provide tax benefits to charitable organizations, to encourage the development of private institutions that serve a useful public purpose or supplement or take the place of public institutions of the same kind.

Tax exemptions for certain institutions thought beneficial to the social order of the country as a whole, or to a particular community, are deeply rooted in our history, as in that of England. The origins of such exemptions lie in the special privileges that have long been extended to charitable trusts. More than a century ago, this Court announced the caveat that is critical in this case:

> [I]t has now become an established principle of American law that courts of chancery will sustain and protect . . . a gift . . . to public charitable uses, provided the same is consistent with local laws and public policy. . . .

Perin v. Carey, 24 How. 465, 501 (1861) (emphasis added). * * * *

These statements clearly reveal the legal background against which Congress enacted the first charitable exemption statute in 1894: charities were to be given preferential treatment because they provide a benefit to society.

What little floor debate occurred on the charitable exemption provision of the 1894 Act and similar sections of later statutes leaves no doubt that Congress deemed the specified organizations entitled to tax benefits because they served desirable public purposes. See, e.g., 26 Cong.Rec. 585–586 [p590] (1894); id. at 1727. [The Court recites additional history of the charitable exemption.]

A corollary to the public benefit principle is the requirement, long recognized in the law of trusts, that the purpose of a charitable trust may not be illegal or violate established public policy. In 1861, this Court stated that a public charitable use must be "consistent with local laws and public policy," Perin v. Carey, 24 How. At 501. * * * *

When the Government grants exemptions or allows deductions all taxpayers are affected; the very fact of the exemption or deduction for the donor means that other taxpayers can be said to be indirect and vicarious "donors." Charitable exemptions are justified on the basis that the exempt entity confers a public benefit—a benefit which the society or the community may not itself choose or be able to provide, or which supplements and advances the work of public institutions already supported by tax revenues. History buttresses logic to make clear that, to warrant exemption under § 501(c)(3), an institution must fall within a category specified in that section and must demonstrably serve and be in harmony with the public interest. The institution's purpose must not be so at odds with the common community conscience as to undermine any public benefit that might otherwise be conferred.

We are bound to approach these questions with full awareness that determinations of public benefit and public policy are sensitive matters with serious implications for the institutions affected; a declaration that a given institution is not "charitable" should be made only where there can be no doubt that the activity involved is contrary to a fundamental public policy. But there can no longer be any doubt that racial discrimination in education violates deeply and widely accepted views of elementary justice. Prior to 1954, public education in many places still was conducted under the pall of Plessy v. Ferguson, 163 U.S. 537; racial segregation in primary and secondary education prevailed in many parts of the country. This Court's decision in Brown v. Board of Education, 347 U.S. 483 (1954), signaled an end to that era. Over the past quarter of a century, every pronouncement of this Court and myriad Acts of Congress and Executive Orders attest a firm national policy to prohibit racial segregation and discrimination in public education.

An unbroken line of cases following Brown v. Board of Education establishes beyond doubt this Court's view that racial discrimination in education violates a most fundamental national public policy, as well as rights of individuals. * * * * [The Court also references various congressional enactments as well as Executive Orders from the Executive branch prohibiting racial discrimination.]

Few social or political issues in our history have been more vigorously debated and more extensively ventilated than the issue of racial discrimination, particularly in education. Given the stress and anguish of the history of efforts to escape from the shackles of the "separate but equal" doctrine of Plessy v. Ferguson, it cannot be said that educational institutions that, for whatever reasons, practice racial discrimination, are institutions exercising "beneficial and stabilizing influences in community life," Walz v. Tax Comm'n, 397 U.S. 664, 673 (1970), or should be encouraged by having all taxpayers share in their support by way of special tax status.

There can thus be no question that the interpretation of § 170 and § 501(c)(3) announced by the IRS in 1970 was correct. That it may be seen as belated does not undermine its soundness. It would be wholly incompatible with the concepts underlying tax exemption to grant the benefit of tax-exempt status to racially discriminatory educational entities, which "exer[t] a pervasive influence on the entire educational process." Whatever may be the rationale for such private schools' policies, and however sincere the rationale may be, racial discrimination in education is contrary to public policy. * * * *

Petitioners contend that, regardless of whether the IRS properly concluded that racially discriminatory private schools violate public policy, only Congress can alter the scope of § 170 and § 501(c)(3). Petitioners accordingly argue that the IRS overstepped its lawful bounds in issuing its 1970 and 1971 rulings.

Yet ever since the inception of the Tax Code, Congress has seen fit to vest in those administering the tax laws very broad authority to interpret those laws. In an area as complex as the tax system, the agency Congress vests with administrative responsibility must be able to

exercise its authority to meet changing conditions and new problems.
* * * *

Congress, the source of IRS authority, can modify IRS rulings it considers improper; and courts exercise review over IRS actions. In the first instance, however, the responsibility for construing the Code falls to the IRS. Since Congress cannot be expected to anticipate every conceivable problem that can arise or to carry out day-to-day oversight, it relies on the administrators and on the courts to implement the legislative will. Administrators, like judges, are under oath to do so.
* * * *

Guided, of course, by the Code, the IRS has the responsibility, in the first instance, to determine whether a particular entity is "charitable" for purposes of § 170 and § 501(c)(3). This in turn may necessitate later determinations of whether given activities so violate public policy that the entities involved cannot be deemed to provide a public benefit worthy of "charitable" status. We emphasize, however, that these sensitive determinations should be made only where there is no doubt that the organization's activities violate fundamental public policy.

On the record before us, there can be no doubt as to the national policy. In 1970, when the IRS first issued the ruling challenged here, the position of all three branches of the Federal Government was unmistakably clear. The correctness of the Commissioner's conclusion that a racially discriminatory private school "is not 'charitable' within the common law concepts reflected in . . . the Code," is wholly consistent with what Congress, the Executive, and the courts had repeatedly declared before 1970. Indeed, it would be anomalous for the Executive, Legislative, and Judicial Branches to reach conclusions that add up to a firm public policy on racial discrimination, and at the same time have the IRS blissfully ignore what all three branches of the Federal Government had declared. * * * * We therefore hold that the IRS did not exceed its authority when it announced its interpretation of § 170 and § 501(c)(3) in 1970 and 1971.

The actions of Congress since 1970 leave no doubt that the IRS reached the correct conclusion in exercising its authority. It is, of course, not unknown for independent agencies or the Executive Branch to misconstrue the intent of a statute; Congress can and often does correct such misconceptions, if the courts have not done so. Yet, for a dozen years, Congress has been made aware—acutely aware—of the IRS rulings of 1970 and 1971. As we noted earlier, few issues have been the subject of more vigorous and widespread debate and discussion in and out of Congress than those related to racial segregation in education. Sincere adherents advocating contrary views have ventilated the subject for well over three decades. Failure of Congress to modify the IRS rulings of 1970 and 1971, of which Congress was, by its own studies and by public discourse, constantly reminded, and Congress' awareness of the denial of tax-exempt status for racially discriminatory schools when enacting other and related legislation make out an unusually strong case of legislative acquiescence in and ratification by implication of the 1970 and 1971 rulings. * * * *.

The evidence of congressional approval of the policy embodied in Revenue Ruling 71–447 goes well beyond the failure of Congress to act on legislative proposals. Congress affirmatively manifested its acquiescence in the IRS policy when it enacted the present § 501(i) of the Code * * * *

III

Petitioners contend that, even if the Commissioner's policy is valid as to nonreligious private schools, that policy cannot constitutionally be applied to schools that engage in racial discrimination on the basis of sincerely held religious beliefs. As to such schools, it is argued that the IRS construction of § 170 and § 501(c)(3) violates their free exercise rights under the Religion Clauses of the First Amendment. This contention presents claims not heretofore considered by this Court in precisely this context.

This Court has long held the Free Exercise Clause of the First Amendment to be an absolute prohibition against governmental regulation of religious beliefs. As interpreted by this Court, moreover, the Free Exercise Clause provides substantial protection for lawful conduct grounded in religious belief. However,

> [n]ot all burdens on religion are unconstitutional. . . . The state may justify a limitation on religious liberty by showing that it is essential to accomplish an overriding governmental interest.

United States v. Lee, 455 U.S. 252, 257–258 (1982).

The governmental interest at stake here is compelling. * * *[T] Government has a fundamental, overriding interest in eradicating racial discrimination in education—discrimination that prevailed, with official approval, for the first 165 years of this Nation's constitutional history. That governmental interest substantially outweighs whatever burden denial of tax benefits places on petitioners' exercise of their religious beliefs. The interests asserted by petitioners cannot be accommodated with that compelling governmental interest, and no "less restrictive means," are available to achieve the governmental interest. * * * *

Affirmed.

■ JUSTICE POWELL, concurring in part and concurring in the judgement

I write separately because I am troubled by the broader implications of the Court's opinion with respect to the authority of the Internal Revenue Service (IRS) and its construction of 170(c) and 501(c)(3) of the Internal Revenue Code. * * * *

I therefore concur in the Court's judgment that tax-exempt status under 170(c) and 501(c)(3) is not available to private schools that concededly are racially discriminatory. I do not agree, however, with the

Court's more general explanation of the justifications for the tax exemptions provided to charitable organizations. * * * *

With all respect, I am unconvinced that the critical question in determining tax-exempt status is whether an individual organization provides a clear "public benefit" as defined by the Court. Over 106,000 organizations filed 501(c)(3) returns in 1981. I find it impossible to believe that all or even most of those organizations could prove that they "demonstrably serve and [are] in harmony with the public interest" or that they are "beneficial and stabilizing influences in community life." Nor am I prepared to say that petitioners, because of their racially discriminatory policies, necessarily contribute nothing of benefit to the community. It is clear from the substantially secular character of the curricula and degrees offered that petitioners provide educational benefits.

Even more troubling to me is the element of conformity that appears to inform the Court's analysis. The Court asserts that an exempt organization must "demonstrably serve and be in harmony with the public interest," must have a purpose that comports with "the common community conscience," and must not act in a manner "affirmatively at odds with [the] declared position of the whole Government." Taken together, these passages suggest that the primary function of a tax-exempt organization is to act on behalf of the Government in carrying out governmentally approved policies. In my opinion, such a view of 501(c)(3) ignores the important role played by tax exemptions in encouraging diverse, indeed often sharply conflicting, activities and viewpoints. * * * * The Court's decision upholds IRS Revenue Ruling 71–447, and thus resolves the question whether tax-exempt status is available to private schools that openly maintain racially discriminatory admissions policies. There no longer is any justification for Congress to hesitate—as it apparently has—in articulating and codifying its desired policy as to tax exemptions for discriminatory organizations. Many questions remain, such as whether organizations that violate other policies should receive tax-exempt status under 501(c)(3). These should be legislative policy choices. * * * * The contours of public policy should be determined by Congress, not by judges or the IRS.

■ JUSTICE REHNQUIST, dissenting

The Court points out that there is a strong national policy in this country against racial discrimination. To the extent that the Court states that Congress in furtherance of this policy could deny tax-exempt status to educational institutions that promote racial discrimination, I readily agree. But, unlike the Court, I am convinced that Congress simply has failed to take this action and, as this Court has said over and over again, regardless of our view on the propriety of Congress' failure to legislate we are not constitutionally empowered to act for it.

In approaching this statutory construction question the Court quite adeptly avoids the statute it is construing. This I am sure is no accident, for there is nothing in the language of 501(c)(3) that supports the result obtained by the Court. * * * * With undeniable clarity, Congress has explicitly defined the requirements for 501(c)(3) status. An entity must be (1) a corporation, or community chest, fund, or foundation, (2) organized for one of the eight enumerated purposes, (3) operated on a nonprofit basis, and (4) free from involvement in lobbying activities and political campaigns. Nowhere is there to be found some additional, undefined public policy requirement.

* * * * Another way to read the Court's opinion leads to the conclusion that even though Congress has set forth some of the requirements of a 501(c)(3) organization, it intended that the IRS additionally require that organizations meet a higher standard of public interest, not stated by Congress, but to be determined and defined by the IRS and the courts. This view I find equally unsupportable. Almost a century of statutory history proves that Congress itself intended to decide what 501(c)(3) requires. * * * * The IRS certainly is empowered to adopt regulations for the enforcement of these specified requirements, and the courts have authority to resolve challenges to the IRS's exercise of this power, but Congress has left it to neither the IRS nor the courts to select or add to the requirements of 501(c)(3).

I have no disagreement with the Court's finding that there is a strong national policy in this country opposed to racial discrimination. I agree with the Court that Congress has the power to further this policy by denying 501(c)(3) status to organizations that practice racial discrimination. But as of yet Congress has failed to do so. Whatever the reasons for the failure, this Court should not legislate for Congress.

NOTES

(A) *Statutory Construction.* Is the majority opinion in *Bob Jones* consistent with the Court's opinion in *Chevron* discussed supra at page 60? Recall that the Court had said that where a statute was unambiguous, there was no gap for the IRS to fill by regulation or ruling. What is ambiguous about § 170? Is Justice Rehnquist correct that the statute's meaning is plain on its face? In *Chevron* the Court rejected an agency interpretation of the statute. In *Bob Jones,* the Court upheld an agency determination. Do you think that influenced the Court's finding that the statute required interpretation?

(B) *Meaning of Charity.* The Court adopts a very broad definition of charity that seems to make the addition of "educational" superfluous. If that word were deleted from § 501(c)(3), would it make any difference? The Court suggests that charities "demonstrably serve and [are] in harmony with the public interest" and that they are "beneficial and stabilizing influences in community life." Justice Powell is convinced that some organizations given tax exemptions fail that test. One could imagine a difference of opinion as to whether the ACLU or the National Rifle Association, whatever their contributions, are stabilizing influences in community life. Note that the

Court cites § 501(i) as manifesting approval of IRS policy. Section 501(i) denies tax exemption to social clubs that discriminate based on race, color, or religion. It does not refer to discrimination based on gender or sexual orientation. Could the IRS adopt a regulation denying tax exemption to a social club that discriminated on those grounds if it believed such discrimination caused the organization not to be "charitable"?

(C) *Educational Organizations.* There has been great controversy over what is "educational" within § 501(c)(3). Charitable organizations that publish newspapers and magazines often obtain tax-exempt status because they are considered educational. In Big Mama Rag, Inc. v. United States, 631 F.2d 1030 (D.C. Cir. 1980), however, the IRS denied the organization tax-exempt status on the ground that its newspaper was not "educational," because it included articles and editorials promoting lesbianism. The Court of Appeals accepted Big Mama Rag's contention that the "full and fair exposition" test used by the IRS to define "educational" was unconstitutionally vague and thus led to discriminatory application.

After *Big Mama Rag,* the IRS formulated a new "methodology test," which focuses on the method of presentation, rather than the content, to define "educational" within § 501(c)(3). This test was upheld by the same circuit that decided *Big Mama Rag* in National Alliance v. United States, 710 F.2d 868 (D.C. Cir. 1983). The court characterized the new test as a carefully-charted middle course that reduces the vagueness found unconstitutional in *Big Mama Rag* and thereby the potential censorship of the content of expression. The court denied tax-exempt status after finding the National Alliance's racist publication to be outside the range of any definition of "educational" promulgated by Congress or the IRS. The newsletter was found to advocate violence to "disadvantage or to injure persons who are members of named racial, religious or ethnic groups."

(D) *Lobbying.* Most public charities may elect to engage in a limited amount of lobbying without losing their tax exemptions. See §§ 501(h) and 4911. The amount of lobbying expenses permissible by an organization that makes the election is a varying percentage of the total exempt expenditures of the charity up to $1 million. Of this amount, no more than 25 percent of the lobbying expenditures may be for "grassroots" lobbying. § 4911(c). An organization that elects to use these rules is subject to an excise tax if the lobbying expenditures exceed the allowable amount, § 4911(a), and may lose its tax-exempt status for excessive repeated violations, § 501(h)(1). An organization that does not or cannot make the § 501(h) election is subject to the general "insubstantial" test. Such an organization may lose its tax-exempt status if it evinces a pattern of excessive lobbying expenditures. An excise tax is imposed on lobbying expenditures of those organizations in any year in which the organization is not exempt because of excessive lobbying expenditures. § 4912. The Supreme Court in Regan v. Taxation With Representation of Washington, 461 U.S. 540 (1983), held that the Code's prohibition against substantial lobbying by tax-exempt organizations does not violate the First Amendment or the Equal Protection Clause of the Fifth Amendment

(E) *Other Restrictions.* No part of the net earnings of the organization may inure to the benefit of any private shareholder or individual. No substantial part of its activities may consist of carrying on propaganda, attempting to influence legislation (except as otherwise provided), or participating in, or intervening in (including the publishing or distributing of statements), any political campaign on behalf of any candidate for public office. Such an organization may not participate in any political campaign in opposition to any candidate for public office.

If an organization fails to comply with these requirements, its exemption will be revoked unless the prohibited activities are insubstantial or incidental to the organization's primary function. The existence of a substantial nonexempt purpose will defeat an organization's tax exemption even if it also has many exempt purposes.

Other organizations are exempt from tax under § 501, but contributions to these organizations do not qualify for deduction under § 170. See §§ 501(c)(2), (c)(4), and (c)(19). These organizations include, for example, certain social welfare organizations, labor unions, business leagues, agricultural organizations, professional football leagues, fraternal lodges and nonprofit cemetery companies. The critical restriction here, as under § 501(c)(3), is the prohibition against inurement to private individuals.

Section 502 denies exemption to any organization operated for the primary purpose of carrying on a trade or business for profit even if the organization pays all of its profits to another organization that is exempt under § 501. These so-called "feeder organizations" are subject to tax unless their eligibility for an exemption is preserved by one of the three special rules in § 502. Sections 511–514 impose an unrelated business income tax (UBIT)—designed to match the corporate income tax—on income received by an exempt organization from an unrelated trade or business, which is defined as a regular activity that is not substantially related to the organization's performance of its exempt function. An organization does not lose its exempt status by engaging in such an unrelated trade or business, but it must pay tax on the proportion of its total income derived from nonexempt activities.

Organizations exempt from tax under § 501(c)(3) are divided into two general categories: private foundations and publicly supported organizations. See § 509 for the definition of private foundation. The law governing the taxation of private foundations is detailed and complex. Private foundations are subject to an excise tax on their net investment income and are required to distribute a specified portion of their income. Limitations are imposed on certain business holdings by private foundations, and self-dealing provisions prohibit specific transactions between foundations and certain "disqualified" persons. Foundations cannot engage in certain political activities, including lobbying and electioneering. The penalties for failure to comply with these restrictions are onerous, generally taking the form of a three-tiered set of taxes. See §§ 4940–4948.

(F) *The Controversy over University Endowments.* Some universities have literally billions of dollars in endowments, and, thanks to § 501, they pay no income taxes on either the contributions they receive or the investment income they earn. Critics of large endowments have argued that they represent funds that should be actively used for the universities' tax-exempt purposes. Endowments, some critics worry, are misused when they enhance the power of university administrators and faculty members and insulate them from the discipline of the marketplace. Defenders of endowments reply that donors often approve of endowments, which offer financial stability to universities and their students.

In 2017, Congress enacted § 4968, which imposes a 1.4 percent excise tax on the net investment income of private universities with at least 500 students and an endowment of at least $500,000 per student. Early estimates suggested that the new tax would apply to about 30 universities, including Harvard, Stanford, and Yale, but the tax will have some odd effects. For example, the Juilliard School, New York's premier school for the performing arts, with an endowment of about $1 billion will owe the tax, while Columbia University, three miles north with a $10 billion endowment will not, because its larger student body means that its endowment does not meet the $500,000 per student test. Likewise, New York University, Vanderbilt, The University of Southern California, and Johns Hopkins—all with endowments over $3 billion—will escape the tax, while small liberal arts colleges, such as Bowdoin in Maine, Claremont McKenna in California and Berea College in Kentucky, with endowments of about $1.5 billion but many fewer students, will have to pay it. In a 2018 budget bill to keep government open, Berea College was excluded from the endowment tax at the behest of Kentucky Senator (and Majority Leader) Mitch McConnell.

C. MEDICAL EXPENSES

Section 213 allows deductions for medical and dental expenses paid during the taxable year for the taxpayer, her spouse, her children, and her other dependents. The deduction includes payments for medical care, defined as the diagnosis, cure, mitigation, treatment, or prevention of disease. Amounts paid for medical insurance are also deductible, as are the costs of transportation primarily for and essential to medical care. Medical expenses can be deducted only if they are not compensated by insurance or reimbursed by employers. Medical expenses are deductible only to the extent they exceed a floor of 7.5 percent of adjusted gross income (rising to 10 percent in 2019). § 213(f). This floor is intended to disallow deduction for normal medical expenses such as annual physical and dental check-ups and supplies for the home medicine chest. The deduction is therefore limited to those taxable years when a person's medical expenses uncompensated by insurance are extraordinary. Furthermore, medical expenses are deductible only if together with other itemized deductions they exceed the standard deduction.

Is the medical expense deduction a subsidy to health care? Or is it a proper means of calculating an individual's net income?

The tax treatment of medical expenses is not consistent. Contrast the treatment of medical expenses covered by a tortfeasor due to an accident or injury and payment made pursuant to a health insurance plan funded by the taxpayer, § 104, or by the taxpayer's employer, § 105. Recall that these payments are excluded from income without limitation. This is equivalent to including the payments in income and deducting the full amount. Self-employed individuals can deduct the cost of health insurance and medical care provided the plan is exempt. § 162(*l*). These rules create an incentive for health insurance, particularly that with a low deductible, which ordinarily would not exceed the deduction threshold. Congress apparently believes that this has the result of over-spending for medical care since taxpayers are not really spending their own money. In response, Congress has created a tax incentive for high-deductible policies. An employee with a policy with a deductible of at least $1,000 (and not more than $5,000; twice that for families) can take a deduction for a contribution to a Health Savings Account. The deduction is limited to the lesser of the deductible or $2,250 ($4,500 for a family). These amounts are adjusted for inflation. The amounts earned in an HSA are not taxable and amounts paid out for medical care are tax-free as well. § 223. While the use of an HSA may cause taxpayers to monitor their spending on items covered by the deductible, it will do nothing to decrease demand for more expensive care funded by insurance.

Millions of Americans cannot use these provisions, however, either because their employers do not provide health insurance or because they do not work. If they purchase health insurance, the premiums are deductible each year only to the extent they itemize deductions and the costs exceed 10 percent (7.5 percent for tax years 2017 and 2018) of adjusted gross income. For many, this means no deduction. As a result, the after-tax cost of health insurance for these taxpayers is much greater than it is for those whose employers provide this benefit. In an effort to deal with this problem the 2010 Affordable Care Act required most individuals not covered by Medicare or Medicaid to obtain minimum health care coverage for themselves and their dependents or pay a penalty. § 5000A. However, the 2017 legislation eliminated this individual mandate by setting the penalty amount to zero beginning in 2019. Low-income individuals are eligible for a refundable premium assistance tax credit, § 36B, which is designed to ensure that qualifying individuals do not spend more than a specific percentage of their incomes on health insurance premiums. Large employers (those with 50 or more employees) are subject to a penalty if they do not offer full-time employees minimum essential health care coverage. Small employers (no more than 25 employees and average wages of less than $50,000) are eligible for a temporary small employer tax credit to help offset the cost of employer-provided insurance so long as the employer contributes at least one-half of the cost of the insurance.

Section 35 (which expires after 2019) permits workers who lose their jobs due to import competition to take a tax credit of 65 percent of the cost of health insurance for themselves and their families. Eligible taxpayers are those who receive trade adjustment assistance. How does this compare to the tax treatment of workers who purchase health insurance when they lose coverage because their employer goes out of business due to domestic competition?

The Code's definition of medical care is easily applied to most payments to doctors, nurses, and hospitals. But there are cases where particular expenses do not fit within the statutory definition as the next case illustrates.

Morrissey v. United States

United States Court of Appeals, Eleventh Circuit, 2017. 871 F.3d 1260.

■ NEWSOM, CIRCUIT JUDGE

This is a tax case. Fear not, keep reading. In determining whether the IRS properly denied a taxpayer's claimed deduction on his 2011 return, we must decide two important and (as it turns out) interesting questions. First up: Was the money that a homosexual man paid to father children through in vitro fertilization—and in particular, to identify, retain, compensate, and care for the women who served as an egg donor and a gestational surrogate—spent "for the purpose of affecting" his body's reproductive "function" within the meaning of I.R.C. § 213? And second: In answering the statutory question "no," and thus in disallowing the taxpayer's deduction of his IVF-related expenses, did the IRS violate his right to equal protection of the laws either by infringing a "fundamental right" or by engaging in unconstitutional discrimination?

Issue

We hold that the costs of the IVF-related procedures at issue were not paid for the purpose of affecting the taxpayer's own reproductive function—and therefore are not deductible—and that the IRS did not violate the Constitution in disallowing the deduction.

Judgement

Plaintiff-Appellant Joseph F. Morrissey is a homosexual man. He has been in a monogamous relationship with his male partner since 2000. Although Mr. Morrissey concedes that he is not medically infertile, he characterizes himself as "effectively" infertile because he is homosexual and because it is physiologically impossible for two men to conceive a child through sexual relations.

facts

In 2010, Mr. Morrissey and his partner decided to try to have children through IVF, with Mr. Morrissey serving as the biological father. The IVF process involved collecting Mr. Morrissey's sperm, using that sperm to fertilize eggs donated by one woman, and then implanting the resulting embryos into the uterus of a second woman who served as a gestational surrogate. Between 2010 and 2014, Mr. Morrissey paid expenses related to (among other things) seven IVF procedures, three egg donors, three surrogates, and two fertility specialists. All told, the IVF process cost Mr. Morrissey more than $100,000. In 2011 alone—the tax year at issue in this case—Mr. Morrissey paid nearly $57,000 out of pocket for IVF-related expenses.

Of that total, only about $1,500 went toward procedures performed directly on Mr. Morrissey's body—namely, blood tests and sperm collection. He spent the remaining $55,000 to identify and retain the women who served as the egg donor and the gestational surrogate, to compensate those women for their services, to reimburse their travel and other expenses, and to provide medical care for them. * * * Mr. Morrissey timely filed an amended 2011 return that claimed a medical-expenses deduction in the amount of $36,538. * * *

213 (a)

In pertinent part, I.R.C. § 213(a) states as follows: "There shall be allowed as a deduction the expenses paid during the taxable year, not compensated by insurance or otherwise, for medical care of the taxpayer, his spouse, or a dependent." Particularly important to this appeal is Section 213(d)'s definition of the term "medical care" as it is used in Section 213(a)—as relevant here, "[t]he term 'medical care' means amounts paid for the diagnosis, cure, mitigation, treatment, or prevention of disease, or for the purpose of affecting any structure or function of the body." I.R.C § 213(d).

Mr. Morrissey rests his statutory argument on a specific portion of Section 213(d)'s definition. He doesn't contend that his claimed deduction fits within Section 213(d)'s first, "disease" clause. Nor does he rely on the phrase "structure of the body" in Section 213(d)'s second clause. Rather, Mr. Morrissey asserts that all of the IVF-related expenses that he incurred in 2011 are deductible as "medical care" on the ground that they constitute amounts paid "for the purpose of affecting any . function of the body." Significantly, because (as applicable here) Section 213(a) allows a deduction for medical care "of the taxpayer," all agree that "the body" at issue in Section 213(d)'s definition is the taxpayer's own—not a third party's. Accordingly, the lone statutory question before us is whether the $36,538 in IVF-related expenses for which Mr. Morrissey claims a deduction constitute amounts paid for the purpose of "affecting any function of [Mr. Morrissey's] body."

Morrissey

In an effort to bring his case within Section 213(d)'s terms, Mr. Morrissey contends that all of the IVF-related expenses that he incurred—including the costs attributable to the identification, retention, compensation, and care of the women who served as the egg donor and the surrogate—were made for the purpose of affecting his body's reproductive function. In particular, Mr. Morrissey asserts that because he and his male partner are physiologically incapable of reproducing together, IVF was his only means of fathering his own biological children. Accordingly, Mr. Morrissey claims, it was medically necessary to involve third parties—a female egg donor and a female surrogate—in order to enable his own body to fulfill its reproductive function.

Section 213's plain language—and particularly the ordinary meaning of the statutory terms "affecting" and "function"—forecloses Mr. Morrissey's argument. First, "affecting." The word "affect" means to "produce an effect upon" or (less tautologically) "to produce a material influence upon or alteration in." Webster's Third New International Dictionary 35 (2002); see also Webster's Second New International Dictionary 42 (1959) (defining "affect" as "to lay hold of or attack (as a disease does); to act, or produce an effect, upon; to impress or influence (the mind or feelings); to touch"). Tracing Section 213(d)'s language, we must therefore determine whether the IVF expenses at issue were paid for the purpose of materially influencing or altering some function of Mr. Morrissey's body.

Now, to "function." The term "function" is defined as "the action for which a person or thing is specifically fitted, used, or responsible or for which a thing exists"; "the activity appropriate to the nature or position of a person or thing"; or "one of a group of related actions contributing to a larger action," such as "the normal and specific contribution of any bodily part (as a tissue, organ, or system) to the economy of a living organism." Webster's Third New International Dictionary 920–21 (2002); see also Webster's Second New International Dictionary 1019 (1959) (defining "function" as "the natural and characteristic action of any power or faculty" or "action; activity; doing; performance"). Stated less technically, it seems fair to summarize—and the parties don't disagree—that the term "function" denotes a person's or thing's unique task or role.

Statutory context yields an additional—and important—insight. In Section 213(d), the word "function" is followed by the prepositional phrase "of the body." That limiting modifier, referring as it does to one "body" rather than multiple "bodies," confirms what Section 213(d)'s plain language indicates—that at least in this context, "function" is an attribute of a singular thing and, accordingly, that the statutory definition should be understood to cover medical care that affects the function of one body, while excluding care that might be thought to affect some "function" achieved by the cooperation of multiple bodies.

Plugging in our definitions, then, the question is whether the IVF-related expenses that Mr. Morrissey incurred—including the costs of identifying, retaining, compensating, and caring for an egg donor and a gestational surrogate—were incurred for the purpose of materially influencing or altering (i.e., "affecting") an action for which Mr. Morrissey's own body is specifically fitted, used, or responsible (i.e., his body's "function"). Mr. Morrissey's position—that all aspects of IVF treatment, including those bearing on a woman's distinctive contributions, altered his reproductive function—mistakes the entire reproductive process for his own body's specific function within that process.

We begin, of necessity, with a primer on the science of human reproduction. (Some of this must surely seem so obvious as not to require restatement, but the circumstances of the case—and the parties' competing contentions—demand a brief refresher. So here goes.) [Ed note: The case includes several paragraphs on how a human embryo is made, which we believe does not require including here.]

Which brings us (at long last) back to the statutory language. As a man, Mr. Morrissey's body's specific responsibility in the reproductive process—his particular reproductive "function"—was to produce and provide healthy sperm. The question here is whether the IVF-related expenses for which Mr. Morrissey claimed tax deductions were paid for care that materially influenced or altered—i.e., "affect[ed]"—that function. Overwhelmingly, they were not.

Reasoning

Mr. Morrissey's claimed deduction—and thus this appeal—turns on the far more significant sums (more than $55,000) that he paid to identify, retain, compensate, and care for the women who served as the egg donor and gestational surrogate. The question is whether those expenses were undertaken for treatment or care that materially influenced or altered—affected—Mr. Morrissey's own reproductive function. They weren't. * * * Because the costs attributable to the identification, retention, compensation, and care of the egg donor and the surrogate weren't incurred "for the purpose of affecting any . function of [Mr. Morrissey's] body," he can't deduct them as "medical care" expenses under I.R.C. § 213.

Our understanding of Section 213's plain language is confirmed by existing Tax Court precedent. That court has consistently rejected efforts by male taxpayers to deduct IVF-related expenses that were paid to cover the care of unrelated female egg donors and gestational surrogates. In Magdalin v. Commissioner, for instance, a single man who was not infertile but was (of course) unable to conceive and bear children without a woman's participation sought to claim deductions of IVF-related expenses for an egg donor and a surrogate. 96 T.C.M. 491 (2009) [aff'd 2010–1 USTC ¶ 50,150 (1st Cir. 2009)]. * * *

Similarly, in Longino v. Commissioner, the Tax Court addressed the deductibility of IVF-related costs that a fertile male taxpayer had incurred on behalf of his fiancée. 105 T.C.M. (CCH) 1491, 2013 WL 1104430 (2013), aff'd, 593 Fed. Appx. 965 (11th Cir. 2014). The court held that the expenses were not deductible because (as relevant here) they were not made for the purpose of affecting the structure or function of the taxpayer's own body. * * *

We are thus constrained by I.R.C. § 213's plain language to reject Mr. Morrissey's statutory claim. Because the human reproductive process entails distinct male and female functions, because Mr. Morrissey's body's own function within that process is to produce and provide healthy sperm, and because Mr. Morrissey was and remains capable of performing that function without the aid of IVF-related treatments, those treatments did not "affect[]" any "function of [his] body" within the meaning of Section 213(d)—and accordingly do not qualify as deductible "medical care" within the meaning of Section 213(a).

Holding

[The court also rejects Morrissey's claim that the IRS has violated his right to equal protection of the laws and that the IRS discriminated against him on the basis of his sexual orientation.]

AFFIRMED.

NOTES

(A) *Reproductive Costs.* The IRS has allowed opposite sex married couples to deduct the costs of "fertility enhancements" to overcome the inability to have children. But it also takes the position that surrogacy expenses do not constitute medical care. In Ltr. Rul. 200318017 (2003), the IRS sanctioned a deduction for egg donation because in that case the woman had been unable to conceive a child with her own eggs. The IRS has held that "expenses preparatory to the performance of a procedure that qualifies as medical care that are directly related to the procedure may also constitute medical care for purposes". For example, surgical, hospital, and transportation expenses incurred by a donor in connection with donating a kidney to the taxpayer are deductible. Rev. Rul. 68–452, 1968–2 C.B. 111.

(B) *Birth Control.* In Revenue Ruling 73–200, 1973–1 C.B. 140, the IRS permitted deduction for birth control pills prescribed by a physician. The IRS simultaneously issued Revenue Ruling 73–201, 1973–1 C.B. 140, which holds that the cost of a vasectomy or lawful abortion is a deductible medical expense. Subsequently, the IRS issued Revenue Ruling 73–603, 1973–2 C.B. 76, permitting a medical deduction for female sterilization. Are expenses for birth control methods not covered by these rulings also deductible? What is the authority for allowing deductions only for legal abortions? Reg. § 1.213–1(e)(1)(ii) prohibits deductions for any illegal operation or treatment. Recall the materials on the public policy limitations on business expense deductions, supra at page 259. Is a similar limitation implicit in § 213? In all sections of the Code?

(C) *Expenses to Promote Good Health.* Reg. § 1.213–1(e)(1)(ii) disallows a deduction for an outlay incurred merely to promote general health. For example, the costs of diet food are not deductible. Nor are the costs of participating in a weight loss program to improve general health or appearance. Rev. Rul. 79–151, 1979–1 C.B. 116. On the other hand, the Service has sanctioned deduction of the costs of weight-loss programs as treatment for a specific disease, including obesity. Rev. Rul. 2002–19, 2002–1 C.B. 778. Similarly, the expenses of treatment to combat alcohol and drug abuse have been held deductible. See Rev. Rul. 73–325, 1973–2 C.B. 72 (alcoholism) and Rev. Rul. 72–226, 1972–1 C.B. 96 (drug addiction). The IRS has also held that the costs of smoking-cessation programs are deductible even when the smoker has not been diagnosed with any specific disease. Prescription drugs to combat the effects of nicotine withdrawal are deductible but the cost of non-prescription nicotine gum and patches are not. Rev. Rul. 99–28, 1999–1 C.B. 1269.

Although the costs of psychiatric treatment generally are deductible, the Service has taken the position that marriage counseling is inherently personal. Rev. Rul. 75–319, 1975–2 C.B. 88.

Historically, the IRS did not permit a deduction for breast pumps and supplies unless they were deemed essential to protect the patient's health. This was despite growing research indicating that breast milk could reduce disease among infants. In Announcement 2011–14, 2011–9 I.R.B. 532, the IRS advised that breast pumps and supplies are medical care under § 213(d) and qualify as deductible medical expenses under § 213(a). Could this announcement be used to advocate allowing deductions for food or procedures that promote good health generally? For drinking less soda and eating more fruits and vegetables?

A prescription from a doctor to undertake certain activities to improve health or to prevent medical problems in not sufficient. For example, a taxpayer who must exercise to treat his emphysema could not deduct transportation costs to and from a golf course. See Altman v. Commissioner, 53 T.C. 487 (1969), where a deduction was denied because the taxpayer had failed to prove why he had to golf instead of engaging in another activity that could have been conducted closer to home. In Borgmann v. Commissioner, 438 F.2d 1211 (9th Cir. 1971), the court disallowed expenditures for a housekeeper employed on a doctor's advice by an individual who had suffered a heart attack. The court found that the duties "were not primarily those of a nurse and thus did not constitute 'medical care.'" Does it make sense that a seriously ill person who needs an attendant can obtain the medical deduction only if he hires a trained nurse? How does this rule comport with nontax health care policies? Why do you suppose the court is willing to substitute its judgement for a doctor's as to what constitutes medical care?

(D) *Drugs and Medicine.* In order to be deductible, § 213(b) requires that a drug or medicine be a "prescribed drug" or insulin. Thus, the cost of aspirin is not deductible even if a physician has prescribed it for heart disease. On the other hand, medical supplies that are not medicine or drugs, such as crutches, bandages, and blood sugar tests are not subject to this limitation and are deductible. Rev. Rul. 2003–58, 2003–22 I.R.B. 959. Gross income does not include drugs provided or subsidized under an insurance plan or Medicare. And since § 105 does not require that medical expenses reimbursed under an employer-provided insurance plan be allowable under § 213, gross income would not include non-prescription medicine covered under such a plan. Reimbursements for non-medical items, such as dietary supplements, are not excludible. Rev. Rul. 2003–102, 2003–2 C.B. 559. Note that while the direct cost of a drug may fall when it becomes an over-the-counter medicine, the indirect costs may rise since it is no longer covered by tax-favored insurance plans and no longer may be deductible for tax purposes.

(E) *Cosmetic Improvements.* Cosmetic surgery is generally not deductible and reimbursements for such surgery from an employer-funded medical plan are not excludable from gross income. Cosmetic surgery is defined as any procedure "which is directed at improving the patient's appearance and does not meaningfully promote the proper function of the body or prevent or treat illness or disease." Cosmetic surgery does not include a procedure necessary to ameliorate a deformity attributable to a congenital abnormality, a personal injury due to accident, or a disfiguring disease. § 213(d)(9).

The Service has held that breast reconstruction surgery after a mastectomy and laser eye surgery that corrects vision so that glasses need not be worn are not cosmetic surgery and thus the costs are deductible. In contrast, the cost of a teeth-whitening procedure, even if intended to reverse the ravages of age, is not deductible, because it is intended to improve a taxpayer's appearance. Rev. Rul. 2003–57, 2003–22 I.R.B. 959.

Michael Jackson allegedly had cosmetic surgery to widen his eyes; if so, could he deduct the cost as a business expense?

The Tax Court has held that male-to-female gender reassignment surgery qualifies as a deductible medical expense under § 213. It found that gender identity disorder is a disease and that the taxpayer's hormone therapy and sex reassignment surgery were for the treatment of a disease. The court ruled that her breast augmentation surgery, however, was intended to improve her appearance and did not meaningfully promote the proper function of her body or treat disease and thus was considered nondeductible cosmetic surgery. O'Donnabhain v. Commissioner, 134 T.C. 34 (2010). Nice that the IRS and Tax Court are so expert on these matters, right?

(F) *Meals and Lodging.* Section 213(d)(1)(B) defines medical care to include transportation primarily for and essential to medical care. Commissioner v. Bilder, 369 U.S. 499 (1962), involved an unsuccessful attempt by a taxpayer to include his lodging expenses within this subsection. Bilder had suffered four heart attacks in eight years and was advised by a heart specialist to spend the winter season in a warm climate. He proceeded, along with his wife and three-year-old daughter, to Ft. Lauderdale where he spent a total of five winter months in 1954 and 1955. His transportation costs were considered deductible, but the Supreme Court, overruling the Tax Court and the Court of Appeals, held that the rental payments for the months spent in a Florida apartment were not deductible as medical expenses.

The extent to which costs for care in an institution other than a hospital constitute deductible medical expenses tends to depend upon the services provided. In Kelly v. Commissioner, 440 F.2d 307 (7th Cir. 1971), the taxpayer had suffered an appendicitis attack and was hospitalized. Subsequently, he was discharged because the hospital needed his room but was advised by his doctor to stay in a nearby hotel. The court held that the taxpayer's condition caused him to stay in the hotel, where he received continuous daily nursing care and was near his doctor. The court held that the hotel bill was a deductible medical expense for care rendered in a substitute institution.

In Levine v. Commissioner, 695 F.2d 57 (2d Cir. 1982), the taxpayer's son suffered from mental illness and had been treated at a hospital clinic. When the son became too old to remain in the clinic, he refused to move to another hospital and insisted on remaining close to his original therapist. He stayed in an apartment rented by his parents and used the clinic as an outpatient. The court held that "only those medically necessary away-from-home living arrangements which involve continuous daily medical care on the premises may give rise to favorable tax treatment for the cost of meals and lodging." The court therefore denied the deduction after finding that, in the two-year period at issue, the taxpayer's son had received medical care only once at the apartment.

Distinguishing travel that is itself therapeutic, such as a vacation in a more desirable climate, from travel required to bring a patient to a place of medical care, the Tax Court in Pfersching v. Commissioner, 46 T.C.M. 424 (1983), allowed a deduction for meal and lodging expenses incurred by the taxpayer and his son in traveling from Nevada to Kentucky, where the son was to receive a special operation.

(G) *Medical vs. Business Deductions.* Revenue Ruling 75–316, 1975–2 C.B. 54, held that payments by blind employees to readers for services relating to the employees' work are deductible as business expenses, not as medical expenses. Revenue Ruling 75–317, 1975–2 C.B. 57, provides examples of situations where amounts paid by the handicapped for travel, meals and lodging, and for companions for their business trips, are deductible as business expenses under § 162 or medical expenses under § 213. Why does it matter which section allows the deduction?

The Tax Court has consistently held that § 280E bars a deduction for the business expenses of an organization that among other things provides medical marijuana to those with debilitating illnesses. That section bars deductions for expenditures in connection with the illegal sale of drugs. Although medical marijuana was legal under California law, it was considered a controlled substance for purposes of § 280E. Californians Helping to Alleviate Medical Problems, Inc. v. Commissioner, 128 T.C. 173 (2007). The court did hold, however, that expenses allocable to the organization's counseling services were not barred. See Olive v Commissioner at page 261, supra.

(H) *Medical Expense vs. Capital Expenditure.* Although capital expenditures are generally not deductible, a capital expenditure may qualify as a medical expense if its primary purpose is medical care for the taxpayer. For example, a wheelchair or a seeing eye dog are deductible medical expenses. A capital expenditure that permanently improves property may qualify as a medical expense to the extent the cost exceeds the increase in value of the property. Reg. § 1.213–1(e)(1)(iii). Expenditures that generally do not increase the value of a residence, for example installing ramps to accommodate a handicapped person, are treated as medical expenses. Revenue Ruling 87–106, 1987–2 C.B. 67.

Many of the litigated cases involve swimming pools. Following the regulations, the Service has held that a pool is "an expenditure incurred for the primary purpose of, and is directly related to, the taxpayer's medical care and, to the extent the expenditure exceeds the increase in value of [the taxpayer's] property as a result of the installation, is deductible." Rev. Rul.

83–33, 1983–1 C.B. 70. For example, in Cherry v. Commissioner, 46 T.C.M. 1031 (1983), the taxpayers were allowed deductions under § 213 for operating and maintenance costs of their indoor heated pool even though it had a deep end and a diving board and was also used for recreational purposes. The primary purpose of the 80 degree pool was to mitigate Cherry's emphysema and bronchitis. Thus, heating oil, chemicals, electricity, and insurance costs related to the pool were all deductible in the year incurred.

The costs of building a pool were held not deductible in Evanoff v. Commissioner, 44 T.C.M. 1394 (1982), where taxpayers for $250 a year could have used one of many nearby community swimming pools. The taxpayers in that case built their own pool because their religious beliefs kept their daughter from swimming with children of the opposite sex. The court held that the expenditure was personal rather than medical if motivated by religious convictions and other personal considerations. In Letter Ruling 8326095, the IRS held that the fees and transportation costs related to using a public pool for medically necessary exercise were deductible.

CHAPTER 4

WHOSE INCOME IS IT?

In addition to knowing whether income is taxed, one must know to whom it is taxed. This requires a decision as to the appropriate taxable unit. One possibility is the individual taxpayer, without regard to her marital status or dependents. Alternatively, the income of married couples might be aggregated, or an "economic unit," such as the household, might be used. So long as there is a progressive rate structure, the definition of the taxable unit will be important.

Throughout the history of the income tax, a major tax planning technique has been to shift income from people or entities to whom it would be taxed at a high marginal rate to people or entities subject to low or zero rates of tax. Conversely, tax may be saved by shifting deductions or in some cases, credits from low- or zero-rate taxpayers to high-rate taxpayers.

Shifting of income and deductions is advantageous when there is any progressivity in the rate structure of the income tax. The wider the spread in rates, the greater the incentive to divide income among family members or other entities, such as trusts. It will often be advantageous to create new taxpayers—for example, trusts, partnerships or corporations—to employ income and deduction shifting.

The existence of tax-exempt entities—including pension funds, Native American tribes, educational and religious organizations, and governmental units—produces opportunities for saving tax. As we saw in the last Chapter, so does the existence of businesses with tax losses that they cannot use immediately to offset taxable income. Various financing arrangements, such as those examined in the tax shelter material in Chapter 3 were designed to shift deductions and credits from individuals or corporations that could not use them to high-bracket individuals or profitable corporations that could. Opportunities for moving income and deductions to the taxpayer who can use them to greatest advantage are increased by variations in the effective tax rates that apply to different types of income.

This Chapter explores various efforts by taxpayers to save tax by shifting deductions and splitting income among family members and other entities. First, the basic provisions governing the taxation of the family are described. The following Section deals with gratuitous assignments of both labor and capital income, and the next Section discusses intrafamily assignments for consideration. A final Section describes the use of entities for income shifting.

SECTION 1.   THE TAXABLE UNIT

Many of the questions about assignments of income historically have arisen out of efforts to keep income in lower brackets by dividing it among members of a family. Students therefore must understand the basic provisions governing the taxation of the family before proceeding to the other materials on assignments of income. One of the most fundamental issues, which has plagued the income tax since its inception, is the appropriate treatment of single people, married couples, and dependent children.

A. TAXATION OF THE FAMILY

Druker v. Commissioner

United States Court of Appeals, Second Circuit, 1982. 697 F.2d 46,
certiorari denied 461 U.S. 957 (1983).

■ FRIENDLY, CIRCUIT JUDGE:

* * *

The principal issue on the taxpayers' appeal is the alleged unconstitutionality of the so-called "marriage penalty". The issue relates to the 1975 and 1976 income tax returns of James O. Druker and his wife Joan. During the tax years in question James was employed as a lawyer, first by the United States Attorney for the Eastern District of New York and later by the District Attorney of Nassau County, New York, and Joan was employed as a computer programmer. For each of the two years they filed separate income tax returns, checking the status box entitled "married filing separately". In computing their respective tax liabilities, however, they applied the rates in I.R.C. § 1(c) for "Unmarried individuals" rather than the higher rates prescribed by § 1(d) for "Married individuals filing separate returns". Prior to undertaking this course of action, James consulted with the United States Attorney for the Eastern District and with members of the Intelligence Division of the IRS, explaining that he and his wife wanted to challenge the constitutionality of the "marriage penalty" without incurring liability for fraud or willfulness. Following these conversations they filed their returns as described, attaching to each return a letter explaining that, although married, they were applying the tax tables for single persons because they believed that the "income tax structure unfairly discriminates against working married couples" in violation of the equal protection clause of the fourteenth amendment. The Tax Court rejected this constitutional challenge, sustaining the Commissioner's determination that the Drukers were subject to tax at the rates provided in § 1(d) for married persons filing separately.

Determination of the proper method for federal taxation of the incomes of married and single persons has had a long and stormy history.

See generally, Bittker, Federal Income Taxation and the Family, 27 Stan. L. Rev. 1389, 1399–1416 (1975). From the beginning of the income tax in 1913 until 1948 each individual was taxed on his or her own income regardless of marital status. Thus, as a result of the progressive nature of the tax, two married couples with the same aggregate income would often have very different tax liabilities—larger if most of the income belonged to one spouse, smaller as their incomes tended toward equality. The decision in Poe v. Seaborn, 282 U.S. 101 (1930), that a wife was taxable on one half of community income even if this was earned solely by the husband, introduced a further element of geographical inequality, since it gave married couples in community property states a large tax advantage over similarly situated married couples with the same aggregate income in common law states.

After *Poe* the tax status of a married couple in a community property state differed from that of a married couple in a common law state in two significant respects. First, each community property spouse paid the same tax as an unmarried person with one-half the aggregate community income, whereas each common law spouse paid the same tax as an unmarried person with the same individual income. Consequently, marriage usually reduced a couple's tax burden if they resided in a community property state but was a neutral tax event for couples in common law states. Second, in community property states all married couples with the same aggregate income paid the same tax, whereas in common law states a married couple's tax liability depended on the amount of income each spouse earned. * * *

The decision in *Poe* touched off something of a stampede among common law states to introduce community property regimes and thereby qualify their residents for the privilege of income splitting. The Supreme Court's subsequent decision in Commissioner v. Harmon, 323 U.S. 44 (1944), that the income-splitting privileges did not extend to couples in states whose community property systems were elective, slowed but did not halt this movement. The result was considerable confusion and much upsetting of expectations founded on long experience under the common law. Congress responded in 1948 by extending the benefits of "income splitting" to residents of common law as well as community property states. * * * Pursuant to this Act, every married couple was permitted to file a joint return and pay twice the tax that a single individual would pay on one-half of their total income. This in effect taxed a married couple as if they were two single individuals each of whom earned half of the couple's combined income. The Act not only reduced the tax burden on married couples in common law states; it also ensured that all married couples with the same aggregate income paid the same tax regardless of the state in which they lived ("geographical uniformity") and regardless of the relative income contribution of each spouse ("horizontal equity").

While the 1948 Act was good news for married couples, it placed singles at a serious disadvantage. The tax liability of a single person was now sometimes as much as 41% greater than that of a married couple with the same income. * * * Although constitutional challenges to the "singles' penalty" were uniformly rejected, * * * the single taxpayer obtained some relief from Congress. The Tax Reform Act of 1969 * * * increased the number of tax schedules from two to four: § 1(a) for marrieds filing jointly; § 1(b) for unmarried heads of households; § 1(c) for unmarried individuals; and § 1(d) for married individuals filing separately.[1] The schedules were set so that a single person's tax liability under § 1(c) would never be more than 120% that of a married couple with the same income filing jointly under § 1(a).

The 1969 reform spawned a new class of aggrieved taxpayers—the two wage-earner married couple whose combined tax burden, whether they chose to file jointly under § 1(a) or separately under § 1(d), was now greater than it would have been if they had remained single and filed under § 1(c). It is this last phenomenon which has been characterized, in somewhat loaded fashion, as the "marriage penalty" or "marriage tax".[2] Here, again, while constitutional attack has been unavailing, * * * Congress has acted to provide relief. The Economic Recovery Tax Act of 1981 * * * allows two-earner married couples a deduction from gross income, within specified limits, equal to 10% of the earnings of the lesser-earning spouse.

* * * [T]he Supreme Court made explicit in Zablocki v. Redhail, 434 U.S. 374 (1978), what had been implicit in earlier decisions, that the right to marry is "fundamental". The Court, however, * * * took care to explain that it did "not mean to suggest that every state regulation which relates in any way to the incidents of or prerequisites for marriage must be subjected to rigorous scrutiny. To the contrary, reasonable regulations that do not significantly interfere with decisions to enter into the marital relationship may be legitimately imposed." 434 U.S. at 386. Whereas differences in race, religion, and political affiliation are almost always irrelevant for legislative purposes, "a distinction between married persons and unmarried persons is of a different character". "Both tradition and common experience support the conclusion that marriage is an event which normally marks an important change in economic status."

We do not doubt that the "marriage penalty" has some adverse effect on marriage; indeed, James Druker stated at argument that, having failed thus far in the courts, he and his wife had solved their tax problem

---

[1] The rates set under § 1(d) were the pre-1969 rates for single taxpayers. So disadvantageous is this schedule that only about 1% of married couples file separately. * * * As a general rule, married taxpayers file separately only when they are so estranged from one another that they do not wish to sign a joint return or when separate filing enables one spouse to exceed the [percentage] of income floor for medical deductions. * * *

[2] Not all married couples are so "penalized". For the couple whose income is earned primarily or solely by one partner, marriage still offers significant tax savings. * * *

by divorcing but continuing to live together. The adverse effect of the "marriage penalty", however, * * * is merely "indirect"; while it may to some extent weight the choice whether to marry, it leaves the ultimate decision to the individual. * * * The tax rate structure of I.R.C. § 1 places "no direct legal obstacle in the path of persons desiring to get married". * * * Nor is anyone "absolutely prevented" by it from getting married * * *. Moreover, the "marriage penalty" is most certainly not "an attempt to interfere with the individual's freedom [to marry]". * * * It would be altogether absurd to suppose that Congress, in fixing the rate schedules in 1969, had any invidious intent to discourage or penalize marriage—an estate enjoyed by the vast majority of its members. Indeed, as has been shown, the sole and express purpose of the 1969 reform was to provide some relief for the single taxpayer. * * * Given this purpose Congress had either to abandon the principle of horizontal equity between married couples, a principle which had been established by the 1948 Act and the constitutionality of which has not been challenged, or to impose a "penalty" on some two-earner married couples. It was put to this hard choice because, as Professor Bittker has shown, supra, 27 Stan. L. Rev. at 1395–96, 1429–31, it is simply impossible to design a progressive tax regime in which all married couples of equal aggregate income are taxed equally and in which an individual's tax liability is unaffected by changes in marital status.[3]

* * *

Faced with this choice, Congress in 1969 decided to hold fast to horizontal equity, even at the price of imposing a "penalty" on two-earner married couples like the Drukers. There is nothing in the equal protection clause that required a different choice. Since the objectives sought by the 1969 Act—the maintenance of horizontal equity and progressivity, and the reduction of the differential between single and married taxpayers—were clearly compelling, the tax rate schedules in I.R.C. § 1 can survive even the "rigorous scrutiny" reserved by *Zablocki* for measures which "significantly interfere" with the right to marry. * * *

Clearly, the alternative favored by the Drukers, that married persons be permitted to file under § 1(c) if they so wish, would entail the loss of horizontal equity.

In the area of family taxation every legislative disposition is "virtually fated to be both overinclusive and underinclusive when judged from one perspective or another". The result, as Professor Bittker has well said, is that there "can be no peace in this area, only an uneasy truce." * * * Congress must be accorded wide latitude in striking the

---

[3] Professor Bittker puts it thus, 27 Stan. L. Rev. at 1430–31:

Another way to describe this collision of objectives is that the tax paid by a married couple must be (a) greater than they paid before marriage, in which event they are subject to a marriage penalty, (b) less than they paid before marriage, in which event unmarried persons are subject to a singles penalty, or (c) unchanged by marriage, in which event equal-income married couples are subject to unequal taxes.

terms of that truce. The history we have reviewed makes clear that Congress has worked persistently to accommodate the competing interests and accomplish fairness.

[W]hat the Drukers choose to call the "marriage penalty" deprived them of no constitutional right. Whether policy considerations warrant a further narrowing of the gap between the schedules applied to married and unmarried persons is for Congress to determine in light of all the relevant legislative considerations. * * *

NOTES

(A) *Both Ends of a Seesaw Cannot Be up at the Same Time.* Judge Friendly observes in *Druker* that "it is simply impossible to design a progressive tax regime in which all married couples of equal aggregate income are taxed equally and in which an individual's tax liability is unaffected by changes in marital status." This fact was demonstrated mathematically by Edwin S. Cohen, then Assistant Secretary of the Treasury for Tax Policy, in 1972 testimony before the House Ways and Means Committee:

Case 1 is a single person who earns $20,000.

Case 2, two single persons each earn $10,000.

Case 3, a husband earns $20,000 and a wife earns zero.

Case 4, a husband and wife, each of whom earns $10,000.

If we want no penalty on remaining single—and a large group insists upon this—Case 1 must pay the same tax as Case 3. A single person earning $20,000 pays the same tax as a married couple earning $20,000.

If we want no penalty on marrying, Case 2 must pay the same tax as Case 4. Two single persons earning $10,000 each pay the same tax as a married couple each earning $10,000.

If we want husband and wife to pay the same tax however they contribute to the family earnings Case 3 pays the same tax as Case 4.

To summarize the tax results:

Case 1 equals Case 3.

Case 2 equals Case 4.

Case 3 equals Case 4.

Based on the fundamental mathematical principle that things equal to the same thing must be equal to each other, the result should then be that Case 1 equals Case 2, or in other words, that the tax on a single person earning $20,000 equals the tax on two single persons each earning $10,000.

But that cannot be so if we are going to have a progressive income tax structure, and progressive taxation is a basic tenet of our income tax system. The tax on a single person earning $20,000—

Case 1—must be greater than the total tax on two single persons each earning $10,000 if we are to have a progressive rate structure.

* * *

[I]t becomes apparent from this analysis that you cannot have each of these principles operating simultaneously, and that there is no one principle of equity that covers all of these cases. No algebraic equation, no matter how sophisticated, can solve this dilemma. * * * All that we can hope for is a reasonable compromise.

Tax Treatment of Single Persons and Married Persons Where Both Spouses Are Working: Hearings Before the Committee on Ways and Means, 92d Cong., 2d Sess. (1972).

(B) *The Marriage Penalty.* Under current law, many couples in which each spouse earns relatively equal amounts of income suffer a "marriage penalty," that is, they pay more tax than they would if they remained single or divorced. This is largely due to the relationship between the tax rate schedules applicable to married couples and those applicable to single people and "heads of households." If the size of a tax rate bracket for married couples filing jointly is less than twice the size of the same rate bracket for single people, the couple's taxes will increase if they have relatively equal earnings and they marry. This difference arises because the second earner's salary is taxed at a higher marginal rate when a couple is married. The effect is the same but may be more pronounced when one of the taxpayers would have otherwise filed as "head of household." There are also significant marriage penalties under the earned income tax credit, a large number of specific phase-outs, and in parts of the rate structure. A 2015 report by the Joint Committee on Taxation, "Fairness and Tax Policy," has an interesting discussion of the taxation of married couples. See JCX–48–15, February 27, 2015, at pages 4–6.

The tax penalty is greatly exacerbated for some low-income taxpayers who are eligible for the earned income tax credit, especially those with children. Recall the example on page 439. For a proof that solving the marriage problem under the earned income tax credit is fraught with the same difficulties as achieving neutrality under a progressive income tax generally, see Anne L. Alstott, "The Earned Income Tax Credit and the Limitations of Tax-Based Welfare Reform," 108 Harv. L. Rev. 533, 562 n.1 (1995).

In contrast to the income tax, a married couple's income is not aggregated for purposes of the Social Security payroll tax. The tax is levied on a flat rate up to a ceiling on an individual's earnings. Although taxes are determined on an individual basis, marital status is taken into account in setting benefits and generally single earner couples receive higher benefits relative to their taxes than two-earner couples.

(C) *The Marriage Bonus.* Some taxpayers enjoy a marriage bonus. Where one taxpayer in a couple earns substantially more than the other, their combined taxes will decline if they marry. The tax rate on the earning spouse's income will be less than it would be if he or she had remained single. That is because higher tax rates apply at higher income levels for joint filers than they do for single filers. Under the 2017 legislation, the number of married couples who will enjoy marriage bonuses will increase.

(D) *Eliminating the Marriage Penalty.* Testifying before the House Ways and Means Committee in January, 1995, Speaker of the House Newt Gingrich urged a rewrite of the earned income tax credit to remove its anti-marriage bias. "That's something staff should be able to do in a week." The Speaker had a limited understanding of the necessary political tradeoffs since, more than two decades later, Congress still has been unable entirely to eliminate marriage penalties, and eliminating marriage penalties in the EITC has not been a priority among the marriage penalty proposals seriously considered by Congress. The 2017 tax legislation, however, did eliminate the marriage penalty in the rate structure for couples with combined income of $300,000 or less, relative to single taxpayers.

The marriage penalty could be eliminated entirely by permitting married couples to file separate returns using the single rate schedules. But this would create differences between married couples based on their relative earnings and whether they live in a community property state. The disadvantage for an unmarried person could be eliminated by having mandatory joint returns with a one rate schedule for individuals and married couples, but that would recreate a marriage penalty.

As *Druker* notes, in 1981, Congress enacted a deduction for two-earner couples equal to 10 percent of the earnings of the lesser-earning spouse, up to a maximum of $3,000. This deduction was repealed in 1986. Congress justified repeal because of changes in the standard deduction and rate schedules. This deduction for two-earner couples abandoned the principle that married couples with the same joint income will have the same tax burden, regardless of the division of earnings.

An alternative to the two-earner deduction would be to tax all individuals, whether married or single, on their separate earnings. There are several practical problems with this approach. First, to avoid serious geographical disparities, it would be necessary to provide that, in community property states, earnings would be taxed to the person who earned them, regardless of who owns them as a matter of state law. Second, it might be necessary to prevent couples from diverting investment income to the spouse with the smaller earned income in order to get the maximum benefit out of splitting the income on two separate returns. Finally, it also would be necessary to provide rules for the allocation of certain personal deductions—such as the deduction for the medical expenses of the couple's children—between the two spouses.

On the other hand, mandatory individual filing would achieve marriage neutrality so that important tax consequences would no longer turn on whether a person was single or married. It also would eliminate some of the disincentive of marriage to second earners—a disincentive that now occurs because the marginal tax rate applicable to the second earner in a married couple depends on the marginal rate of the first earner. Such a regime, however, would make income tax equality among married couples depend on the similarity of relative incomes of each spouse rather than similarity in the aggregate income of couples.

(E) *Why Are Married Couples Different?* A number of justifications have been offered for treating married couples differently.

Income Pooling. One historical argument for treating married couples differently is that marriage is an equal partnership in which the couples pool their income and jointly share it. Thus, income should be aggregated for tax purposes regardless of how it is actually earned. This treats the couple as an economic unit. The extent of income pooling within a marriage may have declined over time as spouses are likely to keep separate checking or investment accounts. In addition, there are cohabitation arrangements other than marriage in which income is pooled although it would be very difficult to develop a workable definition for income tax purposes of an economic unit in which income is shared.

Costs of Children. Another argument for treating married couples differently relates to the additional costs of raising children. Thus, for example, a married couple with children should have lower income tax than a single with the same income. As noted in Chapter 3, the child credits and allowances for child care compensate somewhat for differences in family size (except for the high income taxpayers whose credits are phased out).

Does an "additional expenses" rationale suggest that the child care allowance should be a deduction rather than a credit? If the child care credit provides only limited tax relief with respect to these costs, is it appropriate to take these costs into account in setting the rates? How does the special rate schedule in § 1(b) (found in § 1(j) for taxable years 2018 through 2025, and adjusted for inflation after 2018) for unmarried heads of households (defined in § 2(b) as taxpayers who maintain households for certain eligible dependents) relate to these issues? Can that provision's lowering of rates be regarded as a surrogate for additional deductions or credits for dependents? If so, what is the special concern here for unmarried individuals?

Recall the discussion of the dependent care credit supra at page 280. One justification for the credit is to offset dependent care costs that permit a taxpayer to be employed. But another justification is to help to create parity with a stay-at-home parent whose imputed income is untaxed. A prior version of § 21 provided a *deduction* for dependent care expenses incurred by a "woman or widower or * * * a husband whose wife is incapacitated." Charles Moritz, a single man who had never married, paid someone to care for his 89-year-old invalid mother, who lived with him. He challenged the constitutionality of a provision that permitted women and widowers to take a deduction but not a single man. The Tenth Circuit agreed that this was invidious discrimination and invalidated the statute. Moritz v. Commissioner, 469 F.2d 466 (10th Cir. 1972). This was the first time since *Eisner v. Macomber* was decided in 1920 that a court had invalidated a section of the income tax law on constitutional grounds. The case was successfully argued for Mr. Moritz by Ruth Bader Ginsburg—one of several cases that she argued on behalf of men in her campaign to secure equal rights for women. Her husband Martin Ginsburg, an exceptionally talented tax lawyer, collaborated with her on the brief.

Imputed Income. The failure to tax imputed income is also a major factor in the taxation of married couples. The imputed income, typically from domestic services in the case of a married couple where only one spouse works for compensation, is not counted along with the other spouse's income either for purposes of determining the applicable bracket or for purposes of calculating the earned income credit threshold. Which couple has more income—and thus more ability to pay taxes: a couple in which one spouse earns $40,000 and the other "earns" nothing but provides $40,000 of domestic services or a couple in which each spouse earns $40,000 and the second wage earner's salary is used to purchase domestic services? Under current law, the first couple is taxed on only $40,000 of income, while the second couple is taxed on $80,000. An alternative to the impractical task of taxing the imputed income would be to reduce the taxable income of the two-earner couple, with a deduction for the second wage-earner.

This failure to tax imputed income has significant efficiency effects. It may be prohibitively expensive for the second spouse (often the wife) to enter the labor market. Not only would her salary be subject to income tax, but it will be taxed at a rate set by the primary earner's rate, i.e., her wages are placed on top of the husband's wages in determining the rate bracket. This may skew labor market decisions and reinforce gender bias. These issues are discussed in detail in Edward J. McCaffery, "Taxation and the Family: A Fresh Look at Behavioral Gender Biases in the Code," 40 UCLA L. Rev. 983 (1993).

Costs of Working. One argument often made in favor of treating married couples differently is that there are greater costs in earning two incomes than in earning one. Are there such differences that should be taken into account in measuring net income? Is this issue limited to a two-worker couple or does it apply equally well to a single laborer? Aren't these the costs of employment, unrelated to marital status? Doesn't a single person who lives off investment income have greater economic income than a single person who must go to work every day? In certain periods the Code allowed a special earned-income deduction to all taxpayers, without regard to marital status.

(F) *Family or Individual?* If an income tax is to be based on "ability to pay," then an initial question is whose ability to pay is relevant—that of the individual or the family? For equity purposes, this translates to whether we want to compare the economic wherewithal of families or individuals. Even if it might be more equitable to compare families, that might be administratively difficult. What should count as a family for this purpose? An unmarried cohabiting couple? A couple and an elderly mother-in-law?

Those who favor taxing the consolidated income of a family unit emphasize that the ability of parents to pay taxes differs depending on whether their children have income of their own. The parents' obligation to provide food, clothing, and other items of support for their children may well decrease as the children's own earnings increase. The parents of actress

Millie Bobby Brown of the Netflix hit Stranger Things, for example, probably have a greater ability to pay than do the parents of a less well-paid child.

Proposals for a family unit of taxation have been criticized for placing a burden on parents to account for the babysitting and paper route earnings of their children. Who should be penalized if parents unwittingly fail to report the income of their teenager from dealing in marijuana or other drugs? See, e.g., Bassett v. Commissioner, 100 T.C. 650 (1993), aff'd 67 F.3d 29 (2d Cir. 1995), where the child actress Skye Bassett was subject to a negligence penalty because of her negligent failure to file her returns reporting her acting fees. Some have argued that family taxation might create a disincentive to productive employment among the children of wealthy families because the earnings of a rich child with a paper route would be taxed more heavily than would the earnings of a poor child with a paper route.

Under current law, a child is considered a separate taxpayer and the child's earned income is not aggregated with the rest of the family even if it pooled to pay household expenses. § 73. The income tax liability of a minor child generally is computed in the same manner as that of an adult, but with special rates. The child is entitled to a standard deduction, except that this amount cannot exceed the child's earned income if the child can be claimed as a dependent by another taxpayer. If the 2017 legislation is not extended, starting again in 2026, a child will also be entitled to a personal exemption. If the parents are entitled to claim the exemption—even if they do not actually do so—the dependent child may not. § 151(d)(2).

If, however, the taxation of the child were wholly divorced from the parent's treatment, any unearned income of the child, such as dividend or interest income, in excess of the amount of the child's standard deduction would be taxable to the child at his or her marginal rate. This would produce a significant incentive for high income parents (and grandparents) to shift income-producing assets to their lower-bracket children (and grandchildren).

The so-called "kiddie tax" of § 1(g), revised for the years 2018 through 2025 by § 1(j)(4), is a major step in the direction of taxation based on family income, by providing restrictions on the intrafamily shifting of income and tax benefits and a rate structure under which the same rate is likely to apply to the income of all family members. The section provides that "net unearned income" of children under the age of 19 as well as children over age 18 but under age 24 who are full-time students (as of the end of the taxable year) is taxed at the ordinary and capital gains rates applicable to trusts and estates[1], regardless of the source of the unearned income. Net unearned income for this purpose is unearned income in excess of the child's standard deduction plus the amount of allowable deductions that are directly connected with the production of the unearned income. This amount is adjusted for inflation. For those who are 18 or older, the kiddie tax applies only to those whose earned income does not exceed one-half of the amount of their support. Investment income on a gift from dad is treated identically to

---

[1]   After 2025, the applicable rates are scheduled to revert to the parents' top marginal rate, which was the rule under § 1(g) before the 2017 legislation.

interest income on a savings account funded with the earnings of a paper route.

In combination, these rules mean that a minimum of $1,000 (indexed for inflation) of a child's unearned income is taxed at the child's marginal tax rate. Any greater amount of unearned income, however, is taxed at the rate applicable to trusts and estates, thus eliminating the income-shifting incentive.

Under limited circumstances, parents may elect to report the gross income of a child in excess of $2,100 on their own return. § 1(g)(7). Under this election, the first $1,050 of unearned income is still not taxed; the next $1,050 is taxed at 10 percent, and any excess is taxed at the parents' marginal rate. § 1(g)(7)(B). Such an election generally excuses the child from filing her own return. The election is permitted where the child has income between $1,050 and $10,500, only from interest and dividends. These numbers are all indexed for inflation. (A good exercise in reading the Code is to determine where the $10,500 amount comes from.)

(G) *What Constitutes Marriage?* The validity of a marriage for federal tax purposes is usually a matter of state law. Taxpayers are not free to argue that they are not married, so long as the state of the marriage considers it valid. See, e.g., McCarty v. United States, 93 A.F.T.R.2d 2004–634 (D.N.J. 2004). The *McCarty* taxpayers failed to research the economic consequences of their marriage and once they discovered the amount of the marriage penalty, they came to regret their wedding in Fiji. While they may have considered it a symbolic marriage only, the court found that Fiji did not.

Conversely taxpayers cannot argue that they are married and file a joint return if the state does not consider the marriage valid. In the federal "Defense of Marriage Act" (DOMA), Congress barred the IRS and other federal agencies from recognizing same-sex marriages permitted under state laws. In United States v. Windsor, 570 U.S. 744 (2013), an estate tax case, the Supreme Court struck down section 3 of DOMA, which had defined marriage as between one man and one woman. Then in Obergefell v. Hodges, 576 U.S. ___, 135 S.Ct. 2584 (2015), the Court held that all states must permit same-sex couples to marry and must recognize legal same-sex marriages performed in other states. The IRS then issued regulations to the effect that all Code sections in which "spouse," "husband," and "wife" are used now apply to individuals lawfully married to a person of the same sex under state law. Reg. § 301.7701–18. Civil unions or domestic registered partnerships, however, are not treated as marriages for tax purposes. A same-sex couple married under state law must either file as "married filing jointly" or "married filing separately." They can no longer file as single taxpayers. This will affect not only filing status but also eligibility for certain credits, such as the earned income tax credit or the child credit and, as discussed above, may produce income tax marriage penalties.

Under California state law, all income and property acquired during the partnership by registered domestic partners is presumed to be community property. California makes domestic partnership status available only to same-sex couples and opposite-sex couples over age 62. In Private Letter

Ruling 201021048 (May 5, 2010), the IRS held that a taxpayer must report one-half of the combined earned income of the taxpayer and his or her domestic partner as well as one-half of the combined income attributable to their community property assets. Thus, a couple who are registered domestic partners in California may receive better tax treatment than married couples because of their ability to file as single persons and pay lower tax than an unmarried couple who earn different amounts of income but live together and pool their income and assets.

B. DISSOLUTION OF THE FAMILY—SEPARATION AND DIVORCE

Having decided that marital status is relevant in determining tax liability, it is obviously necessary to determine whether a taxpayer is married. The Code provides that a couple will no longer be considered "married" for federal tax purposes if they are divorced. § 7703(a)(2). As we previously saw, where the earnings of both spouses are approximately equal, there will be a marriage penalty if the spouses file jointly. Thus, there is sometimes an incentive to divorce for tax purposes. The following ruling deals with tax-motivated divorces.

Revenue Ruling 76–255

Internal Revenue Service, 1976. 1976–2 C.B. 40.

* * *

Advice has been requested concerning the marital status of certain taxpayers for Federal income tax purposes under the circumstances described below.

SITUATION 1

A and *B* were married in 1975 and filed a joint 1975 Federal income tax return on April 15, 1976, which included their combined incomes. On April 16, 1976, a state court of competent jurisdiction annulled the marriage and decreed that no valid marriage ever existed.

SITUATION 2

C and *D* were married in 1964 and filed joint Federal income tax returns for the years 1964 through 1974. In 1975, *C* and *D* determined that for Federal income tax purposes it would be advantageous for them to be unmarried so that each of them could file a separate Federal income tax return as an unmarried individual.

On December 30, 1975, *C* and *D* secured a divorce under the laws of a foreign jurisdiction. For purposes of this ruling, it is assumed that such divorce was valid. However, at the time of the divorce, they intended to remarry each other and did so in January 1976.

Section 143(a)(1) of the Internal Revenue Code of 1954 provides generally that the determination of whether an individual is married shall be made as of the close of the taxable year.

Section 6013 of the Code permits a husband and wife to file a joint income tax return.

Section 1.143–1(a) and section 1.6013–4(a) of the Income Tax Regulations provide that status as husband and wife under these sections is determined as of the close of the year for two individuals having the same taxable year. These sections also provide that an individual shall be considered as married even though living apart from the individual's spouse unless legally separated under a decree of divorce or separate maintenance.

Rev. Rul. 67–442, 1967–2 C.B. 65, provides that the Internal Revenue Service generally will not question for Federal income tax purposes the validity of any divorce decree until a court of competent jurisdiction declares the divorce to be invalid.

In *Situation 1,* a state court having competent jurisdiction has annulled the marriage and, in accordance with state law, has decreed that no valid marriage ever existed.

Accordingly, since no valid marriage ever existed *A* and *B* were single individuals as of the close of the taxable year 1975. Thus, they must file amended Federal income tax returns for 1975 as unmarried individuals.

In *Situation 2,* although *C* and *D* were divorced under the laws of the foreign jurisdiction, the divorce was not intended by them to have effect except to enable them to qualify as unmarried individuals who would be eligible to file separate returns. In addition, *C* and *D* intended to and did remarry each other early in the succeeding taxable year.

The true nature of a transaction must be considered in light of the plain intent and purpose of the statute. Such transaction should not be given any effect for Federal income tax purposes if it merely serves the purpose of tax avoidance. In determining whether it serves the purpose of tax avoidance all of the surrounding facts and circumstances are to be considered. Neither section 143 nor section 6013 of the Code or the applicable regulations thereunder contemplates a "sham transaction" designed to manipulate for Federal income tax purposes an individual's marital status as of the close of a taxable year. See Gregory v. Helvering, 293 U.S. 465 (1935), XIV–1 C.B. 193 (1935).

Accordingly, *C* and *D* for purposes of sections 143 and 6013 of the Code were married individuals as of the close of the taxable year 1975. Therefore, for 1975 they must file either a joint Federal income tax return or separate returns using rules for married individuals filing separate returns.

NOTES

(A) *Marital Status.* The Code contains special rules for determining marital status and they do not always conform to state law. For example, an individual's marital status is generally determined at year end. Thus, a taxpayer who marries on New Year's Eve is treated as having been married for the entire year. Similarly, a taxpayer whose spouse dies midyear is treated as married at year end. Conversely, a taxpayer who divorces before the end of the year is treated as being unmarried for the entire year. § 7703(a).

In some circumstances, taxpayers who are married for state law purposes are treated as if they were unmarried for federal tax purposes. For example, a taxpayer married to a nonresident alien can qualify for head of household status because he is treated as not being married. § 2(b)(2)(B). In the case of married individuals living apart, the Code often treats one spouse very favorably and the other less so. A married woman, for example, who for the last six months of the taxable year did not live with her husband, but did maintain for more than one-half the taxable year a home in which she lived with a dependent child is not considered married. § 7703(b). Ironically, if the other spouse does not live with a child, he continues to be treated as married. In a scheme Stephen Colbert would appreciate, this results in a taxpayer being married to someone who is not considered his spouse.

A number of Code provisions rely on a determination that the taxpayer and his spouse "live apart." See, e.g., § 21(e)(4) and § 2(c). When it is to his benefit, a taxpayer may argue that he and his spouse are not members of the same household even though they live in the same house. This generally involves the introduction of fairly sordid testimony about sleeping habits and the like. The courts generally decline to weigh such evidence, preferring to take at face value the relationship of a married couple under one roof. See, e.g., McAdams v. Commissioner, 118 T.C. 373 (2002) (in responding to the taxpayer's argument that separate bedrooms constituted "living apart," the judge "declined to explore the quality of a marriage").

(B) *Sham Divorces.* Rev. Rul. 76–255 abandons the notion that local law will be used to determine marital status and instead appears to create a federal definition of "divorce." See also Boyter v. Commissioner, 74 T.C. 989 (1980), remanded 668 F.2d 1382 (4th Cir. 1981), where the facts are similar to situation 2 in the ruling. Although the Tax Court adopted much of the reasoning of Rev. Rul. 76–255, the Fourth Circuit remanded for consideration of the applicability of the sham transaction doctrine. In other contexts, the sham transaction doctrine has been used to invalidate a transaction that has no real economic substance other than the tax consequences. Recall *Knetsch,* discussed supra at page 367. Is a "sham" divorce a transaction in which there are no significant nontax effects? In *Boyter,* the couple was divorced for 32 days during the first year in issue and 79 days during the second year. If Mr. Boyter had died during that period, "Mrs." Boyter may not have been able to collect his pension. Nor would Mr. Boyter have been entitled to a marital deduction on his estate tax return for amounts left to "Mrs." Boyter.

(C) *Decree of Divorce.* What is a "decree of divorce" as that term is used in § 7703? Estate of Borax v. Commissioner, 349 F.2d 666 (2d Cir. 1965), cert. denied, 383 U.S. 935 (1966), involved a couple who had been married in New York. Later they separated and entered into a separation agreement. Thereafter, the husband obtained an ex parte divorce in Mexico. The wife had been notified of the Mexican proceeding, but did not appear there. The husband then married another woman, first in Mexico and later in Connecticut.

The first wife promptly brought an action in New York for a declaratory judgment that she was still married to the husband. This was fully litigated in New York and resulted in a decree in favor of the first wife. The husband nevertheless continued to live with the second wife and to make periodic payments to the first wife as provided in the separation agreement. The IRS disallowed the deduction of alimony payments to the first wife on the ground that they were not made under a separation agreement "incident to * * * a decree of divorce." The Second Circuit ruled that the payments were deductible even though the divorce had been held invalid in New York. (Under the 2017 law, alimony is not deductible for divorce or separation agreements signed after December 31, 2018.)

In Revenue Ruling 67–442, 1967–2 C.B. 65, the IRS announced that it would not follow *Borax* and in Estate of Felt v. Commissioner, 54 T.C.M. 528 (1987), the Tax Court said that it would not follow *Borax*, but nevertheless recognized a Dominican divorce that had not been explicitly invalidated by a New York court. Cf. Ry Cooder, "It's a Sin to Get a Mexican Divorce," Paradise and Lunch (1971); hear also Steely Dan, "Haitian Divorce," The Royal Scam (1976).

Note on the Tax Treatment of Alimony and Child Support Payments and Property Settlements upon Divorce

When the family unit dissolves, difficult issues arise in determining who should be taxed on the income. Suppose, for example, that one spouse is ordered to pay alimony out of her wages to the former spouse and to make child support payments. Should the payor be taxed on the wages because she earned them or should the recipient and/or children be taxed because they enjoyed the consumption? Suppose that the former spouse transfers appreciated property as part of a property settlement in exchange for her spouse's marital rights. Should the gain on the property be taxed? The Code now provides answers to these questions—and due to the 2017 legislation, those answers are quite different for divorce and separation agreements entered into after December 31, 2018 than they are for such agreements entered into before that. Since both parties always are concerned with their after-tax economic position, tax planning may be an important aspect of legal advice relating to divorce.

1. ALIMONY AND SUPPORT PAYMENTS

Throughout most of the history of the income tax, payments made from a spouse to a former spouse have been taxable to one but not both spouses. Prior to 1942, alimony paid to a divorced spouse was not includible in the recipient's gross income and was treated as a nondeductible personal expense of the payor. *Gould v. Gould*, 245 U.S. 151 (1917). In 1942, Congress reversed that rule by requiring that certain alimony payments be included in the recipient spouse's income and permitting the payor-spouse to deduct those payments. In 2017, Congress reversed the rule again for payments incident to divorce or separation agreements executed in 2019 or later. This change aligned the treatment of alimony payments with payments for child support and property settlements, which are generally nondeductible to the payor and excludable by the recipient.

Under the prior rule, which treated alimony as deductible to the payor, there was a considerable incentive to classify payments as alimony instead of child support or a property settlement, which are not deductible. The payor spouse is generally in a higher tax bracket than the recipient, making the deduction more valuable in the hands of the payor. Section 71, now repealed, provided a set of rules for distinguishing alimony payments from property settlements in order to limit the kind of income shifting this rule incentivized. For the definition of alimony under the 2017 legislation, see § 152(d)(5).

Payments to a third party on behalf of one's former spouse—as for tuition, rent, or taxes—may qualify as alimony if made pursuant to a divorce or separation agreement. Premiums for term or whole life insurance on the life of the payor similarly may be treated as alimony to the extent that the former spouse is the owner of the policy.

2. PROPERTY SETTLEMENTS

Under prior law, a taxpayer recognized gain (but not loss) on the transfer of property to a spouse (or former spouse) in exchange for the release of marital claims. The recipient received a basis in the property equal to its fair market value. *United States v. Davis*, 370 U.S. 65 (1962). These rules did not apply to the equal division of community property or to the partition of jointly-held property. This distinction produced considerable litigation and caused some states to amend their property laws in an attempt to avoid the *Davis* result.

Section 1041 now provides that no gain or loss is to be recognized on any transfer of property between spouses or on a transfer incident to divorce between former spouses. This rule applies regardless of whether the transfer was of community or separately-owned property or whether it was for consideration. The recipient takes a carryover basis in the property equal to the adjusted basis of the transferor. This rule differs from the usual rule treating the satisfaction of a debt with appreciated property as a taxable transaction. In effect, the transfer between spouses is treated the same as a gift, regardless of the transferor's motivation or intent. The transferee's basis is a carryover basis regardless of the value of the transferred property. Thus, unlike the gift basis rule of § 1015, one spouse can transfer a loss to another spouse.

The reasons for these changes were explained in the House Ways and Means Committee Report as follows:

> The committee believes that, in general, it is inappropriate to tax transfers between spouses. This policy * * * reflects the fact that a husband and wife are a single economic unit.

> The current rules governing transfers of property between spouses or former spouses incident to divorce have not worked well and have led to much controversy and litigation. Often the rules have proved a trap for the unwary * * *.

> Furthermore, in divorce cases, the government often gets whipsawed. The transferor will not report any gain on the transfer, while the recipient spouse, when he or she sells, is entitled under the *Davis* rule to compute his or her gain or loss by reference to a basis equal to the fair market value of the property at the time received.

H.Rep. 432, 98th Cong., 2d Sess. 1490–92 (1984).

Under § 1041, a transfer is treated as incident to divorce if it occurs within one year after the marriage ceased or if it is related to the cessation of the marriage. Temporary regulations state that a transfer of property generally will be treated as related to the cessation of the marriage if it is made under a divorce or separation instrument and occurs not more than six years after the end of the marriage. Temp. Reg. § 1.1041–1T(b) Q–7.

While the carryover basis rule of § 1041 reduces a divorcing couple's immediate overall tax liability, it is generally favorable to transferors, who do not have to recognize gain on the transfer of appreciated property, and unfavorable to transferees, who are required to recognize larger capital gains or recapture ordinary income when they ultimately dispose of the property in a taxable transaction. Bargaining between the parties should take this consequence into account.

NOTES

(A) *Delinquent Payments.* If the payor spouse fails to make the alimony or child support payments, the disappointed spouse does not obtain a bad debt deduction. Since the recipient, generally a cash basis taxpayer, has not included the missing payments in income, she has no basis and thus is not entitled to a deduction under § 166.

(B) *Child Credits and Medical Deductions.* The tax implications of divorce settlements also involve the entitlement to the child tax credit for the couple's children. This credit clearly goes to the custodial parent. There is some ambiguity, however, about whether the parties can agree that it is to go to the noncustodial parent. This was the rule for dependency exemptions under § 152(e)(1) but the child credit rules in § 24 refer only to § 152(c) and not § 152(e), so it seems that agreements to allocate child credits to the noncustodial former spouse would not be effective.

A parent who pays the medical bills of his or her child can qualify for the medical expense deduction if the child is a dependent of either parent. § 213(a)(4). Because the 10 percent floor for medical expense deductions (reduced to 7.5 percent for 2017 and 2018) bars deduction for most such expenses, it typically will be easier for the parent with the lower adjusted gross income to meet this floor and take the deduction.

(C) *Why Allow an Alimony Deduction?* Are the alimony provisions structured appropriately? The fundamental question is which treatment—deduction/inclusion or nondeduction/exclusion—better reflects the abilities of the former spouses to meet their tax liabilities. Would the deduction for the payor be an inappropriate departure from the notion that earnings should be taxed to the earner? Or is a failure to tax the recipient be a departure from the usual rule that one who consumes or saves should be taxed? Is the no deduction/exclusion rule much simpler?

C. ANTENUPTIAL AGREEMENTS

Farid-Es-Sultaneh v. Commissioner

United States Court of Appeals for the Second Circuit, 1947. 160 F.2d 812.

■ CHASE, JUDGE:

The problem presented by this petition is to fix the cost basis to be used by the petitioner in determining the taxable gain on a sale she made in 1938 of shares of corporate stock. She contends that it is the adjusted value of the shares at the date she acquired them because her acquisition was by purchase. The Commissioner's position is that she must use the adjusted cost basis of her transferor because her acquisition was by gift. * * *

The petitioner * * * reported sales [in 1938] of 12,000 shares of the common stock of the S. S. Kresge Company at varying prices per share, for the total sum of $230,802.36 which admittedly was in excess of their cost to her. How much this excess amounted to for tax purposes depends upon the legal significance of the facts now to be stated.

In December 1923 when the petitioner, then unmarried, and S. S. Kresge, then married, were contemplating their future marriage, he delivered to her 700 shares of the common stock of the S. S. Kresge Company * * * The shares were * * * to be held by the petitioner "for her benefit and protection in the event that the said Kresge should die prior to the contemplated marriage between the petitioner and said Kresge." The latter was divorced from his wife on January 9, 1924, and on or about

January 23, 1924 he delivered to the petitioner 1800 additional common shares of S. S. Kresge Company which * * * were to be held by the petitioner for the same purposes as were the first 700 shares he had delivered to her. On April 24, 1924, and when the petitioner still retained the possession of the stock so delivered to her, she and Mr. Kresge executed a written ante-nuptial agreement wherein she acknowledged the receipt of the shares "as a gift made by the said Sebastian S. Kresge, pursuant to this indenture, and as an ante-nuptial settlement, and in consideration of said gift and said ante-nuptial settlement, in consideration of the promise of said Sebastian S. Kresge to marry her, and in further consideration of the consummation of said promised marriage" she released all dower and other marital rights, including the right to her support to which she otherwise would have been entitled as a matter of law when she became his wife. They were married in New York immediately after the ante-nuptial agreement was executed and continued to be husband and wife until the petitioner obtained a final decree of absolute divorce from him on, or about, May 18, 1928. No alimony was claimed by, or awarded to, her.

* * * Her adjusted basis for the stock she sold in 1938 was $10.66 2/3 per share computed on the basis of the fair market value of the shares which she obtained from Mr. Kresge. * * * His adjusted basis for the shares she sold in 1938 would have been $0.159091.

When the petitioner and Mr. Kresge were married he was 57 years old with a life expectancy of 16 ½ years. She was then 32 years of age with a life expectancy of 33 ³/₄ years. He was then worth approximately $375,000,000 and owned real estate of the approximate value of $100,000,000.

The Commissioner determined the deficiency on the ground that the petitioner's stock * * * was acquired by gift within the meaning of that word as used in [§ 102], and * * * used as the basis for determining the gain on her sale * * * the basis it would have had in the hands of the donor. This was correct if [§ 1015] * * * is applicable, and the Tax Court held it was * * *.

[A] transfer * * * solely in consideration of [a prospective wife's] promise of marriage, and to compensate her for loss of trust income which would cease upon her marriage, was not for an adequate and full consideration in money or money's worth within the meaning of the [the gift tax statute] * * * [T]he Tax Court * * * found that the transfer was not one at arm's length made in the ordinary course of business. But we find nothing in this decision to show that a transfer, taxable as a gift under the gift tax, is ipso facto to be treated as a gift in construing the income tax law.

* * * Although Congress in 1932 also expressly provided that the release of marital rights should not be treated as a consideration in money or money's worth in administering the estate tax law, and failed

to include [such] a provision in the gift tax statute [the Supreme Court] held that the gift tax law should be construed to the same effect.

We find in this decision no indication, however, that the term "gift" as used in the income tax statute should be construed to include a transfer which, if made when the gift tax were effective, would be taxable to the transferor as a gift merely because of the special provisions in the gift tax statute defining and restricting consideration for gift tax purposes. * * *

In our opinion the income tax provisions are not to be construed as though they were in pari materia with either the estate tax law or the gift tax statutes. They are aimed at the gathering of revenue by taking for the public use given percentages of what the statute fixes as net taxable income. Capital gains and losses are * * * factors in determining net taxable income. What is known as the basis for computing gain or loss on transfers of property is established by statute in those instances when the resulting gain or loss is recognized for income tax purposes. * * * When Congress provided that gifts should not be treated as taxable income to the donee there was, without any correlative provisions fixing the basis of the gift to the donee, a loophole which enabled the donee to make a subsequent transfer of the property and take as the basis for computing gain or loss its value when the gift was made. Thus it was possible to exclude from taxation any increment in value during the donor's holding and the donee might take advantage of any shrinkage in such increment after the acquisition by gift in computing gain or loss upon a subsequent sale or exchange. It was to close this loophole that Congress provided that the donee should take the donor's basis when property was transferred by gift. * * * Because of this we think that a transfer which should be classed as a gift under the gift tax law is not necessarily to be treated as a gift income-tax-wise. Though such a consideration as this petitioner gave for the shares of stock she acquired from Mr. Kresge might not have relieved him from liability for a gift tax, had the present gift tax then been in effect, it was nevertheless a fair consideration which prevented her taking the shares as a gift under the income tax law since it precluded the existence of a donative intent.

Although the transfers of the stock * * * by Mr. Kresge to this taxpayer are called a gift in the ante-nuptial agreement later executed and were to be for the protection of his prospective bride if he died before the marriage was consummated, the "gift" was contingent upon his death before such marriage, an event that did not occur. Consequently, it would appear that no absolute gift was made before the ante-nuptial contract was executed and that she took title to the stock under its terms, viz: in consideration for her promise to marry him coupled with her promise to relinquish all rights in and to his property which she would otherwise acquire by the marriage. Her inchoate interest in the property of her affianced husband greatly exceeded the value of the stock transferred to her. It was a fair consideration under ordinary legal concepts of that term for the transfers of the stock by him. She performed the contract under the terms of which the stock was transferred to her and held the shares not as a donee but as a purchaser for a fair consideration.

* * *

Decision reversed.

■ CLARK, CIRCUIT JUDGE (dissenting):

The opinion accepts two assumptions, both necessary to the result. The first is that definitions of gift under the gift and estate tax statutes are not useful, in fact are directly opposed to, definitions of gift under the capital-gains provision of the income tax statute. The second is that the circumstances here of a transfer of the stock some months before the marriage showed, contrary to the conclusions of the Tax Court, a purchase of dower rights, rather than a gift. The first I regard as doubtful; the second, as untenable.

It is true that [the Supreme Court decisions] which would require the transactions here to be considered a gift, dealt with estate and gift taxes. But no strong reason has been advanced why what is a gift under certain sections of the Revenue Code should not be a gift under yet another section. * * * The Congressional purpose would seem substantially identical—to prevent a gap in the law whereby taxes on gifts or on capital gains could be avoided or reduced by judicious transfers within the family or intimate group.

But decision on that point might well be postponed, since, in my mind, the other point should be decisive. Kresge transferred the stock to petitioner more than three months before their marriage. Part was given when Kresge was married to another woman. At these times petitioner had no dower or other rights in his property. If Kresge died before the wedding, she could never secure dower rights in his lands. Yet she would nevertheless keep the stock. Indeed the specifically stated purpose of the transfer was to protect her against his death prior to marriage. It is therefore difficult to perceive how her not yet acquired rights could be consideration for the stock. Apparently the parties themselves shared this difficulty, for in their subsequent instrument releasing dower rights they referred to the stock transfer as a gift and an antenuptial settlement.

If the transfer be thus considered a sale, as the majority hold, it would seem to follow necessarily that this valuable consideration (equivalent to one-third for life in land valued at one hundred million dollars) should have yielded sizable taxable capital gains to Kresge, as well as a capital loss to petitioner when eventually she sold. I suggest these considerations as pointing to the unreality of holding as a sale what seems clearly only intended as a stimulating cause to eventual matrimony.

NOTES

(A) *Tax Consequences to Doris Farid-Es-Sultaneh.* Ms. Farid-Es-Sultaneh apparently did not realize any gain on the transfer of her marital rights in exchange for the stock. Why? Rev. Rul. 67–221, 1967–2 C.B. 63, held that there is no gain when marital rights are relinquished, but provides no analysis of why there is no gain. Is there any statutory authority for this exclusion? It seems that Ms. Farid-Es-Sultaneh did not strike a particularly good bargain, i.e., the value of what she might have inherited or received on divorce from Kresge was much greater than the value of the Kresge stock. Does that matter?

(B) *Tax Consequences to S.S. Kresge.* What were the tax consequences to Mr. Kresge in 1924 when he transferred the stock to Ms. Farid-Es-Sultaneh? If Mr. Kresge had died after the stock transfer but before marrying Ms. Farid-Es-Sultaneh, what would he have received "in exchange" for the stock? Could Mr. Kresge claim that he had made a gift?

(C) *Section 1041.* Section 1041 only applies to transfers between spouses or transfers incident to a divorce. It generally therefore would not apply to a transfer made prior to marriage pursuant to an antenuptial agreement. Is there any justification for the disparate treatment of antenuptial agreements and transfers between spouses (or former spouses)? Is there a reason why transfers in contemplation of marriage should not be treated similarly to gifts under § 1041?

(D) *Definition of Gift.* The opinion in *Farid-Es-Sultaneh* expressly notes that the definition of gift for income tax purposes does not need to be construed identically with the definition of gift for gift tax purposes. Furthermore, the definition of gift for tax purposes need not be the same as the definition for state law purposes. Consider Blagaich v. Commissioner, 111 T.C.M. 1006 (2016). In that case the petitioner was involved in a romantic relationship with a Mr. Burns, who gave her more than $270,000 and a Corvette. Subsequently they entered into a written agreement to confirm their commitment to each other and Mr. Burns transferred another $400,000 to the petitioner. But it wasn't long before they broke up and Mr. Burns filed a suit asking for it all back. (He also filed a Form 1099 reporting to the IRS that he had provided petitioner with more than $700,000 of income.) The state court found that all the payments preceding the agreement were gifts, which she was entitled to keep. The Tax Court, however, found that the IRS was not estopped from arguing that the payments were not gifts despite the state court ruling.

(E) *Unmarried Cohabitants.* There are no special provisions to govern the tax treatment of payments or property settlements when unmarried cohabitants separate. Payments thus would not be deductible to the payor and would be taxable to the recipient if determined to be something other than a gift.

Cohabitants sometimes own property jointly and must divide it up when they separate. If they split the jointly held property equally, there probably is no gain or loss. But what if one party took some pieces of jointly-held property while the other party took the remainder? The principle of the *Davis* case presumably would require the recognition of gain or loss on the transfer of separately-held property. It is possible that the full value of the property might have to be included in the income of the recipient as a contractual payment or a "windfall" or compensation, rather than a gift, especially if the property division was hotly disputed. Of course, if they had married, the issue would not arise because § 1041 would apply.

SECTION 2. ASSIGNMENTS OF INCOME IN GENERAL

This Section of this Chapter details the basic income tax rules that govern the attribution of income to taxpayers. In general, two basic principles emerge from the materials that follow: (1) earned income is taxable to the person who earns it and (2) income from property is taxable to the owner of the property. The classic cases that produced these basic rules are presented here along with some modern applications.

A. INCOME FROM SERVICES

Lucas v. Earl

Supreme Court of the United States, 1930. 281 U.S. 111.

■ MR. JUSTICE HOLMES delivered the opinion of the Court.

This case presents the question whether the respondent, Earl, could be taxed for the whole of the salary and attorney's fees earned by him in the years 1920 and 1921, or should be taxed for only a half of them in view of a contract with his wife which we shall mention. The Commissioner of Internal Revenue and the Board of Tax Appeals imposed a tax upon the whole, but their decision was reversed by the Circuit Court of Appeals, 30 F.(2d) 898. * * *

By the contract, made in 1901, Earl and his wife agreed "that any property either of us now has or may hereafter acquire * * * in any way, either by earnings (including salaries, fees, etc.), or any rights by contract or otherwise, during the existence of our marriage, or which we or either of us may receive by gift, bequest, devise, or inheritance, and all the proceeds, issues, and profits of any and all such property shall be treated and considered, and hereby is declared to be received, held, taken, and owned by us as joint tenants, and not otherwise, with the right of survivorship." The validity of the contract is not questioned, and we assume it to be unquestionable under the law of the State of California, in which the parties lived. Nevertheless we are of opinion that the Commissioner and Board of Tax Appeals were right.

The Revenue Act of 1918 * * * imposes a tax upon the net income of every individual including "income derived from salaries, wages, or compensation for personal service * * * of whatever kind and in whatever form paid," sec. 213(a). The provisions of the Revenue Act of 1921 * * * are similar to those of the above. A very forcible argument is presented to the effect that the statute seeks to tax only income beneficially received, and that taking the question more technically the salary and fees become the joint property of Earl and his wife on the very first instant on which they were received. We well might hesitate upon the latter proposition, because however the matter might stand between husband and wife he was the only party to the contracts by which the salary and fees were earned, and it is somewhat hard to say that the last step in the performance of those contracts could be taken by anyone but himself alone. But this case is not to be decided by attenuated subtleties. It turns on the import and reasonable construction of the taxing act. There is no doubt that the statute could tax salaries to those who earned them and provide that the tax could not be escaped by anticipatory arrangements and contracts however skillfully devised to prevent the salary when paid from vesting even for a second in the man who earned it. That seems to us the import of the statute before us and we think that no distinction can be taken according to the motives leading to the arrangement by which the fruits are attributed to a different tree from that on which they grew.

Judgment reversed.

■ THE CHIEF JUSTICE took no part in this case.

NOTES

(A) *Relationship to the Joint Return Provisions.* The tax results that Mr. and Mrs. Earl could not achieve by contract routinely are achieved today by married couples through use of the joint return provisions described in the first section of this Chapter. Consider also the decision of the Supreme Court in Poe v. Seaborn, 282 U.S. 101 (1930), discussed in the *Druker* case, supra at page 496, which held that, in community property states, each spouse was taxable on one-half of community income, even if it was earned solely by one of the spouses. The principle of *Lucas v. Earl* nonetheless continues to prevent taxpayers from otherwise assigning earned income to those whose services did not produce the income. Given the kiddie tax, see supra at page 505, and the narrow rate brackets for trusts, enacted in the 1986 Tax Reform Act, there are many fewer cases where an assignment would save taxes. Legislation in 2017, however, opened new opportunities for using partnerships and corporations to shift income to lower tax rates. See the discussion at page 531.

Was Mrs. Earl also taxed on the receipt of the income? If not, why not?

(B) *Income Splitting and Assignments Between Unmarried Cohabitants.* As we have described, unmarried cohabitants are required to file separate tax returns using the single or head of household rate schedule, whichever is appropriate. This rule may operate to their advantage if their incomes are relatively equal because they might incur a "marriage penalty" if they formalized their relationship.

What if cohabitants entered into an income-pooling agreement similar to that in *Lucas v. Earl*? Income shifted as a result of such an arrangement would be taxed to the person who earned it and again to the person who received it unless the payments could be shown to have resulted from "detached and disinterested generosity" and therefore be excluded under § 102 as a gift.

(C) *Who Is the Earner?* In Hundley v. Commissioner, 48 T.C. 339 (1967), the taxpayer had entered into an agreement with his father to share equally any bonus he might receive for signing a professional baseball contract. This amount was to compensate Hundley's father for coaching efforts and for acting as Hundley's agent in contract negotiations. In 1960, Hundley entered into a contract providing for a bonus of $110,000 to be paid over five years. The Commissioner contended that the amount paid to his father was includible in Hundley's gross income. The Tax Court determined that the amount paid by Hundley to his father was reasonable in amount and held that Hundley, while required to include the entire payment in his gross income, was entitled to a business expense deduction under § 162 for the payment to his father. The younger Hundley, Randy, was a catcher for the Chicago Cubs, the same position his son Todd would go on to play. In 1960 $110,000 was considered a huge bonus.

(D) *Unique Factual Situations.* In some cases, law school faculty members who are the attorney of record in matters handled by law school clinics receive court-ordered or statutorily-provided compensation, which the faculty member then assigns to the law school. Although citing *Lucas v. Earl*, the IRS in a revenue ruling said that it recognized that that amounts that would otherwise be deemed income are not, in certain unique factual situations, subject to the broad rule of inclusion provided by § 61. Rev. Rul. 74–581, 1974–2 C.B. 25. Similarly, Rev. Rul. 65–282, 1965–2 C.B. 21, holds that statutory legal fees received by attorneys for representing indigent defendants are not includible in gross income where the attorneys, pursuant to their employment contracts, immediately turn the fees over to their employer, a legal aid society. Can the position of the IRS in these rulings and other "unique factual situations" be reconciled with *Lucas v. Earl* and its progeny?

Compare Rev. Rul. 66–377, 1966–2 C.B. 21 (fees received from private professional practice by faculty members of a university's school of medicine are includible in the gross income of those earning the fee even though under the contracts of employment such fees are required to be turned over promptly to the school), and Rev. Rul. 70–161, 1970–1 C.B. 15, holding that Medicare fees earned by staff physicians of a hospital, but collected and used by a tax-exempt hospital, are includible in the physicians' gross income, but that such amounts are deductible as charitable contributions. How can these rulings be distinguished from Revenue Ruling 74–581? While allowing deductions as charitable contributions will often result in the same amount of taxable income to the doctors as if these earnings had been excluded from the doctors' gross income, that would not be true in all cases: the doctors will have to itemize their deductions, and the amounts will have to be small enough relative to their income not to trigger the 60 percent limitation on charitable deductions under § 170.[2] In addition, the doctors' adjusted gross

---

[2]   For tax years starting in 2026, this limitation is scheduled to revert to 50 percent.

income will be higher, and that may produce other consequences, such as increasing the floors that limit deductions for medical expenses.

Allowing an employee to deduct as a business expense the fees turned over to the employer might result in tax to the employee. Before 2018, employee business expenses were deductible only as itemized deductions and were subject to the 2 percent floor on itemized deductions under § 67. These deductions were eliminated through 2025 by the 2017 tax legislation. See the discussion supra at page 233.

(E) *Assignments to Charities.* The IRS has tended to reject an "agency" theory to determine whether earnings received by members of a religious order who have taken vows of poverty must be included in their gross income. For example, Rev. Rul. 76–323, 1976–2 C.B. 18, concerned two such individuals who turned over to their tax-exempt religious order all of their earnings from outside employment less an amount necessary for living expenses. The IRS required the members to include all of their earnings in gross income because they were not acting as agents of the order. The Service explained that a member performs services as an agent of a religious order only if the order itself performs the services as a principal. The members were entitled to charitable contribution deductions (to the extent allowable under § 170) for amounts turned over to the order.

The Second Circuit has held that to prove an assignment of income on an agency theory, the taxpayer "must show that a contractual relationship existed between their secular employer and the religious order and that the religious order controlled or restricted the taxpayer's use of the money purportedly turned over to the order." Mone v. Commissioner, 774 F.2d 570 (2d Cir. 1985). In that case and a number of others, tax protesters set up churches and turned over all their property and earnings to a church that then paid all of the taxpayer's living expenses. In *Mone*, one of the taxpayers was an electrical engineer with Con Ed in New York and assigned all of his wages to the Order of Almighty God of the Life Science Church. The court found that Con Ed had paid his wages to him in his individual capacity, rather than as an agent of the church. The courts usually also deny charitable deductions in such cases, sometimes expressing skepticism about the validity of the church. For example, in Gunkle v. Commissioner, 753 F.3d 502 (5th Cir. 2014), the court taxed the Gunkle couple on their retirement income assigned to the City of Refuge Christian Fellowship Pastoral Expense Account, which they used to pay their personal expenses. The Gunkles had concocted this scheme after Brice Gunkle had attended a "church leadership conference" where Frederic Gardner and his wife Elizabeth Gardner were marketing a pre-packaged kit for implementing this tax scam. Nearly three years later, in Gardner v Commissioner, 845 F.3d 971 (9th Cir. 2017), the Ninth Circuit upheld a Tax Court decision concluding that the fees earned by the Bethel Aram Ministries (BAM), a "church" that the Gardners controlled, were taxable to the Gardners. BAM had no congregation and all of its funds came from the Gardners' sales (for $1900 each) of more than 300 tax avoidance schemes to people like the Gunkles. Rejecting the Gardners' argument that the court should respect the separate identity of BAM, the court observed that this "seems a little like arguing that Clark Kent is not

Superman." And with more than a little irony, the court relied on the Fifth Circuit's decision in *Gunkle* to require the taxation of the Gardners' promotional fees.

B. INCOME FROM PROPERTY

As noted previously, the general rule is that income from property is taxed to the owner. A gift of property serves to shift the income from the property to the transferee. A gift of the income from property, however, does not shift the tax. In reading the next two cases, see if you can determine why the transfer in *Blair* was respected but the transfer in *Horst* was not.

Blair v. Commissioner

Supreme Court of the United States, 1937. 300 U.S. 5.

■ MR. CHIEF JUSTICE HUGHES delivered the opinion of the Court.

This case presents the question of the liability of a beneficiary of a testamentary trust for a tax upon the income which he had assigned to his children prior to the tax years and which the trustees had paid to them accordingly.

The trust was created by the will of William Blair, a resident of Illinois who died in 1899, and was of property located in that State. One-half of the net income was to be paid to the donor's widow during her life. His son, the petitioner Edward Tyler Blair, was to receive the other one-half and, after the death of the widow, the whole of the net income during his life. In 1923, after the widow's death, petitioner assigned to his [children], an interest amounting to * * * $9000 in each calendar year thereafter, in the net income which the petitioner was then or might thereafter be entitled to receive during his life. * * * In later years, by similar instruments, he assigned to these children additional interests * * * in the net income. The trustees accepted the assignments and distributed the income directly to the assignees.

The * * * Commissioner of Internal Revenue ruled that the income was taxable to the petitioner. The Board of Tax Appeals held the contrary. 18 B.T.A. 69. The Circuit Court of Appeals reversed the Board, holding that under the law of Illinois the trust was a spendthrift trust and the assignments were invalid. Commissioner v. Blair, 60 F.2d 340. We denied certiorari. 288 U.S. 602.

[Subsequent litigation in the Illinois Courts held that the assignments were valid and the Court acknowledged that it must respect that decision.]

* * * The question remains whether, treating the assignments as valid, the assignor was still taxable upon the income under the federal income tax act. That is a federal question.

Our decisions in *Lucas v. Earl*, 281 U.S. 111, and *Burnet v. Leininger*, 285 U.S. 136, are cited. In the Lucas case the question was whether an attorney was taxable for the whole of his salary and fees earned by him in the tax years or only upon one-half by reason of an agreement with his wife by which his earnings were to be received and owned by them jointly. We were of the opinion that the case turned upon the construction of the taxing act. We said that "the statute could tax salaries to those who earned them and provide that the tax could not be escaped by anticipatory arrangements and contracts however skillfully devised to prevent the same when paid from vesting even for a second in the man who earned it." That was deemed to be the meaning of the statute as to compensation for personal service and the one who earned the income was held to be subject to the tax. In *Burnet v. Leininger*, supra, a husband, a member of a firm, assigned future partnership income to his wife. We found that the revenue act dealt explicitly with the liability of partners as such. The wife did not become a member of the firm; the act specifically taxed the distributive share of each partner in the net income of the firm; and the husband by the fair import of the act remained taxable upon his distributive share. These cases are not in point. The tax here is not upon earnings which are taxed to the one who earns them. Nor is it a case of income attributable to a taxpayer by reason of the application of the income to the discharge of his obligation. * * * There is here no question of evasion or of giving effect to statutory provisions designed to forestall evasion; or of the taxpayer's retention of control. * * *

In the instant case, the tax is upon income as to which, in the general application of the revenue acts, the tax liability attaches to ownership. * * *

The Government points to the provisions of the revenue acts imposing upon the beneficiary of a trust the liability for the tax upon the income distributable to the beneficiary. But the term is merely descriptive of the one entitled to the beneficial interest. These provisions cannot be taken to preclude valid assignments of the beneficial interest, or to affect the duty of the trustee to distribute income to the owner of the beneficial interest, whether he was such initially or becomes such by valid assignment. The one who is to receive the income as the owner of the beneficial interest is to pay the tax. If under the law governing the trust the beneficial interest is assignable, and if it has been assigned without reservation, the assignee thus becomes the beneficiary and is entitled to rights and remedies accordingly. We find nothing in the revenue acts which denies him that status.

The decision of the Circuit Court of Appeals turned upon the effect to be ascribed to the assignments. The court held that the petitioner had no interest in the corpus of the estate and could not dispose of the income until he received it. Hence it was said that "the income was *his*" and his assignment was merely a direction to pay over to others what was due to himself. The question was considered to involve "the date when the income became transferable." * * * The Government refers to the terms of the assignment—that it was of the interest in the income "which the said party of the first part now is, or may hereafter be, entitled to receive during his life from the trustees." From this it is urged that the assignments "dealt only with a right to receive the income" and that "no attempt was made to assign any equitable right, title or interest in the trust itself." This construction seems to us to be a strained one. We think it apparent that the conveyancer was not seeking to limit the assignment so as to make it anything less than a complete transfer of the specified interest of the petitioner as the life beneficiary of the trust, but that with ample caution he was using words to effect such a transfer. That the state court so construed the assignments appears from the final decree which described them as voluntary assignments of interests of the petitioner "in said trust estate," and it was in that aspect that petitioner's right to make the assignments was sustained.

The will creating the trust entitled the petitioner during his life to the net income of the property held in trust. He thus became the owner of an equitable interest in the corpus of the property. * * * By virtue of that interest he was entitled to enforce the trust, to have a breach of trust enjoined and to obtain redress in case of breach. The interest was present property alienable like any other, in the absence of a valid restraint upon alienation * * *. The beneficiary may thus transfer a part of his interest as well as the whole. * * *

We conclude that the assignments were valid, that the assignees thereby became the owners of the specified beneficial interests in the income, and that as to these interests they and not the petitioner were taxable for the tax years in question. * * *

Reversed.

Helvering v. Horst

Supreme Court of the United States, 1940. 311 U.S. 112.

■ MR. JUSTICE STONE delivered the opinion of the Court.

The sole question for decision is whether the gift, during the donor's taxable year, of interest coupons detached from the bonds, delivered to the donee and later in the year paid at maturity, is the realization of income taxable to the donor.

In 1934 and 1935 respondent, the owner of negotiable bonds, detached from them negotiable interest coupons shortly before their due date and delivered them as a gift to his son who in the same year collected them at maturity. The Commissioner ruled that * * * the interest payments were taxable, in the years when paid, to the respondent donor who reported his income on the cash receipts basis. The circuit court of appeals reversed the order of the Board of Tax Appeals sustaining the tax. We granted certiorari, because of the importance of the question in the administration of the revenue laws and because of an asserted conflict in principle of the decision below with that of Lucas v. Earl, 281 U.S. 111, and with that of decisions by other circuit courts of appeals. * * *

The Court below thought that as the consideration for the coupons had passed to the obligor, the donor had, by the gift, parted with all control over them and their payment, and for that reason the case was distinguishable from *Lucas v. Earl, supra,* and *Burnet v. Leininger*, 285 U.S. 136, where the assignment of compensation for services had preceded the rendition of the services, and where the income was held taxable to the donor.

The holder of a coupon bond is the owner of two independent and separable kinds of right. One is the right to demand and receive at maturity the principal amount of the bond representing capital investment. The other is the right to demand and receive interim payments of interest on the investment in the amounts and on the dates specified by the coupons. Together they are an obligation to pay principal and interest given in exchange for money or property which was presumably the consideration for the obligation of the bond. Here respondent, as owner of the bonds, had acquired the legal right to demand payment at maturity of the interest specified by the coupons and the power to command its payment to others which constituted an economic gain to him.

Admittedly not all economic gain of the taxpayer is taxable income. From the beginning the revenue laws have been interpreted as defining "realization" of income as the taxable event rather than the acquisition of the right to receive it. And "realization" is not deemed to occur until the income is paid. But the decisions and regulations have consistently recognized that receipt in cash or property is not the only characteristic of realization of income to a taxpayer on the cash receipts basis. Where the taxpayer does not receive payment of income in money or property realization may occur when the last step is taken by which he obtains the fruition of the economic gain which has already accrued to him. * * * This may occur when he has made such use or disposition of his power to receive or control the income as to procure in its place other satisfactions which are of economic worth. The question here is, whether because one who in fact receives payment for services or interest payments is taxable only on his receipt of the payments, he can escape all tax by giving away his right to income in advance of payment. If the taxpayer procures payment directly to his creditors of the items of interest or earnings due him, * * * or if he sets up a revocable trust with income payable to the objects of his bounty, * * * he does not escape taxation because he did not actually receive the money. * * *

Underlying [this] reasoning * * * is the thought that income is "realized" by the assignor because he, who owns or controls the source of the income, also controls the disposition of that which he could have received himself and diverts the payment from himself to others as the means of procuring the satisfaction of his wants. The taxpayer has equally enjoyed the fruits of his labor or investment and obtained the satisfaction of his desires whether he collects and uses the income to procure those satisfactions, or whether he disposes of his right to collect it as the means of procuring them. * * *

Although the donor here, by the transfer of the coupons, has precluded any possibility of his collecting them himself he has nevertheless, by his act, procured payment of the interest, as a valuable gift to a member of his family. Such a use of his economic gain, the right to receive income, to procure a satisfaction which can be obtained only by the expenditure of money or property, would seem to be the enjoyment of the income whether the satisfaction is the purchase of goods at the corner grocery, the payment of his debt there, or such non-material satisfactions as may result from the payment of a campaign or community chest contribution, or a gift to his favorite son. Even though he never receives the money he derives money's worth from the disposition of the coupons which he has used as money or money's worth in the procuring of a satisfaction which is procurable only by the expenditure of money or money's worth. The enjoyment of the economic benefit accruing to him by virtue of his acquisition of the coupons is realized as completely as it would have been if he had collected the interest in dollars and expended them for any of the purposes named. * * *

In a real sense he has enjoyed compensation for money loaned or services rendered and not any the less so because it is his only reward for them. To say that one who has made a gift thus derived from interest or earnings paid to his donee has never enjoyed or realized the fruits of his investment or labor because he has assigned them instead of collecting them himself and then paying them over to the donee, is to affront common understanding and to deny the facts of common experience. Common understanding and experience are the touchstones for the interpretation of the revenue laws.

The power to dispose of income is the equivalent of ownership of it. The exercise of that power to procure the payment of income to another is the enjoyment and hence the realization of the income by him who exercises it. We have had no difficulty in applying that proposition where the assignment preceded the rendition of the services, *Lucas v. Earl, supra; Burnet v. Leininger, supra,* for it was recognized in the *Leininger* case that in such a case the rendition of the service by the assignor was the means by which the income was controlled by the donor and of making his assignment effective. But it is the assignment by which the disposition of income is controlled when the service precedes the assignment and in both cases it is the exercise of the power of disposition of the interest or compensation with the resulting payment to the donee which is the enjoyment by the donor of income derived from them.

This was emphasized in *Blair v. Commissioner*, 300 U.S. 5, on which respondent relies, where the distinction was taken between a gift of income derived from an obligation to pay compensation and a gift of income-producing property. In the circumstances of that case the right to income from the trust property was thought to be so identified with the equitable ownership of the property from which alone the beneficiary derived his right to receive the income and his power to command disposition of it that a gift of the income by the beneficiary became effective only as a gift of his ownership of the property producing it. Since the gift was deemed to be a gift of the property, the income from it was held to be the income of the owner of the property, who was the donee, not the donor, a refinement which was unnecessary if respondent's contention here is right, but one clearly inapplicable to gifts of interest or wages. Unlike income thus derived from an obligation to pay interest or compensation, the income of the trust was regarded as no more the income of the donor than would be the rent from a lease or a crop raised on a farm after the leasehold or the farm had been given away. * * * We have held without deviation that where the donor retains control of the trust property the income is taxable to him although paid to the donee. * * *

The dominant purpose of the revenue laws is the taxation of income to those who earn or otherwise create the right to receive it and enjoy the benefit of it when paid. * * * The tax laid by the 1934 Revenue Act upon income "derived from * * * wages or compensation for personal service, of whatever kind and in whatever form paid, * * *; also from interest * * *" therefore cannot fairly be interpreted as not applying to income derived from interest or compensation when he who is entitled to receive it makes use of his power to dispose of it in procuring satisfactions which he would otherwise procure only by the use of the money when received.

* * *

Reversed.

■ The separate opinion of MR. JUSTICE MCREYNOLDS.

* * *

The unmatured coupons given to the son were independent negotiable instruments, complete in themselves. Through the gift they became at once the absolute property of the donee, free from the donor's control and in no way dependent upon ownership of the bonds. No question of actual fraud or purpose to defraud the revenue is presented.

Neither Lucas v. Earl, 281 U.S. 111, nor Burnet v. Leininger, 285 U.S. 136, support petitioner's view. Blair v. Commissioner, 300 U.S. 5, 11, 12, shows that neither involved an unrestricted completed transfer of property.

* * *

The general principles approved in Blair v. Commissioner, 300 U.S. 5, are applicable and controlling. The challenged judgment should be affirmed.

■ The CHIEF JUSTICE and MR. JUSTICE ROBERTS concur in this opinion.

NOTES

(A) *Taxation of Bonds and Other Income Producing Property.* The specific result in *Horst* has been overruled by statute. Section 1286 now provides that where a taxpayer disposes of unmatured coupons or the naked bond, the basis of the bond is allocated between the retained portion and the portion sold. The transferor and the transferee are then subject to the original issue discount rules, discussed infra at page 757. Each year, the holder of the coupons reports the increase in value of each coupon as it nears payment. The holder of the bond reports annually the increase in value as it moves toward maturity. The total amount of income reported is the same as in *Horst*, but, instead of being taxed solely to the transferor, it is allocated between the transferor and transferee.

Section 1286 is limited to bonds. Should *Horst* continue to apply where the property transferred is neither a bond nor its coupons? What would the result be if Dad gives stock to his son? What if he gives the stock to his daughter and the dividend rights to his son? What if the son subsequently transfers the dividend rights to his child? The *Horst* Court apparently felt compelled to find that either the transferor or the transferee (but not both) should be taxed on the income. This reflects the Court's assumption that there is only one owner of the bond. As a financial matter, however, both the transferor and the transferee own an interest in the property, each of which produces economic income annually. Requiring the transferor to report all of the income permits the transferee to shift income to the transferor. The realization rule, however, currently prevents taxation of the increase in value in the remainder interest and this may explain the need to tax the transferor on the entire income. For criticism of *Horst* and a recommendation that the § 1286 approach be extended far more widely, see Noël B. Cunningham & Deborah H. Schenk, "Taxation Without Realization: A 'Revolutionary' Approach to Ownership," 47 Tax L. Rev. 725 (1992).

In Irwin v. Gavit, 268 U.S. 161 (1925), the Court held that the beneficiary of an income interest in a trust could not exclude the gift under § 102. One implication of the decision is that § 102 applies only to the remainderman of a trust. If the Court had permitted the exclusion of *both* the corpus and the income, the § 102 exclusion would be greater for divided interests than it would be for a single gift of the property. As with the holder of the bond in *Horst*, the increase in value of the remainder escapes tax. The holding in *Gavit* is codified in § 102(b)(2). Section 1.102–1(e) of the regulations makes clear that "Section 102 is not intended to tax a donee upon the same income which is taxed to the grantor of a trust or assignor of income under section 61 or sections 671 through 677 [regarding the taxation of trusts]. . . ."

(B) *Trees and Fruits.* Justice Holmes' metaphor—the fruits of a taxpayer's labor cannot be attributed "to a different tree from that on which they grew"—has given rise to a whole body of case law that has attempted to jam the facts into the metaphor. *Blair,* for example, is said to stand for the proposition that one cannot avoid taxation by giving away simply the fruit (i.e., the income). If, however, the entire tree (i.e., the property) is transferred, the fruit (income) is taxable to the transferee. *Blair* should be contrasted with Harrison v. Schaffner, 312 U.S. 579 (1941), in which a trust income beneficiary assigned a portion of the income for one year with the donor retaining subsequent trust income. There the Court found that only fruit—and not the tree—had been transferred. In *Schaffner* and *Horst,* the taxpayer carved out an interest, retaining a remainder, whereas in *Blair,* there was no carve-out. Distinguishing the cases where there has been a carve-out and where there has been a complete transfer is not easy. For example, in McGinnis v. Commissioner, 65 T.C.M. 1870 (1993), the taxpayer transferred a 45 percent interest in a leasehold to a trust and argued that he had transferred a share of the entire property, a part of the tree. The court disagreed, finding that the income came not from the leasehold, but from the property itself, which the taxpayer retained.

Even where the taxpayer has transferred the entire tree, any "ripe fruit" usually is taxable to the transferor. For example, the donor of an apartment building is taxed on any accrued but unpaid rents. This concept applies as well to income from services. In Helvering v. Eubank, 311 U.S. 122 (1940), decided on the same day as *Horst,* a taxpayer who had been an agent for a life insurance company, was taxed on renewal commissions that he had assigned after he left employment. As the Supreme Court noted in *Schaffner:*

> one who is entitled to receive, at a future date, interest or compensation for services and who makes a gift of it by an anticipatory assignment, realizes taxable income quite as much as if he had collected the income and paid it over to the object of his bounty.

A taxpayer owned stock in a closely-held corporation. After the declaration of a dividend, but before the record date, he made a gift of the shares. The Tax Court held that the dividend was taxable to the donor. Anton v. Commissioner, 34 T.C. 842 (1960), affirmed sub nom. Smith's Estate v. Commissioner, 292 F.2d 478 (3d Cir. 1961). The Fifth Circuit reached the opposite conclusion, rejecting the notion that the taxpayer had earned the income. Disparaging, but nevertheless using, the fruit and tree metaphor, the court noted: "We fail to see why the ripeness of the fruit matters, so long as the entire tree is transplanted before the fruit is harvested." Caruth v. United States, 865 F.2d 644 (5th Cir. 1989).

(C) *Transfer of Appreciated Property.* Consider the Court's statement in *Horst* that

> [t]o say that one who has made a gift thus derived from interest or earnings paid to his donee has never enjoyed or realized the fruits of his investment or labor, because he has assigned them instead of collecting them himself and then paying them over to the donee, is

to affront common understanding and to deny the facts of common experience.

Does not the same reasoning apply to any gift of appreciated property? Recall the carryover of basis under § 1015, discussed at page 141.

(D) *Life Imitates Art and Vice Versa.* In the 1994 film, "It Could Happen to You" a New York police officer (played by Nicholas Cage), unable to leave a tip, promises to share his lottery winnings with a poor waitress (played by Bridget Fonda). He wins $4 million, gives her half, she buys the diner, and, with many complications, romance ensues. The crucial question, completely ignored by the film, is, of course, who is taxable on the $4 million winnings. The real-life incident on which the film was based, presents an easier question: in 1984 New York police officer Robert Cunningham had suggested that, in lieu of a tip, he and Phyllis Penzo, a waitress at a pizza restaurant he regularly visited, each pick three of six numbers on a lottery ticket and split the winnings. Although Penzo forgot about the incident, the ticket was a winner and Cunningham split the $6 million prize with her. No romance followed. In the real-life case, Penzo had contributed her forgone tip and picked half of the winning numbers so the winnings were taxed half to her and half to Cunningham.

In Riebe v. Commissioner, 41 B.T.A. 935 (1940), aff'd 124 F.2d 399 (6th Cir. 1941), the holder of a sweepstakes ticket made an oral assignment of a two-thirds interest to members of his family. He made the assignment after the ticket was selected but before the sweepstakes. The proceeds were paid according to the transfer. The court held that all of the proceeds were taxable to the transferor. Compare Braunstein v. Commissioner, 21 T.C.M. 1132 (1962), where the taxpayers transferred their interest in an Irish Sweepstakes ticket to a trust for their children two days before the race; the donors were taxable on the $2,137 guaranteed value of the ticket, but not on the remainder of their $136,000 prize.

In Dickerson v. Commissioner, 103 T.C.M. 1280 (2012), a customer, Edward Sweard, had given a Florida lottery ticket worth more than $5 million to Tonya Lynn Dickerson, a waitress at a Waffle House in Grand Bay, Alabama. Seward didn't know that the ticket was a winner, and since Dickerson had not waited on him that day, the court agreed that the winnings were a gift, not a taxable tip.

(E) *Is Income from Property or Services?* By transferring property, the taxpayer ordinarily may shift the tax on income from the property to the transferee. In some cases, however, it is difficult to determine whether income is from property or from services, or whether the property has been transferred or retained. These problems arise frequently in the context of patents and copyrights. For example, in Heim v. Fitzpatrick, 262 F.2d 887 (2d Cir. 1959), the court upheld as a valid assignment of income from property the taxpayer's transfer to his wife and children of 25 percent of the royalties from patents on his inventions of new types of rods and bearings. The court specifically found that *Blair* was applicable and not *Horst* or *Eubank.*

If a parent transfers a patent or copyright to children, the income typically will be taxed to the children. Rev. Rul. 54–599, 1954–2 C.B. 52. This may occur even if the patent or copyright has been licensed prior to the transfer to the children. But if the patent or copyright has been transferred to a third party, a further transfer of only the right to the receipts from that transfer is not a valid assignment of income. And a bare license of a patent or copyright produces royalties that are taxable as ordinary income to the transferor.

Due to the many variations of such arrangements, there may be considerable difficulty in telling whether a given transaction is properly treated as a gift or sale or as a license with royalties reserved. There has been a tendency of courts to hold that patents and copyrights are divisible. Thus, the transferor is not taxable on income shifted by means of an exclusive right to use the patent in a particular area, or to use a copyright in a particular medium (such as a book, radio, or movies) for the life of the patent or copyright. This question is considered further infra at page 594 in connection with capital gains issues.

SECTION 3.   USING ENTITIES

Taxpayers sometimes have created corporations, partnerships, or trusts for the purpose of shifting income to later years or to lower tax brackets.

Corporations generally are treated as separate taxable entities distinct from their shareholders. In contrast, partnerships (along with limited liability companies, which may be taxed as partnerships and S corporations) are treated as conduits through which items of income and deduction flow to the various partners to be reported on their individual tax returns. The income of some trusts is taxed to an individual (or individuals) who is treated as the "owner" of the trust property; the income of other trusts is taxed to the beneficiaries if it is currently distributed but, at least initially, to the trust as a separate taxpayer if it is accumulated at the trust level.

The taxation of corporations, partnerships, and trusts is generally not considered in this book, but the rate changes of the 2017 legislation have made issues of entity taxation much more important to many people. For example, notwithstanding the general prohibition of *Lucas v. Earl* against the shifting of income from one's labor, the Code sometimes affords taxpayers opportunities to accumulate personal services income in a corporation or partnership. The desirability of such a shift depends on the relationships of the various tax rates that apply. As the following material describes, the 2017 legislation made major changes to these relationships.

Note Providing an Overview of Taxation of Business Income

Business income is taxed under rules relating to the type of entity conducting the business. The principal business entities for federal income tax purposes are C corporations, partnerships (including limited liability companies (LLCs)), S corporations, and sole proprietorships. Partnerships and S corporations are often referred to as "pass-through" entities because, like sole proprietorships, their income is included in the gross income of the owners of the entities rather than in the income of the entities themselves. C corporations are taxed at the entity level at a rate of 21 percent beginning in 2018. § 11. When C corporations distribute earnings to their individual shareholders as dividends, the dividends are usually taxed at the shareholder level at the capital gains rate. § 1(h)(11). And when corporate shares are sold, any gains are typically taxed as capital gains.

In 2014 more than two-thirds of all business returns were nonfarm sole proprietorships, S corporations accounted for 12.2 percent of business returns, and partnerships represented an all-time high of 10 percent of business returns. C Corporations accounted for approximately five percent of returns. In 2014 there were approximately 1.6 million C corporations, 3.6 million partnerships, 4.4 million S corporations, 24.6 million nonfarm sole proprietorships, and 1.8 million farm sole proprietorships.[3]

Before 1987, when C corporation tax rates were lower than individual rates, there were more C corporations than S corporations and partnerships combined. But the 1986 Tax Reform Act changed the tax rates significantly, and in 1987 the number of S corporations and partnerships exceeded the number of C corporations. Since 1987 the combined number of pass-through entities has more than tripled. The growth has been led by large increases in the number of small S corporations (those with less than $100,000 in assets) and limited liability companies taxed as partnerships. Since 1996, LLCs have grown at a rate of approximately 14 percent per year.

---

[3]   The data in this overview are taken from Joint Committee on Taxation, Present Law and Data Related to the Taxation of Business Income, JCX–42–17, September 15, 2017.

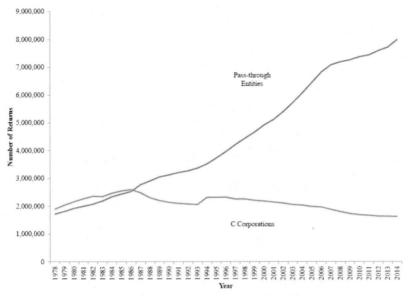

Source: JCT staff calculations on SOI data.

Distributing by the number of returns, for C corporations, the three most prevalent industries are professional, scientific, and technical services, real estate and rental leasing, and retail trade. These three industries account for approximately 33 percent of all C corporations. Over half of all entities taxed as partnerships are in the real estate and rental leasing industry, with finance and insurance and professional, scientific, and technical services rounding out the three most prevalent industries. These three industries account for approximately two-thirds of all partnerships. Nonfarm sole proprietorships are most likely to be in the industry of professional, scientific, and technical services, other services, or construction. These three industries account for almost 38 percent of all nonfarm sole proprietorships.

Looking at the distribution of business entities by assets, however, paints a different picture. For C corporations, the three largest sectors are finance and insurance, holding companies and manufacturing. These three sectors account for more than 83 percent of all assets reported by all C corporations. For S corporations, the three largest sectors are holding companies, manufacturing, and wholesale trade. These three sectors account for 37 percent of all assets reported by all S corporations. For partnerships, the two largest industries by far are finance and insurance and real estate, followed by manufacturing at a distant third. These three industries account for more than 81 percent of all assets reported on all partnership returns.

The advent and growth of private equity, sovereign wealth funds, and business investments by pension funds and the endowments of universities and other tax-exempt organizations have allowed very large business entities to amass large amounts of capital while avoiding the public capital markets. This allows many large entities to be organized as partnerships or S corporations, but most net income is earned by very large entities that are still C corporations.

Distribution of Net Income by Business Entity Type, 2014

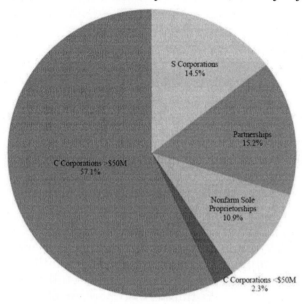

While the majority of business returns are filed by nonfarm sole proprietorships, such businesses represent only 10.9 percent of business net income. In contrast, although they file 4.5 percent of business returns, C Corporations represent more than half of all business income. In fact, the 1.3 percent of C corporations with gross receipts in excess of $50 million reported 57.1 percent of all business net income for 2014, while the remaining 98.7 percent reported 2.3 percent of all business net income.

S Corporations and partnerships are responsible for about the same share of overall business net income. And that income is concentrated near the top: over 70 percent of the net income of S corporations and partnerships is reported on tax returns of the top one percent of taxpayers.

As the foregoing pie chart illustrates, before the 2017 legislation U.S. business income was roughly evenly split between C corporations and flow-through business entities (partnerships, LLCs, and S corporations). The 2017 legislation dramatically reduced the tax rate differentials between investments in C corporations and flow-through entities. The new law has also created new differences in tax rates between employees and sole proprietorships (including independent contractors) and among flow-through entities based on their income levels and their types of business.

In 2017, the U.S. corporate rate at 35 percent plus the maximum individual dividend (or capital gains) rate of 23.8 percent totaled approximately 50 percent on corporate income (35 percent + 23.8 percent of the 65 percent remaining after tax). (This shareholder rate applies only to taxable U.S. shareholders, but only about one third of U.S. corporate shares is owned by taxable U.S. shareholders; the remaining two thirds is owned by foreigners or tax-exempt investors.) Thus, until 2018 the top tax rate on flow-through entities of 39.6 percent was significantly advantageous. Beginning in 2018, the corporate rate of 21 percent plus the unchanged dividend (or capital gains) rate of 23.8 percent on the after-tax income totals 39.8 percent, much closer to the top individual rate of 37 percent.[4] Because the dividend and capital gains taxes can be deferred, however, the total tax liability can be significantly reduced if the corporation directly invests and reinvests its after-tax income and later distributes it to its shareholders. Holding shares until death will avoid the shareholder's tax on earnings retained by the corporation entirely.

There are also new incentives for employees to incorporate and become employees of a wholly-owned corporation that then contracts with the former employer or a new entity for services. Not only does a lower tax rate apply, but some business deductions (including state income taxes) are available only to corporations. § 164. Anti-abuse rules, such as special taxes on unreasonable accumulations of earnings, have largely been ineffective.

The 2017 law also adds a special unique and unprecedented 20 percent deduction from the taxable income of certain qualified business income of partnerships (including LLCs), S corporations, and sole proprietorships. § 199A. This deduction is available at all levels of income: for example, it will reduce the lowest tax bracket from 10 percent to 8 percent and the top tax bracket from 37 percent to 29.6 percent. This deduction will expire after December 31, 2025 unless extended in subsequent legislation.

Note on Qualified Business Income of Pass-Through Entities

With the reduction of the corporate tax rate to 21 percent, representatives of non-corporate businesses whose owners would be taxed at higher individual tax rates if they did not convert to C corporations persuaded Congress to enact § 199A, which provides a special deduction with respect to "qualified business income" from non-

---

[4]   Dividends paid by corporations and capital gains with respect to corporate stock are generally taxed a rate of 20 percent (and may be subject to the additional 3.8 percent "Medicare tax" on net investment income). The total combined rate on corporations and shareholders may thus be 36.8 percent (or 39.8 percent if the Medicare tax applies).

corporate enterprises, including partnerships, limited liability companies, S corporations, and sole proprietorships.

Broadly speaking, as a result of the special deduction under § 199A, the top individual tax rate on business income may be reduced from 37 percent to as low as 29.6 percent. This should be compared to the combination of the flat 21 percent tax rate applicable to a C corporation plus the second level of tax imposed on dividends or capital gains realized by the corporation's shareholders, which as the previous note describes, can be as high as 39.8 percent. The 20 percent deduction is available without regard to the taxpayer's marginal rate on other ordinary income and therefore encourages substantial tax planning both to qualify for and to maximize the lower tax rate available as a result of the § 199A deduction. As with other changes in individual taxation, § 199A terminates for taxable years beginning after December 31, 2025. Thus, unless extended, § 199A will apply only for eight years.

Section 199A generally provides a special deduction from taxable income equal to 20 percent of the "qualified business income" ("QBI") arising from a "qualified trade or business." Simply illustrated, if the sole owner of a supermarket (otherwise taxable at the top marginal rate) realizes taxable income of $150,000 from the store's operations, the owner would be entitled to a special $30,000 § 199A deduction, reducing the owner's marginal income tax rate by 20 percent. With such a meaningful tax savings available, it is important to understand what income qualifies for this special § 199A deduction and what limits apply to it.

Never before 2018 have such sharp distinctions in tax rates been applied broadly to varying industries and lines of business. Congress justified this change as: (1) encouraging the growth of all non-corporate businesses, including those owned by lower-income taxpayers; (2) encouraging job creation and capital investment by non-corporate businesses, except for a specified group of service businesses owned by higher-income taxpayers; and (3) reducing the incentive for non-corporate businesses to switch to corporate status to qualify for the 21 percent rate.

In order to limit the disparity between the tax treatment of wage-earning employees, whose top rate is set at 37 percent, and qualifying non-corporate business owners, whose top rate would be as low as 29.6 percent as a result of § 199A, and to curb the scope of the tax reduction in favor of non-corporate businesses owned by higher-income taxpayers, Congress adopted two limitations on the favorable tax treatment afforded by § 199A. If the business is owned by higher-income taxpayers: (1) the 20 percent deduction does not apply to specified types of service businesses or any other business "where the principal asset is the reputation or skill of one or more of its employees;" and (2) the 20 percent deduction cannot exceed the *greater* of two "wage limits:" (i) 50 percent of the wages paid to employees of the trade or business *or* (ii) the total of 25 percent of such wages and 2.5 percent of the unadjusted basis immediately after acquisition of depreciable tangible property used in the trade or business.

The denial of § 199A to "specified service businesses" owned by higher-income taxpayers, but not to other businesses owned by such taxpayers, is one of its most noteworthy aspects. The specified service businesses that are not eligible for the § 199A deduction, if they are owned by higher-income taxpayers, generally include the performance of services in the fields of health, law, accounting, actuarial science, performing arts, consulting, athletics, financial services, brokerage services, investing, investment management, and securities trading or dealing. (While this disfavored litany of specified services business generally follows the list in § 1202(e)(3)(A), Congress decided that businesses disqualified under § 199A should not include architecture or engineering, both of which appear in § 1202(e)(3)(A).)

In addition, while § 199A does not generally apply to financial services, brokerage services, investing, investment management, or securities trading or dealing when such trades or business are owned by higher-income taxpayers, the special § 199A deduction is expressly allowed for 20 percent of any taxpayer's aggregate amount of investment income from (i) dividends paid by a real estate investment trust (REIT) or a cooperative and (ii) the net allocable share of each item of ordinary income attributable to a publicly traded partnership, unless any such investment income would otherwise be taxed as capital gains and thus taxed at an even lower rate. § 199A(b)(1)(B). This feature of § 199A applies to such investment income without regard to the taxpayer's taxable income or the amount of wages paid by the REIT, cooperative, or publicly traded partnership.

In contrast to the favorable tax treatment provided by omitting architecture and engineering from the list of disqualified "specified service trade or business" and allowing a deduction for ordinary investment income from publicly traded partnerships, REITs and cooperatives, § 199A critically denies its benefit not only to the specified services businesses, but also to both: (1) the trade or business of performing services as an employee, regardless of the employee's taxable income, and (2) any trade or business where the principal asset of the trade or business is the reputation or skill of one or more of its employees or owners, if such businesses are owned by higher-income taxpayers. In this regard, QBI does not include any amount paid to business owners as reasonable compensation for their services, whether as employees of S corporations or as guaranteed payments for services rendered with respect to the trade or business by a partner in a partnership.

As described above, the two additional limitations on the § 199A deduction (the exclusion of certain specified businesses and the wage requirements) are imposed only on businesses owned by higher-income taxpayers—those with taxable income in excess of a "threshold amount."

The threshold amount is $157,500 for single taxpayers and $315,000 for married couples filing a joint return. These threshold amounts are indexed for inflation occurring after 2018. § 199A(e)(2). In order to ameliorate a "cliff effect" for those higher-income taxpayers with taxable income just above the threshold amounts, each of the two limitations is "phased in" gradually for taxpayers with taxable income up to either (a) $50,000 over the threshold amount for single taxpayers or (b) $100,000 over the threshold amount for taxpayers filing a joint tax return. See § 199A(b)(3) and § 199A(d)(3).

Example:[5] The taxpayers husband (H) and wife (W) file a joint tax return on which they include taxable income of $520,000 (before any special deduction under § 199A). Husband is a partner in an automobile dealership partnership. Wife is a lawyer in sole practice, specializing in tax law and litigation with the IRS. Husband's share of QBI from the automobile dealership is $300,000. Husband's share of wages paid by the dealership is $100,000. Husband's share of the unadjusted basis of all qualified property used in the dealership business is $4,000,000. Because H&W family's income is more than $100,000 above the threshold amount for a joint tax return of $315,000, the wage limits must be applied in full to H's automobile dealership income to calculate the § 199A deduction, as follows:

Lesser of:

(A)   20% of H's share of the dealership's QBI; or $60,000

(B)   Greater of:

    (1)   50% of H's share of W-2 wages; or $50,000

    (2)   25% of H's share of W-2 wages, plus $25,000

       2.5% of H's share of the cost basis of $100,000
    qualified property.

                            $125,000

Hence, H's § 199A deduction with respect to the automobile dealership is $60,000.

W's QBI from her law practice is $325,000 and the wages paid to her associate, paralegal and clerical employees are $150,000. The unadjusted basis of depreciable property used in W's law practice is $100,000. The H&W family has taxable income more than $100,000 above the threshold amount of $315,000. As a result, W has no eligible QBI taxable income from her law practice because the term "qualified trade or business" does not include the practice of law (or any other service listed in § 199A(d)) for such high-income taxpayers.

H and W's combined QBI deduction amount is thus comprised of the deductible amount of $60,000 for H's automobile dealership and $0 for

---

[5]   This example is derived from Example 1 in H.R. Rep. No. 115–466, at 220 (2017).

W's solo law practice, reducing their taxable income from $520,000 to $460,000.

If H and W's combined taxable income had been below the $315,000 taxable threshold for married couples filing joint returns, W's law practice would also have qualified for the QBI deduction and neither of the wage limitations would have been applicable in determining H's QBI deduction from his automobile partnership.

NOTES

(A) *Trade or Business of Performing Services as an Employee.* Consider T, a law firm partner earning $175,000 per year. One of T's law school classmates, G, is employed as the general counsel of one of the clients of T's law firm. G earns a salary of $200,000 per year and files a joint tax return with her stay-at-home husband on which they report the same $175,000 of taxable income as T and her spouse Z report. Under § 199A(d)(1)(B), the trade or business of performing services as an employee is not a qualified trade or business. As a result, G is not entitled to any deduction under § 199A. But T is eligible for the 20 percent QBI deduction. Does it make sense for T and her spouse to enjoy the 20 percent deduction not available to G and her spouse? Why should Congress favor individual business owners over similarly situated individual employees?

(B) *W-2 Wages.* The wage limits applicable to qualified trades or businesses owned by taxpayers with taxable income above the applicable thresholds ($315,000 for joint returns or $157,500 for singles) are determined with respect to W-2 wages paid to employees. See § 199A(b)(4), § 6051(a). The wage limit does not include any amounts paid to independent contractors. Should businesses seek to convert from using independent contractors to hiring employees to increase the § 199A deduction? Consider the potential effect of such a reclassification of employment status or compensation on each independent contractor's own § 199A and § 162 business expense deduction. Similarly, in a business where tips are important, such as a restaurant, should the owner add a service charge to all of the customer's bills in lieu of tips and pay such amounts as wages to increase the QBI deduction limitation?

(C) *Unadjusted Basis of Qualified Property.* For purposes of § 199A, qualified property includes tangible real or personal property of a character subject to depreciation. If a business owner has acquired property in which the business is operated as an inheritance, the unadjusted basis under § 1014 would be the fair market value of the property at the date of the decedent's death. Does it make sense to provide for an increase in the § 199A deduction with respect to the untaxed appreciation reflected in a stepped-up basis under § 1014?

(D) *"Good" and "Bad" Service Businesses.* Assume that B operates a barber salon, which is a qualified trade or business for purposes of § 199A and is thus eligible for the special deduction under § 199A. If B had instead been a dentist, or engaged in any other specified service trade or business, such as being a doctor, actor, tennis player or investment banker, he would not have been entitled to any deduction under § 199A. § 199A(d). Why did Congress lower taxes on barbers, but not these other service businesses? Are barbers more beneficial to society than doctors or dentists? Are barbers who own their businesses more beneficial to society than barbers who are employees?

While § 199A clearly applies to barbers, the legislative history of § 199A suggests that it does not apply to anyone engaged in trades or businesses of providing services by physicians, nurses, dentists and other "similar healthcare professionals." Does the catchall phrase "similar healthcare professionals" includes the operation of health or health spas that provide physical exercise or conditioning to their customers? The legislative history cites Reg. § 1.448–1T(e)(4)(ii) to confirm that such trades or businesses qualify for § 199A. Why would Congress prefer health spas and gyms over doctors and dentists?

(E) *Skill or Reputation of a Single Person.* The term "specified service trade or business" used in § 199A to disqualify certain businesses owned by higher-income taxpayers includes any trade or business where the principal asset of the trade or business is the reputation or skill of one or more of its employees or owners. See § 1202(e)(3)(A). If a barber's skill is so well known that it brings customers to her salon, would the § 199A deduction be denied to the barber?

Notice the article "the," in the phrase "where *the* principal asset of such trade or business is the reputation or skill of one or more of its employees." See § 1202(e)(3)(A). What is the difference, if any, between "a" principal asset and "the" principal asset? Do taxpayers have to prove that their reputation or skill (or the reputation or skill of their employees) is not the biggest asset of their trade or business in order to qualify for the § 199A deduction? Do they have to prove there is a bigger asset than the owner's or employees' reputation or skill used in the trade or business?

(F) *Skill or Reputation of a Single Person, Again.* The legislative history states that business owners who *support* performing artists qualify for § 199A, even though the performing artists themselves may not so qualify: "the performance of services in the field of the performing arts does not include the provision of services by persons who themselves are not performing artists (e.g. persons who may manage or promote such artists) . . . ." The legislative history thus implies strongly that agents who manage performers are not disqualified from the benefit of § 199A simply by virtue of working with actors, musicians, or athletes. But, if an agent or manager of performing artists runs a talent agency, with no tangible assets other than a mobile phone and other office equipment, is "the principal asset" of the trade or business, indeed the only real asset, the "skill or reputation" of the owner-agent?

For example, after having a "breakthrough" about his role as a sports agent, in the classic 1996 movie "*Jerry McGuire*," Jerry (played by Tom Cruise, who received an Oscar nomination for his performance) published a mission statement—"The Things We Think and Do Not Say: The Future of Our Business"—describing perceived dishonesty in the sports management business and expressing his desire to work on his own as a sole proprietor with fewer clients to achieve superior results for them. In response, his boss at the large agency where he had been employed fired Jerry, who then quickly called all of his clients trying to convince them to retain his services in his new sole proprietorship. The only client who agrees to hire Jerry is Arizona Cardinals receiver Rod Tidwell, played by Cuba Gooding, Jr. (who won an Oscar for his performance). Rod "needs" a $10 million contract, as he sees the end of his athletic career approaching, so he retains Jerry to represent him because of the approach described by Jerry in the mission statement and Jerry's strong personal connection with Rod and his family. As the movie reaches its climax, Jerry secures Rod an $11.2 million contract, for which Jerry earns a fee of approximately $1.5 million. After Rod then thanks Jerry profusely, Jerry speaks with several other pro athletes who have read his earlier mission statement and respect his work with Rod. Does the mission statement support Jerry's qualification for the § 199A deduction? If Jerry were a real person and the action took place in 2018, is "the principal asset" of Jerry's sports management agency proprietorship his "skill or reputation"? If so, would Jerry McGuire be denied the benefit of § 199A, notwithstanding the favorable legislative history regarding "persons who manage or promote" performing artists in the legislative history?

(G) *Reasonable Compensation.* Section 199A(c)(4) provides that QBI does not include "reasonable compensation paid to the taxpayer by a qualified trade or business for services rendered with respect to the trade or business." If a business owner decides not to pay himself any compensation, perhaps because such compensation will reduce the amount of his QBI and would be taxed at his full ordinary income tax rate, should the IRS be able to impute an amount of reasonable compensation to the owner to achieve the same result? Compare the reverse situation described in *Exacto Spring*, supra at page 243, where the IRS attempted to disallow a deduction under § 162 for any "unreasonable compensation" paid by a corporation to a shareholder in order to reduce the amount of corporate tax.

(H) *Financial Services or Banking?* The list of "specified service trade or business," disqualified for higher-income taxpayers, includes "financial services," but not "banking." The Independent Community Banking Association claims to have been "in ongoing contact with lawmakers and staff during the crafting of the law and was repeatedly assured that shareholders in S-corp community banks would be eligible for the pass-through deduction." See http://www.icba.org/news/news-details/2018/01/17/s-corp-shareholders-eligible-for-new-20-percent-deduction. Are such assurances relevant for statutory analysis? Isn't "banking" merely an example of "financial services"?

(I) *Does Enormous Size Matter?* Many enormous business enterprises clearly are eligible for the special QBI deduction under § 199A. For example, it has been reported that Bechtel, an enormous construction and civil engineering company, is organized as an S corporation. (See https://think progress.org/are-the-small-businesses-republicans-claim-to-be-protecting-from-a-tax-increase-really-small-cf21b0be339e/.) If Bechtel is indeed an S corporation, its owners would be entitled to the § 199A deduction, even though it was reportedly the 8th largest privately owned American company in 2017 (https://www.forbes.com/companies/bechtel/). Does it make sense to allow very large businesses to choose whether to be taxed as a pass-through entity or a taxable corporation?

———

The following case illustrates the tension between the basic assignment of income doctrine and the corporation as a separate taxpaying entity.

Sargent v. Commissioner

United States Court of Appeals, Eighth Circuit, 1991. 929 F.2d 1252.

■ BOGUE, SENIOR DISTRICT JUDGE:

This case, on appeal from the United States Tax Court, is one of first impression for this Court. * * *

Sargent and Christoff (hereinafter "Appellants") were hockey players with the Minnesota North Stars Hockey Club (hereinafter the "Club"). Appellants' personal service corporations (PSC), created to represent the business associations of each Appellant, contracted with the Club to provide each Appellant's services to the Club as a hockey player and, in the case of Sargent, also as a consultant. The North Stars paid each PSC for the use of each Appellant's services; each PSC, in turn, paid each Appellant a salary and contributed the remainder to each PSC's qualified pension plan. The Commissioner proposed to disallow these pension deductions and elected to tax Appellants on the entire amount paid by the Club to the PSC.

* * * The case was tried in the United States Tax Court, [and] Judge Tannenwald, writing for the majority, issued an opinion upholding the deficiencies proposed by the Commissioner. We reverse the decision of the Tax Court and hold that Appellants were employees of their respective personal service corporations; and, therefore, Appellants should not be taxed on the pension deductions of their PSCs.

* * *

The determination of an employer-employee relationship involves a mixed question of law and fact. Because, however, the decision is predominantly one of determining whether the established facts fall within the relevant legal definition, and does not involve constitutional issues, we apply a clearly erroneous standard of review. * * *

BACKGROUND

* * * Appellants were both professional hockey players with the Minnesota North Stars Hockey Club. Prior to signing with the North Stars, Appellant Sargent sought out the assistance of Attorney Arthur Kaminsky concerning the benefits of incorporation. Kaminsky advised Sargent that incorporation provided two primary benefits: increased

bargaining power and the possibility of placing money into a pension plan.

Based upon his consultations with Kaminsky, Sargent incorporated Chiefy-Cat, Inc. (Chiefy-Cat) on July 20, 1978. Sargent was the sole shareholder, president, and sole director of this personal service corporation. On July 20, 1978, Sargent entered into an Employment Contract with Chiefy-Cat wherein he agreed to provide his services as a professional hockey player and consultant exclusively for Chiefy-Cat for the period July 1, 1978, to June 30, 1984. At the same time, Chiefy-Cat agreed to furnish the services of Sargent as both a hockey player and consultant to the Club. In exchange, the Club agreed to pay Chiefy-Cat a set salary during each respective playing season. Further, Sargent's employment agreement with Chiefy-Cat provided that Chiefy-Cat agreed to pay Sargent a set salary during each respective season.

* * *

Christoff followed substantially the same route toward incorporation. * * *

During the years at issue, neither Sargent nor Christoff were considered employees of the Club for purposes of the National Hockey League Players' Pension Plan. In each case, the Club paid Chiefy-Cat and RIF, respectively, the amounts that it would otherwise have contributed to the Players' Pension Plan on their behalf. The sole issue before this Court is whether Sargent and Christoff should be taxed now on those amounts contributed by their respective PSC's to each PSC's qualified pension plan.

I.

The Tax Court takes the position that because Sargent and Christoff were members of a hockey "team," the requisite control over them-for purposes of taxation-was lodged in the hockey Club, and not in their respective PSCs, with which they had a contractual employment relationship. We reject this contention.

With respect to the "control" factor, which is heavily relied upon by the Tax Court, the Regulations state:

> In this connection, it is not necessary that the employer actually direct or control the manner in which the services are performed; it is sufficient if he has the right to do so. Treasury Regulation § 31.3121(d)–1(c)(2) (1980).

It seems to this Court that legal analysis is forgotten if we simply measure the control element of an employment relationship by whether the employee is or is not a member of a superficially defined "team." Eventually, the issue becomes mired in a game of definitions: If the organizational structure is itself mislabeled a "team," a personal service corporation, as a matter of law, is a forbidden tax deferment tool for each and every person providing his or her services to that organization. On the other hand, if the organization to which the services are provided is not defined as a "team," then those same service-providers are free to create a PSC and subject that PSC's legitimacy to traditional common law and tax code analysis, regardless of the level of control exerted over those persons by the organization. Such an arbitrary approach is specious at best.

Accordingly, within Regulation § 31.3121(d)–(1)(c)(2), two necessary elements must be met before the corporation, rather than the service-recipient, in this case the North Stars Hockey Club, may be considered the true controller of the service-provider. First, the service-provider must be just that-an employee of the corporation whom the corporation has the right to direct or control in some meaningful sense. Johnson v. Commissioner, 78 T.C. 882 (1982). Second, there must exist between the corporation and the person or entity (Club) using the services a contract or similar indicium recognizing the corporation's controlling position. See *Johnson,* supra.

These two elements were applied in a case strikingly similar to the one before us. In *Johnson,* supra, Charles Johnson, a professional basketball player with the San Francisco Warriors, created a PSC and the IRS sought to tax Johnson for the entire amount paid to his PSC by the Warriors. Without ever addressing whether Johnson was or was not a member of a "team," the Tax Court ultimately held the contracts to be dispositive of the issue of control:

> In the case before us, we accept arguendo that the [PSC-Johnson] agreement was a valid contract which required the payments with respect to [Johnson's] performance as a basketball player ultimately to be made to the [PSC]. *We also accept arguendo that the [PSC-Johnson] agreement gave [the PSC] a right of control over [Johnson's] services, . . .* Thus, the first element [of control] is satisfied. [emphasis added] *Johnson,* 78 T.C. at 883.

Ultimately, Johnson was required to pay individual income tax on the entire amount paid to his PSC, but only because his PSC had no contractual arrangement with the Warriors basketball team. Said the Tax Court regarding the second prong of the "control" test: "[c]rucial is the fact that there was no contract or agreement between the Warriors and [the PSC]." We are not faced with such a dilemma in this case. Not only did Appellants have a contractual arrangement with their respective PSCs, thereby passing the first prong of the analysis, each PSC also had a contractual relationship with the North Stars Hockey Club. Consistent with its analysis in the past, the Tax Court in *Johnson* concluded that the existence of bona fide contracts between the parties satisfied the requisite elements of control. Indeed, the Tax Court at no time concerned itself with whether Johnson was or was not a member of a "team."

The Tax Court's "team" analysis further breaks down when one looks at a decision handed down by the Tax Court just one day after the case before us. In *Pflug v. Commissioner,* 58 T.C.M. 685 (1989), an actress entered into an exclusive employment contract with her husband's corporation, Charwool Production, Inc. ("Charwool"), of which she was an officer. Subsequently, Charwool entered into a contract with 20th Century Fox Studios, agreeing to provide the services of Ms. Pflug for a new TV series. Although the ultimate issue was whether Ms. Pflug was subject to self-employment taxes on income received from Charwool, the Court was first required to decide whether Ms. Pflug was an employee of Charwool. In holding that Ms. Pflug was an employee of Charwool, and not an employee of 20th Century Fox Studios, the Tax Court held the contracts between the respective parties to be dispositive and stated:

> The fundamental question is whether Charwool had the right to exercise dominion and control over the activities of [Pflug], not only as to results but also as to the means and methods used to accomplish the result. We find, by virtue of the contract [Pflug] entered with Charwool, Charwool had the requisite right to control [Pflug].

This Court is perplexed to find that those same contractual arrangements which were dispositive of the issue of "control" in *Pflug* were summarily discarded in the case before us. By the same token, those same "team" factors which were dispositive of the issue of control in the case before us were not even discussed in *Pflug.*

Was not Joanne Pflug a part of a team every bit as "controlled" as Sargent and Christoff? Like a hockey team in which different players assume different roles to insure success, the members of Pflug's team included the cast, writers, directors, and producers all working toward the common goal of producing a successful TV series. More importantly, just as a hockey player has a generalized set of plays tailored to fit his talents and the talents of his teammates, so, too, Ms. Pflug's "plays" included movements carefully choreographed to mesh with other cast members, a script prepared for her to follow, cue cards to insure that little or no deviation from the designed "play" occurred, and numerous retakes to guarantee that ultimate control vested in the hands of the studio, not Ms. Pflug's PSC. Nevertheless, the Tax Court concluded that Ms. Pflug was an employee of her PSC.

There can be little question that Ms. Pflug was part of a team under more stringent production controls than those placed on either Sargent or Christoff by the Club. But, as the Tax Court concluded, ". . . by virtue of the contract [Pflug] entered with Charwool, Charwool had the requisite right to control [Pflug]." Appellants' contractual arrangements, which were every bit as bona fide as those entered into by Ms. Pflug, should and do provide the requisite control for Appellants to be considered employees of their respective PSCs.

Once the "team" analysis of control is disregarded, this Court is able to fall back on ample Tax Court precedent which upholds the sanctity of contractual relations between taxpayers and their respective personal service corporations. * * *

Although the Commissioner argues that in each of these cases the employer-employee relationship was never addressed, this Court thinks otherwise. Each time the legitimacy of the employee's relationship with the corporation was raised, the Tax Court pointed to the existence of a contractual relationship between the corporation and the employee/service-provider as the rationale for upholding the legal significance of the PSC. * * *

Appellants in this case entered into bona fide arms lengths [sic] agreements with their respective PSCs. For this reason, each is considered to be an employee of that PSC, and not an employee of the North Stars Hockey Club.

II.

By rejecting the Tax Court's "team" test, and embracing the viability of the contractual relations between Appellants and their personal service corporations, we have effectively decided the only issue presented for our deliberation: By whom were Appellants employed? Thus, because Appellants were employees of their respective PSCs, they were improperly taxed on the entire amount paid by the North Stars Hockey Club to the PSCs.

Furthermore, by embracing the "contract" theory of this case, we are at the same time discarding the Tax Court's conclusion that this case involves the "assignment of income" doctrine, as articulated in *Lucas v. Earl,* 281 U.S. 111, 50 S.Ct. 241, 74 L.Ed. 731 (1930), and its progeny, and Section 61 of the Tax Code. The Tax Court's contention that Appellants were attempting to employ a corporate "assignment of income" scheme to evade their income tax responsibility is without merit.

We do not doubt that the "assignment of income" doctrine serves a useful tax purpose. For example, as the Tax Court [has] observed: "The assignment of income doctrine * * * constitutes an essential tool * * * where the corporation is not respected by the taxpayer/shareholder as a separate entity which carries on business activities." Overuse of the assignment of income doctrine, however, has met with stiff resistance.

In *Foglesong v. Commissioner,* 35 T.C.M. 1309 (1976), rev'd and remanded at 621 F.2d 865 (7th Cir.1980), the IRS attempted to set aside the transactions entered into by a corporation without ever looking at the validity of the corporation itself. Said the Seventh Circuit:

> We believe that, where the issue is application of the assignment of income doctrine to effectively set aside the corporation, under the particular circumstances of this case * * *, an attempt to strike a balance between tax avoidance motives and "legitimate" business purposes is an unproductive and inappropriate exercise. Such an approach places too low a

value on the policy of the law to recognize corporations as economic actors except in exceptional circumstances.

In *Johnson, supra,* a case whose facts run parallel to the facts of this case, the Tax Court also observed, regarding the blind application of *Lucas v. Earl:*

> However, the realities of the business world present an overly simplistic application of the *Lucas v. Earl* rule whereby the true earner may be identified by pointing to the one actually turning the spade or dribbling the ball. Recognition must be given to corporations as taxable entities which, to a great extent, rely upon the personal services of their employees to produce corporate income. Where a corporate employee performs labors which give rise to income, it solves little merely to identify the actual laborer. Thus, a tension has evolved between the basic tenets of *Lucas v. Earl* and recognition of the nature of the corporation business form.

As long as a corporation carries on some form of business, the Supreme Court has concluded that the tax advantages which properly flow from incorporation should not be questioned. The Supreme Court reasoned:

> The doctrine of corporate entity fills a useful purpose in business life. Whether the purpose be to gain an advantage under the law of the state of incorporation or to avoid or to comply with the demands of creditors or to serve the creator's personal or undisclosed convenience, so long as that purpose is the equivalent of business activity or is followed by the carrying on of business by the corporation, the corporation remains a separate taxable entity. *Moline Prop. Inc. v. Commissioner,* 319 U.S. 436, 438–39 (1943).

The Tax Court voiced this same conclusion almost forty years later, when it stated that "[t]he policy favoring the recognition of corporations as entities independent of their shareholders requires that we not ignore the corporate form so long as the corporation actually conducts business." Indeed, at no time has the Commissioner questioned the legitimacy of Appellants' corporate business activities. According to the record, both [PSCs] withheld income and employment taxes from the salary payments to Appellants; paid contributions to the [Pension Plans of the PSCs] on account of their employment of Sargent and Christoff, respectively; filed forms 940 and 941 with respect to the withholding taxes; and filed corporate tax returns and paid corporate income taxes. Such obvious business activity by Appellants' PSCs is far removed from that conduct which is forbidden under the "assignment of income" doctrine.

Neither will this Court question the motivation behind Appellants' desire to incorporate. That each Appellant has taken steps to enhance his retirement through a richer corporate sponsored pension plan is of no consequence to this court. The Code provisions relating to qualified retirement plans are a deliberate congressional bestowal of benefits upon employers and employees; efforts to obtain the advantages of these benefits, by way of conducting business in the corporate form, are not to be deemed to render the taxpayer culpable of illegal tax avoidance or evasion. Thus, "[o]nce a corporation is formed and all organizational and operational requirements are met, it should be recognized for tax purposes regardless of the fact that it was formed to take advantage of richer corporate retirement plans."

Unfortunately, taxpayers will often go to great lengths to evade unlawfully the payment of income taxes. Whether it simply be lying on their tax forms, assigning income to those who have not earned it, or sheltering income in non-existent or improper tax-avoidance investments, each is destructive to the often painful revenue-production responsibility of the IRS. In this case, however, we are presented with taxpayers who have fulfilled each and every task required of them in order to become properly incorporated. More importantly, for purposes of this case, Appellants took steps to insure that each was a contractually-bound employee of his respective PSC. That these contracts of employment were recognized and respected by the North Stars Hockey Club, the National Hockey League and the Minnesota Office of Administrative Hearings lends substantial credibility to the fact that Appellants were employees of their respective PSCs-and not the North Stars Hockey Club.

* * *

In conclusion, this Court finds that Appellants were, at all times relevant to this case, employees of their respective personal service corporations. Furthermore, the PSCs established by Appellants are legitimate corporate entities, created to conduct Appellants' business. Appellants, therefore, are obligated to pay income tax only on those amounts paid to them as salary by their respective PSC. For all of the reasons articulated above, the decision of the United States Tax Court is

Reversed.

■ ARNOLD, CIRCUIT JUDGE (dissenting):

I would affirm, essentially for the reasons given in Judge Tannenwald's thorough opinion for the Tax Court, 93 T.C. 572 (1989). In my view, the finding that the taxpayers were employed by the Minnesota North Stars Hockey Club, rather than by their respective personal-service corporations, is not clearly erroneous. The coach of the North Stars had the right to control, and actually did control, the conduct of Sargent and Christoff on the ice. The idea that the coach issued orders to Sargent and Christoff in their capacity as corporate officers, which orders they then relayed to themselves as corporate employees, is fanciful.

NOTES

(A) *Formalities.* As *Sargent* indicates, shifting personal service income to a corporation therefore clearly depends on complying with the formalities and, at a minimum, requires the person or entity that obtains services to do business with the corporation rather than with the individual who actually provides the services. Often this requires an actual contract between the "employer" and the corporation. See, e.g., Evatt v. Commissioner, 63 T.C.M. 3194 (1992) (real estate commissions taxable to sole shareholder and not personal services corporation in the absence of a contract between corporation and entity using the services).

In a subsequent case appealable to a different circuit, the Tax Court refused to follow the formalities approach adopted by the Eighth Circuit in *Sargent.* Leavell v. Commissioner, 104 T.C. 140 (1995). Leavell, a guard with the Houston Rockets basketball team, formed a personal service corporation that entered into an arrangement that was very similar to the one used by Sargent. The Tax Court, obviously believing that the language in the standard contract with the PSC did not reflect reality, stuck to a control approach, quoting the dissenting opinion of Judge Arnold in *Sargent.*

(B) *Sections 482 and 269A.* Section 482 allows the Commissioner to reallocate income between two or more businesses (whether or not incorporated) controlled by the same interests where "necessary in order to prevent evasion of taxes or clearly to reflect * * * income." Although § 482 has its most significant application in attempting to monitor prices among related multinational companies, its application has been upheld in cases involving closely held and family corporations, but in a portion of the *Sargent* opinion omitted here, was held not to change the result there.

Section 269A allows the IRS to allocate income, deductions, credits, and other tax benefits between certain personal service corporations and their employee-owners if (1) the principal purpose for the formation or use of the corporation is tax avoidance, (2) substantially all of the services of the corporation are performed for one other corporation or business entity, and (3) allocation is necessary to prevent avoidance or evasion of taxes or to clearly reflect the income of the personal service corporation or any of its employee-owners. An employee-owner is defined as any employee who owns more than 10 percent of the stock of the corporation.

————

The tension between the partnership provisions (including the post-2017 deduction for 20 percent of QBI described above) and the assignment of income doctrine is illustrated by the next case.

Schneer v. Commissioner

United States Tax Court, 1991. 97 T.C. 643.

■ GERBER, JUDGE:

Until February 25, 1983, petitioner was an associate with the law firm of Ballon, Stoll & Itzler (BSI). BSI was a partnership. Petitioner was not a partner in BSI and he did not share in general partnership profits. Petitioner's financial arrangement with BSI consisted of a fixed or set salary and a percentage of any fees which arose from clients petitioner brought or referred to the firm. * * *

When petitioner left BSI he had an understanding that he would continue to receive his percentage of fees which arose from clients he had referred when he was an associate with BSI. Petitioner was expected to consult regarding clients he referred to BSI and whose fees were to be shared by petitioner. Petitioner would have become entitled to his percentage of the fees even if he had not been called upon to consult.

After petitioner left BSI and while he was a partner of two other law partnerships (other than BSI) he consulted on numerous occasions concerning BSI clients. * * * The services provided by petitioner to BSI consisted of legal advice and consultation on legal matters.

Late in February 1983, petitioner became a partner in the law firm of Bandler & Kass (B & K), and on August 1, 1985, petitioner became a partner in the law firm of Sylvor, Schneer, Gold & Morelli (SSG & M). * * * [P]etitioner agreed to turn over to the [B & K and SSG & M] partnership all legal fees received after joining the partnership, regardless of whether the fees were earned in the partnership's name or from the partnership's contractual relationship with the client. The same agreement existed between the partners of SSG & M, including petitioner.

During 1984 and 1985, BSI remitted $21,329 and $10,585 to petitioner. The amounts represented petitioner's percentage of fees from BSI clients that he had referred to BSI at a time when he was an associate with BSI. * * * Petitioner, pursuant to his agreements with B & K and SSG & M, turned those amounts over to the appropriate partnership. B & K and SSG & M, in turn, treated the amounts as partnership income which was distributed to each partner (including petitioner) according to the partner's percentage share of partnership profits. * * *

We consider here basic principles of income taxation. There is agreement that the amounts paid to petitioner by his former employer-law firm are income in the year of receipt. The question is whether petitioner (individually) or the partners of petitioner's partnerships (including petitioner) should report the income in their respective shares.

The parties have couched the issue in terms of the anticipatory assignment-of-income principles. See Lucas v. Earl, 281 U.S. 111 (1930). Equally important to this case, however, is the viability of the principle that partners may pool their earnings and report partnership income in amounts different from their contribution to the pool. See sec. 704(a) and (b). The parties' arguments bring into focus potential conflict between these two principles and compel us to address both.

First, we examine the parties' arguments with respect to the assignment-of-income doctrine. Respondent argues that petitioner earned the income in question before leaving BSI, despite the fact that petitioner did not receive that income until he was a partner in B & K and, later, SSG & M. According to respondent, by entering into partnership agreements requiring payment of all legal fees to his new partnerships, petitioner anticipatorily assigned to those partnerships the income earned but not yet received from BSI. * * *

Petitioner contends that the income in question was not earned until after he left BSI and joined B & K and SSG & M. He argues that the income received from BSI is reportable by the partners of the B & K and SSG & M partnerships (including petitioner) in their respective shares. * * *

[The court then finds that the majority of the fees were earned after the taxpayer left BSI and while he was a partner of B & K or SSG & M.]

Two additional related questions remain for our consideration. First, respondent argues that irrespective of when petitioner earned the income from BSI, "there was no relationship * * * [between] the past activity of introducing a client to * * * [BSI], and the petitioner's work as a partner with * * * [B & K or SSG & M]." According to respondent, petitioner should not be allowed to characterize as partnership income fees that did not have a requisite or direct relationship to a partnership's business. In making this argument, respondent attempts to limit and modify his longstanding and judicially approved position in Rev. Rul. 64–90, 1964–1 C.B. 226 (Part 1). [In Rev. Rul. 64–90, the IRS ruled that "fees received by a partner for similar services performed in his individual capacity" are partnership income if paid to the partnership]. See also Bufalino v. Commissioner, T.C.Memo. 1976–110; Brandschain v. Commissioner, 80 T.C. 746 (1983), both involving partnership agreements similar to the one described in Rev. Rul. 64–90. * * *

These final two questions bring into focus the true nature of the potential conflict in this case—between respondent's revenue ruling and the assignment-of-income doctrine. Both questions, in their own way, ask whether any partnership agreement—under which partners agree in advance to turn over to the partnership all income from their individual efforts—can survive scrutiny under the assignment-of-income principles.

Respondent's rulings have approved as partnership income fees generated by partners serving in individual capacities only tangentially related to the partner's employment in his or her partnership. See Rev. Rul. 80–338, 1980–2 C.B. 30 (accounting partner serving as executor); Rev. Rul. 54–223, 1954–1 C.B. 174 (partner working for another organization as a school bus driver).

There is no need for us to adopt a broader view of petitioner's partnership in this case. His referral fee income was clearly earned through activities "within the ambit" of the business of his new partnerships. Their business was the practice of law as was petitioner's consulting activity for BSI. His work was incident to the conduct of the business of his partnerships. * * *

Thus, we arrive at the final question in this case. We have already held that petitioner had not yet earned the majority of the income in question when he joined his new partnerships. Additionally, petitioner's fee income from his BSI clients qualifies, under the case law and respondent's rulings, as income generated by services sufficiently related to the business conducted by petitioner's new partnerships. If we decide that petitioner's partnerships should report the income in question, petitioner would be taxable only to the extent of his respective partnership share. This would allow petitioner, through his partnership agreements with B & K and SSG & M, to assign income not yet earned from BSI. Thus, the case law and respondent's rulings permit (without explanation), in a partnership setting, the type of assignment addressed by Lucas v. Earl, 281 U.S. 111 (1930). We must reconcile the principle behind Rev. Rul. 64–90, 1964–1 C.B. 226 (Part 1), with *Lucas v. Earl,* supra. The question is whether income not yet earned and anticipatorily assigned under certain partnership agreements are without the reach of the assignment-of-income principle.

The Internal Revenue Code of 1954 provided the first comprehensive statutory scheme for the tax treatment of partners and partnerships. No section of the 1954 Code, successive amendments or acts, nor the legislative history specifically addresses the treatment of income earned by partners in their individual capacity but which is pooled with other partnership income. It is implicit in subchapter K, however, that the pooling of income and losses of partners was intended by Congress. This question is more easily answered where the partnership contracts with the client for services which are then performed by the partner. The question becomes more complex where the partner contracts and performs the services when he is a partner.

Moreover, no opinion contains a satisfactory rationale as to why partnership pooling agreements do not come within the holding of *Lucas v. Earl.*

The fundamental theme penned by Justice Holmes [in *Lucas v. Earl*] provides that the individual who earns income is liable for the tax. It is obvious that the partnership, as an abstract entity, does not provide the physical and mental activity that facilitates the process of "earning" income. Only a partner can do so. The income earned is turned over to the partnership due solely to a contractual agreement, i.e., an assignment, in advance, of income.

The provisions of subchapter K tacitly imply that the pooling of income is permissible. Said implication may provide sufficient reason to conclude that a partnership should be treated as an entity for the purpose of pooling the income of its partners. Under an entity approach, the income would be considered that of the partnership rather than the partner, even though the partner's individual efforts may have earned the income. If the partnership is treated as an entity earning the income, then assignment-of-income concepts would not come into play.

In this regard, an analysis of personal service corporations (PSC's) may provide, by way of analogy, some assistance in reconciling the principles inherent in Rev. Rul. 64–90 with those underlying *Lucas v. Earl*. Keeping in mind Justice Holmes' desire to tax the "earner" of the income, we consider the assignment-of-income doctrine in the context of personal service corporation cases. In partnerships and personal service corporations an individual performs the services that earn income. In both, a separate entity—the partnership or personal service corporation—is cast as the "earner" for tax purposes. That characterization in both situations is, in essence, an assignment of income. If, in either situation, the transfer to the entity is of income earned before an agreement to turn it over is entered into, the assignment-of-income doctrine will serve to invalidate the transfer. In both the context of a PSC or partnership, transfers prior to the performance of a partner's services may be subject to the partner's or employee's control—in that either may refuse to perform.

* * *

Thus, an employee of a personal service corporation, or other corporate entity, is outside the holding of Lucas v. Earl, to some degree because of the "entity concept." The business entity is cast as the earner of the income, obviating the need to analyze whether there has been an assignment of income.

The same type of approach may be used with respect to partners of a partnership. In the same manner that a corporation is considered the earner of income gained through the labor of its employees, a partnership, with an appropriate partnership agreement, may be considered the earner of income. Income earned prior to such an agreement, of course, remains within the principles and holding of *Lucas v. Earl*, supra. The link between respondent's Rev. Rul. 64–90 and *Lucas v. Earl* must be the entity concept as it relates to partnerships. * * *

The principle we must analyze in this case involves the role of the partnership with respect to the function of earning income. A general partnership is "an association of two or more persons to carry on as co-owners a business for profit." Either a partnership or a corporation may enter into a contract with clients to perform services. In a partnership, however, either the entity or the individual may enter into contracts. The question we seek to answer is whether this distinction should be treated differently.

For purposes of an entity concept approach to partnerships, we must consider the type and source of income which should be included. Because we have already determined that the type of activity generating the income is relevant to an assignment-of-income analysis in the partnership setting, we focus our analysis of partnerships as entities in situations where the income is of a type normally earned by the partnership. Only in such situations has a partner acted as part of the partnership entity.

The entity concept as it relates to partnerships is based, in part, on the concept that a partner may further the business of the partnership by performing services in the name of the partnership or individually. The name and reputation of a professional partnership plays a role in the financial success of the partnership business. If the partners perform services in the name of the partnership or individually they are, nonetheless, associated with the partnership as a partner. This is the very essence of a professional service partnership, because each partner, although acting individually, is furthering the business of the partnership. * * *

The lack of structure inherent in the partnership form does not lend itself to easy resolution of the assignment-of-income question. A partnership's characteristics do, however, militate in favor of treating a partner's income from services performed in an individual capacity, which are contractually obligated to the partnership for allocation in accord with the pre-established distributive shares, in the same manner as income earned through partnership engagement.

Accordingly, in circumstances where individuals are not joining in a venture merely to avoid the effect of *Lucas v. Earl*, supra, it is appropriate to treat income earned by partners individually, as income earned by the partnership entity, i.e., partnership income, to be allocated to partners in their respective shares. To provide the essential continuity necessary for the use of an entity concept in the partnership setting, the income should be earned from an activity which can reasonably be associated with the partnership's business activity. * * *

There is no apparent attempt to avoid the incidence of tax by the formation or operation of the partnerships in this case. Petitioner, in performing legal work for clients of another firm, was a partner with the law firms of B & K and SSG & M. In view of the foregoing, we hold that, * * * the fee income from BSI was correctly returned by the two partnerships in accord with the respective partnership agreements.

■ HALPERN, J., dissenting:

[The majority's] analysis wholly ignores the doctrine of agency. When a partner, acting as agent for the partnership, performs services for a client, the partnership is the earner of the income: the instrumentality (in this case the partner) through which the partnership has earned its fee is of no consequence. Therefore, the focus of the anticipatory assignment-of-income analysis ought to be on whether the partner acted for himself individually or as agent of the partnership. This is entirely consistent with the latitude accorded partnerships to disproportionately distribute partnership income: the pertinent requirement is merely that the partnership income so distributed have been earned by the partnership. In this case, it is quite clear that petitioner earned the fees in question pursuant to an agreement he entered into, on his own behalf, with Ballon, Stoll & Itzler—an agreement that was consummated before petitioner's relationship with Bandler & Kass. Consequently, petitioner is the true earner of the income and should not escape taxation by means of an anticipatory assignment. Lucas v. Earl, 281 U.S. 111 (1930).

The majority's "resolution" of the perceived conflict is unsatisfactory. The majority considers the determinative question to be whether the income is "of a type normally earned by the partnership. Only in such situations has the partner acted as part of the partnership entity."

The majority's distinction is unprincipled. The majority observes that "The name and reputation of a professional partnership plays a role in the financial success of a partnership business" suggesting that partners, even acting individually, can further the business of the partnership by adding to its reputation. But, that may be so even if the partner acts individually, doing work entirely dissimilar to that normally performed by the partnership. In any event, the majority fails to explain why such an obviously incidental benefit to the partnership should permit us to frustrate the assignment-of-income doctrine. * * *

NOTES

(A) *More Fruit.* In the usual case, two lawyers may join together to form a partnership and will be taxed on their share of the partnership income according to the agreement, regardless of who performed the services. How well does Justice Holmes' oft-cited statement about not attributing fruit to "a different tree from that on which it grew" apply to those common facts?

(B) *Scope of Schneer.* Law firm partnership agreements often require lawyers to turn over lecture fees, teaching compensation or book royalties to the firm. After *Schneer,* is the income taxable to the partner? Does it matter what the lecture or book topic is?

(C) *Family Partnerships.* The family partnership has been a popular means by which taxpayers have attempted to shift income generated by their own property or services to their children or to other individuals in lower tax brackets. A particularly egregious case involved a former IRS agent who attempted—ultimately unsuccessfully—to form a law and accounting partnership with his one-day-old child. See Tinkoff v. Commissioner, 120 F.2d 564 (7th Cir. 1941).

In the famous case of Commissioner v. Culbertson, 337 U.S. 733 (1949), the taxpayer transferred a partnership interest in his cattle ranch to his four sons in return for their interest-bearing notes payable out of proceeds from the operation of the ranch. The Tax Court held that the entire income from the partnership could be taxed to the father on the ground that the sons had contributed neither vital services nor capital originating with them.

These tests were deemed by the Supreme Court to be persuasive but not determinative. Instead, the Court held that:

> [i]f, upon a consideration of all the facts, it is found that the partners joined together in good faith to conduct a business, having agreed that the services or capital to be contributed presently by each is of such value to the partnership that the contributor should participate in the distribution of profits, that is sufficient.

The *Culbertson* decision, while intended to clarify the tax treatment of family partnerships, produced much confusion among the lower courts.

Congress responded to this confusion in 1951 by enacting § 704(e) that recognizes for tax purposes a partnership in which the partner owns a capital interest, whether or not that interest was acquired by purchase or gift from any other person, including a member of the family. The Committee Report emphasized that the purpose of the provision was "to harmonize the rules governing interests in the so-called family partnership with those generally applicable to other forms of property or business * * * [and to make clear] that, however the owner of a partnership interest may have acquired such interest, the income is taxable to the owner, if he is the real owner." Thus, in effect, family partnerships are recognized under the Code.

The rule applies only to partnerships in which "capital is a material income-producing factor." The *Culbertson* case continues to govern whenever a donee owns an interest in a partnership in which capital is not a significant factor. The regulations provide that capital is not considered a material income-producing factor if the partnership earns its income primarily from "fees, commissions or other compensation for personal services." It therefore must be demonstrated that the members of such a partnership "in good faith and acting with a business purpose intended to join together in the present conduct of the enterprise" as required by *Culbertson*.

The family partnership rules, therefore, generally incorporate the distinction previously observed in this Chapter between assignments of income from services and assignments of income from property: (1) income from property is taxed to the owner of the property and (2) income from services is taxed to the person who renders the services. Taxpayers have a far greater ability to shift earnings to others if the family partnership is one in which capital is a "material income-producing factor."

(D) *S Corporations and Limited Liability Companies.* As we have discussed, certain corporations may elect to be taxed under a pass-through regime. These corporations, known as S corporations because the rules governing them are found in Subchapter S of the Code, are not subject to tax at the entity level. Instead, the income or loss flows through and is taxed to the shareholders. Although an S corporation is taxed somewhat like a partnership, it is not able to use some of the more advantageous, although complicated, provisions available to partnerships.

All states have enacted legislation permitting the creation of a form of business organization designed to combine the federal tax advantages of partnerships with the limited liability of a corporation. The IRS has held that a limited liability company (LLC) is to be treated as a partnership for federal tax purposes. Thus, it is not subject to the corporate tax at the entity level and the tax benefits flow through to the owners. An LLC may be more advantageous than an S corporation because there are no limitations on the number and types of owners and no restrictions on its capital structure.

(E) *Gift-Leasebacks.* Taxpayers have sometimes used gift-leasebacks as a mechanism for shifting income among family members. For example, a taxpayer may give business property—such as an office building or professional equipment—to his adult children. The taxpayer then might lease back the equipment and deduct his payments as an ordinary and necessary business expense. He thus may succeed in shifting an amount of income equal to the annual rental expense to his children, who will include that amount in their income.

The basic purpose of most gift-leaseback arrangements is to shift income to family members in lower brackets. Most professionals will have equipment or furniture, if not real property, that may be used in a gift-leaseback. In some instances—for example, where fully depreciated business property is transferred—a gift-leaseback also may produce additional business deductions for rent that otherwise would not be available.

The circuits are divided as to whether family gift-leasebacks may give rise to business deductions. The majority of the circuits that have addressed the issue, have allowed the deduction if the leaseback was motivated by a "business purpose." Rosenfeld v. Commissioner, 706 F.2d 1277 (2d Cir. 1983). Some circuits, most notably the Fourth and Fifth, allow the deduction only where the entire transaction was motivated by a business purpose. See, e.g., Perry v. United States, 520 F.2d 235 (4th Cir. 1975), cert. denied, 423 U.S. 1052 (1976); Van Zandt v. Commissioner, 341 F.2d 440 (5th Cir. 1965), cert. denied, 382 U.S. 814 (1965).

(F) *Sale-Leasebacks.* The validity of a sale-leaseback in a family setting was upheld, for example, in Hudspeth v. Commissioner, 509 F.2d 1224 (9th Cir. 1975). The taxpayer parents in that case were farmers who were restricted by law to owning no more than 320 acres of federally irrigated land. The government could withdraw irrigation from any excess land and force the farmer to sell the land at a bargain price. The taxpayers sought to avoid this rule by transferring their additional land to their three sons in exchange for notes and mortgages representing the fair market value of the land. The children's indebtedness was to be satisfied by cash gifts and rental payments that they were to receive each year from their parents.

The Tax Court upheld the IRS's disallowance of interest deductions to the children on the ground that the transaction was not a bona fide sale but an installment gift designed to take advantage of the annual gift tax exclusion. The Tax Court also noted that the children would have lacked sufficient funds to meet their repayment obligations had they not received the annual payments from their parents.

The Ninth Circuit reversed on the ground that the children were legally obligated to continue their mortgage payments regardless of whether the parents continued to make their gifts. The children were allowed interest deductions equal to the amount of the rental payments received from their parents. (For example, one son received a $3,000 rental payment and a $9,000 gift: $5,760 of his mortgage obligation for the year represented interest and the balance represented principal. He was allowed an interest deduction of $3,000.)

CHAPTER 5

CAPITAL GAINS AND LOSSES

Probably no subject relating to income taxation has been as much discussed and debated as the taxation of capital gains. During the early years of the federal income tax, leading economists disagreed sharply whether a comprehensive definition of income encompassed capital gains. And for some time there was uncertainty whether the power granted to Congress by the Sixteenth Amendment to tax "income" was broad enough to authorize a tax on gains derived from a sale of property. The issue was settled in favor of the power to tax in Merchants' Loan and Trust Co. v. Smietanka, 255 U.S. 509 (1921). Thus, the sale or exchange of an asset for more than its cost generally produces taxable income.

Throughout almost the entire history of the income tax, however, Congress has treated certain gains preferentially. These gains have been labeled "capital gains." Congress has never satisfactorily explained why certain gains should be treated better than other types of income. Congressional actions over the years reveal a lack of any comprehensive theoretical framework for taxing capital gains, and there is every reason to suspect that Congress's rather bewildering tinkering will continue in the future.

The distinction between capital gain (and loss) and ordinary income (and loss) has been one of the major sources of income tax complexity. That is in part because the concept of a "capital gain" is a creature of the tax law, without a direct analogue in either economics or accounting. If you are able to discern a bright-line distinction between capital gain and ordinary income after reading this Chapter, you should remove your rose-colored glasses and take another look at the cases.

Note: An Historical Overview of Capital Gains Taxation

Capital gains have been accorded some sort of preferential tax treatment since 1921, when the tax was limited to 12½ percent on gains from sales of capital assets held for more than two years. In 1924, the deduction for capital losses was correspondingly limited to a maximum of 12½ percent of the loss. This basic pattern of preferential treatment for capital gains and limited deductibility of capital losses has continued in effect for most of the period the income tax has been in place.

Since the 1920s, the Congress has pursued two basic goals, although with a wide variety of technical details. First is the preferential treatment of capital gains on assets held for some specific period of time (e.g., six months, one year, two years, or ten years). In 1934, for instance, the Congress provided for a decreasing percentage of gain to be taxable the longer the asset was held, ranging from 100 percent if the asset were held a year or less to only 30 percent of the gain if the asset had been held for more than 10 years. Second is the limitation on the deduction of capital losses that exceed capital gains. To continue with the 1934 example: losses were deductible only to the extent of recognized gains plus $2,000.

The legislative outlier, historically speaking, was the Tax Reform Act of 1986. As part of an effort to significantly broaden the tax base in exchange for lower rates, Congress repealed the preferential tax rate for capital gains. The top tax rate on ordinary income as well as capital gains was 28 percent. Capital losses continued to be deductible without limit against capital gains and the limitation on net capital losses of individuals deductible annually against ordinary income was $3,000, meaning capital losses (whether short-term or long-term) offset ordinary income dollar for dollar up to that limit.

The repeal of the capital gains preference was short-lived, however, lasting only until 1990, when Congress increased the maximum marginal tax rate for individuals to 31 percent but left the maximum rate on capital gains at 28 percent.

Today's capital gains rules feature a maximum rate of 20 percent for high-income individuals, but, as the detailed description that follows shows, many taxpayers are subject to capital gain rates ranging from zero to 15 percent. Most dividends received by individuals are taxed at the capital gains rates. And capital losses of individuals are deductible only to the extent of capital gains plus $3,000. These low rates on capital gains create a substantial opportunity for tax planning.

Under current law, there are now several different rates on capital gains, as summarized below:

0% If the taxpayer's adjusted gross income is below the inflation-adjusted zero-percent threshold: (1) assets held for more than one year (2) gain on small business stock (§ 1202) after 50 percent exclusion, and (3) dividends. The 2018 zero-percent threshold amounts are $77,200 for married couples filing jointly, $51,700 for heads of household, and $38,600 for single filers.

10% If taxpayer is otherwise in the 10 percent bracket: (1) assets held for one year or less, (2) gain to the extent of depreciation on real estate held for more than one year, and (3) gain on collectibles.

11% or 12% If the taxpayer is otherwise in the 22 or 24 percent bracket, respectively, gain on small business stock (§ 1202) after 50 percent exclusion.

12% If taxpayer is otherwise in the 12 percent bracket: (1) assets held for one year or less, (2) gain to the extent of depreciation on real estate held for more than one year, and (3) gain on collectibles.

14% If the taxpayer is otherwise in the 32, 35 or 37 percent bracket, gain on small business stock (§ 1202) after 50 percent exclusion.

15% If the taxpayer's adjusted gross income is above the zero-percent threshold and below the inflation-adjusted fifteen-percent threshold: (1) assets held for more than one year and (2) dividends. The 2018 fifteen-percent threshold amounts are $479,000 for married couples filing jointly, $452,400 for heads of household, and $425,800 for single filers.

20% If the taxpayer's adjusted gross income is above the fifteen-percent threshold: (1) assets held for more than one year and (2) dividends.

22% or 24% If the taxpayer is otherwise taxable at a 22 or 24 percent rate, respectively, gain on collectibles.

25% Gain to the extent of depreciation on real estate held for more than one year if the taxpayer is otherwise taxable at a 25 percent or higher rate.

28% Gain on collectibles held for more than one year if the taxpayer is otherwise taxable at a 28 percent or higher rate.

Capital gains are not distributed evenly across income classes. In 2015, nearly three-quarters of net taxable gains were received by taxpayers with incomes of $500,000 or more. They are even more concentrated at the very top. More than one-third of taxable gains were reported by taxpayers with adjusted gross income exceeding $10 million. For that group of taxpayers, capital gains were more than twice as large as wages.

The tax advantages accorded capital gains coupled with the tax disadvantages of capital losses have generated many contests between the government and taxpayers concerning whether a particular item qualifies as a capital gain or loss. The interpretation of the general statutory definition has been left to the Treasury, the courts, and in the first instance to taxpayers (and their attorneys). The task has been made more difficult by the failure of Congress to adopt any consistent theory of what should qualify as capital gains and losses.

As you will see from the following material, both the mechanics and the attempt to distinguish capital gains from ordinary income are extremely complicated. Furthermore, the rate differentials create a powerful incentive to structure transactions to obtain capital gains. Although it is far from clear on which kinds of gains Congress wishes to bestow preferential treatment, Congress wants to limit the ability of taxpayers to convert ordinary income into capital gain.

SECTION 1. THE MECHANICS OF THE TREATMENT OF CAPITAL GAINS AND LOSSES

The mechanics of the taxation of capital gains and losses are found in §§ 1001–1288 of the Code. Particularly important for present purposes are §§ 1(h), 1001, 1011, 1012, 1016, 1211, 1212, 1221–1231, and 1245 and 1250. These sections should be read carefully.

First, the Code requires a taxable event that causes the taxpayer to "realize" a gain or loss, as taxation is limited to realized gains. The Code contains no definition of "realization," but gain is defined in § 1001(a) as the "excess of the amount realized * * * over the adjusted basis of the property." No realization occurs when property merely appreciates in value; the property must be sold or otherwise disposed of for a taxable event to occur. Recall the discussion of the realization requirement in Chapter 2.

In some cases, there may be a realization event, but the resulting gain or loss nevertheless is not "recognized." Section 1001(c) provides that all gains or losses are recognized in full unless "otherwise provided." Congress has provided a number of nonrecognition provisions and these are discussed later in this Chapter.

After it has been determined that the taxpayer has realized gain or loss and that the gain or loss is recognized, the character of the gain or loss must be determined. All gains and losses are divided into two classes: capital and ordinary. All gains and losses that are not capital in nature fall into the "ordinary" classification. Taxpayers generally prefer capital gains because they are taxed at lower rates, but they also prefer ordinary losses, which are deductible in full from ordinary income while capital losses generally are deductible only to the extent of capital gains plus (for individuals) a limited amount of ordinary income.

Securities brokers are required to file information returns that must report the customer's adjusted basis and whether and gain or loss is short-term or long-term. § 6045(g). This makes it more difficult for taxpayers to understate gains and overstate losses on the sale of stock. It also makes life easier for those who are prone to bad record-keeping.

But there are limits to the slack the IRS will cut taxpayers. In one disastrous example of poor record-keeping, Dean Youngquist was an amateur stock trader who opened a brokerage account in November of 1996 and funded it with $73,000. He traded very actively and borrowed money to increase the amount he invested. In fact, in his first month, he sold a total of $1.4 million of securities. By December of that year, his balance was down to $67,322, and he closed his account. His brokerage firm reported the $1.4 million of sales to the IRS. Mr. Youngquist did not file returns or respond to the IRS until 2010 when the U.S. moved to foreclose on tax liens against his property. By that time, Youngquist did not have any records of the purchases that corresponded to his $1.4 million in stock sales to substantiate his basis. The court rejected his argument that his bank statements showing the amount he used to fund his account and the amount he received when he cashed it out could be used to prove that he had an aggregate loss of $5,677 on the sales. Without any substantiation of his basis, Youngquist was left with the tax bill on $1.4 million of income. United States v. Youngquist, 609 Fed. Appx. 524 (9th Cir. 2015), affirming United States v. Youngquist, 111 A.F.T.R.2d (RIA) 2467.

A. NONCORPORATE TAXPAYERS

Capital gains and losses are subdivided into two classes—short-term and long-term. The current dividing line (known as the holding period) is twelve months. The taxpayer must have held property for more than twelve months before any gain from its sale qualifies as a long-term capital gain subject to the lowest rates. §§ 1222 and 1223.

Because short-term gains and losses historically have been treated differently from long-term gains and losses, determining the tax on an individual's capital gains involves a two-stage netting process. First, the taxpayer must separately net short-term gains against short-term losses. If short-term gains exceed short-term losses, there is a net short-term gain; if short-term losses are greater, there is a net short-term loss. § 1222(5) and (6). Likewise, unless they net to zero, the netting of long-term gains and long-term losses produces either a net long-term gain or net long-term loss. § 1222(7) and (8) .

The short-term gain or loss then is netted against the long-term gain or loss. If the net short-term capital gain exceeds net long-term capital losses, the excess short-term gain is taxable in full as ordinary income. If the net long-term capital gain exceeds the net short-term capital loss, the excess ("net capital gain") is taxed at the preferential capital gains rate. When the taxpayer has both a net short-term gain and a net long-term gain, the former is taxed in full as ordinary income, and the latter is subject to the favorable rate.

Where the losses exceed the gains, the excess capital loss offsets up to $3,000 of ordinary income each taxable year. Any excess not allowed in one taxable year is carried forward indefinitely until it is completely utilized. The losses carried over keep their character; for example, the excess of net short-term capital loss over net long-term capital gain is a short-term capital loss in the following year. For this purpose, the "excess capital loss" is the lesser of the amount that exceeds the ordinary income deduction or "adjusted taxable income." Adjusted taxable income for this purpose is taxable income increased by the amount of ordinary income deductions. §§ 1211 and 1212. If the taxpayer's taxable income is less than $3,000, the ordinary deduction for capital losses is limited to the taxable income. In that case, the amount that is carried over is the full amount of net losses minus the amount of the ordinary deduction.

Examples of the Mechanics of Capital Gains and Losses

Example 1: The taxpayer has taxable income of $100,000 for the year excluding capital gains and losses. His capital gains and losses are as follows:

Long-term capital gain	$5,000	
Long-term capital loss	($1,000)	
Net long-term capital gain		$4,000
Short-term capital gain	$2,000	
Short-term capital loss	($3,500)	
Net short-term capital loss		($1,500)
Net capital gain		$2,500

The taxable income of $100,000 (excluding the capital gains) is taxed at the ordinary income rates. The rate at which the net capital gain is taxed depends on the amount of taxable income. In this example the net capital gain of $2,500 is taxed at a 15 percent rate.

Example 2: The taxpayer has taxable income of $500,000 for the taxable year excluding capital gains and losses. Her capital gains and losses are as follows:

Long-term capital gain	$5,000	
Long-term capital loss	($1,000)	
Net long-term capital gain		$4,000
Short-term capital gain	$2,000	
Short-term capital loss	($500)	
Net short-term capital gain		$1,500

The taxpayer's taxable income of $500,000 plus the net short-term capital gain of $1,500 is taxed at the ordinary income rates. The net long-term capital gain of $4,000 is taxed at a 20 percent rate.

Example 3: The taxpayer has taxable income for the taxable year of $100,000 excluding capital gains and losses. His capital gains and losses are as follows:

Long-term capital gain	$1,000	
Long-term capital loss	($5,000)	
Net long-term capital loss		($4,000)
Short-term capital gain	$2,000	
Short-term capital loss	($500)	
Net short-term capital gain		$1,500
Net capital loss		($2,500)

The taxpayer is permitted to net the $2,500 capital loss against up to $3,000 of ordinary income. Thus, the taxpayer has $97,500 taxable income taxed at ordinary income rates.

Example 4: The taxpayer has taxable income for the taxable year of $100,000 excluding capital gains and losses. Her capital gains and losses are as follows:

Long-term capital gain	$1,000	
Long-term capital loss	($5,000)	
Net long-term capital loss		($4,000)
Short-term capital gain	$1,000	
Short-term capital loss	($3,000)	
Net short-term capital loss		($2,000)
Net capital loss		($6,000)

The taxpayer is permitted to use $3,000 of the $6,000 capital loss against up to $3,000 of ordinary income. Thus, the taxpayer has $97,000 of taxable income taxed at ordinary income rates. In addition, she will carry over to the following year $3,000 of long-term capital loss. For purposes of determining the character of the losses carried over to a subsequent year, any short-term losses are deemed to offset ordinary income before long-term losses. § 1212(b)(2). This is bad news for taxpayers, who would prefer to use long-term losses first. (Long-term losses are worth less, because they offset long-term gains taxable at the preferential rate. Short-term losses are worth more, because they offset gains taxable at the higher ordinary rate.)

B.   CORPORATE TAXPAYERS

Net capital gains and losses are calculated in the same way by corporate and noncorporate taxpayers, but they produce different tax consequences.

There is no rate difference between ordinary income and capital gains for corporations. A corporation's taxable income is taxed at the rate listed in § 11, now 21 percent.

Still, capital losses are only deductible to the extent of capital gains. Corporations are permitted a three-year carryback and a five-year carryover of capital losses to be used against past or future capital gains. Each amount carried back or carried forward is treated as a short-term capital loss. It must be carried back to the earliest permitted year, with the unused excess then carried to more recent years and then carried forward until it is fully used. The corporation forfeits losses not used within the permissible period.

C. A WORD OF CAUTION

The preceding discussion of the mechanics of capital gains taxation is intended merely to provide beginning students of federal taxation with a straightforward overview. Many details ignored here may complicate the taxation of a particular transaction. In addition, there may be important interactions with other provisions of the Code. For example, capital gains and losses may be passive gains or losses, subject to the limitation on passive losses of § 469, discussed supra at page 424.

SECTION 2.   THE POLICY OF PREFERENTIAL TREATMENT OF CAPITAL GAINS

Although preferential treatment for capital gains has been a distinctive feature of the U.S. income tax since 1921, the congressional purposes for the favorable treatment always have seemed uncertain and often contradictory. Congress has never clearly articulated a set of policy objectives for this preference. The note that follows sets forth the most commonly raised policy arguments and examines some of their implications for defining "capital" transactions. A more detailed discussion of each of the arguments can be found in Noël B. Cunningham & Deborah H. Schenk, "The Case for a Capital Gains Preference," 48 Tax L. Rev. 319 (1993).

Note on Policy Arguments for and Against Preferential Treatment of Capital Gains

Arguments Favoring Preferential Treatment:

(1) *Capital gains are not income.* This is the most fundamental ground offered for excluding capital gains from the income tax base. The argument concentrates on two common features of capital gains: (a) they are not recurring and (b) they sometimes simply reflect changes in interest rates.

(a) *Capital gains are nonrecurring.* This argument reflects the view that a progressive income tax should be imposed only on recurring items, and generally should exclude extraordinary gains or windfalls.

The critic's response. This narrow view of income, which enjoyed considerable favor in the early days of the income tax, was rejected in the Supreme Court's decision in *Glenshaw Glass* (treating punitive damage awards as income, discussed supra at page 84). Including only recurring items in income would conflict with the notion that the income tax base should reflect differences in people's ability to pay tax, even where one person's greater ability is due to a windfall or other extraordinary event. A dollar of capital gain has the same purchasing power as any other dollar of income and this implies no special treatment for capital gains (or for capital losses).

(b) *Asset value changes due to interest rate fluctuations are not income.* The notion that changes in asset values that simply reflect changes in interest rates should not be considered income is more complicated. When interest rates fall, the price of a bond or other fixed-income asset will rise so that its yield will be comparable to that of similar assets paying the new lower rate of interest. The rise in price does not affect the owner's interest income. For example, assume that a bond paying a 12 percent rate of interest rises in value from $1,000 to $1,200 when the market rate of interest falls to 10 percent. The taxpayer who sells such a bond and invests the entire proceeds in a new bond yielding 10 percent will continue to earn interest income of $120 a year (10 percent on a principal amount of $1,200). He will be no better off, notwithstanding the price rise (i.e. the capital gain).

The critic's response. That much is true. However, the investor who has enjoyed the price increase is in a better economic position than people whose capital value remained unchanged. He can now purchase $1,200 rather than $1,000 of goods or services and, if he keeps it invested, his capital will produce a greater return than the capital of people who had not invested in such fixed-income assets before the drop in interest rates. Those people, with only $1,000 of capital, will be able to earn only the lower interest rate on new investments, but will not have enjoyed the increase in capital value. The fact that he invested sooner and reaped the benefits in the form of an increase in capital value made him better off.

(2) *Bunching.* Proponents of a capital gains preference often defend it as ameliorating bunching: the realization rule forces a taxpayer to report in the year of the asset's sale capital gains that have accrued over a period of years, and thus the gain on the sale may be subject to a higher marginal rate than would have applied had the gains been reported each year as they accrued.

The critic's response. First, bunching is a problem only in a system with graduated tax rates and only if the taxpayer is in a higher bracket on the disposition date than she was when the income accrued. Second, the argument fails to take into account the benefit the taxpayer enjoyed from deferring the tax on the gain until the asset was sold; the deferral attributable to the realization requirement may offset the bunching effect completely. Finally, a lower capital gains rate is an extremely crude mechanism for what is essentially income averaging. A better solution would be to permit the taxpayer to allocate the gain or loss realized to the number of years the asset has been held and compute the tax liability on that fraction at the appropriate marginal rate.

(3) *Inflation.* In an inflationary period, a portion of the capital gain is inflation, rather than "real" gain, and, to the extent it merely reflects the rise in general prices, it does not add to one's economic purchasing power. Thus, it does not represent economic income, and should not be part of the tax base. For example, if A purchases an asset for $100 and prices rise 5 percent during the year, A will report $5 of gain on a sale of

the asset even though the $105 sales proceeds reflect no real economic gain. To reflect true economic gain, A's basis should be increased by 5 percent to $105 to reflect the rate of inflation.

The critic's response. It is true that gain on assets held during a long period of inflation will be mismeasured when current dollars realized on sale are compared to prior years' dollars of basis. The amount of overtaxation of inflationary gains therefore depends on the rate of inflation per year and the period the asset was held, which determines the amount by which basis was understated. A rate preference for capital gains is a poor solution because it bears no relation to this factor. Furthermore, the inflation may be offset by the benefit of deferring the tax on the gain until realization. The lower tax rate will be of no use to a taxpayer who experiences an economic loss.

Finally, it is somewhat hard to defend an adjustment for inflationary capital gains without comprehensive income tax adjustments for inflation. Accelerated depreciation is sometimes defended on the ground that it ameliorates the effects of inflation, but Congress has never adopted inflation indexing of the basis of assets (or debt), i.e., adjusting the basis to reflect general price increases during the holding period. Such indexation is widely viewed as being extraordinarily complex. Congress has taken some steps to ameliorate inflation by indexing certain items, such as tax brackets, the standard deduction, and the earned income credit, to keep the amounts constant in real terms. These adjustments do not affect the basis of assets.

(4) *Taxation of capital gains on corporate stock is double taxation.* This is because gains that typically have been taxed once as income to the corporation are taxed again when a shareholder realizes them on the sale of stock when the increase in the stock value reflects retained earnings of the corporation, which have already been taxed.

The critic's response. Taxing gains on the sale of stock constitutes double taxation when the retained earnings already have been subject to corporate income tax. A more equitable and more efficient solution to this problem would be to integrate corporate and personal income taxes, with the aim of taxing all corporate income alike and taxing corporate source income in the same manner as all other income. Lowering the tax on the sale of stock and dividends (which Congress did in 2003) and a reduction in corporate rates (which Congress did in 2017) could be viewed as an indirect, albeit imperfect effort to integrate corporate and personal income. See Daniel Halperin, "Mitigating the Potential Inequity of Reducing Corporate Rates," 126 Tax Notes 641 (2010). In any event, even if this argument were accepted, it would support a preference for gains only on corporate stock attributable to retained earnings, not other capital assets or gains attributable to untaxed appreciation at the corporate level.

(5) *Disincentive to risk taking.* Taxing capital gains makes investors less willing to make risky investments because the tax reduces the

expected return. This reduces economic welfare because investors may shift their portfolios toward less risky assets from those they would retain in a nontax world. High-risk investments are sometimes thought to perform particularly valuable social functions, such as funding new businesses, which are a source of jobs and innovation, and inherently risky, but essential ventures, such as agriculture.

The critic's response. It is not clear that an income tax would significantly discourage risk taking if there is a complete tax offset for losses. If losses are fully deductible, the government shares in the downside risk as well as the upside potential of investments. But generally neither business losses nor capital losses always produce tax refunds. There are significant limitations on the deduction for capital losses in order to limit "cherrypicking," i.e., realizing losses to obtain deductions but deferring gains. A more generous allowance of loss offsets against ordinary income might provide a better incentive for risk taking. Furthermore, the general capital gains preference is not limited to risky assets. The special advantage of § 1202 for small business stock, however, is one attempt to target a capital gains preference toward risky investments.

(6) *Disincentive to saving.* People's consumption behavior generally is thought to depend more on average lifetime income, or expected long-term income, than on annual income. Thus, a once-in-a-lifetime capital gain is likely to be spent, if at all, over the entire lifetime of a rational spender. Gain that is taxed immediately will be spent by the government whereas it would have been saved (at least temporarily) by the taxpayer. In a growing economy, that means a continuing drain on savings. Taxation of capital gains impinges more heavily on savings than on consumption, since these gains would tend to be saved. Such taxation is therefore more likely to reduce overall savings and investment than other means of raising revenue.

The critic's response. The concern that capital gains taxation impinges on savings generally supports taxation of consumption, rather than income. A consumption tax would exclude all savings from the tax base without regard to the taxpayer's sources of income. Limiting the favorable treatment of savings to capital gain income may be particularly unfair, because assets eligible for capital gains treatment may be more likely than other forms of savings to be held by upper-income taxpayers. This concern would offset the argument, even if it is true, that favoring capital gains has a more powerful effect on savings since upper-income taxpayers are those most likely to save in any event.

Furthermore, it is not clear that raising the rate of return on savings by not taxing amounts saved would increase the amount of private savings. Some savers are target savers—they save to accumulate a certain amount, say for education or retirement—and will save only until they reach their goal. An increase in the rate of return would enable these savers to achieve their goal more quickly and thus, they might save less.

Even assuming an increase in private savings, it is not certain that this would lower the cost of capital and increase domestic investment. In an open economy, foreign investment might be increased instead.

(7) *Lock-in.* To avoid the taxation of the gain on appreciated assets, taxpayers will refrain from selling assets, even when market conditions otherwise would favor sales. This "lock-in" effect reduces liquidity, impairs the mobility of capital, and may lead to broader fluctuations in market prices. A preference for capital gains reduces the tax barriers to economically-motivated shifts in investments.

The critic's response. The lock-in effect is real, but a large percentage of capital gains are never subject to tax. The small number of realizations is due primarily to § 1014, which in many cases permits heirs to step up the basis of inherited property to its fair market value, thus permitting the gain to escape tax permanently, and to the exclusion of a significant amount of gain on the sale of a personal residence. (This provision is discussed infra at page 650.) The gain on a personal residence is their largest capital gain for most taxpayers and for many, the only significant capital gain outside of nontaxable retirement savings funds.

The lock-in problem could be eliminated either by not taxing gains on the sales of assets or by taxing unrealized gains as they accrue. Under a so-called mark-to-market system, a taxpayer would be required to report the value of his property at the end of each year and treat as gain (or loss) the increase (or decrease) in value since the end of the preceding year. Although many proponents of an income tax contend that taxing accrued gains is theoretically correct, they have long considered proposals to do so administratively impractical. But some advocates of cutting back or eliminating the realization requirement do not regard the administrative problems as insurmountable. In fact, some commentators argue that such a system would simplify the income tax; they contend that although accrual taxation would be complicated by valuation and liquidity problems, these disadvantages would be outweighed by the reduction in tax planning complexities, the simplification of adjustments for inflation, and the possible elimination of the corporate income tax.

Not taxing capital gains at all is inappropriate in an income tax. An alternative to not taxing gains is nonrecognition or rollover of gain on sales. Rollover proposals are designed to encourage capital mobility, but they would be a major step toward taxing consumption rather than income, since gains would be taxed only when they were consumed, not when they are reinvested. A consumption tax, however, would exclude all savings from the tax base, not just capital gains.

Arguments Opposing Preferential Treatment:

(1) *A dollar of capital gain is the same as any other dollar of economic gain.* Because a dollar of capital gain has the same purchasing power as any other dollar of income, there should be no special treatment for capital gains (or for capital losses).

The critic's response. A dollar of capital gain is different for all of the reasons set forth above.

(2) *The preferential treatment of capital gains is a great source of income tax complexity.* Many provisions in the Code deal with the special treatment of capital gains and losses. Tax planning to achieve capital gain status, including "conversion" of ordinary income into capital gain, has induced bizarre and complex arrangements and transactions.

The critic's response. Much of the complexity attributed to the special treatment of capital gains does not disappear by taxing capital gains as ordinary income. The complexity largely is due to the need to measure gain or loss—for example, through basis computations and adjustments—and to determine when income should be taxed (or loss allowed). Moreover, if the realization requirement is retained, some limitations on capital loss deductions remain necessary; otherwise, individuals with accrued gains and losses would realize only the losses, which they could offset without limitation against salaries or other unrelated income. Any remaining restriction on capital losses would require that "capital" transactions be distinguished from "ordinary" transactions, thereby retaining much of the definitional complexity.

(3) *The capital gains preference creates too much inequity and too little "bang for the buck."* The preference for capital gains primarily benefits high-bracket taxpayers. In addition, it produces too little additional savings and risk taking for the revenue cost.

The critic's response. The revenue cost from capital gains taxation is overstated. When capital gains rates are high, people defer realizations of gains, thereby both decreasing revenues and inhibiting economic growth. Indeed, no matter what the capital gains tax rate, wealthy people, who have a sizable portfolio of stocks and other capital assets, have always enjoyed great discretion about when to pay capital gains taxes or even whether to pay them. This occurs because they control the timing of their sales of assets and thereby the timing of the payment of capital gains tax. If they need cash, they can borrow against assets that have appreciated in value, rather than selling them, and avoid capital gains taxes. People who have assets with both capital gains and capital losses in their portfolios, a common occurrence among the wealthy, can avoid or postpone capital gains taxes by timing their sales of the loss assets.

Given the great flexibility many people have in selling or holding appreciated assets, what rate of capital gains taxation maximizes the government's revenue? Although one cannot be certain about the precise level of the revenue-maximizing tax rate for capital gains, considerable economic evidence suggests that it currently lies somewhere between 19 and 28 percent. Treasury Department economists have believed this rate to be about 20 percent, while key congressional staff economists have regarded it as closer to 28 percent. Perhaps the 25 percent top rate in effect during the 1940s, 1950s, and 1960s was a pretty good approximation. In fact, when the top tax rates on ordinary income were increased above that level in both the 1990 and 1993 Budget Acts, the maximum capital gains rate was retained at 28 percent in order not to lose revenue.

Note on Justification for the Limitation on Losses

In a system without a realization requirement, there would be no need for a limitation on losses—all gains and losses would be taxed as they accrue. If, however, gains are deferred until realized, loss limitations are thought to be necessary to prevent selective realization of losses. Otherwise, taxpayers could dispose of assets with losses and hold on to those with gains and use the losses to offset other income. Although the taxpayer's portfolio may reflect a net gain overall, she may realize a loss. If allowed, this practice would be especially egregious when the taxpayer has hedged her investments, i.e., she has purchased assets expected to move in opposite directions.

Assume, for example, that A acquires an asset that has a 50 percent chance of increasing in value by 10 and a 50 percent chance of decreasing in value by 10. Assume A also acquires an asset that is a perfect hedge of the first asset, that is, if the first asset increases in value by 10, the second asset will decline in value by 10 and vice versa. A has no chance of an overall loss. Suppose the first asset increases in value and the second asset declines in value. Absent limitations on losses, A would sell the second asset but retain the first, thereby creating a tax loss although she has no economic loss.

In order to limit cherrypicking of losses, § 1211 generally limits the deduction for capital losses to the amount of realized capital gains during a taxable year plus $3,000. Corporations may deduct capital losses only to the extent of capital gains. Thus, taxpayers who want to deduct capital losses will have to also realize gains in order to enjoy the current value of the loss deduction. The capital loss limitation rules apply, however, regardless of whether the taxpayer has appreciated assets in his portfolio or has ever enjoyed the capital gains preference.

The limitation on losses applies to both short-term and long-term capital losses whereas the capital gains preference applies only to long-term capital gains. In addition, capital losses in excess of capital gains are deductible dollar for dollar against $3,000 whereas capital gains generally are now taxed at a maximum of 55 percent of the rate on ordinary income and historically have been taxed at about 50 to 60 percent of the regular rate. Finally, the limit on losses creates a bias against risky investments whereas one of the arguments for preferential treatment for gains was to encourage risk taking. The justification for the capital loss limitation and alternative approaches to the cherrypicking problem are discussed in Robert H. Scarborough, "Risk,

Diversification and the Design of Loss Limitations Under a Realization-Based Income Tax," 48 Tax L. Rev. 677 (1993).

Note on Defining a "Capital" Transaction

That the words "capital," "gain," and "loss" have a familiar ring often misleads students into feeling unduly comfortable with the phrase "capital gain or loss." The capital gain concept is an artificial creation of the tax law that has no firm theoretical grounding in accounting or economics.

Moreover, the Code provides only a skeletal guide for drawing the necessary distinctions between transactions that produce capital gain (or loss) and those that produce ordinary gain (or loss). Congress has identified those transactions qualifying for favorable capital gains treatment by requiring that a transaction meet three conditions: (1) the transaction must involve "property" that is a "capital asset," (2) the property must be transferred in a "sale or exchange," and (3) the minimum holding period must be met.

A lower tax on capital gains than on ordinary income induces taxpayers to endeavor mightily to qualify profitable transactions for capital gains treatment, and the loss limitations encourage attempting to qualify losing transactions for ordinary treatment. The courts have played an important role in drawing the capital-ordinary distinction, but their results often seem inconsistent, even contradictory.

These inconsistencies are to be expected, given the general nature of the statutory rules and the variety of policy justifications for the preferential income tax treatment of capital gains. The diverse justifications for the capital gains preference, set forth in the preceding Note, have each contributed in some way to the issues that have emerged. Courts often endeavor to match a relevant policy argument to their conclusions characterizing particular transactions as capital or ordinary. For example, the desire to prevent "bunching" has been used to support capital gains treatment for income that accrues over time but is recognized in one period. The concern about "lock-in" has been advanced to limit capital gain treatment to situations involving a "transfer" of the underlying property rather than those involving a sale of a "carved-out" portion of a larger interest. The policy of creating incentives for savings, investment, and risk taking has been argued to limit preferential treatment to gains from an investment rather than compensation for services, to rewards for risk rather than interest resulting from the mere passage of time, and to market fluctuations rather than normal business profits. For example, the sale of stock typically produces capital gain, while the compensation earned by the corporation's employees, the interest earned by the corporation's creditors, and the profits earned by the corporation on its sales of inventory all give rise to ordinary income. In determining whether the requisite "investment" or "property" is present, the courts often seek guidance not from tax policy concerns but rather from common law concepts of "property" and "ownership."

The distinction between capital gain and ordinary income cannot be so flexible as to allow taxpayers unlimited freedom to structure transactions to their best advantage. Taxpayers must be restricted from converting ordinary income into capital gain and recharacterizing capital losses as ordinary deductions. Many such restrictions are contained in the Code, the regulations, and the case law. The entire process is greatly complicated by the ability of taxpayers to create a variety of ownership-like legal relationships (sale-leasebacks, for example) as well as by the existence of corporations and other legal entities, whose ordinary income transactions (dividends, for example) must be distinguished from capital transactions (certain redemptions, reorganizations, liquidations, and recapitalizations, for example).

This problem is illustrated nicely by "carried interest." Hedge funds invest pools of money from wealthy individuals in fairly risky ways that sometimes produce above-market returns. For that, those who manage the money are paid handsomely, usually by a formula known as "2 and 20." Funds generally take a management fee equal to 2 percent of the amount invested and a 20 percent commission on portfolio gains above a predetermined benchmark. This return is referred to as "carried interest." Although the 2 percent management fee is clearly taxed as ordinary income, the 20 percent is currently taxed at the lower capital gains rate.

Critics of the current rule argue that the carried interest is compensation for the services they render—managing companies and selling them at a profit. It is akin to a bonus or performance reward, and like others who receive a bonus for service, it should be taxed as ordinary income. The investment gains that the managers share are generally not on the managers' own money, and they bear no downside risk. They get a share of the gains but are not responsible for a share of the losses.

Hedge funds, not surprisingly, say that "the 20" is investment gain, pure and simple, and should be taxed like all other investment gains. They also argue that this compensation isn't salary because it is especially risky. But that is true of a lot of compensation—those who lose their jobs in a recession or others whose compensation is contingent on profits. The 2017 legislation retained the treatment of carried interest as capital gains, but requires generally that to be eligible for long-term capital gains treatment, the interest must be held for three years. See § 1061. In February 2018, Bloomberg reported that, because corporations were exempt from the new rules (including the three-year holding period), certain private equity firms have been setting up LLCs in Delaware. For example, the report found more than 70 LLCs connected with private equity firm Starwood Capital Group had been established in Delaware since the end of 2017. That afternoon, Treasury Secretary Steve Mnuchin told Congress that Treasury could fix it even though it was not clear that Treasury's "fix" would be upheld by courts. The following day, Ways and Means Committee Chairman Kevin Brady announced that he would make an effort to enact technical corrections legislation to correct this problem and others that already had started bubbling to the surface. Stay tuned. . .

The distinction between capital gains and ordinary income is hard to draw and as we have seen, there is some inconsistency. Proponents of the current treatment argue that they should be treated like others who enjoy preferential treatment. For example, when Jeff Bezos sells shares of Amazon, his gain reflects market appreciation but it surely also reflects his labor and business acumen. Nevertheless his entire gain is taxed at preferential capital gains rates. While it might be very difficult to figure out what portion of stock gain is attributable to personal effort, it is relatively easy to tax carried interest as ordinary income.

Big money is involved. The top 25 hedge fund managers earned an average of $440 million each in 2016, and the top earner received $1.6 billion. The combined income of this group was $11 billion. Congress, looking for ways to close the tax gap, has considered legislation that would tax the fees earned by private equity and hedge funds as ordinary income. That brings the lobbyists out in droves who try to convince Congress that keeping the rates low is important to reward risk to create economic growth. So far at least the lobbyists have won. So have members of Congress who obtain donations from these affluent taxpayers.

SECTION 3.   WHAT IS A CAPITAL ASSET?

We now turn to an examination of the statutory provisions and judicial opinions that have attempted to distinguish capital gain from ordinary income. The statutory scheme is intricate and complex. Capital gains or losses are derived only from the "sale or exchange" of property constituting a "capital asset." § 1222. Section 1221 defines capital assets broadly to include all property held by the taxpayers with certain exceptions. The general statutory exceptions are:

1)   the stock in trade or inventory of a business, or property that is held primarily for sale to customers in the ordinary course of a trade or business,

2)   depreciable or real property used in a trade or business,

3)   literary or artistic property held by its creator, unless the creator of a musical composition or a copyright in musical works elects to treat it as a capital asset,

4)   accounts or notes receivable acquired in the ordinary course of the taxpayer's trade or business,

5) U.S. government publications received from the government at a price less than that which the general public is charged,

6) commodities derivative financial instruments held by commodities derivative dealers,

7) identified hedging transactions under rules provided in regulations, and

8) supplies regularly consumed by the taxpayer in the ordinary course of the trade or business.

The exclusion provided by § 1221(a)(2) for real and depreciable property used in the taxpayer's trade or business is affected by § 1231. The principal effect of § 1231 is to characterize net gain on sales of depreciable or real property used in a business as capital gain and net losses on sales of such assets as ordinary losses. Section 1245, however, often "recaptures" as ordinary income amounts that otherwise would be treated as capital gain under § 1231. Sections 1231 and 1245 are considered explicitly, infra at page 593.

The exclusions of § 1221, in general, are intended to produce ordinary income treatment for proceeds from everyday business activities and from personal labor and capital gains treatment for investment gains. The scope of the statutory exclusions under § 1221 and their application to varying factual contexts have been the subject of much litigation. Taxpayers have exerted great efforts to structure transactions to avoid the statutory exclusions and thus to obtain capital gain treatment. As a result, the courts have construed the exclusions broadly and, in some cases, expanded them beyond the statutory language. These interpretations then have been used by other taxpayers to obtain ordinary—rather than capital—loss treatment on transactions involving property that otherwise would qualify under the statute as a capital asset. The materials that follow will give the student a feel for some of the problems that the courts have faced. This Section considers first the specific statutory exceptions and then the cases that expand the exceptions beyond a literal construction of the statutory language.

A. THE STATUTORY FRAMEWORK

1. PROPERTY HELD FOR SALE TO CUSTOMERS

Section 1221(a)(1) exempts from the definition of capital asset property "held by the taxpayer primarily for sale to customers in the ordinary course of his trade or business." Section 1231(b)(1)(B) likewise excludes such assets from § 1231 treatment. Thus, any gain or loss from the sale or exchange of such property will be ordinary gain or loss. These exclusions apply only if the taxpayer is engaged in a trade or business that ordinarily sells the property in question.

NOTES

(A) *The Meaning of "Primarily."* The Code uses everyday words that sometimes have multiple meanings, which could affect the tax treatment of transactions. In Malat v. Riddell, 383 U.S. 569 (1966), the Supreme Court had to determine which meaning of "primarily" was intended in § 1221(a)(1). The Court said:

> The [Commissioner] urges upon us a construction of "primarily" as meaning that a purpose may be "primary" if it is a "substantial" one.
>
> As we have often said, "the words of statutes—including revenue acts—should be interpreted where possible in their ordinary, everyday senses." Crane v. Commissioner, 331 U.S. 1, 6. * * * Departure from a literal reading of statutory language may, on occasion, be indicated by relevant internal evidence of the statute itself and necessary in order to effect the legislative purpose. * * * But this is not such an occasion. The purpose of the statutory provision with which we deal is to differentiate between the "profits and losses arising from the everyday operation of a business" on the one hand (Corn Products Refining Co. v. Commissioner, 350 U.S. 46, 52) and "the realization of appreciation in value accrued over a substantial period of time" on the other. * * * A literal reading of the statute is consistent with this legislative purpose. We hold that, as used in [§ 1221(a)(1)], "primarily" means "of first importance" or "principally."

The Court noted that the purpose of the § 1221(a)(1) exclusion is to distinguish profits and losses "arising from the everyday operation of a business" from those resulting from changes "in value accrued over a substantial period of time."

Application of the exclusion to particular facts has caused great difficulty for the courts. At what point do investment activities become business activities? Contrary to the initial expectations of some analysts, *Malat* has had little impact on later lower court determinations. In situations involving a change of purpose from rental to sale, lower courts often have indicated that the time for determining the taxpayer's "purpose" is the time of sale. It is tautological that at the time of sale, sale is "of first importance." See, e.g., Bynum v. Commissioner, 46 T.C. 295 (1966), where the Tax Court, finding ordinary income in a real estate case, noted: "[W]e are not dealing with * * * a dual purpose as concerned the Supreme Court in *Malat,* but with a change in purpose * * *."

Malat was thought to have the most significance in the "dual-purpose" context involving assets held for both rental and sale, but the lower courts have had little difficulty in molding the semantics of *Malat* to avoid characterizing "everyday business profits" as capital gains. Sometimes the courts find two "businesses"—a rental business and a sales business. It naturally follows that the sale is "of first importance" to the sales business. See, e.g., Continental Can Co. v. United States, 190 Ct.Cl. 811, 422 F.2d 405 (1970), cert. denied, 400 U.S. 819 (1970), where the taxpayer manufactured and sold cans for food and other products and leased to its customers machines for sealing the cans. An antitrust decree then required Continental to permit its customers to purchase the canning machines. The taxpayer contended that capital gains treatment was proper on sales of machines to customers who previously had leased the machines. The machines purchased by these lessees averaged 16.6 years of age. The court distinguished *Malat:*

> Where there is a change in the purpose of the holding of an asset, as there was here * * * [t]he basic question is the primary purpose of holding as of the date of the sale * * *. And where a company is, at such date, regularly engaged in the dual business of selling and renting its machines, then income resulting from either activity satisfies the "primarily" concept since it is "a part of" the "normal stream * * * of the taxpayer's business" and not "outside" * * * [or] separate from the main-stream of the enterprise.

See also Rev. Rul. 80–37, 1980–1 C.B. 51, requiring ordinary income treatment for sales of equipment to leasing customers by a taxpayer "regularly engaged in the dual business of renting and selling such equipment;" International Shoe Machine Corp. v. United States, 491 F.2d 157 (1st Cir. 1974), cert. denied, 419 U.S. 834 (1974), finding ordinary income where sales to customers were an ongoing and regular part of the business even though the taxpayer's major source of revenue was rental of machines, and sales accounted for only 7 and 2 percent of gross revenues in the years at issue.

Courts often allow capital gain treatment in "rental obsolescence" cases, where equipment is sold only after its rental income producing potential has ended. See, e.g., Mafco Equipment Co. v. Commissioner, 47 T.C.M. 88 (1983), where the Tax Court treated as capital gain the proceeds received by an equipment lessor from sales of equipment that was no longer appropriate for rental because of age, condition, or obsolescence.

(B) *The Present Value of a Stream of Ordinary Income.* In *International Shoe Machine,* supra, the court distinguished the sale of machinery that retained the potential of rental income from the liquidation of inventory that generally produced capital gain. The court observed that "the sale of such machinery, for a price which included the present value of [the] future ordinary income [that the machines would generate], cannot be considered the liquidation of an investment outside the scope of the ordinary course of * * * business." Is not the sales price of any asset—whether a patent, a share of stock, or a piece of real estate—the present value of an expected stream of future ordinary income? Would this rationale, if carried to an extreme, deny capital gains treatment on any asset sale?

The cases interpreting § 1221(a)(1), many of which involve real estate, tend to turn on their facts, but three issues predominate. Often the issue is whether the nature of the taxpayer's dealings in property classify the taxpayer as a dealer who is holding the property primarily for sale to customers in the ordinary course of business. In other cases, it is clear that the taxpayer acquired the property for investment but changed his purpose and the issue is whether the change resulted in his being treated as a dealer.

And third, in some cases, the taxpayer has a dual purpose—perhaps to sell or to rent or to hold for appreciation or sell to customers—or perhaps no set purpose other than to make money. The issue is which purpose controls. The case that follows illustrates the difficulties.

Bramblett v. Commissioner

United States Court of Appeals, Fifth Circuit, 1992. 960 F.2d 526.

■ E. GRADY JOLLY, CIRCUIT JUDGE:

This tax appeal arises out of a series of transactions entered into by a partnership and a related corporation. The partnership, Mesquite East, and the corporation, Town East, are owned by the same four people, and each person has the same ownership interest in the corporation as he does in the partnership. Mesquite East bought several parcels of land for the stated purpose of investment. It then sold almost all of this land to Town East, which developed it and sold it to various third parties. Mesquite East reported the income from the sale of land at issue as capital gain, arguing that it held the land as a capital asset. The commissioner asserted a deficiency * * * arguing that the profit should be taxed as ordinary income, because in the light of the activities of Town East and their relationship to Mesquite East, Mesquite East was really in the business of selling land. The tax court affirmed the deficiency, holding that the totality of circumstances supported the conclusion that Mesquite East was in the business of selling land.

We hold that Mesquite East was not directly in the business of selling land, that Town East was not the agent of Mesquite East, and that the activities of Town East cannot be attributed to Mesquite East. Thus, Mesquite did hold the land as a capital asset and is entitled to capital gains treatment. Therefore, we reverse the decision of the tax court.

I

On May 16, 1979, William Baker, Richard Bramblett, Robert Walker, and John Sexton formed the Mesquite East Joint Venture. Baker, Bramblett, Walker, and Sexton had respective 50%, 22%, 18%, and 10% interests in the joint venture. The stated purpose of the joint venture was to acquire vacant land for investment purposes. On June 4, 1979, the same four individuals formed Town East Development Company, a Texas corporation, for the purpose of developing and selling real estate in the Mesquite, Texas area. The shareholders' interests in Town East mirrored their interests in Mesquite East.

In late 1979 and early 1980, Mesquite East acquired 180.06 acres of land from Bramco, a corporation of which Bramblett was the sole shareholder. Also, in late 1979, Mesquite East acquired 84.5 acres of land from an unrelated third party, bringing its acquisitions to a total of 264.56 acres. Subsequent to its acquisition of the property and prior to the sale at issue here, Mesquite East made four separate sales of its acquired land. In three of the four instances, Mesquite East initially sold the property to Town East, which then developed it and sold it to third parties. In each of these instances, prior to the time Town East purchased the property from Mesquite East, it already had a binding sales agreement with the third party. In the fourth transaction, Mesquite East sold property directly to Langston R & B Financial Joint Venture No. 1. Mesquite East's gross profit on these four transactions was $68,394.80 and it reported this amount as ordinary income on its 1981 partnership tax return.

Following these transactions, [Mesquite] East still owned 121 acres. In 1982, Baker * * * entered into five contingent contracts of sale for portions of this property. Mesquite East consulted its attorneys and accountants seeking advice on how to structure the transactions to avoid ordinary income tax on the sale. In December 1982, Mesquite East sold the property to Town East in exchange for two promissory notes totaling $9,830,000.00, the amount an appraiser determined to be the fair market value of the land. The notes provided for an interest rate of twelve percent per annum on the unpaid balance and an annual principle payment of $1.5 million. Town East proceeded to develop the property and sold most of it to unrelated third parties in eight different transactions. Town East made no payments on the notes until after the property had been sold to third parties. Town East paid the entire principal amount by the end of 1984, but it did not make the required interest payments.

Mesquite East characterized its profits from this sale as long-term capital gain on its 1983 and 1984 partnership tax returns. On audit, the Commissioner of Internal Revenue determined that the profits constituted ordinary income * * *.

II

* * * The tax court upheld the deficiencies, finding that the sale of land was the business of Mesquite East, and that, therefore, the profits were ordinary income. The tax court stated that this was true whether the business was conducted directly or through Town East. The tax court noted that the businessmen were owners in proportionate shares of the joint venture and the corporation, that the corporation was formed less than a month after the joint venture, that the corporation routinely entered into contracts of sale to third parties before buying the property from the joint venture, that the corporation made no payments to the joint venture until funds were received from third parties, that the corporation did not make the required interest payments and that the corporation only developed land that it bought from the joint venture. * * * The court * * * stated that "the point to be made here, however, is that evidence of the corporation's activities and their correlation with activities of the joint venture is proof of the nature of the business of the joint venture. * * * The totality of the evidence supports the conclusion that the business of the joint venture was the sale of land and that the

resulting gains should be taxed as ordinary income." The Brambletts now appeal the decision of the tax court.

III

On appeal, the Brambletts argue that Town East was not the agent of Mesquite East, and that, therefore, its activities cannot be attributed to Mesquite East. They further argue that Mesquite East itself was not in the business of selling property, making the tax court's determination that the profits are ordinary income incorrect. The commissioner argues that under the well-known principle of "substance over form," the business of Town East, selling property, can be attributed to Mesquite East, making its profits ordinary income.

IV

In order to qualify for favorable treatment as long-term capital gain, * * * the gain must arise from the sale or exchange of a "capital asset" held more than one year. "Property held by the taxpayer primarily for sale to customers in the ordinary course of his trade or business" cannot be a capital asset. It is well settled that the definition of a capital asset is to be construed narrowly. Corn Products Refining Co. v. Commissioner, 350 U.S. 46, 52, 76 S. Ct. 20, 24, 100 L. Ed. 29 (1955). The determination of whether Mesquite East was directly involved in the business of selling land is a factual determination, to be reversed only if clearly erroneous. Byram v. United States, 705 F.2d 1418, 1423–24 (5th Cir.1983).

The tax court's opinion is in some respects, not very clear. At one point, the court stated that the facts support the conclusion that Mesquite East was in the business of selling land, directly or through Town East. Later, the court mentioned the agency principle, but did not specifically hold that Town East was the agent of Mesquite East. Finally, the court stated that the totality of evidence supports the conclusion that the business of the joint venture was the sale of land. The commissioner argues that what the tax court meant, was that under the substance over form principle, the activities of Town East can be attributed to Mesquite East.

* * *

V

The tax court held that Mesquite East was in the business of selling land, either directly or through Town East. This court has developed a framework to be used in determining whether sales of land are considered sales of a capital asset or sales of property held primarily for sale to customers in the ordinary course of a taxpayer's business. Three principal questions must be considered:

(1) Was the taxpayer engaged in a trade or business, and if so, what business?

(2) Was the taxpayer holding the property primarily for sale in that business?

(3)   Were the sales contemplated by the taxpayer "ordinary" in the course of that business?

Seven factors which should be considered when answering these three questions are: (1) the nature and purpose of the acquisition of the property and the duration of the ownership, (2) the extent and nature of the taxpayer's efforts to sell the property, (3) the number, extent, continuity and substantiality of the sales, (4) the extent of subdividing, developing, and advertising to increase sales, (5) the use of a business office for the sale of the property, (6) the character and degree of supervision or control exercised by the taxpayer over any representative selling the property, and (7) the time and effort the taxpayer habitually devoted to the sales. The frequency and substantiality of sales is the most important factor.

A review of these factors indicates that any finding by the tax court that Mesquite East was directly in the business of selling land is clearly erroneous. Mesquite East did not sell land frequently and the only substantial sale was the sale at issue. It conducted a total of five sales over a three-year period; two in 1979, one in 1980, one in 1981, and the one at issue in 1982. As a result of the first four transactions, Mesquite East made a profit of $68,394.80. On the sale at issue, Mesquite East made a profit of over seven million dollars. This record of frequency does not rise to the level necessary to reach the conclusion that the taxpayer held the property for sale rather than for investment Suburban Realty Co. v. U.S., 615 F.2d 171, 174 (5th Cir.1980) (taxpayer made 244 sales over a thirty-two year period); Biedenharn Realty Co. v. U.S., 526 F.2d 409, 411–12 (5th Cir.1976) (during thirty-one year period, taxpayer sold 208 lots and twelve individual parcels from subdivision in question; 477 lots were sold from other properties); U.S. v. Winthrop, 417 F.2d 905, 907 (5th Cir.1969) (taxpayer sold 456 lots over a nineteen-year period).

In *Byram*, this court affirmed the district court's finding that even though taxpayer made twenty-two sales over a three-year period, netting $3.4 million, he did not hold the property in question for sale: Though these amounts are substantial by anyone's yardstick, the district court did not clearly err in determining that 22 such sales in three years were not sufficiently frequent or continuous to compel an inference of intent to hold the property for sale rather than investment. This is particularly true in a case where the other factors weigh so heavily in favor of the taxpayer. "Substantial and frequent sales activity, standing alone, has never been held to automatically trigger ordinary income treatment."

In *Byram*, the taxpayer did not initiate the sales, he did not maintain an office, he did not develop the property and he did not devote a great deal of time to the transactions. The taxpayer held the property for six to nine months. In the case at hand, all of the other factors also weigh heavily in favor of the taxpayers. The stated purpose of Mesquite East was to acquire the property for investment purposes. It sought advice as to how to structure the transaction to preserve its investment purpose.

Mesquite East held the property in question for over three years. Mesquite East did not advertise or hire brokers, it did not develop the property and it did not maintain an office. The partners did not spend more than a minimal amount of time on the activities of Mesquite East. In the light of the fact that all of these factors weigh so heavily in favor of the taxpayers, and in the light of the fact that Mesquite East made only one substantial sale and four insubstantial sales over a three-year period, any finding by the tax court that Mesquite East was directly in the business of selling land is clearly erroneous. Therefore, we cannot affirm the tax court's decision on this ground.

VI

It is not clear from the tax court's opinion whether the court found that Town East was the agent of Mesquite East, and that therefore, Mesquite East was in the business of selling land through Town East, or whether it attributed the activities of Town East to Mesquite East based on a "substance over form" principle.

* * *

Whether the corporation operates in the name and for the account of the principal, binds the principal by its actions, transmits money received to the principal, and whether the receipt of income is attributable to the services of the employees of the principle [sic] and to assets belonging to the principal are some of the relevant considerations in determining whether a true agency exists. If the corporation is a true agent, its relations with its principal must not be dependent upon the fact that it is owned by the principal, if such is the case. Its business purpose must be the carrying on of the normal duties of an agent.

The Supreme Court [has] held that the subsidiaries were not agents of the corporation simply when the business arrangement arose because of ownership and domination by the parent. The Court acknowledged that the arrangement would not have been the same if third parties owned the subsidiaries.

* * * There is no evidence that Town East ever acted in the name of or for the account of Mesquite East. Town East did not have authority to bind Mesquite East. Town East did transfer money to Mesquite East, but it was the amount of the agreed upon fair market value of the property at the time of the sale. Town East realized a profit from its development that was much larger than a typical agency fee. The receipt of income by Town East was not attributable to the services of employees of Mesquite East or assets belonging to the joint venture. * * * [C]ommon ownership of both entities is not enough to prove an agency relationship. * * * It is clear that Town East was not carrying on the normal duties of an agent; it was not selling or developing the property on behalf of Mesquite East because Town East retained all of the profit from development. Thus, * * * Town East was not an agent of Mesquite East. Nor are there any other factors * * * that indicate that Town East was the agent of

Mesquite East. Therefore, we cannot affirm the tax court's decision on the grounds that Town East was the agent of Mesquite East.

VII

The Commissioner argues that the tax court correctly attributed the activities of Town East to Mesquite East. He further argues that the well known principle of substance over form supports this attribution. The Supreme Court recently stated that in applying the principle of substance over form: the Court has looked to the objective economic realities of a transaction, rather than to the particular form the parties employed. The Court has never regarded "the simple expedient drawing up of papers," as controlling for tax purposes when the objective economic realities are to the contrary. "In the field of taxation, administrators of the laws and the courts are concerned with substance and realities, and formal rigid documents are not rigidly binding." Nor is the parties' desire to achieve a particular tax result necessarily relevant. Frank Lyon Co. v. United States, 435 U.S. 561, 573, 98 S. Ct. 1291, 1298, 55 L. Ed. 2d 550 (1978) (internal citations omitted). The Supreme Court further stated, however, that in cases where the form chosen by the taxpayer has a genuine economic substance, "is compelled or encouraged by business or regulatory realities, is imbued with tax-independent considerations, and is not shaped solely by tax-avoidance features," *Frank Lyon*, 435 U.S. at 583–84, the government should honor the tax consequences effectuated by the taxpayer.

The Commissioner argues that when determining what the partnership's purpose was for holding the land, the tax court correctly looked to the economic substance of the transactions as a whole and attributed the activity of Town East to Mesquite East. We disagree. The business of a corporation is not ordinarily attributable to its shareholders. Neither the tax court nor the Commissioner argue that Town East is a sham corporation whose corporate shield can be pierced. Indeed, the tax court recognized and the Commissioner contends that both are separate taxable entities. Moreover, there was clearly at least one major independent business reason to form the corporation and have it develop the land and sell it—that reason being to insulate the partnership and the partners from unlimited liability from a multitude of sources. Furthermore, there is no substantial evidence that the transaction was not an arm's length transaction or that business and legal formalities were not observed. Finally, the partnership bought the real estate as an investment, hoping its value would appreciate. The partnership, however, bore the risk that the land would not appreciate. Therefore, the tax court erred in finding that the activity of Town East can be attributed to Mesquite East and, consequently, that Mesquite East was in the business of selling land. Mesquite East held the land as an investment and is therefore entitled to capital gains treatment on the gain realized by the sale.

VIII

Thus, we conclude. Any finding by the tax court that Mesquite East was directly in the business of selling land is clearly erroneous. Neither the frequency nor the substantiality of the sales made by Mesquite East supports the conclusion that Mesquite East was directly in the business of selling land. The tax court's opinion cannot be affirmed on the grounds that Town East was the agent of Mesquite East. * * * Town East was not acting as the agent of Mesquite East. * * * Finally, the activities of Town East may not be attributed to Mesquite East when determining whether Mesquite East was in the business of selling land. The corporation is not a sham; there was at least one major independent reason to form the corporation. Furthermore, the partners did invest in a capital asset in the sense that they bore the risk that the land would not appreciate. Therefore, the partnership held the land as a capital asset and is entitled to capital gains treatment. The decision of the tax court is

REVERSED.

NOTES

(A) *General Approach.* In the *Byram* case, discussed in *Bramblett*, the appellate court's opinion begins, "If a client asks you in any but an extreme case whether, in your opinion, his sale will result in capital gain, your answer should probably be, 'I don't know, and no one else in town can tell you.'" The *Bramblett* case once again confirms this "hackneyed truism," in the context of sales of real estate. Why should this be so? Is there no logic to when capital gains treatment is appropriate? A grocery store earns ordinary income. Since a box of cereal does not appreciate in value, what enables a grocery store to make a profit? Does this help with the analysis of the real estate cases?

Determinations whether real estate is "held for sale to customers" tend to turn on their particular facts, and there is diversity among the courts concerning the precise factors to be considered and much diversity over the relative importance of each.

In Boree v. Commissioner, 837 F.3d 1093 (11th Cir. 2016), for example, the court found that a tract of land was held for sale in the ordinary course of business even after county zoning ordinances made it commercially impractical to develop as the owners originally intended. The taxpayers in that case sold the undeveloped land after the zoning decisions. The court held that the Tax Court properly considered Boree's intent over the time he held the property, not just at the time that he sold it. Further, the court found that Boree continued development activities after the ordinances by seeking variances from the county planner.

(B) *Frequency and Substantiality of Sales.* The most important factor cited in many cases is the number, frequency, and substantiality of sales. Courts suggest that numerous sales that extend over a long period of time are more likely to have occurred in the ordinary course of business, while sales that are few and isolated are more likely to have resulted from investment activity.

For example, in emphasizing the importance of frequent and substantial sales, the Fifth Circuit in *Suburban Realty Co.* noted,

> The frequency and substantiality of sales are highly probative on the issue of holding purpose because the presence of frequent sales ordinarily belies the contention that property is being held "for investment" rather than "for sale."

615 F.2d at 174.

The court was following the Fifth Circuit's en banc decision in *Biedenharn Realty Co.,* which held that a realty company had realized ordinary income rather than capital gain from the sale of subdivided real estate. Biedenharn Realty Co. v. United States, 526 F.2d 409 (5th Cir. 1976).

Although frequency of sales is clearly an important factor, the fact that the taxpayer engaged in only occasional sales does not guarantee that she is not a dealer. Other factors are important as well.

(C) *The Seller's Passivity.* In Adam v. Commissioner, 60 T.C. 996 (1973), the court suggested that a taxpayer would seldom be found to have engaged in a trade or business where he had done little, if anything, to acquire, improve, or market his properties. A rather extreme case emphasizing the taxpayer's passivity, Williams v. United States, 84–1 U.S.T.C. ¶ 9384 (N.D.Tex. 1983), refused to impute the activity of the seller's usual broker and partner to the taxpayer. The court found it significant that he (1) did not seek out sellers or buyers of property (brokers brought him sellers and buyers without his asking), (2) rarely negotiated prices but merely accepted or rejected bids, (3) did not have a real estate license, and (4) devoted no more than 56 hours over the several years to his real estate holdings. As *Williams* involved sales of 118 parcels over a seven-year period, the case illustrates the proposition that "the frequency and substantiality of sales activity *standing alone"* does not "*automatically* * * * trigger ordinary income treatment" (emphasis added).

Williams should be contrasted with *Biedenharn Realty,* where the Fifth Circuit, after the taxpayer had attempted to minimize the importance of its own sales and advertising activities, observed that "even one inarguably in the real estate business need not engage in promotional exertions in the face of a favorable market. * * * [W]e do not always require a showing of active solicitation where 'business * * * [is] good, indeed brisk.' " 526 F.2d at 418.

(D) *Relative Earnings.* The court in *Adam* attached considerable importance to the fact that the taxpayer's real estate activities produced relatively little of his income. In the three years at issue, the net gain from real estate activities constituted 5 percent, 16 percent, and 30 percent of the taxpayer's income. The court noted, "The significant difference in income generated by the two activities tends to show that [the taxpayer's] real estate dealings were investment activities." Why does the difference in relative incomes matter? Adam was an accountant. Should the outcome have differed if Adam was a mechanic earning only $10,000 a year from employment? Compare Goodman v. United States, 390 F.2d 915 (Ct.Cl.1968), (involving sales by attorneys of 32 real estate interests over a three-year period, with the court noting that individuals may be engaged in more than one trade or business and concluding that buying and selling real estate was one of the businesses of the attorneys).

(E) *What Is the Asset?* In Long v. Commissioner, 772 F.3d 670 (11th Cir. 2014), the taxpayer sold a judgment that entitled him to purchase land. The judgment was a state court order for specific performance of a purchase agreement between Long and a landowner. Rather than purchase and develop the property, Long decided to sell his position in the lawsuit to another developer for $5.75 million. The Tax Court determined that the sale produced ordinary income because Long, a developer, originally intended to build condominiums on the property for sale to customers. The Eleventh Circuit held that the asset Long sold was not the land itself, but rather the judgment granting the right to purchase land. Since Long did not hold it for sale in the ordinary course of business, the judgment was a capital asset.

(F) *Bulk Sales.* The emphasis in cases such as *Suburban Realty* and *Biedenharn* on the frequency and substantiality of sales suggests that taxpayers are more likely to obtain capital gains treatment if they dispose of their land in a single bulk sale rather than in many smaller sales. This lesson obviously was taken seriously by the taxpayers in *Bramblett.* The *Biedenharn* court observed in a footnote, however, that it was "not prepared to tell taxpayers that in all cases a single bulk sale provides the only road to capital gains." The court suggested that capital gains treatment might remain appropriate when "the change from investment holding to sales activity results from unanticipated, externally induced factors which make impossible the continued pre-existing use of the realty." These factors might include, for example, "acts of God, condemnation of part of one's property, new and unfavorable zoning regulations, or other events forcing alteration of taxpayer's plans * * *." 526 F.2d at 420–21 & n.39.

Would an "externally induced factor" that increased the property's value be compatible with capital gains treatment on sales of parcels of the property? Suppose that creeping suburbanization so increases the value of farmland held as investment property that the owner cannot pay her property taxes without selling pieces of the property. Is it appropriate to require the investor to sell the land in bulk to others who will develop it in order to obtain favorable treatment?

The "bulk sales" exception does not apply when a taxpayer sells a going business. In Williams v. McGowan, 152 F. 2d 570 (2d Cir. 1945), the taxpayer sold his hardware store for $64,000. Among the assets sold were inventory, fixtures, and receivables. The taxpayer reported the transaction as a sale of one asset, the business. But the Second Circuit held that the taxpayer must treat the sale as a disposition of each asset, with capital or ordinary status determined under Section 1221. (In contrast, a sale of all of the shares of a corporate business typically will produce capital gain.)

(G) *Stock and Securities.* The same asset can be either capital or ordinary depending on the holder's relationship to the asset. Since most assets ultimately are held for sale, the courts must distinguish between those held "primarily for sale to customers" and those that are not. Particularly in dealing with stocks or securities, the courts have identified three classes of taxpayers holding stock—dealers, traders, and investors. Consider the following definitions:

> A dealer is a person who purchases the securities or commodities with the expectation of realizing a profit not because of a rise in value during the interval of time between purchase and resale, but merely because they have or hope to find a market of buyers who will purchase from them at a price in excess of their cost. This excess or mark-up represents remuneration for their labors as a middle man bringing together buyer and seller, and performing the usual services of retailer or wholesaler of goods. Dealers have customers for purposes of section 1221.

> Traders, on the other hand, are sellers of securities or commodities who "depend upon such circumstances as a rise in value or an advantageous purchase to enable them to sell at a price in excess of cost." A trader performs no merchandising functions nor any other service which warrants compensation by a price mark-up of the securities he or she sells. "[A] trader will be deemed to be engaged in a trade or business if his or her trading is frequent and substantial." Generally, both dealers and traders will be engaged in a trade or business; only a dealer, however, has customers.

> An investor is very similar to a trader. Like a trader, an investor "makes purchases for capital appreciation and income." Unlike a trader, however, an investor makes such purchases "usually without regard to short-term developments that would influence prices on the daily market." An investor, on the other hand, will never be considered to be engaged in a trade or business with respect to his or her investment activities, no matter how extensive his or her activities might be.

United States v. Wood, 943 F.2d 1048 (9th Cir. 1991) (citations omitted).

Section 1236 permits securities dealers to receive capital gains treatment on securities they earmark as investment assets. Most dealers must identify their investment securities by the end of the day of acquisition, while floor traders have seven business days to designate securities in which they are registered specialists. An ordinary loss cannot be taken on any security that previously has been identified as an investment asset.

In Bielfeldt v. Commissioner, 231 F.3d 1035 (7th Cir. 2000), the court refused to treat a large trader in U.S. treasury bonds as a dealer. Bielfeldt was not a floor specialist so he could not utilize § 1236. He hoarded Treasury bonds bought at auction with the intention of re-selling them when the temporary glut created by the auction disappeared. He argued that he performed a valuable market function. Judge Posner, however, found that he was "a mere speculator, period * * *That activity may have been socially beneficial, as he argues, but it is no different from the social benefits of speculation generally. His argument if accepted would turn every speculator into a dealer for purposes of the Internal Revenue Code."

(H) *Bifurcated Ordinary Income and Capital Gain Treatment.* Where the taxpayer has a dual or changed motive, it might be theoretically preferable to bifurcate the character of the gain. For example, the gain that accrued while the taxpayer held the property as an investment would be capital and the gain that accrued during the period the taxpayer held the property primarily for sale to customers would be ordinary. Such a provision would be extremely difficult to administer. Section 1237, however, under which a taxpayer can preserve capital gains treatment for at least a portion of the profits when she subdivides or develops land, does take a bifurcated approach. Section 1237 establishes conditions under which land will not be deemed to have been "held primarily for sale to customers in the ordinary course of trade or business" solely because it has been subdivided. The taxpayer must have held the land for at least five years. He must not have previously held the land primarily for sale to customers in the ordinary course of business and must not have made any improvement "that substantially enhances the value of the lot or parcel." If there are more than five parcels in the same tract of land, the gain from any sale that occurs in the taxable year in which the sixth parcel is sold or thereafter will be taxed as ordinary income to the extent of 5 percent of the selling price.

2. DEPRECIABLE PERSONAL PROPERTY AND REAL PROPERTY USED IN A TRADE OR BUSINESS

Note on the Mechanics of § 1231

Section 1221(a)(2) excludes from the definition of capital assets depreciable personal property and real property used in a trade or business. Section 1231, however, allows real and depreciable property used in a trade or business to yield capital gain when disposed of at a net gain and ordinary loss when disposed of at a net loss. This combination of options "constitutes in the tax solar system, the best of all possible worlds."

The predecessor to § 1231 was enacted in 1942 to provide for favorable treatment on dispositions of ships and other property used in the war effort, which due to war needs had greatly appreciated in value. At the same time, Congress retained ordinary treatment for losses on business assets in order to encourage the replacement of obsolete assets.

Section 1231 applies to the disposition of real or depreciable property—such as land, buildings, machinery, and fixtures—excluded from the definition of capital assets by § 1221(a)(2) . The property must have been held by the taxpayer for at least one year.

These so-called "quasi-capital assets" do not include, however, other business assets that are denied capital gains treatment by § 1221; thus, § 1231 does not apply to inventory or other property held primarily for sale to customers, copyrights, artistic compositions, or letters produced by or for the taxpayer, government documents obtained below cost, commodity derivatives held by dealers, hedging transactions, or supplies consumed in the business. On the other hand, several types of business property—including certain livestock, timber, coal, minerals, and unharvested crops sold with the land—are specifically made eligible for "quasi-capital asset" treatment by § 1231. See § 1231(b)(2), (3), and (4).

Three types of dispositions may give rise to § 1231 treatment: (1) gain or loss from sales and exchanges of property used in a trade or business, (2) gain or loss arising from condemnations and involuntary conversions (such as casualty or theft losses) of property used in a trade or business, and (3) gain or loss from condemnations and involuntary conversions of capital assets held in connection with a trade or business or in a profit-seeking activity.

Section 1231 requires a two-stage netting process. First, the taxpayer nets her gains from casualty and theft losses (from insurance proceeds, for example) against her losses from such involuntary conversions. If losses exceed gains, § 1231 does not apply to either the losses or the gains. There is no "sale or exchange," so the gains are taxable as ordinary income and the losses are deductible from ordinary income. Bringing net losses into § 1231 in these circumstances has no upside. See Example 1. But it could have a downside if the § 1231 pot also includes gain because if gains exceed losses both gains and losses are carried over into the second stage of the netting process. See § 1231(a)(4) and Example 2. Since there is no sale or exchange, in the absence of § 1231, the gain would be ordinary so bringing this gain into § 1231 could help. This first stage of netting is often called the "firepot," since it deals with conversions from fire, storm, or other similar casualties.

Second, the taxpayer compares her total gains with her total losses from (1) involuntary conversions carried over from the first stage "firepot," (2) condemnations, sales, and exchanges of business property, and (3) condemnations of capital assets used in a trade or business or an income-producing property. This second stage of netting is often referred to as the "hotchpot." If losses exceed gains, the gains are includible in ordinary income and the losses are deductible from ordinary income. If gains exceed losses, however, the gains are treated as long-term capital gains and the losses are treated as long-term capital losses; these gains and losses then are carried to the tax return to be combined with long-term capital gains and long-term capital losses from other sources. See § 1231(a)(1), (2), and (3).

The recapture provisions described below may require amounts that otherwise would be capital gain (or § 1231 gain) on depreciable property nevertheless to be reported as ordinary income. Amounts that are recaptured as ordinary income do not enter into either the firepot or the hodgepot. See the Note on Recapture Provisions, infra at page 593.

The following examples illustrate the application of § 1231.

Example 1:

Involuntary Dispositions		Gains	Losses
Factory building destroyed by fire			
Adjusted basis of building	$100,000		
Insurance proceeds	50,000		
(Loss)	($50,000)		($50,000)
Theft of uninsured equipment			(10,000)
Total in firepot			($60,000)
Other Dispositions			
Sale of real estate used in business		$100,000	
Sale of truck used in business			($5,000)
Condemnation of rental property			
Adjusted basis of building	$30,000		
Compensation	35,000		
Gain	$5,000	5,000	
Total in hotchpot		$105,000	($5,000)

In this example, the application of § 1231 leaves the taxpayer with a long-term capital gain of $105,000 to be added to other long-term capital gains (from the sale of stock, for example) and $5,000 of long-term capital losses to be added to other long-term capital losses. The $60,000 of theft and casualty losses in the firepot is not added to the hotchpot because there is a net loss. Thus, the $60,000 loss is deductible from ordinary income.

Example 2:

Involuntary Dispositions		Gains	Losses
Factory building destroyed by fire			
Adjusted basis of building	$100,000		
Insurance proceeds	160,000		
Gain	$60,000	$60,000	
Theft of uninsured equipment			($5,000)
Other Dispositions			
Sale of real estate used in business			($75,000)
Sale of truck used in business			(5,000)
Condemnation of rental property			
Adjusted basis of building	$30,000		
Compensation	35,000		

Gain	$5,000	5,000	
Total in hotchpot		$65,000	($85,000)

In Example 2, the application of § 1231 leaves the taxpayer with a gain of $65,000 that is taxed as ordinary income and a loss of $85,000 deductible from ordinary income. Note that the gains and loss from the firepot are included in the hotchpot because there was a net gain.

Section 1231 is said to be tax nirvana in that net losses are ordinary and net gains are capital gains. Because of the netting process, however, this is not always the case. Therefore, the application of § 1231 is limited in order to prevent taxpayers from bunching their gains from "quasi-capital assets" into one year and their losses into another. A taxpayer may be required to treat as ordinary income the excess in any year of his gains on § 1231 property over his losses on § 1231 property. This provision applies to the extent of the taxpayer's net § 1231 losses for the preceding five years. § 1231(c). Suppose, for example, that T has a net § 1231 loss of $5,000 in Year 1, which is treated as ordinary and in Year 2 has a net § 1231 gain of $8,000. Only $3,000 of that gain is capital and $5,000 is "recaptured" as ordinary. Note that is the identical result if the net loss and net gain had occurred in the same year.

The two-stage netting process and the carryover of ordinary losses leads to significant complexity and the netting process itself creates uncertainty as to whether a particular transaction will result in ordinary or capital treatment. It is worth considering how much would change if § 1231 were repealed and whether repeal would be consistent with good tax policy. As to depreciable assets and land used in a trade or business, gains and losses would be ordinary under § 1221(a)(2). Because of recapture under § 1245 (discussed in the next Note), however, even with § 1231, personal property would produce ordinary income under most circumstances (where the gain is attributable to depreciation). Gains on depreciable real property, to extent the selling price did not exceed original cost, would be taxed at no more than 25 percent under §§ 1250 and 1(h)(6). This would have no impact on taxpayers in 25 percent bracket or lower and a relatively small impact on others. Gains on involuntary conversions and condemnation could be deferred under § 1033 by investing in similar use property (or for condemnation of real estate in like kind property as well). See page 648, infra. The treatment of property considered used in a trade or business under § 1231(b)(2)–(4) would also change. The major effect of repeal would be ordinary income rates on profits from the sale of land or from sale of buildings held in a business to the extent proceeds exceeded original cost. Would it be sensible to amend § 1221(a)(2) to exclude real estate? One benefit of making all real estate capital assets would be that it would be unnecessary to determine whether real estate activity amounts to a trade or business, which could be an issue, for example, for a taxpayer who owns one or a limited number of buildings.

As to involuntary conversion of capital assets used in trade or business or a transaction for profit, since there is no sale or exchange, gains and losses would be ordinary. For depreciable assets, the recapture rules would minimize the change. Further, as noted above, § 1033 would allow gains to be deferred. Condemnation of capital assets used in a trade or business or a transaction for profit could lead to a capital loss, which might seem unfair but one could certainly allow ordinary loss on condemnation without resort to the complexity of § 1231.

Note on Recapture Provisions

If depreciation accurately measured the actual decline in value of an asset, a taxpayer's basis would be approximately equal to its fair market value and thus a sale would produce neither gain nor loss. Current depreciation rules, however, make no real attempt to accurately measure decline in value, and thus a taxpayer may realize a gain or loss. When the taxpayer realizes a gain on depreciable property, he has been permitted to take depreciation exceeding the economic cost of holding the asset. (Conversely, if a loss is realized, the depreciation allowance was too limited.)

If the taxpayer were able to enjoy depreciation deductions (which offset ordinary income) and obtain capital gain treatment on sale via § 1231, he would be able to convert ordinary income into capital gain. Section 1245 was enacted to prohibit such conversion on the sale of depreciable property at a gain by requiring the "recapture" of previously deducted depreciation as ordinary income. The ordinary gain "pays back" the excess depreciation, although the taxpayer has enjoyed the time value of the earlier depreciation deductions.

If depreciable property is sold for more than its adjusted basis, any gain not exceeding the total depreciation allowed is taxed as ordinary income. Section 1245 also recaptures as ordinary income amounts deducted under § 179 in lieu of depreciation, amortization deductions (such as under § 197), and other deductions under §§ 190 or 193. Generally, depreciable personal property is subject to recapture under § 1245. § 1245(a)(3).

The following example illustrates the application of § 1245:

In Year 1, A purchased a machine for $100,000 to use in his manufacturing business. After taking depreciation deductions of $61,600, A sells the machine in Year 3 for $90,000. His entire gain of $51,600 on the sale ($90,000 sales proceeds minus his $38,400 adjusted basis) will be taxed as ordinary income because the amount of his depreciation deductions exceeds the amount of the gain. The depreciation deductions that he has taken against ordinary income must be fully "recaptured"—that is, taxed as ordinary income.

Section 1250 provides a comparable, but less complete, "recapture" mechanism for dispositions of virtually all kinds of real property. It recaptures the excess of accelerated depreciation over straight line depreciation on certain real estate. Real estate currently is only depreciated using the straight line method, and thus there is no § 1250 recapture on property that has been allowed only straight line depreciation. Gain up to the amount of depreciation allowed on real property held for more than twelve months is taxed at a special capital gains rate of 25 percent. While this is more advantageous than taxing the gain at ordinary rates, which can be as high as 37 percent it is not as beneficial as the usual maximum capital gains rate of 15 or 20 percent.

Other recapture provisions aimed at limiting the conversion of ordinary income into long-term capital gains include § 1258, discussed infra at page 612, which explicitly denies capital gain treatment for a specific category of "conversion" transactions.

3.   Copyrights, Literary, Musical, and Artistic Compositions, and Patents

Note on the Treatment of Copyrights, Literary, Musical, and Artistic Compositions, and Patents

Sections 1221(a)(3) and 1231(b)(1)(C) exclude from the definition of a capital asset patents, inventions, models or designs (whether or not patented), secret formulas or processes, copyrights, literary, musical, and artistic compositions, and letters or memoranda prepared by or for the taxpayer. The exclusion from capital gains treatment is limited to dispositions of property held by its creator or by a taxpayer whose basis is determined by reference to the creator's basis (for example, the recipient of a gift of the copyright). This creates parity between one who is paid for his services in creating an artistic composition and one who sells the actual composition. Copyrights and literary, musical, or artistic creations are capital assets, however, in the hands of buyers or most legatees unless they are held for sale to customers in the ordinary course of a trade or business.

Shortly after Congress originally enacted § 1221(a)(3) , it enacted § 1235, which permits capital gain treatment on the sale of a patent by the holder even when he is a "professional" who makes the sale in the ordinary course of his business. Section 1235 allows capital gain treatment even if the consideration received by the holder is dependent upon the transferee's sales or use and even if the minimum holding period is not satisfied. The favorable treatment of § 1235 also applies to those who have financed the inventor's work.

Section 1235 requires that the patent holder transfer "all substantial rights" in a patent in order to qualify for capital gains treatment. The regulations provide that this requirement will not be satisfied by a transfer of a patent for a period less than its remaining term or by a transfer of rights limited geographically within the country of issuance or limited to less than all the economic fields of use. See Reg. § 1.1235–2(b).

The 2017 legislation amended § 1221(a)(3) to deny capital gain treatment for self-created inventions disposed of in 2018 or after, but unlike the House version of the bill, did not repeal § 1235.

NOTES

(A) *Scope of § 1221(a)(3)*. The exclusion applies not only to letters and memoranda, but also to "similar property." The regulations define this broadly to include "a draft of a speech, a manuscript, a research paper, an oral recording, * * * a personal or business diary, a log or journal, a corporate archive, * * * office correspondence, a financial record, a drawing, a photograph or a dispatch." Reg. § 1.1221–1(c)(2). The taxpayer in Jones v. Commissioner, 560 F.3d 1196 (10th Cir. 2009), tried to claim a charitable deduction for the donation of discovery material he received as lead counsel for Timothy McVeigh. The court held that discovery material is excepted from capital asset treatment by § 1221(a)(3)(B) and thus the charitable deduction would be limited to the taxpayer's basis. The court also noted that the taxpayer had no basis in the discovery material prepared for him.

The "similar property" exclusion is now important with respect to computer software, whether or not it is copyrighted. The software creator has ordinary income on the sale of the program.

In an attempt to claim capital gains treatment on income from patents, the taxpayers in Cooper v. Commissioner, 143 T.C. 194 (2014), transferred patents to a corporation they formed with Ms. Cooper's sister and friend in exchange for a large percentage of any royalties the corporation earned from licensing them. Although the Coopers owned only 24 percent of the corporation, Mr. Cooper made essentially all decisions on business matters. Because of this effective control, the Tax Court found that the Coopers did not transfer all substantial rights to the patents, and so the royalties were not eligible for capital gains treatment under § 1235.

(B) *Songwriter's Benefit*. In 2005 Congress amended § 1221 to provide that the creator of a music composition or copyright in musical works who sells or exchanges the work can elect to treat the gain or loss as capital. § 1221(b)(3). A songwriter who sells a song, just like a furniture maker who sells a chair, is receiving compensation for his labor. So why would Congress provide special treatment for composers and not authors, sculptors, or painters? Apparently because a Southern congressman responded to the plaintive cries of country and western singers and created a Songwriting Caucus on Capitol Hill. Limiting the provision to only those who sing about heartbreak and pick-up trucks was not practical, so Congress extended the special treatment to budding Mahlers but not Tolstoys or Rembrandts. Go figure.

(C) *Inventor-Employees.* Where the inventor is an employee who has contracted to assign any patents to her employer, payments from the employer to the employee typically will be treated as compensation.

4.   ACCOUNTS AND NOTES RECEIVABLE

Section 1221(a)(4) excludes from the definition of capital assets "accounts or notes receivable acquired in the ordinary course of trade or business for services rendered or from the sale of property" held for sale to customers in the ordinary course of business. The provision further illustrates the general congressional intent to exclude from capital gain or loss treatment transactions arising out of a taxpayer's everyday business activities.

An accrual basis taxpayer includes an account receivable as ordinary income at the time of its receipt; a cash basis taxpayer would include the payments on the receivable as ordinary income. (Accounting methods are discussed in detail in Chapter 7, infra.) Thus, if the note is subsequently sold for less than the amount included, there will be an ordinary loss. If sold for more than basis, there will be an ordinary gain.

Section 1221(a)(4) requires that the notes or receivables be received in exchange for services. When a mortgage lender provides loans, are the notes receivable acquired for services or money? Burbank Liquidating Co. v. Commissioner, 335 F.2d 125 (9th Cir. 1964), found that the receivables were received for services. Federal National Mortgage Association v. Commissioner, 100 T.C. 541 (1993), held that the notes received by Fannie Mae in the secondary market also fell under § 1221(a)(4). The IRS proposed and then withdrew a rule that would have treated notes purchased in the secondary market as capital assets, rather than receivables received in exchange for services. What is the appropriate treatment for investors in debt instruments that lose value in a recession or when interest rates rise?

5.   GOVERNMENT PUBLICATIONS RECEIVED FREE OR AT A DISCOUNT

Section 1221(a)(5) excludes from the capital asset definition government publications received by taxpayers without charge or at a reduced price. An example would be copies of the Congressional Record received free by members of Congress. This provision, as well as the exclusion of § 1221(a)(3) for letters and memoranda prepared by or for the holder, was designed to deprive taxpayers of charitable deductions for the fair market value of such materials when they are contributed to a charity such as a university or a library. Before these provisions were enacted, politicians routinely took charitable deductions for the fair market value of gifts of such items to charities. Recall § 170(e), discussed supra at page 467.

6.   DERIVATIVES, HEDGING TRANSACTIONS, AND SUPPLIES USED IN A
     BUSINESS

Section 1221(a)(1) and (2) excludes from capital gains treatment
many, but not all, of the assets used in a trade or business. Suppose an
airline purchases jet fuel and subsequently sells the fuel that it discovers
it does not need. Or suppose the airline is concerned about the price of
fuel and purchases a derivative (a financial contract with a value tied to
the price of fuel) to hedge its costs. Neither the fuel nor the derivative is
inventory or depreciable property. They generally, however, would be
ordinary assets under §§ 1221(a)(7) and (8), provisions adopted in the
wake of the *Arkansas Best* case, which appears below. See also the Note
on Hedging Transactions, at page 604, infra.

Arkansas Best Corporation v. Commissioner

Supreme Court of the United States, 1988. 485 U.S. 212.

■ JUSTICE MARSHALL delivered the opinion of the Court.

The issue presented in this case is whether capital stock held by
petitioner Arkansas Best Corporation (Arkansas Best) is a "capital asset"
as defined in § 1221 of the Internal Revenue Code regardless of whether
the stock was purchased and held for a business purpose or for an
investment purpose.

I

Arkansas Best is a diversified holding company. In 1968 it acquired
approximately 65% of the stock of the National Bank of Commerce (Bank)
in Dallas, Texas. Between 1969 and 1974, Arkansas Best more than
tripled the number of shares it owned in the Bank, although its
percentage interest in the Bank remained relatively stable. These
acquisitions were prompted principally by the Bank's need for added
capital. Until 1972, the Bank appeared to be prosperous and growing,
and the added capital was necessary to accommodate this growth. As the
Dallas real estate market declined, however, so too did the financial
health of the Bank, which had a heavy concentration of loans in the local
real estate industry. In 1972, federal examiners classified the Bank as a
problem bank. The infusion of capital after 1972 was prompted by the
loan portfolio problems of the bank.

Petitioner sold the bulk of its Bank stock on June 30, 1975, leaving
it with only a 14.7% stake in the Bank. On its federal income tax return
for 1975, petitioner claimed a deduction for an ordinary loss of $9,995,688
resulting from the sale of the stock. The Commissioner of Internal
Revenue disallowed the deduction, finding that the loss from the sale of
stock was a capital loss, rather than an ordinary loss, and that it
therefore was subject to the capital loss limitations in the Internal
Revenue Code.

Arkansas Best challenged the Commissioner's determination in the United States Tax Court. The Tax Court, relying on cases interpreting Corn Products Refining Co. v. Commissioner, 350 U.S. 46 (1955), held that stock purchased with a substantial investment purpose is a capital asset which, when sold, gives rise to a capital gain or loss, whereas stock purchased and held for a business purpose, without any substantial investment motive, is an ordinary asset whose sale gives rise to ordinary gains or losses. See 83 T.C. 640, 653–654 (1984). The court characterized Arkansas Best's acquisitions through 1972 as occurring during the Bank's " 'growth' phase," and found that these acquisitions "were motivated primarily by investment purpose and only incidentally by some business purpose." Id., at 654. The stock acquired during this period therefore constituted a capital asset, which gave rise to a capital loss when sold in 1975. The court determined, however, that the acquisitions after 1972 occurred during the Bank's " 'problem' phase," and, except for certain minor exceptions, "were made exclusively for business purposes and subsequently held for the same reason." These acquisitions, the court found, were designed to preserve petitioner's business reputation, because without the added capital the Bank probably would have failed. The loss realized on the sale of this stock was thus held to be an ordinary loss.

The Court of Appeals for the Eighth Circuit reversed the Tax Court's determination that the loss realized on stock purchased after 1972 was subject to ordinary-loss treatment, holding that all of the Bank stock sold in 1975 was subject to capital-loss treatment. 800 F.2d 215 (1986). The court reasoned that the Bank stock clearly fell within the general definition of "capital asset" in Internal Revenue Code section 1221, and that the stock did not fall within any of the specific statutory exceptions to this definition. The court concluded that Arkansas Best's purpose in acquiring and holding the stock was irrelevant to the determination whether the stock was a capital asset. We granted certiorari, 480 U.S. 930, and now affirm.

II

Section 1221 of the Internal Revenue Code defines "capital asset" broadly, as "property held by the taxpayer (whether or not connected with his trade or business)," and then excludes five specific classes of property from capital-asset status. In the statute's present form, the classes of property exempted from the broad definition are (1) "property of a kind which would properly be included in the inventory of the taxpayer", (2) real property or other depreciable property used in the taxpayer's trade or business, (3) "a copyright, a literary, musical, or artistic composition," or similar property, (4) "accounts or notes receivable acquired in the ordinary course of trade or business for services rendered" or from the sale of inventory, and (5) publications of the Federal Government. Arkansas Best acknowledges that the Bank stock falls within the literal definition of capital asset in section 1221, and is outside of the statutory exclusions. It asserts, however, that this determination does not end the inquiry. Petitioner argues that in *Corn Products Refining Co. v. Commissioner, supra,* this Court rejected a literal reading of section 1221, and concluded that assets acquired and sold for ordinary business purposes rather than for investment purposes should be given ordinary-asset treatment. Petitioner's reading of *Corn Products* finds much support in the academic literature and in the courts. Unfortunately for petitioner, this broad reading finds no support in the language of § 1221.

In essence, petitioner argues that "property held by the taxpayer (whether or not connected with his trade or business)" does not include property that is acquired and held for a business purpose. In petitioner's view an asset's status as "property" thus turns on the motivation behind its acquisition. This motive test, however, is not only nowhere mentioned in § 1221, but it is also in direct conflict with the parenthetical phrase "whether or not connected with his trade or business." The broad definition of the term "capital asset" explicitly makes irrelevant any consideration of the property's connection with the taxpayer's business, whereas petitioner's rule would make this factor dispositive.[5]

In a related argument, petitioner contends that the five exceptions listed in § 1221 for certain kinds of property are illustrative, rather than exhaustive, and that courts are therefore free to fashion additional exceptions in order to further the general purposes of the capital-asset provisions. The language of the statute refutes petitioner's construction. Section 1221 provides that "capital asset" means "property held by the taxpayer, * * * but does not include" the five classes of property listed as exceptions. We believe this locution signifies that the listed exceptions are exclusive. The body of section 1221 establishes a general definition of the term "capital asset," and the phrase "does not include" takes out of that broad definition only the classes of property that are specifically mentioned. The legislative history of the capital asset definition supports this interpretation, see H.R.Rep. 704, 73d Cong., 2d Sess., 31 (1934) ("[T]he definition includes all property, except as specifically excluded"); H.R.Rep. 1337, 83d Cong., 2d Sess., A273 (1954) ("[A] capital asset is property held by the taxpayer with certain exceptions"), as does the applicable Treasury regulation, see 26 CFR section 1.1221–1(a) (1987) ("The term 'capital assets' includes all classes of property not specifically excluded by section 1221").

---

[5] Petitioner mistakenly relies on cases in which this Court, in narrowly applying the general definition of "capital asset," has "construed 'capital asset' to exclude property representing income items or accretions to the value of a capital asset themselves properly attributable to income," even though these items are property in the broad sense of the word. United States v. Midland-Ross Corp., 381 U.S. 54, 57 (1965). See, e.g., Commissioner v. Gillette Motor Co., 364 U.S. 130 (1960) ("capital asset" does not include compensation awarded taxpayer that represented fair rental value of its facilities); Commissioner v. P.G. Lake, Inc., 356 U.S. 260 (1958) ("capital asset" does not include proceeds from sale of oil payment rights); Hort v. Commissioner, 313 U.S. 28 (1941) ("capital asset" does not include payment to lessor for cancellation of unexpired portion of a lease). This line of cases, based on the premise that section 1221 "property" does not include claims or rights to ordinary income, has no application in the present context. Petitioner sold capital stock, not a claim to ordinary income.

Petitioner's reading of the statute is also in tension with the exceptions listed in section 1221. These exclusions would be largely superfluous if assets acquired primarily or exclusively for business purposes were not capital assets. Inventory, real or depreciable property used in the taxpayer's trade or business, and accounts or notes receivable acquired in the ordinary course of business, would undoubtedly satisfy such a business-motive test. Yet these exceptions were created by Congress in separate enactments spanning 30 years. Without any express direction from Congress, we are unwilling to read section 1221 in a manner that makes surplusage of these statutory exclusions.

In the end, petitioner places all reliance on its reading of Corn Products Refining Co. v. Commissioner, 350 U.S. 46 (1955)—a reading we believe is too expansive. In *Corn Products*, the Court considered whether income arising from a taxpayer's dealings in corn futures was entitled to capital-gains treatment. The taxpayer was a company that converted corn into starches, sugars, and other products. After droughts in the 1930's caused sharp increases in corn prices, the company began a program of buying corn futures to assure itself an adequate supply of corn and protect against price increases. The company "would take delivery on such contracts as it found necessary to its manufacturing operations and sell the remainder in early summer if no shortage was imminent. If shortages appeared, however, it sold futures only as it bought spot corn for grinding." The Court characterized the company's dealing in corn futures as "hedging." As explained by the Court of Appeals in *Corn Products,* "[h]edging is a method of dealing in commodity futures whereby a person or business protects itself against price fluctuations at the time of delivery of the product which it sells or buys." In evaluating the company's claim that the sales of corn futures resulted in capital gains and losses, this Court stated:

> "Nor can we find support for petitioner's contention that hedging is not within the exclusions of [§ 1221]. Admittedly, petitioner's corn futures do not come within the literal language of the exclusions set out in that section. They were not stock in trade, actual inventory, property held for sale to customers or depreciable property used in a trade or business. But the capital-asset provision of section 1221 must not be so broadly applied as to defeat rather than further the purpose of Congress. Congress intended that profits and losses arising from the everyday operation of a business be considered as ordinary income or loss rather than capital gain or loss. * * * Since this section is an exception from the normal tax requirements of the Internal Revenue Code, the definition of a capital asset must be narrowly applied and its exclusions interpreted broadly." 350 U.S., at 51–52 (citations omitted).

The Court went on to note that hedging transactions consistently had been considered to give rise to ordinary gains and losses, and then concluded that the corn futures were subject to ordinary-asset treatment. Id., at 52–53.

The Court in *Corn Products* proffered the oft-quoted rule of construction that the definition of "capital asset" must be narrowly applied and its exclusions interpreted broadly, but it did not state explicitly whether the holding was based on a narrow reading of the phrase "property held by the taxpayer," or on a broad reading of the inventory exclusion of § 1221. In light of the stark language of § 1221, however, we believe that *Corn Products* is properly interpreted as involving an application of section 1221's inventory exception. Such a reading is consistent both with the Court's reasoning in that case and with § 1221. The Court stated in *Corn Products* that the company's futures transactions were "an integral part of its business designed to protect its manufacturing operations against a price increase in its principal raw material and to assure a ready supply for future manufacturing requirements." The company bought, sold, and took delivery under the futures contracts as required by the company's manufacturing needs. As Professor Bittker notes, under these circumstances, the futures can "easily be viewed as surrogates for the raw material itself." 2 B. Bittker, Federal Taxation of Income, Estates and Gifts paragraph 51.10.3, p. 51–62 (1981). The Court of Appeals for the Second Circuit in *Corn Products* clearly took this approach. That court stated that when commodity futures are "utilized solely for the purpose of stabilizing inventory cost, * * * they cannot reasonably be separated from the inventory items," and concluded that "property used in hedging transactions properly comes within the exclusions of section 1221." This Court indicated its acceptance of the Second Circuit's reasoning when it began the central paragraph of its opinion: "Nor can we find support for petitioner's contention that hedging is not within the exclusions of [§ 1221]." In the following paragraph, the Court argued that the Treasury had consistently viewed such hedging transactions as a form of insurance to stabilize the cost of inventory, and cited a Treasury ruling which concluded that the value of a manufacturer's raw-material inventory should be adjusted to take into account hedging transactions in futures contracts. 350 U.S. at 52–53 (citing G.C.M. 17322, XV–2 Cum.Bull. 151 (1936)). This discussion, read in light of the Second Circuit's holding and the plain language of § 1221, convinces us that although the corn futures were not "actual inventory," their use as an integral part of the taxpayer's inventory-purchase system led the Court to treat them as substitutes for the corn inventory such that they came within a broad reading of "property of a kind which would properly be included in the inventory of the taxpayer" in § 1221.

Petitioner argues that by focusing attention on whether the asset was acquired and sold as an integral part of the taxpayer's everyday business operations, the Court in *Corn Products* intended to create a general exemption from capital-asset status for assets acquired for business purposes. We believe petitioner misunderstands the relevance of the Court's inquiry. A business connection, although irrelevant to the initial determination of whether an item is a capital asset, is relevant in determining the applicability of certain of the statutory exceptions, including the inventory exception. The close connection between the futures transactions and the taxpayer's business in *Corn Products* was crucial to whether the corn futures could be considered surrogates for the stored inventory of raw corn. For if the futures dealings were not part of the company's inventory-purchase system, and instead amounted simply to speculation in corn futures, they could not be considered substitutes for the company's corn inventory, and would fall outside even a broad reading of the inventory exclusion. We conclude that *Corn Products* is properly interpreted as standing for the narrow proposition that hedging transactions that are an integral part of a business' inventory-purchase system fall within the inventory exclusion of § 1221.[7] Arkansas Best, which is not a dealer in securities, has never suggested that the Bank stock falls within the inventory exclusion. *Corn Products* thus has no application to this case.

It is also important to note that the business-motive test advocated by petitioner is subject to the same kind of abuse that the Court condemned in *Corn Products*. The Court explained in *Corn Products* that unless hedging transactions were subject to ordinary gain and loss treatment, taxpayers engaged in such transactions could "transmute ordinary income into capital gain at will." The hedger could garner capital-asset treatment by selling the futures and purchasing the commodity on the spot market, or ordinary-asset treatment by taking delivery under the futures contract. In a similar vein, if capital stock purchased and held for a business purpose is an ordinary asset, whereas the same stock purchased and held with an investment motive is a capital asset, a taxpayer such as Arkansas Best could have significant influence over whether the asset would receive capital or ordinary treatment. Because stock is most naturally viewed as a capital asset, the Internal Revenue Service would be hard pressed to challenge a taxpayer's claim that stock was acquired as an investment, and that a gain arising from the sale of such stock was therefore a capital gain. Indeed, we are unaware of a single decision that has applied the business-motive test so as to require a taxpayer to report a gain from the sale of stock as an ordinary gain. If the same stock is sold at a loss, however, the taxpayer may be able to garner ordinary-loss treatment by emphasizing the business purpose behind the stock's acquisition. The potential for such

---

[7] Although congressional inaction is generally a poor measure of congressional intent, we are given some pause by the fact that over 25 years have passed since Corn Products Refining Co. v. Commissioner was initially interpreted as excluding assets acquired for business purposes from the definition of "capital asset," see Booth Newspapers, Inc. v. United States, 157 Ct.Cl. 886, 303 F.2d 916 (1962), without any sign of disfavor from Congress. We cannot ignore the unambiguous language of § 1221, however, no matter how reticent Congress has been. If a broad exclusion from capital-asset status is to be created for assets acquired for business purposes, it must come from congressional action, not silence.

abuse was evidenced in this case by the fact that as late as 1974, when Arkansas Best still hoped to sell the Bank stock at a profit, Arkansas Best apparently expected to report the gain as a capital gain. See 83 T.C. at 647–648.

III

We conclude that a taxpayer's motivation in purchasing an asset is irrelevant to the question whether the asset is "property held by a taxpayer (whether or not connected with his business)" and is thus within section 1221's general definition of "capital asset." Because the capital stock held by petitioner falls within the broad definition of the term "capital asset" in § 1221 and is outside the classes of property excluded from capital-asset status, the loss arising from the sale of the stock is a capital loss. *Corn Products Refining Co. v. Commissioner,* supra, which we interpret as involving a broad reading of the inventory exclusion of § 1221, has no application in the present context. Accordingly, the judgment of the Court of Appeals is affirmed.

It is so ordered.

■ JUSTICE KENNEDY took no part in the consideration or decision of this case.

NOTE

Corn Products and Its Aftermath. The taxpayer in Corn Products Refining Co. v. Commissioner, 350 U.S. 46 (1950), discussed in *Arkansas Best,* manufactured various products, including corn sugar, out of raw corn. To hedge the risk that the price of corn would rise, the company purchased corn futures. (Corn futures are contracts for the future purchase of corn at a fixed price set in the contract. That is, even if "spot" market prices rise, the owner of the futures contract can still purchase at the lower contract price.) Corn Products sold some of its futures contracts at a substantial profit in 1940 and contended in court that its futures were "capital assets."

The Supreme Court rejected the taxpayer's claim and held that the futures contracts were ordinary assets. Analyzing the predecessor of § 1221, the Court wrote:

> Admittedly, petitioner's corn futures do not come within the literal language of the exclusions set out in that section. They were not stock in trade, actual inventory, property held for sale to customers or depreciable property used in a trade or business. But the capital-asset provision of § [1221] must not be so broadly applied as to defeat rather than further the purpose of Congress. * * * Congress intended that profits and losses arising from the everyday operation of a business be considered as ordinary income or loss rather than capital gain or loss. The preferential treatment provided by § [1221] applies to transactions in property which are not the normal source of business income. It was intended "to relieve the taxpayer from * * * excessive tax burdens on gains resulting from a conversion of capital investments, and to remove

the deterrent effect of those burdens on such conversions." * * * Since this section is an exception from the normal tax requirements of the Internal Revenue Code, the definition of a capital asset must be narrowly applied and its exclusions interpreted broadly. * * *

The IRS subsequently discovered that it had won the battle but lost the war with its *Corn Products* victory. The decision repeatedly was invoked to treat losses as ordinary, but seldom used to treat gains as ordinary income. This was largely because revenue agents are unlikely to suspect that anything is amiss when a taxpayer reports capital gain from the sale of property that is typically considered to be a capital asset (a share of stock, for example), but that actually would be ordinary income property under *Corn Products* in the particular circumstances. Revenue agents are more likely to question taxpayers who reported ordinary loss on the sale of such an asset. The Court's decision in *Arkansas Best* severely limited the scope of *Corn Products* and thus the cases where the taxpayer might claim an ordinary loss.

Note on Hedging Transactions

The Supreme Court's decision in *Arkansas Best* has had important implications for the treatment of hedging transactions, such as that entered into by Corn Products Refining Co. When *Corn Products* originally was decided, the determination whether an asset was a capital asset in the hedging context had significance only in terms of characterizing the loss or gain on disposition. With the addition of certain mark-to-market and loss deferral rules, however, the determination of what constitutes a capital asset also became important with respect to the timing of income and deductions because the applicability of these timing rules depends in part on whether a transaction produces ordinary income and loss. See § 1256.

Hedging is a risk management technique widely used by businesses to reduce or eliminate certain risks, for example, fluctuations in commodity prices, the relative value of different currencies, or interest rates. Consider the following simple example. T is a corn farmer who plants a crop of corn each spring at a cost of $10 a bushel. T is uncertain about the price at which he can sell the corn at the end of summer, but would like to lock in a $2 profit (i.e., he is willing to sacrifice any additional profit in order to eliminate the risk of a loss.) In order to hedge this price risk, T sells a forward contract for the amount of corn he expects to harvest. A forward contract is the right to purchase a certain quantity of a commodity at a fixed date in the future. T agrees to deliver a certain amount of corn in August for $12 a bushel. Thus, no matter what happens to the price of corn, T knows he can sell his crop for $12 a bushel. Suppose corn prices rise to $14 a bushel. T could sell his corn at the market price (making a $4 profit per bushel) and purchase corn on the market at $14 a bushel to satisfy the forward contract obligation. The loss on the forward contract transaction ($2) offsets the $4 profit on the corn, netting a $2 profit. If the market price falls to $10 a bushel, T will use his own corn to satisfy the forward contract, obtaining a price of $12 and profiting $2 a bushel.

In reality, T almost never actually delivers the corn. Instead, T will sell both the corn and the forward contract at their market prices. For example, if corn prices rise to $14 a bushel, T will sell the corn (producing a profit of $4), and buy out the holder of the contract for $2, the difference between the forward price ($12) and the market price ($14) (producing a $2 loss). If the price drops to $10, T will sell the corn and have no profit, but will have an offsetting gain on the sale of the forward contract of $2.

Notice that in each case, the gain (or loss) on the sale of the corn is reflected in the revenues on the sale of the inventory, which produces ordinary gain or loss. The offsetting loss (or gain) arises on a business hedge, which, for parity, also should produce an ordinary gain or loss. If, however, the loss is capital, the taxpayer may not be able to deduct it; on the other hand, if the gain is capital, the taxpayer obtains an unwarranted benefit.

Almost everyone agreed that supplies used by a business (cattle feed or jet fuel for example) as well as business hedges (the corn farmer's forward contract) should be treated as ordinary assets. But after *Arkansas Best*, there was a good deal of uncertainty and concern that taxpayers would be whipsawed, for example, by being required to report ordinary income on the sale of the inventory and a capital loss on a forward contract used to hedge the inventory price. Congress amended § 1221 in 1999 to clarify the law to exclude business hedges from the capital asset definition. § 1221(a)(7) and (8) and (b). The taxpayer must identify a hedging transaction as such on the day it is entered into to qualify for the exclusion. Recall that corporate capital gains are taxed at the same rate as ordinary income so, for a corporation, identifying a business hedging transaction as such operates to allow ordinary loss treatment if the value of the hedge declines.

NOTES

(A) *Timing and Character.* The character of a business hedge also may affect its timing. Section 1256 requires the holder of certain financial contracts and options to mark them to market at year end, requiring gain or loss to be recognized at that time. A business hedge that qualifies for ordinary treatment, however, generally is not subject to these mark-to-market rules. § 1256(e). Business hedges that are not eligible for ordinary income treatment are subject to the mark-to-market rules. The gain or loss is reported annually as 40 percent short-term gain or loss and 60 percent long-term gain or loss. § 1256(a). Furthermore, in some cases, taxpayers would not be permitted to take loss positions into account if the gain position was postponed.

(B) *Ongoing Vitality of* Corn Products? Although the Supreme Court's opinion in *Arkansas Best* appeared to sound a death knell for the *Corn*

Products doctrine, *Corn Products* continued to have some vitality although the addition to the Code of § 1221(a)(7) and (8) has eliminated its role in hedging cases. Because the opinion did not explicitly overrule *Corn Products*, the lower courts were left to determine the extent of the Supreme Court's retreat in *Arkansas Best*. For example, the Fifth Circuit treated a loss sustained by an employer on the sale of an employee's home as a capital loss. The employer had entered into an agreement to purchase the home if it fired the employee and it argued that the expense was a form of employee compensation. Relying on *Arkansas Best* for the view that a business purpose for acquisition was irrelevant, the court found that the house was not "used in the trade or business" as required by § 1221(a)(2). Azar Nut Co. v. Commissioner, 931 F.2d 314 (5th Cir. 1991). Note that if the employer simply had reimbursed the employee for his loss on the sale of the house, the payment would have been deductible as compensation.

7.   CAPITAL GAIN ON SMALL BUSINESS STOCK

In order to encourage investment in "small" companies, Congress has conferred capital gains treatment on a special kind of stock. § 1202. An individual can exclude 50 percent of the gain on the sale or exchange of "qualified small business stock" held for at least five years (60 percent if the stock is sold before the end of 2018). The includible portion is taxed at a maximum 28 percent rate; thus, the maximum effective tax rate on the gain is 14 percent. The amount of gain eligible for exclusion is the greater of ten times the taxpayer's basis in the stock or $10 million of gain on stock in the corporation. In order to use the exclusion, the taxpayer must have acquired the stock at its original issuance.

An eligible corporation is one whose net worth at the time of the issuance of the stock is $50 million or less. Furthermore, at least 80 percent of its assets must be used in the conduct of an active trade or business during substantially all of the taxpayer's holding period. Finally, the business conducted by the corporation must be something other than one where one of the principal assets of the business is the reputation of one or more of its employees (such as law, accounting, architecture, athletics, and financial services). The business also cannot involve banking, insurance, leasing, financing, investing, farming, or operating a hotel or restaurant. A taxpayer can elect to roll over the taxable portion of the gain on the sale of qualified small business stock by investing the proceeds in new qualified stock. The new stock must meet the active business requirement for the six-month period following the purchase. The holding period of the old stock is tacked to the new stock so that a total holding period of five years will qualify.

8.   DIVIDENDS

Dividends received on corporate stock are taxed as capital gains. Thus, they are also taxed at a maximum rate of 20 percent or a lower rate depending on the taxpayer's ordinary income tax rate. § 1(h)(11). "Dividend" is a term of art and refers to a distribution made by a corporation with respect to its stock. §§ 301, 316. Thus, salary, payments to creditors, and other transfers by corporations are not "dividends."

9. MEDICARE INVESTMENT TAX

As part of health care reform in 2010, Congress enacted a new Medicare tax on investment income. While the tax was enacted to help fund Medicare, eligibility and computation of the tax are dependent on income.

The tax applies to taxpayers who file jointly with adjusted gross income exceeding $250,000 and single taxpayers with adjusted gross income exceeding $200,000. The tax is equal to 3.8 percent of the lesser of (1) net investment income or (2) the excess of adjusted gross income over the threshold. Net investment income includes interest, dividends, royalties, rents, capital gains, and income and gains from a passive activity minus deductions attributable to that income. For example, a couple with an AGI of $500,000 and a $100,000 net capital gain would owe an income tax on the capital gain of $20,000 and an investment tax of $3,800. This is still significantly less than the maximum 37 percent tax on ordinary income or wages (which would also be subject to the payroll taxes).

Note that this tax also contains a marriage penalty. Two single taxpayers with adjusted gross incomes of $200,000 would not owe any Medicare tax on their capital gains and dividends, regardless of their size. If they married, however, they would owe the 3.8 percent Medicare tax.

B. JUDICIAL GLOSS ON THE STATUTE—THE COMMON LAW OF CAPITAL GAINS

The language of § 1221 implies that all property qualifies as a capital asset unless it is specifically excluded under the exceptions enumerated in paragraphs (a)(1) to (8) of that section. The favorable tax rates and the vagaries that would result from applying § 1221 literally have prompted the courts to narrow the scope of the definition of capital asset beyond the statutory requirements although, as we have seen, the Court in *Arkansas Best* rejected that approach.

Before the *Arkansas Best* decision, courts had adopted two general approaches to decide whether assets that literally come within the scope of § 1221 nevertheless should be denied capital gains treatment. These approaches were described in Michot v. Commissioner, 43 T.C.M. 792, 794 (1982):

> First, some cases derive from [Commissioner v.] Gillette Motor Co., [364 U.S. 130 (1960),] the rule that all that is property in a common sense is not property within the meaning of Section 1221. See, *e.g., Commissioner v. Ferrer,* 304 F.2d 125 (2d Cir. 1962) * * *. Second, other cases, relying on *Commissioner v. P.G.*

Lake, Inc., 356 U.S. 260 (1958) and *Hort v. Commissioner*, 313 U.S. 28 (1941), deny capital asset status when a substitute for future ordinary income is perceived.

Importantly, all of the cases cited above in *Michot* maintained their vitality after the *Arkansas Best* decision.

1.   DISPOSITIONS OF LEASES, LIFE ESTATES, CONTRACTS, AND OTHER INTERESTS

This Section examines a variety of controversies over eligibility for capital gain treatment for dispositions of leases, life estates, contracts, and other interests. Often these cases turn on the relationship of the interest transferred to the property retained by the taxpayer. Sometimes, this is done by asking whether there has been a "sale or exchange" of a capital asset. Although there must be both a "sale or exchange" and a capital asset, the two doctrines are often intermingled. Cases dealing explicitly with the sale or exchange requirement are discussed infra at page 628.

The courts' reluctance to find capital gain when the interest disposed of is a portion of a larger property resembles their reluctance to permit effective assignments of income when something less than the taxpayer's entire property interest is transferred. Recall *Horst* and *Blair* from the preceding Chapter. Distinctions routinely are drawn between so-called "vertical slices," transfers of an interest coterminous with the seller's rights, and "horizontal slices," where the disposition involves a right "carved out" of a larger interest for a shorter period of time. Capital gain treatment is more likely for the former than the latter. As in the assignment of income context, the cases here are haunted by the "fruit v. tree" metaphor.

Hort v. Commissioner
This case appears supra at page 146.

NOTES

(A) *Rights to Future Income.* The court in *Hort* characterized the lump sum payment for cancellation of the lease as a substitute for "nothing more than the relinquishment of the right to future rental payments." Why should this characterization be dispositive of the capital gains issue? Isn't the value of property generally the present value of its future income stream and thus are not all sales of capital assets essentially relinquishments of the right to future ordinary income?

This "substitute for ordinary income" standard, while frequently adopted by the courts, can provide at most only a clue whether ordinary income or capital gains treatment is appropriate. In a rough way, the capital gains provisions require distinguishing returns to capital (interest, rents, royalties, and the like), which should be taxed as ordinary income, from appreciation in the value of an asset, which should qualify as capital gain when the asset is sold.

(B) *Changes in Value Due to Changes in the Economy—the Landlord.* Suppose the tenant in *Hort* had simply prepaid the rent by transferring the present value of all the rental payments. The landlord clearly would have reported ordinary income. In *Hort* the general decline in rental prices caused by the Depression made the lease more valuable to the lessor at the time of the cancellation in 1934 than it had been when entered into in 1927. Is this the kind of appreciation that should be subject to capital gains rates? Is it any different from appreciation of a bond bearing a high interest rate during a period when interest rates are falling? If Hort had sold the building and land subject to the lease, he would have received capital gains treatment. Why does the sale of the lease alone suggest a different result?

(C) *Changes in Value Due to Changes in the Economy—the Tenant.* Suppose the tenant has a lease with terms more favorable than the current market and the tenant sells the leasehold for a premium. The amount received is a capital gain. Rev. Rul. 72–85, 1972–1 C.B. 234. Why are the landlord and the tenant treated differently? Is it because the lease is a "tree" to the tenant but a "fruit" to the landlord? What if the tenant sold only several years' worth of his leasehold for a premium?

Commissioner v. P.G. Lake, Inc.

Supreme Court of the United States, 1958. 356 U.S. 260.

■ MR. JUSTICE DOUGLAS delivered the opinion of the Court.

* * *

Lake is a corporation engaged in the business of producing oil and gas. It has a seven-eighths working interest[1] in two commercial oil and gas leases. In 1950 it was indebted to its president in the sum of $600,000 and in consideration of his cancellation of the debt assigned him an oil payment right in the amount of $600,000, plus an amount equal to interest at 3 percent a year on the unpaid balance remaining from month to month, payable out of 25 percent of the oil attributable to the taxpayer's working interest in the two leases. At the time of the assignment it could have been estimated with reasonable accuracy that the assigned oil payment right would pay out in three or more years. It did in fact pay out in a little over three years.

---

[1] An oil and gas lease ordinarily conveys the entire mineral interest less any royalty interest retained by the lessor. The owner of the lease is said to own the "working interest" because he has the right to develop and produce the minerals.

In Anderson v. Helvering, 310 U.S. 404, we described an oil payment as "the right to a specified sum of money, payable out of a specified percentage of the oil, or the proceeds received from the sale of such oil, if, as and when produced." Id., at 410. A royalty interest is "a right to receive a specified percentage of all oil and gas produced" but, unlike the oil payment, is not limited to a specified sum of money. The royalty interest lasts during the entire term of the lease. Id. at 409.

In its 1950 tax return Lake reported the oil payment assignment as a sale of property producing a profit of $600,000 and taxable as a long-term capital gain under § 117 of the Internal Revenue Code of 1939. The Commissioner determined a deficiency, ruling that the purchase price (less deductions not material here) was taxable as ordinary income, subject to depletion. * * *

First, as to whether the proceeds were taxable as long-term capital gains * * * or as ordinary income subject to depletion. The Court of Appeals started from the premise, laid down in Texas decisions, see especially Tennant v. Dunn, 130 Tex. 285, 110 S.W.2d 53, that oil payments are interests in land. We too proceed on that basis; and yet we conclude that the consideration received for these oil payment rights * * * was taxable as ordinary income, subject to depletion.

The purpose of [the capital gains provision] was "to relieve the taxpayer from * * * excessive tax burdens on gains resulting from a conversion of capital investments, and to remove the deterrent effect of those burdens on such conversions." See Burnet v. Harmel, 287 U.S. 103, 106. And this exception has always been narrowly construed so as to protect the revenue against artful devices. See Corn Products Refining Co. v. Commissioner, 350 U.S. 46, 52.

We do not see here any conversion of a capital investment. The lump sum consideration seems essentially a substitute for what would otherwise be received at a future time as ordinary income. The payout of these particular assigned oil payment rights could be ascertained with considerable accuracy. Such are the stipulations, findings, or clear inferences. * * * [C]ash was received which was equal to the amount of the income to accrue during the term of the assignment, the assignee being compensated by interest on his advance. The substance of what was assigned was the right to receive future income. The substance of what was received was the present value of income which the recipient would otherwise obtain in the future. In short, consideration was paid for the right to receive future income, not for an increase in the value of the income-producing property.

These arrangements seem to us transparent devices. Their forms do not control. Their essence is determined not by subtleties of draftsmanship but by their total effect. * * * We have held that if one, entitled to receive at a future date interest on a bond or compensation for services, makes a grant of it by anticipatory assignment, he realizes taxable income as if he had collected the interest or received the salary and then paid it over. That is the teaching of Helvering v. Horst, 311 U.S. 112, * * * and it is applicable here. As we stated in Helvering v. Horst, supra, 117, "The taxpayer has equally enjoyed the fruits of his labor or investment and obtained the satisfaction of his desires whether he collects and uses the income to procure those satisfactions, or whether he disposes of his right to collect it as the means of procuring them." There the taxpayer detached interest coupons from negotiable bonds and presented them as a gift to his son. The interest when paid was held taxable to the father. Here, even more clearly than there, the taxpayer is converting future income into present income.

* * *

Reversed.

NOTES

(A) *Nature of the Asset vs. Method of Payment.* Why is the ability to estimate accurately the future payout of the assigned oil payment important to the Court? Has the Court applied *Corn Products* to find no capital asset in this case? Or is the Court relying on the lack of a sale or exchange, that is, the lack of "any conversion of a capital asset?" In other words, is the nature of the assets sold or the method of payment determinative here?

(B) *Sales of Income. P.G. Lake* should be compared with Rhodes' Estate v. Commissioner, 131 F.2d 50 (6th Cir. 1942), in which the taxpayer owned 600 shares on which a dividend of $20 per share had been declared. He sold his dividend rights for $11,925 before the dividend was payable. The taxpayer argued that the sale of the dividend rights constituted capital gains. In a per curiam opinion, citing assignment of income cases, the court held that the sale of the dividend rights produced ordinary income. In both *P.G. Lake* and *Rhodes' Estate,* future ordinary income was sold for its present value, and the income interest was sold while the income-generating asset was retained. In neither case did the sales price reflect market appreciation or depreciation. Only if one is concerned about bunching of income—in these cases, a taxpayer's voluntary bunching of income—is there an argument for treating the amount received as capital gain.

(C) *Section 636.* Congress changed the specific result of the *P.G. Lake* case when it enacted § 636 in 1969 to provide new rules governing production payments. The sale of a carved-out production payment is treated as a loan. The seller remains taxable on the income from the oil produced and is entitled to deductions for depletion. He can deduct the interest element of the payments. The purchaser of the payment is taxable only on the interest and cannot deduct depletion. An owner who sells a well and retains a production payment is treated as having made a sale subject to a mortgage. The purchaser is taxable on the proceeds of production and is entitled to depletion deductions.

(D) *Slicing the Asset: Horizontal vs. Vertical Slices.* What if the taxpayer in *P.G. Lake* had sold the entire leasehold interest? In United States v. Dresser Industries, Inc., 324 F.2d 56 (5th Cir. 1963), the taxpayer had been granted an exclusive right to practice a patent on a new method of surveying for oil wells. The taxpayer later relinquished the "exclusive" feature of the contract in exchange for $500,000. The court distinguished *P.G. Lake:*

> The taxpayer here is cutting off a "vertical slice" of its rights, rather than carving out an interest from the totality of its rights under the grant. The interest transferred was not to terminate when a certain

amount was paid, as was so in *Lake,* and taxpayer retained no reversionary interest in the "exclusivity" feature transferred. The tree was sold along with the fruit, at least insofar as that branch was concerned.

* * *

We conclude, therefore, that the sale was not merely the present sale of the right to earned income, to be paid in the future. Taxpayer had an asset, a right, a property which would produce income. The fact that the income which *could* be earned would be ordinary income is immaterial; such would be true of the sale of all income-producing property.

(E) *Disposition of a Life Estate.* In Bell's Estate v. Commissioner, 137 F.2d 454 (8th Cir. 1943), the court held that a transfer by a life tenant of his interest in a trust to the remainderman produced capital gain. The court found that the taxpayers sold interests in property and not "income or the naked rights to receive income." What distinguishes the life estate in *Bell's Estate* (which was treated as a capital asset) from the oil production payment in *P.G. Lake* or from the lease in *Hort* (which were treated as ordinary assets)? Is it the probable term of the future interest? The method of the transfer? The nature of the property transferred? The fact that the transferor conveyed all that he had? Suppose the consideration for the life estate had been paid in installments over a number of years. Should that have affected the result? Suppose it had been paid in the form of an annuity, payable to the life tenant each year as long as she lived. Would there still be capital gain or loss? Suppose the life tenants had not sold the life estate but collected the income (their only right)?

(F) *Conversion Transactions.* The difference between the maximum tax rate on ordinary income and that on capital gains creates an incentive to convert ordinary income into capital gains. One of the most common ways to do this is to disguise interest—or payments attributable to the time value of money—as capital gain. Increasingly, Congress has adopted statutory provisions designed to prevent this conversion.

Section 1258, for example, recharacterizes the capital gain on a so-called "conversion transaction" as ordinary income. The general idea is to target transactions in which the taxpayer's economic position is similar to that of a lender and thus the return should be treated as ordinary income, as interest is. Broadly speaking, a conversion transaction is one consisting of two or more positions taken with regard to the same or similar property, where substantially all of the taxpayer's return is attributable to the time value of the net investment. The taxpayer bears no significant risks other than those usually borne by a lender. Conversion transactions include straddles, transactions marketed or sold on the basis that they produce capital gain, and the acquisition of property and a contemporaneous agreement to sell the same property in the future. Treasury may designate other conversion transactions. § 1258(c)(2).

The amount of the gain that is treated as ordinary income cannot exceed the interest the taxpayer would have earned if the rate were 120 percent of the applicable federal rate. For example, suppose T purchases stock for $100 on January 1 and, at the same time, enters into a forward contract to sell the stock for $105 on January 1 of the following year. This is economically similar to a loan for a year where T is to receive 5 percent interest. Assuming the applicable federal rate is greater than 4 percent, $5 of the sales price is ordinary income. If the applicable federal rate was less than 4 percent, part of the gain would be capital gain and, in any event, the gain, unlike interest, would be deferred until the sale takes place.

2. WHAT IS THE MEANING OF PROPERTY?

Taxpayers commonly receive payments pursuant to contracts. In some settings, questions arise whether the payments represent gain (or loss) on the exchange of property—or whether, instead, the payments represent ordinary income.

One famous instance involved the noted actor José Ferrer. In 1950, Ferrer entered into a contract that granted him the right to stage a production of a play based on a novel called "Moulin Rouge." The well-known film director John Huston became interested in the project, and the parties agreed to abandon the stage play in favor of a motion picture (starring Ferrer, of course). Ferrer's contract with Huston's film production company called for the actor to receive a number of payments, including salary plus a percentage of net profits.

In the tax year 1953, Ferrer received total payments of roughly $100,000 in salary and $200,000 in "Participating Interests" payments based on net profits. On his tax return, Ferrer reported the former as ordinary income and the latter as a long-term capital gain on the sale of his rights to the stage play (which he surrendered in agreeing to make the film).

The film was a success, garnering seven Academy Award nominations, including one for Best Actor for Ferrer. Ferrer was surely less thrilled when the IRS took an interest. The IRS asserted that all of the amounts Ferrer received constituted ordinary income.

In Commissioner v. Ferrer, 304 F. 2d 125 (2d Cir. 1962), the Second Circuit split the $200,000 payment into two parts, one capital and one ordinary, based on the court's analysis of the terms of the initial contract for the production of the stage play. The contract, the court found, had granted Ferrer ownership of the rights to produce the stage play, and the Huston company's payment for these, accordingly, was capital gain. But the initial contract did not vest in Ferrer ownership of the motion picture rights; instead, the author of the play retained those rights and granted Ferrer only a contingent right to participate in the proceeds of a sale of motion picture rights. The payment Ferrer received in exchange for this participation right, accordingly, represented compensation for a stream of ordinary income and, as such, was itself ordinary.

Ferrer remains good law to this day, but the legal distinction between capital and ordinary contract payments remains difficult to explain, as the next case illustrates.

Lattera v. Commissioner

United States Court of Appeals, Third Circuit, 2006. 437 F.3d 399.

■ AMBRO, CIRCUIT JUDGE:

Lottery winners, after receiving several annual installments of their lottery prize, sold for a lump sum the right to their remaining payments. They reported their sale proceeds as capital gains on their tax return, but the Internal Revenue Service (IRS) classified those proceeds as ordinary income. The substitute-for-ordinary-income doctrine holds that lump-sum consideration substituting for something that would otherwise be received at a future time as ordinary income should be taxed the same way. We agree with the Commissioner of the IRS that the lump-sum consideration paid for the right to lottery payments is ordinary income.

I.   Factual Background and Procedural History

In June 1991 George and Angeline Lattera turned a one-dollar lottery ticket into $9,595,326 [payable over 26 years] in the Pennsylvania Lottery. They did not then have the option to take the prize in a single lump-sum payment, so they were entitled to 26 annual installments of $369,051.

In September 1999 the Latteras sold their rights to the 17 remaining lottery payments to Singer Asset Finance Co., LLC for $3,372,342. * * * On their joint tax return, the Latteras reported this sale as the sale of a capital asset held for more than one year. They reported a sale price of $3,372,342, a cost or other basis of zero, and a long-term capital gain of the full sale price. The Commissioner determined that this sale price was ordinary income.

* * *

III. Discussion

The lottery payments the Latteras had a right to receive were gambling winnings, and the parties agree that the annual payments were ordinary income. * * * But the Latteras argue that when they sold the right to their remaining lottery payments, that sale gave rise to a long-term capital gain.

Whether the sale of a right to lottery payments by a lottery winner can be treated as a capital gain under the Internal Revenue Code is one of first impression in our Circuit. But it is not a new question. Both the Tax Court and the Ninth Circuit Court of Appeals have held that such sales deserve ordinary-income treatment. *United States v. Maginnis*, 356 F.3d 1179, 1181 (9th Cir. 2004) *Davis v. Comm'r*, 119 T.C. 1, 1 (2002).

* * * [W]e propose a different approach. We begin with a discussion of basic concepts that underlie our reasoning.

A.   Definition of a capital asset

A long-term capital gain (or loss) is created by the "sale or exchange of a capital asset held for more than 1 year." I.R.C. § 1222(3). Section 1221 of the Internal Revenue Code defines a capital asset as "property held by the taxpayer (whether or not connected with his trade or business)." This provision excludes from the definition certain property categories, none of which is applicable here.

A 1960 Supreme Court decision suggested that this definition can be construed too broadly, stating that "it is evident that not everything which can be called property in the ordinary sense and which is outside the statutory exclusions qualifies as a capital asset." *Comm'r v. Gillette Motor Transp., Inc.*, 364 U.S. 130, 134 (1960). The Court noted that it had "long held that the term 'capital asset' is to be construed narrowly in accordance with the purpose of Congress to afford capital-gains treatment only in situations typically involving the realization of appreciation in value accrued over a substantial period of time, and thus to ameliorate the hardship of taxation of the entire gain in one year." *Id.* But the Supreme Court's decision in *Arkansas Best Corp. v. Commissioner*, 485 U.S. 212 (1988), at least at first blush, seems to have reversed that narrow reading. *Arkansas Best* suggests instead that the capital-asset definition is to be broadly construed. *See id.* at 218.

B.   The substitute-for-ordinary-income doctrine

The problem with an overly broad definition for capital assets is that it could "encompass some things Congress did not intend to be taxed as capital gains." *Maginnis*, 356 F.3d at 1181. An overly broad definition, linked with favorable capital-gains tax treatment, would encourage transactions designed to convert ordinary income into capital gains. *See id.* at 1182. For example, a salary is taxed as ordinary income, and the right to be paid for work is a person's property. But it is hard to conceive that Congress intends for taxpayers to get capital-gains treatment if they were to sell their rights (*i.e.*, "property held by the taxpayer") to their future paychecks.

To get around this problem, courts have created the substitute-for-ordinary-income doctrine. This doctrine says, in effect, that " 'lump sum consideration [that] seems essentially a substitute for what would otherwise be received at a future time as ordinary income' may not be taxed as a capital gain." *Maginnis*, 356 F.3d at 1182 (quoting *Commissioner v. P. G. Lake, Inc.*, 356 U.S. 260, 265, 78 S. Ct. 691, 2 L. Ed. 2d 743, 1958–1 C.B. 516 (1958)) (alteration in original).

The seminal substitute-for-ordinary-income case is the 1941 Supreme Court decision in *Hort v. Commissioner*, 313 U.S. 28, 61 S. Ct. 757, 85 L. Ed. 1168, 1941–1 C.B. 319 (1941). * * * The Supreme Court bolstered the doctrine in *Lake*. * * *

The Latteras argue that the substitute-for-ordinary-income doctrine, which takes "property held by the taxpayer" outside the statutory capital-asset definition, did not survive *Arkansas Best*. But although *Arkansas Best* ostensibly cabined the exceptions to the statutory definition, it made clear that the *Hort-Lake* "line of cases, based on the premise that § 1221 'property' does not include claims or rights to ordinary income, had no application in the present context." *Arkansas Best*, 485 U.S. at 217 n.5. The Tax Court has several times confirmed that *Arkansas Best* "in no way affected the viability of the principle established in the [*Hort-Lake*] line of cases." *Davis*, 119 T.C. at 6 (citing cases). And the Ninth Circuit agrees. *Maginnis*, 356 F.3d at 1185. We follow suit, holding that the substitute-for-ordinary-income doctrine remains viable in the wake of *Arkansas Best*.

But there is a tension in the doctrine: in theory, all capital assets are substitutes for ordinary income. * * * For example, a stock's value is the present discounted value of the company's future profits. *See, e.g., Maginnis*, 356 F.3d at 1182; *cf. United States v. Dresser Indus., Inc.*, 324 F.2d 56, 59 (5th Cir. 1963) (applying this concept to the value of land). [A]n "overbroad 'substitute for ordinary income' doctrine, besides being analytically unsatisfactory, would create the potential for the abuse of treating capital losses as ordinary." The doctrine must therefore be limited so as not to err on either side.

C.   The lottery cases

* * *

In 2004 the Ninth Circuit decided *Maginnis*, the first (and so far only) appellate opinion to deal with this question. Maginnis won $9 million [payable over time] in a lottery and, after receiving five of his lottery payments, assigned all of his remaining future lottery payments to a third party for a lump-sum payment of $3,950,000. *Maginnis*, 356 F.3d at 1180. The Ninth Circuit held that Maginnis's right to future lottery payments was not a capital asset and that the lump-sum payment was to be taxed as ordinary income. *Id.* at 1182.

The Court relied on the substitute-for-ordinary-income doctrine, but it was concerned about taking an "approach that could potentially convert all capital gains into ordinary income [or] one that could convert all ordinary income into capital gains." *Id.* The Court opted instead for "case-by-case judgments as to whether the conversion of income rights into lump-sum payments reflects the sale of a capital asset that produces a capital gain, or whether it produces ordinary income." *Id.* It set out two factors, which it characterized as "crucial to [its] conclusion," but not "dispositive in all cases": "Maginnis (1) did not make any underlying investment of capital in return for the receipt of his lottery right, and (2) the sale of his right did not reflect an accretion in value over cost to any underlying asset Maginnis held." *Id.* at 1183.

* * * The first factor—underlying investment of capital—would theoretically subject all inherited and gifted property (which involves no investment at all) to ordinary-income treatment. It also does not explain the result in *Lake*, where the company presumably made an investment in its working interest in oil and gas leases, yet the Supreme Court applied ordinary-income treatment. *Id.*

The second factor also presents analytical problems. Not all capital assets experience an accretion in value over cost. For example, cars typically depreciate, but they are often capital assets. * * * The *Maginnis* Court held that there was no accretion of value over cost in lottery winnings because there was no cost, as "Maginnis did not make any capital investment in exchange for his lottery right." 356 F.3d at 1184. But if Maginnis's purchase of a lottery ticket had been a capital investment, would the second factor automatically have been satisfied? (That is, the "cost" in that scenario would have been $1, and the increase would have been $3,949,999.) Our first instinct is no. Moreover, the second factor does not seem to predict correctly the result in both *Hort* (where a building was inherited for no "cost") and *Lake* (where the working interest in the oil lease presumably had a "cost"), in both of which the taxpayer got ordinary-income treatment.

Thus, while we agree with *Maginnis*'s result, we do not simply adopt its reasoning. And it is both unsatisfying and unhelpful to future litigants to declare that we know this to be ordinary income when we see it. * * *

We therefore proceed to our case-by-case analysis, but in doing so we set out a method for analysis that guides our result. At the same time, however, we recognize that any rule we create could not account for every contemplated transactional variation.

D.   Substitute-for-ordinary-income analysis

In our attempt to craft a rubric, we find helpful a Second Circuit securities case and a recent student comment. The Second Circuit dealt with a similarly "seamless spectrum" in 1976 when it needed to decide whether a note was a security for purposes of section 10(b) of the 1934 Securities and Exchange Act. *See Exch. Nat'l Bank of Chi. v. Touche Ross & Co.*, 544 F.2d 1126, 1138 (2d Cir. 1976). The Court created a "family resemblance" test. * * * We adopt an analogous analysis. Several types of assets we know to be capital: stocks, bonds, options, and currency contracts, for example. *See, e.g., Arkansas Best*, 485 U.S. at 222–23 (holding—even though, as noted above, the value of a stock is really the present discounted value of the company's future profits—that "stock is most naturally viewed as a capital asset"). We could also include in this category physical assets like land and automobiles.

Similarly, there are several types of rights that we know to be ordinary income, *e.g.*, rental income and interest income. In *Gillette Motor*, the Supreme Court held that ordinary-income treatment was indicated for the right to use another's property—rent, in other words.

See 364 U.S. at 135. Similarly, in *Midland-Ross*, the Supreme Court held that earned original issue discount should be taxed as ordinary income. *See United States v. Midland-Ross Corp.*, 381 U.S. 54, 58, 85 S. Ct. 1308, 14 L. Ed. 2d 214 (1965). There, the taxpayer purchased non-interest-bearing notes at a discount from the face amount and sold them for more than their issue price (but still less than the face amount). *Id.* at 55. This gain was conceded to be equivalent to interest, and the Court held it taxable as ordinary income. *Id.* at 55–56, 58. For the "family resemblance" test, we can set those two categories at the opposite poles of our analysis. For example, we presume that stock, and things that look and act like stock, will receive capital-gains treatment. For the in-between transactions that do not bear a family resemblance to the items in either category, like contracts and payment rights, we use two factors to assist in our analysis: (1) type of "carve-out" and (2) character of asset.[4]

1.   *Type of carve-out*

The notion of the carve-out, or partial sale, has significant explanatory power in the context of the *Hort-Lake* line of cases. * * * There are two ways of carving out interests from property: horizontally and vertically. A horizontal carve-out is one in which "temporal divisions [are made] in a property interest in which the person owning the interest disposes of part of his interest but also retains a portion of it." In lottery terms, this is what happened in *Davis* * * *—the lottery winners sold some of their future lottery payment rights (*e.g.*, their 2006 and 2007 payments) but retained the rights to payments further in the future (*e.g.*, their 2008 and 2009 payments). *Davis*, 119 T.C. at 3. This is also what happened in *Hort* and *Lake*; portions of the total interest (a term of years carved out from a fee simple and a three-year payment right from a working interest in an oil lease, respectively) were carved out from the whole.

A vertical carve-out is one in which "a complete disposition of a person's interest in property" is made. In lottery terms, this is what happened in *Maginnis*—the lottery winners sold the rights to all their remaining lottery payments. *See Maginnis*, 356 F.3d at 1181 (noting that the lottery winner assigned his right to receive all his remaining lottery payments). Horizontal carve-outs typically lead to ordinary-income treatment. *See, e.g., Maginnis*, 356 F.3d at 1185–86 ("Maginnis is correct that transactions in which a taxpayer transfers an income right without transferring his entire interest in an underlying asset will often be occasions for applying the substitute for ordinary income doctrine."). This was also the result reached in *Hort* and *Lake*. *Lake*, 356 U.S. at 264; *Hort*, 313 U.S. at 32.

---

[4]   We borrow these factors from Thomas Sinclair, Comment, *Limiting the Substitute-for-Ordinary Income Doctrine: An Analysis Through Its Most Recent Application Involving the Sale of Future Lottery Rights*, 56 S.C. L. Rev. 387, 401–03, but we differ from him slightly in the way we apply the character factor. [Ed. Note: This case should give hope to all those who believe that law review student comments go unread.]

Vertical carve-outs are different. In *Dresser Industries*, for example, the Fifth Circuit distinguished *Lake* because the taxpayer in *Dresser* had "cut[ ] off a 'vertical slice' of its rights, rather than carved out an interest from the totality of its rights." *Dresser Indus.*, 324 F.2d at 58. But as the results in *Maginnis* and *Watkins* demonstrate, a vertical carve-out does not necessarily mean that the transaction receives capital-gains treatment. * * *

Because a vertical carve-out could signal either capital-gains or ordinary-income treatment, we must make another determination to conclude with certainty which treatment should apply. Therefore, when we see a vertical carve-out, we proceed to the second factor—character of the asset—to determine whether the sale proceeds should be taxed as ordinary income or capital gain.

2.   *Character of the asset*

The Fifth Circuit in *Dresser Industries* noted that "there is, in law and fact, a vast difference between the present sale of the future right to *earn* income and the present sale of the future right to *earned* income." *Dresser Indus.*, 324 F.2d at 59 (emphasis in original). The taxpayer in *Dresser Industries* had assigned its right to an exclusive patent license back to the patent holder in exchange for a share of the licensing fees from third-party licensees. *Id.* at 57. The Court used this "right to earn income"/"right to earned income" distinction to hold that capital-gains treatment was applicable. It noted that the asset sold was not a "right to earned income, to be paid in the future," but was "a property which would produce income." *Id.* at 59. Further, it disregarded the ordinary nature of the income generated by the asset; because "all income-producing property" produces ordinary income, the sale of such property does not result in ordinary-income treatment. *Id.* (This can be seen in the sale of stocks or bonds, both of which produce ordinary income, but the sale of which is treated as capital gain.)

Sinclair explains the concept in this way: "Earned income conveys the concept that the income has already been earned and the holder of the right to this income only has to collect it. In other words, the owner of the right to earned income is entitled to the income merely by virtue of owning the property." Sinclair, *supra*, at 406. He gives as examples of this concept rental income, stock dividends, and rights to future lottery payments. For the right to earn income, on the other hand, "the holder of such right must do something further to earn the income . . . [because] mere ownership of the right to earn income does not entitle the owner to income." Sinclair, *supra*, at 406. Following *Dresser Industries*, Sinclair gives a patent as an example of this concept. *Id.* Assets that constitute a right to earn income merit capital-gains treatment, while those that are a right to earned income merit ordinary-income treatment. * * *

Similarly, when an erstwhile employee is paid a termination fee for a personal-services contract, that employee still possesses the asset (the right to provide certain personal services) and the money (the termination fee) has already been "earned" and will simply be paid. The employee no longer has to perform any more services in exchange for the fee, so this is not like *Dresser Industries*'s "right to earn income." These termination fees are therefore rights to earned income and should be treated as ordinary income.

* * *

E.   Application of the "family resemblance" test

Applied to this case, the "family resemblance" test draws out as follows. First, we try to determine whether an asset is like either the "capital asset" category of assets (*e.g.*, stocks, bonds, or land) or like the "income items" category (*e.g.*, rental income or interest income). If the asset does not bear a family resemblance to items in either of those categories, we move to the following factors.

We look at the nature of the sale. If the sale or assignment constitutes a horizontal carve-out, then ordinary-income treatment presumably applies. If, on the other hand, it constitutes a vertical carve-out, then we look to the character-of-the-asset factor. There, if the sale is a lump-sum payment for a future right to *earned* income, we apply ordinary-income treatment, but if it is a lump-sum payment for a future right to *earn* income, we apply capital-gains treatment.

Turning back to the Latteras, the right to receive annual lottery payments does not bear a strong family resemblance to either the "capital assets" or the "income items" listed at the polar ends of the analytical spectrum. The Latteras sold their right to all their remaining lottery payments, so this is a vertical carve-out, which could indicate either capital-gains or ordinary-income treatment. But because a right to lottery payments is a right to earned income (*i.e.*, the payments will keep arriving due simply to ownership of the asset), the lump-sum payment received by the Latteras should receive ordinary-income treatment.

This result comports with *Davis* and *Maginnis*. It also ensures that the Latteras do not "receive a tax advantage as compared to those taxpayers who would simply choose originally to accept their lottery winning in the form of a lump sum payment," something that was also important to the *Maginnis* Court. *Maginnis*, 356 F.3d at 1184.

IV. Conclusion

The lump-sum consideration paid to the Latteras in exchange for the right to their future lottery payments is ordinary income. We therefore affirm.

NOTES

(A) *More Winners and Losers*. Five circuit courts have issued opinions on facts substantially identical to those in *Lattera*. All five courts agreed that the sale of future lottery proceeds clearly produced ordinary income, but they could not agree on the reason. The Ninth Circuit in *Maginnis* (discussed in

Lattera) placed great emphasis on the lack of an underlying investment and the fact that the sale did not reflect an accretion in value over the cost of any underlying asset. The Eleventh Circuit also focused on the differences between lottery rights and the typical capital asset—an increase in value of an original investment. Womack v. Commissioner, 510 F.3d 1295 (11th Cir. 2007). The Tenth Circuit decided that it did not need to formulate any specific test under the substitute-for-ordinary-income doctrine. Watkins v. Commissioner, 447 F.3d 1269 (10th Cir. 2006). The Second Circuit adopted a "you will know it when you see it approach," noting "whatever the doctrine's outer limits, this case falls squarely within them." Prebola v. Commissioner, 482 F.3d 610 (2d Cir. 2007).

(B) *The Purchaser.* The purchaser of the lottery payments from the Latteras presumably paid the present value of the stream of payments. Suppose interest rates change and the value of the payments increases and the purchaser re-sells them. Would he have ordinary income or capital gains?

(C) *Body Parts.* Suppose a taxpayer sells blood, eggs, an embryo, or other body parts. The cash received is clearly income, but is it capital or ordinary? That depends on whether the donor has transferred property or has rendered services. In Rev. Rul. 53–162, 1953–2 C.B. 127, the Service held that the donation of blood is a contribution of services and thus not eligible for a charitable contribution deduction. Green v. Commissioner, 74 T.C. 1229 (1980), however, held that a sale of blood constituted the sale of property rather than a transfer of services. In dictum, the court noted that the taxpayer, who had a rare type of blood that was much in demand was in the trade or business of selling her blood plasma and therefore the gain was ordinary under § 1221(a)(1). If a body part is property, and the taxpayer contributes only once or rarely, the statute seems to treat it as a capital asset. Is this the type of property that should receive favorable capital gains treatment?

In Perez v. Commissioner, 144 T.C. 51 (2015), the Tax Court required an egg donor to report income received under a contract as a payment for services rendered rather than for a sale of property. The court distinguished *Green* by noting that the taxpayer in that case was paid by the quantity and quality of plasma produced whereas Perez's payments were based solely on how far into the egg-retrieval process she went. Perez had also argued that the payments should be exempt from income under § 104(a)(2) as damages for pain and suffering, but the court rejected that argument since she had voluntarily contracted to endure the pain.

(D) *Bitcoin.* The IRS has determined that Bitcoin is property and not currency. Notice 2014–21, 2014–16 I.R.B. 938. Thus, Bitcoin received in exchange for services or property is taxable at the time of receipt—the value is the U.S. dollar value of the Bitcoin. If a buyer uses Bitcoin to pay for services or property, she may have gain recognition if the value of the Bitcoin has increased since acquisition. For example, if she bought Bitcoin for $700 and uses it when it is worth $800 to buy an $800 computer, she has $100 of gain on the disposition of property, i.e., the Bitcoin. If she had "mined" the Bitcoin when it was worth $700, she would have the same result because mined Bitcoins are taxable on receipt and thus she would have a basis of

$700. The IRS and other tax agencies around the world have expressed concerns that Bitcoin and its progeny are being used to evade income taxes.

3.   EFFECT OF PRIOR TRANSACTIONS

Cummings v. Commissioner

United States Court of Appeals, Second Circuit, 1974. 506 F.2d 449,
cert. denied 421 U.S. 913 (1975).

■ IRVING R. KAUFMAN, CHIEF JUDGE:

The interplay of two distinct statutory schemes often gives rise to some engrossing legal questions. In this case, we are called upon to consider the relationship of the Internal Revenue Code and the securities laws—in particular, the proper tax treatment of a payment made in satisfaction of an apparent liability under § 16(b) of the Securities Exchange Act. We find that the policies of both statutes support the determination of the Commissioner of Internal Revenue that § 16(b) repayments should be treated as long term capital losses, and reverse the decision of the Tax Court allowing a deduction as an ordinary and necessary business expense.

I

Unlike those in many tax cases, the facts here are relatively straightforward. Nathan Cummings, chairman of the board and chief executive officer of Consolidated Food Corporation, was offered a large bloc of stock in Metro-Goldwyn-Mayer, Inc. [MGM] during 1959. He was told that the company was experiencing management problems, and that if he would become a director, three members of the board who were involved in controversy would resign. Cummings then purchased 51,500 shares of MGM stock for something more than $1,030,000, and was elected to the board after the three directors resigned.

The price of MGM stock rose, and on April 17, 1961, Cummings sold 3400 shares for a total of $227,648.28. His profit was properly reported as a long term capital gain on the 1961 tax return which he and his wife jointly filed. Between September 18 and October 2, 1961, however, Cummings bought back 3000 shares for $146,960.89. This purchase, within six months after the sale, brought him within the likely purview of § 16(b) of the Securities Exchange Act, making the difference between the sale price and the purchase price, $53,870.81, recoverable by MGM. Cummings was apparently unaware of his liability until soon after MGM, in preparation for its 1962 annual meeting, submitted its proxy material to the Securities and Exchange Commission. On January 16, 1962, the Division of Corporate Finance of the SEC informed Joseph A. Macchia, secretary of MGM, that if Cummings had realized profits from his sale and purchase, that fact would have to be noted in the proxy statement. Macchia promptly communicated this to Cummings and although Cummings believed that any violation, if it did occur, was inadvertent, he nevertheless decided to remit the $53,870.81 to MGM. Cummings testified that the purpose of the payment was to prevent any delay in the issuance of MGM's proxy statement and also to protect his business reputation, which might be injured by a disclosure of his potential liability because of an alleged securities laws violation. The Tax Court gave credence to Cummings' version. In any event, MGM issued its proxy statement dated January 18, 1962, without reference to any potential liability outstanding from Cummings.

Cummings and his wife treated his repayment as a deduction against ordinary income on their 1962 income tax return, but the Commissioner disallowed this and assessed a deficiency of $45,790.18, maintaining that long term capital loss treatment was appropriate. The Tax Court, 60 T.C. 91 (1973) held that the payment was properly characterized as an ordinary and necessary business expense, incurred to protect Cummings' business reputation. * * *

II

We are not required in this case to write on a tabula rasa, for the Courts of Appeals of two circuits have already rejected the Tax Court's treatment of § 16(b) repayments as ordinary and necessary business expenses. Anderson v. C.I.R., 480 F.2d 1304 (7th Cir.1973), reversing 56 T.C. 1370 (1971); Mitchell v. C.I.R., 428 F.2d 259 (6th Cir.1970), certiorari denied 401 U.S. 909 (1971), rev'g 52 T.C. 170 (1969). Our starting point, as was theirs, is Arrowsmith v. C.I.R., 344 U.S. 6 (1952), which held that an expenditure made for a business purpose will not be treated as an ordinary and necessary business expense if it is sufficiently related to an earlier capital gains transaction. * * *

The *Arrowsmith* rule was explained and applied in United States v. Skelly Oil Co., 394 U.S. 678 (1969).* There, a corporation repaid money which it had recorded in an earlier taxable year as income reduced by the 27½% oil depletion allowance. The Court held that the corporation could not deduct 100% of the repayment as a business expense since only 72½% of the income had been subject to taxation. *Arrowsmith* was held to forbid the windfall which would result if income taxed at a special lower rate when received were deductible on repayment at a different and more favorable rate.

The nexus between the § 16(b) repayment and the earlier capital gains is apparent. The repayment "had its genesis" in the earlier sale, see *Mitchell,* 428 F.2d at 261, which was a prerequisite for § 16(b) liability. As the *Anderson* court noted, 480 F.2d at 1307, "The amount of liability is calculated by subtracting from the sales proceeds the lowest purchase price within the six-month period" so the repayment may properly be viewed as a return of a portion of the sales proceeds or an adjustment of the sales price. In addition, the capital gain appears to include the profits from the sale and purchase. Cummings experienced a gain in the

---

*   [Ed Note: *Skelly Oil* is set out infra at page 696.]

economic sense when he repurchased the stock at a lower price than that at which it was sold. But the only gain which he recognized for tax purposes was the capital gain on his original sale. Thus, for tax purposes, his payment of $53,870.81 profit from the sale and purchase may appropriately be regarded as an adjustment to the amount of that capital gain.

It is apparent, also, that Cummings would obtain a windfall like that condemned in *Skelly Oil* if we were to treat his § 16(b) repayment as an ordinary and necessary business expense. Both before and after the events at issue he owned the 3000 shares of MGM. In the interim, however, he consummated a sale which resulted in the recognition of a gain and a subsequent repurchase within six months—the combination of which violated § 16(b). The § 16(b) repayment was designed, so far as practicable, to restore the status quo prior to the offending sale and purchase. We would be remiss, therefore, if we allowed Cummings a windfall which would flow from permitting his gain to be taxed at a lower capital gains rate and his repayment—designed to erase the improper § 16(b) gains—to be deducted at the more favorable ordinary income rate.

The result we reach is supported not only by a proper interpretation of the tax laws, but by the policy of § 16(b) as well. Our longstanding interpretation of that provision, noted over 30 years ago, is that " * * * the statute was intended to be thoroughgoing, to squeeze all possible profits out of stock transactions" within its purview, in order to remove the incentive for short-term trading by corporate insiders. It would defeat this policy if insiders could reap a tax advantage by enjoying the low capital gains rate on realized gains while obtaining a deduction against ordinary income when they surrendered those gains in satisfaction of a § 16(b) liability. In this case, for example, Cummings would benefit by $45,790.18 if he were permitted to deduct his repayment as a business expense, although (assuming that he elected the 25% alternate capital gains tax) he paid taxes of only $13,467.70 when he reported the comparable gain in 1961. Thus, he seeks to profit by $32,322.48 as a result of his § 16(b) transaction. We agree with the Seventh Circuit that, "Without good reason, we are unwilling to interpret the Internal Revenue Code so as to allow this anomalous result which severely and directly frustrates the purpose of Section 16(b)." * * *

Cummings maintains, however, that the statutory policy is irrelevant to this proceeding because he was never adjudicated to be in violation of § 16(b). * * * In particular, he notes two possible defenses— that the MGM board had the discretion not to demand repayment of Cummings's insider profits, and that the "opportunity for speculative abuse," described as the keystone of § 16(b) liability in Kern County Land Co. v. Occidental Petroleum Corp., 411 U.S. 582 (1973), was lacking because the decision to repurchase was made by Cummings's personal financial assistant.

Even a fledgling securities lawyer would recognize that these "defenses" border on the frivolous. There is no evidence that MGM would not have demanded payment. Moreover, the failure of a board of directors to demand repayment of § 16(b) profits scarcely extinguishes an insider's liability, which may readily be collected in a shareholder derivative action that is inevitable when stock is as widely held as MGM's. Nor is Cummings's reliance on *Kern County* plausible. * * * [It involved] a situation hardly comparable to the garden variety sale and purchase which was executed by Cummings.

In any event, we need not conclusively determine that Cummings violated or intended to violate § 16(b) in order to deny him an ordinary and necessary business expense deduction. Section 16(b) is a placid inlet in the chaotic sea of securities law—a statute designed for easy application. The elements of the cause of action are simple, and information about possible violations is widely disseminated. Thus, no proof need be forthcoming that the insider intended at the time he sold to repurchase the securities within six months, or that inside information was actually used. * * * One can hardly imagine a scheme better designed to insure the almost automatic enforcement of a statute, and we decline to subvert it by refusing to squeeze all profits from inside transactions unless liability has been established by a court adjudication.

III

In viewing Cummings's § 16(b) repayment as a long term capital loss rather than a business expense, we do not ignore a third alternative. As Judge Drennan suggested in his dissenting opinion in the Tax Court, the repayment may be viewed as linked to the repurchase, and treated for tax purposes as an addition to the basis of the purchased stock. The effective net result is that the repayment would be treated as a long term capital loss in the year that the repurchased stock is finally sold. It may be that such treatment would in an appropriate case better effectuate the policy of § 16(b) than that which we adopt today. But, by deferring the tax benefit of a payment currently made, the addition to basis would exact a penalty beyond that specified by Congress from an insider whose violation might be only inadvertent. Since neither party urges adoption of Judge Drennan's formula, however, we decline to resolve the issue. Reversed.

■ JOSEPH SMITH, CIRCUIT JUDGE (concurring in the result):

I concur in the reversal of the judgment, but respectfully differ from the rationale adopted.

I do not agree that this case is controlled by Arrowsmith v. C.I.R., 344 U.S. 6 (1952) and United States v. Skelly Oil Co., 394 U.S. 678 (1969). Both of those cases held that, when income is taxed at a reduced rate when received, it cannot be deducted at a more favorable rate if for some reason it has to be repaid. At the heart of those cases is the repayment of an amount which had previously been included in income. * * *

This case, involving a probable sale and repurchase violation of § 16(b), simply does not present that kind of situation. The mere fact that there could be no liability under § 16(b) were there not a sale which (in this case) resulted in taxable income is irrelevant, because the money paid out by Cummings to MGM cannot be treated as an item previously included in income. The amount of income on the sale (determined by the difference between the original purchase price and the sale price) has no bearing on the calculation of the insider's profit (determined, roughly, by the difference between the sale price and the repurchase price). In fact, it is perfectly clear that there can be an insider's profit even if the sale resulted in a loss, because the sale assumes relevance for tax purposes only when linked with the original purchase and the repurchase will not have tax significance until a subsequent sale occurs. The sale and repurchase, which result in § 16(b) liability, do not constitute a transaction with any tax significance whatever, and the insider's profit is not income for tax purposes, regardless of whether it may be considered, as my brother Kaufman considers it, as "gain in the economic sense."

I also disagree with the characterization of the payment to MGM as an adjustment to the sale price of the stock. I cannot subscribe to the view that "the capital gain appears to include the profits from the sale and purchase," * * * because the transaction resulting in capital gain terminated with the sale, and the purchase was the initiation of a new transaction that should be considered entirely separate and independent for tax purposes. * * *

This reasoning applies, of course, only to sale and repurchase violations of § 16(b). The tax significance of a purchase and sale violation would be entirely different. In that case, the insider's profit obviously should be treated as the repayment of an amount included in income. But the fact that one kind of violation of § 16(b) leads to *Arrowsmith/Skelly Oil* treatment does not require that all kinds of violations of § 16(b) be so treated. * * *

Nor do I think Tank Truck Rentals, Inc. v. C.I.R., 356 U.S. 30 (1958) relevant to the litigation before us. That decision—which is to be applied only in a "sharply limited and carefully defined category" of cases, Commissioner v. Tellier, 383 U.S. 687, 694 (1966)—involved the payment of punitive fines assessed after an adjudication of liability. Since the payment here—made in contemplation of potential liability—was remedial and not punitive, * * * this is not an appropriate case for applying a policy designed to avoid the dilution of punishment. * * *

For these reasons, I would not hold that the ordinary loss deduction should be disallowed and treated instead as a capital loss deduction. These transactions should more properly be treated in accordance with the opinion of Judge Drennen below: For tax purposes, the proper treatment would be to add to the repurchase price as the basis for the new shares the amount paid over, and to recognize neither capital gain or loss nor ordinary business expense until the tax year in which the shares are sold.

NOTES

(A) *Post*-Arrowsmith *Cases.* In *Arrowsmith,* relied on by the court in *Cummings,* the taxpayer liquidated a corporation and properly reported the gain on the redemption of the stock as a capital gain. Subsequently, the taxpayer was required to satisfy a judgment against the corporation. The Court treated the payment as a capital loss because it was linked to the earlier liquidation proceedings, thereby creating the so-called *Arrowsmith* doctrine which, as the *Cummings* court notes, has been read to require capital loss treatment for transactions "sufficiently related" to an earlier capital gains transaction.

For example, in Kimbell v. United States, 490 F.2d 203 (5th Cir. 1974), the taxpayer sold an interest in two oil and gas leases and reported capital gains. When it was discovered that the wells on the leases were constructed illegally, he settled a claim by making a payment. The court found that the payment was not an ordinary and necessary business expense, but rather was a capital loss because it related back to the earlier transaction. See also the special provisions covering the reacquisitions of real property in § 1038.

(B) *Post*-Cummings *Cases. Cummings* was the third in a series of appellate court reversals of Tax Court decisions on § 16(b) payments. It was followed by the Tenth Circuit in Brown v. Commissioner, 529 F.2d 609 (10th Cir. 1976), and by the IRS in Rev. Rul. 75–210, 1975–1 C.B. 72. In that ruling, a government regulatory agency announced in 1974 that all employees working in its licensing and regulatory functions must divest themselves of stocks, bonds, and other securities in regulated companies. The IRS required the employees to treat their losses on the subsequent sales as capital losses. The securities were deemed to be capital assets because they had been purchased and held for investment purposes even if they had been sold for business purposes.

In Smith v. Commissioner, 67 T.C. 570 (1976), the Tax Court considered payment of a § 12(a) penalty for violation of registration requirements of the Securities Act of 1933. The Court found *Arrowsmith* to be applicable because there was a "direct relationship" between the sale of stock and the taxpayer's settlement payments. The Tax Court cases involving payments under § 16(b) were distinguished. In Bradford v. Commissioner, 70 T.C. 584 (1978), the Tax Court required capitalization of expenditures paid in connection with stock in violation of § 10(b) of the Securities Exchange Act. The Tax Court also denied deduction as an ordinary and necessary business expense under § 162 and required capitalization in connection with a payment due to a possible violation of § 16(b) in Mitchell v. Commissioner, 67 T.C.M. 3015 (1994). Thus, in the Tax Court at least, the position urged by Judge Smith in his concurring opinion in *Cummings* has apparently taken hold.

(C) *Loss Followed by Gain.* The principles of *Arrowsmith* may apply to the reverse situation as well, i.e., a loss followed by a subsequent gain.

SECTION 4.   WHAT IS A SALE OR EXCHANGE?

In order to report a capital gain or loss, there not only must be a capital asset, but it must be sold or exchanged. Under the various provisions of § 1222, the several types of capital gain and loss all arise on "the sale or exchange of a capital asset." The need for a sale or exchange is also important under § 1231.

The sale or exchange requirement undoubtedly arises because of concern about the "lock-in" problem. Taxpayers are thought to be more likely to dispose of assets if given an incentive to do so. Courts have sometimes invoked the sale or exchange requirement to prevent favorable capital gains treatment when they considered such treatment to be inappropriate. The requirement also has been viewed as a means of preventing the conversion of interest and dividends into capital gain.

Although this Chapter deals with the questions "What is a capital asset?" and "What is a sale or exchange?" as separate issues, the distinction is not as clear in the judicial opinions. For example, in *Hort,* supra at page 146, the taxpayer realized ordinary income and not capital gain when he sold the right to future rental income and retained the underlying property. It is not clear, however, whether ordinary income treatment resulted from the nature of the asset transferred or because the taxpayer had divided—rather than sold or exchanged—his property interest. In other words, did the retention of the underlying property mean that no capital asset had been transferred or that no sale or exchange occurred?

The *P.G. Lake* case, supra at page 609, and related decisions in the natural resources context, also illustrate the analytical confusion between the nature of the asset and the sale or exchange requirement. In these cases, the taxpayer typically transferred the right to future business income—a production payment or royalties—but retained the operation of the underlying business. The decisions in this area have not turned, however, on the taxpayer's retention of a working interest in the property. In general, whether a transaction has produced capital gain or ordinary income has turned on whether the "carved-out" interest disposed of is coterminous with the interest owned by the taxpayer. If the carved-out interest is coterminous, capital gain results; if not, the taxpayer has ordinary income. Again, it is not clear analytically whether the courts deny capital gains treatment because no capital asset was transferred or because no sale or exchange occurred.

Although the issue often is framed as a narrow question—whether there has been a sale or exchange so that the gain is capital—it often has broader implications that would arise even in the absence of a capital gains preference. For example, the form of a transaction may be a "sale" even though the substance is a "gift" or a "lease," the tax consequences of which may be quite different from those if the transaction is treated as a sale.

Many of the problems relating to the "sale or exchange" requirement have been resolved by specific statutory provisions. For example, § 1231 ignores the need for a sale or exchange on a gain arising from an involuntary conversion. Other examples are discussed infra at page 635.

The materials that follow consider some of the more important applications of the "sale or exchange" requirement. The student should be aware, however, that in most cases, the question of whether a sale or exchange has occurred is an easy one.

Note on "Short Sales Against the Box" and "Constructive Realization"

Concerned about taxpayers' ability to engage in transactions that allow them to diversify their portfolio of assets and also to eliminate future benefits of appreciation or risks of depreciation in assets they currently hold without incurring a current capital gains tax, Congress adopted § 1259. The longstanding technique to accomplish diversification without tax had been the short sale against the box. This note provides a brief description of this technique and of § 1259.

The following definition of a short sale, given by the Supreme Court in Provost v. United States, 269 U.S. 443, 450–51 (1926), is as good as any:

> [A] short sale is a contract for the sale of shares which the seller does not own or the certificates for which are not within his control so as to be available for delivery at the time when, under the rules of the [New York Stock] Exchange, delivery must be made.

Tax-oriented short sales usually were made by taxpayers who hold a long position in the same securities (short sales against the box). Generally the taxpayer borrows securities, usually from a broker, and sells them. The taxpayer subsequently closes out the transaction by delivering identical securities to the lender. (The box apparently refers to the historical practice of holding pieces of paper evincing long positions in securities in a dealer's strongbox.)

Under current law, when a taxpayer sells securities, she generally is allowed to identify the securities sold for purposes of determining gain or loss on the disposition. If the taxpayer does not make an adequate identification, she is deemed to have disposed of the securities first acquired. Reg. § 1.1012–1(c)(1). Mutual fund investors, however, are allowed to determine the adjusted bases of their shares based on the average cost of all such shares.

Under prior law, when a taxpayer sold securities specifically identified as borrowed securities, gain or loss could not be computed because the taxpayer's cost for the securities was not known. The recognition of gain or loss generally was postponed until the taxpayer closed the sale by returning identical property to the lender. See Reg. § 1.1233–1(a) ("a short sale is not deemed to be consummated until delivery of property to close the short sale"). The rationale was that the taxpayer had the option of delivering the securities held or newly purchased securities.

These rules allowed a taxpayer to lock in gain on securities when he entered into a short sale against the box, which eliminated risk of loss on the securities. Any decline in the value of the investor's long position was offset by an increase in the value of the short position, just as any increase in the value of the long position resulted in a loss on the short position. In addition, a short-against-the-box sale often monetized the taxpayer's position because it produced cash almost equal to the value of the long position.

For example, suppose T owns 100 shares of Ford stock that it purchased for $40 per share and that currently are worth $100 per share. Rather than selling the stock for cash, which would produce taxable gain of $60, T could deposit the Ford stock with a broker. The broker then would borrow another 100 shares of Ford stock from a third party and sell the borrowed shares short on the open market on behalf of T. To close out this short sale, T would have to repay the third party 100 shares of Ford stock. Since T already owns 100 shares of Ford stock, any appreciation or depreciation in the Ford stock would have no economic relevance to T because T is both long and short at the same time with respect to 100 shares of Ford stock. Moreover, T could borrow (generally up to 95 percent) of the short sale proceeds and reinvest this cash in assets of its choosing. (Section 1233 limits these transactions to prevent taxpayers from using short sales against the box to accelerate losses or to convert short-term capital gain into long-term capital gain or long-term capital loss into short-term capital loss.) T locked in $60 of profit and converted his Ford stock into cash or another asset, deferring tax on the gain until the short sale was closed.

Another way to hedge appreciated securities is to enter into a short forward contract. Such a contract both obligates and entitles the investor to sell the security for a fixed price on a specified date in the future. Because the sales price is fixed, the investor is no longer exposed to movements in the price of the security. The forward contract might be satisfied by the delivery of the securities or settled with cash.

Alternatively, the investor can buy a put option on the security (the right to sell the security) at a price equal to its current price, thereby hedging against declines in the price of the security. The option might be cash settled. In contrast to an investor that sells short against the box or enters into a short forward contract, an investor that uses a put option retains the potential for gain from further appreciation. If the value of the security rises above the option strike price, the holder will fail to exercise the put and can sell on the open market. This upside potential comes at the cost of the option premium.

Short forwards and put options hedge against risk of loss, but do not necessarily monetize a long position. An investor who wishes to monetize a long position, as well as hedge against risk of loss, of course, can borrow money in a separate transaction.

In general, whether these other transactions were successful in avoiding gain recognition seemed to depend on whether the investor remained the owner of the appreciated security for tax purposes or whether the other party to the transaction became the owner. If the other party did not become the owner, the taxpayer probably would not be deemed to have sold the property.

Retention of the ability to transfer property to a third party suggests that the taxpayer continues to own the property. Assume, for example, that a taxpayer owning appreciated securities enters into a forward contract that obligates and entitles the taxpayer to sell those securities on a date in the future. Assume further that identical securities are available in the market (e.g., shares of publicly traded stock) and that the taxpayer's obligations under the contract are not secured by the particular securities owned by the taxpayer at the time that the contract is entered into. The taxpayer is free to transfer the securities it owns to a third party and later to acquire identical securities in the market to perform under the forward contract. In this case, the taxpayer was not viewed as having transferred ownership by entering into the forward contract.

The tax advantage of these types of transactions was substantially curtailed by § 1259, which taxes the holder on any gain where there is deemed to be a constructive sale of an appreciated financial position. A financial position includes a futures or forward contract, a short sale, or an option with respect to stock, debt, or a partnership interest. A constructive sale is deemed to occur when the taxpayer (or a related person) enters into a short sale or an offsetting notional principal contract with respect to the same or substantially identical property, or enters into a futures or forward contract to deliver the same or substantially identical property. A constructive sale also occurs where the taxpayer holds an appreciated short position in property and acquires a long position in the same property. Sales of nonpublicly traded property, however, are not subject to this rule.

Thus, § 1259 eliminates the tax advantage of a short against the box—upon entering into the short sale, the gain on the underlying appreciated stock is taxed. A taxpayer who enters into a forward contract to sell property, that is, a contract "to deliver a substantially fixed amount of property for a substantially fixed price," also is taxed on the gain on the underlying property. For example, suppose X holds 100 shares of Techno stock with an adjusted basis of $1,000 and a fair market value of $10,000. He enters into a contract to sell the shares one year hence for $11,000. On entering the contract, he is deemed to have sold

CAPITAL GAINS AND LOSSES

the shares for $10,000 and must report a gain of $9,000. The remaining $1,000 is reported when the forward contract is closed.

An offsetting notional principal contract is an agreement to pay or credit the investment yield (including appreciation) on such property for a specified period, and a right to be reimbursed for (or receive credit for) any decline in the value of such property. A popular example is an equity swap. Suppose A owns 100 shares of Digico stock worth $20,000 that have appreciated $5,000. Under prior law, an equity swap permitted her to lock in the appreciation on the Digico stock and invest in another asset without reporting the gain on Digico. Here's how: for a five-year period, A agrees to transfer to B annually an amount equal to the dividends paid on the Digico stock plus the amount by which the value of the stock has increased. B agrees to transfer to A annually an amount equal to a market rate of interest on $20,000 plus the amount by which the value of the Digico stock has decreased. A has essentially sold the Digico stock— she will neither enjoy the appreciation or risk a loss in value—and invested in a $20,000 bond. Because the agreement with B is an offsetting notional principal contract, A now is taxed on the gain on the Digico stock on entering into the contract. When A actually sells the stock, she is credited with the gain already taxed.

There are many financial positions and offsetting contracts that could accomplish essentially the same thing as the forward contract or the equity swap. Section 1259 gives the IRS the authority to draft regulations that would treat as constructive sales other transactions that have the same effect as those described above. The committee report suggests that transactions have the same effect if they eliminate substantially all of the risk of loss and the opportunity for gain. Does the put option described above meet this condition? There are many open questions that the regulations must resolve. For example, what is substantially identical property? What if a taxpayer holds the short position and his wholly-owned corporation owns the long position? For a discussion of many of these questions, see Deborah H. Schenk, "Taxation of Equity Derivatives: A Partial Integration Proposal", 50 Tax L. Rev. 571 (1995); for further discussion of similar techniques, see Edward Kleinbard, "Risky and Riskless Positions in Securities", 71 Taxes 783 (1993); Robert Scarborough, "Proposal Would Tax Short-Against-the-Box Sales, But May Encourage Alternatives That Use Derivatives," Derivatives Magazine (May, 1996), at 217.

Many other complex rules apply to derivatives and economically similar instruments are often not treated identically. Taxpayers are able to take advantage of these inconsistencies. In 2013 Rep. David Camp, chairman of the House Ways and Means Committee, offered a proposal to tax all derivatives on a mark-to-market basis, meaning that holders of derivatives would report gain or loss each year on the change in market value without waiting for a sale or other disposition.

A. SALE VS. ABANDONMENT OR EXTINGUISHMENT OF RIGHTS

Suppose that a taxpayer abandons unimproved real estate subject to a nonrecourse mortgage exceeding the fair market value and thereby suffers a tax loss? What is the character of the loss? In Helvering v. Hammel, 311 U.S. 504 (1941), the Supreme Court held that the loss on a foreclosure sale was capital even though the mortgagee received nothing on the sale. In Yarbro v. Commissioner, 737 F.2d 479 (5th Cir. 1984), the court determined that a similar rule should apply on abandonment of such property. Because the taxpayer gave up the property in exchange for being relieved of the debt, the transaction was deemed an exchange. The court noted that this created parity: had the property appreciated in value, the taxpayer would have reported a capital gain on disposition.

Does the receipt of a payment in exchange for the termination of contract rights constitute a sale or exchange giving rise to capital gain or loss? The Tax Court's position is that it does not because the asset disappears on the payment. For example, in Foote v. Commissioner, 81 T.C. 930 (1983), the taxpayer resigned his tenured appointment to a university faculty in exchange for a cash payment. The court ruled that, even if tenure has significant economic value and thus could have been considered an intangible capital asset, the voluntary extinction of tenure did not constitute a sale or exchange. As the court explained:

> The agreement in question simply terminated [the taxpayer's] rights; his tenure did not pass to the university, but was extinguished. Tenure is a personal right. It cannot be transferred to, or utilized by another. * * * Under these circumstances, there is no sale or exchange.

In *Commissioner v. Ferrer,* discussed supra at page 613, the Second Circuit explicitly rejected the disappearing asset approach. The court argued that there was no substantive distinction between transfers that resulted in the immediate extinguishment of contract rights and transfers of rights to third parties who could transfer them again through agreements that would then lead to their extinguishment. In a subsequent case, however, the Second Circuit found that a release of rights did not produce capital gain. Taxpayers have sought to take advantage of the sale or exchange requirement to create ordinary instead of capital losses, for example, by cancelling rather than selling their interest. This ploy led to the enactment of § 1234A, which treats gain or loss from the extinguishment or cancellation of contracts rights as capital, despite the lack of a sale or exchange.

B. SALE VS. LOAN

Some sales are very similar to a loan. Nonrecourse financing arrangements in particular bear many of the same characteristics as a sale but the tax consequences are quite different. A taxpayer who transfers appreciated property as collateral for a loan does not recognize gain on the transfer of the property. On the sale of the property of course, the taxpayer recognizes the gain. This creates an incentive to structure the transfer of appreciated property as a loan rather than a sale. Because the two structures are often so similar, the courts must determine whether what purports to be a financing arrangement is actually a loan. Generally with respect to nonfungible property, the test is who has the benefits and burdens of ownership. See, e.g., Grodt & McKay Realty, Inc. v. Commissioner, 77 T.C. 1221 (1981), in which the court determined tax ownership by looking at multiple factors, such as legal title, who bore the risk of loss, who benefited from any appreciation or profits, how the parties treated the transaction, and who had possession. Other courts have tried to establish whether the indicia of an indebtedness—such an obligation to pay interest, a fixed maturity date, and whether there is an obligation to repay—are present in the transaction. See, e.g., Welch v. Commissioner, 204 F.3d 1228, 1230 (9th Cir. 2000).

Securities present a special difficulty because they are fungible—the transferor does not care which shares of stock are ultimately returned because all shares of stock in a corporation are identical. Consider the facts of Calloway v. Commissioner, 691 F.3d 1315 (11th Cir. 2012). Calloway transferred his appreciated shares of IBM stock in exchange for cash. The transaction was characterized by the parties as a nonrecourse loan of 90 percent of the value of the IBM stock pledged as collateral but Calloway was prohibited from making any interest or principal payments during the term of the "loan." The amount of the loan proceeds was determined by the amount the transferee received when it sold the stock immediately after receipt. At maturity Calloway could either pay off the "loan" and have an equivalent amount of IBM stock returned to him or forfeit the stock as payment for the "loan." The value of IBM fell and at maturity Calloway forfeited the stock. In effect Calloway received 90 percent of the value of his stock and hoped to avoid paying tax on his gain. The Tax Court determined, however, that he had sold his stock. In a very similar case, the Ninth Circuit also found such an arrangement was a sale, not a loan. The court noted that while the list of factors in Grodt & McKay, supra, was a good place to start, "creating an exclusive lists of factors risks over-formaliz[ing] the concept of a 'sale,' hamstringing a court's effort to discern a transaction's substance and realities in evaluating tax consequences." Sollberger v. Commissioner, 691 F.3d 1119 (9th Cir. 2012).

Recall the use of securities lending in connection with short sales supra at page 629. That discussion focused on the person who borrowed the securities. The taxpayer in Calloway is the equivalent of the securities lender. The Supreme Court long ago held that the securities lender in a short sale had a taxable disposition of the stock. Provost v. United States, 269 U.S. 443 (1926). The key factor in determining that there had been a disposition was not who bore the market risk—the lender did—but rather the fact that the borrower had the right to dispose of the stock and thus had control over the stock. For a good analysis of the various ways of determining tax ownership, see Alex Raskolnikov, "Contextual Analysis of Tax Ownership", 85 B.U. L. Rev. 431, 481–82 (2005).

C. STATUTORY "SALES OR EXCHANGES"

Loss by Casualty or Government Seizure. Does a taxpayer suffer an ordinary loss or a capital loss upon the destruction by fire of an uninsured building used for business purposes? Does he recognize ordinary income or capital gain if he receives an amount of insurance in excess of the adjusted basis of the building? What if the government seizes the taxpayer's property under its power of eminent domain? Do such events constitute sales or exchanges?

These questions are covered by § 1231, discussed supra at page 589, which treats aggregate losses on involuntary conversions of business assets as ordinary losses. Aggregate gains may be capital gains, depending on the mix of assets in the § 1231 hotchpot.

Stocks and Bonds That Become Worthless. Instead of being redeemed or paid off, stocks and bonds may become worthless. Although the owner has suffered a loss, there is no "transaction," and therefore nothing that may be regarded as a realization event (much less a sale or exchange). The owner still has the stocks or bonds; they simply have no value. Sections 165(a) and (c)(2) allow the deduction of the loss in such a case. Section 165(g) provides that such losses are capital losses where the security is a capital asset in the hands of the taxpayer. Ordinary loss treatment, however, is provided under § 1244 for loss on worthlessness or sale of certain stock of a "small business corporation."

Nonbusiness Debt Held by an Individual. The deduction of a nonbusiness bad debt by an individual is treated as a short-term capital loss. The treatment of these losses is discussed supra at page 428.

Cancellation of Lease or Distributor's Agreement. Section 1241 treats as capital gain or loss amounts received by a lessee (not a lessor) for the cancellation of a lease, or by a distributor (not his supplier) for the cancellation of his distributor's agreement. This provision applies to distributors only if the distributor has a substantial capital investment in the distributorship. There is no similar requirement for a lessee, and the provision thus applies whether or not the lessee has a substantial investment.

This list of statutory sales or exchanges is not exhaustive. There are other provisions in the Code that permit capital gains treatment on certain types of transactions. Often the signal is that the statute says that an amount received "shall be regarded as received on the sale or exchange" of property.

D. Settlements

Freda v. Commissioner

United States Court of Appeals, Seventh Circuit, 2011. 656 F.3d 570.

■ Tinder, Circuit Judge.

* * *

C & F is an Illinois-based meat processing company. In the early 1980s, C & F developed a process for making and freezing pre-cooked sausage that had the appearance and taste of home-cooked sausage. C & F applied for and obtained a patent protecting its new process. C & F treated as trade secrets all subsequent refinements to the process. In 1985, one of C & F's long-time customers, Pizza Hut, expressed an interest in using sausage made pursuant to the C & F process in its outlets nationwide, which would result in purchases of at least 200,000 pounds per week. The catch was that C & F had to agree to share the C & F process with Pizza Hut's other sausage suppliers so that Pizza Hut could offer its customers a uniform product. Later that year, Pizza Hut and C & F signed an agreement pursuant to which C & F disclosed to Pizza Hut information relating to the C & F process, and Pizza Hut promised to keep mum about those details. * * *

Pizza Hut faltered on its end of the bargain: it failed to buy sufficient quantities of sausage from C & F and allegedly—it has never admitted wrongdoing—divulged crucial information regarding the C & F process to IBP, Inc., another meat processing company with whom C & F had not signed a confidentiality or licensing agreement. IBP replicated the C & F process, set its prices below C & F's, and began selling large quantities of sausage to Pizza Hut. Pizza Hut bought less and less sausage from C & F, and C & F suffered financially. C & F eventually filed suit against both Pizza Hut and IBP * * *. C & F alleged, inter alia, that Pizza Hut "misappropriated [its] trade secrets by, among other things: (a) acquiring the trade secrets through fraudulent misrepresentations and omissions, and (b) disclosing and using such trade secrets, after notice, without express or implied consent of C & F." "As a result," the complaint continued, "C & F has been damaged, and has suffered, among other things, lost profits, lost opportunities, operating losses, and expenditures." * * *

Pizza Hut and C & F settled the trade secret misappropriation claim for $15.3 million in January 2002. The settlement agreement provided for "a lump-sum payment in full and complete discharge and settlement of the Lawsuit and all other past, present, and future claims that could be asserted now or in the future by the C & F Parties and Pizza Hut related to the events or circumstances described in the Lawsuit." After deducting attorneys' fees, expenses, * * * from the settlement, C & F walked away with $6.12 million.

C & F characterized the $6.12 million as gain from a "trade secret sale" and reported the entire amount as long-term capital gain. * * * [T]he sole issue remaining * * * was whether the $6.12 million should have been reported as ordinary income or long-term capital gain.

* * *

The shareholders first "ask this Court to adopt a rule that, as a matter of law, settlement proceeds received as a result of a sole claim for misappropriation of a capital asset are taxed as capital gains." Because C & F's claim had at its center a capital asset, they contend, all compensation C & F (and they) received in settlement of that claim must also be treated as capital in nature. This broad-brush approach obscures some crucial finer points of the so-called "origin of the claim" doctrine, the underlying principles of which are applicable here. (It also elevates form over substance, which is generally frowned upon in tax jurisprudence, see, e.g., Frank Lyon, 435 U.S. at 583–84, and potentially opens the door to exploitation of the beneficial—and exceptional—capital gains tax rate. * * *

The origin of the claim doctrine had its roots in a dispute over legal expenses a taxpayer incurred while defending his income-producing property during a divorce dispute. See United States v. Gilmore, 372 U.S. 39 (1963). * * *

While the doctrine in its purest form is not directly applicable here, the principles underlying it long have been. That is, "the [tax] classification of amounts received in settlement of litigation is to be determined by the nature and basis of the action settled, and amounts received in compromise of a claim must be considered as having the same nature as the right compromised." * * * Where "the recovery represents damages for lost profits, it is taxable as ordinary income. However, if it represents a replacement of capital destroyed or injured, the money received . . . is a return of capital and not taxable." * * * We look to what the settlement payment in question is "in lieu of."

Here, the tax court, after reviewing the record and hearing testimony on the matter at trial, found that "Pizza Hut paid the amount at issue to C & F for 'lost profits, lost opportunities, operating losses and expenditures.' * * * The tax court implicitly recognized that trade secret misappropriation claims—and recoveries associated with them—are rather chameleonic. Injuries caused by trade secret misappropriation can take many forms and may be remedied by many types of relief. * * * Among these remedies are a variety of damages, including lost profits and royalties, that are properly characterized as ordinary income for tax purposes. The [taxpayer] had the burden of demonstrating that the Commissioner was wrong when he concluded that the settlement payment was in lieu of one or more of these ordinary income streams. Based on the record before it, the tax court did not err in upholding the Commissioner's presumptively correct determination that the settlement was not "in lieu of" a replacement of capital.

We are similarly unmoved by the shareholders' alternative argument, that the alleged misappropriation and subsequent settlement payment in fact constituted a protracted commercial transaction in which a capital asset held for more than a year was exchanged for money. In their view, Pizza Hut "bought" a capital asset when it misappropriated the C & F process, then completed the sale or exchange years later by "paying" C & F with the settlement. * * *

This argument grows out of 26 U.S.C. § 1222(3), which defines as "long-term capital gain" proceeds from the "sale or exchange of a capital asset held for more than 1 year," and 26 U.S.C. § 1235, which provides that "[a] transfer . . . of property consisting of all substantial rights to a patent . . . shall be considered the sale or exchange of a capital asset held for more than 1 year." (The parties agree that trade secrets are analogous to patents for purposes of § 1235.

The [taxpayer contends] that Pizza Hut deprived C & F of all the economic value of, and thus almost all of the substantial rights to, its trade secret when it misappropriated the C & F process back in the 1980s. * * * The only valuable right C & F had left in their view was "the right to pursue a claim against Pizza Hut for unauthorized use or disclosure," which C & F gave up in exchange for the settlement payment in 2002.

The facts of the case undermine their position, however. The tax court found that Pizza Hut disclosed the C & F process to IBP in 1989. Four years later, C & F filed suit against both Pizza Hut and IBP. It secured a sizeable jury verdict against IBP for trade secret misappropriation. To achieve such a result, C & F had to have possessed—and exercised—its right to exclude others, not just Pizza Hut, from using or disclosing its protected process. * * * C & F necessarily retained a rather valuable right associated with its trade secret * * * one that was not transferred to Pizza Hut at any point during the 13 years separating the misappropriation from the settlement payment. C & F could not have transferred all substantial rights in its trade secret while simultaneously keeping a $10.9 million right to exclude IBP in its back pocket. Moreover, the settlement agreement gives no indication that Pizza Hut believed it was compensating C & F for the sale or even the use of its trade secrets. * * * It states only that $15.3 million was tendered "in consideration of the dismissal with prejudice of the lawsuit," not in exchange for anything else Pizza Hut previously or concurrently received. Transactions involving the transfer of capital assets must be "in the nature of a sale" to qualify for capital gains treatment. Here, the tax court expressly concluded that "Pizza Hut did not pay the amount at issue under the settlement agreement for C & F's sale or exchange of the C & F trade secret to Pizza Hut." Without at least some hallmarks of a sale, C & F's transfer to Pizza Hut of its trade secrets should not be considered one for tax purposes.

The tax court rightly concluded that the settlement payment did not represent the final phase of a 13-year-long transfer of a capital asset. Because there was not a complete transfer of all substantial rights, there was no "sale" of a capital asset or long-term capital gain resulting therefrom.

AFFIRMED.

■ MANION, CIRCUIT JUDGE, dissenting.

* * *

It is with respect to C & F's primary argument that I part ways with the court. * * *

The Tax Court concluded that the settlement proceeds were for lost profits. But C & F did not lose profits to Pizza Hut—it lost them to IBP when Pizza Hut transferred the business to IBP. * * * What C & F did lose to Pizza Hut was value to its trade secret when Pizza Hut misappropriated it. In light of the IBP verdict, the profits lost to C & F from purchases that Pizza Hut made with IBP instead of C & F have already been accounted for in the jury award, and any additional money recovered from Pizza Hut cannot correspond to money from lost sales. In its opinion, the Tax Court dismissed this issue, saying that C & F could have also lost profits attributable to Pizza Hut that were not attributable to IBP. Nothing in the record supports that finding: instead, C & F's case is limited to Pizza Hut giving the secret to one competitor, IBP; C & F's lost profits went to IBP from IBP's sausage sales to Pizza Hut; and these profits were recovered as part of the jury award against IBP.

The Tax Court is wrong because it misread the complaint. In the complaint, after describing the elements of its trade secret misappropriation claim against Pizza Hut, C & F alleged that "[a]s a result, C & F has been damaged, and has suffered, among other things, lost profits, lost opportunities, operating losses and expenditures." * * * From this one phrase of "lost profits," the Tax Court concluded that C & F was only seeking lost profits against Pizza Hut. This is an incorrect way of reading the complaint. Recall, the complaint when first filed was against Pizza Hut and IBP. The nature of the claim that C & F was bringing against Pizza Hut was that Pizza Hut had wrongfully acquired and then disclosed a trade secret to C & F's competitor, IBP. This undoubtedly damaged C & F's property interest in the trade secret. Accordingly, in the complaint, the phrase "lost profits" was part of a non-exclusive list describing ways C & F had been injured by Pizza Hut's trade secret misappropriation. But this phrase "lost profits" did not negate the fact that C & F's trade secret had been severely damaged and that C & F was also seeking compensation for this damage. The Tax Court erroneously discarded the neighboring phrase "lost opportunities" which easily includes, for example, the lost opportunity to negotiate a transfer of the secret process to another pizza giant after Pizza Hut cut C & F off. The Tax Court was clearly wrong to conclude that the claim against Pizza Hut could only be for lost profits and that it wasn't also to compensate the injury to its trade secret, when the only profits lost were those transferred to IBP.

* * *

Although the Tax Court concluded that Pizza Hut paid the settlement to C & F for lost profits, there is nothing in the record indicating that the parties understood the settlement proceeds to be a payment equivalent to C & F's lost profits—there are no calculations indicating the equivalency between C & F's lost profits and the settlement amount. Instead, Pizza Hut paid the settlement proceeds to C & F in an agreement to settle all past, present, and future claims against Pizza Hut, in typical boilerplate language contained in any litigation-ending release agreement. And the only issue in that final phase of the litigation following the IBP verdict was the damage to the trade secret asset.

Other than its reliance on the single "lost profits" reference in the complaint, the Tax Court does not cite to anything in the record which supports the position that C & F's remaining claim against Pizza Hut was for lost profits. In fact, the record contained direct testimonial evidence to the contrary, which the Tax Court rejected as unreliable based on its reading of the "lost profits" phrase.

In sum, the "nature and basis" of the trade secret misappropriation claim, at the time when Pizza Hut entered into its settlement agreement following the IBP verdict, was a claim seeking compensation for the substantially diminished value inflicted upon the trade secret. And since a trade secret is a capital asset, the settlement should be characterized as capital gain. I respectfully dissent.

NOTES

(A) *Sausage Making.* It is often said that the process of making sausage, as suggested by the facts in *Freda,* is a messy business. The same might be said of understanding judicial opinions about capital gains. Why did the taxpayer in *Freda* receive ordinary income treatment? Because of the lack of a sale or exchange? Because it failed to transfer a capital asset? Because the payment it received was a substitute for ordinary income?

(B) *The Importance of the Complaint.* The court is clear that if the complainant sued for nothing more than damages for lost profits, any payment would have been ordinary income. Could C & F have changed the tax results by alleging instead damages arising from the destruction of a capital asset? Would it have mattered if the complaint had used lost profits as a metric to calculate the damages?

SECTION 5.   HOLDING PERIOD

The dividing line between short-term and long-term capital gains and losses currently is fixed at one year. At other times it has been only six months.

NOTES

(A) *What a Difference a Day Makes.* A capital asset must be held for *more than* one year to produce a long-term gain. Holding for exactly one year will not suffice—as some taxpayers have learned the hard way. Because the sellers sold securities one day too early in Caspe v. United States, 694 F.2d 1116 (8th Cir. 1982), they were assessed a $95,553 deficiency on a gain of $1,186,424 (the difference between long-term and short-term capital gains treatment) and interest of $18,861 on the deficiency.

(B) *Seemed So Simple, Didn't It?* In Rev. Rul. 70–598, 1970–2 C.B. 168, the Service ruled that in counting the holding period, the day an asset is purchased is excluded and the day the asset is sold is included.

In his comprehensive district court opinion in Caspe v. United States, 82–1 U.S.T.C. ¶ 9247 (S.D.Iowa 1982), Judge Vietor explained the logic behind the "less one" rule:

> To avoid duplication of days and to eliminate the need to calculate fractions of days, the holding period is measured by determining the interval between the date of acquisition and the date of disposition and then subtracting one day. This eliminates the need of calculating the actual hours of ownership on the date of acquisition and the actual hours on the date of disposition, and basically evidences a recognition that the ownership of the asset for two partial days would average one whole day.

(C) *Then "Less One" Became "Plus One."* The IRS has ruled that the "less one" rule becomes a "plus one" rule where the period is counted backward from a designated event. See Rev. Rul. 66–6, 1966–1 C.B. 160. That ruling involved § 631(a), which provides capital gains treatment on the sale of timber if the taxpayer owned the timber or had a contract right to cut it for more than one year before the beginning of the taxable year. At the time of the ruling, the required holding period was six months. At issue was whether a taxpayer who acquired timber on December 31 had owned it for more than six months before the beginning of his taxable year on the following July 1. The IRS ruled that:

> [w]hen a prescribed period of months is before a designated day * * *, it is properly computed * * * by excluding the day so designated and computing the period backward to, and including the day designated as its beginning. * * *

> For example, the first day of a period six months before June 16, 1963, would be December 16, 1962, determined by excluding June 16, and computing backward from June 15 to the corresponding date of the appropriate preceding month, i.e. December 15, plus one day, to December 16, 1962.

Moreover, when the date before which something must have occurred is the first day of a month, the date which begins the period is determined by going backward to the last day of the appropriate preceding month, plus one.

The taxpayer was therefore eligible for capital gains treatment since he had acquired the timber by January 1.

(D) *Inherited Property.* Capital assets acquired by inheritance are exempted from the holding period requirement by § 1223(11). The inherited property therefore can be sold immediately upon receipt in a transaction that will result in long-term capital gain or loss.

(E) *"Tacking" of Holding Periods.* Section 1223 allows taxpayers in some circumstances to "tack on" to their own holding period a period of time before their acquisition of the capital asset. For example, a taxpayer who receives property by gift combines her own holding period with the holding period of her donor. § 1223(2). See also the discussion of tacking in nonrecognition transactions at page 647, infra.

SECTION 6.   NONRECOGNITION OF GAIN OR LOSS

There are numerous situations where gain or loss realized on the sale, exchange, or other disposition of property is not recognized. Sections 1031–1042 deal with many such transactions. There are a number of corporate and partnership nonrecognition provisions as well.

Where such provisions apply, recognition generally is postponed until the taxpayer's investment is significantly altered. Usually, the basis of the property disposed of becomes the basis of the property acquired, thus preserving the gain or loss. The deferral of tax accomplished by the nonrecognition provisions can be very valuable. Recall the discussion of deferral, supra at page 313. Moreover, if the recognition of gain can be deferred until the taxpayer's death, the tax may be eliminated completely because the basis of the property often will be stepped up to its fair market value at the decedent's death. § 1014. The nonrecognition provisions of § 1031 (like kind exchanges) and § 1033 (involuntary conversion) are discussed in the materials that follow. The special rule of § 121 (sale of a principal residence) is also discussed here.

A.   EXCHANGES OF "LIKE KIND" PROPERTIES

Under § 1031, no gain or loss is recognized when real property held for productive use in a trade or business or for investment is exchanged for real property "of a like kind." The gain or loss on many common investments cannot be deferred. Personal property, such as machinery, stock, certificates of trust or beneficial interests, other securities or evidences of indebtedness, and partnership interests are not eligible for nonrecognition treatment under § 1031. Inventory or other property held primarily for sale is also excluded from § 1031.

When like kind properties of equal value are exchanged in a nonrecognition transaction, the basis of the property given up becomes the basis of the property received. § 1031(d). A like kind exchange also may include the transfer of "boot"—that is, money or other nonqualifying property received in addition (or "to boot")—from one party to the other in order to equalize the exchange. In such cases, the taxpayer will recognize gain, but not loss, on the transaction to the extent of any boot received. §§ 1031(b), (c). His transferred basis in the new property is decreased by any money received and increased by any gain recognized. § 1031(d). If the new property is depreciable, it is depreciated over the remaining recovery period, using the same depreciation method as the relinquished property.

For example, suppose A transfers real property with a basis of $150 and a fair market value of $200 in exchange for $20 in cash and B's real property with a basis of $120 and a value of $180. A realizes gain of $50 on the transaction—$200 fair market value of property received [$180 building + $20 cash] minus $150 basis—but recognizes gain of only $20 (the cash boot). A's basis in the property received remains $150. (His old basis of $150 is decreased by $20 cash received and increased by the $20 gain recognized.) B realizes gain of $60—$200 fair market value of property received minus $140 basis (property and cash)—but recognizes no gain because he received no boot. The basis of the property he receives is $140.

The term "like kind" refers to the nature of the property exchanged rather than to its grade or quality. The transfer of real property for personal property does not qualify for § 1031 treatment because the two are not of similar character. The transfer of improved realty for unimproved realty, however, does qualify as a like kind exchange. A leasehold for 30 years or more is considered to be of like kind to a fee interest in real property. Reg. § 1.1031(a)–1. The 2017 legislation makes clear that a transfer of U.S. real property for foreign real property or vice versa does not qualify as an exchange of like kind property. § 1031(h).

Quite often, the property will be subject to a mortgage. When a mortgage is assumed, or the property is taken subject to the mortgage, the outstanding mortgage is treated as cash received and is recognized as boot to the extent it exceeds any mortgage the seller must assume or to which the property he receives is subject.

The following example from Reg. § 1.1031(d)–2 illustrates the application of this rule:

> B, an individual, owns an apartment house which has an adjusted basis in his hands of $500,000, but which is subject to a mortgage of $150,000. On September 1, 1954, he transfers the apartment house to C, receiving in exchange therefor $50,000 in cash and another apartment house with a fair market value on that date of $600,000. The transfer to C is made subject to the

$150,000 mortgage. B realizes a gain of $300,000 on the exchange, computed as follows:

Value of property received	$600,000
Cash	$50,000
Liabilities subject to which old property was transferred	$150,000
Total consideration received	$800,000
Less: Adjusted basis of property transferred	$500,000
Gain realized	$300,000

Under section 1031(b) $200,000 of the $300,000 is recognized. The basis of the apartment house acquired by B upon the exchange is $500,000, computed as follows:

Adjusted basis of property transferred	$500,000
Less: Amount of money received	$200,000
Cash	$50,000
Amount of liabilities subject to which property was transferred	$150,000
Difference	$300,000
Plus: Amount of gain realized upon the exchange	$200,000
Basis of property acquired upon the exchange	$500,000

There may be relatively few situations where two taxpayers simply want to trade property with each other. Thus, it is likely that several parties will have to become involved to achieve a like kind exchange transaction. For example, assume A wants to dispose of Blackacre in a like kind exchange. B wants to purchase Blackacre for cash. In order to satisfy both objectives, A directs B to purchase Whiteacre, held by C, which B will then swap with A for Blackacre. The traditional position of the IRS and the courts was that multi-party transactions would not qualify for nonrecognition if they had the formal appearance of a sale of property followed by a reinvestment of the proceeds. The application of § 1031 also might be challenged if it appeared that one of the parties was acting as an agent of the other.

Today, however, the courts and the IRS are more liberal in permitting multiparty exchanges to qualify for § 1031 nonrecognition treatment. See, e.g., Rev. Rul. 77–297, 1977–2 C.B. 304 (three-party exchange of real property qualifies for § 1031 treatment). They often focus on whether the parties intended to enter into a like kind exchange and whether the several steps in the transaction were part of a single integrated plan. Given the policy discussion in Note (I), infra, is this the right approach? Would it make more sense to repeal § 1031 or extend nonrecognition treatment to all sale and repurchase transactions?

NOTES

(A) *Intent.* The intent of the taxpayer is important, but not necessarily dispositive, in determining whether a transaction is a sale or a nontaxable exchange. A transaction that is structured as an exchange may be recharacterized as a sale if the taxpayer receives not the property itself but cash that he uses to purchase the property. For example, in Carlton v. United States, 385 F.2d 238 (5th Cir. 1967), the taxpayers intended to exchange their ranch for another ranch so that their gain would go unrecognized under 1031. The court conceded that had the purchasers actually transferred title to the properties located by the sellers, no gain would have been reported. Since, however, the sellers received cash and an assignment of the purchaser's contract rights to the property, they were required to report their entire gain. *Carlton* should be contrasted with another Fifth Circuit case, Biggs v. Commissioner, 632 F.2d 1171 (1980), in which the court rejected the Commissioner's argument that a failure of the transferor to obtain title to the replacement property precluded the use of § 1031. In *Biggs*, the transferor had a contractual obligation to purchase the replacement property. Although he transferred this obligation to Biggs, the court noted that at least for a short period of time, he bore the risk of being required to make payment on promissory notes of a significant amount. The court also emphasized the fact that all the steps in *Biggs* were part of an integrated plan intended to be a like kind exchange.

Note that the taxpayer who purchases the property to swap generally has no gain or loss. If, however, there is a delay and the property increases in value, he cannot use § 1031 because he was not holding the property for use in his business or for investment.

In Reesink v. Commissioner, T.C. Memo 2012–118, the court held that the intent of the taxpayer is considered at the time of the sale. In this case, the taxpayers sold an apartment building and purchased a single family home they intended to rent out as an investment property. After eight months, they had not found a renter. They then sold their house and moved into the new property. § 1031 only applies to property held for productive use in a trade or business or for investment, which generally excludes a taxpayer's primary residence. Because the taxpayers intended the property to be an investment when they exchanged their apartment building for it, the court held that the transaction was eligible for § 1031 treatment.

(B) *Delayed Exchanges and Options to Receive Cash.* Often, the seller may locate a buyer for his property before finding a replacement property for the buyer to exchange. The taxpayers in Starker v. United States, 602 F.2d 1341 (9th Cir. 1979), transferred their interest in timber acreage in exchange for a corporation's promise to transfer suitable property within five years or to pay the outstanding balance in cash. The Ninth Circuit found a like kind exchange despite the possible five-year delay in effectuating the property exchanges and the possibility of a cash transaction. The court observed that:

[e]ven if the contract right includes the possibility of the taxpayer receiving something other than ownership of like kind property * * * it is still of a like kind with ownership for tax purposes when the taxpayer prefers property to cash before and throughout the executory period, and only like kind property is ultimately received.

In order to prevent the tax planning made possible by the use of long delays with options to receive cash or non-like kind property, the Code now requires the like kind exchange to be completed within 180 days after the taxpayer relinquishes property. In addition, the property to be received in exchange must be designated as such within 45 days after the transfer. The contract may designate a limited number of possible properties within the 45-day period if the particular property to be transferred is to be determined by contingencies beyond the control of both parties. § 1031(a)(3). An industry has been created to facilitate these transactions. For a feel for the complexity, see Reg. § 1.1031(k)–1.

(C) *"Productive Use in a Trade or Business or for Investment."* Real property is eligible for § 1031 treatment only if it, as well as the replacement property, are "held for productive use in a trade or business or for investment." Investment property may be exchanged for property to be used in a trade or business or vice versa. Reg. § 1.1031(a)–1(a).

(D) *Loss Transactions.* Where like kind property is exchanged, § 1031 is mandatory, not elective. Taxpayers sometimes have sought to avoid its provisions where, for example, they wish to recognize a loss on the property transferred or to obtain a fair market value basis for depreciation of the property received. Section 1031 may be avoided by structuring a transaction as a sale and reinvestment of sale proceeds, rather than as an exchange. Unless the seller has other losses to offset the income triggered by a sale and reinvestment, the tax deferral accorded by a like kind exchange under § 1031 is more advantageous than the step-up to fair market value of basis that would occur in a sale and reinvestment transaction. This may not be so, however, if there is a wide differential between capital and ordinary income rates and very accelerated depreciation, as was once the case.

On the other hand, a taxpayer may be forced to forgo loss recognition if a transaction intended to be a sale is instead deemed to be a like kind exchange. See, e.g., Godine v. Commissioner, 36 T.C.M. 1595 (1977), where the taxpayers were prevented from recognizing loss on their transfer of an unprofitable residential building in exchange for a duplex.

(E) *Sale-Leasebacks.* As noted previously, an exchange of a fee interest for a leasehold of 30 years or longer is treated as a nonrecognition exchange. Reg. § 1.1031(a)–1(c). Suppose the taxpayer transfers a fee interest in property for cash and a 30-year leasehold in the same property. Is the gain or loss recognized? In Jordan Marsh Co. v. Commissioner, 269 F.2d 453 (2d Cir. 1959), the Second Circuit found that a sale-leaseback with a 30-year and 30-day lease was in substance a sale and thus a loss was recognized. In Century Electric Co. v. Commissioner, 192 F.2d 155 (8th Cir. 1951), however, the Eighth Circuit treated a sale for cash and a 95-year lease as a like kind exchange and disallowed the loss.

Does it make a difference whether the cash received for the assets is equal to the fair market value or whether the rent is a market rent? In this situation, the leasehold has no market value to be exchanged for the property. Note, however, that § 1031 would apply even though cash equaled 99 percent of the value of the property exchanged. See Leslie Co. v. Commissioner, 539 F.2d 943 (3d Cir. 1976), which found a "sale-leaseback" to be a nonrecognition exchange where the "sales" price and rent were both at market value.

(F) *Sales to Related Parties.* The ability to use the deferral provided by § 1031 is severely limited where the exchange is between two related parties. Where a taxpayer exchanges like kind property with a related party (as defined in § 267) and either party disposes of the property within two years, the gain on the original transfer is recognized on the date of the disposition. § 1031(f). (Although the statute technically permits a loss to be recognized as well, it usually will not be because a loss to a related party is disallowed under § 267(a)(1).) A disposition by death, an involuntary conversion, or a disposition that does not have a tax avoidance purpose does not trigger recognition.

In a multi-party exchange taxpayers often use "qualified intermediaries" to acquire the relinquished and replacement properties and transfer them to the proper parties without being considered the agent of any party. In Teruya Bros. v. Commissioner, 580 F.3d 1038 (9th Cir. 2009), the Ninth Circuit considered a very complicated transaction in which the taxpayer used qualified intermediaries to avoid the limitation of § 1031(f) by cashing out its investment without gain recognition. Although the transactions literally qualified as nonrecognition exchanges, the court found that they were entered into in order to shift basis so that the built-in gain on the relinquished property was not recognized when a related party sold the replacement property. The court found that "part of a transaction (or series of transactions) [was] structured to avoid the purposes of [§ 1031(f)]." See § 1031(f)(4).

And in North Central Rental & Leasing, LLC v. United States, 779 F.3d 738 (8th Cir. 2015), affirming North Central Rental & Leasing, LLC v. United States, 112 A.F.T.R.2d 2013–7045 (D. N.D. 9/3/13), related taxpayers transacted through an unnecessary intermediary in order to avoid the restrictions of § 1031(f). The court determined that, because the transactions could have been accomplished more simply, they appear to have been designed to avoid § 1031(f). Because the transactions were designed with this purpose, they did not qualify for § 1031 like kind exchange treatment.

(G) *Holding Period.* A taxpayer who receives property in a tax-free exchange (such as an exchange of like kind property) tacks his holding period for the property that he relinquished onto his holding period for the newly acquired property. § 1223(1). This rule applies only if the taxpayer's basis in the property given up is the same as his basis in the property received and if the property given up was a capital asset or a § 1231 asset at the time of the exchange. The latter requirement is intended to prevent the conversion of ordinary income into capital gain.

(H) *Policy.* What is the justification for not requiring the taxpayer to recognize the appreciation that has been realized on the exchange of real estate property? Legislative history indicates that Congress was concerned with imposing a tax when the transaction produced no cash with which to pay the tax. But that cannot be the only motivation. In a swap of non-like kind properties (such as a truck for land), the taxpayer must pay tax on any gain on the truck despite the lack of cash. Congress also was apparently troubled about the difficulty of valuing property. Valuation is also not a sufficient explanation because in any case in which there is boot, the property must be valued. Valuation is also required in all non-like kind exchanges.

Courts often justify § 1031 by noting that the taxpayer has changed only the form and not the substance of his investment and thus there is a continuity of interest in the investment. Does that justification work when the taxpayer swaps an apartment building for a farm? Has the substance of the investment changed when the taxpayer sells for cash and immediately reinvests in similar property? Does the elevation of form over substance enable taxpayers who own real property that qualifies for § 1031 treatment in effect to elect whichever tax result—recognition or nonrecognition—is most advantageous? Should nonrecognition be extended to all sale and repurchase transactions? What would be the effect of such an extension on the taxation of capital appreciation generally?

B. INVOLUNTARY CONVERSIONS

Section 1033 permits nonrecognition of gain resulting from involuntary conversions, such as where property is taken by eminent domain or destroyed by fire or other casualty. The taxpayer must use the proceeds to acquire "property similar or related in service or use" to the property converted, or, in the case of real estate, to acquire property for business or investment use that is of "like kind" to property condemned by the government. See § 1033(a) and (g). This suggests that "similar or related in service or use" does not mean the same thing as "like kind."

The taxpayer must acquire the new property by the end of the second year following the taxable year in which the involuntary conversion occurred. This time limit is extended to the end of the third year for condemnations of real property used for business or investment.

Section 1033, unlike § 1031, is elective if the taxpayer has received money (rather than property) in exchange for the converted property. This is common, for example, when insurance proceeds are received. The section does not apply to losses resulting from involuntary conversions. (The recognition of such losses on property held for personal use is limited by § 165, discussed in Chapter 3, supra at page 382.)

The purpose of § 1033 is to provide relief where "the taxpayer's property, through some outside force or agency beyond his control, is no longer useful or available to him for his purposes." C.G. Willis, Inc. v. Commissioner, 41 T.C. 468 (1964). Congress considered it unfair to impose tax on those who probably did not intend to dispose of property and thereby realize gains, who may have suffered hardship, and who reinvest any conversion proceeds in replacement property. The taxpayer must recognize gain, however, to the extent that proceeds from involuntary conversions exceed the amount reinvested in replacement property.

NOTES

(A) *Relationship of § 1033 to Other Provisions.* Note that § 1033(g) (like § 1031(a)) excludes from eligibility for nonrecognition treatment real property which is "stock in trade or property held primarily for sale," an exception obviously derived from the § 1221(a)(1) exclusion from the capital asset definition. Note also the relationship between § 1033 and § 1231. The treatment of involuntary conversions under § 1231 is discussed supra at page 590.

(B) *Definition of "Involuntary Conversion."* An involuntary conversion of the taxpayer's property may qualify for nonrecognition under § 1033(a) if it is the result of destruction (complete or partial), theft, seizure, requisition, or condemnation, or a sale or exchange under threat of condemnation. Generally, if an event would constitute a casualty for purposes of § 165(c), it constitutes an involuntary conversion, but the events covered by § 1033 are broader. See, e.g., Rev. Rul. 89–2, 1989–1 C.B. 753, where property rendered unsafe for its intended use by chemical contamination was considered "destroyed."

Some sales of property to the government—or to third parties under what the taxpayer might characterize as a threat of government condemnation—may not qualify for nonrecognition under § 1033. The government must have decided to acquire the property for a public purpose and the taxpayer must have had reasonable grounds to believe that the property would be taken. The "reasonable belief" requirement typically is satisfied if the taxpayer has been notified by a responsible public official that a governmental body has decided to acquire his property and if he reasonably concludes that the body will do so by condemnation if it cannot do so by purchase. For example, the taxpayer was denied nonrecognition treatment in Tecumseh Corrugated Box Co. v. Commissioner, 932 F.2d 526 (6th Cir. 1991). The taxpayer owned property that was on a list of lots to be condemned by the National Park Service, but the taxpayer's property had a low priority and the NPS and the taxpayer had been unable to negotiate a transfer price. Section 1033 treatment will be denied where the disposition of property appears to have been a matter of business discretion rather than of practical necessity. For example, selling pursuant to a state court order of specific performance on a contract for the sale of a property the taxpayer no longer wanted to sell is not an involuntary conversion for purposes of § 1033. United States v. Peters, 113 A.F.T.R.2d 2014–2501 (E.D.Mo. 2014).

(C) *Definition of "Replacement Property."* There is often uncertainty whether replacement property is sufficiently similar to the property replaced for gain on the conversion to go unrecognized under § 1033. Several courts have adopted a "similar use test" that focuses not on the two pieces of property themselves but on the uses to which they were put by the taxpayer. For example, in Clifton Investment Co. v. Commissioner, 312 F.2d 719 (6th Cir. 1963), a taxpayer invested proceeds from the condemnation of an office building in a hotel. The taxpayer, which had operated the office building itself with the help of two employees, hired professional management to operate the hotel. The court held that the taxpayer's responsibilities with respect to the two properties differed so greatly that they could not be held to be "similar or related in service or use."

Technological, economic, or political factors may sometimes make it difficult—if not impossible—for the taxpayer to reinvest condemnation proceeds in similar property. For example, the taxpayer in Davis v. United States, 589 F.2d 446 (9th Cir. 1979), for several decades had owned and leased out agricultural property and an adjoining sea fishery in Hawaii. The proceeds from the condemnation of this property were used to improve property that the taxpayer was developing for lease to an industrial customer. The district court had observed that replacement land could not be purchased and rented out profitably in light of the state's shift over time from an exclusively agricultural economy to a mixed industrial, commercial, resort, and agricultural economy. It also noted that acquisition of a replacement sea fishery was virtually impossible because the state had a declared public policy of absorbing ownership of sea fisheries. The Ninth Circuit held that the conversion qualified for nonrecognition under § 1033(a) because of the similarity of the taxpayer's relationship to the two investments. The court made the appropriate link to the underlying policy of § 1033 when it observed that the test was whether

> the taxpayer has achieved a sufficient continuity of investment to justify non-recognition of the gain, or whether the differences in the relationship of the taxpayer to the two investments are such as to compel the conclusion that he has taken advantage of the condemnation to alter the nature of his investment for his own purposes.

Section 1033(g) provides for nonrecognition of gain where real property held for business or investment use is condemned and the proceeds are reinvested in real property of a "like kind" as defined by § 1031. This amendment was added to § 1033 primarily "in order to conform the standard for condemned property to that of voluntary exchanges" under § 1031.

C. SALE OR EXCHANGE OF TAXPAYER'S RESIDENCE

Section 121 allows the taxpayer to exclude $250,000 (or $500,000 if married filing jointly) of gain from the sale of her principal residence provided it had been used by the taxpayer as such for two of the previous five years. A failure to meet this requirement due to a change in the place of employment, health, or other unforeseen circumstances results in the taxpayer excluding a fraction of $250,000 of gain equal to the fraction of the two-year requirement met.

The regulations provide that the factors that indicate that the sale was caused by unforeseen circumstances include whether "the circumstances giving rise to the sale are not reasonably foreseeable when the taxpayer begins using the property as the taxpayer's principal residence." In Letter Ruling 201628002, the IRS held that the birth of a second child to a couple who were living in their two-bedroom condo with another child was such an unforeseen circumstance.

A taxpayer generally can use this provision no more frequently than every two years. If a taxpayer marries a person who used the provision within the previous two years, she nevertheless may exclude up to $250,000 of gain. Similarly, if spouses file jointly but do not share a residence, each may exclude up to $250,000 of gain. If both reside in the residence, they may exclude $500,000 of gain even if only one of them has lived in the home for two of the previous five years. A surviving spouse can exclude $500,000 of gain if the residence is sold within two years of the decedent spouse's death and the use requirement was satisfied before the spouse's death. Section 121 also provides that members of the uniformed services and the Foreign Service may elect to suspend for a maximum of ten years the five-year ownership period for use of the principal residence during certain absences due to service.

For example, if a taxpayer purchases a residence for $50,000 and occupies it as his principal residence for three years before selling it for $90,000, he can exclude all $40,000 of gain. If he then purchases a home for $100,000 and sells it six years later for $500,000, he can exclude $250,000 of the $400,000 of gain. If he files a joint return with his spouse who also occupies the residence, he can exclude all $400,000 of gain. A wealthy taxpayer can avoid paying any tax on the appreciation in a residence simply by selling one home and purchasing another as the gain nears $500,000. For example, if a couple purchases a home for $1 million and sells it after four years for $1.5 million, they pay no tax. If they buy a new home for $1.5 million and sell it after six years for $2 million, they pay no tax again. The exclusion is worth $100,000 on each occasion (at a 20 percent capital gains rate). That's a big incentive to move. For those for whom the transaction costs outweigh the tax benefits or for whom moving is just a big hassle, they may be able to hold on to the house until death, when the property will pass free of income tax to their beneficiaries.

A taxpayer may have only one principal residence for purposes of Section 121 even if he owns several residences. The property where he spends the majority of his time will ordinarily be considered his principal residence.

Gain attributable to periods of nonqualified use is not eligible for exclusion. A period of nonqualified use is any period in which the taxpayer does not use the house as a principal residence. To determine the amount that is taxable, the gain is multiplied by a fraction the numerator of which is the aggregate periods of nonqualified use during the period the property was owned by the taxpayer and the denominator is the period the taxpayer owned the property. Any period after the taxpayer last uses the property as a principal residence is not treated as nonqualified use. For example, suppose a couple purchases a house for $300,000 and rents it for two years, after which they use it as a principal residence for two years and sell it the following year for $900,000. The two years the property was rented is a nonqualified use and therefore 40 percent of the $600,000 gain (two years/five years) or $240,000 must be reported. The taxpayer may exclude the remaining $360,000 of gain.

NOTES

(A) *Principal Residence.* The taxpayer in Revenue Ruling 77–298, 1977–2 C.B. 308, was a member of Congress, who owned residences in both Washington, D.C. and her congressional district. The taxpayer and her family occupied the Washington residence and the taxpayer's minor children attended school in the Washington area. The taxpayer occasionally used the other residence for lodging during visits to her district. The IRS held that the taxpayer was entitled to nonrecognition of gain on the sale of the Washington residence.

Is an elected official who resides for most of the year in what President Reagan once jokingly called "public housing" entitled to nonrecognition on the sale of a home? One of President Nixon's many tax problems arose out of an ultimately unsuccessful attempt early in his Presidency to exclude gain from the sale of his New York apartment. At the time, the law required that the taxpayer purchase a new principal residence in order to defer the gain. Nixon purchased a San Clemente estate and claimed it as his principal residence. The staff of the Joint Committee on Taxation, which examined the Nixon tax returns in 1974, concluded that the President spent too little time at his "Western White House" for it to qualify as his principal residence. Joint Committee on Internal Revenue Taxation, Examination of President Nixon's Tax Returns for 1969 through 1972. H. Rep. No. 93–996, 93d Cong. 117–18 (1974).

(B) *Conversion Transactions.* Where a taxpayer acquires the house in a § 1031 like kind exchange and then converts it to his personal residence, it must be held for five years before § 121 can be used. § 121(d)(11). Section 121 also provides that where the taxpayer depreciated a portion of the house because it was rented or used as a home office, the excluded gain must be reduced by the amount of depreciation deductions. Reg. § 1.121–1(e). Because the taxpayer need not have resided in the house immediately prior to its sale, he may rent it for a period provided he occupied it as a principal residence for two of the previous five years. If the taxpayer does rent her "principal residence" prior to sale, can she take deductions for depreciation and rental expenses? The Ninth Circuit ruled that she could both deduct the expenses and exclude the gain. The court held that she did not convert the house from "personal use." The dissent agreed with the IRS that depreciation deductions and use of the exclusion were mutually exclusive as a matter of law. Bolaris v. Commissioner, 776 F.2d 1428 (9th Cir. 1985).

(C) *Tax Expenditures for Housing.* There are multiple tax expenditure provisions in the Code designed to incentivize the ownership of a home. The exclusion of gain on the sale of a residence, together with the deductions for real estate taxes and for home mortgage interest, are significant tax expenditures. These items were estimated to involve $124.1 billion in lost revenue in 2016. (Recall, however, that the 2017 legislation limits the deduction for state and local taxes to $10,000 from 2018 through 2025.) In addition, the imputed income from living in one's own house is excluded from gross income.

D. SMALL BUSINESS INVESTMENT COMPANIES

Section 1044 permits the nonrecognition of gain on the sale of publicly-traded securities provided the proceeds are invested in common stock or a partnership interest in a "specialized small business investment" company within 60 days of the sale of the securities. An SSBIC must be licensed by the Small Business Administration. To the extent the proceeds are not so invested, gain is recognized. The taxpayer's basis in the SSBIC stock or partnership interest is reduced by the gain not recognized on the sale of the securities.

E. QUALIFIED SMALL BUSINESS STOCK

Taxpayers can elect to defer recognition of gain on the sale of "qualified small business stock" so long as the stock has been held for more than six months and the taxpayer purchases replacement stock in another qualified small business. § 1045. Qualified small business stock is defined in § 1202 and is discussed supra at page 606. The gain on the sale of the original stock is recognized only to the extent that the sales proceeds exceed the purchase price of the replacement stock. The basis of the replacement stock is the purchase price minus the deferred gain on the sale of the original stock. Note that § 1044 and § 1045, unlike § 1031, are elective and allow for sale and reinvestment rather than requiring an exchange, at least in form. Although the basis adjustment rule is formally different from § 1031(d), the result should be the same.

CHAPTER 6

DEFERRED COMPENSATION: THE VALUE OF TAX DEFERRAL REVISITED

As we have seen, tax deferral can be valuable, akin to an interest-free loan to the taxpayer from Uncle Sam. See the Note on Tax Deferral, supra at page 313. And we've seen that tax deferral is pervasive in the tax law. The realization requirement (introduced in Chapter 2) authorizes the deferral of investment gains. The rules on annuities (also in Chapter 2) defer taxable income by hastening basis recovery. Accelerated depreciation, introduced in Chapter 3, also defers tax by immediate expensing of capital expenditures or frontloading depreciation deductions relative to economic depreciation.

In this chapter, we take a closer look at the value of tax deferral in the context of retirement savings and executive compensation. The analysis here will require a little bit of patience with some numerical examples, but the intellectual and practical payoff is big. It turns out that deferred compensation takes a variety of forms, and the value of tax deferral in each case depends on the timing of income and deductions, the tax rates of workers and firms, and the investment options of workers and firms.

Put another way, tax deferral comes in fifty shades of, well, green. Deferral is (almost) always valuable to the parties and costly to the Treasury. But a savvy policy maker (or tax lawyer) needs to understand just how valuable the deferral is, and under what conditions.

Understanding tax deferral at this deeper level reveals some unexpected conclusions. For instance, we typically think that deferred compensation offers a tax benefit to workers, because they can include income later rather than now. But, as we shall see, the tax benefit to workers may be offset, in whole or in part, when the Code defers the employer's deduction. In many cases, the tax benefit to workers turns entirely on the rate of tax (sometimes zero) that applies to the investment earnings on the amount of compensation that has been deferred. The net value of deferred compensation to workers and employers often is a complex function of relative tax rates and investment options.

SECTION 1.   INDIVIDUAL RETIREMENT ACCOUNTS ("IRAS")

Note on Individual Retirement Accounts ("IRAs")

With the Employee Retirement Income Security Act of 1974, Congress established a tax-advantaged savings account, the IRA, to encourage taxpayers to save money for retirement by providing an optional deduction for contributions to an IRA up to an annual cap. These accounts are now called traditional IRAs. Distributions from a traditional IRA are taxable as ordinary income when they are attributable to deductible contributions and earnings from investments. The traditional IRA thus combines an immediate deduction for savings with deferred taxation of the contributions and earnings.

Savers now have a second option for tax-advantaged retirement accounts, the Roth IRA. Contributions to Roth IRAs are not deductible, so that contributions are made in after-tax dollars. But distributions from a Roth IRA, including earnings from investments, are not included in a taxpayer's income. The Roth IRA thus provides no upfront deduction for contributions but exempts from tax all earnings in the account.

When a taxpayer's marginal tax rates are constant, the two forms of IRA are generally economically equivalent. (This conclusion should be no surprise, since it simply applies the insights developed in the Note on Tax Deferral, supra at page 313.) For example, assume that T, who is in the 37 percent tax bracket, earns $5,000, which he invests in a traditional IRA for which he receives a deduction. Assume that the yield on the IRA is 10 percent, so that, at the end of 10 years, the account has grown to $12,969. After paying a tax of $4,799, T is left with $8,170. Alternatively, T could have contributed $3,150 to a Roth IRA, after paying $1,850 in taxes on his $5,000 of wages. At 10 percent, the $3,150 will grow to $8,170, which he can withdraw tax-free. If it isn't yet intuitive why the two IRA arrangements generally provide the same tax benefit, consult the next Section of this Chapter, which explores this concept in greater detail.

If investment yields are not constant, the Roth IRA has the curious effect of taxing two individuals with wildly different amounts of income at the same rate. This result follows from the fact that the Roth IRA exempts from tax all earnings on contributions, whether the taxpayer makes a huge profit or none at all. Suppose, for example, that A and B (both in the 37 percent bracket) each earn $10,000 in wages, pay $3,700 in income tax, and contribute the remaining $6,300 to a Roth IRA. A's investments perform so badly that she has only her original $6,300 in her Roth IRA at retirement. B, by contrast, has earned a healthy return and has $20,000. Under normal income tax principles, B has $13,700 of income, and A has zero. But the Roth IRA does not tax either taxpayer on the amounts she withdraws from her account.

Under current law, the maximum amount that can be contributed annually to a traditional IRA and deducted is $5,000 (indexed for inflation). At age 50, people are allowed to contribute an extra $1,000. If, however, the individual is an active participant in a qualified plan (that is, an employer plan), the IRA deduction is phased out for taxpayers with income between $80,000–$100,000 ($50,000–$60,000 for single taxpayers). Generally, taxpayers who withdraw savings from an IRA before age 59½ are subject to a 10 percent withdrawal penalty. This penalty does not apply to withdrawals to pay medical expenses, health insurance premiums, or education expenses.

The Roth IRA reverses the usual deduction/inclusion picture. A nondeductible contribution of up to $5,000 (indexed for inflation) annually may be made to a Roth IRA, and distributions for certain purposes are excludible. § 408A. Qualified distributions are those made at least five years after the first contribution and that are either made after the taxpayer reaches age 59½, made to a beneficiary after the death of the contributor, or made because the contributor is disabled or to a first-time homebuyer. The use of a Roth IRA is phased out for single taxpayers with income between $95,000–$110,000 ($150,000–$160,000 if married filing jointly). A taxpayer can contribute to both a regular and a Roth IRA, but total contributions cannot exceed $5,000 annually. The early withdrawal penalty does not apply to a distribution to a first-time homebuyer, capped at $10,000. See § 72(t)(2)(D).

There is no income limitation on conversion of a regular IRA to a Roth IRA. Paying the tax now to avoid paying tax in the future is a real advantage if you think tax rates will be higher when payouts begin from a regular IRA. Apparently, many well-heeled IRA owners have concluded that the future holds tax increases to deal with the deficit and therefore converting to a Roth IRA makes sense.

Taxpayers may convert a traditional IRA to a Roth IRA by treating the value of their IRA as income in the current period. In order to benefit from the conversion, the entire conversion amount must be moved from the traditional to the Roth IRA, and the taxpayer must pay the tax due on the conversion out of non-IRA funds. As Note (B) below implies, one benefit of the conversion is an increase in the total investment that becomes eligible for the nontaxation of investment earnings. What impact do conversions have on current government revenues? (Recall that government revenues are treated as cash receipts for budgetary purposes.) What impact do conversions today have on government revenues in the future? Given that Congress uses cash-flow budgeting rules focused on the short term, what incentives do the current members of Congress have to promote or deter conversions?

NOTES

(A) *Youth, Age, and the IRA Choice.* Traditional and Roth IRAs are equivalent for any taxpayer only if her marginal tax rate remains the same over time. But most people face a predictable trajectory of income. Earnings tend to be lowest in one's 20s and peak in one's 50s, and decline after retirement. Combine that pattern with progressive marginal tax rates, and the typical taxpayer will face relatively low marginal tax rates in her 20s and after retirement and her highest marginal rates in her 50s. If these predictions hold (and they do for most workers), the result is that taxpayers in their 20s should contribute to Roth IRAs, because the deduction is worth relatively little (given their low marginal tax rate). By contrast, taxpayers in their 50s generally should opt for a traditional IRA, since their peak earnings place them in a peak marginal tax rate, which makes the deduction most valuable.

(B) *Pre-Tax and After-Tax Dollars Differ—Obviously.* A given dollar that is contributed to a Roth IRA represents an after-tax contribution, and therefore requires a greater reduction in current consumption (since the contribution is not deductible) than would the same amount contributed in deductible (before-tax) dollars. As a result, an after-tax contribution (such as a Roth IRA) represents more saving than the same dollar contribution to a deductible IRA, which is made with pre-tax dollars. One way to think about this result is to realize that the U.S. Treasury owns, in effect, 37 percent or so of the balance in a traditional IRA (with the percentage equal to the taxpayer's marginal tax rate). By contrast, the taxpayer owns 100 percent of the balance in her Roth IRA.

(C) *401(k).* Section 401(k) allows employees to elect to defer a portion of their compensation if their employer sponsors a plan. While not Congress' intent when it created this section, 401(k) plans have become a major retirement savings vehicle. Like IRAs, these accounts can be made available in traditional or Roth varieties. Contributions to a traditional 401(k) are deductible in the year they are made, and the full amount of any distribution is taxed as ordinary income. Roth contributions are made with after-tax dollars, and all distributions, including gains, are tax free. This is the same immediate deduction-yield exemption scheme we saw with IRAs. When a taxpayer has a constant marginal tax rate, traditional and Roth 401(k)s are also generally economically equivalent. Most employers also contribute to their employees' 401(k) plans. Employees of tax-exempt entities can have generally similar plans, just under different Code sections. See §§ 403(b) and 457.

(D) *Cui Bono?* IRAs, 401(k)s, and other tax-preferred forms of pension savings disproportionately benefit higher-income workers. The tax expenditure amounts to nearly $300 billion per year. And roughly two-thirds of those tax expenditure dollars benefit the richest 20 percent of taxpayers. In large part, this distribution is predictable: recall that tax expenditures taking the form of deductions or exclusions will produce greater tax savings to those in higher marginal rate brackets. And some taxpayers are able to take advantage of investment opportunities not available to the public. For instance, in the 2012 presidential election, candidate Mitt Romney disclosed that he had an IRA potentially worth as much as $100 million. The report generated commentary and controversy, with speculation that Romney had (legally) used his IRA funds to make risky (and highly profitable) investments in private companies. Romney will owe tax on distributions from this account at ordinary income rates, which are higher than the preferential capital gains rates he would have paid outside of an IRA.

The way the Joint Committee on Taxation estimates the tax expenditure is controversial. Following the standard federal budget use of cash revenues and outlays, the estimate counts amounts that are paid into a plan and therefore are not taxed as compensation in any given year; for Roth IRAs, the revenue forgone in any year results from the untaxed distributions. Economically, the "tax expenditure" from these retirement savings plans would be better measured by the taxes forgone annually on the investment earnings of these tax-advantaged savings plans.

(E) *Limits on Contributions.* Traditional and Roth IRAs can be seen as economically equivalent savings instruments. Note that this does not mean that a dollar contributed to a Roth IRA has the same value as a dollar contributed to a traditional IRA because income taxes have already been paid on the Roth contribution. In the earlier example (supra at page 656), this was exactly offset by the fact that Roth contributions are more expensive to make for the same reason. However, the cap on IRA contributions is the same for both types of IRA, which means that taxpayers are effectively allowed to save more in a Roth IRA.

(F) *Reform Proposals.* Policy makers have offered several proposals to extend the benefits of tax-favored retirement savings to lower earners. Some proposals would automatically enroll all workers in government-sponsored retirement savings plans. Other proposals would replace traditional and Roth IRAs with an IRA that provides a tax credit for contributions. (Recall that a dollar of tax credit has a similar value to each taxpayer, regardless of marginal tax rate.)

Note on IRAs and the Immediate Deduction-Yield Exemption Equivalence

The equivalence between an immediate deduction and a yield exemption helps explain the value of deferred compensation in its various incarnations. We have just seen that a traditional IRA and a Roth IRA can produce tax deferral of equal value to the taxpayer under certain conditions. That result is one application of the more general equivalence we first introduced in Chapter 3 supra at pages 313–318. To refresh your memory, and to set the stage for the remainder of this chapter, consider the following example.

Example. Assume that a taxpayer earns $100 in wages and faces a 30 percent marginal tax rate. The pre-tax yield, or return, on investments is 10 percent, and the taxpayer will hold her investment for 10 years.

Under a standard income tax, her wages are immediately taxable, leaving $70 to invest. The annual interest would be taxable, yielding an after-tax return of 7 percent (10 percent return less 30 percent tax). After 10 years, the taxpayer would have $137.70 to spend—that is, free and clear of further income taxes.

By contrast, either an immediate deduction or a yield exemption leaves the taxpayer better off than under the income tax. An immediate deduction, recall, permits the taxpayer to deduct her investment. The deduction of $100 offsets the taxpayer's $100 of income, leaving zero net income and zero tax to be paid. The immediate deduction also imposes no tax on investment income while the taxpayer holds her investment; instead, the full amount is taxed only when she withdraws her money. After 10 years, the taxpayer's $100 investment has compounded to $259.37, leaving her $181.56 after paying tax at the 30 percent marginal rate.

A yield exemption reaches the same result. The taxpayer's wages are fully taxable, because there is no deduction for saving. So she could invest $70 after paying her income taxes. After 10 years, the taxpayer's investment is worth $181.56, and no further tax is due since, by assumption, the yield is exempt from tax.

As we noted in Chapter 3, the assumptions underlying this result are important to note. These include:

(1)   A Constant Marginal Tax Rate. The equivalence holds only if the marginal tax rate remains the same over time. This assumption includes the idea that the marginal tax rate doesn't change if the taxpayer's income changes (within the parameters of the example).

(2)   Immediate Tax Savings. The deduction produces an immediate tax savings equal to the taxpayer's marginal tax rate times the deducted amount.

(3)   Reinvestment at the Same Rate of Return. The tax savings is reinvested so as to yield the same return as the original investment.

So far, this is all review, but it's important review. Even the Joint Committee on Taxation doesn't always get these assumptions quite right. In its 2012 report on the tax treatment of retirement savings, it said that that only the 'normal' rate of return is exempted from tax under an immediate deduction scheme.[1] This statement distorts the third condition outlined here. As long as all earnings are reinvested at the same rate of return, it doesn't matter how high the return may be: it is still tax-exempt. What the Joint Committee should have said is that the third condition may be violated if the initial investment earns a higher return than subsequent investments.

In the materials that follow, we will examine an additional assumption that turns out to be important when we are analyzing deferred compensation paid in an employer-employee relationship. When we move from isolated investments (as in the examples above) to the context of executive compensation and retirement savings, new variables

---

[1]   Joint Committee on Taxation, JCX 32–12, Present Law and Background Relating to the Tax Treatment of Retirement Savings (April 13, 2012).

become important. As you know, employers typically can deduct compensation paid under § 162. So it turns out that the employer's financial situation matters too. The employer's marginal tax rate and the employer's investment returns can affect the value of tax deferral.

SECTION 2.   NONQUALIFIED AND QUALIFIED DEFERRED COMPENSATION

Employers frequently pay compensation for personal services not as the services are rendered but instead in a later year. Compensation may be deferred in order to spread over a number of years the income of those whose earnings are concentrated in a few years. Thus, an inventor may receive royalties over a period of time instead of as his designs are sold, or a professional athlete may receive payments over several years instead of in the year that she plays. In one of the worst examples of deferred compensation in sports, the New York Mets agreed to pay right fielder Bobby Bonilla 25 annual installments of $1.19 million, deferring the first payment for 10 years, instead of immediately paying the $5.9 million remaining on his contract. The Mets were apparently happy to defer the payouts because ownership believed they were making excellent investment returns with their fund manager, Bernie Madoff, who served time in prison after his investment Ponzi scheme collapsed. Compensation also may be deferred to provide employees income during retirement and, in some cases, so that employees will be taxed on the income after they retire, when they may be in lower tax brackets.

There are two types of deferred compensation arrangements: nonqualified and qualified plans. Qualified plans are subject to a number of stringent statutory rules in both the Internal Revenue Code and under the Employee Retirement Income Security Act of 1974 (ERISA) in exchange for favorable tax treatment. For example, qualified plans are forbidden to discriminate in favor of highly compensated employees and are subject to ERISA's vesting and funding standards. Most nonqualified plans, by contrast, are not subject to ERISA's vesting and funding standards. With qualified plans, employers are allowed to deduct deferred compensation currently, and employees are not taxed currently, but instead are taxed only when the compensation is paid during retirement. Importantly, the investment income on the deferred compensation is not taxed to the "pension trust" that invests the money that has been set aside to fund the deferred compensation. Thus, in the case of qualified plans, the investment income is untaxed. This treatment is similar to that of an IRA, discussed supra at page 656.

As the following ruling indicates, it is possible under certain circumstances to achieve deferral under nonqualified plans. In 2004, as described in the notes following the ruling, Congress tightened the rules regulating when income can be deferred under a nonqualified plan. § 409A.

Revenue Ruling 60–31

Internal Revenue Service, 1960. 1960–1 C.B. 174.

Advice has been requested regarding the taxable year of inclusion in gross income of a taxpayer, using the cash receipts and disbursements method of accounting, of compensation for services received under the circumstances described below.

(1) On January 1, 1958, the taxpayer and corporation X executed an employment contract under which the taxpayer is to be employed by the corporation in an executive capacity for a period of five years. Under the contract, the taxpayer is entitled to a stated annual salary and to additional compensation of 10x dollars for each year. The additional compensation will be credited to a bookkeeping reserve account and will be deferred, accumulated, and paid in annual installments equal to one-fifth of the amount in the reserve as of the close of the year immediately preceding the year of first payment. The payments are to begin only upon (a) termination of the taxpayer's employment by the corporation; (b) the taxpayer's becoming a part-time employee of the corporation; or (c) the taxpayer's becoming partially or totally incapacitated. Under the terms of the agreement, corporation X is under a merely contractual obligation to make the payments when due, and the parties did not intend that the amounts in the reserve be held by the corporation in trust for the taxpayer.

The contract further provides that if the taxpayer should fail or refuse to perform his duties, the corporation will be relieved of any obligation to make further credits to the reserve (but not of the obligation to distribute amounts previously contributed) * * *. There is no specific provision in the contract for forfeiture by the taxpayer of his right to distribution from the reserve; and, in the event he should die prior to his receipt in full of the balance in the account, the remaining balance is distributable to his personal representative at the rate of one-fifth per year for five years, beginning three months after his death.

* * *

(4) In June 1957, the taxpayer, a football player, entered into a two-year standard player's contract with a football club in which he agreed to play football and engage in activities related to football during the two-year term only for the club. In addition to a specified salary for the two-year term, it was mutually agreed that as an inducement for signing the contract the taxpayer would be paid a bonus of 150x dollars. The taxpayer could have demanded and received payment of this bonus at the time of signing the contract, but at his suggestion * * * an escrow agreement was executed on June 25, 1957, in which the club agreed to pay 150x dollars on that date to the Y bank, as escrow agent; and the escrow agent agreed to pay this amount, plus interest, to the taxpayer in installments over a period of five years. The escrow agreement also provides that the account established by the escrow agent is to bear the taxpayer's name; that

payments from such account may be made only in accordance with the terms of the agreement; that the agreement is binding upon the parties thereto and their successors or assigns; and that in the event of the taxpayer's death during the escrow period the balance due will become part of his estate.

* * *

[T]he individual concerned in each of the situations described above, employs the cash receipts and disbursements method of accounting. Under that method, * * * he is required to include the compensation * * * in gross income only for the taxable year in which it is actually or constructively received. Consequently, the question for resolution is whether in each of the situations described the income in question was constructively received in a taxable year prior to the taxable year of actual receipt.

A mere promise to pay, not represented by notes or secured in any way, is not regarded as a receipt of income within the intendment of the cash receipts and disbursements method. * * *

This should not be construed to mean that under the cash receipts and disbursements method income may be taxed only when realized in cash. For, under that method a taxpayer is required to include in income that which is received in cash or cash equivalent. * * * And, as stated in the * * * regulations, the "receipt" contemplated by the cash method may be actual or constructive.

* * *

[U]nder the doctrine of constructive receipt, a taxpayer may not deliberately turn his back upon income and thereby select the year for which he will report it. * * * Nor may a taxpayer, by a private agreement, postpone receipt of income from one taxable year to another. * * *

However, the statute cannot be administered by speculating whether the payor would have been willing to agree to an earlier payment. See * * * C.E. Gullett, et al. v. Commissioner, 31 B.T.A. 1067, in which the court, citing a number of authorities for its holding, stated:

> It is clear that the doctrine of constructive receipt is to be sparingly used; that amounts due from a corporation but unpaid, are not to be included in the income of an individual reporting his income on a cash receipts basis unless it appears that the money was available to him, that the corporation was able and ready to pay him, that his right to receive was not restricted, and that his failure to receive resulted from exercise of his own choice.

Consequently, it seems clear that in each case involving a deferral of compensation a determination of whether the doctrine of constructive receipt is applicable must be made upon the basis of the specific factual situation involved.

Applying the foregoing criteria to the situations described above, the following conclusions have been reached:

(1) The additional compensation to be received by the taxpayer under the employment contract concerned will be includible in his gross income only in the taxable years in which the taxpayer actually receives installment payments in cash or other property previously credited to his account.

* * *

(4) In arriving at a determination as to the includibility of the 150x dollars concerned in the gross income of the football player, under the circumstances described, in addition to the authorities cited above, consideration also has been given to Revenue Ruling 55–727, C.B. 1955–2, 25, and to the decision in E.T. Sproull v. Commissioner, 16 T.C. 244.

[The IRS distinguished Rev. Rul. 55–727 on the ground that the bonus received by a baseball player in that situation had not been placed in an escrow account.]

In E.T. Sproull v. Commissioner, 16 T.C. 244, affirmed 194 F.2d 541, the petitioner's employer in 1945 transferred in trust for the petitioner the amount of $10,500. The trustee was directed to pay out of principal to the petitioner the sum of $5,250 in 1946 and the balance, including income, in 1947. In the event of the petitioner's prior death, the amounts were to be paid to his administrator, executor, or heirs. The petitioner contended that the Commissioner erred in including the sum of $10,500 in his taxable income for 1945. In this connection, the court stated:

The question then becomes * * * was "any economic or financial benefit conferred on the employee as compensation" in the taxable year. If so, it was taxable to him in that year. This question we must answer in the affirmative. The employer's part of the transaction terminated in 1945. It was then that the amount of the compensation was fixed at $10,500 and irrevocably paid out for petitioner's sole benefit.

Applying the principles stated in the *Sproull* decision to the facts here, it is concluded that the 150x-dollar bonus is includible in the gross income of the football player concerned in 1957, the year in which the club unconditionally paid such amount to the escrow agent.

* * *

With respect to deductions for payments made by an employer under a deferred compensation plan, see section 404(a)(5) of the 1954 Code and section 1.404(a)–12 of the Income Tax Regulations.

In the application of those sections to unfunded plans, no deduction is allowable for any compensation paid or accrued by an employer on account of any employee under such a plan except in the year when paid and then only to the extent allowable under section 404(a). Thus, under an unfunded plan, if compensation is paid by an employer directly to a former employee, such amounts are deductible under section 404(a)(5) when *actually* paid *in cash or other property to the employee,* provided that such amounts meet the requirements of section 162 or section 212.

NOTES

(A) *Section § 409A.* In 2004 Congress adopted rules limiting the circumstances when income can be deferred under a nonqualified plan. If a plan meets the requirements of this provision, the employee is not taxed currently but, as under prior law, the employer must defer deduction of the compensation until it is included in the employee's income. § 404(a)(5). Nonqualified deferred compensation is included in the employee's income when distributed unless it is subject to a substantial risk of forfeiture. Note therefore that a transfer of restricted property subject to § 83 (see supra at page 121) would not be "deferred compensation." If a plan subsequently fails to meet the requirements of § 409A, the employee is not taxed so long as the compensation is subject to a substantial risk of forfeiture, that is "if such person's rights to such compensation are conditioned on the future performance of substantial services." § 409A(d)(4). If, however, the employee can control the lapse of the risk or if the risk is illusory, the compensation will be taxed.

(B) *Cash Equivalency.* Although Revenue Ruling 60–31 states that a "mere promise to pay, not . . . secured in any way is not regarded as a receipt of income" under the cash method (the method of accounting, discussed in Chapter 7, that most individuals use), the ruling does indicate that the cash equivalency doctrine might apply if something more than a mere promise guarantees the employee's right to receive payment. In case (4) of the ruling, the football player is subject to immediate taxation when his bonus was placed in escrow. In general, nonforfeitable "funded" deferred compensation—for example, amounts transferred in trust or to an escrow account—must be included in current income. Funds may be set aside in a trust to provide for deferred compensation, however, if the terms of the trust make the trust assets available to satisfy creditors' claims on insolvency or bankruptcy of the employer. Section 409A, which was in part a response to arrangements to avoid the requirement of Rev. Rul. 60–31 that nonqualified deferred compensation not be funded, makes clear that if a plan includes a provision that provides for immediate distribution or that restricts funds based on changes in the employer's financial health, the result is immediate taxation to the employee.

(C) *Constructive Receipt.* As indicated in Rev. Rul. 60–31, the Service will not urge application of the constructive receipt doctrine (discussed at length in Chapter 7) merely because the employee made an election to defer receipt. While prior rules were more generous, under § 409A(a)(4)(B) an election to defer compensation must generally be made in a year before the year in which the services are to be performed. An election with respect to a bonus covering services of at least 12 months, however, can be made up to six months before the end of the service period.

There is also much less flexibility on the timing of distributions. In a nonqualified plan, deferred compensation generally cannot be distributed earlier than a fixed time or under a fixed schedule unless there is separation from service, disability, death, an unforeseeable emergency, or a change in ownership control of the employer. The plan cannot provide for acceleration of distributions on certain events nor can it provide for a distribution based on some contingent event.

(D) *Nonforfeitable Compensation.* Should the law be changed to include in current income an employee's nonforfeitable deferred compensation benefits whenever the employer is solvent?

Consider the following excerpt from the report of the Ways and Means Committee on its version of the Tax Reform Act of 1969:

> It is anomalous that the tax treatment of deferred compensation should depend on whether the amount to be deferred is placed in a trust or whether it is merely accumulated as a reserve on the books of the employer corporation. An employee who receives additional compensation in the form of a promise to pay him that compensation in the future made by a large, financially sound corporation, is probably as likely to receive the compensation as an employee whose deferred compensation is placed in trust.

H.Rep. No. 91–413, 91st Cong., 1st Sess. 90 (1969).

Employees of corporations that were sound when deferred compensation was awarded but subsequently went bankrupt before that compensation could be paid might question the committee's conclusion.

Note on Nonqualified Deferred Compensation

As the preceding materials in the Chapter have detailed, deferral can be equivalent to tax exemption of investment income. In the case of nonqualified deferred compensation, however, any "missing" tax on investment income may be supplied by the employer. One way to achieve this is to defer any deduction of the salary payment until the amount is includible in the employee's income, as is required by § 404(a)(5). This is an example of substitute or surrogate taxation. For an extended explanation of this point, see Daniel I. Halperin and Alvin C. Warren, "Understanding Income Tax Deferral," 67 Tax L. Rev. 317, 327–30 (2014).

This is illustrated by the following example in which it is assumed that an employee is entitled to a $10,000 bonus, the rate of return is 10 percent, and both the employer and the employee are subject to tax at a marginal rate of 37 percent. It is also assumed that the amounts of the bonus and the tax savings are invested as is any interest earned thereon.

Case 1: Bonus Paid Currently

In this case, the employee includes and the employer deducts the compensation immediately. We assume a constant rate of return on investments of 10 percent. In this hypothetical, we assume that the employer invests the tax savings for two years, earning an investment return in the meantime.

	Employee	Employer	
Employee Receives	$10,000		
Tax at 37 percent	3,700	$3,700	Tax Savings
After-Tax Investment	6,300		
Year 1 Interest Earned	630	370	
Tax Liability	233	137	
After-Tax Interest	397	233	
Total Accumulation	6,697	3,933	
Year 2 Interest Earned	670	393	
Tax Liability	248	145	
After-Tax Interest	422	248	
Total Accumulation	$7,119	$4,181	

Case 2: Bonus Deferred for Two Years

In this case, the employee inclusion and the employer deduction are both delayed for two years, and (importantly!) the interest earned is taxable on a current basis.

	Employee	Employer	
Employer Invests	$10,000		
Year 1 Interest Earned	1,000		
Tax Liability	370		
After-Tax Interest	630		
Total Accumulation	10,630		
Year 2 Interest Earned	1,063		
Tax Liability	393		
After-Tax Interest	670		
Total Accumulation/			
Paid to Employee	$11,300		
		$4,181	Tax Savings
Tax at 37 percent	4,181		
Net to Employee	$7,119		

Under these conditions, tax deferral is not valuable to either the employee or to the employer (relative to current taxation).

If, however, the employer is tax-exempt or subject to a lower marginal tax rate than the employee, or if the employer can earn a higher rate of return than the employee, the fund will grow at a faster rate in the hands of the employer. Consequently, there will be more money available if the employee defers compensation. After the 2017 act, because of the reduction of the corporate tax rate to 21 percent and the new deduction for 20 percent of "qualified business income" under § 199A (both discussed in Chapter 4), it is much more likely that the employer's tax rate will be lower than the employee's, especially when nonqualified deferred compensation is provided to high-income employees.

Congress required employees to include deferred compensation on a current basis and pay a further tax on investment income when distributed when compensation is received from a tax indifferent party. §§ 457 and 457A. See generally Daniel I. Halperin, "Interest in Disguise: Taxing the 'Time Value of Money,' " 95 Yale L.J. 506 (1986).

NOTES

(A) *Investment Income Is the Key.* The example should make clear that the key factor is the tax rate applied to investment income, not the matching of the deduction and inclusion. The employer would be taxed on the investment income even if it were permitted to deduct $10,000 when the bonus is earned as long as no further deduction was allowed to reflect the larger subsequent distribution.

(B) *A Hidden Tax Benefit.* As explained in the Note, nonqualified deferred compensation provides a net tax benefit to workers only if the employer faces a lower marginal tax rate on investment income (or earns a higher investment return). But taxable companies can fund deferred compensation via tax-preferred investments, including investing in a company's own stock (tax-exempt under § 1032) and investing in tax-advantaged life insurance policies. For an investigation of employer investment patterns, see David I. Walker, "The Practice and Tax Consequences of Nonqualified Deferred Compensation," Boston University School of Law, Law & Economics Research Paper (2016).

Note on Qualified Pension Plans

Sections 401–404 and 410–416 provide more favorable tax treatment for pension, profit-sharing, and "stock bonus" plans that are "qualified." Employees are not taxed on their interests in qualified plans until they actually receive benefits even though the plans are funded. On the other hand, contributions to the plan are immediately deductible by the employer. Thus, unlike nonqualified plans subject to § 404(a)(5), qualified plans do not provide for "matching" of income and deductions. Moreover, the pension trust or fund is itself tax-exempt. As the previous note shows, while failure to match can be an advantage, the principal advantage for qualified plans is the exemption of the investment income.

Case 3: Qualified Deferred Compensation

In this case, the employee's inclusion is deferred for two years. Here we have assumed that the employer is taxed at a 21 percent rate and the employee is taxed at 37 percent. The employer takes an immediate deduction. The investment income earned by the qualified plan is tax-exempt in the meantime and in the example is shown as the employee's earnings.

	Employee	*Employer*	
Employer Invests	$10,000	$2,100	Tax Savings
Year 1 Interest Earned	1,000	210	
Tax Liability	0	44	
After-Tax Interest	1,000	166	
Total Accumulation	11,000	2,266	
Year 2 Interest Earned	1,100	227	
Tax Liability	0	48	
After-Tax Interest	1,100	179	
Total Accumulation/			
Paid to Employee	$12,100	$2,445	
Tax at 37 percent	4,477		
Net to Employee	$7,623		

Note that the employee would have received only $6,300 if the $10,000 had been paid to her currently, and the example allows the investment earnings to compound tax-free only for two years, thus understating the benefit of the tax-free earnings.

To be "qualified," the plan must meet certain prescribed conditions, for example, that it not discriminate in favor of officers, stockholders, or other highly compensated employees. §§ 401(a)(4), (5), and 410(b). See also § 414(a).

Retirement plans can be divided into two main categories:

(1) "Defined benefit plans," under which the employee is entitled to specified benefits (e.g., $20 per month per year of service or 40 percent of average earnings for the three years prior to retirement) and the employer makes whatever contributions are required to provide such benefits.

(2) "Defined contribution plans," under which the employer makes a specific contribution (e.g., 10 percent of pay), the contributions are credited to an employee's account, and the retirement benefit is whatever amount can be provided by the accumulated fund.

Nondiscrimination Requirements for Qualified Plans. Extensive legislative efforts since 1974 have required qualified plans to provide more protection for rank-and-file employees and limited the total amount that can be set aside for highly-paid employees. These efforts, including the nondiscrimination test, have been aimed at encouraging employers to supplement the Social Security retirement benefits provided to their low- and moderate-income employees. For example, the 1986 Act strengthened the nondiscrimination standards and rules permitting integration of employer-provided pension plans and Social Security.

In theory, the nondiscrimination requirements are present in the Code for the purpose of inhibiting tax abuses and ensuring that employer-provided pensions satisfy retirement income security goals. These requirements operate by permitting pension plan contributions and earnings to qualify for tax-advantaged treatment only if a substantial number of lower-paid employees participate in the plan. The basic requirement is stated as a minimum level of coverage necessary for a plan to qualify for favorable tax treatment. Specifically, the nondiscrimination requirement is satisfied if the percentage of employees covered under the plan who do not earn high wages is at least 70 percent of the percentage of highly compensated employees covered under the plan and, for defined benefit plans, if the lesser of 50 employees or 40 percent of all employees are covered by the plan. See §§ 410(b)(1) and 401(a)(26).

These rules seem inadequate to ensure that the tax advantages of qualified plans provide retirement security for rank-and-file workers. A number of important exceptions to the nondiscrimination requirements remain, and coverage of low- and moderate-income employees remains restricted by the ability of employers to "integrate" their pension plans with Social Security benefits. Such "integration" allows employers to treat retirement benefits provided under Social Security as if they were provided by the employer in testing whether the employer's pension plan satisfies the Code's nondiscrimination tests. See § 401(*l*). Many plans meet the nondiscrimination standards only if the Social Security benefits or payments by an employer are taken into account as if they were pension benefits provided under a pension plan, thereby allowing employer plans to take into account the disproportionately larger benefits of Social Security for low- and moderate-income workers and earners.

Vesting Requirements for Qualified Plans. Employers have some flexibility in giving employees vested rights to benefits, i.e., the right to receive benefits if the employee leaves or loses his job before retirement. An employer must either fully vest pension benefits in workers after five years of service or vest 20 percent of benefits each year beginning at the end of three years of service, so that such employees will be fully vested at the end of seven years of service. Under legislation enacted in 2001, faster vesting of benefits is required for employer contributions matching those of employees. Either 100 percent of such contributions must vest after three years of service or 20 percent must vest each year beginning with the second year of service so that 100 percent is vested after six years of service. See § 411. These requirements represent a substantial improvement on the pre-1986 ERISA standards. If a five-year standard had been applicable in 1985, almost 21 million additional workers would have been entitled to vested benefits—a 7 percent increase in the number of men and a 10 percent increase in women. Greater coverage requirements would have made 6.3 million more women eligible for pension benefits than under prior law. The length of employment conditions is a means of promoting stability in the workforce and avoiding the additional administrative costs of an immediate vesting standard. These rules, however, do not seem likely to attain either the retirement security or tax justice advantages of an immediate vesting rule.

Pre-Retirement Withdrawals. Tax penalties are imposed when employees withdraw their pension funds prior to retirement. The Code imposes tax penalties for most early distributions from qualified plans to recoup the initial tax advantage gained. With some exceptions, the Code applies an additional 10 percent income tax to all early distributions included in gross income. § 72(t). These provisions were adopted principally as a means of ensuring that tax advantages intended for retirement savings will be recaptured whenever such savings do not satisfy the retirement security goal and to create a disincentive for early withdrawals. There are also restrictions on borrowing against pension assets. § 72(p). In both cases, Congress seemed to be concerned principally with the tax abuse potential inherent in a regime that would allow pre-retirement withdrawals.

It should be noted, however, that the uniform 10 percent penalty is far more likely to recapture the tax advantage for employees taxed at low marginal rates, which may suggest that Congress cared most about deterring withdrawals that would be more likely to jeopardize retirement security.

Funding and Termination of Qualified Plans. To guard against inadequate funding by employers of pension benefits promised to their employees, § 412 imposes funding requirements as a condition of favorable tax treatment. Employers also are required to guarantee benefits to protect employees when plans are terminated before they are completely funded, and a government agency, the Pension Benefit Guaranty Corporation ("PBGC") has been created to provide "plan termination insurance" when neither funding nor the employer guarantee is sufficient. PBGC is funded by mandatory employer premiums. Note that these protections do not apply to the most common providers of defined-benefit pension plans, federal, state and local governments. The Brookings Institute estimated the unfunded portion of the obligation to these employees was $3 trillion in 2016.

Limits on Contributions and Benefits. Section 415 limits the maximum amount of contributions to pension plans and pension benefits. These limits were lowered from time to time in the 1980s and 1990s, principally to increase current revenues in connection with deficit reduction efforts. The 2001 legislation, however, raised these limits. Generally, the maximum annual contribution is $40,000 for defined contribution plans and the maximum annual benefit is $160,000 for defined-benefit plans. These limits are indexed for inflation. The same limitations apply to self-employed people and partners as to corporate employees.

SECTION 3.   STOCK OPTIONS

A stock option is a very popular form of deferred compensation. Generally, executives in consideration for services are given an option to purchase a set number of shares of the employer's stock at a fixed price at given date in the future. These options may be taxed in two different ways, as incentive stock options or nonqualified options. We consider each in turn.

A.   INCENTIVE STOCK OPTIONS

Under §§ 421 and 422 of the Code, "incentive stock options" are not taxable at the time they are granted or exercised, and the employee usually obtains capital gain treatment when she ultimately sells the stock. The employer ordinarily may not deduct the option as compensation.

To qualify as an ISO, the option price cannot be less than the fair market value of the stock at the time the option is granted. The taxpayer cannot dispose of the stock within two years after receiving the option or within one year after exercising the option. If she does not meet these holding requirements, the portion of gain that represents the difference between the value of the stock when the option was exercised and her purchase price will constitute ordinary income. The employer will receive a deduction at that time to the extent that the employee recognizes ordinary income. The holding period requirements do not apply if the employee dies. Further, to qualify as an ISO, the aggregate fair market value of stock subject to options that are exercisable for the first time in any calendar year cannot exceed $100,000. § 422(d). Accordingly such options are not an important tool for senior executives.

Suppose, for example, that X Co. granted an option to its CEO to acquire 100 shares of X Co. stock for $10 each in two years at a time when the stock is worth $10. When the CEO exercises the option, the stock is worth $100. A year later, the stock is worth $120 and the CEO sells the shares for $12,000. The CEO has no income at the time he receives the option even though he has received a valuable right. Although the option is not "in the money," the CEO will enjoy the benefit of any increase in the value of the stock above $10 and suffers no loss if the stock price declines below $10. Furthermore, he recognizes no income on the spread between $10 and $100 when he exercises the option. He would report the difference between the sales price of $12,000 and his basis of $1,000 as capital gain on the disposition of the stock.

The alternative minimum tax ("AMT"), a regime adopted by Congress to limit the benefits of certain tax preferences to very high-income taxpayers, may limit the tax advantages of ISOs by requiring taxpayers to pay up to a 28 percent tax on the spread between exercise price and fair market value at the time of exercise. See § 56(b)(3).

The AMT is due even if the stock later plummets in value, a tax fact that many executives learn with dismay. For example, the taxpayers in Speltz v. Commissioner, 454 F.3d 782 (8th Cir. 2006), owed AMT of more than $200,000 after exercising options when the employer's stock price was over $100 per share. After the company's stock fell to just 80 cents per share, the entire block of stock was worth just $1,647.

B. EMPLOYEE STOCK OWNERSHIP PLANS ("ESOPS")

ERISA and subsequent legislation have provided special advantages for the Employee Stock Ownership Plans (ESOPs) that promote employee ownership of businesses. An ESOP is a qualified deferred compensation employee trust fund that invests in the company's stock and gives employees a right to demand distribution of the stock on retirement or other termination of employment. § 409. As qualified plans, ESOPs are subject to the general rules applicable to such plans. Certain special tax advantages are available to ESOPs, however. See, e.g., § 1042 (providing nonrecognition treatment for certain ESOP transactions). In addition, the standard qualified deferred compensation plan benefits of an immediate deduction to employers and deferral of employee recognition of income until withdrawals from the trust actually made are still available and somewhat widely used. The Code also provides special estate tax benefits for ESOPs.

C. NONQUALIFIED STOCK OPTIONS

Companies may issue stock options that do not qualify as ISOs. These so-called nonqualified stock options fall under the provisions of § 83.

Alves v. Commissioner

Court of Appeals for the 9th Circuit, 1984. 734 F. 2d 478.

■ KENNEDY, SCHROEDER, and BOOCHEVER, CIRCUIT JUDGES.

* * *The appeal raises an unusual question under section 83 of the Internal Revenue Code, 26 U.S.C. Sec. 83 (1982). Section 83 requires that an employee who has purchased restricted stock in connection with his

"performance of services" must include as ordinary income the stock's appreciation in value between the time of purchase and the time the restrictions lapse, unless at the time he purchased the stock he elected to include as income the difference between the purchase price and the fair market value at that time. The issue here is whether section 83 applies to an employee's purchase of restricted stock when, according to the stipulation of the parties, the amount paid for the stock equaled its full fair market value, without regard to any restrictions. The Tax Court, with two dissenting opinions, held that section 83 applies to all restricted stock that is transferred "in connection with the performance of services," regardless of the amount paid for it. * * * We affirm.

FACTS

General Digital Corporation (the company) was formed in April, 1970, to manufacture and market micro-electronic circuits. At its first meeting, the company's board of directors * * * voted to sell an additional 264,000 shares of common stock to seven named individuals, including Alves. All seven became company employees.

Alves joined the company as vice-president for finance and administration. As part of an employment and stock purchase agreement dated May 22, 1970, the company agreed to sell Alves 40,000 shares of common stock at ten cents per share "in order to raise capital for the Company's initial operations while at the same time providing the Employee with an additional interest in the Company. . . ." * * * The agreement divided Alves's shares into three categories: one-third were subject to repurchase by the company at ten cents per share if Alves left within four years; one-third were subject to repurchase if he left the company within five years; and one-third were unrestricted. * * *

[In 1973 and 1974, Alves sold shares, and in 1974 and 1975, restrictions on the remaining stock lapsed.]

Although Alves reported the $8,736 of gain on the sale of the 2,240 five-year shares * * * as ordinary income on his 1974 tax return, he did not report the difference between the fair market value of the four and five-year shares when the restrictions ended, and the purchase price paid for the shares. The Commissioner treated the difference as ordinary income in 1974 and 1975, pursuant to section 83(a).

In proceedings before the Tax Court, the parties stipulated that: (1) General Digital's common stock had a fair market value of 10 cents per share on the date Alves entered into the employment and stock purchase agreement; (2) the stock restrictions were imposed to "provide some assurance that key personnel would remain with the company for a number of years;" (3) Alves did not make an election under section 83(b) when the restricted stock was received * * *

DISCUSSION

* * * By its terms, [section 83] applies when property is: (1) transferred in connection with the performance of services; (2) subject to

a substantial risk of forfeiture; and (3) not disposed of in an arm's length transaction before the property becomes transferable or the risk of forfeiture is removed. In the present case, it is undisputed that the stock in question was subject to a substantial risk of forfeiture, that it was not disposed of before the restrictions lapsed, and that Alves made no section 83(b) election. Alves's contention is that because he paid full fair market value for the shares, they were issued as an investment, rather than in connection with the performance of services.

The Tax Court concluded that Alves obtained the stock "in connection with the performance of services" as company vice-president. To the extent that this conclusion is a finding of fact, it is not clearly erroneous. * * * Although payment of full fair market value may be one indication that stock was not transferred in connection with the performance of services, the record shows that * * * Alves purchased the stock when he signed his employment agreement and the stock restrictions were linked explicitly to his tenure with the company. In addition, the parties stipulated that the restricted stock's purpose was to ensure that key personnel would remain with the company. Nothing in the record suggests that Alves could have purchased the stock had he not agreed to join the company.

Alves maintains that, as a matter of law, section 83(a) should not extend to purchases for full fair market value. He argues that "in connection with" means that the employee is receiving compensation for his performance of services. In the unusual situation where the employee pays the same amount for restricted and unrestricted stock, the restriction has no effect on value, and hence, Alves contends, there is no compensation.

The plain language of section 83(a) belies Alves's argument. The statute applies to all property transferred in connection with the performance of services. No reference is made to the term "compensation." Nor is there any statutory requirement that property have a fair market value in excess of the amount paid at the time of transfer. Indeed, if Congress intended section 83(a) to apply solely to restricted stock used to compensate employees, it could have used much narrower language. * * *

Alves suggests that the language of section 83(b) indicates that Congress meant for that section to apply only to bargain purchases and that section 83(a) should be interpreted in the same way. Section 83(b) allows taxpayers to elect to include as income in the year of transfer "the excess" of the full fair market value over the purchase price. Alves contends that a taxpayer who pays full fair market value would have "zero excess," and would fall outside the terms of section 83(b).

Section 83(b), however, is not a limitation upon section 83(a). Congress designed section 83(b) merely to add "flexibility," not to condition section 83(a) on the presence or absence of an "excess." * * *

Moreover, nothing in section 83(b) precludes a taxpayer who has paid full market value for restricted stock from making an 83(b) election. Treasury Regulations promulgated in 1978 and made retroactive to 1969 specifically provide that section 83(b) is available in situations of zero excess [See Regs. Section 1.83–2(a).] * * *

Alves last contends that since every taxpayer who pays full fair market value for restricted stock would, if well informed, choose the section 83(b) election to hedge against any appreciation, applying section 83(a) to the unfortunate taxpayer who made no election is simply a trap for the unwary. The tax laws often make an affirmative election necessary. Section 83(b) is but one example of a provision requiring taxpayers to act or suffer less attractive tax consequences. A taxpayer wishing to avoid treatment of appreciation as ordinary income must make an affirmative election under 83(b) in the year the stock was acquired. * * *

Note on Section 83 and Elective Tax Deferral

Section 83, introduced in Chapter 2, may offer an employee who receives restricted stock (or stock options) a choice between two tax regimes. Often, employers grant or sell stock (or stock options) to workers but require forfeiture if the worker leaves the firm before a set period has elapsed. In these cases, the taxpayer can choose between two different tax timing rules, both found in § 83.

Under § 83(a), the key event is the time that the employee may transfer the property or, if earlier, when the property is no longer subject to a "substantial risk of forfeiture." In that year, the taxpayer must report, as ordinary income, the difference between the amount she paid for the stock (or stock option) and its fair market value. The employer receives a deduction for the same amount.

By contrast, if the employee makes a § 83(b) election, she reports income in the year she receives the stock, equal to the difference between the amount paid for the stock and its fair market value at that time.

For example, suppose that a taxpayer pays $10 in Year 1 for employer stock with a fair market value of $60. The stock is subject to forfeiture until the end of Year 2, when the fair market value is $100. The taxpayer sells the stock in Year 3 for $120.

Under § 83(a), because the stock is subject to a substantial risk of forfeiture, the taxpayer has no income on receipt. When the stock vests in Year 2, the taxpayer includes $90 at that time (the difference between the fair market value of the stock, $100, and the amount the taxpayer paid, $10). When the taxpayer sells the stock, she has additional gain of $20.

If, however, the taxpayer makes a § 83(b) election, the timing of her income is different. She would be taxed on $50 immediately in Year 1 (the difference between purchase price and fair market value in that year).

She would pay no tax in Year 2 and would pay tax on gain of $60 when she sells the stock in Year 3.

Should the taxpayer make the election? Her total income subject to tax is the same in either case ($110), but the timing of income varies. So her decision should take into account the value of one year's tax deferral. Using a 10 percent discount rate and a 37 percent tax rate, the tax payments due under § 83(a) have a present value (as of Year 1) of $36.39. The tax due under § 83(b) has a present value of $36.85, making the election unattractive in this case.

Of course, these results depend on the trajectory of the stock price relative to the timing of vesting and sale. Change the example so that the fair market value of the stock is initially $10, rising (as in the prior example) to $100 in Year 2 and $120 in Year 3. In that case, the present value of the tax due on the $110 total income is still $36.39 under § 83(a) but only $33.64 under § 83(b).

In general, a § 83(b) election will tend to be valuable if the immediate inclusion is small (because there is a small spread between the price paid and the value of the stock) and if the date of sale is far in the future.

The tax treatment of capital gains further complicates matters. Recall that long-term capital gains are taxed at a preferential rate, generally 20 percent for high-income taxpayers. Capital losses are tax-disadvantaged, deductible only to the extent of capital gains. See Chapter 5.

A taxpayer subject to § 83(a) reports ordinary income when the stock is no longer subject to a substantial risk of forfeiture. She then takes a basis equal to fair market value, and any subsequent gains are capital gains. In the first example above, the initial $90 of income would be ordinary, and the later $20 would be capital gains. When a taxpayer elects to apply § 83(b), the immediate inclusion is ordinary, and subsequent inclusions are capital gains. Generally, the long-term capital gains preference makes a Section 83(b) election more attractive, especially when the initial inclusion is small.

NOTES

(A) *Joint Tax Planning.* Recall that the timing of the employee's inclusion under § 83 also affects the employer. See § 83(h). In principle, then, firms and workers could maximize their joint tax savings by coordinating with one another in deciding whether to make a § 83(b) election. The planning problem is complex, however. See Michael S. Knoll, "The Section 83(b) Election for Restricted Stock: A Joint Tax Perspective," 59 S.M.U. L. Rev. 721 (2006).

(B) *Equity Compensation in Private Companies.* When workers receive stock in a private company, they may owe federal income taxes even though the stock is not readily saleable. The 2017 tax act responded by creating a special tax deferral regime for equity compensation in companies with stock that is not publicly traded. Employees receiving such stock can elect to defer income (attributable to the receipt of stock upon the exercise of nonqualified stock options or the settlement of restricted stock units) for up to 5 years, provided a number of conditions are met. § 83(i). Notably, the private company must adopt a plan granting equity compensation to 80 percent of its U.S. employees. It is unclear how many eligible employers will comply with the new regime.

CHAPTER 7

WHEN IS IT INCOME? OR DEDUCTIBLE?—ACCOUNTING PROBLEMS

It is obviously not reasonable to wait until a person's death to add up his accounts for his entire lifetime and collect income tax on the net result. As a practical matter, income taxes must be collected on a periodic basis. The period normally selected is the taxable year. The allocation of income to a particular taxable year necessarily involves the application of accounting conventions that often produce controversial results. This Chapter considers the problems that arise from the necessity of assigning particular items of income or deduction to one taxable year or another.

Tax accounting problems are not merely mechanical exercises necessary to calculate taxable income; they present some of the most difficult theoretical and policy issues in income taxation. Two people who have the same economic income and who engage in the same transactions may have different taxable income and tax liabilities, depending only on how they keep their books. As you study the materials in this Chapter, evaluate the policy considerations advanced in support of this "inequality" among similarly situated taxpayers.

The basic statutory provisions on accounting matters are found in §§ 441–483 of the Code. Sections 441, 446, 451(a), and 461(a) and (h) are particularly important and should be examined carefully. They provide, as a general rule, that the accounting method used on the taxpayer's books ordinarily determines when an item of income is taxed or a deduction allowed. There are two basic methods of accounting—the cash method and the accrual method.

Determining when income is taxed and when deductions are permitted is often as important, in terms of a taxpayer's tax liability, as determining what is income and what is deductible. Even in an era of modest interest rates, the economic value of delaying tax liability can be considerable. (This is demonstrated in some detail in the Note on Tax Deferral, page 313, supra, which might profitably be reviewed at this point.) If, for example, tax-exempt interest rates are 3 percent, a taxpayer in the 37 percent bracket who can delay the inclusion of $1 million for a year, or advance a deduction of $1 million by a year, can earn $11,100 in tax-exempt interest on the $370,000 that eventually will go to the government in taxes. Furthermore, if an item produces opposite tax consequences for the two parties involved (e.g., a payment is deductible by the payor and includible by the payee) and each uses different accounting rules, the possibility of generating tax savings through deferral can lead to tax-motivated transactions that lack economic purpose. Conversely, if each party is in the same tax bracket and must apply identical accounting rules, the importance of timing issues diminishes, since any advantage to one party produces an offsetting disadvantage to the other. During the past few decades, taxpayers, the Treasury, and Congress have become more sensitive to time value of money and accounting issues.

Other considerations besides the time value of money can influence timing questions. Tax rates may change from year to year because of tax legislation or changes in the taxpayer's income. Sometimes important tax consequences flow from a shift of one or two years in the inclusion of income or allowance of deductions. Tax rates have changed frequently in recent decades. In 1963, for example, the top tax rate for individuals was a whopping 91 percent of taxable income. After tax reform in 1986, the top rate was just 28 percent. Most recently, in 2017, legislation cut the top individual tax rate from 39.6 percent to 37 percent and cut the top corporate rate from 35 percent to 21 percent.

Even if tax rates remain constant, the progressive rate structure means that an individual may be taxed at a higher marginal rate if her income is received in one year rather than spread over several years. Thus, she might wish to shift deductions to a high-income year or postpone income to a low-income year. So-called "income-averaging" rules, which mitigated the effect of the progressive rate structure to some extent, were repealed when the Tax Reform Act of 1986 flattened tax rates.

There are other factors that make timing important. For example, the statute of limitations may have run on a particular year; if income can be allocated to that year, the Commissioner is precluded from collecting tax. The taxpayer's status may change in a manner that substantially affects tax liability. For example, he may be unmarried in one year and married in the next. Changes in the Internal Revenue Code, the Regulations, or the case law may require different treatment of items of income or deduction in different years.

In sum, the allocation of income or deduction to particular years is quite important in determining tax liability. The significance of these accounting issues, and the broad discretion delegated to the Commissioner to resolve them, have produced considerable dispute over when income is taxable or deductions are allowable. For example, of the thousands of letter rulings issued to taxpayers annually, more than half typically involve requests by taxpayers to change their method of accounting.

It is important to remember that timing issues generally are discrete from the questions "What is income?" and "What is deductible?" If an item does not represent taxable income, there is no question as to *when* it is taxed. The appropriate time to take into account an expenditure arises only for those expenses that are deductible. Nevertheless, some "timing" rules are imbedded in substantive provisions that apply to all taxpayers regardless of accounting method. See, e.g., § 168 (determining when depreciation deductions are taken); § 165 (providing for a deduction when losses are "sustained"); § 166 (providing for a deduction when a bad debt becomes "worthless").

Although there is considerable similarity between tax accounting and financial accounting, there are also significant differences. This reflects the different goals between financial accounting and tax accounting. As the Supreme Court noted in Thor Power Tool Co. v. Commissioner, 439 U.S. 522 (1979):

> The primary goal of financial accounting is to provide useful information to management, shareholders, creditors, and others properly interested; the major responsibility of the accountant is to protect these parties from being misled. The primary goal of the income tax system, in contrast, is the equitable collection of revenue; the major responsibility of the Internal Revenue Service is to protect the public fisc. Consistently with its goals and responsibilities, financial accounting has as its foundation the principle of conservatism, with its corollary that "possible errors in measurement [should] be in the direction of understatement rather than overstatement of net income and net assets." In view of the Treasury's markedly different goals and responsibilities, understatement of income is not destined to be its guiding light. Given this diversity, even contrariety, of objective, any presumptive equivalency between tax and financial accounting would be unacceptable.

This Chapter deals with the problems that arise because of the necessity of assigning particular elements of income or deductions to one tax year or another. In general, the question of when income is taxed depends on two factors: (1) the taxable year and (2) the taxpayer's method of accounting. Problems relating to the taxable year are considered first.

SECTION 1.   THE TAXABLE YEAR

A. IN GENERAL

Burnet v. Sanford & Brooks Co.
Supreme Court of the United States, 1931. 282 U.S. 359.

■ MR. JUSTICE STONE delivered the opinion of the Court.

* * *

From 1913 to 1916, inclusive, respondent, a Delaware corporation engaged in business for profit, was acting for the Atlantic Dredging Company in carrying out a contract for dredging the Delaware River, entered into by that company with the United States. In making its income tax returns for the years 1913 to 1916, respondent added to gross income for each year the payments made under the contract that year, and deducted its expenses paid that year in performing the contract. The total expenses exceeded the payments received by $176,271.88. The tax returns for 1913, 1915, and 1916 showed net losses. That for 1914 showed net income.

In 1915 work under the contract was abandoned, and in 1916 suit was brought in the Court of Claims to recover for a breach of warranty of the character of the material to be dredged. Judgment for the claimant, 53 Ct.Cl. 490, was affirmed by this Court in 1920. United States v. Atlantic Dredging Co., 253 U.S. 1. * * * From the total recovery, respondent received in that year the sum of $192,577.59, which included the $176,271.88 by which its expenses under the contract had exceeded receipts from it, and accrued interest amounting to $16,305.71. Respondent having failed to include these amounts as gross income in its tax returns for 1920, the Commissioner made the deficiency assessment here involved, based on the addition of both items to gross income for that year.

The Court of Appeals ruled that only the item of interest was properly included, holding, erroneously as the government contends, that the item of $176,271.88 was a return of losses suffered by respondent in earlier years and hence was wrongly assessed as income. Notwithstanding this conclusion, its judgment of reversal and the consequent elimination of this item from gross income for 1920 were made contingent upon the filing by respondent of amended returns for the years 1913 to 1916, from which were to be omitted the deductions of the related items of expenses paid in those years. Respondent insists that as the Sixteenth Amendment and the Revenue Act of 1918, which was in force in 1920, plainly contemplate a tax only on net income or profits, any application of the statute which operates to impose a tax with respect to the present transaction, from which respondent received no profit, cannot be upheld.

If respondent's contention that only gain or profit may be taxed under the Sixteenth Amendment be accepted without qualification, see Eisner v. Macomber, 252 U.S. 189 * * *, the question remains whether the gain or profit which is the subject of the tax may be ascertained, as here, on the basis of fixed accounting periods, or whether, as is pressed upon us, it can only be net profit ascertained on the basis of particular transactions of the taxpayer when they are brought to a conclusion.

All the revenue acts which have been enacted since the adoption of the Sixteenth Amendment have uniformly assessed the tax on the basis of annual returns showing the net result of all the taxpayer's transactions during a fixed accounting period, either the calendar year, or, at the option of the taxpayer, the particular fiscal year which he may adopt. Under sections 230, 232 and 234(a) of the Revenue Act of 1918, 40 Stat. 1057, respondent was subject to tax upon its annual net income, arrived at by deducting from gross income for each taxable year all the ordinary and necessary expenses paid during that year in carrying on any trade or business, interest and taxes paid, and losses sustained, during the year. * * *

That the recovery made by respondent in 1920 was gross income for that year within the meaning of these sections cannot, we think, be doubted. The money received was derived from a contract entered into in the course of respondent's business operations for profit. While it equalled, and in a loose sense was a return of, expenditures made in performing the contract, still, as the Board of Tax Appeals found, the expenditures were made in defraying the expenses incurred in the prosecution of the work under the contract, for the purposes of earning profits. * * * Only by including these items of gross income in the 1920 return would it have been possible to ascertain respondent's net income for the period covered by the return, which is what the statute taxes. The excess of gross income over deductions did not any the less constitute net income for the taxable period because respondent, in an earlier period, suffered net losses in the conduct of its business which were in some measure attributable to expenditures made to produce the net income of the later period.

* * *

But respondent insists that if the sum which it recovered is the income defined by the statute, still it is not income, taxation of which without apportionment is permitted by the Sixteenth Amendment, since the particular transaction from which it was derived did not result in any net gain or profit. But we do not think the amendment is to be so narrowly construed. A taxpayer may be in receipt of net income in one year and not in another. The net result of the two years, if combined in a single taxable period, might still be a loss; but it has never been supposed that that fact would relieve him from a tax on the first, or that it affords any reason for postponing the assessment of the tax until the end of a lifetime, or for some other indefinite period, to ascertain more precisely whether the final outcome of the period, or of a given transaction, will be a gain or a loss.

The Sixteenth Amendment was adopted to enable the government to raise revenue by taxation. It is the essence of any system of taxation that it should produce revenue ascertainable, and payable to the government, at regular intervals. Only by such a system is it practicable to produce a regular flow of income and apply methods of accounting, assessment, and collection capable of practical operation. It is not suggested that there has ever been any general scheme for taxing income on any other basis. * * * While, conceivably, a different system might be devised by which the tax could be assessed, wholly or in part, on the basis of the finally ascertained results of particular transactions, Congress is not required by the amendment to adopt such a system in preference to the more familiar method, even if it were practicable. It would not necessarily obviate the kind of inequalities of which respondent complains. If losses from particular transactions were to be set off against gains in others, there would still be the practical necessity of computing the tax on the basis of annual or other fixed taxable periods, which might result in the taxpayer being required to pay a tax on income in one period exceeded by net losses in another. * * *

The assessment was properly made under the statutes. Relief from their alleged burdensome operation which may not be secured under these provisions, can be afforded only by legislation, not by the courts.

Reversed.

NOTES

(A) *Fiscal Years.* The basic statutory provision on the taxable year is § 441 of the Code. (Note that §§ 1 and 11 impose the individual and corporate income taxes "for each taxable year.") Ordinarily, the taxable year is a relatively simple concept. For most individuals and a great many businesses, it is the calendar year—from January 1 through December 31. Individuals and businesses, however, may use a fiscal year ending on the last day of any other month. A fiscal year ordinarily cannot end on a day other than the last day of a month, but taxpayers may report tax based on a year of 52 or 53 weeks that always ends on the same day of the week if they regularly keep their books on this basis. § 441(f).

Usually business factors control the decision to use a fiscal year rather than a calendar year. If the natural business cycle of a taxpayer is slowest during the summer, as with ski resorts, a June 30 fiscal year end may be appropriate for a variety of reasons—for example, inventories will be relatively small and easy to evaluate at that time, adjustments for items spanning two years will be minimized, and there may be more time to deal with bookkeeping matters.

Many restrictions apply to the election of a fiscal year. For example, a sole proprietor of a business may use a fiscal year for reporting her business income only if she also uses the same fiscal year for reporting her personal income. There are similar restrictions on the use of a fiscal year by a partnership or S corporation. A person may use a calendar year for reporting his personal income and a fiscal year for his business income if he incorporates his business, and the corporation is taxable under subchapter C. Are there advantages to the use of a fiscal year that might lead you to advise a client to incorporate?

(B) *The Importance of Changing Tax Rates.* The holding in *Sanford & Brooks* required the taxpayer to include roughly $200,000 in income in 1920, after having deducted roughly $175,000 over the years 1913–1916. Normally, the time value of money works in the taxpayer's favor when it can deduct amounts early and include the same amounts in income later. But, here, the taxpayer fought all the way to the Supreme Court to avoid this result. Can you infer why? It helps to know that the highest corporate tax bracket in the years 1913–1916 was 2 percent, while the top rate in 1920 was 10 percent.

(C) *Short Taxable Years.* Returns may have to be filed on the basis of a short taxable year as a result of a taxpayer's death, the creation or dissolution of a corporation, or a change in accounting period. A short taxable year generally is treated as a full taxable year for all purposes. See § 443.

(D) *Changes in Accounting Periods.* Changes from one accounting period to another are governed by §§ 442 and 443 of the Code. Section 442 provides that a taxpayer may change his taxable year only with the permission of the Commissioner. The change will not be permitted unless the taxpayer establishes a substantial nontax business purpose for the change. In addition, the Commissioner may require the taxpayer to make certain adjustments so that the change does not produce a substantial reduction or deferral of tax liability. § 481.

B.   MODIFICATIONS OF THE EFFECTS OF THE ANNUAL ACCOUNTING PERIOD CONCEPT

As indicated by the Court's opinion in *Burnet v. Sanford & Brooks Co.,* supra, the concept of the taxable year is fundamental. Tax computations are made with respect to taxable years; Congress has rejected a general transactional approach.

As suggested by the Supreme Court in *Sanford & Brooks,* however, there are situations in which strict application of the annual accounting period would produce hardship. The most frequent problems involve transactions that occur or have effects in two or more years. This may be the case when an item is deducted in one taxable year and recovered in another, when money received in one year must be repaid in a later year, or when income earned over a number of years is paid in one year, or, as in *Sanford & Brooks,* when a taxpayer experiences losses in one year and profits in another. A number of specific statutory provisions and administrative and judicial interpretations have been developed to ameliorate the effect of strict adherence to the taxable year concept.

1.   THE "TAX BENEFIT" CONCEPT

Generally, where a taxpayer deducts an amount from income in one year and recovers or fails to pay the deducted item in a later taxable year, the amount recovered or not paid must be included in income in the later year. This rule commonly is referred to as the "tax benefit" rule (or the "inclusionary" component of the tax benefit rule). For example, in a typical application of the tax benefit rule, in National Bank of Commerce v. Commissioner, 115 F.2d 875 (9th Cir. 1940), a bank was found to have income from recoveries on loans that it had previously written off because it had deducted those losses in the year it wrote off the loans.

There is a second aspect to the tax benefit rule that generally is labeled the "exclusionary" component. Originally developed by the courts, and now partially codified in § 111, this rule provides that where a deduction in a prior year produced no "tax benefit"—as, for example, where the taxpayer had no income and hence no tax liability—subsequent recovery or eventual nonpayment of the previously deducted item does not produce taxable income in the year of recovery or nonpayment. Section 111 initially was limited to the recovery of bad debts and taxes, but now extends to recovery of any deduction taken in a prior year to the extent that the deduction did not reduce "the amount of tax imposed by this Chapter." This permits taxpayers to exclude recoveries of amounts that may have reduced taxable income, but not the amount of tax imposed (for example, due to excess tax credits). Suppose the taxpayer paid a $10,000 medical bill that should have been issued for $1,000. When the physician returns $9,000 to the taxpayer, the patient has no income if he did not deduct medical expenses as an itemized deduction in the year of payment because he would have received no tax benefit from the medical expense.

Section 111 also applies to tax credits. Except for the foreign tax credit and the investment tax credit, which have their own recapture rules, § 111 requires an increase in tax imposed in any year in which there was a subsequent recovery with respect to any item for which a tax credit was allowable in a prior year. If a credit did not reduce income taxes in the earlier year, it does not increase income taxes in the later year. § 111(b). For example, assume an individual in one year claims a 25 percent credit for $1,000 of wages paid to a child caretaker (§ 21), but in a subsequent year, $200 of the wages are refunded. Under § 111(b), tax would be increased in the subsequent year by $50 (25 percent of $200) unless the prior year's credit had not reduced tax.

A somewhat related provision is § 186 of the Code, which deals with damage recoveries for antitrust violations, breach of contract, and patent infringement. This section allows a taxpayer to deduct from damage recoveries those losses that did not produce any earlier tax benefit.

The tax benefit rule provides only rough justice. It does not eliminate differences in tax that result if tax liability was reduced by one rate in the earlier year, but increased by the later recovery at a different rate. See Alice Phelan Sullivan Corp. v. United States, 381 F.2d 399 (Ct.Cl. 1967) (taxing the recovery at the rate applicable in the later year regardless of the size of the tax benefit in the earlier year). Suppose, for example, that the taxpayer, who is in a 24 percent bracket, takes a deduction for a $1,000 painting donated to charity. If the charity returns the painting in a year in which he is in a 37 percent bracket, he will pay an additional $370 of taxes on the $1,000 recovery although he saved only $240 in taxes when he took the deduction in the prior year.

Even if the rate brackets remain the same, and the taxpayer's total tax is zero—the position he would have been in by never having donated the painting—he enjoys the advantage of the time value of the earlier savings of taxes.

Hillsboro National Bank v. Commissioner and United States v. Bliss Dairy, Inc.

Supreme Court of the United States, 1983. 460 U.S. 370.

■ JUSTICE O'CONNOR delivered the opinion of the Court.

These consolidated cases present the question of the applicability of the tax benefit rule to two corporate tax situations: the repayment to the shareholders of taxes for which they were liable but that were originally paid by the corporation; and the distribution of expensed assets in a corporate liquidation. We conclude that, unless a nonrecognition provision of the Internal Revenue Code prevents it, the tax benefit rule ordinarily applies to require the inclusion of income when events occur that are fundamentally inconsistent with an earlier deduction. Our examination of the provisions granting the deductions and governing the liquidation in these cases lead us to hold that the rule requires the recognition of income in the case of the liquidation but not in the case of the tax refund.

I

[Illinois had imposed a property tax on shares of incorporated banks doing business in the state. Hillsboro National Bank paid this tax on behalf of its shareholders, taking the deduction for taxes permitted by § 164(e). The state refunded some of these payments directly to shareholders after the Supreme Court upheld a state constitutional amendment prohibiting ad valorem taxation of personal property owned by individuals. The IRS sought to include the repayment in Hillsboro's income.

Bliss Dairy deducted under § 162 the full cost of cattle feed purchased for use in its operations. Bliss adopted a plan of liquidation in the next taxable year and distributed a substantial amount of remaining feed to its shareholders in a nontaxable transaction. The IRS asserted that Bliss should have taken into income the value of the feed distributed to its shareholders.]

II

The Government in each case relies solely on the tax benefit rule—a judicially developed principle[8] that allays some of the inflexibilities of the annual accounting system. An annual accounting system is a practical necessity if the federal income tax is to produce revenue ascertainable and payable at regular intervals. Burnet v. Sanford & Brooks Co., 282 U.S. 359, 365 (1931). Nevertheless, strict adherence to an annual accounting system would create transactional inequities. Often an apparently completed transaction will reopen unexpectedly in a subsequent tax year, rendering the initial reporting improper. For instance, if a taxpayer held a note that became apparently uncollectible

---

[8] Although the rule originated in the courts, it has the implicit approval of Congress, which enacted § 111 as a limitation on the rule.

early in the taxable year, but the debtor made an unexpected financial recovery before the close of the year and paid the debt, the transaction would have no tax consequences for the taxpayer, for the repayment of the principal would be recovery of capital. If, however, the debtor's financial recovery and the resulting repayment took place after the close of the taxable year, the taxpayer would have a deduction for the apparently bad debt in the first year under § 166(a) of the Code. * * * Without the tax benefit rule, the repayment in the second year, representing a return of capital, would not be taxable. The second transaction, then, although economically identical to the first, could, because of the differences in accounting, yield drastically different tax consequences. The Government, by allowing a deduction that it could not have known to be improper at the time, would be foreclosed from recouping any of the tax saved because of the improper deduction.[10] Recognizing and seeking to avoid the possible distortions of income,[11] the courts have long required the taxpayer to recognize the repayment in the second year as income.

The taxpayers and the Government in these cases propose different formulations of the tax benefit rule. The taxpayers contend that the rule requires the inclusion of amounts *recovered* in later years, and they do not view the events in these cases as "recoveries." The Government, on the other hand, urges that the tax benefit rule requires the inclusion of amounts previously deducted if later events are inconsistent with the deductions; it insists that no "recovery" is necessary to the application of the rule. Further, it asserts that the events in these cases are inconsistent with the deductions taken by the taxpayers. We are not in complete agreement with either view.

An examination of the purpose and accepted applications of the tax benefit rule reveals that a "recovery" will not always be necessary to invoke the tax benefit rule. The purpose of the rule is not simply to tax "recoveries." On the contrary, it is to * * * achieve rough transactional parity in tax, and to protect the Government and the taxpayer from the adverse effects of reporting a transaction on the basis of assumptions that an event in a subsequent year proves to have been erroneous. Such an event, unforeseen at the time of an earlier deduction, may in many cases

---

[10] When the event proving the deduction improper occurs after the close of the taxable year, even if the statute of limitations has not run, the Commissioner's proper remedy is to invoke the tax benefit rule and require inclusion in the later year rather than to re-open the earlier year. * * *

[11] As the rule developed, a number of theories supported taxation in the later year. One explained that the taxpayer who had taken the deduction "consented" to "return" it if events proved him not entitled to it, while another explained that the deduction offset income in the earlier year, which became "latent" income that might be recaptured. Still a third view maintained that the later recognition of income was a balancing entry. All these views reflected that the initial accounting for the item must be corrected to present a true picture of income. While annual accounting precludes reopening the earlier year, it does not prevent a less precise correction—far superior to none—in the current year, analogous to the practice of financial accountants. This concern with more accurate measurement of income underlies the tax benefit rule and always has.

require the application of the tax benefit rule. We do not, however, agree that this consequence invariably follows. Not every unforeseen event will require the taxpayer to report income in the amount of his earlier deduction. On the contrary, the tax benefit rule will "cancel out" an earlier deduction only when a careful examination shows that the later event is indeed fundamentally inconsistent with the premise on which the deduction was initially based. That is, if that event had occurred within the same taxable year, it would have foreclosed the deduction. In some cases, a subsequent recovery by the taxpayer will be the only event that would be fundamentally inconsistent with the provision granting the deduction. In such a case, only actual recovery by the taxpayer would justify application of the tax benefit rule. For example, if a calendar-year taxpayer made a rental payment on December 15 for a 30-day lease deductible in the current year under § 162(a)(3), * * * the tax benefit rule would not require the recognition of income if the leased premises were destroyed by fire on January 10. The resulting inability of the taxpayer to occupy the building would be an event not fundamentally inconsistent with his prior deduction as an ordinary and necessary business expense under § 162(a). The loss is attributable to the business and therefore is consistent with the deduction of the rental payment as an ordinary and necessary business expense. On the other hand, had the premises not burned and, in January, the taxpayer decided to use them to house his family rather than to continue the operation of his business, he would have converted the leasehold to personal use. This would be an event fundamentally inconsistent with the business use on which the deduction was based. In the case of the fire, only if the lessor—by virtue of some provision in the lease—had refunded the rental payment would the taxpayer be required under the tax benefit rule to recognize income on the subsequent destruction of the building. In other words, the subsequent recovery of the previously deducted rental payment would be the only event inconsistent with the provision allowing the deduction. It therefore is evident that the tax benefit rule must be applied on a case-by-case basis. A court must consider the facts and circumstances of each case in the light of the purpose and function of the provisions granting the deductions.

When the later event takes place in the context of a nonrecognition provision of the Code, there will be an inherent tension between the tax benefit rule and the nonrecognition provision. * * * We cannot resolve that tension with a blanket rule that the tax benefit rule will always prevail. Instead, we must focus on the particular provisions of the Code at issue in any case.

* * *

In the cases currently before us, then, we must undertake an examination of the particular provisions of the Code that govern these transactions to determine whether the deductions taken by the taxpayers were actually inconsistent with later events and whether specific nonrecognition provisions prevail over the principle of the tax benefit rule.

III

In *Hillsboro,* the key provision is § 164(e). That section grants the corporation a deduction for taxes imposed on its shareholders but paid by the corporation. It also denies the shareholders any deduction for the tax. In this case, the Commissioner has argued that the refund of the taxes by the state to the shareholders is the equivalent of the payment of a dividend from Hillsboro to its shareholders. If Hillsboro does not recognize income in the amount of the earlier deduction, it will have deducted a dividend. Since the general structure of the corporate tax provisions does not permit deduction of dividends, the Commissioner concludes that the payment to the shareholders must be inconsistent with the original deduction and therefore requires the inclusion of the amount of the taxes as income under the tax benefit rule.

In evaluating this argument, it is instructive to consider what the tax consequences of the payment of a shareholder tax by the corporation would be without § 164(e) and compare them to the consequences under § 164(e). Without § 164(e), the corporation would not be entitled to a deduction, for the tax is not imposed on it. * * * If the corporation has earnings and profits, the shareholder would have to recognize income in the amount of the taxes, because a payment by a corporation for the benefit of its shareholders is a constructive dividend. * * * The shareholder, however, would be entitled to a deduction since the constructive dividend is used to satisfy his tax liability. Section 164(a)(2). Thus, for the shareholder, the transaction would be a wash: he would recognize the amount of the tax as income, but he would have an offsetting deduction for the tax. For the corporation, there would be no tax consequences, for the payment of a dividend gives rise to neither income nor a deduction. Section 311(a).

Under § 164(e), the economics of the transaction of course remain unchanged: the corporation is still satisfying a liability of the shareholder and is therefore paying a constructive dividend. The tax consequences are, however, significantly different, at least for the corporation. The transaction is still a wash for the shareholder, although § 164(e) denies him the deduction to which he would otherwise be entitled, he need not recognize income on the constructive dividend, Treas. Reg. § 1.164–7, 26 CFR § 1.164–7 (1982). But the corporation is entitled to a deduction that would not otherwise be available. In other words, the only effect of § 164(e) is to permit the corporation to deduct a dividend. Thus, we cannot agree with the Commissioner that, simply because the events here give rise to a deductible dividend, they cannot be consistent with the deduction. In at least some circumstances, a deductible dividend is within the contemplation of the Code. The question we must answer is whether § 164(e) permits a deductible dividend in these circumstances— when the money, though initially paid into the state treasury, ultimately reaches the shareholder—or whether the deductible dividend is available, as the Commissioner urges, only when the money remains in the state treasury, as properly assessed and collected tax revenue.

Rephrased, our question now is whether Congress, in granting this special favor to corporations that paid dividends by satisfying the liability of their shareholders, was concerned with the *reason* the money was paid out by the corporation or with the *use* to which it was ultimately put. Since § 164(e) represents a break with the usual rules governing corporate distributions, the structure of the Code does not provide any guidance on the reach of the provision. This Court has described the provision as "prompted by the plight of various banking corporations which paid and voluntarily absorbed the burden of certain local taxes imposed upon their shareholders, but were not permitted to deduct those payments from gross income." The section, in substantially similar form, has been part of the Code since the Revenue Act of 1921 * * *. The only discussion of the provision appears to be that between Dr. T.S. Adams and Senator Smoot at the Senate hearings. Dr. Adams' statement explains why the States imposed the property tax on the shareholders and collected it from the banks, but it does not cast light on the reason for the deduction. Senator Smoot's response, however, is more revealing:

> "I have been a director in a bank * * * for over 20 years. They have paid that tax ever since I have owned a share of stock in the bank. * * * I know nothing about it. I do not take 1 cent of credit for deductions, and the banks are entitled to it. They pay it out."

The payment by the corporations of a liability that Congress knew was not a tax imposed on them gave rise to the entitlement to a deduction; Congress was unconcerned that the corporations took a deduction for amounts that did not satisfy their tax liability. It apparently perceived the shareholders and the corporations as independent of one another, each "[knowing] nothing about" the payments by the other. In those circumstances, it is difficult to conclude that Congress intended that the corporation have no deduction if the State turned the tax revenues over to these independent parties. We conclude that the purpose of § 164(e) was to provide relief for corporations making these payments, and the focus of Congress was on the act of payment rather than on the ultimate use of the funds by the state. As long as the payment itself was not negated by a refund to the corporation, the change in the character of the funds in the hands of the state does not require the corporation to recognize income, and we reverse the judgment below.

IV

The problem in *Bliss* is more complicated. Bliss took a deduction under § 162(a), so we must begin by examining that provision. Section 162(a) permits a deduction for the "ordinary and necessary expenses" of carrying on a trade or business. The deduction is predicated on the consumption of the asset in the trade or business. See Treas. Reg.

§ 1.162–3 (1982) ("Taxpayers * * * should include in expenses the charges for materials and supplies only in the amount that they are *actually consumed and used in operation* in the taxable year. * * * ") (emphasis added). If the taxpayer later sells the assets rather than consuming it in furtherance of his trade or business, it is quite clear that he would lose his deduction, for the basis of the asset would be zero, * * * so he would recognize the full amount of the proceeds on sale as gain. See § 1001(a) , (c). In general, if the taxpayer converts the expensed asset to some other, non-business use, that action is inconsistent with his earlier deduction, and the tax benefit rule would require inclusion in income of the amount of the unwarranted deduction. That non-business use is inconsistent with a deduction for an ordinary and necessary business expense is clear from an examination of the Code. While § 162(a) permits a deduction for ordinary and necessary business expenses, § 262 explicitly denies a deduction for personal expenses. * * * Thus, if a corporation turns expensed assets to the analog of personal consumption, as Bliss did here—distribution to shareholders—it would seem that it should take into income the amount of the earlier deduction.

That conclusion, however, does not resolve this case, for the distribution by Bliss to its shareholders is governed by a provision of the Code that specifically shields the taxpayer from recognition of gain— § 336.* We must therefore proceed to inquire whether this is the sort of gain that goes unrecognized under § 336. Our examination of the background of § 336 and its place within the framework of tax law convinces us that it does not prevent the application of the tax benefit rule.

[The Court's discussion of § 336 is omitted.]

Thus, the legislative history of § 336, the application of other general rules of tax law, and the construction of the identical language in § 337 all indicate that § 336 does not permit a liquidating corporation to avoid the tax benefit rule. Consequently, we reverse the judgment of the Court of Appeals and hold that, on liquidation, Bliss must include in income the amount of the unwarranted deduction.

V

Bliss paid the assessment on an increase of $60,000 in its taxable income. In the District Court, the parties stipulated that the value of the grain was $56,565, but the record does not show what the original cost of the grain was or what portion of it remained at the time of liquidation. The proper increase in taxable income is the portion of the cost of the grain attributable to the amount of grain on hand at the time of liquidation. In *Bliss,* then, we remand for a determination of that amount. In *Hillsboro,* the taxpayer sought a redetermination in the Tax

---

*   [Ed Note: This "gain-shielding" quality of § 336 was removed by the Tax Reform Act of 1986.]

Court rather than paying the tax, so no further proceedings are necessary, and the judgment of the Court of Appeals is reversed.

It is so ordered.

■ [The dissenting opinion of JUSTICE BRENNAN in *Hillsboro National Bank* and the opinion of JUSTICE STEVENS joined by JUSTICE MARSHALL, concurring in *Hillsboro National Bank* and dissenting in *Bliss Dairy* have been omitted.]

■ [JUSTICE BLACKMUN, dissenting in both cases, would have required the corporations in both cases to have amended their tax returns and remove the deductions for the year in which the deductions were claimed. An excerpt from his dissent follows.]

I have no difficulty in favoring some kind of "tax benefit" adjustment in favor of the Government for each of these situations. An adjustment should be made, for in each case the beneficial deduction turned out to be improper and undeserved because its factual premise proved to be incorrect. Each taxpayer thus was not entitled to the claimed deduction, or a portion of it, and this nonentitlement should be reflected among its tax obligations.

This takes me, however, to the difficulty I encounter with * * * the unraveling or rectification of the situation. The Commissioner and the United States in these respective cases insist that the Bank and the Dairy should be regarded as receiving income in the very next tax year when the factual premise for the prior year's deduction proved to be incorrect. I could understand that position, if, in the interim, the bar of a statute of limitations had become effective or if there were some other valid reason why the preceding year's return could not be better corrected and additional tax collected. But it seems to me that the better resolution of these two particular cases and others like them—and a resolution that should produce little complaint from the taxpayer—is to make the necessary adjustment, whenever it can be made, in the tax year for which the deduction was originally claimed. This makes the correction where the correction is due and it makes the amount of the net income for each year a true amount and one that accords with the facts, not one that is unstructured, imprecise, and fictional. This normally would be accomplished either by the taxpayer's filing an amended return for the earlier year, with payment of the resulting additional tax, or by the Commissioner's assertion of a deficiency followed by collection. This actually is the kind of thing that is done all the time, for when a taxpayer's return is audited and a deficiency is asserted due to an overstated deduction, the process equates with the filing of an amended return.

* * *

This, in my view, is the way these two particular tax controversies should be resolved. I see no need for anything more complex in their resolution than what I have outlined. Of course, if a statute of limitations problem existed, or if the facts in some other way prevented reparation to the Government, the cases and their resolution might well be different.

I realize that my position is simplistic, but I doubt if the judge-made tax benefit rule really was intended, at its origin, to be regarded as applicable in simple situations of the kind presented in these successive-tax-year cases. So often a judge-made rule, understandably conceived, ultimately is used to carry us further than it should.

I would vacate the judgment in each of these cases and remand each case for further proceedings consistent with this analysis.

NOTES

(A) *"Fundamentally Inconsistent" Events.* The Supreme Court's decisions in *Hillsboro* and *Bliss Dairy* make it clear—contrary to some prior appellate court decisions—that the tax benefit rule does not require an economic or physical "recovery" of an item or a cancellation of a liability; all that is required is an event "fundamentally inconsistent" with the earlier deduction. Beyond that, however, the majority opinion does little to define a "fundamentally inconsistent event." The refund of taxes to shareholders in *Hillsboro* was deemed not to trigger the tax benefit rule because of the majority's reading of the legislative history of § 164(e). The dissenting Justices disagreed with the conclusion of the majority that the "focus of Congress was on the act of payment rather than on the ultimate use of the funds by the state;" even granting the majority's conclusion, the dissent argued that the refund of the taxes to the shareholders could easily have been classified as "fundamentally inconsistent" with the earlier deduction. The facts of *Hillsboro* seem unique (as does the debate over the legislative purpose of § 164(e)), and the Court here provides little guidance for the application of the tax benefit doctrine in future cases.

The Court's opinion in *Bliss Dairy* creates considerable uncertainty about when courts will intervene to recapture other "fundamentally inconsistent" deductions. For example, the Ninth Circuit refused to treat as a fundamentally inconsistent event the distribution on liquidation of unharvested crops, where the corporation had previously deducted the costs of production. Rojas v. Commissioner, 901 F.2d 810 (9th Cir. 1990). The Court distinguished *Bliss Dairy* on the ground that in that case, the feed that had been deducted was distributed, whereas in *Rojas* the seed, fertilizer, and other expensed assets were consumed. It rejected the Service's position that consumption required the production of income, stating that this would "extend the tax benefit rule well beyond the parameters outlined in *Bliss Dairy.*" If the feed in *Bliss Dairy* had been eaten by the cattle, which were then distributed, what result? If the cattle in *Bliss Dairy* had been eaten by a horse, which in turn, was eaten by an old lady who had swallowed a fly, what result? (She died, of course.)

(B) *A Transactional Approach.* Would Justice Blackmun's position have the effect of replacing annual accounting with a full transactional system? Compare § 1341, discussed infra at page 699, which allows taxpayers who take a deduction for the surrender of an item previously included in income to calculate their tax savings by reference to either the year of inclusion or the year of deduction. Why should this option be allowed only where a taxpayer first pays taxes and later seeks a refund, and not where the taxpayer first lowers taxes through a deduction and subsequently increases income?

(C) *Items Erroneously Deducted in the Earlier Year.* What if the taxpayer erroneously claimed a deduction in the earlier year? In Mayfair Minerals, Inc. v. Commissioner, 56 T.C. 82 (1971), aff'd 456 F.2d 622 (5th Cir. 1972), the Tax Court required a subsequent recovery to be included in income even though the original deduction had been improperly taken. The court held that the taxpayer had "misled" the revenue agents by treating the deduction improperly in the earlier year.

In Unvert v. Commissioner, 72 T.C. 807 (1979), aff'd 656 F.2d 483 (9th Cir. 1981), cert. denied, 456 U.S. 961 (1982), the taxpayer first deducted as prepaid interest an initial payment for the purchase of condominium units. He later recovered this sum. He argued that the initial outlay really had been a nondeductible deposit and that its recovery constituted a nontaxable restoration of capital. He attempted to invoke the erroneous deduction exception to defeat the application of the tax benefit rule to the recovery. The Tax Court invoked *Mayfair's* estoppel rule and required the taxpayer to include the returned money in income. On appeal, the Ninth Circuit ignored the Tax Court's "quasi-estoppel" theory and affirmed on the ground that the statute of limitations should never bar the inclusion of the recovery of an earlier erroneous deduction. The Fifth Circuit also has rejected the erroneous deduction exception. In Hughes & Luce L.L.P. v. Commissioner, 70 F.3d 16 (5th Cir. 1995), a law firm deducted "service costs" that the IRS determined were nondeductible loans. The Fifth Circuit found that reimbursement of the loans triggered income under the tax benefit rule.

(D) *Amount of the Inclusion.* Where the taxpayer transfers property and takes a deduction and the property is later returned to her, the fair market value of the property may have increased or decreased. In *Alice Phelan Sullivan Corp.,* supra, the IRS only attempted to tax the later recovery of property previously donated to charity to the extent of fair market value at the time of the deduction, which was the amount deducted. The Tax Court has held that the inclusion is the lesser of the amount of the deduction or the fair market value of the property when returned. Rosen v. Commissioner, 71 T.C. 226 (1978), aff'd 611 F.2d 942 (1st Cir. 1980). If the taxpayer had previously received no tax benefit from the deduction, but the property had increased in value, should there be any taxable income on the return of the property?

2.   CLAIM OF RIGHT—INCOME RECEIVED SUBJECT TO CONTINGENCIES
     OR LIABILITIES

Problems similar to those discussed in connection with the tax benefit rule arise in the converse situation where a taxpayer receives income in one year and is required to repay the amount received in a later year. The courts have had to decide how rigorously to apply the taxable year concept as described in *Sanford & Brooks*.

The issue arises whenever it turns out that the taxpayer did not have an absolute right to the money or property, but only a "claim of right." The general rule is that amounts received under a "claim of right" must be included in income when received and may be deducted if subsequently repaid. The subsequent repayment does not affect the initial inclusion. United States v. Lewis, 340 U.S. 590 (1951).

The case that follows discusses § 1341, which in some cases affects the amount of the deduction, and seems to add a "tax detriment" limitation to the subsequent deduction.

United States v. Skelly Oil Co.

Supreme Court of the United States, 1969. 394 U.S. 678.

■ MR. JUSTICE MARSHALL delivered the opinion of the Court.

During its tax year ending December 31, 1958, respondent refunded $505,536.54 to two of its customers for overcharges during the six preceding years. Respondent, an Oklahoma producer of natural gas, had set its prices during the earlier years in accordance with a minimum price order of the Oklahoma Corporation Commission. After that order was vacated as a result of a decision of this Court, * * * respondent found it necessary to settle a number of claims filed by its customers; the repayments in question represent settlements of two of those claims. Since respondent had claimed an unrestricted right to its sales receipts during the years 1952 through 1957, it had included the $505,536.54 in its gross income in those years. The amount was also included in respondent's "gross income from the property" as defined in § 613 of the Internal Revenue Code of 1954, the section which allows taxpayers to deduct a fixed percentage of certain receipts to compensate for the depletion of natural resources from which they derive income. Allowable percentage depletion for receipts from oil and gas wells is fixed at 27½% of the "gross income from the property." Since respondent claimed and the Commissioner allowed percentage depletion deductions during these years, 27½% of the receipts in question was added to the depletion allowances to which respondent would otherwise have been entitled. Accordingly, the actual increase in respondent's taxable income attributable to the receipts in question was not $505,536.54, but only $366,513.99. Yet, when respondent made its refunds in 1958, it attempted to deduct the full $505,536.54. The Commissioner objected and assessed a deficiency. * * * The Government won in the District Court, but the Court of Appeals for the Tenth Circuit reversed, 392 F.2d 128 (1968). Upon petition by the Government, we granted certiorari, 393 U.S. 820 (1968), to consider whether the Court of Appeals decision had allowed respondent "the practical equivalent of double deduction," * * * in conflict with past decisions of this Court and sound principles of tax law. We reverse.

I

The present problem is an outgrowth of the so-called "claim-of-right" doctrine. Mr. Justice Brandeis, speaking for a unanimous Court in North American Oil Consolidated v. Burnet, 286 U.S. 417, 424 (1932), gave that doctrine its classic formulation. "If a taxpayer receives earnings under a claim of right and without restriction as to its disposition, he has received income which he is required to [report on his tax return], even though it may still be claimed that he is not entitled to retain the money, and even though he may still be adjudged liable to restore its equivalent." Should it later appear that the taxpayer was not entitled to keep the money, Mr. Justice Brandeis explained, he would be entitled to a deduction in the year of repayment; the taxes due for the year of receipt would not be affected. This approach was dictated by Congress' adoption of an annual accounting system as an integral part of the tax code. See Burnet v. Sanford & Brooks Co., 282 U.S. 359, 365–366 (1931). Of course, the tax benefit from the deduction in the year of repayment might differ from the increase in taxes attributable to the receipt; for example, tax rates might have changed, or the taxpayer might be in a different tax "bracket." * * *

Section 1341 of the 1954 Code was enacted to alleviate some of the inequities which Congress felt existed in this area.[1] * * * As an alternative to the deduction in the year of repayment which prior law allowed, § 1341(a)(5) permits certain taxpayers to recompute their taxes for the year of receipt. Whenever § 1341(a)(5) applies, taxes for the current year are to be reduced by the amount taxes were increased in the year or years of receipt because the disputed items were included in gross income. Nevertheless, it is clear that Congress did not intend to tamper with the underlying claim-of-right doctrine; it only provided an alternative for certain cases in which the new approach favored the taxpayer. When the new approach was not advantageous to the taxpayer, the old law was to apply under § 1341(a)(4).

In this case, the parties have stipulated that § 1341(a)(5) does not apply. Accordingly, as the courts below recognized, respondent's taxes must be computed under § 1341(a)(4) and thus, in effect, without regard to the special relief Congress provided through the enactment of § 1341. Nevertheless, respondent argues, and the Court of Appeals seems to have held, that the language used in § 1341 requires that respondent be allowed a deduction for the full amount it refunded to its customers. We think the section has no such significance.

In describing the situations in which the section applies, § 1341(a)(2) talks of cases in which "a deduction is allowable for the taxable year

---

[1] * * * Section 1341(b)(2) contains an exclusion covering certain cases involving sales of stock in trade or inventory. However, because of special treatment given refunds made by regulated public utilities, both parties agree that § 1341(b)(2) is inapplicable to this case and that, accordingly, § 1341(a) applies.

because it was established after the close of [the year or years of receipt] that the taxpayer did not have an unrestricted right to such item. * * * " The "item" referred to is first mentioned in § 1341(a)(1); it is the item included in gross income in the year of receipt. The section does not imply in any way that the "deduction" and the "item" must necessarily be equal in amount. In fact, the use of the words "a deduction" and the placement of § 1341 in subchapter Q—the subchapter dealing largely with side-effects of the annual accounting system—make it clear that it is necessary to refer to other portions of the Code to discover how much of a deduction is allowable. The regulations promulgated under the section make the necessity for such a cross-reference clear. Treas. Reg. § 1.1341–1 (1957). * * *

II

Under the annual accounting system dictated by the Code, each year's tax must be definitively calculable at the end of the tax year. * * * In cases arising under the claim-of-right doctrine, this emphasis on the annual accounting period normally requires that the tax consequences of a receipt should not determine the size of the deduction allowable in the year of repayment. There is no requirement that the deduction save the taxpayer the exact amount of taxes he paid because of the inclusion of the item in income for a prior year. * * *

Nevertheless, the annual accounting concept does not require us to close our eyes to what happened in prior years. For instance, it is well settled that the prior year may be examined to determine whether the repayment gives rise to a regular loss or a capital loss. Arrowsmith v. Commissioner, 344 U.S. 6 (1952). The rationale for the *Arrowsmith* rule is easy to see; if money was taxed at a special lower rate when received, the taxpayer would be accorded an unfair tax windfall if repayments were generally deductible from receipts taxable at the higher rate applicable to ordinary income. The Court in *Arrowsmith* was unwilling to infer that Congress intended such a result.

This case is really no different. In essence, oil, and gas producers are taxed on only 72½% of their "gross income from the property" whenever they claim percentage depletion. The remainder of their oil and gas receipts is in reality tax exempt. We cannot believe that Congress intended to give taxpayers a deduction for refunding money that was not taxed when received. * * * Accordingly, *Arrowsmith* teaches that the full amount of the repayment cannot, in the circumstances of this case, be allowed as a deduction.

This result does no violence to the annual accounting system. Here, as in *Arrowsmith,* the earlier returns are not being reopened. And no attempt is being made to require the tax savings from the deduction to equal the tax consequences of the receipts in prior years.[3] In addition, the

---

[3] Compare the analogous approach utilized under the "tax benefit" rule. Alice Phelan Sullivan Corp. v. United States, 381 F.2d 399 (Ct.Cl.1967); see Internal Revenue Code of 1954 § 111. In keeping with the analogy, the Commissioner has indicated that the Government will

approach here adopted will affect only a few cases. The percentage depletion allowance is quite unusual; unlike most other deductions provided by the Code, it allows a fixed portion of gross income to go untaxed. As a result, the depletion allowance increases in years when disputed amounts are received under claim of right; there is no corresponding decrease in the allowance because of later deductions for repayments. Therefore, if a deduction for 100% of the repayments were allowed, every time money is received and later repaid the taxpayer would make a profit equivalent to the taxes on 27½% of the amount refunded. In other situations when the taxes on a receipt do not equal the tax benefits of a repayment, either the taxpayer or the Government may, depending on circumstances, be the beneficiary. Here, the taxpayer always wins and the Government always loses. We cannot believe that Congress would have intended such an inequitable result. * * *

Reversed.

■ [The dissenting opinion of JUSTICE DOUGLAS and the dissenting opinion of JUSTICE STEWART in which JUSTICE HARLAN and JUSTICE DOUGLAS joined are omitted.]

NOTES

(A) *A "Tax Detriment" Rule?* Does the Supreme Court's opinion in *Skelly Oil* suggest a "tax detriment" rule, i.e., that the tax benefit in the subsequent year of deduction should correspond to the tax detriment of the income inclusion in the earlier year? Does the Court's reasoning suggest that rate differentials generally should be taken into account under the claim of right doctrine? When the tax benefit rule is applied? Or could disenchantment with the percentage depletion deduction distinguish *Skelly Oil* from other situations?

The *Arrowsmith* case relied upon by the Court in *Skelly Oil* is discussed supra at page 627.

(B) *Section 1341.* As suggested in *Skelly Oil*, § 1341 overruled the prior case law that permitted the subsequent deduction to reduce taxes only at the rate applicable in the year of repayment. Section 1341 allows taxpayers to reduce tax liability in the year of repayment by the amount of the tax on the income in the year of inclusion. This eliminates discrepancies due to different years and thereby effects a more thorough revision of the taxable year concept than does the tax benefit rule.

Section 1341, however, operates only where it "appeared" in the earlier year "that the taxpayer had an unrestricted right" to the income. In Rev. Rul. 68–153, 1968–1 C.B. 371, the IRS ruled that refunds made to customers by a railroad because of subsequent administrative findings that the rates were excessive or because of retroactive rate changes qualified for the favorable treatment of § 1341 because the railroad appeared to have an unrestricted right to the income in the year of inclusion. The ruling also holds that refunds

---

only seek to reduce the deduction in the year of repayment to the extent that the depletion allowance attributable to the receipt directly or indirectly reduced taxable income. * * *.

because of erroneous billing or as a result of subsequent events, such as passenger ticket refunds, do not qualify for the benefits of § 1341. Similarly, Rev. Rul. 65–254, 1965–2 C.B. 50, held that § 1341 was not applicable to the repayment of embezzled funds since the taxpayer had no "unrestricted right" to the funds in the year of embezzlement. The taxpayer would have only a loss deduction under § 165 in the year of repayment.

In addition, voluntary repayments do not qualify for § 1341 treatment. In Pike v. Commissioner, 44 T.C. 787 (1965), acq. 1968–2 C.B. 2, a lawyer received a payment in 1957 from a corporation represented by his law firm. In 1958, a controversy arose about this payment. The lawyer contended that his position was sound, but he repaid the amount in order to preserve the good relations of the parties involved. The Tax Court held that the repayment, while deductible when made, did not come within § 1341 since it was never "established * * * [that the taxpayer] 'did not have an unrestricted right'" to the original payment as provided in § 1341. It is not necessary that the taxpayer contest the repayment to qualify under § 1341, however.

(C) *Repayment of "Unreasonable" Salaries.* Recall that under § 162 a deduction is permitted for "reasonable" salaries. It is not uncommon for a business to have a contractual provision requiring repayment of any salary that is determined by the IRS to be "unreasonable." In Revenue Ruling 69–115, 1969–1 C.B. 50, the Service held that § 1341 does not apply to such a payment. In Van Cleave v. United States, 718 F.2d 193 (6th Cir. 1983), the court held that the § 1341 adjustment was available for such a repayment by a controlling stockholder-employee. In reversing the district court opinion, the court remarked:

> The district court seemed to be persuaded by the argument that, if Mr. Van Cleave were allowed section 1341 treatment under these circumstances, this would open the door to tax avoidance in that taxpayers who controlled corporations could "test the waters" in setting their compensation without risk of an adverse tax result. We believe, however, that such possibility of tax avoidance is not a proper consideration in applying this statute, and that the consideration is a legislative rather than a judicial consideration. Moreover, as Mr. Van Cleave suggests, the possibility of tax avoidance could be reduced by requiring the corporation and recipient of compensation to state in their returns that such compensation was paid subject to an obligation to reimburse in the event a deduction is disallowed to the corporation.

(D) *Source of the Deduction.* As the Court in *Skelly Oil* points out, the taxpayer must first find a source for the deduction of the repayment before turning to § 1341. If the deduction is not permitted, § 1341 has no application. For example, in Nacchio v. United States, 824 F.3d 1370 (Fed. Cir. 2016), the court refused to permit a taxpayer to use § 1341 to take a deduction for the forfeiture of $44 million of insider trading profits because a deduction was denied under § 165 on public policy grounds.

Similarly, even though the taxpayer is unable to use the deduction, no adjustment is made to the earlier income inclusion. In Butchko v.

Commissioner, 638 F.2d 1214 (9th Cir. 1981), a racetrack teller had shortage amounts deducted from his wages by the racetrack. He was required to include these amounts in income, although he had not received them, because they were used to satisfy his obligations for shortages under his employment contract. Because they were employee business expenses, they were deductible from adjusted gross income and thus no deduction was permitted unless the taxpayer itemized deductions.

Section 2.   Methods of Accounting

The allocation of items of income and deduction to the proper taxable year generally is governed by the taxpayer's method of accounting. Section 446 of the Code provides that taxpayers shall compute taxable income "under the method of accounting on the basis of which the taxpayer regularly computes his income in keeping his books" so long as that method "clearly reflects income." Books include records kept solely for tax purposes as well as books used for financial reporting purposes.

Section 451 of the Code requires taxpayers to include items in gross income in the taxable year of receipt unless their method of accounting requires that the income be included in a different taxable year. Section 461 provides that deductions and credits "shall be taken for the taxable year which is the proper taxable year under the method of accounting used in computing taxable income."

The methods most commonly used are the cash method and the accrual method. There are, in addition, special rules for particular types of transactions, such as installment sales. See § 453 of the Code, and infra at page 751. Moreover, some Code sections provide rules for determining the timing of particular deductions. For example, § 213 provides that medical expenses are deductible when "paid."

Under the accrual method, in contrast, items generally are included in income in the year in which they are earned, regardless of when they are received, and, in general, items are taken as deductions in the year in which they are incurred, regardless of when they are paid, although as discussed infra at page 744, deductions are often deferred until economic performance occurs. Most corporations and some individuals, partnerships, and trusts use the accrual method.

Under the accrual method, in contrast, items generally are included in income in the year in which they are earned, regardless of when they are received, and, in general, items are taken as deductions in the year in which they are incurred, regardless of when they are paid, although as discussed at page 735, infra, deductions are often deferred until economic performance occurs. Most corporations and some individuals, partnerships, and trusts use the accrual method.

The 2017 tax act significantly expanded the universe of taxpayers able to use the cash method. Under prior law, any corporation or partnership with gross receipts averaging less than $5 million was permitted to use the cash method. The 2017 legislation raised the threshold to $25 million, promoting the change as small business tax reform. § 448(c)(1). The $25 million amount is indexed for inflation after 2018.

The taxpayer's accounting method will govern, however, only if the method "clearly reflects income." The Commissioner is given broad authority to ensure that a taxpayer's accounting method "clearly reflects income" and to permit or refuse changes in methods. If the taxpayer keeps no books, or if his method of accounting does not clearly reflect income, the Commissioner selects an accounting method. § 446(b).

Although the cash method is relatively simple, many commentators believe that it fails to measure income accurately when the taxpayer's activities are more complex. Examples include when expenses accrue in one year that are not paid until the following year, income is earned in one year and cash will not be received until a future year, or cash is prepaid for services and goods to be received in the future.

The accrual method is widely thought to give a more accurate reflection of economic gain and is used by most businesses in presenting the results of operations to management, investors, and creditors. Nevertheless, historically the regulations mandated the accrual method only when inventories are required, i.e., whenever the sale of goods is a material income-producing factor.

Perhaps responding to considerable academic sentiment, Congress limited the categories of taxpayers who are permitted to use the cash method. Subchapter C corporations, partnerships with a C corporation as a partner, and tax shelters must use the accrual method. § 448. Subchapter C corporations and partnerships with C corporation partners are exempt from this rule if they average less than $25 million in gross receipts annually over the period of three taxable years before the taxable year in question. See § 448(b)(3) and (c). There is also an exception—the fruit of much lobbying, including some rather aggressive lawyering by a large group of former IRS commissioners and Treasury assistant secretaries for tax policy who are now partners in large law firms—for "qualified personal service corporations," which may continue to use the cash method (as may partnerships with such corporations as a partner) regardless of the amount of their annual gross receipts. To qualify, substantially all of an entity's activities must be within one of a number of specified fields, including law, health, engineering, architecture, accounting, actuarial science, performing arts, and consulting. See § 448(d)(2).

Although the accrual method of accounting generally is considered more accurate in measuring economic income, it is not without problems. Historically, the accrual method has taken income and deduction items into account at their stated amount rather than at their discounted present value even if they are to be received or paid in the future. The ability, for example, to deduct now amounts to be paid far in the future creates a time value of money advantage for taxpayers and, in effect, mismeasures income. On the other hand, because income sometimes is subject to tax before cash is received, there may be liquidity problems for the taxpayer. The government may face enforcement obstacles if tax liability is deferred to the point of accrual at which time the cash may have been spent. As you review the materials on the accrual method, you will discover that the Service and the courts have responded by creating what is, in fact, a hybrid method of accounting, departing from accrual accounting where it would create problems for tax collection.

In upholding the Commissioner's authority to require a newspaper company to change from the cash to the accrual method of accounting in Knight-Ridder Newspapers, Inc. v. United States, 743 F.2d 781 (11th Cir. 1984), Judge Goldberg waxed eloquent (or went off the deep end) in characterizing the two methods and the tax law's attitude toward them:

> These * * * two most common accounting methods * * * could be said to emblematize the polar nature of the human spirit. The cash method—simple, plodding, elemental—stands firmly in the physical realm. It responds only through the physical senses, recognizing only the tangible flow of currency. Money is income when this raw beast actually feels the coins in its primal paw; expenditures are made only when the beast can see that it has given the coins away.

> The accrual method, however, moves in a more ethereal, mystical realm. The visionary prophet, it recognizes the impact of the future on the present, and with grave foreboding or ecstatic anticipation, announces the world to be. When it becomes sure enough of its prophecies, it actually conducts life as if the new age has already come to pass. Transactions producing income or deductions spring to life in the eyes of the seer though nary a dollar has moved.

> The Internal Revenue Code, the ultimate arbiter, stands to the side, shifting its eyes uneasily from the one being to the other. The Code is possessed of great wisdom and tolerance. It knows that man must generally choose his own way. Therefore, it leaves to the Taxpayer the original choice of which accounting method to use. Section 446(c) specifically authorizes both the cash and accrual methods.

> Yet the Code also understands that either extreme possesses inherent weaknesses and can become blinded to reality. Thus the Code and subsequent Treasury Regulations empower the Secretary of the Treasury and the Commissioner of Internal Revenue to cure the blindness. * * *

> Of course, in deciding whether the Commissioner has abused his discretion, we immediately face an age-old philosopher's dilemma: how can we mere mortals know who sees the truth

most vividly? How can we know whether the primal cash method or the mystical accrual method sees income more clearly without knowing what income really is?

This Section considers the methods of accounting, beginning with the cash method. This Chapter generally ignores accounting methods of special and limited application, such as the special method of accounting for long-term contracts, which has wide application in the construction industry.

A. CASH METHOD

Under the cash method of accounting, items of income ordinarily are included in the year in which they are "received," and items of deduction are taken in the year in which they are "paid." Usually, there is not much doubt about the time for inclusion or deduction for a cash basis taxpayer.

In order to prevent cash basis taxpayers from having complete freedom to decide when to report income, the receipt concept has been expanded to include the notion of "constructive receipt." Under certain circumstances, however, a contract that defers payments will be honored even though the other party would have been willing to pay earlier. There also have been disputes concerning the treatment under the cash method of payments received by a third person (such as an escrow agent) on the taxpayer's behalf. Also, other issues concern whether an amount received is income or a "deposit."

Special problems also arise when a taxpayer receives something other than cash, such as a check or a note. When the receipt of property would be taxable, there is often a question of whether the receipt is the equivalent of cash. Checks, which are mechanisms for making payment, are treated like cash. On the other hand, since notes (and accounts receivable) are mechanisms to defer payment, rather than mechanisms of payment, their inclusion in income immediately upon receipt, in all circumstances, would have the effect of obliterating the basic distinction between the cash and accrual methods of accounting. Thus, special rules are needed to preserve the distinction, yet prevent abuse. Questions also arise as to whether payment by credit card or use of other borrowed funds constitute payment.

Finally, there are important limitations on a taxpayer's flexibility under the cash method to accelerate deductions (by making deductible expenditures before the close of the taxable year). The materials that follow illustrate some of these issues.

1.   THE "CONSTRUCTIVE RECEIPT" DOCTRINE

Cash, property, and services are taxable to cash method taxpayers when "actually or constructively received." Reg. § 1.446–1(c)(1). The "constructive receipt" doctrine, set forth in § 1.451–2(a) of the

Regulations, requires inclusion of income when a taxpayer has the immediate power to receive the income:

> Income although not actually reduced to a taxpayer's possession is constructively received by him in the taxable year during which it is credited to his account, set apart for him, or otherwise made available so that he may draw upon it at any time, or so that he could have drawn upon it during the taxable year if notice of intention to withdraw had been given. However, income is not constructively received if the taxpayer's control of its receipt is subject to substantial limitations or restrictions.

In Ross v. Commissioner, 169 F.2d 483, 491 (1st Cir. 1948), the court described the purpose of the constructive receipt doctrine:

> The doctrine of constructive receipt was, no doubt, conceived by the Treasury in order to prevent taxpayers from choosing the year in which to return income merely by choosing the year in which to reduce it to possession. Thereby the Treasury may subject income to taxation when the only thing preventing its reduction to possession is the volition of the taxpayer.

The government typically raises constructive receipt issues in urging that an item be included in income earlier than desired by the taxpayer. The following case, however, illustrates that taxpayers sometimes urge that the doctrine apply.

Carter v. Commissioner

Tax Court of the United States, 1980. 40 T.C.M. 654.

■ WILBUR, JUDGE:

     * * * The only issue for decision is whether $1,073.01 in wages for services rendered during November and December 1974 but not received by petitioner until 1975, were constructively received by petitioner in 1974 within the meaning of section 451.

* * *

Robert J. Carter * * * reported his income for 1975 as a cash basis taxpayer. Mr. Carter was unemployed from January through September 1974. He began working for the city of New York as a laboratory technician in the Office of the Chief Medical Examiner in October 1974. Several weeks later, he transferred to the City Health Department. Petitioner worked as a laboratory technician at the Health Department also, with the added benefit of a permanent job title. He received continuous service credit for the time he was with the Chief Medical Examiner. Subsequent to Mr. Carter's transfer, there was a delay in processing his payroll checks, arising out of tardiness in forwarding his records from the Chief Medical Examiner and a backlog in payroll processing in the Health Department. Consequently, despite numerous protests and demands for his past due salary, Mr. Carter did not get paid for 6 weeks. He was paid $1,073.01 in gross wages on January 3, 1975. This represented 4 weeks back pay ($715.34) and 2 weeks timely pay ($357.67). From this point, his paycheck was up to date.

Had Mr. Carter received the 4 weeks back wages on time, in 1974, he would have owed no extra taxes. His total income for 1974 would have been $818.30. Petitioner was advised by an Internal Revenue employee who assisted him in preparing his 1975 Federal income tax return to exclude the $1,073.01 from his 1975 wages because it was attributable to 1974. Petitioner did so. Respondent assessed a $195 deficiency in petitioner's 1975 taxes.

Petitioner contends that he constructively received the income in 1974, because the work was performed in 1974. He argues that he had a permanent job title, and the funds necessary to pay him were in the city budget. He argues that this constitutes constructive receipt since all that was necessary was for the city to transfer the funds from its budget to his budget. Respondent's position is that Mr. Carter must be taxed when he actually received the money in 1975. While we sympathize with petitioner's plight, we hold that there was no constructive receipt of income in 1974 and petitioner must be taxed in 1975 when he was finally paid.

Petitioner is a cash basis taxpayer. All items which constitute gross income are to be included for the taxable year in which actually or constructively received. * * *

The petitioner did not have the free and unrestricted control of his wages prior to actual receipt that this Court has required in order to find constructive receipt. * * * Indeed, he tried repeatedly to obtain his back wages during the month of December but was unsuccessful. His control over his wages was clearly subject to substantial limitations or restrictions. Their mere presence in the New York City budget is insufficient to find constructive receipt.

Petitioner appears to recognize that this is the rule of law applicable to his case, but urges that we make an exception in his case that the average man would expect in view of the compelling equities involved. However, as we explained to petitioner at trial, the typical taxpayer expects to pay tax when he receives the income, because only then does he have the money in hand to make the payment. This is the essence of the cash system—an item is income when received and a deduction when paid—and it accords with the practical exigencies as well as obviates requiring the average taxpayer to deal with the complex concepts of more sophisticated accounting systems.

Petitioner would have owed no tax on the income had he received it in 1974, rather than in 1975. But under the cash basis of reporting income, it is taxable in the year received and not in the year producing the smallest tax burden. The rules are clear and must be so for the convenience of all citizens subject to the tax.

While it is truly unfortunate that Mr. Carter became a victim of bureaucratic inefficiency, he clearly did not constructively receive the income in 1974, and as a cash basis taxpayer is taxable on the wages when he actually received them in 1975. We sustain respondent's determination.

holding

NOTES

(A) *Other Taxpayers Urging Constructive Receipt.* In Hornung v. Commissioner, 47 T.C. 428 (1967), the taxpayer was awarded a 1962 Corvette by Sport Magazine for his outstanding performance in a football game held in Green Bay, Wisconsin on Sunday, December 31, 1961. The award was announced at 4:30 p.m. that day in Green Bay, but the person who announced the award had neither the title nor the keys to the car. Hornung actually received the car in New York on January 3, 1962. Hornung's claim that the award was taxable income in 1961 (a year closed by the statute of limitations) was rejected by the Tax Court:

> [S]ince December 31, 1961, was a Sunday, it is doubtful whether the car could have been transferred to petitioner before Monday even with the cooperation of the editor in chief of Sport. The New York dealership at which the car was located was closed. The car had not been set aside for petitioner's use and delivery was not dependent solely upon the volition of petitioner. The doctrine of constructive receipt is therefore inapplicable, and we hold that petitioner received the Corvette for income tax purposes in 1962.

(B) *Refusing to Take Compensation.* In Commissioner v. Mott, 85 F.2d 315 (6th Cir. 1936), the taxpayer was entitled to take three percent of the income from a trust as compensation for his services as trustee. In fact, he took nothing. The court found that he was not taxable on the amount that he might have taken.

(C) *Refusing to Take a Prize.* If a taxpayer wins a prize and refuses to accept it, he has no income. But suppose the taxpayer waits awhile before declining the prize or directs that the prize be given to someone else? At the end of the 2015 Super Bowl game, New England Patriots quarterback Tom Brady was announced as the winner of the MVP award that came with a fully loaded Chevy pick-up truck. Subsequently, Brady "gave" the prize (i.e. the truck) to Malcolm Butler, an unsung cornerback who caught his first interception on a Russell Wilson pass to steal the Super Bowl from the Seattle Seahawks. Media outlets reported that Chevrolet would give the truck directly to Butler, not Brady, so that Butler would be taxed on the value of the truck (and Brady would owe no income taxes). Is that correct? Does it matter that Brady was present at the post-game award ceremony and accepted the MVP award? Does it matter that it wasn't until two days after the Super Bowl that Brady told a reporter: "I would love to give him the truck. I would love to do that. I'm going to figure out how to make that work"?

(D) *Delaying Payment by Contract.* In Schniers v. Commissioner, 69 T.C. 511 (1977), the Tax Court upheld for tax purposes a deferred payment arrangement entered into in December 1973, whereby a cotton farmer delayed until January 1974 receipt of income from crops harvested and warehoused in 1973. The Commissioner had argued for constructive receipt on the ground that the deferred payment contracts were entered into voluntarily by the taxpayer for the sole purpose of delaying the reporting of income. The Tax Court found that the contracts were valid and binding on the taxpayer and remarked:

> The point is that income is not realized by a cash basis farmer from merely harvesting his crops. He receives income only when he actually or constructively receives income from the sale of those crops. He is not required to sell the crops in the year in which he harvests them. He may decide not to sell them until the following year. Nor is he required, if he decides to sell them in the year of harvest, to contract for immediate payment for his crops. The contract may call for payment after the close of the harvest year and he does not realize income in the year of sale if the contract is a valid, enforceable one.

Taxpayers do not have constructive receipt merely because they could have entered into an arrangement to receive payment earlier. Thus, the fact that the payor is solvent or would have been willing to enter into a contract to pay earlier is irrelevant.

(E) *Delaying Payment by Amending Contracts.* In Oates v. Commissioner, 18 T.C. 570 (1952), aff'd 207 F.2d 711 (7th Cir. 1953), the taxpayers were insurance agents who, at retirement, amended their agency contracts with the insurance company to provide for the payment of future renewal commissions in equal monthly installments over a 15-year period, regardless of when and in what amounts the renewal commissions would have become due under the original agency agreement. The amounts payable for any year, however, were limited to amounts that already had been earned. The Commissioner asserted that the agents were taxable on the renewal commissions as they accrued under the original contract. Both the Tax Court and the Seventh Circuit rejected the Commissioner's position. They found that the amended contract constituted a novation, that the old contract had been extinguished, and that the taxpayers had no right to demand compensation for services other than as set out in the new contract. The Tax Court pointed out that the taxpayers "under their amended contracts * * * were not entitled to receive any more than they did in fact receive and that being on the cash basis they can only be taxed on [those amounts actually received]."

In Commissioner v. Olmsted Inc. Life Agency, 304 F.2d 16 (8th Cir. 1962), aff'g 35 T.C. 429 (1960), a life insurance agency assigned to an insurance company all rights to renewal commissions on previously written life insurance policies. In return, the agency was to receive fixed monthly payments based on the estimated present value of the renewals over a 15-year period. Finding *Oates* to be controlling, both the Tax Court and the Eighth Circuit held the transaction to be a novation rather than a "sale or other disposition" within the meaning of § 1001 of the Code. The cash method agency could be taxed on the payments only as received. In *Oates,* the contract was not transferable, the contractual rights were not assignable, and the total payment per year was limited to the renewal commissions actually earned; in *Olmsted,* there were no such limitations. The courts, however, did not agree with the IRS that the difference between *Olmsted* and *Oates* justified different results. The IRS announced its acquiescence in *Oates,* 1960–1 C.B. 5, but its nonacquiescence in *Olmsted,* 1961–2 C.B. 6.

Oates and *Olmsted* should be revisited in connection with the materials on nonqualified deferred compensation, supra at page 666. The result in similar cases may be affected by § 409A. This section, which generally requires a deferral election to be made before services are performed, applies to independent contractors providing services to one party.

(F) *Agency Arrangements.* The general rule that receipt by an agent is receipt by the principal is normally followed in tax cases. Escrows can be distinguished from agency arrangements because the escrow intermediary often has obligations to both parties to a transaction while an agent normally acts exclusively for his principal. Cases frequently state that a "deferred escrow arrangement that is not part of a bona fide agreement between the buyer and the seller-taxpayer, but rather is a 'self-imposed limitation' created by the seller-taxpayer, is legally ineffective to shift tax liability from one year to the next." A number of cases, however, illustrate that a legally binding sale via an escrow arrangement often will be effective to shift income to the following year. See, e.g., Busby v. United States, 679 F.2d 48 (5th Cir. 1982) (bank holding payments for sale of cotton held to be agent of the buyer not the seller; therefore no constructive receipt).

2. RECEIPT OF THE EQUIVALENT OF CASH OR "ECONOMIC BENEFIT"

Generally, when a taxpayer actually receives cash or property, no timing question arises; taxation occurs on receipt. But where the taxpayer receives a right to receive money in the future, a persistent problem is whether this right is "equivalent" to cash. For example, the taxpayer may receive a check or a note or a contract right. It may be nontransferable or negotiable only at a substantial discount. It may be placed in escrow or secured by other property. Although the courts are uniform in holding that a "cash equivalent" is taxable on receipt, there is disagreement as to what types of property interests are cash equivalents.

Revenue Ruling 80–52

Internal Revenue Service, 1980. 1980–1 C.B. 100.

ISSUE

What is the amount includible in gross income as a result of the bartering transactions described below, and when is the amount includible in gross income?

FACTS

A and *B* are both members of a barter club. The barter club operates as a vehicle for the exchange of property and services among the members. The club uses "credit units" as a medium of exchange and makes available to members information concerning property and services other members are offering for exchange. The club debits or credits members' accounts for goods or services received from or rendered to other members. Exchanges are made on the basis that one credit unit equals one dollar of value. The rules of the club require that the value placed on goods or services exchanged be equal to the member seller's normal retail price. The transfer of credit units between members is accomplished by various source documents, such as invoices, and the club charges the member purchaser a 10 percent commission payable in cash on barter purchases. Any barter transaction between members is reflected in the form of bookkeeping entries on the books and records of the club. The club does not guarantee that a member will be able to use all of that member's credit units and does not pay a member cash for any credit units not used. However, a member's credit units can be used immediately to purchase goods or services offered by other members of the club, and the member may transfer or sell the member's credit units to another member of the club.

Situation 1. Both *A* and *B* use the cash receipts and disbursements method of accounting. Through the club, *A* bartered to *B* for 200 credit units services that *A* would normally perform for $200. During the same taxable year, *B* bartered to *A* for 200 credit units services that *B* would normally perform for $200.

Situation 2. C is an employee of the barter club. During the taxable year, *C,* who uses the cash receipts and disbursements method of accounting, received from the club in exchange for *C's* services gross wages of $20,000, $10,000 in cash and 10,000 credit units. *C* is entitled to use the credit units in the same manner as other members of the club. However, the club does not charge *C* a commission on *C's* barter purchases.

LAW AND ANALYSIS

Section 61 of the Internal Revenue Code and regulations thereunder provide that, except as otherwise provided by law, gross income means all income from whatever source derived.

Section 1.61–1 of the Income Tax Regulations provides, in part, that gross income includes income realized in any form, whether in money, property, or services.

Section 1.61–2(d)(1) of the regulations provides that, if services are paid for other than in money, the fair market value of the property or services taken in payment must be included in income as compensation.

* * *

Section 451 of the Code provides that the amount of any item of gross income is includible in the gross income for the taxable year in which received by the taxpayer, unless, under the method of accounting used in computing taxable income, such amount is to be properly accounted for as of a different period.

Section 1.451–1(a) of the regulations provides that income is includible in gross income for the taxable year in which it is actually or constructively received by the taxpayer, unless it is includible in a different year in accordance with the taxpayer's method of accounting.

Rev. Rul. 70–331, 1970–1 C.B. 14, concerns "prize points" that are earned by salespersons and are redeemable for merchandise prizes listed in a catalog. That revenue ruling holds that the fair market value of the prize points awarded to a salesperson who uses the cash receipts and disbursements method of accounting is includible in the salesperson's gross income when the prize points are paid or otherwise made available to the salesperson, whichever is earlier. The prize points in Rev. Rul. 70–331 and the credit units in this revenue ruling both represent payment for services in a form other than money.

In this case *A, B,* and *C* received income in the form of a valuable right represented by credit units that can be used immediately to purchase goods or services offered by other members of the barter club. There are no restrictions on their use of the credit units because *A, B,* and *C* are free to use the credit units to purchase goods or services when the credit units are credited to their accounts.

HOLDINGS

Situation 1. A and *B* must include $200 in their gross incomes for the taxable year in which the credit units are credited to their accounts. * * *

Situation 2. C must include $20,000 in *C*'s gross income for the taxable year. * * *

If the commission paid to the barter club by a member purchaser was paid to acquire an item for use in connection with the member purchaser's trade or business, the amount of the commission is deductible as a business expense under section 162 of the Code, provided the item received in the barter transaction meets the requirements of that section. If the commission was paid to acquire a capital item, the amount of the commission must be capitalized pursuant to section 263. If the commission was paid to acquire an item for personal purposes, the amount of the commission is not deductible, pursuant to section 262.

* * *

NOTES

(A) *Checks.* A check, which is a mechanism for making payment, rather than a promise to pay, generally is treated as cash. A number of disputes, however, have arisen when a taxpayer received a check at year end but did not cash the check until early in the following year. For example, in Lavery v. Commissioner, 158 F.2d 859 (7th Cir. 1946), a taxpayer who received a check on December 30 that was not deposited until January 2 had income in the earlier year because the taxpayer could have cashed the check in the year it was received. See also Bright v. United States, 926 F.2d 383 (5th Cir. 1991), where the taxpayer had income in 1985 due to a check deposited with a bank, although the bank withheld funds until it had collected from the drawee bank in 1986. The court noted that the taxpayer could have had access to the funds in 1985 by opening an account at the drawee bank. Compare Baxter v. Commissioner, 816 F.2d 493 (9th Cir. 1987), where the court held that a check constituted income in 1980 when the funds could not have been credited to the cash basis taxpayer by his bank until January 2, 1980. The facts that the monies were earned in 1979, the check was dated December 30, 1979, and the check could have been picked up by the taxpayer on that date if he had driven to its location 40 miles from his home did not make the amount taxable in 1979. The court pointed out that December 30 was a Saturday and the banks were not open until January 2. These cases appear to be based on constructive receipt—that is, the taxpayer could have "actually" received the cash and thus constructively was deemed to have received it. In Millard v. Commissioner, 90 T.C.M. 136 (2005), the court held that a retirement account distribution was income in the year the taxpayer received the check even though the taxpayer changed his mind about the distribution and refused to cash the check.

Other cases take the position that a check is a cash equivalent and whether the taxpayer has the ability to turn it into cash is irrelevant. For example, in Revenue Ruling 73–486, 1973–2 C.B. 153, the taxpayer received a check made out for the wrong amount. He returned the check and received one for the correct amount in the following taxable year. The IRS held that a check for the wrong amount is income when received unless the recipient either was not entitled to any excess or would prejudice a further claim by cashing the check for less than the amount due.

On the other hand, constructive receipt questions can arise with regard to checks when the taxpayer does not actually obtain possession of the check in the first year. For example, in Revenue Ruling 76–3, 1976–1 C.B. 114, the Post Office attempted to deliver a check sent by certified mail on December 31, 1974, but the taxpayer was not home to sign for the check. Nevertheless, the Service held that the check was taxable in the first year because the fact that the taxpayer could not sign for the check was not a "limitation or restriction on receipt of the payment." Davis v. Commissioner, 37 T.C.M. 42 (1978), holds to the contrary.

(B) *The "Cash Equivalence" Doctrine.* Unlike the constructive receipt doctrine, the "cash equivalence" or "economic benefit" doctrine requires the *actual* receipt of property or of a right to receive property in the future. This doctrine inquires whether the property or right received confers a present—and often marketable—economic benefit. The doctrine originated in deferred compensation cases, where taxpayers had attempted to receive benefits without recognizing income, but has been applied in a variety of other contexts. Compare, for example, Kuehner v. Commissioner, 214 F.2d 437 (1st Cir. 1954), which required the taxpayer to recognize income on the deposit of amounts into an escrow account that he controlled on the ground that his property interest in the escrow account was "equivalent to cash," with Reed v. Commissioner, 723 F.2d 138, 146–47 (1st Cir. 1983), reversing 45 T.C.M. 398 (1982), where the court of appeals refused to follow a Tax Court decision applying the "economic benefit" doctrine to an escrow agreement. The court stated in the latter case that to do so "would be at odds with the well-established principle that a deferred payment arrangement is effective to defer income recognition to a cash basis taxpayer, provided it is part of an arms-length agreement between the purchaser and seller." The court asserted that extension of the economic benefit doctrine to such cases "would significantly erode the distinction between the cash and accrual methods of accounting."

(C) *Virtual Currencies.* The advent of virtual currencies like Bitcoin raises questions about how gains and losses from changes in the currency's value will be taxed. The IRS issued a notice in 2014 stating that virtual currencies will be treated as property for tax purposes, unlike foreign currencies. 2014–16 I.R.B. 938. This treatment makes spending virtual currency a taxable exchange.

(D) *Notes.* Much of the difficulty with the "economic benefit" or "cash equivalence" doctrine has involved transfers of notes or other transferable contract rights. In Cowden v. Commissioner, 289 F.2d 20 (5th Cir. 1961), the Fifth Circuit found the receipt of a contract right to receive amounts in the next two years to be immediately taxable as the receipt of the equivalent of cash. The court enumerated the qualities that would make a contract or note (or other debt instrument) the equivalent of cash:

> A promissory note, negotiable in form, is not necessarily the equivalent of cash. Such an instrument may have been issued by a maker of doubtful solvency or for other reasons such paper might be denied a ready acceptance in the market place. We think the converse of this principle ought to be applicable. We are convinced that if a promise to pay of a solvent obligor is unconditional and assignable, not subject to set-offs and is of a kind that is frequently transferred to lenders or investors at a discount not substantially greater than the generally prevailing premium for the use of money, such promise is the equivalent of cash and taxable in like manner as cash would have been taxable had it been received by the taxpayer rather than the obligation. The principle that negotiability is not the test of taxability in an equivalent of cash case such as is before us, is consistent with the rule that men may, if they can, so order their affairs as to minimize taxes, and points up the doctrine that substance and not form should control in the application of income tax laws.

On remand, the Tax Court found that the taxpayers "received income in the form of the equivalent of cash in the amount of the then fair market value" of the contracts upon the execution of the agreement. Cowden v. Commissioner, 20 T.C.M. 1134 (1961).

By contrast, in Williams v. Commissioner, 28 T.C. 1000 (1957), the taxpayer received a note at a time when its maker was without funds; he tried to sell it without success. The court held that the note was not the equivalent of cash, and not income when received. The Commissioner acquiesced in this decision. 1958–1 C.B. 6.

(E) *Accounts Receivable.* A law firm on the cash method of accounting performs services for a large solvent bank and notifies the client of the amount due. Is this account receivable taxable to the law firm under the cash equivalency doctrine prior to collection? Accounts receivable, non-negotiable notes, or other debt instruments typically are not included in income when received by a cash method taxpayer. Requiring all debt instruments to be included immediately in income would obliterate the fundamental distinction between the cash and accrual methods of accounting.

3.   PAYMENTS

Section 1.461–1(a)(1) of the regulations provides that under the cash method, allowable deductions are taken into account for the taxable year in which paid. As the following ruling and notes illustrate, controversies sometimes arise as to what constitutes "payment."

Revenue Ruling 78–38

Internal Revenue Service, 1978. 1978–1 C.B. 67.

The Internal Revenue Service has given further consideration to Rev. Rul. 71–216, 1971–1 C.B. 96, which holds that a taxpayer who used a bank credit card to contribute to a qualified charity may not deduct any part of the contribution under section 170(a)(1) of the Internal Revenue Code of 1954 until the year the cardholder makes payment of the amount of the contribution to the bank.

Rev. Rul. 71–216 cites [the predecessor to current § 1.170A–1(a)(1) of the regulations] which provides that a deduction is only allowable to an individual under section 170 of the Code for charitable contributions "actually paid" during the taxable year, regardless of when pledged and regardless of the method of accounting employed by the taxpayer in keeping books and records.

In Rev. Rul. 71–216 the assumption was made that a charitable contribution made by a taxpayer by use of a credit card was tantamount to a charitable contribution made by the issuance and delivery of a debenture bond or a promissory note by the obligor to a charitable organization * * *.

Upon further study, it has been concluded that there are major distinctions between contributions made by the use of credit cards and contributions made by debenture bonds and promissory notes. In Rev. Rul. 68–174, the charitable organization that received the debenture bond or promissory note from the obligor received no more than a mere promise to pay. Conversely, the credit card holder in Rev. Rul. 71–216, by using the credit card to make the contribution, became immediately indebted to a third party (the bank) in such a way that the cardholder could not thereafter prevent the charitable organization from receiving payment. The credit card draft received by the charitable organization from the credit card holder in Rev. Rul. 71–216 was immediately creditable by the bank to the organization's account as if it were a check.

Since the cardholder's use of the credit card creates the cardholder's own debt to a third party, the use of a bank credit card to make a charitable contribution is equivalent to the use of borrowed funds to make a contribution.

The general rule is that when a deductible payment is made with borrowed money, the deduction is not postponed until the year in which the borrowed money is repaid. Such expenses must be deducted in the year they are paid and not when the loans are repaid. * * *

Accordingly, the taxpayer discussed in Rev. Rul. 71–216, who made a contribution to a qualified charity by a charge to the taxpayer's bank credit card, is entitled to a charitable contribution deduction under section 170(a) of the Code in the year the charge was made and the deduction may not be postponed until the taxpayer pays the indebtedness resulting from such charge.

NOTES

(A) *Payments Made by Borrowing from Third Parties.* Checks, pay-by-phone devices, and electronic fund transfers are means for making payment and, as Revenue Ruling 80–335 indicates, are treated as such for tax purposes. Typically, accounts and notes payable are means for deferring payment, and a cash method taxpayer will not be allowed deductions until such items are paid. Difficulties may arise, however, because a deduction is normally allowed when an item is paid with funds borrowed from a third party. Revenue Ruling 78–38, while reflecting this general rule, allows a deduction for charitable contributions made by credit card; the ruling distinguishes contributions made by a promissory note, which it describes as a "mere promise to pay." See also Rev. Rul. 78–39, 1978–1 C.B. 73, where the IRS held that a cash basis taxpayer had made a "payment," deductible under § 213, upon charging medical expenses on a bank credit card.

This distinction for borrowing from third parties led the Service to the conclusion that payments of deductible expenses were deductible when charged to a bank credit card but not deductible until paid if charged to a credit card issued by the vendor. Thus, for example, whether gasoline purchased by a traveling salesman was deductible turned on which credit card he used. Despite the "tax logic" of the IRS position, it was incomprehensible—or even viewed as a bad joke—by normal people and ultimately was abandoned to allow deduction when the charge appears on the taxpayer's credit card statement. A small triumph for common sense.

(B) *"Paying" by Delivering a Note.* The Supreme Court has held that the transfer of the taxpayer's own note does not constitute payment. Helvering v. Price, 309 U.S. 409 (1940) (a secured note satisfying taxpayer's guaranty obligation did not give rise to a deduction because it was not the equivalent of cash).

(C) *Payment by Borrowing from the Payee.* In Cleaver v. Commissioner, 158 F.2d 342 (7th Cir. 1946), the taxpayer borrowed money by giving a note to a bank. He received from the bank the face amount of the note, less a discount. The court held that he was not entitled to an interest deduction until he paid the note. But compare Burgess v. Commissioner, 8 T.C. 47 (1947), where the taxpayer borrowed money to pay interest on another note and was entitled to a deduction for interest paid, with Battelstein v. Internal Revenue Service, 631 F.2d 1182 (5th Cir. 1980) (en banc), which disallowed interest deductions by a cash basis taxpayer who borrowed the interest from the original lender.

What if the debtor goes to a second bank and borrows funds to pay the interest? See Crown v. Commissioner, 77 T.C. 582 (1981) (permitting a deduction).

Note that the test for whether a note is income to a cash basis taxpayer is different from the test for whether it constitutes payment. This is illustrated by Revenue Ruling 76–135, 1976–1 C.B. 114, in which a client paid a lawyer with a negotiable promissory note. The ruling held that the cash basis lawyer, who discounted the note at a bank, had income on the discounted value of the note when received. The cash basis client had a deduction only when he made actual payments to the bank.

4.   EXPENSES PAID IN ADVANCE—PREPAYMENTS

Commissioner v. Boylston Market Ass'n

United States Circuit Court of Appeals, First Circuit, 1942. 131 F.2d 966.

■ MAHONEY, CIRCUIT JUDGE:

* * *

The taxpayer in the course of its business, which is the management of real estate owned by it, purchased from time to time fire and other insurance policies covering periods of three or more years. It keeps its books and makes its returns on a cash receipts and disbursements basis. The taxpayer has since 1915 deducted each year as insurance expenses the amount of insurance premiums applicable to carrying insurance for that year regardless of the year in which the premium was actually paid. This method was required by the Treasury Department prior to 1938 * * *.

We are asked to determine whether a taxpayer who keeps his books and files his returns on a cash basis is limited to the deduction of the insurance premiums actually paid in any year or whether he should deduct for each tax year the pro rata portion of the prepaid insurance applicable to that year. * * *

The arguments * * * in favor of treating prepaid insurance as an ordinary and necessary business expense are persuasive. We are, nevertheless, unable to find a real basis for distinguishing between prepayment of rentals, Baton Coal Co. v. Commissioner, 3 Cir., 1931, 51 F.2d 469, certiorari denied 284 U.S. 674; * * * bonuses for the acquisition of leases, Home Trust Co. v. Commissioner, 8 Cir., 1933, 65 F.2d 532; * * * bonuses for the cancellation of leases, Steele-Wedeles Co. v. Commissioner, 30 B.T.A. 841, 842; * * * commissions for negotiating leases, see Bonwit Teller & Co. v. Commissioner, 2 Cir., 1931, 53 F.2d 381, 384, 82 A.L.R. 325, and prepaid insurance. Some distinctions may be drawn in the cases cited on the basis of the facts contained therein, but we are of the opinion that there is no justification for treating them differently insofar as deductions are concerned. All of the cases cited are readily distinguishable from such a clear-cut case as a permanent improvement to a building. This latter is clearly a capital expenditure. * * * In such a case there is the creation of a capital asset which has a life extending beyond the taxable year and which depreciates over a period of years. The taxpayer regardless of his method of accounting can only take deductions for depreciation over the life of the asset.

Advance rentals, payments of bonuses for acquisition and cancellation of leases, and commissions for negotiating leases are all matters which the taxpayer amortizes over the life of the lease. Whether we consider these payments to be the cost of the exhaustible asset, as in the case of advance rentals, or the cost of acquiring the asset, as in the case of bonuses, the payments are prorated primarily because the life of the asset extends beyond the taxable year. To permit the taxpayer to take a full deduction in the year of payment would distort his income. Prepaid insurance presents the same problem and should be solved in the same way. Prepaid insurance for a period of three years may be easily allocated. It is protection for the entire period and the taxpayer may, if he desires, at any time surrender the insurance policy. It thus is clearly an asset having a longer life than a single taxable year. The line to be drawn between capital expenditures and ordinary and necessary business expenses is not always an easy one, but we are satisfied that in treating prepaid insurance as a capital expense we are obtaining some degree of consistency in these matters. * * *

The decision of Board of Tax Appeals is affirmed.

NOTES

(A) *Capital Expenditures.* A cash basis taxpayer may not be able to deduct all payments in the year made. As *Boylston* indicates, a cash basis taxpayer clearly cannot deduct capital expenditures, such as a building or a substantial improvement to a building, merely because she pays cash for it. Reg. § 1.461–1(a) in this regard does not distinguish between cash and accrual method taxpayers. If an expenditure results in the creation of an asset having a useful life that extends substantially beyond the close of the taxable year, such an expenditure may not be deductible, or may be deductible only in part, for the taxable year in which made. See Chapter 3, at page 318, supra.

(B) *The One-Year Exception.* The regulations dealing with the capitalization of intangibles permit deduction of payments whose benefit lasts 12 months after the taxpayer first realizes the benefit or the end of the taxable year following the taxable year in which the payment was made, whichever period is shorter. Reg. § 1.263(a)–4(f). Thus, for example, a taxpayer who pays for a license that spans two taxable years can deduct the full amount in the first year.

This exception tracks prior case law in which the courts permitted a deduction of expenses that did not provide benefits lasting for more than a year. In Zaninovich v. Commissioner, 616 F.2d 429 (9th Cir. 1980), the court adopted a "one-year" guidepost to determine whether an expenditure results in the creation of an asset having a useful life extending substantially beyond the end of the taxable year. Under this formulation, prepayments generally were deducted if they did not provide benefits that extend beyond one year. *Zaninovich* itself approved the deduction of a lease payment in December for the following year. The Tax Court refused to follow *Zaninovich*, finding that there is no generally accepted one-year rule as adopted by that case. The court maintained that there was no current deduction for expenses with a useful life of less than 12 months that provide benefits beyond the current taxable year. U.S. Freightways v. Commissioner, 113 T.C. 329 (1999). The Tax Court also took the position that the one-year exception does not apply to an accrual basis taxpayer in any event. The Seventh Circuit rejected both positions. It concluded that an accrual basis taxpayer can expense short-term items, including those whose benefits extend into the next taxable year. The court permitted deduction of "ordinary" one-year items that recur "with clockwork regularity." 270 F.3d 1137 (7th Cir. 2001). The Tax Court, however, has been unwilling to let this one go. In Lattice Semiconductor Corp. v. Commissioner, 101 T.C.M. 1483 (2011), it held that accrual basis taxpayers in the Ninth Circuit were not eligible to use the one-year exception, notwithstanding the Seventh Circuit's holding in *U.S. Freightways*.

(C) *Materials and Supplies.* The regulations also provide that a taxpayer's materials and supplies are deductible in the year consumed in many cases. § 1.162–3(a). A prior version of § 1.162–3 was worded differently. It said taxpayers should include as expenses only the costs of materials and supplies actually consumed during the year "provided that the costs of such materials and supplies have not been deducted" in a previous year. In Agro-Jal Farming Enters. v. Commissioner, 145 T.C. 145 (2015), the Tax Court interpreted this to mean that a cash basis taxpayer is not required to defer the expense because, under the cash method of accounting, it took the deduction in the year it paid for them. The current regulation eliminates the "provided that" language. Of course, even if capitalized, many such expenditures might be eligible for immediate expensing, at least for several years following the 2017 legislation. See page 348, supra.

(D) *Interest.* Prepayments of deductible items by cash method taxpayers have caused problems for the income tax for a long time.

Prepayments of interest, for example, were a common method of tax deferral and in the 1970s and 1980s became an important component of tax shelter investments in real estate, farming, motion pictures, and the like. Section 461(g) now requires a cash method taxpayer to allocate and deduct prepaid interest over the loan period, in effect, putting cash method taxpayers on an accrual method for interest deductions. This rule applies to all prepayments of interest, whether on a business or investment debt or on a home mortgage. An exception is provided for "points" on the taxpayer's home mortgage in certain cases.

(E) *The Economics of Prepayments.* A taxpayer who arranges to prepay for goods or services to be delivered in the future may be viewed as having engaged in two transactions: (1) a purchase of goods or services and (2) a loan to the transferee of the prepaid funds until the goods are delivered or the services performed. The transferee has the use of the funds during the interval between payment and economic performance. In the prepayment case, however, the interest on the "loan" typically is reflected in the price of the goods and services and is not separately stated. Since the payor cannot earn the interest income on the funds, she will be unwilling to prepay the amount that normally would be required at the time of economic performance; she will insist on paying a lower amount. By the same token, since the seller has the use of the money in the interval (thereby earning interest income or avoiding interest charges on alternative borrowing), he should be willing to reduce the amount that he otherwise would ask at the later date. The payor thus obtains the benefit of at least nominally tax-free interest income and the recipient forgoes the explicit deduction of an interest expense. When both parties are subject to the same marginal tax rate, the Treasury gains as much from the interest deduction forgone by the seller as it loses from the interest income excluded by the buyer. Thus, the extent to which a prepayment results in tax avoidance depends upon whether the payor can deduct the expenditure (and the timing of the deduction) or, if the expenditure is nondeductible, on when the seller, if taxable, includes the payment in income and the comparative tax rates of the buyer and seller.

As a result, the benefits of avoiding taxation of the interest income may be eliminated by delaying the payor's deduction until economic performance occurs. For example, assume A would normally pay B $110 for deductible services, but pays only $100 when the services are to be rendered one year in the future. Separating the transaction into a sale of services and a loan suggests that A has loaned B $100 for one year, at the end of which B will repay A $100 and $10 interest, which A will retransfer to B as payment for the services. In the year the services are performed, A should be allowed a deduction for $110 and charged with $10 interest income. The net result is the same as allowing a deduction of $100 in the year the services are performed.

If, however, the prepayment was for two years—at a 10 percent interest rate the $100 charge would be $121 if paid at the later date—the results will not be exactly equivalent. Separating the transaction into its two components, a loan and a sale of services, would produce interest income to A of $10 in the first year and $11 in the second year and a deduction of $121 in the second year. Permitting A to deduct $100 in the second year is not the same.

Similar opportunities for shifting interest income may involve prepayments of nondeductible amounts. Consider, for example, a tax-exempt university that charges $11,000 a year for tuition but will accept $10,000 if paid one year in advance. A high-bracket taxpayer, in effect, can avoid the tax on the interest income by prepaying the expense.

If, however, the payee were subject to the same marginal rate as the payor and was required to include the payment in income when received, the tax avoided on the interest income would be offset by effectively denying the payee an interest deduction. Thus, if the transaction were separated into its two components, the payee would have $11,000 of income in Year 2 and a $1,000 interest expense or net income of $10,000. Including $10,000 in income in Year 2 would, thus, correctly measure the payee's income. Including $10,000 in income in Year 1, instead, effectively denies the payee an interest deduction since it is equivalent in present value to including $11,000 in Year 2.

Since the circumstances where the avoidance of tax on interest income is effectively offset will not cover all potential transactions, a comprehensive approach to the economics of prepayments would require recharacterizing such transactions to reflect the existence of a loan. Interest then would be imputed on the loan part of the transaction. The below-market and interest-free loan provisions of § 7872 (described infra at page 761) seem to provide the IRS with authority to adopt such an approach where the potential for tax avoidance is substantial, but only at the cost of significant additional complexity. For a comprehensive analysis of prepayments and related transactions, see Daniel I. Halperin, "Interest in Disguise: Taxing the Time Value of Money," 95 Yale L.J. 506 (1986).

B. ACCRUAL METHOD

We now turn to the accrual method, which is the method of accounting used by most corporate taxpayers and some individuals, partnerships, and trusts. The accrual method generally requires that items of income be taxed in the year in which they are earned, regardless of when they are received, and that items of expense be deducted in the year in which they are incurred, regardless of when they are paid. In studying the materials that follow, consider the proper role of the accrual method of accounting in the tax system. There are two basic positions. One view is that accrual accounting is necessary to determine net income properly. That is because generally accepted techniques of accrual accounting are thought to reflect taxpayers' reasonable expectations of revenues and expenses and thereby to match income with any related expenses. This view regards the cash method of accounting simply as a concession to the unsophisticated.

A second view is that the amount by which a taxpayer's current receipts exceed his current expenses properly reflects his current ability to pay taxes, without regard to whether this excess reflects income earned in the current year or in some other year. Given this view, accrual accounting for tax purposes may be regarded as merely a convenience for taxpayers who keep their business records on an accrual basis.

One's acceptance of one or the other of these radically different views towards accrual accounting for tax purposes significantly influences one's perception of the cases and statutory provisions in this Section. Most of the problems of applying the accrual method arise in three contexts: (1) where uncertainty exists as to whether an amount will be received or paid, (2) where an amount is received before it has been earned, and (3) where an obligation to pay an amount is fixed long before the time when payment will be made.

1. THE "ALL EVENTS" TEST

The "all events" test is the general test for determining whether items of income and deduction have accrued for tax purposes. A statutory definition can be found in § 461(h)(4), which provides that the "all events" test is met with respect to a deductible item if "all events have occurred which determine the fact of liability and the amount of such liability can be determined with reasonable accuracy." The statute codified longstanding regulatory provisions defining the test for deductions, § 1.461–1(a)(2), and parallels complementary regulatory language requiring items to be included in income under the accrual method "when all the events have occurred which fix the right to receive such income and the amount thereof can be determined with reasonable accuracy." Reg. § 1.451–1(a).

The "all events" test originated in United States v. Anderson, 269 U.S. 422 (1926), where the munitions tax on the profits from a munitions manufacturer's 1916 sales became due and was paid in 1917. The taxpayer deducted this amount from its 1917 income (preferring that year of high tax rates). The Supreme Court held that the taxpayer's books were kept on the accrual basis and that the tax was deductible in 1916, not 1917. The Court said:

> In a technical legal sense it may be argued that a tax does not accrue until it has been assessed and becomes due; but it is also true that in advance of the assessment of a tax, all the events may occur which fix the amount of the tax and determine the liability of the taxpayer to pay it. In this respect, for purposes of accounting and of ascertaining true income for a given accounting period, the munitions tax here in question did not stand on any different footing than other accrued expenses appearing on appellee's books. In the economic and bookkeeping sense with which the statute and Treasury decision were concerned, the taxes had accrued.

In Spring City Foundry Co. v. Commissioner, 292 U.S. 182 (1934), the Supreme Court applied the "all events test" to require inclusion of items in income. In that case, the taxpayer shipped goods during the year 1920, but it did not receive payment. Before the close of the year, a bankruptcy petition was filed against the purchaser. Several years later, the taxpayer received a little more than a quarter of the sales price from the trustee in bankruptcy of the purchaser. The Court held that the entire sales price was accrued income in 1920, stating: "[I]t is the *right* to receive and not the actual receipt that determines the inclusion of the amount in gross income. When the right to receive an amount becomes fixed, the right accrues." The law applicable to that year contained no provision (as there is now in § 166(a)(2)) for the deduction of a partially worthless debt. As the claim still had some value, no adjustment could be made with respect to it during 1920.

Businesses typically prefer to maximize income reported on financial statements provided to investors, but the rules of financial accounting are often different than those of the Code. In the 2017 tax act, Congress linked the all events test to financial accounting, providing that the all events test is met with respect to an item of gross income no later than the time the income item is taken into account on the taxpayer's financial statements. § 451(b). The rule contains an exception for taxpayers without an "applicable financial statement," defined to include statements prepared for securities offerings or provided to investors. § 451(b)(3). The rule should have little impact on businesses with less than $25 million in gross receipts, which may now use the cash method. § 448. Thus, the rule will primarily affect larger companies that sell securities to the public or solicit capital from private investors.

The requirement that accrual occur when the amount of income or liability can be determined with "reasonable accuracy" naturally raises issues of what kinds and degrees of uncertainty will preclude accrual. The "all events" test is less precise in application than its language might suggest. Moreover, to divorce the time of accrual from the time of payment raises questions as to the effect of income received prior to the normal time for accrual and of payments made long after the "all events" test has been satisfied. We consider each of these issues in turn.

2.   ACCRUAL OF INCOME

Hallmark Cards, Inc. v. Commissioner

United States Tax Court, 1988. 90 T.C. 26.

■ KORNER, JUDGE:

* * * Petitioner's primary business is the manufacture and sale of greeting cards, giftwrap, ribbon, stationery, and related products. * * * [P]etitioner embarked on a policy of shipping seasonal merchandise to customers in advance of the period during which the merchandise would normally be displayed and sold. As to Christmas merchandise, customers were generally willing to accept this merchandise in advance. * * *

[P]etitioner's customers were less disposed to receiving Valentine shipments in advance. St. Valentine's Day falls shortly after Christmas, the busiest retail season of the year. Merchants were unwilling to accept large shipments of Valentine merchandise while their stores were filled with Christmas merchandise. Additionally, many calendar year customers were concerned over the financial impact of inclusion of large amounts of Valentine merchandise in their yearend inventories. There also was an unwillingness to bear the cost of personal property tax on Valentine merchandise included in yearend inventory. * * *

In 1958, petitioner concluded that it could * * * satisfy customer concerns over its early shipment (other than physical storage) by changing its terms of sale as regards Valentine merchandise. Shipments of Valentine merchandise would be made during the later part of the year preceding Valentine's Day; however, the terms of sale were that title to the goods and risk of loss would not pass to the buyer until January 1 of the following year. Although customers were in physical possession of the merchandise at yearend, they did not own it and therefore were not required to include it in yearend inventory or pay personal property taxes on it. The terms of sale of all other merchandise remained the same (i.e., title and risk of loss passed at time of shipment). Petitioner revised its order forms, sales invoices, and shipping documents to reflect this change in sales terms for Valentine merchandise, and made substantial efforts to apprise its customers of the new policy. Customer reaction to the revised sales terms was generally favorable. * * *

Respondent * * * determined deficiencies in tax [for the years 1975, 1976, 1977 and 1978] attributable to petitioner's allegedly improper deferral of income from Valentine sales until the calendar year following the year of shipment. The notices determined that this practice was inconsistent with petitioner's method of accounting for sales of other merchandise and resulted in a distortion of income. * * *

Petitioner utilizes the calendar year as its accounting period and has employed an accrual method of accounting for both tax and financial accounting purposes. When an accrual method of accounting is utilized, an item of income is included in the taxpayer's gross income for the accounting period during which all the events have occurred which fix the taxpayer's right to receive the item of income, and the amount thereof can be determined with reasonable accuracy. Petitioner contends that, as regards Valentine merchandise shipped prior to yearend, this "all events" test is not satisfied until January 1 of the following year when title to the merchandise and risk of loss pass to the customer. Respondent argues that the all events test is satisfied, at the very latest, at midnight on December 31 of the year in which the merchandise was shipped. We agree with petitioner.

At what point in time a sale takes place is to be determined from the totality of the circumstances. While no single factor is controlling, passage of title is perhaps the most significant factor to be considered, although the transfer of possession is also significant. The objective is to determine at what point in time the seller acquired an unconditional right to receive payment under the contract. Lucas v. North Texas Lumber, 281 U.S. 11, 13 (1930).

Based on the record before us, it is indisputable that petitioner's rights under the sales contracts for Valentine merchandise do not mature until January 1 of the new year. Not until this point in time did petitioner relinquish the benefits and burdens of ownership of the merchandise in exchange for a right to receive payment. Since petitioner had no right to income prior to January 1, the first prong of the all-events test is not met until that date.[4] We cannot agree with respondent's characterization of the passage of title and risk of loss on January 1 as a mere "ministerial act" or "formality." Far from being a ministerial act, the passage of title and risk of loss to the buyer constitutes the very heart of the transaction and is the sine qua non to petitioner's right to receive payment. Until that moment in time when title passes, the potential buyer has mere possession of the merchandise and nothing more. Should it be destroyed while in his possession, the loss is suffered by petitioner. Should he decide that he does not wish to proceed with the transaction, he may return the merchandise to petitioner without penalty. The fact that customers rarely exercised this right is of no consequence; it is existence of the right which controls.

Respondent's heavy reliance on United States v. Hughes Properties, Inc., 476 U.S. 593 (1986), is in our view misplaced. That case concerned the deductibility by the taxpayer, a casino operator, of properly accrued progressive slot machine jackpots which remained unpaid at yearend. The Court allowed the deductions, holding that at the end of its taxable year, the taxpayer's liability for the accrued amounts was definite and fixed pursuant to Nevada law. The Court held that the remote possibility that the casino would cease operations—or the even more remote possibility that people would cease to gamble—went to whether the liability would eventually be paid—not to whether it had been incurred.

Respondent argues that since the Court in *Hughes* ignored these highly remote contingencies in allowing expense accruals, we should accrue Valentine income as of midnight, December 31, of the year of shipment, since at that point of time, there is no doubt that the sale will occur in the next instant.

Respondent misinterprets *Hughes*. In that case, all the events necessary to make the taxpayer's liability for the accrued amounts fixed and definite had occurred by the end of its tax year. The remote contingencies in *Hughes* were found to go to whether the liability would be paid; as to the liability itself, there were no contingencies. Here, in contrast, petitioner does not possess any fixed and definite rights to

---

[4] Since no right to receive income exists in the year of shipment, the second prong of the all-events test—whether the value of that right can be reasonably estimated—is never reached.

payment at yearend. The fact that at the stroke of midnight petitioner knows with absolute certainty, that in the next instant, these rights will arise, cannot compensate for the fact that as of the close of the old year, they do not exist. The all-events test is based on the existence or nonexistence of legal rights or obligations at the close of a particular accounting period, not on the probability—or even absolute certainty—that such right or obligation will arise at some point in the future. We thus hold that as to merchandise sold by petitioner pursuant to its deferred Valentine program, the all-events test is not satisfied until January 1, and that income from those sales is not accruable by petitioner until that date.[6]

*　*　*

Respondent's theory that petitioner employs a hybrid accounting method is premised on a basic misunderstanding of [the regulations under section 446]. Respondent alleges that the "shipment method" is petitioner's predominant method of accounting which it uses for the sale of all merchandise with the exception of Valentine merchandise, income from the sale of which is accounted for using the "title method." However, the regulation reference to accounting for the sale of an item when shipped, delivered, accepted, or when title to the merchandise passes, does not refer to different accounting methods, but is merely illustrative of the different points in time at which an accrual method taxpayer may accrue an item of income. The touchstone for determining when an item may be accrued is the all-events test. For any given manufacturer, this test may be satisfied when merchandise is shipped, accepted, delivered, or at some other point in time, depending upon the particular circumstances. Petitioner's change in the point of time at which it recognizes income from Valentine sales was in recognition of a change in the contractual terms under which it sold Valentine merchandise. A change in treatment of an item of income resulting from a change in underlying facts does not constitute a change in method of accounting. Sec. 1.446–1(e)(2)(ii)(b), Income Tax Regs. To hold otherwise would effectively give respondent the right to dictate to petitioner the terms under which it may sell its merchandise, clearly "an odious propagation of the tentacles of the government anemone." We therefore conclude that petitioner has consistently used an accrual method of accounting for all sales both before and after its 1958 adoption of revised terms of sale as to Valentine merchandise. Since petitioner has consistently utilized a permissible method of accounting which is deemed to clearly reflect income, respondent abused his discretion in requiring petitioner to adopt a different method of accounting for Valentine sales.

---

[6] The business reasons for petitioner's adoption of the Jan. 1 passage of title and risk of loss are sound and have not been disputed. Thus, this is not a case where a taxpayer has deliberately manipulated the terms of sale so as to prevent income from accruing that it would otherwise become entitled to prior to the end of its taxable year. We express no opinion as to the tax consequences of such a situation.

NOTES

(A) *Time of Accrual of Sales of Goods*. When does income accrue from a sale of goods? When the order is given or accepted, when the goods are billed or shipped, or at some other time? See Reg. § 1.446–1(c)(1)(ii)(C), which provides:

> The method used by the taxpayer in determining when income is to be accounted for will generally be acceptable if it accords with generally accepted accounting principles, is consistently used by the taxpayer from year to year, and is consistent with the Income Tax Regulations. For example, a taxpayer engaged in a manufacturing business may account for sales of the taxpayer's product when the goods are shipped, when the product is delivered or accepted, or when title to the goods passes to the customers, whether or not billed, depending upon the method regularly employed in keeping the taxpayer's books.

This requirement of consistency with the seller's standard method of accounting provides greater flexibility than is suggested by the requirement of the "all events" test that income be reported when the seller's "right to payment" becomes "fixed."

Section 458 permits accrual method taxpayers to exclude from income amounts attributable to sales price adjustments for records, magazines, and paperback books returned within a specified period ending shortly after the close of the taxable year.

(B) *Collecting Judgments*. At the end of 1984, the taxpayer in Schlumberger Technology Corp. v. United States, 82 A.F.T.R.2d 98–7384 (S.D. Tex. 1998), was pursuing an action in a French court to enforce a Swiss arbitration award it had won against a former joint venture partner. Although the Swiss judgment was final, the opposing party did not have significant assets in Switzerland, leaving Schlumberger Technology unable to enforce the judgment there. The parties reached a tentative agreement to settle the French litigation in 1984, but did not finalize it until 1985. Schlumberger Tech. reported the settlement as income in 1985. The Commissioner argued that the arbitration award should be included in income in 1984 because the Swiss arbitration award became final in that year. The Court disagreed and held that income is not fixed under the all events test until the award is reduced to a final judgment in a jurisdiction where it is enforceable or the parties enter into a binding settlement agreement.

(C) *Relation to Expenses*. Many taxpayers, faced with the refusal of courts to permit deferral of income, have attempted to offset the immediate inclusion of income by immediately deducting the costs that would be incurred in earning the income. The courts have been more inclined to defer the accrual of deductions than to defer the accrual of income. But see ABKCO Industries, Inc. v. Commissioner, 482 F.2d 150 (3d Cir. 1973), aff'g 56 T.C. 1083 (1971) (amount of royalty payments owed to Chubby Checker—the inventor of "The Twist"—sufficiently contingent to require postponement of accrual).

(D) *Substantial Uncertainty About Collectability.* There is a difference between a contingent receivable, which an accrual basis taxpayer does not include because it is unclear whether she has earned it, and an amount that has been earned, which must be accrued unless the financial condition of the debtor creates a substantial likelihood that the debt will not be paid. Mere doubt about collectability is not sufficient to prevent accrual. Similarly, legal unenforceability of the debt does not prevent accrual. See, e.g., Flamingo Resort, Inc. v. United States, 664 F.2d 1387 (9th Cir. 1982), and Rev. Rul. 83–106, 1983–2 C.B. 77 (casino required to accrue gambling winnings from patrons using credit when gambling occurred despite unenforceability of markers representing the debt because debts typically are paid).

The accrual of income is not required when a fixed right to receive it arises if there is not a reasonable expectancy that the claim will be paid. In Georgia School-Book Depository, Inc. v. Commissioner, 1 T.C. 463 (1943), the taxpayer was a broker for the purchase of school books for the state of Georgia. For a commission of 8 percent of the sales price, the taxpayer arranged for books to be shipped, stored them until needed, and distributed them to the schools. The commissions were payable only from the "Free Textbook Fund," a trust fund comprised solely of revenues from the state's excise tax on beer. During the years in question, the amount in the fund was inadequate to pay the liabilities. The taxpayer argued that its commissions should not be accrued until payment. The court rejected the taxpayer's argument on the ground that, under the accrual method, the right to receive rather than actual receipt determines the time of accrual. Since the taxpayer had earned its commissions, it had to accrue the income unless it could show "a reasonable expectancy that the claim will never be paid." This exception to accrual was limited to situations where "the right itself is in litigation or * * * the debtor is insolvent." The court concluded that, even though the fund was inadequate, there was no reasonable expectation that the commissions would not be paid:

> Georgia is a state possessing great resources and a fine record of fiscal probity, and undoubtedly it can and will meet its obligations. The fact that petitioner * * * continued to sell and deliver school books to the state indicates that there was no serious doubt as to the ultimate collection of the amounts here involved.

In the *Georgia School-Book Depository* case, there were legal restrictions preventing payment in the year in which the court required accrual. Should legal restrictions on payment be given greater weight by the courts and the IRS? Or should accrual be deferred only where there is a substantial economic uncertainty that the amount will be paid?

3.   ADVANCE PAYMENTS FOR UNEARNED ITEMS

One of the most intensely disputed issues in tax law is when an accrual basis taxpayer must include in income amounts that actually have been received but have not yet been earned. Under generally accepted accounting principles, the income is properly accrued when earned by delivery of goods or services. The Commissioner has taken the position, however, that such amounts are income when received. In the early cases, the inclusion of unearned items in income was based on the claim of right doctrine established in North American Oil Consolidated v. Burnet, 286 U.S. 417 (1932), discussed in *Skelly Oil* supra at page 697.

After the repeal of § 452, which excluded prepaid receipts from income until earned, taxpayers enjoyed some success in court challenging the Commissioner's policy of requiring immediate reporting of prepaid amounts. See, e.g., Beacon Publishing Co. v. Commissioner, 218 F.2d 697 (10th Cir. 1955), rev'g 21 T.C. 610 (1954), which permitted an accrual basis taxpayer to defer income from prepaid subscriptions until the year when the liability to furnish the newspaper, magazine, or other periodical arose. (Deferral or prepaid subscription income is now permitted under § 455, and deferral of prepaid dues of nonprofit membership organizations is permitted under § 456.)

But three Supreme Court decisions in 1957, 1961, and 1963 required accrual basis taxpayers to include advance payments in income when received, even though accounting principles would indicate deferral. The case that follows discusses two of these cases and illustrates the difficulty that the lower courts have had in applying these Supreme Court decisions.

Westpac Pacific Food v. Commissioner

United States Court of Appeals, Ninth Circuit, 2006. 451 F.3d 970.

■ ANDREW J. KLEINFELD, JUDGE.

We must decide whether cash paid in advance by a wholesaler to a retailer, in exchange for a volume commitment, is "gross income" under 26 U.S.C. § 61. In the grocery trade, these are called "advance trade discounts."

It is hard to think of a way to make money by buying things. A child may think buying things is how one makes money: he sees his father give a clerk a single piece of paper money, and receive in exchange the goods purchased, several pieces of paper money, and a number of coins. And a person may jokingly say to a spouse "I made $100 today" after buying something on sale for $100 off. But everyone knows these are merely amusing remarks, not real ways to make money.

The facts outlined below sound more complicated than they are, so imagine a simple hypothetical. Harry Homeowner goes to the furniture store, spots just the right dining room chairs for $500 each, and says "I'll take four, if you give me a discount." Negotiating a 25% discount, he pays only $1,500 for the chairs. He has not made $500, he has spent $1,500. Now suppose Harry Homeowner is short on cash, and negotiates a deal where the furniture store gives him a 20% discount as a cash advance instead of the 25% off. This means the store gives him $400 "cash back" today, and he pays $2,000 for the four chairs when they are delivered shortly after the first of the year. Harry cannot go home and say "I made $400 today" unless he plans to skip out on his obligation to pay for the four chairs. Even though he receives the cash, he has not made money by buying the chairs. He has to sell the chairs for more than $1,600 if he wants to make money on them. The reason why the $400 "cash back" is not income is that, like a loan, the money is encumbered with a repayment obligation to the furniture store and the "cash back" must be repaid if Harry does not perform his obligation.

This case is that simple, except that it involves a little more math and a lot more money. The taxpayer promised to buy a lot of items and received cash in advance as its discount on its future, high-volume purchases. Using accrual accounting, the taxpayer treated the up front cash discount as a liability when it was received, just like a loan. As goods were sold, the taxpayer applied the discount *pro rata* to the full purchase price it paid. The net effect was that Westpac reduced its cost of goods sold and increased its reported profit (and thus its taxable income). * * * *

The government concedes, and the Tax Court agreed, that Westpac's method was consistent with generally accepted accounting principles. * * * * Nevertheless, the Tax Court concluded that the cash discount received in advance was income, noting that tax principles do not serve the same purposes as accounting principles, such as reflecting to shareholders how their company is performing.

A company would indeed have a major problem if it accounted to its shareholders as the Tax Court would have it account to the government. Were a company to get very significant amounts of up front cash discounts on its obligation to purchase goods in the future and tell stockholders and prospective stock purchasers that it had "made" this much "income," investors would be sorely disappointed to learn that all the money had to be paid back if their company did not sell all the goods it had promised to sell in the future. The company would be like Harry Homeowner claiming to have "made" $400 when he received his cash advance discount on the four chairs. Harry might have to spend the night on the couch, but the CEO could spend the night in jail.

Facts

Three grocery store chains—Raley's, Save Mart, and Bel Air—organized the taxpayer, Westpac, as a partnership to purchase and warehouse inventory. Westpac is an accrual basis taxpayer.

During 1990 and 1991, Westpac made four contracts to buy inventory and receive cash in advance: (1) lightbulbs from GTE Sylvania; (2) Hallmark cards from Ambassador; (3) bows, wrapping paper, and other products from American Greetings; and (4) spices from McCormick. Under each contract, Westpac promised to buy a minimum quantity of merchandise and received a volume discount in the form of cash up front. If Westpac bought too few lightbulbs, spices, greeting cards, etc., then it was obligated to pay back the cash advance *pro rata*. Conversely,

Westpac's obligation to repay the cash advance was extinguished if Westpac purchased the required volume. Westpac made other promises as well, such as exclusivity and shelf space, but the volume purchased determined whether it had to refund the cash advance and, if so, how much it had to refund.

GTE Sylvania Contract

In July of 1990, Westpac made a deal with the Sylvania Lighting division of GTE Products Corp. to (1) make GTE Sylvania its exclusive lightbulb supplier for Westpac and its member stores for four years; (2) "aggressively and regularly" advertise and promote GTE Sylvania's products; (3) dedicate on average at least 12 lineal feet of shelf space to GTE Sylvania's products in its member stores; and (4) purchase $17 million in lightbulbs during the term of the agreement. Given Westpac's volume purchase commitment, GTE Sylvania agreed to pay Westpac $1.1 million as an "unearned advance allowance." GTE Sylvania paid this to Westpac by check, and agreed to pay Westpac another $200,000 on the first, second, and third anniversaries of the agreement, provided that GTE Sylvania was satisfied with Westpac's warehouse distribution arrangement. The contract refers to the total $1.7 million in payments as the "Westpac Allowance" and contains the following clause:

> Upon termination of this Agreement, Westpac will reimburse GTE Sylvania on a pro-rated basis for any portion of the Westpac Allowance advanced to Westpac but not earned due to the failure by Westpac to purchase at least $17.0 million in lamps.

During Westpac's 1991 tax year, GTE Sylvania paid the first $200,000 to Westpac.

Westpac could not resell enough lightbulbs to meet the minimum volume the contract called for, so it terminated the arrangement in October of 1994. Westpac's termination letter acknowledged its obligation to pay back a pro-rated portion of the Westpac Allowance, and it repaid $861,857 to GTE Sylvania in December. * * * *

[Discussion of the other contracts, which are similar arrangements, is omitted.]

Westpac's Tax Reporting

In accord with standard accounting principles, Westpac accounted for the up front cash as a liability at the time it received the cash. The cash advance got translated into taxable income through Westpac's inventory accounting. As Westpac purchased the goods for which it had the volume obligations, it subtracted *pro rata* portions of the advance cash discounts from what it paid. This had the effect of reducing the cost of goods sold (and increasing the taxable profits from sales) by the amount of the cash advances attributable to the goods sold.

The government took the position that Westpac * * * under-reported over $5.5 million in gross income for 1990 and over $4.9 million for 1991 because [it] did not report the cash advances as gross income. Westpac filed a petition for readjustment and the government opposed it. Relying on *Commissioner of Internal Revenue v. Glenshaw Glass Co.*, the Tax Court held that the cash advance discounts were "income" under section 61 of the Internal Revenue Code. Westpac timely filed this appeal.

The sole issue before us is whether advance trade discounts constitute gross income when received. We hold that they do not and reverse the Tax Court.

ANALYSIS

* * *

B. Is A Discount in the Form of A Cash Advance Income When Received?

There appears to be no circuit court authority on point, but the Supreme Court authorities bracketing the question compel our answer: Cash advances in exchange for volume purchase commitments, subject to *pro rata* repayment if the volume commitments are not met, are not income when received.

The statutory definition of gross income is expansive. *Commissioner v. Glenshaw Glass Co.* held that punitive damages received by a successful litigant were "income" because they were "accessions to wealth, clearly realized, and over which the taxpayers have complete dominion." The government argues that the cash advances in this case fit that definition because Westpac had "complete dominion" over the money. It did not have to put the cash in a trust account and could spend the money as it chose. But that leaves out [the] *sine qua non* of income: that it be an "accession to wealth." One may have "complete dominion" over money but it does not become income until it is an "accession to wealth." That is why borrowed money is not income, even though the borrower has "complete dominion" over the cash. * * *

The Supreme Court decisions bracketing this case are *CIR v. Indianapolis Power & Light Co.* [493 U.S. 203, 110 S. Ct. 589, 107 L. Ed. 2d 591 (1990)] on one side, and *Automobile Club of Michigan v. CIR* [353 U.S. 180, 77 S. Ct. 707, 1 L. Ed. 2d 746 (1957)] and *Schlude v. CIR* [372 U.S. 128, 83 S. Ct. 601, 9 L. Ed. 2d 633 (1963)] on the other.

Indianapolis Power held that utility customers' security deposits are not income to the utility because of the obligation to repay the money when service ended. The decision analogizes the security deposits to loans because of the repayment obligation. *Automobile Club of Michigan* holds that prepaid membership dues are income when received, despite the association's obligation to provide membership services—maps, tire repair and the like—during the subsequent year. The reason was that *pro rata* application of the dues to each month "bears no relation to the services" the club had to perform. Drivers do not call AAA once a month to repair a flat or send a map, and AAA is entitled to keep the membership dues regardless of whether the member ever requests any goods or services. *Schlude* held that cash paid to a dance studio for ballroom dancing lessons was income when received, not when the lessons were provided. The Court applied *Automobile Club of Michigan*, because the money was not refundable and the studio could keep it even if the student did not show up for dance lessons.

This case is like *Indianapolis Power*, not *Automobile Club of Michigan* or *Schlude*. The cash advance trade discounts are like the security deposits in that they are subject to repayment, and unlike the membership dues in that the recipient cannot keep the money regardless of what happens after receipt. Westpac could only retain the full, up front trade discount if it met the volume requirements. Like the security deposit, the cash advance is subject to repayment. The only difference is that the repayment amount in this case may not be the full amount advanced by the vendor, but that is because the repayment amount is reduced *pro rata* to the extent Westpac fails to fulfill its volume commitment.

Because the taxpayer here has to pay the money back if the volume commitments are not met, it is not an "accession to wealth" as required by *Glenshaw Glass*. Westpac either has to buy a specified volume of goods for more than it would otherwise pay or pay back the money, just like Harry Homeowner. Thus the cash advance discounts are, like a loan or customer security deposit, liabilities rather than income when received.

The Tax Court found that Westpac's accounting for the cash advances as affecting cost of goods sold complied with generally accepted accounting principles, but correctly held that accounting rules are not necessarily controlling for tax purposes. The regulations require that inventory accounting conform to best accounting practices *and* clearly reflect income. But that does not go far enough to transform the cash into "income" in the face of *Indianapolis Power*. We cannot agree with the government that Westpac's "unfettered use" of the money makes it income, because it was not an accession to wealth. Rather, it was merely an advance against an obligation, repayable if the obligation was not performed.

* * *

Our decision in *Milenbach* [v. Commissioner, 318 F.3d 924 (9th Cir. 2003)] is more analogous to this case than *Schlude* or *Automobile Club of Michigan*. In *Milenbach*, a Los Angeles entity loaned the Oakland Raiders $6.7 million, repayable only out of revenue from the luxury suites to be built in the future, to induce the team to move to Los Angeles. Even though it was a non-recourse loan with no certain repayment date, and even though the Raiders neither built the suites nor made any payments, we held that the $6.7 million was not income because the repayment obligation was genuine. The case at bar is easier than *Milenbach* because the cash advances here are more plainly subject to repayment in calculable amounts by a set date. Westpac not only had a duty to repay the discounts, it actually did repay them when it did not meet the volume commitments. When Westpac did buy the required volume of goods, it paid list price rather than a discounted price, and realized the income for tax purposes.

It works out about the same as with Harry Homeowner: He has to sell the chairs for more than he paid in order to make money on them. Westpac had to sell the lightbulbs, ribbons, greeting cards, and such for more than they paid in order to make money on them. It remains exceedingly difficult to make money merely by buying things. Westpac did not get any richer when it received its volume discount in the form of cash up front than Harry Homeowner did when he got the $400 from the furniture store. There was no accession to wealth when Westpac got the cash, just an increase in cash assets offset by an equal liability for the advance trade discounts.

REVERSED.

NOTES

(A) *Codification of Deferral Rules.* The 2017 tax legislation codified IRS practice in permitting accrual-basis taxpayers to defer some advance payments, provided that the payments are also deferred for financial reporting purposes. Section 451(c) now provides that an accrual basis taxpayer who receives an advance payment must report it as income at the earlier of the time it is included in revenue on financial statements or the taxable year of receipt. Taxpayers who received a payment but have not included the payment as revenue on financial statements may elect to defer inclusion of the advance payment to the next taxable year. For purposes of these rules, an advance payment is defined to exclude rents, payments with respect to financial instruments, and payments subject to § 83, among other items. § 451(c)(4)(B). These rules are intended to mirror those announced by the IRS in Rev. Proc. 2004–34, as modified and clarified by Rev. Proc. 2011–18 and Rev. Proc. 2013–33, which permitted certain advance payments to be deferred until the subsequent year or until reported for financial accounting purposes, whichever is earlier.

(B) *Advance Trade Discounts.* Following *Westpac*, the IRS announced that it would apply the holding of the case to all taxpayers who receive "advance trade discounts." Rev. Proc. 2007–53, 2007–2 C.B. 233. The ruling says nothing about other situations. The Third Circuit distinguished *Westpac* in a case with similar facts. There, another grocery received a sum of money from its primary lender. It signed a promissory note but payments on the note were forgiven so long as the grocery purchased a fixed amount of inventory from the vendor. Although the taxpayer argued the amounts received were loan proceeds, the court found that so long as the grocery upheld its end of the bargain, it could keep the money, and therefore it was taxable. Karns Prime & Fancy Food Ltd. v. Commissioner, 494 F.3d 404 (3d Cir. 2007).

(C) *Prepayments vs. Security Deposits.* Often the issue arises whether a receipt is an advance payment for services, which is taxable on receipt, or a security deposit, which is not. For example, in Commissioner v. Indianapolis Power and Light Co., 493 U.S. 203 (1990), discussed in *Westpac,* the Supreme Court treated as nontaxable security deposits amounts received by a utility from its customers to secure their performance. The Court distinguished advance payments from security deposits by looking at the rights and obligations of the parties at the time the payments were made. An individual who makes an advance payment has no right to a refund if the recipient fulfills the contract. A customer who gives a security deposit to a utility, like a lender, retains the right to repayment in cash. The Court noted that the customer has no obligation to buy electricity even if he may apply his deposit against such purchases. The Tax Court has broadly interpreted *Indianapolis Power & Light.* For example, in Oak Industries, Inc. v. Commissioner, 96 T.C. 559 (1991), the court treated as excludable security deposits amounts received by a cable television service even though they were noninterest bearing because they were conditionally refundable.

(D) *Gift Cards.* Reg. § 1.451–5 treats sales of gift cards as advance payments. Taxpayers may defer recognition of income from gift card sales until the gift cards are redeemed by customers if certain conditions are met. § 451(b) limits deferral for advance payments by requiring that income be included no later than it is included for financial accounting purposes. As discussed in Note (A), taxpayers may defer recognition of this income only until the next tax year. § 451(c).

(E) *Other Litigation.* Following the Supreme Court decisions described in *Westpac,* the Commissioner enjoyed great success in taxing prepaid but unearned income. In RCA Corp. v. United States, 664 F.2d 881 (2d Cir. 1981), the taxpayer serviced TV sets that it sold. Purchasers paid a lump sum that entitled them to receive service and repairs for a stated period. Relying on the Supreme Court cases, the court held that payments were taxable, noting that RCA could not "know the extent of the performance that the customer might ultimately require, and it could not be certain of the amount of income that it would ultimately earn from the contract." The court noted that such uncertainty was sufficient to delay the inclusion of income for financial accounting but not for tax accounting.

The Seventh Circuit permitted deferral, however, in Artnell Co. v. Commissioner, 400 F.2d 981 (7th Cir. 1968), rev'g 48 T.C. 411 (1967). *Artnell* involved receipts by the Chicago White Sox in one taxable year for tickets, parking, and broadcasting rights for baseball games to be played in the following taxable year. The court sustained the taxpayer's deferral on the ground that the time and extent of the future services were so definite that the taxpayer's method could "so clearly reflect income" that the Commissioner's refusal to permit deferral would be an abuse of his discretion under § 446. The Supreme Court decisions were distinguished on the basis of uncertainty in those cases about the time and extent of the performance of services. The court remanded the case to the Tax Court for a determination whether the White Sox method of accounting clearly reflected income. On remand, the Tax Court found that the White Sox method, while not perfect in matching income with expenses, was more desirable than the Commissioner's proposed method and approved deferral. 29 T.C.M. 403 (1970). For a case illustrating that *Artnell* was not a one-inning wonder, see Tampa Bay Devil Rays, Ltd. v. Commissioner, 84 T.C.M. 394 (2002). The Devil Rays successfully deferred reporting season ticket income received in 1995 and 1996 for their first season. When the tickets were bought it was unclear whether Tampa Bay would even acquire a major league team; the first major league pitch by a Tampa Bay player was thrown in 1998.

(F) *Non-Cash Prepayments.* The prepayment need not always be in the form of cash. In T.F.H. Publications, Inc. v. Commissioner, 72 T.C. 623 (1979), an accrual basis taxpayer acquired printing and publishing assets in 1971 for a price that included a credit on the first $40,000 of advertising placed by the seller in the taxpayer's publications. The Tax Court held that the assets received in 1971 constituted payment for future advertising services that must be included in income under *Schlude.*

(G) *Policy of Treatment of Prepayments.* If the accrual method generally is superior to the cash method in accurately measuring income, why does the Commissioner urge the courts to abandon the accrual method with regard to prepayments? Does the answer lie in administrative concerns? The IRS is often troubled when the tax liability arises after the taxpayer has received cash or property. Questions of collectability and enforcement inevitably arise. This is not the first time we have seen administrative concerns trump accurate income measurement. The cash method generally and the realization requirement, which permit taxpayers to defer income until receipt, also are often justified on similar grounds. With a solvent taxpayer like Westpac, do concerns about collectability justify the Commissioner's position?

As discussed supra at page 719 taxing prepayments on receipt, which over-taxes the recipient, could offset the ability of the payor to avoid tax on interest income by prepaying a nondeductible expenditure. Can the IRS argue that this is a justification for taxing prepayments?

4. EXPENSES

The timing of the deduction for an accrual method taxpayer turns on the "all events" test. Section 461(h)(4) states that the all events test is met "if all events have occurred which determine the fact of liability and the amount of such liability can be determined with reasonable accuracy." This test is limited by § 461(h)(1), which provides that the all events test will not be deemed to be satisfied until there is "economic performance."

The following case illustrates the kind of problem that gave rise to § 461(h). The taxpayer attempted to accrue current deductions for an amount to be paid far in the future. The claimed deduction totaled $24.6 million, but the obligation had a present value of only $4.4 million. The case was decided after § 461(h) was amended to add economic performance to the all events test but involves taxable years before that amendment.

Ford Motor Company v. Commissioner
United States Court of Appeals, Sixth Circuit, 1995. 71 F.3d 209.

■ MILBURN, CIRCUIT JUDGE:

Petitioner Ford Motor Company ("Ford") appeals the decision of the United States Tax Court upholding respondent Commissioner of Internal Revenue's ("Commissioner") reduction of petitioner's deductions for its obligations under agreements it entered into in settlement of tort lawsuits against it. On appeal, the issue is whether respondent Commissioner abused her discretion in determining that petitioner's method of accounting for its structured settlements was not a clear reflection of income under 26 U.S.C. § 446(b) and in ordering petitioner to limit its deduction in 1980 to the cost of the annuity contracts it purchased to fund the settlements. For the reasons that follow, we affirm.

I

A

Petitioner Ford Motor Company is engaged in a number of businesses, including the manufacture of cars and trucks, and it maintains its books and records and files its income taxes using the accrual method of accounting. In the years preceding 1980, some of Ford's cars and trucks were involved in automobile accidents, and in 1980, Ford entered into 20 structured settlement agreements in settlement of personal injury or accidental death claims with persons who were injured in the accidents and with survivors of persons who died as a result of the accidents. In these structured settlement agreements, Ford agreed to make periodic payments of tort damages, yearly or monthly, in exchange for a release of all claims against it. The payments were to be made over various periods of time, the longest of which was 58 years. All but three of the settlements provided for payments over a period of 40 years or more. The agreements were of three types: (I) those that required petitioner to make periodic payments for a period certain ("Type I settlements"); (II) those that required petitioner to make periodic payments for the remainder of a claimant's life ("Type II settlements"); and (III) those that required petitioner to make periodic payments for the longer of a period certain or the remainder of a claimant's life ("Type III settlements"). In total, the structured settlement agreements provided for payments of $24,477,699.

To provide it with funds to cover the periodic payments, Ford purchased single premium annuity contracts at a cost of $4,424,587. The annuity contracts were structured so that the yearly annuity payments would equal the yearly amount owed to the claimants under the structured settlement agreements. None of the settlement agreements released petitioner from liability following the purchase of the annuity contract, and, in the event of a default on an annuity, petitioner would be required to pay the remaining balance owed to the tort claimants. The parties stipulated that the present value of the deferred payments that petitioner agreed to make to the claimants did not exceed the cost of the annuity contracts.

On its 1980 tax return, petitioner claimed deductions for the various types of structured settlements as follows: for the Type I settlements, it claimed the total amount of all periodic payments due; for the Type II settlements, it claimed the amounts it actually paid during 1980; and for the Type III settlements, it claimed the total amount of all payments due for the period certain portion of the settlement. These deductions totaled $10,636,994, which petitioner included as part of a product liability loss that it carried back to its 1970 taxable year pursuant to 26 U.S.C. § 172(b)(1)(I). It also reported the annuity income on its 1980 federal income tax return under 26 U.S.C. § 72. For financial accounting purposes, petitioner reported the 1980 structured settlements by expensing the cost of the annuity in the year of the settlement. * * *

Respondent Commissioner determined that Ford's method of accounting for its structured settlements did not clearly reflect income under 26 U.S.C. § 446(b) and disallowed the deductions petitioner claimed in excess of the cost of the annuities petitioner purchased. Respondent also excluded from petitioner's income the amounts required to be reported as income from annuity contracts, which was $323,340 in 1980. As a result, respondent determined a deficiency in petitioner's 1970 federal income tax liability of $3,300,151.

B

Petitioner Ford * * * claimed that it was entitled to deduct in 1980 the full amount of all payments to be made under the structured settlements, basing its valuation of the life settlements on the life expectancies of the claimants. The total deduction Ford claimed was $24,477,699.

The parties submitted the case to the United States Tax Court with all facts fully stipulated. A divided court upheld the Commissioner's position. * * *

II

A

Section 446 of the Internal Revenue Code provides the general rule governing use of methods of accounting by taxpayers. Section 446(b) provides that, if the method of accounting used by the taxpayer to compute income does not clearly reflect income, "the computation of taxable income shall be made under such method as, in the opinion of the Secretary or his delegate, does clearly reflect income." The Commissioner has broad discretion under § 446(b) to determine whether a particular method of accounting clearly reflects income. Thor Power Tool Co. v.

Commissioner, 439 U.S. 522 (1979). "Since the Commissioner has 'much latitude for discretion,' his interpretation of the statute's clear-reflection standard 'should not be interfered with unless clearly unlawful.'" 439 U.S. at 532 (quoting Lucas v. American Code Co., 280 U.S. 445, 449 (1930)). Once the Commissioner has determined that a method of accounting does not clearly reflect income, she may substitute a method that, in her opinion, does clearly reflect income.

* * * All facts in this case were stipulated, and the issue before us is a question of ultimate fact, which we review de novo.

B

There are three stages to our analysis in this case: first, we decide whether the application of § 446(b) was appropriate; second, we decide whether the tax court correctly determined that petitioner's method of accounting did not clearly reflect income; and third, we address the appropriateness of the method of accounting that the Commissioner imposed in its place.

First, petitioner argues that the tax court erred in allowing the Commissioner to require Ford to change its method of accounting because, in the absence of abuse or manipulation, an accrual method taxpayer clearly reflects its income when its reporting satisfies the "all events" test. Therefore, it argues that, because its accrual of deductions satisfied the all events test, the Commissioner had no authority to invoke § 446(b) .

Ford Motor Company is an accrual method taxpayer. The accrual method of accounting takes income into account when the right to payment is earned, even if payment is not received until later, and expenses into account when they are incurred, even if payment is not made until a later time. Financial accounting systems differ regarding the time that an expense is "incurred" and therefore should be accrued, but, under the tax law, the standard for determining when an expense is "incurred" is the "all events" test. This test provides that an accrual method taxpayer must deduct an expense in the taxable year when all the events have occurred that establish the fact of liability giving rise to the deduction and the amount of the liability can be determined with reasonable accuracy. Id. The tax court assumed for purposes of discussion that Ford's deductions satisfied the all events test, and for purposes of our review, we will make this assumption as well.

It is a well established principle that the Commissioner may not invoke her authority under § 446(b) to require a taxpayer to change from an accounting method that clearly reflects income, even if she believes that a second method might more clearly reflect income. However, we hold that satisfaction of the all events test by an accrual method taxpayer does not preempt the Commissioner's authority under § 446(b) to determine that a taxpayer's method of accounting does not clearly reflect income.

Section 446(c) of the Internal Revenue Code provides that, subject to the provisions of subsections (a) and (b), a taxpayer may compute taxable income under the accrual method of accounting. The all events test, which is merely a means devised to define the years in which income and deductions accrue, clearly is subordinate to the clear reflection standard contained in subsection (b). The tax court stated:

> The provisions of section 446 make it clear that a taxpayer's ability to use one or more of the methods of accounting listed in 446(c) is contingent upon the satisfaction of subsections 446(a) and (b). The statute does not limit the Commissioner's discretion under section 446(b) by the taxpayer's mere compliance with the methods of accounting generally permitted under section 446(c). * * * In short, the statute clearly provides that the taxpayers may use an accrual method so long as it clearly reflects income.

The language of § 446 is clear on its face, and we agree with the tax court's interpretation of the statute. See Mooney Aircraft, Inc. v. United States, 420 F.2d 400, 406 (5th Cir.1969) ("The 'all events test,' however, is not the only basis upon which the Commissioner can disallow a deduction. Under 446(b) he has discretion to disallow any accounting method which does not clearly reflect income.").

Petitioner argues that Congress acknowledged that the Commissioner's discretion under § 446(b) does not extend to situations such as the present case when it changed the Internal Revenue Code, effective in 1984, to provide in § 461(h)(2)(C) that accrual method taxpayers cannot deduct tort liabilities until the year in which payment is made. Ford points to the legislative history of § 461, which states that "the rules relating to the time for accrual of a deduction by a taxpayer using the accrual method of accounting should be changed to take into account the time value of money." It argues that this statement indicates a recognition by Congress that the Commissioner was not authorized to deny the sort of accrual that Ford is attempting prior to 1984.

The tax court held that the change in prior law to which the legislative history refers is the all events test contained in the Income Tax Regulations and that Congress did not intend "to limit respondent's authority under section 446(b) in any way by enacting section 461(h) in 1984." We agree that the change that this passage references is a modification of the all events test and conclude that nothing in the legislative history of § 461(h) limits the Commissioner's authority under § 446(b). Section 461(h) was a Congressional effort to remedy an accounting distortion by placing all accrual method taxpayers on the cash method of accounting for tort liabilities, regardless of the length of the payout period and without any consideration of whether accrual of an expense in an earlier year would distort income. Its enactment does not preclude the Commissioner from applying the clear reflection standard of § 446(b) on a case-by-case basis to taxpayers in tax years prior to 1984.

C

Having determined that expenses that satisfy the all events test can be disallowed when accrual would not result in a clear reflection of income, we now examine the correctness of the Commissioner's determination that Ford's method of accounting for its tort obligations did not clearly reflect income. * * *

[The court's discussion of the Tax Court's conclusion, by way of an example, that the tax savings from a current deduction would make Ford better off financially by having accidents is omitted. The court accepted Ford's contention that the Tax Court's calculation was incorrect, but concluded that this factor was not determinative to the Tax Court but merely highlighted the distortion of income.]

[E]ven viewing petitioner's numerical example as correct, the gross distortion of income that it demonstrates between the economic and tax results persuades us that the tax court's decision was not improper. Given the length of the payment periods, allowing a deduction for the full amount of liability in 1980 could lead to the result that the tax benefit from the deduction would fund the full amounts due in future years and leave petitioner with a profit. Such a result extends the accrual method of accounting beyond its inherent limitations.

Our task on appeal is to determine whether there is an adequate basis in law for the Commissioner's conclusion that Ford's method of accounting did not clearly reflect income. See RCA Corp., 664 F.2d at 886. We find several cases from other circuits that support our finding that the Commissioner's exercise of her discretion was proper. * * *

[I]n this case, assuming that the all events test for accrual is satisfied, the long time period between the deductions and eventual payment of the obligations causes a distortion of petitioner's income.

Petitioner also argues that the tax court's decision that petitioner's method of accounting did not clearly reflect income was improper because it "authorizes arbitrary and unprincipled use of the Commissioner's section 446(b) power." It asserts that the tax court failed to provide any principles "to delineate the scope of section 446(b)," and that, in doing so, it created an "arbitrary system * * * that requires all accrual taxpayers to account for their liabilities when they become fixed, yet makes the validity of that reporting method subject to the unconstrained whim of the Commissioner."

We are not persuaded by this policy-based argument. The tax court concluded its opinion stating:

> Finally, we want to make clear that the mere fact that a deduction which accrues prior to the time payment is made (the timing factor) does not, by itself, cause the accrual to run afoul of the clear reflection of income requirement. Inherent in the use of an accrual method is the fact that a deduction may be allowed in advance of payment. Our holding in the instant case is not

intended to draw a bright line that can be applied mechanically in other circumstances. We decide only the ultimate question of fact in the instant case; namely, whether, for tax purposes, petitioner's method of accounting for its obligations under the structured settlements clearly reflects income. We hold that it does not and that the Government did not abuse its discretion in making that determination.

As the tax court observed, "the issue of whether the taxpayer's method of accounting clearly reflects income is a question of fact to be determined on a case-by-case basis." We find the tax court's language sufficient to limit its holding to extreme cases such as this one in which the economic results are grossly different from the tax results and therefore conclude that the tax court's decision does not allow the Commissioner arbitrary or unprincipled discretion.

D

Given that a change was necessary because Ford's accrual of its settlement obligations in 1980 did not clearly reflect income, Ford argues that the method of accounting that the Commissioner imposed in its place was improper. Ford asserts that the Commissioner lacked the authority to impose the method of accounting that she did because it is "inconsistent with the plain dictates of the Code and regulations and the undisputed facts of this case."

The method of accounting that the Commissioner imposed was to allow Ford a deduction for the amount that it paid for the annuities with no further deductions for the future payments that Ford will make to the claimants. To offset her disallowance of future deductions, the Commissioner will permit Ford to exclude its income from the annuity contracts. Petitioner asserts that this scheme violates established tax law for several reasons and forces Ford to use a tax treatment that it could not have adopted on its own.

First, petitioner argues that the Commissioner is imposing on it a present value method of accounting which should only be imposed in the presence of a directive by Congress to do so. Ford additionally argues that this method impermissibly allows it only to deduct the approximately $4 million it paid for the annuities without ever allowing a deduction for the additional approximately $20 million it will pay to the claimants and that the Commissioner's method is arbitrary because it is not a method that Ford could have adopted on its own.

Respondent counters that its method of accounting is a modified cash basis method that allows Ford "a dollar for dollar deduction, albeit in the form of an offset against its annuity income, for the full face amount of its future payments of approximately $24 million." Respondent points out that, because she allowed Ford to deduct the full cost of the annuity contracts in 1980, it has no basis in the contracts and would be fully taxable on the annuity income of $24,477,699 as it is received. However, the payments Ford is required to make to the tort claimants, which correspond exactly to the amount of its annuity income, give rise to deductions that offset the income and create a wash. Respondent argues that, because she has relieved taxpayer of the obligation to report the annuity income as it is received, she should not allow Ford any deductions for the required payments.

We find no merit in petitioner's assertion that this methodology is improper because it reduces the amount of the deductions to the present value of the payments petitioner is obligated to make. The Commissioner reduced petitioner's deduction to the cost of the annuity contracts. The stipulated facts provided only that the present value of the payments petitioner is obligated to make did not exceed this amount. There is no indication that respondent was imposing a present value method of accounting on petitioner.

Furthermore, we find no authority that prohibits the tax accounting treatment that the Commissioner and the tax court imposed here. The Commissioner's discretion to impose an alternate method of accounting under § 446(b) is not limited to methods that Ford could have adopted on its own. While we recognize that to require Ford to account for its tort obligations on the cash method might have been a more logical alternative, we cannot find that the Commissioner's exercise of her discretion was arbitrary because it resulted in an accounting treatment more favorable to Ford that a straight cash method would be. The only difference between the Commissioner's method of accounting and the cash basis method is that petitioner receives an immediate deduction for the cost of its annuities rather than recovering that cost over the terms of the annuities under 26 U.S.C. § 72, and this difference inures to Ford's benefit. We therefore conclude that the tax court's decision regarding the accounting method the Commissioner imposed was proper.

III

For the reasons stated, the judgment of the tax court is AFFIRMED.

NOTES

(A) *Time Value of Money and Accrual Accounting.* Prior to *Ford Motor Co.*, the government had little success in convincing courts to apply time value of money principles (and three Tax Court judges even dissented in *Ford*). Congress responded in 1984 by enacting § 461(h), which allows deductions for tort liabilities only as payments are made, but that statute was not applicable in the *Ford* case. The government's only previous significant victory on time value of money grounds had been in Mooney Aircraft, Inc. v. United States, 420 F.2d 400 (5th Cir. 1969), which involved an average twenty-year delay between accrual and payment. In that case, the court acknowledged that the "all events" test was satisfied but held that a long delay between accrual and payment would necessarily violate the requirement that accounting methods "clearly reflect income."

More typical was the Supreme Court's opinion in *Hughes Properties, Inc.,* distinguished in *Ford,* in which the Supreme Court dismissed the Commissioner's time value concerns. The court in *Ford Motor Co.* notes that the Commissioner's tax avoidance concerns in *Hughes* might not have been dismissed so easily if the "progressive" slot machine payouts at issue there had been extended for a longer period. But it is not clear that the Supreme Court would have ruled differently. The Supreme Court apparently believed there was no "potential for tax avoidance" despite the Commissioner's urging that the taxpayer's discretion to set very high odds against progressive payoffs and to place into operation additional progressive slot machines at the end of each taxable year created opportunities to inflate deductions for amounts that would not be paid until sometime in the distant future. The Court found no tax avoidance motive or behavior in the case and, in an extraordinary exercise of judicial non-notice, concluded that it was not in the casino's self interest to set the odds so high as to defer payoffs too far in the future because "customers will refuse to play and will gamble elsewhere." It is difficult to imagine where the Court might have been looking when it reached that conclusion. Are the Justices so insulated from ordinary life that they do not know of the extraordinary economic success of state lotteries that routinely raise enormous sums of money from untold numbers of people who avidly want—rather than shrink from—gambles that couple huge payoffs with extremely long odds? Could their law clerks also live lives so sheltered that they too are oblivious to this phenomenon?

In *Mooney Aircraft,* the court noted that the longer the delay between accrual and payment, the less probable the payment. In *Mooney Aircraft,* the taxpayer had made no payments and the court apparently feared it would never do so. In *Ford Motor Co.,* however, the taxpayer had purchased an annuity equal to the present value of its obligations. If it had not done so, how might the Tax Court have determined the present value of Ford's future liability?

Concerns over the inability to determine present value for lack of a discount rate prompted Congress to choose the approach of § 461(h) that denies a deduction until there is economic performance (defined to be payment in the case of structured settlements) rather than permitting a current deduction for the present value of the liability. The equivalency of various methods is discussed in the Note on the Economic Equivalence of §§ 461(h), 468A, and 468: The Concept of Non-Advantageous Tax Deferral, *infra* at page 746.

(B) *Relationship of Section 461(h) to the Cash Method.* Although § 461(h) technically changes the "all events test" applicable to accrual basis taxpayers, its effect is essentially to move those taxpayers closer to the cash method for expenditures. The House Report accompanying the 1984 Act, which adopted § 461(h), explained the reasons for change:

> The committee believes that the rules relating to the time for accrual of a deduction by a taxpayer using the accrual method accounting should be changed to take into account the time value of money. * * * Allowing a taxpayer to take deductions currently for an amount to be paid in the future overstates the true cost of the

expense to the extent the time value of money is not taken into account; the deduction is overstated by the amount the face value exceeds the present value of the expense.

H.R.Rep. 98–432, 9th Cong., 2d Sess. 1254 (1984).

Under § 461(h), all the events that establish liability for a deductible expenditure for an accrual basis taxpayer are not treated as having occurred any earlier than the time "economic performance" occurs.

On its face, § 461(h) does not apply to all premature accruals. It is limited to liabilities arising out of the provision of services or property, or a payment arising from workers' compensation or a tort. The statute, however, gives the Service the authority to issue regulations determining economic performance for other liabilities. The regulations provide that economic performance occurs only on payment arising out of breach of contract or violation of law, rebates and refunds, awards, prizes, and jackpots, amounts paid for insurance, warranty and service contracts, and taxes. Reg. § 1.461–4(g). Cash basis principles are used to determine payment. Reg. § 1.461–4(g)(1)(ii)(A).

(C) *Economic Performance.* Neither the statute nor the regulations define "economic performance," but the House Report explains that "[e]conomic performance with respect to a particular liability generally occurs when the activities that the taxpayer is obligated to do to satisfy the liability actually are performed." Section 461(h) provides specific rules for certain situations. For example, if the liability of the taxpayer arises out of the receipt of services or property by the taxpayer, economic performance occurs as the taxpayer receives the services or property. Thus, if A in Year 1 incurs a fixed liability to pay B $100 in Year 3 for services to be performed in Year 3, A may deduct the $100 only in Year 3. Even if A paid the $100 in Year 1, the deduction could only be taken in Year 3 when economic performance occurs.

(D) *Recurring Items Exception.* The principal exception to the economic performance rule is for recurring items. A taxpayer may deduct expenditures for recurring items as soon as the "all events" test is met, so long as economic performance occurs no later than eight and a half months after the close of the taxable year and either the item is immaterial or all events accounting results in a better matching of the liability with the income to which it relates than would result from accruing the liability when economic performance occurs. § 461(h)(3). The Conference Committee Report for the 1984 Act gives the following examples of when the "all events" test does a better job than the "economic performance" test of picking the taxable year for deduction:

> For example, a sales commission agreement may require certain collection activities to be performed in a year subsequent to the year in which sales income is reported. In such a case, economic performance with respect to some portion of the liability to pay the commission may not occur until the following year. Nevertheless, deducting the commission expense in the year in which the sales income is reported results in a better matching of the commission expense with the sales income. Likewise, if income from the sale of

goods is recognized in one year, but the goods are not shipped until the following year, the shipping costs are more properly matched to income in the year the goods are sold rather than in the year the goods are shipped.

In applying the recurring items exception, the consistency of the taxpayer's tax and financial statement accounting methods is taken into account. Tort and workers' compensation liabilities are not eligible for the exception. See § 461(h)(3). The regulations also exempt from the recurring items rule fines and liabilities arising out of breach of contract. Reg. § 1.461–5(c).

The recurring expense exception does not eliminate the general requirement that all events must have occurred that determine the fact of the liability. Courts have continued to struggle with the question of whether the fact of the liability has been established when there is some possibility that the taxpayer will not have to make payment. For example, in Giant Eagle, Inc. v. Commissioner, 822 F.3d 666 (3d Cir. 2016), the taxpayer met all the requirements of the § 461(h) recurring expense exception, but the IRS argued that the fact of the liability had not been established. The taxpayer was a grocery store chain that gave gas awards for grocery purchases that could only be redeemed by purchasing gas. Even though some of the awards would not be redeemed within the permitted time period, the court found that the offer of the rewards was a unilateral contract that established liability at the time of the groceries were purchased.

(E) *Special Rules for Nuclear Decommissioning and Coal Mine Reclamation Expenses.* The potential lapse of long periods between accrual and payment is addressed in specific Code provisions that govern expenses of decommissioning nuclear power plants, reclaiming coal mines, and for certain waste disposal sites. See §§ 468A and 468 of the Code. Under § 468A, taxpayers may deduct, subject to an annual limitation, contributions to a qualified nuclear decommissioning reserve fund. The taxpayer must obtain an IRS ruling in order to take such deductions. The taxpayer must actually set aside the amounts in a segregated fund to be used exclusively for the payment of decommissioning costs or taxes and management costs of the fund. The reserve fund is treated as a separate taxable entity and was originally taxed at the maximum corporate tax rate unless exempt under another provision of the Code. (The tax rate has been reduced to 20 percent). Contributions to the fund are not subject to tax. Other rules prohibit self-dealing or the purchase of assets of a related party. Withdrawals from the fund for any purpose except payment of taxes and management costs are includible in the income of the nuclear plant. The withdrawal then may be deducted from the gross income of the plant if paid for reasonable decommissioning expenditures. Any funds remaining in the reserve when the decommissioning is complete must be included in the taxable income of the plant.

Section 468 provides an elective method for deducting the costs of future reclamation and closing costs of coal mines or certain waste disposal sites required by federal or state law. Taxpayers are allowed a current deduction for reasonable additions to a reserve based upon the amount of surface disturbed by the mining or solid waste activity. An annual interest charge, specified by statute, is imputed on the reserve account and serves to limit future deductions. Amounts charged against the reserve at the time of reclamation or closing are not deductible and any excess of the reserve balance over the estimated or actual costs is immediately taxable. In effect, the taxpayer is treated as realizing taxable income equal to a statutorily imputed rate of interest on amounts held for future expenditures as measured by the reserve. The relationship of §§ 468 and 468A to the economic performance requirement of § 461(h) is discussed in the following note.

Note on the Economic Equivalence of §§ 461(h), 468A, and 468: The Concept of Non-Advantageous Tax Deferral

Offsetting the Advantage of Deferral. We have previously discussed the equivalence of allowing a deduction earlier than it should be allowed and providing an interest-free loan from the government to the taxpayer of the tax savings resulting from the accelerated deduction. See the Note on Tax Deferral in Chapter 3 supra at page 313 and the further discussion in Chapter 6 at 655.[1] Taxpayers could achieve similar tax advantages before 1984 by the use of what the tax-writing committees of Congress labeled "premature accruals"—immediate deduction of nominal costs to be paid in the future. Thus, taxpayers who could deduct expenses to be paid many years hence were able to earn interest (or other investment income) on the tax saved without paying offsetting interest (or increased taxes) to the government. "Structured settlements," such as those at issue in the *Ford Motor Co.* case, are one such example. As we suggested above, by failing to account for the time value of money, Ford was effectively trying to accelerate an interest deduction.

The Code uses a number of approaches to offset the benefit of deferral. One approach would explicitly increase the amount of tax deferred by an interest charge. For example, the taxpayer would be allowed a full-value current deduction but also would be charged to compensate the government for the delay in the collection of tax. This would convert the "interest-free" loan into an interest-bearing loan and thereby eliminate the advantage of tax deferral. See, e.g., § 668 (charging interest on tax deferred on income received by a U.S. beneficiary of an "accumulation distribution" from a foreign trust); § 453A (charging interest on deferred tax liability on installment notes); § 1291 (charging interest on deferred tax on "passive foreign investment companies"); § 460(b) (charging or paying interest on deferred (or accelerated) tax on

---

[1]   That Note also points out that, under certain conditions, the immediate deduction of capital expenditures is equivalent to the exemption from tax of the yield from the capital asset. This suggests the important relationship between the timing of tax deductions and the taxation of investment income, a matter that is discussed in some detail in Chapter 6 and this Note.

completed contract project). Sections 668, 453A, and 1291 use the tax underpayment rule; § 460(b) uses the tax overpayment rule.

Alternatively, the taxpayer might be allowed to take the deduction at the earlier time but be required to invest the tax savings in a zero-interest bond issued by the federal government. This would recapture for the government the value of the "interest-free loan." This approach can be found in § 832(e), which relates to certain mortgage guarantee insurance companies; this rather obscure provision requires that tax benefits from current deductions be invested in special-issue U.S. bonds that are not transferable and pay no interest.

Payments that are accelerated or deferred often could be separated into two transactions: first, a purchase of goods or services, and second, a loan from one party to the other (depending on whether the payment is accelerated or deferred). If interest income and deductions on the "loan" were imputed and allocated to the parties, the time value of money would be appropriately reflected. This approach is discussed supra at page 719.

Finally, the advantage of tax deferral might be redressed by imposing a substitute tax on another taxpayer. This approach produces results that would be equivalent to the government and to the taxpayers if the same tax rates and rates of return apply to both taxpayers. These notions seem to inform those provisions that require "matching" of the time of the payor's deduction with the time of the recipient's inclusion of the payment in income. See, e.g., §§ 267(a)(2), 404(d) and the discussion of nonqualified deferred compensation in Chapter 6.

The rules of §§ 461(h), 468A, and 468 are all attempts to correct the failure of prior law to take into account the "time value of money." Moreover, as discussed in Chapter 6, relating to deferred compensation, they could be considered to have a further goal: to impose a substitute tax to compensate for tax avoided by another party.

These provisions respond to the problem of premature accruals either by deferring the deduction or discounting it to the present value. Section 461(h) defers the deduction until "economic performance." Section 468A allows a current deduction, limited to an amount that is expected to grow in time to provide the needed decommissioning funds, but requires the deducted amount to be set aside in a special fund whose earnings were originally taxed at the top corporate rate. Section 468 allows the immediate deduction of the full amount estimated to be needed for reclamation expenses but, in effect, taxes imputed interest on the amount deducted. In theory, despite the earlier deduction, which is even larger in the case of § 468, §§ 468A, and 468 are under certain conditions[2] economically equivalent to the delay in deduction required by

---

[2] The examples in this Note all assume that economic performance and payment occur at the same time, but § 461(h) usually turns on the time of economic performance rather than the time of payment (except in the case of certain liabilities where § 461(h)(2)(C) provides that economic performance occurs as payments are made). Since the present value of future costs turns on the time of payment, the House Report implies (by equating the deferral of deduction

§ 461(h) and therefore should not be viewed as intended to provide special advantages to nuclear decommissioning or coal mine reclamation expenses.

The Concept of Non-Advantageous Deferral. The alternative approaches described above, as well as those of §§ 461(h), 468A, and 468, seem to imply that we can be indifferent to the timing of income or deductions so long as no tax advantage results. Non-advantageous tax deferral occurs when the tax base increases over time by the after-tax return applicable to the taxpayer's investment. In that case a taxpayer is no better off in present value terms than he would have been by taking the deduction in an earlier year. For example, accelerating deductions will not be advantageous if the amount deducted in a later year is larger in amount than, and equal in present value to, the amount that would have been deducted in the earlier year. More precisely, taxpayers will not benefit if the investment return is taxed currently and the amount of the deduction that would have been available in the later year is equal to the earlier deduction adjusted to reflect the after-tax investment return. Taxpayers will be advantaged, however, if tax deferral permits either compounding of income at something greater than the taxpayer's after-tax rate of return (for example, because the pretax investment income is tax-exempt or is taxed at a lower rate as it now is in the case of nuclear decommissioning funds) or if excessive deferral is not compensated for either by subsequently including in income an amount compounded at the after-tax rate of return or by discounting the earlier deduction at the after-tax rate of return.[3]

Demonstrating that this is so is best done by reviewing three examples that rely on a number of common assumptions. (Following the examples, the significance of these assumptions is explored.) First, the taxpayer is assumed to be subject to a 30 percent marginal tax rate on all relevant amounts (and for offsetting all relevant deductions) for all taxable years. Second, pretax rates of return are assumed to be 10 percent per year, therefore yielding a 7 percent after-tax rate of return. Third, it is assumed that "economic performance" occurs in Year 4 and that $100 will be spent in Year 4 on the activity giving rise to the deduction.

Example 1: The Equivalence of Delaying Deductions and Allowing Immediate Deduction of Present Value.

---

until economic performance to the current deduction of the present value of the future payment) that economic performance and payment will occur at approximately the same time.

[3] Even if the taxpayer receives no advantage from deferring tax, the government may independently care about the timing of tax collections. The government may be concerned, for example, because of the size of an annual deficit or surplus or because the government discount rate is different from the taxpayer's after-tax rate of return or other compensating charge imposed by the Code. Since government revenues are calculated on a cash basis, consequences under federal budget legislation often turn on which year taxes will be paid.

(1) The taxpayer saves $30 of tax in Year 4—the year of economic performance and payment—if the $100 deduction is delayed until that year. This would be required under § 461(h).

(2) Allowing a deduction currently for the present value of the Year 4 deduction—$100 discounted at the *after-tax* rate of return of 7 percent—would produce a deduction in Year 1 of $81.60.[4] At a 30 percent tax rate, an $81.60 deduction saves $24.48 in tax in Year 1. At a 7 percent after-tax rate of return, compounded annually, the Year 1 tax savings of $24.48 would grow to $30 in Year 4. This amount is equal to the tax that would be saved in Year 4 if the deduction were deferred until that time.[5]

Example 2: The Equivalence of § 461(h) and § 468A (Nuclear Decommissioning Expenses).

(1) Under § 461(h), as above, the $100 deduction is deferred until Year 4; the tax savings is $30 at that time at a 30 percent tax rate.

(2) Under § 468A, the present value of future nuclear decommissioning expenses ($81.60) can be deducted currently and set aside in a fund taxable at a rate (assumed to be 30 percent). As noted above, the current rate under § 468A is 20 percent, slightly below the current top corporate rate of 21 percent. At a 7 percent after-tax rate of return the fund will grow to $100 in year 4. The tax saved in Year 1 from the $81.60 deduction is $24.48; that amount will grow to $30 in Year 4 (at a 7 percent after-tax rate of return).[6]

Example 3: The Equivalence of § 461(h) and § 468 (Coal Mine Reclamation Expenses).

(1) Again, as above, a $100 deduction in Year 4 under § 461(h) saves $30 in taxes that year.

(2) Under § 468, an amount equal to the present estimate of future coal mine reclamation expenses can be deducted currently. The "present value" concept is accomplished by annually adding an imputed interest return to the reserve. The reserve is taxable in any year to the extent that the reserve amount exceeds the estimated reclamation costs; any remaining excess in the reserve is taxed at the time of reclamation.

---

[4]   Tables of Present Value are set forth in the Appendix infra at page 803.

[5]   Legislative history indicates that Congress was unclear whether the perceived problem with pre-1984 law was that deductions were taken too soon or that the deductions allowed were too large. The House Report seems to imply that the timing was correct but the amount wrong. In this light, the economic performance test is a mechanism to avoid the administrative difficulties of allowing current deductions at present value. As discussed subsequently in this Note, that conclusion seems correct for some items covered by § 461(h), but wrong for others.

[6]   Perhaps surprisingly, *so long as the assumptions hold,* the value of the tax savings under § 468A will not vary, regardless of the amount put into the fund. Assume, for example, that $200 instead of $84 is set aside in the fund in Year 1. The results will be as follows:

Year 1	Amount into fund	$200
	Earnings of fund (at 10 percent)	20
	Less tax (at 30 percent)	6
	Addition to fund	14
Fund in Year 2		$214

Amounts charged against the reserve for reclamation costs are not deductible at that time. The results under § 468 are as follows:

Year 1:	Amount deducted and added to the reserve	$100
	Tax savings to a 30 percent taxpayer	$30

Year 2: If the imputed interest rate were equal to the *after-tax* rate of return, $7 of imputed interest would be taxed in Year 2 (since the fund would exceed the estimated reclamation expenses by that amount). This would increase taxes by $2.10 in Year 2. The tax savings of $30 in Year 1 would earn $2.10 (at a 7 percent after-tax rate of return) leaving a net savings of $30. Identical results would occur in Years 3 and 4 ($7 imputed income, increasing taxes by $2.10, exactly offsetting the $2.10 after-tax earnings on the $30 tax savings of Year 1), leaving a net tax savings in Year 4 of $30, an amount identical to that under § 461(h).[7]

(3) The results would not change if, instead of taxing the imputed return of the reserve annually, the imputed return were allowed to compound and the compounded return were all taxed in Year 4. The additional tax in Year 4 would then fully offset the after-tax return earned on the $30 tax savings in Year 1. The net effect would be $30 of tax saved in Year 4.

(4) If the return imputed to the § 468 reserve is different from the after-tax rate of return, results identical to delaying the deduction will not occur. Under § 468, the imputed return, after a phase-in period, is a "federal" rate, which is defined in § 1274 of the Code as a rate on U.S. Treasury bonds and, in that section and elsewhere in the Code, is regarded as a pretax rate of return. If the taxpayer's after-tax rate of return is less than the imputed rate (which it will be if the taxpayer earns a pretax rate equal to the federal funds rate), § 468 will produce a lesser tax savings in present value terms than either § 461(h) or § 468A. On the other hand, if the taxpayer earns an after-tax return greater than the rate imputed under § 468, the provision will result in a greater tax savings in present value terms than under either § 461(h) or § 468A. Some of the problems resulting from variations of the actual and imputed returns are avoided in § 468A, which requires the deducted amount actually to be set aside in a fund.

Conditions Required for the Equivalences to Hold. It is no coincidence that the examples demonstrating the equivalence among §§ 461(h), 468A, and 468 assumed that (1) the same tax rate applied to

[7] This result should not be surprising in light of the previous Note which shows that, in the nuclear decommissioning approach, the after-tax savings does not increase in present value terms so long as the investment return is taxed, allowing the fund to compound at an after-tax amount that is then taxed if not spent on the deductible activity.

all relevant income in each relevant taxable year and (2) that pretax rates of return were invariant and that they were taxable currently, yielding an after-tax rate of return equal to the (unchanging) pretax rate reduced by the (unchanging) tax rate. When these conditions do not hold, the timing of income and deductions may produce greater or lesser tax in present value terms than is shown in the examples. Alternative approaches to time value of money issues therefore must be sensitive to the assumptions necessary to such economic equivalence so that tax-avoidance opportunities will be minimized.

Relationship to the Taxation of Interest Income. Both this Note and prior materials indicate that the timing of deductions relates directly to the timing of the taxation of interest income.

The concepts discussed in this Note are discussed in greater detail in Daniel I. Halperin, "Interest in Disguise: Taxing the 'Time Value of Money,'" 95 Yale L.J. 506 (1986); Noël Cunningham, "A Theoretical Analysis of the Tax Treatment of Future Costs," 40 Tax L. Rev. 577 (1985), and are generalized in Alvin Warren, "The Timing of Taxes," 34 Nat'l Tax J. 499 (1986), and in Daniel I. Halperin and Alvin C. Warren, "Understanding Income Tax Deferral", 67 Tax L. Rev. 317, 327–30 (2014).

C. INSTALLMENT METHOD

Note on Installment Sales

Where a taxpayer receives a note or installment obligation on the sale of appreciated property, there may be a liquidity concern in imposing tax on the gain immediately because the seller has not received cash or other property, but merely a right to receive cash in the future. Congress has provided special rules for the disposition of property where at least one payment is to be received in a year after the year of sale. Section 453 typically permits sellers to defer payment of tax by spreading the gain over a number of years, treating a portion of each payment as gain and a portion as a recovery of the taxpayer's basis in the property. The rule has broad application, applying not only to taxpayers with liquidity problems, but also to those who simply want to defer payment of taxes.

Election Not to Use the Installment Method. What does the taxpayer report who receives notes in a transaction not covered by the installment method or for which the taxpayer elects not to use the installment method? The Supreme Court in Burnet v. Logan, 283 U.S. 404 (1931), had permitted even more favorable treatment than under the installment method where a sales price was contingent on future events. In that case, the cash method taxpayer sold stock for cash and a right to receive 60 cents for each ton of ore removed from a certain mine. The Court held that there was no income until her basis had been recovered fully, saying:

The promise was in no proper sense equivalent to cash. It had no ascertainable fair market value. The transaction was not a closed one. Respondent might never recoup her capital investment from payments only conditionally promised. * * * She properly demanded the return of her capital investment before assessment of any taxable profit based on conjecture.

The continued vitality of that case is not clear. In Warren Jones Co. v. Commissioner, 524 F.2d 788 (9th Cir. 1975), the taxpayer sold property under a transferable contract that had a fair market value, but the contract could be sold only at a discount of about 50 percent. The court held that if the contract had a fair market value, it had to be included in the amount realized regardless of the discount. The court took the view that the cash equivalency doctrine does not apply to cash basis taxpayers on deferred payment sales. The court's position in *Warren Jones* as to the inapplicability of the cash equivalency doctrine is reflected in the regulations. Temp. Reg. § 15A.453–1(d)(2) provides that where a taxpayer has elected out of the installment sale rules, the "[r]eceipt of an installment obligation shall be treated as a receipt of property, in an amount equal to the fair market value of the installment obligation, whether or not such obligation is the equivalent of cash." The regulations also say that the fair market value of the obligation cannot be less than the fair market value of the property, minus any other consideration received. Even where substantial uncertainty or contingent payments exist, the IRS tends to treat contingent price sales as if they involved a fixed price equal to the fair market value of the property sold. Temp. Reg. § 15A.453–1(d)(2)(iii). According to the regulations, only in "rare and extraordinary" cases will a contingent obligation be treated as not having a fair market value.

Availability of the Installment Method. Section 453 makes the installment method available to any nondealer who sells real property or non-inventory personal property if payment of at least part of the purchase price is deferred to a future year even if there is only one payment. § 453(b)(1). Section 453(k) denies installment sales treatment to any installment obligations arising from the sale of stock or securities that are traded on an established securities market or arising from sales of other property of a kind regularly traded on an established market and from sales under a revolving credit plan. Furthermore, dealers in personal or real property cannot use the installment method. §§ 453(b)(2) and 453(*l*).

The installment method applies where the seller has a recognized gain; it does not apply to losses. The taxpayer may file an election to opt out of the installment method. § 453(d). If this election is made, gain is recognized in accordance with the seller's regular method of accounting. This probably results in more, or perhaps all, of the gain being recognized in the year of sale.

Computation of Reported Gain. Where the installment method applies, a portion of every "payment" is treated as gain and a portion is treated as a recovery of basis. The reportable gain equals the "payments" received in the taxable year multiplied by the ratio of "gross profit" on the sale to the "contract price." § 453(c). The "gross profit" is the "selling price" of the property minus its adjusted basis. The "contract price" is the total amount paid for the property. (Adjustments for any indebtedness that the buyer assumes or takes subject to are discussed later in this Note). Temp. Reg. § 15A.453–1(b)(2). The installment obligation itself does not constitute a "payment" unless the buyer's note is payable on demand or is readily tradable. § 453(f)(4).

If there is no interest on the obligation or an insufficient amount of stated interest is payable annually, part of the principal will be redesignated as interest and taxed as accrued. The imputation of interest is discussed in the next principal Note.

Example. S has a basis in Blackacre of $200. In Year 1, he transfers it to B for a $500 note, with adequately stated interest.[8] B is to pay $100 in Year 1, $150 (plus interest) in Year 2, and $250 (plus interest) in Year 3. S's gain and gross profit is $300 ($500 sales price minus $200 adjusted basis) and the contract price is $500. Because the gross profit ratio is 60 percent of the contract price, 60 percent of each payment is recognized as gain.

	Year 1	Year 2	Year 3
Payment	$100	$150	$250
Basis	40	60	100
Taxable Gain	60	90	150

Note that the total taxable gain is the same as it would have been if only cash were received, but the timing of the gain differs. In this example, S is able to defer taxes on $240 of the gain.

Where the sales price is uncertain due to contingencies, Reg. § 15A.453–1(c) provides a number of alternatives for basis recovery including permitting basis to be recovered ratably in each year of payment. For an unsuccessful effort by taxpayers to manipulate this rule to their advantage see the *ACM Partnership* case, infra at page 774.

Mortgaged Property. An assumption of a "qualifying indebtedness" on the property is not treated as a payment. A "qualifying indebtedness" is a mortgage or other encumbrance on the property that the purchaser assumes or takes subject to as part of the acquisition cost of the property. It does not include indebtedness that is unrelated to the property. Temp. Reg. § 15A.453–1(b)(2)(iv).

---

[8] Interest at a rate equal to the rate on bonds of the federal government.

The full mortgage is included in the selling price for purposes of calculating the gross profit. The contract price does not include the mortgage except to the extent it exceeds the seller's adjusted basis, thus generally reflecting cash payments. The excess of the mortgage over the seller's adjusted basis is treated as a payment in the year of sale. Temp. Reg. § 15A.453–1(b)(3)(i). The effect of these rules is to permit the seller to offset his entire basis against the mortgage, thus allocating more (or all) of the gain to the future cash payments.

Example. In Year 1 S sells Blackacre, in which he has a basis of $200 and which is subject to a $100 mortgage. The value of the property is $600. B assumes the mortgage and gives S a note for $500 with $300 to be paid in Year 2 and $200 to be paid in Year 3. S's gain and gross profit is $400 ($600 selling price minus $200 adjusted basis) and the contract price is $500 (the selling price, excluding the mortgage). The gross profit ratio is 80 percent ($400/$500). Assuming the mortgage is qualified indebtedness, the amount of gain to be recognized on each payment is:

	Year 1		Year 2	Year 3	Total
Payment	$100	(mortgage)	$300	$200	$600
Basis	100		60	40	200
Reported Gain	0		240	160	400

Suppose instead that the mortgage were $250 and B paid $350 on the notes ($200 in Year 2 and $150 in Year 3). The gross profit remains $400 and the contract price is also $400 because it includes the notes ($350) and the amount by which the mortgage exceeds the basis or $50 ($250 − $200). The gross profit ratio therefore is 100 percent and the gain is reported:

	Year 1		Year 2	Year 3	Total
Payment	$250	(mortgage)	$200	$150	$600
Basis	200		0	0	200
Reported Gain	50		200	150	400

Character of Gain. Whether the reported gain is capital gain or ordinary income generally is governed by the normal capital gain rules, including the "recapture rules," which produce ordinary income. See Chapter 5. Any recapture income, however, must be recognized in the year of disposition of the property. § 453(i) . Therefore, only gain in excess of recapture income may be taken into account under the installment method. The seller must report the recapture income in the year of sale even if no payments are received that year. The basis of the property is increased by the recapture income in computing the gross profit ratio so that the gain will not be taxed twice.

Further, if the buyer's note is payable on demand or is readily tradable, it is considered paid in the year of sale, eliminating any deferral. § 453(f)(4).

Disposition of Installment Obligations. The disposition of an installment obligation generally triggers any remaining gain on the original sale, in many cases even if the disposition is not a taxable event. § 453B. This section applies on the sale, exchange, transfer, gift, cancellation, or unenforceability of the installment obligation. It does not apply to a transfer at death or to a transfer between spouses or former spouses subject to § 1041. There is, however, no step-up in the basis of an installment obligation at the decedent's death, § 1014(c), and the estate or the beneficiary reports the gain as payments are received using the decedent's profit ratio.

On the disposition of an installation obligation, gain or loss is recognized equal to the difference between the amount realized on the disposition and the taxpayer's basis in the installment obligation. The amount realized on a transfer other than a sale or exchange is the fair market value of the obligation. The taxpayer's basis in the obligation is the difference between the face value of the obligation and the amount that would be reported as income if the obligation were satisfied in full.

Example. S transfers Blackacre in exchange for an installment obligation of $100,000 to be paid in equal installments over 10 years. S's adjusted basis in Blackacre is $20,000. The gross profit ratio is 80 percent. After three payments have been made, S sells the installment obligation for $65,000. S's adjusted basis in the installment obligation is the face value ($70,000) minus the income that would be reported if paid in full ($70,000 × 80 percent = $56,000) or $14,000. Thus, S's gain on the sale of the note is $51,000 ($65,000 − $14,000).

NOTES

(A) *Payments.* A guarantee of the buyer's obligation does not create a payment; nor does a standby letter of credit issued as security for the sale. § 453(f)(3); Temp. Reg. § 15A.453–1(b)(3)(i). If, however, the security is provided by an escrow account funded with cash or a cash equivalent, the secured indebtedness is treated as a payment. Temp. Reg. § 15A.453–1(b)(3)(i). If the buyer's note is payable on demand or is readily tradable, it is considered paid in the year of sale, eliminating any deferral. § 453(f)(4).

(B) *Interest on Deferred Tax Liability.* The installment method essentially provides the taxpayer with an interest-free loan from the government for the period the taxes are deferred on the gain. In order to limit this significant advantage to casual sellers of property, § 453A imposes an interest charge on the deferred tax liability on any sale where the sales price exceeds $150,000 and the taxpayer has outstanding installment obligations that arose during the taxable year exceeding $5 million. The interest rate is the rate on tax deficiencies under § 6621(a)(2). This rule does not apply to the sale of farms.

Sellers of time-share units and other residential lots are permitted to use the installment method—unlike other dealers in real property—but they must pay interest on the deferred tax liability.

SECTION 3.   UNSTATED OR IMPUTED INTEREST

Note on Unstated or Imputed Interest

The time value of money typically is reflected in financial transactions as interest. If money is to be paid at a future time, the amount to be paid will reflect the ability of the payor to earn interest in the interim on the deferred payment. Interest that is not paid as it is earned may be reinvested to earn more interest, which is why interest normally accrues at a compound rate.

By the same token, amounts to be paid currently can be compared to amounts to be paid in the future by "discounting" the future amount to its "present value." Present discounted value is the value now of money to be paid in the future. The value is determined by asking how much money would have to be put aside today—assuming it can earn a specified rate of compound interest—to fund the future payment. Discounting to present value, therefore, is merely the reverse of compounding to future value. Both computations compare amounts to be paid at different times by adjusting these amounts to reflect the ability to earn a compound rate of interest over the relevant period. The accrual of compound interest is typically referred to as "economic," "actuarial," or "constant" interest, terms regarded here as interchangeable. Any pattern of cash payments can be valued with reference to an economic accrual of compound interest to reflect either present value or future value.[9]

The Internal Revenue Code generally did not recognize the significance of compound interest until 1982 and even now uses compound interest concepts only in certain contexts. Identifying the economic interest element in a transaction is important under the income tax for four reasons. First, it provides a theoretically consistent method for comparing cash flows at different times—of measuring and adjusting income and deductions (and therefore tax liability) to take into account the time value of money. Second, interest income is taxed as ordinary income and thus must be distinguished from appreciation in the value of assets over time, which often is eligible for favorable capital gain treatment. Third, interest expense is often (although not always) deductible whereas a repayment of principal is not. Fourth, interest income and expense must be allocated to the proper taxpayer to prevent shifting of these items among taxpayers subject to different tax rates. The relevant income tax rules can be seen in four contexts: (1) original

---

[9]   Tables of discounted present values and compounded future values can be found in the Appendix infra at page 803.

issue discount, (2) market discount, (3) deferred payment sales, and (4) interest-free or below-market loans.

Original Issue Discount. Original issue discount (OID) exists when the original "issue price" of a debt instrument (a bond, note, or other evidence of indebtedness) is less than the amount to be paid at maturity. Original issue discount typically is present when bonds are issued with no interest payable currently (zero coupon bonds) or a below-market rate of interest payable currently. The difference between the amount received by the borrower (the "issue price") and the amount to be repaid (the "stated redemption price at maturity") is compensation to the lender for the use of money and is functionally equivalent to interest.

Initially, the rules were limited to ensuring that OID would be taxed to the lender as ordinary income, not capital gains. The current rules are designed to treat an original issue discount bond equivalently to one currently paying a market rate of interest. In general, they require the lender to report as interest income annually the amount of OID that economically accrues on the debt instrument. The borrower treats an identical amount as interest that he may deduct, subject to the limitations on interest deductions.

Although the OID rules apply in a number of contexts, we first consider their application when a debt instrument is issued in exchange for cash. Then we will turn to debt instruments issued for property.

If a debt obligation is subject to the OID rules of § 1272, imputed interest is required to be included in income and may be deducted annually on an economic accrual basis, whether or not paid. A debt obligation is subject to the rules if it has OID, which is defined as the excess of the stated redemption price at maturity over the issue price. § 1273(a)(1). Where a debt instrument is issued for cash, the "issue price" is the cash paid by the buyer (the lender). § 1273(b)(2). The "stated redemption price at maturity" is the amount to be paid by the borrower on the maturity date, but excludes any interest payments made at regular intervals of a year or less. § 1273(a)(2). The lender is required to include the "daily portions" of OID in its income for each taxable year it holds the bond. § 1272(a)(1). The OID for each accrual period is determined by multiplying the adjusted issue price at the beginning of the period by the yield to maturity. § 1272(a)(3). The OID that is reported for each accrual period is added to the adjusted issue price of the bond (and to the holder's adjusted basis). § 1272(a)(4)(B). Generally, the accrual period is six months. § 1272(a)(5). The borrower deducts the same amount as interest. § 163(e). It is helpful to think of an OID obligation as being like a bank savings account from which there are no withdrawals; interest accrues on the original principal as well as on the interest from prior periods that was not withdrawn.

Example. B issues a bond for $7,462 with a redemption price of $10,000 on the maturity date three years from the issue date. As the issue price is $7,462 and the redemption price is $10,000, there is $2,538 of

OID. L, who purchases the bond, must include the "daily portions" of OID in income for each six-month accrual period. As the yield to maturity on this instrument is 10 percent compounded semiannually, the OID for each six-month period is:

Period	Adjusted Issue Price	Yield	OID
First	$7,462	.05	$373
Second	7,835	.05	392
Third	8,227	.05	411
Fourth	8,638	.05	432
Fifth	9,070	.05	454
Sixth	9,524	.05	476
Redemption	$10,000		

Thus, in the first year, L would report $765 of interest (the OID for the first two accrual periods). If, for example, B used the proceeds of the loan for business purposes, B would deduct $765 of interest in the first year.

Note that the borrower's and lender's methods of accounting are irrelevant. The effect of §§ 1272 and 163(e) is to put both parties on the accrual method with respect to original issue discount.

The OID rules do not apply to tax-exempt obligations, U.S. savings bonds, or short-term obligations (those with a term of a year or less). They also do not apply to loans between natural persons if the total outstanding loans between the borrower and the lender are $10,000 or less, the loan has not been made as part of the lender's trade or business, and there is no tax avoidance purpose. § 1272(a)(2).

These rules are quite complex, as even this simple example illustrates. What is the harm if the borrower and lender want to treat all interest as accruing on the maturity date or interest as accruing ratably over the term of the loan? As students should by now know well, taxpayers will take advantage of such mismeasurements of taxable income. For example, suppose an accrual basis borrower issues an OID obligation to a cash basis lender. Absent § 1272, the borrower would accrue interest deductions annually, but the lender would include nothing in income until he was paid interest at maturity. Any method of accounting for OID interest other than as it economically accrues will mismeasure income. A ratable allocation of interest would attribute more interest to earlier periods than economically accrues. Thus, both interest income and interest deductions would be accelerated. This would lead to transactions between accrual basis borrowers, who would take advantage of the accelerated deductions and tax-exempt lenders, who would be unaffected by the earlier inclusion of income.

Deferred Payment Sales. Suppose a taxpayer sells property with an adjusted basis of $5,000 that is worth $7,462 today in exchange for a note with a face value of $10,000 to be paid in three years. The seller, of course, has demanded more for the property than he would receive currently because he is to receive the cash in the future. If, however, the seller and the buyer were permitted simply to characterize the sales price as $10,000, the sales price would be overstated, and income would be measured incorrectly in several ways. Characterizing the full $10,000 as the sales price would benefit the seller if the property was a capital asset, by transforming ordinary interest income into capital gain. The seller also would be able to report his income only when payments were received rather than accruing interest over time. The buyer also might benefit, if the property was eligible for depreciation deductions, because depreciation would be calculated on an overstated basis, and because depreciation is often accelerated, the buyer might save taxes by substituting depreciation deductions for the interest deductions that otherwise might be available. In effect, the seller has both sold an asset and made a loan to the buyer; by paying $10,000 rather than the property's $7,462 value, the buyer is compensating the seller for the use of the purchase price for three years.

The original issue discount rules apply to impute interest to deferred payment sales to prevent these sorts of machinations. If a debt instrument is issued in exchange for property, the OID rules apply whenever there is unstated interest. The OID rules, in effect, recharacterize a portion of the "sales price" as interest. Interest is imputed, however, only if "adequate stated interest" is not provided in the debt instrument. There is adequate stated interest if the imputed principal amount (that is, the present discounted value of all payments under the debt instrument) is at least equal to the stated principal amount. §§ 1274(c)(2); 1274(b)(1). In the example, the stated principal amount is $10,000 and the imputed principal amount is $7,462. In calculating this amount, the stream of payments is discounted using the current interest rate on federal debt of a comparable term, compounded semiannually. This rate is known as the applicable federal rate or the AFR. Therefore, there will be adequate stated interest (and none will be imputed) whenever the debt instrument provides stated interest at a rate equal to at least the AFR, compounded semiannually.

In the example above, there is no stated interest because the buyer is to make one $10,000 payment three years hence. If the applicable discount rate (the AFR) is 10 percent, the imputed principal amount would be $7,462 (the present value of all payments). This becomes the issue price of the debt instrument, and thus because the issue price of $7,462 is less than the redemption price of $10,000, the debt instrument is an OID obligation. The issue price of the debt instrument is treated as the sales price of the property; the timing of the taxation of the gain or loss on the sale depends upon whether the installment method applies. Unless the seller elects out of the installment method, he will report as gain or loss the difference between his adjusted basis in the property,

$5,000, and the sales price of $7,462 at the time the payment is made ($2,462 of gain). During the three years the note is outstanding, he will include in income the interest that economically accrues (as shown in the table supra on page 758). The buyer will have an adjusted basis in the property of $7,462 and will deduct as interest the OID that economically accrues during each accrual period.

The rules of § 1274 do not apply to the sale of a principal residence, a debt instrument traded or issued for publicly traded property, a sale of a patent where part of the sales price is contingent on use, or the sale of a farm by an individual or small business for $1 million or less. § 1274(c). With the exception of patents, these transactions are subject to § 483. Section 483, rather than § 1274, also applies to sales of property involving total payments of $250,000 or less. If the transaction is governed by § 483, the imputed interest is allocated among the principal payments under the contract using an economic accrual computation, but the amounts so allocated are reported as interest by cash basis taxpayers at the time of payment rather than when they accrue. The other major difference between § 1274 and § 483 is that in the case of a sale of land between related individuals, a discount rate of 6 percent or less is used under § 483 to determine whether there is unstated interest, so long as the total sales price for all such sales between the individuals during the year does not exceed $500,000.

Section 1274A provides that the discount rate for purposes of §§ 483 and 1274 cannot exceed 9 percent for seller-financed sales of property where the stated principal does not exceed $2.8 million. In addition, a borrower and lender may jointly elect to have § 1274 not apply and to report interest under the cash method. To qualify for this election, the stated principal of the debt instrument cannot exceed $2 million and the lender can neither be a dealer with respect to the property sold nor use the accrual method of accounting.

Market Discount. Market discount occurs when the value of a debt obligation declines after it is issued, typically because market rates of interest increase. For example, a $1,000 bond paying 10 percent interest will decline in value if the market rate of interest rises from 10 percent to 12 percent. The purchaser of such a bond who, for example, might pay only $900 for the bond, will—absent tax considerations—be indifferent whether the discount is market or original; the total amount of "interest" income will be the same. The tax treatment of original and market discount, however, is not identical. Whereas the OID rules affect both the timing and the character of the "interest," the market discount rules affect only the character. Section 1276 treats the market discount as ordinary interest income on a compound interest basis, but does not require cash basis holders of market discount obligations to report the interest until the bond is disposed of. On retirement or sale of the bond, the accrued market discount is reported as ordinary income. Furthermore, unless the holder elects otherwise, the interest is deemed to accrue on a ratable, rather than a constant interest basis. A market discount bond is one in which the stated redemption price exceeds the holder's basis in the bond at the time of its acquisition. § 1278(a)(2). Where a bond originally was issued with OID, the determination of market discount is more complex.

Example. Assume T buys a $1,000 bond, which was originally issued at its face value, for $850. Because the stated redemption price of $1,000 exceeds T's adjusted basis of $850, the bond has market discount of $150. The market discount is allocated ratably over the remaining three-year term. If T holds the bond until redemption, he would report $150 of ordinary income. If T sold the bond at the end of one year for $930, he would report $50 as ordinary interest income (one-third of the market discount) and $30 of capital gain.

Low-Interest or Interest-Free Loans. Ordinarily, a lender will demand a market rate of interest for the use of his money. But there are situations where the lender may agree to forgo market interest. For example, where an employer makes an interest-free loan to an employee, the employee has received an economic benefit equal to the market rate of interest she otherwise would have paid. It is as if the employer paid the employee additional wages, which the employee then remitted to the employer as interest on the loan. Similarly, when a parent makes an interest-free loan to a child, the child has received a gift equal to the forgone interest.

Section 7872 generally precludes the use of interest-free or low-interest loans between employers and employees to avoid employment taxes or limitations on interest deductions, between family members to shift income from high-rate taxpayers to low-rate taxpayers, and between corporations and their shareholders to disguise dividends. Section 7872 applies to below-market loans that are characterized as gift loans, compensation-related loans, corporate-shareholder loans, and tax avoidance loans. § 7872(c).

A below-market *demand loan* (any gift loan or a loan payable on demand) is one in which the interest payable on the loan is less than the applicable federal rate. § 7872(f). Under § 7872(a), for each taxable year the loan is outstanding, the amount of interest that would have been payable if the interest rate had been the AFR is treated as if it had been transferred by the lender to the borrower and then retransferred to the lender as interest.

Example: An employer lends an employee $100,000 payable on demand at a time when the AFR is 10 percent. On the last day of the year, the employer is deemed to transfer $10,250 to the employee (the amount of interest that would have been due if interest had been stated at 10 percent compounded semiannually). This is treated as taxable compensation income to the employee and deductible compensation to the employer. The employee is then deemed to transfer $10,250 of interest to the employer. This will be deductible to the employee only if the interest is deductible under § 163. The employer reports $10,250 of interest income.

In many cases the income tax consequences of employer loans will net out to zero, but employment taxes will apply to the additional compensation. There may be significant income tax consequences, however, if the loan is a gift loan. In the above example, the deemed transfer of $10,250 from a donor to a donee would be a gift, not taxable for income tax purposes. The donor would have no deduction for the transfer of the gift, but would be taxable on the deemed interest income. The donee may be entitled to a deduction for the deemed interest paid under § 163, but may not be, for example, if she does not itemize deductions or if the interest is not deductible even for itemizers. Where the total outstanding loans between the donor and the donee are less than $100,000, the amount of interest deemed transferred by the borrower is limited to the borrower's net investment income. This appropriately taxes the lender on the income produced by the principal, rather than shifting it to a lower-bracket donee.

A *term loan* is a below-market loan if the amount loaned exceeds the present value of all payments to be made under the loan, using the AFR at the date the loan is entered into as the discount rate. § 7872(e). If there is no interest, or if the interest (either stated or OID) is less than the AFR, § 7872 will apply. On the date of the loan, the lender is treated under § 7872 as having transferred cash equal to the amount loaned over the present value of all payments required to be made. The latter amount becomes the issue price of the debt obligation, which will be less than the redemption price, creating OID. The borrower is treated as paying interest at the statutory rate for each accrual period; this results in income that is taxed to the lender on an economic accrual basis and, generally, in a deduction for the borrower. The compensation (in an employer-employee context) or a dividend (in a corporation-shareholder context) is treated as being fully paid in the year a term loan is made, while the interest accrues economically over the loan period. This results in a tax advantage in terms of the time value of money to the lender, who spreads out interest income over the life of the loan, and a disadvantage to the borrower, who realizes the entire amount of compensation or dividend in the initial year of the loan.

Example. An employer loans an employee $100,000 to be repaid at the end of three years. There is no stated interest; the AFR is 10 percent compounded semiannually. Because this is a below-market loan, the employer is treated under § 7872 as if it loaned the employee $74,620 and transferred $25,380 of additional compensation on the date of the loan. The employer deducts and the employee includes $25,380 of additional compensation, which is subject to any applicable employment taxes. In addition, because the issue price of the loan ($74,620) is less than the redemption price ($100,000), it is an OID obligation. The employee is treated as if he paid to the employer interest each six months at the AFR.

For the first year, the employee would be deemed to have paid $7,650 in interest and the employer is treated as if it received $7,650 of interest income, which is taxable. (See the table supra on page 758.)

Section 7872 does not apply to any gift loan between individuals so long as the outstanding amount of loans between them does not exceed $10,000 and the proceeds are not used to purchase or carry income-producing assets. There is also a de minimis exception for compensation and corporate-shareholder loans not exceeding $10,000 so long as one of the principal purposes of the loan arrangement is not tax avoidance.

NOTES

(A) *Relationship of § 7872 to Income Shifting Rules.* Section 7872 is necessary to prevent avoidance of the assignment of income (and grantor trust) rules. If the lender had assigned the income from an amount equal to the proceeds of the loan to the borrower, the assignment of income doctrine would tax the lender on the income. Similarly, if the lender had created a revocable grantor trust, he would continue to be taxed on the income.

(B) *Low-Interest Loans Not Covered by § 7872.* Section 7872 does not cover all below-market loans. The legislative history indicates that Congress thought that gift loans, compensation-related loans, and corporate-shareholder loans were most susceptible to abuse. Under proposed regulations, § 7872 generally does not apply to loans in connection with the sale or exchange of property. Would a prepayment for services be within § 7872?

A plan popular at a number of universities has been to permit prepayment of tuition. Suppose tuition is $10,000, but if tuition is paid one year in advance, the fee is $9,000. The payor shifts the interest income on the $9,000 to the tax-exempt university for one year. How would the payor be treated if she loaned $9,000 to the university and received $10,000 one year later? Is this an example of a tax avoidance loan under § 7872(c)(1)(D)?

All states and some private educational institutions adopted similar plans. Parents or other interested individuals can make contributions to a state fund that will be used to pay tuition at universities many years hence. Section 529 provides for tax-free accumulations of income and so long as the withdrawals are used to pay education expenses, the distribution is taxed neither to the contributor nor the student. A parent who saves for college expenses by investing in a normal bank account, for example, would need to save a larger amount since the investment return would be subject to tax.

(C) *Recharacterizing Transactions as Loans.* Recharacterizing transactions involving deferred payment or prepayment as routinely involving a loan with interest imputed on an economic accrual basis might produce a theoretically consistent method for dealing with time value of money issues. These might include situations where an accrual basis taxpayer accrues a liability to be paid in the future (see, for example, *Ford Motor Co.,* supra at page 736), where a cash basis taxpayer prepays for services or goods (see *Boylston Market,* supra at page 716), or where an accrual basis taxpayer receives payment before services are performed (see the discussion of *RCA Corp.,* supra at page 734). Compare the tax results that would follow from recharacterizing these transactions as loans with an economic accrual of interest.

(D) *Rent.* A concept similar to the OID rules applies to rental payments. Suppose a lessor agrees to accept a single payment of $300,000 at the end of a three-year lease. Absent special rules, an accrual basis lessee would deduct $100,000 each year. A cash basis lessor would include nothing until the $300,000 payment was made. Section 467 requires the parties to calculate the rent that economically accrues, by determining what the constant rental stream would have to be for the three years so that the present value would be equal to the present value of $300,000 to be paid in three years. The lessor includes and the lessee deducts that amount each year. Of course, the lessee does not actually pay that amount so § 467 treats the lessor as having loaned that amount to the lessee, triggering imputed interest. The details are far too complex to relate here.

SECTION 4.   CHANGE OF ACCOUNTING METHOD

Note on Change of Accounting Method

A taxpayer may seek to change its method of accounting; for example, a growing business might seek to shift from the cash method to the accrual method. Or the taxpayer may be required by the IRS to abandon an accounting method that does not accurately reflect income.

Taxpayers would have many opportunities to avoid tax if they had unconstrained ability to shift from one accounting method to another. Consider, for example, a taxpayer with $1,000 in accounts receivable earned in Year 1 but not collected until Year 2. The receivables might never be included in income if the taxpayer changed from the cash method of accounting in Year 1 to the accrual method in Year 2. (That is because the cash method would defer inclusion until Year 2, while the accrual method would treat the receivables as having already been realized in Year 1.) The Code contains two provisions, however, that are designed to limit such opportunities.

Section 446(e) gives the IRS broad discretion to approve or deny requests by taxpayers who desire to change their methods of accounting. This discretion applies both when taxpayers seek to change from an incorrect accounting method to a correct method and when they seek to change from one correct method to another. This treatment of changes of accounting method should be contrasted with the treatment of an initial selection of accounting method; a taxpayer selecting an accounting method for the first time may choose any approved method that accurately reflects income without first obtaining the consent of the IRS.

Issues often arise over whether a procedure used to calculate tax liability constitutes a "method of accounting" that cannot be changed without IRS approval. The regulations define a change of accounting method as a "change in the overall plan of accounting for gross income or deductions or a change in the treatment of any material item used in such overall plan." The regulations further explain that a method of accounting is generally not established with respect to an item without "a pattern of consistent treatment." Reg. § 1.446–1(e)(2)(ii)(a).

The IRS considers a change in "the overall plan of accounting" to include, for example, a change from the cash method of accounting to the accrual method (or vice versa), a change in the method of valuing inventories, a change in depreciation method, or a change involving the adoption, use or discontinuance of a special method of computing taxable income, such as the long-term contract method. A change in "the treatment of any material item" includes, for example, a change by an accrual basis taxpayer from accruing property taxes when paid to accruing them when due. The regulations provide that "a material item is any item which involves the proper time for the inclusion of the item in income or the taking of a deduction." Reg. § 1.446–1(e)(2)(ii)(a). Thus, a change in the timing of income or deduction may constitute a change of accounting method even where the dollar amount of income or deduction remains constant in nominal terms. The correction of a mathematical error in the computation of tax liability is not a change of accounting method.

The IRS decides whether to permit the taxpayer to change his accounting method on the basis of all the facts and circumstances. The courts have indicated that the IRS cannot attach unreasonable conditions to a grant of permission to a taxpayer to change his method of accounting. In practice, the IRS routinely grants requests for a change in accounting method if based on adequate business reasons and if the taxpayer agrees to adjust taxable income to compensate for the change.

The ability of the IRS to insist on adjustments as a condition for its consent to a taxpayer's change in accounting method is complemented by the adjustment rules of § 481. These rules apply both to taxpayers who are required by the IRS to abandon an incorrect method and to taxpayers who change methods voluntarily (sometimes without IRS consent, for example, where the Code allows changes at the taxpayer's option). Section 481 requires such taxpayers to take into account "those adjustments which are determined to be necessary solely by reason of the change in order to prevent amounts from being duplicated or omitted." To see the necessity of § 481, return to the example of the cash basis taxpayer with $1,000 in accounts receivable earned in Year 1 but collected in Year 2. When the taxpayer switches to the accrual method in Year 2, an inclusion of $1,000 is necessary to avoid the omission of the $1,000 from the tax base altogether.

The period over which the adjustment may be taken into account depends on several factors. If the taxpayer is changing from an impermissible to a permissible method and the adjustment results in increasing taxable income for the adjustment year, the spread period is three years. In some situations, shorter periods are mandated to encourage use of a permissible period initially. If the taxpayer is changing from one permissible method to another, the spread period is six years. If the adjustment results in decreasing taxable income for the year of adjustment, the adjustment is taken into account that year. The IRS frequently issues revenue procedures governing changes in methods of accounting. Sometimes these set forth procedures that are generally applicable; sometimes they describe specific changes common to a particular industry.

CHAPTER 8

CORPORATE TAX SHELTERS AND ETHICAL RESPONSIBILITIES OF TAX LAWYERS

In the last decades, corporations increasingly used tax shelters to produce losses or credits that may be used to shelter income or to offset tax liability. There is widespread agreement that the proliferation of shelters poses a serious problem for the government, but there is far less agreement about exactly what constitutes a tax shelter and how best to combat them. The government has enjoyed considerable success litigating against them, and large penalties and new reporting requirements have apparently begun to dampen many companies' enthusiasm for them.

This Chapter explores this phenomenon. It considers several definitions of tax shelters and the various ways that Congress and the Treasury sought to end them. A look at this development provides an opportunity to delve into some questions and doctrines that cut across materials considered separately in the preceding chapters. For example, tax shelters often raise difficult statutory interpretation questions. If a transaction literally falls within the language of a section of the Code, should that control even if it is unlikely Congress intended the provision to apply in the circumstances at issue? Sometimes the courts use judicial doctrines to find that a transaction will be respected only if it has a "business purpose" or "economic substance." This Chapter explores whether it is better for the IRS and the courts to have these flexible standards or whether specific statutory rules would foster more compliance and greater certainty.

Taxpayers might be willing to take the risk of losing a case if challenged whenever they believe they will, in addition to taxes that would have been paid in the absence of the shelter transaction, just owe interest on the tax liability that should have been paid. This Chapter explores the need for greater penalties on abusive transactions, or perhaps just more assurance that penalties will apply. Even though the taxpayer might lose if the transaction were discovered and challenged in court, the IRS might not have the resources to find and challenge all "abusive" transactions. This Chapter also explores whether more disclosure of these transactions on tax returns or otherwise would be helpful.

Lawyers and other tax professionals have played a major role in the proliferation of tax shelters, in part by providing opinions that enable taxpayers to avoid penalties. This is a good place to consider a lawyer's legal and ethical responsibilities with respect to tax matters. This Chapter provides a brief introduction to the statutory, regulatory, and ethical standards that apply to lawyers engaged in tax practice.

SECTION 1.   CORPORATE TAX SHELTERS

Excerpt from the Problem of Corporate Tax Shelters: Discussion, Analysis and Legislative Proposals

United States Treasury Department, 1999.

There is widespread agreement and concern among tax professionals that the corporate tax shelter problem is large and growing.

The American Bar Association, in an appearance before the House Ways and Means Committee, noted its "growing alarm [at] the aggressive use by large corporate taxpayers of tax 'products' that have little or no purpose other than the reduction of Federal income taxes," and its concern at the "blatant, yet secretive marketing" of such products.

The New York State Bar Association, in testimony before the Senate Finance Committee, stated: "We believe that there are serious, and growing, problems with aggressive, sophisticated and, we believe in some cases, artificial transactions designed principally to achieve a particular tax advantage. * * * There is obviously an effect on revenue. While we are unable to estimate the amount of this revenue loss, anecdotal evidence and personal experience leads us to believe that it is likely to be quite significant." * * *

A recent cover story in Forbes magazine was devoted to the "thriving industry of hustling corporate tax shelters." This article quoted a partner in a major accounting firm who described the development and highly selective marketing of "black box" strategies for tax avoidance that can save its purchasers from tens of millions to hundreds of millions of dollars at the expense of other U.S. taxpayers.

While corporate tax payments have been rising, taxes have not grown as fast as have corporate profits. One hallmark of corporate tax shelters is a reduction in taxable income with no concomitant reduction in book income. The ratio of book income to taxable income has risen fairly sharply in the last few years. Some of this decline may be due to tax shelter activity. * * *

There are several reasons to be concerned about the proliferation of corporate tax shelters. These concerns range from the short-term revenue loss to the tax system, to the potentially more troubling long-term effects on our voluntary income tax system.

Short-term revenue loss

Corporate tax shelters reduce the corporate tax base, raising the tax burden on other taxpayers.

Disrespect for the system

Corporate tax shelters breed disrespect for the tax system—both by the people who participate in the tax shelter market and by others who perceive unfairness. A view that well-advised corporations can and do avoid their legal tax liabilities by engaging in these tax-engineered transactions may cause a "race to the bottom." If unabated, this could have long-term consequences to our voluntary tax system far more important than the short-term revenue loss we are experiencing.

The New York State Bar Association recently noted the "corrosive effect" of tax shelters: "The constant promotion of these frequently artificial transactions breeds significant disrespect for the tax system, encouraging responsible corporate taxpayers to expect this type of activity to be the norm, and to follow the lead of other taxpayers who have engaged in tax advantaged transactions."

Complexity

Piecemeal legislative remedies complicate the Code and call into question the viability of common law tax doctrines. In the past few years alone, nearly 30 narrow statutory provisions have been adopted responding to perceived abuses.

Uneconomic use of resources

Significant resources, both in the private sector and the Government, are currently being wasted on this uneconomic activity. Private sector resources used to create, implement and defend complex sheltering transactions could be better used in productive activities. Similarly, the Congress (particularly the tax-writing committees and their staffs), the Treasury Department, and the IRS must expend significant resources to address and combat these transactions.

The ACM Partnership v. Commissioner case alone cost the Federal Government over $2 million to litigate. In addition, there are a number of docketed cases involving almost identical shelter products.

Peter Cobb, former Deputy Chief of Staff of the Joint Committee on Taxation recently stated: "You can't underestimate how many of America's greatest minds are being devoted to what economists would all say is totally useless economic activity."

* * *

Because corporate tax shelters take many different forms and utilize many different structures, they are difficult to define with a single formulation. A number of common characteristics, however, can be identified that are useful in crafting an approach to solving the corporate tax shelter problem.

Lack of economic substance—Professor Michael Graetz recently defined a tax shelter as "a deal done by very smart people that, absent tax considerations, would be very stupid." This definition highlights one of the most important characteristics common to most corporate tax shelters—the lack of any significant economic substance or risk to the participating parties. Through hedges, circular cash flows, defeasements and the like, the participant in a shelter is insulated from any significant economic risk.

Inconsistent financial accounting and tax treatments—There is a current trend among public companies to treat corporate in-house tax departments as profit centers that strive to keep the corporation's effective tax rate (i.e., the ratio of corporate tax liability to book income) low and in line with that of competitors. Accordingly, in most recent corporate tax shelters involving public companies, the financial accounting treatment of the shelter item has been inconsistent with the claimed Federal income tax treatment.

Tax-indifferent parties—Many recent shelters have relied on the use of "tax-indifferent" parties—such as foreign or tax-exempt entities—who participate in the transaction in exchange for a fee to absorb taxable income or otherwise deflect tax liability from the taxable party.

Marketing activity—Promoters often design tax shelters so that they can be replicated multiple times for use by different participants, rather than to address the tax planning issues of a single taxpayer. This allows the shelter "product" to be marketed and sold to many different corporate participants, thereby maximizing the promoter's return from its shelter idea.

Confidentiality—Similar to marketing, maintaining confidentiality of a tax shelter transaction helps to maximize the promoter's return from its shelter idea—it prevents expropriation by others and it protects the efficacy of the idea by preventing or delaying discovery of the idea by the Treasury Department and the IRS. In the past, promoters have required prospective participants to sign a non-disclosure agreement that provides for million dollar payments for any disclosure of the "proprietary" advice.
* * *

Contingent or refundable fees and rescission or insurance arrangement—Corporate tax shelters often involve contingent or refundable fees in order to reduce the cost and risk of the shelter to the participants. In a contingent fee arrangement, the promoter's fee depends on the level of tax savings realized by the corporate participant. Some corporate tax shelters also involve insurance or rescission arrangements. Like contingent or refundable fees, insurance or rescission arrangements reduce the cost and risk of the shelter to the participants.

High transaction costs—Corporate tax shelters carry unusually high transaction costs. For example, the transaction costs in the ASA case

($24,783,800) were approximately 26.5 percent of the purported tax savings (approximately $93,500,000).

NOTES

(A) *The Threat.* Tax-motivated transactions have a long history. Recall *Cottage Savings*, supra at page 163, in which taxpayers swapped mortgages to realize losses, *Knetsch*, supra at page 367, in which the taxpayer attempted to deduct interest on a non-economic transaction, or *P.G. Lake*, supra at page 609, in which a taxpayer accelerated income to offset losses. Uneasiness over individual tax shelters abated after the Tax Reform Act of 1986, which added the passive loss rules. In recent years, however, there has been renewed concern about the current crop of tax shelters, generally marketed to corporations, which are not subject to § 469. There is some disagreement about whether corporate tax shelters present a serious threat. Treasury, as well as many academics and practitioners, have argued that the tax system faces a crisis, contending that these shelters, many of which would fail if detected, threaten to undermine the corporate tax. Supporters of this view tend to favor giving the IRS broad additional discretionary power to attack shelters. Critics—many of whom are the promoters selling the shelters—argue that there is not a serious problem and that it is a bad idea to give the IRS additional broad powers. Both sides agree that this is a problem that cannot be solved in an easy or straightforward manner.

(B) *You Know It When You See It.* The corporate tax shelter controversy is mired in definitional issues, not the least of which is defining "tax shelter." A definition is essential if statutory penalties or loss or tax credit disallowance rules are to apply only to tax shelters. A tax shelter is somewhat like pornography—you know it when you see it—but that will not work as a statutory definition. Many observers describe a tax shelter as a transaction that would not happen were it not for the tax advantages, as opposed to business deals that do not depend on the tax consequences. Both Treasury and the Staff of the Joint Committee on Taxation have offered definitions that try to draw that line.

JCT Staff Definition:

> Corporate tax shelter—A partnership, entity, plan, or arrangement (collectively referred to as an "arrangement") involving a corporate participant will be considered to have a significant purpose of Federal income tax avoidance or evasion under section 6662 if it satisfies *one* of five corporate tax shelter indicators. The mere purchase or sale of an asset will not constitute an arrangement for these purposes.

Corporate tax shelter indicators—

(1) The present value of the reasonably expected pre-tax profit from the arrangement is insignificant relative to the present value of the reasonably expected net tax benefits.

(2) The arrangement involves a tax-indifferent participant, and (a) results in taxable income materially in excess of economic

income to the tax-indifferent participant, (b) permits a corporate participant to characterize items of income, gain, loss, deductions, or credits in a more favorable manner than it otherwise could without the involvement of the tax-indifferent participant, or (c) results in a noneconomic increase, creation, multiplication, or shifting of basis for the benefit of the corporate participant, and results in the recognition of income or gain that is not subject to Federal income tax because the tax consequences are borne by the tax-indifferent participant.

(3)   The arrangement involves significant reasonably expected net tax benefits and a tax indemnity or similar agreement.

(4)   The arrangement involves significant reasonably expected net tax benefits and a reasonably expected "permanent difference" for U.S. financial reporting purposes under generally accepted accounting principles.

(5)   The arrangement involves significant reasonably expected net tax benefits and the corporate participant incurs little (if any) additional economic risk.

Treasury Definition:

Corporate tax shelter—Any entity, plan, or arrangement in which a direct or indirect corporate participant attempts to obtain a "tax benefit" in a "tax avoidance transaction."

Tax benefit—Includes any reduction, exclusion, avoidance, or deferral of tax, or an increase in a refund, but would not include a tax benefit clearly contemplated by the applicable provision.

Tax avoidance transaction—(1) Any transaction in which the present value of the reasonably expected pre-tax profit of the transaction is insignificant relative to the present value of the reasonably expected net tax benefits, and (2) In the case of financing transactions, any transaction in which the present value of the tax benefits of the taxpayer to whom the financing is provided is significantly in excess of the present value of the pre-tax profit or return of the person providing the financing.

How would the transaction entered into by the bank in *Cottage Savings*, supra at page 163, fare under the Treasury definition? Is the "transaction" in that case the swap of the mortgages, where there is no expectation of pre-tax profit and thus tax benefits clearly dominate, or is the "transaction" the original loan?

(C)   *Literalism.* One of the problems in crafting a definition of "tax shelter" (or for that matter "tax avoidance") is that many of these transactions are based on a literal reading of the Code or a regulation to obtain tax benefits that were not intended by Congress. A serious question is whether taxpayers should be able to rely on the literal language of the statutes and regulations. This view has been expressed by former Senator John Breaux who noted that many taxpayers and their advisors do not have access to sophisticated professional advice and ought to be able to assume that a statute means what it says.

But those who believe that literal compliance with the statute and regulations is not sufficient cannot agree on how to implement this principle. Some favor leaving it up to the courts to use common law doctrines that would deny tax benefits—relying in particular on the requirements that a transaction have economic substance and a business purpose to be respected for tax purposes.

(D) *Why Now?* The dramatic increase in corporate tax shelters is probably due to a variety of factors, not all tax related. For example, many express the view that corporate tax departments have become potential profit centers due to a change in the culture of corporate management that encourages corporations to look favorably on shelters. Others cite the enlarged role played in tax planning by investment banks and accounting firms and the huge fees to be earned by peddling shelters. The development of more complete capital markets that enable corporations to use derivatives to hedge away almost all economic risk has surely made these transactions more attractive to risk-averse firms.

But the tax system itself clearly is at fault as well. As the Code has become more and more complex, it has become less coherent, less understandable, and more open to manipulation. Even when Congress responds to abuses, it often does so in broad-brush ways that open the door to additional abuses. Recall the IRS position in *Corn Products*, supra at page 597. This is an example where the government won the battle but lost the war. In its decision to eliminate tax advantages for one taxpayer, the government often creates advantages for others. And there are structural aspects of the Code that invite creative tax planning. The realization rule, for example, often makes the timing of gains and losses elective. A major change made by the Tax Reform Act of 1986 may also have spurred corporations to look for shelters. That Act caused corporations to recognize gain on distributions and dispositions of appreciated assets and many companies began to search for losses (preferably non-economic, artificial losses) to offset these gains.

In the final analysis, however, the decline in audit rates and the inability of the IRS to detect shelters during audits of large companies kept the tax shelter industry afloat. As noted in Chapter 1, the audit rate has declined precipitously, encouraging otherwise risk-averse taxpayers to play the audit lottery. And even large corporations, who are constantly under audit, play their own sophisticated form of the audit lottery. IRS agents frequently do not have the training or resources to ferret out shelters that are not disclosed on the corporation's return. The IRS in recent years has reorganized its audit functions for large corporations and now requires disclosure of "uncertain" positions. Along with increased penalties, these efforts seem to be enjoying some success.

The following case illustrates how the economic substance requirements have been used to attack an abusive corporate tax shelter.

ACM Partnership v. Commissioner

United States Court of Appeals, Third Circuit, 1998. 157 F.3d 231.

■ GREENBERG, JUDGE:

This appeal concerns the tax consequences of a series of transactions executed between November 1989 and December 1991 by appellant ACM, a partnership formed on October 27, 1989, with its principal place of business in Curacao, Netherlands Antilles. Each of ACM's three partners was created as a subsidiary of a larger entity several days before ACM's formation. Southampton was incorporated under Delaware law on October 24, 1989, as a wholly-owned subsidiary of Colgate-Palmolive Company ("Colgate"), an international consumer products company. Kannex Corporation N.V. ("Kannex") was incorporated under Netherlands Antilles law on October 25, 1989, as an entity controlled by Algemene Bank Nederland N.V. ("ABN"), a major Dutch bank. ACM's third partner, Merrill Lynch MLCS, Inc. ("MLCS"), was incorporated under Delaware law on October 27, 1989, as a wholly owned subsidiary of Merrill Lynch Capital Services, an affiliate of the financial services holding company Merrill Lynch & Co., Inc. ("Merrill Lynch"). * * *

The concept behind the ACM partnership originated in a proposal which Merrill Lynch presented to Colgate in May 1989. During the previous year, Colgate had reported $104,743,250 in long-term capital gains which were attributable in significant part to the sale of its wholly owned subsidiary The Kendall Company ("Kendall"). Colgate had considered and rejected several proposals to reduce the tax liability arising from those 1988 capital gains, when Merrill Lynch * * * approached Colgate * * * in May 1989 and proposed an investment partnership that would generate capital losses which Colgate could use to offset some of its 1988 capital gains.[1]

Colgate's Vice President of Taxation * * * expressed reservations because the plan entailed substantial costs, might not be recognized for tax purposes, and did not seem to serve Colgate's non-tax business purposes, and thus might not be well-received by Colgate's legal, financial, and accounting departments who would be required to participate in the plan. Colgate consulted a law firm for advice on the proposed transaction, which the law firm summarized as follows:

A (a foreign entity), B, and C form the ABC Partnership (ABC) on June 30, 1989 with respective cash contributions of $75, $24 and $1. Immediately thereafter, ABC invests $100 in short-term securities which it sells on December 30, 1989, to an unrelated party. The fair market value and face amount of the short-term securities at the time of the sale is still $100. In consideration for the sale, ABC receives $70 cash and an installment note that provides for six semiannual payments. * * * Each payment equals the sum of a notional principal amount multiplied by the

---

[1] The proposal was premised on I.R.C. § 1212(a), which permits a [corporate] taxpayer to carry back a capital loss to offset capital gains recognized within the preceding three years.

London Interbank Offering Rate (LIBOR) at the start of the semiannual period.[2] ABC uses the $70 cash and the first payment on the installment note to liquidate A's interest in ABC and uses the subsequent interest payments to purchase long-term securities.

The law firm advised that the sale of the short-term securities would be reported as a contingent installment sale under the installment method which governs "disposition[s] of property where at least 1 payment is to be received after the close of the taxable year in which the disposition occurs," I.R.C. § 453, and the ratable basis recovery rule which provides that, [w]hen a stated maximum selling price cannot be determined as of the close of the taxable year in which the sale or other disposition occurs, but the maximum period over which payments may be received under the contingent sale price agreement is fixed, the taxpayer's basis (inclusive of selling expenses) shall be allocated to the taxable years in which payment may be received under the agreement in equal annual increments. Temp. Treas. Reg. § 15a.453–1(c)(3)(i). Thus, the law firm advised, ABC would recover $25 of its basis in each of the 4 taxable years from 1989 through 1992, and ABC would recognize gain to the extent that the payments received in any year exceeded the $25 or loss to the extent that the payments fell below the $25, but only if the loss were carried over to a year with sufficient reported gains against which to offset that loss.

* * * Colgate was interested in the concept of using the proposed partnership to invest in its own debt because of recent developments which had weighted Colgate's debt portfolio toward fixed-rate long-term debt, leaving Colgate vulnerable to a decline in interest rates. Moreover, persistent rumors that Colgate was a likely target for a hostile takeover or leveraged buyout had decreased the value of Colgate's debt issues due to the risk that Colgate's credit rating would be downgraded if Colgate became more highly leveraged. Because of these factors, Colgate perceived an opportunity to rebalance its debt profile, thus decreasing its exposure to falling interest rates, by acquiring its long-term debt issues at their presently discounted prices.

Colgate and Merrill Lynch discussed the possibility of using the proposed partnership to achieve these objectives. The acquisition of its own debt issues would decrease Colgate's exposure to falling interest rates because by acquiring those debt issues as an asset, Colgate effectively would reap the benefits of receiving the above-market interest payments due on those issues, thus hedging against the burdens associated with owing those payments. Acquiring the debt through the partnership instead of directly would keep the acquisitions off Colgate's books, thus permitting Colgate to carry out its debt acquisition strategy without alerting potential acquirors to the internal accumulation of debt issues which, by increasing the capacity for internal leverage, would

---

[2] The LIBOR [London Interbank Offering Rate] is the primary fixed income index reference rate used in [European financial] markets.

increase Colgate's vulnerability to a hostile takeover bid. Thus, the acquisition of Colgate debt through the partnership would allow Colgate to use partnership capital to acquire its debt issues immediately at advantageous prices, then to retire and reissue the debt when market conditions were more favorable. In the interim, the debt effectively would be retired because Colgate would not owe the obligations thereon to third parties, yet the debt would remain outstanding for accounting purposes, reducing Colgate's vulnerability to potential acquirors.

On July 28, 1989, Merrill Lynch presented a proposed partnership transaction summary which incorporated Colgate's debt acquisition objectives into the tax reduction proposal involving the contingent installment sale which Merrill Lynch had presented to Colgate in May 1989. Merrill Lynch revised its proposals throughout the summer and approached ABN about participating in the partnership with Colgate and Merrill Lynch. Merrill Lynch explained to ABN that the partnership would invest in Colgate long-term debt to serve Colgate's debt management objectives, would engage in a contingent installment sale, and would require ABN's participation for no more than 2–3 years.

* * *

A representative of ABN's legal department testified that the partnership, as he understood it, was to:

> enter into transactions that would create a capital gain and in a later stage a capital loss, and that * * * depending on the percentage of your participation, you would either take part in the gain or the loss. So by having us being the majority partner at the start, we would take the majority of the gain, while in a later stage one of the other partners would take the loss.

* * *

A September 20, 1989 document delineated the details of the proposed partnership transactions and their anticipated tax consequences under I.R.C. § 453 and the ratable basis recovery rule, Temp. Treas. Reg. § 15a.453. The document contemplated using the partnership's $200 million in cash investments to acquire short-term notes, disposing of the short-term notes in exchange for $140 million in cash and LIBOR instruments which would generate contingent payments with a present value of $60 million, and using the $140 million in cash to purchase Colgate debt. Because the partnership was to receive payments on the exchange over the course of six years, the $200 million basis in the short-term notes was to be recovered ratably over six tax years in equal increments of $33.3 million per year pursuant to § 15a.453. Thus, according to this document, the transaction would result in significant capital gains in the first year, consisting of the $106.7 million difference between the $140 million cash received that year and the $33.3 million basis recovered that year, and would result in capital losses in each of the ensuing years because the contingent payments received in each of those years * * * would fall short of the $33.3 million basis to be recovered in each of those years. The aggregate projected capital losses in the ensuing years equaled precisely the amount of capital gains reported in the first year, and the document stated that the recognition of those losses "may be accelerated in any year subsequent to 1989 by sale of the remaining LIBOR notes."

The document also contemplates Colgate's increasing its share in the partnership from 15% to 97% after the partnership recognized the $106.7 million capital gain in the year 1 but before it recognized the capital losses in the ensuing years. According to the document, the LIBOR notes eventually would be sold for a capital loss of $80 million, 97% of which would be allocated to Colgate based on its 97% partnership interest by the time the loss was incurred.

Between October 24 and October 27, 1989, ABN established Kannex, Colgate established Southampton, and Merrill Lynch established MLCS to participate in the ACM partnership. The October 27, 1989 partnership agreement among these newly created entities provided that Kannex was to receive a preferred return of the first $1.24 million in any partnership profits otherwise allocable to Southampton.

[The partnership was subsequently formed and the amounts contributed by the partners were used to purchase Citicorp notes. These notes were subsequently sold for cash and installment notes whose interest rate was based on LIBOR.* In exchange for the $175 million Citicorp notes, ACM received total consideration of $174.4 million, consisting of $140 million in cash and the LIBOR notes, which had a present value of $34.4 million. The payments on the notes were used to purchase Colgate debt. In 1991, through a series of transactions involving Colgate, Southampton, and the ACM partnership, Kannex's interest in the partnership was purchased and redeemed, leaving Colgate-Southampton with a combined 99.7 ownership interest in the partnership.]

On its partnership return for the tax year ended November 30, 1989, ACM treated the [sale] of the Citicorp notes as an installment sale under I.R.C. § 453, as ACM was to receive part of the consideration for that exchange "after the close of the taxable year in which the disposition occurs" pursuant to § 453(b)(1). Because the quarterly LIBOR note payments would vary based on fluctuations in the LIBOR, there was no "stated maximum selling price" that could be identified "as of the close of the taxable year in which the * * * disposition occurs." Thus, the transaction came within the terms of Temp. Treas. Reg. § 15a.453–1(c), whose ratable basis recovery rule provides that the taxpayer's basis

---

* [Ed. Note: The LIBOR notes provided for a stream of 20 quarterly contingent payments beginning March 1, 1990, whose amount was derived from multiplying the LIBOR rate times a notional principal amount of $97.76 million. The notional principal amount did not represent an amount owed but was simply a multiplier to determine the amount of the LIBOR-based contingent payments.]

"shall be allocated to the taxable years in which payment may be received under the agreement in equal annual increments."

Accordingly, ACM divided its $175,504,564 basis in the Citicorp notes * * * equally among the six years over which payments were to be received in exchange for those notes, and thus recovered one sixth of that basis, or $29,250,761, during 1989. Subtracting this basis from the $140 million in cash consideration for the Citicorp notes, ACM reported a 1989 capital gain of $110,749,239.42 which it allocated among its partners according to their partnership shares, resulting in an allocation of $91,516,689 of the gain to Kannex, $18,908,407 to Southampton, and $324,144 to MLCS. Southampton and MLCS were subject to United States income tax on their respective shares of the gain, but Kannex as a foreign corporation was not.[17]

Under the ratable basis recovery rule the tax basis remaining to be recovered over the following five years became $146,253,803, representing the difference between the $175,504,564 value of the Citicorp notes which ACM relinquished to acquire those notes and the $29,250,761 in basis recovered during the first year of the transaction. * * * [This left $146,253,803 remaining basis attributable to the LIBOR notes, whose actual cost totaled $35,504,564. ACM subsequently sold or distributed the LIBOR notes, which produced an $85 million capital loss in 1991. Some of the LIBOR notes were distributed to Southampton, Colgate's partnership entity, and Southampton sold them at roughly a $34 million capital loss in 1989, the same year in which it was allocated a gain, resulting in a net capital loss of about $13.5 million. During the time ACM held the LIBOR notes, they declined in value by nearly $6 million due to declining interest rates.]

[T]he Commissioner of Internal Revenue ("Commissioner") issued ACM a Notice * * * eliminating ACM's $110,749,239.42 installment gain from the sale of the Citicorp notes in November 1989, redetermining ACM's tax basis in the * * * LIBOR notes distributed in December 1989, and disallowing the $84,997,111 capital loss deduction which ACM reported in 1991. In writing this opinion we primarily focus on the capital loss aspects of the case, though it should be understood that the gain and loss are part of a single integrated plan. The Commissioner asserted * * * that the transactions involving the purchase and sale of the Citicorp notes in exchange for cash and LIBOR notes, "were shams in that they were prearranged and predetermined. * * * [S]aid transactions were devoid of economic substance necessary for recognition for federal income tax purposes and were totally lacking in economic reality. The transactions were created solely for tax motivated purposes without any realistic expectation of profit."

---

[17] According to the Tax Court the share allocated to Kannex was not taxed in any jurisdiction but we, of course, are focusing only on the United States tax aspects of the transaction.

The Tax Court * * * issued a memorandum opinion upholding the Commissioner's adjustments on the grounds that "[a] taxpayer is not entitled to recognize a phantom loss from a transaction that lacks economic substance." In reaching the conclusion that ACM was not entitled to deduct its claimed capital losses, the court examined the stated purposes and anticipated economic consequences of the transaction, and found that the claimed losses were "not economically inherent in" the transactions but rather were "created artificially" by machinations whose only purpose and effect was to give rise to the desired tax consequences. * * *

ACM contends that, because its transactions on their face satisfied each requirement of the contingent installment sale provisions and regulations thereunder, it properly deducted the losses arising from its "straightforward application" of these provisions, which required it to recover only one sixth of the basis in the Citicorp notes during the first of the six years over which it was to receive payments. * * * Thus, ACM contends, it properly subtracted the basis in the LIBOR notes to include the remaining five-sixths of the basis in the Citicorp notes used to acquire them. Consequently, ACM argues it properly subtracted the approximately $96 million remaining unrecovered basis in the LIBOR notes from the approximately $11 million consideration it received upon disposition of those notes, and correctly recognized and reported the gains and losses arising from its sale or exchange of property in accordance with I.R.C. § 1001.

While ACM's transactions, at least in form, satisfied each requirement of the contingent installment sale provisions and ratable basis recovery rule, ACM acknowledges that even where the "form of the taxpayer's activities indisputably satisfie[s] the literal requirements" of the relevant statutory language, the courts must examine "whether the substance of those transactions was consistent with their form," because a transaction that is "devoid of economic substance * * * simply is not recognized for federal taxation purposes."

We begin our economic substance analysis with Gregory v. Helvering, the Supreme Court's foundational exposition of economic substance principles under the Internal Revenue Code. In *Gregory*, as in this case, the transactions on their face satisfied "every element required by" the relevant statutory language. The taxpayer, instead of transferring stock from her wholly owned corporation directly to herself which would have generated taxable dividends, created a new corporation, transferred the stock to the new corporation, then liquidated the new corporation, transferred the stock to herself, and asserted that she had not recognized any taxable gain because she had received the stock "in pursuance of a plan of reorganization" within the meaning of I.R.C. § 112(g). Although the transactions satisfied each element of the statute, which defined "reorganization" as a transfer of assets between corporations under common control, the Court found that "[t]he whole undertaking, though conducted according to the [statutory] terms * * * was in fact an elaborate and devious form of conveyance masquerading as a corporate reorganization."

The Court stated that "if a reorganization in reality was effected" any "ulterior [tax avoidance] purpose * * * will be disregarded" and the transaction will be respected for tax purposes. The Court emphasized, however, that where the transactions merely "put on the form of a corporate reorganization as a disguise for concealing its real character" which was a "preconceived plan * * * not to reorganize a business," but rather "to transfer * * * shares to the [taxpayer]," the transaction was not, in reality, "the thing which the statute intended." Viewed according to their substance rather than their form, the Court found, the transactions fell "outside the plain intent of the statute" and therefore could not be treated in accordance with their form without "exalt[ing] artifice above reality." Thus, pursuant to *Gregory*, we must "look beyond the form of [the] transaction" to determine whether it has the "economic substance that [its] form represents," because regardless of its form, a transaction that is "devoid of economic substance" must be disregarded for tax purposes and "cannot be the basis for a deductible loss."[30]

In applying these principles, we must view the transactions "as a whole, and each step, from the commencement * * * to the consummation * * * is relevant." The inquiry into whether the taxpayer's transactions had sufficient economic substance to be respected for tax purposes turns on both the "objective economic substance of the transactions" and the "subjective business motivation" behind them. However, these distinct aspects of the economic sham inquiry do not constitute discrete prongs of a "rigid two-step analysis," but rather represent related factors both of which inform the analysis of whether the transaction had sufficient substance, apart from its tax consequences, to be respected for tax purposes. For the reasons that follow, we find that both the objective analysis of the actual economic consequences of ACM's transactions and the subjective analysis of their intended purposes support the Tax Court's conclusion that ACM's transactions did not have sufficient economic substance to be respected for tax purposes.[31]

---

[30] The courts have distinguished between "shams in fact" where the reported transactions never occurred and "shams in substance" which "actually occurred but that lack the substance their form represents." Because it is undisputed that ACM's transactions actually occurred, we confine our inquiry to the question of whether their economic substance corresponds to their form.

[31] While it is clear that a transaction such as ACM's that has neither objective non-tax economic effects nor subjective non-tax purposes constitutes an economic sham whose tax consequences must be disregarded, and equally clear that a transaction that has both objective non-tax economic significance and subjective non-tax purposes constitutes an economically substantive transaction whose tax consequences must be respected, it is also well established that where a transaction objectively affects the taxpayer's net economic position, legal relations, or non-tax business interests, it will not be disregarded merely because it was motivated by tax considerations. * * *

1.   Objective Aspects of the Economic Sham Analysis

In assessing the economic substance of a taxpayer's transactions, the courts have examined "whether the transaction has any practical economic effects other than the creation of income tax losses," and have refused to recognize the tax consequences of transactions that were devoid of "nontax substance" because they "did not appreciably affect [the taxpayer's] beneficial interest except to reduce his tax." Knetsch v. United States, 364 U.S. 361, 366 (1960). [The court then discusses *Knetsch*, set forth at page 367, and similar cases.]

* * * In light of these cases, we must determine whether the Tax Court erred in concluding that ACM's exchange of the Citicorp notes for contingent-payment LIBOR notes which gave rise to the tax consequences at issue generated only "a phantom loss" that was not "economically inherent in the object of the sale" and did not have "economic substance separate and distinct from economic benefit achieved solely by tax reduction." For the following reasons, we conclude that it did not.

2.   Objective Economic Consequences of ACM's Transactions

While the Tax Court's analysis focused on the lack of non-tax purposes behind ACM's transactions rather than on their objective economic consequences, the court made numerous findings that were indicative of the lack of objective economic consequences arising from ACM's shortswing acquisition and disposition of the Citicorp notes. * * * The court noted that ACM sold the Citicorp notes "for consideration equal to [their] purchase price" and thus did not realize any gain or loss in the notes' principal value. Moreover, as the court observed, the lack of change in principal value was not merely coincidental, but was inherent in the terms of the notes and of the transactions in which they were traded. Likewise, the court found that the interest income generated by the notes could not have a material effect on ACM's financial position because the Citicorp notes paid interest at a rate that varied only nominally from the rate that ACM's cash contributions "were already earning * * * in * * * deposit accounts before the notes were acquired," resulting in only a $3,500 difference in yield over the 24-day holding period, a difference which was obliterated by the transaction costs associated with marketing private placement notes to third parties. * * * These transactions, which generated the disputed capital losses by triggering the application of the ratable basis recovery rule, offset one another with no net effect on ACM's financial position. Examining the sequence of ACM's transactions as a whole as we must in assessing their economic substance, we find that these transactions had only nominal, incidental effects on ACM's net economic position.

Viewed according to their objective economic effects rather than their form, ACM's transactions involved only a fleeting and economically inconsequential investment in and offsetting divestment from the Citicorp notes. In the course of this brief interim investment, ACM passed $175 million of its available cash through the Citicorp notes before converting 80% of them, or $140 million, back into cash while using the remaining 20%, or $35 million, to acquire an amount of LIBOR notes that was identical, apart from transaction costs, to the amount of such notes that ACM could have acquired by investing its $35 million in cash directly into such assets. Thus, the transactions with respect to the Citicorp notes left ACM in the same position it had occupied before engaging in the offsetting acquisition and disposition of those notes.[35]

* * *

Gregory requires us to determine the tax consequences of a series of transactions based on what "actually occurred." Just as the *Gregory* Court found that the intervening creation and dissolution of a corporation and transfer of stock thereto and therefrom was a "mere device which put on the form of a corporate reorganization as a disguise for concealing its real character" which amounts to a mere "transfer * * * of corporate shares to the [taxpayer]," so we find that ACM's intervening acquisition and disposition of the Citicorp notes was a mere device to create the appearance of a contingent installment sale despite the transaction's actual character as an investment of $35 million in cash into a roughly equivalent amount of LIBOR notes. Thus, the acquisition and disposition of the qualifying private placement Citicorp notes, based upon which ACM characterized its transactions as a contingent installment sale subject to the ratable basis recovery rule, had no effect on ACM's net economic position or non-tax business interests and thus, as the Tax Court properly found, did not constitute an economically substantive transaction that may be respected for tax purposes.[37]

ACM contends that the Tax Court was bound to respect the tax consequences of ACM's exchange of Citicorp notes for LIBOR notes because, under Cottage Sav. Ass'n v. Commissioner, 499 U.S. 554, an exchange of property for "materially different" assets is a substantive disposition whose tax effects must be recognized. We find Cottage Savings inapposite. * * * The distinctions between the exchange at issue in this case and the exchange before the Court in *Cottage Savings* predominate over any superficial similarities between the two transactions. The taxpayer in *Cottage Savings* had an economically

---

[35] The variable rate on the Citicorp notes presented a theoretical possibility that the consequences of owning those notes would vary from the consequences of leaving ACM's funds on deposit at a rate of interest virtually identical to the initial rate on the Citicorp notes. However, ACM's exposure to any fluctuation in the rate of return on its Citicorp note investment was illusory, as the interest rates were scheduled to be reset only once per month and ACM had arranged to hold the notes for only 24 days, encompassing only one interest rate adjustment on November 15 that would affect the notes for only 12 days before their disposition.

[37] [Each of the cases discussed above] involved objective acts which satisfied the technical requirements of the Internal Revenue Code provisions that the taxpayer sought to invoke, but which the courts disregarded for tax purposes because they lacked any net effect on the taxpayer's economic position or non-tax business interests. Accordingly, we are unpersuaded by ACM's argument that its transactions must be regarded as economically substantive because it actually and objectively engaged in them.

substantive investment in assets which it had acquired a number of years earlier in the course of its ordinary business operations and which had declined in actual economic value by over $2 million from approximately $6.9 million to approximately $4.5 million from the time of acquisition to the time of disposition. The taxpayer's relinquishment of assets so altered in actual economic value over the course of a long-term investment stands in stark contrast to ACM's relinquishment of assets that it had acquired 24 days earlier under circumstances which assured that their principal value would remain constant and that their interest payments would not vary materially from those generated by ACM's cash deposits.

While the dispositions in *Cottage Savings* and in this case appear similar in that the taxpayer exchanged the assets for other assets with the same net present value, beneath this similarity lies the more fundamental distinction that the disposition in *Cottage Savings* precipitated the realization of actual economic losses arising from a long-term, economically significant investment, while the disposition in this case was without economic effect as it merely terminated a fleeting and economically inconsequential investment, effectively returning ACM to the same economic position it had occupied before the notes' acquisition 24 days earlier.[39]

As the Supreme Court emphasized in *Cottage Savings*, deductions are allowable only where the taxpayer has sustained a " 'bona fide' " loss as determined by its " '[s]ubstance and not mere form.' " According to ACM's own synopsis of the transactions, the contingent installment exchange would not generate actual economic losses. Rather, ACM would sell the Citicorp notes for the same price at which they were acquired, generating only tax losses which offset precisely the tax gains reported earlier in the transaction with no net loss or gain from the disposition.[40] Tax losses such as these, which are purely an artifact of tax accounting methods and which do not correspond to any actual economic losses, do not constitute the type of "bona fide" losses that are deductible under the Internal Revenue Code and regulations.

While ACM contends that "it would be absurd to conclude that the application of the Commissioner's own [ratable basis recovery] regulations results in gains or losses that the Commissioner can then deem to be other than 'bona fide,' " its argument confounds a tax accounting regulation which merely prescribes a method for reporting

---

[39] ACM contends that its disposition of the Citicorp notes was substantive because it "relinquished the benefits and burdens of owning the Citicorp notes for the distinct benefits and burdens of owning $140 million of cash and the LIBOR notes." This argument, however, erroneously assumes that ACM had acquired the benefits and burdens associated with the Citicorp notes in an economically substantive sense, when in reality ACM's brief investment in and offsetting divestment from these assets exposed ACM only to de minimis risk of changes in principal value or interest rates.

[40] The participation of a foreign partner that was impervious to tax considerations and that claimed most of the reported gains while allocating to Colgate virtually all of the losses allowed Colgate as ACM's major U.S. partner to reap the benefits of the tax losses without sustaining the burdens of the offsetting tax gains.

otherwise existing deductible losses that are realized over several years with a substantive deductibility provision authorizing the deduction of certain losses. In order to be deductible, a loss must reflect actual economic consequences sustained in an economically substantive transaction and cannot result solely from the application of a tax accounting rule to bifurcate a loss component of a transaction from its offsetting gain component to generate an artificial loss which, as the Tax Court found, is "not economically inherent in" the transaction.[41] Based on our review of the record regarding the objective economic consequences of ACM's short-swing, offsetting investment in and divestment from the Citicorp notes, we find ample support for the Tax Court's determination that ACM's transactions generated only "phantom losses" which cannot form the basis of a capital loss deduction under the Internal Revenue Code.[42]

3. Subjective Aspects of the Economic Sham Analysis

* * *

We * * * find that the Tax Court's analysis properly rested on economic substance cases applying provisions which, like those relevant in this case, do not by their terms require a business purpose or profit motive. [The court then discusses cases where an inquiry into profit motive or business purpose was undertaken despite the lack of such a requirement in the statute.] [W]e find no merit in ACM's argument that the Tax Court erred as a matter of law by scrutinizing the asserted business purposes and profit motives behind ACM's transactions.

* * *

4. Intended Purposes and Anticipated Profitability of ACM's Transactions

Before the Tax Court, ACM conceded that there were tax objectives behind its transactions but contended that "tax independent considerations informed and justified each step of the strategy." ACM asserted that its transactions, in addition to presenting "a realistic prospect that ACM would have made a profit" on a pre-tax basis, also

---

[41] Because the ratable basis recovery rule simply provides a method for reporting otherwise existing economically substantive losses, we find it irrelevant that the rule recognizes that its application could "inappropriately defer or accelerate recovery of the taxpayer's basis," resulting in " 'substantial distortion' " of the tax consequences realized in any particular year of a transaction. Temp. Treas. Reg. §§ 15a.453–1(c)(3), (c)(7). While the rule contemplates some distortion as to the timing of when actual gains or losses are reported over the span of a contingent installment sale, it does not contemplate the reporting of losses which are not the bona fide result of an economically substantive transaction. Thus, contrary to ACM's argument, the tax losses it reported are not "precisely what the [regulations] intended."

[42] Having found ample support for the Tax Court's conclusion that ACM's transactions lacked economic substance and thus cannot give rise to taxable gains or deductible losses regardless of how those gains and losses are allocated, we need not address the Commissioner's alternative argument that the tax consequences of the transaction must be disregarded because ACM's partnership structure artificially "bifurcated the tax consequences of the transaction" by allocating taxable gains to a foreign partner and offsetting tax losses to the taxpayer in a manner which the relevant statute and regulations did not intend.

served the tax-independent purposes of providing an interim investment until ACM needed its cash to acquire Colgate debt and a hedge against interest rate risk within the partnership. The Tax Court, however, found that the record did not support ACM's assertions that the transactions were designed either to serve these non-tax objectives or to generate a pre-tax profit, and * * * we agree.

* * *

In addition to rejecting ACM's asserted non-tax justifications for its sequence of investments and dispositions, the Tax Court also rejected ACM's contention that its transactions were reasonably expected to yield a pre-tax profit because the court found ACM had planned and executed its transactions without regard to their pretax economic consequences. The evidence in the record overwhelmingly supports this conclusion. The documents outlining the proposed transactions, while quite detailed in their explication of expected tax consequences, are devoid of such detailed projections as to the expected rate of return on the private placement notes and contingent payment notes that were essential components of each proposal.

Moreover, ACM's partners were aware before they entered the partnership that the planned sequence of investments would entail over $3 million in transaction costs. Yet Colgate, which effectively bore virtually all of these costs pursuant to the terms of the partnership agreement, did not attempt to assess whether the transactions would be profitable after accounting for these significant transaction costs. Furthermore, while ACM planned to dispose of the Citicorp notes after a brief holding period for an amount equal to their purchase price, its proposed transactions contemplated holding for two years the LIBOR notes whose principal value would decline in the event of the falling interest rates which ACM's partners predicted.

Thus, while the Citicorp note investment which was essential to structuring the transaction as a contingent installment sale was economically inconsequential, the LIBOR note investment which was equally essential to achieving the desired tax structure was economically disadvantageous under the market conditions which Colgate predicted and which actually transpired. ACM's lack of regard for the relative costs and benefits of the contemplated transaction and its failure to conduct a contemporaneous profitability analysis support the Tax Court's conclusion that ACM's transactions were not designed or reasonably anticipated to yield a pre-tax profit, particularly in view of the significant transactions costs involved in exchanging illiquid private placement instruments. * * *

ACM also argues that the Tax Court's profitability analysis was flawed because the court adjusted the income expected to be generated by the LIBOR notes to its net present value. * * * In transactions that are designed to yield deferred rather than immediate returns, present value adjustments are, as the courts have recognized, an appropriate means of assessing the transaction's actual and anticipated economic effects. * * * We find no basis in the law for precluding a tax court's reliance on a present value adjustment where such an adjustment, under the surrounding circumstances, will serve as an accurate gauge of the reasonably expected economic consequences of the transaction.

* * *

[The portion of the court's opinion allowing a deduction for the approximately $6 million economic loss on the LIBOR notes, due to a decline in interest rates while the partnership held them, is omitted.]

■ McKEE, CIRCUIT JUDGE, dissenting.

By finding that ACM's sales of the Citicorp notes for cash and LIBOR Notes "satisfied each requirement of the contingent installment sales provisions and the ratable basis recovery rule," yet, simultaneously subjecting these transactions to an economic substance and sham transaction analysis, the majority has ignored the plain language of IRC § 1001, and controlling Supreme Court precedent. We have injected the "economic substance" analysis into an inquiry where it does not belong. Therefore, I respectfully dissent.

ACM, like all taxpayers, has the absolute right to decrease or to avoid the payment of taxes so long as that goal is achieved legally. Gregory v. Helvering. * * * [In *Gregory*] the Court disregarded the transaction, even though the form of the transaction satisfied the literal requirements of the IRC's reorganization provisions, because it found that the entire transaction was nothing but "an elaborate and devious form of conveyance masquerading as a corporate reorganization, and nothing else." In other words, the transaction was one which "upon its face lies outside the plain intent of the statute." Consequently, "the rule which excludes from consideration the motive of tax avoidance" did not apply.

Accordingly, I am not as persuaded as my colleagues that *Gregory* should guide our inquiry into these transactions. Here, the sales of the Citicorp Notes for cash and LIBOR Notes were clearly "legitimate" sales in the nontax sense. Under IRC § 1001, the tax consequences of a gain or loss in the value of property are deferred until the taxpayer realizes the gain or loss. *Cottage Savings Assoc. v. Commissioner.* * * * I believe that, under *Cottage Savings*, the tax loss here should have been allowed. ACM's sales of the Citicorp Notes for cash and LIBOR Notes resulted in the exchange of materially different property with "legally distinct entitlements." Consequently, the sales were substantive dispositions, and the tax effects of those transactions should be recognized. *Cottage Savings*, as well as the plain language of IRC § 1001, demands that result. * * * Here, the "economic substance" inquiry must be governed by the "material difference requirement" of *Cottage Savings*, not by the tax avoidance intent of the taxpayers. As recited earlier, ACM's sales of the

Citicorp Notes for cash and LIBOR Notes resulted in the exchange of materially different property. I believe our inquiry should proceed no further, and reverse the holding of the Tax Court eliminating the capital gains and losses attributable to ACM's application of the contingent installment sale provisions and the ratable basis recovery rule to its disposition of the Citicorp Notes.

I can't help but suspect that the majority's conclusion to the contrary is, in its essence, something akin to a "smell test." If the scheme in question smells bad, the intent to avoid taxes defines the result as we do not want the taxpayer to "put one over." However, the issue clearly is not whether ACM put one over on the Commissioner, or used LIBOR notes to "pull the wool over his eyes." The issue is whether what ACM did qualifies for the tax treatment it seeks under § 1001. The fact that ACM may have "put one over" in crafting these transactions ought not to influence our inquiry. Our inquiry is cerebral, not visceral. To the extent that the Commissioner is offended by these transactions he should address Congress and/or the rulemaking process, and not the courts.

NOTES

(A) *Just the Facts, Ma'am.* The D.C. Circuit denied the tax losses in a transaction identical to the one in *ACM Partnership* but on the ground that the partnership was a sham. In ASA Investerings Partnership v. Commissioner, 201 F.3d 505 (D.C. Cir. 2000), Allied Signal also entered into a transaction peddled by Merrill Lynch in which the gains on an installment sale were allocated to a foreign tax-exempt entity. As in *ACM*, by using the basis-recovery rule, large losses were created and allocated to Allied Signal, who used them to offset a capital gain on the sale of its interests in another company. The court found that the partnership was created solely to avoid taxes and therefore was not a valid separate entity. Although the court basically found it was not necessary to pursue the economic substance doctrine once it found the partnership was a sham, its analysis in making the determination that the partnership had no purpose other than tax avoidance is very similar to that used by the Third Circuit in *ACM*.

Judge Williams, who wrote the circuit court's opinion in *ASA*, remarked that "[t]he hardest aspect of this case is simply getting a handle on the facts." He attempted to make them manageable in the following simplified summary, which may be helpful in understanding the essence of the transaction in *ACM*:

> [S]uppose A finds a way of allocating the nominal tax gain to a tax-free entity, reserving for himself a nominal tax loss? Here is how he might do it: He forms a partnership with a foreign entity not subject to U.S. tax, supplying the partnership with $100,000 and inducing the "partner" to supply $900,000. The "partnership" buys for $1,000,000 property eligible for installment sale treatment under § 453, and, as the ink is drying on the purchase documents, sells the property * * * for $500,000 in cash and an indefinite five-year debt instrument. The cash payment produces a gain of

> $300,000, 90% of which goes to the nontaxable foreign entity. Then ownership adjustments are made so that A owns 90% of the partnership. In Year 2 the instrument is sold, yielding a tax loss of $300,000, 90% of which is allocable to A. Presto: A has generated a tax loss of $240,000 ($270,000 loss in Year 2, offset by $30,000 gain in Year 1), with no material change in his financial position—other than receipt of the valuable tax loss. This example is [this] case stripped to its essentials.

201 F.3d at 507–08. The D.C. Circuit court also rejected another transaction very similar to that in *ACM*. Boca Investerings Partnership v. United States, 314 F.3d 625 (D.C. Cir. 2003).

(B) *You Win Many, You Lose Some.* The IRS has been successful in convincing courts to disallow the benefits claimed under various shelters. Still, the IRS has also lost major cases, creating concern that litigation could not stem the tide of tax shelters. For example, in The Limited, Inc. v. Commissioner, 113 T.C. 169 (1999), the Tax Court refused to let the taxpayer characterize a related company as "carrying on the banking business" because of its limited activities and in the context of a structured transaction intended to defer U.S. taxes. But the Sixth Circuit reversed, holding that "banking business" included credit-card companies, which was part of the ordinary and natural meaning of the phrase. 286 F.3d 324 (6th Cir. 2002). Another major loss involved a shelter entered into by United Parcel Service. The Tax Court found that the transactions were done for "the purpose of avoiding taxes," "had no economic substance or business purpose," and were "sham transaction[s] with no economic effect." United Parcel Service of America v. Commissioner, 78 T.C.M. 262 (1999). The Eleventh Circuit disagreed, however, finding that there was enough economic substance to the activity to avoid labeling it a sham. 254 F.3d 1014 (11th Cir. 2001).

(C) *The Economic Substance Doctrine.* The IRS has won a number of major victories with respect to judicial doctrines, with the court in each case upholding the use of the economic substance doctrine to override literal compliance with statutory language. Despite its label as a "doctrine," the courts have differing views of what it means and how it should be applied.

The courts sometimes distinguish two strands to the doctrine: objective economic substance and subjective business purpose. The first strand generally requires that the transaction offered an opportunity for pre-tax profit, although how to calculate that profit and how much profit is required is subject to much debate. Sometimes the court will find that there is not sufficient economic substance to a transaction unless a rational economic actor would have accepted the deal. In a case involving deductions generated by a complex and Byzantine structure put together by two Nobel Laureates (among others), the court accepted the testimony of another Nobel Laureate that a rational economic actor would not have entered into the transaction but for the tax benefits. Long Term Capital Holdings v. United States, 330 F.Supp.2d 122 (D. Conn. 2004), affirmed in an unpublished opinion, 150 Fed.Appx. 40 (2d Cir. 2005). The court also found that the expected cash receipts of $1.9 million were swallowed up by the $3.5 million in fees to put the deal together. The second strand of the economic substance doctrine requires that there be a subjective business purpose for the transaction (other than tax avoidance). In *Long Term Capital Holdings*, the court rejected the taxpayer's attempt to spin a business purpose.

Still, economic substance remains a flexible doctrine intended to empower the IRS and courts to take a hard look at taxpayer-created formalities. As Second Circuit Judge Denny Chin wrote, in a 2015 opinion disallowing foreign tax credits claimed by a large bank in a structured transaction, "The economic substance doctrine exists to provide courts a "second look" to ensure that particular uses of tax benefits comply with Congress's purpose in creating that benefit." Bank of New York Mellon Company v. Commissioner, No. 14–704 (2d Cir. 2015). One of a series of cases disallowing the tax benefits of a transaction, known as STARS, designed by Barclays and KPMG to take advantage (through the use of foreign tax credits) of different tax treatment of the same transaction under U.S. and U.K. law. Along with the *Bank of New York* case, three additional litigated cases involve $1.4 billion in credits claimed against U.S. tax. Like the Second Circuit, the other courts that have heard these cases have held for the government. See, e.g. Santander Holdings USA, Inc. v. United States, 844 F.3d 15, 26 (1st Cir. 2016); Salem Fin., Inc. v. United States, 786 F.3d 932, 948 (Fed. Cir. 2015).

(D) *Related Doctrines.* The case law also makes use of doctrines related to the economic substance doctrine, often applying them in conjunction with the economic substance doctrine. Substance over form, sham, and step transaction are, essentially, variants of the economic substance idea, although courts sometimes present them as distinct doctrines. Some of these doctrines appear in cases earlier in this book, notably *Knetsch* (sham transaction doctrine), supra at page 367.

For examples of these doctrines in the tax shelter context, see BB&T Corp. v. United States, 523 F.3d 461 (4th Cir. 2008) (holding that in substance the transaction was a financing arrangement, not a true lease, and thus denying the deductions); RJT Investments X v. Commissioner, 491 F.3d 732 (8th Cir. 2007) (holding that a partnership used to carry out a complicated shelter was a sham); H.J. Heinz Co. v. United States, 76 Fed.Cl. 570 (Fed.Cl. 2007) (denying a claimed loss, holding that where the taxpayer intended a series of actions to be part of a single, integrated transaction, the tax consequences would be determined by the end result).

(E) *Codification of the Economic Substance Doctrine.* As part of the Health Care and Education Reconciliation Act of 2010, Congress codified the economic substance doctrine (which has nothing to do with health care but was estimated to raise some revenue to help pay for it.) Under the codified doctrine, in order to have economic substance, a transaction must change "in a meaningful way (apart from Federal income tax effects) the taxpayer's economic position" and the taxpayer must have "a substantial purpose (apart from Federal income tax effects) for entering into such transaction." § 7701(*o*). Note that this test is in the conjunctive and therefore resolves the split in the courts over whether a taxpayer had to meet both or only one of the two tests.

Section 7701(*o*) does not require the taxpayer to show a potential profit from a transaction in order to establish economic substance under the first prong of the test but if the taxpayer does so, it must demonstrate that "the present value of the reasonably expected pre-tax profit from the transaction is substantial in relation to the present value of the expected net tax benefits that would be allowed if the transaction were respected." Fees and other transaction costs must be taken into account in determining pre-tax profit. § 7701(*o*)(2).

Codification of the doctrine was accompanied by the threat of a large strict liability penalty of 20 percent for any underpayment attributable to disallowing tax benefits because a transaction lacked economic substance. § 6662(b)(6). The § 6664(c) "reasonable cause" exception is unavailable. Reliance on the opinion of a lawyer or tax advisor will not insulate a taxpayer from the penalty. (The role of legal opinion letters is discussed in the Note on the Role of Lawyers, Accountants, and Other Experts supra at page 793.) The penalty is increased to 40 percent if the taxpayer does not adequately disclose the relevant facts on its tax return. These penalty provisions greatly increase the stakes of deciding where and when the doctrine applies.

The statute limits the use of the doctrine to cases in "which the economic substance doctrine is relevant" and indicates that "the determination of whether the economic substance doctrine is relevant to a transaction shall be made in the same manner as if this subsection had never been enacted." Thus application is not mandatory—although a court cannot claim it has no authority to apply the doctrine, it can choose whether and when to apply § 7701(*o*). This provision is also intended to mollify those who opposed codification on the grounds that it would have a sweeping application to transactions that would never have been subject to the common law doctrine, although it is far from clear how the IRS and courts will actually apply it. The congressional intent appears to be that the statutory provision should not apply in cases where the courts have not historically applied it. Furthermore, according to the Report of the Staff of the Joint Committee on Taxation, § 7701(*o*) "is not intended to alter the tax treatment of certain basic business transactions that, under longstanding judicial and administrative practice are respected, merely because the choice between meaningful economic alternatives is largely or entirely based on comparative tax advantages." That report includes a nonexclusive "angel list" of transactions that would not be invalidated by the doctrine, but its scope remains uncertain.

Legislative history indicates that the codification of the economic substance doctrine was not intended to alter or supplant any other common law doctrine, which would include the doctrines discussed in the prior Notes.

SECTION 2.   PENALTIES

Note on Penalties and Tax Shelters

Litigation based on doctrines like economic substance is not the only weapon in the government's arsenal. A complementary approach is to

change the cost-benefit analysis of tax shelters by increasing the costs if
the shelter fails. To this end, a variety of penalties on understatements
attributable to tax shelters have been enacted. The penalty structure for
taxpayers has developed in several stages. The result is a set of complex
and sometimes overlapping penalties, with unclear deterrence effects.

Initially Congress imposed a penalty for "negligence," that is, the
failure to make a reasonable attempt to comply with the tax laws. § 6662.
A taxpayer can avoid the 20 percent penalty for negligence if he discloses
his position on the return and the position has a reasonable basis. For
background on the development of the meaning of reasonable basis, see
page 800, infra.

Congress then attempted to add a "no-fault" standard when it
substantially revised the penalty structure in 1984. A 20 percent penalty
applies to a substantial understatement of income, that is, where the
underpayment of tax exceeds the greater of 10 percent of the correct tax
liability or $5,000 ($10,000 for a corporation). § 6662(d). No penalty is
imposed, however, to the extent the understatement is attributable to a
position for which substantial authority exists or the relevant facts are
adequately disclosed and there is a reasonable basis for the position. The
penalty is not actually a no-fault penalty, however, because it may be
avoided if the taxpayer acts in good faith and has reasonable cause.
§ 6664(c). As discussed below, a legal opinion often provided this
protection.

Because these penalties did not stem the use of tax shelters, in 2004
Congress responded by adding a new, higher accuracy-related penalty,
on "reportable avoidance transactions," which are listed transactions and
reportable transactions with a significant tax avoidance purpose. If the
investor adequately discloses the transaction, the penalty is 20 percent;
if not adequately disclosed, the penalty is 30 percent. § 6662A. The
definition of reportable transactions tracks those transactions that must
be disclosed. The penalty can be waived if the taxpayer had reasonable
cause and acted in good faith. That requires disclosure of the transaction,
substantial authority for the position taken, and a reasonable belief that
the treatment was "more likely than not" correct. That belief must be
based on the facts and law that exist at the time the tax return is filed
and must relate solely to the taxpayer's chance of success on the merits,
regardless of likelihood of audit. The investor cannot rely on a
disqualified opinion for penalty protection, i.e. an opinion based on
unreasonable factual or legal assumptions, that unreasonably relies on
the taxpayer for factual representations, and that does not identify or
consider all of the relevant facts. Taxpayers also cannot rely on opinions
issued by a promoter or someone who has an involvement with the
transaction, including a material advisor. § 6664(d). These two penalties
are not likely to have much of an impact on a corporation's risk-reward
calculus. The disclosure penalty itself is so small that it hardly makes a
dent in the expected tax benefits. On the other hand, a failure to disclose

would increase the understatement penalty to 30 percent. But if a corporation does a cost-benefit analysis that weighs the benefits against the odds of detection and the probability of penalties, it may well find that a 30 percent penalty is not sufficient to deter investment in the shelter, particularly if the penalty can be waived or is not imposed.

At the same time, § 6707A imposes a penalty on taxpayers who fail to disclose "reportable transactions." The penalty is $10,000 on individuals and $50,000 on all others. The penalties are significantly higher—$100,000 and $200,000—on listed transactions, i.e. those transactions the IRS has identified as abusive in a published notice. The penalty applies regardless of whether the taxpayer's position is sustained on the merits and cannot be waived with respect to listed transactions. It can be waived for other reportable transactions or if rescission would promote compliance with the tax laws and effective tax administration.

There are five types of reportable transactions that are subject to penalty for failure to disclose:

1.   listed transactions and those with substantially similar consequences;

2.   confidential transactions;

3.   transactions with contractual protection, i.e. those where fees with respect to the transaction are contingent on achieving the intended consequences;

4.   excessive loss transactions that result in a deductible loss exceeding $10 million in a single tax year or $20 million in multiple tax years ($2 million/$4 million for individuals);

5.   transactions involving assets with holding periods of 45 days or less and a tax credit exceeding $250,000.

The regulations give Treasury the authority to issue a private ruling that a particular transaction need not be disclosed. Reg. § 1.6011–4; Notice 2006–6, 2006–1 C.B. 358.

The § 6707A penalty is premised on the notion that if tax shelters were exposed to scrutiny, taxpayers might be less likely to invest in questionable transactions. In any event, their likely discovery and challenge by the IRS would become part of the taxpayer's cost-benefit analysis. At the very least, they would give the IRS a good sense as to where the tax gambits are buried.

In 2010 Congress adopted a new strict liability penalty when it codified the economic substance doctrine. See Note (C) supra at page 788. The 20 percent penalty (40 percent if no disclosure) has no reasonable cause exception and cannot be waived by asserting the blessings of an attorney's opinion letter. It remains to be seen how often it will apply, however. Judges may be reluctant to find that there is no economic substance to a transaction if there is an automatic 20 percent penalty, particularly if the taxpayer has relied on a legal opinion letter or on a literal reading of the statute.

Congress has also imposed penalties on those who promote and advise with respect to tax shelters in the hope that they will be dissuaded from doing so. Section 6111 requires a "material advisor" with respect to a reportable transaction to notify the service with details about the transaction. Material advisors are not only promoters but also those who earn substantial fees from advising about promoting or implementing the transaction. In addition material advisors are required to maintain a list of the names of all persons for whom the advisor provided advice with respect to reportable transactions. § 6112.

In order to enforce these disclosure rules, the government issued summonses to law firms and accounting firms to force them to disclose client lists and promotional materials. Although some complied, others have vigorously resisted, often claiming attorney-client privilege. The accounting and law firms are also under attack by disgruntled clients. Several whose shelters have been disallowed have sued alleging everything from aggressive marking to racketeering to ethics violations. The lawsuits have provided a look into the highly secretive tax shelter world. The released documents include hard-sell promotional materials (including forms that let the client specify the amount and nature of the desired loss) as well as apparently canned penalty protection opinion letters.

In an extremely controversial move, the IRS issued a notice requiring large corporations to reveal so-called "uncertain tax positions." Corporations that issue audited financial statements are required to file a schedule of uncertain tax positions ("Schedule UTP") with their tax returns. Announcement 2010–30, 2010–19 I.R.B. 668. Uncertain positions are those for which the taxpayer has recorded a reserve in an audited financial statement. Under financial accounting rules (known as Fin 48), taxpayers must record a reserve in audited financial statements for any tax position that is not "more likely than not to be sustained," and for any portion of a tax position that is not greater than 50 percent likely of being realized upon ultimate settlement with the Service. In layman's terms, that means any position the taxpayer expects to lose if the IRS finds out about it. Consider United States v. Textron Inc., 577 F.3d 21, 25 (1st Cir. 2009), where the taxpayer unsuccessfully claimed a work product privilege for tax accrual papers describing the taxpayer's tax reserves. The taxpayer assessed the Service's likelihood of success on some "uncertain positions" as 100 percent.

Note on the Role of Lawyers, Accountants, and Other Experts

Lawyers have become key players in the tax shelter world. Many tax shelters have also been designed and promoted by accounting firms and investment bankers. Very large fees have been paid to promoters for these tax products. Lawyers may provide some insurance that penalties will not be imposed if the shelter collapses. Although a penalty can be imposed on a substantial understatement of income with respect to a tax shelter under § 6662, the penalty can be avoided if the taxpayer reasonably believed that the tax treatment claimed was more likely than not the proper treatment. Section 6664(c) provides an exception if the taxpayer has reasonable cause and acted in good faith. Generally, a lawyer's opinion that the shelter "works" protects the investors against the penalty, and they are willing to pay top dollar for such an opinion. But not always.

In the fall of 2003 the Senate Subcommittee on Investigations held hearings about the tax shelter industry and the role of accounting firms, banks, investment advisors, and law firms. It issued a report with detailed evidence about four shelters marketed by KMPG. The Committee described the way the industry was operating:

> First, the investigation has found that the tax shelter industry is not focused primarily on providing individualized tax advice to persons who initiate contact with a tax advisor. Instead, the industry focus has expanded to developing a steady supply of generic "tax products" that can be aggressively marketed to multiple clients. In short, the tax shelter industry has moved from providing one-on-one tax advice in response to tax inquiries also to initiating, designing, and mass marketing tax shelter products.

> Secondly, the investigation has found that numerous respected members of the American business community are now heavily involved in the development, marketing, and implementation of generic tax products whose objective is not to achieve a business or economic purpose, but to reduce or eliminate a client's U.S. tax liability. Dubious tax shelter sales are no longer the province of shady, fly-by-night companies with limited resources. They are big business, assigned to talented professionals at the top of their fields and able to draw upon the vast resources and reputations of the country's largest accounting firms, law firms, investment advisory firms, and banks.

The report details "the intense pressure on the firm's tax professionals" to sell tax products, even to its own audit and tax preparation clients. Internal e-mails encouraged partners to "SELL, SELL, SELL" products that "the firm knew were potentially abusive or illegal." KPMG worked closely with Brown & Wood (now Sidley Austin LLP), informing clients that the law firm would provide an opinion letter that would protect them from penalties. According to the report, Brown & Wood gave 600 opinions, charging $50,000 per opinion, and each and every one of those opinions assumed that there was a possibility for profit as well as a business purpose. Many of the opinions were identical, with no individualized tax advice, and were partially drafted by KPMG. The "client" usually was not consulted. The report notes that there was a real question about the accuracy and reliability of the factual representations made by the firm.

While the purchaser might have been protected from penalties by the law firm's opinion letter, what about KPMG? Section 6111 requires promoters to disclose tax shelters that they market to investors. The firm concluded that the tax products were not shelters and concealed them from the IRS. And even if they were shelters, at least one partner explicitly recommended not registering them for business reasons.

> [A] senior KPMG tax professional advocated in very explicit terms that, for business reasons, KPMG ought to ignore federal tax shelter requirements and not register the * * * tax product with the IRS, even if required by law. In an email sent to several senior colleagues, this KPMG tax professional explained his reasoning. In that email, he assumed that [the tax product] qualified as a tax shelter, and then explained why the firm should not, even in this case, register it with the IRS as required by law. Among other reasons, he observed that the IRS was not vigorously enforcing the registration requirement, the penalties for noncompliance were much less than the potential profits from selling the tax product, and "industry norms" were not to register any tax products at all. The KPMG tax professional coldly calculated the penalties for noncompliance compared to potential fees from selling [the shelter]: "Based upon our analysis of the applicable penalty sections, we conclude that the penalties would be no greater than $14,000 per $100,000 in KPMG fees. . . . For example, our average deal would result in KPMG fees of $360,000 with a maximum penalty exposure of only $31,000." The senior tax professional also warned that if KPMG were to comply with the tax shelter registration requirement, this action would place the firm at such a competitive disadvantage in its sales that KPMG would "not be able to compete in the tax advantaged products market." In short, he urged KPMG to knowingly, purposefully, and willfully violate the federal tax shelter law.

(KPMG's tax shelter business ultimately proved very costly to the firm. See infra, Note (C), at page 798.)

The sometimes hidden role of these experts also comes to light when the IRS challenges a tax shelter in court. One of the most revealing cases is Long Term Capital Holdings v. United States, 330 F.Supp.2d. 122 (D. Conn. 2005), aff'd 150 F.Appx. 40 (2d Cir. 2005). If tax cases were made into movies, this would be a good place to start. As described by Professor Alvin Warren:

> The intended result of the convoluted transaction in Long Term
> Capital Holdings was the creation of an artificial loss of $400
> million that was cloned, sold twice, and deducted by two
> different groups of U.S. taxpayers. * * * We will encounter
> dubious behavior by public companies (taking millions in
> artificial deductions), Nobel Laureates (taking the same
> deductions a second time), prominent law firms (providing
> opinions that the court found superficial and devoid of legal
> analysis), and major accounting firms (counseling taxpayers to
> hide the deductions on the tax return).

Alvin C. Warren Jr., "Understanding Long Term Capital," 106 Tax Notes
681 (Feb. 7, 2005). One of the principals of LTCH who managed a part of
the deal was the Nobel Laureate (in economics) Myron Scholes, who
testified about the economic substance of the transaction. The district
court judge did not mince words in rejecting his testimony. She found
portions of it unsupported, farfetched, and "more likely a contrivance to
show expected profitability and objective economic substance than a
serious economic analysis." 330 F.Supp.2d 122 at 162. LTCH tried to
avoid penalties by relying on the opinions of two law firms, King &
Spalding and Shearman & Sterling. The court ignored the King &
Spalding opinion, which was received after LTCH filed its tax return,
calling it shallow, superficial, and lacking in legal analysis. The
Shearman & Sterling opinion fared no better. It was described as
containing no legal analysis or reasoning. But even if there had been good
legal advice, the court refused to apply the reasonable cause exception
because LTCH concealed its losses on the return in a misleading way. It
did so at the suggestion of its accountants Price Waterhouse and Coopers
& Lybrand. In the end the judge threw the book at LTCH, imposing $16
million in penalties, which were upheld on appeal. If LTCH believed that
it was protected from penalties by the legal opinions, it had a major
economic incentive to enter into the transaction. The $400 million of
losses (deducted twice) dwarfed its costs. As Professor Warren notes:

> [T]he penalties are central to the case. This was an extremely
> aggressive transaction, which was marketed by tax
> professionals as a tax product and blessed by opinions from
> prominent law firms that, according to the court, did not provide
> the quality of legal work expected from such firms. The
> taxpayers managed their participation in the transaction as a
> tax product and, on the advice of major accounting firms,
> concealed the results on the relevant tax return. Unfortunately,
> that pattern of behavior is not limited to Long Term and its
> advisers. Given the sums of money involved, such conduct by
> major professional firms and their clients will change only if the
> courts are willing to sustain penalties imposed by the
> government when justified.

Taxpayers against whom the IRS asserts a penalty routinely rely on § 6664(c) under which the penalty can be waived if the taxpayer had reasonable cause and acted in good faith. Sometimes this works. See, e.g., Klamath Strategic Investment Fund v. United States, 568 F.3d 537 (5th Cir. 2009) (waiving the penalty because the taxpayer had in good faith relied on the advice of "qualified" accountants and tax attorneys); American Boat Company v. United States, 583 F.3d 471 (7th Cir. 2009) (waiving the penalty because of the quality and objectivity of the tax advice on which the taxpayer relied) But often, as in LTCH, it does not. Where the lawyer issuing the opinion is also the promoter, the taxpayer is more likely to get hit with penalties. See New Phoenix Sunrise Corp. v. Commissioner, 132 T.C. 161 (2009); Palm Canyon X Investments, LLC. v. Commissioner, 98 T.C.M. 574 (2009) (firm that wrote the opinion was part of the promoter team); Stobie Creek Investments, LLC v. United States, 82 Fed. Cl. 636 (2008) (taxpayers knew of the conflict of interest of the lawyers promoting the transaction and writing the opinion so reliance on the legal opinions was not reasonable.) In Murfam Farms, LLC v. United States, 94 Fed. Cl. 235 (2010), the court refused to waive the penalty because the tax advisor in question was Ernst & Young, the firm that sold the taxpayer the shelter. It noted that there was a conflict of interest because E & Y's fee was a percentage of the tax loss, which made it unreasonable for the taxpayer to rely on the accounting firm.

NOTES

(A) *Good Faith and the Tax Lawyer.* In Bobrow v. Commissioner, 107 T.C.M. 1110 (2014), the court refused to waive an accuracy-related penalty under § 6662 for reasonable cause and good faith because the taxpayer was a tax attorney and concluded that the taxpayer must have read the statute. The issue in the case was whether the rule that a taxpayer is limited to only one rollover distribution from one IRA to another during a one-year period applies to all of the taxpayer's IRAs or to each one separately. The court held that the plain language of the statute precluded the taxpayer's interpretation. Should a tax attorney ever be able to use the reasonable cause and good faith exception with respect to her own return?

(B) *Reining in the Tax Experts.* Opinion letters drafted by attorneys are often the linchpin of shelter offerings because they provide the taxpayer an assurance that a certain tax consequence will prevail, and perhaps more importantly, may provide penalty protection if the transaction fails. Under 31 U.S.C. § 230, the Secretary of the Treasury has the authority to establish practice standards for those who practice before the IRS. The Secretary has exercised this authority by issuing regulations known as "Circular 230." Violation of Circular 230 standards can result in disbarment from practice before the IRS. The regulations under Circular 230 apply to all tax advice but anticipate some of the shady practices that were characteristic of many tax shelter opinions.

Specifically, § 10.37 ("Requirements for Written Advice") requires those giving written advice to:

(i)   Base the written advice on reasonable factual and legal assumptions (including assumptions as to future events);

(ii) Reasonably consider all relevant facts and circumstances that the practitioner knows or reasonably should know;

(iii) Use reasonable efforts to identify and ascertain the facts relevant to written advice on each Federal tax matter;

(iv) Not rely upon representations, statements, findings, or agreements (including projections, financial forecasts, or appraisals) of the taxpayer or any other person if reliance on them would be unreasonable;

(v)   Relate applicable law and authorities to facts; and

(vi) Not, in evaluating a Federal tax matter, take into account the possibility that a tax return will not be audited or that a matter will not be raised on audit.

The Circular 230 rules apply only to written advice. Is that because there is less concern that practitioners will overstep in providing oral advice? Or that clients will insist on advice in writing in questionable situations? Or is it a problem of enforcement?

After shoddy opinions came to light, some firms argued that the offending opinion writer was a rogue partner and other partners were unaware of his activity. In an attempt to spread the responsibility, Circular 230 now requires the head of tax practice at a firm to ensure that the firm has procedures in place to see that all affected parties comply with these rules. See Circular 230, § 10.36. Such a practitioner is subject to discipline if through willfulness, recklessness, or gross incompetence, he does not take steps to impose such procedures and one or more individuals have engaged in a pattern or practice of failing to comply with these rules. The new rules, however, do not provide for vicarious liability despite some discussion of that possibility. Even if a tax advisor is disciplined under the rules, the firm escapes liability.

It is difficult to know how much the Circular 230 rules help to staunch the flow of tax shelters. Most shelters already come with a more-likely-than-not opinion, although it is not often based on the type of factual and legal analysis called for by the Circular 230 opinion rules. In cases where the shelter depends on a literal reading of the statute, regulations, or a ruling, invalidation may depend on a vague doctrine such as economic substance and practitioners may well differ as to the likely results. And it is likely that practitioners would not have much difficulty arguing that a transaction is consistent with the statute and congressional purpose so as to avoid being a "principal purpose transaction" subject to the stringent opinion regulations.

(C) *Criminal Charges.* In what may be its most potent weapon in the tax shelter wars, however, the government began criminal proceedings against some of those who sold tax shelters. In 2005 the government indicted nineteen tax professionals with KPMG, charging them with criminal tax conspiracy in designing, marketing, and implementing tax shelters. The government charged that the KPMG executives prepared false tax returns, documentation, and tax opinions, failed to register tax shelter transactions, and failed to produce documents covered by summonses. The possibility of prison time or other criminal penalties may have more of an impact on those who peddle shelters than civil nondisclosure penalties or ethics rules. In addition, the government had earlier entered into a deferred prosecution agreement with KPMG in a tax fraud conspiracy case against the firm. The firm admitted criminal wrongdoing and agreed to pay $465 million in fines, restitution, and penalties to the government and to accept permanent restrictions on the firm's tax practice. Subsequently the underlying criminal trial of the individual accountants was bogged down with procedural matters, including a ruling that the firm's refusal to pay legal fees for the executives was a constitutional violation that justified a dismissal of the indictment of most of the defendants. Talk around the accounting and law firm communities suggests that KPMG's experience had a chilling effect on the production and marketing of tax shelters. Few law or accounting firms are willing to take the risk of a criminal indictment.

The government has also sought to penalize law firms that wrote opinion letters for tax shelters. It levied a $76 million promoter penalty on Jenkens & Gilchrist (which subsequently went paws up and disbanded) and a $39.4 million penalty on Sidley Austin. In both cases the government agreed not to prosecute the firms on criminal charges. In an unpublished opinion the Fifth Circuit upheld a district court's finding that a lawyer who wrote a tax opinion (for which he was paid $25,000) supporting a Jenkens & Gilchrist tax shelter was civilly liable to an investor in the tax shelter for breach of fiduciary duty, negligent misrepresentation, fraud, and civil conspiracy. For several reasons no damages were awarded, but $75,000 of attorney fees were shifted. Ducote Jax Holdings LLC v. Bradley, 2009 U.S. App. LEXIS 13445.

(D) *Reining in the Taxpayers.* Taxpayers may be willing to invest in a tax shelter that seems highly problematic because they assume that no penalty will be imposed so long as they can show their reliance on a tax advisor as evidence that they had reasonable cause to believe that the treatment was more likely than not correct. As the opinion in *Long Term Capital Holdings,* supra at pages 788 and 795, indicates, some courts are no longer willing to waive the penalty just because the taxpayer has a legal opinion. Other courts are beginning to put some responsibility on the investor. In Mortensen v. Commissioner, 440 F.3d 375 (6th Cir. 2006), the judge upheld a penalty and rejected the so-called "ostrich defense." The taxpayer relied entirely on the promoters of the shelter and neglected to consult an independent tax advisor even when the promoters told him to do so. The court found his behavior unacceptable, noting that "when predators are circling, no reasonable ostrich sticks its head in the sand . . . The ostrich that does pays the penalty." And, as the Note on Penalties and Tax Shelters, supra at page 790, describes, failing the economic substance requirements of § 7701(*o*) is supposed to trigger an automatic 20 percent (40 percent if no disclosure) penalty.

SECTION 3.   ETHICAL RESPONSIBILITIES OF TAX PRACTITIONERS

The organized bar promulgates ethical standards for its members, and tax lawyers, like other lawyers, are subject to the ethical codes of the state in which they are admitted. Tax lawyers are also subject to the practice standards established by the Treasury Department under Circular 230 for all those who engage in practice before the Internal Revenue Service. These standards describe minimum acceptable conduct. Finally, lawyers who are also "tax return preparers" are subject to rules and penalties imposed by the Internal Revenue Code itself.

One of the most important and controversial ethical issues facing tax practitioners involves the standard to be applied in giving tax advice. For many years, the most important authority delineating the tax lawyer's ethical obligations was ABA Opinion 314. It provided:

> In practice before the Internal Revenue Service, which is itself an adversary party rather than a judicial tribunal, the lawyer is under a duty not to mislead the Service, either by misstatement, silence, or through his client, but is under no duty to disclose the weaknesses of his client's case. He must be candid and fair, and his defense of his client must be exercised within the bounds of the law and without resort to any manner of fraud or chicane.

The opinion permitted lawyers who advised clients on the preparation of tax returns to urge positions favorable to the client as long as there was a "reasonable basis" for doing so. The opinion explained:

> [W]here the lawyer believes there is a reasonable basis for a position that a particular transaction does not result in taxable income, or that certain expenditures are properly deductible as expenses, the lawyer has no duty to advise that riders be attached to the client's tax return explaining the circumstances surrounding the transaction or the expenditure.

The "reasonable basis" standard was widely criticized, and in response, the ABA issued Opinion 85–352, which provides that:

> [A]lawyer, in representing a client in the course of the preparation of the client's tax return, may advise the statement of positions most favorable to the client if the lawyer has a good faith belief that those positions are warranted in existing law or can be supported by a good faith argument for an extension, modification or reversal of existing law. A lawyer can have a good faith belief in this context even if the lawyer believes the client's position probably will not prevail. * * * However, good faith requires that there be some realistic possibility of success if the matter is litigated. * * *

> In the role of advisor, the lawyer should counsel the client as to whether the position is likely to be sustained by a court if

challenged by the IRS, as well as of the potential penalty consequences to the client if the position is taken on the tax return without disclosure. * * * If after receiving such advice the client decides to risk the penalty by making no disclosure and to take the position initially advised by the lawyer in accordance with the standard stated above, the lawyer has met his or her ethical responsibility with respect to the advice.

In all cases, however, with regard both to the preparation of returns and negotiating administrative settlements, the lawyer is under a duty not to mislead the Internal Revenue Service deliberately, either by misstatements or by silence or by permitting the client to mislead.

What is "some realistic possibility of success if the matter is litigated?" A task force of the ABA Section of Taxation expressed the view that "a position having only a 5 percent or 10 percent likelihood of success, if litigated, should not meet this new standard. A position having a likelihood of success closely approaching one-third should meet the standard." Paul Sax, James P. Holden, Theodore Tannenwald Jr., David Watts & Bernard Wolfman, "Report of the Special Task Force Report on Formal Opinion 85–352," reprinted in 39 Tax Lawyer 633, 638–39 (1986). How easy is it to quantify the likelihood of success? Surely a lawyer can differentiate between a one-third chance and a 10 percent chance, but is it helpful to distinguish a one-quarter chance from a one-third chance?

The reasonable basis standard of ABA Opinion 314 was often referred to as a "laugh aloud" standard, suggesting an attorney could urge any position that he could state without laughing aloud. Although the "realistic possibility of success" standard expressed in Opinion 85–352 is surely more stringent than the reasonable basis standard, is it anything more than a "giggle test?"

Whether or not Opinion 85–352 is an improvement, it may have little practical effect because no one is enforcing it. Provisions of the law and administrative requirements are more apt to have a real impact.

APPENDIX

THE CONCEPT OF PRESENT VALUE

The concept of present value can be summed up in the notion that a dollar today is worth more than a dollar tomorrow. That is because today's dollar can be invested immediately to earn interest for the recipient. Likewise, a dollar that one must pay tomorrow—as income tax, for example—is worth less to the payor than a dollar that must be paid today.

For example, assume that a person could receive a payment either today or 12 months from today. Also assume that he could earn a 6 percent rate of interest on any funds that he invested. If he would accept $100 if the payment were made today, he should demand $106 if the payment were deferred to the later year. Or, assume that the same person owes $500 of tax. Assuming an after-tax interest rate of 6 percent, his tax liability would cost only $471.70 in present value if he could defer payment until the next taxable year.

It follows that a dollar tomorrow is worth more than a dollar the day after tomorrow. The taxpayer in the previous example would thus demand $112.36 if the payment was not to be received for two years; he would reduce his tax liability to $445.00 if he did not have to settle up with the IRS for two years.

Present value is thus the amount that one would have to invest today at a specified interest rate in order to have a specified amount at a specified future date. This amount is calculated by discounting the future payment by the rate of return available to the investor over the relevant period. This formula may be expressed as:

$$PV = \frac{C}{(1 + r)^n}$$

where PV equals the present value, r equals the rate of return, C equals the future payment and n equals the number of years of deferral.

The difference in value between a dollar today and a dollar in the future thus depends both upon interest rates and upon the length of deferral. in the context of the income tax it also depends on the marginal rate of the taxpayer in the two periods.

The following tables list the present value of a dollar received after different lengths of time and at different rates of interest (Table 1) and the future value of a dollar that compounds for different periods of time and at different rates of interest (Table 2).

APPENDIX TABLE 1

Discount factors: Present value of $1 to be received after n years $= 1/(1 + r)^n$

Number of years	Interest rate per year									
	1%	2%	3%	4%	5%	6%	7%	8%	9%	10%
1	.990	.980	.971	.962	.952	.943	.935	.926	.917	.909
2	.980	.961	.943	.925	.907	.890	.873	.857	.842	.826
3	.971	.942	.915	.889	.864	.840	.816	.794	.772	.751
4	.961	.924	.888	.855	.823	.792	.763	.735	.708	.683
5	.951	.906	.863	.822	.784	.747	.713	.681	.650	.621
6	.942	.888	.837	.790	.746	.705	.666	.630	.596	.564
7	.933	.871	.813	.760	.711	.665	.623	.583	.547	.513
8	.923	.853	.789	.731	.677	.627	.582	.540	.502	.467
9	.914	.837	.766	.703	.645	.592	.544	.500	.460	.424
10	.905	.820	.744	.676	.614	.558	.508	.463	.422	.386
11	.896	.804	.722	.650	.585	.527	.475	.429	.388	.350
12	.887	.788	.701	.625	.557	.497	.444	.397	.356	.319
13	.879	.773	.681	.601	.530	.469	.415	.368	.326	.290
14	.870	.758	.661	.577	.505	.442	.388	.340	.299	.263
15	.861	.743	.642	.555	.481	.417	.362	.315	.275	.239
16	.853	.728	.623	.534	.458	.394	.339	.292	.252	.218
17	.844	.714	.605	.513	.436	.371	.317	.270	.231	.198
18	.836	.700	.587	.494	.416	.350	.296	.250	.212	.180
19	.828	.686	.570	.475	.396	.331	.277	.232	.194	.164
20	.820	.673	.554	.456	.377	.312	.258	.215	.178	.149
25	.780	.610	.478	.375	.295	.233	.184	.146	.116	.092
30	.742	.552	.412	.308	.231	.174	.131	.099	.075	.057

Number of years	Interest rate per year									
	11%	12%	13%	14%	15%	16%	17%	18%	19%	20%
1	.901	.893	.885	.877	.870	.862	.855	.847	.840	.833
2	.812	.797	.783	.769	.756	.743	.731	.718	.706	.694
3	.731	.712	.693	.675	.658	.641	.624	.609	.593	.579
4	.659	.636	.613	.592	.572	.552	.534	.516	.499	.482
5	.593	.567	.543	.519	.497	.476	.456	.437	.419	.402

Number of years	Interest rate per year									
	11%	12%	13%	14%	15%	16%	17%	18%	19%	20%
6	.535	.507	.480	.456	.432	.410	.390	.370	.352	.335
7	.482	.452	.425	.400	.376	.354	.333	.314	.296	.279
8	.434	.404	.376	.351	.327	.305	.285	.266	.249	.233
9	.391	.361	.333	.308	.284	.263	.243	.225	.209	.194
10	.352	.322	.295	.270	.247	.227	.208	.191	.176	.162
11	.317	.287	.261	.237	.215	.195	.178	.162	.148	.135
12	.286	.257	.231	.208	.187	.168	.152	.137	.124	.112
13	.258	.229	.204	.182	.163	.145	.130	.116	.104	.093
14	.232	.205	.181	.160	.141	.125	.111	.099	.088	.078
15	.209	.183	.160	.140	.123	.108	.095	.084	.074	.065
16	.188	.163	.141	.123	.107	.093	.081	.071	.062	.054
17	.170	.146	.125	.108	.093	.080	.069	.060	.052	.045
18	.153	.130	.111	.095	.081	.069	.059	.051	.044	.038
19	.138	.116	.098	.083	.070	.060	.051	.043	.037	.031
20	.124	.104	.087	.073	.061	.051	.043	.037	.031	.026
25	.074	.059	.047	.038	.030	.024	.020	.016	.013	.010
30	.044	.033	.026	.020	.015	.012	.009	.007	.005	.004

Number of years	Interest rate per year									
	21%	22%	23%	24%	25%	26%	27%	28%	29%	30%
1	.826	.820	.813	.806	.800	.794	.787	.781	.775	.769
2	.683	.672	.661	.650	.640	.630	.620	.610	.601	.592
3	.564	.551	.537	.524	.512	.500	.488	.477	.466	.455
4	.467	.451	.437	.423	.410	.397	.384	.373	.361	.350
5	.386	.370	.355	.341	.328	.315	.303	.291	.280	.269
6	.319	.303	.289	.275	.262	.250	.238	.227	.217	.207
7	.263	.249	.235	.222	.210	.198	.188	.178	.168	.159
8	.218	.204	.191	.179	.168	.157	.148	.139	.130	.123
9	.180	.167	.155	.144	.134	.125	.116	.108	.101	.094
10	.149	.137	.126	.116	.107	.099	.092	.085	.078	.073
11	.123	.112	.103	.094	.086	.079	.072	.066	.061	.056
12	.102	.092	.083	.076	.069	.062	.057	.052	.047	.043
13	.084	.075	.068	.061	.055	.050	.045	.040	.037	.033

Number of years	Interest rate per year									
	21%	22%	23%	24%	25%	26%	27%	28%	29%	30%
14	.069	.062	.055	.049	.044	.039	.035	.032	.028	.025
15	.057	.051	.045	.040	.035	.031	.028	.025	.022	.020
16	.047	.042	.036	.032	.028	.025	.022	.019	.017	.015
17	.039	.034	.030	.026	.023	.020	.017	.015	.013	.012
18	.032	.028	.024	.021	.018	.016	.014	.012	.010	.009
19	.027	.023	.020	.017	.014	.012	.011	.009	.008	.007
20	.022	.019	.016	.014	.012	.010	.008	.007	.006	.005
25	.009	.007	.006	.005	.004	.003	.003	.002	.002	.001
30	.003	.003	.002	.002	.001	.001	.001	.001	.000	.000

For example: If the interest rate is 10 percent per year, the present value of $1 to be received in 5 years is $0.621

APPENDIX TABLE 2

Future value of $1 by the end of n years $= (1 + r)^n$

Number of years	Interest rate per year									
	1%	2%	3%	4%	5%	6%	7%	8%	9%	10%
1	1.010	1.020	1.030	1.040	1.050	1.060	1.070	1.080	1.090	1.100
2	1.020	1.040	1.061	1.082	1.102	1.124	1.145	1.166	1.188	1.210
3	1.030	1.061	1.093	1.125	1.158	1.191	1.225	1.260	1.295	1.331
4	1.041	1.082	1.126	1.170	1.216	1.262	1.311	1.360	1.412	1.464
5	1.051	1.104	1.159	1.217	1.276	1.338	1.403	1.469	1.539	1.611
6	1.062	1.126	1.194	1.265	1.340	1.419	1.501	1.587	1.677	1.772
7	1.072	1.149	1.230	1.316	1.407	1.504	1.606	1.714	1.828	1.949
8	1.083	1.172	1.267	1.369	1.477	1.594	1.718	1.851	1.993	2.144
9	1.094	1.195	1.305	1.423	1.551	1.689	1.838	1.999	2.172	2.358
10	1.105	1.219	1.344	1.480	1.629	1.791	1.967	2.159	2.367	2.594
11	1.116	1.243	1.384	1.539	1.710	1.898	2.105	2.332	2.580	2.853
12	1.127	1.268	1.426	1.601	1.796	2.012	2.252	2.518	2.813	3.138
13	1.138	1.294	1.469	1.665	1.886	2.133	2.410	2.720	3.066	3.452
14	1.149	1.319	1.513	1.732	1.980	2.261	2.579	2.937	3.342	3.797
15	1.161	1.346	1.558	1.801	2.079	2.397	2.759	3.172	3.642	4.177
16	1.173	1.373	1.605	1.873	2.183	2.540	2.952	3.426	3.970	4.595
17	1.184	1.400	1.653	1.948	2.292	2.693	3.159	3.700	4.328	5.054

Number of years	Interest rate per year									
	1%	2%	3%	4%	5%	6%	7%	8%	9%	10%
18	1.196	1.428	1.702	2.026	2.407	2.854	3.380	3.996	4.717	5.560
19	1.208	1.457	1.754	2.107	2.527	3.026	3.617	4.316	5.142	6.116
20	1.220	1.486	1.806	2.191	2.653	3.207	3.870	4.661	5.604	6.727
25	1.282	1.641	2.094	2.666	3.386	4.292	5.427	6.848	8.623	10.83
30	1.348	1.811	2.427	3.243	4.322	5.743	7.612	10.06	13.27	17.45

Number of years	Interest rate per year									
	11%	12%	13%	14%	15%	16%	17%	18%	19%	20%
1	1.110	1.120	1.130	1.140	1.150	1.160	1.170	1.180	1.190	1.200
2	1.232	1.254	1.277	1.300	1.323	1.346	1.369	1.392	1.416	1.440
3	1.368	1.405	1.443	1.482	1.521	1.561	1.602	1.643	1.685	1.728
4	1.518	1.574	1.630	1.689	1.749	1.811	1.874	1.939	2.005	2.074
5	1.685	1.762	1.842	1.925	2.011	2.100	2.192	2.288	2.386	2.488
6	1.870	1.974	2.082	2.195	2.313	2.436	2.565	2.700	2.840	2.986
7	2.076	2.211	2.353	2.502	2.660	2.826	3.001	3.185	3.379	3.583
8	2.305	2.476	2.658	2.853	3.059	3.278	3.511	3.759	4.021	4.300
9	2.558	2.773	3.004	3.252	3.518	3.803	4.108	4.435	4.785	5.160
10	2.839	3.106	3.395	3.707	4.046	4.411	4.807	5.234	5.695	6.192
11	3.152	3.479	3.836	4.226	4.652	5.117	5.624	6.176	6.777	7.430
12	3.498	3.896	4.335	4.818	5.350	5.936	6.580	7.288	8.064	8.916
13	3.883	4.363	4.898	5.492	6.153	6.886	7.699	8.599	9.596	10.70
14	4.310	4.887	5.535	6.261	7.076	7.988	9.007	10.15	11.42	12.84
15	4.785	5.474	6.254	7.138	8.137	9.266	10.54	11.97	13.59	15.41
16	5.311	6.130	7.067	8.137	9.358	10.75	12.33	14.13	16.17	18.49
17	5.895	6.866	7.986	9.276	10.76	12.47	14.43	16.67	19.24	22.19
18	6.544	7.690	9.024	10.58	12.38	14.46	16.88	19.67	22.90	26.62
19	7.263	8.613	10.20	12.06	14.23	16.78	19.75	23.21	27.25	31.95
20	8.062	9.646	11.52	13.74	16.37	19.46	23.11	27.39	32.43	38.34
25	13.59	17.00	21.23	26.46	32.92	40.87	50.66	62.67	77.39	95.40
30	22.89	29.96	39.12	50.95	66.21	85.85	111.1	143.4	184.7	237.4

Number	Interest rate per year									
of years	21%	22%	23%	24%	25%	26%	27%	28%	29%	30%
1	1.210	1.220	1.230	1.240	1.250	1.260	1.270	1.280	1.290	1.300
2	1.464	1.488	1.513	1.538	1.563	1.588	1.613	1.638	1.664	1.690
3	1.772	1.816	1.861	1.907	1.953	2.000	2.048	2.097	2.147	2.197
4	2.144	2.215	2.289	2.364	2.441	2.520	2.601	2.684	2.769	2.856
5	2.594	2.703	2.815	2.932	3.052	3.176	3.304	3.436	3.572	3.713
6	3.138	3.297	3.463	3.635	3.815	4.002	4.196	4.398	4.608	4.827
7	3.797	4.023	4.259	4.508	4.768	5.042	5.329	5.629	5.945	6.275
8	4.595	4.908	5.239	5.590	5.960	6.353	6.768	7.206	7.669	8.157
9	5.560	5.987	6.444	6.931	7.451	8.005	8.595	9.223	9.893	10.60
10	6.728	7.305	7.926	8.594	9.313	10.09	10.92	11.81	12.76	13.79
11	8.140	8.912	9.749	10.66	11.64	12.71	13.86	15.11	16.46	17.92
12	9.850	10.87	11.99	13.21	14.55	16.01	17.61	19.34	21.24	23.30
13	11.92	13.26	14.75	16.39	18.19	20.18	22.36	24.76	27.39	30.29
14	14.42	16.18	18.14	20.32	22.74	25.42	28.40	31.69	35.34	39.37
15	17.45	19.74	22.31	25.20	28.42	32.03	36.06	40.56	45.59	51.19
16	21.11	24.09	27.45	31.24	35.53	40.36	45.80	51.92	58.81	66.54
17	25.55	29.38	33.76	38.74	44.41	50.85	58.17	66.46	75.86	86.50
18	30.91	35.85	41.52	48.04	55.51	64.07	73.87	85.07	97.86	112.5
19	37.40	43.74	51.07	59.57	69.39	80.73	93.81	108.9	126.2	146.2
20	45.26	53.36	62.82	73.86	86.74	101.7	119.1	139.4	162.9	190.0
25	117.4	144.2	176.9	216.5	264.7	323.0	393.6	478.9	581.8	705.6
30	304.5	389.8	497.9	634.8	807.8	1026	1301	1646	2078	2620

For example: If the interest rate is 10 percent per year, the investment of $1 today will be worth $1.611 at the end of year 5.

INDEX

References are to Pages